MW00344444

FEDERAL RULES OF EVIDENCE
Rules, Legislative History, Commentary and Authority

FEDERAL RULES OF EVIDENCE

Rules, Legislative History, Commentary and Authority

GLEN WEISSENBERGER
Professor of Law
DePaul University College of Law

JAMES J. DUANE
Professor of Law
Regent University School of Law

Seventh Edition

 LexisNexis®

ISBN: 978-1-4224-9563-6

Library of Congress Cataloging-in-Publication Data
Weissenberger, Glen.
  Weissenberger's federal evidence / Glen Weissenberger, James J. Duane. — 7th ed.
p. cm.
  Includes bibliographical references and index.
  ISBN: 978-1-59345-814-0 (hardbound)
  ISBN: 978-1-5791-1500-5 (eBook)
  ISBN: 978-1-4224-9563-6 (Law school edition)
1. Evidence (Law)—United States. I. Duane, James J. II. Title. III. Title: Federal evidence.
  KF8935.W42 2011
  347.73'6—dc23

2011041534

NOTE TO USERS

To ensure that you are using the latest materials available in this area, please be sure to periodically check the LexisNexis Law School web site for downloadable updates and supplements at www.lexisnexis.com/lawschool.

Editorial Offices
121 Chanlon Rd., New Providence, NJ 07974 (908) 464-6800
201 Mission St., San Francisco, CA 94105-1831 (415) 908-3200
www.lexisnexis.com

MATTHEW◆BENDER

(2011-Pub.3545)

Table of Contents

Table of Contents

Table of Contents

Table of Contents

Table of Contents

Table of Contents

Table of Contents

Table of Contents

Table of Contents

Table of Contents

Table of Contents

Table of Contents

Table of Contents

Table of Contents

Chapter 804 **Rule 804. Exceptions to the Rule Against Hearsay — When the Declarant Is Unavailable as a Witness**

Table of Contents

Chapter 805   Rule 805. Hearsay Within Hearsay

Table of Contents

Table of Contents

Table of Contents

Table of Contents

Table of Contents

Table of Authorities

Jack B. Weinstein, WEINSTEIN'S FEDERAL EVIDENCE, Second Edition, Matthew Bender & Co. (1987), hereinafter WEINSTEIN'S FEDERAL EVIDENCE, § —

James Wm. Moore, MOORE'S FEDERAL PRACTICE, Third Edition, Matthew Bender & Co. (1997), hereinafter MOORE'S FEDERAL PRACTICE , § —

Graham C. Lilly, AN INTRODUCTION TO THE LAW OF EVIDENCE, Third Edition, West Publishing Co. (1966), hereinafter LILLY, § —

Christopher B. Mueller and Laird C. Kirkpatrick, FEDERAL EVIDENCE, Second Edition, Aspen Publishing Co. (1999), hereinafter MUELLER & KIRKPATRICK, § —

MCCORMICK ON EVIDENCE, 5th edition, Practitioner's edition, West Publishing Co. (1999), hereinafter MCCORMICK § —

Stephen A. Saltzburg, Michael M. Martin, and Daniel J. Capra, FEDERAL RULES OF EVIDENCE MANUAL, 7th edition, Lexis (1998), hereinafter SALTZBURG & MARTIN, Rule —

John Henry Wigmore, EVIDENCE IN TRIALS AT COMMON LAW, Volume 1, Aspen Publishing Co. (Tillers Rev. 1983), hereinafter 1 WIGMORE, § —

John Henry Wigmore, EVIDENCE IN TRIALS AT COMMON LAW, Volume 1A, Aspen Publishing Co. (Tillers Rev. 1983), hereinafter 1A WIGMORE § —

John Henry Wigmore, EVIDENCE IN TRIALS AT COMMON LAW, Volume 2, Aspen Publishing Co. (Tillers Rev. 1979), hereinafter 2 WIGMORE § —

John Henry Wigmore, EVIDENCE IN TRIALS AT COMMON LAW, Volume 3, Aspen Publishing Co. (Chadbourne Rev. 1970), hereinafter 3 WIGMORE § —

John Henry Wigmore, EVIDENCE IN TRIALS AT COMMON LAW, Volume 3A, Aspen Publishing Co. (Chadbourne Rev. 1970), hereinafter 3A WIGMORE, § —

John Henry Wigmore, EVIDENCE IN TRIALS AT COMMON LAW, Volume 4 Aspen Publishing Co. (Chadbourne Rev. 1972), hereinafter 4 WIGMORE § —

John Henry Wigmore, EVIDENCE IN TRIALS AT COMMON LAW, Volume 5, Aspen Publishing Co. (Chadbourne Rev. 1974), hereinafter 5 WIGMORE § —

John Henry Wigmore, EVIDENCE IN TRIALS AT COMMON LAW, Volume 6, Aspen Publishing Co. (Chadbourne Rev. 1976), hereinafter 6 WIGMORE § —

John Henry Wigmore, EVIDENCE IN TRIALS AT COMMON LAW, Volume 7, Aspen Publishing Co. (Chadbourne Rev. 1978), hereinafter 7 WIGMORE § —

John Henry Wigmore, EVIDENCE IN TRIALS AT COMMON LAW, Volume 8, Aspen Publishing Co. (McNaughton Rev. 1961), hereinafter 8 WIGMORE § —

John Henry Wigmore, EVIDENCE IN TRIALS AT COMMON LAW, Volume 9, Aspen Publishing Co. (Chadbourne Rev. 1981), hereinafter 9 WIGMORE § —

About the Authors

Glen Weissenberger is a Professor at DePaul University College of Law. He previously taught at the University of Cincinnati Law School for 27 years, rising to become the Judge Joseph P. Kinneary Professor of Law. During this time, he served as special counsel to the university president and as director of the university's Center for Studies in Professional Skills. He received many teaching and scholarship awards, including the Ohio State Bar Foundation Outstanding Research Award, the University of Cincinnati Faculty Achievement Award, and the Jerome P. Goldman Prize for Teaching Excellence. In 2005, he was appointed chair of the Editorial Advisory Board of LexisNexis Legal Publishing, one of the largest legal publishers in the United States. Weissenberger earned his Juris Doctor from Harvard University in 1972 and a Bachelor of Arts degree from the University of Cincinnati in 1969. A prolific scholar, Weissenberger is the author of many works found in libraries and classrooms across the nation. WEISSENBERGER'S FEDERAL EVIDENCE is commonly cited in law review articles and texts on evidence law, while its companion work, WEISSENBERGER'S FEDERAL EVIDENCE COURTROOM MANUAL, has been published annually since 1992.

James J. Duane is a Professor at Regent Law School in Virginia Beach, Virginia. He has taught as a Visiting Professor at William & Mary Law School, and at the National Trial Advocacy College conducted each year at the University of Virginia School of Law. He was awarded the Distinguished Faculty Achievement Award by the Virginia State Council of Higher Education in 2002. Professor Duane is a member of the Panel of Academic Contributors to *Black's Law Dictionary,* and has published more than thirty articles in the field of evidence law. He is admitted to practice in New York and Virginia, and before the Supreme Court of the United States and several other federal courts. He received his A.B. *magna cum laude* from Harvard College in 1981, where he was Phi Beta Kappa, and his J.D. *cum laude* from Harvard Law School in 1984. He clerked for the Hon. Michael A. Telesca of the United States District Court for the Western District of New York, and the Hon. Ellsworth A. Van Graafeiland on the United States Court of Appeals for the Second Circuit, before practicing with Connors & Vilardo in Buffalo, New York.

Preface to the Seventh Edition

This is the seventh edition of a comprehensive, one volume treatise on the Federal Rules of Evidence. Like the previous editions, this work is intended to serve as a succinct yet scholarly analysis of the Federal Rules of Evidence for judges, practitioners, and students. Although this edition expands upon the contents of the previous editions, we have made every effort to retain the clarity and brevity of the previous editions, as well as our commitment to integrating theory with a practical understanding of how these rules operate in the real world.

Much has changed in the world of federal evidence law in the last few years. Three years ago, Congress enacted Rule 502, the first new Federal Rule of Evidence in fifteen years, and the first privilege rule written into the rules since their original adoption. This book includes a detailed line-by-line summary and analysis of Rule 502, which sets forth certain important new limitations on the waiver of the attorney-client privilege and work product protection. This edition also contains the comprehensive stylistic amendments to the rules that went into effect on December 1 of this year.

And of course we continue our coverage of the extensive body of case law developing in the wake of *Crawford v. Washington* (2004), *Davis v. Washington* (2006), *Whorton v. Bockting* (2007), *Giles v. California* (2008), *Melendez-Diaz v. Massachusetts* (2009), *Michigan v. Bryant* (2011), and *Bullcoming v. New Mexico* (2011). These landmark Supreme Court decisions have almost completely rewritten the law governing the extent to which the Confrontation Clause of the Sixth Amendment restricts and sometimes forbids the admission of hearsay against the accused in a criminal case.

It remains our hope that this book will continue to make a significant contribution to the development and understanding of the Federal Rules of Evidence.

Glen Weissenberger
Professor of Law
DePaul University College of Law

James J. Duane
Professor of Law
Regent University School of Law
December, 2011

Acknowledgments

Professor Weissenberger would like to acknowledge the research contributions of Michael G. Frey, Daniel J. Donnellon, Jean C. Donath, V. Ellen Graham, Carole Kellerman, Marilyn Magg, Wade Kocovsky, Susan Demidovich, Brenda N. Dunlap, Elizabeth Fox, A.J. Stephani, Joseph A. Stegbauer, and Mark E. Elsner

Professor Duane gratefully acknowledges the invaluable assistance of Tracy Hasse, Jadinah Sejour, Colleen Holmes, Elisabeth MacBride Hopkins, Christine Moore, Bruce Page, Mark Moseley, Christopher Brownwell, Sharon Noonan, and Shayne Picard.

FEDERAL RULES OF EVIDENCE

ARTICLE I.
GENERAL PROVISIONS

Rule 101. Scope; Definitions

(a) **Scope.** These rules apply to proceedings in United States courts. The specific courts and proceedings to which the rules apply, along with exceptions, are set out in Rule 1101.

(b) **Definitions.** In these rules:

(1) "civil case" means a civil action or proceeding;

(2) "criminal case" includes a criminal proceeding;

(3) "public office" includes a public agency;

(4) "record" includes a memorandum, report, or data compilation;

(5) a "rule prescribed by the Supreme Court" means a rule adopted by the Supreme Court under statutory authority; and

(6) a reference to any kind of written material or any other medium includes electronically stored information.

(Amended, eff 10-1-87; 11-1-88; 12-1-93; 12-1-11)

Rule 102. Purpose

These rules should be construed so as to administer every proceeding fairly, eliminate unjustifiable expense and delay, and promote the development of evidence law, to the end of ascertaining the truth and securing a just determination.

(Amended, eff 12-1-11)

Rule 103. Rulings on Evidence

(a) **Preserving a Claim of Error.** A party may claim error in a ruling to admit or exclude evidence only if the error affects a substantial right of the party and:

(1) if the ruling admits evidence, a party, on the record:

(A) timely objects or moves to strike; and

(B) states the specific ground, unless it was apparent from the context; or

(2) if the ruling excludes evidence, a party informs the court of its substance by an offer of proof, unless the substance was apparent from the context.

(b) **Not Needing to Renew an Objection or Offer of Proof.** Once the court rules definitively on the record — either before or at trial — a party need not renew an objection or offer of proof to preserve a claim of error for appeal.

(c) **Court's Statement About the Ruling; Directing an Offer of Proof.** The court may make any statement about the character or form of the evidence, the objection made, and the ruling. The court may direct that an offer of proof be made in question-and-answer form.

(d) **Preventing the Jury from Hearing Inadmissible Evidence.** To the extent practicable, the court must conduct a jury trial so that inadmissible evidence is not suggested to the jury by any means.

(e) **Taking Notice of Plain Error.** A court may take notice of a plain error affecting a substantial right, even if the claim of error was not properly preserved.

(Amended, eff 12-1-00; 12-1-11)

Rule 104. Preliminary Questions

(a) **In General.** The court must decide any preliminary question about whether a witness is qualified, a privilege exists, or evidence is admissible. In so deciding, the court is not bound by evidence rules, except those on privilege.

(b) **Relevance That Depends on a Fact.** When the relevance of evidence depends on whether a fact exists, proof must be introduced sufficient to support a finding that the fact does exist. The court may admit the proposed evidence on the condition that the proof be introduced later.

(c) **Conducting a Hearing So That the Jury Cannot Hear It.** The court must conduct any hearing on a preliminary question so that the jury cannot hear it if:

(1) the hearing involves the admissibility of a confession;

(2) a defendant in a criminal case is a witness and so requests; or

(3) justice so requires.

(d) **Cross-Examining a Defendant in a Criminal Case.** By testifying on a preliminary question, a defendant in a criminal case does not become subject to cross-examination on other issues in the case.

(e) **Evidence Relevant to Weight and Credibility.** This rule does not limit a party's right to introduce before the jury evidence that is relevant to the weight or credibility of other evidence.

(Amended, eff 10-1-87; 12-1-11)

Rule 105. Limiting Evidence That Is Not Admissible Against Other Parties or for Other Purposes

If the court admits evidence that is admissible against a party or for a purpose — but not against another party or for another purpose — the court, on timely request, must restrict the evidence to its proper scope and instruct the jury accordingly.

(Amended, eff 12-1-11)

Rule 106. Remainder of or Related Writings or Recorded Statements

If a party introduces all or part of a writing or recorded statement, an adverse party may require the introduction, at that time, of any other part — or any other writing or recorded statement — that in fairness ought to be considered at the same time.

(Amended, eff 10-1-87; 12-1-11)

ARTICLE II.
JUDICIAL NOTICE

Rule 201. Judicial Notice of Adjudicative Facts

(a) Scope. This rule governs judicial notice of an adjudicative fact only, not a legislative fact.

(b) Kinds of Facts That May Be Judicially Noticed. The court may judicially notice a fact that is not subject to reasonable dispute because it:

(1) is generally known within the trial court's territorial jurisdiction; or

(2) can be accurately and readily determined from sources whose accuracy cannot reasonably be questioned.

(c) Taking Notice. The court:

(1) may take judicial notice on its own; or

(2) must take judicial notice if a party requests it and the court is supplied with the necessary information.

(d) Timing. The court may take judicial notice at any stage of the proceeding.

(e) Opportunity to Be Heard. On timely request, a party is entitled to be heard on the propriety of taking judicial notice and the nature of the fact to be noticed. If the court takes judicial notice before notifying a party, the party, on request, is still entitled to be heard.

(f) Instructing the Jury. In a civil case, the court must instruct the jury to accept the noticed fact as conclusive. In a criminal case, the court must instruct the jury that it may or may not accept the noticed fact as conclusive.

(Amended, eff 12-1-11)

ARTICLE III.
PRESUMPTIONS IN CIVIL CASES

Rule 301. Presumptions in Civil Cases Generally

In a civil case, unless a federal statute or these rules provide otherwise, the party against whom a presumption is directed has the burden of producing evidence to rebut the presumption. But this rule does not shift the burden of persuasion, which remains on the party who had it originally.

(Amended, eff 12-1-11)

Rule 302. Applying State Law to Presumptions in Civil Cases

In a civil case, state law governs the effect of a presumption regarding a claim or defense for which state law supplies the rule of decision.

(Amended, eff 12-1-11)

ARTICLE IV.
RELEVANCE AND ITS LIMITS

Rule 401. Test for Relevant Evidence

Evidence is relevant if:

(a) it has any tendency to make a fact more or less probable than it would be without the evidence; and

(b) the fact is of consequence in determining the action.

(Amended, eff 12-1-11)

Rule 402. General Admissibility of Relevant Evidence

Relevant evidence is admissible unless any of the following provides otherwise:

• the United States Constitution;

• a federal statute;

• these rules; or

• other rules prescribed by the Supreme Court.

Irrelevant evidence is not admissible.

(Amended, eff 12-1-11)

Rule 403. Excluding Relevant Evidence for Prejudice, Confusion, Waste of Time, or Other Reasons

The court may exclude relevant evidence if its probative value is substantially outweighed by a danger of one or more of the following: unfair prejudice, confusing the issues, misleading the jury, undue delay, wasting time, or needlessly presenting cumulative evidence.

(Amended, eff 12-1-11)

Rule 404. Character Evidence; Crimes or Other Acts

(a) Character Evidence.

(1) *Prohibited Uses.*   Evidence of a person's character or character trait is not admissible to prove that on a particular occasion the person acted in accordance with the character or trait.

(2) *Exceptions for a Defendant or Victim in a Criminal Case.*   The following exceptions apply in a criminal case:

(A)   a defendant may offer evidence of the defendant's pertinent trait, and if the evidence is admitted, the prosecutor may offer evidence to rebut it;

(B)   subject to the limitations in Rule 412, a defendant may offer evidence of an alleged victim's pertinent trait, and if the evidence is admitted, the prosecutor may:

(i)   offer evidence to rebut it; and

(ii)   offer evidence of the defendant's same trait; and

(C)   in a homicide case, the prosecutor may offer evidence of the alleged victim's trait of peacefulness to rebut evidence that the victim was the first aggressor.

(3) *Exceptions for a Witness.*   Evidence of a witness's character may be admitted under Rules 607, 608, and 609.

(b) Crimes, Wrongs, or Other Acts.

(1) *Prohibited Uses.*   Evidence of a crime, wrong, or other act is not admissible to prove a person's character in order to show that on a particular occasion the person acted in accordance with the character.

(2) *Permitted Uses; Notice in a Criminal Case.*   This evidence may be admissible for another purpose, such as proving motive, opportunity, intent, preparation, plan, knowledge, identity, absence of mistake, or lack of accident. On request by a defendant in a criminal case, the prosecutor must:

(A)   provide reasonable notice of the general nature of any such evidence that the prosecutor intends to offer at trial; and

(B)   do so before trial — or during trial if the court, for good cause, excuses lack of pretrial notice.

(Amended, eff 10-1-87; 12-1-91; 12-1-00; 12-1-06; 12-1-11)

Rule 405. Methods of Proving Character

(a) By Reputation or Opinion.   When evidence of a person's character or character trait is admissible, it may be proved by testimony about the person's reputation or by testimony in the form of an opinion. On cross-examination of the character witness, the court may allow an inquiry into relevant specific instances of the person's conduct.

(b) By Specific Instances of Conduct. When a person's character or character trait is an essential element of a charge, claim, or defense, the character or trait may also be proved by relevant specific instances of the person's conduct.

(Amended, eff 10-1-87; 12-1-11)

Rule 406. Habit; Routine Practice

Evidence of a person's habit or an organization's routine practice may be admitted to prove that on a particular occasion the person or organization acted in accordance with the habit or routine practice. The court may admit this evidence regardless of whether it is corroborated or whether there was an eyewitness.

(Amended, eff 12-1-11)

Rule 407. Subsequent Remedial Measures

When measures are taken that would have made an earlier injury or harm less likely to occur, evidence of the subsequent measures is not admissible to prove:

• negligence;

• culpable conduct;

• a defect in a product or its design; or

• a need for a warning or instruction.

But the court may admit this evidence for another purpose, such as impeachment or — if disputed — proving ownership, control, or the feasibility of precautionary measures.

(Amended, eff 12-1-97; 12-1-11)

Rule 408. Compromise Offers and Negotiations

(a) Prohibited Uses. Evidence of the following is not admissible — on behalf of any party — either to prove or disprove the validity or amount of a disputed claim or to impeach by a prior inconsistent statement or a contradiction:

(1) furnishing, promising, or offering — or accepting, promising to accept, or offering to accept — a valuable consideration in compromising or attempting to compromise the claim; and

(2) conduct or a statement made during compromise negotiations about the claim — except when offered in a criminal case and when the negotiations related to a claim by a public office in the exercise of its regulatory, investigative, or enforcement authority.

(b) Exceptions. The court may admit this evidence for another purpose, such as proving a witness's bias or prejudice, negating a contention of undue delay, or proving an effort to obstruct a criminal investigation or prosecution.

(Amended, eff 12-1-06; 12-1-11)

Rule 409. Offers to Pay Medical and Similar Expenses

Evidence of furnishing, promising to pay, or offering to pay medical, hospital, or similar expenses resulting from an injury is not admissible to prove liability for the injury.

(Amended, eff 12-1-11)

Rule 410. Pleas, Plea Discussions, and Related Statements

(a) Prohibited Uses. In a civil or criminal case, evidence of the following is not admissible against the defendant who made the plea or participated in the plea discussions:

(1) a guilty plea that was later withdrawn;

(2) a nolo contendere plea;

(3) a statement made during a proceeding on either of those pleas under Federal Rule of Criminal Procedure 11 or a comparable state procedure; or

(4) a statement made during plea discussions with an attorney for the prosecuting authority if the discussions did not result in a guilty plea or they resulted in a later-withdrawn guilty plea.

(b) Exceptions. The court may admit a statement described in Rule 410(a)(3) or (4):

(1) in any proceeding in which another statement made during the same plea or plea discussions has been introduced, if in fairness the statements ought to be considered together; or

(2) in a criminal proceeding for perjury or false statement, if the defendant made the statement under oath, on the record, and with counsel present.

(Amended, 12-12-75; 4-30-79, eff 12-1-80; 12-1-11)

Rule 411. Liability Insurance

Evidence that a person was or was not insured against liability is not admissible to prove whether the person acted negligently or otherwise wrongfully. But the court may admit this evidence for another purpose, such as proving a witness's bias or prejudice or proving agency, ownership, or control.

(Amended, eff 10-1-87; 12-1-11)

Rule 412. Sex-Offense Cases: The Victim's Sexual Behavior or Predisposition

(a) Prohibited Uses. The following evidence is not admissible in a civil or criminal proceeding involving alleged sexual misconduct:

(1) evidence offered to prove that a victim engaged in other sexual behavior; or

(2) evidence offered to prove a victim's sexual predisposition.

(b) Exceptions.

(1) *Criminal Cases.* The court may admit the following evidence in a criminal case:

(A) evidence of specific instances of a victim's sexual behavior, if offered to prove that someone other than the defendant was the source of semen, injury, or other physical evidence;

(B) evidence of specific instances of a victim's sexual behavior with respect to the person accused of the sexual misconduct, if offered by the defendant to prove consent or if offered by the prosecutor; and

(C) evidence whose exclusion would violate the defendant's constitutional rights.

(2) *Civil Cases.* In a civil case, the court may admit evidence offered to prove a victim's sexual behavior or sexual predisposition if its probative value substantially outweighs the danger of harm to any victim and of unfair prejudice to any party. The court may admit evidence of a victim's reputation only if the victim has placed it in controversy.

(c) Procedure   to   Determine Admissibility.

(1) *Motion.*   If a party intends to offer evidence under Rule 412(b), the party must:

(A) file a motion that specifically describes the evidence and states the purpose for which it is to be offered;

(B) do so at least 14 days before trial unless the court, for good cause, sets a different time;

(C) serve the motion on all parties; and

(D) notify the victim or, when appropriate, the victim's guardian or representative.

(2) *Hearing.*   Before admitting evidence under this rule, the court must conduct an in camera hearing and give the victim and parties a right to attend and be heard. Unless the court orders otherwise, the motion, related materials, and the record of the hearing must be and remain sealed.

(d) Definition of "Victim." In this rule, "victim" includes an alleged victim.

(Effective 10-28-78; amended, eff 11-18-88; 12-1-94; 12-1-11)

Rule 413. Similar Crimes in Sexual-Assault Cases

(a) Permitted Uses. In a criminal case in which a defendant is accused of a sexual assault, the court may admit evidence that the defendant committed any other sexual assault. The evidence may be considered on any matter to which it is relevant.

(b) Disclosure to the Defendant. If the prosecutor intends to offer this evidence, the prosecutor must disclose it to the defendant, including witnesses' statements or a summary of the expected testimony. The pros-

ecutor must do so at least 15 days before trial or at a later time that the court allows for good cause.

(c) Effect on Other Rules. This rule does not limit the admission or consideration of evidence under any other rule.

(d) Definition of "Sexual Assault." In this rule and Rule 415, "sexual assault" means a crime under federal law or under state law (as "state" is defined in 18 U.S.C. § 513) involving:

(1) any conduct prohibited by 18 U.S.C. chapter 109A;

(2) contact, without consent, between any part of the defendant's body — or an object — and another person's genitals or anus;

(3) contact, without consent, between the defendant's genitals or anus and any part of another person's body;

(4) deriving sexual pleasure or gratification from inflicting death, bodily injury, or physical pain on another person; or

(5) an attempt or conspiracy to engage in conduct described in subparagraphs (1)–(4).

(Effective 7-9-95; amended, eff 12-1-11)

Rule 414. Similar Crimes in Child-Molestation Cases

(a) Permitted Uses. In a criminal case in which a defendant is accused of child molestation, the court may admit evidence that the defendant committed any other child molestation. The evidence may be considered on any matter to which it is relevant.

(b) Disclosure to the Defendant. If the prosecutor intends to offer this evidence, the prosecutor must disclose it to the defendant, including witnesses' statements or a summary of the expected testimony. The prosecutor must do so at least 15 days before trial or at a later time that the court allows for good cause.

(c) Effect on Other Rules. This rule does not limit the admission or consideration of evidence under any other rule.

(d) Definition of "Child" and "Child Molestation." In this rule and Rule 415:

(1) "child" means a person below the age of 14; and

(2) "child molestation" means a crime under federal law or under state law (as "state" is defined in 18 U.S.C. § 513) involving:

(A) any conduct prohibited by 18 U.S.C. chapter 109A and committed with a child;

(B) any conduct prohibited by 18 U.S.C. chapter 110;

(C) contact between any part of the defendant's body — or an object — and a child's genitals or anus;

(D) contact between the defendant's genitals or anus and any part of a child's body;

(E) deriving sexual pleasure or gratification from inflicting death, bodily injury, or physical pain on a child; or

(F) an attempt or conspiracy to engage in conduct described in subparagraphs (A)–(E).
(Effective 7-9-95; amended, eff 12-1-11)

Rule 415. Similar Acts in Civil Cases Involving Sexual Assault or Child Molestation

(a) Permitted Uses. In a civil case involving a claim for relief based on a party's alleged sexual assault or child molestation, the court may admit evidence that the party committed any other sexual assault or child molestation. The evidence may be considered as provided in Rules 413 and 414.

(b) Disclosure to the Opponent. If a party intends to offer this evidence, the party must disclose it to the party against whom it will be offered, including witnesses' statements or a summary of the expected testimony. The party must do so at least 15 days before trial or at a later time that the court allows for good cause.

(c) Effect on Other Rules. This rule does not limit the admission or consideration of evidence under any other rule.
(Effective 7-9-95; amended, eff 12-1-11)

ARTICLE V. PRIVILEGES

Rule 501. Privilege in General

The common law — as interpreted by United States courts in the light of reason and experience — governs a claim of privilege unless any of the following provides otherwise:

• the United States Constitution;

• a federal statute; or

• rules prescribed by the Supreme Court.
But in a civil case, state law governs privilege regarding a claim or defense for which state law supplies the rule of decision.
(Amended, eff 12-1-11)

Rule 502. Attorney-Client Privilege and Work Product; Limitations on Waiver

The following provisions apply, in the circumstances set out, to disclosure of a communication or information covered by the attorney-client privilege or work-product protection.

(a) Disclosure Made in a Federal Proceeding or to a Federal Office or Agency; Scope of a Waiver. When the disclosure is made in a federal proceeding or to a federal office or agency and waives the attorney-client privilege or work-product protection, the waiver extends to an undisclosed communication or information in a federal or state proceeding only if:

(1) the waiver is intentional;

(2) the disclosed and undisclosed communications or information concern the same subject matter; and

(3) they ought in fairness to be considered together.

(b) Inadvertent Disclosure. When made in a federal proceeding or to a federal office or agency, the disclosure does not operate as a waiver in a federal or state proceeding if:

(1) the disclosure is inadvertent;

(2) the holder of the privilege or protection took reasonable steps to prevent disclosure; and

(3) the holder promptly took reasonable steps to rectify the error, including (if applicable) following Federal Rule of Civil Procedure 26(b)(5)(B).

(c) Disclosure Made in a State Proceeding. When the disclosure is made in a state proceeding and is not the subject of a state-court order concerning waiver, the disclosure does not operate as a waiver in a federal proceeding if the disclosure:

(1) would not be a waiver under this rule if it had been made in a federal proceeding; or

(2) is not a waiver under the law of the state where the disclosure occurred.

(d) Controlling Effect of a Court Order. A federal court may order that the privilege or protection is not waived by disclosure connected with the litigation pending before the court — in which event the disclosure is also not a waiver in any other federal or state proceeding.

(e) Controlling Effect of a Party Agreement. An agreement on the effect of disclosure in a federal proceeding is binding only on the parties to the agreement, unless it is incorporated into a court order.

(f) Controlling Effect of this Rule. Notwithstanding Rules 101 and 1101, this rule applies to state proceedings and to federal court-annexed and federal court-mandated arbitration proceedings, in the circumstances set out in the rule. And notwithstanding Rule 501, this rule applies even if state law provides the rule of decision.

(g) Definitions. In this rule:

(1) "attorney-client privilege" means the protection that applicable law provides for confidential attorney-client communications; and

(2) "work-product protection" means the protection that applicable law provides for tangible material (or its intangible equivalent) prepared in anticipation of litigation or for trial.

(Effective 12-19-2008; amended, eff 12-1-11)

ARTICLE VI.
WITNESSES

Rule 601. Competency to Testify in General

Every person is competent to be a witness unless these rules provide otherwise. But in a civil case, state law governs the witness's competency regarding a claim or defense for which state law supplies the rule of decision.

(Amended, eff 12-1-11)

Rule 602. Need for Personal Knowledge

A witness may testify to a matter only if evidence is introduced sufficient to support a finding that the witness has personal knowledge of the matter. Evidence to prove personal knowledge may consist of the witness's own testimony. This rule does not apply to a witness's expert testimony under Rule 703.

(Amended, eff 10-1-87; 11-1-88; 12-1-11)

Rule 603. Oath or Affirmation to Testify Truthfully

Before testifying, a witness must give an oath or affirmation to testify truthfully. It must be in a form designed to impress that duty on the witness's conscience.

(Amended, eff 10-1-87; 12-1-11)

Rule 604. Interpreter

An interpreter must be qualified and must give an oath or affirmation to make a true translation.

(Amended, eff 10-1-87; 12-1-11)

Rule 605. Judge's Competency as a Witness

The presiding judge may not testify as a witness at the trial. A party need not object to preserve the issue.

(Amended, eff 12-1-11)

Rule 606. Juror's Competency as a Witness

(a) At the Trial. A juror may not testify as a witness before the other jurors at the trial. If a juror is called to testify, the court must give a party an opportunity to object outside the jury's presence.

(b) During an Inquiry into the Validity of a Verdict or Indictment.

(1) *Prohibited Testimony or Other Evidence.* During an inquiry into the validity of a verdict or indictment, a juror may not testify about any statement made or incident that occurred during the jury's deliberations; the effect of anything on that juror's or another juror's vote; or any juror's mental processes concerning the verdict or indictment. The court may not receive a juror's affidavit or evidence of a juror's statement on these matters.

(2) *Exceptions.* A juror may testify about whether:

(A) extraneous prejudicial information was improperly brought to the jury's attention;

(B) an outside influence was improperly brought to bear on any juror; or

(C) a mistake was made in entering the verdict on the verdict form.

(Amended, eff 10-1-87; 11-1-88; 12-1-03; 12-1-11)

Rule 607. Who May Impeach a Witness

Any party, including the party that called the witness, may attack the witness's credibility.

(Amended, eff 10-1-87; 12-1-11)

Rule 608. A Witness's Character for Truthfulness or Untruthfulness

(a) Reputation or Opinion Evidence. A witness's credibility may be attacked or supported by testimony about the witness's reputation for having a character for truthfulness or untruthfulness, or by testimony in the form of an opinion about that character. But evidence of truthful character is admissible only after the witness's character for truthfulness has been attacked.

(b) Specific Instances of Conduct. Except for a criminal conviction under Rule 609, extrinsic evidence is not admissible to prove specific instances of a witness's conduct in order to attack or support the witness's character for truthfulness. But the court may, on cross-examination, allow them to be inquired into if they are probative of the character for truthfulness or untruthfulness of:

(1) the witness; or

(2) another witness whose character the witness being cross-examined has testified about.

By testifying on another matter, a witness does not waive any privilege against self-incrimination for testimony that relates only to the witness's character for truthfulness.

(Amended, eff 10-1-87; 11-1-88; 12-1-03; 12-1-11)

Rule 609. Impeachment by Evidence of a Criminal Conviction

(a) In General. The following rules apply to attacking a witness's character for truthfulness by evidence of a criminal conviction:

(1) for a crime that, in the convicting jurisdiction, was punishable by death or by imprisonment for more than one year, the evidence:

(A) must be admitted, subject to Rule 403, in a civil case or in a criminal case in which the witness is not a defendant; and

(B) must be admitted in a criminal case in which the witness is a defendant, if the probative value of the evidence outweighs its prejudicial effect to that defendant; and

(2) for any crime regardless of the punishment, the evidence must be admitted if the court can readily determine that establishing the elements of the crime required proving — or the witness's admitting — a dishonest act or false statement.

(b) Limit on Using the Evidence After 10 Years. This subdivision (b) applies if more than 10 years have passed since the witness's conviction or release from confinement for it, whichever is later. Evidence of the conviction is admissible only if:

(1) its probative value, supported by specific facts and circumstances, substantially outweighs its prejudicial effect; and

(2) the proponent gives an adverse party reasonable written notice of the intent to use it so that the party has a fair opportunity to contest its use.

(c) Effect of a Pardon, Annulment, or Certificate of Rehabilitation. Evidence of a conviction is not admissible if:

(1) the conviction has been the subject of a pardon, annulment, certificate of rehabilitation, or other equivalent procedure based on a finding that the person has been rehabilitated, and the person has not been convicted of a later crime punishable by death or by imprisonment for more than one year; or

(2) the conviction has been the subject of a pardon, annulment, or other equivalent procedure based on a finding of innocence.

(d) Juvenile Adjudications. Evidence of a juvenile adjudication is admissible under this rule only if:

(1) it is offered in a criminal case;

(2) the adjudication was of a witness other than the defendant;

(3) an adult's conviction for that offense would be admissible to attack the adult's credibility; and

(4) admitting the evidence is necessary to fairly determine guilt or innocence.

(e) Pendency of an Appeal. A conviction that satisfies this rule is admissible even if an appeal is pending. Evidence of the pendency is also admissible.

(Amended, eff 10-1-87; 12-1-90; 12-1-06; 12-1-11)

Rule 610. Religious Beliefs or Opinions

Evidence of a witness's religious beliefs or opinions is not admissible to attack or support the witness's credibility.

(Amended, eff 10-1-87; 12-1-11)

Rule 611. Mode and Order of Examining Witnesses and Presenting Evidence

(a) Control by the Court; Purposes. The court should exercise reasonable control over the mode and order of examining witnesses and presenting evidence so as to:

(1) make those procedures effective for determining the truth;

(2) avoid wasting time; and

(3) protect witnesses from harassment or undue embarrassment.

(b) Scope of Cross-Examination. Cross-examination should not go beyond the subject matter of the direct examination and matters affecting the witness's credibility. The court may allow inquiry into additional matters as if on direct examination.

(c) Leading Questions. Leading questions should not be used on direct examination except as necessary to develop the witness's testimony. Ordinarily, the court should allow leading questions:

(1) on cross-examination; and

(2) when a party calls a hostile witness, an adverse party, or a witness identified with an adverse party.

(Amended, eff 10-1-87; 12-1-11)

Rule 612. Writing Used to Refresh a Witness's Memory

(a) Scope. This rule gives an adverse party certain options when a witness uses a writing to refresh memory:

(1) while testifying; or

(2) before testifying, if the court decides that justice requires the party to have those options.

(b) Adverse Party's Options; Deleting Unrelated Matter. Unless 18 U.S.C. § 3500 provides otherwise in a criminal case, an adverse party is entitled to have the writing produced at the hearing, to inspect it, to cross-examine the witness about it, and to introduce in evidence any portion that relates to the witness's testimony. If the producing party claims that the writing includes unrelated matter, the court must examine the writing in camera, delete any unrelated portion, and order that the rest be delivered to the adverse party. Any portion deleted over objection must be preserved for the record.

(c) Failure to Produce or Deliver the Writing. If a writing is not produced or is not delivered as ordered, the court may issue any appropriate order. But if the prosecution does not comply in a criminal case, the court must strike the witness's testimony or — if justice so requires — declare a mistrial.

(Amended, eff 10-1-87; 12-1-11)

Rule 613. Witness's Prior Statement

(a) Showing or Disclosing the Statement During Examination. When examining a witness about the witness's prior statement, a party need not show it or disclose its contents to the witness. But the party must, on request, show it or disclose its contents to an adverse party's attorney.

(b) Extrinsic Evidence of a Prior Inconsistent Statement. Extrinsic evidence of a witness's prior inconsistent statement is admissible only if the witness is given an opportunity to explain or deny the statement and an adverse party is given an opportunity to examine the witness about it, or if justice so requires. This subdivision (b) does not apply to an opposing party's statement under Rule 801(d)(2).

(Amended, eff 10-1-87; 11-1-88; 12-1-11)

Rule 614. Court's Calling or Examining a Witness

(a) Calling. The court may call a witness on its own or at a party's request. Each party is entitled to cross-examine the witness.

(b) Examining. The court may examine a witness regardless of who calls the witness.

(c) Objections. A party may object to the court's calling or examining a witness either at that time or at the next opportunity when the jury is not present.

(Amended, eff 12-1-11)

Rule 615. Excluding Witnesses

At a party's request, the court must order witnesses excluded so that they cannot hear other witnesses' testimony. Or the court may do so on its own. But this rule does not authorize excluding:

(a) a party who is a natural person;

(b) an officer or employee of a party that is not a natural person, after being designated as the party's representative by its attorney;

(c) a person whose presence a party shows to be essential to presenting the party's claim or defense; or

(d) a person authorized by statute to be present.

(Amended, eff 10-1-87; 11-1-88; 11-18-88; 12-1-98; 12-1-11)

ARTICLE VII.
OPINIONS AND EXPERT TESTIMONY

Rule 701. Opinion Testimony by Lay Witnesses

If a witness is not testifying as an expert, testimony in the form of an opinion is limited to one that is:

(a) rationally based on the witness's perception;

(b) helpful to clearly understanding the witness's testimony or to determining a fact in issue; and

(c) not based on scientific, technical, or other specialized knowledge within the scope of Rule 702.

(Amended, eff 10-1-87; 12-1-00; 12-1-11)

Rule 702. Testimony by Expert Witnesses

A witness who is qualified as an expert by knowledge, skill, experience, training, or education may testify in the form of an opinion or otherwise if:

(a) the expert's scientific, technical, or other specialized knowledge will help the trier of fact to understand the evidence or to determine a fact in issue;

(b) the testimony is based on sufficient facts or data;

(c) the testimony is the product of reliable principles and methods; and

(d) the expert has reliably applied the principles and methods to the facts of the case.

(Amended, eff 12-1-00; 12-1-11)

Rule 703. Bases of an Expert's Opinion Testimony

An expert may base an opinion on facts or data in the case that the expert has been made aware of or personally observed. If experts in the particular field would reasonably rely on those kinds of facts or data in forming an opinion on the subject, they need not be admissible for the opinion to be admitted. But if the facts or data would otherwise be inadmissible, the proponent of the opinion may disclose them to the jury only if their probative value in helping the jury evaluate the opinion substantially outweighs their prejudicial effect.

(Amended, eff 10-1-87; 12-1-00; 12-1-11)

Rule 704. Opinion on an Ultimate Issue

(a) In General — Not Automatically Objectionable. An opinion is not objectionable just because it embraces an ultimate issue.

(b) Exception. In a criminal case, an expert witness must not state an opinion about whether the defendant did or did not have a mental state or condition that constitutes an element of the crime charged or of a defense. Those matters are for the trier of fact alone.

(Amended, eff 10-12-84; 12-1-11)

Rule 705. Disclosing the Facts or Data Underlying an Expert's Opinion

Unless the court orders otherwise, an expert may state an opinion — and give the reasons for it — without first testifying to the underlying facts or data. But the expert may be required to disclose those facts or data on cross-examination.

(Amended, eff 10-1-87; 12-1-93; 12-1-11)

Rule 706. Court-Appointed Expert Witnesses

(a) Appointment Process. On a party's motion or on its own, the court may order the parties to show cause why expert witnesses should not be appointed and may ask the parties to submit nominations. The court may appoint any expert that the parties agree on and any of its own choosing. But the court may only appoint someone who consents to act.

(b) Expert's Role.   The court must inform the expert of the expert's duties. The court may do so in writing and have a copy filed with the clerk or may do so orally at a conference in which the parties have an opportunity to participate. The expert:

(1)   must advise the parties of any findings the expert makes;

(2)   may be deposed by any party;

(3)   may be called to testify by the court or any party; and

(4)   may be cross-examined by any party, including the party that called the expert.

(c) Compensation.   The expert is entitled to a reasonable compensation, as set by the court. The compensation is payable as follows:

(1)   in a criminal case or in a civil case involving just compensation under the Fifth Amendment, from any funds that are provided by law; and

(2)   in any other civil case, by the parties in the proportion and at the time that the court directs — and the compensation is then charged like other costs.

(d) Disclosing the Appointment to the Jury.   The court may authorize disclosure to the jury that the court appointed the expert.

(e) Parties' Choice of Their Own Experts.   This rule does not limit a party in calling its own experts.

(Amended, eff 10-1-87; 12-1-11)

ARTICLE VIII.
HEARSAY

Rule 801. Definitions That Apply to This Article; Exclusions from Hearsay

(a) Statement.   "Statement" means a person's oral assertion, written assertion, or nonverbal conduct, if the person intended it as an assertion.

(b) Declarant.   "Declarant" means the person who made the statement.

(c) Hearsay.   "Hearsay" means a statement that:

(1)   the declarant does not make while testifying at the current trial or hearing; and

(2)   a party offers in evidence to prove the truth of the matter asserted in the statement.

(d) Statements That Are Not Hearsay. A statement that meets the following conditions is not hearsay:

(1) *A Declarant-Witness's Prior Statement.*   The declarant testifies and is subject to cross-examination about a prior statement, and the statement:

(A)   is inconsistent with the declarant's testimony and was given under penalty of perjury at a trial, hearing, or other proceeding or in a deposition;

(B)   is consistent with the declarant's testimony and is offered to rebut an express or implied charge that the declarant recently fabricated it or acted from a recent improper influence or motive in so testifying; or

(C)   identifies a person as someone the declarant perceived earlier.

(2) *An Opposing Party's Statement.*   The statement is offered against an opposing party and:

(A)   was made by the party in an individual or representative capacity;

(B)   is one the party manifested that it adopted or believed to be true;

(C)   was made by a person whom the party authorized to make a statement on the subject;

(D)   was made by the party's agent or employee on a matter within the scope of that relationship and while it existed; or

(E)   was made by the party's coconspirator during and in furtherance of the conspiracy.

The statement must be considered but does not by itself establish the declarant's authority under (C); the existence or scope of the relationship under (D); or the existence of the conspiracy or participation in it under (E).

(Amended, eff 10-31-75; 10-1-87; 12-1-97; 12-1-11)

Rule 802. The Rule Against Hearsay

Hearsay is not admissible unless any of the following provides otherwise:

- a federal statute;
- these rules; or

• other rules prescribed by the Supreme Court.

(Amended, eff 12-1-11)

Rule 803. Exceptions to the Rule Against Hearsay — Regardless of Whether the Declarant Is Available as a Witness

The following are not excluded by the rule against hearsay, regardless of whether the declarant is available as a witness:

(1) *Present Sense Impression.* A statement describing or explaining an event or condition, made while or immediately after the declarant perceived it.

(2) *Excited Utterance.* A statement relating to a startling event or condition, made while the declarant was under the stress of excitement that it caused.

(3) *Then-Existing Mental, Emotional, or Physical Condition.* A statement of the declarant's then-existing state of mind (such as motive, intent, or plan) or emotional, sensory, or physical condition (such as mental feeling, pain, or bodily health), but not including a statement of memory or belief to prove the fact remembered or believed unless it relates to the validity or terms of the declarant's will.

(4) *Statement Made for Medical Diagnosis or Treatment.* A statement that:

(A) is made for — and is reasonably pertinent to — medical diagnosis or treatment; and

(B) describes medical history; past or present symptoms or sensations; their inception; or their general cause.

(5) *Recorded Recollection.* A record that:

(A) is on a matter the witness once knew about but now cannot recall well enough to testify fully and accurately;

(B) was made or adopted by the witness when the matter was fresh in the witness's memory; and

(C) accurately reflects the witness's knowledge.

If admitted, the record may be read into evidence but may be received as an exhibit only if offered by an adverse party.

(6) *Records of a Regularly Conducted Activity.* A record of an act, event, condition, opinion, or diagnosis if:

(A) the record was made at or near the time by — or from information transmitted by — someone with knowledge;

(B) the record was kept in the course of a regularly conducted activity of a business, organization, occupation, or calling, whether or not for profit;

(C) making the record was a regular practice of that activity;

(D) all these conditions are shown by the testimony of the custodian or another qualified witness, or by a certification that complies with Rule 902(11) or (12) or with a statute permitting certification; and

(E) neither the source of information nor the method or circumstances of preparation indicate a lack of trustworthiness.

(7) *Absence of a Record of a Regularly Conducted Activity.* Evidence that a matter is not included in a record described in paragraph (6) if:

(A) the evidence is admitted to prove that the matter did not occur or exist;

(B) a record was regularly kept for a matter of that kind; and

(C) neither the possible source of the information nor other circumstances indicate a lack of trustworthiness.

(8) *Public Records.* A record or statement of a public office if:

(A) it sets out:

(i) the office's activities;

(ii) a matter observed while under a legal duty to report, but not including, in a criminal case, a matter observed by law-enforcement personnel; or

(iii) in a civil case or against the government in a criminal case, factual findings from a legally authorized investigation; and

(B) neither the source of information nor other circumstances indicate a lack of trustworthiness.

(9) *Public Records of Vital Statistics.* A record of a birth, death, or marriage, if reported to a public office in accordance with a legal duty.

(10) *Absence of a Public Record.* Testimony — or a certification under Rule 902 — that a diligent search failed to disclose a public record or statement if the testimony or certification is admitted to prove that:

(A)   the record or statement does not exist; or

(B)   a matter did not occur or exist, if a public office regularly kept a record or statement for a matter of that kind.

(11) *Records of Religious Organizations Concerning Personal or Family History.* A statement of birth, legitimacy, ancestry, marriage, divorce, death, relationship by blood or marriage, or similar facts of personal or family history, contained in a regularly kept record of a religious organization.

(12) *Certificates of Marriage, Baptism, and Similar Ceremonies.* A statement of fact contained in a certificate:

(A)   made by a person who is authorized by a religious organization or by law to perform the act certified;

(B)   attesting that the person performed a marriage or similar ceremony or administered a sacrament; and

(C)   purporting to have been issued at the time of the act or within a reasonable time after it.

(13) *Family Records.* A statement of fact about personal or family history contained in a family record, such as a Bible, genealogy, chart, engraving on a ring, inscription on a portrait, or engraving on an urn or burial marker.

(14) *Records of Documents That Affect an Interest in Property.* The record of a document that purports to establish or affect an interest in property if:

(A)   the record is admitted to prove the content of the original recorded document, along with its signing and its delivery by each person who purports to have signed it;

(B)   the record is kept in a public office; and

(C)   a statute authorizes recording documents of that kind in that office.

(15) *Statements in Documents That Affect an Interest in Property.* A statement contained in a document that purports to establish or affect an interest in property if

the matter stated was relevant to the document's purpose — unless later dealings with the property are inconsistent with the truth of the statement or the purport of the document.

(16) *Statements in Ancient Documents.* A statement in a document that is at least 20 years old and whose authenticity is established.

(17) *Market Reports and Similar Commercial Publications.* Market quotations, lists, directories, or other compilations that are generally relied on by the public or by persons in particular occupations.

(18) *Statements in Learned Treatises, Periodicals, or Pamphlets.* A statement contained in a treatise, periodical, or pamphlet if:

(A)   the statement is called to the attention of an expert witness on cross-examination or relied on by the expert on direct examination; and

(B)   the publication is established as a reliable authority by the expert's admission or testimony, by another expert's testimony, or by judicial notice.

If admitted, the statement may be read into evidence but not received as an exhibit.

(19) *Reputation Concerning Personal or Family History.* A reputation among a person's family by blood, adoption, or marriage — or among a person's associates or in the community — concerning the person's birth, adoption, legitimacy, ancestry, marriage, divorce, death, relationship by blood, adoption, or marriage, or similar facts of personal or family history.

(20) *Reputation Concerning Boundaries or General History.* A reputation in a community — arising before the controversy — concerning boundaries of land in the community or customs that affect the land, or concerning general historical events important to that community, state, or nation.

(21) *Reputation Concerning Character.* A reputation among a person's associates or in the community concerning the person's character.

(22) *Judgment of a Previous Conviction.* Evidence of a final judgment of conviction if:

(A)   the judgment was entered after a trial

or guilty plea, but not a nolo contendere plea;

(B)   the conviction was for a crime punishable by death or by imprisonment for more than a year;

(C)   the evidence is admitted to prove any fact essential to the judgment; and

(D)   The pendency of an appeal may be shown but does not affect admissibility.

The pendency of an appeal may be shown but does not affect admissibility.

(23) *Judgments Involving Personal, Family, or General History, or a Boundary.* A judgment that is admitted to prove a matter of personal, family, or general history, or boundaries, if the matter:

(A)   was essential to the judgment; and

(B)   could be proved by evidence of reputation.

(24) *[Other Exceptions.]* [Transferred to Rule 807]

(Amended, eff 12-12-75; 10-1-87; 12-1-97; 12-1-00; 12-1-11)

Rule 804. Exceptions to the Rule Against Hearsay — When the Declarant Is Unavailable as a Witness

(a) Criteria for Being Unavailable. A declarant is considered to be unavailable as a witness if the declarant:

(1)   is exempted from testifying about the subject matter of the declarant's statement because the court rules that a privilege applies;

(2)   refuses to testify about the subject matter despite a court order to do so;

(3)   testifies to not remembering the subject matter;

(4)   cannot be present or testify at the trial or hearing because of death or a then-existing infirmity, physical illness, or mental illness; or

(5)   is absent from the trial or hearing and the statement's proponent has not been able, by process or other reasonable means, to procure:

(A)   the declarant's attendance, in the case of a hearsay exception under Rule 804(b)(1) or (6); or

(B)   the declarant's attendance or testimony, in the case of a hearsay exception under Rule 804(b)(2), (3), or (4).

But this subdivision (a) does not apply if the statement's proponent procured or wrongfully caused the declarant's unavailability as a witness in order to prevent the declarant from attending or testifying.

(b) The Exceptions.   The following are not excluded by the rule against hearsay if the declarant is unavailable as a witness:

(1) *Former Testimony.*   Testimony that:

(A)   was given as a witness at a trial, hearing, or lawful deposition, whether given during the current proceeding or a different one; an

(B)   is now offered against a party who had — or, in a civil case, whose predecessor in interest had — an opportunity and similar motive to develop it by direct, cross-, or redirect examination.

(2) *Statement Under the Belief of Imminent Death.*   In a prosecution for homicide or in a civil case, a statement that the declarant, while believing the declarant's death to be imminent, made about its cause or circumstances.

(3) *Statement Against Interest.*   A statement that:

(A)   a reasonable person in the declarant's position would have made only if the person believed it to be true because, when made, it was so contrary to the declarant's proprietary or pecuniary interest or had so great a tendency to invalidate the declarant's claim against someone else or to expose the declarant to civil or criminal liability; and

(B)   is supported by corroborating circumstances that clearly indicate its trustworthiness, if it is offered in a criminal case as one that tends to expose the declarant to criminal liability.

(4) *Statement of Personal or Family History.*   A statement about:

(A)   the declarant's own birth, adoption, legitimacy, ancestry, marriage, divorce, relationship by blood, adoption, or marriage, or similar facts of personal or family history, even though the declarant had no way of acquiring personal knowledge about that fact; or

(B)   another person concerning any of

these facts, as well as death, if the declarant was related to the person by blood, adoption, or marriage or was so intimately associated with the person's family that the declarant's information is likely to be accurate.

(5) *[Other Exceptions.]* [Transferred to Rule 807.]

(6) *Statement Offered Against a Party That Wrongfully Caused the Declarant's Unavailability.* A statement offered against a party that wrongfully caused — or acquiesced in wrongfully causing — the declarant's unavailability as a witness, and did so intending that result.

(Amended, eff 12-12-75; 10-1-87; 11-18-88; 12-1-97; 12-1-10; 12-1-11)

Rule 805. Hearsay Within Hearsay

Hearsay within hearsay is not excluded by the rule against hearsay if each part of the combined statements conforms with an exception to the rule.

(Amended, eff 12-1-11)

Rule 806. Attacking and Supporting the Declarant's Credibility

When a hearsay statement — or a statement described in Rule 801(d)(2)(C), (D), or (E) — has been admitted in evidence, the declarant's credibility may be attacked, and then supported, by any evidence that would be admissible for those purposes if the declarant had testified as a witness. The court may admit evidence of the declarant's inconsistent statement or conduct, regardless of when it occurred or whether the declarant had an opportunity to explain or deny it. If the party against whom the statement was admitted calls the declarant as a witness, the party may examine the declarant on the statement as if on cross-examination.

(Amended, eff 10-1-87; 12-1-97; 12-1-11)

Rule 807. Residual Exception

(a) **In General.**   Under the following circumstances, a hearsay statement is not excluded by the rule against hearsay even if the statement is not specifically covered by a hearsay exception in Rule 803 or 804:

(1) the statement has equivalent circumstantial guarantees of trustworthiness;

(2) it is offered as evidence of a material fact;

(3) it is more probative on the point for which it is offered than any other evidence that the proponent can obtain through reasonable efforts; and

(4) admitting it will best serve the purposes of these rules and the interests of justice.

(b) **Notice.**   The statement is admissible only if, before the trial or hearing, the proponent gives an adverse party reasonable notice of the intent to offer the statement and its particulars, including the declarant's name and address, so that the party has a fair opportunity to meet it.

(Effective 12-1-97; amended, eff 12-1-11)

ARTICLE IX. AUTHENTICATION AND IDENTIFICATION

Rule 901. Authenticating or Identifying Evidence

(a) **In General.**   To satisfy the requirement of authenticating or identifying an item of evidence, the proponent must produce evidence sufficient to support a finding that the item is what the proponent claims it is.

(b) **Examples.**   The following are examples only — not a complete list — of evidence that satisfies the requirement:

(1) *Testimony of a Witness with Knowledge.* Testimony that an item is what it is claimed to be.

(2) *Nonexpert Opinion About Handwriting.* A nonexpert's opinion that handwriting is genuine, based on a familiarity with it that was not acquired for the current litigation.

(3) *Comparison by an Expert Witness or the Trier of Fact.* A comparison with an authenticated specimen by an expert witness or the trier of fact.

(4) *Distinctive Characteristics and the Like.* The appearance, contents, substance, internal patterns, or other distinctive characteristics of the item, taken together with all the circumstances.

(5) *Opinion About a Voice.* An opinion identifying a person's voice — whether heard firsthand or through mechanical or electronic transmission or recording — based on hearing the voice at any time under circumstances that connect it with the alleged speaker.

(6) *Evidence About a Telephone Conversation.* For a telephone conversation, evidence that a call was made to the number assigned at the time to:

(A) a particular person, if circumstances, including self-identification, show that the person answering was the one called; or

(B) a particular business, if the call was made to a business and the call related to business reasonably transacted over the telephone.

(7) *Evidence About Public Records.* Evidence that:

(A) a document was recorded or filed in a public office as authorized by law; or

(B) a purported public record or statement is from the office where items of this kind are kept.

(8) *Evidence About Ancient Documents or Data Compilations.* For a document or data compilation, evidence that it:

(A) is in a condition that creates no suspicion about its authenticity;

(B) was in a place where, if authentic, it would likely be; and

(C) is at least 20 years old when offered.

(9) *Evidence About a Process or System.* Evidence describing a process or system and showing that it produces an accurate result.

(10) *Methods Provided by a Statute or Rule.* Any method of authentication or identification allowed by a federal statute or a rule prescribed by the Supreme Court.

(Amended, eff 12-1-11)

Rule 902. Evidence That Is Self-Authenticating

The following items of evidence are self-authenticating; they require no extrinsic evidence of authenticity in order to be admitted:

(1) *Domestic Public Documents That Are Sealed and Signed.* A document that bears:

(A) a seal purporting to be that of the United States; any state, district, commonwealth, territory, or insular possession of the United States; the former Panama Canal Zone; the Trust Territory of the Pacific Islands; a political subdivision of any of these entities; or a department, agency, or officer of any entity named above; and

(B) a signature purporting to be an execution or attestation.

(2) *Domestic Public Documents That Are Not Sealed but Are Signed and Certified.* A document that bears no seal if:

(A) it bears the signature of an officer or employee of an entity named in Rule 902(1)(A); and

(B) another public officer who has a seal and official duties within that same entity certifies under seal — or its equivalent — that the signer has the official capacity and that the signature is genuine.

(3) *Foreign Public Documents.* A document that purports to be signed or attested by a person who is authorized by a foreign country's law to do so. The document must be accompanied by a final certification that certifies the genuineness of the signature and official position of the signer or attester — or of any foreign official whose certificate of genuineness relates to the signature or attestation or is in a chain of certificates of genuineness relating to the signature or attestation. The certification may be made by a secretary of a United States embassy or legation; by a consul general, vice consul, or consular agent of the United States; or by a diplomatic or consular official of the foreign country assigned or accredited to the United States. If all parties have been given a reasonable opportunity to investigate the document's authenticity and accuracy, the court may, for good cause, either:

(A) order that it be treated as presumptively authentic without final certification; or

(B) allow it to be evidenced by an attested summary with or without final certification.

(4) *Certified Copies of Public Records.* A copy of an official record — or a copy of a document that was recorded or filed in a public office as authorized by law — if the copy is certified as correct by:

(A) the custodian or another person authorized to make the certification; or

(B) a certificate that complies with Rule 902(1), (2), or (3), a federal statute, or a rule prescribed by the Supreme Court.

(5) *Official Publications.* A book, pamphlet, or other publication purporting to be issued by a public authority.

(6) *Newspapers and Periodicals.* Printed material purporting to be a newspaper or periodical.

(7) *Trade Inscriptions and the Like.* An inscription, sign, tag, or label purporting to have been affixed in the course of business and indicating origin, ownership, or control.

(8) *Acknowledged Documents.* A document accompanied by a certificate of acknowledgment that is lawfully executed by a notary public or another officer who is authorized to take acknowledgments.

(9) *Commercial Paper and Related Documents.* Commercial paper, a signature on it, and related documents, to the extent allowed by general commercial law.

(10) *Presumptions Under a Federal Statute.* A signature, document, or anything else that a federal statute declares to be presumptively or prima facie genuine or authentic.

(11) *Certified Domestic Records of a Regularly Conducted Activity.* The original or a copy of a domestic record that meets the requirements of Rule 803(6)(A)-(C), as shown by a certification of the custodian or another qualified person that complies with a federal statute or a rule prescribed by the Supreme Court. Before the trial or hearing, the proponent must give an adverse party reasonable written notice of the intent to offer the record — and must make the record and certification available for inspection — so that the party has a fair opportunity to challenge them.

(12) *Certified Foreign Records of a Regularly Conducted Activity.* In a civil case, the original or a copy of a foreign record that meets the requirements of Rule 902(11), modified as follows: the certification, rather than complying with a federal statute or Supreme Court rule, must be signed in a manner that, if falsely made, would subject the maker to a criminal penalty in the country where the certification is signed. The proponent must also meet the notice requirements of Rule 902(11).

(Amended effective 10-1-87; 11-1-88; 12-1-00; 12-1-11)

Rule 903. Subscribing Witness's Testimony

A subscribing witness's testimony is neces-sary to authenticate a writing only if required by the law of the jurisdiction that governs its validity.

(Amended eff 12-1-11)

ARTICLE X.
CONTENTS OF WRITINGS, RECORDINGS, AND PHOTOGRAPHS

Rule 1001. Definitions That Apply to This Article

In this article:

(a) A "writing" consists of letters, words, numbers, or their equivalent set down in any form.

(b) A "recording" consists of letters, words, numbers, or their equivalent recorded in any manner.

(c) A "photograph" means a photographic image or its equivalent stored in any form.

(d) An "original" of a writing or recording means the writing or recording itself or any counterpart intended to have the same effect by the person who executed or issued it. For electronically stored information, "original" means any printout — or other output readable by sight — if it accurately reflects the information. An "original" of a photograph includes the negative or a print from it.

(e) A "duplicate" means a counterpart produced by a mechanical, photographic, chemical, electronic, or other equivalent process or technique that accurately reproduces the original.

(Amended eff 12-1-11)

Rule 1002. Requirement of the Original

An original writing, recording, or photograph is required in order to prove its content unless these rules or a federal statute provides otherwise.

(Amended eff 12-1-11)

Rule 1003. Admissibility of Duplicates

A duplicate is admissible to the same extent as the original unless a genuine question is raised about the original's authenticity or the circumstances make it unfair to admit the duplicate.

(Amended eff 12-1-11)

Rule 1004. Admissibility of Other Evidence of Content

An original is not required and other evidence of the content of a writing, recording, or photograph is admissible if:

(a) all the originals are lost or destroyed, and not by the proponent acting in bad faith;

(b) an original cannot be obtained by any available judicial process;

(c) the party against whom the original would be offered had control of the original; was at that time put on notice, by pleadings or otherwise, that the original would be a subject of proof at the trial or hearing; and fails to produce it at the trial or hearing; or

(d) the writing, recording, or photograph is not closely related to a controlling issue.

(Amended, eff 10-1-87; 12-1-11)

Rule 1005. Copies of Public Records to Prove Content

The proponent may use a copy to prove the content of an official record — or of a document that was recorded or filed in a public office as authorized by law — if these conditions are met: the record or document is otherwise admissible; and the copy is certified as correct in accordance with Rule 902(4) or is testified to be correct by a witness who has compared it with the original. If no such copy can be obtained by reasonable diligence, then the proponent may use other evidence to prove the content.

(Amended, eff 12-1-11)

Rule 1006. Summaries to Prove Content

The proponent may use a summary, chart, or calculation to prove the content of voluminous writings, recordings, or photographs that cannot be conveniently examined in court. The proponent must make the originals or duplicates available for examination or copying, or both, by other parties at a reasonable time and place. And the court may order the proponent to produce them in court.

(Amended, eff 12-1-11)

Rule 1007. Testimony or Statement of a Party to Prove Content

The proponent may prove the content of a writing, recording, or photograph by the testimony, deposition, or written statement of the party against whom the evidence is offered. The proponent need not account for the original.

(Amended, eff 10-1-87; 12-1-11)

Rule 1008. Functions of the Court and Jury

Ordinarily, the court determines whether the proponent has fulfilled the factual conditions for admitting other evidence of the content of a writing, recording, or photograph under Rule 1004 or 1005. But in a jury trial, the jury determines — in accordance with Rule 104(b) — any issue about whether:

(a) an asserted writing, recording, or photograph ever existed;

(b) another one produced at the trial or hearing is the original; or

(c) other evidence of content accurately reflects the content.

(Amended, eff 12-1-11)

ARTICLE XI.
MISCELLANEOUS RULES

Rule 1101. Applicability of the Rules

(a) To Courts and Judges. These rules apply to proceedings before:

• United States district courts;

• United States bankruptcy and magistrate judges;

• United States courts of appeals;

• the United States Court of Federal Court Claims; and

• the District courts of Guam, the Virgin Islands, and the Northern Mariana Islands.

(b) To Cases and Proceedings. These rules apply in:

• civil cases and proceedings, including bankruptcy, admiralty and maritime cases;

• criminal cases and proceedings; and

• contempt proceedings, except those in which the court may act summarily.

(c) Rules on Privilege. The rules on privilege apply to all stages of a case or proceeding.

(d) Exceptions. The rules — except for those on privilege — do not apply to the following:

(1) The court's determination, under Rule 104(a), on a preliminary question of a fact governing admissibility;

(2) grand-jury proceedings;

(3) miscellaneous proceedings such as:

• extradition or rendition;

• issuing an arrest warrant, criminal summons, or search warrant;

• a preliminary examination in a criminal case;

• sentencing;

• granting or revoking probation or supervised release; and

• considering whether to release on bail or otherwise.

(e) Other Statutes and Rules. A federal statute or a rule prescribed by the Supreme Court may provide for admitting or excluding evidence independently from these rules.

(Amended, eff 12-12-75; 10-1-79; 10-1-82; 10-1-87; 11-1-88; 11-18-88; 12-1-93; 12-1-11)

Rule 1102. Amendments

These rules may be amended as provided in 28 U.S.C. § 2072.

(Amended, eff 12-1-91; 12-1-11)

Rule 1103. Title

These rules may be cited as the Federal Rules of Evidence.

(Amended, eff 12-1-11)

ARTICLE I.
GENERAL PROVISIONS

Synopsis

§ 106.1   Function and Purpose of the Rule

Chapter 101

Rule 101. Scope; Definitions

Rule 101. Scope; Definitions

(a) **Scope.** These rules apply to proceedings in United States courts. The specific courts and proceedings to which the rules apply, along with exceptions, are set out in Rule 1101.

(b) **Definitions.** In these rules:

    (1) "civil case" means a civil action or proceeding;

    (2) "criminal case" includes a criminal proceeding;

    (3) "public office" includes a public agency;

    (4) "record" includes a memorandum, report, or data compilation;

    (5) a "rule prescribed by the Supreme Court" means a rule adopted by the Supreme Court under statutory authority; and

    (6) a reference to any kind of written material or any other medium includes electronically stored information.

---

§ 101.1   General Applicability

Rule 101 is fundamentally a statement of the scope of the Federal Rules of Evidence. Rule 101 provides that, as a general principle, the Federal Rules of Evidence apply in all courts of the United States as well as in proceedings before United States magistrates.[1] Rule 1101 must be consulted to determine the particular limitations and refinements of this statement.[2]

Rule 101 is designed to contain a general introduction to the applicability of the Rules of Evidence. The intent of the drafters was to provide detail in Rule 1101. Consequently, specific exceptions are set forth at the end of the

---

[1] *See generally,* 1 WEINSTEIN'S FEDERAL EVIDENCE §§ 101.01–101.03; 1 MUELLER & KIRKPATRICK, § 1. *See also* Degnan, *The Law of Federal Evidence Reform,* 76 HARV. L. REV. 275 (1962); Goldberg, *The Supreme Court, Congress, and Rules of Evidence,* 5 SETON HALL L. REV. 667 (Spring, 1974); Powell and Burns, *A Discussion of the New Federal Rules of Evidence,* 8 GONZ. L. REV. 1 (1972); Weinberg, *Choice of Law and the Proposed Federal Rules of Evidence: New Perspectives,* 122 U. PA. L. REV. 594 (1974).

[2] *See* the discussion of Rule 1101, *infra,* at Chapter 1101.

Rules where, as the Advisory Committee has stated, they "will not discourage the reader of the rules by confronting him at the outset with a rule filled with minute detail."[3]

It should be noted that the Rules of Evidence generally apply in both civil and criminal cases and in both jury and bench trials.

---

[3] Rule 101, Advisory Committee Note to first draft. *See* Chapter 1101 for a discussion of the specific exceptions to the applicability of the Rules of Evidence.

Chapter 102

Rule 102. Purpose

Rule 102. Purpose

These rules should be construed so as to administer every proceeding fairly, eliminate unjustifiable expense and delay, and promote the development of evidence law, to the end of ascertaining the truth and securing a just determination.

---

§ 102.1   In General

Rule 102 directs courts to apply a construction to the Rules of Evidence that will attain the stated goals of fairness to the parties and the elimination of unjustifiable expense and delay.[1] The Rule also provides courts with at least limited power to supplement the Rules of Evidence through case law to ensure growth and refinement of the Rules of Evidence in order that truth may be ascertained and fair results obtained.[2] By granting a certain degree of discretion to the trial court in admitting evidence, at least in areas where the rules have not plainly spoken, the drafters tacitly recognized that the inflexible application of any system of rules may result in unfairness.

A system of rules that does not allow for some discretion on the part of a

---

[1] *See generally,* 1 WEINSTEIN'S FEDERAL EVIDENCE §§ 102.02–102.06; 1 MUELLER & KIRKPATRICK, §§ 2–3. *See also* Weissenberger, *Are the Federal Rules of Evidence a Statute?* 55 OHIO ST. L. J. 393 (1994); Weissenberger, *The Supreme Court and the Interpretation of the Federal Rules of Evidence,* 53 OHIO ST. L. J. 1307 (1992); Imwinkelried, *A Brief Defense of the Supreme Court's Approach to the Interpretation of the Federal Rules of Evidence,* 27 IND. L. REV. 267 (1993); Christian, *The Proposed Federal Rules of Evidence,* 33 FED. B.J. 96 (1974); Rothstein, *The Proposed Amendments to the Federal Rules of Evidence,* 62 GEO. L.J. 125 (1973); Ladd, *Some Highlights of the New Federal Rules of Evidence,* 1 FLA. ST. U. L. REV. 191 (1973); Atkins, *Significant Changes in the Proposed Federal Rules of Evidence,* 9 FORUM 175 (1973).

[2] *See* United States v. Bibbs, 564 F.2d 1165 (5th Cir. 1977) (court is free to fashion an evidentiary procedure with regard to subsequent inconsistent statements that will accord with objectives of Rule 102); United States v. King, 73 F.R.D. 103 (E.D.N.Y. 1977) (reliance on Rule 102 to hold that the need for full revelation of all pertinent evidence was the most powerful factor in privilege matter); *see also In re* Richter & Phillips Jewelers & Distrib., 31 B.R. 512 (Bankr. Ct. Ohio 1983) (after stating reasons for admitting into evidence an original check stamped "Paid" under Rule 803(6) and (24), the court also cited Rule 102, to refuse to admit the check would thwart the general purpose of the rules and the interests of justice).

trial judge in making evidentiary rulings lays the groundwork for its own obsolescence. As methods of communication and interaction between individuals change, the Rules of Evidence must accommodate this progress. Rule 102 is designed to ensure the continued viability of the Federal Rules of Evidence by providing that the evidence as to the disputed relationship between the parties is available to the trier of fact.

Rule 102 relies on the discretion of the trial court to fulfill its stated objectives. The court's discretion is, of course, subject to review under Rule 103.[3]

§ 102.2   Interpretation and Construction

The proper method for interpreting the Federal Rules of Evidence is a subject open to debate.[4] In one sense, the Rules are a product of Congressional action, and hence should be interpreted according to normal principles of statutory interpretation. On the other hand, the Rules are the end product of centuries of common-law development. When Congress enacted the Federal Rules, its primary role was to review and ratify laws developed by the judiciary.[5] Because of the special nature of the Federal Rules, Professor Edward Cleary believed that the meaning of the Rules could not be understood without reference to their historical background and drafting history.[6]

Despite this argument, the primary approach employed by the Supreme Court in deciding interpretive questions about the Federal Rules of Evidence

---

[3] *See, e.g.,* United States v. Thorne, 547 F.2d 56 (8th Cir. 1976) (rules permit exercise of discretion by trial judge in finding witness rehabilitated, and therefore limiting cross-examination under Rule 609 so as to implement objectives of Rule 102); *see also* Weinstein & Berger, *Basic Rules of Relevancy in the Proposed Federal Rules of Evidence,* 4 GA. L. REV. 43 (1969).

[4] *See* CARLSON ET AL., EVIDENCE: TEACHING MATERIALS FOR AN AGE OF SCIENCE AND STATUTES 24 (4th ed. 1997); *see also* Becker & Orenstein, *The Federal Rules of Evidence after Sixteen Years,* 60 GEO. WASH. L. REV. 857 (1992); Imwinkelried, *A Brief Defense of the Supreme Court's Approach to the Federal Rules of Evidence,* 27 IND. L. REV. 267 (1993); Jonakait, *The Supreme Court, Plain Meaning, and the Changed Rules of Evidence,* 68 TEX. L. REV. 745 (1990) [hereinafter Jonakait, *Supreme Court, Plain Meaning*]; Jonakait, *Text, Texts, or Ad Hoc Determinations: Interpretation of the Federal Rules of Evidence,* 71 IND. L.J. 551, 557 (1996) [hereinafter Jonakait, *Text, Texts, or Ad Hoc Determinations*]; Scallen, *Classical Rhetoric, Practical Reasoning and the Law of Evidence,* 44 AM. U. L. REV. 1717 (1995); Taslitz, *Interpretive Method and the Federal Rules of Evidence: A Call for a Politically Realistic Hermeneutics,* 32 HARV. J. ON LEGIS. 329 (1995); Weissenberger, *The Supreme Court and the Interpretation of the Federal Rules of Evidence,* 52 OHIO ST. L.J. 1307 (1992).

[5] *See* Weissenberger, *The Supreme Court and the Interpretation of the Federal Rules of Evidence,* 52 OHIO ST. L.J. 1307, 1309 (1992).

[6] *See* CARLSON ET AL., EVIDENCE: TEACHING MATERIALS FOR AN AGE OF SCIENCE AND STATUTES 24 (4th ed. 1997); *see also* Cleary, *Preliminary Notes on Reading the Rules of Evidence,* 57 NEB. L. REV. 908 (1978).

has been a textual or plain meaning approach. Under the plain meaning approach, the plain language of a Rule controls the interpretation of that Rule. As the Court stated in *Caminetti v. United States* in formulating the plain meaning approach, "[i]f the words are plain, they give meaning to the act, and it is neither the duty nor the privilege of the courts to enter speculative fields in search of a different meaning."[7] However, the Supreme Court has not always rigidly applied plain meaning to the Federal Rules. For a time at least, the Court apparently "adopted a moderate textualist approach to the construction of the Rules."[8] This moderate position suggested that the plain language of a Rule controls unless the result would be either absurd or unconstitutional.[9] The moderate approach would also allow for a limited inquiry into legislative history; where that history clearly indicates that legislators intended a different meaning than the plain meaning, the intended meaning will prevail.[10]

For a time, it appeared that the Court was willing to adopt a moderate approach under which even the plain language of a rule would not always be decisive, at least not in extreme cases where such a reading would lead to absurd results. As recently as 1989, in the case of *Green v. Bock Laundry Machine Co.,* the Court refused to literally apply the plain meaning of Rule 609 (as it was then written) in a civil case, as the result would have arbitrarily favored civil defendants over civil plaintiffs. The Court announced its unwillingness to enforce a rule that "can't mean what it says."[11]

It is not clear, however, whether the Court's decision in *Green* is still an accurate reflection of the Court's willingness to engage in a moderate construction of the rules. It has been more than a decade since *Green* was decided, and not once since 1989 has the Court been willing to disregard the plain meaning of any rule of Evidence or Procedure. On the contrary, other recent decisions have suggested an uncompromising commitment to attaching controlling significance to the text of any rule that is written in plain language. For example, in *Bourjaily v. United States*, the Court, basing its decision on the plain meaning of Rules 104 and 801(d)(2)(E), held that the Rules eliminated the requirement of independent corroboration of the

---

[7] Caminetti v. United States, 242 U.S. 470, 490 (1917).

[8] Imwinkelried, *A Brief Defense of the Supreme Court's Approach to the Federal Rules of Evidence,* 27 IND. L. REV. 267 (1993).

[9] *See* Green v. Bock Laundry Machine Co., 490 U.S. 504 (1989).

[10] *See* Jonakait, *The Supreme Court, Plain Meaning, and the Changed Rules of Evidence,* 68 TEX. L. REV. 745, 746–747 (1990). *See, e.g.,* United States v. Dowdell, 595 F.3d 50 (1st Cir. 2010) (a Federal Rule of Evidence need not be interpreted in accordance with its plain language, if a literal and unqualified enforcement of the rule would violate its plain purpose; a court should go beyond the literal language of a statute if reliance on that language would defeat the plain purpose of the statute).

[11] Green v. Bock Laundry Machine Co., 490 U.S. 504 (1989).

existence of a conspiracy before a conspirator's statement can be admitted under the hearsay rules.[12] Plain meaning analysis was also used in *Huddleston v. United States,* to hold that evidence of other acts under Rule 404(b) was admissible so long as the jury could reasonably conclude that the act had occurred. The Court refused to apply the common-law tradition requiring a preliminary showing that the other act actually occurred before the evidence could be admitted because the language of the Rules does not require such a showing.[13] In *United States v. Owens,* the Court interpreted Rule 801(d)(1)(C), which allows the admission of an out-of-court identification as long as the declarant is subject to cross-examination about the identification. Applying the "natural reading" of the Rule, the Supreme Court held that as long as the declarant was present and available to answer questions, even though he could not provide any meaningful answers due to memory loss, then he was subject to cross about the identification.[14]

In *Daubert v. Merrell Dow Pharmaceuticals, Inc.,* the Court employed a plain meaning approach to hold that the common-law *Frye* test controlling the admission of novel scientific evidence was no longer applicable following the adoption of the Federal Rules. The Supreme Court noted that nowhere does the text of Rule 702 mention the words "general acceptance," the *Frye* standard, as a prerequisite for admissibility. The Court supported its decision by referring to the liberal policy underlying the Rules and the general policy relaxing traditional barriers to expert testimony. In place of the *Frye* test, the Court created the reliability standard, which, as one commentator suggests, while arguably consonant with the plain text of the Rules, is not mandated by their language.[15]

These cases show that the Court favors the plain language of the Rules, and that the plain language enjoys a place of preeminence that is not set aside even in the face of overwhelming common-law tradition to the contrary.

Rule 102 clearly affords the district judge some discretion in interpreting ambiguous rules of evidence, or in choosing among reasonable alternative interpretations of a rule. But it would be a mistake to regard Rule 102 as a

---

[12] Bourjaily v. United States, 483 U.S. 171 (1987); *see also* Becker & Orenstein, *The Federal Rules of Evidence after Sixteen Years,* 60 GEO. WASH. L. REV. 857, 864–865 (1992).

[13] *See* Huddleston v. United States, 485 U.S. 681 (1988); *see also* Jonakait, *The Supreme Court, Plain Meaning, and the Changed Rules of Evidence,* 68 TEX. L. REV. 745, 752–755 (1990).

[14] *See* United States v. Owens, 484 U.S. 554 (1988); *see also* Jonakait, *The Supreme Court, Plain Meaning, and the Changed Rules of Evidence,* 68 TEX. L. REV. 745, 755–757 (1990).

[15] *See* Daubert v. Merrell Dow Pharmaceuticals, Inc., 509 U.S. 579 (1993); *see also* Jonakait, *Text, Texts, or Ad Hoc Determinations: Interpretation of the Federal Rules of Evidence,* 71 IND. L.J. 551, 557–559 (1996).

license for a district judge to disregard or overlook the plain language of rules that are unambiguous. The Federal Rules of Criminal Procedure contain a virtually identical provision as an aid to their construction, declaring that "These rules are intended to provide for the just determination of every criminal proceeding. They shall be construed to secure simplicity in procedure, fairness in administration, and the elimination of unjustifiable expense and delay."[16] Despite that seeming grant of flexibility and discretion, however, the Supreme Court has held that such interpretive principles could not be used by the district judge to excuse the late filing of a defendant's motion for a judgment of acquittal, in violation of a rule requiring that such motions be filed "within seven days" after the jury is discharged, even though the motion was filed only one day late because of attorney error.[17] Despite the existence of compelling factors arguing in favor of a lenient enforcement of the seven-day requirement, the Supreme Court held that the functional equivalent of Federal Rule of Evidence 102 "sets forth a principle of interpretation to be used in construing ambiguous rules, not a principle of law superseding clear rules that do not achieve the stated objectives."[18]

For more than a decade, the Court has never once construed a Rule of Evidence in a way that would violate or contradict its plain language. But the Court has been willing to look to considerations of legal history and policy in adopting interpretations of rules that supplement or go beyond the literal terms of their plain language. For example, in *Tome v. United States,* the Supreme Court, interpreting Rule 801(d)(1)(B), looked beyond the plain language of the Rule to determine its meaning.[19] The Court looked to the common law, the similarity between the language of the Rule and that used in many pre-Rule cases, and the Advisory Committee Note to determine the proper interpretation. From this analysis, the Court concluded that the Rule codified the common-law requirement that the statement offered to rebut a charge of recent fabrication must have been made before the declarant's

---

[16] Fed. R. Crim. Proc. 2.

[17] Carlisle v. United States, 517 U.S. 416 (1996).

[18] *Carlisle,* 517 U.S. at 424 (interpreting Fed. R. Crim. Proc. 2). The Court reached this result despite an extraordinary collection of facts weighing in favor of a lenient interpretation of the rules: the motion for judgment of acquittal was filed only one day late, the delay was the result of attorney error, the conviction (conspiracy to distribute marijuana) was for a serious offense, and the district judge — who was willing to forgive the late filing — found there was insufficient evidence of guilt to support the jury's verdict and that the denial of the motion would result in "grave injustice." *Id.* at 419. Despite all this, the Supreme Court ruled that the plain language of the Rules of Criminal Procedure could not be bent in the slightest, not even to release a possibly innocent man from prison, despite the Rules' admonition that they be interpreted to comport with fairness and justice.

[19] *See* Tome v. United States, 513 U.S. 150 (1995).

motive to fabricate evidence arose, although the Rule does not mention the pre-motive requirement.[20]

The justices of the Supreme Court have not always spoken with one voice in deciding how much weight to give to the Advisory Committee Notes as a guide to interpreting the rules. Although Justice Scalia has argued that the notes ought to be given no weight,[21] the Court has been willing to give at least some weight to those Notes "as a reliable source of insight into the meaning of a rule,"[22] at least when construing a rule that is ambiguous. But the Notes are not authoritative, however, and there are times when "the policy expressed in the Rule's text points clearly enough in one direction that it outweighs whatever force the Notes may have."[23]

For the most part, the Supreme Court has adopted a moderate textualistic approach to interpreting the Federal Rules of Evidence, departing from the plain language of the Rule only in cases where a contrary legislative intent is clearly expressed in the Rule's drafting history. Although the Advisory Committee Notes and even the common-law precedents may provide guidance in some cases, at least when construing ambiguous rules, the Court appears to have embraced an interpretive scheme that affords a strong (if not conclusive) presumption that any clear and unambiguous Rules must be interpreted according to their plain meaning.[24]

---

[20] *See Tome*, 513 U.S. at 156–163.

[21] Green v. Bock Laundry Machine Co., 490 U.S. 504, 528 (1989) (Scalia, J., concurring in judgment).

[22] United States v. Vonn, 535 U.S. 55, 64, n.6 (2002) (construing the Federal Rules of Criminal Procedure; "In the absence of a clear legislative mandate, the Advisory Committee Notes provide a reliable source of insight into the meaning of a rule, especially when, as here, the rule was enacted precisely as the Advisory Committee proposed . . . . Although the Notes are the product of the Advisory Committee, and not Congress, they are transmitted to Congress before the Rule is enacted into law"); *see also* Schiavone v. Fortune, 477 U.S. 21, 31 (1986) (Committee Notes are to be given some weight).

[23] Williamson v. United States, 512 U.S. 594 (1994).

[24] *See* CARLSON ET AL., EVIDENCE: TEACHING MATERIALS FOR AN AGE OF SCIENCE AND STATUTES 24, 30 (4th ed. 1997).

Chapter 103

Rule 103. Rulings on Evidence

Rule 103. Rulings on Evidence

(a) **Preserving a Claim of Error.** A party may claim error in a ruling to admit or exclude evidence only if the error affects a substantial right of the party and:

   (1) if the ruling admits evidence, a party, on the record:

      (A) timely objects or moves to strike; and

      (B) states the specific ground, unless it was apparent from the context; or

   (2) if the ruling excludes evidence, a party informs the court of its substance by an offer of proof, unless the substance was apparent from the context.

(b) **Not Needing to Renew an Objection or Offer of Proof.** Once the court rules definitively on the record — either before or at trial — a party need not renew an objection or offer of proof to preserve a claim of error for appeal.

(c) **Court's Statement About the Ruling; Directing an Offer of Proof.** The court may make any statement about the character or form of the evidence, the objection made, and the ruling. The court may direct that an offer of proof be made in question-and-answer form.

(d) **Preventing the Jury from Hearing Inadmissible Evidence.** To the extent practicable, the court must conduct a jury trial so that inadmissible evidence is not suggested to the jury by any means.

(e) **Taking Notice of Plain Error.** A court may take notice of a plain error affecting a substantial right, even if the claim of error was not properly preserved.

---

§ 103.1   Rulings on Evidence — In General

Rule 103 embodies the general procedures pertaining to appellate review of errors in evidentiary rulings.[1] It should be noted that the Rule addresses

---

[1] *See generally,* 1 McCormick §§ 51–52, 55, 58, 59; 2 McCormick § 351; 1 Weinstein's Federal Evidence §§ 103.01–103.43; 1 Mueller & Kirkpatrick §§ 4–23; 1

only the issue of identifying evidentiary rulings that are subject to review, and does not provide substantive standards governing the circumstances under which a reversal is required. A ruling on the admissibility of evidence is entitled to great deference on appeal, and will only be set aside if the lower court's ruling was an abuse of discretion,[2] which is only the case if the district judge's application of the rules was "arbitrary and irrational."[3] A mistaken *interpretation* of one of the Federal Rules of Evidence, on the other hand, is always an abuse of discretion because "[a] district court by definition abuses its discretion when it makes an error of law."[4]

Rule 103 is unique among the Federal Rules of Evidence, most of which only concern the law governing the kinds of evidence that are admissible at the trial. Rule 103, by contrast, is primarily written for lawyers and judges involved with appeals from evidentiary rulings. It defines the general circumstances under which an appeals court is authorized to reverse a lower court judgment on the basis of errors committed in the trial court, and also defines some of the steps that careful lawyers must take at the trial level to protect their rights on appeal.

Rule 103(a) identifies two necessary conditions that must be met before a lawyer may bring a successful appeal and overturn a judgment on the basis of an error in a ruling by the lower court on an issue of evidence law. The rule puts this point in fairly archaic language when it defines the circumstances under which a party "may claim error in a ruling," which means simply to cite some ruling by the lower court in an appellate argument as a ground for reversal. The error must have been both (1) prejudicial, meaning that "the error affects a substantial right of the party" claiming the error,[5] and (2) preserved for appeal, meaning that the party took all appropriate steps to ensure that the lower court was given a reasonable opportunity to avoid the

---

WIGMORE, §§ 17, 18. *See also* Poulos, *The Trial of Celebrated Criminal Cases: An Analysis of Evidentiary Objections,* 56 TUL. L. REV. 602 (1982); Note, *Harmful Use of Harmless Error in Criminal Cases,* 64 CORNELL L. REV. 538 (1979); Note, *Harmless Error: The Need for a Uniform Standard,* 53 ST. JOHN'S L. REV. 541 (1979); Note, *Ineffective Assistance of Counsel and the Harmless Error Rule: The Eighth Circuit Abandons Chapman,* 43 GEO. WASH. L. REV. 1384 (1975).

[2] General Electric Co. v. Joiner, 522 U.S. 136, 141–142 (1997). Appellate courts must "give the trial court the deference that is the hallmark of abuse-of-discretion review," and therefore must not subject the lower court's ruling to an overly "stringent" review. *Id.* at 143.

[3] United States v. Cole, 631 F.3d 146 (4th Cir. 2011); United States v. Vosburgh, 602 F.3d 512 (3d Cir. 2010); United States v. Mejia, 545 F.3d 179 (2d Cir. 2008). One Circuit Court of Appeals has held that evidentiary rulings in criminal cases should be subject to a "heightened" standard of review and will therefore be more closely examined on appeal, United States v. Valencia, 600 F.3d 389 (5th Cir. 2010), although the Supreme Court of the United States has shown no indication of a willingness to apply a different standard of review to evidentiary rulings in criminal cases.

[4] Koon v. United States, 518 U.S. 81, 100 (1996).

[5] Rule 103(a); *see* discussion of this requirement at § 103.2, *infra.*

error that allegedly justifies reversal.[6] These are only necessary conditions for reversal, however, and not by themselves sufficient conditions to guarantee success on appeal.[7] These two conditions are discussed, respectively, in the next two sections of this treatise.

§ 103.2 Degrees of Error in Evidentiary Rulings

Rule 103(a) lays down the rule that any party seeking reversal of a judgment because of a violation of any of the Federal Rules of Evidence at trial must persuade the Court of Appeals that "the error affects a substantial right of the party" by the violation.[8] This rule has been consistently interpreted by the courts much more narrowly than it sounds.[9] In practice, this means that the appellant must persuade the appeals court not merely that some rule of evidence was violated at the trial (that will be the case at almost every trial), but that there was at least some reasonable likelihood that the error affected the *outcome* of the trial, so that a retrial without the error might well produce a different result.[10] For example, the Court of Appeals will never reverse and order a retrial merely because a criminal defendant can show that some item of evidence was erroneously admitted or excluded, as long as the admissible evidence of guilt is so overwhelming that a conviction at any retrial without that error would be a foregone conclusion. Unless there

---

[6] See the discussion of this requirement at § 103.3, *infra.* Rule 103(d) codifies the "plain error" doctrine, which acts as an exception to the general rule requiring preservation of error as a condition to a successful appeal.

[7] For example, even a lawyer who literally complies with all the requirements of Rule 103(a)(1) may find that his rights to appeal were nevertheless waived by his conduct at trial after complying with those rules, as the defendant did in *Ohler v. United States,* 529 U.S. 753 (2000), discussed more fully at § 103.4, *infra.* But an appellant who does not comply with all the requirements of Rule 103 is almost certain to lose on appeal even if he can otherwise show that there was some error committed at trial on an issue of evidence law.

[8] Even the "plain error" doctrine, which serves as an important exception to the most basic rules governing preservation of error, is limited to "plain errors affecting substantial rights." *See* § 103.3, *infra,* Rule 103(d).

[9] After all, every rule of evidence gives the parties a right to insist on the admission of certain helpful evidence or the exclusion of certain prejudicial evidence — for example, the right to object to letting the jury hear about inadmissible hearsay — and those rights are binding upon trial judges, who are not free to disregard them as they wish. At the moment those rights are being asserted at a trial, they usually involve matters of considerable significance to the objecting party, and the sort of thing that most objective observers would naturally describe as "a substantial right." But this language of Rule 103(a) was intended to clarify that a party seeking reversal must show something much more significant than the mere denial of the right to the exclusion of a single piece of evidence.

[10] *See* Satcher v. Honda Motor Co., 52 F.3d 1311, 1317 (5th Cir. 1995) (an appellate court should reverse only if the complaining party establishes that the erroneous evidentiary ruling affected a substantial right); Jordan v. Medley, 711 F.2d 211 (D.C. Cir. 1983) (an assessment of whether an error affected a substantial right "involves an assessment of the likelihood that the error affected the outcome of the case"). The terms "prejudicial error'" and "reversible error" are synonymous. *See* 1 WEINSTEIN'S FEDERAL EVIDENCE § 103.02.

is some chance that a retrial might turn out differently, there is no point in reversing a judgment merely because some item of evidence was erroneously admitted or excluded in violation of one of the rules of evidence. There are no exceptions to this rule.[11] As the Supreme Court never tires of reminding appellants in criminal cases, "the Constitution entitles a criminal defendant to a fair trial, not a perfect one."[12]

Courts interpreting this requirement routinely distinguish between two types of error: harmless and prejudicial. Harmless error involves an incorrect ruling, either the erroneous admission or exclusion of evidence, that does not affect the final determination of the case (for example, in a jury trial, the verdict).[13] Any error in an evidentiary ruling will never lead to reversal if the error is deemed to be harmless.[14] Prejudicial error, by contrast, entails an erroneous ruling that is found, on appeal, to have affected a substantial right by possibly distorting the outcome of the case. In deciding whether an error was prejudicial or harmless, the Court of Appeals will consider, among other factors, the strength of the prevailing party's case, the length and complexity of the trial, whether the trial court gave an effective curative instruction, and whether the evidence was referred to in closing argument.[15] Error is also

---

[11] The Supreme Court has identified a limited number of constitutional violations that are so fundamental to the integrity of the trial process that they are not subject to harmless error analysis, meaning that a violation of such rights requires automatic reversal regardless of whether such errors can be shown to have affected the outcome of the trial. But none of those rights involve the admission or exclusion of evidence. These special rights, the violation of which can never be dismissed as "harmless error," include the right of a criminal defendant to counsel, Gideon v. Wainwright, 372 U.S. 335 (1963), counsel of the defendant's choice, United States v. Gonzalez-Lopez, 548 U.S. 140 (2006); the right of defendants to represent themselves, McKaskle v. Wiggins, 465 U.S. 168, 177–178, n. 8 (1984), a public trial, Waller v. Georgia, 467 U.S. 39, 49, n. 9 (1984), an accurate instruction on the requirement of reasonable doubt, Sullivan v. Louisiana, 508 U.S. 275 (1993), an unbiased trial judge, Tumey v. Ohio, 273 U.S. 510 (1927), and a grand jury selected without racial discrimination. Vasquez v. Hillery, 474 U.S. 254 (1986). Because the denial of these special rights leads to an automatic reversal, cunning criminal defendants count themselves most fortunate when such errors are committed over their objection, because then their first trial becomes a no-lose proposition: an acquittal will be the end of the prosecution because of the Double Jeopardy Clause, but a conviction will be certainly set aside for an automatic "do-over."

[12] Delaware v. Van Arsdall, 475 U.S. 673 (1986).

[13] See, e.g., Government of Virgin Islands v. Archibald, 987 F.2d 180 (3d Cir. 1993) (in rape case, the admission of hearsay evidence on redirect was not harmless error where the evidence was the only independent evidence of defendant's motive).

[14] See United States v. Madden, 38 F.3d 747, 753 (4th Cir. 1994) (an error is harmless and reversal is not required unless it is "highly probable" that the error affected the outcome).

[15] United States v. Mejia, 597 F.3d 1329 (D.C. Cir. 2010) (in drug conspiracy prosecution, error in admitting evidence that defendant, a former police officer, possessed a firearm permit and that two handguns were seized from his driver, was harmless, even though evidence had limited probative value and carried a risk that the jury would presume that guns and drug trafficking go together; the driver was not charged as a member of the conspiracy,

more likely to be deemed harmless if the jury returns a mixed verdict — for example, convicting the accused on some counts but acquitting on others — that suggests the jury was not unfairly prejudiced or unreasonably inflamed against the defendant by the erroneous admission of some evidence the jurors should not have heard.

§ 103.3   Requirements for Preservation of Error for Appeal

Rule 103(a) identifies two situations in which the record of the trial proceedings must clearly reflect the alleged prejudicial error if the appellate court is to review the propriety of an evidentiary ruling: (1) where error is predicated on an improperly overruled objection to the admission of evidence and (2) where error is predicated on the improper exclusion of evidence. Provided such alleged error is not merely harmless (*i.e.,* provided the alleged error affects a substantial right of the complaining party), the error may serve as a proper basis for appeal.[16] In order to preserve the issue for appeal, the complaining party must comply with the procedural requirements of Rule 103.

According to Rule 103(a)(1), errors in rulings admitting evidence are forfeited if there is no timely motion to strike or objection in the record stating the supporting reasons.[17] This rule is derived from the general principle that a reviewing court will consider an issue only if it was raised in a manner that gave the lower court ample opportunity to consider its own ruling and pass on the issue.[18] For an issue to be preserved for appeal, both

---

the jury was made aware of fact that defendant did not possess a gun at any meetings, the defendant confessed, and there was other strong evidence of guilt); City of Long Beach v. Standard Oil Co. of California, 46 F.3d 929, 937 (9th Cir. 1995) (error in excluding evidence was harmless because evidence had low probative value and was cumulative of other evidence).

[16] *See* § 103.2, *supra.*

[17] *See, e.g.,* United States v. Carrillo-Figueroa, 34 F.3d 33, 39–40 (1st Cir. 1994) (an objection without a stated basis will not serve as the basis for an appeal unless the basis is apparent from the context); Prymer v. Ogden, 29 F.3d 1208, 1213–1214 (7th Cir. 1994) (where plaintiff failed to object at trial on ground raised on appeal, he has forfeited the right to argue that issue); United States v. Castro-Lara, 970 F.2d 976 (1st Cir. 1992) (appellate court declined to consider defendant's hearsay objection to certain testimony where he had failed to object at trial); United States v. McQuisten, 795 F.2d 858 (9th Cir. 1986) (defendant who did not object to admission of photograph was held to have waived issue for appeal); United States v. Mascio, 774 F.2d 219 (7th Cir. 1985) (defendant who did not object at evidentiary hearing to testimony about other acts similar to the offense at trial was not permitted to raise issue on appeal).

[18] *See, e.g.,* United States v. DeBiasi, 712 F.2d 785 (2d Cir. 1983) (defendant's complaint was not reviewable on appeal where defense counsel withdrew his motion to strike and failed to seek a curative instruction regarding trial testimony's purported implication that defendants had threatened the witness); United States v. Richardson, 562 F.2d 476 (7th Cir. 1977) (admission of unobjected-to FBI photograph and palm print did not constitute plain error, and accordingly, was not cognizable on appeal).

the objection and its grounds must be stated in the record; however, if the grounds for objection are apparent from the context, the specific grounds need not be stated.[19]

Rule 103(a)(2) functions similarly for rulings excluding evidence. The error will be deemed forfeited unless the party offering such evidence, the proponent, makes a proffer of the substance of the evidence (an "offer of proof") to ensure that the reviewing court is presented with a complete record on appeal.[20] If, however, the substance of the excluded evidence is apparent from the context within which it was sought to be introduced — such as where it is clear from the question what the answer would have been — a proffer is unnecessary.[21] No special form for a proffer is set forth in the Rules. The only requirement is that the substance of the excluded evidence must be made clear in the offer of proof.[22] Although common law often relaxed the requirement for an offer of proof when dealing with evidence

---

[19] *See* United States v. Hutcher, 622 F.2d 1083, 1087 (2d Cir. 1980) (mere statement of objection without stating grounds was insufficient to preserve error, where the specific ground was not apparent).

[20] *See* Dupre v. Fru-Con Eng'g, Inc., 112 F.3d 329, 336–337 (8th Cir. 1997) (where the record does not reflect an offer of proof, the party will not be heard to complain about the exclusion of evidence on appeal); Strong v. Mercantile Trust, 816 F.2d 429 (8th Cir. 1987) (plaintiff's offer of proof at trial was not sufficient to preserve right to appeal exclusion where the offer did not indicate that evidence was other than cumulative, even though the evidence as detailed in appeal would have been admissible); McQuaig v. McCoy, 806 F.2d 1298 (5th Cir. 1987) (plaintiffs preserved right to appeal exclusion of evidence where the plaintiffs made both the substance and the purpose of the evidence clear at a pretrial conference and made some effort to introduce the evidence into the record at trial); Merrill v. Southern Methodist Univ., 806 F.2d 600 (5th Cir. 1986) (party waived right to argue the admissibility of evidence on appeal where she failed to make an offer of proof during trial); Saltzman v. Fullerton Metals Co., 661 F.2d 647 (7th Cir. 1981) (court refused to entertain plaintiff's argument that judge erroneously denied cross-examination where plaintiff's "conclusory offer of proof disclosed neither of plaintiff's particular needs for cross-examination argued on appeal and failed to set out any testimony not cumulative of that already provided"). *See also* Heyne v. Caruso, 69 F.3d 1475, 1481–1482 (9th Cir. 1995) ("The lack of an offer of proof . . . is excused where 'an entire class of evidence has been in advance formally declared inadmissible by the trial court.' ").

[21] Beech Aircraft Corp. v. Rainey, 488 U.S. 153 (1988) (where "the nature of the proposed testimony was abundantly apparent from the very question put by [plaintiff's] counsel," the plaintiff had not waived the issue for appeal).

[22] *See* United States v. Amaya-Manzanares, 377 F.3d 39 (1st Cir. 2004) (a ruling excluding evidence is preserved for appellate review where the proponent merely told the district judge that its evidence was relevant, because that party "was not asked to elaborate on the reasoning behind its relevance argument nor given much opportunity to do so"); United States v. Brown, 303 F.3d 582 (5th Cir. 2002) (an order excluding a witness from testifying was preserved for appeal even though defense counsel had said in district court he would submit a written proffer of the testimony but never did so; counsel provided an "adequate oral description" of the proposed testimony before the district judge definitely excluded it, and "[a]n oral proffer may be sufficient to preserve an error for appellate review"); United States v. Adams, 271 F.3d 1236 (10th Cir. 2001) (sending a facsimile of a

excluded on cross-examination due to the fact that an adverse party may not be able to state what evidence the witness would have provided, courts applying Rule 103 have generally required some type of proffer even in such a situation. However, a party may be able to satisfy this requirement by informing the trial court as to the substance of the evidence sought to be elicited.[23]

Rule 103(a) carries with it a specificity requirement. Attorneys should take care to be specific when making objections. The admission of evidence over a general objection is not a basis for reversal if any significant part of the evidence is admissible. Likewise, if it is admissible for any purpose, admission of evidence over a general objection will not constitute reversible

---

psychologist's report to the trial judge the day before a hearing does not generally suffice as an offer of proof of the contents of the report, but an exception was made and the report was considered proffered since the trial judge referenced having received the report and opposing counsel did not object to its inclusion in the court record); United States v. Jimenez, 256 F.3d 330 (5th Cir. 2001) (potential error concerning exclusion of witness's mental health records was preserved even though proponents made no offer of proof during trial, since district court explained that its ruling on admissibility would be subject to appellate review); Tiller v. Baghdady, 244 F.3d 9 (1st Cir. 2001) (an offer of proof need not be made in writing, or in any particular form, to preserve error); United States v. Morales, 108 F.3d 1031 (9th Cir. 1997) (since the proffer made known the substance of the excluded testimony, the issue was properly preserved for appeal); United States v. Ballis, 28 F.3d 1399, 1406 (5th Cir. 1994) (the proffer should show "what counsel intends to show by the evidence and why it should be admitted").

[23] *See* United States v. Lopez, 944 F.2d 33, 41 (1st Cir. 1991); United States v. Martinez, 776 F.2d 1481, 1485 (10th Cir. 1985) (although counsel informed the court that he was not pursuing one line of inquiry, he did not specify what he sought to elicit from the witness on cross-examination, and because the substance of the sought-after testimony was not apparent from the context, the court was not required to consider the issue on appeal); United States v. Lavallie, 666 F.2d 1217, 1220 (8th Cir. 1981) ("Absent an offer of proof as required by Rule 103(a)(2) of the Federal Rules of Evidence, neither the trial court nor the appellate court on review can truly ascertain what response was expected at the time"); United States v. Vitale, 596 F.2d 688, 689–690 (5th Cir. 1979); Wright v. Hartford Acc. & Indem. Co., 580 F.2d 809 (5th Cir. 1978) ("The arguments for a more relaxed requirement of an offer of proof on cross-examination . . . are inapplicable when, as in this case, the evidence is deposition testimony . . . and the trial judge specifically requests that counsel provide support for admitting the evidence"). *See also* Fairfield Scientific Corp. v. United States, 611 F.2d 854 (Ct. Cl. 1979) (explaining that although no offer of proof regarding the substance of the witness's excluded testimony was made, the attorney had stated the question he wished to ask to give the court some idea of the information sought). The common-law doctrine was noted by the Supreme Court in Alford v. United States, 282 U.S. 687, 692 (1931) (citations omitted):

> Counsel often cannot know in advance what pertinent facts may be elicited on cross-examination . . . . [T]he rule that the examiner must indicate the purpose of his inquiry does not, in general, apply. It is the essence of a fair trial that reasonable latitude be given the cross-examiner, even though he is unable to state to the court what facts a reasonable cross-examination might develop.

error.[24] The Rule provides a limited exception to the requirement of specificity, for a lawyer must state the specific ground of objection unless it was apparent from the context.[25] This means that a general objection will suffice to preserve error in the exceptional situations where it is obvious to the appeals court what the objecting attorney intended, but that is a perilous gambit that careful lawyers will virtually never take, since it is so much easier and safer to state the "obvious" objection on the record.[26]

In a similar fashion, attorneys should take care when stating the grounds of the objection. When a party advances a specific ground for an objection, whether of its own volition or at the request of the court, the party will have forfeited its right to seek reversal on appeal based on any other legal grounds.[27] Like all of the details laid out in Rule 103, however, this

---

[24] United States v. Gentile, 525 F.2d 252 (2d Cir. 1975) (no error in overruling *Miranda*-based defense objections in bribery prosecution, since there was no warrant for suppression of all the statements and defendant made no effort to differentiate the statements at trial or on appeal; trial judge was not required to separate out the statements which were arguably excludable on the objection); *e.g.,* United States v. Abou-Saada, 785 F.2d 1 (1st Cir. 1986) (a general objection to the finding that a conspiracy existed was not sufficient to object to hearsay); United States v. Sandini, 803 F.2d 123 (3d Cir. 1986) (a general objection was not sufficient where defendant should have invoked specific Rules of Evidence). *See generally,* 1 WEINSTEIN'S FEDERAL EVIDENCE §§ 103.10–103.13;1 MUELLER & KIRKPATRICK §§ 7–8.

[25] Rule 103(a)(1)(B). United States v. Joseph, 310 F.3d 975 (7th Cir. 2002) (defense counsel's pretrial objection to evidence of other criminal acts was preserved for appeal where he said enough to make it "clear to everyone at the hearing that the parties were arguing about Rule 404(b)," even though he did not explicitly cite that rule).

[26] *See* United States v. Phillips, 596 F.3d 414 (7th Cir. 2010) (when accused objected to the admission of redacted audio recording merely on the grounds that it was redacted, she forfeited her right on appeal to argue that the district court must review a complete recording before admitting a redacted version into evidence. The Court of Appeals could not say that her specific ground of objection, requiring the district court to review the complete recording in its entirety, was "apparent from the context" of her objection, especially since she pointed to no precedent requiring a district court to perform the *sua sponte* labor-intensive review she requested on appeal); Bandera v. City of Quincy, 344 F.3d 47 (1st Cir. 2003) (even though testimony was "wholly inappropriate opinion testimony" that "should certainly not have been admitted," that objection was not obvious from the context of a general objection, and therefore was not preserved, given other specific objections that were specifically made during the testimony and before trial. The "testimony, although clearly inappropriate, was at the tag end of other testimony to which different objections had been litigated pretrial"). In truth, the "escape valve" of Rule 103(a)(1), which sometimes allows a general objection to suffice as well as a specific objection for preserving error for appeal, was written not for trial lawyers but for desperate appellant's lawyers, who are on rare occasions able to use it as a last resort in seeking relief from the unfortunate and ill-advised decision of their client's trial counsel to make nothing more than a general objection.

[27] *See, e.g.,* United States v. Mardirosian, 602 F.3d 1 (1st Cir. 2010) (where defendant objected to a statement as hearsay and raised only general objections to the remainder of the disputed testimony, he did not preserve for appeal a challenge to the probative value of the evidence); Desai v. Hersh, 954 F.2d 1408 (7th Cir. 1992) (in a diversity libel suit, a

requirement of specificity only limits the prospects for reversal in the Court of Appeals, and does not limit the power of the trial judge to exclude evidence for reasons not raised by the objecting party.[28] Where, however, the court assigns the wrong reason for admitting evidence yet a proper reason exists, a reviewing court generally will not reverse since the lower court's receipt of the evidence was nevertheless proper.[29]

Rule 103(a) also bears a timeliness requirement for objections and motions to strike. Although the Rule does not clearly state when an objection is considered timely, the prevailing view is that an objection must be made as soon as the ground of objection becomes apparent.[30] For example, an objection to an improper question must be made before the answer is given in order to constitute a timely objection; a motion to strike an improper answer should be made immediately following the objectionable answer.

A party who fails to strictly comply with the preservation of error requirements of Rule 103(a) may still have a slim chance of reversal under the doctrine of plain error, provided that the error was not waived in the lower court. This possibility requires a careful examination of the subtle distinction between forfeiture and waiver of an error.

---

meritorious claim to disclosure of the identities of journalistic sources was waived under Rule 103(a)(1) by the failure to raise specific objection); Williams v. Jader Fuel Co., 944 F.2d 1388 (7th Cir. 1991) (a specific objection made on the wrong grounds and consequently overruled precludes a party from raising a specific objection on other tenable grounds on appeal); Thomas v. Booker, 784 F.2d 299 (8th Cir. 1986) (defendant's objection to jury instruction based on lack of sufficient evidence did not preserve right to argue on appeal that the instruction applied an improper legal standard); K-B Trucking Co. v. Riss Int'l Corp., 763 F.2d 1148 (10th Cir. 1985) (objection to exhibit based on lack of foundation did not preserve objection on appeal that evidence was inadmissible under Rule 403).

[28] United States v. Wilder, 597 F.3d 926 (8th Cir. 2010) (even though an attorney objected to a document merely on hearsay grounds, the trial court acted within its power to exclude the evidence instead on the basis of its inadequate foundation, because a trial court is allowed to exclude evidence for reasons not raised by the objecting party).

[29] 1 WIGMORE, §18.

[30] *See* United States v. Perez-Ruiz, 353 F.3d 1 (1st Cir. 2003) (although lawyers normally must object before an improper question is answered, they are not required to object to proper questions in anticipation of unresponsive or otherwise inappropriate answers. "When a proper question elicits an untoward reply, the failure to object to the question is excused so long as the aggrieved party promptly moves to strike the offending answer"); United States v. Meserve, 271 F.3d 314 (1st Cir. 2001) (when defense attorney "objected as soon as it became obvious that the government's line of questioning was in violation of Rule 609," the objection was "sufficiently contemporaneous" to be timely and to preserve error for appeal, even though the objection came after the question was answered and the accused made no motion to strike. "The general principle that an objection should be made after a question has been asked but before an answer has been given . . . is flexible in deference to the heat of a hotly contested criminal trial"); United States v. Saccoccia, 58 F.3d 754, 780–781 (1st Cir. 1995); McKnight v. Johnson Controls, Inc., 36 F.3d 1396, 1407–1408 (8th Cir. 1994) (where the speculative nature of evidence was obvious when given, a motion to strike at the end of direct examination was not timely).

If an alleged error has not been properly preserved for appeal through a proper objection or offer of proof, the error is said, by definition, to have been forfeited. Forfeiture of an error must be carefully distinguished from waiver. Forfeiture results from the mere failure to make a timely and sufficient assertion of some right, while waiver is an intentional relinquishment of a known right, and normally requires some affirmative action by the party.[31] For example, when an arguably inadmissible piece of evidence is offered by a prosecutor, a criminal defense attorney who says nothing and merely fails to object has forfeited but not waived the client's claim of error. But if the lawyer stands and states to the judge on the record "We have no objection to this evidence," any claim of error in its admission has been not merely forfeited but also waived.[32]

This distinction between waiver and mere forfeiture is critical to appellants who seek reversal under the doctrine of plain error. A party who had waived a possible claim of error in the admission of some evidence cannot obtain reversal by arguing that the admission of the evidence was plain error. But if the error has been merely forfeited and not waived, the complaining party still has at least a slim chance of obtaining reversal by persuading the Court of Appeals that the lower court's ruling was "plain error."[33] The plain error doctrine, reflected in Rule 103(d), represents an important but narrow exception to the general rule that trial errors will not lead to reversal unless

---

[31] United States v. Olano, 507 U.S. 725, 732–733 (1993).

[32] The courts have identified a subcategory of waived errors: some (although not all) waived errors are also described as "invited error." Instances of "invited error" typically arise where the party seeking reversal on appeal for the allegedly erroneous admission of some evidence was the same party who either offered the evidence himself or opened the door to its admission. Errors that have been invited by the objecting party's action are virtually never a proper basis for appeal, not even on the basis of plain error, or it would otherwise be far too easy for parties who are losing at trial to sabotage the case by planting the seeds for reversal in the record by their own actions. *See* Ohler v. United States, 529 U.S. 753, 755 (2000) ("Generally, a party introducing evidence cannot complain on appeal that the evidence was erroneously admitted"); United States v. Wells, 519 U.S. 482, 488 (1997) (under doctrine of "invited error," parties may not complain on appeal of errors they themselves invited or provoked the lower court to commit); United States v. Cowart, 90 F.3d 154, 158 (6th Cir. 1996) (defendant will not be heard to complain about the introduction of evidence of his nolo plea when he referred to plea during his own testimony, effectively arguing that he admits his guilt when he has done something wrong; the fact that the defendant's strategy backfired did not give him the right to raise the issue of the admissibility of his nolo plea); Hoselton v. Metz Baking Co., 48 F.3d 1056, 1062 (8th Cir. 1995) (because the plaintiffs had insisted that an entire deposition be read into evidence, any error in admitting inadmissible portions was invited).

[33] *See* United States v. Olano, 507 U.S. 725, 732–733 (1993). The difference between the two cases, as the Supreme Court has explained, is that an unpreserved error is still an error as long as it has not been waived. But when a party makes an explicit and affirmative waiver of some right by announcing on the record that he has no objection to some course of action proposed by opposing counsel, the willingness of the trial judge to take that course cannot be error at all, much less plain error. *Id.*

they are properly preserved for appeal. As long as the error was not waived, an appellate court is empowered to review the issue and redress the wrong where the error complained of, though not raised at trial, is sufficiently plain and egregious.[34] The error must also be prejudicial; that is, it must have created an obvious possibility that the outcome of the case would have been different but for the error.[35] On these grounds, it has been held that a mere error in the form of the questions put to a witness can never be reversible as plain error, and that ruling seems correct.[36] The doctrine provides a reviewing court with a device which it may use in its discretion to review instances in which, perhaps through inexperience or incompetence of counsel, a party adversely affected by a significant evidentiary error has not properly preserved its position on the record.

The threshold for invocation of the plain error doctrine is higher in civil cases than in criminal matters, and erroneous rulings in civil cases are susceptible to reversal as plain error only in extreme situations.[37] Because the doctrine of plain error is discretionary, however, the appeals court is not obligated to reverse on the basis of unpreserved errors even if the court concludes that there was some plain violation of the rights of the complaining party.[38] For example, if the appellate court believes that a party

---

[34] Rogers v. United States, 422 U.S. 35, 40 (1975) (after trial court, in absence of counsel, instructed jury on effect of a recommendation of mercy, "the combined effect of the District Court's errors was so fraught with potential prejudice as to require us to notice them, notwithstanding petitioner's failure to raise the issue in the court of appeals or in this court"); United States v. Restivo, 8 F.3d 274, 279 (5th Cir 1993) ("Plain error is error so obvious and substantial that failure to notice it would affect the fairness, integrity, or public reputation of the judicial proceedings and would result in manifest injustice"); United States v. Roenigk, 810 F.2d 809 (8th Cir. 1987) (despite defendant's failure to object to the prosecutor's description of a drug conspiracy in violation of a pretrial order by the trial judge, appeals court reversed perjury conviction based on plain error).

[35] Rule 103(e) makes this point explicit by limiting plain error review to "a plain error affecting a substantial right." *See also* Angelo v. Armstrong World Indus., Inc., 11 F.3d 957, 961 (10th Cir. 1993) (the party claiming error "bear[s] the burden of proving plain error and that it 'almost surely affected the outcome of the case' ").

[36] United States v. Meza-Urtado, 351 F.3d 301 (7th Cir. 2003) (errors involving only the form of the question, such as "leading," are never reversible as plain error; without an objection at trial, reversal would be unfair to the party who was denied the chance to rephrase the question and elicit the same evidence, presumably with the same outcome at the end of the trial. "Any reasonably good lawyer worth his salt can accomplish this little trick").

[37] *See* Committee Note to Rule 103 (application of the plain error doctrine "more pronounced" in criminal cases). *See also* United States v. Valencia, 600 F.3d 389 (5th Cir. 2010) (in a criminal case, evidentiary rulings are subject to a "heightened" level of appellate review and will therefore be more closely examined on appeal).

[38] Building Serv. Local 47 v. Grandview Raceway, 46 F.3d 1392, 1397 (6th Cir. 1995) ("A court's power to review a claim of error under the plain error doctrine is discretionary and should be exercised only in those situations in which the failure to do so would result in a manifest miscarriage of justice") (internal quotations omitted); cf. United States v. Olano, 507

consciously refrained from objecting as a tactical matter, that action will virtually rule out any possibility that the appeals court will choose to reverse under its discretionary power of plain error review, regardless of how obvious the lower court's violation of the rules may have been.[39]

§ 103.4   Objections in Special Circumstances

Although Rule 103 requires an objection to preserve an evidentiary error on appeal, the manner in which this objection is made may vary from the traditional notion in certain situations. For example, when a party has an objection to an entire line of questions, neither counsel nor the court may find it productive for the attorney to continually restate the objection as each question is asked. In such a situation, where a party has what amounts to a continuous objection, the attorney should clearly state that he or she has a continuing objection to the testimony or other evidence and state the ground for that objection. The continuing objection will then cover all subsequent evidence admitted within the scope of the initial ruling.[40] However, unless a new objection is made, the continuing objection will be limited to the grounds stated in the original objection.

A similar situation may arise where two or more codefendants are being tried together. If the interests of the defendants are sufficiently aligned and each has the same evidentiary objection to the evidence, each defendant need not state a separate objection. Where one defendant objects to the admitted testimony or other evidence, the objection serves to preserve the issue for all defendants.[41] Of course, each defendant is then limited to arguing against the

---

U.S. 725 (1993) (construing Fed. R. Crim. P. 52(b), which is substantially identical to the plain error provision of Rule 103, and stating that plain error affecting substantial rights does not require reversal or the discretion inherent in the rule "would be rendered illusory").

[39] United States v. Yu-Leung, 51 F.3d 1116, 1123 (2d Cir. 1995) (finding it reasonable to infer that a strategic decision had been made to forgo any objection to the evidence of defendant's other acts of misconduct; considering the amount of evidence introduced regarding the defendant's past conduct, defense counsel "would have had to have suffered from aggravated narcolepsy for us to believe that this failure to object did not reflect a clear and conscious tactical decision").

[40] *See* United States v. Marshall, 762 F.2d 419, 425 (5th Cir. 1985) (a "party is entitled to rely upon the trial judge's ruling as the law of the case, without waiving his rights under the continuing objection, to question subsequently on appeal the admission of any evidence of the nature specifically objected to by him initially"); *see also* United States v. Gomez-Norena, 908 F.2d 497 (9th Cir. 1990) (continuing objection merely avoids "repeated objections to evidence admitted within the scope of the court's specific evidentiary ruling"; it does not provide basis for appeal on grounds not stated at time of original objection).

[41] *See* United States v. Gatling, 96 F.3d 1511, 1521 (D.C. Cir. 1996) ("Trial judges have discretion to determine whether each defendant must individually object or whether objections raised by one defendant will count as having been raised for all similarly situated defendants"); United States v. Church, 970 F.2d 401 (7th Cir. 1992) (holding that codefendants could rely on objection raised by codefendant's attorney); Howard v. Gonzales, 658 F.2d 352 (5th Cir. 1981) ("Unless the identity of the objector somehow affects the

evidence on the grounds stated in the original objection.

A different situation is presented where a party files a motion *in limine* for a ruling on the admissibility of evidence before it is actually offered at trial. Such motions may be made by either the party seeking admission or the party seeking exclusion, and are usually (although not always) made before trial.[42] Rule 103(b) provides that a definitive advance ruling excluding or admitting evidence, either before or during trial, is sufficient to preserve a claim of error; the objection or offer of proof need not be renewed at trial, much less before the jury. This amendment changed the law in all but three federal circuits.[43]

The rule does not specify when a ruling is "definitive." If the judge's ruling is tentative or provisional, or if the judge indicates that the ruling might change if the judge is asked to reconsider the matter during trial, the ruling is not definitive, and no claim of error is preserved for appeal unless the losing party renews its objection or offer of proof at an appropriate time during trial.[44] When there is any doubt about the finality of a pretrial ruling,

---

admissibility of the evidence, no reason appears why a party should be required to join in the objection or offer of another litigant aligned with him, in order to raise the issue on appeal").

[42] *In limine* means "[o]n or at the threshold; at the very beginning; preliminarily." BLACK'S LAW DICTIONARY 708 (5th ed. 1979). The Supreme Court has defined a motion *in limine* "in a broad sense to refer to any motion, whether made before or during trial, to exclude anticipated prejudicial evidence before the evidence is actually offered," Luce v. United States, 469 U.S. 38, 40 n.2 (1984), although of course it would also include a motion for a pretrial ruling *admitting* evidence, which parties are sometimes required to make. *See, e.g.,* Rule 412(c).

[43] Before the amendment to Rule 103, only three federal circuits never required renewal of a pretrial objection that had been definitively overruled. Rice v. Community Health Ass'n, 203 F.3d 283, 286 (4th Cir. 2000); Wilson v. Williams, 182 F.3d 562 (7th Cir. 1999) (en banc); Anderson v. Group Hospitalization, Inc., 820 F.2d 465, 470 n.2 (D.C. Cir. 1987) (dictum); United States v. Williams, 561 F.2d 859, 862–863 (D.C. Cir. 1977). For a thorough review of the law in every circuit and how it changed under the new rule, and for a discussion of the tactical aspects of motion *in limine* practice under the new rule, see Duane, *Appellate Review of* In Limine *Rulings,* 182 F.R.D. 666 (Jan. 1999); Duane, *Pretrial Motions and Preservation of Error: Recent Developments in State and Federal Law and Their Tactical Implications,* 63 TEXAS BAR JOURNAL 616 (July 2000).

[44] *See* United States v. Phillips, 596 F.3d 414 (7th Cir. 2010) (appellant could not rely on the denial of her motion *in limine* to preserve her objection to the admission of a redacted recording, even though the trial court denied the motion based on the government's representation that the complete recording would be available at the time of trial, when she never renewed that objection at the time the redacted version was offered at trial); Tennison v. Circus Circus Enters., 244 F.3d 684 (9th Cir. 2001) (following a tentative ruling excluding evidence of sexual harassment and complaints, plaintiff who did not attempt to reintroduce testimony at trial did not preserve claim of error in ruling and would not be allowed to challenge it on appeal); Udemba v. Nicoli, 237 F.3d 8 (1st Cir. 2001) (after trial judge makes only a provisional ruling on a motion *in limine* and the unsuccessful party does not renew the objection at trial, no error is preserved and the ruling is reviewable on appeal only for plain error).

as there often is, the losing party must take the initiative to obtain clarification.[45] Even after a definitive ruling, the judge may revisit the matter at any time. When this happens, or when an opposing party or the judge violates an earlier ruling, the lawyer aggrieved by that course must renew the objection, and may not rely on a motion *in limine* to preserve the contention for appeal.[46]

It is critical to underscore two things Rule 103(b) does not do. It does not preserve error in a pretrial ruling, even one that is final and definitive, if the ruling is based upon a condition that does not materialize at trial. For example, if a court rules that the criminal record of an accused will be admissible for impeachment if the accused testifies, and he or she therefore decides not to testify, any error in the ruling is not preserved for appellate review.[47] Nor is error preserved by a pretrial motion to exclude evidence, even if the motion is definitively denied, if the losing party then bites the

---

[45] Crowe v. Bolduc, 334 F.3d 124 (1st Cir. 2003) (it is "not uncommon" for trial courts to make *in limine* ruling that is ambiguous as to whether "the ruling was only tentative, or that it was final unless circumstances at trial changed"; still, the burden is on the aggrieved party to clarify whether the ruling is final); *but see* Cook v. Sheriff of Monroe County, Florida, 402 F.3d 1092 n.6 (11th Cir. 2005) (although a tentative pretrial ruling excluding evidence generally does not preserve error for appeal unless the evidence is offered again at trial, the failure to do so would be overlooked because the judge told the losing party that "Your record is protected on that. There is no difficulty at all in taking this to the Eleventh Circuit," because "these comments by the trial court created the clear impression that [the proponent] had done all she needed to do to preserve her objection").

[46] Rule 103(a), Advisory Committee Note, reproduced *infra*, at Appendix A.

[47] Luce v. United States, 469 U.S. 38 (1984). The Advisory Committee noted that *Luce* has been extended by lower federal courts to many other situations involving conditional rulings, and the Committee expressly disclaimed any intent to affect *Luce* with its 2000 amendment to the rule. *See* Rule 103(a), Advisory Committee Note. *See also* United States v. Culver, 598 F.3d 740 (11th Cir. 2010) (in child pornography prosecution, because the accused never called any character witnesses, the Court of Appeals would not decide whether the district court erred in its pretrial ruling that his child pornography convictions could be used to impeach any character witnesses that he might have called); United States v. Fallon, 348 F.3d 248 (7th Cir. 2003) (after pretrial ruling that accused could be impeached with his convictions under Rule 609, accused who did not testify waived his right to challenge that ruling under *Luce*, even though he explicitly informed the district court that his decision was based on the denial of the motion *in limine*; "Neither *Luce* nor its rationale makes exception for a defendant who informs the trial judge that the denial of his motion *in limine* is the basis for his decision not to take the stand"); United States v. Hall, 312 F.3d 1250 (11th Cir. 2002) (in prosecution for possession of child pornography, district court ruled before trial that evidence of accused's molestation of a minor would be admitted if he raised the defense of lack of intent; because accused raised no such defense at trial, evidence of the other crime was never admitted, so no issue was preserved for review, notwithstanding defendant's claim that erroneous pretrial ruling forced him to relinquish the right to testify and present his defense). For a criticism of *Luce* and a description of some of the reasons why many States have declined to follow it, see Duane, *Appellate Review of In Limine Rulings*, 182 F.R.D. 666, 679–690 (Jan. 1999) (urging Advisory Committee to refrain from codifying *Luce* in Rule 103(a)).

bullet and offers the evidence in an effort to remove its sting. Under an extension of the invited error doctrine, the party who offers the evidence that the party tried in vain to exclude has waived any claim of error in its admission, under the Supreme Court's ruling in *Ohler v. United States.*[48] Thus, even if your pretrial motion to exclude evidence is definitively denied, no claim of error is preserved for appeal if you then adopt a trial strategy to make the ruling moot or if you bring out the evidence yourself — regardless of whether you did such things only because of the ruling to make the best of a very bad situation.

§ 103.5   Record of Offer and Ruling

As a corollary to the duty of the parties to make a record concerning rulings on the admission and exclusion of evidence, Rule 103(c) provides that the court *may* comment for the record on the circumstances surrounding its ruling. This procedure is especially useful where evidence is received on a limited basis and the trial court feels constrained to instruct the jury accordingly. By so instructing the jury, the trial judge simultaneously ensures that the reasons for the ruling appear in the record for review on appeal.

§ 103.6   Hearing of Jury

Rule 103(d) provides that, whenever practicable, discussions concerning rulings on evidence should be conducted outside the hearing of the jury. Quite obviously, the purpose of the procedures set out in Rule 103(a), (b), and (c) could be wholly defeated if the jury were permitted to overhear a proffer of excluded evidence or a lengthy discourse on, *e.g.,* the highly prejudicial nature of evidence admitted over objection.

----

[48] Ohler v. United States, 529 U.S. 753 (2000) (where accused testified and brought out her criminal history on direct examination after a pretrial ruling that the prosecutor could do so on cross-examination for impeachment, she waived any claim of error in the pretrial ruling). *Ohler* thus answers a question that the Advisory Committee had said would remain open after the 2000 amendment to Rule 103(a).

Chapter 104

Rule 104. Preliminary Questions

Rule 104. Preliminary Questions

- **(a)** **In General.** The court must decide any preliminary question about whether a witness is qualified, a privilege exists, or evidence is admissible. In so deciding, the court is not bound by evidence rules, except those on privilege.

- **(b)** **Relevance That Depends on a Fact.** When the relevance of evidence depends on whether a fact exists, proof must be introduced sufficient to support a finding that the fact does exist. The court may admit the proposed evidence on the condition that the proof be introduced later.

- **(c)** **Conducting a Hearing So That the Jury Cannot Hear It.** The court must conduct any hearing on a preliminary question so that the jury cannot hear it if:

  - **(1)** the hearing involves the admissibility of a confession;

  - **(2)** a defendant in a criminal case is a witness and so requests; or

  - **(3)** justice so requires.

- **(d)** **Cross-Examining a Defendant in a Criminal Case.** By testifying on a preliminary question, a defendant in a criminal case does not become subject to cross-examination on other issues in the case.

- **(e)** **Evidence Relevant to Weight and Credibility.** This rule does not limit a party's right to introduce before the jury evidence that is relevant to the weight or credibility of other evidence.

---

§ 104.1   Rule 104 — In General

Rule 104 governs the basic division of labor between the judge and the jurors with respect to the evidence offered at a trial. In a nonjury trial, sometimes called a "bench trial," the judge will of course perform all of the responsibilities that would otherwise be handled by the jury, and so all of the issues governed by Rule 104 become moot.

Rule 104 is titled "Preliminary Questions," which in this context refers to questions that are raised pertaining to the admissibility of evidence, and which must somehow be resolved, at least on a provisional basis, before the trial may proceed. Such questions typically are raised by the following sequence of events, which is played out many times at every trial. One party offers evidence of some fact; the Federal Rules of Evidence refer to this party as the *proponent* of the evidence.[1] By "offering" the evidence, the proponent is indicating his belief that the evidence should be admitted, so that the jurors will be allowed to hear or see or somehow learn about it. The other party sometimes objects to its admission, and argues that the evidence is inadmissible. The objecting party does not necessarily contend that the evidence is unreliable or inaccurate — although he might — but he may nevertheless argue that there is some technical reason why the evidence is inadmissible under the rules of evidence or some other legal rule.

When evidence is offered and objected to in this fashion, the competing positions of the parties necessarily raise one or more "preliminary questions" that must be resolved before the trial may proceed. Who decides those disputes? By what standard? These are the sorts of issues governed by Rule 104. The primary focus of the rule is on situations in which either the law or logic requires some sort of a preliminary showing to be made before evidence can be properly admitted. In many contexts, this procedure is commonly described by the familiar phrase, "laying the foundation" for the admission of some evidence.

The most basic distinction between the duties of the judge and the jury, reflected in several different ways in Rule 104, can be simply stated as follows. The judge decides all aspects of every dispute with respect to the *admissibility* of the evidence: that is, the court decides whether the jurors will be allowed to hear and see the evidence. The jurors, in turn, have the fundamental responsibility to decide the *weight and credibility* of the testimony and the other evidence admitted for their consideration, for not all evidence that may be admissible is equally deserving of credence, and not all credible testimony has the same degree of logical value in deciding the issues presented at a trial. As the Supreme Court of the United States recently observed, our legal system "is built on the premise that it is the province of the jury to weigh the credibility of competing witnesses."[2]

Rule 104 is designed to preserve this basic division of responsibility. It ensures that the trial judge reserves the power to make all necessary rulings on disputes over admissibility, while minimizing the risk that inadmissible evidence might be put before the jury.

---

[1] The word *proponent* is used in this way in Rules 609(b), 703, 804(a), 807, 901(a), and 1004.

[2] Kansas v. Ventris, — U.S. —, 129 S. Ct. 1841, 173 L. Ed. 2d 801, 809 n.* (2009). On that basis, the Court declined to use the United States Constitution as a basis for fashioning a special rule to regulate the admissibility of uncorroborated testimony from "jailhouse snitches," despite the existence of reason to believe that such testimony is often notoriously unreliable. *Ibid.*

§ 104.2   Role of the Judge in Determining Admissibility

An objection to the admission of evidence always raises one or more preliminary questions that must be resolved. These questions may involve either matters of law or fact. Rule 104(a) provides that all these preliminary questions regarding the admissibility of evidence, regardless of whether they involve issues of law or fact, shall always be determined by the trial judge. That is of course what any ordinary observer would expect with respect to the law, for the judge decides all legal issues raised during the course of a trial. The newcomer to the study of evidence law is far more likely to be surprised to learn that the judge also decides any *factual* disputes between the parties on which admissibility may depend.

As the Rule specifies, preliminary questions may involve the qualifications of a person to be a witness (*e.g.,* whether a witness is qualified to testify as an expert, or whether a lay witness is competent to testify under Rule 601), or the existence of a privilege (*e.g.,* whether a communication was made in confidence), or any other question pertaining to the admissibility of some testimony or other evidence (*e.g.,* whether a hearsay statement is admissible under some exception to the hearsay rules). In each of these situations and countless similar examples, the law provides that evidence of some fact is admissible only if the party offering the evidence can also prove that some *other* fact is true. For example, evidence about a witness's opinion on the cause of some disease is usually admissible only if the witness is shown to be a qualified expert. Likewise, evidence of the contents of a criminal defendant's statement to the police is sometimes admissible only if the statement was made voluntarily after the police warned him of certain rights. In all these cases, Rule 104(a) provides that the judge shall admit the disputed evidence only if the proponent of the evidence can satisfy the judge that the required preliminary foundation can be established.[3]

How much proof is necessary with respect to the foundational facts relevant to admissibility? Although Rule 104 is silent as to appropriate burden of persuasion, the Supreme Court has concluded that the relevant facts need be proved only by a "preponderance of the evidence," even in criminal cases where the ultimate substantive facts must be proved beyond a reasonable doubt.[4] The Court reasoned that this standard is adequate to

---

[3] The power of the judge to decide all issues pertaining to admissibility is subject to one important qualification. In the context of an objection under the so-called "best evidence rule," Rule 1008 ensures that certain fundamental issues concerning the existence and details of an original document must ultimately be preserved for resolution by the jury, because such questions may "go beyond the mere administration of the [evidence] rule preferring the original and into the merits of the controversy." Committee Notes to Rule 1008. This scheme ensures that the disposition of the case is not effectively taken away from the jury by a judicial ruling that is ostensibly limited to a single narrow issue of admissibility

[4] Daubert v. Merrell Dow Pharmaceuticals, Inc., 509 U.S. 579, 592 n.10 (1993); Bourjaily

ensure "that before admitting evidence, the court will have found it more likely than not that the technical issues and policy concerns addressed by the Federal Rules of Evidence have been afforded due consideration."[5]

In making its resolution of any disputed preliminary question, the court "is not bound by evidence rules except those on privilege."[6] This means that a court may base its ruling on admissibility by considering evidence that is inadmissible or that has not yet been shown to be admissible. Indeed, a judge ruling upon the admissibility of some exhibit can actually consider and give appropriate weight to that very exhibit, which can therefore serve as at least part of the basis for a ruling that the exhibit is in fact admissible.[7]

The framers of Rule 104 concluded that there was no need to make the rules of evidence binding upon a judge who is resolving a dispute as their applicability to some item of evidence, noting that the exclusionary rules of evidence have been described as "the child of the jury system."[8] Indeed, most of the rules of evidence are a reflection of a general judicial mistrust for the capacity of jurors to sensibly appreciate the limitations of certain kinds of evidence, which is why the rules have been made inapplicable to a host of other important decisions made by the judge.[9] The Committee also justified this rule in part on the basis of "practical necessity,"[10] pointing out that many important preliminary questions under the rules logically cannot be decided unless the judge has the authority to scrutinize the very exhibit whose admissibility he is trying to resolve. For example, the hearsay rules contain exceptions that allow the admission of out-of-court statements if the

---

v. United States, 483 U.S. 171, 175–176 (1987).

[5] *Bourjaily,* 483 U.S. at 175. The Court acknowledged that the burden of persuasion may sometimes be placed upon the party who seeks to demonstrate the applicability of some Rule of Evidence requiring exclusion of the evidence, but the Court declined to "address the circumstances in which the burden of coming forward to show that the proffered evidence is inadmissible is appropriately placed on the nonoffering party." *Id.* at 176 n.1.

[6] Rule 104(a). This provision is also reflected in Rule 1101(d)(1), which states that the rules, other than the privilege rules, do not apply to "the court's determination, under Rule 104(a), on a preliminary question of fact governing admissibility."

[7] *Bourjaily,* 483 U.S. at 171.

[8] Committee Note to Rule 104(a) (citation omitted).

[9] *See, e.g.,* the many other contexts set forth in Rule 1101(d)(3), which involve factual issues decided by a judge without the constraints of the rules of evidence. *See also* Rule 1101(b) (providing that the evidence rules apply to contempt proceedings "except those in which the court may act summarily," which means that the rules are only binding on contempt proceedings in which there is a right to a jury trial). *See* Al-Bihani v. Obama, 590 F.3d 866 (D.C. Cir. 2010) (because district judges are experienced and sophisticated fact finders, they need not be protected from unreliable information in the manner in which the Rules of Evidence aim to shield the eyes of impressionable juries; the law of evidence is "the child of the jury system" in that it seeks to exclude probative evidence because of its possible adverse effects on a lay jury).

[10] Committee Notes to Rule 104(a), set out in Appendix A, *infra.*

speaker was intentionally making that statement to further the purposes of a conspiracy, or describing the details surrounding his imminent death.[11] It is almost always impossible to resolve disputes over the applicability of rules like those unless the judge has the ability to examine and consider the contents of the statement itself.

The privilege rules, however, are explicitly made binding upon the judge while ruling on questions pertaining to admissibility. This is in keeping with the fact that privilege laws, unlike all other rules of evidence, have been made applicable to "all stages of a case or proceeding."[12] The privilege rules have been made binding on the judge just as much as the jurors, because the privilege rules (unlike the other evidence rules) are intended not to keep certain kinds of untrustworthy evidence from the jury, but rather to keep certain kinds of sensitive and confidential information entirely immune from public disclosure to anyone other than those who are lawfully entitled to knowledge of those secrets.[13]

§ 104.3   Conditional Relevance

Rule 104(b) governs "conditional relevance" — situations in which the relevance of some evidence logically "depends on whether a fact exists."[14] This refers to the common scenario in which the relevance of the evidence depends on some factual dispute between the parties, and whether the proponent can offer sufficient evidence to resolve that preliminary factual question in its favor. The process of laying that foundation typically involves a showing that the evidence being offered can be connected somehow to the other facts and participants involved in the case.[15]

The elemental and self-evident requirements of logic frequently dictate that evidence of some fact is simply not relevant unless the party offering the evidence can also prove some other fact. This task of demonstrating the

---

[11] *See* Rules 801(d)(2)(E) and 804(b)(2), respectively.

[12] Rule 1101(c). *See also* Fed. R. Civ. P. 26(b)(1) (even inadmissible evidence may be subject to a pretrial discovery request, but only if it is "nonprivileged").

[13] This prohibition is not absolute, however, for even materials arguably protected by the attorney-client privilege may be subjected to the limited intrusion of a confidential *in camera* review by the court once there has been a prima facie showing that the materials may fall within the crime-fraud exception to that privilege. United States v. Zolin, 491 U.S. 554 (1989). *See* § 501.5, *infra.*

[14] Rule 104(b).

[15] King v. McMillan, 594 F.3d 301 (4th Cir. 2010) (in sexual harassment case by female deputy sheriff against her supervisor, testimony by other women who were sexually harassed by the same sheriff was properly admitted with a limiting instruction that it could be used to prove that the defendant's conduct was sufficiently severe or pervasive to create a hostile work environment, but only if the plaintiff was aware of the harassment described by those other women while she employed. Such testimony was also admissible, however, without regard to whether she was aware of such facts at the time of her employment, to prove her claim that the sheriff's unwelcome conduct was because of her sex).

relevance of one's proffered evidence, which is regulated by Rule 104(b), is also part of the process of "laying a foundation" for the admission of disputed evidence. For example, simple logic teaches that evidence of a written death threat received by a murder victim normally has no relevance to the prosecution's case unless the threat was made or authorized by the accused on trial. Another example: the fact that a plaintiff made an oral statement giving notice of a defect in the defendant's stairway is not relevant in a case, and therefore not admissible, unless the defendant was present and able to hear the statement when the statement was made. In these and countless similar examples of "conditional relevance," the question arises: What if the party objecting to the evidence denies that its relevance has been adequately proved?

In all cases where the relevance of some evidence — let's call it Exhibit A — depends on the answer to some factual dispute, Rule 104(b) assigns different roles to the judge and the jury in deciding what is to be done with that evidence. The judge will first perform the preliminary role of screening the evidence, both pro and con, on the answer to that preliminary factual question, to determine whether the proponent has sufficient admissible evidence to permit a rational jury to resolve that factual question in favor of the proponent. In this context, unlike other admissibility disputes governed by Rule 104(a), the judge does not resolve the factual dispute presented, but merely decides whether proof has been introduced "sufficient to support a finding that the fact does exist."[16] Exhibit A will be admitted only if the *judge* first makes the preliminary determination that the proponent has offered (or will offer) evidence sufficient to permit (although perhaps not require) a finding by the *jury* that the exhibit is relevant to the case. If the exhibit is admitted, the proper weight to be given to that exhibit will be argued by the parties in closing argument and decided by the jurors. This point is underscored by Rule 104(e), which clarifies that the powers assigned to the court by Rule 104 cannot be employed in a manner that would undermine the power of the jury to resolve issues of weight and credibility in the context of problems involving conditional relevance.[17]

When deciding whether there is sufficient evidence to fulfill the condition that would make some other evidence relevant under Rule 104(b), is the

---

[16] Rule 104(b). This process bears an instructive resemblance to the role played by a judge in resolving a motion for summary judgment, Fed. R. Civ. P. 56, or a motion during trial for judgment as a matter of law, Fed. R. Civ. P. 50. In those analogous settings as well, the judge does not decide the factual disputes between the parties, but merely examines the evidence to see if there is enough to create a genuine issue for the jury to resolve.

[17] United States v. Nadeau, 598 F.3d 966 (8th Cir. 2010) (in assault prosecution, trial court did not err in admitting a metal pipe found in a car in which the accused was riding, because witnesses identified it as similar to a pipe they saw in the defendant's hands; the fact that no blood, tissue, or fingerprints were found on the pipe was something for the jury to consider in determining how much weight to give the pipe but did not make it inadmissible).

judge entitled to consider inadmissible evidence, as he might do when deciding any other issue of admissibility under Rule 104(a)? The rule contains no explicit answer to that question, but the answer is obvious. A judge ruling on a conditional relevance objection under Rule 104(b) is limited to determining whether there is sufficient evidence to support a finding by the *jury* on the preliminary factual condition. That evidence therefore must be admissible by definition, for inadmissible evidence cannot be considered by the jury (assuming there is a proper objection), and therefore could never support a finding by them of any conclusion. Thus, for example, if a prosecutor wishes to offer an alleged confession and has a fair amount of evidence that the letter was written by the accused but all of that foundational evidence consists of inadmissible hearsay, the letter simply cannot be admitted.

In one critical respect, Rule 104(b) is not discretionary. If the judge concludes that there is sufficient admissible evidence to permit a rational jury to possibly conclude that some exhibit or testimony is relevant to the case at trial, the court shall admit it.[18] For example, if a police officer testifies that a written confession was signed by the accused, and that testimony is not inherently incredible, the court has no discretion to exclude the confession merely because the judge is personally persuaded that it is more probable that the officer is mistaken or lying. The trial court cannot arrogate to itself the power to decide debatable issues of conditional relevance, or the constitutional power of the jury would become meaningless; there is not much value in a jury that is only allowed to hear the exhibits that the judge finds believable. As the framers of the rules insisted in another context, it would be extraordinary to allow "a judge to exclude evidence because he does not believe it."[19]

The Federal Rules give a trial judge a fair amount of discretion in regulating the method and order in which evidence is presented.[20] Accordingly, Rule 104(b) likewise grants the judge the power to admit evidence of debatable relevance "on the condition that the proof be introduced later."[21] This possibility of admitting evidence before the proof of its connection to the case involves a process often described as "connecting up." When a party

---

[18] Until its recent stylistic revision, Rule 104(b) made this point clear by providing that "the court *shall* admit" any evidence if the offering party submits the required foundational evidence that would be adequate to permit a jury to find that the relevant condition had been fulfilled (emphasis added). This language was deleted from the rule when it was revised in 2011, but no contrary language has been inserted in the rule to suggest that a different result should now follow in such circumstances.

[19] Introductory Advisory Committee Note to Article VIII, Hearsay ("Introductory Note: the Hearsay Problem").

[20] Rule 611(a).

[21] Rule 104(b).

offering an exhibit assures that she will "connect it up," the proponent is telling the court, in effect, "If you will take my word for it as an officer of the court and admit this document now, I promise that I will later produce sufficient admissible evidence to demonstrate that this document can be connected to the parties and the facts of this case, although there is some good reason why that foundational evidence cannot be supplied at this moment."[22] If the trial judge agrees to accept that assurance at face value, the court will essentially be granting the proponent the ability to lay some or all of the foundation for the admissibility of the evidence after the evidence is admitted. The evidence is then admitted "subject to" the promise by the proponent to connect it up at some later point in the trial. If the proponent forgets or fails to make good on that promise before resting its case, the opposing party must renew its objection and ask that the evidence be stricken from the record, at which point the jury will be told to disregard that evidence.[23]

Why do Rules 104(a) and 104(b) provide such different methods for resolving preliminary questions concerning (1) ordinary issues of admissibility and (2) conditional relevance? The difference in treatment can be explained by one basic underlying distinction. All admissibility rulings delegated to the court by Rule 104(a) involve questions, both factual and legal, that are made controlling by the *law*. For example, it is a rule of law — not an abstract principle of self-evident logic — that dictates that the voluntariness and admissibility of a confession sometimes depends on whether the accused was read his rights, or that a confidential conversation with one's spouse is privileged. These disputes, even when they turn on the resolution of some factual question, are therefore best suited to a judge, who should ordinarily be much less prone than the jurors to regard the rules of evidence as irrational technicalities that should be circumvented, when need be, to get at the truth. But conditional relevance disputes, on the other hand, simply require the application of self-evident principles of *logic,* which can be much more safely entrusted to jurors with no special legal training or allegiance to the system of evidence rules. There is good reason to doubt that a jury can be trusted to faithfully follow the legal rule that makes an

---

[22] What would count as a good reason will be up to the judge. Sometimes it will be the fact that an important foundational witness for some exhibit is not available to testify until some later point in the trial, although the proponent believes that it will promote clarity to allow the jury to see that exhibit right now, perhaps while some other witness is on the stand and ready to answer other questions about the exhibit. Or sometimes the foundation cannot be laid without the testimony of two different witnesses (for example, one witness who will verify that Government Exhibit One is the same weapon that was used to commit some crime, and another witness who will verify that it was found on a search of the defendant), only one of whom can be called at a time.

[23] *See* United States v. Dougherty, 895 F.2d 399, 403 (7th Cir. 1990) ("If a condition attached to the admission of evidence is not satisfied by the offering party, the burden properly rests with the objecting party to renew the objection.").

otherwise trustworthy confession inadmissible because of some "technicality" in the way the police obtained the statement, as the Supreme Court has recognized.[24] But nobody would doubt the ability of any jury to follow the dictates of the common-sense logical proposition that an otherwise "incriminating" letter should be given no weight if there is no evidence that the letter was actually written by the accused.

§ 104.4   Procedure for Resolving Preliminary Questions

When a court resolves preliminary factual and legal questions presented by an evidentiary objection, the court will frequently entertain legal argument by counsel and may even need to consider live testimony or other evidence. Of course, as long as the arguments and evidence presented at such at a hearing are being considered to resolve a dispute over admissibility, there is no requirement that the jury be allowed to remain in the room to overhear such matters. But it would be time-consuming and inefficient to excuse the jury from the room every time an evidentiary objection is raised and argued during the course of a trial. Of course, these issues become moot any time an evidentiary objection is resolved before the trial begins, which is one more advantage for counsel and the court when important issues can be disposed of through a motion *in limine*.[25]

When an evidentiary objection is raised in the middle of a jury trial, Rule 104(c) addresses whether the jury should be allowed to remain in the courtroom. In every case, of course, the judge must be sensitive to the risk that the jury might hear discussions about the admissibility of evidence that may later be excluded but which has the potential to adversely influence the jury's verdict. In almost every case, Rule 104(c) gives the trial judge a broad grant of discretion as to whether arguments over the admissibility of evidence should be conducted in the presence of the jury. But the Rule also identifies two situations in which that discretion is eliminated, and in which the hearing must be held "so that the jury cannot hear it." In those two situations, the judge will usually hear the matter either before trial or while the jury has been excused from the room. If the argument will not require the presentation of testimony or extensive evidence, the court may prefer to save time by hearing argument from counsel at a "sidebar conference," at which the judge and the lawyers will meet briefly for a quiet discussion at the end of the judge's bench that is farthest from the jury and out of the range of their hearing.

The first situation in which argument must be held outside the hearing of the jury involves all hearings involving "the admissibility of a confession."[26] This provision reflects the inherently inflammatory effect of even a passing

---

[24] *See* Jackson v. Denno, 378 U.S. 368 (1966), discussed in § 104.4, *infra.*

[25] *See* § 103.4, *supra,* for a more detailed discussion of such motions.

[26] Rule 104(c).

mention of such evidence. It is essentially a codification of *Jackson v. Denno,*[27] which held that the Constitution forbids a trial court from allowing a jury to resolve disputes over the voluntariness and admissibility of a confession. In *Jackson,* the Supreme Court reasoned that jurors entrusted with such an assignment will (1) be unduly influenced by their knowledge of the confession's existence in trying to resolve the supposedly independent issue of its voluntariness, and (2) might well be unable to put the confession out of their minds even if they conclude that it is inadmissible. If jurors are allowed to hear even a brief mention of the existence of an alleged confession in a criminal trial, it is likely to exert a terribly prejudicial influence on their deliberations, even if the judge concludes that the confession is inadmissible, excludes it from evidence, and instructs the jurors to forget anything they heard on the subject.[28] To a very large extent, the objectives of this Rule are now more directly accomplished by Federal Rule of Criminal Procedure 12(b), which requires almost any motion to suppress a confession to be made and decided before the trial begins — thus eliminating the need to agonize over exclusion of the jury.[29]

Rule 104(c) also mandates that hearings on preliminary questions be held outside the presence of the jurors in a criminal case, even if it involves some evidence other than a confession, any time the accused wishes to testify at the hearing and so requests. This provision was added to the Rule by the House Committee on the Judiciary out of a "proper regard for the right of an accused not to testify generally in the case."[30] If a jury is allowed, over the objection of the accused, to hear and see him testify on any preliminary issue in the trial — even a matter as innocuous as whether a certain signature was his, or whether the police had a warrant before they entered his home — those jurors would almost inevitably draw an adverse inference from the fact

---

[27] Jackson v. Denno, 378 U.S. 368 (1966).

[28] Of course, if the jurors were improperly allowed to remain in the courtroom during the argument over the admissibility of a confession but the judge ultimately ruled the confession *admissible,* the jury would then hear and see the confession for themselves, so there would have been no harm done in allowing them to have heard about it before it was admitted. As long as the confession is properly deemed admissible, the court's violation of Rule 104(c) would always be harmless error. *See* § 103.2, *supra,* for a discussion of "harmless error."

[29] In federal court, a motion to "suppress" any evidence in a criminal case, including a confession, must be made before trial. Fed. R. Crim. P. 12(b)(3)(C). (*Suppression* refers to the exclusion of evidence on the grounds that it was obtained in violation of some constitutional right.) The failure to do so constitutes a waiver of the objection, unless the court finds "good cause" to grant relief from the waiver. Fed. R. Crim. P. 12(e). The trial court is also obligated to decide the motion before trial unless it finds good cause to defer the ruling until the time of trial. Fed. R. Crim. P. 12(d). When those requirements are honored, the matter will be decided long before any jury has been selected, and so the requirements of Rule 104(c) will usually become moot.

[30] Report of the House Comm. on the Judiciary on Rule 104(c), reproduced in Appendix A, *infra.*

that the accused did not choose during the trial to take the stand and answer any questions about the accusations against him. In addition, such an arrangement would also entail the intolerable risk that the jury might hear the court, in the course of making its ruling, find that the accused testified falsely on the preliminary matter, which would be devastating to the right of the accused to a fair trial.[31]

In all other cases not covered by those two special rules, the judge has discretion whether to allow the jury to remain in the room to overhear arguments or evidence that is presented to assist the judge in resolving some dispute over admissibility. Hearing on these other preliminary matters must be conducted out of the hearing of the jury if "justice so requires."[32] In making that decision, the court will be guided primarily by two factors.

(1) First, the judge will be concerned primarily with whether the preliminary foundational proof or arguments could be heard by the jury with no adverse effect.[33] Some legal requirements for admissibility have nothing to do with the merits of the case, so there is no real harm to either side if the jury is allowed to hear the foundational evidence, regardless of what the judge decides to do. For example, there is rarely much risk of prejudice to either party if the judge allows a few brief questions in front of the jury as to whether a hearsay document was written by someone in the ordinary course of his employment, and therefore admissible under the hearsay exception for business records.[34] Even if the judge concludes that the document was not a "business record" and therefore excludes any further mention of the document at the trial, there is likely to be little if any prejudice to the objecting party from the fact that the jury learned briefly about the existence of some alleged office record that they never saw. Other preliminary factual issues, such as the voluntariness of an accused's confession, are so intimately related to the merits of the case that it would have a terribly prejudicial impact to allow the jury to hear any evidence on

---

[31] It is of course unlikely that any judge would ever be clumsy or unguarded enough, in the presence of the jury, to make an explicit announcement that "I find that the defendant's testimony is not truthful." But the jury will get the point. If the jurors were allowed to sit through a brief hearing at which the accused and the officer gave obviously conflicting testimony as to whether the officer had a search warrant, and the judge then made a ruling that favored the prosecutor, the jury would almost certainly understand that the judge found the testimony of the accused not credible. Indeed, even if the judge takes pains to avoid making many explicit findings of fact in the hearing of the jury and all they hear him say is "objection overruled," the jurors might well mistakenly conclude that the judge had concluded that the accused was lying or dishonest, when perhaps the judge had merely concluded that the accused was mistaken or confused.

[32] Rule 104(c).

[33] "Much evidence on preliminary questions, though not relevant to jury issues, may be heard by the jury with no adverse effect." Committee Notes to Rule 104(c).

[34] *See* Rule 803(6).

such matters, even if the judge subsequently decides that the actual contents of the confession are inadmissible. Once the jury gets wind of the fact that the defendant made a "confession," it does the defendant little good if the confession is ruled inadmissible and the jury therefore does not see its details. Indeed, the jurors might well be tempted to imagine that the confession was more incriminating than it really was, especially if they know that it was concealed from them at the request of the defense — which is why Rule 104(c) wisely creates a special rule for disputes over confessions.

(2) The second primary issue the judge needs to consider is whether the foundational evidence might be of any possible value to the jury if the challenged evidence is admitted.[35] Sometimes the evidence that governs the *admissibility* of testimony or an exhibit might also be relevant to its *weight or credibility*. For example, the qualifications of a supposed "expert witness" are important to the judge — who must decide whether the witness is truly an "expert" as that term is defined in Rule 702 and whether she will therefore be allowed to testify — but may also be important to the jurors in deciding how much weight to give the expert's opinion if she is allowed to testify. In such a case, it makes sense to take the preliminary foundational proof on the expertise of the witness in the hearing of the jurors, so that it will not need to be repeated for them if the judge rules that the witness is entitled to testify and offer an opinion as an expert. More often, however, the foundational evidence relevant to the legal admissibility of some exhibit has little or nothing to do with its logical persuasiveness or force. For example, if a judge needs to hear conflicting testimony as to whether a statement made to a lawyer was confidential and therefore protected as privileged, that testimony has nothing to do with the weight or credibility of the allegedly privileged statement. Allowing the jury to stay in the room while the judge hears such foundational proof therefore does not have the potential to save much time, because there would be no need to repeat it for the jury's benefit if the challenged exhibit is admitted.

§ 104.5   Testimony by the Accused on Preliminary Matters

In a criminal case, the accused will often wish to testify on some preliminary matter outside the hearing of the jury, perhaps at a pretrial hearing, as Rule 104(c) allows.[36] For example, he might wish to be heard by

---

[35] "Not infrequently the same evidence which is relevant to the issue of establishment of fulfillment of a condition precedent to admissibility is also relevant to weight or credibility, and time is saved by taking foundation proof in the presence of the jury." Committee Notes to Rule 104(c). If the challenged evidence is excluded, on the other hand, the judge will never regret having taken a chance and asking the jury to leave the room while she heard foundational proof pertaining to its admissibility. There is no need for the jury to know anything about the details pertaining to evidence that the judge ultimately declined to admit.

[36] It should be noted, however, that the term *preliminary questions,* as it is used in Rule

the court at a suppression hearing on whether the police produced a warrant before they entered his home. But often that same defendant might not be willing to testify if there was any risk that the judge would allow the prosecutor on cross-examination to get into other matters in the case more directly involving guilt or innocence. To encourage the accused to offer such testimony without fear, Rule 104(d) guarantees that an accused who chooses to testify on a preliminary matter will not be "subject to cross-examination on other issues in the case." This provision operates as an exception to Rule 611(b), which gives a trial judge in any other context the discretion to allow a cross-examiner to ask questions outside the subject matter of the direct examination. It is intended to safeguard the critical ability of an accused to testify on preliminary matters bearing on the admissibility of evidence without forsaking his Fifth Amendment right to refuse to answer any questions about his guilt or innocence.

Of course, the accused cannot have it both ways. If he chooses, while testifying during a pretrial hearing on a preliminary question, to offer gratuitous comments on other matters, he will then be subject to cross-examination on those topics. Just like any other witness, the accused is subject to cross-examination on any matters that he or she introduces that exceed the scope of the evidence necessary to resolve the preliminary matter. This is consistent with the rule that makes every topic fair game for the cross-examiner if it was raised during, or made a part of, "the subject matter of the direct examination."[37]

Rules 104(c) and 104(d) are both "designed to encourage participation by the accused in the determination of preliminary matters,"[38] by assuring the accused that his testimony will be heard outside the presence of the jury, and that he will not be forced to answer questions on other matters that he chooses to not discuss. But the decision of the accused to be heard on some preliminary question is not entirely without risk. Under prevailing law, the testimony given by the accused before trial on a preliminary matter cannot be used as evidence against him at trial, at least if he does not testify at the trial.[39] But can the testimony given by the accused, if it tends to incriminate him, be used to impeach his credibility as a "prior inconsistent statement" if he later elects to testify at trial in a way that contradicts what he said at the

---

104 and throughout this Chapter, had nothing to do with the questions that arise at a "preliminary hearing," a pretrial stage in a criminal prosecution at which a magistrate or other judicial official must determine whether there is probable cause to believe that a criminal offense was committed by the accused. *See* Fed. R. Crim. P. 5.1 ("Preliminary Hearing").

[37] Rule 611(b).

[38] Committee Note to Rule 104(d).

[39] Simmons v. United States, 390 U.S. 377 (1968) (where accused testified that he was the owner of a suitcase at a suppression hearing to show his standing to contest the legality of its seizure, that testimony could not be admitted against him at trial as part of the Government's case in chief as proof of his guilt).

suppression hearing?[40] Rule 104 does not answer that question,[41] and the Supreme Court has not yet squarely resolved it.[42] But lower courts to consider the matter have uniformly found that such evidence may be used to impeach the later inconsistent testimony by the accused,[43] and that conclusion is almost surely correct. In almost every context in which the issue has arisen, the Supreme Court of the United States has held that "tainted evidence" obtained in violation of the constitution, and therefore inadmissible as part of the Government's case in chief, is admissible for impeachment if the accused testifies at trial in a manner that is arguably inconsistent with that earlier testimony.[44]

§ 104.6   Rule 104 and Preserving the Role of the Jury

Rule 104 gives a trial judge a vast degree of control over the resolution of the many important "preliminary questions" pertaining to admissibility that arise during the course of any trial — including even those questions of fact that are bitterly disputed and the subject of conflicting testimony. This is true even with respect to preliminary questions that involve little more than the sort of "credibility determinations" that have always been thought, in most other contexts, to be particularly well suited for resolution by a jury.[45] Indeed, most of those issues will be resolved by the court in a manner that will leave the jury ignorant that the issue was ever disputed or decided.

But the control given to the court over such matters is not unlimited. The rule concludes with the important reminder that, at least with respect to evidence that is admitted after an objection has been overruled, Rule 104 does not limit the right of either party to insist that the jury be allowed to consider all evidence that is relevant to the weight or credibility of the evidence that the jury has been allowed to consider.[46]

---

[40] *See* Chapter 613, *infra,* for a detailed discussion of this method of impeachment.

[41] This point is made explicit in the Committee Notes to Rule 104(d) ("The rule does not address itself to questions of the subsequent use of testimony given by an accused at a hearing on a preliminary matter").

[42] United States v. Salvucci, 448 U.S. 83, 93–94 (1980) (collecting cases holding that testimony from a suppression hearing may be used for impeachment, but declining to resolve the issue).

[43] United States v. Jaswal, 47 F.3d 539, 543 (2d Cir. 1995); United States v. Beltran-Gutierrez, 19 F.3d 1287, 1291 (9th Cir. 1994); United States v. Quesada-Rosadal, 685 F.2d 1281, 1283 (11th Cir. 1982).

[44] Kansas v. Ventris, — U.S. —, 129 S. Ct. 1841, 173 L. Ed. 2d 801, 809 (2009) (collecting cases).

[45] Kansas v. Ventris, — U.S. —, 129 S. Ct. 1841, 173 L. Ed. 2d 801, 809 n.* (2009) (our legal system "is built on the premise that it is the province of the jury to weigh the credibility of competing witnesses").

[46] The Rule puts the point, perhaps not as clearly as could be imagined, when it states that it "does not limit the right of a party to introduce before the jury evidence relevant to weight or credibility." Rule 104(e).

This provision is written primarily for the benefit of the objecting party who has tried without success to persuade the judge that some evidence ought to be excluded, in those cases where the asserted *legal* grounds for exclusion would also have some *logical* bearing on the weight or credibility of the evidence. For example, the law provides that a confession is inadmissible if the judge believes the defendant's testimony that the confession was coerced through physical duress, and common sense confirms that the same confession, if admitted, should be disregarded and given no weight if the jury can be persuaded by that same testimony. This will also be true in those fairly unusual situations in which the rules give the court discretion to admit or exclude evidence based on the court's assessment of its reliability or trustworthiness.[47] For example, if a judge entertains extensive argument before overruling an objection that a business record lacks "trustworthiness,"[48] or that the opinion of an alleged expert is not sufficiently "reliable,"[49] the objecting party will not be precluded from renewing those *same* arguments before the jurors in an effort to demonstrate that the admitted evidence is not deserving of belief or trust. In effect, Rule 104(e) gives the unsuccessful objecting party a chance to rescue victory from the jaws of defeat by persuading the jury that the judge was wrong to admit the evidence. The judge is not allowed to preclude such arguments on the theory that "I have already considered and resolved that matter." But great care must always be taken to ensure that the jury will not learn or infer that they are, in effect, being asked to reconsider a factual issue that has already been considered and decided by the judge, or there would be little chance that the jury could consider the question with an open mind.

Rule 104(e) also sometimes operates, although less rarely, in favor of the proponent who successfully sought admission of some evidence by persuading the judge that the details of the evidence justified its admission. For example, if a judge considers and overrules an objection to the testimony of an witness after concluding that the witness is an expert, following a hearing that was conducted outside the hearing of the jury, the offering party has the right to ask the witness about her credentials and expertise once again in the presence of the jurors, in an effort to persuade them that the opinion of the witness is deserving of respect. The judge cannot deprive the lawyer of that

---

[47] The Federal Rules of Evidence sometimes — although only very rarely — give the judge the discretion to exclude certain forms of evidence if the judge concludes that the evidence is not sufficiently reliable or trustworthy.

[48] *See* Rule 803(6) (hearsay statements made in the regular course of a business may be excluded if "the source of information or circumstances of preparation indicate lack of trustworthiness").

[49] *See* Rule 702 (expert opinion testimony may be excluded it is not sufficiently "reliable").

opportunity merely because the court has already concluded that the witness is an expert.[50]

Rule 104(e) probably does not make it sufficiently explicit that this right — the ability to ask the jury to essentially reconsider a preliminary question that has already been decided by the judge — only pertains to the weight or credibility of the evidence that has been *admitted*. The somewhat ambiguous language of the Rule might lead the uninitiated observer to mistakenly suppose that it also gives parties a right to ask the jury to reconsider a judge's ruling when an objection has been sustained and some evidence has therefore been *excluded*. For example, a party might be tempted to ask a judge: "I know you have concluded that Exhibit A is so unreliable that it is not admissible, despite my arguments and evidence to the contrary, but I still want the jury to hear that evidence so they can consider and decide the matter for themselves." But that request will never be granted. Once a judge sustains an objection and concludes that some exhibit or testimony is *not* admissible, even in those rare cases where the judge is allowed to make that ruling based on her assessment that the evidence is not sufficiently reliable or trustworthy, that is the end of the matter. If the judge concludes that some exhibit is not admissible, any evidence submitted by the offering party in its unsuccessful attempt to persuade the judge to admit that exhibit will also be excluded from the jury's consideration on the grounds that it has simply become irrelevant. As long as the jurors will not be allowed to see or hear about some document, they have no need to know anything about the manner in which it was created.

---

[50] Indeed, the Advisory Committee has sensibly recommended in this context that the judge not tell the jurors that he has determined that a particular witness is qualified to testify as an "expert" as that term is used in Rule 702, or even use the word "expert" in the presence of the jury, so that the jury will not be unduly influenced by the knowledge that the issue before them has been considered and passed upon by the court in an analogous context. *See* Committee Note to 2000 Amendment to Rule 702, reproduced in Appendix A, *infra*.

Chapter 105

Rule 105. Limiting Evidence That Is Not Admissible Against Other Parties or for Other Purposes

Rule 105. Limiting Evidence That Is Not Admissible Against Other Parties or for Other Purposes

If the court admits evidence that is admissible against a party or for a purpose — but not against another party or for another purpose — the court, on timely request, must restrict the evidence to its proper scope and instruct the jury accordingly.

---

§ 105.1   The Concept of Limited Admissibility

The Rules of Evidence recognize the concept of limited admissibility. A number of evidentiary rules state that evidence which is generally inadmissible may nevertheless be admissible when offered for a certain, specific purpose. For example, Rule 404(b) generally excludes evidence of other crimes, wrongs, or acts. However, the Rule also states that evidence of prior bad acts may be admissible for the limited purpose of proving motive, opportunity, intent, etc.[1] When offered for this limited purpose, the evidence should not be considered broadly as it relates to any issue or party, but should be considered only for the narrow purpose for which the Rules allow its admission. Other rules which provide for the admission of evidence for a limited purpose include Rules 106, 407, 408, 409, 411 and 801.[2] Each of

---

[1] *See* Rule 404(b); § 404.11 *et seq., infra.*

[2] *See* Rule 106; § 106.1, *infra* (evidence admitted to satisfy the rule of completeness may be inadmissible for purposes other than placing the primary writing or recording in context); Rule 407; § 407.4, *infra* (evidence of subsequent remedial measures may be admissible to prove ownership, control or feasibility of precautionary measures); Rule 408; § 408.5, *infra* (evidence of compromise offer may be admissible to prove bias or prejudice of a witness, etc.); Rule 409; § 409.4, *infra* (evidence of payment of medical expenses may be admissible to establish control, identity, responsibility, etc.); Rule 411; § 411.4, *infra* (evidence of insurance may be admissible where a consequential fact other than negligence or wrongful conduct is the object of proof); Rule 608 (evidence of a witness's character or specific acts of conduct may be admissible to attack the credibility of a witness); Rule 609 (evidence of a conviction may be admissible to impeach a witness's credibility); Rule 801 (hearsay statements may be admissible as non-hearsay if offered for purpose other than for the truth of the matter asserted).

these Rules illustrate that evidence may be admissible for one purpose while simultaneously remaining inadmissible for another.[3]

Rule 105 embodies the doctrine of limited admissibility.[4] It recognizes that, where evidence of limited admissibility is admitted by the trial judge, there exists an almost certain risk that the jury, unless instructed otherwise, will consider the evidence beyond its limited purpose. Hence the Rule provides the trial judge with a mechanism — the limiting instruction — to educate the jury as to the permissible use of the evidence it has heard or seen, and thus control the use to which the trier of fact will put the admitted evidence.[5]

§ 105.2   Limiting Instructions

A limiting instruction allows the judge to instruct the jury as to the proper scope of the evidence. The most effective instructions are those that specify and prohibit the impermissible use of the admitted evidence; however, the Rule imposes on the trial judge no duty to provide such a prohibited-use instruction.[6] Instead, the judge has the discretion to craft what he or she feels to be an appropriate limiting instruction.[7] For example, in some instances, a judge may deem it wiser to state the instruction in terms of the permissible uses to which the evidence may be put, rather than state the uses to which the evidence may not be put, so as to avoid planting a seed in the jury's mind

---

[3] Evidence admitted under any of these Rules may be subject to a limiting instruction upon the request of the opposing party. *See generally* United States v. Brown, 707 F.2d 125 (5th Cir. 1983).

[4] *See generally,* 1 MCCORMICK §§ 56, 59; 1 WEINSTEIN'S FEDERAL EVIDENCE §§ 105.01–105.07; 1 MUELLER & KIRKPATRICK §§ 38–41; 1, 1A WIGMORE, §§ 13, 216. *See also* Note, *Co-defendant's Confessions,* 3 COLUM. L.J. & SOC. PROBS. 80 (1967); Note, *The Limiting Instruction—Its Effectiveness and Effect,* 51 MINN. L. REV. 264 (1966); Note, *Evidence Admissible for a Limited Purpose—The Risk of Confusion Upsetting the Balance of Advantage,* 16 SYRACUSE L. REV. 81 (1964).

[5] *See, e.g.,* Thronson v. Meisels, 800 F.2d 136 (7th Cir. 1986) (in a housing discrimination suit, the court gave instructions that evidence of the defendant's rejection of plaintiffs' rental application because they were a "mixed couple" was relevant only to the damages the plaintiffs suffered and that it "must be considered for that limited purpose and for no other"); United States v. Eddy, 597 F.2d 430 (5th Cir. 1979) (testimony by agent that co-defendant had told him he received forged checks from defendants was admissible to impeach co-defendant who had testified that he received checks from someone else; evidence was therefore not hearsay; trial court had properly instructed jury twice not to use testimony as evidence of defendant's guilt).

[6] *Cf.* Government of the Virgin Islands v. Mujahid, 990 F.2d 111 (3d Cir. 1993) ("The instruction to the jury must deal precisely with the issue of how the . . . evidence can and cannot be used").

[7] *See* Borunda v. Richmond, 885 F.2d 1384 (1989) (a "forbidden use" instruction, although preferred, is not required by Rule 105); Hale v. Firestone Tire & Rubber Co., 820 F.2d 928 (8th Cir. 1987) (stating that Rule 105 "does not require all limiting instructions to contain prohibited use language").

as to the impermissible use.[8]

Rule 105 is triggered by a request for a limiting instruction,[9] — and it imposes a mandatory duty ("the court . . . must restrict the evidence to its proper scope") upon the court to issue the instruction when such a request is made.[10] The request may be made during the course of the trial or prior to trial when a party anticipates that an issue of limited admissibility will arise. In either case, the request should be specific and in conformity with the directives of Rule 103(a) pertaining to rulings on evidence.[11] Failure to request a limiting instruction generally means that the proffered evidence can be used for any purpose.[12] Although it is preferable that a trial court provide the limiting instruction at the time the challenged evidence is introduced, so as to maximize the effectiveness of the instruction, the actual timing of an instruction is an issue left to the discretion of the trial court.[13] In some cases, however, where a delayed instruction would effectively be the

---

[8] *See* Federal Judicial Center Pattern Jury Instruction No. 18 (limiting the jury's consideration to one purpose without disclosing impermissible purposes).

[9] Rule 105 does not specify that the request must be made by a party. However, it is not clear from the Rule or from the Advisory Committee Note who, other than a party, might make such a request. *See* United States v. Christian, 786 F.2d 203 (6th Cir. 1986) (trial court's failure to give limiting instruction *sua sponte* where defendant failed to request one was not plain error). *But cf.* Ferguson v. Knight, 809 F.2d 1239 (6th Cir. 1987) (trial court's failure to give limiting instruction *sua sponte* on the purpose for which defendant's prior conviction could be used was plain error of constitutional proportions despite defendant's failure to request such instruction).

[10] *See* Lubbock Feed Lots, Inc. v. Iowa Beef Processors, 630 F.2d 250 (5th Cir. 1980) (but finding error harmless). *But cf.* United States v. Thirion, 813 F.2d 146 (8th Cir. 1987) (trial court properly denied request for limiting instruction regarding government witness's testimony where the request did not specifically identify portions of testimony to be limited and the request was not made until after co-defendants' cross-examination).

[11] *See* United States v. Thirion, 813 F.2d 146 (8th Cir. 1987) (a request for a limiting instruction was properly denied where the request was not specific and not timely made); United States v. Dozier, 672 F.2d 531 (5th Cir. 1982).

[12] *See* United States v. Walter, 434 F.3d 30, 35 (1st Cir. 2006) (a party who is entitled to a limiting instruction but fails to request one thereby waives any objection to the judge's failure to give such an instruction); Gray v. Busch Entertainment Corp., 886 F.2d 14 (2d Cir. 1989) (because opposing party failed to request a limiting instruction, the proffered evidence could be considered for any purpose). *See also* United States v. Johnson, 46 F.3d 1166, 1171 (D.C. Cir. 1995) (to provide a limiting instruction where one is not requested might undermine a strategy to minimize jury recollection of unfavorable evidence).

[13] *See* United States v. Chance, 306 F.3d 356 (6th Cir. 2002) (when admitting evidence that is admissible as to only one party or purpose, it is within the judge's discretion whether to give a requested limiting instruction contemporaneous with introduction of the evidence or to wait until just before jury deliberations); United States v. Sliker, 751 F.2d 477 (2d Cir. 1984) (finding no error where the judge "chose to delay the limiting instruction until the final charge"); Lubbock Feed Lots, Inc. v. Iowa Beef Processors, Inc., 630 F.2d 250 (5th Cir. 1980) ("Although generally more effective at the time the evidence is presented, limiting instructions may be requested and given as part of the court's final instructions to the jury").

equivalent of no instruction at all, the trial court may be required to provide an immediate limiting instruction.

Although Rule 105 places the burden of requesting a limiting instruction on the party who wishes it, nothing in the Rule *prevents* the trial judge from providing a limiting instruction *sua sponte* in the absence of a request by a party. Similarly, nothing in the Rule *requires* the judge to provide a limiting instruction when no request is made.[14]

§ 105.3   Relationship with Rule 403

The function of Rule 105 must be considered in light of Rule 403, which provides for the exclusion of otherwise relevant evidence where the probative value is substantially outweighed by countervailing negative influences. Accordingly, where, for example, the admission of evidence would cause unfair prejudice or confusion of the issues, such evidence may be excluded under Rule 403.[15] Part of the court's consideration in deciding whether to exclude evidence under Rule 403 should address an evaluation of the effectiveness of a limiting instruction under Rule 105 if the evidence were admitted.[16] Consequently, the proponent of evidence who evokes an objection based on Rule 403 should suggest that the court may obviate the adverse effect by giving the jury a limiting instruction.[17] Conversely, a party who requests the exclusion of evidence under Rule 403 should be prepared to seek a limiting instruction should the court overrule the initial objection.

It should be noted that a limiting instruction may not be used in criminal trials in situations where an accused's constitutional rights would be jeopardized by the admission of evidence for a limited purpose. For example, a limiting instruction will not correct the constitutional error of

---

[14] *See* LILLY, § 1.5 (3d ed.); *see also* United States v. Johnson, 46 F.3d 1166, 1171 (D.C. Cir. 1995) (to provide a limiting instruction where one is not requested might undermine a strategy to minimize jury recollection of unfavorable evidence).

[15] Rule 403; *see* 1 WEINSTEIN'S FEDERAL EVIDENCE § 105.02; 1 MUELLER & KIRKPATRICK § 38; 1 MCCORMICK, § 59; *but cf.* United States v. De Carlo, 458 F.2d 358 (3d Cir. 1972) (in extortion prosecution, evidence that alleged victim died of arsenic poisoning was received to shed light on state of mind of alleged victim, who was portrayed by other testimony as being "possessed by fear and capable of taking extreme action to secure the money needed to pay his debt and to protect his family"; since victim's fear was provable as a necessary element of the crime, it was proper to receive this evidence even though it might lead jury to wonder if defendants had murdered the alleged extortion victim or played a role in having him killed).

[16] *See* Rule 403, Advisory Committee Note; *see also* Mauldin v. Upjohn Co., 697 F.2d 644 (5th Cir. 1983).

[17] United States v. Lujan, 603 F.3d 850 (10th Cir. 2010) (because jurors can usually be trusted to follow the limiting instructions given by the trial judge, the risk of jury confusion should not normally justify exclusion of even potentially prejudicial evidence where there is some way to fashion an appropriate limiting instruction that will identify the proper use of the evidence).

admitting into evidence the confession of a non-testifying co-defendant when that confession implicates another defendant.[18]

---

[18] *See* Cruz v. New York, 481 U.S. 186 (1987) (where a non-testifying co-defendant's confession facially incriminating the defendant is not directly admissible against the defendant, the Confrontation Clause bars its admission at their joint trial, even if the jury is instructed not to consider it against the defendant, and even if the defendant's own confession is admitted against him); *but cf.* Richardson v. Marsh, 481 U.S. 200 (1987) (the Confrontation Clause is not violated when the non-testifying co-defendant's confession is redacted to eliminate not only the defendant's name, but any reference to her existence, and proper limiting instructions are provided); *see also* Bruton v. United States, 391 U.S. 123 (1968). For an extensive discussion of *Bruton* and its progeny, *see* 1 WEINSTEIN'S FEDERAL EVIDENCE § 105.06; *see also* Thomas v. Hubbard, 273 F.3d 1164 (9th Cir. 2001) (in most circumstances, a court can safely trust a jury to follow instructions that out-of-court statements may be considered only for some limited purpose other than the truth of the statements, but there are some cases "in which out-of-court statements are so prejudicial that a jury would be unable to disregard their substantive content regardless of the purpose for which they are introduced and regardless of any curative instruction," thus resulting in a Confrontation Clause violation).

Chapter 106

Rule 106. Remainder of or Related Writings or Recorded Statements

Rule 106. Remainder of or Related Writings or Recorded Statements

If a party introduces all or part of a writing or recorded statement, an adverse party may require the introduction, at that time, of any other part — or any other writing or recorded statement — that in fairness ought to be considered at the same time.

---

§ 106.1 Function and Purpose of the Rule

Rule 106 is the federal codification of the common-law rule of completeness. Under the Rule, when a proponent introduces a writing or recording, or part thereof, into evidence, the adverse party may require the proponent to introduce any other writing or recording, or the remainder of the proponent's excerpt, if the trial court determines that fairness requires that the remainder ought to be considered contemporaneously with the excerpt.[1] The Rule does not require that the remainder of a written or recorded statement be introduced when an excerpt of the statement is admitted; it only requires the admission of the complementary evidence when it would be unfair not to do so.[2] If the court decides that "fairness" mandates the admission of additional evidence, the proponent may be given the option to decide whether to proceed with all the evidence required by the court or to forgo introducing any of the evidence.[3]

---

[1] United States v. Phillips, 596 F.3d 414 (7th Cir. 2010) (even if a redacted recording tells an incomplete story, this does not render the recording inadmissible; the proper remedy would not be to exclude the redacted recording but to supplement it with the other portions necessary to complete the context). *See generally,* 1 McCormick § 56; 1 Weinstein's Federal Evidence §§ 106.01–106.08; 1 Mueller & Kirkpatrick, §§ 42–46; 7 Wigmore, §§ 2094–2125; *see* Fed. R. Civ. P. 32(a)(6) (regarding depositions).

[2] *See* United States v. Branch, 91 F.3d 699, 727 (5th Cir. 1996) ("Neither the Constitution or Rule 106 . . . require the admission of the entire statement once any portion is admitted . . . .").

[3] *See* American Bald Eagle v. Bhatti 9 F.3d 163 (1st Cir. 1993) (it was not an error for the trial court, when it had found portions of a document had been taken out of context, to instruct

Obviously, the Rule contemplates a high degree of discretion to be exercised by the trial judge in determining when "fairness" mandates the admission of additional evidence.[4] In deciding whether fairness requires additional evidence, a judge should consider whether the complementary evidence is needed "to (1) explain the admitted portion, (2) place the admitted portion in context, (3) avoid misleading the trier of fact, or (4) ensure a fair and impartial understanding" of the primary evidence.[5] The party objecting to the partial reading of a document must ordinarily do more than insist on a reading of the entire document, and must specify which portion is relevant and why it should be presented to qualify or explain the portions that the jury has heard.[6]

When some evidence is judged to be incomplete, Rule 106 requires the proponent to introduce complementary evidence at a time when it is needed to place the primary writing or recording into the proper context or perspective.[7] Hence the Rule is essentially a timing rule. It operates to avoid

---

the proponent of the excerpt to "choose whether the entire document or no portions thereof would be admitted").

[4] United States v. Weisman, 624 F.2d 1118 (2d Cir. 1980) (trial court did not err in refusing to admit tape recordings introduced by the prosecution in their entirety where the omitted portions were not "necessary to clarify, or make not misleading, that which is introduced"); *see also* United States v. Velasco, 953 F.2d 1467 (7th Cir. 1992) (the district court properly denied defendant's motion to introduce the remaining portion of his statement to authorities since it did not satisfy the court's standards and would have potentially misled the jury); United States v. Sweiss, 814 F.2d 1208 (7th Cir. 1987) (prejudicial impact of exclusion did not rise to the level of abuse of discretion); United States v. Larranaga, 787 F.2d 489 (10th Cir. 1986) (where defendant failed to request the introduction of his entire grand jury testimony at the time the government introduced part of it, but only offered it on redirect, it was not an abuse of discretion for the trial court to refuse its admission, and would not have been an abuse even if defendant had followed proper procedure because the omitted portions were not necessary for fairness); United States v. Enright, 579 F.2d 980 (6th Cir. 1978). *See generally,* 7 WIGMORE, § 2094. Failure to apply Rule 106 to an accused's recorded statement can result in reversible error despite the high level of discretion afforded the trial judge; *see, e.g.,* United States v. Walker, 652 F.2d 708 (7th Cir. 1981).

[5] United States v. Soures, 736 F.2d 87, 91 (3d Cir. 1984). *See also* United States v. Branch, 91 F.3d 699 (5th Cir. 1996) (denying defendant the right to introduce exculpatory portions of his post-arrest statement when the government introduced inculpatory portions because the exculpatory portions did not contradict, explain or qualify the introduced portions); United States v. Haddad, 10 F.3d 1252, 1259 (7th Cir. 1993) ("the trial judge need only admit the remaining portions of the statement which are needed to clarify or explain the portion already received").

[6] McCoy v. Augusta Fiberglass Coatings, Inc., 593 F.3d 737 (8th Cir. 2010) (when a lawyer objects under Rule 106 by merely requesting, "Your Honor, if counsel's going to read part of the report, I request that he reads all of the report," without specifying why the entire report should be admitted or which portions of the report would be relevant, the objecting party has not met its burden under Rule 106 and the district court does not err in refusing that request).

[7] *See* Beech Aircraft Corp. v. Rainey, 488 U.S. 153 (1988) (stating that the rule of

the need for an adverse party to wait until cross-examination or rebuttal to introduce the complementary writings or recordings, and it is intended to prevent consideration of matters out of context.[8] Some courts have held that Rule 106 has a purpose beyond functioning as a timing rule, stating that a party who offers an incomplete statement forfeits any objection that the complementary evidence is inadmissible, *e.g.*, on hearsay grounds.[9] Evidence admissible solely under Rule 106 is to be used for the limited purpose expressed in the Rule. A limiting instruction, if requested under Rule 105, is

---

completeness guards against the "danger that an out-of-context statement may create such prejudice that it is impossible to repair by a subsequent presentation of additional material").

[8] *See, e.g.,* Harris v. Browning Ferris Indus., 635 F. Supp. 1202 (D. La. 1986), *aff'd,* 806 F.2d 259 (5th Cir. 1986) (where plaintiff introduced police officer's testimony explaining an auto accident, defendant could introduce testimony of another officer completing the statement of the first officer as to how the accident occurred); Huddleston v. Herman & MacLean, 640 F.2d 534 (5th Cir. 1981), *modified on other grounds,* 456 U.S. 914 (1982) (en banc) (since Rule 106 is made specifically applicable to depositions, defendants were entitled to introduce other portions of deposition relating to same matter dealt with in portion of deposition introduced by plaintiff; hearsay objections may be made when deposition is introduced into evidence). *Compare* Beech Aircraft Corp. v. Rainey, 488 U.S. 153 (1988) (the common-law "rule of completeness" was not circumscribed by Rule 106, and therefore the remainder of a document may be introduced on cross-examination or as part of the adversary's own case). *See generally,* 1 WEINSTEIN'S FEDERAL EVIDENCE § 106.02; *see also* United States v. Jamar, 561 F.2d 1103, 1108–1109 (4th Cir. 1977) (on perjury charge growing out of defendant's testimony at preliminary hearing it was not error for government to introduce transcript of defendant's testimony without introducing testimony of other witnesses, including defendant's daughter; "the purpose of Rule 106 . . . is to permit the contemporaneous introduction of recorded statements that place in context other writings admitted into evidence, which, viewed alone, may be misleading . . . there is no such problem here").

[9] *See* United States v. Lopez-Medina, 596 F.3d 716 (10th Cir. 2010) (even if evidence would otherwise be subject to a hearsay objection, that does not block its use when it is needed to provide context for a statement already admitted; the rule of completeness may be invoked to justify the introduction of otherwise inadmissible evidence when the court finds in fairness that the proffered evidence should be considered contemporaneously); United States v. Sutton, 801 F.2d 1346, 1368–1369 (D.C. Cir. 1986) ("Rule 106 can adequately fulfill its function only by permitting the admission of some otherwise admissible evidence when the court finds in fairness that the proffered evidence should be considered contemporaneously. A contrary construction raises the specter of distorted and misleading trials . . . ."); United States v. LeFevour, 798 F.2d 977, 980–981 (7th Cir. 1986) ("if otherwise inadmissible evidence is necessary to correct a misleading impression, then either it is admissible for this limited purpose by force of Rule 106 . . . or, if it is inadmissible, . . . the misleading evidence must be excluded too"). *But see* United States v. Wilkerson, 84 F.3d 692 (4th Cir. 1996) (Rule 106 does not "render admissible the evidence which is otherwise inadmissible under the hearsay rule"); United States Football League v. National Football League, 842 F.2d 1335 (2d Cir. 1988) (the Rule "does not compel admission of otherwise inadmissible hearsay evidence"). While this issue is not without debate, it appears that otherwise inadmissible evidence may be exposed to the jury where "in fairness" the trier of fact should receive the evidence under Rule 106. *See* 1 MUELLER & KIRKPATRICK, § 42 (noting that Rule 403 may operate to preempt the application of Rule 106 in this context).

appropriate to prevent the jury from improperly using the evidence.[10]

On its face, Rule 106 is limited to writing and recordings; hence the Rule does not expressly govern the admission of complementary evidence to oral statements.[11] Many courts have recognized that Rule 611 grants a trial court the authority to apply the Rule 106 principle of completeness to oral statements.[12]

---

[10] *See* Chapter 105, *supra*; *see also* United States v. LeFevour, 798 F.2d 977, 980–981 (7th Cir. 1986) (explaining that evidence admitted solely for the purpose of correcting a misleading impression under Rule 106 is admissible only for a "limited purpose").

[11] *See* United States v. Terry, 702 F.2d 299 (2d Cir. 1983); *see also* United States v. Pintar, 630 F.2d 1270 (8th Cir. 1980) (doctrine of verbal completeness expressed in Rule 106 has no application where prosecution witness impeached for bias, and government witness seeks to show additional reasons for her hostility to defendants).

[12] *See* Rule 611; *see also* United States v. Lopez-Medina, 596 F.3d 716 (10th Cir. 2010) (while Rule 106 applies only to writings and recorded statements, the rule of completeness embodied in the Rule is substantially applicable to oral testimony, and by virtue of Rule 611(a), which obligates the court to make the interrogation and presentation effective for the ascertainment of the truth. But the rule of completeness does not require admission of an entire statement, writing or recording; rather, only those portions that are necessary to clarify or explain the portion already received need be admitted); United States v. Branch, 91 F.3d 699, 727 (5th Cir. 1996); United States v. Li, 55 F.3d 325, 329 (7th Cir. 1995) ("[Rule] 611(a) grants district courts the same authority regarding oral statements which [Rule] 106 grants regarding written and recorded statements."); United States v. Haddad, 10 F.3d 1252, 1258–1259 (7th Cir. 1993).

ARTICLE II.
JUDICIAL NOTICE

Synopsis

Chapter 201

Rule 201. *Judicial Notice of Adjudicative Facts*

Rule 201. Judicial Notice of Adjudicative Facts

(a) Scope. This rule governs judicial notice of an adjudicative fact only, not a legislative fact.

(b) Kinds of Facts That May Be Judicially Noticed. The court may judicially notice a fact that is not subject to reasonable dispute because it:

(1) is generally known within the trial court's territorial jurisdiction; or

(2) can be accurately and readily determined from sources whose accuracy cannot reasonably be questioned.

(c) Taking Notice. The court:

(1) may take judicial notice on its own; or

(2) must take judicial notice if a party requests it and the court is supplied with the necessary information.

(d) Timing. The court may take judicial notice at any stage of the proceeding.

(e) Opportunity to Be Heard. On timely request, a party is entitled to be heard on the propriety of taking judicial notice and the nature of the fact to be noticed. If the court takes judicial notice before notifying a party, the party, on request, is still entitled to be heard.

(f) Instructing the Jury. In a civil case, the court must instruct the jury to accept the noticed fact as conclusive. In a criminal case, the court must instruct the jury that it may or may not accept the noticed fact as conclusive.

---

§ 201.1 Judicial Notice of Adjudicative Facts — In General

Judicial notice is the evidentiary process by which a court recognizes a fact in the absence of any antecedent, formal proof.[1] It is a substitute for

---

[1] *See generally,* 2 McCormick, §§ 328–335; 1 Weinstein's Federal Evidence §§ 201.01–201.34; 1 Mueller & Kirkpatrick, §§ 47–60; 9 Wigmore, §§ 2565–2583;

formal proof where, under the circumstances of a particular case, an adjudicative fact sought to be proved is reasonably beyond dispute. Where the fact sought to be noticed is reasonably indisputable, the normal standards of formal proof, if held to apply, would impede judicial efficiency by erecting unwarranted barriers to the party seeking to establish the fact. In this regard, the policy of judicial notice permits the court to accept evidence through an alternate process of admission without sacrificing the fundamental safeguards of the adversary system.[2] In operation, judicial notice does nothing to cast aside the basic standards upon which the system of evidence is predicated. Rather, judicial notice represents a realistic appraisal that certain facts present virtually none of the risks that the usual safeguards are designed to protect, and consequently, the need for formal proof is largely absent where the standard of Rule 201 is satisfied.[3]

In essence, judicial notice supersedes formal proof, yet it carries equal force. As such, the doctrine of judicial notice is applicable to circumstantially relevant facts as well as to ultimate facts of any case, civil or criminal, although the jury may be under varying instructions depending upon the nature and significance of the fact judicially noticed.

§ 201.2   "Adjudicative" versus "Legislative" Facts

On its face, Rule 201(a) limits the scope of the Rule to the judicial notice of "adjudicative facts." Put simply, adjudicative facts are those facts that concern the burdens of proof of the case as they pertain to the immediate parties and to the outcome of the litigation. Such facts reveal who did what to whom, when and where it occurred, and how and why it occurred.[4]

O'Brien, *Of Judicial Myths, Motivations and Justifications: A Postscript on Social Science and the Law,* 64 JUDICATURE 285 (1981); Comment, *The Presently Expanding Concept of Judicial Notice,* 13 VILL. L. REV. 528 (1969); Roberts, *Preliminary Notes Toward a Study of Judicial Notice,* 52 CORNELL L.Q. 210 (1967). As Rule 201(a) expressly provides, the Rule only pertains to judicial notice of "adjudicative facts." This chapter is likewise limited in scope. Rule 44.1, Federal Rules of Civil Procedure, and Rule 26.1, Federal Rules of Criminal Procedure, pertain to judicial notice of foreign law. Judicial notice of "legislative facts" is not codified. *See* Rule 201, Advisory Committee Note. Other types of facts, of which a court may take cognizance in the absence of formal proof, are also outside the scope of the Rule; *see generally,* Morgan, *Judicial Notice,* 36 HARV. L. REV. 269 (1944).

[2] *See* Rule 201, Advisory Committee Note.

[3] *See* 1 MUELLER & KIRKPATRICK, § 47; 1 WEINSTEIN'S FEDERAL EVIDENCE § 201.02; *see also* Davis, *A System of Judicial Notice Based on Fairness and Convenience,* PERSP. OF LAW 69 (1964); Davis, *Judicial Notice,* 55 COLUM. L. REV. 945 (1955).

[4] *E.g.,* Finley v. United States, 314 F. Supp. 905, 28 Ohio Misc. 1 (D. Ohio 1970); 2 DAVIS, ADMINISTRATIVE LAW TREATISE, § 15.03 (1958); *see also* Snell v. Suffolk County, 782 F.2d 1094, 1105–1106 (2d Cir. 1986) ("adjudicative facts are 'the ultimate facts in the case, plus those evidential facts sufficiently central to the controversy that they should be left to the jury.' " (quoting 21 C. Wright & K. Graham, *Federal Practice & Procedure: Evidence* § 5103, at 478 (1977)).

Adjudicative facts are normally established through formal proof and only exceptionally through judicial notice.

By comparison, "legislative" facts are those facts that are employed by the court in the decisional process of a case in the expansion of the common law or in the interpretation, construction, and extension of legislative enactments.[5] When courts make new law, or "legislate," they inevitably rely upon policy assumptions concerning the operation of the law and its impact on society. These policy assumptions, which are largely factual in nature, are denominated "legislative facts." Generally, these factual assumptions are not made the subject of formal proof and the court takes cognizance of them merely by "noticing" them.

The label "legislative fact" is primarily significant in distinguishing such facts from adjudicative facts in the context of judicial notice. This distinction is important because "indisputability" is a requirement only for notice of adjudicative facts. The indisputability standard does not attach to legislative facts that a court might judicially notice in extending or expanding the law.[6]

§ 201.3   Qualification of Adjudicative Facts

Subdivision (b) of Rule 201 delineates the necessary conditions for a court to take judicial notice of adjudicative facts. An adjudicative fact is subject to judicial notice if it is not subject to dispute or uncertainty[7] because it is

---

[5] Davis, *Judicial Notice*, 55 COLUM. L. REV. 945 (1955). *See generally,* 1 WEINSTEIN'S FEDERAL EVIDENCE §§ 201.03, 201.51. Judge Weinstein points out that: "Requiring formal proof of legislative facts would be inhibiting, time consuming and expensive . . . . The judges may seek information from the parties via briefs, request the aid of amicus curiae or conduct independent research of their own." 1 WEINSTEIN'S FEDERAL EVIDENCE § 201.51; *see also* United States v. Hernandez-Fundora, 58 F.3d 802 (2d Cir. 1995) (judicial notice of a fact that impacts a jurisdictional issue involves judicial notice of a legislative, not adjudicative, fact); Siderius, Inc. v. M.V. Amilla, 880 F.2d 662 (2d Cir. 1989) (doubting applicability of Rule 201 to the New York Produce Exchange Interclub Agreement, which is probably governing law for potential disputes between parties); Personnel Adm. of Mass. v. Feeney, 442 U.S. 256 (1979); Alexander v. Youngstown Bd. of Educ., 454 F. Supp. 985 (D.C. Ohio 1978).

[6] *See* 1 WEINSTEIN'S FEDERAL EVIDENCE § 201.51; 1 MUELLER & KIRKPATRICK, § 47; *see also* Karst, *Legislative Facts in Constitutional Litigation*, 1960 SUP. CT. REV. 75. *See generally,* 2 MCCORMICK, § 331.

[7] *See, e.g.,* Datlof v. United States, 252 F. Supp. 11 (E.D. Pa. 1966) (judicial notice taken that October 5, 1955, was a Wednesday); Wansley v. Wilkerson, 263 F. Supp. 54 (W.D. Va. 1967) (judicial notice taken of 4-year delay before trial being due to efforts of petitioner rather than the government). *Compare* Oneida Indian Nation of New York v. State of New York, 691 F.2d 1070, 1086 (2d Cir. 1982) ("judicial notice of a disputed fact should not ordinarily be taken as the basis for dismissal of a complaint on its face," and therefore, trial court erred in dismissing claims); *see also* General Electric Capital Corp. v. Lease Resolution Corp., 128 F.3d 1074 (7th Cir. 1997) (trial court improperly took judicial notice of finding made in prior unrelated proceeding without first establishing that the facts of the earlier proceeding and the application of the earlier finding to the present case were undisputed).

well-known within the trial court's jurisdiction.[8] In the alternative, notice is appropriate if the fact is capable of ready and accurate determination by resort to a reasonably reliable source.[9]

Rule 201(b)(1) applies to reasonably indisputable adjudicative facts generally known within the trial court's jurisdiction. Certain kinds of facts are part of the structure and function of the court itself and are peculiarly within the purview of judicial notice.[10] Beyond facts relating specifically to the court, the appropriateness of judicial notice is measured by the general notoriety of facts. The fact subject to notice must be within the general knowledge of reasonably well-informed people within the territorial juris-

---

[8] *See* Shahar v. Bowers, 120 F.3d 211 (11th Cir. 1997) (court refused to take judicial notice of the conduct of a person based upon newspaper accounts about that conduct; the court did not find that the newspaper accounts transformed the fact into one "not subject to reasonable dispute"); Eden Toys, Inc. v. Marshall Field & Co., 675 F.2d 498 (2d Cir. 1982); *see also* Transorient Navigators Co., S.A. v. M/S Southwind, 788 F.2d 288 (5th Cir. 1986) (appellate court held trial court properly took notice of prevailing interest rates); United States v. Whitely, 734 F.2d 1129 (6th Cir. 1984) (appellate court noted in dictum that trial court properly took notice that cocaine is made from coca leaves and accordingly is a controlled substance); In re Auto-Pak, Inc., 63 B.R. 321 (Bankr. D.D.C. 1986), *rev'd on other grounds,* 73 B.R. 52 (D.D.C. 1987) (cashier's check equivalent to cash in commercial usage); *see, e.g.,* Otto v. Alper, 489 F. Supp. 953 (D. Del. 1980); Caulfield v. Board of Ed. of City of New York, 486 F. Supp. 862 (E.D.N.Y. 1980); United States v. Fatico, 441 F. Supp. 1285 (E.D.N.Y. 1977), *rev'd on other grounds,* 579 F.2d 707 (2d Cir. 1978), *on remand,* 458 F. Supp. 388 (E.D.N.Y. 1978).

[9] *E.g.,* United States v. Garland, 991 F.2d 328 (6th Cir. 1993) (where defendant was charged with interstate fraud, the Ghanian convictions of two Ghanian citizens for defrauding defendant in a cocoa bean transaction was judicially noticeable and justified the grant of a new trial); Kramer v. Time Warner, Inc., 937 F.2d 767 (2d Cir. 1991) (the trial court may properly take judicial notice of the contents of public documents filed with the SEC as this is a "resort to sources whose accuracy cannot reasonably be questioned"); In re Ahlers, 794 F.2d 388 (8th Cir. 1986), *rev'd on other grounds,* 485 U.S. 197 (1988) (appellate court took judicial notice of a "highly respected publication" by the University of Minnesota detailing the pattern of land values in the region over a decade); United States v. Perez, 776 F.2d 797 (9th Cir. 1985) (appellate court took judicial notice that the minimum distance between Rota and Guam was 31 nautical miles, "a fact subject to accurate determination from a map," and hence any trip between the two islands must involve travel through international waters); KVUE, Inc. v. Moore, 709 F.2d 922 (5th Cir. 1983); Reiner v. Washington Plate Glass Co., 711 F.2d 414 (D.C. Cir. 1983).

[10] United States v. Daychild, 357 F.3d 1082 (9th Cir. 2004) (in denying motion to dismiss indictment, district judge could take judicial notice that the indictment was returned in open court before a magistrate and that the required number of grand jurors concurred in the indictment, based on the court's familiarity with its own grand jury records and procedures for the return of grand jury indictments); Kowalski v. Gagne, 914 F.2d 299 (1st Cir. 1990) (court took judicial notice of convictions of defendant); Commodity Futures Trading Comm'n v. Co/Petro Mktg. Group, 680 F.2d 573 (9th Cir. 1982) (judicial notice taken of prior judgments entered against defendant); ITT Rayonier, Inc. v. United States, 651 F.2d 343 (5th Cir. 1981) (court may take judicial notice of its own records or of those of inferior courts).

diction of the trial court. The Rule should be interpreted to permit the court to take judicial notice of those adjudicative facts that are, or should be, known to people of reasonable intelligence within the trial court's jurisdiction.[11]

Where general notoriety within the jurisdiction does not attend the fact sought to be noticed, Rule 201(b)(2) provides for judicial notice if the fact is subject to accurate and ready determination. The critical feature of this provision is that it shifts the test from common knowledge to that of verifiable accuracy.[12] If the fact is not commonly known, it may nevertheless be noticed so long as it is capable of instant and reasonable demonstration.[13] Most notably, this application of judicial notice has been used to obtain recognition of historical and geographical facts or scientific and medical principles. It has been used to justify, for example, the evidentiary use of dates, natural and political boundaries, positions of public figures, blood tests, ballistics, fingerprints, handwriting, and typewriter analysis.[14] Federal courts will routinely take judicial notice of pertinent federal or state law, including statutes and judicial opinions, because such matters are readily ascertained through universally available sources, but that is not true of municipal ordinances and private codes referred to in state statutes, which

---

[11] 2 McCORMICK, § 329. *See* N.D. v. Hawaii Department of Education, 600 F.3d 1104 (9th Cir. 2010) (in action challenging closure of public schools on certain dates, the Court of Appeals would not take judicial notice of declarations filed on appeal by parents of disabled minor students, describing how their children were emotionally affected by the closure. "The status of the disabled children is not generally known throughout the jurisdiction of the Ninth Circuit nor are the parents sources whose accuracy cannot reasonably be questioned."); *In re* Mora, 199 F.3d 1024 (9th Cir. 1999) (one day before filing for bankruptcy, debtors mailed a cashier's check for over $24, 000 to their mortgage lender and asked the court of appeals to take judicial notice that first class mail is delivered overnight; the court declined to so note, holding that the advertised goal of delivering first class mail overnight locally is far from being "beyond reasonable dispute").

[12] *See* United States v. Wood, 925 F.2d 1580 (7th Cir. 1991) (on motion for judgment on the pleadings, the district court may take judicial notice of matters of public record); Northern Heel Corp. v. Compo Indus., 851 F.2d 456 (1st Cir. 1988) (judicial notice of OSHA regulations); Massachusetts v. Westcott, 431 U.S. 322 (1977) (judicial notice taken of Coast Guard Records); Coast Indian Community v. United States, 550 F.2d 639 (Ct. Cl. 1977) (judicial notice taken of voter's roster that was published in the newspaper); Government of Canal Zone v. Burjan, 596 F.2d 690 (5th Cir. 1979); Davis v. Freels, 583 F.2d 337 (7th Cir. 1978); United States v. Hawkins, 566 F.2d 1006 (5th Cir. 1978).

[13] *See* United States v. Garcia, 672 F.2d 1349 (11th Cir. 1982) (judicial notice taken, relying on testimony and map, that place at which defendant's airplane was intercepted by the Air Force was beyond the three-mile territorial limit recognized as United States border for purposes of ocean border-crossing cases); Baker v. City of Kissimmee, 645 F. Supp. 571 (M.D. Fla. 1986) (judicial notice of data obtained from United States Census).

[14] *See* 1 WEINSTEIN'S FEDERAL EVIDENCE §§ 201.10–201.13; *see also* Browning-Ferris Indus. v. Muszynski, 899 F.2d 151 (2d Cir. 1990) (judicial notice of scientific literature on proper well-casing materials); Patrick v. Sharon Steel Corp., 549 F. Supp. 1259 (N.D.W. Va. 1982). *See generally,* 1 MUELLER & KIRKPATRICK, §§ 49–50.

generally must be placed in evidence and need not be judicially noticed unless they are readily available.[15]

Representative authoritative sources for verification include such reference materials as historical works, science and art books, language and medical journals and dictionaries, calendars, encyclopedias, commercial lists and directories, maps and charts, statutes, and legislative reports.[16]

§ 201.4   Judicial Knowledge versus Judicial Notice

Judicial notice of adjudicative facts in any particular case is not determined or circumscribed by the personal knowledge of the individual court. It is inconsequential that matters of judicial cognizance are actually known or unknown to the judge. As long as the facts are a proper subject for notice, the judge may be informed of the indisputability of the facts in any reasonable way. Likewise, facts that are not subject to judicial cognizance must be proved, even though personally known to the court to be true.[17]

The rule is similar with respect to jurors. Unlike the early stages of common law, under modern practice jurors are selected because of their supposed unfamiliarity with, and disinterest in the litigation. Accordingly, in the absence of admissible evidence on the subject, jurors may not predicate a finding of fact upon their peculiar knowledge or experience.[18] In according weight to the evidence and credibility to witnesses, however, jurors are expected to employ their own common experience and observation of human nature.

§ 201.5   Discretionary versus Mandatory Judicial Notice

In subdivision (c)(1), Rule 201 provides that the court may *sua sponte*

---

[15] Getty Petroleum Marketing, Inc. v. Capital Terminal Co., 391 F.3d 312 (1st Cir. 2004).

[16] *See* 1 MUELLER & KIRKPATRICK, §§ 49–50.

[17] *See* LaSalle Nat'l Bank v. First Conn. Holding Group, L.L.C., 287 F.3d 279 (3d Cir. 2002) (judicial notice of the contents of conversations between plaintiff's attorney and the district judge's law clerk was inappropriate; the contents of the conversations were neither a matter of common knowledge nor provable from a source of unquestioned accuracy, and the judge was not a party to the conversations); United States v. Mariscal, 285 F.3d 1127 (9th Cir. 2002) (judicial notice that a local road was "heavily traveled" was an inappropriate reference to personal driving experience); Storm Plastics v. United States, 770 F.2d 148 (10th Cir. 1985) (trial judge erred in taking judicial notice that items manufactured by Storm were "a good product"; the district court's personal appraisal of the "quality and reputation" of the taxpayer's product is not within the purview of Rule 201); United States v. Sorrells, 714 F.2d 1522 (11th Cir. 1983) (trial judge's finding that his personal knowledge of an informant's reliability could cure an otherwise defective affidavit on which a search warrant was based was contrary to Rule 201(b); however, the court found that there was no Fourth Amendment violation); United States v. Bramble, 641 F.2d 681 (9th Cir. 1981) (no judicial notice taken that 21 marijuana plants in a hot house in defendant's yard must have been grown for purposes of sale; not common knowledge to members of panel); United States v. Baker, 641 F.2d 1311 (9th Cir. 1981) (no judicial notice taken that anyone who is a gill netter and resident of Washington knows of injunction).

[18] *In re* Beverly Hills Fire Litig., 695 F.2d 207 (6th Cir. 1982).

take judicial notice of adjudicative facts under the proper circumstances at any time during the course of the proceedings.[19] The taking of judicial notice under this provision rests within the sound discretion of the trial court, and such determinations may only be disturbed upon a finding of an abuse of the discretion.[20]

Subdivision (c)(2) places upon the trial court the express duty of taking judicial notice of any adjudicative fact where the proponent of the evidence advances information or documentation demonstrating the fact to be reasonably indisputable. Naturally, this provision operates almost exclusively within the context of proving those facts that are capable of ready and accurate verification, since, in the main, such supporting data would not be useful or required where the fact is commonly known by persons of reasonable intelligence in the community.[21] While Rule 201(c)(2) mandates the court to take judicial notice when it is "supplied with the necessary information," the nature and quality of information or documentation that is sufficient to establish the veracity of a fact is, in the end, a matter of discretion with the trial court. As is the case under Rule 201(c)(1), this function of the trial court, and any subsequent rulings on the admission of adjudicative facts, will not be invaded by a reviewing court absent a clear showing of an abuse of discretion and prejudice.[22]

§ 201.6 Hearing in Support or Opposition

Basic considerations of procedural fairness demand an opportunity to be heard on the propriety of taking judicial notice and the nature of the matter to be noticed. On its face, the Rule requires the granting of an opportunity to be heard upon request. The Rule is not limited to the party against whom the fact is offered, and it is equally available to the party offering the matter to be noticed. No formal scheme of hearing nor any procedure for giving

---

[19] *See* Eden Toys, Inc. v. Marshall Field & Company, 675 F.2d 498 (2d Cir. 1982) (summary judgment). *But see* United States v. Bliss, 642 F.2d 390 (10th Cir. 1981) (court declined to take judicial notice at appellate level).

[20] *See, e.g.,* Oneida Indian Nation of New York v. State of New York, 691 F.2d 1070 (2d Cir. 1982) (trial court erred in dismissing Indian land claims on basis of judicial notice of meaning of Articles of Confederation, Proclamation of 1783 and 1784 Fort Stanwix Treaty; disputed facts are not appropriate subjects for judicial notice). *See also* FDIC v. Houde, 90 F.3d 600 (1st Cir. 1996) (although the trial court could have taken judicial notice that the banking association failed and the FDIC took over through receivership, as it had in two prior opinions, the court was not required to take judicial notice *sua sponte* and in the absence of a request from either party, the court was not compelled to take judicial notice). *See generally,* Eagle-Picher Indus. v. Liberty Mutual Ins. Co., 682 F.2d 12 (1st Cir. 1982).

[21] *See* Clark v. South Central Bell Tel. Co., 419 F. Supp. 697 (W.D. La. 1976) (no judicial notice taken of black/white labor force in race employment discrimination case, since it was not a matter of general knowledge; no facts or reliable sources placed before the court).

[22] *See generally,* M/V American Queen v. San Diego Marine Constr. Corp., 708 F.2d 1483 (9th Cir. 1983) (district court did not abuse its discretion).

notice to adverse parties is provided or contemplated.[23] Consequently, the Rule is flexible in its nonspecificity, and it is clearly intended to permit the trial court, in the exercise of its sound discretion, to manage such matters in an *ad hoc* fashion. Accordingly, the time for making a request to be heard on the subject, depending upon the peculiarities of any given case, is also flexible. Accordingly, in the absence of advance notice, an adversely affected party may request a hearing either contemporaneously with the taking of notice or even after the fact. And, in the absence of prior notice, a request made after the fact could not fairly be held to be untimely.[24]

The requirement that a hearing be afforded the affected parties is fundamentally consistent with the directive contained in Rule 201(b) that requires that only those adjudicative facts reasonably beyond dispute are amenable to judicial notice.

§ 201.7   Time of Taking Judicial Notice

In accord with the prevailing view and pre-Rule Federal law, judicial notice of adjudicative facts may be taken at any stage in the proceedings, whether during the trial or on appeal.[25] Judicial notice may be taken during

---

[23] *See* 1 WEINSTEIN'S FEDERAL EVIDENCE § 201.31; 1 MUELLER & KIRKPATRICK, § 54; *see also* Lussier v. Runyon, 50 F.3d 1103, 1114 (1st Cir. 1995) (trial court inappropriately took judicial notice of information regarding a wrongfully-discharged postal employee's disability benefits that it received "through untested unilateral submissions" after the record had been closed and not by means of an adversary hearing).

[24] 1 MUELLER & KIRKPATRICK, § 48.

[25] *E.g.,* Grason Elec. v. Sacramento Municipal Util. Dist., 571 F. Supp. 1504 (E.D. Cal. 1983), *rev'd on other grounds,* 770 F.2d 833 (9th Cir. 1985) (judicial notice of adjudicative fact was taken in deciding motion for summary judgment). For examples of judicial notice taken on appeal, *see* Central Green Co. v. United States, 531 U.S. 425 (2001) (Supreme Court took judicial notice of certain geographic facts); United States v. Esquivel, 88 F.3d 722, 726–727 (9th Cir. 1996) (court took judicial notice of Government's census data on appeal where offered to rebut similar data presented by the defendant, despite the admonition that "the Government could and should have presented the refined census material in the district court"); Gustafson v. Cornelius Co., 724 F.2d 75 (8th Cir. 1983); Reiner v. Washington Plate Glass Co., 711 F.2d 414 (D.C. Cir. 1983); Jones v. Illinois Dep't of Rehabilitation Servs., 689 F.2d 724 (7th Cir. 1982). *But see* Colonial Leasing v. Logistics Control Group Int'l, 762 F.2d 454 (5th Cir. 1985), *reh'g granted in part, denied in part,* 770 F.2d 479 (5th Cir. 1985) (in a suit alleging that a transfer of assets defrauded creditors, the trial judge erred in taking judicial notice of plaintiff's judgment against the transferor more than a month after a verdict was returned; the provision in Rule 201(f) regarding the court's instructions to the jury assumes that notice will be taken prior to jury deliberation; moreover, in this case, state law required the plaintiff to establish the validity of the transferor's debt to him and the defendant relied on plaintiff's failure to do this in declining to produce any evidence of its own; remanded for new trial on the issue of creditor status); United States v. Dior, 671 F.2d 351 (9th Cir. 1982) ("for a court to take notice of an adjudicative fact after a jury's discharge in a criminal case would cast the court in the role of fact finder and violate the defendant's Sixth Amendment right to trial by jury"). However, the Ninth Circuit may have modified its position in *Dior.* In United States v. Perez, 776 F.2d 797 (9th Cir. 1985), the court affirmed

the course of the presentation of formal evidence, during pretrial conference, or after the evidence is closed. Subdivision (f) is a natural complement to subdivision (e) in providing that judicial notice remains available to any court, subject only to subdivision (b)(1) on the appellate level, *i.e.,* the common knowledge basis for notice applies to the territorial jurisdiction of the trial court, not the appellate court.

Although the procedure may be applied to any adjudicative fact, reviewing courts frequently resort to judicial notice of adjudicative facts to fill in trivial factual gaps in the record as transmitted by the parties. An appellate court may judicially notice any fact that the lower court could have noticed, and where the appellate court is presented with an appeal from a judgment that is entirely correct, except for the absence of some indisputable but essential fact, the court may affirm the judgment by taking judicial notice of the missing fact.[26] This procedure is considered preferable to remanding the cause on the basis of the defect in the record; the trial court and the parties are not made to suffer an unreasonable and time-consuming impediment to final disposition of the matter on the merits. However, where the adjudicative fact is of such magnitude as to be critical to the outcome of the case, and the fact is not commonly known but arguably capable of accurate demonstration, appellate courts tend to avoid the available curative route of judicial notice. Most frequently in this situation, the case is remanded so that a complete record may be presented to the reviewing court.[27]

§ 201.8 Jury Instructions

Subdivision (f) of Rule 201 follows the common-law principle that once

---

a conviction for importation of controlled substances into Guam "from a place outside [the United States]," despite the lower court's incorrect instructions to the jury that Rota is outside the United States for this purpose, by taking judicial notice that the minimum distance between Rota and Guam is 31 nautical miles and any trip between the two must involve travel through international waters.

[26] *See* Ives Labs. v. Darby Drug Co., 638 F.2d 538 (2d Cir. 1981) (appellate court took notice of facts indicating that premise of trial judge's decision had no support); Government of Canal Zone v. Burjan, 596 F.2d 690 (5th Cir. 1979) (appellate court took judicial notice of geographical boundaries). *But cf.* Johnson v. Chater, 108 F.3d 942, 946 (8th Cir. 1997) (for an appellate court reviewing an administrative law judge's decision regarding Social Security benefits to take judicial notice of a fact not in the record would undermine the administrative law judge's role as the factfinder under the Social Security Act); Melong v. Micronesian Claims Comm'n, 643 F.2d 10 (D.C. Cir. 1980) (appellate court did not take judicial notice of 172 pages of unauthenticated documentary material; material submitted did not satisfy Rule 201).

[27] *See, e.g.,* Central Green Co. v. United States, 531 U.S. 425 (2001) (Supreme Court took judicial notice of certain geographic facts "for the purposes of this opinion," while leaving the objecting party "an opportunity to challenge those details on remand"); Reiner v. Washington Plate Glass Co., 711 F.2d 414 (D.C. Cir. 1983) (in action involving stockholder's petition to collect monies owed by insolvent corporation, court of appeals stated that any objection to its taking of judicial notice should be addressed on remand).

a fact has been judicially noticed in a civil action, it is conclusive. The adverse party may not introduce evidence to contradict the noticed fact.[28] Accordingly, the jury in a civil case must be specifically instructed as to the conclusive nature of the evidence received pursuant to judicial notice. Because judicial notice of a given fact relieves the proponent of the burden of presenting formal proof, it might seem that the opposing party should be at liberty to present contradictory evidence to the trier of fact on the point in an attempt to defeat the noticed fact. Nevertheless, it is clear under the Rule that the appropriate time for such contradictory evidence is when the matter is heard by the trial judge in the first instance under Rule 201(d).

It should be noted that when the court hears evidence in opposition to judicial notice, the evidence heard in this context goes to the limited issue of whether notice should be made. Frequently, however, in addressing the issue, the opponent of the noticed fact will offer evidence that seeks to demonstrate the falsity of the fact in question. Consequently, the issue of appropriateness of judicial notice in a civil case is always won or lost before the judge, not the trier of fact. But in deciding whether notice is warranted, the court often considers whether the opponent of the fact has contradicting evidence available that might be presented through the medium of formal proof. Such contradicting evidence would demonstrate that the fact is disputable and not subject to notice. Nevertheless, in civil cases where the judge has ruled on the appropriateness of notice and has determined that notice is proper, the jury will be instructed that judicially noticed facts are conclusive upon the parties to the litigation.[29]

In criminal cases, the Rule reinforces the principle that a conviction may only rest upon a finding that each element of the charged offense has been proved beyond a reasonable doubt and that a verdict will not be directed against the accused.[30] Accordingly, Rule 201 provides that where the

---

[28] 1 WEINSTEIN'S FEDERAL EVIDENCE § 201.33; 1 MUELLER & KIRKPATRICK, § 55; *see also* Davis, *A System of Judicial Notice Based on Fairness and Convenience,* PERSP. OF LAW 69 (1964).

[29] 1 WEINSTEIN'S FEDERAL EVIDENCE § 201.33; *see, e.g.,* Morgan, *Judicial Notice,* 57 HARV. L. REV. 269 (1944); Keefe, Landis, and Shaad, *Sense and Nonsense About Judicial Notice,* 2 STAN. L. REV. 664 (1950); 2 MCCORMICK, § 332.

[30] United Brotherhood of Carpenters & Joiners of America v. United States, 330 U.S. 395 (1947) (the trial court cannot constitutionally direct a verdict of guilty against the accused); *see also* United States v. Dior, 671 F.2d 351 (9th Cir. 1982) (where the government was required to prove, as an element of the charge, that the value of the items in question was more than $5,000, and it had only shown that the items were worth $13,690 in Canadian dollars ($12,006 United States on the relevant date), the trial court would not have been permitted to take judicial notice of the relevant exchange rate in ruling on defendant's motion for acquittal; "[f]or a court, however, to take notice of an adjudicative fact after a jury's discharge in a criminal case would cast the court in the role of fact finder and violate the defendant's Sixth Amendment right to trial by jury"). *But cf.* United States v. Perez, 776 F.2d 797 (9th Cir. 1985) (appellate court affirmed conviction for importation of controlled

judicially noticed fact represents an element of the charged crime, the jury must be instructed that the taking of judicial notice provides that the jury may, but is not required to, accept as conclusive any fact judicially noticed.[31] Despite the conceptual foundation that judicially noticed facts are only those that are notorious or beyond reasonable dispute, the accused has the procedural opportunity to present evidence to the trier of fact that is directly contradictory to the judicially noticed fact. For example, where an essential element of rape is the fact that the victim is not the spouse of the accused, the court may take judicial notice of the fact that the two have no marriage license on file with the county clerk. Nonetheless, the accused may introduce evidence to show that the records were destroyed or that a common-law marriage existed at the time of the alleged offense. Under the Rule, the jury may resolve this issue in favor of either party and the judge must instruct the jury accordingly.

§ 201.9 Selected Matters Judicially Noticed

Under the rubric of judicial notice, courts have taken notice of facts concerning cities, towns, villages, and school districts, such as their populations[32] or the effect of the national economy upon the region,[33] prevailing financial rates,[34] centers of specific types of industrial or commercial enterprises,[35] locations of buildings, parks, streets, and com-

---

substances into Guam "from a place outside [the United States]" despite the lower court's improper jury instruction that Rota is outside the United States for this purpose by taking notice that the minimum distance between Rota and Guam is 31 nautical miles and so any trip between the two must involve travel through international waters).

[31] *See* United States v. Hernandez-Fundora, 58 F.3d 802, 812 (2d Cir. 1995) (jury instruction that penitentiary where assault occurred was within the territorial jurisdiction of the United States did not improperly remove factual issues from the province of the jury; the court held that a factual issue "whose resolution is necessary to a determination of . . . jurisdictional issue" involved judicial notice of a legislative, not adjudicative, fact, making the procedural safeguards of Rule 201 inapplicable); United States v. Chapel, 41 F.3d 1338, 1342 (9th Cir. 1994) (the trial court did not usurp the jury's role as factfinder by taking judicial notice, referring to the trial judge's repeated instruction that the jury could, but was not required to, accept the court's declaration regarding the judicially-noticed fact).

[32] Castilleja v. Southern Pac. Co., 445 F.2d 183 (5th Cir. 1971) (court noticed the population of Dallas).

[33] Mainline Inv. Corp. v. Gaines, 407 F. Supp. 423 (D.C. Tex. 1976) (court noticed economic events in 1973 and their probable impact on oil industry and party's ability to perform); Fox v. Kane-Miller Corp., 398 F. Supp. 609 (D.C. Md. 1975) (court took judicial notice of the decline of purchasing power due to inflation).

[34] Transorient Navigators Co., S.A. v. M/S Southwind, 788 F.2d 288 (5th Cir. 1986) (judicial notice of prevailing interest rates); Varlack v. SWC Caribbean, Inc., 550 F.2d 171 (3d Cir. 1977) (judicial notice of discount rate for reducing anticipated future earnings to present worth).

[35] United States v. Ramirez, 910 F.2d 1069 (2d Cir. 1990) (judicial notice that there are no firearms manufacturers in New York); United States v. Underwood, 344 F. Supp. 486

mercial centers,[36] and the condition of prisons.[37] Judicial notice may be taken either because the fact offered is commonly known within the jurisdiction or because it is readily capable of being accurately demonstrated to a reasonable certainty.[38]

Similarly, facts relating to the course and laws of nature, qualities and properties of organic or inorganic matter, scientific, technological, or mechanical principles and processes, and normal human experiences are all readily susceptible to being noticed judicially as adjudicative facts in any appropriate case. Accordingly, notice has been taken of such things as the effects of certain drugs, alcohol, and medicinal compounds,[39] general statistical data on the distance required to permit a car to stop,[40] the phenomena of animal and vegetable life,[41] and the development of disease in humans.[42] Geographical, historical, and political and linguistic facts, such

---

(D.C. Fla. 1972) (judicial notice that tourism is one of the largest commercial interests and revenue sources for the State of Florida).

[36] United States v. Hughes, 542 F.2d 246 (5th Cir. 1976) (judicial notice that streets where arrest took place were located on federal enclave).

[37] Falzerano v. Collier, 535 F. Supp. 800 (D.N.J. 1982) (judicial notice of overcrowding of state prisons, temporary relocation of state prisoners, and plans to construct new state facilities).

[38] *See also* Ritter v. Hughes Aircraft Co., 58 F.3d 454, 458–459 (9th Cir. 1995) (it was proper for the trial court to take judicial notice that there had been widespread layoffs at defendant's plant because it was a fact generally known and was also capable of accurate and ready determination).

[39] United States v. Howard, 381 F.3d 873 (9th Cir. 2004) (Court of Appeals would take judicial notice of well-known and common side effects of narcotic painkillers, set forth in the Physician's Desk Reference and quoted in a party's appellate memorandum of law); Jaffee v. United States, 592 F.2d 712 (3d Cir. 1979) (judicial notice that the dangers of radiation from nuclear detonation are a matter of public knowledge); Miller Brewing Co. v. G. Heileman Brewing Co., 561 F.2d 75 (7th Cir. 1977) (judicial notice that alcoholic and caloric content go hand in hand).

[40] Jamison v. Kline, 454 F.2d 1256 (3d Cir. 1972) (proper to receive in evidence testimony by a state trooper based in part upon a speed chart; the chart was a reduction to usable form of the speed of the vehicle, and was a proper subject for judicial notice); *see also* Clayton v. Rimmer, 262 N.C. 302 (1964); Brown v. Hale, 263 N.C. 176 (1964).

[41] Golaris v. Jewel Tea Co., 22 F.R.D. 16 (D.C. Ill. 1958) (user of pork charged with obligation of cooking meat to the point of killing the trichinae; courts adhere to the concept of caveat emptor in this particular circumstance); Long v. United States, 241 F. Supp. 286 (D.C.S.C. 1965) (court took judicial notice of fact that livestock are easily frightened by sudden loud noises and by objects that are propelled directly over their heads, thereby making defendant guilty of negligence that was the proximate cause of plaintiff's injuries when an armed forces helicopter passed overhead at tree level, causing the blades of a mule-drawn mower to almost amputate plaintiff's leg).

[42] Bey v. Bolger, 540 F. Supp. 910 (E.D. Pa. 1982); *see also* Franklin Life Ins. Co. v. William J. Champion & Co., 350 F.2d 115 (6th Cir. 1965) (judicial notice taken of the fact that cancer does not manifest itself to the person afflicted with it until it suddenly affects a vital part of the body, rather than making itself known in the beginning stages; therefore it

as the location and topographical characteristics of lakes, streams, mountains, and navigable waters,[43] distance between places,[44] public events of local or worldwide notoriety,[45] time, days and dates,[46] weights, measures and values,[47] offices held by persons,[48] are all subject to judicial notice. Further, notice may be taken of human life, health, habits, customs, and usages as well as sociological matters.[49] The court may also be willing to take judicial notice of the doctrine or purpose of an organization.[50]

---

often results in death even though the best treatment available is given upon discovery of the disease). *But see* Rivera v. Philip Morris, Inc., 395 F.3d 1142 (9th Cir. 2005) (judicial notice should not be used to resolve whether the link between smoking and specific illnesses was "common knowledge" in 1969, as that issue was for the jury to resolve); United States v. Mitchell, 365 F.3d 215 (3d Cir. 2004) (judicial notice of a scientific conclusion was inappropriate, especially in light of a five-day *Daubert* hearing in which the defendant directed showed that the matter was subject to reasonable dispute).

[43] *See* Central Green Co. v. United States, 531 U.S. 425 (2001) (Supreme Court took judicial notice of geographic and physical features of flood control and irrigation project); United States v. Garcia, 672 F.2d 1349 (11th Cir. 1982) (judicial notice of territorial boundary); Farmland Preservation Asso. v. Goldschmidt, 611 F.2d 233 (8th Cir. 1979) (judicial notice that rural area between Cedar Rapids and Waterloo consisted of valuable farm lands adapted to various agricultural uses).

[44] Berkshire Fashions, Inc., v. The M.V. Hakusan II, 954 F.2d 874 (3d Cir. 1992) (judicial notice of relative distance of alternative maritime routes); United States v. Perez, 776 F.2d 797 (9th Cir. 1985) (judicial notice of the minimum distance between Rota and Guam).

[45] Washington Post v. Robinson, 935 F.2d 282 (D.C. Cir. 1991) (judicial notice of newspaper articles publicizing ongoing criminal investigation of Mayor Marion Barry); Pratt v. Kelly, 585 F.2d 692 (4th Cir. 1978) (judicial notice of deed by which Virginia conveyed to the United States title to certain land).

[46] Platts v. United States, 658 F. Supp. 850 (D. Me. 1987) (court noticed that September 4, 1984, was a Tuesday, the day after Labor Day); *see* Allen v. Allen, 518 F. Supp. 1234 (E.D. Pa. 1981) (court noticed that date of Father's Day, 1979, was June 17).

[47] *See* Varlack v. SWC Caribbean, Inc., 550 F.2d 171 (3d Cir. 1977) (court noticed discount rate for reducing anticipated future earnings to present worth).

[48] Orlando v. Wizel, 443 F. Supp. 744 (W.D. Ark. 1978) (judicial notice of the name of the elected Chancery and Probate Judge of the Fourteenth Chancery District of Arkansas).

[49] United States v. Evans, 404 F.3d 227 (4th Cir. 2005) (district court permissibly took "judicial notice of the fact that memories may fade over time"); Dippin' Dots, Inc. v. Frosty Bites Distribution, L.L.C., 369 F.3d 1197 (11th Cir. 2004) (trial court properly took judicial notice that color is indicative of flavor in ice cream, an adjudicative fact generally known among consumers); Knox v. Butler, 884 F.2d 849 (5th Cir. 1989) (judicial notice of data proving that "many young black men lived in the area"); Snell v. Suffolk County, 782 F.2d 1094 (2d Cir. 1986) (judicial notice of adjudicative fact of "conduct rising to the level of racial hatred existing in Suffolk County"). *But see* United States v. Hoyts Cinemas Corp., 380 F.3d 558 (1st Cir. 2004) (in Americans with Disabilities Act case, it was improper to take judicial notice of the fact that movie patrons prefer the middle or back of the theater; the issue of seating preference was central to the case, was subject to reasonable dispute, and would be resolved differently in each case depending upon the individual characteristics of each theater).

[50] United Klans of America v. McGovern, 453 F. Supp. 836 (N.D. Ala. 1978), *aff'd,* 621

Under limited circumstances, courts may also take judicial notice of proceedings in other courts, both within and outside the federal court system.[51] A court may take judicial notice of another court's documents and orders "only for the limited purpose of recognizing the 'judicial act' that the order represents or the subject matter of the litigation."[52] A court may not take judicial notice of another court's documents "for the truth of the matters asserted in the other litigation, but rather [judicial notice is only appropriate] to establish the fact of such litigation and related filings."[53] For a court to be able to take judicial notice of the facts found to be true in another litigation would preclude a party from introducing contrary evidence regarding that fact, thus circumventing the doctrine of collateral estoppel.[54]

F.2d 152 (5th Cir. 1980) (judicial notice that United Klans of America would be regarded as a "white hate group" pursuant to FBI's counterintelligence program); United States v. Crenshaw County Unit of United Klans, 290 F. Supp. 181 (D.D.C. 1968) (judicial notice of the historical reputation of the Ku Klux Klan).

[51] *See* United States v. Hope, 906 F.2d 254, 260 n.1 (7th Cir. 1990); United States v. Jones, 29 F.3d 1549, 1553 (11th Cir. 1994); Liberty Mutual Ins. Co. v. Rotches Pork Packers, Inc., 969 F.2d 1384, 1388 (2d Cir. 1992).

[52] *Jones,* 29 F.3d at 1553. *See also* Lasar v. Ford Motor Co., 399 F.3d 1101 (9th Cir. 2005) (court could not take judicial notice of an order of an Ohio state court to prove the truth of the factual findings contained in that order; "Factual findings in one case ordinarily are not admissible for their truth in another case through judicial notice"); Nolte v. Capital One Financial Corp., 390 F.3d 311 (4th Cir. 2004) (a court may take judicial notice of the fact that the SEC has filed a civil complaint, where the mere fact of its filing is relevant to the case before the court, but it may not take judicial notice of the truth of the facts alleged in that complaint); Kushner v. Beverly Enters., 317 F.3d 820 (8th Cir. 2003) (courts may take judicial notice of allegations in government filings if those documents are not being offered to prove the truth of those allegations; in civil fraud action, the court could not take judicial notice of disputed allegations in sentencing memorandum by the government in related criminal case); Herrick v. Garvey, 298 F.3d 1184 (10th Cir. 2002) (judicial findings of fact in an unrelated action cannot serve as the basis for judicial notice where the parties had a reasonable dispute as to the truth of those findings); Werner v. Werner, 267 F.3d 288 (3d Cir. 2001) (although the court refused to take judicial notice of the truth of the contents of company meeting minutes "filed in a separate action involving separate parties, in a different court, in a different state," judicial notice was taken of both the existence and the filing of the minutes).

[53] *Liberty Mutual,* 969 F.2d at 1388. *See also* Bryant v. Avado Brands, Inc., 187 F.3d 1271 (11th Cir. 1999) (court considering a motion to dismiss a securities fraud case may take judicial notice of relevant public documents required to be filed with the SEC and actually filed). American Stores Co. v. Commissioner of IRS, 170 F.3d 1267 (10th Cir. 1999) (holding by implication that unpublished private rulings by IRS and administrative practice manuals of the IRS were not appropriate items for judicial notice, because notice would serve only to fill in gaps in appellant's trial preparation).

[54] *See Jones,* 29 F.3d at 1553 (citing WRIGHT & GRAHAM, FEDERAL PRACTICE & PROCEDURE: EVIDENCE § 5104 (1977 & Supp. 1994)); *see also* International Star Class Yacht Racing Ass'n v. Tommy Hilfiger U.S.A., Inc., 146 F.3d 66 (2d Cir. 1998) (statements of fact concerning trademark search practices set forth in a court opinion in an unrelated action were not subject to judicial notice because they were not common knowledge and were not derived

from unimpeachable source); General Electric Capital Corp. v. Lease Resolution Corp., 128 F.3d 1074, 1083 (7th Cir. 1997).

ARTICLE III.
PRESUMPTIONS IN CIVIL CASES

Synopsis

Chapter 301

Rule 301. Presumptions in Civil Cases Generally

Rule 301. Presumptions in Civil Cases Generally

In a civil case, unless a federal statute or these rules provide otherwise, the party against whom a presumption is directed has the burden of producing evidence to rebut the presumption. But this rule does not shift the burden of persuasion, which remains on the party who had it originally.

§ 301.1 Presumptions in Civil Actions — In General

Rule 301 governs the effect of presumptions on the allocation of the burden of proof in civil actions and other civil proceedings.[1] Its scope is limited, and in conjunction with Rule 302, its provisions are inapplicable to: (a) presumptions governed by state law; (b) presumptions directed against a criminal defendant; and (c) presumptions governed by congressional enactments.[2] Moreover, the Rule addresses only one aspect of the law of presumptions, *i.e.,* the question of the impact of a presumption on the burden of going forward and the burden of persuasion. The Rule leaves to case law the resolution of corollary issues that are raised by the invocation of a presumption.[3]

As enacted by Congress, Rule 301 greatly differs from the version of the rule recommended by the Advisory Committee and promulgated by the Supreme Court. The Supreme Court's rule followed the approach advocated

---

[1] *See generally,* 2 McCORMICK, §§ 336–348; 1 WEINSTEIN'S FEDERAL EVIDENCE §§ 301.01–301.30; 1 MUELLER & KIRKPATRICK, §§ 61–72; 9 WIGMORE, §§ 2483–2493. *See also* Allen, *Presumptions, Inferences and Burden of Proof in Federal Civil Actions—An Anatomy of Unnecessary Ambiguity and a Proposal for Reform,* 75 NW. U. L. REV. 892 (1983); Allen, *Presumptions in Civil Actions Reconsidered,* 66 IOWA L. REV. 843 (1981); Gordon and Tenebaum, *Conclusive Presumption Analysis: The Principle of Individual Opportunity,* 71 NW. U.L. REV. 579 (1977); Louisell, *Construing Rule 301: Instructing the Jury on Presumptions in Civil Actions and Proceedings,* 63 VA. L. REV. 281 (1977).

[2] *See generally,* 1 WEINSTEIN'S FEDERAL EVIDENCE § 301.03. *See* § 301.4, *infra,* as to "Scope of the Rules."

[3] *See* § 301.4, *infra.*

by Professor Morgan, which shifted both the burden of going forward and the burden of persuasion to the opponent of the presumption after its proponent established the base facts.[4] Supporters of this rule argued that a rule that shifted only the burden of production gave too "slight and evanescent" an effect to a presumption because it disappeared from the case and might not have been mentioned to the jury once its opponent introduced evidence sufficient to support a finding of the nonexistence of the presumed fact.[5] Despite this criticism, Congress adopted a rule that shifts only the burden of going forward.

Under Rule 301, a presumption is a procedural device that operates to shift the evidentiary burden of producing evidence (*i.e.,* the burden of going forward) to the party against whom the presumption is directed.[6] The burden of producing evidence operates generally to expose a party to an adverse result on a directed verdict where evidence on the issue has not been advanced. The burden of persuasion, *i.e.,* the risk of nonpersuasion, is not affected under the Rule, and it remains on the party to whom it was originally allocated by the substantive law and the pleadings.[7] Under Rule 301, a presumption has a modest effect; it is not applied where substantial rebuttal evidence regarding the fact or facts to be presumed is provided by the opponent of the presumption, but it may still have an affect on the outcome of the trial where the rebuttal evidence only questions the validity of the basic facts that would lead to the presumption.[8]

§ 301.2   Definitional Distinctions

Confusion in the area of presumptions has been generated by the imprecise usage of a variety of terms such as burden of persuasion, burden of production, rebuttable presumption, irrebuttable or conclusive presumption and inference. The terms should be distinguished as follows:

Burden of Persuasion.

The "burden of persuasion" is the "risk of non-persuasion." It is the burden of persuading the trier of fact of the elements of a claim or a defense

---

[4] The Supreme Court's Rule 301 read:

In all cases not otherwise provided for by Act of Congress or by these rules a presumption imposes on the party against whom it is directed the burden of proving that the nonexistence of the presumed fact is more probable than its existence.

See 1 WEINSTEIN'S FEDERAL EVIDENCE § 301.03.

[5] Rule 301, Advisory Committee Note (quoting Morgan and Maguire, *Looking Backward and Forward at Evidence,* 50 HARV. L. REV. 909 (1937)); *see* 2 MCCORMICK, § 344.

[6] Earlier versions of the Rule would have had a more dramatic effect on the burden of proof. *See* 1 MUELLER & KIRKPATRICK, § 61.

[7] Hood v. Knappton Corp., 986 F.2d 329 (9th Cir. 1993) (admiralty law rule required shifting the burden of persuasion to defendant and this result was not affected by Rule 301).

[8] LILLY, § 3.4.

in accordance with the degree of proof mandated by the substantive law, *i.e.,* "preponderance of the evidence," "clear and convincing evidence," or "beyond a reasonable doubt."[9] Under Rule 301 the burden of persuasion is not affected by a presumption, and it remains upon the party to whom it was originally allocated by the substantive law.

Burden of Going Forward.

The "burden of going forward" is the "burden of production" or the "burden of producing evidence." It is the burden to come forward with evidence to avoid an adverse resolution by the judge that would preempt consideration by the trier of fact of the issue,[10] usually through the device of a directed verdict.[11] It is the obligation, initially, to produce sufficient evidence to support a rational jury decision in favor of the factual element sought to be proven.[12] Under Rule 301 the burden of production may be affected by a presumption. A presumption operates to shift the burden of production on a factual element where the proponent of the presumption submits evidence as to the base facts (the fundament) of the presumption. Having proved the base facts of the presumption, the burden of production as to the presumed fact is satisfied for the proponent. The burden of production to disprove the presumed fact shifts to the opponent by virtue of the operation of the presumption, *i.e.,* the opponent risks a preemptive verdict by failing to counter the presumption.

Inference.

An "inference" is a permissible deduction or induction that the trier of fact may draw from facts that are established according to the rules of evidence. An inference is typically based on logic or common human experience, and it is the essential component of circumstantial proof. A jury may attach weight to the inferred fact in the same manner as it does to the direct evidence upon which the inferred fact is based.[13]

Rebuttable Presumption.

A "rebuttable presumption" is a presumption that the law requires the trier of fact to make where the prerequisite base facts have been established and where no contrary evidence has been produced.[14] A common example is the presumption of delivery and receipt that derives from the establishment of

---

[9] LILLY, § 3.1, at 48–49.

[10] LILLY, § 3.1, at 51.

[11] 2 McCORMICK, § 336.

[12] 2 McCORMICK, § 338.

[13] *See, e.g.,* United States v. Roglieri, 700 F.2d 883 (2d Cir. 1983); United States v. Leonard, 524 F.2d 1076 (2d Cir. 1975); *see generally,* 1 MUELLER & KIRKPATRICK, §§ 66–72.

[14] Gausewitz, *Presumptions in a One Rule World,* 5 VAND. L. REV. 324 (1952).

the base fact that a letter was mailed. Once a proponent establishes that a letter was properly addressed and posted, a rebuttable presumption arises that the letter was delivered and received by the addressee. Under Rule 301, the burden of production would then shift to the opposing party, who must either produce evidence that the letter was not received by the addressee or suffer the adverse ruling that the letter was received.[15] If the opposing party does produce sufficient evidence to rebut the presumption, the issue then proceeds to the jury, with the burden of persuasion remaining with the party on whom the substantive law and pleadings had originally cast it.

Rule 301, which governs rebuttable presumptions, only directs the manner in which presumptions operate, and it does not dictate whether a particular presumption applies or obtains. Substantive law must provide a particular presumption. Presumptions are based upon a variety of rationales, and as creatures of deliberate legal formulation, presumptions may or may not coincide with logic or common experience. Consequently, while in some cases a presumption may be based upon or coincide with an inference indicated by logic and experience, the terms "inference" and "presumption" are not synonymous.

Conclusive Presumption.

The term "conclusive presumption" denotes what is more properly considered a rule of substantive law as opposed to an evidentiary, procedural device. For example, where the law declares that a child of less than seven years is incapable of committing a felony, such a rule forecloses the legal questions involved.[16] It raises no proof problems, and consequently is not within the purview of Rule 301.

§ 301.3 The Policy of Presumptions

Presumptions are largely products of evidentiary necessity or convenience that operate to assist a party in satisfying the risk of nonpersuasion. They are derived from varied rationales and serve such purposes as: (1) counterbalancing one party's superior access to proof; (2) advancing deep-seated social or economic policies; (3) avoiding a legal impasse; and (4) acknowledging the high probability of a given conclusion that experience has demonstrated (*i.e.,* giving formal effect to an inference).[17] Frequently, a presumption is

---

[15] *See* Anderson v. United States, 966 F.2d 487 (9th Cir. 1992) (explaining that because taxpayer had presented credible evidence that income tax return had been properly mailed and because the IRS did not produce sufficient evidence it had not received the return, the trial court did not err by allowing the presumption that the return had been received to stand against the IRS). *But see* Carroll v. Commissioner, 71 F.3d 1228 (6th Cir. 1995) (the common-law presumption that a letter mailed was received had no application regarding the mailing of tax documents to the IRS; "a taxpayer who sends a document to the IRS by regular mail, as opposed to registered or certified mail, does so at his own peril").

[16] MORGAN, BASIC PROBLEMS OF EVIDENCE, 31 (1962).

[17] *See* 2 McCORMICK, § 343.

based on some combination of the foregoing factors, and it almost always is indicated by a modicum of rational, intrinsic probability.

The common-law doctrine of bailee liability is illustrative of the policy regarding accessibility of evidence: Where property is delivered to a bailee, and the bailee on demand fails to deliver the property to the bailor, a common-law presumption of liability may arise on the part of the bailee. Social or economic policies supporting presumptions are reflected by the frequently recognized presumption of legitimacy that attaches to a child born during lawful wedlock. Likewise, the presumption against a finding of suicide is also illustrative of a social policy underpinning. Presumptions dealing with the order of death of persons involved in a common disaster illustrate the use of a presumption to avoid a legal impasse in a situation where the proof is equally inaccessible to all parties and the presumption is imposed to facilitate a final result.

§ 301.4   Effect of the Rule

Rule 301 comes into play where the party bearing the burden of persuasion on a given issue introduces base facts that are supportive of a presumption supplied by substantive law. At this point the burden of production shifts to the opposing party, who is required to come forward with evidence that is contrary to the presumed fact. The risk of nonpersuasion, however, is not affected, and it remains on the party to whom it was originally allocated.

In practice, this distinction between shifting the burden of production but not that of persuasion translates into an evaluation of the quantity and quality of rebuttal evidence required of the party opposing the presumption in order to avoid an instruction to the trier of fact on the presumption. In accordance with the traditional Thayer-Wigmore theory of presumptions,[18] the opponent of the presumption need only offer credible evidence sufficient to support a finding that is contrary to the presumed fact in order to dislodge the presumption from the case.[19] The standard does not place upon the opponent

---

[18] 9 WIGMORE, § 2490 *et seq.*

[19] *See* Rabon v. Great S.W. Fire Ins. Co., 818 F.2d 306 (4th Cir. 1987) (in suit against insurance company for failure to pay claim, trial judge erred in instructing jury that parties to civil suits are presumed innocent of criminal acts where the insurance company had introduced evidence from which arson could be inferred; a supplemental instruction that the presumption exists until evidence to the contrary is presented did not cure error); Breeden v. Weinberger, 493 F.2d 1002 (4th Cir. 1974) (court relied on proposed Rule 301 as persuasive, though not controlling, in an administrative proceeding concerning Social Security disability benefits, and noted that the party against whom the presumption operates need only persuade the trier that the contrary of the presumed fact is more probable than not; there is no increased measure of persuasion; "[A]s a general rule, presumptions do not operate to raise the standard of proof"); Sinatra v. Heckler, 566 F. Supp. 1354 (E.D.N.Y. 1983). *See generally,* 1 WEINSTEIN'S FEDERAL EVIDENCE § 301.02; 2 MCCORMICK § 344; *see also* United States v. Chicago, 411 F. Supp. 218 (1976) (civil rights action involving sexual and racial discrimi-

the burden of proving the contrary finding, for example, by a preponderance of the evidence or beyond a reasonable doubt. In the language of the terms defined in Section 301.2, *supra,* the opposing party must only satisfy its burden of going forward in order to defeat its operation, but a growing minority has also required the burden of persuasion to be met.[20]

Interestingly, Rule 301 itself does not dictate the procedural result that attends compliance or non-compliance with the requirement of producing evidence to rebut the presumption. Case law continues to govern in this regard, and case law provides that if the party opposing the presumption fails to come forward with sufficient credible evidence, as determined by the court, the presumption is crystallized, and the jury is instructed to find the presumed fact if it believes the base facts to be true.[21] If, however, the party against whom the presumption is directed produces sufficient rebuttal evidence, the presumption never takes effect and it is not mentioned to the jury. No instruction is given.[22] Fundamentally, the impact of a presumption turns on whether the instruction will be given: "If you find X (base facts), then you must find Y (presumed facts)."

Although internally consistent, application of the "bubble-bursting effect"[23] of presumptions under Rule 301 has been criticized for according too little weight to presumptions, many of which are forged of significant policy considerations. Consequently, some proponents of such criticism would allow the presumption to be mentioned to the jury in such cases, even where evidence contrary to the presumed fact has been introduced.[24] The express language of Rule 301 does not prohibit courts from carving out limited areas where the existence of a presumption might be mentioned to the jury even though credible rebuttal evidence has been introduced.

§ 301.5   Presumptions in Criminal Cases

The procedures delineated in Rule 301 are inapplicable to criminal cases.

---

nation in Chicago's police department, where employers argued that Rule 301 precluded the placement on them of the burden of persuasion respecting the job-relatedness of the questioned testing; the court rejected this contention on the ground that the pertinent provision of the Civil Rights Act of 1974, as interpreted by the Supreme Court, placed the burden of proof of job-relatedness of testing on the employer, and that the statutory prescription prevailed over Rule 301).

[20] LILLY, § 3.4.

[21] *See generally,* 9 WIGMORE, § 2490; 1 MUELLER & KIRKPATRICK, §§ 69–72.

[22] 2 MCCORMICK, § 344; *see* Rabon v. Great S.W. Fire Ins. Co., 818 F.2d 306 (4th Cir. 1987) (in suit against insurance company for failure to pay claim, trial judge erred in instructing jury that parties to civil suits are presumed innocent of criminal acts where the insurance company had introduced evidence from which arson could be inferred; a supplemental instruction that the presumption exists until evidence to the contrary is presented did not cure error).

[23] 2 MCCORMICK, § 345; *see also* 1 MUELLER & KIRKPATRICK, §§ 69–72 *et seq.*

[24] *See* 2 MCCORMICK, § 344; 1 MUELLER & KIRKPATRICK, §§ 69–70.

Although the Supreme Court promulgated Proposed Rule 303 which, if adopted, would have governed the instructions attendant to and circumstances under which a presumption could be submitted to the jury in a criminal action, the Rule was deleted by Congress because the subject of presumptions in criminal cases was addressed in several bills pending to amend the pertinent provisions of the federal criminal code.[25]

The revision of the federal code pertaining to these matters was not adopted, however, and thus in federal criminal cases the operation of presumptions currently is controlled by principles of federal common law as circumscribed by constitutional limitations.[26]

At the common law prior to the adoption of the Federal Rules of Evidence, presumption instructions were often employed by trial courts even in criminal cases. But an important line of constitutional decisions by the Supreme Court has virtually eliminated any role for such instructions in criminal cases.

The Due Process Clause of the Fourteenth Amendment denies States the power to deprive the accused of his liberty unless the prosecution proves every element of the charged offense beyond a reasonable doubt,[27] and therefore absolutely forbids a judge from directing a jury to make certain findings no matter how conclusive the evidence may appear.[28] "Jury

---

[25] Proposed Rule 303 (now Standard 303) reads:

(a) Scope. Except as otherwise provided by Act of Congress, in criminal cases, presumptions against an accused, recognized at common law or created by statute, including statutory provisions that certain facts are prima facie evidence of other facts or guilt, are governed by this rule.

(b) Submission to Jury. The judge is not authorized to direct the jury to find a presumed fact against the accused. When the presumed fact establishes guilt or is an element of the offense or negatives a defense, the judge may submit the question of guilt or of the existence of the presumed fact to the jury, if, but only if, a reasonable juror on the evidence as a whole, including the evidence of the basic facts, could find the guilt or the presumed fact beyond a reasonable doubt. When the presumed fact has a lesser effect, its existence may be submitted to the jury if the basic facts are supported by substantial evidence, or are otherwise established, unless the evidence as a whole negatives the existence of the presumed fact.

(c) Instructing the Jury. Whenever the existence of a presumed fact against the accused is submitted to the jury, the judge shall give an instruction that the law declares that the jury may regard the basic facts as sufficient evidence of the presumed fact but does not require it to do so. In addition, if the presumed fact establishes guilt or is an element of the offense or negatives a defense, the judge shall instruct the jury that its existence must, on all the evidence, be proved beyond a reasonable doubt.

[26] 1 MUELLER & KIRKPATRICK, 61.

[27] *In re* Winship, 397 U.S. 358, 364 (1970).

[28] United States v. Martin Linen Supply Co., 430 U.S. 564, 572–573 (1977) ("a trial judge is prohibited from entering a judgment of conviction or directing the jury to come forward with such a verdict . . . regardless of how overwhelmingly the evidence may point in that

instructions relieving States of this burden violate a defendant's due process rights," because they "subvert the presumption of innocence accorded to accused persons and also invade the truth-finding task assigned solely to juries in criminal cases."[29] The Due Process Clause of the United States Constitution therefore forbids the use of any jury instruction that is reasonably likely to be understood by the jury as relieving the prosecution of this burden of persuasion with respect to any of the essential elements of the charged offense.[30]

Thus, for example, the Supreme Court has held that it is a violation of Due Process and reversible error for a trial judge to instruct a jury (1) that if the defendant removed property he thought to be abandoned on government property, his "felonious intent . . . is presumed by his own act,"[31] or (2) that "the law presumes that a person intends the ordinary consequences of his voluntary acts,"[32] or (3) that the defendant's "intent to commit theft by fraud is presumed" if he failed to return a rented vehicle within twenty days after the owner demanded its return, and he "shall be presumed to have embezzled the vehicle" if he intentionally failed to return the vehicle within five days after the rental agreement expired.[33] Even where the trial judge explicitly states that a presumption is "rebuttable," the Due Process Clause forbids the use of any jury instruction that is reasonably likely to be interpreted by the jury as creating either a conclusive or a rebuttable presumption that shifts the burden of persuasion to the accused on an essential element of the offense.[34]

---

direction"); *see also* Crawford v. Washington, 541 U.S. 36, 62 (2004) (ridiculing the idea of "dispensing with jury trial because a defendant is obviously guilty"); Rose v. Clark, 478 U.S. 570, 578 (1986) (dictum) (it would never be harmless error "if a court directed a verdict for the prosecution in a criminal trial by jury").

[29] Carella v. California, 491 U.S. 263, 265 (1989).

[30] If a challenged jury instruction is ambiguous and can possibly be interpreted in two or more ways, as will often be true, an appellate court is required to decide whether there is "a reasonable likelihood" that the jury applied the challenged instruction in an unconstitutional manner. Boyde v. California, 494 U.S. 370, 378–381 (1990). This standard does not require the defendant to prove that the jury probably adopted an interpretation that would be unconstitutional, *id.* at 380 ("a defendant need not establish that the jury was more likely than not to have been impermissibly inhibited by the instruction"), but he will not prevail if the possibility of the forbidden interpretation of the instruction was not reasonable or "no more than speculation." *Id.*

[31] Morisette v. United States, 342 U.S. 246, 249 (1952).

[32] Sandstrom v. Montana, 442 U.S. 510, 513 (1979).

[33] Carella v. California, 491 U.S. 263, 265 (1989).

[34] Francis v. Franklin, 471 U.S. 307, 309 (1985) (reversing conviction obtained because of jury instruction that "[a] person of sound mind and discretion is presumed to intend the natural and probable consequences of his acts but the presumption may be rebutted"). At least in theory, the Court has claimed that it has not yet formally decided "whether a mandatory presumption that shifts only a burden of production to the defendant is consistent with the Due Process Clause," *id.* at 314 n.3, although scholarly commentators appear to be

As a practical matter, these cases have all but abolished any use of presumptions against the accused in a criminal jury trial, as well as any judicial instruction suggesting that some aspect of the Government's case may be "presumed" from the proof of other facts.[35] Many states have responded to these cases through the more widespread use of the so-called "permissive inference" instruction, which "suggests to the jury a possible conclusion to be drawn if the State proves predicate facts, but does not require the jury to draw that conclusion."[36] The Supreme Court has approved the use of a permissive instruction, which is therefore much more likely to survive constitutional challenge,[37] but such instructions should be employed with great caution. They must not be worded in a manner that will convey any sense that the law requires or expects the jurors to reach a certain result, nor interfere with the jury's independent assessment of the evidence.[38] Indeed, in lieu of giving jurors any instructions about permissive inferences in criminal cases, it is usually "best to keep the instructions concise" by "leaving inferences to arguments of counsel."[39] Moreover,

---

unanimous in agreeing that in light of the Court's holdings it "seems safe to say that presumptions simply cannot be used to shift to defendants the burden of production on an element of a charged crime." Christopher B. Mueller & Laird Kirkpatrick, I FEDERAL EVIDENCE 522 & nn. 19–20 (3d ed. 2007) (collecting authorities).

[35] Of course, these cases do not restrict in any way those relatively rare situations in which a presumption in a criminal case is used in ways that might benefit the *accused,* nor do they cast any doubt on the constitutional right of the accused to an instruction on the so-called "presumption of innocence," Taylor v. Kentucky, 436 U.S. 478, 483 (1978), which "is not technically a 'presumption' — a mandatory inference drawn from a fact in evidence," but "is better characterized as an 'assumption' that is indulged in the absence of contrary evidence." *Id.* at 483 n.12.

[36] *Francis,* 471 U.S. at 314 & n.2 (1985).

[37] *Id.* at 314–315 (1985) ("A permissive inference violates the Due Process Clause only if the suggested conclusion is not one that reason and common sense justify in light of the proven facts before the jury.").

[38] County Court of Ulster County v. Allen, 442 U.S. 140, 156 (1979) (an inference instruction and a presumption are alike in that "their validity under the Due Process Clause" is determined, among other things, by "the degree to which the device curtails the factfinder's freedom to assess the evidence independently"); *see also* Quercia v. United States, 289 U.S. 466, 470 (1933) (a trial judge has a duty "to use great care that an expression of opinion upon the evidence 'should be so given as not to mislead, and especially that it should not be one-sided'; that 'deductions and theories not warranted by the evidence should be studiously avoided.'").

[39] United States v. Hill, 252 F.3d 919, 923 (7th Cir. 2001). The Pattern Criminal Jury Instructions published by the Federal Judicial Center recommend that the following time-honored permissive inferences should no longer be explained by the trial court in its jury instructions: "Use of Witness's Prior Consistent Statements" (Instr. 34), "Inference from Fact that Witness Not Called" (Instr. 39), "Defendant's Incriminating Actions After the Crime" (Instr. 43), "Defendant's False Exculpatory Statements" (Instr. 44), and "Defendant's Failure to Respond to Accusatory Statements" (Instr. 45). The Commentary to each of those proposed instructions specifically recommends that such matters should not be routinely covered by the

entrusting such matters to counsel is always much less likely to compromise the fairness of the proceeding, since an "instruction on the subject gives undue weight to a particular piece of evidence."[40]

---

court in its charge to the jury but should instead be left to counsel in closing argument. *See* FEDERAL JUDICIAL CENTER, PATTERN CRIMINAL JURY INSTRUCTIONS (1988).

[40] FEDERAL CRIMINAL JURY INSTRUCTIONS OF THE SEVENTH CIRCUIT COURT, Comment on Instruction 3.20 (1999) (explaining why evidence of the defendant's flight, although "a relevant circumstance evidencing a consciousness of guilt," is best left to counsel to discuss in closing argument and should not be the subject of a judicial instruction).

Chapter 302

Rule 302. Applying State Law to Presumptions in Civil Cases

Rule 302. Applying State Law to Presumptions in Civil Cases

In a civil case, state law governs the effect of a presumption regarding a claim or defense for which state law supplies the rule of decision.

---

§ 302.1   In General

Rule 302 provides that a court must apply state law to determine the effect of a presumption where a fact to which the presumption applies is an element of a claim or defense as to which state law provides the rule of decision.[1] The Rule as enacted applies only to civil actions and proceedings.

Rule 302 is in essence an embodiment of the *"Erie* doctrine."[2] Under *Erie Railroad Company v. Tompkins,* rules governing presumptions and burdens of proof may in certain applications be treated as substantive because of a clear and direct effect on the litigation's outcome.[3] The *Erie* doctrine

---

[1] *See generally,* 2 McCORMICK, § 349; 1 WEINSTEIN'S FEDERAL EVIDENCE §§ 302.01–302.05; 1 MUELLER & KIRKPATRICK, §§ 73–76. *See also* Berger, *Privileges, Presumptions and Competency of Witnesses in Federal Court: A Federal Choice of Laws Rule,* 42 BROOK. L. REV. 417 (1976); Wellborn, *The Federal Rules of Evidence and the Application of State Law in Federal Courts,* 5 TEX. L. REV. 3 (1977); Weinstein, *The Uniformity-Conformity Dilemma Facing Draftsmen of Federal Rules of Evidence,* 69 COLUM. L. REV. 353 (1969).

[2] *See generally,* 17A MOORE'S FEDERAL PRACTICE, § 124.09.

> Except in matters governed by the Federal Constitution or by Acts of Congress, the law to be applied in any case is the law of the state. And whether the law of the state shall be declared by its legislature in a statute or by its highest court in a decision is not a matter of federal concern. There is no federal general common law. Congress has no power to declare substantive rules of common law applicable in a state whether they be local in their nature or "general."

Erie Railroad Company v. Tompkins, 304 U.S. 64, 78 (1938).

[3] Dick v. New York Life Ins. Co., 359 U.S. 437 (1959); Palmer v. Hoffman, 318 U.S. 109, 117 (1943) ("the question of the burden of establishing contributory negligence is a question of local law which federal courts in diversity of citizenship cases . . . must apply"); Johnson

continues to control the circumstances under which a federal court is to apply a state-created presumption.[4]

The scope of Rule 302 is coextensive with the scope of the *Erie* doctrine. Therefore, Rule 302 requires application of state law to presumptions that affect claims or defenses arising from state law, regardless of the basis of federal jurisdiction. Even if jurisdiction is based upon diversity, Rule 302 will not apply state law to cases involving federal claims or issues. Only if the source of the claim is governed by state law will Rule 302 apply.[5]

§ 302.2   Application of State Law

Rule 302 draws a distinction between presumptions that operate upon a substantive element of a claim or defense and those that serve only tactical purposes. Rule 302 requires application of state law only as to the former type of presumption.[6] Examples of presumptions that commonly relate to a substantive element of a claim or defense include the presumption that death resulted from accidental causes in an action to recover accidental death benefits[7] and the presumption of lack of consideration for a conveyance from a bankrupt to a family member in a proceeding to set aside the conveyance.[8] In comparison the following example illustrates a tactical use of a presumption:

---

v. Pierce Packing Co., 550 F.2d 474, 476 n.1 (9th Cir. 1977) ("[R]ules governing presumptions and burdens of proof are generally regarded as substantive for purposes of *Erie*.").

[4] 1 MUELLER & KIRKPATRICK, § 73.

[5] Rule 302, Advisory Committee Note; *see, e.g.,* Steele v. Richardson, 472 F.2d 49 (2d Cir. 1972) (in action to review decision denying benefits under Social Security Act, New York law of presumptions as to validity of marriages applied; the court seemed affected by the general federal policy in favor of claimants of the type involved); Maternally Yours, Inc. v. Your Maternity Shop, Inc., 234 F.2d 538, 540–541 n.1 (2d Cir. 1956) ("it is the source of the right sued upon, and the ground on which federal jurisdiction over the case is founded, which determines the governing law . . . thus the *Erie* doctrine applies, whatever the ground for federal jurisdiction to any issue or claim which has its source in state law"); *see also* Monger v. Cessna Aircraft Co., 812 F.2d 402 (8th Cir. 1987) (in a diversity action for wrongful death against an aircraft manufacturer, state law determined what effect to give a presumption of due care where manufacturer had introduced evidence that the pilot did not conduct proper pre-flight inspection).

[6] *See* Rule 302, Advisory Committee Note; *see also* 1 WEINSTEIN'S FEDERAL EVIDENCE § 302.02; 1 MUELLER & KIRKPATRICK, § 73; 2 MCCORMICK, § 349.

[7] Melville v. American Home Assur. Co., 584 F.2d 1306 (3d Cir. 1978) (following a forum non conveniens dismissal in New York state court, beneficiary under accident policy brought diversity action to recover proceeds following insured's death in airplane crash; insurance company claimed that insured had committed suicide; District Court found that Pennsylvania would classify presumption against suicide as substantive, and then found that Pennsylvania's choice of law in contract cases was in utter disarray and confusion and that either the traditional choice of law rule for contracts or an interest analysis — Restatement II approach would lead to choosing New York rather than Delaware or Pennsylvania law).

[8] *In re* Bahre, 23 B.R. 460 (Bankr. D. Conn. 1982).

In an action upon an account, plaintiff, desiring to prove defendant's failure to deny as an admission of liability, may prove the mailing of a statement of account to defendant and rely upon the presumption that it was received by him in due course of the mails. The presumed fact of delivery is much smaller than an element in the case.[9]

Whether a presumption is of tactical or substantive importance may not at all times be clear, but there are characteristics that indicate a purely tactical use of a presumption. If the presumption can be raised by either a defendant or plaintiff in any factual context in which the presumption would be applicable, then the presumption probably does not attempt to create a substantive right in a particular type of plaintiff or defendant and was created by the state merely to facilitate the litigation process.[10] In this situation the state presumption would serve merely a tactical purpose in the federal litigation, and consequently, neither the *Erie* doctrine nor Rule 302 would require the federal court to apply state law.[11] In cases in which it remains unclear whether a presumption is substantive or tactical, the narrow interpretation of the *Erie* doctrine contained in Rule 302 suggests federal law should be applied to advance the policy of uniformity in federal courts.[12]

---

[9] Cleary, *Presuming and Pleading: An Essay on Juristic Immaturity,* 12 STAN. L. REV. 5 (1959).

[10] *See generally,* 1 WEINSTEIN'S FEDERAL EVIDENCE § 302.02.

[11] *But cf.* Dodson v. Imperial Motors, Inc., 295 F.2d 609 (6th Cir. 1961) (court applied Michigan's statutory presumption that a notarial certificate constitutes presumptive evidence of the facts contained therein, and affirmed a judgment against defendant).

[12] 1 WEINSTEIN'S FEDERAL EVIDENCE § 302.02.

ARTICLE IV.
RELEVANCE AND ITS LIMITS

Synopsis

Chapter 401

Rule 401. Test for Relevant Evidence

Rule 401. Test for Relevant Evidence

Evidence is relevant if:

    (a)   it has any tendency to make a fact more or less probable than it would be without the evidence; and

    (b)   the fact is of consequence in determining the action.

---

§ 401.1   Test for Relevant Evidence — In General

Considered in conjunction with Rule 402, Rule 401 constitutes the cornerstone of the federal evidentiary system. In essence, Rule 401 provides that in order for evidence to qualify for admission, such evidence must meet the threshold test of relevance.[1] Once relevance is established, however, evidence may be excluded for affirmative reasons identified in Rule 402. The bases for exclusion identified in Rule 402 are the Constitution of the United States, statutes enacted by the Congress, the Federal Rules of Evidence, and other rules prescribed by the Supreme Court pursuant to statutory authority.

Accordingly, relevant evidence is "assumptively" admissible.[2] The proponent of evidence must be prepared to establish its relevance, and if appropriate, the opponent of the evidence must be prepared to establish its inadmissibility predicated on one of the bases cited in Rule 402.

---

[1] The Advisory Committee Notes that were written with the original draft of the Federal Rules of Evidence in 1969 refer to this as "relevancy," an archaic term that is still used in this nation by many older lawyers and law professors but nobody else. "*Relevancy* was the predominant form in American and British writings on evidence of the 19th century, but now *relevance* is more common except in Scotland." Bryan Garner, A Dictionary of Modern Legal Usage 750 (2d ed. 1995). In recent decades, *relevancy* has appeared in only a handful of opinions written by a justice of the Supreme Court of the United States (not counting cases in which a justice was quoting someone else), but *relevance* in literally hundreds of Supreme Court opinions. Aspiring lawyers should therefore avoid the archaic word *relevancy* unless they plan to practice law in Scotland — or in the 19th century.

[2] Lilly, § 2.4. Professor Lilly uses the term "assumptive," as opposed to "presumptive," admissibility in order to avoid confusion with the operation of "presumption" as a term of art.

§ 401.2   Determination of Relevance

Determining whether a particular item of evidence is relevant is ordinarily not a question of law. Rather, the process of determining relevance is based on experience, logic, and common sense. Consequently, many cases applying the concept of relevance fall into no set pattern, and the trial lawyer can only rarely rely upon specific precedent to establish the relevance of a particular item of evidence. While certain cases tend to fall into recurring patterns from which some guidance can be gleaned,[3] cases dealing with

---

[3] *See* 2 WEINSTEIN'S FEDERAL EVIDENCE § 410.08, for a thorough discussion of the categories mentioned in this note. For example, evidence of similar accidents or incidents is frequently offered to establish notice, Mauldin v. Upjohn Co., 697 F.2d 644 (5th Cir. 1983), the gravity of the danger involved, Collins By and Through Kay v. Seaboard Coastline R.R., 675 F.2d 1185 (11th Cir. 1982), or the foreseeability of the product defect in question, Joy v. Bell Helicopter Textron, 999 F.2d 549 (D.C. Cir. 1993) (in a products liability action, evidence of similar part failures in two unrelated accidents was properly admitted); Wagner v. Int'l Harvester Co., 611 F.2d 224 (8th Cir. 1979), or causation, Walker v. Fairchild Indus., 554 F. Supp. 650 (D. Nev. 1982). In cases falling within these categories the similarity between the prior accident or incident and the present crime will be the determining factor of relevance.

If misunderstanding or distortion can only be avoided through admission of the remainder of a document, a portion of which was previously introduced, the material required for completeness is *ipso facto* relevant and therefore admissible under Rule 401 and 402. Beech Aircraft Corp. v. Rainey, 488 U.S. 153 (1988).

Videotaped evidence of a defendant's slurred speech and lack of muscular coordination obtained without *Miranda* warnings is not testimonial and is admissible evidence. A defendant's videotaped response when asked if he knew the date of his sixth birthday also obtained without *Miranda* warnings is testimonial and is not admissible evidence. Pennsylvania v. Muniz, 496 U.S. 582 (1990).

Prior complaints offered to prove notice of design defects where sufficient facts were not presented for a court to be able to determine if the circumstances were "substantially similar" to the case at bar were properly excluded. Rye v. Black & Decker Mfg. Co., 889 F.2d 100 (6th Cir. 1989).

In a suit for gender discrimination and unlawful retaliation, plaintiff may present evidence of "condoned sexual harassment in a workplace." Hawkins v. Hennepin Technical Ctr., 900 F.2d 153 (8th Cir. 1990). *See also* Perry v. Ethan Allen, Inc., 115 F.3d 143 (2d Cir. 1997) (evidence that other female employees of the defendant had been sexually harassed was relevant in a harassment case even if the plaintiff had no personal knowledge of the instances as a claim of hostile workplace involves an examination of the totality of the circumstances).

Evidence of a defendant's actions or speech may also be relevant as bearing on his consciousness of guilt. Reeves v. Sanderson Plumbing Products, Inc., 530 U.S. 133, 147 (2000) (in keeping with "the general principle of evidence law that the factfinder is entitled to consider a party's dishonesty about a material fact as affirmative evidence of guilt," jury in age discrimination case may infer that falsity of employer's explanation for firing is evidence of discriminatory motive).

Also, physical evidence offered by the prosecution to show a defendant possessed a weapon used in a crime is highly relevant and falls into a category of generally admissible evidence. United States v. Arnott, 704 F.2d 322 (6th Cir. 1983); *see also* United States v. Byers, 603 F.3d 503 (8th Cir. 2010) (when accused was charged with possession of a firearm

relevance more frequently involve the reasoning of the court in a specific instance that is of little precedential value because of its intimate relationship with the unique facts of the case.[4]

§ 401.3 Standard of Relevance

Evidence is relevant if it merely alters the probabilities of the existence or nonexistence of a fact properly before the court. The offered evidence need only make the fact sought to be proven more probable or less probable in order to satisfy Rule 401. A single item of relevant evidence need not in itself be sufficient to support a jury verdict in order to satisfy the threshold standard of relevance. Accordingly, in stating, "[a] brick is not a wall,"[5] McCormick points out that each item of evidence need only alter the probabilities of a factual issue to a slight extent, whereas the totality of the evidence must support the factual proposition sought to be proven if the proponent is to prevail on the issue.

Evidence is not subject to exclusion solely because its probative value is extremely low. If evidence has any probative value whatsoever, it is relevant and admissible unless otherwise excludable for an affirmative reason.[6] The

---

as a convicted felon, evidence that he was found in possession of particularly lethal "hollow tip" ammunition was relevant and properly admitted, even if only to show the "background" behind the charged offense).

Evidence of the defendant's acquisition of a large amount of wealth following a crime is relevant. United States v. Mangan, 575 F.2d 32 (2d Cir. 1978). Other categories of generally admissible relevant evidence include evidence of a defendant's wealth in assessing punitive damages. Fury Imports Inc. v. Shakespeare Co., 554 F.2d 1376 (5th Cir. 1977).

Governmental, industrial, or professional regulations, customs, and practices are highly probative in some instances when a party's knowledge of such procedures is relevant. Johnson v. Niagara Mach. & Tool Works, 666 F.2d 1223 (8th Cir. 1981). Statistics are highly relevant in discrimination cases, Gay v. Waiters' & Dairy Lunchmen's Union, 694 F.2d 531 (9th Cir. 1982), and the sale of a comparable piece of real estate may be relevant in judging the market value of a piece of real property. United States v. 79.20 Acres of Land, More or Less, 710 F.2d 1352 (8th Cir. 1983).

[4] See, e.g., Jay Edwards, Inc. v. New England Toyota Distrib., 708 F.2d 814 (1st Cir. 1983); Gootee v. Colt Industries, 712 F.2d 1057 (5th Cir. 1983); United States v. Washington, 705 F.2d 489 (D.C. Cir. 1983); United States v. Clifford, 704 F.2d 86 (3d Cir. 1983).

[5] 1 McCormick, § 185, at 776.

[6] See Blinzler v. Marriott Int'l, Inc., 81 F.3d 1148 (1st Cir. 1996) (in a negligence action arising out of a hotel's alleged failure to promptly summon aid for a guest suffering a heart attack, the trial court did not abuse its discretion in admitting evidence that the defendant had destroyed a relevant printout of all outgoing calls made around the time of the incident; the court explained that the defendant knew of the report's significance and the need to preserve it as evidence at trial, and thus the jury could reasonably infer that the defendant destroyed the report because it was harmful to its case); Kirchoff v. American Cas. Co., 997 F.2d 401 (8th Cir. 1993) (no abuse of discretion found in admitting evidence of a low settlement offer by an insurance company where evidence of the insurance company's valuation of plaintiff's claim was introduced; because their valuation of the claim was significantly higher than the settlement offer, both figures were relevant to the issue of whether the offer was made in good

practical consequence is that the opponent of the evidence cannot properly argue exclusion on the basis of minimal probative value alone. Evidence with low probative value, however, may be subject to exclusion under Rule 403, which balances probative value against such countervailing considerations as unfair prejudice and confusion of the issues.[7] Consequently, where the probative value of evidence is low, an argument coupling the minimal probative value with a counterweight, *e.g.,* confusion, may justify exclusion under Rule 403.

The establishment of a connection between the evidence and the fact sought to be proved is usually not a scientific process.[8] The Rule is more customarily applied by the trial judge in a highly discretionary manner based upon experiential perceptions of the way in which the world operates.[9]

---

faith); Pfeiffer v. Marion Ctr. Area Sch. Dist., 917 F.2d 779 (3d Cir. 1990) (in sex discrimination case, plaintiff sued National Honor Society after she was dismissed from the society because of her pregnancy; trial court erred in excluding evidence that two years later a male member was permitted to remain in the society after impregnating his girlfriend; evidence might have been relevant to state of mind of Society's local council); and discussion of Rule 402, at § 402.1 *et seq., infra. But see* Kelly v. Boeing Petroleum Services, Inc., 61 F.3d 350 (5th Cir. 1995) (in action alleging that the defendant did not reasonably accommodate the plaintiff's handicap during his employment, the trial court did not abuse its discretion in excluding testimony that the plaintiff's supervisor made derogatory remarks toward certain sick or handicapped employees; the court found that the relationship between the bias that the supervisor's remarks might suggest and the plaintiff's claim of discrimination was nebulous).

[7] *See* discussion of Rule 403, at § 403.1 *et seq., infra.*

[8] *See* 2 WEINSTEIN'S FEDERAL EVIDENCE § 401.04. Scientific evidence may be admissible in some situations to enhance the relevance of another piece of evidence. For example, statistical evidence of the small probability that a given disease would occur in a normal individual not exposed to a caustic substance would enhance the relevance of a claim that X had been exposed to Y and had suffered a disease as a result. When statistical evidence of the probability of an occurrence is utilized, great care must be taken to lay a foundation that establishes the accuracy of the probability admitted into evidence. United States v. Green, 680 F.2d 520 (7th Cir. 1982).

[9] *See, e.g.,* Redman v. John D. Brush & Co., 111 F.3d 1174 (4th Cir. 1997) (trial court erred in admitting advertisement proclaiming defendant's safe to be "burglar deterrent" in action against the manufacturer of a safe after it was burglarized; court noted that the ad was issued several years after the plaintiff had bought his safe and promoted a different model than the one owned by the plaintiff); Blinzler v. Marriott Int'l, Inc., 81 F.3d 1148 (1st Cir. 1996) (in a negligence action arising out of a hotel's alleged failure to promptly summon aid for a guest suffering a heart attack, the trial court did not abuse its discretion in admitting evidence that the defendant had destroyed a relevant printout of all outgoing calls made around the time of the incident; the court explained that the defendant knew of the report's significance and the need to preserve it as evidence at trial, and thus the jury could reasonably infer that the defendant destroyed the report because it was harmful to its case); Baker v. Delta Airlines, Inc., 6 F.3d 632 (9th Cir. 1993) (in an age discrimination action, where defendant claimed that its policy barring pilots over age 60 from certain positions was based upon safety concerns, trial court erred in excluding certain memoranda that discussed the policy but failed to mention safety as the underlying basis); Horne v. Owens-Corning Fiberglas Corp., 4 F.3d 276

Application of the standard of relevance consequently calls upon the trial lawyer to use persuasion in establishing the necessary logical or experiential nexus between the offered evidence and the consequential facts sought to be established.

§ 401.4   Direct and Circumstantial Evidence

The definition of relevance in Rule 401 comprehends both direct and circumstantial evidence. Direct evidence does not rely upon an inference; it usually involves an eyewitness account of the ultimate, consequential facts sought to be proven.[10] Circumstantial evidence consists of proof of facts from which other connected facts are established.[11] As noted by Professor Lilly, direct evidence raises only issues of credibility of the testifying witness, whereas circumstantial evidence additionally involves an assessment by the trier of fact of the inference connecting the evidence and the consequential fact sought to be proven.[12]

§ 401.5   Conditional Relevance

By its terms, Rule 401 does not purport to deal with the concept of "conditional relevance." Where evidence is conditionally relevant, its probative value depends upon not only satisfying the basic requirement of

---

(1993) (where plaintiff filed an action alleging that the decedent got cancer from his thirteen years of exposure to asbestos, trial court did not abuse its discretion in admitting evidence of OSHA regulations in effect after decedent was exposed to asbestos; court held that such "state-of-the-art" evidence was relevant to show that defendant was labeling asbestos products under its own safety guidelines before the OSHA guidelines were in effect); Malarkey v. Texaco, Inc., 983 F.2d 1204 (2d Cir. 1993) (evidence of plaintiff's prior employment success and plaintiff's office memorandum alleging sex discrimination were relevant to plaintiff's age and sex discrimination claim); United States v. Searing, 984 F.2d 960 (8th Cir. 1993) (where defendant was charged with cocaine-related conspiracy offenses, neighbor's testimony about defendant's bagging of an unknown white substance in his kitchen was held to be relevant); Whalen v. Unit Rig. Inc., 974 F.2d 1248 (10th Cir. 1992) (where plaintiff filed an age discrimination claim after defendant fired him, trial court properly permitted plaintiff to introduce lists of employees that defendant had asked for in declining order of age); Douglass v. Eaton Corp., 956 F.2d 1339 (6th Cir. 1992) (in a discrimination case, evidence of prior fights similar to the plaintiff's held admissible); Bruno v. W.B. Saunders Co., 882 F.2d 760 (3d Cir. 1989) (in an ADEA suit, though studies comparing whether employees over 40 received promotions at the same rate as employees under 40 would not have been admissible in class action disparate treatment/impact litigation, it was helpful to the jury, and therefore admissible, because it bolstered plaintiff's case that the employer's basis for discharging plaintiff was pretextual); United States v. Sweeney, 688 F.2d 1131 (7th Cir. 1982); United States v. Bouye, 688 F.2d 471 (7th Cir. 1982).

[10] *See* United States v. Brady, 579 F.2d 1121 (9th Cir. 1978); United States v. Pelton, 578 F.2d 701 (8th Cir. 1978).

[11] *See* United States v. Bycer, 593 F.2d 549 (3d Cir. 1979); United States v. Knife, 592 F.2d 472 (8th Cir. 1979); *see also* United States v. Fairchild, 526 F.2d 185 (7th Cir. 1975) (illustrates use of circumstantial proof to support elements of prosecution's charges and to defeat elements of a defense).

[12] LILLY, § 2.7.

relevance, but also upon establishing the existence of some other fact. Under conditional relevance one item of evidence is relevant only if another item of evidence is established. The discussion of conditional relevance appears in connection with Rule 104, which specifically addresses the concept.[13]

§ 401.6 Relevance and Materiality

Rule 401 designates a properly provable fact as one "that is of consequence in determining the action." "Of consequence" is a term of art that embraces the traditional concept of materiality.

Material evidence, under traditional terminology, is evidence offered to establish a matter that is properly an issue in the case according to the substantive law.[14] Analysis of the pleadings and substantive law generally indicates whether a fact is material. Under the traditional analysis, if the evidence offered is not directed to a factual proposition that substantive law indicates is a matter in issue, the evidence was said to be "immaterial."

Relevance and materiality have frequently been used interchangeably, because the concepts are nearly impossible to distinguish in many situations. Because of this blurring between relevance and materiality, the Federal Rules of Evidence have abandoned the term materiality in favor of the more comprehensive term of relevance. Accordingly, under the terminology of Rule 401, the term relevance applies both to traditional relevance and traditional materiality. The result is a change only in terminology, and as a result of this change, evidence may be irrelevant, and subject to exclusion on this basis, in two distinct ways. First, evidence may be irrelevant if it is directed to a fact not properly at issue under the substantive law of the case. This is the application of the concept of materiality under traditional terminology. Under modern federal terminology the factual proposition is said to be irrelevant because it is not "of consequence" or "consequential" in the law suit.[15] Second, an item of evidence may fail to alter the probabilities

---

[13] *See* § 104.1 *et seq., supra. See generally,* MORGAN, BASIC PROBLEMS OF EVIDENCE, 45 (1962).

[14] *See* United States v. Duff, 707 F.2d 1315 (11th Cir. 1983); Rossi v. Mobil Oil Corp., 710 F.2d 821 (Temp. Emer. Ct. App. 1983); *see also* Stonehocker v. General Motors Corp., 587 F.2d 151 (4th Cir. 1978) (in diversity action based on crashworthiness or second collision products liability theory, evidence of automobile manufacturer's compliance with subsequently enacted federal safety standard should have been admitted as relevant on issue of due care).

[15] United States v. Hofus, 598 F.3d 1171 (9th Cir. 2010) (when accused was charged with attempting to coerce and entice a minor to engage in sexual activity, in violation of 18 U.S.C. § 2422(b), the government was merely required to prove that the accused tried to persuade a minor to assent to sexual contact; the trial court therefore properly excluded testimony from a defense expert that the accused engaged in sexual texting "in fantasy alone" and was unlikely to actually engage in sex with the minor victim, on the grounds that such facts, even if true, were not relevant); Cameron v. City of New York, 598 F.3d 50 (2d Cir. 2010) (if a party's belief as to some legal issue is relevant to the outcome of a case — or example, where

of the existence or nonexistence of a consequential fact, *i.e.,* a fact to be proven pursuant to the substantive law. This evidence, while directed toward a proper factual target, is irrelevant because of a failure of logical or experiential connection with the target, consequential fact.[16]

Accordingly, a "fact of consequence" or a "consequential fact" is an ultimate fact because it is a substantive element of a charge, claim or defense, or it is a fact that is logically or experientially connected with such an ultimate fact by an inference that satisfies the "more or less probable" standard.

§ 401.7   Relevant Facts Need Not Be Contested Facts

Rule 401 presents no requirement that the consequential facts sought to be proved are contested or disputed in the law suit. Evidence is relevant even if it is directed to a fact that is conceded by the opposing party to be true. Background evidence, for example evidence of a person's name, address and profession, is undisputed and usually admitted without questions. Likewise, charts and illustrations are examples of evidence that usually involve undisputed matters that are yet relevant and admissible. Accordingly, if trial counsel wishes to exclude an opponent's evidence merely by conceding its truth, the evidence will not be rendered irrelevant and inadmissible. Nevertheless, evidence that is directed to a consequential fact that is not contested in the law suit has minimal probative value and may be subject to

---

a police officer is sued for false arrest, and claims that she believed she possessed probable cause to arrest — that party's testimony about her own subjective belief may be admissible. But opinions by other witnesses, such as a prosecutor, as to the existence of probable cause and the officers' credibility are irrelevant in virtually all malicious prosecution cases); United States v. Wilder, 597 F.3d 936 (8th Cir. 2010) (defendant in drug conspiracy prosecution was properly precluded from playing for the jury a recording of exculpatory statements he made to a friend after the two were arrested and held in police car; even if his statements about the unfairness of the police actions were related to show his "state of mind," that issue was not relevant to the charges in the case).

[16] *See* United States v. Akers, 702 F.2d 1145 (D.C. Cir. 1983); United States v. Bifield, 702 F.2d 342 (2d Cir. 1983); *see also* Rule 401; Redman v. John D. Brush & Co., 111 F.3d 1174 (4th Cir. 1997) (trial court erred in admitting advertisement proclaiming defendant's safe to be "burglar deterrent" in action against the manufacturer of a safe after it was burglarized; court noted that the ad was issued several years after the plaintiff had bought his safe and promoted a different model than the one owned by the plaintiff); Blinzler v. Marriott Int'l, Inc., 81 F.3d 1148 (1st Cir. 1996) (in a negligence action arising out of a hotel's alleged failure to promptly summon aid for a guest suffering a heart attack, the trial court did not abuse its discretion in admitting evidence that the defendant had destroyed a relevant printout of all outgoing calls made around the time of the incident; the court explained that the defendant knew of the report's significance and the need to preserve it as evidence at trial, and thus the jury could reasonably infer that the defendant destroyed the report because it was harmful to its case); Baker v. Delta Airlines, Inc., 6 F.3d 632 (9th Cir. 1993) (in an age discrimination action, where defendant claimed that its policy barring pilots over age 60 from certain positions was based upon safety concerns, trial court erred in excluding certain memoranda that discussed the policy but failed to mention safety as the underlying basis).

exclusion under Rule 403 where a stipulated counterweight is applicable.[17]

§ 401.8   Relevance Compared with Competency

Relevance and competency are distinguishable. Relevance, considered in Rule 401, is defined in terms of the minimal qualifications an item of evidence must possess in order to be admissible. "Competency" usually refers to the appropriateness of testimony from a particular witness. Competency is generally addressed in Rule 601 and 602.[18] Also, the term competency is occasionally used as a synonym for admissible evidence, *i.e.,* evidence that is admissible on a particular subject or in regard to a particular fact, as in the expression, "A is competent proof of B."

§ 401.9   Relevance Compared with Weight and Sufficiency of the Evidence

Relevance, weight, and sufficiency should be distinguished. Relevance, a standard to be administered by the trial judge, is the threshold qualification for evidence. Sufficiency, by comparison, is a term that refers to the totality of the evidence that must be admitted in order to advance an issue to the jury.[19] Relevance deals primarily with admissibility or inadmissibility. Sufficiency deals primarily with whether a party has submitted sufficient evidence to warrant jury consideration of the matter. The weight of evidence is the believability of the evidence as evaluated by the jury.[20]

---

[17] *See* discussion of Rule 403, at § 403.1, *infra.*

[18] *See* discussion of Rule 601, at § 601.1, *infra.*

[19] It is for the trial judge to determine if there is any evidence to establish a fact in issue that should go to the jury. To comply with the requirements of sufficiency is tantamount to the defeat of a motion for a directed verdict.

[20] Some courts have failed to observe these distinctions. United States v. Kreimer, 609 F.2d 126 (5th Cir. 1980) (confusion of relevance with sufficiency); United States v. McCoy, 517 F.2d 41 (7th Cir. 1975) (trial court confused relevance with the weight of the evidence); Lehrman v. Gulf Oil Corp., 464 F.2d 26 (5th Cir. 1972) (confusion of relevance with sufficiency to prove a contested proposition of fact).

Chapter 402

Rule 402. General Admissibility of Relevant Evidence

Rule 402. General Admissibility of Relevant Evidence

Relevant evidence is admissible unless any of the following provides otherwise:

- the United States Constitution;
- a federal statute;
- these rules; or
- other rules prescribed by the Supreme Court.

Irrelevant evidence is not admissible.

---

§ 402.1   Admissibility — In General

Rule 402 is the pivotal provision of the federal evidentiary system by connecting Rule 401, which defines relevance, with all rules of exclusion.[1] Thayer identified the concept embodied in Rule 402 as the "pre-supposition involved in the very conception of the rational system of evidence."[2] The essence of Rule 402 is that irrelevant evidence is not admissible, and that all relevant evidence will be admitted subject to specific identified exceptions. The opponent must advance a specific exclusionary rule or principle to justify the exclusion of relevant evidence.

Rule 402 indicates that the bases for excluding evidence may be internal to the Rules or they may be extrinsic authority. In the latter category, Rule 402 specifically identifies authorities that are to be given the equivalent force of express exclusionary rules set forth in the Rules of Evidence.

§ 402.2   Conceptual Basis for Rule 402

Most fundamentally, relevant evidence will be admitted to the trier of fact unless there is a specific reason to exclude it, and the policies supporting the exclusion of evidence are manifold. For example, exclusion may be

---

[1] *See generally,* 1 WEINSTEIN'S FEDERAL EVIDENCE §§ 402.01–402.06; 1 MUELLER & KIRKPATRICK, §§ 90–91. *See also* Martin, *Inherent Judicial Power, Flexibility Congress Did Not Write Into the Federal Rules of Evidence,* 57 TEX. L. REV. 167 (1979).

[2] THAYER, PRELIMINARY TREATISE ON EVIDENCE, 264 (1898).

predicated on social policy. Certain social policies are paramount to the accurate determination of the facts in a law suit and require suppression of relevant and otherwise trustworthy evidence. Obvious examples of such values are those associated with privileges, presumptions, subsequent remedial actions and compromise negotiations.[3] Other reasons for excluding evidence may relate to the inherent trustworthiness or lack of trustworthiness of the evidence, and obvious examples would include the authentication rules,[4] the hearsay rules,[5] and the so-called "best evidence rule."[6] Likewise, accuracy may be affected by the evidence's psychological or emotional impact on the trier of fact. Character evidence is an example of relevant evidence that may be excluded because of its untoward inflammatory effect upon the trier of fact.[7]

§ 402.3   The Rules of Evidence: Constitutional Inadmissibility

Rule 402 implicitly indicates that no attempt is made within the Rules of Evidence to codify constitutional principles of exclusion. Evidence that is relevant may appear to be admissible because no specific Rule within the Rules of Evidence would require its exclusion. Nevertheless, the evidence may be subject to exclusion in order to protect the constitutional rights of a litigant. Consequently, constitutional inadmissibility may be a distinct basis for denying the admission of evidence, and like other bases, the opponent of the evidence generally must be prepared to assert the constitutional doctrine in an effort to exclude the evidence in question.[8] While there is no embodiment within the Rules of constitutional doctrines, such as those pertaining to unlawful search and seizure or self-incriminating statements, such doctrines of constitutional inadmissibility obviously may be the basis for excluding evidence in federal courts.

§ 402.4   The Rules of Evidence: Statutory Inadmissibility

Rule 402 provides that statutes governing the inadmissibility of evidence have not been abrogated by the adoption of the Rules.

Statutes that would commonly have the effect of rendering evidence inadmissible include: sections of the Omnibus Crime Control and Safe Streets Act of 1979 that determine the appropriateness of admitting wiretap evidence;[9] Section 605 of the Communications Act, which protects indi-

---

[3] *See* Articles III, IV, and V.

[4] *See* Article IX.

[5] *See* Article VIII.

[6] *See* Article X.

[7] *See* Chapter 404, *infra.*

[8] *See, e.g.,* Dickerson v. United States, 530 U.S. 428 (2000) (Constitution forbids use of custodial statement not preceded by warning to suspect of his rights); Katz v. United States, 389 U.S. 347 (1967); Miranda v. Arizona, 384 U.S. 436 (1966).

[9] 28 U.S.C. §§ 2510–2520 (1979) (§ 2514 was repealed in 1974); *see also* Weiss v. United

viduals' privacy by preventing the unauthorized interception of wire or radio transmissions, or by an electronic means;[10] and statutes that prevent the admissibility of originals as retained copies of data sheets submitted to the Census Bureau.[11]

§ 402.5   Other Rules of Inadmissibility

Other Rules promulgated by the Supreme Court will render relevant evidence in a proceeding inadmissible. The Federal Rules of Criminal Procedure, the Federal Rules of Civil Procedure, the Bankruptcy Rules, and the Rules of Admiralty are the most notable sources of Rules that determine the admissibility of evidence.

Also, in light of the incorporation of state law in Rule 501, state law may also render evidence inadmissible, when the state's law of privileges govern a claim or defense in a civil action.[12]

States, 308 U.S. 321 (1939); Nardone v. United States, 302 U.S. 379 (1937); United States v. Dote, 371 F.2d 176 (7th Cir. 1966).

[10] 47 U.S.C. § 605 (1970).

[11] 13 U.S.C. § 9(a) (1970).

[12] *See* the discussion of Rule 501, Chapter 501, *infra.*

Chapter 403

Rule 403. Excluding Relevant Evidence for Prejudice, Confusion, Waste of Time, or Other Reasons

Rule 403. Excluding Relevant Evidence for Prejudice, Confusion, Waste of Time, or Other Reasons

The court may exclude relevant evidence if its probative value is substantially outweighed by a danger of one or more of the following: unfair prejudice, confusing the issues, misleading the jury, undue delay, wasting time, or needlessly presenting cumulative evidence.

---

§ 403.1   In General

Rule 403 codifies the long-standing authority of the trial judge to exclude relevant evidence where the probative value of the offered evidence is outweighed by one or more of certain identified countervailing considerations.[1] The underlying premise of the Rule is that certain relevant evidence should not be admitted to the trier of fact where the admission would result in an adverse effect upon the effectiveness or integrity of the fact finding process.[2] This same policy generally underpins the succeeding Rules contained in Article IV, and Rules 404 through 415 represent applications of the balancing of relevance and countervailing adverse effects that have recurred with sufficient frequency to have resulted in a specific rule.

Like most rules of exclusion in the Federal Rules of Evidence, Rule 403 may be applied as the authority for objection at trial, or alternatively, it may be the basis for a motion *in limine* submitted prior to trial pursuant to Rule

---

[1] *See generally,* 1 MCCORMICK, § 185; 2 WEINSTEIN'S FEDERAL EVIDENCE §§ 403.01–403.07; 1 MUELLER & KIRKPATRICK, §§ 92–98; 2 WIGMORE, §§ 443–444; 6 WIGMORE, §§ 1904–1907; Graham, *Observation—The Relationship Among Federal Rules of Evidence 607, 801(d)(1)(A) and 403: A Reply to Weinstein,* 55 TEX. L. REV. 573 (1977); Wellborn, *The Federal Rules of Evidence and the Application of State Law in Federal Courts,* 55 TEX. L. REV. 3 (1977); Travers, *An Essay on the Determination of Relevancy Under the Federal Rules of Evidence,* 1977 ARIZ. ST. L.J. 327 (1977); Weinstein & Berger, *Basic Rules of Relevancy in the Proposed Rules of Evidence,* 4 GA. L. REV. 43 (1969).

[2] Rule 611 codifies parallel authority regarding the trial judge's control of the interrogation of witnesses.

104. A pretrial ruling on evidence potentially subject to exclusion under Rule 403 may be particularly desirable. If raised at trial as a basis for exclusion, objections citing prejudice and confusion — even if granted — may not absolutely prevent the jury from being exposed to inflammatory or misleading evidence. Through the device of a pretrial motion *in limine, i.e.,* a motion for an advance ruling on the admissibility of evidence, the trial judge can consider both sides' positions on probative value as well as the counterweight in question without exposing the jury to evidence that may be ultimately excluded.[3]

The Supreme Court has repeatedly reaffirmed the constitutionality of evidence rules, like Rule 403, that permit judges "to exclude evidence that is repetitive, only marginally relevant or poses an undue risk of harassment, prejudice, or confusion of the issues."[4] State and federal rulemakers have broad latitude under the Constitution to establish rules excluding evidence from trials, but that latitude has constitutional limits in a criminal case. "Whether rooted directly in the Due Process Clause of the Fourteenth Amendment or in the Compulsory Process or Confrontation clauses of the Sixth Amendment, the Constitution guarantees criminal defendants a meaningful opportunity to present a complete defense"[5] and "prohibits the exclusion of defense evidence under rules that serve no legitimate purpose or that are disproportionate to the ends that they are asserted to promote."[6] This right "is abridged by evidence rules that infringe upon a weighty interest of the accused and are arbitrary or disproportionate to the purposes they are designed to serve."[7] On that basis, the Supreme Court has repeatedly struck down as "arbitrary" rules of evidence that "excluded important defense evidence but that did not serve any legitimate interests."[8]

---

[3] *See, e.g.,* Litton Sys. v. Am. Tel. & Tel. Co., 700 F.2d 785 (2d Cir. 1983); United States v. Southard, 700 F.2d 1 (1st Cir. 1983); Mauldin v. Upjohn Co., 697 F.2d 644 (5th Cir. 1983).

[4] Holmes v. South Carolina, 547 U.S. 319, 326–327 (2006) (citations and internal punctuation omitted).

[5] *Holmes,* 547 U.S. at 324 (citations and internal punctuation omitted).

[6] *Id.* at 326.

[7] *Id.* at 325 (citations and internal punctuation omitted).

[8] *Id.* at 325 (a rule precluding the accused from introducing proof of someone else's guilt in cases where the prosecution has introduced forensic evidence that, if believed, strongly supports a guilty verdict, was illogical, arbitrary, and did not rationally advance any legitimate state interest in restricting the admission of evidence on collateral matters); Rock v. Arkansas, 483 U.S. 44, 61 (1987) (a rule prohibiting hypnotically refreshed testimony was unconstitutional because "[w]holesale inadmissibility of a defendant's testimony is an arbitrary restriction on the right to testify in the absence of clear evidence by the State repudiating the validity of all post-hypnotic recollections"); Crane v. Kentucky, 476 U.S. 683, 691 (1986) (defendant was prevented from attempting to show at trial that his confession was unreliable because of the circumstances under which it was obtained, and the state could not advance "any rational justification for the wholesale exclusion of this body of potentially exculpatory evidence"); Chambers v. Mississippi, 410 U.S. 284, 302–303 (1973) (after

§ 403.2 Balance of Probative Values versus Counterweight, Discretion of Trial Judge

When the court is requested to exclude evidence for one of the reasons specified under Rule 403, the trial judge must determine whether the adverse effect *substantially* outweighs the probative value of the evidence. The word "substantial" is undoubtedly a word of some elasticity, and ultimately in applying that standard, the trial judge has broad discretion. Consequently, it is generally held that a trial judge's determination based on Rule 403 will be overturned only upon a showing of abuse of discretion.[9] No precise definition of the term "substantial" appears in the Rules, yet it is clear that, at least symbolically, Rule 403 favors a presumption of admissibility by mandating that the negative attribute of the evidence must substantially outweigh its probative value before exclusion is justified.[10] Even evidence that carries some small risk of unfair prejudice should be admitted if its potential probative value is at least equally substantial.[11] At a minimum, a

---

murder defendant called a witness who had previously confessed to the murder but the witness repudiated the confession, defendant was denied due process by state "voucher rule" that precluded him from impeaching any witness he called to the stand, and by state hearsay rules that did not include an exception for statements against penal interest, where state was unable to defend the rationale for those rules of evidence); Washington v. Texas, 388 U.S. 14, 22–23 (1967) (murder defendant was denied his right to fair trial when he was precluded from calling as a witness a person who had been convicted of committing the same murder because of state law restricting alleged participants in a crime from testifying in defense of each other; the rule could not "even be defended on the ground that it rationally sets apart a group of persons who are particularly likely to commit perjury" since the rule allowed an alleged participant to testify if he or she had been acquitted or was called by the prosecution); *but see* United States v. Scheffer, 523 U.S. 303, 309 (1998) (a rule excluding all polygraph evidence did not abridge the right to present a defense because the rule "serve[d] several legitimate interests in the criminal trial process," was "neither arbitrary nor disproportionate in promoting these ends," and did not "implicate a sufficiently weighty interest of the defendant").

[9] *See* Foley v. City of Lowell, 948 F.2d 10 (1st Cir. 1991) (it was not an abuse of discretion to admit evidence of a similar though isolated incident of police brutality since the prejudicial effect of the evidence was outweighed by its high probative value in determining a policy of tolerance); Wierstak v. Heffernan, 789 F.2d 968 (1st Cir. 1986) (the District Court did not abuse its discretion in excluding plaintiff's prior conviction since evidence was not probative); United States v. McDowell, 762 F.2d 1072 (D.C. Cir. 1985) (the District Court did not abuse its discretion by admitting bulletproof vest into evidence since it could be used to prove intent to distribute drugs); United States v. Abel, 469 U.S. 45 (1984) (no abuse of discretion to allow highly probative yet prejudicial testimony of membership in a prisoners' group dedicated to commit perjury on behalf of members where court took precautions, *i.e.,* limiting instruction, to prevent undue prejudice).

[10] *See* LILLY, § 2.5; *e.g.,* Estate of Larkins v. Farrell Lines, Inc., 806 F.2d 510 (4th Cir. 1986); United States v. Calbas, 821 F.2d 887 (2d Cir. 1987) (evidence offered not allowed because it was confusing and of doubtful relevance).

[11] United States v. Diaz, 592 F.3d 467 (3d Cir. 2010) (in prosecution for drug and firearms charges, the district court did not err in allowing limited testimony by Government witnesses

litigant seeking exclusion based on Rule 403 should never argue that the balance is a "close question."

As indicated by the Advisory Committee Note, Rule 403 essentially states a principle broadly recognized in prior law.[12] While the trial judge has always possessed substantial discretion to exclude evidence, the Rule sharpens this analysis and provides a framework for clearer argument as to admissibility or inadmissibility. Prior case law often evaluated counterbalancing factors as merely part of the function of assessing probative value, and pre-Rule case law might, for example, assess probative value as non-existent because of concomitant unfair prejudice or confusion. As McCormick has stated, the better approach is to distinguish between probative value on one hand, and the counterbalancing danger on the other:

> Some courts and textwriters have described this process of weighing marginal costs and benefits as a matter of "legal relevance," in that "legally relevant" evidence must have a "plus value" beyond a bare minimum of probative value. This notion of "plus value" is at best an imprecise way to say that the probative value and the need for the evidence must outweigh the harm likely to result from admission . . .[13]

In applying Rule 403, the trial judge should consider alternate means by which the fact sought to be proven can be established. Obviously, if the same consequential fact can be proven by evidence unattended by the risk of prejudice, confusion or inefficiency, the trial court should exercise its

---

that they feared being labeled a "snitch" and what members of their community would do to them in retaliation for their cooperation with the Government; the evidence had little probative value, as it only helped explain why those witnesses were uncooperative, but its potential for prejudice was not substantial, because no witness stated directly that the defendant was violent, and the testimony merely reflected the general dangerousness of the housing project); United States v. Nadeau, 598 F.3d 966 (8th Cir. 2010) (in assault prosecution, trial court did not err in admitting a metal pipe found in a car in which the accused was riding, despite possible questions as to whether it was the same pipe used in the assault, as there was "no reason to believe that the pipe would have lured the jury into declaring guilt on an improper basis"); United States v. Vosburgh, 602 F.3d 512 (3d Cir. 2010) (in prosecution for possession of child pornography, it was not an abuse of discretion to admit Government evidence that the accused was found in possession of "child erotica," which suggested that he harbored a sexual interest in children, and tended to disprove any argument that he unknowingly possessed child pornography found on his computer, or that he had attempted to access a certain website by accident).

[12] *See* Rule 403, Advisory Committee Note; *see also* United States v. Brown, 547 F.2d 1264 (5th Cir. 1977).

[13] 1 McCormick, § 185, at 784–85; *see, e.g.,* United States v. Ellis, 156 F.3d 493 (3d Cir. 1998) (no abuse of discretion to disallow impeachment of Government witness, who was called solely for the purpose of authenticating tape recordings, with evidence that the witness had testified falsely at a hearing; the proposed "impeachment" had no probative value because the accused had already stipulated to the truth of the matters testified to on direct examination, *i.e.,* the authenticity of the tapes).

inherent power under Rule 403 to compel the use of the alternate method of proof.[14] For example, in a prosecution of a man accused of being a convicted felon in unlawful possession of a firearm, the Supreme Court ruled in *Old Chief v. United States* that a trial court abuses its discretion in refusing the defendant's offer to stipulate that he was previously convicted of a felony and admitting evidence concerning the nature of the previous offense where the nature of that offense raises the danger of unfair prejudice to the defendant. The Court found that the sole purpose for admitting evidence of the prior conviction was to establish that the defendant had previously been convicted of a felony — an element of the statute he was charged with violating — and held that the trial court should have excluded the defendant's conviction record, because other, less prejudicial evidence (*i.e.,* the defendant's admission) was available.[15]

A judge should also determine whether a limiting instruction pursuant to Rule 105 would sufficiently diminish the danger of an adverse effect. Where the use of a limiting instruction cannot adequately neutralize the negative attribute of the evidence, exclusion under Rule 403 may be warranted.[16] In any case in which Rule 403 is invoked, it is appropriate for a trial lawyer to ask the trial judge to provide a statement on the record that explicates the court's analysis of probative value and the countervailing adverse effect.[17]

§ 403.3   Exclusion of Relevant Evidence Based upon Unfair Prejudice

Exclusion on the basis of unfair prejudice involves more than a balance of adverse prejudice. If unfair prejudice referred to any evidence prejudicial to a party's case, anything adverse to a litigant's position at trial would be excludable under Rule 403. Emphasis must be placed on the word "unfair." Evidence is not *unfairly* prejudicial, however, even if it has some tendency

---

[14] Roshan v. Fard, 705 F.2d 102 (7th Cir. 1981); United States v. Mills, 704 F.2d 1553 (11th Cir. 1980).

[15] *See* Old Chief v. United States, 519 U.S. 172 (1997). For a critical analysis of the Court's reasoning in *Old Chief,* and for a discussion of its tactical implications for trial lawyers and judges, *see* Duane, *"Screw Your Courage to the Sticking-Place": The Roles of Evidence, Stipulations, and Jury Instructions in Criminal Verdicts,* 49 HASTINGS L. J. 463 (Jan. 1998); Duane, *Litigating Felon-with-a-Firearm Cases After* Old Chief: *Trial Strategies for Lawyers and Judges,* 12 CRIMINAL JUSTICE NO. 3, 18 (Fall 1997); Duane, *Stipulations, Judicial Notice, and a Prosecutor's Supposed "Right" to Prove Undisputed Facts: Oral Argument from an Amicus Curiae in* Old Chief v. United States, 168 F.R.D. 405 (Nov. 1996). *See also* United States v. DeLeon, 170 F.3d 494 (5th Cir. 1999) (convicted felon was accused of being in possession of ammunition found by police with a parole document bearing his name in his girlfriend's home; admission of the redacted parole document was not an abuse of discretion because of its tendency to tie defendant to the ammunition).

[16] Harris v. Illinois-California Express Inc., 687 F.2d 1361 (10th Cir. 1982); United States v. Figueroa, 618 F.2d 934 (2d Cir. 1980).

[17] *See* United States v. Dwyer, 539 F.2d 924 (2d Cir. 1976).

to arouse the horror or antipathy of the jurors, as long as the evidence goes directly to proving the defendant's commission of the offenses for which he is on trial.[18] Unfair prejudice is that quality of evidence that might result in an improper, usually irrational, basis for a jury decision.[19] Consequently, if

---

[18] United States v. Schneider, 594 F.3d 1219 (10th Cir. 2010) (in criminal prosecution for prescribing controlled medications without a legitimate medical purpose, thereby causing the death of over twenty patients, the trial court could not use its discretion under Rule 403 to limit the prosecution to proof of just a few deaths; evidence of a doctor's responsibility for the deaths of over twenty patients may have a profound effect on the jury, but when that is the precise conduct for which the defendant is charged, such facts are not collateral activity or prior bad acts, and while the evidence was certainly prejudicial, it was not unfairly prejudicial).

[19] *See* United States v. Dierling, 131 F.3d 722, 730 (8th Cir. 1997) ("The critical issue is the degree of unfairness of the prejudicial evidence and whether it tends to support a decision on an improper basis"); *see also* United States v. Saccoccia, 58 F.3d 754 (1st Cir. 1995) (testimony by a dog handler that the trained drug dog had been alerted to the presence of drugs was found to be relevant and not unfairly prejudicial where corroborated by other evidence); United States v. Chandler, 996 F.2d 1073 (11th Cir. 1993) (in drug conspiracy case, evidence that defendant had made threats against two people he suspected of stealing his drugs was not unfairly prejudicial to defendant); United States v. Harvey, 991 F.2d 981 (2d Cir. 1993) (where defendant was charged with purchasing child pornography through the mail, evidence of graphic adult pornography found at defendant's home was unfairly prejudicial because it may have inflamed the jury); Bilal v. Lockhart, 993 F.2d 643 (8th Cir. 1993) (in § 1983 action, no unfair prejudice resulted where trial court admitted testimony by prison officials concerning an unwritten prison policy); United States v. Khan, 993 F.2d 1368 (9th Cir. 1993) (evidence of defendants' involvement in a prior drug transaction was not unfairly prejudicial because it was very similar to the charged crime, so the probative value was great); Johnson v. Ford Motor Co., 988 F.2d 573 (5th Cir. 1993) (in products liability action, trial court properly excluded evidence of other lawsuits filed against defendant and of correspondence between defendant and a federal safety agency where there was a danger of prejudice to defendant and of misleading the jury); United States v. Donovan, 984 F.2d 507 (1st Cir. 1993) (where defendant bank president was charged with failure to file certain transaction reports, evidence of other related misconduct by defendant was not unfairly prejudicial because defendant testified that the failure to file the reports was an honest mistake); United States v. Hitt, 981 F.2d 422 (9th Cir. 1992) (where defendant in a firearms case claimed that a rifle fired automatic rounds because of an internal malfunction, admission of a photograph showing the outside of the rifle along with nine other guns owned by defendant's housemate was unfairly prejudicial to defendant and lacked probative value); Four Corners Helicopters v. Turbomeca, 979 F.2d 1434 (10th Cir. 1992) (in products liability action, trial court did not abuse its discretion in admitting evidence of other similar accidents); Whalen v. Unit Rig, Inc., 974 F.2d 1248 (10th Cir. 1992) (in an age discrimination action, defendant was not unfairly prejudiced by the admission of lists of employees that defendant had asked for in declining order of age); Wallace v. Mulholland, 957 F.2d 333 (7th Cir. 1992) (in a civil rights case involving police injury to a mental patient, it was proper to exclude evidence of patient's schizophrenia since its prejudicial effect outweighed the probative value); United States v. Kang, 934 F.2d 621 (5th Cir. 1991) (where the accused had stipulated to criminal intent, evidence of his flight from justice was improperly admitted because its prejudicial effect substantially outweighed its probative value). *But see* United States v. Hankins, 931 F.2d 1256 (8th Cir. 1991) (the court used a four-step analysis of inferential reasoning to determine that evidence of flight from justice was circumstantial evidence of

the evidence arouses the jury's emotional sympathies, evokes a sense of horror, or appeals to an instinct to punish, the evidence may be unfairly prejudicial.[20] Usually, although not always, unfairly prejudicial evidence appeals to the jury's emotions rather than intellect.[21]

Unfair prejudice may be present when inflammatory or otherwise shocking real proof or photographs are offered.[22] Likewise, the subject matter of testimony may be excessively prejudicial and subject to exclusion under Rule 403.[23] It must be remembered that Rule 403 calls for a balancing of

---

consciousness of guilt, and its probative value outweighed its prejudicial effect); *In re* Richardson-Merrell, Inc. "Bendectin" Products Liability Litigation, 624 F. Supp. 1212 (S.D. Ohio 1985) (allowing deformed child in courtroom caused unfair prejudice to defendant); Le Boeuf v. K-Mart Corp., 888 F.2d 330 (5th Cir. 1989) (evidence that a store manager's bonus was proportional to the store profits after tort judgments was unfairly prejudicial); United States v. Masters, 924 F.2d 1362 (7th Cir. 1991) (defendant could not explore third party's transvestism in murder case because danger of unfair prejudice was substantial); United States v. Eason, 920 F.2d 731 (11th Cir. 1990) (cross-examination of defense witness by prosecutor, in which it was revealed that defendant's father was convicted of similar offense, was unfairly prejudicial and cause for reversal); United States v. Gibbs, 174 F.3d 762 (6th Cir. 1999) (in a prosecution of forty-one persons involved in an alleged conspiracy to distribute crack cocaine, trial court properly admitted photographs of t-shirts referring to the group as they tied one defendant to the conspiracy, but erred in admitting photographs of graffiti-covered buildings with references to cop killings and gang names; the prejudicial effect of the graffiti photographs greatly outweighed their very low probative value).

[20] 1 McCORMICK, § 185.

[21] *See* Advisory Committee Note, Rule 403; *see, e.g.,* United States v. Cooper, 591 F.3d 582 (7th Cir. 2010) (in prosecution for possession of heroin with the intent to distribute, the district court erred in allowing the Government to prove that many of those who purchased the defendant's heroin died as a result, and that he exhibited a lack of remorse for the deaths. This evidence was "explosive" and the jury was probably repulsed by the evidence of his callousness about the consequences of his sales, and its potential for unfair prejudice greatly exceeded its probative value at the guilt stage of the trial — even though it would have been unquestionably admissible during the later sentencing proceeding, where the court would have been concerned with the nature and circumstances of his offense, his history and characteristics).

[22] *See, e.g.,* United States v. Qamar, 671 F.2d 732 (2d Cir. 1982); United States v. Bowers, 660 F.2d 527 (5th Cir. 1981); *but see* United States v. Kime, 99 F.3d 870 (8th Cir. 1996) (photographs of the scene of a robbery, including gunshot wounds suffered by the victim, tended to corroborate trial testimony and were not unduly gruesome; trial court did not abuse its discretion in admitting them).

[23] *See, e.g.,* United States v. Fulmer, 108 F.3d 1486 (1st Cir. 1997) (where defendant was convicted of threatening a federal agent after sending a voice-mail stating, "silver bullets are coming," the trial court erred in allowing prejudicial testimony from the victim that he feared defendant's threats because of the Oklahoma City bombing; also, the admission of bullets taken from defendant's desk to show they are silvery in color was unduly prejudicial; finally, although a certain amount of testimony about a victim's reaction is customary, it was unfairly prejudicial to admit testimony that the victim was glad he had brought home extra ammunition that night); United States v. Thomas, 49 F.3d 253 (6th Cir. 1995) (trial court erred in admitting a sawed-off shotgun where that shotgun was not used in any of the drug

probative value against the case counterweight, and no evidence is inadmissible simply because it is sensational or prejudicial.[24]

Rule 403 frequently operates in conjunction with other Rules of Evidence to fine tune their application, and reference will be made through this Treatise to the interplay between Rule 403 and other Rules.

§ 403.4   Exclusion of Relevant Evidence Based upon Confusion of the Issues or Misleading the Jury

Exclusion based upon confusion usually is justified where the offered evidence would require the trier of fact to engage in intricate, extraordinary, or impossible mental gymnastics in order to comprehend the import of the evidence or to assess its weight.[25] Likewise, if the jury is likely to ascribe

---

transactions for which the defendant was being prosecuted); *In re* Bendectin, 857 F.2d 290 (6th Cir. 1988) (in a consolidated proceeding limited to the issue of whether Bendectin caused birth defects, trial judge did not abuse discretion in forbidding plaintiffs' counsel from using the term "Thalidomide" when referring to plaintiffs' comparative research studies or the qualifications of plaintiffs' experts); United States v. Quigley, 890 F.2d 1019 (8th Cir. 1989) (district court erred by admitting testimony comparing defendants' conduct to a drug courier profile as evidence of defendant's guilt); United States v. Abel, 469 U.S. 45 (1984) (use of name "Aryan Brotherhood" excluded as unduly prejudicial); United States v. Milstead, 671 F.2d 950 (5th Cir. 1980); Cohn v. Papke, 655 F.2d 191 (9th Cir. 1981); Ware v. Reed, 709 F.2d 345 (5th Cir. 1983).

[24] *See* Mullen v. Princess Anne Volunteer Fire Co., 853 F.2d 1130 (4th Cir. 1988) (in a civil rights suit, trial judge erred in excluding evidence that defendants commonly referred to blacks as "niggers"); United States v. Gatto, 924 F.2d 491 (3d Cir. 1991) (hypnotism of eyewitness ten years prior to trial does not preclude admission of his testimony against accused; potential prejudice resulting from effect of hypnosis does not substantially outweigh probative value of eyewitness identification); United States v. Dazzo, 672 F.2d 284 (2d Cir. 1982); Ballou v. Henri Studios Inc., 656 F.2d 1147 (5th Cir. 1981); United States v. Thompson, 710 F.2d 915 (2d Cir. 1983); Leopold v. Baccarat, Inc., 174 F.3d 261 (2d Cir. 1999) (where the defense claimed that an age and sex discrimination plaintiff had been fired for her difficulty in getting along with other employees, there was no abuse of discretion in allowing testimony about plaintiff's racist and bigoted comments to co-workers years before her discharge; although both the probative value and the danger of unfair prejudice were significant, neither was overwhelming).

[25] *See* United States v. Hartley, 678 F.2d 961 (11th Cir. 1982); United States v. Schmidt, 711 F.2d 595 (5th Cir. 1983); United States v. Flitcraft, 803 F.2d 184 (5th Cir. 1986). *But see* Karns v. Emerson Electric Co., 817 F.2d 1452 (10th Cir. 1987) (evidence not excluded because it was helpful to the jury in deciding the case); Freund v. Fleetwood Enterprises, 956 F.2d 354 (1st Cir. 1991) (evidence of propane leakages from refrigerators significantly different from the plaintiff's was properly excluded as potentially confusing or misleading); United States v. Rewald, 889 F.2d 836 (9th Cir. 1989), *amended,* 902 F.2d 18 (9th Cir. 1990) (in a trial for swindling investors out of millions of dollars, extensive evidence tending to prove the defendant was a CIA agent, rather than proving defendant's contention that the CIA instructed him to spend the investor's money, was properly excluded to prevent confusion of issues or misleading the jury); Le Boeuf v. K-Mart Corp., 888 F.2d 330 (5th Cir. 1989) (the probative value of evidence regarding the condition of defendant's floors two years after plaintiff slipped and fell was outweighed by its potential to mislead the jury; the probative value of a K-Mart video regarding the number of in-store accidents nationwide each year,

excessive, unwarranted weight to the evidence, the offered proof is a candidate for exclusion under Rule 403.[26] In any situation in which the evidence must be accompanied by a limiting instruction so convoluted or tortured that the jury will be at a loss to gauge the proper application or weight of the evidence, Rule 403 may operate to exclude the evidence.[27]

While the bases of exclusion relating to confusion of the issues or misleading of the jury find precedent in pre-Rule case law,[28] some pre-Rule cases address the analysis in terms of "remoteness," *i.e.,* remoteness resulting because the offered facts are temporarily or spatially separated from the event sought to be established.[29] In actuality, any evidence that alters the probabilities of a fact of consequence in the law suit is relevant even though substantial time or space separates the facts offered from the transaction or occurrence sought to be established. However, as a general-

---

with no direct relationship to the particular store where the accident occurred, was also outweighed by its potential to mislead the jury).

[26] *See* Johnson v. Ford Motor Co., 988 F.2d 573 (5th Cir. 1993) (in products liability action, trial court properly excluded evidence of other lawsuits filed against defendant and of correspondence between defendant and a federal safety agency where there was a danger of misleading the jury); United States v. Bowen, 876 F.2d 897 (9th Cir. 1988) (in a prosecution of two border patrol agents for violating an individual's civil rights and for conspiring to falsify the results of an internal investigation of the charges, the trial court did not abuse its discretion in excluding the circumstances surrounding and the results of a polygraph exam; although the evidence would have been admissible to show the operative facts of the conspiracy, the jury may have inferred that the defendants had failed the exam and so were guilty, and its admission would have opened the door to evidence that the defendants had passed other polygraphs in violation of general circuit ban against the use of polygraph test results); Brumley Estate v. Iowa Beef Processors, 704 F.2d 1351 (5th Cir. 1983); United States v. Landes, 704 F.2d 152 (5th Cir. 1983); Golden Bear Distr. Sys. of Texas v. Chase Revel, Inc., 708 F.2d 944 (5th Cir. 1983); Faigin v. Kelly, 184 F.3d 67 (1st Cir. 1999) (athlete sued his former advisors for misleading him about investments but failed to prosecute and took a voluntary dismissal; one advisor then moved for and was awarded sanctions under Fed. R. Civ. P. 11; later, the athlete wrote an autobiography that portrayed the advisors as disreputable; when one of the advisors sued for libel, the trial court properly refused to admit evidence of the sanction order under Fed. R. Evid. 403, because a jury might give special weight to such judicial findings).

[27] *See* Walker v. Nations Bank of Florida N.A., 53 F.3d 1548 (11th Cir. 1995) (in an action for age and sex discrimination, the trial court did not abuse its discretion in excluding a letter from the Washington branch of the Equal Employment Opportunity Commission that found reasonable cause to believe that defendant had discriminated against plaintiff; the Miami branch of the EEOC had concluded that there was no discrimination; court found that admission of such evidence would have been prejudicial because it would have forced the jury to resolve the conflicting findings from two different administrative officials on the same issue); F.H. Krear & Co. v. Nineteen Named Trustees, 810 F.2d 1250 (2d Cir. 1987); Kim v. Coppin State College, 662 F.2d 1055 (4th Cir. 1981); United States v. Steffen, 641 F.2d 591 (8th Cir. 1980); United States v. Ness, 665 F.2d 248 (8th Cir. 1981).

[28] *See, e.g.,* Shepard v. United States, 290 U.S. 96 (1933); United States v. 25.406 Acres of Land, 172 F.2d 990 (4th Cir. 1949).

[29] *See, e.g.,* Cotton v. United States, 361 F.2d 673 (8th Cir. 1966).

ization, the more remote a fact from the event sought to be proven, the lower its probative value, and an extremely remote fact possessing extremely low probative value may be easily excluded under Rule 403 where an appropriate counterweight is present, *e.g.*, confusion or prejudice. "A specific application of this principle is found in rules regulating the admission of evidence proffered by criminal defendants to show that someone else committed the crime with which they are charged,"[30] since such evidence may be excluded if "it does not sufficiently connect the other person to the crime, as, for example, where the evidence is speculative or remote."[31] It should be emphasized, however, that no evidence is inadmissible simply because its probative value is extremely low. An express exclusionary rule must be invoked. Nevertheless, when probative value is extremely low, Rule 403 may be an appropriate basis for exclusion of the minimally helpful evidence where a negative attribute identified in Rule 403 can be cited.[32]

Confusion of the issues and misleading the jury may also be bases for exclusion of evidence in instances where evidence is inadmissible in part or where evidence is admissible for one purpose and not for another.[33] Pursuant to Rule 105, evidence is not rendered inadmissible simply because it is admissible for one purpose but not for another, and the court may admit such evidence subject to a limiting instruction to the jury. Rule 403 may be the basis for exclusion of evidence falling within this category where its admission would have such a misleading effect that the jury's decision-making process would be compromised.[34] Again, it should be emphasized that the danger must *substantially* outweigh the probative value, and the

---

[30] Holmes v. South Carolina, 547 U.S. 319, 327 (2006) (citations and internal punctuation omitted).

[31] *Holmes,* 547 U.S. at 327 (quoting 40A AM. JUR. 2D, HOMICIDE § 286 (1999).

[32] *E.g.,* Chamberlin v. Town of Stoughton, 601 F.3d 25 (1st Cir. 2010) (district court properly excluded report that town commissioned from an attorney who concluded that explanation by the town's chief of police was not credible, because the limited probative value of that attorney's opinion was outweighed by its prejudicial effect; the report contained no factual details that were not otherwise available to plaintiffs, and attorney's evaluation of what the jury was expected to decide served no useful purpose); Starrett v. Wadley, 876 F.2d 808 (10th Cir. 1989) (in an employment discrimination case in which both sides had agreed before trial not to discuss unemployment compensation pursuant to the "collateral source" rule, the trial court properly excluded plaintiff's application for unemployment insurance; although plaintiff had indicated on the form that she left her employment due to lack of work, she also indicated on the form that she was fired in retaliation for filing a harassment claim, and therefore the form's probative (impeachment) value was very slight and the risk of jury confusion was great, and so the trial court was within its discretion in excluding the form).

[33] Jamison v. Storer Broadcasting Co., 511 F. Supp. 1286 (E.D. Mich. 1981); United States v. Terebecki, 692 F.2d 1345 (11th Cir. 1982); United States v. Green, 548 F.2d 1261 (6th Cir. 1977).

[34] Larue v. National Union Elec. Corp., 571 F.2d 51 (1st Cir. 1978); Marx & Co. v. Diners' Club Inc., 550 F.2d 505 (2d Cir. 1977).

mere possibility of confusion will not be a basis for exclusion of evidence under Rule 403.

§ 403.5 Exclusion of Relevant Evidence Based upon Waste of Time, Undue Delay and Needless Presentation of Cumulative Evidence

A trial judge possesses discretion under Rule 403 to exclude evidence based upon such efficiency and considerations as undue delay, needless presentation of cumulative evidence and waste of time.[35] Because of the similarity between waste of time, undue delay, and presentation of cumulative evidence as grounds for exclusion, courts rarely distinguish among these factors.[36] Nevertheless, it is clear that in this context, Rule 403 may be the basis for limiting the number of witnesses to prove a fact,[37] repetitious evidence,[38] and evidence that represents an inefficient use of the court's time when compared with its probative value.[39] But relevant evidence with

---

[35] *See* Goldberg v. Nat'l Life Ins. Co. of Vermont, 774 F.2d 559 (2d Cir. 1985) (court of appeals held that district court did not abuse its discretion in excluding psychiatric testimony due to undue delay); Lucas v. Bechtel Corp., 800 F.2d 839 (9th Cir. 1986) (testimony offered to impeach the official minutes of the conventions constituted waste of time); United States v. Rewald, 889 F.2d 836 (9th Cir. 1989), *amended,* 902 F.2d 18 (9th Cir. 1990) (extensive evidence tending to prove that the defendant was a CIA agent, rather than proving the defendant's contention that the CIA instructed him to spend investor money, was properly excluded to avoid undue delay); Abernathy v. Superior Hardwoods, Inc., 704 F.2d 963 (7th Cir. 1983); United States v. Bouye, 688 F.2d 471 (7th Cir. 1982).

[36] *See, e.g.,* United States v. Cole, 622 F.2d 98 (4th Cir. 1980); United States v. Johnson, 605 F.2d 1025 (7th Cir. 1979).

[37] *See, e.g.,* Leefe v. Air Logistics, Inc., 876 F.2d 409 (5th Cir. 1989) (in a personal injury suit in which liability was not contested, trial court properly excluded the testimony of a physician from whom plaintiff twice sought a second opinion because the primary physician had already testified regarding the extent of plaintiff's injuries; the "cumulative effect of testimony by several experts" was not necessary even though the second physician was willing to give plaintiff a specific disability rating the primary physician could not supply); Donovan v. Burger King Corp., 672 F.2d 221 (1st Cir. 1982); Wetherill v. University of Chicago, 565 F. Supp. 1553 (N.D. Ill. 1983).

[38] *See, e.g.,* International Minerals & Resources S.A. v. Pappas, 96 F.3d 586 (2d Cir. 1996) (in case alleging that the defendant tortiously interfered with plaintiff's contract to buy a ship, the trial court did not abuse its discretion in excluding letters relating to the plaintiff's plans for the ship, as the jury had already heard similar evidence regarding damages through witness testimony); Elwood v. Pina, 815 F.2d 173 (1st. Cir. 1987) (testimony of the substance of conversations between administrative assistant and investigator excluded because they had already been introduced); Gibson v. Mohawk Rubber Co., 695 F.2d 1093 (8th Cir. 1982); United States v. Ackal, 706 F.2d 523 (5th Cir. 1983).

[39] *See* Scaggs v. Consolidated Rail Corp., 6 F.3d 1290 (7th Cir. 1993) (plaintiff filed an action against his employer for injuries sustained in an accident on the job; trial court properly excluded as excessively prejudicial and time consuming evidence that the employer kept plaintiff under surveillance after the claim was filed but failed to find anything fraudulent concerning plaintiff's claims); United States v. Tindle, 808 F.2d 319 (4th Cir. 1986) (allowing defendant to call an undercover DEA agent as a witness was inefficient use of the court's

substantial probative value may not be arbitrarily limited solely for the purpose of shortening the trial.[40]

§ 403.6   Exclusion of Relevant Evidence and the Role of "Surprise"

In not designating unfair surprise as a ground for exclusion, Rule 403 comports with Wigmore's view.[41] While surprise may undoubtedly result in injustice in certain situations, the granting of a continuance is considered to be the more appropriate method of achieving fairness in this context.[42]

§ 403.7   Relationship of Rule 403 and Rule 105

The interrelationship between Rule 105, "Limited Admissibility," and Rule 403 cannot be overemphasized. Rule 105 provides for a limiting instruction from the trial judge, and a limiting instruction is frequently used as the second line of defense when trial counsel has unsuccessfully attempted to exclude evidence under Rule 403.[43] Likewise, the trial judge should consider the efficacy of a limiting instruction in addressing the counterweight in evaluating a claim of exclusion based on Rule 403.

---

time); MCI Communications, Inc. v. Am. Tel. & Tel. Co., 708 F.2d 1081 (7th Cir. 1983); Kontz v. K-Mart Corp., 712 F.2d 1302 (8th Cir. 1983); *see also* Abernathy v. Superior Hardwoods, 704 F.2d 963 (7th Cir. 1983).

[40] United States v. Schneider, 594 F.3d 1219 (10th Cir. 2010) (in criminal prosecution of defendants charged with prescribing controlled medications without a legitimate medical purpose, thereby causing the death of over twenty patients, the trial court could not use its discretion under Rule 403 or 404 to shorten the trial by limiting the prosecution to proof of just a few of those deaths, given the probative value of that evidence to the prosecution's case).

[41] *See* 6 WIGMORE, § 1848; *see generally,* 2 MUELLER & KIRKPATRICK, § 98; LILLY, § 2.5.

[42] *See* Shad v. Dean Witter Reynolds, Inc., 799 F.2d 525 (9th Cir. 1986); Rule 403, Advisory Committee Note.

[43] *See* discussion of Rule 105, Chapter 105, *supra.*

Chapter 404

Rule 404. Character Evidence; Crimes or Other Acts

Rule 404. Character Evidence; Crimes or Other Acts

(a) **Character Evidence.**

    (1) *Prohibited Uses.* Evidence of a person's character or character trait is not admissible to prove that on a particular occasion the person acted in accordance with the character or trait.

    (2) *Exceptions for a Defendant or Victim in a Criminal Case.* The following exceptions apply in a criminal case:

        (A) a defendant may offer evidence of the defendant's pertinent trait, and if the evidence is admitted, the prosecutor may offer evidence to rebut it;

        (B) subject to the limitations in Rule 412, a defendant may offer evidence of an alleged victim's pertinent trait, and if the evidence is admitted, the prosecutor may:

            (i) offer evidence to rebut it; and

            (ii) offer evidence of the defendant's same trait; and

        (C) in a homicide case, the prosecutor may offer evidence of the alleged victim's trait of peacefulness to rebut evidence that the victim was the first aggressor.

    (3) *Exceptions for a Witness.* Evidence of a witness's character may be admitted under Rules 607, 608, and 609.

(b) **Crimes, Wrongs, or Other Acts.**

    (1) *Prohibited Uses.* Evidence of a crime, wrong, or other act is not admissible to prove a person's character in order to show that on a particular occasion the person acted in accordance with the character.

    (2) *Permitted Uses; Notice in a Criminal Case.* This evidence may be admissible for another purpose, such as proving motive, opportunity, intent, preparation, plan, knowledge, identity, absence of mistake, or lack of accident. On request by a defendant in a criminal case, the prosecutor must:

        (A) provide reasonable notice of the general nature of any such evidence that the prosecutor intends to offer at trial; and

(B)   do so before trial — or during trial if the court, for good cause, excuses lack of pretrial notice.

§ 404.1   Character Evidence — In General

Rule 404 addresses the circumstances under which evidence of character or a trait of character is admissible.[1] Once it is determined that character evidence is admissible, consideration of Rule 405 is necessary to determine the methodology of proof. However, where character evidence is admissible to affect the credibility of a witness, Rules 608 and 609 should be considered for methodology of proof.

§ 404.2   Policy Supporting Rule 404(a)

Rules 401 through 403 define relevance and provide for the function of relevance as the threshold standard of admissibility.[2] The remainder of the Rules in Article IV relate to applications of relevance in specific situations that have recurred with sufficient frequency to warrant the development of specialized principles. The considerations underlying the limited admissibility of character evidence embody the same policy contained in Rule 403.[3] Essentially, character evidence is, in many instances, inadmissible because its probative value is *substantially* outweighed by its potential adverse effect on the integrity of the litigation process.[4] Accordingly, it should be noted that character evidence may be highly relevant, but nevertheless inadmissible under Rule 404.[5]

§ 404.3   Definitions

The term "character" refers to a generalized description of a person's disposition or a general trait such as honesty, temperance, or peacefulness.[6] Generally speaking, character refers to an aspect of an individual's personality that is usually described in evidentiary law as a "propensity."[7] The term

---

[1] *See generally,* 1 McCormick, §§ 186–193; 2 Weinstein's Federal Evidence §§ 404.01–404.11; 1 Mueller & Kirkpatrick, §§ 99–118; 1A Wigmore, §§ 52–81; *see also* Uviller, *Evidence of Character to Prove Conduct: Illusion, Illogic and Injustice in the Courtroom,* 130 U. Pa. L. Rev. 845 (1982); Weissenberger, *Character Evidence Under the Federal Rules; A Puzzle with Missing Pieces,* 48 U. Cin. L. Rev. 1 (1979); Comment, *Collateral Estoppel Effect of Prior Acquittals: United States v. Mespoulede,* 46 Brooklyn L. Rev. 781 (1980); Annot., *When is Evidence of a Trait of Accused Character "Pertinent" for Purposes of Admissibility under Rule 404(a)(1) of the Federal Rules of Evidence,* 49 A.L.R. Fed. 478 (1980).

[2] *See generally,* § 401.1 *et seq., supra.*

[3] *See generally,* § 403.3 *et seq., supra.*

[4] *See* 1 McCormick, § 188; *see generally,* 2 Weinstein's Federal Evidence § 404.21.

[5] 1 Mueller & Kirkpatrick, § 99.

[6] 1 McCormick, § 195.

[7] *See generally,* 2 Weinstein's Federal Evidence § 404.10.

propensity is perhaps misleading when used synonymously with "character," because "propensity" may refer to character or habit.

"Habit" is a person's regular practice of meeting a particular kind of situation with a specific type of responsive conduct.[8] In behavioral terms, habit refers to the tendency of a person to exhibit a regular response to a specific stimulus.[9] Habit is unquestionably a form of propensity, and consequently, it is, in many cases, difficult to distinguish habit from what evidentiary law would designate as character.[10] The distinction, nevertheless, is important, because the admissibility of character evidence is highly restricted by Rule 404, whereas the admissibility of habit evidence is authorized under Rule 406.[11] Where the form of propensity is general and represents a behavioral inclination, it constitutes character governed by Rule 404; where the form of propensity is specific and connected with an identifiable prompting circumstance, it constitutes habit[12] governed by Rule 406. While gradations of gray undoubtedly exist between these polar concepts, the law requires designation of the propensity as either character or habit to determine whether Rule 404 or Rule 406 applies.[13] Consequently, sensitive appreciation of the policy of this sector of the law of evidence is important to ensure a proper resolution in difficult cases.

Likewise, reputation and character are distinguishable, despite occasional blurring of the concepts.[14] Character is a trait of personality, whereas reputation is the collective perception of an individual by persons in an identifiable community.[15] As discussed in conjunction with Rule 405, reputation is a specific means of proving the character of an individual after character evidence is deemed generally admissible.

§ 404.4 Exclusionary Rule as to Character Evidence

Rule 404(a) codifies the basic principle that evidence of a person's character is not admissible for the purpose of proving that such person acted in conformity with that character on a particular occasion.[16] This basic

---

[8] *See generally,* 2 WEINSTEIN'S FEDERAL EVIDENCE § 404.02; 2 MUELLER & KIRKPATRICK, § 156; 1 McCORMICK, § 195; 1A WIGMORE, §§ 92–97.

[9] It is perhaps useful to distinguish the concepts in terms of psychological differentiation. For example, it has been surmised that "character" carries Freudian connotations, while "habit" is properly viewed in Pavlovian terms. 2 WEINSTEIN'S FEDERAL EVIDENCE § 404.02.

[10] *See* 1 McCORMICK, § 195.

[11] *See* § 406.1, *infra.*

[12] 1 McCORMICK, § 195.

[13] *See, e.g.,* Browne v. Maxfield, 663 F. Supp. 1193 (E.D. Pa. 1987) (degree of regularity of conduct necessary for admissible habit evidence under Rule 406 was lacking).

[14] *See* 2 WEINSTEIN'S FEDERAL EVIDENCE § 404.02.

[15] Rule 405, Advisory Committee Note.

[16] *See generally,* McKinney v. Rees, 993 F.2d 1378 (9th Cir. 1993); United States v.

prohibition is often called "the propensity rule"[17] because it prohibits the use of evidence of a person's propensity to behave in a particular fashion to prove that the person behaved in that fashion on a particular occasion.[18]

Under the prohibition of Rule 404(a), a person's character, or general propensity to act in a particular way, may not be offered as a basis for the inference that, on a specific occasion, the person acted in conformity with the propensity or trait. Subject to the express exceptions in Rule 404(a)(2), and Rules 413 through 415, the prohibition applies in civil and criminal proceedings to any person, party or non-party, principal actor or minor player.

There is only one area of the law where Rule 404 does not control the admission of character evidence in federal court. Since 1994, Rule 404 no longer governs criminal and civil cases where the defendant is charged with sexual assault or child molestation. In those two contexts, Rule 404 has been superseded by the adoption of Rule 413 through 415, which freely allow the prosecution or plaintiff to offer evidence that the defendant has committed such offenses in the past for any relevant purpose, including the (ordinarily impermissible) inference that the defendant committed such an act on the particular occasion described in the indictment or complaint.[19] It must be remembered that everything said in this chapter is subject to those qualifications. Almost nothing that follows in this chapter is still true in federal cases involving allegations of sexual assault or child molestation.

Evidence of a person's character or traits of character possesses the inherent risk of distracting the trier of fact from the primary issues of the case.[20] Character evidence has a tendency to invite a finding based upon the trier's attitude toward a person's character, rather than upon an objective evaluation of the operative facts of the case.[21] Consequently, the prohibition of Rule 404(a)(1) is aimed at the tactic of attempting to prove a person's action on a particular occasion by offering evidence that the person has an ingrained tendency to act in a certain manner.

In order to comprehend the application of Rule 404(a)(1), it is important

---

Simpson, 992 F.2d 1224 (D.C. Cir. 1993). *See also* 2 WEINSTEIN'S FEDERAL EVIDENCE § 404.02; 1 McCORMICK, § 188; 1 MUELLER & KIRKPATRICK, § 100.

[17] 2 WEINSTEIN'S FEDERAL EVIDENCE § 404.10.

[18] The appellation, however, is somewhat of a misnomer because character is only one form of propensity. Other forms of propensity, such as habit, are governed by distinct rules; *see* § 404.3, *supra.*

[19] *See* Rules 413 through 415, discussed in Chapters 413–415 *infra.*

[20] 1 McCORMICK, § 186; *see also* Garraghty v. Jordan, 830 F.2d 1295 (4th Cir. 1987) (even if evidence was relevant, which it wasn't, it was still confusing); Carter v. District of Columbia, 795 F.2d 116 (D.C. Cir. 1986) (error to admit evidence that may have confused the jury or convinced them to accept forbidden character inference).

[21] *See generally,* 1 MUELLER & KIRKPATRICK, § 100.

to recognize two considerations. First, a person's character, *e.g.*, violence, is unquestionably (indeed, by definition) relevant in proving an act consistent with the general form of propensity, *e.g.*, murder. Consequently, the policy of Rule 404(a)(1) is not based upon non-existent relevance. Rather, the policy is based upon the relatively low probative value of character evidence and its potential for unfair prejudice.[22] Second, where the proponent of the prohibited evidence is seeking to prove an act, the proponent is not deprived of all means to prove the act. A generalized propensity to commit an act is but one item of relevant evidence that might be employed to alter the probabilities of the occurrence of the act. Other lines of proof are unaffected by Rule 404(a)(1) and remain available, *e.g.*, eyewitness testimony of the occurrence, circumstantial evidence such as motive, opportunity, and habit. In the case of the proof of murder, for example, myriad forms of proof are available to prove the act, other than the violent character of the alleged perpetrator. Consequently, the effect of Rule 404(a)(1) is to preclude but one line of circumstantial evidence to prove an act.

As noted, Rule 404(a)(1) is applicable in both civil and criminal cases, but its prohibitory effect will most frequently arise in a criminal case.[23] Accordingly, the prosecution may not offer evidence of a negative trait of character of the accused to establish that the accused acted in conformity with the character trait and committed the crime in question.[24] While, for example, a general propensity to be violent is probative of an assault, such evidence is excluded under Rule 404(a)(1) because it may unduly excite the emotions and prejudices of the jury and invite an irrational verdict. The trier of fact might seek to penalize a person who has a violent character rather than making a dispassionate and objective evaluation of the operative facts of the case.[25]

While Rule 404(a)(1) arises most frequently in criminal cases, the basic proposition that character evidence is inadmissible has equal force in civil cases. Accordingly, accident proneness or a generalized propensity toward

---

[22] 1 McCORMICK, § 188; *see also* Spencer v. Texas, 385 U.S. 554, 560–561 (1967) ("the defendant's interests are protected by . . . the discretion residing with the trial judge to limit or forbid the admission of particularly prejudicial evidence even though admissible under an acceptable rule of evidence"). The relatively low probative value and importance of character evidence is also reflected in the ethical rule that "[a] judge should not testify voluntarily as a character witness." CODE OF CONDUCT FOR UNITED STATES JUDGES, Canon 2(B). There is no similar ethical restriction that would excuse a judge, even a sitting justice of the Supreme Court, from the duty to testify if he or she is an *eyewitness* to the events that gave rise to some civil or criminal trial.

[23] *See* 1 MUELLER & KIRKPATRICK, § 100.

[24] 1 McCORMICK, § 191.

[25] The doctrine embodied in Rule 404(a) has been generally recognized in pre-Rule case law; *see* 1A WIGMORE, §§ 57, 64; 1 McCORMICK, § 159.

negligence is not admissible to establish that a person failed to exercise due care on a particular occasion.[26]

Rule 404(a)(2) sets forth three exceptions where the exclusionary principle will not apply and where character may be used to prove conforming conduct. In effect, these exceptions authorize use of the otherwise forbidden inference in limited contexts. The otherwise prohibited inferential pattern may be used only where these three exceptions apply. When character evidence is used pursuant to one of these exceptions, it is introduced pursuant to the procedure designated in Rule 405, *i.e.,* through the testimony of character witnesses.

§ 404.5 · Character of the Accused, Rule 404(a)(2)(A)

Rule 404(a)(2)(A) provides that an accused in a criminal case may elect to introduce evidence of his or her own character. The exception is therefore not available to a defendant in a civil case, even if the civil claims involve allegations that would also amount to criminal acts.[27] When authorized by Rule 404(a)(2)(A), evidence of an accused's character is introduced pursuant to the procedures in Rule 405 governing the use of character witness testimony. In a criminal matter, the accused may offer appropriate evidence supporting his or her good character to establish that, on the particular occasion involving the crime charged, the accused acted in conformity with this good character and did not commit the crime in question.[28] For example,

---

[26] *See In re* Aircrash in Bali, Indonesia, 684 F.2d 1301 (9th Cir. 1982); Reyes v. Missouri P. R. Co., 589 F.2d 791 (5th Cir. 1979); George v. Morgan Constr. Co., 389 F. Supp. 253 (E.D. Pa. 1975). *But cf.* Gray v. Sherril, 542 F.2d 953 (5th Cir. 1976) (since plaintiff had put his character in issue by testifying that he was calm and temperate, no error in permitting testimony by witness concerning plaintiff's emotional outbursts and being argumentative; no mention of Federal Rules); *see generally,* 1 McCORMICK, § 189; 2 WEINSTEIN'S FEDERAL EVIDENCE § 404.22.

[27] Rule 404(a)(1) always made this point clear enough, at least by implication, because of its reference to evidence offered by the "accused" and by the "prosecution" in response. At least a few courts had reasoned, however, that the policy underlying the rule ought to apply to certain civil cases as well, at least if the allegations were of a criminal nature. *See* Carson v. Polley, 689 F.2d 562, 576 (5th Cir. 1982) ("when a central issue in a case is close to one of a criminal nature, the exceptions to the Rule 404(a) ban on character evidence may be invoked"). That suggestion was rejected by an amendment to the rule in 2006, which explicitly limits the exceptions of 404(a)–404(a)(2) to evidence offered "in a criminal case." Regrettably, however, the Committee Notes inaccurately state that this change will "clarify that in a civil case evidence of a person's character is *never* admissible to prove that the person acted in conformity with the character trait." *See* Committee Notes to the 2006 amendment to Rule 404 (emphasis added). That is not true, since evidence of the character of a witness may still be used under Rule 404(a)(3), even in a civil case, to prove that the witness acted in keeping with his character while lying or telling the truth during his trial testimony.

[28] *See* United States v. Diaz, 961 F.2d 1417 (9th Cir. 1992) (though harmless, it was error to disallow defense witness testimony that defendant was not prone to commit criminal activity, as this is merely the converse of an inquiry into defendant's law abiding character);

where the criminal defendant is charged with an assault, the accused may offer evidence of a "pertinent trait" in accordance with Rule 404(2)(A).[29] A "pertinent trait" in this context would be peacefulness, *i.e.,* a general propensity that is consistent with the accused's theory of the case and behaviorally incompatible with the crime charged. Rule 404(a)(2)(A) requires evidence of a *pertinent* trait, and evidence of the accused's general good character is not authorized.[30] Likewise, introduction of general good character in this context is tactically unwise because it invites a wide range of rebuttal evidence from the prosecution.[31]

The prosecution, as part of its case-in-chief, may not offer evidence of the accused's character to show a general propensity to commit the acts underlying the crime charged.[32] Rule 404(a)(2)(A) embodies this policy.[33] Only the accused may introduce character evidence by offering appropriate testimony in accordance with Rule 405 regarding his own character. Once, however, the accused has introduced such evidence, the prosecution, in its case in rebuttal, may offer evidence attacking the character of the accused.[34]

United States v. Roberts, 887 F.2d 534 (5th Cir. 1989) (in a trial for possessing and importing cocaine, trial court erred by excluding expert psychological testimony that the defendant's personality was consistent with his defense that he was acting as a "self-appointed vigilante" to "ferret out drug dealers"); *see also* United States v. Lechoco, 542 F.2d 84 (D.C. Cir. 1976); *see generally,* 1 MCCORMICK, § 191.

[29] *See* 1 MCCORMICK, § 191.

[30] *See* 1 MUELLER & KIRKPATRICK, § 101.

[31] *See generally,* 1 MCCORMICK, § 191.

[32] *See, e.g.,* United States v. Karas, 950 F.2d 31 (1st Cir. 1991) (evidence that defendant admitted cocaine trafficking constituted forbidden "propensity evidence"); United States v. Temple, 862 F.2d 821 (10th Cir. 1988) (reversible error to allow government to introduce evidence that showed defendant's "bad character or a propensity to commit crimes"). This is now subject to an exception in federal cases where the accused is charged with sexual assault or child molestation. *See* Rules 413 and 414.

[33] United States v. Lechoco, 542 F.2d 84, 88 n.5 (D.C. Cir. 1976) ("Rule 404(a)(1) merely codified the then prevailing practice").

[34] *See* discussion of Rule 405, Chapter 405, *infra,* which governs the methodology of proof by both the accused and the prosecution; *see also* United States v. Lopez-Medina, 596 F.3d 716 (10th Cir. 2010) (evidence that the accused was present in the United States illegally was not admissible as proof that he committed the charged offense of drug possession with intent to distribute, but after he testified that he was a law-abiding citizen with a clean record, he opened the door for prosecutor to ask about the illegal immigration status to rebut that misleading suggestion); United States v. Green, 180 F.3d 216 (5th Cir. 1999) (where a former police officer charged with conspiracy to distribute cocaine and with harboring a fugitive offered testimony from officers who worked under him that they thought him to be a "good cop," the government was properly allowed to counter with evidence from another officer of the defendant's reputation as untrustworthy); Carson v. Polley, 689 F.2d 562 (5th Cir. 1982) (reversible error for court to allow defendant's purported eyewitness, who was also his stepson, to be cross-examined about defendant's convictions where witness had not been called as a character witness).

Again, this evidence must conform to the directives of Rule 405.[35]

An accused will often elect to use character evidence where the prosecution's case is largely circumstantial. The use of character evidence in this situation may serve to establish reasonable doubt that the accused committed the crime. Reasonable doubt, of course, may be created by evidence that it is unlikely that the accused is the type of person who would commit the crime in question, *i.e.,* that the accused lacks the general propensity to commit such a crime.[36]

When evidence of an accused's good character is offered, three critical tactical considerations must be addressed.[37] First, consistent with Rule 405, any character witness offered may be cross-examined as to acts of the accused that are relevant to the pertinent trait advanced.[38] These acts might otherwise never be exposed to the jury. Second, the accused should usually seek to advance a narrow trait, rather than a general endorsement of law-abiding character; the narrower the trait, the narrower the rebuttal by the prosecution.[39] Third, the accused must weigh the possibility of negative character witnesses called by the prosecution during its case in rebuttal.[40] Pre-Rule case law generally supports the principles embodied in Rule 404(a)(2)(A).[41]

Until recently, a federal prosecutor could only offer evidence of the defendant's bad character if the accused first "opened the door" by offering evidence of his supposedly good character. That is no longer true. The 2000

---

[35] *See* 2 WEINSTEIN'S FEDERAL EVIDENCE § 404.11.

[36] Edgington v. United States, 164 U.S. 361 (1896); *see* Michelson v. United States, 335 U.S. 469 (1948); *see also* United States v. Pujana-Mena, 949 F.2d 24 (2d Cir. 1991) (the district court did not err in refusing to instruct the jury that evidence of defendant's good character "standing alone" could generate a reasonable doubt); 1 MUELLER & KIRKPATRICK, § 101.

[37] *See generally,* 1 MUELLER & KIRKPATRICK, § 102.

[38] Rule 405 reads as follows:

(a) **By Reputation or Opinion.** When evidence of a person's character or character trait is admissible, it may be proved by testimony about the person's reputation or by testimony in the form of an opinion. On cross-examination of the character witness, the court may allow an inquiry into relevant specific instances of the person's conduct.

(b) **By Specific Instances of Conduct.** When a person's character or character trait is an essential element of a charge, claim, or defense, the character or trait may also be proved by relevant specific instances of the person's conduct.

See United States v. Apfelbaum, 621 F.2d 62 (3d Cir. 1980); United States v. Glass, 709 F.2d 669 (11th Cir. 1983); 1 McCORMICK, § 191.

[39] *See* United States v. Reed, 700 F.2d 638 (11th Cir. 1983).

[40] *See* United States v. Reese, 568 F.2d 1246 (6th Cir. 1976).

[41] *See* Michelson v. United States, 335 U.S. 469 (1948); United States v. Lechoco, 542 F.2d 84 (D.C. Cir. 1976).

amendment to Rule 404(a)(2)(A) creates a second way for the accused to open the door. Now the Government may prove a character trait of the accused if he or she first introduces evidence of "the same trait of character" in the alleged victim to prove the conduct of the victim on a particular occasion, as an accused is allowed to do under Rule 404(a)(2)(B). For example, if a man accused of assault claims self-defense and offers evidence of his alleged victim's violent character, the prosecutor can respond with rebuttal evidence to show that the *accused* had a reputation for violence to show that he was actually the first aggressor.[42]

§ 404.6   Character of the Accused, Policy for Admissibility

While character evidence is generally thought to have an adverse effect on the fact-finding process, character evidence is nonetheless available to the accused. This rule is based upon three complementary policies. First, a criminal defendant should have every opportunity to disprove guilt. This rule, like the constitutional rule requiring proof of guilt beyond a reasonable doubt in a criminal case, indicates the relative importance attached to the risks of erroneous convictions and acquittals in our society, which has chosen to impose "almost the entire risk of error upon itself"[43] because of the "fundamental value determination . . . [that] it is far worse to convict an innocent man than to let a guilty man go free."[44] It must be emphasized, however, that if the accused exercises the option to utilize character evidence, it results in possible admission of prosecution evidence to rebut the accused's evidence of a beneficial trait of character.

Second, there is relatively little risk of unfair prejudice to the opposing party when the defendant is allowed to call favorable character witnesses. In a typical criminal case involving conduct that poses a significant danger to the community, as long as the Government's evidence of guilt is otherwise strong enough to convict, there is little chance that the jury will be moved to change its verdict and acquit after hearing that the accused's friends and relatives do not believe he or she was the kind of person who could have done such a thing. Given the generally secretive nature of the criminal personality, a jury is much more likely to discount such evidence on the grounds that those character witnesses apparently did not really know the

---

[42] *See* § 404.7, *infra.*

[43] Addington v. Texas, 441 U.S. 418, 423–424 (1979).

[44] Francis v. Franklin, 471 U.S. 307, 313 (1985) (quoting *In re* Winship, 397 U.S. 358, 372 (1970) (Harlan, J., concurring)). How much worse is a matter of some debate. In *Coffin v. United States*, the Supreme Court cited Blackstone for the venerable maxim that "it is better that ten guilty persons escape than that one innocent suffer," but the Court also listed other common-law authorities suggesting, at least in capital cases, that the conviction of one innocent man is somewhere between five to twenty times worse than the acquittal of a guilty man. Coffin v. United States, 156 U.S. 432, 455–456 (1895). The common ground, of course, is clear.

accused so well after all.[45] And even if the jury accepts the testimony of the defendant's character witnesses and concludes that it was really quite "out of character" for the defendant to have committed this crime, there is little risk that a jury will acquit a criminal if the evidence of guilt was otherwise strong enough to convict; no murderer or rapist gets mercy just because the jury concluded it was probably the accused's first offense.[46]

Third, when evidence of an accused's trait of character is offered by the accused, the risk of prejudice is subject to the control of the accused,[47] and the defense is afforded the opportunity to apply a cost-benefit analysis of the risk of prejudice.[48] By allowing the defendant to choose whether to admit such evidence, the risks of prejudice and other possible dangers are subsumed in the decision to use the evidence.

But why should the right to call favorable character witnesses — the so-called "mercy rule" — be limited to criminal defendants, and not extend to the defendant in a civil case? One common explanation is that the criminal accused may need "a counterweight against the strong investigative and prosecutorial resources of the government."[49] There is much force to that

---

[45] Even when criminals are caught red-handed during the commission of the most vile crimes, sometimes on videotape and after having confessed, news reporters (just like defense attorneys) seemingly never have any difficulty locating friends and relatives and neighbors who are ready and willing to sincerely verify that "I never saw anything unusual about him, and can't believe he could have done such a thing." Nobody is surprised to read these sorts of worthless accounts, because that's just what even the worst criminals go out of their way to deceive their neighbors into thinking.

[46] By contrast, a jury may well choose to convict a man if they know he has been guilty of terrible crimes in the past and suspect that he was evidently not punished enough for those offenses, even if the jury has some lingering doubts about whether he is guilty this time as well. In this sense, evidence of the criminal character of the accused, if it were allowed, would give the prosecution literally two different ways to win: either by persuading the jury that the defendant is guilty, or else that the community would benefit from his incarceration regardless of whether he might be innocent this time. Evidence of the defendant's good character, on the other hand, will not result in an acquittal unless it persuades the jury that the defendant is innocent, and so does not carry a similar risk of an unjust acquittal, or the same risk of "unfair prejudice" to the opposing party. This is presumably the point the Advisory Committee had in mind when it said somewhat cryptically, in its explanation of the original version of Rule 404, that "[w]hile its basis lies more in history and experience than in logic an underlying justification can fairly be found in terms of the relative presence and absence of prejudice in the various situations."

[47] *See* 1 McCORMICK, § 191; 1 MUELLER & KIRKPATRICK, § 100.

[48] *See* Michelson v. United States, 335 U.S. 469, 478–479 (1948) ("[T]he law extends helpful but illogical options to a defendant. Experience taught a necessity that they be counterweighted with equally illogical conditions to keep the advantage from becoming an unfair and unreasonable one. The price a defendant must pay for attempting to prove his good name is to throw open the entire subject which the law has kept closed for his benefit and to make himself vulnerable where the law otherwise shields him").

[49] Committee Notes to the 2006 amendment to Rule 404 (quoting Mueller & Kirkpatrick,

generalization, although it is of course not always true.[50] A more consistently impressive explanation is the fact that the parties in a civil case, unlike a criminal case, are supposed to be starting the trial on a roughly level playing field, as reflected in the rule that the verdict in a civil case is generally awarded to the party whose case is proved by a preponderance of the evidence. In a civil case there is no reason for the law to extend any significant "mercy" or assistance to either side more than the other. Moreover, the reluctance to extend the mercy rule to civil defendants probably reflects the relative risk of unfair prejudice to the defendant's opposing parties in civil and criminal cases. In contrast with civil litigation, criminal cases are much more likely to involve sensational allegations of vile and intentional misconduct posing a significant danger to the community. That is why, as long as the Government's evidence of guilt is otherwise strong enough to convict, there is little chance that jurors will be moved to acquit out of mercy merely because they conclude that the defendant, although guilty this time, may have committed no earlier offense. Civil cases are more likely to involve allegations of less dramatic or even unintentional actions on the part of the defendant, thus increasing the likelihood that favorable character evidence might tempt the jury to err on the side of mercy, for example, if they learn that a defendant in a negligence case had an long and impeccable record of safe and careful driving and that it was quite out of character for him or her to be guilty of a fairly minor act of negligence.

§ 404.7 Character of the Alleged Victim, Rule 404(a)(2)(B)

The second exception to the exclusionary principle of Rule 404(a)(1) provides that an accused may introduce pertinent evidence of the character of the alleged crime victim.[51] Again, the term "accused" indicates that, like

---

EVIDENCE: PRACTICE UNDER THE RULES, 264–265 (2d ed. 1999). The Committee categorically asserted, a bit implausibly, that "[t]hese concerns do not apply to parties in civil cases." Committee Notes to the 2006 amendment to Rule 404.

[50] After all, if that were the best explanation for the rule, the trial judge surely ought to be given the discretion to extend the "mercy rule" to defendants with limited resources who find themselves pitted against the government or other wealthy adversaries in *civil* litigation, especially when the defendant faces serious civil charges of conduct that would also be a crime. But the rule does not allow that, as the Advisory Committee explicitly reaffirmed with its most recent amendment to the rule. Nor does this explanation account very well for the fact that the right to call character witnesses is freely available to extremely wealthy criminal defendants, some of whom have more investigative resources and witnesses than the prosecutor.

[51] Lagasse v. Vestal, 671 F.2d 668 (1st Cir. 1982); United States v. Greschner, 647 F.2d 740 (7th Cir. 1981); Government of Virgin Islands v. Carino, 631 F.2d 226 (3d Cir. 1980); *see also* United States v. Bailey, 834 F.2d 218 (1st Cir. 1987) (in trial for attempting to influence a juror, defendant attempted to introduce evidence that the juror had violated his oath by discussing the case with neighbors; the trial court properly excluded this evidence, because the juror is a non-victim, and because the connection between the juror's

the first exception to Rule 404, Rule 404(a)(2)(B) is applicable only in a criminal case.

In practical terms, the right of the accused to offer evidence about the character of the alleged victim under Rule 404(a)(2)(B) is limited almost entirely to crimes of violence where the accused argues a claim of self-defense and that the alleged victim was actually the first aggressor. In virtually every other context, evidence of an alleged crime victim's conduct and character is simply not even relevant, and is therefore excluded by Rule 402 even without regard to the character rule. The only other example originally given by the Advisory Committee is the defense of "consent in a case of rape,"[52] but Rule 404(a)(2)(B) no longer governs such cases since the subsequent adoption of Rule 412, enacted three years after the Federal Rules went into effect. In prosecutions for rape and other forms of sexual assault and misconduct, Rule 412 preempts Rule 404(a)(2)(B) in governing the admissibility of the alleged victim's sexual behavior and reputation.[53]

Under Rule 404(a)(2), the prosecutor may not offer evidence of the character of the alleged victim unless the accused first "opens the door" to such evidence. The defense may do this in two ways. First, in any criminal case where the conduct of the victim is relevant, most notably self-defense cases, an accused who first offers evidence of the character of the alleged victim (for example, violence) thereby allows the prosecutor to respond in kind with evidence that the victim did not have that character trait, although both sides will be subject to the limitations of Rule 405.[54] Second, under a special provision applicable only to homicide cases, even if the accused offers no evidence about the character of the victim, he will still open the door to allow the prosecution to offer such evidence if he raises a claim of self-defense and offers evidence that the deceased was in fact the first aggressor.[55] (An accused who raises a self-defense claim is not necessarily offering evidence about the character of the deceased; he could try to prove his claims about who started the fight through the testimony of eyewitnesses without calling a single character witness.) In homicide prosecutions, "a plea of self-defense, coupled with evidence that the deceased was the first aggressor, is sufficient to trigger the prosecutor's right to offer rebuttal evidence that the victim was a person of peaceful character."[56] This

---

talkativeness and the crime was too tenuous for the evidence to be "pertinent" under Rule 404(a)(2)).

[52] *See* Rule 404(a), Advisory Committee Note.

[53] *See* the discussion of Rule 412, Chapter 412, *infra.*

[54] Rule 404(a)(2)(B)(ii).

[55] Rule 404(a)(2)(C).

[56] LILLY, § 5.8, at 140; *see* United States v. Greschner, 647 F.2d 740 (7th Cir. 1981) (where accused inmate claimed self-defense, error to exclude evidence that victim had previously stabbed another inmate); United States v. Kelley, 545 F.2d 619 (8th Cir. 1976) (if

provision is based upon the peculiar need for this kind of evidence in situations where the victim, by the nature of the crime, is unavailable.[57] Evidence that the victim was the first aggressor may be of any competent type to avail the prosecution of the opportunity to offer evidence of the victim's peaceful character. Any evidence so offered by the prosecution must, of course, conform to the directives of Rule 405.[58]

Until recently, there was no connection between the operation of Rule 404(a)(2)(A) and 404(a)(2)(B) in a particular case. Those two rules, respectively, ordinarily make it impossible for the prosecutor to offer any evidence about the character of either the accused or his alleged victim for the purpose of proving what either did on the date of the charged crime, unless the accused somehow "opens the door" to the admission of such evidence. It is as if evidence of such matters was hidden at the beginning of each criminal trial behind two different locked doors, and the keys to each were given only to the accused, who had the exclusive say as to whether to unlock either or both. Until December 2000, the accused also had the protection of knowing that he could choose to open one door while keeping the other locked tight. That is no longer true.

Under the 2000 Amendment to Rule 404, an accused who chooses to offer evidence of the alleged victim's character under Rule 404(a)(2)(B) opens the door to allow the prosecution to offer evidence of "the defendant's same trait."[59] For example, if a man accused of assault claims self-defense and offers evidence of his alleged victim's violent character, the prosecutor can respond with rebuttal evidence to show the accused had a reputation for violence to show that he was actually the first aggressor. This change was designed to rectify a perceived imbalance in the Rules, which had previously allowed a criminal defendant to attack the character of his alleged victim while keeping evidence of his identical character traits from the jury.

The Advisory Committee emphasizes, however, that the prosecution is not permitted to offer evidence of the accused's character under this new amendment unless defense evidence about the character of the victim is

---

no self-defense plea, question of first aggressor irrelevant).

[57] LILLY, § 5.8.

[58] *See, e.g.,* United States v. Waloke, 962 F.2d 824 (8th Cir. 1992) (court properly admitted evidence of victim's reputation and excluded evidence of specific acts).

[59] *See* Rule 404(a)(2)(B)(ii). Indeed, it should be remembered that when an accused offers evidence of the character of his alleged victim to prove the conduct of the victim, he is now simultaneously opening *both* doors, and making it possible for the prosecutor to respond with evidence on whether that alleged trait of character (for example, violence) is true of the alleged victim *and* the accused. Even before the 2000 amendment to Rule 404, it has long been the rule that defense evidence offered on the character of the victim would allow the prosecution to respond in kind with its evidence of the character of the victim. *See* Rule 404(a)(2)(B)(i) (allowing the prosecution, after the defense raises the issue of the character of the alleged victim, to offer evidence about the victim "to rebut it").

admitted to prove the alleged victim committed some specific act in accordance with that character trait. In rare cases, an accused will sometimes use character evidence about his alleged victim for some purpose other than to prove the conduct of the victim, such as where the evidence is offered only to support a claim that the accused *thought,* perhaps mistakenly, that he was in danger of imminent bodily harm because of what he knew of his apparent attacker's violent reputation.[60] In such a case, the evidence of the character of the alleged victim is offered to prove something about the accused's state of mind, not the conduct of the alleged victim. It therefore does not open the door to rebuttal evidence by the prosecution concerning the character of the accused.[61]

§ 404.8   Character of Witness, Rule 404(a)(3)

The third exception to the exclusionary principle of Rule 404(a) relates to the character of a witness who takes the stand to testify. Rule 404(a)(3) provides that the character of a witness may be explored as to the witness's traits of veracity or truth-telling. Unlike the exceptions of Rule 404(a)(2) for evidence about the character of the accused and the victim in a *criminal* case, this exception is not so limited and applies to witnesses who testify in either a criminal or a civil case.[62] This exception to the basic exclusionary rule is more specifically codified in Rules 607, 608, and 609, which relate to impeachment, and this subsection serves as a cross-reference to them.

Just like the exceptions set forth in Rule 404(a)(2), subdivision 404(a)(3) defines an exceptional situation in which the law allows a party to offer evidence about the character of a person even for the ordinarily forbidden purpose of trying to persuade the jury that the person committed some act on

---

[60] *See* United States v. Gregg, 451 F.3d 930, 933–936 (8th Cir. 2006) (when a murder defendant claims self-defense, evidence of specific instances of violent conduct by the alleged victim may be admissible under Rule 404(b)(2), not to prove the conduct of the victim but to explain the accused's state of mind and why he reasonably feared that he needed to act in self-defense, but only if the defendant offers evidence that he was aware of such prior violent conduct at the time of his alleged act of self-defense); United States v. Burks, 470 F.2d 432, 434–435 (D.C. Cir. 1972) (evidence of the alleged victim's violent character, when known by the accused, was admissible "on the issue of whether or not the defendant reasonably feared he was in danger of imminent great bodily harm"). Evidence about the character of the victim in such a case is freely admissible without regard to any of the restrictions in Rules 404 and 405, simply because it is relevant to some issue in the case other than the conduct of the alleged victim. *See* § 404.9, *infra.*

[61] *See* Rule 404(a)(2)(A), Committee Note.

[62] This is why the Advisory Committee was mistaken to state, in connection with the most recent amendment to Rule 404(a)(2)(A) and (a)(2)(B), that "in a civil case evidence of a person's character is *never* admissible to prove that the person acted in conformity with the character trait." Committee Note to the 2006 amendment to Rule 404 (emphasis added). As noted above, evidence of the character of a witness may be used under Rule 404(a)(3), even in a civil case, to prove that the witness acted in keeping with his character while lying or telling the truth during his trial testimony.

a particular occasion in keeping with that character trait. In this case, however, the "person" is a witness, and the "occasion" refers not to what someone did back at the scene of the alleged crime, but whether the witness told the truth or a lie on direct examination during the trial.

It must be noted that Rule 404(a)(3) sometimes overlaps in its operation with subdivision (a)(2)(A) in criminal cases if the accused chooses to waive his or her Fifth Amendment rights and take the witness stand. But those two rules refer to different aspects of the character of the accused, and refer to doors that are opened in different ways. Rule 404(a)(2)(A) gives criminal defendants the right to decide whether to open the door to evidence by both sides as to whether they have the sort of character that would make them more likely to have committed the crime charged back at the time and place described in the indictment. They will usually open that door, if they open it at all, by calling "character witnesses" or offering testimony from any witness about whether they have the character trait that is pertinent to that charged offense (for example, in a murder case, whether the accused is peaceful or violent).[63] Rule 404(a)(3), on the other hand, gives the accused the distinct right to decide whether to open the door to evidence about whether he is generally the sort of dishonest person who would be more likely than most individuals to lie on the witness stand at trial. Whether the accused will open this door depends almost entirely on whether he chooses to take the witness stand, and has nothing to do with whether he talks about his character while testifying on direct examination.[64]

§ 404.9   Character in Issue — In General

While the basic exclusionary principle of Rule 404(a)(1) prohibits the use of a specific type of inference, it does not forbid the use of all character evidence. Consequently, when character evidence is offered to establish consequential facts other than conforming conduct of the applicable person, the character evidence is not proscribed by Rule 404(a)(1).[65] The great

---

[63] Note that this "character witness" may be either the accused or any other witness. Whether defendants open the door to evidence of their law-abiding or criminal character under Rule 404(a)(1) does not depend on whom the defense calls to the stand, but whether any witness offers an opinion about those issues at the request of the defense lawyer. This could even happen on cross-examination of government witnesses, if the accused so wishes, although a defense lawyer will rarely wish to invite a potentially hostile witness to offer an opinion or details on the defendant's propensity for criminality. Defendants who open this door on cross-examination usually do so through clumsiness or inadvertence.

[64] To be precise, there is one other way that the accused could open this door. In the rare case in which a defendant does not testify but is able to offer evidence of statements that he made out of court under some exception to the hearsay rules, the Government would be allowed to offer evidence to impeach his character for truthfulness under Rule 806 just as if he had testified. *See* Chapter 806, *infra*.

[65] While character evidence that does not capitalize on the forbidden inference of Rule 404(a)(1) usually falls within the category of "character in issue," a third, relatively rare,

majority of uses of character evidence, however, attempts to capitalize upon the forbidden inference, and consequently, the prohibition and its limited exceptions will apply in most situations. While "character in issue" is not expressly addressed by Rule 404, the admissibility of such evidence arises by implication because it is relevant (indeed, substantively mandated), and not excluded under Rule 404.[66]

§ 404.10   Character in Issue — Test for Application

Essentially, character evidence is not caught within the net of the Rule 404(a)(1) exclusionary principle wherever character evidence is offered to prove anything other than conforming conduct. When character is "in issue," the character evidence is not being offered to prove facts to be inferred from the character evidence. Rather, character, itself, is a consequential fact of a party's burden as mandated by substantive law. Where character or a trait of character is an essential element of a crime, claim, or defense, character is "in issue."[67] For example, actions for libel and slander have been identified as cases in which character may be "in issue."[68] The character of the accused is also an essential element in a criminal prosecution where the accused raises the defense of entrapment, which requires the prosecution to prove that he was predisposed to commit the charged offense before his contact with government agents.[69] It should be strongly emphasized, however, that

---

application of character evidence is also analytically possible. This third, distinct application of character evidence (*i.e.,* not "character in issue" and not the prohibited inference of Rule 404(a)(1)), is the use of character as the basis for an inference other than conforming conduct. *See* LILLY, § 5.10, at 144–145. For example, evidence of a victim's character may be relevant not by showing any conforming conduct, but rather by showing the accused's reasonable reaction to the character trait known to the accused; *see* 1A WIGMORE, § 54 ("a deceased's character to show that the defendant was reasonably afraid of an attack by the deceased.") This rare use of character evidence is admissible because it is not caught by the exclusionary net of Rule 404(a)(1); Senra v. Cunningham, 9 F.3d 168 (1st Cir. 1993) (in a civil rights action filed against police officers, evidence of prior personal contacts between the officers and the plaintiff were admissible to prove the reasonableness of the officers' action); Weissenberger, *Character Evidence Under the Federal Rules: A Puzzle with Missing Pieces,* 48 U. CIN. L. REV. 1 (1979); 2 WEINSTEIN'S FEDERAL EVIDENCE § 404.11. *See generally,* 1 MUELLER & KIRKPATRICK, § 105.

[66] *See generally,* Weissenberger, *Character Evidence under the Federal Rules: A Puzzle with Missing Pieces,* 48 U. CIN. L. REV. 1 (1979).

[67] *See, e.g.,* United States v. Shaw, 714 F.2d 544 (5th Cir. 1983) (to rebut claim that shooting was accidental, no error to admit evidence that defendant became violent when drunk, as it speaks to intent); *see generally,* 2 WEINSTEIN'S FEDERAL EVIDENCE § 404.10.

[68] *See* 1 MCCORMICK, § 187; 1 WIGMORE, § 66.

[69] United States v. Duran, 596 F.3d 1283 (11th Cir. 2010) (in a prosecution for acting as agent of foreign government without notice to the Attorney General, evidence of defendant's payment of illegal kickbacks to Venezuelan government officials was admissible to counter his claim of entrapment by showing his predisposition to commit the crime charged. By raising the defense of entrapment, the defendant shifts to the Government the burden to show that he was predisposed to commit the offense charged beyond a reasonable doubt; the

the nature of the case is not always determinative of whether character is "in issue." Instead, the question is always whether character or a trait of character is the basis for an inference to prove conforming conduct. Quite simply, if character is used in an inferential manner to prove conforming conduct in any case, then the prohibition of Rule 404 applies. Where Rule 404 applies, character is admissible only pursuant to the express exceptions in the Rule. If, on the other hand, character or a trait of character is an essential element of a party's case, character is "in issue" as compelled by the substantive law, and its use is not prohibited by Rule 404.[70]

The "essential element" formulation, which finds its source in Rule 405, however, can be misleading if it is not fully appreciated. The cause of the problem is that the term "essential" can have various connotations. For example, "essential" evidence could be construed to mean evidence that is necessary because alternative, sufficient means of proof are unavailable for some unforeseen reason. This, however, is not the intent of the Rule or the "character in issue" principle. The essential element test demands that character evidence be substantively required as the terminal point of proof.[71] The substantive law must give the party no choice but to prove character if the claim or defense is to be substantiated. For example, where plaintiff charges defendant with a slander claiming that the defendant said "Plaintiff is dishonest," and the defendant subsequently pleads truth as a defense, the defendant must prove plaintiff's dishonesty (a trait of character) in order to prevail.[72] The dishonesty trait of the plaintiff becomes an element of the defendant's affirmative defense. Plaintiff's dishonesty is not being utilized as proof of any conforming conduct. Rather, it is an essential element of the defense, and plaintiff's trait of character is properly "in issue."

§ 404.11   Other Crimes, Wrongs, or Acts — In General

Rule 404. Character Evidence; Crimes or Other Acts

***

(b)   **Crimes, Wrongs, or Other Acts.**

(1)   *Prohibited Uses.* Evidence of a crime, wrong, or other act is not admissible to prove a person's character in order to show that on a particular occasion the person acted in accordance

---

defendant therefore puts his character at issue by raising an entrapment defense); United States v. Thomas, 134 F.3d 975 (9th Cir. 1998) (to support entrapment defense, defendant may present evidence of the absence of a criminal or arrest record to demonstrate a lack of criminal predisposition).

[70] Likewise, any use of character other than to prove conforming conduct is not prohibited; *see* § 404.9, *supra.*

[71] *See* Spell v. McDaniel, 604 F. Supp. 641 (E.D.N.C. 1985) (evidence admissible not as character evidence but as an element of plaintiff's substantive claim).

[72] *See* 1 McCormick, § 187.

with the character.

(2) ***Permitted Uses; Notice in a Criminal Case.*** This evidence may be admissible for another purpose, such as proving motive, opportunity, intent, preparation, plan, knowledge, identity, absence of mistake, or lack of accident. On request by a defendant in a criminal case, the prosecutor must:

(A) provide reasonable notice of the general nature of any such evidence that the prosecutor intends to offer at trial; and

(B) do so before trial — or during trial if the court, for good cause, excuses lack of pretrial notice.

Rule 404(b)(1) codifies an extension of the exclusionary principle of Rule 404(a)(1), and it is a restatement of implicit limitations on the proof of character evidence set forth in Rule 405. Rule 404(b)(1) provides that evidence of other crimes, wrongs, or acts is not admissible to prove the character of a person in order to show that the person acted in conformity with the character on a particular occasion.[73] As in the application of Rule 404(a)(1), Rule 404(b)(1) embraces the customary construction of the term "character," *i.e.,* a form of propensity. Accordingly, the term "character" essentially pertains to a person's distinct traits or propensities to act in a particular way, and it applies to such traits of character as dishonesty, violence, peacefulness, and veracity.[74] It is important to note that the Rule applies in both civil and criminal cases, and its scope encompasses any extrinsic act, not merely acts resulting in criminal conviction or subject to criminal prosecution.[75] As used in Rule 404(b)(1), an "other act" or an "extrinsic act" is simply any act that is not part of the operative facts or episode of the case; *i.e.,* it is "extrinsic" usually because of a separation in time, space, or both.[76]

---

[73] *See* Weissenberger, *Making Sense of Extrinsic Act Evidence: Federal Rules of Evidence 404(b),* 70 Iowa L. Rev. 579 (1985); Orfield, *The Defense of Entrapment in the Federal Courts,* 1967 Duke L.J. 39 (1978); Annot., *Admissibility Under Rule 404(b) of Federal Rules of Evidence, of Evidence of Other Crimes, Wrongs, or Acts not Similar to Offense Charged,* 41 A.L.R. Fed. 497 (1979); *cf.* United States v. Bibo-Rodriguez, 922 F.2d 1398 (9th Cir. 1991) ("other" crime evidence in Rule 404(b) can be evidence of a crime subsequent to the charged crime as well as a previous one). *See generally,* 1 McCormick, §§ 190–193; 2 Weinstein's Federal Evidence §§ 404.20–404.22; 1 Mueller & Kirkpatrick, §§ 110–118; 2 Wigmore, §§ 300–373.

[74] *See* discussion at § 404.3, *supra.*

[75] *See* 1 Mueller & Kirkpatrick, §§ 110–115.

[76] United States v. Becton, 601 F.3d 588 (D.C. Cir. 2010) (in criminal drug conspiracy prosecution, Rule 404(b) did not bar the admission of evidence that the accused continued to manage the drug operation while he was incarcerated for two years on unrelated charges,

Like Rule 404(a)(1), Rule 404(b)(1) creates a prohibited inferential pattern, but the pattern forbidden in Rule 404(b)(1) extends one step further than the forbidden inferential pattern of Rule 404(a)(1).[77] Rule 404(b)(1) creates a forbidden two-step inference pursuant to which an extrinsic specific act inferentially indicates a character trait or general propensity, which in turn inferentially indicates commission of the act that is part of the operative facts of the case.[78] Actually, Rule 404(b)(1) is largely redundant, because the final inferential step of Rule 404(b)(1) is identical to the forbidden inferential pattern of Rule 404(a)(1).[79] The Rule, in essence, prohibits the argument that would suggest that because a person acted in a particular way on a distinct, specific occasion unconnected with the operative facts, that person likely acted in the same way with regard to operative facts of the instant litigation. The force of such an argument relies upon the intermediate operative inference of character.[80]

Rule 404(b) contains three distinct functions. The Rule first sets forth the basic rule of exclusion. A clarifying provision is then added to emphasize the limited scope of the basic exclusionary rule contained in the first sentence and to outline the sort of purposes for which such evidence may be admissible. Finally, the Rule establishes a notice requirement for the prosecution in a criminal case when attempting to use such evidence.

§ 404.12   Policy of Rule 404(b)(1) in Criminal Cases

The prohibition of Rule 404(b)(1) pertains to the establishment of extrinsic acts as a basis for the inference that an individual acted in conformity with "other" actions and the indicated character or form of propensity.[81] While applicable in both civil and criminal cases, Rule 404(b)(1) arises most frequently in criminal cases to exclude evidence of the accused's antisocial acts that are not subject to the instant charge or indictment. In this context the evidence of the extrinsic act is excluded

---

since such evidence was direct evidence of his continuing participation in the charged conspiracy and was therefore "intrinsic evidence" outside the scope of Rule 404(b)); United States v. Navarro, 169 F.3d 228 (5th Cir. 1999) (drug evidence found in a different state three months after charged conspiracy ended was not extrinsic and therefore was not excluded by Rule 404(b) where it showed the structure of the drug organization and the continuing contact between defendants).

[77] Here the forbidden inference can be diagrammed:

| Extrinsic | —>> | Character | —>> | Conforming |
| Act | | (Propensity) | | Conduct |

[78] *See* 1 MUELLER & KIRKPATRICK, § 110–115.

[79] *See* 2 WEINSTEIN'S FEDERAL EVIDENCE § 404.20.

[80] *See* Bryden and Park, *"Other Crimes" Evidence in Sex Offense Cases,* 78 U. MINN. L. REV. 529 (1994).

[81] *See* 1 McCORMICK, § 190.

because it is thought that the jury might punish an individual for the discrete conduct rather than weighing only the direct evidence of the charged crime.[82] Another policy supporting Rule 404(b)(1) is a recognition of the danger that the jury may overestimate the probative value of the extrinsic act evidence in evaluating its significance:[83]

> [Extrinsic act evidence is excluded] not because it has no appreciable probative value, but because it has too much. The natural and inevitable tendency of the tribunal—whether judge or jury—is to give excessive weight to the vicious record of crime thus exhibited, and either to allow it to bear too strongly on the present charge, or to take proof of it as justifying a condemnation irrespective of guilt of the present charge.[84]

Rule 404(b)(1) recognizes the frequent unpredictability of human behavior, and consequently excludes extrinsic act evidence to prevent the tendency of a jury to believe that the defendant is guilty of committing the crime merely because the defendant is purportedly a bad person with a criminal disposition.[85]

Rule 404(b)(1) is also based on the fundamental premise of our accusatory mode of trial, as opposed to an inquisitorial mode often representative of civil law countries. The accusatory model generally embraces the policy that a person should be free from past misdeeds when facing a charge for a specific criminal act and should not be expected to defend an entire past life. As Justice Rutledge has stated:

> General bad character, much less general bad reputation, has not yet become a criminal offense in our scheme. Our whole tradition is that a man can be punished by criminal sanctions only for specific acts defined beforehand to be criminal, not for general misconduct or bearing a reputation for such misconduct.[86]

It should be noted that the prohibition of Rule 404(b)(1) applies to all

---

[82] *See generally,* 1 MUELLER & KIRKPATRICK, §§ 110–115.

[83] *See, e.g.,* United States v. McCourt, 925 F.2d 1229 (9th Cir. 1991) (Rule 404 doesn't allow the inference that "because someone was a bad guy once, he is likely to be a bad guy again"); United States v. Lewis, 787 F.2d 1318 (9th Cir. 1986) (noting "danger that a jury will infer present guilt from prior convictions"); *see generally,* 1 MUELLER & KIRKPATRICK, §§ 110–115.

[84] 1A WIGMORE, § 58.2, at 1212.

[85] *See* 2 WEINSTEIN'S FEDERAL EVIDENCE § 404.20; *see, e.g.,* United States v. Hodges, 770 F.2d 1475 (9th Cir. 1985) ("defendant must be tried for what he did, not for who he is").

[86] Michelson v. United States, 335 U.S. 469, 489 (1948) (Rutledge, J., dissenting); *see* United States v. Arias-Montoya, 967 F.2d 708 (1st Cir. 1992) (evidence of an eight-year-old conviction for possession of a minor amount of cocaine was erroneously admitted at defendant's trial for possession of cocaine where defendant was arrested when driving someone else's car that contained a kilogram of cocaine).

parties, including the criminal defendant, and the Rule therefore operates to prevent the accused from introducing evidence of extrinsic *good* acts to show action in conformity with the accused's good character on the occasion in question. Consistent with the express provisions of Rule 405, character may never be established with specific act evidence where it is offered to prove conforming conduct.

§ 404.13 Admissible Extrinsic Acts — In General

After stating the basic rule of exclusion, Rule 404(b)(2) indicates that evidence of other crimes, wrongs, or acts may be admissible where offered to prove consequential facts other than conforming conduct. It should be appreciated that although a specific inference involving extrinsic acts is prohibited in Rule 404(b)(1), the Rule does not, by its terms, absolutely prohibit the admissibility of extrinsic crimes, wrongs, or acts. A person's extrinsic acts, including criminal acts, may be relevant for a purpose other than demonstrating a general propensity to commit a similar act.[87] Some of these purposes are suggested in Rule 404(b)(2). Evidence of such acts used for these purposes would not be subject to the exclusionary principle expressed in Rule 404(b)(1).[88]

The list of bases for properly offering an extrinsic act set forth in Rule 404(b)(2) is not exhaustive,[89] and the fundamental issue is whether the act is offered only to prove character and conforming conduct. If so, the evidence is rendered inadmissible by Rule 404(b)(1). Moreover, the list of possible bases for offering an extrinsic act should not be seen as a list of exceptions to the Rule, but rather as a suggestive, nonexhaustive catalogue of bases that do not violate the exclusionary principle of Rule 404(b)(1).[90] The ultimate issue is a determination of the way in which the extrinsic act

---

[87] For example, one such purpose may be the satisfaction of a specific jurisdictional requirement. 2 WEINSTEIN'S FEDERAL EVIDENCE § 404.22; *see, e.g.,* Sanabria v. United States, 437 U.S. 54 (1978) (conduct violative of state law admissible because state law violation is jurisdictionally required before federal prosecution).

[88] *See generally,* 2 WEINSTEIN'S FEDERAL EVIDENCE § 404.22; 1 MUELLER & KIRKPATRICK, §§ 110–115; 1 McCORMICK, § 190.

[89] *See* 1 McCORMICK, § 190.

[90] *See* 2 WEINSTEIN'S FEDERAL EVIDENCE § 404.20; *see, e.g.,* United States v. Sarracino, 131 F.3d 943 (10th Cir. 1997) (evidence of defendant's attack on two individuals babysitting his children was admissible in murder prosecution to explain the context in which the defendant had admitted to killing the victim and not to show that the defendant was a violent person); United States v. Powers, 59 F.3d 1460 (4th Cir. 1995) (where defendant was charged with raping and sexually abusing his daughter over a period of nine months, trial court admitted testimony that defendant was extremely violent and threatening towards his entire family; evidence did not violate Rule 404(b) because evidence of defendant's violent behavior was necessary to place sexual abuse in context and to explain the victim's delay in reporting the sexual abuse); United States v. Stockton, 788 F.2d 210 (4th Cir. 1986) (impeachment is a proper "other purpose" of the Rule; Rule is not exhaustive); United States v. Williams, 577 F.2d 188 (2d Cir. 1978) (while Rule 404(b)(2) does not mention

is relevant, because the Rule specifically authorizes the use of extrinsic acts where the evidence is offered to prove a relevant fact other than propensity and conforming conduct.[91] The burden is accordingly on the proponent of the extrinsic act evidence to demonstrate that the relevance of the extrinsic act does not pertain to character and conforming conduct.[92]

Criminal cases often raise the question of the admissibility of extrinsic act evidence relating to an element of a charged crime when that element is not contested by the defendant.[93] The willingness of the accused to concede some essential element of the charged offense (or at least to not contest that issue at trial) does not automatically render evidence irrelevant when offered to prove that uncontested point, and does not necessarily preclude the admission of evidence of "other acts" to prove that point.[94] But the case for admission of such evidence is obviously weakest when it is offered to prove some point that is conceded or undisputed, and in such circumstances it is much more likely that the probative value of the evidence will be substantially outweighed by its potential for unfair prejudice,[95] especially

---

corroboration, the list is not exhaustive; evidence of prior conviction admitted only for corroborative purposes).

[91] Of course, the ultimate admissibility of the evidence is subject to the balancing provisions of Rule 403. *See* § 404.21, *infra*. The exclusionary principle merely reflects the judgment that evidence caught within the net of Rule 404(b)(1) is not subject to further balancing and should be excluded. However, if evidence bypasses the net of Rule 404(b)(1), it does not automatically qualify for admission. "That the general rule mandating exclusion does not dictate the outcome merely means that the decision as to admission must be made in light of the general principle that relevant evidence is admissible unless its probative value is substantially outweighed by countervailing considerations." 1 MCCORMICK, § 186, at 787 n.4. *See, e.g.,* State v. Goebel, 36 Wn.2d 367, 379 (1950) ("this class of evidence . . . should not be admitted even though falling within the generally recognized exceptions (sic) to the rule of exclusion, when the trial court is convinced that its effect would be to generate heat instead of diffusing light, or . . . where the minute peg of relevancy will be completely obscured by the dirty linen hung upon it").

[92] *See, e.g.,* Morris v. Washington Metro. Area Transit Auth., 702 F.2d 1037 (D.C. Cir. 1983); United States v. Scott, 701 F.2d 1340 (11th Cir. 1983); United States v. Bice-Bey, 701 F.2d 1086 (4th Cir. 1983); *see also* United States v. Miller, 895 F.2d 1431 (D.C. Cir. 1990) (evidence of defendant's conviction was admissible to prove the state of mind of a witness other than the defendant where the defendant put the witness's state of mind in issue).

[93] *See* LILLY, § 5.15; 2 WEINSTEIN'S FEDERAL EVIDENCE §§ 404.22–404.23; *see generally,* 1 MUELLER & KIRKPATRICK, §§ 110–115.

[94] United States v. Thomas, 593 F.3d 752 (8th Cir. 2010) (in prosecution of man charged with drug offenses committed in 2004, district court properly admitted evidence of his "subsequent bad acts" consisting of his commission of highly similar drug transactions in the same vicinity in 2008; even though the defense made a complete denial of any participation in the charged offense — as opposed to asserting that he had become embroiled in the charged offense through accident or ignorance — the evidence was properly admitted with a "limiting instruction" that the evidence "could be used only to establish [his] intent, knowledge, or lack of mistake").

[95] *See* Old Chief v. United States, 519 U.S. 172 (1997) (when the accused was charged

when the undisputed fact is clearly established through other evidence in the case.[96]

§ 404.14   Degree of Proof Necessary to Establish Extrinsic Act

Where an extrinsic act is properly admitted pursuant to Rule 404(b)(2), the proponent of the extrinsic act evidence must of course show (*i.e.*, offer evidence) that the act has, in fact, occurred. Moreover, in criminal cases where the alleged extrinsic act is that of the accused, the proponent must demonstrate a sufficient connection between the criminal defendant and the commission of the extrinsic act.[97] For a period after the adoption of the Rules, the Circuit Courts did not agree on the degree of proof necessary to establish this connection, with requirements varying from a "beyond a reasonable doubt" standard[98] to a threshold "sufficient for the jury to reasonably find that the offense occurred" test.[99]

---

as a felon in possession of a firearm, the trial court abused its discretion in admitting prejudicial and detailed evidence about the nature of the defendant's felony convictions when he was willing to stipulate to the fact of his conviction); United States v. Sumner, 119 F.3d 658 (8th Cir. 1997) (trial court erred in admitting evidence of prior bad acts of defendant; although the prosecution contended that the prior acts evidence was necessary to show intent, the court found intent was not at issue, and thus no evidence was needed, where the defendant specifically denies only the criminal act; moreover, the defendant had offered to stipulate to the intent element).

[96] United States v. Jenkins, 593 F.3d 480 (6th Cir. 2010) (in prosecution for constructive possession of drugs and guns found all over a house shared by several individuals, the defendant's conviction for possession of marijuana with intent to distribute eight years earlier was more unfairly prejudicial than probative when allegedly offered to show the defendant's knowledge or intent, because those issues were so clearly proved through the other evidence at trial. "We do not think the issue of knowledge was at issue in any meaningful sense. Whoever possessed all these drugs laying in plain view throughout the house obviously did not do so inadvertently.")

[97] In Dowling v. United States, 493 U.S. 342 (1990), the Supreme Court denied a Due Process and Double Jeopardy challenge against the rule that evidence of other crimes for which the defendant has been previously acquitted is admissible. Because an acquittal merely resolves the issue of whether the crime has been committed beyond a reasonable doubt, it does not preclude use of evidence of the act in future cases, which admissibility is governed by a lower standard of proof. *See also* United States v. Marshall, 173 F.3d 1312 (11th Cir. 1999) (evidence of prior arrest of two defendants in a crack cocaine production facility and large amounts of cash was improperly admitted in a prosecution for conspiracy to possess crack cocaine with intent to distribute, where no connection was made between the defendants and the production in the house in which they were arrested).

[98] United States v. Testa, 548 F.2d 847, 852 n.1 (9th Cir. 1977) (court charged jury that "prior events could not be considered for any purpose unless the jury first found beyond a reasonable doubt that the accused did the act charged"). *But cf.* United States v. Herrera-Medina, 609 F.2d 376 (9th Cir. 1979) (clear and convincing).

[99] United States v. Mortazavi, 702 F.2d 526 (5th Cir. 1983); United States v. Beechum, 582 F.2d 898 (5th Cir. 1978); *see generally,* 1 MCCORMICK, § 190; 2 WEINSTEIN'S FEDERAL EVIDENCE § 404.21.

In *Huddleston v. United States,*[100] the Supreme Court specified the analysis to be used by district courts when ruling on "other acts" evidence pertaining to the accused in a criminal case.[101] A unanimous Court held that a threshold inquiry must be made by the court as to whether the evidence is "probative of a material issue other than character."[102] If the evidence is being used for a proper purpose, it is "subject only to general strictures limiting admissibility such as Rules 402 and 403,"[103] and relevant "only if the jury can reasonably conclude that the act occurred and that the defendant was the actor."[104] This kind of conditional relevance based upon fact is addressed under Rule 104(b). The Court reasoned that Rule 104(b) requires only that a court determine whether the jury could reasonably find the conditional fact by a preponderance of the evidence, not that the court itself find that the preponderance has been met.[105] The Court emphasized that, in making the assessment whether the evidence is sufficient for the jury to find the conditional fact by a preponderance of the evidence, the trial court must consider all the evidence presented to the jury. " '[I]ndividual pieces of evidence, insufficient in themselves to prove a point, may in cumulation prove it. The sum of an evidentiary presentation may well be greater than its constituent parts'."[106] If the court finds that the jury could find the conditional fact by a preponderance of the evidence, the evidence of the prior act may be admitted.[107]

In deciding that Rule 404(b) rulings fall within Rule 104(b), the Court rejected the argument that the potential danger of prejudice requires a preliminary determination by the court on the admissibility of the evidence

---

[100] Huddleston v. United States, 485 U.S. 681 (1988). The defendant, charged with possession of stolen property, challenged the admission of evidence offered by the government to demonstrate defendant's knowledge the items were stolen. This evidence concerned defendant's previous offer to sell televisions for $28 apiece, and the government's only support for the fact that the televisions were stolen was the low price of the televisions and failure of the defendant to produce a bill of sale at trial. *Id.* at 684.

[101] *See* § 404.20, *infra,* for a discussion of the analysis and the balancing process to be used by the district courts.

[102] *Huddleston,* 485 U.S. at 686.

[103] *Id.* at 688.

[104] *Id.* at 689. In *Huddleston,* the fact that the defendant was selling the televisions was relevant only if the jury found that the televisions were, in fact, stolen.

[105] *Id.* at 689–690. *See* Rule 104 and § 104.1 *et seq., supra.*

[106] *Id.* at 691 (quoting Bourjaily v. United States, 483 U.S. 171, 179–180 (1987)). In *Huddleston,* this included not only the direct evidence that the televisions were stolen — the low price, large quantity, and failure to produce a bill of sale — but also the evidence concerning defendant's similar activity regarding stolen property, including the charged items. *Huddleston* 485 at 691.

[107] *Id.* at 691; *see, e.g.,* discussion of Dowling v. United States, 493 U.S. 342 (1990), *supra.*

pursuant to Rule 104(a).[108] The Court noted the self-contained structure of Article IV, which sets forth the general exclusionary principle and provides bases for the exclusion of evidence in Rule 403. Citing legislative history supporting the proposition that Congress intended to "plac[e] greater emphasis on admissibility" of Rule 404(b) evidence than an earlier draft of the promulgated Rule,[109] the Court also relied on the absence of any language in Rule 404 making reference to a preliminary determination on the admissibility of evidence or Rule 104(a).[110]

The Court noted a concern for possible prejudice inherent in Rule 404(b) evidence, but felt that such fears were adequately addressed: first, through the threshold requirement of Rule 404(b) that the evidence be offered for a proper purpose; second, through the relevance protections of Rule 104(b); third, through the balancing process mandated by Rule 403;[111] and finally, through the limiting instruction pursuant to Rule 105.[112]

§ 404.15   Extrinsic Act Evidence Offered to Show Intent, Knowledge, or Absence of Mistake in a Criminal Case

Cases have generally held that extrinsic acts of the accused are admissible to establish the mental state of the accused in situations in which such an issue is properly before the court. Nevertheless, while intent must be a genuine issue in the litigation before extrinsic acts are admitted, courts differ in their determination of when intent is in issue.[113] The notion of intent is

---

[108] *Huddleston,* 485 U.S. at 686–687. In a subsidiary holding, the Court found that such a determination must be made by a preponderance of the evidence, not a clear and convincing standard, as some Circuit courts had held. *Id.* at 687 n.5.

[109] *Id.* at 687–689.

[110] *Id.* at 688.

[111] *See* § 404.21, *infra.*

[112] *See* § 404.22, *infra.*

[113] *See* United States v. Rooks, 596 F.3d 204 (4th Cir. 2010) (in prosecution for possession of crack with intent to distribute, defendant's three earlier convictions for drug sales were admissible to prove his knowledge of the drug trade, as well as his intent to distribute the crack found in a small bag he threw away when chased by the police); United States v. Sumner, 119 F.3d 658 (8th Cir. 1997) (trial court erred in admitting evidence of prior bad acts of defendant as proof of defendant's intent as intent was not at issue where the defendant's only defense was that the criminal act never occurred); United States v. Colon, 880 F.2d 650 (2d Cir. 1989) (in a drug "steering" prosecution, the trial court erred in admitting evidence that defendant had previously engaged in similar activity; defendant had not yet made clear whether lack of intent was his defense; the "prior acts" evidence should not have been admitted until and unless it was clear that defendant was disputing intent); United States v. Franklin, 704 F.2d 1183 (10th Cir. 1983); United States v. Hamilton, 684 F.2d 380 (6th Cir. 1982) (evidence of prior crimes is admissible when specific intent is an issue); United States v. Reed, 639 F.2d 896 (2d Cir. 1981) (no issue of intent when defendant denies commission of the act instead of admitting the act and arguing lack of intent); *see also* Sparks v. Gilley Trucking Co., 992 F.2d 50 (4th Cir. 1993) (in a vehicular contributory negligence claim against plaintiff, the admission of plaintiff's prior speeding tickets was a

closely related to that of knowledge, and courts often admit evidence under the dual theory of knowledge and intent without differentiating between the two.[114] Both concepts involve the absence of mistake or accident, and are implicated when a person claims innocence in a criminal act. It is said that knowledge indicates awareness of the criminality of an act,[115] while intent includes not only an awareness of the criminality of an act, but also a desire to achieve the particular criminal act.[116] Still, it is important to distinguish the two concepts, because intent is an element of virtually every crime,[117] while knowledge has elemental application in specific contexts.[118]

Evidence of extrinsic acts of the accused that are similar to the crime charged may tend to show that the accused purposefully, as opposed to accidentally, committed the acts.[119] Courts vary in the degree of requisite

---

violation of Rule 404(b); this was a negligence case and intent was not a factor); United States v. McLamb, 985 F.2d 1284 (4th Cir. 1993) (evidence of three similar money laundering transactions by defendant held to be admissible to show defendant had the necessary specific intent); United States v. Robison, 904 F.2d 365 (6th Cir. 1990) (in a trial for conspiracy to distribute cocaine where defendant claimed he was only a drug user, evidence of previous drug transactions was probative of an intent to distribute). *See generally,* 2 WEINSTEIN'S FEDERAL EVIDENCE § 404.23.

[114] *See, e.g.,* United States v. Betts, 16 F.3d 748 (7th Cir. 1994) (in a drug conspiracy case, trial court erroneously admitted evidence of drugs found in a search of defendant's home eighteen months after the end of the conspiracy to show defendant's knowledge and intent concerning the prior conspiracy; error found to be harmless where other evidence of defendant's guilt was overwhelming). For a collection of cases illustrating the lack of differentiation between intent and knowledge, *see* 2 WEINSTEIN'S FEDERAL EVIDENCE § 404.22.

[115] 1 MUELLER & KIRKPATRICK, § 112; *see* 2 WEINSTEIN'S FEDERAL EVIDENCE § 404.22.

[116] *Id.*

[117] 2 WEINSTEIN'S FEDERAL EVIDENCE § 404.22.

[118] Some examples include possession of stolen property, possession of unregistered firearms, and harboring or transporting an illegal alien. *See* 2 WEINSTEIN'S FEDERAL EVIDENCE § 404.22.

[119] *See* 1 MUELLER & KIRKPATRICK, § 112. *See* United States v. Littlewind, 595 F.3d 876 (8th Cir. 2010) (in prosecution of man for assaulting his girlfriend, the Government was properly allowed to prove that he had been convicted three times of assaulting the same woman, to rebut his claims that he lacked criminal intent and that she was possibly hurt in an accident; the probative value of prior crime evidence, when offered to prove the intent of the accused, is greatest when both offenses were under similar circumstances and associated with the same victim); Jannotta v. Subway Sandwich Shops, 125 F.3d 503 (7th Cir. 1997) (holding that evidence of the defendant's prior fraudulent acts was admissible to show intent where the defendant's intent to commit fraud was relevant for the purpose of determining whether to award punitive damages); United States v. Segien, 114 F.3d 1014 (10th Cir. 1997) (where defendant was charged with spitting on and injuring a corrections officer and testified that any spitting or other injury was an unintended by-product of a verbal argument, prosecution was permitted to introduce evidence of previous incidents where the defendant had beaten and spit on other prison officers); United States v. Haukaas, 172 F.3d 542 (8th Cir.

similarity between the prior act and charged crime as a precondition to admitting the evidence.[120] Many courts have required only a very low degree of similarity between the extrinsic acts and the charged act, possibly because the likelihood that one mental state will produce a similar mental state is stronger than the possibility that a mental state will produce a subsequent act.[121] This low threshold requirement of similarity is especially prevalent in narcotics cases[122] and cases involving child abuse.[123]

When a party seeks to admit evidence of "other acts" to prove intent, some courts have held that, to be sufficiently probative, the other act should have similar criminal elements to the crime with which the accused is charged.[124] However, at least one Circuit has rejected a strict matching requirement between elements of the prior act and the charged act.[125] The Fifth Circuit has held that the degree to which the elements match might be relevant to its overall probative value, but not to the threshold issue of relevance for admissibility purposes.[126] Rather, evidence is relevant once it appears "to alter the probabilities of a consequential fact."[127]

Where admissible, the acts might tend to prove that the accused understood that certain acts would result in the wrongful nature of the act by virtue of the fact that prior similar wrongful conduct has been the subject of

---

1999) (evidence of prior domestic assault admissible to show absence of mistake or accident and to rebut claim of self-defense, where defendant claimed that he was holding knife stationary when victims thrust themselves on to the knife); United States v. Gellene, 182 F.3d 578 (7th Cir. 1999) (in prosecution of attorney for knowingly and fraudulently making a false material declaration in a bankruptcy proceeding, evidence of four prior misrepresentations to courts was properly admitted under Rule 404(b), as it showed his "cavalier disregard" for the truth in his dealings with courts and went to prove whether he had the requisite fraudulent intent).

[120] *See, e.g.,* United States v. Dixon, 698 F.2d 445 (11th Cir. 1983); United States v. Evans, 697 F.2d 240 (8th Cir. 1983); *see also* United States v. Hill, 898 F.2d 72 (7th Cir. 1990) (at a pretrial hearing for conspiracy to cultivate marijuana, a prior arrest for possession of marijuana seeds was highly probative of defendant's intent to cultivate); United States v. Levario Quiroz, 854 F.2d 69 (5th Cir. 1988) (where defendant claimed self-defense for shooting a border patrol officer, it was plain error to admit evidence that defendant had shot at three persons at a dance two months earlier, because there were almost no characteristics in common between the two incidents).

[121] Bryden and Park, *"Other Crimes" Evidence in Sex Offense Cases,* 78 U. MINN. L. REV. 529 (1994).

[122] 2 WEINSTEIN'S FEDERAL EVIDENCE § 404.22.

[123] Bryden and Park, *"Other Crimes" Evidence in Sex Offense Cases,* 78 U. MINN. L. REV. 529 (1994).

[124] *See* 2 WEINSTEIN'S FEDERAL EVIDENCE § 404.22.

[125] United States v. Beechum, 582 F.2d 898 (5th Cir. 1978).

[126] *Beechum,* 582 F.2d at 911.

[127] *Id.* at 913.

arrest or conviction.[128] Consequently, a disclaimer of knowledge of the criminal nature of an act may be rebutted by proof of prior law enforcement encounters involving similar acts.[129]

Extrinsic act evidence may be admissible to negate a mistake or accident, and obviously, this theory is closely linked with a demonstration of intent. Under this theory, the proponent of the extrinsic evidence must establish a relationship between the mode, time and situation involved in the extrinsic act and the act sought to be proven to show that the person in question acted purposefully, rather than mistakenly or accidentally.[130] Professor Lilly provides this example:

---

[128] *See* United States v. Nabors, 707 F.2d 1294 (11th Cir. 1983); United States v. Dudley, 562 F.2d 965 (5th Cir. 1977); *cf.* United States v. Robison, 904 F.2d 365 (6th Cir. 1990) (in defense to possession with intent to distribute charge, defendant argued that he possessed drugs for personal use only; once intent issue was raised, evidence of previous drug transactions was probative); United States v. Rubio-Estrada, 857 F.2d 845 (1st Cir. 1988) (in prosecution for possession of cocaine with intent to distribute in which the defendant claimed to use an electronic scale and a ledger that recorded large cash transactions for legitimate business purposes, no error to admit prior conviction, since it made defendant more likely to know that scale and ledger were commonly used in drug transactions; dissent argued that the only inference to be made from the conviction was the "character" inference forbidden by Rule 404(b)).

[129] United States v. Wilford, 710 F.2d 439 (8th Cir. 1983); *see also* Turley v. State Farm Mutual Ins. Co., 944 F.2d 669 (10th Cir. 1991) (evidence of a prior fake slip-and-fall claim held admissible on the issue of whether plaintiff committed insurance fraud in the present case); United States v. Murphy, 935 F.2d 899 (7th Cir. 1991) (disability checks received by accused beyond limitations period held admissible to show fraudulent intent and pattern of deception); United States v. Paulino, 935 F.2d 739 (6th Cir. 1991) (evidence of an Uzi handgun found in defendant's apartment was admissible because it tended to prove intent to promote and protect a narcotics conspiracy); United States v. Crump, 934 F.2d 947 (8th Cir. 1991) (witness testimony that she often had sex with defendant in exchange for drugs properly admitted to show defendant's predisposition to distribute cocaine); United States v. Roper, 874 F.2d 782 (11th Cir. 1989) (once defendant raises the possibility of entrapment, the government may introduce similar prior acts to show that the defendant was predisposed to commit the crime and thereby rebut the entrapment theory); United States v. Mazzanti, 888 F.2d 1165 (7th Cir. 1989) (in conspiracy to distribute cocaine charge, defendant denied any involvement or wrongdoing in order to negate intent, the government was properly allowed to reestablish intent with evidence of defendant's prior discussions regarding cocaine purchases and defendant's knowledge of the slang term 'z' referring to cocaine); United States v. Castillo, 181 F.3d 1129 (9th Cir. 1999) (evidence of a 1995 conviction for possession of marijuana was admissible in a 1997 prosecution for the same offense, to show knowledge and absence of mistake or accident).

[130] *See, e.g.,* United States v. Mejia, 600 F.3d 12 (1st Cir. 2010) (in drug conspiracy prosecution, the district court did not err in admitting the defendant's alleged "drug ledgers" containing names, quantities and amounts that correspond to the market rate for drugs, as proof of the existence of the conspiracy; the evidence was highly probative given the defense claim that he was "merely present" at the drug deal and otherwise uninvolved in the conspiracy); United States v. Satterfield, 644 F.2d 1092 (5th Cir. 1981); United States v. Sciortino, 601 F.2d 680 (2d Cir. 1979); United States v. Fairchild, 526 F.2d 185 (7th Cir. 1975) (in prosecution for distributing counterfeit bills, no error to receive evidence that

In the trial of D for receiving stolen property from A, evidence that on other occasions and under similar circumstances A had supplied D with goods known by D to have been stolen is relevant to show that D had "knowledge" that the goods in question were stolen.[131]

§ 404.16   Extrinsic Act Evidence Offered to Show Motive in a Criminal Case

Where an extrinsic act is used to establish motive, the act should demonstrate that the accused possesses a specific reason to commit the crime charged.[132] An extrinsic act used to prove motive is illustrated by the hypothetical fact pattern in which an accused is charged with the murder of a person who witnessed the commission of a prior crime. The fact that the victim is a known witness to the prior crime may be admissible, rendering

---

defendant had other bills in his possession, as tending to negative "mere accident or mistake").

[131] LILLY, § 5.14, at 158; *see also* Huddleston v. United States, 485 U.S. 681 (1988) (in a trial for possession of stolen goods, where the only disputed issue was whether the defendant knew that the goods were stolen, the trial court properly admitted evidence that defendant had twice offered to sell goods in large quantities at prices substantially below their fair value); United States v. Kindred, 931 F.2d 609 (9th Cir. 1991) (evidence of defendant's prior conviction that trial court admitted to show knowledge was not sufficiently probative where knowledge was not a material element of the offense).

[132] *See* United States v. Seale, 600 F.3d 473 (5th Cir. 2010) (in prosecution for conspiracy to commit kidnapping, other bad acts related to defendant's racial animus and membership in the Ku Klux Klan were admissible to show his motive, intent, and his relationship with others in the conspiracy, where the evidence made it clear that victims were abducted because of the color of their skin by men who shared membership in a group hostile to African Americans and the Civil Rights movement); United States v. Sriyuth, 98 F.3d 739 (3d Cir. 1996) (evidence of sexual assault against a victim of a kidnapping is relevant during trial for kidnapping as to the issue of the defendant's motive and the victim's lack of consent; evidence was offered in rebuttal to the defendant's claim that the victim consented to the defendant's action under the Laotian custom of arranged marriages); United States v. Southwest Bus Sales, Inc., 20 F.3d 1449 (8th Cir. 1994) (where defendant was charged with violations of the Sherman Act for fixing prices of buses sold to school districts, evidence of a similar scheme in another market was admissible as evidence of defendant's motive and plan); United States v. Palmer, 3 F.3d 300 (9th Cir. 1993) (statement implicating defendant's involvement in other drug offenses was inadmissible because motive was not a material element of the offense charged but error was harmless); Johnson v. Hugo's Skateway, 974 F.2d 1408 (4th Cir. 1992) (in racially motivated discrimination action, evidence of defendant's ten-year-old consent decree with the Department of Justice in a prior unrelated race matter was properly admitted); United States v. McMahon, 938 F.2d 1501 (1st Cir. 1991) (evidence of financial difficulty was admissible to prove motive to accept a bribe); United States v. Shriver, 842 F.2d 968 (7th Cir. 1988) (no error in admitting evidence that defendant, charged with making false statements to obtain a loan, was in default on his franchise agreement for failure to make payments; the need for funds provided a motive for misrepresenting his financial status); United States v. Fraser, 709 F.2d 1556 (6th Cir. 1983); Phillips v. Smalley Maintenance Serv., 711 F.2d 1524 (11th Cir. 1983); Bohannon v. Pegelow, 652 F.2d 729 (7th Cir. 1981); *see generally,* 2 WEINSTEIN'S FEDERAL EVIDENCE § 404.22; 1 MUELLER & KIRKPATRICK, § 110.

the prior crime admissible, because it would be relevant in establishing a motive for the accused to murder the victim in question, as part of an effort to "cover up" the prior crime. Likewise, evidence of specific acts of misconduct by the accused may be admissible under this rule when they are offered to show the motive of others to act as they did — for example, acts of violence by the accused may be admitted to explain why a prosecution witness did not disclose certain information to the police.[133]

Courts do not require any specific quantum of similarity between prior acts and charged crimes when accepting evidence under a motive theory. Obviously, a dissimilar prior act is just as feasible in supplying a motive for committing a crime as is a similar prior act.

It should be noted that although motive is usually relevant in all criminal cases, it is not a necessary element of the crime. Nevertheless, extrinsic act evidence of motive may be admissible in cases in which it is probative.[134]

§ 404.17 Extrinsic Act Evidence Offered to Show Identity in a Criminal Case

Extrinsic act evidence may be used to establish the defendant's identity as the perpetrator of the offense in question by showing that the defendant committed similar crimes in which a distinct modus operandi was commonly utilized in the commission of the crimes.[135] This pattern of similarity is often

---

[133] United States v. York, 600 F.3d 347 (5th Cir. 2010) (in arson prosecution, after defendant's former girlfriend testified against him and he sought to impeach her with the fact that some details of her testimony had not been disclosed earlier to the police, trial court properly allowed her to explain her silence by describing her fear of the accused and an assault he had once committed against her. This act was relevant to her credibility, and its potential for unfair prejudice was relatively low because of the lack of similarity between the domestic abuse episode and the charged offense of arson).

[134] *See, e.g.,* United States v. Birney, 686 F.2d 102 (2d Cir. 1982); United States v. Engleman, 648 F.2d 473 (8th Cir. 1981).

[135] *See* United States v. Carrillo, 981 F.2d 772 (5th Cir. 1993) (where defendant, charged with selling drugs, carried them in a balloon in his mouth, evidence of defendant's two prior drug balloon sales were inadmissible because the method was not sufficiently distinctive to establish defendant's modus operandi); United States v. Khan, 993 F.2d 1368 (9th Cir. 1993) (evidence of drug defendant's involvement in a prior drug transaction was of substantial probative value because it showed the preparation, planning and background of the drug transaction charged); United States v. Sneezer, 983 F.2d 920 (9th Cir. 1992) (evidence of a prior rape attempt was sufficiently similar to the charged rape to show defendant's plan); United States v. Miller, 959 F.2d 1535 (11th Cir. 1992) (the district court properly admitted evidence of a later extrinsic act that was remarkably similar to the evidence of the charged act); United States v. Feinman, 930 F.2d 495 (6th Cir. 1991) (evidence of an uncharged incident involving the transport of marijuana in defendant's truck was admissible as evidence of an ongoing scheme since it was similar and near in time to the charged offense); *see also* United States v. Messersmith, 692 F.2d 1315 (11th Cir. 1982); United States v. Andrini, 685 F.2d 1094 (9th Cir. 1982). *But see* Grady v. Corbin, 495 U.S. 508 (1990) (O'Connor, J., dissenting) (doubting the "continued vitality of Rule 404(b)"); *see generally,* 2 WEINSTEIN'S

referred to as a "signature" or "print" left by the perpetrator of the crime.[136] Any unique pattern should tend to show that the crimes were committed by the same person, and consequently, the defendant's extrinsic acts may be relevant to evidence a unique modus operandi where identity of the perpetrator is an issue.[137]

When admitting evidence for the purpose of establishing identity, courts have required a higher degree of similarity between the prior act and the charged crime than for such purposes as establishing intent or motive. Since the distinctive similarity between the prior acts and charged crimes constitutes the very basis for admission under an identity theory, a high requisite of similarity is appropriate.

Courts are not always precise in their analysis and often admit evidence under a guise of identity that actually demonstrate a separate basis for admission, such as scheme or plan.[138] The reverse is also true. In certain cases, courts will admit evidence showing a unique modus operandi, or

---

FEDERAL EVIDENCE § 404.22; 1 MUELLER & KIRKPATRICK, § 114.

[136] *See* United States v. McQuiston, 998 F.2d 627 (8th Cir. 1993) (evidence of other robberies admissible to prove identity because robberies were all committed in similar ways); United States v. Sanchez, 988 F.2d 1384 (5th Cir. 1993) (evidence of prior drug transaction was admissible because it was so similar to charged crime as to "evince a signature quality"); United States v. Silva, 580 F.2d 144 (5th Cir. 1978) (in narcotics prosecution, error to admit evidence of subsequent sale that did not bear "such a high degree of similarity as to mark it as the handiwork of the accused"); *see generally,* 2 WEINSTEIN'S FEDERAL EVIDENCE § 404.22; 1 MUELLER & KIRKPATRICK, § 114.

[137] *See* United States v. Murray, 103 F.3d 310 (3d Cir. 1997) (in prosecution for murder, the trial court erred in admitting evidence that the defendant had killed someone before because the similarities between the two killings were insufficient to make the first killing relevant on the issue of identity); United States v. Kern, 12 F.3d 122 (8th Cir. 1993) (evidence that defendant previously robbed a hotel was properly admitted at defendant's bank robbery trial where the circumstances of the two robberies were similar and close in time); United States v. Miller, 883 F.2d 1540 (11th Cir. 1989) (where the only similarities between the prior act and the crime charged were the use of a beeper and delivery by car, which are common drug trafficking methods, and the similarities could be attributed to government intervention, extrinsic acts were not admissible to show a distinctive modus operandi), *vacated,* 923 F.2d 158 (11th Cir. 1991); United States v. Hudson, 843 F.2d 1062 (7th Cir. 1988) (in a trial for entering a credit union with intent to commit larceny, no error to admit evidence of a similar act where the details of the modus operandi were similar to that in the charged crime); *see, e.g.,* Adail v. Wyrick, 711 F.2d 99 (8th Cir. 1983); United States v. Means, 695 F.2d 811 (5th Cir. 1983).

[138] *See* United States v. Treff, 924 F.2d 975 (10th Cir. 1991) (in prosecution for throwing molotov cocktails at house of ex-supervisor, court properly admitted stipulation that defendant killed wife and fled with children to motel in same episode, which helped show it was he who threw firebombs); United States v. Waldron, 568 F.2d 185 (10th Cir. 1977) (in bank robbery prosecution, proof that defendant had been involved in a theft of guns from a house a year earlier was admissible to prove identity, where the same guns were allegedly used in the bank robbery itself).

"signature," even though identity of the perpetrator is not in issue.[139]

§ 404.18   Extrinsic Act Evidence Offered to Show Scheme, Plan, or System in a Criminal Case

Extrinsic acts may be part of the immediate background of the act that is the fundament of the crime charged. In this situation, the extrinsic act evidence must show events that are "inextricably related" to the crime charged.[140] Occasionally, this admissibility theory is known as the "res gestae" doctrine.[141] Under this doctrine, the acts must rationally constitute the same transaction or episode as the act that is the object of proof.[142]

Also, extrinsic acts may be admissible on a theory that utilizes the distinct acts of the accused as elements of a sequence of events logically or inevitably leading up to the crime charged.[143] Consequently, where evidence is presented that the accused previously stole a gun to facilitate the commission of a charged robbery, the extrinsic act of the theft of the gun is probative of a plan to commit the armed robbery.[144] Cases utilizing this basis for admissibility vary greatly in the range of acts constituting part of a scheme or plan relevant to the act constituting the crime charged.[145]

It is counterintuitive to require a specific degree of similarity between the prior acts and the charged crime when accepting evidence under a scheme or plan theory. The shoplifting of a gun is more probative of an ongoing plan to commit a future armed robbery than is a prior armed robbery. Nevertheless, the acts may, in fact, be similar, especially under a "res gestae"

---

[139] *See, e.g.,* State v. Willis, 370 N.W.2d 193 (S.D. 1985) (in a rape case where defendant argues consent and identity is not in issue, modus operandi evidence is nonetheless admissible as showing intent and plan).

[140] *E.g.,* United States v. Costa, 691 F.2d 1358 (11th Cir. 1982); United States v. Wooten, 688 F.2d 941 (4th Cir. 1983).

[141] United States v. Blewitt, 538 F.2d 1099 (5th Cir. 1976) (court properly admitted allegedly forged checks where payor, payee, and endorsement were the same as on checks that defendant was charged with aiding and abetting their interstate transportation; all checks constituted part of the system of criminal action involved in the entire fraudulent scheme); *see* 2 WIGMORE, § 218, for a criticism of this concept. *See generally,* 1 MUELLER & KIRKPATRICK, § 113.

[142] 1 MCCORMICK, § 193.

[143] *See generally,* 2 WEINSTEIN'S FEDERAL EVIDENCE § 404.22.

[144] *See* LILLY, § 5.14.

[145] *See, e.g.,* United States v. Nadler, 698 F.2d 995 (9th Cir. 1983); United States v. McCrary, 699 F.2d 1308 (11th Cir. 1983); United States v. Roylance, 690 F.2d 164 (10th Cir. 1982). *But see* United States v. Blackstone, 56 F.3d 1143 (9th Cir. 1995) (where defendant was charged with gun possession, trial court erred in admitting evidence of defendant's methamphetamine recipes and marijuana for personal use; while evidence of drug trafficking has been held to be relevant to the possession of a firearm, the court found that evidence of marijuana for personal use was not authorized; resulting prejudice to defendant outweighed the probative value).

doctrine.[146]

§ 404.19 Extrinsic Acts in Civil Cases

While Rule 404(b) will most frequently arise in the context of a criminal case, the Rule is nonetheless applicable in civil cases. For example, pursuant to Rule 404(b)(1), evidence of other instances of negligence of a defendant is not admissible to establish the defendant's negligence on the particular occasion that forms the basis for the cause of action.[147] Extrinsic acts may not be used to establish a person's generalized negligent propensity or high degree of accident proneness. While the extrinsic acts might be relevant, they would fall squarely within the prohibition set forth in Rule 404(b)(1).[148] For example, distinct automobile accidents are not admissible when offered against a civil defendant who is sued for vehicular negligence to demonstrate a generalized pattern of negligent propensity.

Under Rule 404(b)(2), evidence of extrinsic acts of an individual are admissible in civil cases where the acts are not offered to establish conforming conduct.[149] Again, Rule 404(b)(1) does not prohibit evidence of all extrinsic acts for any reason; the Rule only prohibits use of a specific inferential pattern. Consequently, evidence of extrinsic acts may be used to show the existence of a dangerous condition.[150] Likewise, evidence of extrinsic acts may be offered to show that notice was provided to a defendant that a dangerous condition or nuisance existed.[151]

---

[146] *See, e.g.,* United States v. Southwest Bus Sales, Inc., 20 F.3d 1449 (8th Cir. 1994) (where defendant was charged with violations of the Sherman Act for fixing prices of buses sold to school districts, evidence of a similar scheme in another market was admissible as evidence of defendant's motive and plan); United States v. Rodriguez-Estrada, 877 F.2d 153 (1st Cir. 1989) (in embezzlement prosecution, no error to admit evidence that defendant previously drew 231 other checks to his own order, since the checks were "virtual replicas" of the checks that were the basis for the indictment).

[147] *See* Buford v. Howe, 10 F.3d 1184 (5th Cir. 1994) (in a medical malpractice case, where plaintiff claimed that defendant performed unnecessary surgery, trial court did not abuse its discretion in excluding evidence of surgical procedures performed by defendant on other patients). *See generally,* 2 WEINSTEIN'S FEDERAL EVIDENCE § 404.22.

[148] *See In re* Aircrash in Bali, Indonesia, 684 F.2d 1301 (9th Cir. 1982); Reyes v. Missouri P. R. Co., 589 F.2d 791 (5th Cir. 1979); George v. Morgan Constr. Co., 389 F. Supp. 253 (E.D. Pa. 1975); *see also* Trautman, *Logical or Legal Relevancy—A Conflict in Theory.* 5 VAND. L. REV. 385 (1952); James and Dickinson, *Accident Proneness and Accident Law,* 63 HARV. L. REV. 769 (1950).

[149] *See* Morgan v. Foretich, 846 F.2d 941 (4th Cir. 1988) (in a child abuse case, it was reversible error to exclude plaintiff's evidence that the victim's sister had suffered similar injuries, where the evidence would have rebutted defendant's explanation of the victim's injuries by showing that he was the only individual with access to both girls).

[150] Young v. Illinois Cent. Gulf R.R., 618 F.2d 332 (5th Cir. 1980); Bailey v. Southern Pac. Transp. Co., 613 F.2d 1385 (5th Cir. 1980); *see generally,* LILLY, § 5.16; 2 WEINSTEIN'S FEDERAL EVIDENCE § 404.22.

[151] LILLY, § 5.16.

§ 404.20   The Interplay of Rule 404(b) with Rule 403

Since *Huddleston* was decided, many district courts have followed the analysis used in that case.[152] The courts use a four-part test:[153] the evidence must be: offered for a proper purpose under Rule 404(b)(2);[154] relevant as viewed through Rule 104(b);[155] balanced under Rule 403 to determine the relative weights of the probative value and risk of prejudice of the evidence;[156] and limited through proper instruction pursuant to Rule 105.[157]

With regard to the third prong of the test identified in the previous paragraph, it must be emphasized that Rule 404(b)(2) presents a special context that almost invariably raises Rule 403 consideration.[158] Because of the potential risk of prejudice and confusion presented by extrinsic act evidence, coupled with the varying degree of probative value of extrinsic acts, there is a special need for careful application of the Rule 403 balance in this context.

§ 404.21   Notice Requirement for the Prosecution in a Criminal Case; Procedure

Upon request by the accused, the prosecution must provide the defense with notice of the extrinsic act evidence it intends to introduce, as part of its case-in-chief, rebuttal, or for impeachment purposes.[159] While there are no strict time limits, and no specific form of notice is required, the Rule anticipates that both counsel will proceed in a reasonable and timely fashion and that the prosecution will apprise the defense of the nature of the evidence with something more specific than a "boilerplate assertion" or a laundry list of the possible uses permitted under Rule 404(b).[160] The court

---

[152] Huddleston v. United States, 485 U.S. 681, 691–692 (1988).

[153] *See, e.g.,* United States v. Gilan, 967 F.2d 776 (2d Cir. 1992); United States v. Bakke, 942 F.2d 977 (6th Cir. 1991); United States v. Morgan, 936 F.2d 1561 (10th Cir. 1991).

[154] *See* §§ 404.15–404.18, *supra.*

[155] *See* § 104.1 *et seq., supra.*

[156] *E.g.,* United States v. Lewis, 693 F.2d 189 (D.C. Cir. 1982); United States v. Melia, 691 F.2d 672 (4th Cir. 1982); United States v. Bailleaux, 685 F.2d 1105 (9th Cir. 1982). *But cf.* United States v. Yeagin, 927 F.2d 798 (5th Cir. 1991) (defendant's recanted claim of innocence in prior prosecution too prejudicial to be admitted; jury could have convicted on that evidence alone); United States v. Jackson, 886 F.2d 838 (7th Cir. 1989) (defendant's prior refusal to provide handwriting exemplars was admissible to prove knowledge of a scheme to alter postal money orders; danger of unfair prejudice too "conjectural;" evidence was unlikely to elicit an emotional response from the jury).

[157] *See* § 404.22, *infra.*

[158] *See generally,* 2 WEINSTEIN'S FEDERAL EVIDENCE § 404.21.

[159] Rule 404(b), Advisory Committee Note (concerning amendment effective December 1, 1991). *See generally,* 2 WEINSTEIN'S FEDERAL EVIDENCE § 404.23.

[160] United States v. Cardinas Garcia, 596 F.3d 788 (10th Cir. 2010) (when the Government's Rule 404(b) notice contained only the boilerplate assertion that an earlier drug

retains the discretion to disallow the evidence because of a lack of timeliness or completeness.

Rule 404(b) requires the Government to give notice of its intent to use evidence of "extrinsic acts" to reduce surprise and promote early resolution on the issue of admissibility, but that notice requirement does not apply to other acts of misconduct that are intrinsic — that is, part of the charged offense.[161]

The notice provision will afford the defense with the opportunity to prepare to seek possible exclusion of the evidence. If the evidence is admitted the notice provision will reduce surprise at trial, and it should allow the defense to prepare an effective cross-examination and rebuttal of the prosecution's evidence, thereby lessening the possibility that the jury will miscalculate the weight of such evidence.[162]

Also, any determination by the court on matters of probative worth or the concern for unfair prejudice should occur outside the hearing of the jury.[163]

§ 404.22   Limiting Instruction

In any case in which the court accepts the proponent's theory of the admissibility of evidence of an extrinsic act and proceeds to admit the act, the trial judge should be requested to provide the jury with a limiting instruction pursuant to Rule 105.[164] Such a limiting instruction would restrict the jury's consideration to the proper basis for admission. The instruction should admonish the jury that the evidence of the extrinsic act may not be considered as a basis for an inference that the individual in question acted in conformity with the individual's extrinsic conduct or with

---

sale was admissible to prove the defendant's "motive, opportunity, intent, preparation, plan, knowledge, identity, absence of mistake or accident and his consciousness of guilt," this scattershot approach failed to adequately frame the issue for opposing counsel and the court).

[161] United States v. Mahdi, 598 F.3d 883 (D.C. Cir. 2010) (evidence of drug conspiracy defendant's threatening use of a knife was properly admitted, even without pretrial notification to the defense, since it showed his organizational management and how he kept his subordinates in line, and was therefore "intrinsic" evidence with respect to the manner in which he committed the charged offense for which he was on trial).

[162] Rule 404(b), Advisory Committee Note (concerning amendment effective December 1, 1991).

[163] *See, e.g.,* United States v. Harrison, 679 F.2d 942 (D.C. Cir. 1982); United States v. Day, 591 F.2d 861 (D.C. Cir. 1978); *see also* Rule 103(d), which provides:

> **(d) Preventing the Jury from Hearing Inadmissible Evidence.** To the extent practicable, the court must conduct a jury trial so that inadmissible evidence is not suggested to the jury by any means.

See generally, 1 MCCORMICK, § 191.

[164] *See* United States v. Phillips, 599 F.2d 134 (6th Cir. 1979); United States v. Woods, 484 F.2d 127 (4th Cir. 1973).

the indicated character.[165]

---

[165] The limiting instruction should be narrowly tailored to indicate the special relevance to some consequential fact other than a propensity to engage in crime. A "laundry-list" instruction that merely recites the text of Rule 404(b)(2) may be insufficient to channel the jury's use of the criminal history. *See* United States v. Cortijo-Diaz, 875 F.2d 13 (1st Cir. 1989).

Chapter 405

Rule 405. Methods of Proving Character

Rule 405. Methods of Proving Character.

(a) **By Reputation or Opinion.** When evidence of a person's character or character trait is admissible, it may be proved by testimony about the person's reputation or by testimony in the form of an opinion. On cross-examination of the character witness, the court may allow an inquiry into relevant specific instances of the person's conduct.

(b) **By Specific Instances of Conduct.** When a person's character or character trait is an essential element of a charge, claim, or defense, the character or trait may also be proved by relevant specific instances of the person's conduct.

---

§ 405.1 Methods of Proving Character — In General

The function of Rule 405 is to designate the permissible method of proving character or a character trait.[1] Rule 405 does not address the issue of the admissibility of character evidence, and Rule 404 should be consulted for determining whether character evidence may be introduced in a particular case.

Rule 405 recognizes three devices for proving a person's character or character trait, but it should be noted that all methodologies of proof are not necessarily available to prove character in each instance in which character is admissible. The three contemplated methods of proof are: first, reputation within a pertinent community may be used to establish circumstantially the character of an individual; second, a person familiar with the character of an individual may provide opinion testimony as to the character in question;

---

[1] *See generally,* 1 McCORMICK, § 191; 2 WEINSTEIN'S FEDERAL EVIDENCE §§ 405.01–405.05; 1 MUELLER & KIRKPATRICK, §§ 119–122; 7 WIGMORE, §§ 1981–1986. *See also* Dunforth, Jr., *Death Knell for Pre-Trial Mental Examination? Privilege Against Self-Incrimination,* 19 RUTGERS L. REV. 489 (1965); Slough, *Relevancy Unraveled—Part II, Character and Habit Evidence,* 5 U. KAN. L. REV. 404 (1957); Curran, *Expert Psychiatric Evidence of Personality Traits,* 103 U. PA. L. REV. 999 (1955); Falknor & Steffey, *Evidence of Character: From the Crucible of the Community to the Couch of Psychiatrist,* 102 U. PA. L. REV. 980 (1954).

third, specific instances of conduct may be offered to establish the character of an individual. The use of a particular methodology depends upon the way in which character is used in conjunction with the issues of a case. Where character is "in issue,"[2] all methodologies of proving character are available.[3] Where character is used circumstantially to establish conforming conduct, only reputation and opinion evidence are available.[4] Where, however, character evidence is utilized to impeach the credibility of a witness, methodology of proof is governed by Rules 608 and 609.

Specific instances of conduct are available to prove character only when character is in issue because, as a general proposition, proof of specific instances of conduct has the greatest capacity to arouse prejudice, to confuse, to surprise, and to consume unnecessary time.[5] Consequently, such methodology of proof is reserved for the situation where character plays a pivotal role in the litigation, *i.e.,* when character is an *essential* element of a claim, charge, or a defense, and not merely because it is relevant to a claim or a defense.[6]

§ 405.2   Reputation Evidence Used to Prove Character

Reputation evidence is available to establish and rebut character in all situations where character is admissible under Rule 404. Reputation evidence, which is used to prove circumstantially the character trait sought to be proven, is the collective opinion of a particular community in regard to a person's character or trait.

The reputation of a person sought to be characterized is established through the testimony of a character witness. A person qualifies as a character witness where he or she is a member of a pertinent community in

---

[2] *See* Chapter 404, §§ 404.9, 404.10, *supra.*

[3] *See, e.g.,* Crumpton v. Confederation Life Ins. Co., 672 F.2d 1248 (5th Cir. 1982); Christy v. United States, 68 F.R.D. 375 (N.D. Tex. 1975); United States v. Dennis, 625 F.2d 782 (8th Cir. 1980).

[4] *See* United States v. Benedetto, 571 F.2d 1246 (2d Cir. 1978) (fact that defendant improperly attempted to establish his good character by reference to specific good acts did not justify prosecution's use of testimony concerning bad acts either in its direct case or on rebuttal); *accord* United States v. Herman, 589 F.2d 1191 (3d Cir. 1978); *see also* 2 WEINSTEIN'S FEDERAL EVIDENCE § 405.02; 1 MCCORMICK, § 191.

[5] *See* United States v. Lewis, 693 F.2d 189 (D.C. Cir. 1982); United States v. Cook, 538 F.2d 1000 (3d Cir. 1976); *see also* 1A WIGMORE, § 58.2.

[6] Gibson v. Mayor & Council of Wilmington, 355 F.3d 215 (3d Cir. 2004) (in wrongful termination action by police officer, the City did not make the officer's character "an essential element" of its defense; in explaining the reason for his dismissal, the City only offered evidence of the untruthful statements he made on one day he falsely called in sick, and "[t]here were no overarching allegations that he was otherwise a dishonest or lying cop," so the trial court correctly excluded rebuttal evidence by the plaintiff to show from his performance evaluations that he was commended for honesty and other good qualities on other occasions).

which the person characterized is known, and the character witness must know the reputation of the person sought to be characterized and be prepared to testify to such reputation within the community.[7] Traditionally, character witnesses must be familiar with a person's reputation in his or her residential community, but contemporary practice permits knowledge of the person's reputation in any relevant community, for example, a business community.[8]

The character witness testifying as to reputation should provide testimony specifically directed to a "pertinent trait" of the person characterized.[9] Accordingly, character evidence of a defendant's truth or veracity is not probative in a case charging him with conspiracy to sell drugs.[10] Nor is evidence of a witness's use of illegal drugs admissible in a case concerned with bank embezzlement.[11] Typically, evidence of a peaceful trait is appropriate for consideration in an assault case; similarly, the trait of honesty is pertinent in a perjury case.[12]

Limiting the scope of the character witness's testimony is critical, because it will ultimately define and limit the scope of cross-examination by opposing counsel. Reputation testimony should also relate to reputation at the time of the facts of the case rather than at the time of the trial.

§ 405.3   Opinion Evidence Used to Prove Character

Rule 405 departs from prior practice in providing for the availability of opinion testimony to establish and rebut the character of an individual. As stated in the Advisory Committee Note to Rule 405: "It seems likely that the persistence of reputation evidence is due to its largely being opinion in disguise."

The justification for opinion testimony is discussed by Wigmore:

---

[7] *See, e.g.,* United States v. Perry, 643 F.2d 38 (2d Cir. 1981).

[8] *See, e.g.,* United States v. Oliver, 492 F.2d 943 (8th Cir. 1974) ("courts have readily extended the concept of community to include the community in which one works, as well as where one lives"); *see also* United States v. Parker, 447 F.2d 826 (7th Cir. 1971) (error to exclude evidence of defendant's reputation among his co-workers, which may well be more significant than his reputation among neighbors, particularly if they are apartment dwellers).

[9] *See* United States v. Collins, 779 F.2d 1520 (11th Cir. 1986) (prosecution allowed to ask whether witness had heard of defendant's arrests when witness testified defendant was a law-abiding citizen); United States v. Angelini, 678 F.2d 380 (1st Cir. 1982); United States v. Hewitt, 634 F.2d 277 (5th Cir. 1981); *see also* Chapter 404 and § 404.8, *supra.*

[10] United States v. Jackson, 588 F.2d 1046 (5th Cir. 1979) (in prosecution for conspiracy to distribute and possess heroin, trial judge did not err in excluding character evidence as to defendant's truth and veracity); *see also* Aaron v. United States, 397 F.2d 584 (5th Cir. 1968) (false bank entries and embezzlement; improper to inquire of illicit affair with woman as wholly immaterial to the character traits involved, but instruction to disregard evidence cured error).

[11] Aaron v. United States, 397 F.2d 584 (5th Cir. 1968).

[12] *See* 1A WIGMORE, § 59; 1 MCCORMICK, § 191.

The Anglo-American rules of evidence have occasionally taken some curious twistings in the course of their development; but they have never done anything so curious in the way of shutting out evidential light as when they decided to exclude the person who knows as much as humanly can be known about the character of another [*i.e.,* firsthand opinion], and have still admitted the second-hand, irresponsible product of multiplied guesses and gossip which we term "reputation."[13]

While reputation is generally thought to be an effective method of proving character because it collects and summarizes all the minute details of a person's life, opinion evidence can be more effective in situations where a person is not well known within a community or where the community is so large that an individual's reputation is only minimally developed.

Opinion evidence is available in all cases where evidence of character or a trait of character is admissible. Like reputation evidence, opinion evidence must be offered through the testimony of a properly qualified character witness who possesses a firsthand basis for his or her opinion. A substantial familiarity with the person characterized is necessary.[14]

§ 405.4   Cross-examination of a Character Witness

The cross-examination of a character witness is governed by the second sentence of Rule 405(a), and on cross-examination, inquiry into relevant specific instances of conduct of the person characterized is permissible.[15] The purpose of cross-examination relating to specific instances of conduct is to test the qualifications of the character witness as to the basis for the reputation or opinion testimony. As stated by Professor Lilly:

Note that if the character witness has not heard of an unfavorable event, his familiarity with the accused's character is brought into question; if he has heard of the unfavorable event, but nonetheless states that the accused enjoys a good reputation, his standard for determining that the reputation is favorable is brought into question.[16]

---

[13] 7 WIGMORE, § 1986, at 244.

[14] *See, e.g.,* United States v. Perry, 643 F.2d 38 (2d Cir. 1981); United States v. Straughan, 453 F.2d 422 (8th Cir. 1972).

[15] *See* United States v. Mason, 993 F.2d 406 (4th Cir. 1993) (cross-examination of defendant's character witnesses as to whether defendant's assumed guilt of crime charged would affect their opinion was error); United States v. Wilson, 983 F.2d 221 (11th Cir. 1993) (where defendant admitted the wrongful charged conduct but denied having criminal intent, prosecution was permitted to ask defense character witnesses whether knowledge of defendant's wrongful conduct would change their opinions).

[16] LILLY, § 5.7, at 135. *See* United States v. Holt, 170 F.3d 698 (7th Cir. 1999) (prosecution may cross-examine defense character witnesses about specific acts by the defendant to test those witnesses' familiarity with his reputation).

Specific instances of conduct may be inquired into on cross-examination only if two criteria are satisfied. First, the instance of conduct must be relevant to the pertinent character trait in question.[17] Accordingly, an act of marital infidelity would not be appropriate for inquiry where the essential issue in the case is embezzlement.[18] Second, before cross-examination, the opponent of the character witness must satisfy the judge that he or she is proceeding in good faith in inquiring into the specific event. The cross-examiner must have a good-faith basis for the contention that the event actually occurred.[19] It should be noted that the cross-examiner may not introduce into evidence independent proof that the events occurred, and he or she is limited to inquiring about such events on cross-examination of the character witness where he or she has a good-faith basis for the inquiry.[20]

Questioning the character witness concerning prior instances of conduct of the person characterized may assume the traditional form: "Have you heard that Mr. X was caught in December of 1998 in an act of embezzlement?" Alternatively the cross-examiner may use the more contemporary form: "Do you know that Mr. X was caught in December of 1998 in an act of embezzlement?"[21]

Specific instances of conduct, where pertinent and supported by a demonstration of good faith, may include acts,[22] arrests,[23] and convictions.[24]

---

[17] *See* United States v. Adair, 951 F.2d 316 (11th Cir. 1992) (once a witness has testified as to the defendant's good character on direct, Rule 405 allows cross-examination as to the witness's knowledge of particular instances of conduct relevant to the trait in question).

[18] Aaron v. United States, 397 F.2d 584 (5th Cir. 1968) (false bank entries and embezzlement; improper to inquire of illicit affair with woman, since it was wholly immaterial to the character traits involved).

[19] United States v. Bright, 588 F.2d 504 (5th Cir. 1979); *see also* United States v. Reese, 568 F.2d 1246 (6th Cir. 1977) (court suggested that before permitting character witnesses to be asked whether they had heard of defendant previously buying stolen merchandise, better practice would have been for the trial judge to have had a voir dire examination to determine whether there were actually such rumors before permitting the cross-examination).

[20] *See* Michelson v. United States, 335 U.S. 469 (1948) (the Supreme Court, in a case that approaches constitutional significance, thoroughly discussed the theory and procedure for the cross-examination of character witnesses in criminal cases).

[21] *See* Advisory Committee Note, Rule 405; *see also* 1 MCCORMICK, § 191; Securities and Exchange Commission v. Peters, 978 F.2d 1162 (10th Cir. 1992) (opinion witnesses could be cross-examined as to specific instances of defendant's conduct in the form of "have you heard" questions).

[22] United States v. Glass, 709 F.2d 669 (11th Cir. 1983); United States v. Brown, 547 F.2d 438 (8th Cir. 1977).

[23] United States v. Watson, 587 F.2d 365 (7th Cir. 1978) (where defendant's character witness was asked about honesty of defendant, door was opened to cross-examination of witness concerning defendant's arrests; no error where defendant then withdrew character witness' testimony on direct and court advised jury of its final rule); United States v. Duhon, 565 F.2d 345 (5th Cir. 1978) (within trial judge's discretion to decide whether character

§ 405.5   Cross-examination of a Character Witness; Rule 105 and Rule 403

The questioning of a character witness concerning prior instances of conduct of the person characterized may result in unfair prejudice, confusion of the issues, and misleading the jury, *i.e.,* the trier of fact may inappropriately consider the prior instances of conduct in conjunction with making a determination of the operative facts of the case, rather than merely considering the conduct in ascribing weight to the testimony of the character witness. To minimize the prejudicial impact, a limiting instruction under Rule 105 may be requested.[25]

In the alternative, Rule 403 may be invoked in an attempt to preclude the inquiry entirely. Where the probative value of the evidence is extremely low in assessing the credibility of the character witness, and the risk of prejudice is high, exclusion under Rule 403 is appropriate.[26]

§ 405.6   Prior Instances of Conduct to Prove Character

According to Rule 405(b), prior instances of conduct may be used to prove or rebut character where character or a trait of character operates as an essential element of a charge, claim or defense, *i.e.,* where character is "in issue."[27] Where character is in issue, all methods of proving character are available.

---

witness could be cross-examined about defendant's arrest and indictment on an independent charge subsequent to events in instant case); United States v. Bermudez, 526 F.2d 89 (2d Cir. 1975) (proper to ask character witnesses in a cocaine case whether they had heard that defendant had been arrested the year before on a marijuana charge).

[24] Government of Virgin Islands v. Roldan, 612 F.2d 775 (3d Cir. 1979) (where limiting instruction not requested, failure to give an instruction does not constitute plain error); United States v. Edwards, 549 F.2d 362 (5th Cir. 1977) (court on cross-examination permitted character witness who testified he had known defendant for over 20 years to be asked if he had heard of 1950 conviction and arrests occurring more than 10 years prior to trial; court expressly refused to apply 10-year limitation of Rule 609); Harbin v. Interlake S.S. Co., 570 F.2d 99 (6th Cir. 1978).

[25] Government of Virgin Islands v. Roldan, 612 F.2d 775 (3d Cir. 1979); *see also* United States v. Tempesta, 587 F.2d 931 (8th Cir. 1978) (where there was no indication that trial court did not weigh the probative value against prejudice, no error in allowing inquiry about 1958 burglary).

[26] United States v. Polsinelli, 649 F.2d 793 (10th Cir. 1981); United States v. Hewitt, 663 F.2d 1381 (11th Cir. 1983); United States v. Davis, 546 F.2d 583 (5th Cir. 1977) (rarely and only upon a clear showing of prejudicial abuse will appellate courts disturb the rulings of trial courts in the admissibility of character evidence).

[27] *See, e.g.,* Schafer v. Time, Inc., 142 F.3d 1361 (11th Cir. 1998) (the determination of whether a trait of character is an essential element of a claim or defense is an issue of substantive law; if so, Rule 405 permits evidence of specific instances of conduct to prove that trait of character); United States v. Manzella, 782 F.2d 533 (5th Cir. 1986); Crumpton v. Confederation Life Ins. Co., 672 F.2d 1248 (5th Cir. 1982); Christy v. United States, 68 F.R.D. 375 (N.D. Tex. 1975); United States v. Dennis, 625 F.2d 782 (8th Cir. 1980). *But see* United States v. Gregg, 451 F.3d 930, 933–936 (8th Cir. 2006) (when a murder defendant

Specific instances of conduct may be established through the testimony of any person who has the requisite firsthand knowledge of the relevant specific acts of the person characterized.[28]

---

claims self-defense, evidence of the alleged victim's violent character is admissible to prove he was the first aggressor, but only in the form of opinion and reputation testimony; since "a victim's character is not an essential element of a defense of self-defense, evidence of a victim's character used to demonstrate the victim was the aggressor is circumstantial in nature" and therefore may not be proved with detailed evidence of specific acts of his violent conduct); United States v. Keiser, 57 F.3d 847 (9th Cir. 1995) (where defendant was charged with assault for shooting the victim, defendant claimed that he was acting in defense of his brother; trial court properly excluded testimony from defendant's brother concerning a violent outburst by the victim outside the courtroom during the trial; because victim's violent character was not an essential element of defendant's defense, Rule 405 limits the method of proving victim character evidence to opinion or reputation evidence).

[28] *See, e.g.,* United States v. Oliver, 492 F.2d 943 (8th Cir. 1974); United States v. Parker, 447 F.2d 826 (7th Cir. 1971); *see also* § 405.2, *supra.*

Chapter 406

Rule 406. Habit; Routine Practice

Rule 406. Habit; Routine Practice

Evidence of a person's habit or an organization's routine practice may be admitted to prove that on a particular occasion the person or organization acted in accordance with the habit or routine practice. The court may admit this evidence regardless of whether it is corroborated or whether there was an eyewitness.

---

§ 406.1   Habit Evidence — In General

Rule 406 addresses the admissibility of the habit of a natural person and the routine practice of a business or organization.[1] While the descriptive phrase "routine practice" is used in the Rule, the term "custom" can be used synonymously with "routine practice." Habits of persons and the routine practices or customs of organizations are equivalent in concept for the operation of Rule 406.

Rule 406 essentially serves two functions. First, the Rule confirms the relevance of habit or routine practice when used to establish conduct that conforms with the habit or routine practice. In this regard, Rule 406 is dissimilar from most other evidentiary rules. It essentially states a rule of admissibility rather than inadmissibility. Its function is declaratory in light of any confusion that might have been engendered by pre-Rule case law. The second function of Rule 406 is to abolish the "no-eyewitness" rule, which served to admit habit or routine practice evidence only if there were no eyewitnesses to testify on the matter.[2] Possibly prompted by a suspicion that habit and character evidence are impossible to distinguish, some courts may have employed such a rule as a compromise between admitting all propensity evidence used to show conforming conduct and foreclosing the

---

[1] *See generally,* 1A MCCORMICK, § 195; 2 WEINSTEIN'S FEDERAL EVIDENCE §§ 406.01–406.06; 2 MUELLER & KIRKPATRICK, §§ 123–126; 1A WIGMORE, §§ 92–97. *See also* Green, *Relevancy and Its Limits,* 1969 LAW AND THE SOCIAL ORDER 533 (1969); Lewan, *Rationale of Habit Evidence,* 16 SYRACUSE L. REV. 39 (1964); Slough, *Relevancy Unraveled,* 5 KAN. L. REV. 404 (1957); Note, *Relevancy and its Limits in the Proposed Rules of Evidence,* 16 WAYNE L. REV. 167 (1969).

[2] *See, e.g.,* Hawbaker v. Danner, 226 F.2d 843 (7th Cir. 1955).

admission of all habit and character evidence. Rule 406 wisely eliminates this limitation by its express terms.[3]

It is important to note that although Rule 406 affirms the *relevance*, and the implicit admissibility of habit and routine practice evidence,[4] the threshold admissibility of such evidence is still determined by Rules 402 and 403. Accordingly, Rule 403 may operate to exclude habit or routine practice evidence where its probative value is substantially outweighed by such counterweights as unfair prejudice or confusion of the issues.[5]

§ 406.2   Definition of Habit

McCormick has defined habit in this way:

"Habit" . . . denoted one's regular response to a repeated situation. If we speak of a character for care, we think of the person's tendency to act prudently in all the varying situations of life—in business, at home, in handling automobiles and in walking across the street. A habit, on the other hand, is the person's regular practice of responding to a particular kind of situation with a specific type of conduct. Thus, a person may be in the habit of bounding down a certain stairway two or three steps at a time, or of driving his automobile without using a seatbelt. The doing of the habitual act may become semi-automatic, as with a driver who invariably signals before changing lanes (footnotes omitted).[6]

Much of the analytical imprecision surrounding the admission of habit evidence results from a failure to adhere to a consistently applied definition of habit. In everyday parlance, the word "habit" is used in varying ways. What are frequently called "habitual acts" will only infrequently rise to the dignity of a habit as recognized by Rule 406.[7]

In order to establish the existence of a habit for the purpose of Rule 406, it must be shown that a person reacts to a certain situation with the frequency of a response that approaches invariability. It is critical that a specific stimulus and a corresponding response can be discretely identified.[8] Accord-

---

[3] *See* 2 MUELLER & KIRKPATRICK, § 123; 1 MCCORMICK, § 195.

[4] United States v. Holman, 680 F.2d 1340 (11th Cir. 1982).

[5] *See, e.g.,* United States v. Brechtel, 997 F.2d 1108 (5th Cir. 1993) (where two bank officers were charged with illegal action in savings and loan transactions, trial court excluded evidence that one of the officers habitually played a passive role in his real estate and stock investments because the evidence might have been confusing to the jury); Perrin v. Anderson, 784 F.2d 1040 (10th Cir. 1986) (court limited number of defendant's witnesses, even though the evidence was relevant to show habit, in order to prevent undue prejudice).

[6] 1 MCCORMICK, § 195, at 825–826.

[7] 1 MCCORMICK, § 195.

[8] *See* United States v. Arredondo, 349 F.3d 310 (6th Cir. 2004) (after federal prisoner claimed his lawyer never told him about plea offer from prosecutor, lawyer was properly

ingly, the Advisory Committee Note comments that evidence of intemperate "habits" is generally excluded when offered to establish inebriation on a particular occasion.[9] The fact that a person "habitually" drinks is insufficiently specific to satisfy the concept of habit embraced by Rule 406, because no stimulus can be identified that is specifically connected with a semi-automatic response.[10] Nevertheless, some courts have admitted evidence of intemperance "habits" when the facts have shown a high degree of regularity of the behavior.[11]

§ 406.3   Application of Habit Evidence

The relevance of habit evidence has been traditionally recognized. As discussed by McCormick:

> Character may be thought of as the sum of one's habits, although doubtless it is more than this. Unquestionably, the uniformity of one's response to habit is far greater than the consistency with which one's conduct conforms to character or disposition. Even though character comes in only exceptionally as evidence of an act, surely any sensible person in investigating whether a given individual did

---

allowed to testify that "he always passed on plea offers to clients." Since the lawyer had already represented five to fifteen criminal defendants in federal court at the time of his alleged omission, and had undertaken more representations since then, his testimony was admissible to show that he acted in conformity with that habit in this case); United States v. Angwin, 271 F.3d 786, 799 (9th Cir. 2001) (accused charged with transporting illegal aliens was properly barred from offering evidence of the training he received in the Coast Guard Auxiliary, which had supposedly "taught [him] to take the least confrontational course of action in potentially dangerous situations." The "proffered evidence of his training was not sufficiently reflexive and specific to constitute habit evidence. His response to dangerous situations—prudently taking the least confrontational course of action—is hardly reflexive or semi-automatic"); Camfield v. City of Oklahoma City, 248 F.3d 1214 (10th Cir. 2001) (testimony regarding alleged "habit" of police officer was properly excluded; "Announcing the seizure of child pornography upon walking into a video rental store is not a semi-automatic act and [can] not serve as a basis for habit evidence," and five incidents were insufficient to establish a habit).

[9] See Advisory Committee Note, Rule 406.

[10] See Reyes v. Missouri P. R. Co., 589 F.2d 791 (5th Cir. 1979) (four convictions for public intoxication spanning a three and one-half year period was of insufficient regularity to rise to the level of "habit" evidence). See also Thompson v. Boggs, 33 F.3d 847, 853–855 (7th Cir. 1994) (the plaintiff had failed to show that the defendant, a police officer, had used excessive force as a regular and semi-automatic response when making arrests and thus trial court did not err in not admitting evidence of other acts under Rule 406).

[11] See, e.g., Loughan v. Firestone Tire & Rubber Co., 749 F.2d 1519 (11th Cir. 1985) (testimony of several individuals, including plaintiff, that plaintiff drank between the hours of 9 A.M. and 5 P.M., admissible to show habit of daily inebriation; facts indicated sufficient regularity to rise to the level of "habit" indicated by Rule 406); Keltner v. Ford Motor Co., 748 F.2d 1265 (8th Cir. 1984) (evidence of plaintiff's drinking habits admitted because he regularly drank a six-pack of beer four nights a week; plaintiff characterized his own conduct as a "habit"); see also § 406.5, infra.

a particular act would be greatly helped in his inquiry by evidence as to whether that individual was in the habit of doing it.[12]

Habit evidence usually falls into the format of the proponent seeking to establish that a habitual response occurred on a particular occasion. In order to establish such a conclusion, the proponent of the habit evidence must first establish that the habit in fact exists.[13] After establishing the habit, the proponent of the evidence submits evidence which would prove that the stimulus for the habitual response occurred on a particular occasion. Habit evidence being relevant and presumptively admissible, the habitual response is circumstantially indicated.

Evidence of habit is often offered to demonstrate conduct in negligence cases. In such cases, habit can be offered for a litany of reasons: to prove identity and demonstrate that the defendant was the wrongdoer; to prove that a dangerous condition could not have existed or could not have been known; to prove that defendant had a duty to warn; or to prove that the careless action was actually committed. It is in this last area that confusion frequently arises because of the blurring between character and habit.[14] A specific careless act that is a function of habit is permitted by Rule 406, and consequently, it is crucial to distinguish habit from character in these contexts by identifying a response to a regularly repeated situation.[15]

§ 406.4 Application of Routine Practice Evidence

Evidence of business custom or routine practice offered to prove conforming conduct is generally admissible. Because the efficiency of many businesses and organizations depends upon the repetitive execution of certain acts, there is some assurance of reliability in accepting proof of this kind.

The routine practice of handling the mail is an example of this kind of evidence. If the mailroom procedures of a certain business are established, then these practices serve as proof of both the posting and receipt of individual letters. A requirement that direct testimony be given that an individual letter was received is absurd, especially in large organizations. The Rule expressly provides that such evidence is relevant whether

---

[12] 1 McCORMICK, § 195, at 826 n.7.

[13] *See* United States v. Sampol, 636 F.2d 621 (D.C. Cir. 1980); Reyes v. Missouri P. R. Co., 589 F.2d 791 (5th Cir. 1979).

[14] *See* § 404.1 *et seq., supra.*

[15] *See, e.g.,* Jones v. Southern Pac. R.R., 962 F.2d 447 (5th Cir. 1992) (in railroad accident case, plaintiff tried to establish that engineer had a habit of operating trains negligently because of nine different safety infractions over a twenty-nine year career; no error to exclude such evidence, as the regularity and frequency of the infractions did not rise to the level of habit).

corroborated or not.[16]

Many times, evidence of custom is used to establish an appropriate standard of care. When evidence of this kind is offered to demonstrate a legal standard and not to prove action in conformity with the conduct, Rule 406 is inapplicable. Admissibility would then be a general question of relevance to be determined under Rule 401 and Rule 402.

§ 406.5   Methodology of Proof

In order to capitalize upon habit evidence, the proponent of the evidence must establish the existence of the habit of the person in question or the routine practice of the organization.[17] In establishing the existence of the habit or routine practice, the proponent may utilize opinion testimony, or in the alternative, may establish the habit or routine practice through proof of specific instances of conduct sufficient in number to warrant a conclusion that the habit exists.[18] Proof of the existence of a habit is normally effected through the testimony of a person who has firsthand knowledge of the individual or organization whose habit or custom is sought to be established.[19] Likewise, the stimulus for the habitual response may be established through any witness possessing firsthand knowledge as required by Rule 602. Generally, the trial judge has broad discretion in determining whether

---

[16] Slough, *Relevancy Unraveled*, 5 KAN. L. REV. 404, 450–451 (1957) ("If the basic fact of posting must be proved by the direct testimony of the mailing clerk, then in large offices posting can seldom be proved. In the ordinary course of events no one will be able to testify, as of his own knowledge, that the letter was in fact posted. And if testimony is offered, more likely than not the witness will be perjuring himself . . . . Add to this the very real possibility that the mailing clerk, himself, will be unavailable as a witness. In good times the turnover in positions of this type is considerable, and the task of discovering long-lost mailing clerks will be burdensome as well as futile").

[17] *See* Karme v. Commissioner, 673 F.2d 1062 (9th Cir. 1982); United States v. General Foods Corp., 446 F. Supp. 740 (D.C.N.Y. 1978), *aff'd mem.*, 591 F.2d 1332 (1978) (to rebut allegations of Federal Food, Drug & Cosmetic Act, defendant may introduce evidence of routine customs involving established cleanup, sanitation, and maintenance procedures, if they fall within Rule 406).

[18] *See* Loughan v. Firestone Tire & Rubber Co., 749 F.2d 1519, 1524 (11th Cir. 1985) (it is only when examples offered to establish such pattern of conduct or habit are "numerous enough to base an inference of systematic conduct," that examples are admissible); Keltner v. Ford Motor Co., 748 F.2d 1265 (8th Cir. 1984) (instances of inebriation on specific nights were numerous enough to constitute "habit" evidence; court noted that Advisory Committee Note, in excluding intemperance evidence, is "at odds with the probability theory of habit seemingly adopted elsewhere in the Notes to Rule 406"); United States v. Holman, 680 F.2d 1340 (11th Cir. 1982) (a single instance of behavior does not indicate a habit of performing that behavior); Strauss v. Douglas Aircraft Co., 404 F.2d 1152 (2d Cir. 1968) (a single instance of faulty repairs to a plane not enough to infer habit of improperly repairing the plane in question; however, 191 instances of frayed cables on five different planes sufficient to support such an inference); Wells Fargo Business Credit v. Ben Kozloff Inc., 695 F.2d 940 (5th Cir. 1983).

[19] *See* Rule 602, Chapter 602, *infra.*

the foundation for the existence of the habit or custom is sufficient to warrant the inference of conforming conduct.

Chapter 407

Rule 407. Subsequent Remedial Measures

Rule 407. Subsequent Remedial Measures

When measures are taken that would have made an earlier injury or harm less likely to occur, evidence of the subsequent measures is not admissible to prove:

- negligence;

- culpable conduct;

- a defect in a product or its design; or

- a need for a warning or instruction.

But the court may admit this evidence for another purpose, such as impeachment or — if disputed — proving ownership, control, or the feasibility of precautionary measures.

---

§ 407.1   Subsequent Remedial Measures — In General

Rule 407 provides that evidence of remedial action taken after an alleged negligent act or omission will not be admissible to show negligence at the time the injury occurred.[1] The Rule excludes evidence of the subsequent remedial actions to prove negligence or any type of culpable conduct in connection with the event that caused injury.[2]

§ 407.2   Scope of Rule 407

Virtually any kind of subsequent remedial action is within the purview of Rule 407, and the Rule is not directed simply to the repair of a mechanical

---

[1] *See generally,* 2 McCormick, § 267; 2 Mueller & Kirkpatrick, §§ 127–133; 2 Weinstein's Federal Evidence §§ 407.01–407.10; 2 Wigmore, § 283. *See also* Fincham, *Federal Rule of Evidence 407 and Its State Variations: The Courts Perform Some Subsequent Remedial Measures of Their Own in Products Liability Cases,* 49 UMKC L. Rev. 388 (1981); Twerski, *Post-Accident Design Modification Evidence in Manufacturing Defect Setting: Strict Liability and Beyond,* 4 J. Prod. Liab. 143 (1981); Kaminsky, *Post Transaction Evidence in Securities Litigation,* 19 B.C.L. Rev. 617 (1978); Comment, *Chart v. General Motors Corp: Did It Chart the Way for Admission of Evidence of Subsequent Remedial Measures in Products Liability Actions?.* 41 Ohio St. L.J. 211 (1980).

[2] The Rule is largely declaratory of pre-existing law. *See* New York, L.E. & W.R.R. v. Madison, 123 U.S. 524 (1887); Columbia and P.S. R.R. v. Hawthorne, 144 U.S. 202 (1892).

device after it causes personal injury. For example, the Rule is sufficiently broad to apply to the discharge of an employee subsequent to an accident where it appeared to the employer that the employee was responsible for the accident.[3] Likewise, the Rule includes within its scope a change in company operating procedures after an accident.[4] As a basic principle the Rule will apply to any measure that, if taken prior to the accident, would have made the injury less likely to occur.[5] However, the Rule does not apply to remedial measures undertaken by a third party.[6]

As amended, Rule 407 makes it clear that its exclusionary principle applies only to remedial measures that are taken after the event that gave rise to the injury or harm. Thus, the rule cannot be used to exclude evidence of changes that are made subsequent to the manufacture or design of a product, but prior to the occurrence that causes injury.[7] However, as explained by the

---

[3] *See, e.g.,* Robbins v. Farmers Union Grain Terminal Ass'n, 552 F.2d 788 (5th Cir. 1977).

[4] *See* Hickman v. Gem Ins. Co., Inc., 299 F.3d 1208 (10th Cir. 2002) (in ERISA action against insurance company, the discontinuation of its disputed practice of limiting payment for hospital room and board charges was inadmissible, as the policy change constituted a subsequent remedial measure).

[5] HDM Flugservice GmbH v. Parker Hannifin Corp., 332 F.3d 1025 (6th Cir. 2003) (manufacturer's "service bulletin" advising users to make certain inspections before using equipment was not admissible to prove the inadequacy of the recommendations in the service manual); Stahl v. Novartis Pharms. Corp., 283 F.3d 254 (5th Cir. 2002) (pharmaceutical package insert including a warning that patients should undergo medical testing if they experienced certain side effects, a warning that was not included on the prior package insert, was inadmissible as a subsequent remedial measure); J.B. Hunt Transp. v. GM Corp., 243 F.3d 441 (8th Cir. 2001) (post-accident vehicle design change was inadmissible to prove fault as a subsequent remedial measure).

[6] *See* Diehl v. Blaw-Knox, 360 F.3d 426 (3d Cir. 2004) (Rule 407 does not exclude evidence of subsequent remedial measures taken by a party other than the defendant; in action against machine's manufacturer, evidence was admissible to prove that machine's owner improved its safety by changing its design after it injured plaintiff); Buchanna v. Diehl Machine, Inc., 98 F.3d 366 (8th Cir. 1996) (subsequent repairs by a third party are not covered by the exclusionary principle of Rule 407); Espeaignnette v. Gene Tierney Co., 43 F.3d 1, 5 & n.5 (1st Cir. 1994) (in suit by worker against the manufacturer of a saw, the trial court erred in excluding evidence that plaintiff's employer had added a safety feature to the saw); TLT-Babcock, Inc. v. Emerson Elec. Co., 33 F.3d 397, 400 (4th Cir. 1994) (noting that third parties "will not be inhibited from taking remedial measures if such actions are allowed into evidence against a defendant"); O'Dell v. Hercules, Inc., 904 F.2d 1194 (8th Cir. 1990) ("exception to Rule 407 is recognized for evidence of remedial action mandated by superior government authority or undertaken by a third party because the policy goal of encouraging remediation would not necessarily be furthered by exclusion of such evidence"); Pau v. Yosemite Park and Curry Co., 928 F.2d 880 (9th Cir. 1991) (remedial action taken by third party instead of defendant does not come within Rule 407).

[7] *See* Chase v. General Motors Corp., 856 F.2d 17, 21–22 (4th Cir. 1988) (interpreting Rule 407 to exclude evidence of a product recall that occurred after the date of the accident, but not to exclude evidence of a change in design that occurred prior to the accident). As the *Chase* court explained, the reason for excluding evidence of measures taken after the accident

Advisory Committee, such evidence may still be excluded under Rule 403 if it offers so great a danger of prejudice or confusion so as to outweigh the probative value of the evidence.

§ 407.3   Policy of Rule 407

Rule 407 is supported by two underpinnings. First, evidence of subsequent remedial actions is thought to have low or nonexistent probative value in establishing negligence, *i.e.,* subsequent remedial actions need not be admissions of culpability. Wigmore has analyzed the concept:

> If machines, bridges, sidewalks, or other objects, never caused corporal injury except through the negligence of their owner, then his act of improving their condition, after the happening of an injury thereat, would indicate a belief on his part that the injury was caused by his negligence. But the assumption is plainly false; injuries may be, and constantly are, caused by reason of inevitable accident, and also by reason of contributory negligence of the injured person.[8]

Wigmore's views notwithstanding, subsequent remedial actions may have some degree of probative value under a standard as liberal as Rule 401,[9] and a justification for excluding remedial actions solely on the basis of probative value is unimpressive. Unquestionably, remedial action does alter the probabilities of negligence or culpability in certain cases even in light of the non-culpable motivations that might compel a remedial action.

The second justification for Rule 407 is based upon the extrinsic social policy of encouraging remedial action, and under this policy, truth-seeking through the evidentiary system is subordinated to the higher social value of encouraging remedial action.[10] The justification is not without its critics. As Judge Weinstein has stated:

> The rationale that corrective action will not be taken in the absence of an exclusionary rule of evidence is weak in some respects. The underlying assumption is that defendants will not take remedial measures because their corrective actions might be used in evidence at a future trial. However, not every defendant will be aware of the possibility that subsequent remedial measures might constitute an admission.

> Of those likely to be aware of the rule, it is unlikely that a responsible insured defendant would refrain deliberately from tak-

---

is that the issue in a products liability action is whether "the manufacturer use[d] reasonable care in designing and manufacturing the product at the time it was marketed, not whether it . . . later has been made better or more safe." *See* 856 F.2d at 20.

[8]   2 WIGMORE, § 283, at 174.

[9]   *See* § 401.3, *supra.*

[10]   *See* Rule 407, Advisory Committee Note.

ing action to prevent the recurrence of subsequent serious injuries merely because in any subsequent case, evidence of the earlier accident would be admissible to show that defendant knew of a dangerous condition.[11]

Consistent with Judge Weinstein's evaluation, it should be appreciated that the basic evidentiary principle embodied in Rule 407 was developed primarily to apply to industrial accidents.[12] The litigation of such accidents now is generally governed and limited by workers' compensation where negligence is largely irrelevant.[13] Today, the Rule more frequently applies in the context of manufacturers' liability actions, and the justification for the exclusion of evidence in this area is considerably less impressive.[14]

§ 407.4   Admissible Remedial Actions

As the second sentence of Rule 407 indicates, exclusion of the evidence of subsequent remedial actions is only required where the evidence is offered to establish negligence or culpable conduct. A specific inferential pattern is prohibited,[15] and evidence of the subsequent remedial action may be offered to establish other relevant issues within a case such as ownership, control, or feasibility of precautionary measures.[16] For remedial actions to be admis-

---

[11] 2 WEINSTEIN'S FEDERAL EVIDENCE § 407.03.

[12] *See* 2 WEINSTEIN'S FEDERAL EVIDENCE § 407.02; *see also* General Motors Corp. v. Holler, 150 F.2d 297 (8th Cir. 1945) (glass booth installed to protect employees from noxious fumes; reversal required); Antietam Paper Co. v. Womble, 294 F. 795 (5th Cir. 1923) (machine redesigned).

[13] *See* 2 WEINSTEIN'S FEDERAL EVIDENCE § 407.02; 2 MUELLER & KIRKPATRICK, § 127.

[14] *See* § 407.5, *infra*; Prentiss & Carlisle Co. v. Koehring-Waterous Div. of Timberjack, Inc., 972 F.2d 6 (1st Cir. 1992) (defendant's investigative analysis of tree harvester wiring after the accident was admissible under Rule 407 because it was not a "measure"); Kelly v. Crown Equipment Co., 970 F.2d 1273 (3d Cir. 1992) (in products liability action, Rule 407 bars admission of post-manufacture, pre-accident design change in forklift); Raymond v. Raymond Corp., 938 F.2d 1518 (1st Cir. 1991) (Rule 407 does not apply in cases where the defendant designed the modification); Chase v. General Motors Corp., 856 F.2d 17 (4th Cir. 1988) (involuntary recall held inadmissible in products liability suit against automobile manufacturer; Fourth Circuit noted that Rule 407 is based on the premise that subsequent remedial action is not an admission of past negligence); Cates v. Sears, Roebuck & Co., 928 F.2d 679 (5th Cir. 1991) (defendant's warning issued one year after plaintiff bought item and one year before accident was not a subsequent remedial measure); Vander Missen v. Kellogg-Citizens Nat'l Bank of Green Bay, 481 F. Supp. 742 (E.D. Wis. 1979).

[15] The inferential pattern may be diagrammed as:

| Remedial | —>> | Negligence or |
| Measure | | Culpability |

[16] *See, e.g.,* Public Serv. Co. v. Bath Iron Works, 773 F.2d 783 (7th Cir. 1985); Rimkus v. Northwest Colorado Ski Corp., 706 F.2d 1060 (10th Cir. 1983); Anderson v. Malloy, 700 F.2d 1208 (8th Cir. 1983); Rozier v. Ford Motor Co., 573 F.2d 1332 (5th Cir. 1978)

sible, such issues must be controverted in the case, and, of course, the remedial action must be probative of the controverted consequential facts.[17] Also, a subsequent remedial measure may be offered to contradict and impeach the credibility of a witness where the witness has testified as to the condition of the instrumentality of the injury.[18]

As one commentator has indicated, the breadth of these exceptions creates the potential for the admissibility of subsequent remedial actions in virtually any case:

> Opportunities for circumventing the purpose of the Rule are legion, and it is quite evident that admission or exclusion will be judged on the basis of subtle trial maneuvers. By the process of exaggeration in placing undue emphasis upon the importance of physical details, the plaintiff may force the defendant to dispute his contentions, thus

(document prepared by defendant in anticipation of a revised safety standard to be required by National Highway Traffic Safety Administration did not meet exclusion rationale of Rule 407).

[17] *E.g.,* Albrecht v. Baltimore & O. R.R., 808 F.2d 329 (4th Cir. 1987) (evidence showing the defendant destroyed the ladder immediately after the accident was probative of a showing the defendant was negligent); Hull v. Chevron U.S.A., 812 F.2d 584 (10th Cir. 1987) (trial court properly excluded evidence not in dispute); Grenada Steel Indus. v. Alabama Oxygen Co., 695 F.2d 883 (5th Cir. 1983); Haynes v. American Motors Corp., 691 F.2d 1268 (8th Cir. 1982); Hall v. American S.S. Co., 688 F.2d 1062 (6th Cir. 1982); *see also* Falknor, *Extrinsic Policies Affecting Admissibility,* 10 RUTGERS L. REV. 574 (1956).

[18] *See* Wood v. Morbark Industries, Inc., 70 F.3d 1201 (11th Cir. 1995) (where trial court had granted defendant's motion *in limine* to exclude evidence of a post-accident design change, plaintiff should have been permitted to impeach defendant with evidence of the change after defendant testified that no design changes had been made); Harrison v. Sears, Roebuck and Co., 981 F.2d 25 (1st Cir. 1992) (in products liability action, trial court properly excluded evidence of a design change in the equipment after defendant's tool design expert testified there was nothing hazardous on the equipment; although plaintiff intended to use the evidence only to impeach the expert's testimony, the evidence did not directly impeach the testimony and would have been prejudicial to defendant); Pitasi v. Stratton Corp., 968 F.2d 1558 (2d Cir. 1992) (in ski slope accident, subsequent measures held admissible to rebut defense of contributory negligence and for impeachment); Petree v. Victor Fluid Power, Inc., 887 F.2d 34 (3d Cir. 1989) (defendant's decal warning of a projectile hazard was admissible for impeachment purposes where defendant claimed that the danger had been designed out of the product before the product was sold to the plaintiff's company); Bickerstaff v. South Cent. Bell Tel., 676 F.2d 163 (5th Cir. 1982); *see also* Dollar v. Long Mfg., 561 F.2d 613 (5th Cir. 1977) (reversible error for trial judge not to have permitted plaintiffs to impeach defendant's design engineer in products liability case by asking him about letter he had sent to dealers warning them of "death dealing propensities" of product when used in the fashion employed in instant case). *But see In re* Consolidation Coal Co., 123 F.3d 126, 136–137 (3d Cir. 1997) (although evidence of subsequent remedial measures may be introduced for impeachment purposes, such evidence can only be introduced when the evidence offered directly contradicts the witness's testimony).

paving the way for admission of proof of subsequent repair.[19]

The problems created by admitting remedial action for reasons other than to show negligence or culpable conduct may be tempered by judicious application of Rule 403.[20] Where the subsequent remedial action is only minimally probative of an issue other than negligence or culpability, the trial judge possesses discretion to exclude the evidence of the remedial action on the basis of prejudice, confusion of the issues, or misleading the jury.[21] At the very least, the trial judge should provide a limiting instruction pursuant to Rule 105 where evidence of remedial action is admitted on a theory of relevance outside the inferential pattern prohibited in the first sentence of Rule 407.[22]

The greatest caution must be exercised in interpreting the rule's exception for evidence ostensibly offered for "impeachment" of the defendant's witnesses. As one court has sensibly observed, this exception "must be read narrowly, lest it swallow the rule."[23] If this exception were applied too loosely it would eviscerate the rule, since some might be tempted to argue that evidence of subsequent remedial measures contradicts and in some sense "impeaches" the testimony of the defendant's witnesses in every case.[24] This exception has been narrowly confined to evidence of remedial measures that is "necessary to prevent the jury from being misled," and is available only if the evidence directly contradicts the testimony of the witness being impeached.[25] Even if the defendant's witnesses offer testi-

---

[19] Slough, *Relevancy Unraveled—Art. III: Remote and Prejudicial Evidence,* 5 KAN. L. REV. 675, 707–708 (1956).

[20] *See* Chapter 403, *supra.* As stated in one commentary: "the principal impact of Rule 407 is not so much in keeping evidence out altogether as it is in limiting the uses to which the evidence may be put. Unless outweighed by the 'danger' or 'considerations' described in Rule 403, the proof usually gets in." 2 MUELLER & KIRKPATRICK, § 127.

[21] *See* Gardner v. Chevron U.S.A., 675 F.2d 658 (5th Cir. 1982).

[22] *See* Chapter 105, *supra; see also* Bauman v. Volkswagenwerk Aktiengesellschaft, 621 F.2d 230 (6th Cir. 1980).

[23] Minter v. Prime Equip. Co., 451 F.3d 1196, 1211–1213 (10th Cir. 2006).

[24] Of course, evidence of subsequent remedial measures would not logically do anything to impeach or discredit the defendant's position, or the testimony of defense witnesses, in the extremely common situation in which the defense merely asserts that its products or premises were reasonably safe at the time of the plaintiff's injury. The first sentence of Rule 407 makes it plain that subsequent remedial measures may never be used as evidence to contradict a claim like that. The impeachment exception is limited to situations in which the defense makes the mistake of claiming something much more specific than a bare denial of negligence or fault.

[25] Minter v. Prime Equip. Co., 451 F.3d 1196, 1211–1213 (10th Cir. 2006) (citations omitted); *see also In re* Air Crash Disaster, 86 F.3d 498, 531 (6th Cir. 1996) (subsequent design changes to correct deficiencies is admissible to rebut a witness's claim that the product was "state of the art"); Wood v. Morbark Indus., Inc., 70 F.3d 1201, 1208 (11th Cir. 1995) (subsequent modifications can be introduced to rebut testimony that "left the jury with the

mony that opens the door to the admission of evidence of remedial measures for impeachment purposes under this rule, the trial judge retains the discretion to exclude such evidence under Rule 403 because of its inherent capacity for unfair prejudice.[26]

§ 407.5   Application of Rule 407 in Products Liability Actions

Prior to 1997, there was tension and debate among the circuit courts as to whether Rule 407 should apply in products liability actions. Advocates of admitting evidence of a subsequent remedial measure in a products liability case argued that a strict liability claim does not require proof that a manufacturer was negligent, but only proof that the product was in a defective condition and unreasonably dangerous when it left the possession of the manufacturer.[27] Hence, because the plaintiff need not prove manufacturer negligence, evidence of subsequent remedial measures should be admissible to prove the defect in the product that injured the plaintiff. Further, they argued, a rational business will not risk millions of dollars in liability that may result from further injuries in order to avoid creating evidence of subsequent remedial measures.[28]

As amended, however, Rule 407 sides with those who favored excluding evidence of subsequent remedial measures in products liability actions.[29] Under the Rule, evidence of subsequent remedial measures may not be used to prove either the existence of a defect in a product or in its design or the necessity for a warning or instruction to accompany the product. The Rule

---

impression that [the defendant] had made no modifications to the [product]"); Polythane Sys., Inc. v. Marina Ventures Int'l., Ltd., 993 F.2d 1201, 1210–1211 (5th Cir. 1993) (subsequent modifications are admissible to impeach testimony that the product was "one of the strongest in the world").

[26] Stecyk v. Bell Helicopter Textron, Inc., 295 F.3d 408 (3d Cir. 2002) (even after defendant manufacturer of Osprey aircraft argued at trial that two-way seal was difficult to install and "not suited for the military environment," trial judge retained the discretion to refuse to admit evidence that the manufacturer in fact made such a change in its design after the crash at issue in the case, in light of other evidence already before the jury that could be used to impeach the defendant on this point).

[27] *See* RESTATEMENT (SECOND) OF TORTS, § 402(a).

[28] *See, e.g.,* Haynes v. American Motors Corp., 691 F.2d 1268 (8th Cir. 1982); Unterburger v. Snow Inc., 630 F.2d 599 (8th Cir. 1980).

[29] *E.g.,* Buchanna v. Diehl Machine, Inc., 98 F.3d 366 (8th Cir. 1996); Wood v. Morbark Industries, Inc., 70 F.3d 1201 (11th Cir. 1995); Raymond v. Raymond Corp., 938 F.2d 1518, 1522 (1st Cir. 1991); *In re* Joint Eastern District and Southern District Asbestos Litigation v. Armstrong World Industries, Inc., 995 F.2d 343 (2d Cir. 1993); Cann v. Ford Motor Co., 658 F.2d 54, 60 (2d Cir. 1981); Kelly v. Crown Equipment Co., 970 F.2d 1273, 1275 (3d Cir. 1992); Werner v. Upjohn, Inc., 628 F.2d 848 (4th Cir. 1980); Grenada Steel Industries, Inc. v. Alabama Oxygen Co., Inc., 695 F.2d 883 (5th Cir. 1983); Bauman v. Volkswagenwerk Aktiengesellschaft, 621 F.2d 230, 232 (6th Cir. 1980); Flaminio v. Honda Motor Company, Ltd., 733 F.2d 463, 469 (7th Cir. 1984); Gauthier v. AMF, Inc., 788 F.2d 634, 636–37 (9th Cir. 1986).

thus adopts the traditional Wigmore view and recognizes that this type of evidence is at best irrelevant and at worst highly prejudicial.[30] The Rule also ensures that the plaintiff retains the burden of persuasion in a products liability action.[31]

The scope of the Rule 407 exclusion should not be forgotten, however, particularly in products liability actions. The rule only excludes evidence of subsequent remedial measures when such evidence is offered to prove "a defect in a product or its design; or a need for a warning or instruction." If the evidence is offered for other reasons, including proving the feasibility of precautionary measures or other reasons identified in the second sentence of Rule 407, then its admission is not barred by Rule 407. The evidence may still be deemed inadmissible, though, if its potential for prejudice or confusion substantially outweighs the probative value of the evidence, as discussed under Rule 403.[32]

---

[30] *See, e.g., In re* Asbestos Litigation, 995 F.2d 343 (2d Cir. 1993) (evidence that defendant had placed warnings on products twelve years after decedent's exposure to the products held inadmissible pursuant to Rule 407); Harrison v. Sears, Roebuck and Co., 981 F.2d 25 (1st Cir. 1992) (in products liability action, trial court properly excluded evidence of a design change in the equipment after defendant's tool design expert testified there was nothing hazardous on the equipment; although plaintiff intended to use the evidence only to impeach the expert's testimony, the evidence did not directly impeach the testimony and would have been prejudicial to defendant); Chase v. General Motors Corp., 856 F.2d 17 (4th Cir. 1988) (involuntary recall held inadmissible in products liability suit against automobile manufacturer); Roberts v. Harnischfeger Corp., 901 F.2d 42 (5th Cir. 1989) (Rule 407 does not prohibit testimony regarding remedial measures taken after a product was manufactured and purchased, but prior to the injury; nonetheless, in this products liability case, design changes were found to be irrelevant to the reasonableness of the design at the time of manufacture); Grenada Steel Indus. v. Alabama Oxygen Co., 695 F.2d 883 (5th Cir. 1983); Hall v. American S.S. Co., 688 F.2d 1062 (6th Cir. 1982); Werner v. Upjohn Co., 628 F.2d 848 (4th Cir. 1980); *see also* Knight v. Otis Elevator Co., 596 F.2d 84 (3d Cir. 1979) (evidence of placing guards around elevator buttons subsequent to accident properly excluded).

[31] Opponents of admission of subsequent remedial measures in products liability actions feel that if such evidence is admitted, the defendant would be required to prove its own due care in order to lessen the adverse impact caused by admitting the evidence, thereby improperly placing the burden of persuasion on the defendant. *See* Birnbaum, *Growing Trend to Deny Admission of Post-Accident Remedial Measures,* NAT'L L.J. 18 (July 23, 1979).

[32] *See* Middleton v. Harris Press & Shear, Inc., 796 F.2d 747 (5th Cir. 1986) (employer's modification of baler after the accident excluded under Rule 403 as unfairly prejudicial); *see also* Grenada Steel Indus. v. Alabama Oxygen Co., 695 F.2d 883 (5th Cir. 1983); Lindsay v. Ortho Pharmaceutical Corp., 637 F.2d 87 (2d Cir. 1980); 2 WEINSTEIN'S FEDERAL EVIDENCE § 407.08.

Chapter 408

Rule 408. Compromise Offers and Negotiations

Rule 408. Compromise Offers and Negotiations

   (a) **Prohibited Uses.** Evidence of the following is not admissible — on behalf of any party — either to prove or disprove the validity or amount of a disputed claim or to impeach by a prior inconsistent statement or a contradiction:

       (1) furnishing, promising, or offering — or accepting, promising to accept, or offering to accept — a valuable consideration in compromising or attempting to compromise the claim; and

       (2) conduct or a statement made during compromise negotiations about the claim — except when offered in a criminal case and when the negotiations related to a claim by a public office in the exercise of its regulatory, investigative, or enforcement authority.

   (b) **Exceptions.** The court may admit this evidence for another purpose, such as proving a witness's bias or prejudice, negating a contention of undue delay, or proving an effort to obstruct a criminal investigation or prosecution.

---

§ 408.1 Compromise Offers and Negotiations — In General

The primary purpose of Rule 408 is to provide for the inadmissibility of evidence relating to an offer of compromise or to a completed compromise. Rule 408 also generally precludes the admissibility of evidence of conduct or statements made during the course of compromise negotiation.[1] The Rule is designed to promote free and open discussion in the course of settlement negotiations with the ultimate objective of encouraging settlements,[2] and it

---

[1] Until recently, this prohibition was absolute, although a recent amendment to the rule, effective December 1, 2006, creates a new exception for statements made during attempts to settle "a claim by a public office or agency in the exercise of regulatory, investigative, or enforcement authority," Rule 408(a)(2), if those statements are later offered at a criminal trial. This amendment is discussed in § 408.6, *infra*.

[2] *See* 2 WEINSTEIN'S FEDERAL EVIDENCE § 408.02; *see also* United States v. Davis, 596 F.3d 852 (D.C. Cir. 2010) (trial court erred in permitting fraternity's treasurer to testify that the defendant, after being confronted with allegation of $29,000 in missing funds, supposedly

represents an extension of generally recognized law concerning the admissibility of settlement negotiations.[3]

§ 408.2   Policy of Rule 408

Two policies have been advanced supporting the exclusionary principle of Rule 408. First, it has been suggested that evidence of an offer of settlement has little or no probative value because the offer may be an indication of a desire for resolution rather than an admission of culpability or weakness of position. As Wigmore has stated:

> The true reason for excluding an offer of compromise is that it *does not* ordinarily proceed from and *imply a specific belief that the adversary's claim is well founded*, but rather a belief that the further prosecution of that claim, whether well founded or not, would in any event cause such annoyance as is preferably avoided by the payment of the sum offered. In short, the offer implies merely a desire for peace, not a concession of wrong done.[4]

McCormick, however, has more correctly analyzed the relevance of an offer of settlement as varying in probative value:

> [T]he relevancy of the offer will vary according to circumstances, with a very small offer of payment to settle a very large claim being much more readily construed as a desire for peace rather than an admission of weakness of position. Relevancy would increase, however, as the amount of the offer approached the amount claimed.[5]

Under the liberal standard of relevance contained in Rule 401, it is difficult to argue that offers of settlement have no probative value whatsoever, and a theory of inadmissibility based solely on irrelevance is

---

responded: "Can we just split this $29,000.00 and make this situation just go away?" Government's position that the evidence was admissible to show his consciousness of guilt was a concession that the evidence was improperly used as evidence of his criminal liability, explicitly forbidden by Rule 408); Pierce v. F.R. Tripler & Co., 955 F.2d 820 (2d Cir. 1992) (evidence of a new job offer by employer to an employee who had filed a complaint with the EEOC held inadmissible since it could "inhibit settlement discussions and interfere with the effective administration of justice"); Cassino v. Reichhold Chem., 817 F.2d 1338 (9th Cir. 1987); Ward v. Allegheny Ludlum Steel Corp., 560 F.2d 579 (3d Cir. 1979) (employee charged that labor union and employer had failed to accommodate his religious beliefs; evidence that employee had offered to reimburse company for expenses it would incur in hiring substitutes should not be admitted); *see, e.g.,* Thomas v. Resort Health Related Facility, 539 F. Supp. 630 (E.D.N.Y. 1982).

[3] *See* West v. Smith, 101 U.S. 263 (1879); Insurance Companies v. Weides, 81 U.S. (14 Wall.) 375 (1872) (a compromise, proposed or accepted, is not evidence of an admission of the amount of the debt).

[4] 4 WIGMORE, § 1061, at 36.

[5] 2 MCCORMICK, § 266, at 194.

unimpressive. The better justification advanced for the inadmissibility of settlement negotiations is the extrinsic social policy of promoting the settlement of disputes and resolving conflicts, and this latter policy predominates in supporting Rule 408.[6]

§ 408.3 Scope of Rule 408

Rule 408 provides for the exclusion of settlement offers and demands, regardless of whether they were accepted or rejected. Rule 408 also comprehends "collateral admissions" within its exclusionary scope, and may be invoked to exclude collateral conduct and statements made during compromise negotiations.[7] The policy for including factual statements made in the course of negotiations within the exclusionary scope of Rule 408 is summarized by McCormick:

> This traditional doctrine of denying the protection of the exclusionary rule to statements of fact had serious drawbacks, however. It discouraged freedom of communication in attempting compromise and, taken with its exceptions, involved difficulties of application.[8]

The inadmissibility of collateral admissions alters pre-Rule case law,[9] under which collateral admissions were not insulated from admissibility unless they were stated hypothetically, *i.e.,* "admitted without prejudice" or "admitted for the sake of compromise discussions only."[10] The Advisory Committee rejected this approach as overly formalistic, excessively oppressive and otherwise unsound.[11]

The rule is broadly written to accomplish its objectives of encouraging robust and uninhibited settlement discussions. Evidence of an offer to settle a disputed claim is not admissible, regardless of whether settlement

---

[6] *See* Rule 408, Advisory Committee Note.

[7] *See* American Ins. Co. v. North Am. Co., 697 F.2d 79 (2d Cir. 1982); United States v. Contra Costa County Water Dist., 678 F.2d 90 (9th Cir. 1982); Ramada Dev. Co. v. Rauch, 644 F.2d 1097 (5th Cir. 1981). As to whether Rule 408 applies to plea bargaining, *see* 2 MUELLER & KIRKPATRICK, § 134. *See also* United States v. Verdoorn, 528 F.2d 103 (8th Cir. 1976).

[8] 2 MCCORMICK, § 266, at 196.

[9] *E.g.,* Factor v. Commissioner, 281 F.2d 100 (9th Cir. 1960) (taxpayer's statements at settlement meetings admissible, since offer of payment was not accompanied by denial of liability); Cooper v. Brown, 126 F.2d 874 (3d Cir. 1942) (income statements submitted by defendant during negotiations for compromise of partnership accounting); accord Albert Hanson Lumber Co. v. United States, 261 U.S. 581 (1923); Nebraska Drillers, Inc. v. Westchester Fire Ins. Co., 123 F. Supp. 678 (D. Col. 1954).

[10] *E.g., In re* Evansville Television, 286 F.2d 65 (7th Cir. 1961) (counsel conducted negotiations contingent upon their being inadmissible); Nebraska Drillers, Inc. v. Westchester Fire Ins., 123 F. Supp. 678 (D. Col. 1954) (collected cases). *See generally,* 2 MUELLER & KIRKPATRICK, § 135.

[11] *See* Rule 408, Advisory Committee Note.

negotiations actually follow, and even if the other party immediately replies with a refusal to negotiate.[12]

The rule forbids the use of settlement efforts even if they are only offered "to impeach [a witness] by a prior inconsistent statement or contradiction."[13] Thus, the rule applies if statements made during compromise efforts are offered either as substantive evidence or merely to impeach the testimony of a witness who testifies at trial in a way that is arguably inconsistent with what that witness or his lawyer allegedly said during compromise negotiations.

Nor does it matter which side of the case is offering the evidence. Where compromise evidence is covered by this rule, it may not be offered at trial by either party to the negotiation. Of course, it would usually be the opposing party who would try to bring to the jury's attention the amount that the opponent had offered or demanded to settle the claim, because of the way such facts are usually prejudicial to the party who made such overtures. But Rule 408 applies even in the relatively rare case in which parties seek to admit their own settlement offers or statements made by them during settlement talks.[14] Thus, for example, if the defendant offers a sum of money to settle a claim, neither side — not even the defendant — can advise the jury of that offer for the purpose of trying to prove the true value of the plaintiff's claim.

Rule 408, like most rules of evidence, explicitly defines only when evidence is admissible and not whether it is discoverable.[15] But at least one court has been persuaded that the policies underlying the rule require the recognition of a privilege to shield such statements from discovery by third parties in other litigation.[16]

---

[12] United States v. Davis, 596 F.3d 852 (D.C. Cir. 2010) ("It makes no sense to force the party who initiates negotiations to do so at his peril.")

[13] Rule 408(a). Other forms of impeachment may be allowed, however. Rule 408(b) specifically approves the use of such evidence, for example, to show "a witness's bias or prejudice." See § 408.5, infra.

[14] Allowing parties to admit their own statements would unfairly disclose to the jury that the other party had evidently been willing to participate in compromise negotiations, and would unwisely embroil the courts in motions to disqualify attorneys on the grounds that they had become witnesses to admissible testimony. See Committee Note to the 2006 amendment to Rule 408. The applicability of Rule 408 to such cases is of course very rarely litigated. Defendants rarely desire to let the jury know how much they offered to settle a case, since it will always be more, usually much more, than what they urge the jury to give the plaintiff.

[15] Apart from the special case of the privilege rules, evidence is not ordinarily undiscoverable merely because it is inadmissible. See Rule 1101(c); Fed. R. Civ. P. 26(b)(1) (relevant evidence, unless privileged, is discoverable regardless of its admissibility); Fed. R. Civ. P. 30(c)(2) (a lawyer ordinarily may not instruct his client to refuse to answer a question, except "when necessary to preserve a privilege").

[16] Goodyear Tire & Rubber Co. v. Chiles Power Supply, Inc., 332 F.3d 976 (6th Cir.

While Rule 408 expands upon pre-existing law, the limitations of the scope of the Rule should be appreciated. The rule does not apply to all statements between potential adversaries, but only to those things said between them once they have begun efforts to settle some claim.[17] The exclusionary principle is inapplicable where a dispute does not exist as to liability or the amount of the claim.[18] The Rule cannot be invoked where settlement discussions relate to an amount that is admittedly due.[19] Either the amount or the validity of the claim must be contested in order for the exclusionary principle to apply.[20] As stated by McCormick:

> An offer to pay an admitted claim is not privileged since there is no policy of encouraging compromises of undisputed claims. They should be paid in full. If the validity of the claim and the amount due are undisputed, an offer to pay a lesser sum in settlement or to pay in installments would accordingly be admissible.[21]

Another limitation on the rule should be noted with care. When a party makes a statement within the scope of this rule about information or documents that would otherwise be discoverable, Rule 408 only operates to make that *statement* inadmissible, but not the information or documents described in that statement.[22] Thus this rule may not be used to "immunize

---

2003). This sort of ruling is consistent with the equitable discretion of a federal court to fashion appropriate privileges "in light of reason and experience." Rule 501. *See* § 501.1, *infra.*

[17] *See* Wall Data Inc. v. Los Angeles Co. Sheriff's Dep't, 447 F.3d 769, 783–784 (9th Cir. 2006) (internal memorandum by defense employee outlining dispute with opposing party was not excluded by Rule 408, because the memo was written almost one week before the parties began settlement discussions; that reasoning seems sound, although a much more solid basis for that ruling would be the fact that the rule rather obviously contemplates statements made between the parties, not private internal communications among the employees of one party; the admissibility of the latter is more appropriately governed by the work product doctrine, *see* Fed. R. Civ. P. 26(b)(3)); Josephs v. Pacific Bell, 443 F.3d 1050, 1064 (9th Cir. 2006) (employer's statements during grievance proceeding in which employee sought reinstatement following his discharge were admissible in later disability discrimination action, because Rule 408 governs the settlement of "existing disputes," and the grievance proceeding did not concern his not-yet-filed discrimination claim).

[18] *See* Branch v. Fidelity & Cas. Co. of New York, 783 F.2d 1289 (5th Cir. 1986) (error for trial court to allow evidence for the purpose of showing defendant's liability and amount of damages); Deere & Co. v. International Harvester Co., 710 F.2d 1551 (Fed. Cir. 1983); United States v. Meadows, 598 F.2d 984 (5th Cir. 1979).

[19] *See, e.g.,* United States v. Meadows, 598 F.2d 984 (5th Cir. 1979) (remark made by defendant that he knew checks were issued by mistake was in no sense an offer to compromise claim; although testimony that defendant agreed to repayment schedule might have been barred by Rule 408, defendant's counsel brought this out on cross-examination); *see also* Perzinski v. Chevron Chemical Co., 503 F.2d 654 (7th Cir. 1974).

[20] *See* 2 WEINSTEIN'S FEDERAL EVIDENCE § 408.02.

[21] 2 MCCORMICK, § 266, at 195. (Footnotes omitted).

[22] Until recently, Rule 408 made this point explicit by providing that: "This rule does not

admissible information, such as a pre-existing document, through the pretense of disclosing it during compromise negotiations."[23] Parties who volunteer otherwise discoverable information during settlement negotiations will still be required to fully answer any questions about such matters in response to subsequent discovery demands. For example, if a defense lawyer reveals during settlement talks that the client's brakes had failed a recent inspection before the accident, Rule 408 would not allow that lawyer's statement to be admitted at the trial, but those facts about the brakes and the inspection would still be admissible as long as they were proved in some other way. After volunteering that ill-advised disclosure, the defendant and the lawyer will inevitably receive discovery requests for the inspection records, as well as interrogatories and deposition questions on that same topic. The defendant would have no right to object to those demands, or to the admissibility of such evidence, on the grounds that such matters were first disclosed by the defense during settlement talks.[24]

§ 408.4   Admissible Statements of Compromise — In General

The final sentence of Rule 408 emphasizes that the Rule excludes evidence of compromise negotiations only where such evidence is offered to establish liability for, or invalidity of, a claim or its amount. The principle of exclusion does not operate when compromise-related evidence is used to establish some other fact of consequence in the litigation.[25] For example,

---

require the exclusion of any evidence otherwise discoverable merely because it is presented in the course of compromise negotiations." This sentence was recently deleted from the rule as "superfluous," based on the Advisory Committee's conclusion that "even without the sentence, the Rule [could not] be read to protect pre-existing information simply because it was presented to the adversary in compromise negotiations." Committee Note to the 2006 amendment to Rule 408.

[23] Advisory Committee Note to the 2006 amendment to Rule 408.

[24] In this way, Rule 408 operates much like the privileges governing confidential communications, which (for example) allow a client to refuse to disclose the *statement* that he made to his lawyer in confidence about an accident, but do not give him the right to refuse to answer questions about the accident itself merely because he discussed those same details with his lawyer; *see* § 501.5, *infra*. Rule 408, just like the attorney-client privilege, is not a "burial ground" where one can dispose of otherwise discoverable evidence.

[25] *See* Rising-Moore v. Red Roof Inns, Inc., 435 F.3d 813, 816 (7th Cir. 2006) (after personal injury case was removed to federal court and plaintiff sought a remand, the amount requested by plaintiff in settlement talks was admissible to show that the case met the amount in controversy requirement for federal diversity jurisdiction); Zurich American Ins. Co. v. Watts Industries, Inc., 417 F.3d 682, 688–689 (7th Cir. 2005) (on motion to compel arbitration, correspondence during settlement talks could be considered by district judge in determining whether the parties had a dispute within the scope of arbitration clause); Kraft v. St. John Lutheran Church of Seward, Nebraska, 414 F.3d 943, 947 (8th Cir. 2005) (in determining whether action was brought within the statute of limitations, court could consider prior settlement communications to determine when the plaintiff knew of a connection between his injuries and defendant's conduct); Brandt v. Wand Partners, 242 F.3d 6 (1st Cir. 2001) (evidence that plaintiff initially sued 69 defendants on allegations of fraud did not

statements during settlement negotiations are not rendered inadmissible by Rule 408 where the statements are offered to establish bias or prejudice of a witness[26] or to show an effort to obstruct a criminal investigation or prosecution.[27] The examples provided by the last sentence of Rule 408 are not exhaustive, and any theory of relevance is permissible provided the evidence is not offered to establish liability for, or invalidity of, the claim or its amount. It should be noted, however, that in any case in which compromise-related evidence is offered for any purpose not forbidden by Rule 408, Rule 403 may operate to exclude the evidence where the probative value is low and the risk of prejudice or confusion is substantial.[28]

§ 408.5   Admissible Statements of Compromise to Show Bias

Most frequently, statements derived from settlement negotiations will be admissible where they are utilized to demonstrate the bias of a witness who

---

involve prohibited evidence of offers to settle; evidence was introduced to demonstrate plaintiff sued everyone possible, without regard to individual defendant's responsibility); Athey v. Farmers Ins. Exchange, 234 F.3d 357 (8th Cir. 2000) (settlement offer by insurer admissible to prove insurer's bad faith); Bankcard Am., Inc. v. Universal Bancard Sys., 203 F.3d 477 (7th Cir. 2000) (no error in allowing evidence of party's reliance on what it believed to be a settlement agreement permitting its actions, where the trial court cautioned the attorneys not to use the words "settlement" or "negotiation" and instructed the jury that the evidence was to be used for the limited purpose of explaining the actions of the party; the purposes of Rule 408 will not be served if one party can induce another into breaching their contract by purporting to enter into a settlement agreement, then suing for the breach once the bogus settlement falls apart); Starter Corp v. Converse, Inc., 170 F.3d 286 (2d Cir. 1999) (settlement agreement falls outside of Rule 408 if it is offered for a purpose other than to prove or disprove the validity of the claims being settled; evidence was accordingly admissible to prove an estoppel claim, as the agreement settled only a trademark infringement claim).

[26] *See* United States Aviation Underwriters v. Olympia Wings, Inc., 896 F.2d 949 (5th Cir. 1990) (settlement evidence admitted to resolve inconsistency between mechanic's pre-trial deposition and his testimony at trial to show that the witness had become more neutral); 2 WEINSTEIN'S FEDERAL EVIDENCE § 408.08.

[27] *See* Uforma/Shelby Business Forms, Inc. v. NLRB, 111 F.3d 1284 (6th Cir. 1997) (Rule 408 does not operate to shield wrongful acts, such as where an employer threatens to terminate jobs if the union persisted in pursuing its grievances, that are committed during settlement negotiations); *but see* United States v. Davis, 596 F.3d 852 (D.C. Cir. 2010) (evidence that the accused, after being confronted with allegation of missing fraternity funds, supposedly responded "Can we just split this $29,000.00 and make this situation just go away?" was not admissible as an attempt to obstruct a criminal investigation or to buy off a prosecution witness, since the amount of the offered payment was not excessive, and the circumstances made it reasonably certain that the speaker was offering to pay the money to the fraternity rather than as an attempt to bribe the other individual into silence).

[28] *See, e.g.,* Swan v. Interstate Brands Corp., 333 F.3d 863 (8th Cir. 2003) (in age discrimination action, Rule 408 excluded evidence that employer offered plaintiff severance pay in exchange for his promise to not sue the company for age discrimination; nor could the offer be used to impeach a defense witness as to the date that the decision was made to terminate the plaintiff, since that was too collateral to the central question of whether he was dismissed because of his age).

has compromised his claim with one of the parties. While the right to a good-faith cross-examination of such a witness is recognized as superior to the public policy underpinning the exclusionary principle of Rule 408, pursuant to the balancing principle of Rule 403, the trial judge may restrict the inquiry on cross-examination in order to preserve the integrity of the process.[29] Where the witness sought to be impeached is a party to the litigation, the danger for prejudice is substantial, and limitation of the cross-examination under Rule 403 may be particularly warranted.[30] Critical in determining whether settlement negotiations should be excluded under Rule 403 is the consideration of whether the settlement was one made in good faith, or rather, one designed to invite favorable testimony.[31]

§ 408.6   Applicability of Rule 408 in Multiparty Litigation and Subsequent Actions

It is common for a party to have potential liability to more than one claimant, or for a single plaintiff to seek damages from more than one defendant. This type of lawsuit requires settlement negotiations to occur on more than one front. Rule 408 furthers settlement in this context by providing the necessary protection from the use of the settlement negotiations between the original parties in a lawsuit, as well as in subsequent litigation, to prove the liability, invalidity, or amount of any claim of a party to the original lawsuit against a new opponent.[32]

Defendants in civil litigation often face potential criminal liability for the same claim. For years, courts have been divided as to whether the defendants' offers to settle the civil case, or their related statements made during those settlement negotiations, are protected under Rule 408 from use against them in later criminal prosecutions arising out of the same or related charges. Three federal circuit courts had correctly reasoned that Rule 408 supplies just as much protection from the use of the settlement at either a

---

[29] *See also* Rule 611(a) and Chapter 611, *infra.*

[30] *See generally,* 2 WEINSTEIN'S FEDERAL EVIDENCE § 408.10; 2 McCORMICK, § 266.

[31] Urico v. Parnell Oil Co., 708 F.2d 852 (1st Cir. 1983).

[32] *See, e.g.,* Lampliter Dinner Theater v. Liberty Mut. Ins. Co., 792 F.2d 1036 (11th Cir. 1986) (evidence that the defendant settled with a third party was excluded); *cf.* Fiberglass Insulators, Inc. v. Dupuy, 856 F.2d 652 (4th Cir. 1988) (plaintiffs in an antitrust suit against a former business partner were not permitted to introduce statements made by the defense counsel during settlement efforts for prior litigation between the same parties; although the prior suit did not involve an antitrust claim, the instant suit was a continuation of the feud between the parties and therefore public policy favored exclusion of the statements). *But see* Carota v. Johns Manville Corp., 893 F.2d 448 (1st Cir. 1990) (plaintiff's settlements with other defendants in a wrongful death asbestosis case were admissible under Massachusetts law that entitles a defendant to introduce evidence of out-of-court settlements in joint tortfeasor actions); McHann v. Firestone Tire and Rubber Co., 713 F.2d 161 (5th Cir. 1983); American Ins. Co. v. North Am. Co. for Property & Casualty Ins., 697 F.2d 79 (2d Cir. 1982); United States v. Contra Costa County Water Dist., 678 F.2d 90 (9th Cir. 1982).

civil or a criminal trial,[33] but three others had mistakenly concluded that Rule 408 has no applicability to any evidence offered at a criminal trial.[34]

A 2006 amendment to the rule was designed to resolve this controversy. The amended rule clarifies that it applies to evidence offered at a criminal trial, and that evidence of defendants' offers to settle disputed civil claims are inadmissible against them in any later civil or criminal case. In drafting this amendment to Rule 408, the Advisory Committee correctly observed that an offer of a compromise, unlike a direct statement of fault, "is not very probative of the defendant's guilt," and that its use in a criminal proceeding would "deter a defendant from settling a civil regulatory action, for fear of use in a subsequent criminal action."[35]

For the same reasons, the amended rule provides that statements by defendants made during settlement talks are also inadmissible against them in later criminal proceedings, at least as a general rule. Such statements are not excluded by this rule when made in civil negotiations "related to a claim by a public office in the exercise of its regulatory, investigative, or enforcement authority."[36]

This compromise solution, which had not been adopted in any federal circuit before the rule was amended,[37] was a most unfortunate and unnecessary change that will serve as nothing but a trap for the unwary. The

---

[33] United States v. Arias, 431 F.3d 1327, 1336–1338 (11th Cir. 2005); United States v. Bailey, 327 F.3d 1131, 1146 (10th Cir. 2003); United States v. Hays, 872 F.2d 582, 588–589 (5th Cir. 1989).

[34] United States v. Logan, 250 F.3d 350, 367 (6th Cir. 2001); United States v. Prewitt, 34 F.3d 436, 439 (7th Cir. 1994); United States v. Gonzalez, 748 F.2d 74, 78 (2d Cir. 1984). These cases were clearly erroneous in failing to give proper weight to the command of Rule 1101(b), which declares that the evidence rules apply generally to both civil and criminal cases (except where they explicitly provide otherwise), and in disregarding the plain language of Rule 408, which (at that time) prohibited the use of civil settlement offers and discussions to prove defendants' "liability" for the civil claim they were trying to compromise, a term that is of course broad enough to include either "civil or criminal liability." Rule 804(b)(3)(A). Even before Rule 408 was amended in 2006, a prosecutor's later use of such evidence against the accused was clearly forbidden as an attempt to prove criminal liability for the claim, or (in the words of the current version of the Rule) the "validity" of the claim.

[35] Committee Note to the 2006 amendment to Rule 408. This note is silent as to precisely how the Advisory Committee thought it was reflecting this resolution in the language of the amendment, although it obviously intended to capture that change in the new language of Rule 408's first sentence, which now provides that such evidence is "not admissible — on behalf of *any* party," which would of course include a prosecutor.

[36] Rule 408(a)(2).

[37] Before 2006, as noted above, the federal circuit courts of appeals were evenly divided as to whether Rule 408 applied to criminal cases with full force or not at all. No circuit had adopted or even proposed a compromise solution that would make Rule 408 generally applicable in criminal cases, except as to statements that had been made in civil litigation with government agencies.

Advisory Committee was obviously aware of this new rule's potential for creating unpleasant surprises for litigators, for it asserted that lawyers representing defendants in civil litigation with the government can "protect against the subsequent use of statements in criminal cases by way of private ordering," and through "negotiation and agreement with the civil regulator or an attorney for the government."[38] The Committee's intended implication is that defense attorneys (and defendants) will not be disadvantaged by this new rule unless they knowingly agree to proceed with settlement talks despite their inability to extract a waiver of its provisions from the government attorney handling the civil matter. But such defense lawyers (assuming they exist) would be just as free, and just as likely, to voluntarily enter into the same sort of precarious settlement talks even if not one word of the rule had been amended, because government attorneys in civil litigation had already been perfectly free, if they wished, to insist that they would not participate in compromise negotiations unless the defendants consented to a waiver of their rights under the former version of Rule 408.[39] That is why this amendment to the rule will never give federal prosecutors any admissible evidence they would not have had without the amendment, except in the case of unwary defendants or lawyers who do not know about the change in this rule, and who rely to their detriment on their knowledge of how this rule was worded in federal court and in more than forty states for over a quarter of a century.[40]

Several poorly reasoned opinions have held that Rule 408 is not violated if defendants' settlements of civil claims are later admitted against them, either in a related civil or criminal case, as long as they are supposedly

---

[38] *See* Committee Note to the 2006 amendment to Rule 408.

[39] *See* § 410.4, *supra*; United States v. Mezzanatto, 513 U.S. 196 (1995) (allowing prosecutors to insist upon a waiver of opposing party's analogous rights under Rule 410).

[40] In a further effort to ameliorate the obvious risk that the new provision will serve as a trap, the Advisory Committee also made the remarkably optimistic suggestion that courts may exclude such evidence under Rule 403 "where the circumstances so warrant," such as, "for example, if an individual was unrepresented at the time the statement was made in a civil enforcement proceeding," on the supposed theory that "its probative value in a subsequent criminal case may be minimal." Committee Note to the 2006 amendment to Rule 408. That wishful thinking, if it were valid, would go a long way toward minimizing the unfairness of the change in the rule. But it is extremely dubious that any courts will be persuaded to exclude otherwise admissible statements allegedly made by parties merely because they were not represented by a lawyer; all over the nation every day of the year, judges in criminal and civil cases admit many thousands of highly incriminating admissions made by criminal defendants and other parties who were not represented by counsel when they made those statements to an investigator or the police or an opposing party or a friend or an informant. Extremely few courts, if any, have ever excluded such evidence on the grounds that an alleged admission of guilt or liability has less probative value merely because it was not made in the presence of counsel, and most judges and juries probably suspect (at least privately) just the opposite: that statements are *more* reliable if made in an unguarded moment without the assistance of counsel.

offered only for the limited purpose of proving that the defendants were on "notice" that there was some problem with the legality of their conduct or the conduct of their subordinates.[41] At the same time that Rule 408 was recently amended for unrelated reasons, the Advisory Committee unwisely cited these cases with apparent approval.[42] This was done to placate the Department of Justice, which had insisted that "it is often the case that through settlement of civil proceedings, a defendant is put on notice of the wrongfulness of his conduct," and that, in later criminal cases, such civil settlements can be "critical to prove that the defendant knew that his conduct was illegal or wrongful."[43] But these cases involve an indefensible construction of the Rule. Because a defendant's constructive notice of the law is always presumed, evidence offered to show actual knowledge of the law's requirements is almost always irrelevant.[44] Besides, even in the rare case when it might be relevant for the Government to prove the defendant's actual notice of some legal obligation that was involved in an earlier civil case, the

---

[41] *See, e.g.,* United States v. Austin, 54 F.3d 394 (7th Cir. 1995) (no error to admit evidence of the defendant's settlement with the FTC, because it was offered to prove that he was on notice that subsequent similar conduct was wrongful); Spell v. McDaniel, 824 F.2d 1380 (4th Cir. 1987) (in a civil rights action alleging that an officer used excessive force, a prior settlement by the City of another brutality claim was properly admitted to prove that the City was on notice of aggressive behavior by police officers); United States v. Gilbert, 668 F.2d 94, 97 & n.1 (2d Cir. 1981) (civil defendant's consent decree with the SEC was admissible at his later criminal trial despite Rule 408, because it was supposedly admitted only to show that he "knew of the SEC reporting requirements involved in the decree" and had "knowledge of [his] legal obligations").

[42] The Committee Notes to the 2006 amendment to Rule 408 devote an entire paragraph to the gratuitous assertion, with several citations, that the amendments did not "affect the case law providing that Rule 408 is inapplicable when evidence of the compromise is offered to prove notice." Technically the Committee did not actually approve those cases when it said the amendment will not "affect" them, but that one-paragraph disclaimer will sound close enough to an actual endorsement to most district judges. That is why the Department of Justice cared so much about the inclusion of this paragraph.

[43] Minutes of the Meeting of the Advisory Committee on the Federal Rules of Evidence, April 25, 2003, at 12.

[44] When the shoe is on the other foot and criminal defendants offer evidence that they actually had no knowledge that their conduct was unlawful, perhaps because they were misinformed or ignorant or even affirmatively misled about the law's requirements, the Justice Department always successfully objects on the grounds that the defendant's constructive knowledge of the criminal law is conclusively presumed and so any alleged ignorance of such matters is irrelevant as a matter of law. *E.g.,* United States v. Funches, 135 F.3d 1405, 1407 (11th Cir. 1998) (because "ignorance of the law" is no defense, a felon charged with illegal possession of a firearm was properly precluded from proving that he was told by state corrections official that his civil rights had been automatically restored upon his release from prison). But if a defendant's actual ignorance of the law is irrelevant, so too is his or her actual knowledge; the Government cannot have it both ways. If the logic of these "notice" cases were sound, a prosecutor could easily circumvent Rule 404 by arguing that defendants' convictions for similar offenses are admissible to show they were on "notice" that the law makes such conduct illegal, which would be equally absurd.

defendant received such notice from the civil complaint, any evidence that was offered in its support, and any summary judgment or verdict entered against the defendant on that claim — all of which may be proved without violating Rule 408 — but not the fact of its voluntary settlement. The Advisory Committee reasoned that "compromise efforts can be offered in criminal cases . . . to prove that the defendant by settling was made aware of the *wrongfulness* of his conduct, on the ground that the purpose for this kind of evidence was to prove something other than the *validity* or amount of the underlying claim."[45] But that spurious distinction is an illusion. Defendants are not made more aware of the wrongfulness of their conduct at the moment they decide to settle some claim — unless of course one assumes, as jurors naturally will, that the willingness to pay money in settlement is additional evidence of the validity of the civil charges. But that is precisely the reasoning that Rule 408 has always explicitly forbidden. These "notice" cases cited by the Advisory Committee are such a blatant violation of Rule 408 that they should have been expressly repudiated by the Committee, not ratified and enshrined with a permanent place of seeming honor in the Committee Notes.

---

[45] MINUTES OF THE MEETING OF THE ADVISORY COMMITTEE ON THE FEDERAL RULES OF EVIDENCE, April 29–30, 2004, at 8 (emphasis added).

Chapter 409

Rule 409. Offers to Pay Medical and Similar Expenses

Rule 409. Offers to Pay Medical and Similar Expenses

Evidence of furnishing, promising to pay, or offering to pay medical, hospital, or similar expenses resulting from an injury is not admissible to prove liability for the injury.

---

§ 409.1   Offers to Pay Medical Expenses — In General

Rule 409 renders inadmissible evidence of the furnishing, or the offering, or the promising to pay medical, hospital, or similar expenses occasioned by an injury where such evidence is offered to establish liability for the injury or harm.[1]

§ 409.2   Policy of Rule 409

Rule 409 is supported by essentially the same rationale that underpins Rule 408, "Compromise Offers and Negotiations." Rule 409 is designed to encourage humane impulses regarding expenses occasioned by an injury.[2] Likewise, in many situations, an offer to pay medical or similar expenses has little probative value as an admission of liability.[3] Professors Mueller and Kirkpatrick contend that the Rule is particularly significant in the context of advance payments by insurers to persons injured in accidents, pointing out the obvious importance of encouraging such payments.[4]

§ 409.3   Scope of Rule 409

Unlike Rule 408, which pertains to compromises, Rule 409 does not render inadmissible conduct or statements that are part of the act of furnishing, offering, or promising to pay expenses. As stated in the Advisory Committee Note to Rule 409:

This difference in treatment arises from fundamental differences in

---

[1] *See generally,* 2 McCormick, § 267; 2 Weinstein's Federal Evidence §§ 409.01–409.03; 2 Mueller & Kirkpatrick, §§ 139–141; 2 Wigmore, § 283.

[2] 2 Weinstein's Federal Evidence § 409.01; 2 Mueller & Kirkpatrick, § 139.

[3] *See* Advisory Committee Note, Rule 409; *see also* 2 Mueller & Kirkpatrick, § 140.

[4] 2 Mueller & Kirkpatrick, § 139.

nature. Communication is essential if compromises are to be effected, and consequently broad protection [under Rule 408] of statements is needed. This is not so in cases of payments or offers or promises to pay medical expenses [under Rule 409], where factual statements may be expected to be incidental in nature.

Whenever an express admission of liability arises in conjunction with an offer to pay medical expenses, the trial judge should make an effort to sever any aspect of the statement related to the payment of medical expenses. The express admission of liability is admissible, but to the extent practicable, any offers to pay medical expenses should be insulated from admissibility. Where severance is impossible, the admission should be submitted to the jury with proper instructions,[5] unless excessive prejudice or confusion would justify exclusion under Rule 403.[6] The balancing principle of Rule 403 may ultimately exclude even an express admission of liability in this context where the probative value of such admission is extremely low (perhaps because of its cumulative nature), and where it is inseparable from an offer to pay medical expenses.

§ 409.4   Admissible Evidence Relating to the Payment of Medical Statements

Unlike Rule 408, relating to compromises and offers to compromise, Rule 409 does not expressly address the issue of whether evidence relating to the payment of medical expenses is admissible to establish issues other than proof of liability. Nevertheless, it is abundantly apparent that Rule 409 only limits admissibility where the evidence of payment or offer of payment is directed to liability.[7] Other consequential facts may be established by such evidence, *e.g.,* control, identity, etc. Before admitting evidence relating to medical payments on a theory of relevance outside the prohibition of Rule 409, however, the trial judge should apply the balancing principle of Rule 403. If the probative value of such evidence is substantially outweighed by a designated adverse effect, the evidence may be excluded. Where evidence of the payment of medical or like expenses is received on a relevance theory outside the proscription of Rule 409, a limiting instruction under Rule 105 should accompany the evidence.

---

[5] *See* § 104.1, *supra.*

[6] *See* § 403.1, *supra.*

[7] *See* Advisory Committee Note, Rule 409; 2 WEINSTEIN'S FEDERAL EVIDENCE § 409.03; *see also* Savoie v. Otto Candies, Inc., 692 F.2d 363 (5th Cir. 1982).

Chapter 410

Rule 410. Pleas, Plea Discussions, and Related Statements

Rule 410. Pleas, Plea Discussions, and Related Statements

(a) **Prohibited Uses.** In a civil or criminal case, evidence of the following is not admissible against the defendant who made the plea or participated in the plea discussions:

    (1) a guilty plea that was later withdrawn;

    (2) a nolo contendere plea;

    (3) a statement made during a proceeding on either of those pleas under Federal Rule of Criminal Procedure 11 or a comparable state procedure; or

    (4) a statement made during plea discussions with an attorney for the prosecuting authority if the discussions did not result in a guilty plea or they resulted in a later-withdrawn guilty plea.

(b) **Exceptions.** The court may admit a statement described in Rule 410(a)(3) or (4):

    (1) in any proceeding in which another statement made during the same plea or plea discussions has been introduced, if in fairness the statements ought to be considered together; or

    (2) in a criminal proceeding for perjury or false statement, if the defendant made the statement under oath, on the record, and with counsel present.

---

§ 410.1 Pleas, Plea Discussions, and Related Statements — In General

Rule 410 insulates from admissibility certain pleas and certain statements made in conjunction with plea bargaining.[1] It is the criminal counterpart to

---

[1] *See generally,* 1 MCCORMICK, §§ 41, 159; 2 MCCORMICK, §§ 257, 266; 2 MUELLER & KIRKPATRICK, §§ 142–151; 2 WEINSTEIN'S FEDERAL EVIDENCE §§ 410.01–410.11; 4 WIG-MORE, §§ 1066–1067. *See also When is statement of accused made in connection with plea bargain negotiations so as to render statement inadmissible under Rule 11(e) of the Federal Rules of Criminal Procedure,* 60 A.L.R. FED. 854 (1982); Note, *The Oath in Rule 11*

Rule 408, which relates to the inadmissibility of statements made in conjunction with compromise negotiations in civil actions.[2]

Subject only to Rule 410(b), the pleas or statements identified in the Rule are inadmissible regardless of the issues sought to be established.[3] Unlike Rules 408 and 409, which render certain statements inadmissible only when offered for a specified purpose, Rule 410 comprehensively prohibits the admission of the identified statements, offers, and pleas at trial. However, Rule 410 may not render inadmissible statements made during post-conviction negotiations wherein the defendant offers to cooperate with the state in return for a reduction of sentence.[4]

The Rule prohibits the use for impeachment purposes of statements made in connection with plea bargaining.[5] By eliminating impeachment use of plea bargaining statements, Rule 410 is designed to further the goal of encouraging guilty pleas and plea bargaining discussions.[6]

§ 410.2   Withdrawn Pleas of Guilty

As analyzed by the United States Supreme Court in *Kercheval v. United*

Proceedings, 46 FORDHAM L. REV. 1242 (1978); *Evidence—Guilty Plea Not Admissible in Subsequent Civil Suit Based Upon the Same Occurrences,* 24 KAN. L. REV. 193 (1975). *Compare* United States v. Greene, 995 F.2d 793 (8th Cir. 1993) (defendant's statements to a DEA agent were not excludable pursuant to Rule 410 where the agent had no actual or apparent authority from the prosecution to negotiate a plea agreement); United States v. Porter, 821 F.2d 968 (4th Cir. 1987) United States v. Magee, 821 F.2d 234 (5th Cir. 1987).

[2] *See* Chapter 408, *supra; see also* United States v. Arroyo-Angulo, 580 F.2d 1137, 1148 (2d Cir. 1978) ("the purpose of Rule 410 is to encourage frank discussion in plea bargaining negotiations . . . since plea agreements are essential to the disposition of bulk of cases in our criminal system").

[3] United States v. Sayakhom, 186 F.3d 928 (9th Cir. 1999) (although harmless, it was error to admit for any purpose the defendant's statements during meetings with prosecutors after defense counsel learned that his client was going to be indicted and presented her so she could give her version of the facts; these meetings were clearly plea negotiations protected under Rule 410); *but see* United States v. Hare, 49 F.3d 447, 450–451 (8th Cir. 1995) (statements made before plea bargaining had begun and those made after a plea agreement had been reached cannot be said to have been made "in the course of plea discussions" and therefore are not excluded by Rule 410).

[4] *See* United States v. Graham, 91 F.3d 213, 218–219 (D.C. Cir. 1996) (post-conviction statements made during negotiations to reduce sentence were admissible at sentencing hearing; such statements were not plea bargaining and thus not excludable under Rule 410). Although the court in *Graham* had declared that post-conviction negotiations to reduce sentence are not covered by Rule 410, the court could have reached the same result in this case by reasoning that Rule 410 does not apply to sentencing hearings. *See* Rule 1101(d)(3).

[5] *See* United States v. Mezzanatto, 513 U.S. 196, 200 n.2 (1995) (under Rule 410, statements made during plea discussions may not be used to impeach the accused at trial unless he waived that protection before the plea discussions began); United States v. Acosta-Ballardo, 8 F.3d 1532 (10th Cir. 1993) (statements made by defendant during a plea negotiation are inadmissible to impeach defendant's testimony at trial).

[6] Advisory Committee Note, Rule 410, as amended in 1980.

States,[7] admission of the withdrawn plea would, in practical effect, render meaningless the permission to withdraw the plea in the first instance. As Judge Weinstein notes, the Supreme Court's reasoning in *Kercheval* was based upon an assumption that when a court allows the withdrawal of a guilty plea, it is because the court has found that the plea was not voluntarily or knowingly entered by the defendant.[8] Once a plea has been accepted by a federal judge, it may not be withdrawn merely because the defendant has a change of mind, but only if the defendant can show "a fair and just reason for requesting the withdrawal."[9] Any time a defendant can make such a difficult showing, it necessarily follows that there is some reason to question the plea as a reliable basis for a finding of guilt, and that its subsequent use against the accused would be unjust.

Judge Weinstein believes that a better rationale for denying the prosecution's use of the withdrawn guilty plea is that to allow the use of this type of evidence would make the granting of the trial a meaningless gesture. Allowing the admission of evidence in the prosecution's case that a guilty plea was withdrawn would be irreparably damaging to the defense.[10] This reasoning is consistent with the general practice of ordering a new trial where evidence in violation of Rule 410 is inappropriately elicited from the accused.[11]

A guilty plea that is not withdrawn may be admissible in subsequent litigation as an admission of the person who entered the plea.[12] Unwithdrawn guilty pleas in prior criminal cases are admissible in subsequent civil litigation under exceptions to the hearsay rules, such as an admission of a

---

[7] Kercheval v. United States, 274 U.S. 220 (1927) ("both sides gave evidence as to matters considered by the court in setting aside the conviction").

[8] 2 WEINSTEIN'S FEDERAL EVIDENCE § 410.02.

[9] Fed. R. Crim. P. 11(d)(2)(B). No such showing need be made in the extremely rare case in which a defendant decides to withdraw the plea before it has been accepted by the district court, which may be done "for any reason or no reason," Fed. R. Crim. P. 11(d)(1), but it is fairly unusual that a defendant would have a change of heart sudden enough to prompt withdrawal of a plea between the time it is made and when it is accepted by the court, often only minutes later.

[10] 2 WEINSTEIN'S FEDERAL EVIDENCE § 410.02. Like any other Evidence Rule designed for the benefit of the accused, however, this protection may be waived by the accused. *See* United States v. Burch, 156 F.3d 1315 (D.C. Cir. 1998) (the rule against admitting withdrawn guilty pleas and related discussions can be waived; such waiver permits the use of such evidence in the opposing party's case-in-chief, not only for purposes of impeachment or rebuttal).

[11] Kercheval v. United States, 274 U.S. 220 (1927); United States v. Long, 323 F.2d 468 (6th Cir. 1963); Oliver v. United States, 202 F.2d 521 (6th Cir. 1953).

[12] *See* Rule 801(d)(2); Miller v. United States, 615 F. Supp. 781 (D. Ohio 1985) (plaintiff's criminal plea not excludable under Rule 410).

party or declaration against interest.[13] Likewise, a conviction may be admissible under certain circumstances, *e.g.,* impeachment of a witness under Rule 609.[14] In regard to guilty pleas, Rule 410 only addresses the admissibility of pleas of guilty that are subsequently withdrawn.

§ 410.3   Pleas of Nolo Contendere

Rule 410(a)(2) provides a general rule of inadmissibility for a plea of nolo contendere, meaning literally "I do not contest it." This sort of plea, sometimes also called a plea of "no contest," is "a plea by which a defendant does not expressly admit his guilt, but nonetheless waives his right to a trial and authorizes the court for purposes of the case to treat him as if he were guilty."[15] Even though it is technically only a statement of the defendant's unwillingness to contest the charges and is not an express admission of guilt, a nolo plea, at least in federal court, operates as a tacit admission, for the purposes of that criminal prosecution only, of "every essential element of the offense that is well pleaded in the charge."[16]

Although there is some doubt about the precise scope of Rule 410(a)(2), it is universally agreed that a plea of nolo contendere may not be used against that defendant in any civil case or criminal prosecution arising out of the same allegations. Even if the plea is withdrawn by the accused or

---

[13] *See* Rain v. Pavkov, 357 F.2d 506 (3d Cir. 1966) (admissible despite state statute declaring guilty plea in traffic offenses inadmissible); Interstate Sec. Co. v. United States, 151 F.2d 224 (10th Cir. 1945) (suit for forfeiture of car; owner's guilty plea admissible against chattel mortgagee); *see also* 2 WEINSTEIN'S FEDERAL EVIDENCE § 410.07.

[14] *See* Rule 803(21); *see also* Rules 608 and 609 regarding impeachment, Chapters 608 and 609, *infra.*

[15] North Carolina v. Alford, 400 U.S. 25, 35 n.8 (1970) ("Throughout its history, that is, the plea of nolo contendere has been viewed not as an express admission of guilt but as a consent by the defendant that he may be punished as if he were guilty and a prayer for leniency"); Advisory Committee Note to the 1974 amendment to Federal Rule of Criminal Procedure 11 ("A plea of nolo contendere is, for purposes of punishment, the same as the plea of guilty . . . . Unlike a plea of guilty, however, it cannot be used against a defendant as an admission in a subsequent criminal or civil case").

[16] United States v. Lott, 367 U.S. 421, 426 (1961) ("Although it is said that a plea of nolo contendere means literally 'I do not contest it,' and is a mere statement of unwillingness to contest and no more, it does admit every essential element of the offense that is well pleaded in the charge. Hence, it is tantamount to an admission of guilt for the purposes of the case, and nothing is left but to render judgment, for the obvious reason that in the face of the plea no issue of fact exists, and none can be made while the plea remains of record") (internal punctuation and citations omitted). *See also Alford,* 400 U.S. at 36 (a nolo contendere plea is entered by "an accused who is unwilling expressly to admit his guilt but who, faced with grim alternatives, is willing to waive his trial and accept the sentence"). In establishing the truth of the prosecution's case only for the purposes of the pending case, a plea of no contest operates much like an admission under Federal Rule of Civil Procedure 36, which binds the party who makes that admission "for purposes of the pending action only," Fed. R. Civ. P. 36(a)(1), in order to induce parties to admit things they might refuse to admit if they knew it could back to haunt them in another case.

rejected by the court,[17] it may not be used against the accused when that same criminal charge goes to trial. The plea of nolo contendere is also inadmissible against co-defendants of the accused who choose to plead not guilty and go to trial.[18] This rule is justified by two considerations. First, the nolo contendere plea is "inconclusive"[19] and has less probative value than a plea of guilty as evidence of the guilt of the one who entered the plea.[20] In federal court, for example, a guilty plea may not be accepted unless the court concludes that "there is a factual basis for the plea,"[21] but "there is no similar requirement for pleas of nolo contendere, since it was thought desirable to permit defendants to plead nolo without making any inquiry into their actual guilt."[22] Second, the rule of exclusion is grounded on the public policy of encouraging such pleas as a way of avoiding trials, at least in cases where the accused would otherwise never agree to waive the right to a trial. Without a guarantee that the plea would not be used against them, the nolo contendere plea would be of no value to the accused, and would accordingly lose any value to the system of justice in the promotion of plea bargaining.[23]

---

[17] A defendant has no constitutional or statutory right to insist that a court accept a plea of no contest, which may be entered only "with the court's consent." Fed. R. Crim. P. 11(a).

[18] Rule 410, by its own terms, only forbids the use of a nolo plea "against the defendant who made the plea," so that rule does not require exclusion if the plea is offered against remaining codefendants or alleged conspirators at their trials. But a person's nolo plea and resulting conviction, if offered against partners in crime as evidence of their guilt, is excluded as inadmissible hearsay, *see* Rule 803(22) (forbidding the use of a nolo contendere plea "to prove any fact essential to the judgment"), and is now surely forbidden by the Confrontation Clause; *see* § 801.2, *infra.*

[19] Advisory Committee Notes to Rule 410.

[20] Pleas of no contest, like a so-called *Alford* plea from a defendant who pleads guilty while formally proclaiming innocence, reflect the historical understanding that "since guilt, or the degree of guilt, is at times uncertain and elusive, an accused, though believing in or entertaining doubts respecting his innocence, might reasonably conclude a jury would be convinced of his guilt and that he would fare better in the sentence" by giving up the right to trial. McCoy v. United States, 363 F.2d 306, 308 (D.C. Cir. 1966) (quoted in *Alford,* 400 U.S. at 33) (internal punctuation omitted).

[21] Fed. R. Crim. P. 11(b)(3).

[22] *Alford,* 400 U.S. at 35 n.8. Before a plea of no contest may be accepted in federal court, the court need not determine if there is a factual basis for the plea, but need only "consider the parties' views and the public interest in the effective administration of justice." Fed. R. Crim. P. 11(a)(3). This "public interest" factor will usually compel the judge to reject any nolo contendere plea if it is undisputed that *somebody* committed the crime with which the accused is charged, so that either he is guilty or else the real perpetrator is still at large. As a practical matter, this is why nolo pleas are usually accepted only in cases (such as tax evasion) in which, if the defendant is truly innocent, there was no crime committed by anyone at all.

[23] Advisory Committee Note to the 1974 amendments to Federal Rule of Criminal Procedure 11 ("A defendant who desires to plead nolo contendere will commonly want to avoid pleading guilty because the plea of guilty can be introduced as an admission in

But what if the nolo plea is later offered against the accused in an unrelated case for some other purpose? Unlike all of the other rules in Article IV of the Federal Rules of Evidence, Rule 410(2) contains no hint that its categorical rule of exclusion has anything to do with the purpose for which the evidence is offered.[24] That rule declares, without any apparent qualification or limitation, that evidence of the "nolo contendere plea" in a civil or criminal case, "is not admissible against the defendant who made the plea." Although no court has ever said so out loud, it is universally agreed that this is one of those rare rules that "can't mean what it says,"[25] for it would lead to absurd results if read too literally, and every court and commentator agrees that there are at least some purposes for which a plea of nolo contendere should be admissible against the one who entered the plea, despite the language of the rule.[26] Determining where that line should be drawn has been the subject of some controversy.

Despite the breadth of the exclusion provided in Rule 410, for example, the courts are apparently unanimous in holding that convictions based upon pleas of nolo contendere are admissible against the defendants if they are offered solely to prove that they were *convicted* of some crime, where the relevance of the convictions does not depend upon any assumption that they were guilty of the crime. Thus, a conviction based on a nolo contendere plea was admissible to prove that the man who entered that plea was later guilty of falsely stating, while applying for a visa to gain re-entry into the country,

---

subsequent civil litigation. The prosecution may oppose the plea of nolo contendere because it wants a definite resolution of the defendant's guilty or innocence either for correctional purposes or for reasons of subsequent litigation. ABA Standards Relating to Pleas of Guilty § 1.1(b) Commentary at 16–18 (Approved Draft, 1968)").

[24] With the exception of this rule, Federal Rule 404 through 412 dictate that their general rules of exclusion depend on the *purpose* for which the evidence is offered. (This is not obvious from the wording of Rule 412(a), although subsection (b) of that rule makes that plain.) Even the evidence described in subsections (3) and (4) of Rule 410 depends for its admissibility on the purpose for which it is offered, as the last sentence of that rule clarifies. In this way, Rule 410(a)(2) is only remotely analogous to Rules 413 through 415, which curiously provide that the evidence covered by those rules is *admissible* without regard to what it is offered to prove "and may be considered for its bearing on any matter to which it is relevant," but those rules were drafted much later by Congress through a very different process, and therefore shed little light on the proper construction of Rule 410. Only Rule 410 subdivisions (a)(1) and (a)(2) identify relevant evidence that is ostensibly *inadmissible* without regard to what it is offered to prove.

[25] Green v. Bock Laundry Machine Co., 490 U.S. 504, 510–511 (1987) (interpreting the former version of Rule 609, the Court concluded that a rule need not and should not be read in accordance with its literal terms if it "can't mean what it says").

[26] To take one obvious example: Surely the accused in a criminal case has a constitutional right to cross-examine a key prosecution witness to reveal that the witness recently pled no contest to some criminal charge in a deal with that same prosecutor's office but has not yet been sentenced, not to prove the witness's guilt but merely to show the possible bias of the witness, and Rule 410 would be unconstitutional if it provided otherwise; *see* § 607.4, *infra*.

that he had never been convicted of a felony.[27] The same would also be true in cases where the defendant's status as a convicted felon is itself an essential element of the charge, such as a case in which the prosecution charges that the accused was a felon unlawfully in possession of a firearm, and courts have reached the same conclusion in a wide variety of situations where a nolo contendere conviction is offered merely to prove a person's *status* as a convicted felon.[28]

The result reached in these cases seems sound,[29] but their reasoning is indefensible. Most of these cases rely primarily on the fact that Rule 410 only literally forbids mention of the "nolo contendere *plea*," leading them to reason that the rule says nothing about the admissibility of a *judgment of conviction* based on that plea.[30] We know for a fact that this was not the intention of the rule's drafters, who explicitly declared that it was based on "the inconclusive and compromise nature of *judgments* based on nolo pleas."[31] Moreover, this proposed reading reduces the rule to a meaningless nullity. Its logic proves far too much, because by that reasoning Rule 410(a)(2) could be easily and thoroughly circumvented in *every* case — even in subsequent civil litigation against the defendant who entered the nolo plea — by simply telling the jury about the criminal conviction that was entered against the defendant, without disclosing how the conviction was reached or that it was based on the plea. That arrangement would do nothing to fulfill

---

[27] United States v. Adedoyin, 369 F.3d 337, 345 (3d Cir. 2004).

[28] *See* Olsen v. Correiro, 189 F.3d 52, 61 (1st Cir. 1999) (collecting cases).

[29] After all, if Rule 410 prevented *any* mention of the fact that a person was convicted based on a plea of no contest in *every* later case, the rule would essentially require later courts to pretend for all intents and purposes that the person had no criminal record at all. That could not have been the intent of the rule. If Rule 410 operated that way, virtually no prosecutor or judge would ever again agree to a nolo contendere plea, thus eliminating the value of such pleas to defendants and to the criminal justice system.

[30] *See Adedoyin,* 369 F.3d at 345 (collecting cases); *Olsen,* 189 F.3d at 61 (collecting cases).

[31] Advisory Committee Note to Rule 410 (emphasis added). The drafters of the rules also stated, in explaining the language of Rule 803(22), that "*[j]udgments of conviction* based upon pleas of nolo contendere are not included. This position is consistent with the treatment of nolo pleas *in Rule 410* and the authorities cited in the Advisory Committee's Note in support thereof." Advisory Committee Note to Rule 803(22) (emphasis added). *See also* United States v. Vonn, 535 U.S. 55, 64 n.6 (2002) ("In the absence of a clear legislative mandate, the Advisory Committee Notes provide a reliable source of insight into the meaning of a rule, especially when, as here, the rule was enacted precisely as the Advisory Committee proposed"). There is no possibility that the drafters of this rule intended to exclude evidence of a nolo contendere plea because of the inconclusive nature of such facts as evidence of guilt, but to freely allow the admission of the judgment of conviction based on that same plea. At least when offered to prove the guilt of the one who entered the plea, the judgment of conviction obviously has no greater probative value than the plea itself.

the purposes underlying Rule 410.[32] It is inconceivable that the framers of Rule 410 could have intended this rule to be so utterly meaningless. In addition, this fatuous argument overlooks the fact that Rule 410(a)(2) does not merely exclude the nolo plea itself, but in fact excludes "*evidence of. . . a nolo contendere plea.*"[33] The fact that someone was convicted based on such a plea is indirect evidence of the plea, and inadmissible facts, such as pleas of nolo contendere, are not to be "suggested to the jury by any means."[34] The inescapable conclusion must be that Rule 410, in cases where it applies, excludes evidence of *both* the nolo contendere plea and the judgment of conviction, both of which have equally limited probative value.

Then how should we rationalize those cases holding that Rule 410 does not apply to nolo pleas and convictions that are offered solely to prove a person's *status* as a convicted felon? A far more sensible explanation for these cases, and the only one that accords with the logic behind the rule, is the fact that Rule 410 was obviously intended to provide that pleas of nolo contendere — and convictions on the basis of such pleas — are excluded by that rule only if they are offered to prove "that the defendant is *guilty* of the crime in question."[35] In other words, the plea "cannot be used against a defendant *as an admission* in a subsequent criminal or civil case."[36] This is the only possible interpretation that allows a sensible reconciliation of the Rule's obvious purposes with the universal willingness of the courts to admit judgments of conviction based on such pleas to show only that the defendant has a criminal conviction (and that, for example, a statement to the contrary

---

[32] *Accord* David P. Leonard, THE NEW WIGMORE: A TREATISE ON EVIDENCE, SELECTED RULES OF LIMITED ADMISSIBILITY 642 (2002). Indeed, merely disclosing a judgment of conviction without revealing that the defendant pled no contest would probably sound even *worse* to the jurors, who would then surely assume that the defendant had been convicted at a trial where he falsely pled not guilty.

[33] Rule 410 (emphasis added).

[34] Rule 103(d). This is why, for example, the courts have universally agreed that criminal convictions are frequently excluded by Rule 404 even though that rule technically makes no mention of convictions and only forbids evidence of a person's "character." Criminal convictions are routinely forbidden when offered as indirect circumstantial evidence of facts that are explicitly excluded by some rule of evidence.

[35] United States v. Adedoyin, 369 F.3d 337, 345 (3d Cir. 2004) (the point of Rule 410 is to provide that "pleas of nolo contendere and convictions on the basis of such pleas are not admissible for purposes of proving that the defendant is guilty of the crime in question"). In support of this conclusion, the Third Circuit also sensibly cited Federal Rule of Evidence 803(22), which declares that a judgment of conviction upon a plea of nolo contendere is not admissible under that hearsay exception "to prove any fact essential to sustain the judgment."

[36] Advisory Committee Note to the 1974 amendment to Federal Rule of Criminal Procedure 11 (emphasis added). This accords with the traditional understanding that a nolo contendere plea is designed to ensure that "the defendant retains the right to *deny the charge* in any other judicial proceedings," Bryan Garner, A DICTIONARY OF MODERN LEGAL USAGE 590 (2d ed. 1995) (emphasis added), which of course is not necessarily the same as the right to deny the existence of the conviction based on that charge.

on a visa application was false). If a conviction is offered only to prove that the defendant was *convicted* and not to show guilt (innocent people are sometimes convicted too), the offer does not depend on any assumption that the plea is reliable evidence of guilt, and therefore does not implicate the concerns underlying Rule 410.[37]

A closer question is presented by a judgment of conviction based on a nolo plea used to later impeach the character for truthfulness of the one who entered that plea, when offered to discredit the defendant's later testimony as a witness. Prior to the adoption of the Federal Rules of Evidence, most federal courts had ruled that a conviction could not be used for impeachment if that conviction was based upon a plea of nolo contendere, in keeping with the limited probative value of such pleas and the doctrine that they were generally inadmissible for any purpose against the one who entered the plea.[38] It is an open question whether those cases were overturned by the adoption of the federal rules. Federal Rule of Evidence 609, which generally allows the use of convictions to impeach witnesses by attacking their character for truthfulness, is silent as to whether convictions can be used if based on a plea of nolo contendere. Despite the broad language of Rule 410, several federal circuit courts have concluded that convictions based upon no contest pleas may be used for impeachment under Rule 609,[39] although the logic of those cases is open to serious question. Those courts have relied primarily on the trivial distinction between pleas and convictions, and the assumption that Rule 410 says nothing about the admissibility of a

---

[37] This explanation also permits us to make sense of the fact, as noted above, that Rule 410 surely would not preclude a criminal defendant from exposing the bias of a prosecution witness who had pled nolo contendere but was awaiting sentencing on other charges in a deal with the same prosecution's office, since the relevance of the plea in that case would not depend on any assumption that the witness was guilty of anything. Even an innocent person facing sentencing has a motive to curry the favor of the prosecution. Indeed, the evidence could be sensibly admitted in such a case, if need be, with a coherent limiting instruction that the plea could not be considered as evidence that the witness was guilty of those charges to which he or she had pled no contest, and it is likely that Rule 410 would require such an instruction upon request.

[38] *See* Mickler v. Fahs, 243 F.2d 515, 517 (5th Cir. 1957) ("The same reasons which make the evidence of a plea of nolo contendere inadmissible as an admission will exclude it in a jury trial when offered for the purposes of impeachment. . . . Such plea is, as we have seen, an admission of guilt only in the case where it is made.") *See also* United States v. Morrow, 537 F.2d 120, 142–143 (5th Cir. 1976) (collecting cases).

[39] Brewer v. City of Napa, 210 F.3d 1093, 1095–1096 (9th Cir. 2000); United States v. Williams, 642 F.2d 136, 139–140 (5th Cir. 1981). Another circuit has also agreed with that reasoning but only in dictum, because that case did not involve a nolo plea. United States v. Lipscomb, 702 F.2d 1049, 1070 (D.C. Cir. 1983) (involving a witness who had entered a so-called *Alford* plea of guilty while maintaining his innocence; nothing in Rule 410 implies that such pleas might be inadmissible for any purpose). The holdings of these cases have been uncritically summarized as the law in many leading evidence treatises, although none of those treatises appears to have subjected these cases to close critical examination.

conviction as long as the jury is not told that the conviction was based on a plea of no contest. That reading of the rule is indefensible, as shown above, for it would reduce the rule to a meaningless absurdity. Those courts have also relied on the fact that the final version of Rule 609, mysteriously and without explanation, deleted an exception in an earlier draft that would have explicitly excluded a plea of nolo contendere.[40] That omission might have been based on a deliberate decision to permit the use of such pleas for impeachment, but its deletion might just as likely have been based on the perfectly sensible conclusion that this exception was superfluous and unnecessary in light of Rule 410 and Rule 803(22). We simply do not know, and this kind of pure speculation about unspoken intentions cannot be a sufficient basis for overlooking the plain language and logic of Rule 410.

As noted above, the most sensible interpretation of Rule 410(2), and the only reading that is reasonably faithful to both its language and its obvious purposes, is that "pleas of nolo contendere *and convictions on the basis of such pleas* are not admissible for purposes of proving that the defendant is guilty of the crime in question."[41] But that is precisely what a cross-examiner attempts to do when impeaching witnesses by asking them to admit that they were convicted of crimes based on a plea of nolo contendere. The most defensible conclusion is that Rule 410 preserves the pre-rules law forbidding the use of convictions based on a plea of *nolo contendere* to impeach a witness at either a civil or a criminal trial, at least in cases where the witness being cross-examined is a party to the case.[42] This result protects all of the purposes underlying Rule 410 but poses no great unfairness to the

---

[40] An early Advisory Committee draft of Rule 609 permitted the district court to admit "evidence that [a witness] has been convicted of a crime, except on a plea of *nolo contendere*." Proposed Rule 609(a), 51 F.R.D. 315, 391 (1971). That exception was later deleted from the final draft of the rule without explanation.

[41] United States v. Adedoyin, 369 F.3d 337, 345 (3d Cir. 2004) (emphasis added). The court was not considering whether nolo pleas could be used to impeach a witness's character for truthfulness under Rule 609, although its sound reasoning would plainly compel a negative answer to that question.

[42] Although no federal court has yet noted this point when discussing the interaction of Rule 410 and Rule 609, the more substantial issue in this context is whether the use of a conviction to impeach a witness would amount to use of such evidence "*against* the defendant who made the plea." Rule 410 (emphasis added). It is debatable whether that language is most naturally construed to apply to the use of a conviction to impeach a nonparty witness. It could be plausibly argued that a conviction is used "against" a witness any time it is used to discredit the witness' testimony, even if he or she is not a party to the case; others might insist that it is only used "against him" if it is being used to help persuade a judge or a jury to return a verdict or a judgment against a party. Both positions seem defensible, and no recent judicial opinion has even considered the question. But surely that language is broad enough under any reasonable construction to prohibit the use of such convictions to impeach a witness who is a party to the proceeding. (And if the witness being cross-examined is not a party to the case, a judgment of conviction based on a plea of nolo contendere would presumably be inadmissible hearsay under Rule 803(22).)

cross-examiner, who would still be entitled at least to ask the witness to admit commission of the underlying criminal act.[43] Although this point is anything but settled at the moment, the two or three federal cases holding to the contrary should be viewed with considerable skepticism.

§ 410.4   Statements Attending Pleas and Offers to Plead

Within the exclusionary scope of Rule 410 are statements made in connection with, and relevant to, the specified pleas or offers to plead. Since the rule only applies to "plea discussions with an attorney for the prosecuting authority," it does not make conversations inadmissible if a criminal suspect foolishly tries to engage in plea bargaining with anyone else, such as a prison guard or a police officer.[44] It has also been held that this rule furnishes no protection for plea negotiations with a prosecutorial official in a foreign nation.[45] Such statements are inadmissible except as provided in the final sentence of the Rule.[46] Under the Rule, a statement may only be admitted for the purpose of either clarifying a plea bargaining statement that the accused offers into evidence, or to substantiate a perjury charge subsequently brought against the accused.

The prosecution is afforded the right to present other statements made in

---

[43] Even if the cross-examiner is forbidden by Rule 410 from asking witnesses to admit that they were convicted of some crime if that conviction was based on a plea of no contest, the attorney could still ask the witness under Rule 608(b) to admit the commission of that crime. *See* David P. Leonard, THE NEW WIGMORE: A TREATISE ON EVIDENCE, SELECTED RULES OF LIMITED ADMISSIBILITY 648 (2002) (the most defensible construction of Rule 410 would allow admission of "the *facts* underlying the previous conviction based on the nolo plea," where those facts are somehow relevant, but would "exclude the plea and the resulting judgment of conviction") (emphasis added).

[44] United States v. Mangine, 302 F.3d 819 (8th Cir. 2002) (jailed defendant's incriminating statements to police officer, made in hopes of receiving assistance from the officer, were not inadmissible as plea negotiations).

[45] United States v. Orlandez-Gamboa, 320 F.3d 328 (2d Cir. 2003) (statements by a defendant in the course of the Colombian equivalent to American plea negotiations are admissible because "attorney for the prosecuting authority" does not mean foreign prosecutors and there was no evidence that the United States played any role in obtaining the statements from the defendant).

[46] Where a bargain to plead guilty has been reached pursuant to Criminal Procedure Rule 11 and the defendant has agreed to testify for the government before the grand jury and at trial, if the defendant later dishonors the agreement after providing grand jury testimony, the statements made by the defendant before the grand jury are not protected by Rule 410. *See* United States v. Stirling, 571 F.2d 708 (2d Cir. 1978). The policy underlying Rule 410 is to encourage plea bargaining discussions that result in guilty pleas. In the situation where the defendant violates the bargain and pleads not guilty, protection of the testimony that was covered by the agreement would not promote plea bargaining. *See* United States v. Davis, 617 F.2d 677 (D.C. Cir. 1979). It should be noted that both of these cases involve statements made before the grand jury, not statements made in the course of plea bargaining. Consequently, it may be more appropriate to view these cases as outside of the scope of Rule 410, instead of as an exception to its application.

a plea bargaining session, after the accused has entered into evidence a statement otherwise protected, in order to ensure the evidence of the defense is viewed in the proper context by the trier of fact. When the accused is charged with perjury, plea bargaining statements may only be used where made by the accused on the record, under oath, and in the presence of defense counsel. In these two situations, the operative policy of Rule 410 to encourage fluid and open discussion during plea bargaining is outweighed by the risk that the truth-finding function of the trial would be impaired if the evidence was not admitted.

In *United States v. Mezzanatto,* the United States Supreme Court held that an agreement to waive the exclusionary provisions of Rule 410 is valid and enforceable absent some affirmative indication that the defendant entered the agreement unknowingly or involuntarily.[47] The Court held that, before agreeing to engage in plea discussions that would otherwise be inadmissible under Rule 410, a prosecutor may properly insist that the defense agree to a limited waiver of the protections of that rule, and stipulate that any statements made by the accused during those talks could be used by the prosecution for impeachment if the defendant later testifies at trial to something that is inconsistent with those statements. The Court did not decide whether it would enforce a broader waiver request, such as one asking the defense to agree to the admissibility of any statement by the defendant, even as part of the government's case-in-chief,[48] although lower courts since *Mezzanatto* have been willing to enforce waivers that make defense statements admissible even if the defendant does not testify at trial, as long as the defense presents arguments that are inconsistent with defendant's representations during plea negotiations.[49]

§ 410.5   Co-Offender Pleas

Rule 410 only defines when certain pleas and related statements may be used at trial "against the defendant who made the plea or was a participant in the plea discussions." This rule therefore does not address the admissibility of a criminal defendant's plea of guilty or no contest, or statements made by the defendant during plea discussions, if they are later offered at

---

[47] United States v. Mezzanatto, 513 U.S. 196 (1995).

[48] *Mezzanatto,* 513 U.S. at 211 (Ginsburg, J., concurring).

[49] United States v. Barrow, 400 F.3d 109 (2d Cir. 2005) (defendant made a valid waiver of his rights under Rule 410 by agreeing that statements made by him during plea negotiations could be used "to rebut any evidence offered or elicited, or factual assertions made, by or on behalf of [him] at any stage of a criminal prosecution," and lower court did not err in holding that this waiver was triggered by statements made at trial by defense counsel in opening statement and on cross-examination); United States v. Velez, 354 F.3d 190 (2d Cir. 2004) (prosecutor may properly ask the defense to agree, before entering plea negotiations, to waive any objection under Rule 410 to the admissibility of statements made by him during those negotiations if the defense presents any contradictory "evidence or arguments" at trial — whether or not defendant testifies).

trial against co-defendants. Nevertheless, it is now clearly settled that a defendant's guilty plea or plea of nolo contendere is inadmissible against codefendants and alleged conspirators, on the grounds that the admission of such a statement would violate their constitutional right to confront the witnesses against them.[50]

If a co-offender appears as a witness, it may be appropriate to admit evidence of the guilty plea to impeach his or her credibility.[51] A limiting instruction should be issued by the court to ensure that the evidence is not impermissibly used by the jury.[52] It may also be necessary to instruct the jury not to speculate about the motivation of a co-offender who does not testify. The instruction is necessary to prevent a jury from correctly surmising that the co-offender has pleaded guilty to the charge, and then improperly using this speculation as evidence of the defendant's guilt.[53]

---

[50] Even though guilty pleas are technically hearsay, many federal cases had (until recently) admitted such statements against other defendants under the hearsay exception for statements against interest of the declarant, Rule 804(b)(3). In light of the Supreme Court's recent decision in *Crawford v. Washington,* 541 U.S. 36 (2004), however, it is now clear that the Sixth Amendment Confrontation Clause forbids the use of a guilty plea allocution as evidence against those who did not enter the plea. United States v. Reifler, 446 F.3d 65, 86–87 (2d Cir. 2006); United States v. Al-Sadawi, 432 F.3d 419, 425–426 (2d Cir. 2005); United States v. Zhou, 428 F.3d 361, 374 (2d Cir. 2005). Even before *Crawford,* a plea of nolo contendere and resulting conviction, if offered against his partners in crime as evidence of their guilt, was already excluded as inadmissible hearsay, *see* Rule 803(22) (forbidding the use of a nolo contendere plea "to prove any fact essential to the judgment").

[51] Smith v. United States, 331 F.2d 265 (8th Cir. 1964) (no prejudice where codefendant available for cross-examination and careful admonition); *see also* Walker v. United States, 93 F.2d 383 (8th Cir. 1937) (reception of pleas of nolo contendere before jury; codefendants became witnesses and testified fully); United States v. Universal Rehabilitation Servs. Inc., 205 F.3d 657 (3d Cir. 2000) (where two participants in a Medicare fraud scheme pled guilty and testified against their accomplices, the trial court properly admitted evidence about the two witnesses' guilty pleas, which were probative of witness credibility, selective prosecution of defendants, and the source of the witnesses' first-hand knowledge, even though defendants agreed not to challenge the credibility of those witnesses).

[52] *See* United States v. Light, 394 F.2d 908 (2d Cir. 1968); *see also* 2 WEINSTEIN'S FEDERAL EVIDENCE § 410.08. *But see* Bruton v. United States, 391 U.S. 123 (1968) (even though a limiting instruction was submitted to the jury, the Supreme Court set aside the conviction of a defendant at a joint trial in which a co-defendant's confession implicating the accused was admitted into evidence); *see also* the discussion of *Bruton* in 2 WEINSTEIN'S FEDERAL EVIDENCE § 410.08.

[53] *See* WEINSTEIN'S FEDERAL EVIDENCE § 410.08.

Chapter 411

Rule 411. Liability Insurance

Rule 411. Liability Insurance

Evidence that a person was or was not insured against liability is not admissible to prove whether the person acted negligently or otherwise wrongfully. But the court may admit this evidence for another purpose, such as proving a witness's bias or prejudice or proving agency, ownership, or control.

---

§ 411.1 Liability Insurance Evidence — In General

Rule 411 codifies the exclusionary rule regarding liability insurance.[1] According to Rule 411, the fact that a person was or was not insured against liability is not admissible to establish negligent or wrongful conduct by the individual. This principle of exclusion, however, does not prohibit the admission of evidence of insurance coverage where a consequential fact, other than negligence or wrongful conduct, is the object of proof. Accordingly, the second sentence of Rule 411 sets forth illustrations of the use of evidence of insurance coverage that are not prohibited by the first sentence of the Rule.[2]

---

[1] *See generally,* 1 MCCORMICK, § 201; 2 WEINSTEIN'S FEDERAL EVIDENCE §§ 411.01–411.06; 2 MUELLER & KIRKPATRICK, §§ 152–154; 2 WIGMORE, § 282. *See also* Fannin, *Disclosure of Insurance in Negligence Trials—The Arizona Rule,* 5 ARIZ. L. REV. 83 (1963); Fournier, *Pre-Trial Discovery of Insurance Coverage and Limits,* 28 FORDHAM L. REV. 215 (1959); Jenkins, *Discovery of Automobile Liability Insurance Limits: Quillets of the Law,* 14 KAN. L. REV. 59 (1965); Laverci, *Disclosure of Insurance Policy Limits,* 1957 INS. L.J. 505 (1957); McCurn, *Battleground: Liability Insurance and the Rules of Discovery,* 1 FORUM, Jan. 1966; Slough, *Relevancy Unraveled, Part III—Remote and Prejudicial Evidence,* 5 KAN. L. REV. 675 (1957); Stopher, *Should a Change be Made in Discovery Rules to Permit Inquiry as to Limits of Liability Insurance?,* 35 INS. COUNSEL J. 53 (1968); Vetter, *Voir Dire III: Liability Insurance,* 29 MO. L. REV. 305 (1964); Eichel v. New York Cent. R. R. Co., 375 U.S. 253 (1963) (per curiam) (dictum). Rule 411 is in accord with pre-Rule law.

[2] *See, e.g.,* Posttape Assocs. v. Eastman Kodak Co., 537 F.2d 751, 758 (3d Cir. 1976) ("generally, evidence of liability coverage is not admissible when a party is accused of acting wrongfully, because of the likelihood for spillover between insurance and inference of fault; knowledge that a party is insured may also affect a verdict if the jury knows that some of the loss has been paid by insurance or that it would satisfy a judgment against a defendant"); Brown v. Walter, 62 F.2d 798, 800 (2d Cir. 1933) ("there can be no rational excuse for

§ 411.2 Policy of Rule 411

Rule 411 is designed to minimize unfair prejudice relating to the consideration of liability insurance. On one hand, the probative value of liability insurance is exceedingly low regarding issues of liability, while on the other hand, the risks of prejudice are extremely high.[3] As stated by McCormick:

> [The doctrine against admissibility of liability insurance is based on] the belief that whether one has insurance coverage reveals little about the likelihood that he will act carelessly. Subject to a few pathological exceptions, financial protection will not diminish the normal incentive to be careful, especially where life and limb are at stake. Similarly, the argument that insured individuals or firms are more prudent and careful, as a group, than those who are self-insurers seems tenuous, and also serves to counteract any force than the first argument may have. Thus, the relevance of the evidence of coverage is doubtful.[4]

Consequently, with the probative value of insurance at best equivocal on the issue of negligence or fault, the policy for exclusion is ultimately grounded in the prejudicial risk that awareness by the fact finder of insurance invites a finding based on ability or inability to absorb the loss.[5] Accordingly, knowledge by the trier of fact of insurance coverage possesses the prejudicial risk of inflating damage awards.[6]

---

mentioning insurance, except the flimsy one that a man is more likely to be careless if insured; that is at most the merest guess, much more than outweighed by the probability that the real issues will be obscured"). *See generally,* 2 WEINSTEIN'S FEDERAL EVIDENCE § 411.03.

[3] *See, e.g.,* Posttape Assocs. v. Eastman Kodak Co., 537 F.2d 751 (3d Cir. 1976) (suit claiming damages for increased costs and lost profits because of defective film; Kodak attempted to show that limitation of damages to replacement of film was a custom and usage of trade of which plaintiff had knowledge; error for trial judge to have excluded evidence of plaintiff's insurance coverage indemnifying it against defective film; the proffered evidence was relevant, and it is doubtful there would be any prejudice, because the parties were both commercial entities, the injury was not likely to stir emotions, and the existence of such coverage might have been so unusual that the purchase itself would have significance in the circumstances; the exclusion of this relevant evidence was far more prejudicial to the defense than its admission would have been to the plaintiffs); *see generally,* 2 WEINSTEIN'S FEDERAL EVIDENCE § 411.02.

[4] 1 MCCORMICK, § 201, at 852–853 (footnotes omitted).

[5] *See* 2 MUELLER & KIRKPATRICK, § 153.

[6] *See id.; see also* Ouachita Nat'l Bank v. Tosco Corp., 686 F.2d 1291 (8th Cir. 1982); Posttape Assocs. v. Eastman Kodak Co., 537 F.2d 751 (3d Cir. 1976). The text and the foregoing authority reflect conventional wisdom on the issue of the admissibility of insurance coverage, a position that is not, however, invulnerable to criticism. *See* 2 MUELLER & KIRKPATRICK, § 153; 1 MCCORMICK, § 201; Schevling v. Johnson, 122 F. Supp. 85 (D. Conn. 1953), *aff'd,* 213 F.2d 959 (2d Cir. 1954) ("justice does not require that law suits shall be torn from their context and tried in an artificially produced vacuum").

§ 411.3   Scope of Rule 411

The exclusionary principle of Rule 411 applies by its terms both to the fault of a defendant and to the contributory negligence or other fault of a plaintiff. It should also be noted that Rule 411 specifically excludes evidence of not only the existence, but also the non-existence, of insurance where such evidence is offered to establish negligence or wrongful conduct.[7]

Rule 411 does not address whether liability insurance is subject to pretrial discovery; the issue is beyond the scope of the Rule.[8] Likewise, Rule 411 is not intended to resolve the issue of whether it is proper to question a prospective juror as to possible interest or bias in connection with an insurance carrier.[9] Rule 411 only addresses whether liability insurance is admissible in evidence in order to establish negligence or wrongful conduct.

As McCormick notes, "Witnesses have been known to make unexpected and unresponsive references to insurance."[10] The curative measure is usually a limiting instruction and not a mistrial[11] unless bad faith abuse by trial counsel is evident.[12]

§ 411.4   Admissible Evidence Relating to Liability Insurance

The exclusionary principle of Rule 411 applies only where liability insurance is offered to establish negligence or wrongful conduct. Where

---

[7] Stephenson v. Steinhauer, 188 F.2d 432 (8th Cir. 1951); *see generally,* 2 WEINSTEIN'S FEDERAL EVIDENCE § 411.03; 1 McCORMICK, § 201.

[8] *See* Fed. R. Civ. P. 26(a)(1)(A), which provides in relevant part:

(1) Initial Disclosures. (A) In General. Except . . . as otherwise stipulated or ordered by the court, a party must, without awaiting a discovery request, provide to other parties:

. . .

(iv) for inspection and copying as under Rule 34, any insurance agreement under which an insurance business may be liable to satisfy part or all of a possible judgment in the action or to indemnify or reimburse for payments made to satisfy the judgment.

[9] As stated by McCormick:

In some jurisdictions the trial judge may allow or disallow the questioning, as he sees fit, and in general, many refinements and variations exist as to consultation with the court in advance and as to the questions that may be asked. It is usually said that the questions must be propounded in good faith. Such "good faith" involves establishing that the party is in fact insured, that prospective jurors may be associated with a liability carrier or otherwise unusually concerned with insurance policies or premiums.

1 McCORMICK, § 201 at 856 n.20. *See generally,* Langley v. Turner's Exp. Inc., 375 F.2d 296 (4th Cir. 1967); Kiernan v. Van Schaik, 347 F.2d 775 (3d Cir. 1965); Kaab, *Insurance Questions on Voir Dire,* 17 CLEVELAND MAR. L. REV. 504 (1968).

[10] 1 McCORMICK, § 201, at 855–56; *see generally,* 2 MUELLER & KIRKPATRICK, § 153; 2 WEINSTEIN'S FEDERAL EVIDENCE § 411.03.

[11] 1 McCORMICK, § 201. *But see* Pickwick Stage Lines, Inc. v. Edwards, 64 F.2d 758 (10th Cir. 1933) (bad faith abuse by trial counsel).

[12] 1 McCORMICK, § 201.

liability insurance is offered to establish other consequential controverted issues, the exclusionary principle of Rule 411 will not foreclose the admissibility of the evidence. As the second sentence to Rule 411 confirms, evidence of liability insurance is not excluded under Rule 411 where offered to prove agency, ownership or control, or to establish the bias or prejudice of a witness. The list of alternate issues, of course, is illustrative and not exhaustive.[13]

While Rule 411 does not on its face require that the alternate issue must be controverted, it is clear that if the issue is not contested, exclusion under the balance of Rule 403 will be justified.

Accordingly, where an issue of agency is contested, evidence that the alleged principal carried liability insurance covering the alleged agent is probative of, and not excluded under Rule 411 as to the existence of the relationship.[14] Likewise, where control is contested, the fact that a particular person carried insurance against risks involving the instrumentality of the injury is admissible under Rule 411 as to control by the insured person.[15]

Liability insurance may be permissibly revealed to the trier of fact in the course of an impeachment involving a statement taken from the witness by an insurance adjuster.[16] Likewise, cross-examination as to interest or bias

---

[13] *See, e.g.,* DSC Communs. Corp. v. Next Level Communs., 107 F.3d 322 (5th Cir. 1997) (evidence of an indemnity agreement, although akin to liability insurance, was an integral part of the relationship between the parties and therefore necessary to the jury's understanding of that relationship; hence trial court properly admitted the evidence under Rule 411); Hunziker v. Scheidemantle, 543 F.2d 489 (3d Cir. 1976); *see generally,* 2 WEINSTEIN'S FEDERAL EVIDENCE § 411.03.

[14] *See, e.g.,* Eldridge v. McGeorge, 99 F.2d 835 (8th Cir. 1938) (in suit against contractor for injuries sustained when plaintiff was run over by truck owned by Callan, where contractor claimed Callan was an independent contractor, and Callan testified that he controlled the operation of the truck, it was error to disallow plaintiff from asking Callan whether he carried liability insurance on the truck, since a negative answer would tend circumstantially to indicate that Callan did not control the truck, or at least not solely); *see also* McCoy v. Universal Carloading & Distrib. Co., 82 F.2d 342 (6th Cir. 1936); *see generally,* 2 WEINSTEIN'S FEDERAL EVIDENCE § 411.04.

[15] *E.g.,* Dobbins v. Crain Bros., 432 F. Supp. 1060 (W.D. Pa. 1976), *modified on other grounds,* 567 F.2d 559 (3d Cir. 1977) (ownership; limiting instructions given).

[16] *E.g.,* Palmer v. Krueger, 897 F.2d 1529 (10th Cir. 1990) (the probative value of evidence that the distribution of insurance proceeds was the source of tension between the plaintiff's and the defendant's families was too small to justify admitting evidence regarding the existence of an insurance policy); Varlack v. S.W.C. Caribbean, Inc., 550 F.2d 171 (3d Cir. 1977) (references to insurance were made in course of arguing that the criteria of Civil Rule 15(c) for amending complaint by adding an additional party had been met, since proposed defendant knew of suit because he had provided insurance carrier with information and would not be prejudiced, because carrier was real party in interest; also not error to mention insurance when identifying statement for impeachment use as prior inconsistent statement).

may permissibly reveal sympathies with an insurance company.[17]

In all situations in which liability insurance is offered to establish a consequential issue other than negligence or wrongful conduct, the balancing principle of Rule 403 may be invoked in an effort to exclude the evidence from consideration.[18] Likewise, a limiting instruction is appropriate where evidence of liability insurance is admitted to establish a consequential fact other than wrongful conduct.[19]

---

[17] *E.g.,* Charter v. Chleborad, 551 F.2d 246 (8th Cir. 1977); Majestic v. Louisville & N.R.R. Co., 147 F.2d 621 (6th Cir. 1945); *see generally,* 2 WEINSTEIN'S FEDERAL EVIDENCE § 411.04.

[18] Charter v. Chleborad, 551 F.2d 246 (8th Cir. 1977) (finding balance in favor of admissibility).

[19] *See* § 104.1, *supra; see also* Majestic v. Louisville & N.R.R. Co., 147 F.2d 621 (6th Cir. 1945).

Chapter 412

Rule 412. Sex Offense Cases: The Victim's Sexual Behavior or Predisposition

Rule 412. Sex-Offense Cases: The Victim's Sexual Behavior or Predisposition

(a) **Prohibited Uses.** The following evidence is not admissible in a civil or criminal proceeding involving alleged sexual misconduct:

    (1) evidence offered to prove that a victim engaged in other sexual behavior; or

    (2) evidence offered to prove a victim's sexual predisposition.

(b) **Exceptions.**

    (1) *Criminal Cases.* The court may admit the following evidence in a criminal case:

        (A) evidence of specific instances of a victim's sexual behavior, if offered to prove that someone other than the defendant was the source of semen, injury, or other physical evidence;

        (B) evidence of specific instances of a victim's sexual behavior with respect to the person accused of the sexual misconduct, if offered by the defendant to prove consent or if offered by the prosecutor; and

        (C) evidence whose exclusion would violate the defendant's constitutional rights.

    (2) *Civil Cases.* In a civil case, the court may admit evidence offered to prove a victim's sexual behavior or sexual predisposition if its probative value substantially outweighs the danger of harm to any victim and of unfair prejudice to any party. The court may admit evidence of a victim's reputation only if the victim has placed it in controversy.

(c) **Procedure to Determine Admissibility.**

    (1) *Motion.* If a party intends to offer evidence under Rule 412(b), the party must:

        (A) file a motion that specifically describes the evidence and states the purpose for which it is to be offered;

        (B) do so at least 14 days before trial unless the court, for good cause, sets a different time;

(C)   serve the motion on all parties; and

(D)   notify the victim or, when appropriate, the victim's guardian or representative.

(2) *Hearing.* Before admitting evidence under this rule, the court must conduct an in camera hearing and give the victim and parties a right to attend and be heard. Unless the court orders otherwise, the motion, related materials, and the record of the hearing must be and remain sealed.

(d)   Definition of "Victim." In this rule, "victim" includes an alleged victim.

---

§ 412.1   Legislative History

The legislative history of Rule 412 is unique among the Federal Rules of Evidence. A brief explication of that history is necessary to properly understand the purpose and effect of the Rule.

The original Rule 412, unlike most other Federal Rules of Evidence, was not promulgated by the Supreme Court. Instead, it was initiated in Congress subsequent to the adoption of the original Rules as a separate piece of legislation to protect victims of certain sexual misconduct crimes from the admission of specified types of prejudicial evidence.[1] The original version of Rule 412, popularly known as "The Federal Rape Shield Law," was applicable only to victims of rape or attempted rape, unlike the present version of the Rule.[2] Accordingly, the exclusionary principles of the original Rule were available only in criminal proceedings.

The original Rule was designed to change prior federal practice in several respects. Most notably, it reflected Congressional consensus that the evidence of a rape victim's past sexual behavior is, in most instances, of limited probative value relative to a determination of the ultimate issue of the trial, *i.e.,* whether a rape has occurred.[3] In accordance with this conclusion, Congress altered the prior practice of the federal courts, which admitted evidence of a rape victim's general propensities under Rule 404(a)(2)(B), which generally governs evidence about the character of an alleged victim.[4] This practice produced the undesirable effect of shifting the focus of the trial away from the guilt or innocence of the accused to a determination of the

---

[1]   124 Cong. Rec. H11944–H11945 (daily ed. Oct. 10, 1978).

[2]   *See* Rule 412 and § 412.4, *infra.*

[3]   124 Cong. Rec. S18580 (daily ed. Oct. 12, 1978); *see also* United States v. Kasto, 584 F.2d 268 (8th Cir. 1978).

[4]   124 Cong. Rec. H11944 (daily ed. Oct. 10, 1978); *see generally,* Rule 404 and Chapter 404, *supra.*

morality of the victim.[5] The prior procedure also created the effect of humiliating the victim without measurably furthering the truth-finding function of the jury.[6] The practice provided for the expenditure of valuable judicial resources on a collateral, and sometimes irrelevant, matter. Additionally, from a societal standpoint, a destructive result of this practice was the loss of testimony from victims who wished to avoid public exposure of their past sexual behavior.[7] Moreover, federal case law did not provide clear guidance on the admission of such evidence, and as a consequence, arbitrariness further exacerbated undesirable results.[8]

Congress was also particularly concerned that evidence of a victim's past sexual behavior not be exposed to the public or the jury until the specific evidence was first reviewed and evaluated in chambers by the judge.[9] Accordingly, the original Rule established a detailed set of procedures that the defense was required to follow when it wished to introduce evidence of the rape victim's sexual behavior.

Since its inception in 1978, Rule 412 has engendered a great deal of confusion, largely due to the length and complexity of the Rule. The original version of the Rule was more than twice as long as the current version, and it contained provisions that were confusingly worded and potentially raised Constitutional issues.[10] Scholarly analysis of the Rule revealed many of the

---

[5] *See* 124 Cong. Rec. H11944–H11945 (daily ed. Oct. 10, 1978); *see also* McLean v. United States, 377 A.2d 74 (D.C. Cir. 1977) (supporting trial judge's discretion to exclude testimony concerning a rape victim's sexual contacts on prior occasions with persons other than the defendants).

[6] *See* McLean v. United States, 377 A.2d 74 (D.C. Cir. 1978) (refusing to admit evidence of sexual reputation; citing Rule 404); *see also* United States v. Driver, 581 F.2d 80 (4th Cir. 1978).

[7] *See* California v. Rincon-Pineda, 14 Cal.3d 864 (Cal. 1975) ("rape in particular has been shown by repeated studies to be grossly under-reported"); *see, e.g.,* Lovely v. United States, 175 F.2d 312 (4th Cir. 1949) (providing an example of the prior practice of admitting such evidence).

[8] *See* 2 WEINSTEIN'S FEDERAL EVIDENCE §§ 412.01–412.05; 2 MUELLER & KIRKPATRICK, §§ 156–158.

[9] *See* 124 Cong. Rec. H11944 (daily ed. Oct. 10, 1978).

[10] For example, the original version of the Rule contained the introductory phrase, "Notwithstanding any other provision of law, . . ." before setting forth the general exclusionary rule. This phrase produced confusion in two respects. First, the language of the Rule did not fit into the conceptual scheme of the other Rules. The general exclusionary rule was subject to exceptions under the Rule, but it was unclear whether these exceptions to Rule 412 could be admitted pursuant to "any other provision of law." The language of the present version makes clear that the exceptions in Rule 412 can be admitted only within the context of the general exclusionary rule of Rule 412, and not within the context of another Rule or statute. However, exclusion of the evidence in criminal proceedings may still be appropriate under Rule 403. *See* Rule 412, Advisory Committee Note. Second, the original Rule did not specify which other provisions of law Congress intended Rule 412 to override. Likewise, the

ambiguities and shortcomings inherent in the original version of the Rule.[11]

The original version of Rule 412 also proved to be unwieldy in practice. As previously noted, the original version of the Rule was available only in prosecutions for rape and attempted rape. An amendment in 1988 expanded the scope of the Rule to apply in any proceeding under 18 U.S.C. Chapter 109A, which included additional sexual offenses not expressly covered under the original version of the Rule. The present version of Rule 412 further expands the scope of the Rule and is potentially applicable in the prosecution of a wide variety of crimes.[12] Unlike its predecessor, the present version of the Rule provides for its application in civil proceedings. This addition reflects Congressional concern that a strong social policy exists for the provision of relief to the victim, in addition to the punishment of those who engage in sexual misconduct.[13]

In response to concerns regarding Rule 412 as enacted in 1978, the 102nd Congress considered, but did not pass, legislation that would have circumvented the normal Rule-making process by directly amending Rule 412.[14] Sensing this Congressional need for immediacy, the Advisory Committee on Criminal Rules of the Judicial Conference, in consultation with the Advisory Committee on Civil Rules, quickly drafted amendments to Rule 412 in early 1993.[15] After an expedited process of public review, hearings and revision, the Judicial Conference submitted its version of proposed amendments to Rule 412 to the Supreme Court for approval in October of that year.[16] In an unusual move, the Supreme Court rejected part of the amendment to Rule 412 proposed by the Judicial Conference that would make the Rule applicable in civil cases.[17] In a letter from the Supreme Court to the Chair of the Executive Committee of the Judicial Conference, Chief Justice Rehnquist explained that several Justices felt that the amendment would

---

original Rule raised significant Constitutional issues. The language in the original version of the Rule authorized a trial judge to make findings of fact with regard to the existence of past sexual conduct between the victim and the accused. *See* Rule 412(c)(2) (original version). This authorization might be interpreted as violating a defendant's right to a jury trial under the Sixth and Seventh Amendments. *See* Rule 412, Advisory Committee Note.

[11] *See, e.g.,* 1 SALTZBURG & MARTIN, 396.

[12] *See* Rule 412, Advisory Committee Note (mentioning kidnapping as one of the crimes during the prosecution of which the Rule may be applicable).

[13] *See* Rule 412, Advisory Committee Note.

[14] Excerpt from the Report of the Judicial Conference Committee on Rules of Practice and Procedure, section IV (September, 1993); *see generally,* Rule 1102 and Chapter 1102, *infra.*

[15] Excerpt from the Report of the Judicial Conference Committee on Rules of Practice and Procedure, section IV (September, 1993).

[16] Memorandum from the Judicial Conference to the Supreme Court (October 25, 1993).

[17] Letter from Chief Justice Rehnquist to House Speaker Thomas S. Foley (April 29, 1994).

violate the Rules Enabling Act.[18] Specifically, several Justices thought that proposed Rule 412(b)(2) might bar evidence of an alleged victim's "sexually provocative speech or dress," which may be relevant in workplace harassment cases.[19] Accordingly, the proposed amendment was revised by the Court to eliminate the civil component. The structure and wording of proposed Rule 412 transmitted by the Supreme Court to Congress were changed to reflect these concerns.[20] Pursuant to the rule-making authority of the Supreme Court in 28 U.S.C. § 2072, an order from the Supreme Court dated April 29, 1994 revised Rule 412, effective December 1, 1994.

The deletion of the civil component from Rule 412 by the Supreme Court was not well received by Congress. Despite the revision of the Rule by the Court, Congress extended Rule 412 to civil cases as part of the Violent Crime Control and Law Enforcement Act of 1994, also to take effect on December 1, 1994.[21] Thus, the present version of Rule 412 is identical to the version originally proposed by the Judicial Conference, although it applies with full force and effect through different rule-making processes.[22]

§ 412.2   Scope

Rule 412(a) absolutely prohibits the admission of evidence concerning an alleged victim's past sexual behavior or sexual predisposition, subject to the exceptions provided in the Rule. Before the adoption of Rule 412, such evidence was sometimes admissible as either substantive evidence (that is, to show that the alleged victim, whether testifying at trial or not, was the type of promiscuous person who would be likely to have consented to sexual conduct with the accused) or as impeachment evidence (to show, if the victim chose to testify, that he or she was the type of dishonest person who would lie on direct examination). Under the rule, evidence of sexual behavior or predisposition is no longer admissible for either purpose. Nor is such evidence admissible at the request of the prosecution, for example to show the victim's lack of sexual history.[23] The language of the Rule clearly

---

[18] The Rules Enabling Act forbids the enactment of rules that would "abridge, enlarge or modify any substantive right." 28 U.S.C. § 2072(b).

[19] Letter from Chief Justice Rehnquist to the Honorable John F. Gerry, Chair of the Executive Committee of the Judicial Conference of the United States (April 29, 1994) (quoting Meritor Savings Bank v. Vinson, 477 U.S. 57 (1986)).

[20] Proposed Amendments to Federal Rules of Evidence, Order from the Supreme Court (April 29, 1994).

[21] P.L. 103-322.

[22] See Rule 412, Advisory Committee Note.

[23] United States v. Blue Bird, 372 F.3d 989 (8th Cir. 2004) (Rule 412's prohibition on evidence of "sexual behavior" includes chaste sexual behavior, and bars evidence that sex offense victim was a virgin. "If the defendant in such a case is prohibited from playing on the potential prejudices of a jury by introducing evidence of the alleged victim's promiscuity, the government should also be forbidden to play on potential prejudices by introducing evidence

indicates that the kinds of evidence described in subsection (a) are admissible only under the specific exceptions to that subsection, and only if the requirements of those exceptions are satisfied. Evidence of the kind described in Rule 412(a) is not admissible pursuant to any other statute or Rule of Evidence.[24] The Advisory Committee Note indicates that the alleged victim need not be a party to the litigation to render Rule 412 applicable.[25]

As previously noted, the prohibition of Rule 412(a) applies in both criminal and civil proceedings in all cases involving sexual misconduct. This represents an expansion of the scope of the Rule from the predecessor version. The Advisory Committee Note comments that "[t]he strong social policy of protecting a victim's privacy and encouraging victims to come forward to report criminal acts . . . is equally great when a defendant is charged with kidnapping, and evidence is offered . . . to prove . . . that the defendant sexually assaulted the victim."[26] Likewise, these same concerns do not disappear merely because the context has changed from a criminal proceeding to a proceeding involving a claim for damages or injunctive relief. Accordingly, the exclusionary principle of Rule 412 is no longer confined to criminal cases.

By its strict terms, the exclusionary principle of Rule 412 applies only to evidence offered against alleged victims of sexual misconduct. Evidence of alleged sexual activities or sexual predisposition of a witness who is not an alleged victim is not covered by Rule 412, although a witness is covered by the protections of other Rules of Evidence, such as Rules 403, 404, 608 and 611(a).[27] Likewise, the prohibition of Rule 412 will not apply in cases when the person against whom the evidence is offered cannot reasonably be characterized as a "victim of alleged sexual misconduct."[28] For example, the Rule would be inapplicable in a defamation action involving statements implicating sexual misconduct, because there is no actual "victim" of "alleged sexual misconduct." Instead, evidence offered to show that the alleged defamatory statements were true against a "victim" of defamation, not "alleged sexual misconduct," would be subject to the more general protections of Rule 401 and 403. However, the Advisory Committee Note clearly indicates that the Rule will apply in a Title VII action where the

---

of the alleged victim's chastity" or by suggesting that he "robbed" her of her virginity).

[24] *See* Rule 412, Advisory Committee Note.

[25] *See* Rule 412, Advisory Committee Note.

[26] Rule 412, Advisory Committee Note.

[27] *See* Rule 412, Advisory Committee Note; *see also* Rule 611(a)(3) ("The court shall exercise reasonable control over the mode and order of interrogating the witnesses and presenting evidence so as to . . . protect witnesses from harassment or undue embarrassment") and Chapter 611, *infra. See generally* Chapters 403 and 404, *supra,* and Chapter 608, *infra.*

[28] Rule 412, Advisory Committee Note.

plaintiff has alleged sexual harassment.[29]

§ 412.3   General Exclusionary Rule

Evidence of a victim's past sexual behavior or sexual predisposition that might be admissible under another Rule of Evidence must nonetheless be excluded under Rule 412 if the requirements of that Rule apply. For example, reputation or opinion evidence of a victim's sexual behavior or propensity is inadmissible on the issue of whether a rape has occurred, notwithstanding the general defense right to introduce opinion or reputation evidence concerning the character of a victim under Rule 404(a)(2). Similarly, evidence of this kind would be inadmissible for impeachment purposes if the complainant testifies as a witness at trial, even if it would be admissible pursuant to Rule 608(a).[30] The word "other" is included in the language of Rule 412(a)(1) to imply a degree of flexibility in the admission of evidence that is "intrinsic" to the alleged sexual misconduct.[31]

The term "sexual behavior" in subsection (a)(1) includes not only actual physical contact, such as sexual intercourse, but also any conduct that implies physical contact.[32] The term is also broad enough to encompass activities of the mind, such as fantasies or dreams.[33] For example, admission of an alleged victim's diary or personal journal that indicated a strong generalized sexual desire would be prohibited by the exclusionary principle of Rule 412.

The inclusion of Rule 412(a)(2) and the term "sexual predisposition" is to provide broader protection of the alleged victim than Rule 412(a)(1) provides. By prohibiting any evidence that may obliquely connote the alleged victim's sexual activity to the factfinder, Rule 412(a)(2) serves the Rule's policy objectives of safeguarding the alleged victim from irrelevant stereotyping and protection of the alleged victim from potential embarrass-ment.[34] As the Advisory Committee Note indicates, evidence of an alleged victim's mode of dress, speech or lifestyle will be prohibited by the

---

[29] *See* Rule 412, Advisory Committee Note.

[30] These examples do not imply that Rule 412 is limited in its operation to reputation or opinion evidence or in rape cases, only to be used for impeachment purposes, or constitute exceptions only to Rule 404 or 608. Clearly, the scope of the Rule, by its own terms and the explanation of the Advisory Committee Note, is intended to encompass other kinds of evidence in various cases, civil or criminal, for impeachment or substantive purposes, that would otherwise be admissible under many different Rules of Evidence.

[31] Rule 412, Advisory Committee Note.

[32] *See, e.g.,* United States v. Galloway, 937 F.2d 542 (10th Cir. 1991) (use of contraceptives inadmissible since it implies sexual activity); United States v. One Feather, 702 F.2d 736 (8th Cir. 1983) (birth of illegitimate child inadmissible); Kansas v. Carmichael, 240 Kan. 149, 727 P.2d 918 (Kan. 1986) (evidence of venereal disease inadmissible).

[33] Rule 412, Advisory Committee Note.

[34] *See* Rule 412, Advisory Committee Note.

exclusionary principle of Rule 412 unless one of the exceptions apply.

It must be noted that, subject to the express exceptions in subsection (b), Rule 412(a) bars the use of any kind of evidence used for the purposes stated in that subsection. Thus, reputation evidence and evidence in the form of an opinion are generally excluded, in addition to evidence in the form of specific acts.

§ 412.4   Exceptions to General Exclusionary Rule

The exclusionary principle of Rule 412 will apply to evidence offered for the specific uses identified in that subsection. Once it is determined that evidence would be prohibited under Rule 412(a), reference to subsection (b) is necessary to ascertain whether the otherwise prohibited evidence falls under an exception in that subsection.

The exceptions to the exclusionary principle of subsection (a) in a criminal proceeding are largely unchanged from the predecessor Rule. However, the Rule has expanded the types of criminal cases in which the exclusionary principle of Rule 412 will apply.[35] In addition, an exception for evidence in civil cases subject to the general exclusionary principle of subsection (a) has been added in Rule 412(b)(2).

§ 412.5   Exception: Physical Evidence

The first exception to the general exclusionary principle of Rule 412 is available only in criminal proceedings. The admission of evidence of specific instances of the alleged victim's sexual behavior is allowed when the accused is attempting to prove that someone else was the source of the victim's injury or the semen found on or near the victim. Obviously, the defendant must be permitted to demonstrate that another person was responsible for the physical evidence being offered.[36]

The term "injury" should be interpreted broadly to include cuts, scratches, bruises or other evidence of physical abuse or physical indications of sexual contact.[37] The inclusion of the phrase "other physical evidence" in the Rule lends support to the suggestion concerning the similar provision in the predecessor Rule that the exception extends to the alleged victim's pregnancy.[38] Additionally, the phrase implies that the exception does not extend

---

[35] *See* Rule 412, Advisory Committee Note.

[36] *See* United States v. Begay, 937 F.2d 515 (10th Cir. 1991); *but see* United States v. Richards, 118 F.3d 622 (8th Cir. 1997) (although Rule 412 allows evidence of prior sexual behavior to prove that a person other than the defendant was the source of semen or other physical evidence, the Rule does not allow for the admission of such evidence where it is the defendant and not the prosecutor who first introduces evidence of the existence of semen in the victim).

[37] *See* United States v. Kasto, 584 F.2d 268 (8th Cir. 1978).

[38] *See* 2 MUELLER & KIRKPATRICK, § 157; *see also* 2 WEINSTEIN'S FEDERAL EVIDENCE § 412.03.

to non-physical injuries. If evidence offered to show non-physical injuries were admissible, the defense may argue that the defendant was not responsible for the mental injury of the alleged victim, instead blaming the past sexual behavior of the alleged victim for that specific injury. This would have the effect of presenting to the jury evidence of a nature otherwise inadmissible under the general exclusionary principle of Rule 412(a).[39] Although the Advisory Committee Note is silent on the issue, the phrase "other physical evidence" in Rule 412(b)(1)(A) strongly implies that evidence excepted under that subsection not extend to non-physical injuries.

As previously noted, evidence that may fall within the exception of Rule 412(b)(1)(A) and thus qualify for admission may nonetheless be excluded if it does not satisfy the other Rules of Evidence. Accordingly, the balancing test of Rule 403 may operate to exclude evidence offered for the specific purpose identified in subsection (b)(1)(A).

Only specific instances of sexual behavior by the alleged victim qualify for exception under this subsection. Reputation and opinion evidence offered for the purposes identified in this subsection are absolutely barred through operation of the general exclusionary principle of Rule 412(a).

§ 412.6   Exception: Victim's Past Behavior

Like the first exception, the second exception to the general exclusionary principle of Rule 412 is also available only in criminal proceedings. This exception allows the accused to introduce specific instances of past sexual behavior of the alleged victim with respect to the accused to prove consent. When offered as proof of consent, evidence of past sexual relations between the alleged victim and the defendant of course has incomparably greater probative value than any evidence of sexual relationship she may have had with anyone else. Likewise, specific instances of past sexual behavior by the alleged victim with respect to the accused are admissible if offered by the prosecution for any reason.[40]

It should be noted that this exception allows the admission of evidence of past sexual behavior of the alleged victim only with respect to the accused. Evidence of past sexual behavior of the alleged victim with persons other than the accused falls within the general exclusionary principle of Rule 412 and may be admitted only through the other exceptions to Rule 412. On the other hand, as the Advisory Committee Note illustrates, this exception is not limited to past sexual acts of the alleged victim with the accused. Specific

---

[39] *See* 2 MUELLER & KIRKPATRICK, § 157; 2 WEINSTEIN'S FEDERAL EVIDENCE § 412.03.

[40] The Advisory Committee Note provides an example of this latter possibility. In a child sexual abuse case, evidence offered by the prosecution of uncharged sexual behavior between the alleged victim and the accused may be admissible pursuant to Rule 404(b) to demonstrate a pattern of behavior. Admission of evidence of this kind is not barred by the general exclusionary principle of Rule 412, and is now made admissible by Rules 413 through 415.

instances of past sexual behavior of the alleged victim *toward* the defendant are allowed under this exception. For example, statements by the alleged victim expressing an intent or desire to engage in sexual contact with the accused would qualify for admission under Rule 412(b)(1)(B).[41]

Like subsection (b)(1)(A), this subsection applies only to specific instances of sexual behavior by the alleged victim. Reputation and opinion evidence offered for the purposes identified in this subsection are absolutely barred through operation of the general exclusionary principle of Rule 412.

§ 412.7   Exception: Constitutional Violation

The third exception to the general exclusionary principle of Rule 412 authorizes the admission of "evidence whose exclusion would violate the defendant's constitutional rights" during a criminal proceeding.[42] Obviously, the Federal Rules of Evidence can never limit the admissibility of evidence that is constitutionally compelled, but the provision obviates any arguable constitutional conflict.

The circumstances under which evidence of an alleged victim's past sexual behavior or sexual predisposition is constitutionally compelled are, at best, only capable of a rough assessment. The clearest case for constitutionally compelled admissibility is in regard to impeachment. Evidence tending to show that the alleged victim was biased, prejudiced, or had an ulterior motive for blaming the defendant is likely to be admissible because constitutionally compelled.[43] Exposing the bias of a witness is traditionally a fundamental method of impeaching a witness, and the right to expose the bias of a witness may be constitutionally required under the Confrontation Clause.[44] Evidence of the victim's sexual history is not admissible under this exception, however, merely because it might assist the defense in explaining some collateral or relatively insignificant aspect of the prosecution's case.[45]

---

[41] *See* Rule 412, Advisory Committee Note.

[42] Rule 412(b)(1)(C).

[43] *See generally,* Davis v. Alaska, 415 U.S. 308 (1974); United States v. Nez, 661 F.2d 1203 (10th Cir. 1981). *See also* Chambers v. Mississippi, 410 U.S. 284 (1973) (refusal of trial court to allow criminal defendant to cross-examine witness called by the defendant violative of due process.)

[44] *See, e.g.,* Olden v. Kentucky, 488 U.S. 227 (1988) (defendant in rape case had right to inquire into alleged victim's cohabitation with another man to show that she had a motive to fabricate the claim of rape that she made as soon as she got out of the defendant's car at night and unexpectedly encountered the same man with whom she was cohabitating); United States v. Kasto, 584 F.2d 268 (8th Cir. 1978).

[45] United States v. Culver, 598 F.3d 740 (11th Cir. 2010) (in prosecution for production of child pornography, the accused had no constitutional right to cross-examine the alleged victim, his 13-year old stepdaughter, on her sexual history or her relations with her boyfriend for the purpose of proving that the defendant was not the reason for the condoms found beneath her bed. The admission of such evidence would have confused the jury and harassed the girl, and the explanation for the presence of the condoms was at best marginally relevant

§ 412.8   Exception: Civil Cases

As previously noted, the general exclusionary principle of Rule 412(a) is applicable in civil as well as criminal cases. Likewise, a new exception governs the admissibility of evidence in civil cases, and the applicable subsection employs a balancing test, unlike the specific exceptions available in a criminal proceeding, "in recognition of the difficulty of foreseeing future developments in the law."[46] The evolution of various causes of action in the civil context mandates the need for greater flexibility in the application of the Rule.

The exception is available to specific instances of sexual behavior as well as reputation or opinion evidence.[47] However, the last sentence of Rule 412(b)(2) indicates that reputation evidence of an alleged victim is admissible only if it has been placed in controversy by the alleged victim, and only if it further satisfies the balancing test of the subsection. The Advisory Committee Note indicates that the alleged victim need not make a specific allegation in a pleading to place the issue in controversy. Presumably, statements made by the alleged victim under oath placing his or her reputation in controversy would be encompassed by the exception. This condition should not be interpreted, however, to apply to reputation evidence of the defendant. By its terms, the "placed in controversy" requirement is applicable only with respect to the alleged victim's reputation.

The balancing test employed by Rule 412(b)(2) differs from Rule 403 in three important respects.[48] First, the balancing test of Rule 412 reverses the procedure of Rule 403 by requiring the proponent of the evidence, whether plaintiff or defendant, to demonstrate admissibility rather than requiring the opponent of the evidence to justify exclusion. Second, the standard expressed in the balancing test of Rule 412 is different from the balancing test of Rule 403. Under Rule 403, evidence will be excluded only if its counterweight substantially outweighs its probative value. Under Rule 412, however, that balance is further tilted toward the exclusion of evidence, thereby creating a higher threshold of admissibility. Pursuant to the language of Rule 412, evidence will be admitted only if its probative value

---

to the key issue in this case — whether the girl was the same young female shown on a tape and in photographs found in the possession of the accused).

[46] Rule 412, Advisory Committee Note.

[47] *See* Judd v. Rodman, 105 F.3d 1339, 1342–1343 (11th Cir. 1997) (in suit alleging that the defendant had wrongfully transmitted genital herpes to plaintiff, court held that any error in admitting evidence of plaintiff's breast augmentation surgery, prior sexual history, and nude dancing was not substantially prejudicial to warrant reversal; in particular, given the fact that genital herpes may lie dormant for a considerable period of time, the court found that evidence of the plaintiff's prior sexual history was highly relevant to the defendant's liability and thus should not have been excluded under Rule 412).

[48] *See* Rule 403 and Chapter 403, *supra.*

substantially outweighs the danger of harm to any victim and unfair prejudice to any party.[49] Finally, as noted, the Rule 412 balancing test adds "harm to any victim" to "prejudice to any party" on the scale to be weighed against its probative value.

§ 412.9   Procedural Requirements

Before evidence pursuant to subdivision (b) is admitted, several procedural steps must be followed.[50] First, the accused must file a pretrial motion at least 14 days before the scheduled trial date. This motion must specifically describe the evidence and state the purpose for which it is offered, *i.e.,* which of the exceptions in subdivision (b) applies. The Rule allows, for good cause, a motion to be made after the 14-day deadline before or during the trial. The "good cause" provision is apparently designed to provide some flexibility in the conditions under which a late motion may be filed. Under the prior version of the Rule, the court could only permit an untimely motion if it determined that the evidence was newly discovered and could not have been obtained earlier through the exercise of due diligence or if the issue to which the evidence relates arose at a later date. The present version of the Rule includes these possibilities in its formulation, but does not limit the permission of a later motion to those conditions. The party requesting

---

[49] *See* Jaros v. LodgeNet Entertainment Corp., 294 F.3d 960 (8th Cir. 2002) (in civil action brought by victim of sexual harassment in workplace, trial judge properly excluded defense evidence under Rule 412 that plaintiff wore sexually suggestive clothing; she was never admonished by her employer for dressing inappropriately, the evidence was not shown to be substantially more probative than prejudicial, and defense never even made an offer of proof); B.K.B. v. Maui Police Dep't, 276 F.3d 1091 (9th Cir. 2002) (in sexual harassment litigation, evidence of plaintiff's sexual fantasies concerning a coworker were improperly admitted; the evidence had no probative value, as the coworker was not a defendant in the action); Beard v. Southern Flying J, Inc., 266 F.3d 792 (8th Cir. 2001) (in a sexual harassment suit, evidence of plaintiff employee's sexually suggestive speech and mannerisms was admissible as to whether the alleged harassment was welcome; failure of defendant to file a motion stating an intention to introduce the evidence was harmless, as plaintiff knew defendant planned to offer it); Rodriguez-Hernandez v. Miranda-Velez, 132 F.3d 848 (1st Cir. 1998) (in sexual harassment suit involving a claim of wrongful discharge and in light of the special standard of admissibility provided in Rule 412, trial court struck an acceptable balance between the danger of unfair prejudice and the jury's need for relevant evidence when it excluded evidence of the plaintiff's moral character and promiscuity but allowed evidence directly relevant to the defendant's theory that the plaintiff's relationship had caused her to neglect her job and that the neglect was the reason she was fired, as well as evidence that plaintiff had flirted with one of her employer's customers, which was offered to show that the customer's advances were not unwanted).

[50] *See* United States v. Boyles, 57 F.3d 535 (7th Cir. 1995) (defendant was charged with kidnapping and aggravated sexual abuse for attacking the victim and claimed prior to trial that he had consensual sex with the victim eleven years earlier and also once before in the prior year; no plain error resulted from the trial judge not issuing a ruling on the admission of the sexual evidence where defendant failed to request such a ruling, failed to make an offer of proof as required by Rule 412, and also did not testify concerning the prior consensual intercourse during his trial testimony).

admission of the evidence must also serve the motion on all parties and notify the victim or the victim's guardian or representative.

Before admission of the requested evidence, the court must hold an *in camera* hearing to decide on the motion. At the hearing, all interested parties will be allowed to be present and afforded the opportunity to be heard. The Rule also provides that any motion, related papers, or record of the hearing must be sealed for the duration of the trial unless otherwise ordered by the court. The purpose of this provision is to ensure the privacy of the victim in the event the evidence is ruled inadmissible or refers to matters not ultimately received by the court.[51] Because the hearing is to be closed to the general public and all records to be sealed, the provision might be read as denying the accused a constitutional right to a public trial. However, the inclusion of the phrase "unless the court orders otherwise" suggests a degree of discretion residing with the trial judge, requiring a case-by-case analysis of the necessity of ensuring the privacy of the victim. This kind of discretionary provision has been found constitutional in related cases.[52]

It should be noted that the procedures in this subsection do not apply to discovery of prior sexual conduct or predisposition in civil cases, which continue to be governed by the corresponding Federal Rule of Civil Procedure.[53]

The present version of Rule 412 also eliminates a clause in the predecessor version that might have been understood to require the judge, not the jury, to make determinations of fact when deciding questions of conditional relevance, contrary to the direction of Rule 104(b). Because such an interpretation yields serious constitutional questions regarding the right to a jury trial under the Sixth Amendment, the clause was eliminated.[54] Rule 412 can now no longer be construed as constituting an exception to Rule 104(b), and a jury will decide questions such as credibility.

---

[51] S.M. v. J.K., 262 F.3d 914 (9th Cir. 2001) (where defendant sought pretrial permission to admit evidence of victim's sexual history, denial of motion and exclusion of the evidence were a proper sanction for his failure to file his motion under seal as required by Rule 412).

[52] *See* Press-Enterprise v. Superior Court of Calif., 478 U.S. 1 (1986) (in rape and murder case, Court recognized privacy interests of prospective jurors that might justify in camera proceedings); Globe Newspaper Co. v. Superior Court for County of Norfolk, 457 U.S. 596 (1982) (in rape case against minors, Court noted "compelling" state interest in protection of the "physical and psychological well-being of a minor" that might justify a closed proceeding, if done on a case-by-case basis).

[53] *See* Fed. R. Civ. P. 26. To preserve the privacy of the victim and underlying principle of Rule 412, courts should liberally issue orders pursuant to Federal Rule of Civil Procedure 26(c). This procedure, along with protective orders barring discovery and confidentiality orders, should adequately protect victims in civil cases. *See* Rule 412, Advisory Committee Note.

[54] *See* Rule 412, Advisory Committee Note.

Chapter 413

Rule 413. Similar Crimes in Sexual-Assault Cases

Rule 413. Similar Crimes in Sexual-Assault Cases

(a) **Permitted Uses.** In a criminal case in which a defendant is accused of a sexual assault, the court may admit evidence that the defendant committed any other sexual assault. The evidence may be considered on any matter to which it is relevant.

(b) **Disclosure to the Defendant.** If the prosecutor intends to offer this evidence, the prosecutor must disclose it to the defendant, including witnesses' statements or a summary of the expected testimony. The prosecutor must do so at least 15 days before trial or at a later time that the court allows for good cause.

(c) **Effect on Other Rules.** This rule does not limit the admission or consideration of evidence under any other rule.

(d) **Definition of "Sexual Assault."** In this rule and Rule 415, "sexual assault" means a crime under federal law or under state law (as "state" is defined in 18 U.S.C. § 513) involving:

   (1) any conduct prohibited by 18 U.S.C. chapter 109A;

   (2) contact, without consent, between any part of the defendant's body — or an object — and another person's genitals or anus;

   (3) contact, without consent, between the defendant's genitals or anus and any part of another person's body;

   (4) deriving sexual pleasure or gratification from inflicting death, bodily injury, or physical pain on another person; or

   (5) an attempt or conspiracy to engage in conduct described in subparagraphs (1)–(4)

---

§ 413.1   In General

Rule 413, like Rules 414 and 415, did not come into being through the typical rule-making process.[1] Rather than being promulgated by the Su-

---

[1] *See* 113 CONG. REC. H5439 (Statement of Rep. Hughes) (the "existing rule-making process involves a minimum of six levels of scrutiny or stages of formal review. This has gone through none. This is an amendment offered on the floor of the Senate after about 20

preme Court and approved by Congress, Rules 413–415 were created by Congress as part of the Violent Crime Control and Law Enforcement Act of 1994.[2]

Under Rule 413, evidence of other sexual assaults committed by the defendant is admissible in a criminal trial when the defendant is accused of an offense of sexual assault.[3] Such evidence may be considered in connection with any matter to which it is relevant.[4] Before introducing evidence of this kind, the government must inform the defendant at least fifteen days before the scheduled date of the trial, disclosing the evidence at that time, including witness statements and summaries of the testimony that will be offered. The court can allow disclosure to be made at a later date upon a showing of good cause.

Rule 413(d) defines the term "sexual assault" as any crime under federal or state law involving (1) conduct prohibited by 18 U.S.C. § 109A; (2) contact, without consent, between the defendant's body or an object and the genitals or anus of another; (3) contact, without consent, between the genitals or anus of the defendant and another person's body; (4) deriving sexual pleasure from the infliction of death or other physical harm to another; or (5) an attempt or conspiracy to engage in any conduct described above.[5] The Rule is not limited to convictions; thus it provides for the admissibility of any evidence, including mere allegations, of other offenses of sexual assault committed by the defendant.[6]

---

minutes' debate, without very much thought, and it is procedurally and substantively flawed"); *see also* Rule 1102; § 1102.1, *infra.*

[2] *See* the legislative history to Rule 413 contained in Appendix A of this Treatise.

[3] *See* United States v. Guardia, 135 F.3d 1326 (10th Cir. 1998) (there are three threshold requirements that must be met before evidence can be admitted under Rule 413: first, the court must determine that the defendant is accused of an offense of sexual assault, as defined by the Rule; second, the court must find that the evidence proffered is evidence of the defendant's commission of another offense of sexual assault, and third, the court must find that the evidence is relevant).

[4] *See id.* (Rule 413 allows the admission of prior acts of sexual assault in connection with any matter to which it is relevant). *See also* Duane, *The New Federal Rules of Evidence on Prior Acts of Accused Sex Offenders: A Poorly Drafted Version of a Very Bad Idea,* 157 F.R.D. 95 (1994).

[5] United States v. Blue Bird, 372 F.3d 989 (8th Cir. 2004) (in prosecution for sexual abuse of a minor, Rule 413 did not permit the admission of testimony from other women who, while minors, had been the subjects of sexual advances by the accused, who allegedly approached them in bed, kissed them, and rubbed their stomachs, but who left them alone when they rebuffed his advances, since such actions did not constitute the sort of "sexual contact" defined by this rule, but witness could testify that the defendant once removed his pants and fell asleep on top of her).

[6] *See* Duane, *The New Federal Rules of Evidence on Prior Acts of Accused Sex Offenders: A Poorly Drafted Version of a Very Bad Idea,* 157 F.R.D. 95, 109 (1994).

§ 413.2 Expansion of Prior Acts Evidence; Relationship to Rule 404

The Rule is not to be construed to limit the admission or consideration of evidence. As such, it enlarges the admissibility of evidence of past crimes as restricted by Rule 404.[7] Under that rule, evidence of past wrongs is admissible for limited purposes, including proof of motive or knowledge, but not to allow an inference of conduct in conformity with the past wrong.[8] Under Rule 413, however, evidence of the commission of sexual assaults is admissible for consideration on any matter to which it is relevant, including, as stated by Representative Susan Molinari in support of the legislation, "the defendant's propensity to commit sexual assault or child molestation offenses."[9] The Rule 413 enlargement only applies to criminal trials where the defendant is accused of an offense of sexual assault; it does not allow evidence of other sexual assaults to be used against a defendant accused of a non-sexual assault crime.

The expansion was intended to help protect the public against those who commit offenses of sexual assault, whose conviction frequently depends upon the credibility of the victim, which is often vulnerable to attack.[10] However, as it widens both the scope of evidence that may be admitted and the purposes for which that evidence may be considered, the Rule may create the danger of convicting a defendant for past actions or on reputation alone (*i.e.,* convicting the defendant because he or she is a "bad person").[11]

§ 413.3 Relationship to Rule 403

Representative Molinari, in arguing for the adoption of the Rules, stated that "the general standards of the rules of evidence will continue to apply, including the restrictions on hearsay evidence and the court's authority under Evidence Rule 403 to exclude evidence whose probative value is substantially outweighed by its prejudicial effect."[12] In practice, courts applying the Rule have consistently looked to Rule 403 to gauge the admissibility of evidence proffered under Rule 413.[13]

---

[7] *See* United States v. Guardia, 135 F.3d 1326 (10th Cir. 1998) (Rule 413 differs from Rule 404 in regards to the legitimate purposes for which evidence of prior acts is admissible); United States v. Enjady, 134 F.3d 1427 (10th Cir. 1998) (Rule 413 allows the admission of prior acts evidence to show propensity).

[8] *See* Rule 404 and §§ 404.11–404.18, *supra.*

[9] 140 CONG. REC. H8991 (Aug. 21, 1994) (Remarks of Rep. Molinari).

[10] *See id.*

[11] *See* Duane, *The New Federal Rules of Evidence on Prior Acts of Accused Sex Offenders: A Poorly Drafted Version of a Very Bad Idea,* 157 F.R.D. 95, 106–107 (1994).

[12] 140 CONG. REC. H8991 (Aug. 21, 1994) (Remarks of Rep. Molinari). *See also* Duane, *The New Federal Rules of Evidence on Prior Acts of Accused Sex Offenders: A Poorly Drafted Version of a Very Bad Idea,* 157 F.R.D. 95, 116–120 (1994).

[13] *See* United States v. Batton, 602 F.3d 1191 (10th Cir. 2010) (evidence of earlier acts of sexual assault by the accused are most highly probative, and therefore most likely to be

While Rule 403 should still apply to evidence admitted under Rules 413–415, those rules will affect how courts consider the Rule 403 balancing test. Since Rule 413 allows the trier of fact to consider evidence of other instances of sexual assault for any matter to which it is relevant, Rule 413 imbues the evidence with more probative value than it would have under Rule 404. The evidence can be considered for its probative value establishing the defendant's propensity to engage in such conduct as well as for its probative value in establishing motive, knowledge, or intent. Because of the greater weight given to such evidence, the evidence is less likely to be excluded under Rule 403.[14]

§ 413.4   Judicial Conference Criticism of Rules 413–415

Rule 413 and its companions Rules 414 and 415 were heavily criticized by the Judicial Conference of the United States. The Conference believed that the Rules were poorly drafted, and that the concerns behind these rules were already adequately addressed by the Federal Rules of Evidence, specifically by Rule 404(b).[15] As a result, the Conference proposed amending Rules 404 and 405 to include specific provisions relating to sexual assaults rather than adopting these Rules;[16] however, the proposed amendments were not accepted.[17]

---

admitted, where the earlier assault is most similar to the details of the charged offense for which the accused is now on trial); United States v. Enjady, 134 F.3d 1427 (10th Cir. 1998) (in a case involving sexual assault, the court should determine the admissibility of other sexual assaults by balancing: (1) how clearly the prior act has been proved; (2) how probative the evidence is of the material fact it is admitted to prove; (3) how seriously disputed the material fact is; and (4) whether government can avail itself of any less prejudicial evidence; "without the safeguards embodied in Rule 403, we would hold [Rule 413] unconstitutional"); Frank v. County of Hudson, 924 F. Supp. 620 (D.N.J. 1996) (the court determined that Rule 413–415 are permissive, not mandatory, rules, holding that "evidence proffered under the new rules must still be shown to be relevant, probative and 'legally relevant' under [Rule] 403"). *See also* United States v. Larson, 112 F.3d 600 (2d Cir. 1997) (conducting a Rule 403 analysis on evidence offered under the similar Rule 414 is "consistent with Congress's intent").

[14] *See* SALTZBURG, ET AL., FEDERAL RULES OF EVIDENCE MANUAL § 413.02[3] (9th ed. 2006).

[15] *See* Rule 413 Report of the Judicial Conference of the United States, contained in Appendix A to this Treatise. *See also* Duane, *The New Federal Rules of Evidence on Prior Acts of Accused Sex Offenders: A Poorly Drafted Version of a Very Bad Idea,* 157 F.R.D. 95, 115–117 (1994).

[16] *See* Rule 413 Report of the Judicial Conference of the United States, contained in Appendix A to this Treatise.

[17] *See* 2 MUELLER & KIRKPATRICK, FEDERAL EVIDENCE § 161 (2d ed. 1994 & Supp. 1995).

Chapter 414

Rule 414. Similar Crimes in Child-Molestation Cases

Rule 414. Similar Crimes in Child-Molestation Cases

(a) Permitted Uses. In a criminal case in which a defendant is accused of child molestation, the court may admit evidence that the defendant committed any other child molestation. The evidence may be considered on any matter to which it is relevant.

(b) Disclosure to the Defendant. If the prosecutor intends to offer this evidence, the prosecutor must disclose it to the defendant, including witnesses' statements or a summary of the expected testimony. The prosecutor must do so at least 15 days before trial or at a later time that the court allows for good cause.

(c) Effect on Other Rules. This rule does not limit the admission or consideration of evidence under any other rule.

(d) Definition of "Child" and "Child Molestation." In this rule and Rule 415:

   (1) "child" means a person below the age of 14; and

   (2) "child molestation" means a crime under federal law or under state law (as "state" is defined in 18 U.S.C. § 513) involving:

      (A) any conduct prohibited by 18 U.S.C. chapter 109A and committed with a child;

      (B) any conduct prohibited by 18 U.S.C. chapter 110;

      (C) contact between any part of the defendant's body — or an object — and a child's genitals or anus;

      (D) contact between the defendant's genitals or anus and any part of a child's body;

      (E) deriving sexual pleasure or gratification from inflicting death, bodily injury, or physical pain on a child; or

      (F) an attempt or conspiracy to engage in conduct described in subparagraphs (A)–(E).

---

§ 414.1 In General

Rule 414 provides for the admission in a criminal trial of evidence of other offenses of child molestation committed by the defendant when he or she is accused of an offense of child molestation. Such evidence may be considered in connection with any matter to which it is relevant.[1] Before introducing evidence of this kind, the government must inform the defendant at least fifteen days before the scheduled date of the trial, disclosing the evidence at that time, including witness statements and summaries of the testimony that will be offered. The court can allow disclosure to be made at a later date upon a showing of good cause.

Under Rule 414(d)(1), a "child" is defined as any person below the age of fourteen.[2] And "child molestation" is defined by Rule 414(d)(2) as any crime under federal or state law involving (A) conduct prohibited by chapter 109A of 18 U.S.C. that was committed in relation to a child; (B) conduct proscribed by chapter 110 of 18 U.S.C.; (C) contact between the defendant's body or an object and the genitals or anus of a child; (D) contact between the genitals or anus of the defendant and a child's body; (E) deriving sexual pleasure from the infliction of death or other physical harm to a child; or (F) an attempt or conspiracy to engage in any conduct described above. The Rule is not limited to convictions; thus it renders any evidence, including mere allegations, of other offenses of child molestation committed by the defendant admissible at trial.[3]

§ 414.2   Relationship to Rules 403 and 404

Like Rule 413, this rule is not to be construed to limit the admission or consideration of evidence, and is also an expansion of the admissibility of evidence of past crimes under Rule 404. It is intended to help protect the public from those who engage in child molestation by allowing the court to consider evidence of past offenses in deciding the defendant's propensity to commit the act he or she is accused of.[4] As a result, the rule can also create

---

[1] *See* Duane, *The New Federal Rules of Evidence on Prior Acts of Accused Sex Offenders: A Poorly Drafted Version of a Very Bad Idea,* 157 F.R.D. 95 (1994).

[2] Because of this statutory limitation, this Rule technically does not apply to molestation of a "child" who is fourteen years or older, but such evidence is admissible under Rule 413, regardless of the age of the victim, if the molestation involves sexual assault. *See* United States v. Batton, 602 F.3d 1191 (10th Cir. 2010) (although Rule 414 only authorizes admission of child molestation offenses committed under children under the age of 14, Rule 413 permits admission of evidence that the accused committed offenses of sexual assault against 14-year old victims, even though such offenses might still be described as episodes of child molestation.) The two rules overlap in their scope, and episodes of sexual assault against child victims may therefore be admissible under either of these two rules.

[3] *See id.* at 109.

[4] *See* 140 CONG. REC. H8991 (Aug. 21, 1994) (Remarks of Rep. Molinari). *See also* United States v. LeCompte, 131 F.3d 767 (10th Cir. 1998) (trial court abused its discretion when it excluded evidence of defendant's prior uncharged sex offenses under Rule 403; although Rule 403 remains available in such a case, Rule 414 expresses a strong legislative judgment that such evidence should ordinarily be admissible, and the substantial similarity of

the danger of convicting the defendant on past actions or reputation alone.[5] However, Rule 403 still operates to exclude evidence admissible under Rule 414 when such evidence is found to be unfairly prejudicial to the defendant.[6] Application of the Rule is limited to criminal trials where the defendant is accused of an offense of child molestation.

§ 414.3 Adoption and Judicial Conference Criticism

Rule 414, like Rules 413 and 415, did not come into being through the typical rule-making process. Rather than being promulgated by the Supreme Court and approved by Congress, Rules 413–415 were created by Congress as part of the Violent Crime Control and Law Enforcement Act of 1994.[7] These Rules were heavily criticized by the Judicial Conference of the United States on several points. See Chapter 413 for a discussion of the Conference's criticisms of the Rules.[8]

---

the prior acts to the charged offense renders evidence of the prior acts admissible).

[5] *See* Duane, *The New Federal Rules of Evidence on Prior Acts of Accused Sex Offenders: A Poorly Drafted Version of a Very Bad Idea,* 157 F.R.D. 95, 106–107 (1994).

[6] *See* United States v. Drewry, 365 F.3d 957 (10th Cir. 2004), *vacated and remanded on other grounds,* 543 U.S. 1103 (2005) (defendant's acts of child molestation twenty-five years earlier were admissible because of the striking similarities between the facts alleged and those in the present case. "Sufficient factual similarity can rehabilitate evidence of prior uncharged offenses that might otherwise be inadmissible due to staleness"); United States v. LeMay, 260 F.3d 1018 (9th Cir. 2001) (evidence of prior acts of child molestation admitted under Rule 414 did not violate defendant's constitutional right to due process or undermine his presumption of innocence, because the Rule 403 balancing test is still applicable); United States v. Gabe, 237 F.3d 954 (8th Cir. 2001) (in sex abuse prosecution, other instances of child molestation, occurring 20 years before the crime charged, were highly probative; the form of the alleged prior abuse was nearly identical to the crime charged, both victims were related to the defendant, and both victims were six-or seven-year-old girls; the prior acts were not too remote in time, as victims of child abuse are unlikely to forget such traumatic events); United States v. Charley, 189 F.3d 1251 (10th Cir. 1999) (defendant was convicted of sexually molesting two young girls after his conviction for molesting his granddaughter was admitted under Rule 414; Rule 414 is constitutional because of the application of Rule 403 to keep out evidence so prejudicial that it would violate a defendant's right to a fair trial); United States v. Larson, 112 F.3d 600 (2d Cir. 1997) (conducting a Rule 403 analysis on evidence offered under Rule 414 is "consistent with Congress's intent"); United States v. Sumner, 204 F.3d 1182 (8th Cir. 2000).

[7] *See* 113 CONG. REC. H5439 (Statement of Rep. Hughes) (the "existing rule-making process involves a minimum of six levels of scrutiny or stages of formal review. This has gone through none. This is an amendment offered on the floor of the Senate after about 20 minutes' debate, without very much thought, and it is procedurally and substantively flawed"); *see also* Rule 1102; § 1102.1, *infra,* and the legislative history of Rules 413–415 contained in Appendix A to this Treatise.

[8] *See* § 413.4, *supra.*

Chapter 415

Rule 415. Similar Acts in Civil Cases Involving Sexual Assault or Child Molestation

Rule 415. Similar Acts in Civil Cases Involving Sexual Assault or Child Molestation

(a) **Permitted Uses.** In a civil case involving a claim for relief based on a party's alleged sexual assault or child molestation, the court may admit evidence that the party committed any other sexual assault or child molestation. The evidence may be considered as provided in Rules 413 and 414.

(b) **Disclosure to the Opponent.** If a party intends to offer this evidence, the party must disclose it to the party against whom it will be offered, including witnesses' statements or a summary of the expected testimony. The party must do so at least 15 days before trial or at a later time that the court allows for good cause.

(c) **Effect on Other Rules.** This rule does not limit the admission or consideration of evidence under any other rule.

---

§ 415.1 In General

Rule 415 applies to civil trials where the relief sought is based on a party's alleged conduct that constitutes an offense of either sexual assault or child molestation. Under the rule, evidence of other offenses of sexual assault or child molestation committed by that party is admissible and may be considered in connection with any matter to which it is relevant.[1] Before introducing evidence of this kind, the party introducing the evidence must inform the party it will be offered against at least fifteen days before the scheduled date of the trial, disclosing the evidence at that time, including witness statements and summaries of the testimony that will be offered. The court can allow disclosure to be made at a later date upon a showing of good cause. No formal method of giving such notice is prescribed by the rule, which is generally satisfied as long as the pleadings and the pretrial

---

[1] *See* Duane, *The New Federal Rules of Evidence on Prior Acts of Accused Sex Offenders: A Poorly Drafted Version of a Very Bad Idea,* 157 F.R.D. 95 (1994).

discovery put the defendant on reasonable notice that plaintiff intended to offer such evidence.[2]

For purposes of this rule, the term "sexual assault" carries the same meaning as it does under Rule 413 (*see* Chapter 413) and the terms "child" and "child molestation" share the definitions outlined in Rule 414 (*see* Chapter 414). Like its companion rules, Rule 415 does not limit admissible evidence to evidence of convictions. It is not to be construed to limit the admission or consideration of evidence, and is also an expansion of the admissibility of evidence of crimes under Rule 404.

As Rule 415 applies to civil trials, it does not create the danger that an individual will be convicted based on a propensity to engage in certain conduct. However, as it widens both the scope of evidence that may be admitted and the purposes for which that evidence may be considered, the rule may create the danger of creating liability based on past actions or reputation alone (*i.e.,* penalizing a party because he or she is a "bad person").[3] The rule is therefore subject to the trial judge's discretion to exclude such evidence under Rule 403 if its probative value is substantially outweighed by its capacity for unfair prejudice.[4] The rule does not apply to cases alleging sex discrimination or sexual harassment unless the claim also

---

[2] Johnson v. Elk Lake Sch. Dist., 283 F.3d 138 (3d Cir. 2002) (provision of Rule 415 requiring party to give pretrial notice of its intent to offer evidence under the Rule was not violated, even though plaintiff gave no such notice explicitly, where witness testifying to other sexual misconduct by defendant was listed on plaintiff's witness list, and had already testified and been questioned by defense counsel on the same incident at a pretrial deposition); EEOC v. Harbert-Yeargin, Inc., 266 F.3d 498 (6th Cir. 2001) (plaintiff fulfilled disclosure requirements for admitting evidence of previous incidents of improper "touching" of employees by giving defendant notice it was challenging a pervasive practice of sexual harassment by male supervisors and by alleging in its complaint that a class of employees had been subjected to sexual harassment, "including offensive and unwelcome touching").

[3] *See* Duane, *The New Federal Rules of Evidence on Prior Acts of Accused Sex Offenders: A Poorly Drafted Version of a Very Bad Idea,* 157 F.R.D. 95, 106–107 (1994).

[4] Blind-Doan v. Sanders, 291 F.3d 1079 (9th Cir. 2002) (in civil action for sexual assault, reversal was required where trial judge failed to make a "clear record" concerning the required Rule 403 balancing before excluding evidence of other sexual assaults by defendant); Johnson v. Elk Lake Sch. Dist., 283 F.3d 138 (3d Cir. 2002) (a defendant may be guilty of "an offense of sexual assault" within the meaning of this Rule and Rule 413 even if he was never charged with or convicted of the offense, and even if he touched his victim through her clothing and not on her skin, but the court retains the discretion to exclude the evidence under Rule 403 if the two offenses are so dissimilar that the probative value of the other assault is substantially undermined); Doe v. Glanzer, 232 F.3d 1258 (9th Cir. 2000) (Rule 415 admission of similar acts evidence in child molestation cases remains subject to a Rule 403 balancing analysis, based upon such factors as (1) the similarity between the prior act and the act charged, (2) the closeness in time of the two acts, (3) frequency of prior acts, (4) any relevant intervening circumstances, and (5) necessity of producing the evidence, in light of other evidence presented at trial).

alleges an instance of sexual assault as defined under Rule 413.[5]

§ 415.2   Adoption and Judicial Conference Criticism

Rule 415, like Rules 413 and 414, did not come into being through the typical rule-making process. Rather than being promulgated by the Supreme Court and approved by Congress, Rules 413–415 were created by Congress as part of the Violent Crime Control and Law Enforcement Act of 1994.[6] These Rules were heavily criticized by the Judicial Conference of the United States on several points. See Chapter 413 for a discussion of the Conference's criticisms of the Rules.[7]

---

[5] *See* Frank v. County of Hudson, 924 F. Supp. 620 (D.N.J. 1996); Shea v. Galaxie Lumber & Construction Co., Ltd., 1996 U.S. Dist. LEXIS 2904 (N.D. Ill. Mar. 12, 1996).

[6] *See* 113 CONG. REC. H5439 (Statement of Rep. Hughes) (the "existing rule-making process involves a minimum of six levels of scrutiny or stages of formal review. This has gone through none. This is an amendment offered on the floor of the Senate after about 20 minutes' debate, without very much thought, and it is procedurally and substantively flawed"); *see also* Rule 1102; § 1102.1, *infra,* and the legislative history of Rules 413–415 contained in Appendix A to this Treatise.

[7] *See* § 413.4, *supra.*

ARTICLE V.
PRIVILEGES

Synopsis

Chapter 501

Rule 501. Privilege in General

Rule 501. Privilege in General

The common law — as interpreted by United States courts in the light of reason and experience — governs a claim of privilege unless any of the following provides otherwise:

- the United States Constitution;
- a federal statute; or
- rules prescribed by the Supreme Court.

But in a civil case, state law governs privilege regarding a claim or defense for which state law supplies the rule of decision.

---

§ 501.1   The Rule as to Privilege — In General

Rule 501 reserves the matter of privileges to the common law and statutes for determination, interpretation, and development. Rule 501 in essence provides that privileges are to be governed either by common-law principles as interpreted by the federal courts, or in those civil actions in which state law supplies the rule of decision as to an element of a claim or defense, by principles of state law.[1]

In adopting Rule 501, Congress rejected the Supreme Court's proposed Article V which contained thirteen Rules relating to privilege. The proposed Rules set forth nine substantive areas of privileged communications as well as four procedural provisions. Congress chose, however, to reject this attempt at specification, which included several modifications of common-

---

[1] *See generally,* 1 MCCORMICK, §§ 72–77; 3 WEINSTEIN'S FEDERAL EVIDENCE §§ 501.01–501.05; 2 MUELLER & KIRKPATRICK, §§ 169–231; 8 WIGMORE, §§ 2201–2396. *See also* Weissenberger, *Toward Precision in the Attorney-Client Privilege for Corporations,* 65 IOWA L. REV. 899 (1980); *The Rights of Criminal Defendants and the Subpoena Duces Tecum: The Aftermath of Fisher v. United States,* 95 HARV. L. REV. 683 (1982); Comment, *The Spousal Testimonial Privilege After Trammel v. United States,* 58 DEN. L.J. 357 (1981); Fregant, *Confidentiality of Personnel Files in the Private Sector,* U.C.D. L. REV. 473 (1981); Hill, *Testimonial Privileges and Fair Trial,* 80 COLUM. L. REV. 1173 (1980).

law privileges.[2] It instead promulgated a single Rule that left the law of privilege in *status quo*.[3]

Rule 501 is significant in three respects. First, it acknowledges that privileges are applicable not only to witnesses, but also to any person, state, or political subdivision. This expansive treatment is necessary in view of the broad applicability of the protection traditionally accorded to privileged communications.[4] Thus, while evidentiary rules in general apply only to courtroom proceedings, privileges "apply to all stages of a case or proceeding conducted under these rules," as provided by Rule 1101(c). For example, a privilege may be invoked during the early stages of a lawsuit in order to justify the refusal of a party to comply with a discovery request. Moreover, Rule 501 contemplates that a witness may be precluded from testifying to matters that are privileged when the holder of the privilege is a person other than the witness. For example, while the physician-patient privilege may function to shield the patient from testifying to confidential communications made within a specific relational framework, it also functions to protect the patient when the physician is the witness.

Second, the Rule specifies the sources from which the substantive law governing privileges are to be drawn. As noted above, where state law does not apply, it is necessary to look to Acts of Congress, rules promulgated by the Supreme Court, and federal common-law principles in order to determine whether the cloak of privilege is available. Implicit in the Rule is the common-law concept that, absent statutory or common-law authority, there is no privilege to withhold information in the face of the judicial process, or to force another to withhold such information.[5] The various privileges available under federal law are discussed in subsequent sections of this chapter.

Third, the Rule specifies the manner in which federal common-law principles respecting privilege are to be interpreted by the courts, that is, "in the light of reason and experience." The language is derived from a preliminary draft of Rule 26 of the Federal Rules of Criminal Procedure.[6] In this regard, the Rule contemplates a continuing development in the area of

---

[2] Federal Rule 501, Report of Senate Committee on the Judiciary. There was some concern in Congress and elsewhere that disregard of state privileges might be unconstitutional or, at the least, contrary to the concept of federalism. *See* 3 WEINSTEIN'S FEDERAL EVIDENCE § 501.01.

[3] Federal Rule 501, House Comm. on the Judiciary, 93rd Cong., 1st Sess., Report on Article V (Comm. Print 1950).

[4] *See, e.g.,* Rules 101 and 104(a).

[5] *See generally,* 2 MUELLER & KIRKPATRICK, § 172.

[6] *See* Fed. R. Crim. P. 26 Advisory Committee Note 1; *see also* 3 ORFIELD, § 26:2 at 266, § 26:3 at 268; Rule 501, House Comm. on the Judiciary, 93rd Cong., 1st Sess., Report on Article V (Comm. Print 1950).

privileges, whether by expansion or contraction of the traditional theories of privileges. Under Rule 501, federal courts must develop the federal common law of privileges on a case-by-case basis.[7]

§ 501.2 Other Rules of Evidence That Relate to Privilege

Rules 1101 and 104 relate to procedural aspects of the application of privilege laws. Rule 1101 sets forth the broad applicability of privilege law and it provides in subsection (c) that: "The rules on privilege apply to all stages of a case or proceeding." Reading Rule 1101 in its entirety, it is clear that privilege rules apply even to proceedings not conducted under the Rules of Evidence.

Rule 104 provides that whether privilege exists in a given situation is a preliminary question to be determined by the court. In making this determination, as well as the determination as to all preliminary questions of admissibility, the court remains bound by rules with respect to privilege even though it is not bound at this stage by other evidentiary rules, *e.g.*, rules on admissibility.[8] In this regard, Rule 104 serves to emphasize the Rules' overriding concern with maintaining the protection of privileged communications.

In operation, Rule 104(a) generally requires the judge to make preliminary determinations on the existence of the privilege without invading the area of privileged communications. In deciding, for example, whether a privilege exists, the court will usually consider whether the necessary facts supportive of a privilege exist (*e.g.,* whether a statutorily or judicially recognized confidential relationship has been shown, whether the relevant communication was made in confidence)[9] without exposing the substance of the allegedly privileged subject matter. However, the Supreme Court has ruled that Rule 104(a) does not categorically prohibit *in camera* review of materials for which a privilege has been claimed. For example, materials claimed to be privileged as attorney-client communications may be examined *in camera* to determine if they fall within the crime-fraud exception[10] to the asserted privilege once the opponent of the privilege makes a

---

[7] 3 WEINSTEIN'S FEDERAL EVIDENCE § 501.03; *see, e.g.,* University of Pennsylvania v. E.E.O.C., 493 U.S. 182 (1990) (declining to recognize a privilege against disclosure of peer review information); Desai v. Hersh, 954 F.2d 1408 (7th Cir. 1992) (in defamation actions where the plaintiff must establish malice, a reporter's privilege to protect sources ordinarily must give way to disclosure); Zuckerbraun v. General Dynamics Corp., 935 F.2d 544 (2d Cir. 1991) (the trial court properly dismissed plaintiff's action because the sought-after information essential to his case fell under the state secrets privilege asserted by the government); Powers v. Chicago Transit Auth., 890 F.2d 1355 (7th Cir. 1989) (declining to adopt a confidential-information-in-litigation privilege).

[8] *See, e.g.,* Rule 104(a).

[9] See discussion at § 501.3, *infra.*

[10] See discussion at § 501.5, *infra.*

threshold showing that such review is appropriate.[11]

§ 501.3 The Theory and the Parameters of Privilege Law

Considering privilege within the ambit of the Rules of Evidence is somewhat anomalous; while evidentiary rules are in large part designed to promote the ascertainment of the truth, privileges may be seen as rules that operate to suppress relevant, otherwise helpful evidence. Inadmissibility is an incidental derivative of privilege rules that seek to preserve the confidentiality of certain private communications. Privilege law, then, is anchored in considerations of policy that exist independently of the usual evidentiary concerns with accuracy and reliability of evidence.[12]

As discussed in the preceding section, rules of privilege function beyond the arena of a trial and may be invoked at any stage of any proceeding. A privilege may involve a refusal to testify, a refusal to disclose a matter during the discovery stage, a refusal to produce real proof, or the right to prevent other people from doing any of the foregoing. A privilege allows a person to resist any governmental process aimed at eliciting protected information. As such, it relieves a person from the duty of revealing facts in response to governmental process and from the corollary risks of contempt for failure to do so. However, recent decisions by the Supreme Court indicate that privileges may be limited by constitutional considerations in criminal cases.[13] It is now questionable if a claim of privilege will be upheld where a criminal defendant asserts, for example: (1) a need to use the privileged

---

[11] United States v. Zolin, 491 U.S. 554 (1989).

[12] *See* 1 McCormick, § 72, at 269, in which the author critically compares the general exclusionary rules of evidence that seek "the elucidation of the truth, a purpose which these rules seek to effect by operating to exclude evidence which is unreliable or which is calculated to prejudice or mislead," with rules of privilege that do not aid "the ascertainment of the truth" but rather protect "interests and relationships which, rightly or wrongly, are regarded as of sufficient social importance to justify some incidental sacrifice of availability of evidence relevant to the administration of justice."

[13] United States v. Nixon, 418 U.S. 683 (1974) (claim of absolute privilege for presidential communications "must yield to the demonstrated, specific need for evidence in a pending criminal trial"); Davis v. Alaska, 415 U.S. 308 (1974) (confrontation clause was violated by state privilege protecting juvenile records where privilege deprived defendant of the opportunity to impeach the prosecution's chief witness); Washington v. Texas, 388 U.S. 14 (1967) (compulsory process clause was violated by Texas statute providing that persons charged or convicted as joint participants in the same crime were incompetent to testify for one another). *But cf.* United States v. Smith, 780 F.2d 1102 (4th Cir. 1985) (Classified Procedure Act was enacted to "combat the growing problem of graymail," in which a criminal defendant threatens to reveal classified information during trial to coerce the government into reducing or dropping charges; Fourth Circuit held en banc that CIPA provisions, which permit separate hearings to determine first whether the information sought is classified and then whether it is protected through use of alternative procedures, preserve the underlying privilege claim).

matter as exculpatory, or (2) a need to use the privileged matter to impeach prosecution testimony.[14]

The rationale behind most non-constitutional testimonial privileges is the protection of certain confidential relationships.[15] Wigmore analyzed the operation of privileges as a guarded exception to the obligation to give testimony that would apply under four prerequisite conditions:

(1) The communications must originate in a *confidence* that they will not be discussed;

(2) This element of *confidentiality must be essential* to the full and satisfactory maintenance of the relation between the parties;

(3) The *relation* must be one that in the opinion of the community ought to be sedulously *fostered*;

(4) The *injury* that would inure to the relation by the disclosure of the communications must be *greater than the benefit* thereby gained for the correct disposition of litigation.[16]

Wigmore concluded that these prerequisites serve as justifications for the widely recognized attorney-client, spousal, and clergy-parishioner privileges.[17] Under Wigmore's analysis, no justification could be found for a physician-patient privilege,[18] although many contemporary commentators would disagree.[19] A more recent rationale for privileges is the protection of the privacy interests of the parties, regardless of whether the existence of a privilege affects the behavior of the persons involved in the relationship.[20] Under modern law, privileges that protect confidential relationships attach, for example, to communications between husband and wife,[21] attorney and client,[22] clergy and parishioner,[23] and physician and patient.[24] The goal of protecting and reinforcing the relationship is sought to be achieved by protecting certain communications made within its confines. In this regard, facts incident to the existence of the relationship itself are not within the

---

[14] 1 MCCORMICK, § 72.

[15] *See* 1 MCCORMICK, § 72.

[16] 8 WIGMORE, § 2285, at 527.

[17] *Id.*

[18] 8 WIGMORE, § 2380(a).

[19] *See* 2 MUELLER & KIRKPATRICK, § 209; 1 MCCORMICK, § 99; *see also* Louisell, *Confidentiality, Conformity and Confusion; Privileges in Federal Court Today,* 31 TUL. L. REV. 101 (1956).

[20] *See* 1 MCCORMICK, § 72.

[21] *See generally,* 8 WIGMORE, § 2332; 2 MUELLER & KIRKPATRICK, § 206.

[22] *See generally,* 8 WIGMORE, § 2291; 2 MUELLER & KIRKPATRICK, § 181.

[23] *See generally,* 8 WIGMORE, § 2396; 2 MUELLER & KIRKPATRICK, § 211.

[24] *See generally,* 8 WIGMORE, § 2380(a); 2 MUELLER & KIRKPATRICK, § 209.

privilege. For example, one who invokes the attorney-client privilege may properly refuse to testify concerning the substance of certain communications made to or by the attorney, but must respond to questions, if otherwise relevant, concerning the name of the attorney, the time frame of the attorney-client relationship, etc.[25] Certain principles are common to all privileges. Initially, it must be noted that not all confidential relationships are privileged. Rather, rights incident to privilege law are available only in connection with relationships that are defined and recognized as privileged by legislative enactment or judicial ruling. Privileges will be generally confined to their express limits. For example, the privileged relationship between husband and wife is not extended by implication.[26]

A second common dimension of privilege law is that rights incident to privilege apply only to privileged *communications*.[27] In this regard, the protected status applies to oral or written communications, although it may also extend in certain instances to nonverbal acts[28] and to knowledge gained by means of observation where such observation is not one that can be construed to be of an obvious nature.[29] The protection generally extends to communications made both by and to the holder of the privilege. For example, in the attorney-client relationship, the privilege protects not only statements made by the holder of the privilege, *i.e.*, the client, to the attorney, but also advisory statements made by the attorney to the client.[30] As

---

[25] *See* United States v. Clemons, 676 F.2d 124 (5th Cir. 1982) (attorney's message regarding date of trial not privileged); NLRB v. Harvey, 349 F.2d 900 (4th Cir. 1965) (identity of client not privileged).

[26] The privilege was intended for preservation of marital harmony and tranquility and may only be asserted in a valid marriage. *See* United States v. Acker, 52 F.3d 509, 514 (4th Cir. 1995) (declining to extend spousal communication privilege to a couple who had lived together for 25 years and rejecting an equal protection challenge to the validity of the spousal privilege); United States v. Lustig, 555 F.2d 737 (9th Cir. 1977); United States v. Neeley, 475 F.2d 1136 (4th Cir. 1973); *see also* United States v. Byrd, 750 F.2d 585 (7th Cir. 1984), *aff'd,* 805 F.2d 1038 (7th Cir. 1986) (the spousal communications privilege does not apply to communications between husband and wife who are permanently separated); Port v. Heard, 764 F.2d 423 (5th Cir. 1985) (court rejected parental claims of a constitutional right to refuse to testify against their child, a defendant in a murder trial).

[27] *See, e.g., In re* Martenson, 779 F.2d 461 (8th Cir. 1985) (court overruled spousal privilege where the questions involved no confidential communication but solicited only objective facts regarding personal background and the purchase of a boat); Olender v. United States, 210 F.2d 795 (9th Cir. 1954).

[28] *See generally,* 1 MCCORMICK, § 89 (only if act is intentionally communicative); 8 WIGMORE, § 2306. *See also* United States v. Bahe, 128 F.3d 1440, 1444–1445 (10th Cir. 1997) (although the appellate court declined to decide the issue because it felt an exception permitted the wife to testify about abusive sexual contact, the district court had held that "physical touching between spouses, especially involving sexual activity, is communication within the marital privilege").

[29] United States v. Bahe, 128 F.3d 1440, 1444–1445 (10th Cir. 1997).

[30] *See In re* Ford Motor Co., 110 F.3d 954 (3d Cir. 1997) (no distinction exists between

previously mentioned, the protection accorded privileged communications does not extend to *objective* facts regarding the relationship.

A further common consideration is that privilege attaches only to communications made in confidence. In this regard, one seeking to invoke the husband-wife privilege, for example, is aided by a presumption that communications made within the marital relationship are in fact confidential; in other privilege situations confidentiality is not presumed but the parties' intention must be shown.[31] Confidentiality may be negated by a showing that the communication was made in the presence of a third person whose presence was not essential to the transaction.[32] However, a third person's presence will not preclude a finding of confidentiality where that person is essential to the transaction (*e.g.,* an interpreter or a nurse), in some instances where that person is an agent of one of the principals, or sometimes where the relationship with the third person is itself privileged (*e.g.,* where a wife is present during her husband's consultation with his physician). The second manner in which confidentiality is negated is where the communication is carelessly made, that is, with little or no concern for maintaining confidentiality. For example, a conversation between an attorney and his client in the midst of a social gathering would not be privileged. At common law, confidentiality also could be destroyed through application of the "eavesdropper" rule. Under this doctrine, a person who inadvertently overheard a privileged communication could testify as to the communication even though no carelessness of the holder could be shown.[33] For example, if a telephone operator overheard a telephone conversation between an attorney and her client, the operator could testify as to the contents of the communication even though the attorney would be prohibited from so

---

communications from the client to the attorney and communications from the attorney to the client; both are protected provided they are made for the purpose of obtaining legal advice); Schwimmer v. United States, 232 F.2d 855 (8th Cir. 1956) (attorney has duty to make assertion of privilege upon any attempt to require him to produce documents or testify as a matter of professional responsibility); *cf.* United States v. Silverman, 430 F.2d 106 (2d Cir. 1970), *modified,* 439 F.2d 1198 (2d Cir. 1970) (statements made by attorney should not be privileged unless they reveal confidential statements made by client).

[31] *See* 1 MCCORMICK, § 80, as to assumed confidentiality in the husband-wife situation; *see, e.g.,* Pereira v. United States, 347 U.S. 1 (1954).

[32] *See* United States v. Ackert, 169 F.3d 136 (2d Cir. 1999) (no attorney-client privilege attaches to conversations between an attorney and a third party who has information necessary to the attorney's representation of the client; an investment banker who pitched the investment to the client was not needed to interpret or translate client communications to the attorney); United States v. Evans, 113 F.3d 1457 (7th Cir. 1997) (the attorney-client privilege did not cover conversation between client and his criminal attorney due to the presence of a third party; although the third party was the client's family lawyer, he was present during the conference only as a friend and potential character witness rather than serving as legal counsel).

[33] *See* 1 MCCORMICK, § 74.

testifying. Now, most cases will only extend the "eavesdropper" rule to situations in which it is reasonably foreseeable that the communication would be intercepted.[34] The eavesdropper rule has been abrogated by statute in most jurisdictions.[35]

Another common incident of privileges is that only the owner, *i.e.,* the holder, of the privilege may assert a privilege in order to suppress relevant evidence. The holders in the testimonial privileges are generally both husband and wife in the marital privilege,[36] the client in the attorney-client privilege,[37] the patient in the physician-patient privilege, and the parishioner in the clergy-parishioner privilege.[38] If the holder does not assert the privilege, the otherwise privileged matter may be revealed. In this regard, it should be noted that the holder of a privilege need not be a party to a suit in order to assert the right. The holder may authorize another person to assert the privilege on his or her behalf. Or, the holder may depend in some instances upon the other party in the privileged relationship to assert the privilege. For example, a lawyer is ethically bound to assert the privilege on behalf of the client,[39] and is presumed to have the authority to do so. It may also occur in a given situation that a judge will in effect assert the privilege for an absent holder. In this instance, although the judge has no explicit authorization, the judge functions to protect society's interest by maintaining the status quo until the holder of the privilege can be contacted to assert it personally.

Only the holder of a privilege may waive the right to the protection of the privilege. A waiver may come about in one of two ways: it may result from the express consent of the holder to testimony of a person who would otherwise be bound by the privilege,[40] or it may result from the voluntary disclosure of a substantial portion of the privileged communication by the holder.[41] The disclosure may be made in court or it may be made entirely in

---

[34] 1 McCormick, § 74.

[35] 1 McCormick, § 74.

[36] 1 McCormick, § 83.

[37] 1 McCormick, § 92.

[38] 1 McCormick, § 102.

[39] Code of Professional Responsibility, Canon 4. Ethical Consideration 4-4 provides in part that "[a] lawyer owes an obligation to advise the client of the attorney-client privilege and timely to assert the privilege unless it is waived by the client."

[40] United States v. Blackburn, 446 F.2d 1089 (5th Cir. 1971) (communications between client and attorney in presence of third party were not privileged); *see also* United States v. Crouthers, 669 F.2d 635 (10th Cir. 1982); United States v. Gordon-Nikkar, 518 F.2d 972 (5th Cir. 1975).

[41] United States v. Bump, 605 F.2d 548 (10th Cir. 1979); United States v. Lilley, 581 F.2d 182 (8th Cir. 1978); *see, e.g.,* Powers v. Chicago Transit Auth., 890 F.2d 1355 (7th Cir. 1989) (in a civil rights action for reverse discrimination, where the plaintiff refused to reveal who

the absence of judicial or governmental process. The disclosure, however, must be voluntary, and some jurisdictions have held that a holder who is erroneously compelled to reveal privileged information at one proceeding may reassert the privilege at a subsequent proceeding.[42]

In addition to the foregoing incidents of privilege, most privileges have recognized exceptions where they do not apply. The exceptions generally arise due to a special need for disclosure in certain situations. Generally, for example, in an action between the holder and the confidant, the privilege does not apply. Accordingly, if an attorney sues the client for the payment of fees, or a patient sues the physician for alleged malpractice, the privilege is restricted to permit disclosure of any communications to the extent necessary to resolve such claims.[43] The need for confidentiality no longer exists in such situations, or, at the very least, it has been abrogated or superseded by the need for disclosure of information in order to prosecute the cause of action.

§ 501.4   Ascertaining Applicable Privilege Law in Federal Courts

The two separate sentences of Rule 501 clearly establish that applicable privilege law will vary in federal courts depending upon the surrounding circumstances and the type of action or proceeding. This result reflects the position taken in the House Report that "federal law should not supersede

---

gave him a potentially privileged memo written by defendant's agent, trial court was unable to determine if a privilege had been waived and the case was properly dismissed); E.E.O.C. v. Gen. Tel. Co., 885 F.2d 575 (9th Cir. 1989) (where an employer voluntarily introduces evidence of its equal opportunity programs at trial, the employer waives its qualified privilege against disclosure of its equal opportunity efforts); In re Sealed Case, 877 F.2d 976 (D.C. Cir. 1989) (where one privileged document was inadvertently disclosed to an auditor, attorney-client privilege was waived with respect to all communications relating to the same subject matter); United States v. Suarez, 820 F.2d 1158 (11th Cir. 1987) (where defendant's attorney testified at pretrial hearing, he could not claim attorney-client privilege to refuse to testify at trial); United States v. Jenkins, 785 F.2d 1387 (9th Cir. 1986) (prior civil deposition by defendant was admissible in later criminal trial; Fifth Amendment privilege against self-incrimination was waived by the earlier testimony).

[42] *See* 2 MUELLER & KIRKPATRICK, §§ 201–203, explaining that this view, although departing from the principles of res judicata, represents a "sounder" view as endorsed by the Advisory Committee in proposed-but-rejected Rule 512, 56 F.R.D. 183, 259 (1972); *see also* Appeal of Malfitano, 633 F.2d 276 (3d Cir. 1980) (where foreign-born wife had consistently claimed spousal privilege in refusing to answer questions before a grand jury, but responded in Judge's chambers under the mistaken belief that she must, privilege was not waived); 1 MCCORMICK, § 92, at 222, the privilege should be considered waived where a client testifies on cross-examination concerning communications with the lawyer without asserting the privilege.

[43] Tasby v. United States, 504 F.2d 332 (8th Cir. 1974); *see also* Hunt v. Blackburn, 128 U.S. 464 (1888) (client waived right to object to testimony when she entered upon that line of defense); Haymes v. Smith, 73 F.R.D. 572 (W.D.N.Y. 1976) (attorney-client privilege waived if client injects privileged communication as an issue in the case).

that of the States in substantive areas such as privilege absent a compelling reason."[44]

The Advisory Committee presented two arguments against federal recognition of state-created privileges. First, privileges are in essence exclusionary rules. Even though privileges suppress evidence to preserve a relationship, the Committee noted that when the relationship itself is an issue in a case, exceptions to state-created privileges often apply and therefore:

> [t]he appearance of privilege in the case is quite by accident, and its effect is to block off the tribunal from a source of information. Thus its real impact is on the method of proof in the case, and in comparison any substantive aspect appears tenuous.[45]

The second argument countered the recognition of state-created privileges by the fact that they are not applicable in federal criminal prosecutions. The Committee believed that in light of its absence in criminal cases, a state-created privilege becomes "illusory as a significant aspect of the relationship out of which it arises."[46] The prevailing Congressional position, however, was that deference should be given to state-created privileges.[47]

By giving deference to state-created privileges, the second sentence of Rule 501 serves the purpose of ensuring that all aspects of substantive state law will apply in a claim or defense based on or having a background relation to state law. The expansive interpretation of Rule 501 requiring application of state privilege law to all aspects of a claim or defense controlled by state law is grounded in the legislative history of Rule 501.[48] The Report of the House/Senate Conferees directs a liberal interpretation of what constitutes an element of a claim or defense based on state law:

> If an item of proof tends to support or defeat a claim or defense, or an element of a claim or defense, and if state law supplies the rule of decision for that claim or defense, then state privilege law applies to that item of proof.[49]

This interpretation, which varied somewhat from the Senate proposal, was in accord with case law authority prior to the adoption of the Rules.[50]

---

[44] H.R. Rep. No. 93-650, 93d Cong., 1st Sess. 8–9 (1973).

[45] *See* Rule 501, Advisory Committee Note; *see also* 2 MUELLER & KIRKPATRICK, §§ 175–177.

[46] Rule 501, Advisory Committee Note.

[47] *See* § 501.3, *supra*.

[48] *See* 2 MUELLER & KIRKPATRICK, §§ 175–177.

[49] H.R. Conf. Rep. No. 93-1597, 93d Cong., 2d Sess. 7 (1974).

[50] Massachusetts Mut. Life Ins. Co. v. Brei, 311 F.2d 463 (2d Cir. 1962); Pritchard v. Insurance Co. of N.A., 61 F.R.D. 104 (D. Miss. 1973); Dixon v. 80 Pine St. Corp., 516 F.2d 1278 (2d Cir. 1975) (data obtained not privileged since "societal interest in uncovering the facts which underlie the wrongful death claim" was paramount).

Moreover, the liberal interpretation intended by Congress is currently being followed in federal courts.[51]

Rule 501 attempts to reconcile privilege law with the *Erie* doctrine[52] by directing that principles of federal common law will be applied in federal question litigation and in federal criminal cases. In civil actions where state law supplies the rule of decision, such as diversity cases, the state-created privilege law must be applied.

Rule 501 leaves unanswered the question of which of several state's laws to apply, once it has been determined that a state's law concerning a privilege should govern. In resolving this issue, the federal courts have largely continued to apply the rule established by the Supreme Court in the *Klaxon* case.[53] Consequently, a claim of privilege that is made at trial is governed by the state law that would be applied in the forum in which the federal court sits.[54] When a claim of privilege arises in the course of a deposition taken in a forum other than the one in which the federal court is sitting, that state's law governing privileges will be applied.[55]

§ 501.5   Attorney-Client Privilege

The privilege for confidential communications between clients and their attorneys had its source in English law centuries ago.[56] As the oldest privilege for confidential communications, it has served as a model for other privileges. The purpose and intent behind the attorney-client privilege is to "promote freedom of consultation of legal advisors by clients."[57] In order to accomplish this goal, "the apprehension of compelled disclosure by the legal advisors must be removed; hence the law must prohibit such disclosure

---

[51] *See* 2 MUELLER & KIRKPATRICK, § 174.

[52] *See* 3 WEINSTEIN'S FEDERAL EVIDENCE § 501.02.

[53] Klaxon Co. v. Stentor Elec. Mfg. Co., 313 U.S. 487 (1941).

[54] Miller v. Transamerican Press, 621 F.2d 721 (5th Cir. 1980); Samuelson v. Susen, 576 F.2d 546 (3d Cir. 1978) (neurosurgeon brought diversity action based upon defamation; plaintiff then sought to depose physicians, who in return sought protective orders; district court properly applied state law in granting the protective orders); *see also In re* Tidewater Group, Inc., 65 B.R. 179 (Bankr. Ct. N.D. Ga. 1986) (in bankruptcy proceeding, debtor counter-claimed that plaintiff had breached a contract to buy debtor's subsidiary; court applying Georgia law held that the Georgia accountant-client privilege prevented plaintiff from obtaining subsidiary's audit reports through discovery).

[55] *See In re* Westinghouse Elec. Corp. Uranium Contracts Litig., 76 F.R.D. 47 (W.D. Pa. 1977) (multidistrict litigation; court applied conflict of law rule of the forum rather than the privilege law of the state whose substantive law would apply); *see also* Palmer v. Fisher, 228 F.2d 603 (7th Cir. 1955). *But cf.* Wm. T. Thompson Co. v. General Nutrition Corp., Inc., 671 F.2d 100 (3d Cir. 1982).

[56] 8 WIGMORE, § 2290.

[57] 8 WIGMORE, § 2291, at 545.

except on the client's consent."[58]

Elements of the Privilege.

The privilege may be summarized as follows: "A client holds a privilege to prevent testimonial disclosure of communications made in confidence between himself and his lawyer during the course of a professional lawyer-client relationship."[59] The client need not be an individual, but may be any type of public or private entity, including a corporation, government or governmental agency.[60] It is the client who actually holds the privilege and who may object to the disclosure of confidential communications. The client need not be a party to the action to assert the privilege.[61] The attorney may claim the privilege on the client's behalf[62] and the code of professional ethics obliges the attorney to do so.[63]

In order for the privilege to vest, the client must be represented by a lawyer or by a person whom the client reasonably believes to be an attorney, even if the belief is mistaken.[64] The attorney need not be a member of the bar in the jurisdiction in which the communication takes place but need only be authorized to practice law in some jurisdiction.[65] However, a privilege

---

[58] 8 WIGMORE, § 2291, at 545; *see* Chase Manhattan Bank, N.A. v. Turner & Newall, PLC, 964 F.2d 159 (2d Cir. 1992) (a magistrate's decision to issue an "attorney's-eyes-only" order directing the defense to release documents to plaintiff's counsel constituted error, as it undermined the purpose of the attorney-client privilege).

[59] 2 MUELLER & KIRKPATRICK, §§ 182–186; *see also* United States v. Rowe, 96 F.3d 1294 (9th Cir. 1996) (finding error in the district court's decision that the attorney-client privilege did not cover conversations between a senior partner and two associates in his firm whom the partner had engaged to research the methods another attorney at the firm used in handling client funds; the appellate court reversed the decision as the partner had an eye towards litigation when he assigned the associates to perform legal services for the firm).

[60] 2 MUELLER & KIRKPATRICK, §§ 182–186; *see also In re* Bieter Co., 16 F.3d 929 (8th Cir. 1994) (court found that an individual was an independent consultant of a client's attorney, and that communications between the consultant and the client's attorney were protected by the attorney-client privilege).

[61] 3 WEINSTEIN'S FEDERAL EVIDENCE § 503.20.

[62] Fisher v. United States, 425 U.S. 391 (1976) (it is universally accepted that the attorney-client privilege may be raised by the attorney).

[63] Schwimmer v. United States, 232 F.2d 855 (8th Cir. 1956) (attorney-client privilege exists for the benefit of the client and not the attorney); Baldwin v. Commission, 125 F.2d 812 (9th Cir. 1942) (privilege is that of client rather than of attorney); *see also* American Bar Association, Canon of Professional Ethics, Canon 37.

[64] 2 MUELLER & KIRKPATRICK, §§ 182–186.

[65] Paper Converting Co. v. FMC Corp., 215 F. Supp. 249 (E.D. Wis. 1963) (privilege applied with respect to correspondence from patent counsel, who was a member of Ohio bar, but not the bar of California, where he was located and employed); Georgia-Pacific Plywood Co. v. United States Plywood Corp., 18 F.R.D. 463 (S.D.N.Y. 1956) (privilege applied in regard to house counsel who belonged to District of Columbia bar, but not to bar of New York, in which was pending litigation in which the lawyer was taking active part); *see also*

does not apply to communications between the client and a practitioner such as a patent representative who is not licensed by any bar, even though the identical communication would be privileged if the practitioner were an attorney.[66]

To assert the privilege successfully, the claimant has the burden of proving that the requisite professional relationship existed.[67] The privilege protects a prospective client's preliminary consultation with an attorney concerning possible representation, even if the client does not pay that lawyer or ultimately retains another lawyer.[68] The consultation need not be related to litigation.[69] However, the relationship must be that of attorney and client; the privilege does not apply when the attorney is consulted as a business advisor,[70] accountant,[71] friend[72] or in some other capacity.[73]

Zenith Radio Corp. v. Radio Corp. of America, 121 F. Supp. 792 (D. Del. 1954).

[66] United States v. United Shoe Mach. Corp., 89 F. Supp. 357 (D. Mass. 1958). *But cf.* Renfield Corp. v. E. Remy Martin & Co., 98 F.R.D. 442 (D. Del. 1982) (court found it irrelevant that French in-house attorneys were not members of any bar since they were competent and lawfully able to give legal advice; therefore communications between the attorneys and corporate personnel were within the attorney-client privilege).

[67] United States v. Moscony, 927 F.2d 742 (3d Cir. 1991) (affidavits given by defendant's employees to defendant's law firm, which was later disqualified, came within attorney-client privilege); United States v. Wilson, 798 F.2d 509 (1st Cir. 1986) (trial court did not err in concluding that claimant had not met his burden of showing that the witness had acted as his attorney); United States v. Kelly, 569 F.2d 928 (5th Cir. 1978); *In re* Bonanno, 344 F.2d 830 (2d Cir. 1965); United States v. Blackburn, 538 F. Supp. 1376 (M.D. Fla. 1982).

[68] Westinghouse Elec. Corp. v. Kerr-McGee Corp., 580 F.2d 1311 (7th Cir. 1978) (where law firm represented American Petroleum Institute, which requested its members to provide law firm with confidential information, attorney-client relationship arose even though none of the members had requested the firm to act as its attorney orally or in writing and the firm did not accept such employment orally or in writing); *see also* Note, *Nature of the Professional Relationship Required Under Privileged Communication Rule,* 24 IOWA L. REV. 538 (1939); *see, e.g.,* Kearns v. Fred Lavery/Porsche Audi Co., 573 F. Supp. 91 (E.D. Mich. 1983).

[69] 3 WEINSTEIN'S FEDERAL EVIDENCE § 503.11. *See also* United States v. Chen, 99 F.3d 1495, 1500–1501 (9th Cir. 1996) (the attorney-client privilege applies not only where a lawyer represents the client in litigation, but also where he or she acts in a counseling and planning role; where an attorney serves as a client's spokesperson to government agencies, the attorney is providing professional legal services and therefore the attorney-client privilege applies).

[70] Colton v. United States, 306 F.2d 633 (2d Cir. 1962) (attorney had to supply information concerning the times and general nature of services performed for client, as well as turn over documents given to him by his client which had not been prepared specifically for purpose of communicating with attorney); *see also* Computer Network Corp. v. Spohler, 95 F.R.D. 500 (D.D.C. 1982).

[71] United States v. Gurtner, 474 F.2d 297 (9th Cir. 1973); *In re* Fisher, 51 F.2d 424 (S.D.N.Y. 1931); *In re* Shapiro, 381 F. Supp. 21 (N.D. Ill. 1974); *see also* Couch v. United States, 409 U.S. 322 (1973) (no federal accountant-client privilege).

[72] *See* United States v. Evans, 113 F.3d 1457 (7th Cir. 1997) (where family lawyer is present during conference between client and his criminal lawyer only as a friend, his

As one commentator has stated, "Only the communication is privileged; the client's knowledge is not."[74] The client cannot immunize a fact from discovery or compelled testimony by communicating it to the attorney. However, if the privilege applies, it protects not only the client's communications to the attorney but also statements by the attorney that would tend to reveal what the client had said.[75] Acts or gestures by the client that are intended to be communicative also are within the privilege.[76] An unresolved issue is whether observations by the attorney about the client, such as the client's dress, demeanor, or mental condition, are privileged. The weight of authority denies privileged status if the observations could be made by anyone.[77] Generally, the privilege is inapplicable to basic facts such as the client's identity, the fact that the client has consulted an attorney, the fees paid, and the nature of the services to be rendered.[78] An exception is

---

presence destroys the confidentiality required for the attorney-client privilege); United States v. Tedder, 801 F.2d 1437 (4th Cir. 1986) (attorney's testimony that defendant had perjured himself was properly admitted where the defendant had spoken to her as a friend personally involved in the case rather than as an attorney); Modern Woodmen of America v. Watkins, 132 F.2d 352 (5th Cir. 1942).

[73] *In re* Grand Jury Proceedings of Browning Arms Co., 528 F.2d 1301 (8th Cir. 1976) (privilege inapplicable where attorney served as member of board of directors); Harris v. United States, 413 F.2d 316 (9th Cir. 1969) (privilege inapplicable where attorney performed clerical services related to trust fund); Banks v. United States, 204 F.2d 666 (8th Cir. 1953) (privilege inapplicable where attorney served as agent in IRS negotiations).

[74] 3 WEINSTEIN'S FEDERAL EVIDENCE § 503.14.

[75] Mead Data Central, Inc. v. United States Dep't of Air Force, 566 F.2d 242 (D.C. Cir. 1977); *In re* Fischel, 557 F.2d 209 (9th Cir. 1977); Natta v. Hogan, 392 F.2d 686 (10th Cir. 1968); Schwimmer v. United States, 232 F.2d 855 (8th Cir. 1956).

[76] 1 McCORMICK, § 89(a). *But see* Granviel v. Lynaugh, 881 F.2d 185 (5th Cir. 1989) (attorney-client privilege does not protect testimony that defendant-client struck his attorney).

[77] *In re* Walsh, 623 F.2d 489 (7th Cir. 1980); United States v. Pipkins, 528 F.2d 559 (5th Cir. 1976) (handwriting samples given to handwriting expert retained by defense were not confidential communications within the realm of the attorney-client privilege); United States v. Kendrick, 331 F.2d 110 (4th Cir. 1964); 1 McCORMICK, § 89.

[78] *In re* Shargel, 742 F.2d 61 (2d Cir. 1984); United States v. Clemons, 676 F.2d 124 (5th Cir. 1982); *In re* Grand Jury Proceedings in Matter of Fine, 641 F.2d 199 (5th Cir. 1981); United States v. Strahl, 590 F.2d 10 (1st Cir. 1978); United States v. Haddad, 527 F.2d 537 (6th Cir. 1975); Vingelli v. United States, 992 F.2d 449 (2d Cir. 1993) (in drug investigation, where grand jury wanted to know how one of the convicted conspirators had paid fees to an attorney, questions concerning client and fee information to another attorney who had forwarded the legal fees did not violate the attorney-client privilege); *In re* Grand Jury Subpoena Issued to Gerson S. Horn, 976 F.2d 1314 (9th Cir. 1992) (forcing defendant to identify the individuals named in the subpoena that were his clients was not a violation of the attorney-client privilege); Clarke v. American Commerce Nat'l Bank, 974 F.2d 127 (9th Cir. 1992) (attorney's billing statements did not constitute privileged communications); 1 McCORMICK, § 90. *But see In re* Grand Jury Subpoena Issued to Bierman, 765 F.2d 1014 (11th Cir. 1985) (attorney was not required to answer whether he had advised his client of the surrender date when his appeal from tax fraud case failed; even if the information would not

recognized, however, when the substance of the communication already has been revealed and revelation of the client's identity consequently would amount to disclosure of the communication.[79] The client's identity also is within the privilege when its revelation would implicate the client in the crime for which he or she sought legal advice.[80] Although the privilege protects the existence and terms of a document drawn up by the attorney for the client, documents that already existed or that are intended to be disclosed are not within the privilege.[81]

The attorney-client privilege also is subject to a requirement of confiden-

ordinarily be privileged, privilege applies here since so much of the substance of the conversation was already known that such disclosure would be the "last link" in determining that the client had received notice of the date and willfully failed to appear).

[79] *In re* Grand Jury Proceedings, 600 F.2d 215 (9th Cir. 1979) (attorney entitled to assert attorney-client privilege even though individuals had not paid their fees, in refusing to divulge to the grand jury names of clients who had paid fees for two individuals arrested in connection with narcotics conspiracy); *In re* Grand Jury Proceedings, 517 F.2d 666 (5th Cir. 1975) (court held names of unidentified persons who arranged for bonds and legal fees on behalf of known clients to be privileged, since the names would be directly relevant to supplementing already existent incriminating information about persons suspected of income tax evasion); *see also* United States v. Tratner, 511 F.2d 248 (7th Cir. 1975) (taxpayer-attorney claimed privilege when government sought information regarding $10, 000 check deposited in his escrow account; appellate court found attorney had not sustained burden of proving that transaction was part of relationship and remanded to give attorney opportunity to include in record on appeal any other evidence that would indicate existence of privilege); NLRB v. Harvey, 349 F.2d 900 (4th Cir. 1965) (unfair labor practice charging that employer fired persons visited by union organizer and that company had put organizer under detective surveillance; attorney refused to divulge identity of client but indicated it was not employer involved in NLRB proceeding; appellate court remanded to district court to ascertain whether hiring of detective was in connection with rendition of legal services; district court found that it was and sustained privilege; client was trying to find out if his plant was being organized so that he would know what he could legally do).

[80] United States v. Hodge & Zweig, 548 F.2d 1347 (9th Cir. 1977) (disclosure of facts concerning actions of known person in obtaining legal services for another known person would be required, even though the former made a prima facie showing that he would be implicated by the disclosure in activity for which he had sought legal advice, but only because government made a prima facie showing that the attorney was retained to continue criminal or fraudulent activity); 2 MUELLER & KIRKPATRICK, §§ 187–188; *see also* United States v. Liddy, 509 F.2d 428 (D.C. Cir. 1974) (error, but harmless, to instruct jury that it might draw an appropriate inference from the fact that defendant sought counsel in the small hours of the morning shortly after the break-in forming the subject matter of the prosecution had occurred); United States ex rel. Macon v. Yeager, 476 F.2d 613 (3d Cir. 1973) (reversible error under Sixth Amendment to allow prosecutor to comment to jury that defendant consulted attorney shortly after the murder with which defendant was subsequently charged).

[81] Fisher v. United States, 425 U.S. 391 (1976) (questions of attorney-client privilege in tax investigation are controlled by common-law principles); United States v. Panetta, 436 F. Supp. 114 (E.D. Pa. 1977), *aff'd without op.,* 568 F.2d 771 (3d Cir. 1978) (rules of privilege applied in criminal case); *see also* 1 MCCORMICK, § 89, at 330 ("[I]f a document would be subject to an order for production if it were in the hands of the client it will be equally subject to such an order if it is in the hands of his attorney").

tiality. In determining whether a communication is confidential, the client's intent is controlling. The circumstances surrounding the communication often are indicative of the client's intent.[82] For example, if a disinterested third party is present, the client probably did not intend for his or her statements to the attorney to remain confidential, and thus the privilege is inapplicable.[83] On the other hand, if the transaction requires a third person, such as an interpreter, confidentiality is not destroyed by his presence during the communication.[84] Although at common law an eavesdropper could testify to otherwise privileged communications, in this day of sophisticated listening devices, an eavesdropper's testimony is barred by the privilege provided the client has taken reasonable precautions to ensure confidentiality.[85] Communications that are intended by the client to be disclosed to another person or that the client actually discloses are not privileged.[86]

Corporate Clients.

Application of the attorney-client privilege becomes complicated where the client is a corporation. As McCormick explained, "The difficulty is basically one of extrapolating the essential operating conditions of the privilege from the paradigm case of the traditional individual client who both supplies information to, and receives counsel from, the attorney."[87] In the corporate context these functions typically are divided between several

---

[82] United States v. Lopez, 777 F.2d 543 (10th Cir. 1985) (where codefendants had separate counsel and potentially adverse interests, there could be no expectation that disclosures made by one defendant at a meeting with the other defendant and the latter's attorney would remain confidential); United States v. Noriega, 917 F.2d 1543 (11th Cir. 1990) (in deciding how attorney-client privilege affected media use of recorded prison conversations between defendant and his attorney, appeals court remanded case to district court with test for whether prison release form signed by defendant affected his confidentiality expectation); 3 WEINSTEIN'S FEDERAL EVIDENCE § 503.15; *see also* United States v. Bigos, 459 F.2d 639, 643 (1st Cir. 1972) ("While we agree that the presence of a third party commonly destroys the privilege, it does so only insofar as it is indicative of the intent of the parties that their communication not be confidential").

[83] United States v. Lopez, 777 F.2d 543 (10th Cir. 1985) (where codefendants had separate counsel and potentially adverse interests, there could be no expectation that disclosures made by one defendant at a meeting with the other defendant and the latter's attorney would remain confidential); United States v. Flores, 628 F.2d 521 (9th Cir. 1980); United States v. Cochran, 546 F.2d 27 (5th Cir. 1977); Johnson v. United States, 542 F.2d 941 (5th Cir. 1976); 1 MCCORMICK, § 91.

[84] United States v. Landof, 591 F.2d 36 (9th Cir. 1978); Himmelfarb v. United States, 175 F.2d 924 (9th Cir. 1949); 1 MCCORMICK, § 91.

[85] 3 WEINSTEIN'S FEDERAL EVIDENCE § 503.15.

[86] United States v. Bump, 605 F.2d 548 (10th Cir. 1979); Esposito v. United States, 436 F.2d 603 (9th Cir. 1970); United States v. Tellier, 255 F.2d 441 (2d Cir. 1958); 3 WEINSTEIN'S FEDERAL EVIDENCE § 503.15.

[87] 1 MCCORMICK, § 87; *see also* Weissenberger, *Toward Precision in the Attorney-Client Privilege for Corporations*, 65 IOWA L. REV. 899 (1980).

different individuals of varying rank. While extending the privilege to communications by any officer or employee of the corporation has been acknowledged as unduly broad,[88] the precise parameters of the privilege remain unclear. In 1962 a district court in Pennsylvania formulated the "control group" test, which limited the privilege to communications by corporate personnel in a position to control or even to take a substantial part in a decision about any action that the corporation may take upon the advice of the attorney.[89] Although the control group test was widely followed,[90] the Supreme Court expressly rejected it in its 1981 decision in *Upjohn Co. v. United States.*[91] The Court concluded that the control group test "cannot . . . govern the development of the law in this area"[92] because it "overlooks the fact that the privilege exists to protect not only the giving of professional advice to those who can act on it but also the giving of information to the lawyer to enable him to give sound and informed advice."[93] The Court declined to establish an alternative to the control group test, choosing instead to decide only the case before it. However, the Court's opinion indicates that information communicated to an attorney should be privileged if it is treated as confidential within the corporation, it is communicated to the attorney for the purpose of receiving legal advice and it is closely related to the duties of the corporate employee who conveys it to the attorney.[94]

Another issue in the corporate context is whether otherwise privileged information must be disclosed in suits by the shareholders against the corporation. The leading federal case, *Garner v. Wolfinbarger,* held that the privilege may be overcome by a showing of good cause, at least where the shareholders charge the corporation with "acting inimically to stockholder interests."[95]

---

[88] *See, e.g.,* Philadelphia v. Westinghouse Elec. Corp., 210 F. Supp. 483 (E.D. Pa. 1962).

[89] Philadelphia v. Westinghouse Elec. Corp., 210 F. Supp. 483, 485 (E.D. Pa. 1962).

[90] Many but not all courts adopted the control group test. In 1970, the Seventh Circuit propounded the subject matter test under which corporate communications with an attorney are privileged if the employee "makes the communication at the direction of his superiors in the corporation," even though the employee is not in a position of control, and the subject matter of the communication "is the performance by the employee of the duties of his employment." Harper & Row Publishers, Inc. v. Decker, 423 F.2d 487 (7th Cir. 1970), *aff'd,* 400 U.S. 348 (1971).

[91] Upjohn Co. v. United States, 449 U.S. 383 (1981).

[92] *Upjohn,* 499 U.S. at 402.

[93] *Id.* at 390.

[94] *Id.* at 394.

[95] Garner v. Wolfinbarger, 430 F.2d 1093, 1103 (5th Cir. 1970); *see also* Van Dusen, *The Responsibility of Lawyers Advising Management Under the ABA Code of Professional Responsibility,* N.Y.S. Bar J. 565 (Dec. 1974). *But cf.* Brennan's Inc. v. Brennan's Restaurants, 590 F.2d 168 (5th Cir. 1979); Ward v. Succession of Freeman, 854 F.2d 780 (5th Cir. 1988) (found the "good cause" exception inapplicable because the shareholder suit

Multiple Clients.

When two or more persons consult an attorney about a common matter, each client retains the right to assert the attorney-client privilege against a third party. However, in a dispute between the joint clients the privilege is inapplicable since joint consultation indicates that the clients did not intend for their communications to be confidential.[96] Where several clients, each with separate counsel, meet to plan a joint defense or course of action for their common good, the situation usually is treated as if the clients jointly consulted one attorney.[97] If there is no common interest among the various clients and they meet on a purely adversary basis, however, the privilege does not apply.[98]

Work Product Doctrine Distinguished.

Although the attorney-client privilege and the work product doctrine often are confused, the two doctrines are distinct. A complete discussion of the work product doctrine is beyond the scope of this Treatise, but the major differences between the attorney-client privilege and the work product

---

sought a benefit for only a small group of the company's stockholders, the actions at issue were not unlawful, and the plaintiffs had not attempted to obtain the information from other sources).

[96] FDIC v. Ogden Corp, 202 F.3d 454 (1st Cir. 2000) (no attorney-client privilege under Massachusetts law where the same firm represents two clients with similar interests and goals, as the privilege only protects against disclosure to those outside the "charmed circle" in which relevant communications are made); Simpson v. Motorists Mut. Ins. Co., 494 F.2d 850 (7th Cir. 1974) (when one attorney represents two parties having a common interest, communications of each party with attorney are privileged from third party but not between the two original parties); Baldwin v. Commissioner, 125 F.2d 812 (9th Cir. 1942) (when two or more parties address lawyer as their common agent, their communications are privileged as against strangers, but not among themselves); Grand Trunk W. R. Co. v. H.W. Nelson Co., 116 F.2d 823 (6th Cir. 1941) ("when two persons employ a lawyer as their common agent, their communications to him as to strangers will be privileged, but as to themselves, they stand on the same footing as to the lawyer, and either can compel him to testify against the other as to their negotiations in any litigation between them, when the subject of the conversation is competent").

[97] *In re* Grand Jury Subpoenas 89-3 and 89-4, 902 F.2d 244 (4th Cir. 1990); Eisenberg v. Gagnon, 766 F.2d 770 (3d Cir. 1985) (communications between the defendant firm and the firm's insurer's attorney were privileged even though defendant firm had a separate attorney and the firm and the insurer had potentially adverse interests, where the correspondence was part of "an ongoing and joint effort to set up a common defense strategy" and the parties' interests were not "completely adverse"); United States v. McPartlin, 595 F.2d 1321 (7th Cir. 1979); Hunydee v. United States, 355 F.2d 183 (9th Cir. 1965); 3 WEINSTEIN'S FEDERAL EVIDENCE § 503.21.

[98] United States v. Lopez, 777 F.2d 543 (10th Cir. 1985) (where codefendants had separate counsel and potentially adverse interests, there could be no expectation that disclosures made by one defendant at a meeting with the other defendant and the latter's attorney would remain confidential); United States v. Cariello, 536 F. Supp. 698 (D.N.J. 1982); Magnaleasing, Inc. v. Staten Island Mall, 76 F.R.D. 559 (S.D.N.Y. 1977).

doctrine are briefly summarized here: (1) While the purpose of the attorney-client privilege is to encourage full disclosure by the client, the work product doctrine is designed to protect the privacy of an attorney's course of preparation of cases for trial.[99] (2) When the privilege is applicable its protection is absolute, while the work product doctrine can be overcome by a showing of substantial need.[100]

Waiver.

The attorney-client privilege protects the interests of the client, and is held only by the client. The privilege therefore may be waived only by the client or by a lawyer who is acting on his or her behalf; it is not waived by the actions or omissions of a former attorney or an attorney acting outside the scope of that representation.[101] Waiver may occur by voluntary disclosure of the communication[102] or by express waiver, at a former trial or earlier proceeding,[103] by a trustee of a corporation in bankruptcy[104] or by the representative of a deceased client.[105] The client's failure to object to the disclosure of privileged information despite having had the opportunity to do

---

[99] *See* Hickman v. Taylor, 329 U.S. 495 (1947).

[100] *See id.*

[101] *See* 8 WIGMORE, § 2327; *see also* United States v. Seale, 600 F.3d 473 (5th Cir. 2010) (where the accused wished to impeach a Government witness by calling the witness's former attorney to testify that the witness had privately recanted a statement incriminating the accused, such testimony was barred by the attorney-client privilege; there was no basis for a finding that the witness had impliedly waived the privilege, even if he knew that his former lawyer was conferring with the attorney for the defendant, since the witness did not personally disclose any confidential communications to the defendant's lawyer); United States v. Chen, 99 F.3d 1495, 1500–1501 (9th Cir. 1996) (a former employee of a corporation has no authority to disclose privileged documents or otherwise waive the attorney-client privilege).

[102] Westinghouse Elec. Corp. v. The Republic of the Philippines, 951 F.2d 1414 (3d Cir. 1991) (the court rejected the concept of selective waiver of attorney-client privilege by voluntary disclosure to government agencies); United States v. McCambridge, 551 F.2d 865 (1st Cir. 1977); United States v. Pauldino, 487 F.2d 127 (10th Cir. 1973); *see also* Howell v. United States, 442 F.2d 265 (7th Cir. 1971) (lawyer permitted to testify that his client was competent to stand trial; testimony amounted to nonconfidential matters).

[103] *See, e.g.,* United States v. Suarez, 820 F.2d 1158 (11th Cir. 1987) (where defendant's attorney testified at pretrial hearing, he could not claim attorney-client privilege to refuse to testify at trial); United States v. Jenkins, 785 F.2d 1387 (9th Cir. 1986) (prior civil deposition by defendant in later criminal trial was properly admissible; Fifth Amendment privilege against self-incrimination was (inadvertently) waived by the earlier testimony).

[104] *See* 8 WIGMORE, § 2327.

[105] *See* 8 WIGMORE, § 2329; Commodity Futures Trading Com. v. Weintraub, 471 U.S. 343 (1985) (trustee of a corporation in bankruptcy has the power to waive the debtor corporation's attorney-client privilege with respect to communications that took place before the filing of the petition in bankruptcy; the trustee plays the role most closely analogous to that of a solvent corporation's management).

so also operates as a waiver.[106] Since the privilege protects confidential communications rather than facts, the client can testify about the facts that were the subject of the consultation with the attorney without waiving the privilege.[107] Several narrow but important aspects of the way in which the attorney-client privilege may be waived are now regulated by Federal Rule of Evidence 502, which was approved by Congress and went into effect in 2008.[108]

Exceptions.

The privilege is subject to several exceptions. When the client consults the attorney in the furtherance of a continuing or future crime or fraud, the privilege does not apply. The exception bars the privilege only if the client is knowingly aware of the illegality of his or her conduct, and regardless of whether the attorney has knowledge of the criminal purpose.[109] The exception is inapplicable when the client consults the attorney about a crime or fraudulent act he committed in the past.[110] Although the privilege survives the death of the client and may be asserted by his representative,[111]

---

[106] Steen v. First Nat'l Bank, 298 F. 36 (8th Cir. 1924).

[107] *In re* Ampicillin, Antitrust Litigation, 81 F.R.D. 377 (D.D.C. 1998); Magida v. Continental Can Co., 12 F.R.D. 74 (S.D.N.Y. 1951).

[108] *See* Chapter 502, *infra,* for a more extended discussion of this rule and its provisions.

[109] 2 MUELLER & KIRKPATRICK, §§ 195–198; *see In re* Grand Jury Proceedings, 604 F.2d 798 (3d Cir. 1979); United States v. Calvert, 523 F.2d 895, 909 (8th Cir. 1975) ("[I]t is the client's purpose which is controlling, and it matters not that the attorney was ignorant of the client's purpose in making the statements."); United States v. Aldridge, 484 F.2d 655 (7th Cir. 1973) (same); *see also* United States v. Ballard, 779 F.2d 287, 291 (5th Cir. 1986) (confidences are not privileged where the party seeking disclosure makes "a prima facie case that the attorney-client relationship was used to promote an intended criminal activity"); *In re* Sealed Case, 754 F.2d 395 (D.C. Cir. 1985) (where government made a prima facie case that communications were in furtherance of fraud, there was no privilege, whether or not the attorneys were aware of the crime); United States v. Friedman, 445 F.2d 1076 (9th Cir. 1971); United States v. Chen, 99 F.3d 1495, 1500–1501 (9th Cir. 1996) (in order to set aside the protection of the attorney-client privilege under the crime fraud exception, the government must make a prima facie showing that the communications "were in furtherance of an intended or present illegality and that there is some relationship between the communications and the illegality"; mere allegations are insufficient to pierce the privilege); *In re* Spalding Sports Worldwide, Inc., 203 F.3d 800 (Fed. Cir. 2000) (the invention record behind plaintiff's patent in a particular basketball cover was submitted to plaintiff's legal department for the purpose of obtaining legal advice, which made it a privileged communication; the mere failure to cite prior art falls short of the prima facie showing of plaintiff's intent to defraud the patent office and justify application of the crime-fraud exception to the privilege).

[110] *See In re* Federal Grand Jury Proceedings, 89-10 (MIA), 938 F.2d 1578 (11th Cir. 1991) (since the sought-after communications between attorney and client took place after the illegal activity, the communications did not fall under the crime-fraud exception and were consequently privileged).

[111] Swidler & Berlin v. United States, 524 U.S. 399 (1998) (the attorney-client privilege survives the death of the client, even in criminal cases; the notion that privileges should be

an exception to the privilege arises when there is a dispute between persons who claim a right to property or money through the decedent. In this situation it is unclear which person is entitled to claim the privilege and therefore neither is permitted to assert it.[112] Another exception is recognized when the attorney acts as an attesting witness to a document executed by the client. The privilege does not apply to communications between the client and attorney that are relevant to an issue concerning the document, because the attorney-client privilege does not protect communications to the attorney in the role of attesting witness.[113] The attorney-client privilege is inapplicable in the event of a breach of duty by either the client or the attorney. When the client fails to pay legal fees, or charges the attorney with malpractice, the attorney may reveal otherwise privileged communications to the extent necessary to recover the fee or to protect his or her reputation.[114]

§ 501.6 Spousal Privileges

Federal courts recognize a privilege against adverse spousal testimony and a privilege for confidential marital communications. Both are discussed below.

Privilege Against Adverse Spousal Testimony.

At common law, the spouse of a party was considered incompetent to testify either for or against the party. This practice resulted from the combination of the common-law rule that disqualified a party from testifying in his or her own behalf and the common-law conception, inspired by Judeo-Christian tradition, that husband and wife were one.[115] In federal courts the disqualification of spouses to testify *for* one another was abolished by the Supreme Court in 1933.[116]

The rule excluding testimony by a spouse evolved into a privilege and was justified as a means to preserve marital harmony and tranquility. It was believed that adverse testimony by a spouse would destroy a marriage. In *Hawkins v. United States,* the Supreme Court endorsed this rationale and

---

strictly construed applies primarily to the creation of new privileges, not the narrowing of a well-established privilege).

[112] 2 MUELLER & KIRKPATRICK, §§ 195–198.

[113] 2 MUELLER & KIRKPATRICK, §§ 195–198.

[114] Johnson v. United States, 542 F.2d 941 (5th Cir. 1976); Tasby v. United States, 504 F.2d 332 (8th Cir. 1974); Laughner v. United States, 373 F.2d 326 (5th Cir. 1967); Housler v. First Nat'l Bank of East Islip, 484 F. Supp. 1321 (E.D.N.Y. 1981); *see also* United States v. Woodall, 438 F.2d 1317 (5th Cir. 1970); United States v. Wiggins, 184 F. Supp. 673 (D.D.C. Cir. 1960).

[115] 2 MUELLER & KIRKPATRICK, § 206.

[116] Funk v. United States, 290 U.S. 371 (1933).

established that both spouses held the privilege to bar adverse testimony.[117] However, in *Trammel v. United States,* the Court sharply cut the broad privilege approved in *Hawkins* by ruling that the privilege to exclude adverse spousal testimony is held solely by the witness spouse; the accused cannot object if the witness spouse freely elects to testify.[118] The Court noted that privileges may impede the search for truth by suppressing evidence, and thus must be strictly construed. In the light of reason and experience, the Court found that the goal of preserving marital harmony no longer justified so sweeping a privilege. The Court observed that the willingness of one spouse to testify against the other suggested the marriage already was beyond saving.[119]

The privilege against adverse spousal testimony is well settled in criminal cases, and has even been extended to asset discovery proceedings that are ancillary to a criminal prosecution,[120] but its possible role in federal civil litigation is unclear. The proposed version of Rule 505, which was approved by the Supreme Court but never adopted by Congress, would have restricted its availability to criminal cases.[121] It has been widely assumed and often asserted, at least in dictum, that the privilege is limited to criminal cases and may never be asserted in a civil proceeding, although the most recent appellate federal cases to discuss the issue have all taken care to avoid squarely ruling on that question.[122] Although those courts have indicated a willingness to consider the possible extension of that privilege to a spouse

---

[117] Hawkins v. United States, 358 U.S. 74, 78 (1958) ("Adverse testimony given [by a spouse] in criminal proceedings would, we think, be likely to destroy almost any marriage").

[118] Trammel v. United States, 445 U.S. 40 (1980); United States v. Porter, 986 F.2d 1014 (6th Cir. 1993) (privilege against adverse spousal testimony did not prevent defendant's ex-wife from testifying against him since the couple was divorced at the time of trial and because the wife did not elect to exercise the privilege); *see also* United States v. Jackson, 939 F.2d 625 (8th Cir. 1991) (spouse waived the adverse testimony privilege by stating her willingness to testify); United States v. Wood, 924 F.2d 399 (1st Cir. 1991) (in husband's trial, wife could waive privilege to testify against husband, but could not waive privilege regarding letter from husband to wife).

[119] Trammel v. United States, 445 U.S. 40 (1980); *see also* United States v. Murphy, 65 F.3d 758 (9th Cir. 1995) (defendant was charged with violating environmental laws and his estranged wife testified against him at trial; trial court did not err in admitting the testimony because, although the parties were technically married, the court found that the marriage was irreconcilable where the parties had been separated for seven years and had filed for divorce).

[120] United States v. Yerardi, 192 F.3d 14, 19 (1st Cir. 1999) (even if adverse spousal testimony privilege is generally unavailable in civil proceedings, it could be invoked in a forfeiture proceeding that was ancillary to a criminal case and designed to recover a penalty under criminal forfeiture provisions where those answers raised "an appreciable risk of contributing to future criminal prosecution" of the defendant, despite Government's assertion that the proceeding was "more civil than criminal" and affected only a property interest).

[121] *See* Proposed Rule 505(a), in Appendix B ("An accused in a criminal proceeding has a privilege to prevent his spouse from testifying against him.").

[122] United States v. Yerardi, 192 F.3d 14, 19 (1st Cir. 1999) ("some formulations of the

called to testify in a civil proceeding, at least in an appropriate case, no court has yet been willing to go that far, and the prospect remains uncertain at best.

Unlike the privilege for marital communications, the testimonial privilege is not limited to confidential statements; it covers testimony on all subjects, including matters that occurred before and during the marriage.[123] To claim the privilege, the party and the witness must have a valid marriage at the time of trial, as determined by the law of the state of their domicile.[124] A sham or fraudulent marriage will not support the privilege. In the event of divorce or annulment, the privilege ends.[125] Some decisions suggest that the

---

privilege, and dicta in some of the cases, assume that the privilege could never be asserted in a civil case," although "it is hard to find a square holding to this effect"); United States v. Premises Known as 281 Syosset Woodbury Road, 71 F.3d 1067, 1070 (2d Cir. 1995) (noting that the adverse spousal testimony privilege "has traditionally been limited to criminal cases," but declining to decide whether its invocation would ever be proper in the arguably "quasi-criminal context" of a civil forfeiture proceeding); In re Martenson, 779 F.2d 461, 463 & n.6 (8th Cir. 1985) (collecting authorities suggesting that the privilege is "inapplicable in civil proceedings," but concluding that "[w]e need not decide whether the adverse testimony privilege may be asserted in a civil case to which neither spouse is a party"); Ryan v. Commissioner, 568 F.2d 531, 544 (7th Cir. 1977) (declining to decide whether the privilege might ever be available in a civil case, and concluding that the privilege would at most be available in civil cases only where "a spouse who is neither a victim nor a participant observes evidence of the other spouse's crime").

[123] United States v. Apodaca, 522 F.2d 568 (10th Cir. 1975) (spousal testimonial privilege would apply as to matters occurring prior to the marriage, but affirming denial of the privilege upon ground that marriage was fraudulent); see also United States v. Van Drunen, 501 F.2d 1393 (7th Cir. 1974); 2 LOUISELL & MUELLER, § 207. But see United States v. Clark, 712 F.2d 299 (7th Cir. 1983) (court expressly approved exception to testimonial privilege for pre-marital acts).

[124] See United States v. Acker, 52 F.3d 509, 514 (4th Cir. 1995) (declining to extend spousal communication privilege to a couple who had lived together for 25 years and rejecting an equal protection challenge to the validity of the spousal privilege); United States v. Hamilton, 19 F.3d 350 (7th Cir. 1994) (testimony from defendant's wife was not rendered inadmissible by defendant's assertion of the spousal privilege where defendant failed to prove the validity of the marriage at trial); United States v. Snyder, 707 F.2d 139 (5th Cir. 1983); United States v. McElrath, 377 F.2d 508 (6th Cir. 1967); In re Grand Jury Proceedings Witness Ms. X, 562 F. Supp. 486 (N.D. Cal. 1983); 2 MUELLER & KIRKPATRICK, § 207; see also United States v. Jackson, 939 F.2d 625 (8th Cir. 1991) (defendant could not invoke the marital communication privilege as the information was communicated after the couple had permanently separated); United States v. Byrd, 750 F.2d 585 (7th Cir. 1984) (the spousal communications privilege does not apply to communications between husband and wife who are permanently separated); Port v. Heard, 764 F.2d 423 (5th Cir. 1985) (court rejected parental claims of a constitutional right to refuse to testify against their child, a defendant in a murder trial).

[125] 3 WEINSTEIN'S FEDERAL EVIDENCE § 505.07; see Pereira v. United States, 347 U.S. 1 (1954) (spouses' divorce ends "any bar of incompetency"); Lutwak v. United States, 344 U.S. 604 (1953) (marriage entered into to obtain the illegal entry into the United States of aliens was a sham and therefore did not support the marital privilege); Yaldo v. Immigration & Naturalization Service, 424 F.2d 501 (6th Cir. 1970) (annulment ends the marital

privilege ceases when the marriage is deemed non-existent in substance, even if not in status.[126]

Generally, the privilege only applies in situations where the witness spouse's testimony will have a direct effect upon the marriage. The majority of courts agree that one of the spouses must be a party to the proceedings. Even though the witness's testimony may be damaging to his or her spouse and thus pose a threat to marital harmony, a spouse who is not a party does not have the requisite direct stake in the outcome of the litigation that justifies the privilege.[127] Similarly, although the privilege applies at grand jury proceedings pursuant to Rule 1101(d)(2), in cases in which the spouse is not the focus of the grand jury's inquiry, the witness spouse normally may not refuse to testify regardless of the testimony's negative reflection on his or her spouse.[128] In cases where a witness is asked questions that might incriminate a spouse who is not a party to the proceeding, several federal circuits have reasoned that the privilege does not apply as long as the witness

---

privilege); *see also* United States v. Byrd, 750 F.2d 585 (7th Cir. 1984) (the spousal communications privilege does not apply to communications between husband and wife who are permanently separated); Port v. Heard, 764 F.2d 423 (5th Cir. 1985) (court rejected parental claims of a constitutional right to refuse to testify against their child, a defendant in a murder trial).

[126] *See* United States v. Murphy, 65 F.3d 758 (9th Cir. 1995) (defendant was charged with violating environmental laws and his estranged wife testified against him at trial; trial court did not err in admitting the testimony because, although the parties were technically married, the court found that the marriage was irreconcilable where the parties had been separated for seven years and had filed for divorce); United States v. Brown, 605 F.2d 389 (8th Cir. 1979); United States v. Fisher, 518 F.2d 836 (2d Cir. 1975).

[127] United States v. Premises Known as 281 Syosset Woodbury Road, 71 F.3d 1067, 1070–1071 (2d Cir. 1995) (in civil forfeiture proceeding brought against property held in the name of a married woman, she could not assert the adverse spousal testimony privilege to refuse to answer questions, because her husband was not a party to the proceeding and the possibility that her answers might later be used against him in a criminal proceeding was deemed "far too speculative"); *In re* Martenson, 779 F.2d 461, 463 (8th Cir. 1985) (declining to decide whether the adverse testimony privilege could ever be asserted in a civil case to which neither spouse is a party, because married woman subjected to questioning in civil forfeiture proceeding failed to demonstrate more than a "speculative" risk that her answers would later in fact prove to be adverse to a protected interest of her spouse); United States v. Burks, 470 F.2d 432 (D.C. Cir. 1972) (murder prosecution; privilege inapplicable where interests of spouse of witness "were in no way at stake"); Halback v. Hill, 261 F. 1007 (D.C. Cir. 1919) (father's petition to obtain custody of child from child's grandmother where father had remarried; proper to require him to authenticate letters written by his new wife, offered by grandmother to demonstrate unfitness of this wife to have custody of child). *Contra* United States v. Hoffa, 349 F.2d 20 (6th Cir. 1965), *aff'd,* 385 U.S. 293 (1966) (prosecution for jury tampering; testimony of wife privileged as to whether defendant's encounters with the law and domestic troubles were associated with drug addiction and his association with other women).

[128] *In re* Snoonian, 502 F.2d 110 (1st Cir. 1974) (husband could not invoke spousal testimonial privilege where government had stated that wife was not target of grand jury investigation); *see also* United States v. George, 444 F.2d 310 (6th Cir. 1971).

is given a binding commitment from the government that those answers will not be used either directly or indirectly in any criminal prosecution of that spouse.[129] These courts, without saying so explicitly, have effectively reasoned that this privilege is like the Fifth Amendment privilege: not an unconditional right to "remain silent," but rather a rule providing that a witness can only be compelled to supply information that tends to incriminate the witness (or her spouse) if she is first given reliable assurances that the answers will not be used to even indirectly assist the government in bringing a prosecution against one or the other.

To ensure the effectiveness of the privilege, the witness spouse must be permitted to claim the privilege outside the presence of the jury. The prosecution may not call the witness spouse with the knowledge that the spouse does not wish to testify and force the spouse to claim the privilege in open court.[130] Once the privilege is asserted, most courts prohibit the prosecution from commenting upon its exercise to the jury.[131]

The exceptions to the privilege against adverse spousal testimony were designed to prevent the injustice that would result if the party could prevent his or her spouse from testifying in certain cases. After *Trammel* removed the party's ability to bar adverse testimony by his or her spouse, the exceptions have less significance. The privilege does not apply where one spouse is charged with committing a crime against the other.[132] Recent cases have

---

[129] United States v. Yerardi, 192 F.3d 14, 20 (1st Cir. 1999) (collecting cases) (in discovery proceedings, adverse spousal testimony privilege is overcome "where the government filed an affidavit promising that it would not use either directly or indirectly the compelled grand jury testimony of one spouse in subsequent criminal proceedings against the other spouse"); United States v. Premises Known as 281 Syosset Woodbury Road, 71 F.3d 1067, 1070 (2d Cir. 1995) (in civil forfeiture proceeding brought against property held in the name of a married woman, she could not assert the adverse spousal testimonial privilege because the government "guaranteed that [her] testimony in this case will not be offered as evidence in any other case against her husband").

[130] *See* 3 WEINSTEIN'S FEDERAL EVIDENCE § 505.08.

[131] *See* United States v. Hall, 989 F.2d 711 (4th Cir. 1993) (cross-examination of defendant using a statement given by defendant's wife, but not offered at trial because of the "adverse spousal testimony" privilege was reversible error); United States v. Morris, 988 F.2d 1335 (4th Cir. 1993) (trial court erred in permitting the prosecution to bring out that defendant's wife had invoked the marital privilege before the grand jury); United States v. Chapman, 866 F.2d 1326 (11th Cir. 1989); United States v. Pariente, 558 F.2d 1186 (5th Cir. 1977); United States v. Tapia-Lopez, 521 F.2d 582 (9th Cir. 1975); *see also* Courtney v. United States, 390 F.2d 521 (9th Cir. 1968) (plain error to allow prosecutor to comment upon defendant's failure to call his wife, whom he had married between the first and second trial, to testify, where defendant had properly claimed his privilege not to have her testify against him); 3 WEINSTEIN'S FEDERAL EVIDENCE § 505.08.

[132] Wyatt v. United States, 362 U.S. 525 (1960); United States v. Smith, 533 F.2d 1077 (8th Cir. 1976).

extended this exception to include crimes against a child of either spouse.[133] An exception also arises in cases in which the spouse is one of several victims of a crime committed by the other spouse.[134]

Less clear is whether federal law should recognize an exception to the privilege for cases in which the spouses co-operated as "joint participants" in the commission of some crime. At least one federal circuit has adopted such an exception,[135] concluding that the privilege should therefore be limited to those cases "where a spouse who is neither a victim *nor a participant* observes evidence of the other spouse's crime."[136] But two other circuits have rejected it, persuasively reasoning that the commission of a single criminal act by a married couple does not mean that the marriage has lost all further social value, and noting that the exception is prone to abuse because of the ease with which a prosecutor can make allegations that a married criminal was receiving the active support of his spouse.[137] The matter remains unsettled. Of course, as long as the two spouses were participating jointly in the commission of a crime, the testimony of either one will still be protected by the Fifth Amendment privilege; the applicability of the privilege against adverse spousal testimony in such cases will therefore almost always be moot as a practical matter unless the prosecution is willing to give immunity to one spouse to compel him or her to testify at the trial of the other.

---

[133] *See* United States v. Bahe, 128 F.3d 1440, 1444–1445 (10th Cir. 1997) (recognizing an exception to the spousal communication privilege "for spousal testimony relating to the abuse of a minor child within the household"); United States v. Lilley, 581 F.2d 182 (8th Cir. 1978); United States v. Allery, 526 F.2d 1362 (8th Cir. 1975).

[134] Wilkerson v. United States, 342 F.2d 807 (8th Cir. 1965).

[135] United States v. Keck, 773 F.2d 759, 767 (7th Cir. 1985). The Seventh Circuit has reasoned that (1) the rationale of the privilege does not justify assuring a criminal that he can enlist the aid of a spouse in a criminal enterprise without fear of creating another potential witness, and (2) the rehabilitative effect of a marriage is diminished when both spouses are participants in the crime. United States v. Van Drunen, 501 F.2d 1393, 1396–1397 (7th Cir. 1974). The Uniform Rules of Evidence, drafted for recommended adoption in state courts, would also make the privilege unavailable "in any criminal proceeding in which an unrefuted showing is made that the spouses acted jointly in the commission of the crime charged." UNIF. RULE OF EVIDENCE 505(d)(2).

[136] United States v. Van Drunen, 501 F.2d 1393, 1397 (7th Cir. 1974) (emphasis added).

[137] *In re* Grand Jury Subpoena United States, Appeal of Koecher, 755 F.2d 1022, 1027–1028 (2d Cir. 1985) (agreeing with Third Circuit that "compelling a spouse to testify under a joint participants exception could create exactly the negative impact on the marriage that the privilege was designed to avoid"), *vacated as moot,* 475 U.S. 133 (1986); Appeal of Malfitano, 633 F.2d 276, 278–279 (3d Cir. 1980) (declining to adopt "joint participants in a crime" exception to the testimonial privilege, because the protection of the privilege may tend "to help future integration of the spouse back into society," and noting that "Given the intimacy of marriage and the fact that conspiracy is a rather flexible concept, it will be quite easy to allege that the spouses are partners").

Privilege for Confidential Marital Communications.

In addition to the privilege against adverse spousal testimony, the federal common law has long recognized a privilege for confidential communications between spouses. The privilege is justified as a means to "encourage marital confidences, which confidences in turn promote harmony between husband and wife."[138] Critics contend that the privilege has virtually no effect on the behavior of spouses because most are unaware of its existence.[139] Proposed Federal Evidence Rule 505 sought to change the existing federal practice by eliminating the privilege, but the Rule was rejected by Congress. Lower federal court decisions and dictum in the Supreme Court's opinion in *Trammel* indicate that private communications between spouses remain privileged under Rule 501.[140]

The privilege for confidential communications applies in both federal criminal cases and civil cases in which state law does not provide the rule of decision.[141] Both spouses hold the privilege and both may assert it to bar disclosure of statements made in confidence by either spouse.[142] The privilege does not cover statements made before or after the marriage, but confidential communications during the marriage are protected forever. Death, divorce, and annulment do not end the privilege for communications made during the marriage.[143] Oral and written statements are protected by the privilege, as are gestures or other acts that are intended to communicate.[144] However, federal courts generally do not permit the privilege to be

---

[138] 1 McCormick, § 86, at 309. For a recent review of the theory and application of this privilege, and a comparison of the versions of the privilege as it is enforced in state and federal courts, *see* Duane, *The Bizarre Drafting Errors in the Virginia Statute on Privileged Marital Communications,* 12 Regent L. Rev. 91 (1999).

[139] *See, e.g.,* Hutchins and Slesinger, *Some Observations on the Law of Evidence: Family Relations,* 13 Minn. L. Rev. 675, 682 (1929) ("Marital harmony among lawyers who know about privileged communications is not vastly superior to that of other professional groups.").

[140] Trammel v. United States, 445 U.S. 40, 45 n.5 (1980) ("[T]his Court recognized just such a confidential communications privilege in *Wolfle v. United States,* 291 U.S. 7 (1934), and in *Blau v. United States,* 340 U.S. 332 (1951) . . . The privilege as to confidential marital communications is not at issue in the instant case; accordingly, our holding today does not disturb *Wolfle* and *Blau*"); United States v. Tsinnijinnie, 601 F.2d 1035 (9th Cir. 1979); United States v. Mendoza, 574 F.2d 1373 (5th Cir. 1978).

[141] 2 Mueller & Kirkpatrick, § 207.

[142] *See* Blau v. United States, 340 U.S. 332 (1951) (husband may refuse to disclose what his spouse told him); Wolfle v. United States, 291 U.S. 7 (1934) (assuming that privilege generally permits husband to refuse to disclose what he told his spouse).

[143] Pereira v. United States, 347 U.S. 1 (1954); United States v. Lilley, 581 F.2d 182 (8th Cir. 1978); United States v. Burks, 470 F.2d 432 (D.C. Cir. 1972).

[144] Pereira v. United States, 347 U.S. 1 (1954); United States v. Smith, 533 F.2d 1077 (8th Cir. 1976); *see also* United States v. Bahe, 128 F.3d 1440, 1444–1445 (10th Cir. 1997) (noting that the district court had held that mere "physical touching between spouses, especially involving sexual activity, is communication within the marital privilege").

invoked to prevent disclosure of the circumstances and events of the marriage or acts that are not solely communicative.[145]

The privilege is subject to the requirement of a valid marriage. Federal courts have refused to extend the privilege to married couples who are permanently separated, or involved in relationships claimed to be the functional equivalent of marriage but not technically married.[146]

To invoke the privilege the spouses also must meet the requirement of confidentiality. In this respect they are aided by a presumption that any statements made in the absence of a third person were intended to be confidential. If a third person is present, however, the statements are presumed not to be confidential.[147] Most courts find that communications in the presence of a child who is old enough to understand are not confidential.[148] There is no confidentiality where it is understood by both that the communication will be related to a third person.[149] Communications are not confidential, and therefore not privileged, if the couple's supposedly private

---

[145] United States v. Klayer, 707 F.2d 892 (6th Cir. 1983); United States v. Thomann, 609 F.2d 560 (1st Cir. 1979); United States v. Moore, 604 F.2d 1228 (9th Cir. 1979); United States v. Long, 468 F.2d 755 (8th Cir. 1972); United States v. Harper, 450 F.2d 1032 (5th Cir. 1971).

[146] *See* United States v. Singleton, 260 F.3d 1295, 1301 (11th Cir. 2001) (there is no privilege protecting communications made while two married people, although not divorced, were permanently separated with no reasonable chance of reconciliation; in deciding whether couple was permanently separated, court should consider how long they have been living apart, whether either had filed for divorce, and any other "objective evidence of the parties' intent or lack of intent to reconcile"); United States v. Acker, 52 F.3d 509, 514 (4th Cir. 1995) (declining to extend spousal communication privilege to a couple who had lived together for 25 years and rejecting an equal protection challenge to the validity of the spousal privilege); United States v. Porter, 986 F.2d 1014 (6th Cir. 1993) (because defendant and his wife were permanently separated at the time of the communication, the privilege against confidential communications did not prevent defendant's wife from testifying at defendant's trial); United States v. Jackson, 939 F.2d 625 (8th Cir. 1991) (defendant could not invoke the marital communication privilege, as the information was communicated after the couple had permanently separated); United States v. Lustig, 555 F.2d 737, 748–749 (9th Cir. 1977) (both privileges depend upon the existence of a valid marriage, as determined by state law; since defendant claimed only a common-law marriage to the witness, and since such a marriage is not valid under Alaska law, neither privilege could apply in this case); United States v. Neeley, 475 F.2d 1136 (4th Cir. 1973) (defendant could not rely upon state spousal testimonial privilege to exclude testimony by another woman, since he had never divorced his wife, and the privilege operates only where there is a valid marriage); *see also* United States v. Boatwright, 446 F.2d 913 (5th Cir. 1971).

[147] Pereira v. United States, 347 U.S. 1 (1954); Wolfle v. United States, 291 U.S. 7 (1934).

[148] Wolfle v. United States, 291 U.S. 7 (1934); United States v. Penn, 647 F.2d 876 (9th Cir. 1980); *In re* Kinoy, 326 F. Supp. 400 (S.D.N.Y. 1970); 2 MUELLER & KIRKPATRICK, § 207.

[149] Wolfle v. United States, 291 U.S. 7 (1934); Grulkey v. United States, 394 F.2d 244 (8th Cir. 1968); United States v. Mitchell, 137 F.2d 1006 (2d Cir. 1943).

conversation took place in some place — such as police custody — where they should have foreseen the possibility that they were being recorded without their knowledge.[150]

Exceptions to the privilege for confidential communications include interspousal suits and the prosecution of one spouse for a crime committed against the other or against the minor children of either spouse.[151] There is some authority that the exception also extends to children who are raised by the couple and are the "functional equivalent" of their children, but this would not extend to young relatives who are merely frequent visitors to their home.[152] Another commonly recognized exception arises where one spouse is charged with a crime and wishes to introduce confidential statements made by either spouse to help in the defense.[153]

Under what is sometimes called "the joint participants" exception, there is no privilege for confidential communications between married people who are also partners in crime, even if one of the two is only an accessory after the fact. This exception appears to have been accepted by every federal circuit to consider the issue, although often with little or no analysis.[154] In

---

[150] United States v. Dunbar, 553 F.3d 48 (1st Cir. 2009) (after a man and his wife were placed in the back of a police cruiser, statements made between them and secretly recorded without their knowledge were not protected as privileged, because the privilege only protects conversations in a setting where the participants have a reasonable expectation of privacy, and "the back of a police car is not a place where individuals can reasonably expect to communicate in private").

[151] Wyatt v. United States, 362 U.S. 525, 529 (1960) (declining to recognize marital privilege at trial of man accused of using his wife in prostitution, even where she asserts an objection to testifying against him); United States v. Castillo, 140 F.3d 874, 884–885 (10th Cir. 1998) (no marital privilege where man was accused of sexually assaulting his two daughters); United States v. Bahe, 128 F.3d 1440, 1446 (10th Cir. 1997) (no privilege where defendant was accused of crimes against minor relatives residing in his home); United States v. White, 974 F.2d 1135, 1137–1138 (9th Cir. 1992) (where accused was charged with killing his stepdaughter, wife was allowed to testify that he privately threatened to do so earlier); United States v. Martinez, 44 F. Supp. 2d 835 (W. D. Tex. 1999) (no spousal communications privilege where ex-husband testified against woman accused of abusing her two minor children).

[152] United States v. Banks, 556 F.3d 967 (9th Cir. 2009) (district court erred in allowing the defendant's wife to testify to statements made by him during the course of their marriage as to why he created a pornographic video with their grandson, because such statements were protected by the marital privilege for confidential communications between spouses; there is an exception to the privilege for crimes committed against a minor child who is the "functional equivalent" of the child of either spouse, but that was not the case for this grandchild, who was a frequent visitor to the home of the accused and his wife but was not raised by them).

[153] See Duane, *The Bizarre Drafting Errors in the Virginia Statute on Privileged Marital Communications,* 12 REGENT L. REV. 91, 117 & nn. 111 & 112 (1999).

[154] *E.g.,* United States v. Darif, 446 F.3d 701, 706 (7th Cir. 2006); United States v. Ramirez, 145 F.3d 345, 355–356 (5th Cir. 1998); United States v. Evans, 966 F.2d 398, 401

an effort to limit the scope of this exception, some circuits have held that it applies only to communications involving "patently illegal activity,"[155] and made after both spouses have learned about and agreed to participate in the criminal scheme.[156] Despite the unanimity with which this well-settled exception has been accepted by the federal courts, however, its logic is open to serious question. Most circuits have reasoned that the exception is supposedly justified by a special need to override the privilege in the pursuit of truth and justice,[157] but that reasoning is difficult to take seriously. Under the logic of this exception, a man may prevent his wife from testifying about his detailed confession to a mass murder as long as she was not involved, but he cannot prevent her from testifying to incriminating statements he made while planning a $20 theft with her help. It is absurd to suggest that the need for overriding the privilege is categorically greater in every case in which the listening spouse was also somehow involved (or claims to have been involved) in the planning or commission of some crime.[158] The exception is well settled under current law, although the Supreme Court of the United

---

(8th Cir. 1992); United States v. Estes, 793 F.2d 465, 466–467 (2d Cir. 1986); United States v. Sims, 755 F.2d 1239, 1243 (6th Cir. 1985); United States v. Broome, 732 F.2d 363, 365 (4th Cir. 1984); United States v. Ammar, 714 F.2d 238 (3d Cir. 1983).

[155] United States v. Evans, 966 F.2d 398, 401 (8th Cir. 1992); United States v. Sims, 755 F.2d 1239, 1243 (6th Cir. 1985); *but see* United States v. Parker, 834 F.2d 408, 412 n.7 (4th Cir. 1987) (rejecting the proposed limitation of the exception to "patently illegal" activity because it is too ambiguous; "We think that all communications between a husband and wife that are in any way related to a crime, and made in the course of the spouses' joint planning or participation in that crime, fall within the exception to the marital privilege.").

[156] United States v. Westmoreland, 312 F.3d 302, 308 (7th Cir. 2002) ("The initial disclosure of a crime to one's spouse, without more, is covered by the marital communications privilege. If the spouse later joins the conspiracy, communications from that point certainly should not be protected."); United States v. Estes, 793 F.2d 465, 466–667 (2d Cir. 1986) (same).

[157] *E.g.,* United States v. Parker, 834 F.2d 408, 412 (4th Cir. 1987) ("The exception arises out of a careful balancing of the policies behind protecting the intimacy of private marital communications and the public policy of getting at the truth and attaining justice."); United States v. Evans, 966 F.2d 398, 401 (8th Cir. 1992) ("Where the communications involve the spouses' joint criminal activity, however, the interests of justice outweigh the goal of fostering marital harmony.").

[158] To understand the extent to which this exception threatens the policies underlying the privilege for confidential marital communications, one needs to bear in mind that a prosecutor seeking to entirely circumvent the privilege need only persuade the defendant's spouse (or ex-spouse) to claim that she had some minor role in planning or conspiring in the commission of the charged offense. Imagine the mindset of a woman who is told by a prosecutor: "I know you deny that you had anything to do with your ex-husband's crime, but I intend to charge and prosecute you both. I will drop all charges against you and give you immunity and make sure you do not lose custody of the children, however, if you agree to testify against him about the things he said to you — which the law allows you to do, if and only if you are willing to admit that you helped him plan or cover up his offense. Now think a little bit longer about your claims of innocence and get back to me."

States has not yet expressed any view on its wisdom.[159]

§ 501.7   Clergy-Parishioner Privilege

As a matter of federal common law, a privilege for confidential communications to religious officials for spiritual advice or personal counseling is recognized under Rule 501.[160] The privilege also is widely recognized by the states.[161] The rationale underlying the privilege was described by Judge Fahy in his concurring opinion in *Mullen v. United States*:

> Sound policy — reason and experience — concedes to religious liberty a rule of evidence that a clergyman shall not disclose on a trial the secrets of a penitent's confidential confession to him, at least absent the penitent's consent. Knowledge so acquired in the performance of a spiritual function . . . is not to be transformed into evidence to be given to the whole world. As Wigmore points out, such a confidential communication meets all the requirements that have rendered communications between husband and wife and attorney and client privileged and incompetent. The benefit of preserving these confidences inviolate overbalances the possible

---

[159] Other asserted justifications for the exceptions are even more dubious. Two circuits have reasoned that the privilege is "akin to the attorney-client privilege, also designed to protect the confidences of the communicator, which has been held not to extend to communications in furtherance of criminal activity." United States v. Ammar, 714 F.2d 238, 258 (3d Cir. 1983); *see also* United States v. Mendoza, 574 F.2d 1373, 1381 n.6 (5th Cir. 1978) (making the same analogy). But that analogy is far too simplistic. The attorney-client privilege does not extend to that situation for the same reason that it does not apply to conversations with a lawyer you hire to change your oil filter: there is simply no valid attorney-client relationship recognized by law where a lawyer and a "client" knowingly co-operate in planning a criminal offense. Nobody has ever suggested that a lawfully married man and a woman should no longer be deemed married in the eyes of the law, or that their marriage was a nullity from the outset, merely because one of the countless things they did together after their wedding was a crime.

[160] Totten v. United States, 92 U.S. 105, 23 L. Ed. 605 (1876) ("It may be stated . . . that public policy forbids the maintenance of any suit in a court of justice, the trial of which would inevitably lead to the disclosure of matters which the law itself regards as confidential, and respecting which it will not allow the confidence to be violated. On this principle, suits cannot be maintained which would require a disclosure of the confidences of the confessional, or those between husband and wife, or of communications by a client to his counsel for professional advice, or of a patient to his physician for a similar purpose"); *see also* Mullen v. United States, 263 F.2d 275 (D.C. Cir. 1958); McMann v. Securities and Exchange Comm'n, 87 F.2d 377 (2d Cir. 1937). *But cf.* United States v. Webb, 615 F.2d 828 (9th Cir. 1980) (court declined to discuss whether clergyman-parishioner privilege was applicable in federal courts under Rule 501). Traditionally, the privilege was referred to as the priest-penitent privilege, but in modern times the privilege encompasses communications made in the context of a broader group of religions than the traditional name indicates. *See* 2 MUELLER & KIRKPATRICK, § 211.

[161] *See* Kuhlmann, *Communications to Clergyman—When Are They Privileged?* 2 VAL. U.L. REV. 265 (1968).

benefit of permitting litigation to prosper at the expense of the tranquility of the home, the integrity of the professional relationship, and the spiritual rehabilitation of a penitent. The rules of evidence have always been concerned not only with truth but with the manner of its ascertainment.[162]

Because the clergy-parishioner privilege is so widely and uniformly recognized, it has posed very few problems in litigation. The only problems arise in establishing the outer limits of the privilege; specifically, in establishing standards for the class of religious officials as to whom communications are privileged and for the types of communications that are privileged. Proposed-but-rejected Rule 506 defined a clergyman as "a minister, priest, rabbi, or other similar functionary of a religious organiza-tion, or an individual reasonably believed so to be by the person consulting him."[163] Although this definition is broader than the definition recognized in many states, the Advisory Committee Note indicates it was not intended to be "so broad as to include all self-denominated 'ministers'."[164] To come within the definition, the religious official must "be regularly engaged in activities conforming at least in a general way with those of a Catholic priest, Jewish rabbi, or minister of an established Protestant denomination, though not necessarily on a full-time basis."[165] Proposed-but-rejected Rule 506 also expanded the type of communications that fall within the privilege. Protected communications are not limited to confessions but include any type of personal counseling.[166]

Like the attorney-client privilege, the parishioner must intend for the communication to remain confidential in order for the clergy-parishioner privilege to apply.[167] The privilege is not limited to oral or written communications but also protects observations made by the clergy.[168] The

---

[162] Mullen v. United States, 263 F.2d 275, 280 (D.C. Cir. 1958) (concurring opinion).

[163] Supreme Court Standard 506(a)(1).

[164] Supreme Court Standard 506, Advisory Committee Note.

[165] Supreme Court Standard 506, Advisory Committee Note; *see also* 3 WEINSTEIN'S FEDERAL EVIDENCE § 506.03.

[166] 2 MUELLER & KIRKPATRICK, § 211; *see also* United States v. Gordon, 493 F. Supp. 822 (N.D.N.Y. 1980), *aff'd,* 655 F.2d 478 (2d Cir. 1981) (privilege inapplicable where communication pertained to business).

[167] *In re* Grand Jury Investigation, 918 F.2d 374 (3d Cir. 1990) (in examination of clergy-communicant privilege under federal common law, appeals court remanded case to trial court; four parishioners met with pastor to discuss an alleged arson incident); United States v. Webb, 615 F.2d 828 (9th Cir. 1980); *see also* United States v. Wells, 446 F.2d 2 (2d Cir. 1971) (priest-penitent privilege did not cover letter from defendant to priest requesting priest to ask an FBI agent to see the defendant, since the letter contained no hint that its contents were to be kept secret or that its purpose was to obtain religious or other counsel or advice).

[168] 2 MUELLER & KIRKPATRICK, § 211.

privilege is held by the parishioner but, in the absence of evidence to the contrary, the clergy may claim it on behalf of the parishioner.[169]

§ 501.8 Physician-Patient Privilege

Unlike the attorney-client, spousal and clergy-parishioner privileges, at common law there was no privilege for communications between a physician and patient.[170] The version of Article V proposed by the Supreme Court reflected the common law in that it also did not contain a general physician-patient privilege.[171] However, following the lead of New York and California,[172] the majority of states have established a physician-patient privilege.[173] Although there was no corresponding federal privilege, prior to the enactment of the Federal Rules of Evidence federal courts sitting in diversity cases often applied state-created physician-patient privileges. In addition, federal courts sometimes applied the privilege in federal question but not federal criminal cases.[174] While Rule 501 on its face now prohibits the application of state privileges in these cases, it authorizes federal courts to recognize a federal physician-patient privilege as the federal common law evolves "in the light of reason and experience."[175] Despite this authorization, federal courts have declined to recognize a general physician-patient privilege.[176] However, a number of federal courts have acknowledged that an alternative source of protection for the physician-patient relationship may be the patient's constitutional right to privacy in receiving medical treatment.[177]

---

[169] 3 WEINSTEIN'S FEDERAL EVIDENCE § 506.04.

[170] 1 MCCORMICK, § 98.

[171] The Advisory Committee explained that no general physician-patient privilege was proposed because "the exceptions which have been found necessary in order to obtain information required by the public interest or to avoid fraud are so numerous as to leave little if any basis for the privilege." Supreme Court Standard 504, Advisory Committee Note.

[172] In 1828 New York passed the following statute and became the first state to recognize a physician-patient privilege: "No person authorized to practice physic or surgery shall be allowed to disclose any information which he may have acquired in attending any patient, in a professional character, and which information was necessary to enable him to prescribe for such patient as a physician, or to do any act for him as a surgeon." N.Y. REV. STATS. 1829, vol. II, part III, c. 7, tit. 3, art. eight, 73. In 1872, California passed a similar statute. Cal. Civ. Proc. Code § 1881 par. 4 (1872).

[173] *See* 1 MCCORMICK, § 98.

[174] 2 MUELLER & KIRKPATRICK, § 209.

[175] *Id. See* Doe v. Diamond, 964 F.2d 1325 (2d Cir. 1992) (the court recognized the existence of a qualified psychotherapist-patient privilege as a matter of federal common law).

[176] *See* United States v. Bek, 493 F.3d 790 (7th Cir. 2007); Patterson v. Caterpillar, Inc., 70 F.3d 503 (7th Cir. 1995); Hancock v. Dodson, 958 F.2d 1367 (6th Cir. 1992); United States v. Bercier, 848 F.2d 917 (8th Cir. 1988).

[177] Whalen v. Roe, 429 U.S. 589 (1977); Caesar v. Mountanos, 542 F.2d 1064 (9th Cir. 1976); Hawaii Psychiatric Soc'y v. Ariyoshi, 481 F. Supp. 1028 (D. Haw. 1979); *see also*

The physician-patient privilege is justified as a means to promote quality medical care by encouraging the patient to disclose all information that would help the physician in diagnosing and treating illness and injury.[178] Some scholars have observed that the privilege also may serve to protect the privacy interests of the patient.[179] The privilege has been criticized as not fulfilling the goal of effective medical care because "[t]he ordinary citizen who contemplates consulting a physician not only has no thought of a lawsuit, but he is entirely ignorant of the rules of evidence. He has no idea whether a communication to a physician is or is not privileged."[180] Despite this criticism, an increasing number of states have enacted physician-patient privileges.[181]

The physician-patient privilege commonly includes the following elements: The privilege is available only where the patient consults the doctor for treatment or diagnosis looking toward treatment.[182] It is not available where the patient is examined by a physician in some other context, such as where a plaintiff in the course of personal injury litigation is examined by doctors hired either by the plaintiff's or defendant's attorney in order to determine the extent of injury.[183] As with privileges in general, the physician-patient privilege protects only communications made in confidence. Confidentiality is not destroyed, however, by the presence of a third person who is necessary for the patient's diagnosis or treatment or who is a

---

United States ex rel. Edney v. Smith, 425 F. Supp. 1038 (E.D.N.Y. 1976), aff'd, 556 F.2d 556 (E.D.N.Y. 1977) (petitioner sought habeas corpus review of state conviction on the ground that the prosecution had called a psychiatric expert who had examined the defendant at his attorney's request and who had testified that defendant knew his conduct was wrong at the trial, where sanity was the only significant issue; petitioner argued that the physician-patient privilege is constitutionally compelled; court, after discussing the arguments for and against affording constitutional protection to the privilege, found that even were there a constitutional basis, the privilege could not be supported in the instant case "when the issue as to which the physician has knowledge is placed in question by the party relying on the privilege — typically in negligence cases, but in criminal proceedings as well — the privilege is deemed waived"); Robinson v. Magovern, 83 F.R.D. 79 (W.D. Pa. 1979) (even assuming that there is a constitutional right of privacy protecting the general doctor-patient relationship, this right must be balanced against competing interests).

[178] 1 McCormick, § 98.

[179] See 2 Mueller & Kirkpatrick, § 209 ("[P]ersonal illness often involves matters which patients reasonably prefer to keep confidential, and the privilege may serve a valid social purpose in this regard").

[180] Morgan, Forward to Model Code of Evidence 28 (1942); see also Lora v. Board of Educ., 74 F.R.D. 565 (E.D.N.Y. 1977) (material not protected because it is unlikely that there was an expectation of privacy by students or families since third parties had access to the data).

[181] 1 McCormick, § 98 (fewer than 10 states do not recognize a physician-patient privilege).

[182] 1 McCormick, § 99.

[183] See Catoe v. United States, 131 F.2d 16 (D.C. Cir. 1942).

close family member.[184] According to the better view, the privilege covers both verbal and nonverbal communications, such as the exhibition of body parts to the physician, and also covers observations made by the doctor unless such observations would be patently obvious to any lay person.[185] However, the privilege does not prohibit a physician from testifying to facts incidental to the relationship, *e.g.*, that he was consulted in a professional capacity by a person on a given date.[186] The privilege is held by the patient but the physician is ethically bound to assert it on the patient's behalf.[187]

The privilege is inapplicable in a variety of situations. If the patient consults the physician for an unlawful purpose the privilege does not apply.[188] The patient is considered to have waived the privilege by putting his or her mental or physical condition in issue in a judicial proceeding.[189] Increasingly, state and local laws require that the privilege does not operate to relieve the physician of the duty to report certain diseases or injuries, such as venereal diseases or gunshot wounds, which affect public health and safety.[190] Laws requiring physicians to report these conditions generally have been upheld against constitutional right of privacy challenges and claims that they violate the privilege.[191]

Although the Rules of Evidence promulgated by the Supreme Court did not include a general physician-patient privilege, they did include a psychotherapist-patient privilege. This provision was intended to recognize psychiatrists' and psychologists' special need for confidentiality:

> Among physicians, the psychiatrist has a special need to maintain confidentiality. His or her capacity to help patients is completely dependent upon their willingness and ability to talk freely. This makes it difficult if not impossible for psychiatrists to function without being able to assure their patients of confidentiality and,

---

[184] 2 Mueller & Kirkpatrick, § 209.

[185] *Id.*

[186] Padovani v. Liggett & Myers Tobacco Co., 23 F.R.D. 255 (E.D.N.Y. 1959); 1 McCormick, § 100.

[187] *Id.*

[188] 1 McCormick, § 99; *see also In re* Grand Jury Proceedings (Violette), 183 F.3d 71 (1st Cir. 1999) (grand jury subpoenas were enforced, under the crime-fraud exception, to require two psychiatrists to testify about the activities of a patient accused of fabricating disabilities to defraud health care providers; the government made the necessary showing for the crime-fraud exception, that the patient was engaged in or planning illegal conduct and communications with the two doctors were made to further that conduct).

[189] O'Brien v. General Acc., Fire & Life Assur. Corp., 42 F.2d 48 (8th Cir. 1930); Lind v. Canada Dry Corp., 283 F. Supp. 861 (D. Minn. 1968); Burlage v. Haudenshield, 42 F.R.D. 397 (N.D. Iowa 1967); Awtry v. United States, 27 F.R.D. 399 (S.D.N.Y. 1961).

[190] 1 McCormick, § 101.

[191] 1 McCormick, § 101.

indeed, privileged communication.[192]

Although the Supreme Court's proposed Rule was not adopted by Congress in 1975, federal law now recognizes a privilege protecting confidential communications between patient and psychotherapist. The Supreme Court expressly recognized this privilege in *Jaffee v. Redmond*.[193] The Court noted that Rule 501 allows federal courts to define new evidentiary privileges as dictated by interpretation of the principles of common law and as judged prudent by reason and experience. In that light, the Court found that a psychotherapist privilege is supported by both private and public interests.

The privilege serves private interests by promoting the confidence and trust necessary for effective psychotherapy. The Court recognized that the possibility that confidential information shared with a psychotherapist could be disclosed "may impede development of the confidential relationship needed for successful treatment."[194] The privilege also serves the public interest in that, by facilitating effective treatment, it promotes the mental and emotional health of the citizenry. Further, the Court felt that failure to recognize the privilege may chill the "frank and complete disclosure of facts, emotions, memories and fears" that is necessary to effective treatment.[195]

As recognized by the Supreme Court, the psychotherapist privilege extends not only to psychiatrists and psychologists, but also to social workers performing psychotherapy. Recognizing that a significant amount of mental health treatment is provided by social workers, the Court saw no reason to distinguish between professionals whose counseling services further the same public goals.[196]

As with other privileges, the psychotherapist privilege is destroyed by a lack of confidentiality. Where the patient disclosed to others information he or she had related in confidence to his therapist, or otherwise makes known to others the substance of the privileged communication, the patient waives the protection of the privilege.[197]

---

[192] Report No. 45, Group for the Advancement of Psychiatry 92 (1960).

[193] Jaffee v. Redmond, 518 U.S. 1 (1996). *See also* United States v. Glass, 133 F.3d 1356 (10th Cir. 1998) (where defendant was charged with threatening the life of the President of the United States, the psychotherapist-patient privilege was available to protect confidential communication made in course of seeking treatment). *See also* Amann & Imwinkelried, *The Supreme Court's Decision to Recognize a Psychotherapist Privilege in* Jaffee v. Redmond: *The Meaning of "Experience" and the Role of "Reason" under Federal Rule of Evidence 501*, 65 U. CIN. L. REV. 1019 (1997); Weissenberger, *The Psychotherapist Privilege and the Supreme Court's Misplaced Reliance on State Legislatures*, 49 HASTINGS LAW J. 999 (1998).

[194] *Jaffee,* 518 U.S. at 15.

[195] *Id.* at 15.

[196] *See id.* at 24.

[197] *See* United States v. Snelenberger, 24 F.3d 799, 802 (6th Cir. 1994) (trial court did not

§ 501.9   Recognizing Additional Privileges

For a time after the passage of Rule 501, some doubt existed as to whether federal courts could only enforce those privileges recognized by common law at the time of the adoption of the Federal Rules or whether the courts were empowered to develop privileges that were not in existence at that time.[198] As seen in *Jaffee v. Redmond,* the Supreme Court has interpreted Rule 501 as granting the courts the authority to recognize new privileges suggested by "the principles of common law as they may be interpreted . . . in light of reason and experience."[199] However, *Jaffee* should not be read as creating broad license to carve out new evidentiary privileges. The recognition of a privilege runs counter to the principle that the public has a right to every man's evidence. Hence the recognition of new privilege should not be undertaken lightly, and courts should hesitate to continually expand the bounds of privilege law.

The party who seeks to invoke the new privilege bears the burden of establishing that recognition of such a privilege is necessary. Mere claims that social policy favors such a privilege should not suffice. As was the case in *Jaffee,* a new privilege should be recognized only where the privilege furthers sufficiently important public and private interests to a degree that outweighs the need for relevant evidence.[200] As one court has stated, "privileges are tolerable only to the very limited extent that permitting a refusal to testify or excluding relevant evidence has a public good transcending the normally predominant principle of utilizing all rational means for ascertaining truth."[201]

Courts have been urged to recognize a number of additional privileges,

---

err in admitting psychotherapist's testimony about patient's threats to kill a judge; the patient had waived the privilege because he had disclosed to others his intent to kill the judge and also told an FBI agent that he had informed his therapist of his plan).

[198] *See In re* Grand Jury Proceedings, 867 F.2d 562 (9th Cir. 1989) (the court did not have the power to recognize a psychotherapist-patient privilege because such a privilege was a creature of statute and did not exist at common law).

[199] *See Jaffee,* 518 U.S. at 15 ("[t]he Rule thus did not freeze the law governing the privileges of witnesses in federal trials at a particular point in our history, but rather directed federal courts to 'continue the evolutionary development of testimonial privileges' " (quoting Trammel v. United States, 445 U.S. 40 (1980)).

[200] *See* University of Pennsylvania v. EEOC, 493 U.S. 182, 184 (1990) ("We do not create and apply an evidentiary privilege unless it 'promotes sufficiently important interests to outweigh the need for probative evidence' " (quoting *Trammel,* 445 U.S. 40 (1980)); *see, e.g.,* Gonzales v. National Broadcasting Co., 186 F.3d 102 (2d Cir. 1998) (information a journalist receives from a non-confidential source enjoys only a qualified privilege, and disclosure may be compelled when the information is relevant to a significant issue and not reasonably obtainable elsewhere; privilege did not shield discovery of outtakes from a television program involving a deputy sheriff who allegedly pulled plaintiffs over without probable cause).

[201] *In re* Grand Jury Proceedings, 103 F.3d 1140 (3d Cir. 1997).

and have generally responded by declining to extend the law of privileges. Among those privileges that courts have refused to endorse are relationship privileges including a parent-child privilege,[202] an accountant-client privilege,[203] a bank-customer privilege,[204] a probationer-probation-officer privilege[205] and union member-representative privilege.[206] Additionally, courts have also been reluctant to recognize a common-interest privilege,[207] a privilege to protect the confidentiality of the peer-review process in employment situations,[208] and a self-critical analysis or self-evaluation privilege that would protect an institution's internal reports regarding its assessment of its past performance,[209] or a privilege for information learned by agents of the Secret Service in protecting the President of the United States.[210]

---

[202] *See id.* (declining to recognize the parent-child privilege, citing the fact that the privilege is not vital to the parent-child relationship and that its value is outweighed by the harm it would cause to truthful fact finding).

[203] *See* William T. Thompson Co. v. General Nutrition Corp., 671 F.2d 100 (3d Cir. 1982).

[204] *See* Harris v. United States, 413 F.2d 316 (9th Cir. 1969).

[205] *See* United States v. Holmes, 594 F.2d 1167 (8th Cir. 1979).

[206] *See* Walker v. Huie, 142 F.R.D. 497 (D. Utah 1992).

[207] *See In re* Grand Jury Subpoena Duces Tecum, 112 F.3d 910 (8th Cir. 1997) (the White House could not invoke the common-interest doctrine to extend any form of governmental attorney-client privilege to conversations between First Lady Hillary Rodham Clinton, her personal attorney, and attorneys representing the White House in regard to documents subpoenaed by the grand jury).

[208] *See* University of Pennsylvania v. EEOC, 493 U.S. 182 (1990).

[209] *See* Dowling v. American Hawaii Cruises, Inc., 971 F.2d 423 (9th Cir. 1992) (holding that recognition of the privilege is not necessary to encourage self-evaluation reports); Davidson v. Light, 79 F.R.D. 137 (D. Colo. 1978). *But see In re* Crazy Eddie Sec. Litig., 792 F. Supp. 197 (E.D.N.Y. 1992); Bredice v. Doctors Hospital, Inc., 50 F.R.D. 249 (D.D.C. 1970) (confidential self-criticism fosters an important public policy such that recognition of the privilege outweighs the cost of excluding the evidence).

[210] *In re* Sealed Case, 148 F.3d 1073 (D.C. Cir. 1998) (officers of United States Secret Service are not protected by a "protective function privilege" from being compelled to testify before a grand jury about information obtained in connection with their duties and their protective function with respect to the President of the United States).

Chapter 502

Rule 502. Attorney-Client Privilege and Work Product; Limitations on Waiver

Rule 502. Attorney-Client Privilege and Work Product; Limitations on Waiver

The following provisions apply, in the circumstances set out, to disclosure of a communication or information covered by the attorney-client privilege or work-product protection.

(a) **Disclosure Made in a Federal Proceeding or to a Federal Office or Agency; Scope of a Waiver.** When the disclosure is made in a federal proceeding or to a federal office or agency and waives the attorney-client privilege or work-product protection, the waiver extends to an undisclosed communication or information in a federal or state proceeding only if:

   (1) the waiver is intentional;

   (2) the disclosed and undisclosed communications or information concern the same subject matter; and

   (3) they ought in fairness to be considered together.

(b) **Inadvertent Disclosure.** When made in a federal proceeding or to a federal office or agency, the disclosure does not operate as a waiver in a federal or state proceeding if:

   (1) the disclosure is inadvertent;

   (2) the holder of the privilege or protection took reasonable steps to prevent disclosure; and

   (3) the holder promptly took reasonable steps to rectify the error, including (if applicable) following Federal Rule of Civil Procedure 26(b)(5)(B).

(c) **Disclosure Made in a State Proceeding.** When the disclosure is made in a state proceeding and is not the subject of a state-court order concerning waiver, the disclosure does not operate as a waiver in a federal proceeding if the disclosure:

   (1) would not be a waiver under this rule if it had been made in a federal proceeding; or

   (2) is not a waiver under the law of the state where the disclosure

295

occurred.

(d)   Controlling Effect of a Court Order. A federal court may order that the privilege or protection is not waived by disclosure connected with the litigation pending before the court — in which event the disclosure is also not a waiver in any other federal or state proceeding.

(e)   Controlling Effect of a Party Agreement. An agreement on the effect of disclosure in a federal proceeding is binding only on the parties to the agreement, unless it is incorporated into a court order.

(f)   Controlling Effect of this Rule. Notwithstanding Rules 101 and 1101, this rule applies to state proceedings and to federal court-annexed and federal court-mandated arbitration proceedings, in the circumstances set out in the rule. And notwithstanding Rule 501, this rule applies even if state law provides the rule of decision.

(g)   Definitions. In this rule:

(1)   "attorney-client privilege" means the protection that applicable law provides for confidential attorney-client communications; and

(2)   "work-product protection" means the protection that applicable law provides for tangible material (or its intangible equivalent) prepared in anticipation of litigation or for trial.

---

§ 502.1   Rule 502 — Purpose and Scope

Any newcomer to the study of the Federal Rules would likely be surprised by the remarkable specificity of Rule 502, the newest addition to the Federal Rules of Evidence, and by the narrowness of its scope.[1] The rule is explicitly limited to several important but very narrow aspects of the law concerning the circumstances under which the disclosure of documents may result in the waiver of the attorney-client privilege or the protections of the work product doctrine.[2] It is notable what the rule does *not* address. As the rule and its Committee Note emphasize, the rule says nothing about: (1) the circumstances under which a document or other information might initially come to be protected on the grounds of privilege or work product; or (2) the many

---

[1] Congress has declared that any rule of evidence or procedure "creating, abolishing, or modifying an evidentiary privilege shall have no force or effect unless approved by Act of Congress." 28 U.S.C. § 2074(b). Accordingly, after its drafting and approval by the Advisory Committee and the Judicial Conference, Rule 502 was enacted by Congress pursuant to 2008 Acts. Pub. L. 110-322, § 1(c), 122 Stat. 3538, which provided that Rule 502 shall apply in all proceedings commenced after the date of its enactment, September 19, 2008, "and, insofar as is just and practicable, in all proceedings pending on such date of enactment."

[2] For a helpful general discussion of the ways in which all privileges (not just the attorney-client privilege) can be waived when the holder makes a voluntary disclosure of privileged information in almost any setting (and not merely in pretrial discovery during judicial proceedings), see the text and Committee Notes to proposed Federal Rules 511 and 512, set forth in Appendix B.

ways in which those protections might be waived other than through disclosure in pretrial discovery proceedings, or (3) the ways in which other privileges might be waived through disclosure or other means. All of those three broad topics, which have each given rise to far more litigation and reported opinions than the issues addressed by Rule 502, continue to be governed by Rule 501, and shall therefore be worked out through judicial interpretation of the principles of the common law.[3]

When so many even more fundamental aspects of privilege law have been left for the courts to fashion on a case-by-case basis, it is likely to strike the reader of the Rules as peculiar that a rule would be adopted to resolve the strikingly narrow collection of privilege issues governed by Rule 502. The explanation of that seeming mystery lies chiefly in a letter two years earlier from the Chair of the House Judiciary Committee, suggesting that the Judicial Conference consider a rule dealing with waiver of attorney-client privilege and work product, in order to limit the rapidly rising costs of pretrial discovery in civil litigation. Many observers had complained that the ambiguity in the law of waiver frequently gave parties an incentive to engage in costly "record-by-record pre-production privilege review, on pain of subject matter waiver," often subjecting the parties to "costs of production that bear no proportionality to what is at stake in the litigation."[4] As the Advisory Committee observed, "litigation costs necessary to protect against waiver of attorney-client privilege or work product have become prohibitive due to the concern that any disclosure (however innocent or minimal) will operate as a subject matter waiver of all protected communications or information."[5] The adoption of Rule 502 was thus intended to advance the legal system's commitment to the principle that parties should be given every incentive to ensure that the resources devoted to pretrial discovery are in proportion to "its likely benefit, considering the needs of the case, the amount in controversy, the parties' resources, the importance of the issues at stake in the action, and the importance of the discovery in resolving the issues."[6]

Rule 502 is intended to meet this objective of reducing the costs of pretrial discovery by greatly increasing the certainty and predictability of the law. As the Supreme Court of the United States has observed, the purposes behind privilege law are largely undermined if the holder of the privilege is not "able to predict with some degree of certainty whether particular discussions will be protected. An uncertain privilege, or one which purports to be certain but results in widely varying applications by the courts, is little better than

---

[3] For a detailed discussion of all three of these topics, see Chapter 501, *supra.*

[4] Committee Note to Rule 502 (quoting Hopson v. City of Baltimore, 232 F.R.D. 228, 244 (D. Md. 2005)).

[5] Committee Note to Rule 502, in Appendix A.

[6] Fed. R. Civ. P. 26(b)(2)(C)(iii).

no privilege at all."[7] The purpose of Rule 502 was to reduce the incentive for lawyers to engage in precautionary overkill while screening documents before producing them in response to discovery requests, by minimizing the adverse consequences that could potentially result from an unintended disclosure of protected material.

The rule applies only to the attorney-client privilege and work product. It defines the former, not surprisingly, as "the protection that applicable law provides for confidential attorney-client communications."[8] Work-product is defined, a little more helpfully, as "the protection that applicable law provides for tangible material (or its intangible equivalent) prepared in anticipation of litigation or for trial."[9] This latter standard clarifies that the "work-product" subject to the rule is broader than the class of tangible materials sometimes known as "Materials Prepared in Anticipation of Litigation."[10] For the sake of simplicity, this chapter shall refer to all documents and information protected by either of those doctrines as "protected material."

§ 502.2   Waiver through Inadvertent Disclosure

The primary issue resolved by Rule 502 concerns a conflict among the courts as to when the inadvertent disclosure of protected material during litigation or agency proceedings may operate as a waiver of privilege or work product protection.[11] A few courts had taken the extreme position that inadvertent disclosure is never a waiver, reasoning that "a disclosure must be

---

[7] Jaffee v. Redmond, 518 U.S. 1, 18 (1996) (quoting Upjohn Co. v. United States, 449 U.S. 383, 393 (1981)). For this same reason, the Court has even more recently noted its reluctance to approve any rule of evidence law that would inject "substantial uncertainty into the privilege's application." Swidler & Berlin v. United States, 524 U.S. 399, 409 (1998).

[8] Rule 502(g)(1). This so-called "definition" is almost circular, and of almost no use to anyone seeking clarification of the basic elements of the attorney-client privilege. See, by comparison, the far more detailed provisions of Proposed Rule 503, set forth in Appendix B. But in fairness to the Advisory Committee, Rule 502 was intended only to govern certain aspects of the way in which the attorney-client privilege may be waived, not how it is created.

[9] Rule 502(g)(2).

[10] See Fed. R. Civ. P. 26(b)(3) (defining the scope of the protection for "documents and tangible things that are prepared in anticipation of litigation or for trial"). That civil discovery rule was intended to only partially codify the doctrine set forth in *Hickman v. Taylor*, 329 U.S. 495 (1947), which also extended similar protection to intangible information in the possession of a party and those acting at its direction and under its control.

[11] Although this issue is addressed in subsection (b) of the Rule, and the other major issue resolved by this new rule is contained in subsection (a), this Treatise discusses those two sections in reverse order because the subject of subsection (b) is both more fundamental and logically antecedent to the other. Courts concerned with both issues must logically resolve whether there has been any waiver at all — the subject of subsection (b) — before deciding the extent of the waiver, if any, and whether it extends to undisclosed materials — the subject of subsection (a). That latter issue is discussed in § 502.3, *infra.*

intentional to be a waiver,"[12] and a few going to the other extreme and holding that such disclosure always amounts to a waiver without regard to the precautions taken to avoid such disclosure. Following the majority approach taken by most courts, Rule 502 opts for a middle ground, and provides that an "inadvertent disclosure" of protected material does not constitute a waiver if the holder of the protection "took reasonable steps to prevent disclosure," and then "promptly took reasonable steps to rectify the error, including (if applicable) following Federal Rule of Civil Procedure 26(b)(5)(B)."[13] Under this standard, a waiver will be found only if the disclosing party acted carelessly in disclosing the protected material, or failed to request its return in a timely manner.

It is a bit curious that the Rule and its Committee Notes do not define precisely what is meant by an "inadvertent disclosure," a phrase that appears in both the title and text of Rule 502(b). The Committee Notes describe the operation of this rule in terms of whether there has been an "inadvertent disclosure of protected communications or information," which it contrasts simply with an "intentional" disclosure.[14] But just what does that mean? Under what may be the most natural interpretation of that phrase, it might be limited to the situation where the very act of disclosure was accidental — for example, "I simply did not know that the July 30 memo somehow slipped into the pile of documents we supplied to opposing counsel." Then again, the language of the rule is also subject to another reasonable and broader interpretation, which would also protect a disclosing party whose "inadvertence" merely consisted of failing to study the documents closely enough to realize that one of them was arguably privileged — for example, "I knew the July 30 memo was one of the materials we turned over to opposing counsel, but we did not notice until later that the author of the memo was one of the corporation's attorneys."[15] In either of those cases, the party seeking to avoid a finding of waiver could plausibly claim that he had merely committed an

---

[12] Committee Note to Rule 502(b).

[13] Rule 502(b). As noted in the text, the rule contains an explicit cross-reference to Federal Rule of Civil Procedure 26(b)(5)(B), which provides:

> If information produced in discovery is subject to a claim of privilege or of protection as trial-preparation material, the party making the claim may notify any party that received the information of the claim and the basis for it. After being notified, a party must promptly return, sequester, or destroy the specified information and any copies it has; must not use or disclose the information until the claim is resolved; must take reasonable steps to retrieve the information if the party disclosed it before being notified; and may promptly present the information to the court under seal for a determination of the claim. The producing party must preserve the information until the claim is resolved.

[14] Committee Note to Rule 502(b).

[15] This broader interpretation of the Rule may or may not be the most natural reading of the phrase "inadvertent disclosure," but it is surely the reading of the Rule that is most consistent with the rule's stated purpose of reducing the incentive of lawyers and litigators to engage in extremely expensive forms of pre-production document review. Under this reading,

"inadvertent disclosure of protected communications or information."[16] Either reading of the rule seems plausible, and neither one is clearly dictated by the text or the Committee Notes to the rule. That ambiguity is unfortunate, as the choice between those two standards would have a significant impact on the scope of its protections.

In any event, under the language of Rule 502, it is clear that even a merely "inadvertent disclosure" will sometimes amount to a waiver, depending on whether the disclosing party took "reasonable" steps to both prevent and to later rectify the error. But how much caution will be adequate for that purpose? The Advisory Committee has stated that this Rule envisions the application of a "flexible" and "multi-factor" test for determining whether a waiver should be found, based on "a set of non-determinative guidelines that vary from case to case."[17] These factors include "the reasonableness of precautions taken, the time taken to rectify the error, the scope of discovery, the extent of disclosure and the overriding issue of fairness," which also entails a consideration of "the number of documents to be reviewed and the time constraints for production," and perhaps whether the disclosing party used "advanced analytical software applications and linguistic tools in screening for privilege and work product" or implemented "an efficient system of records management" before the litigation.[18] According to the Advisory Committee, the provision of the Rule requiring reasonable steps to rectify any error does not require disclosing parties "to engage in a post-production review to determine whether any protected communication or information has been produced by mistake," but does require them "to follow up on any obvious indications that a protected communication or information has been produced inadvertently."[19]

The Committee's adoption of such a "flexible" balancing test is natural and understandable, even if only because it was the view taken by a majority of the federal courts to consider the same issue. Still, it is a somewhat surprising choice, especially in light of the Supreme Court's admonition that privilege rules should not be fashioned in ways that would introduce

---

a party's act of producing documents in discovery is not an "intentional disclosure" of protected material unless the party knew that he was disclosing the document *and* that it was privileged. *Cf.* Flores-Figueroa v. United States, — U.S. —, —, 129 S. Ct. 1886, 173 L. Ed. 2d 853, 858 (2009) ("If we say that someone knowingly ate a sandwich with cheese, we normally assume that the person knew both that he was eating a sandwich and that it contained cheese.").

[16] Committee Note to Rule 502(b). The ambiguity, in other words, is whether the protection for "inadvertent disclosures" requires the disclosing party to prove that, at the time of disclosure, he was unaware that (1) he was disclosing *that* document, or (2) he was disclosing a *privileged* document.

[17] Committee Note to Rule 502(b).

[18] *Id.*

[19] Committee Note to Rule 502(b).

"substantial uncertainty into the privilege's application," or that would entail the "use of a balancing test in defining the contours of [a] privilege."[20] The Committee's choice to opt for just such an uncertain and unpredictable balancing test in this context is especially curious when one recalls that the stated purpose behind the Rule was "to provide a predictable, uniform set of standards under which parties can determine the consequences" of their actions, and thereby discourage lawyers from engaging in expensive litigation practices that had become "necessary to protect against waiver of attorney-client privilege or work product."[21] The Committee of course could have virtually eliminated that incentive by simply opting for a broader protection that would have allowed waiver *only* in the case of intentional disclosures. That approach would have had its own imperfections, but would have surely been the best way to all but eliminate the fears that previously drove litigators to undertake unreasonably expensive pre-production precautions out of the concern that a single slip-up in discovery could affect the outcome of the case.[22] Any lawyer who otherwise would have been tempted to "worry too much" about an inadvertent disclosure will be given only relatively limited comfort by Rule 502, which protects him from a finding of waiver only if the trial court is later persuaded that the lawyer undertook "reasonable" precautions against that mistake, after the court applies a test that even its drafters describe as a set of "flexible" set of factors that will "vary from case to case."[23]

§ 502.3   The Scope of Waiver

The second issue resolved by Rule 502 concerns the scope of the waiver that will be found in cases where the attorney-client privilege or work product protection has been waived by the disclosure of protected materials. Before the adoption of Rule 502, courts were occasionally divided as to whether the disclosure of protected material would merely waive the protection for the documents that were actually disclosed, or whether it might amount to a so-called "subject matter waiver" applicable to all documents and materials in the possession of the disclosing party and concerning the same subject matter.[24] From the perspective of the party

---

[20] Swidler & Berlin v. United States, 524 U.S. 399, 409 (1998).

[21] Committee Note to Rule 502.

[22] We say "all but eliminate" because even under that approach, the extremely cautious lawyer might still be tempted to engage in overkill out of fear that if he made an ill-advised disclosure he could never predict with certainty whether a reviewing court would conclude that the disclosure was truly "inadvertent." But the compromise approach codified in Rule 502(b) also leaves the attorney unable to predict with certainty whether the court will be persuaded, if need be, that the precautions against disclosure undertaken by that lawyer were "reasonable."

[23] Committee Note to Rule 502(b).

[24] Of course, a subject matter waiver will extend only to other documents in the

resisting discovery and opposing the claim of waiver, the difference between the two standards can be immense, because case law raised the risk that even the accidental disclosure of a protected document might result in a finding that thousands of other documents had become discoverable, perhaps even in future and unrelated litigation.[25]

Rule 502 severely limits the possibility that the disclosure of protected materials might result in a subject matter waiver. First and most importantly, it declares that the waiver will never extend to undisclosed communications or information unless the waiver was "intentional."[26] This means that the inadvertent or accidental disclosure of protected materials will never operate as a subject matter waiver.[27] That single change in the law will substantially reduce the incentive for parties to engage in disproportionately expensive pre-production document review out of the fear that the accidental production of a single document might result in the waiver of protection for a vast collection of related materials.

Indeed, it seems that the protections of this new rule may sweep much more broadly than its framers intended. Rule 502 provides that no subject matter waiver can result from pretrial disclosure unless, among other things, "the *waiver* is intentional."[28] This provision is perhaps a bit poorly worded, for it plainly implies that such a waiver can be found only if the disclosing party was aware not merely that he was showing a document to his adversary and that it was arguably subject to some privilege, but *also* knew and intended that such disclosure would result in a *waiver* of the privilege. That may or may not have been what the Committee actually had in mind, but it is surely a bit anomalous.[29] By that logic, a party — including even a *pro se*

---

possession of the party who committed the acts leading to the waiver, or as to which he was the holder of the privilege. This common-sense limitation is not reflected in the language of the rule, which merely speaks of when a waiver "extends to an undisclosed communication or information" that "concern[s] the same subject matter." Rule 502(a). But a party's act of disclosing documents protected by the attorney-client privilege, by itself, could never result in a waiver of the privilege for documents in the possession of the *opposing* party and received from its attorney, even if (as will often be true) those documents concern the same subject matter.

[25] *See, e.g., In re* Sealed Case, 877 F.2d 976 (D.C. Cir. 1989) (inadvertent disclosure of documents during discovery automatically constituted a subject matter waiver). The Notes to Rule 502 explicitly note the Committee's intention to overrule that case.

[26] Rule 502(a)(1).

[27] To be precise, the rule states that the *waiver* must have been intentional, but it logically follows that the disclosure itself must also have been intentional. It is not possible for a party to commit an intentional waiver of a privilege except through its knowing and voluntary actions.

[28] Rule 502(a)(1) (emphasis added).

[29] The Committee Notes to Rule 502(a) refer to "voluntary disclosure," as opposed to "inadvertent disclosure," and make no reference — as the Rule does — to whether the very *waiver* resulting from that disclosure was also intentional. It seems probable that the Advisory

litigant — could never be found to have committed a subject matter waiver if he can persuade the court that he knew nothing about the law of waiver, or how it applied to his case. In virtually every analogous setting in the area of privilege law, in keeping with the maxim that "ignorance of the law is no excuse," a finding of waiver does not depend on whether the disclosing party even knew that he had a privilege, much less whether he understood and intended that his actions might amount to its waiver.[30]

Even if the disclosure of protected material was intentional, the Rule provides that no subject matter waiver will result unless "the disclosed and undisclosed communications or information concern the same subject matter," and "they ought in fairness to be considered together."[31] This restriction clarifies that "a subject matter waiver (of either privilege or work product) is reserved for those unusual situations in which fairness requires a further disclosure of related, protected information, in order to prevent a selective and misleading presentation of evidence to the disadvantage of the adversary."[32] Just as in the case of evidence admitted under Rule 106, the intention of this rule is to emphasize a party that makes a selective and misleading presentation that is unfair to the adversary opens itself to a more complete and accurate presentation on rebuttal.

§ 502.4   Applicability of Rule 502 to Arbitration and State Court Proceedings

Rule 502 is unique among all the Federal Rules of Evidence in the extent to which its protections are made controlling outside the context of judicial proceedings in federal courts. The other rules have no applicability, for example, in arbitration proceedings, and have nothing to do with the admissibility of any evidence in the courts of the states,[33] which have otherwise unrestricted freedom to adopt any rules of evidence as they see fit.

Committee actually meant instead to require a showing that "the waiver resulted from an intentional disclosure," or that "the disclosure was intentional." But that is not what the Rule states.

[30] *See* Committee Note to Proposed Rule 511, in Appendix B (in the context of privileges for confidential communications, "knowledge or lack of knowledge of the existence of the privilege appears to be irrelevant" to issues of waiver).

[31] Rule 502(a)(2) and (3).

[32] Committee Note to Rule 502(a). The Committee Note adds: "Thus, subject matter waiver is limited to situations in which a party intentionally puts protected information into the litigation in a selective, misleading and unfair manner." *Id.*

[33] Prior to the adoption of Fed. R. Evid. 502, there was not one word in any provision of the Federal Rules of Evidence that restricted the liberty of the states to decide for themselves whether to follow or reject the example set by those rules. *See* Rules 101 and 1101(a) (both limiting the applicability of the rules to federal judicial proceedings). Indeed, before Rule 502 went into effect, state courts had the right, if they were so disposed, to abolish the attorney-client privilege altogether — indeed, to abolish all rules of evidence. That is no longer true, for state courts must now honor the commands of Rule 502.

The framers of Rule 502 were understandably concerned that its protections might be far less valuable if litigating parties were not certain whether their disclosure of arguably protected materials in federal proceedings might leave them subject to a finding that their disclosure amounted to a waiver, or even a subject-matter waiver, under state law.[34] To eliminate that possibility, Rule 502 declares that its protections shall extend "to State proceedings and to Federal court-annexed and Federal court-mandated arbitration proceedings, in the circumstances set out in the rule."[35]

Rule 502 is unique in a second respect. When a state law claim is litigated in federal court in a civil case,[36] Rule 501 provides that all other privilege issues that arise in the case (other than those involving federal constitutional questions) are governed by state law.[37] But the framers of Rule 502 were justifiably concerned that its salutary protections would be greatly undermined if they were not available to a party who is later involved in a federal diversity case. Consequently, Rule 502 provides that "notwithstanding Rule 501, this rule applies even if state law provides the rule of decision."[38] This clarifies that a party cannot be stripped of Rule's 502 protections merely because he finds himself litigating a state law claim in federal court in a state that provides less generous protection for the attorney-client privilege than that afforded by the new federal law.

Rule 502 contains several other similar provisions deserving of passing mention. When the disclosure of protected material took place in a state court and the issue of possible waiver arises in a later federal proceeding, the federal judge choosing between Rule 502 and state law will apply whichever one is more protective of the privilege, and which more narrowly restricts the scope of any waiver.[39] When a federal court orders that some privilege or protection will not be waived by disclosure connected with litigation

---

[34] It is a familiar principle that a legal rule will sometimes encourage parties to overcome their reluctance to undertake certain actions by giving them assurances that their choice will not be used against them in some later federal proceeding — as in the case of Rules 407–410. *See also* Fed. R. Civ. P. 36(a) (allowing parties to demand an admission of certain facts "for purposes of the pending action only"). Rule 502 is the first federal rule to take that notion and extend it to a guarantee that certain disclosures will have only limited effect in a *state* court proceeding.

[35] Rule 502(f). To this extent, the rule explicitly overrides the contrary provisions of Rules 101 and 1101, which limit the applicability of all the other rules to judicial proceedings in federal court. This point is also made in the language of Rule 502(a) and (b), both of which dictate certain waiver principles binding "in a Federal or State proceeding."

[36] This ordinarily happens only when the claim is filed in federal court on the basis of the court's diversity jurisdiction, 28 U.S.C. § 1332, or supplemental jurisdiction, 28 U.S.C. § 1367, or removed there by the defendants on the same basis, 28 U.S.C. § 1441.

[37] *See* § 501.4, *supra.*

[38] Rule 502(f).

[39] Rule 502(c).

pending before that court, the rule provides that such "confidentiality orders" will be binding in any other federal or state court proceeding.[40] Stipulations between the parties concerning such matters are also encouraged by the rule, although an agreement in a federal proceeding on the effect of disclosure "is binding only on the parties to the agreement, unless it is incorporated into a court order."[41]

Although the expansion of the Rule's protections to state court is a sensible choice and perfectly consistent with the aims of the rule, it does introduce a conspicuous anomaly into the structure and logic of the Federal Rules of Evidence. As previously noted in this treatise, Rule 502 is not the only federal rule aimed at encouraging litigants to take certain actions by giving them assurances that those actions will not come back to haunt them. For example, Rule 408 attempts to serve the judicial system's compelling interest in promoting settlement by assuring defendants that statements and offers made by them while attempting to settle a civil claim ordinarily cannot be used in a later prosecution as proof of their criminal liability.[42] But not every state observes the same rule, and Rule 408 therefore turns out to be a hollow promise for any hapless defendant who relied on its assurances when settling a civil claim in federal court before a later criminal prosecution was brought for the same allegation in the courts of a state that allows such evidence to be used by prosecutors as evidence of guilt.[43] It is far from obvious that the values served by Rule 502 are any more compelling than those underlying Rule 408, or why only the former should therefore be controlling in state court. In fairness to the Advisory Committee, of course, the inconsistency can be explained by the fact that Rule 502 was created as part of a Congressional enactment, while Rule 408 and most other evidence rules were not,[44] and it is most unlikely that the framers of an ordinary federal rule of evidence or procedure could make it binding on state courts.[45]

---

[40] Rule 502(d).

[41] Rule 502(e).

[42] *See* § 408.6, *supra*. For other examples of federal rules that strive to achieve laudable social goals with similar promises that "we won't use it against you," *see* Rules 407, 409, 410, and 411.

[43] Some states make this provision explicit in their statutory evidence code, *e.g.*, Louisiana Code of Evidence 408(B), and others reach this result through judicial interpretation of rules similar to Federal Rule 408, *e.g.*, State v. O'Connor, 119 P.3d 806, 812–813 (Wash. 2005) (en banc); State v. Mead, 27 P.3d 1115, 1128 (Utah 2001); Mayes v. State, 887 P.2d 1288, 1309 (Okla. Crim. App. 1994).

[44] Although some of them were — for example, Rules 412 through 415, all of which were enacted by Congressional legislation and were intended to serve as models for the reform of state evidence law, but none of which were made binding on state courts.

[45] The Supremacy Clause makes state courts subject to the United States Constitution "and the laws of the United States which shall be made in pursuance thereof," U.S. CONST., Art. VI, but it is not obvious that a rule of procedure promulgated by the Judicial Conference

Nevertheless, the fact remains that Rule 502 introduces the anomalous result that only one federal evidence rule has been made binding on state courts, while many other rules serving equally compelling federal objectives are not.

---

and approved by the Supreme Court of the United States would constitute such a "law."

ARTICLE VI.
WITNESSES

Synopsis

Chapter 601

Rule 601. Competency to Testify in General

Rule 601. Competency to Testify in General

Every person is competent to be a witness unless these rules provide otherwise. But in a civil case, state law governs the witness's competency regarding a claim or defense for which state law supplies the rule of decision.

---

§ 601.1 Competency of Witnesses — In General

Federal Evidence Rule 601 declares that all witnesses are competent to testify in federal matters, except where other specified Federal Evidence Rules render a potential witness incompetent.[1] Where the witness is to provide testimony that pertains to claims or defenses as to which state law provides the rule of decision, witness competency is controlled by state law. In the latter category, the statutory or common law of the applicable state law controls the competency of witnesses.[2]

---

[1] *See generally,* 1 McCORMICK, §§ 61–67; 3 WEINSTEIN'S FEDERAL EVIDENCE §§ 601.01–601.05; 3 MUELLER & KIRKPATRICK, §§ 232–235; 2 WIGMORE, §§ 483–686; 3 WIGMORE, §§ 687–721. *See also* Schmertz, *The First Decade under Article VI of the Federal Rules of Evidence; Some Suggested Amendments to Fill Gaps and Cure Confusion,* 30 VILL. L.J. 1367 (1985); Melton, *Children's Competency to Testify,* 5 LAW & HUMAN BEHAVIOR 73 (1981); Brooks, *Treatment of Witnesses in the Proposed Federal Rules of Evidence for the United States District Courts, Article VI,* 25 REC. 632 (1970); Comment, *The Uniformity-Conformity, Dilemma Facing Draftsmen of Federal Rules of Evidence,* 69 COLUM. L. REV. 353 (1969); *see also* Pennsylvania v. Muniz, 496 U.S. 582 (1990) (videotaped evidence of defendant's slurred speech and lack of muscular coordination obtained without *Miranda* warnings is not testimonial and is admissible evidence; the defendant's videotaped response when asked if he knew the date of his sixth birthday also obtained without *Miranda* warnings is testimonial and is not admissible evidence); Rock v Arkansas, 483 U.S. 44 (1987) (Arkansas' *per se* rule excluding all hypnotically refreshed testimony infringes impermissibly on a criminal defendant's right to testify on his or her own behalf).

[2] *See* McKenzie v. Harris, 679 F.2d 8 (3d Cir. 1982) (in a claim for social security benefits, court applied state law to bar husband and wife from testimony tending to indicate that their child was not the legitimate product of their union). The Supreme Court's proposed Rule 601 did not contain the second sentence of the Rule as enacted. This language was added by the House in order to protect strong state policies, such as the so-called Dead Man's Statutes, in cases where the federal court was constitutionally required under the *Erie* doctrine

The purpose of Rule 601 is to create a broad presumption of competency except where other Rules explicitly render a party incompetent or where governing state law disqualifies the witness. Rule 601 abolishes any remnants of federal common-law grounds for incompetency including: religious belief; conviction of a crime; insanity; infancy; and interest in the litigation, *e.g.,* as a party or as a spouse of a party.[3] The Rule also renders inapplicable any so-called Dead Man's Statutes in cases where state law does not control.[4] Rule 601 effectively shifts the focus from witnesses' competency to their credibility in cases where federal principles apply. An alleged infirmity often held to be a threshold question of competency at common law is now frequently considered an issue of credibility for the trier of fact.[5]

§ 601.2   The Court's Power to Exclude Testimony Contained in the Rules of Evidence: The Interplay Between Rule 601 and Rules 104 and 403

Since Rule 601 establishes a general presumption of competency, there is no requirement for a preliminary examination to determine competency under Rule 104.[6] While such a preliminary examination is not mandated, it is advisable in any case in which the trial judge has reason to believe that the

---

to apply state law to an issue or defense. *See* Courtland v. Walston & Co., 340 F. Supp. 1076 (S.D.N.Y. 1972), which the House Judiciary Committee cited in its Report to the House of Representatives.

[3] *See* 3 WEINSTEIN'S FEDERAL EVIDENCE § 601.02.

[4] *See* Advisory Committee Note, Rule 601; *see also* Sundstrand Corp. v. Sun Chemical Corp., 553 F.2d 1033 (7th Cir. 1977) (Illinois Dead Man's Act was not applied in action charging violations of securities laws); Donaldson v. Hovanec, 473 F. Supp. 602 (E.D. Pa. 1979) (in civil rights action, Pennsylvania Dead Man's Act does not apply); United States v. Diehl, 460 F. Supp. 1282 (S.D. Tex. 1978) (Dead Man's Act does not apply in federal question case).

[5] *See, e.g.,* United States v. Allen J., 127 F.3d 1292 (10th Cir. 1997) (any inconsistencies or other problems with the testimony of a juvenile witness with mild mental retardation raised questions of credibility and not competence); United States v. Zizzo, 120 F.3d 1338, 1347 (7th Cir. 1997) ("even the most dastardly scoundrels, cheats, and liars are generally competent to testify"; a witness's penchant for perjury affords the opposing party "an ample opportunity to undermine his credibility on cross-examination"); United States v. Gates, 10 F.3d 765 (11th Cir. 1993) (trial court did not err in refusing to hold a competency hearing before permitting a prosecution witness to testify; although defendant claimed that the witness was mentally unstable, the jury could evaluate the witness's credibility); United States v. Peyro, 786 F.2d 826 (8th Cir. 1986) (judge did not abuse discretion in permitting government witness to testify where she admitted that she had "some very substantial memory problems" and was "emotionally unbalanced"). *See generally,* 1 MCCORMICK, §§ 61–62.

[6] United States v. Roach, 590 F.2d 181 (5th Cir. 1979) (court found there no longer to be an occasion for judicially ordered psychiatric examinations or competency hearings of witnesses); *see also* Kentucky v. Stincer, 482 U.S. 730 (1987) (defendant's exclusion from a hearing to determine the competency of two child witnesses did not violate his rights under

witness's testimony might be impaired by infancy, mental or psychological condition, or chemical influence.[7]

Despite the strong preference for witness competency embodied in Rule 601, a trial judge is not without inherent and express authority to prevent a witness from testifying. The trial judge, of course, retains the power to exclude irrelevant testimony under Rule 401, or to determine that offered evidence is inherently incredible and insufficient to sustain a verdict when asked to rule on a motion for acquittal, a directed verdict, or a motion for a judgment notwithstanding the verdict.[8] Control of witness's testimony is also authorized under Rule 403, which may be invoked where the testimony is relevant but where its probative value is substantially outweighed by the dangers of unfair prejudice, confusion, delay, or when it results in the needless presentation of cumulative evidence.[9] A judge may apply Rule 403 to exclude testimony in a manner effectively similar to a finding of the incompetency of a witness where the judge determines the jury will be misled by the witness due to the jury's inability to assess accurately the credibility of the witness's testimony.[10] While there is a divergence of view as to the restraint that should be exercised in foreclosing a witness's testimony under Rule 403, no question exists that the trial judge has such

---

either the Confrontation Clause of the Sixth Amendment or the Due Process Clause of the Fourteenth Amendment).

[7] *See, e.g.,* United States v. Strahl, 590 F.2d 10 (1st Cir. 1978) (defendant claimed that testimony of prosecution witness should have been struck because his memory faded and he had drunk heavily at time of events in question; appellate court found that objections were suitably treated as questions concerning the credibility of the witness rather than his competency); United States v. Narciso, 446 F. Supp. 252 (E.D. Mich. 1976) (court on motion *in limine* to suppress identification testimony of witness held that witness could testify even though he made his identification after a hypnotic interrogation); *see also* United States v. Raineri, 91 F.R.D. 159 (W.D. Wis. 1980).

[8] *But see* Rock v. Arkansas, 483 U.S. 44 (1987) (in murder prosecution where defendant claimed accidental killing, trial court violated due process clause of 14th Amendment by denying defendant opportunity to testify to hypnotically-refreshed memory of shooting; "a defendant in a criminal case has the right to take the witness stand and to testify in his or her own defense"; Arkansas law completely barred the admission of *any* hypnotically refreshed testimony; Court indicated that if the exclusion had been based on a particularized inquiry rather than a blanket rule, it might have been acceptable).

[9] *See, e.g.,* United States v. Hyson, 721 F.2d 856 (1st Cir. 1983).

[10] United States v. Banks, 520 F.2d 627 (7th Cir. 1975) (line of inquiry involved taking of drugs, including methadone, during the trial; court ruled it was error to preclude this inquiry, since it prevented the jury from assessing credibility); *see also* Commonwealth v. Whitehead, 379 Mass. 640, 400 N.E.2d 821 (Mass. 1980) (in prosecution for rape, armed robbery, armed assault with intent to murder, and assault and battery by means of a dangerous weapon, where defendant moved to strike victim's testimony as incompetent on the grounds of inconsistencies and her limited intelligence, no error in trial judge's decision to allow victim to testify). *But see* Rock v. Arkansas, 483 U.S. 44 (1987).

authority.[11] Application of Rule 403 in this context requires an appreciation of the analytic balance of Rule 403, as well as the preference expressed in Rule 601 for competency. The result should be to permit the jury to consider the witness's testimony in most cases.

As an alternative to preventing a witness from testifying altogether, a trial judge should consider available means of assisting the trier of fact in its role of assessing witness credibility. Appropriate instructions may be given. Also, under Rule 614(b), the court may interrogate witnesses in an impartial manner in order to identify limitations in the witness's testimony. Other pertinent authority is provided in Rule 611(a), which provides the judge with authority over the mode and order of the interrogation of witnesses and in Rule 103(c), which provides:

The court may make any statement about the character or form of the evidence, the objection made, and the ruling. . . .

§ 601.3   Infancy and Psychological and Mental Impairment

It is imperative that the trial judge ascertain any intrinsic limitations on a witness's ability to testify.[12] Rule 611 commands the court to control the presentation of witness's testimony, and discharge of this mandate compels the trial judge to assess inherent limitations in potential testimony and undertake any appropriate corrective measures described in the previous section of this chapter. If the jury cannot make this determination, Rule 403 should be used to exclude the offered testimony.

On voir dire of the witness as authorized by Rule 104(a), the court should determine the witness's ability to state correctly matters that have come within his or her perception;[13] whether the witness can communicate to the

---

[11] Professors Mueller and Kirkpatrick state:

> In our adversary system, it is unlikely that a party would call a witness whose testimony is utterly valueless, and an active role by the judiciary in evaluating witness competency might simply encourage unfounded challenges. Nonetheless, in extreme circumstances the testimony of a raving or incoherent witness could be excluded as irrelevant under FRE 401 and 402, as unfairly prejudicial, misleading, or confusing under FRE 403, as lacking in perception or memory under FRE 602, as lacking in understanding of the duty to tell the truth under FRE 603, or as needlessly consuming time or embarrassing the witness under FRE 611(a).

MUELLER & KIRKPATRICK, Evidence § 6.2 (2d ed. 1999). *Compare* 3 WEINSTEIN'S FEDERAL EVIDENCE § 601.04. *See* Rock v. Arkansas, 483 U.S. 44 (1987).

[12] *See, e.g.,* Borawick v. Shay, 68 F.3d 597 (2d Cir. 1995) (trial court did not err in refusing to permit plaintiff, an alleged victim of childhood sexual abuse, to testify concerning allegedly repressed memories of abuse following therapeutic hypnosis; plaintiff was not a competent witness); United States v. Gutman, 725 F.2d 417 (7th Cir. 1984); United States v. Lightly, 677 F.2d 1027 (4th Cir. 1982).

[13] United States v. Benn, 476 F.2d 1127 (D.C. Cir. 1972).

jury;[14] the witness's ability to tell the difference between truth and falsity;[15] and the likelihood that the witness will be subject to effective cross-examination.[16] The court may also inquire into extrinsic sources to determine the wisdom of excluding the witness's testimony.[17]

While children are generally competent under the broad authorization of the first sentence of Rule 601, a special statute applies to child witnesses in abuse trials.[18] Further, when mental or psychological impairment is evident, there is no requirement that the judge order a psychiatric examination of a witness before the witness testifies. Authority exists, however, for the court to order such an examination where it deems such an evaluation necessary.[19]

Under Rule 601, a witness who is under the influence of alcohol or drugs at the time of testifying is not presumptively incompetent because of this condition.[20] Such a condition will, however, be a basis for impeachment, either to cast doubt on the witnesses' ability to narrate accurately their testimony, or to prove that their ability to accurately remember the event in question has been impaired.[21] Drug or alcohol use may also have the effect of exaggerating the witness's emotional response to what was said, resulting in a bias against a party.[22] The court may order a physical examination of the witness to determine the extent to which the witness's ability to testify

---

[14] United States v. Roach, 590 F.2d 181 (5th Cir. 1979); *see also* United States v. Van Meerbeke, 548 F.2d 415 (2d Cir. 1976) (witness who may have taken drug while on stand could testify where jury observed his actions); United States v. Callahan, 442 F. Supp. 1213 (D. Minn. 1978) (court held competency hearing to determine whether witness's drug use negated minimum level of required competency; found that witness could testify in a clear and lucid manner).

[15] United States v. Perez, 526 F.2d 859 (5th Cir. 1976) (judge had not erred in proceeding without a voir dire or in permitting minors to testify); *see also* Note, *The Child As A Witness,* 37 WASH. L. REV. 303 (1962).

[16] United States v. Benn, 476 F.2d 1127 (D.C. Cir. 1972).

[17] *Id.*

[18] *See* 18 U.S.C. § 3509(c).

[19] United States v. Jackson, 576 F.2d 46 (5th Cir. 1978) (narcotics use goes to credibility, not competency).

[20] *See, e.g.,* United States v. Jackson, 576 F.2d 46 (5th Cir. 1978); *see also* United States v. Killian, 524 F.2d 1268 (5th Cir. 1975) (no error to refuse to strike testimony of prosecution witness who was drug user, where he had not used drugs for several days prior to testifying); United States v. Davis, 486 F.2d 725 (7th Cir. 1973) (no error in failing to inquire into competency of witness where he was not under influence of narcotics while testifying, his testimony was corroborated, and his condition at the time about which he was testifying was developed on cross-examination).

[21] *See, e.g.,* United States v. Hyson, 721 F.2d 856 (1st Cir. 1983); United States v. Banks, 520 F.2d 627 (7th Cir. 1975).

[22] *See* 3 MUELLER & KIRKPATRICK, § 233.

accurately has been impaired.[23] In cases where a real threat to the accuracy of the witness's testimony exists because of the witness's drug or alcohol use, the court should issue an instruction to the jury cautioning it on this potential defect in the witness's testimony.[24] As discussed above, Rule 403 may be applied to exclude the testimony in extreme cases.

In a criminal case, the discretion of the trial judge may be circumscribed by the requirements of the Fourteenth Amendment due process clause. The Supreme Court has ruled that a state could not enforce a blanket proscription against hypnotically-refreshed testimony where the result of the rule was to bar an individual from testifying in her own defense. The Court suggested that, at least with respect to the defendant in a criminal trial, the Constitution requires a particularized inquiry into whether the testimony should be allowed, and that the prosecutor must bear the burden of persuasion.[25]

§ 601.4   Rule 601 — Other Provisions in the Rules

Rule 601 provides that exceptions to the declaration of general competency in the first sentence of the Rule are contained in other provisions of the Rules of Evidence. Accordingly, Rule 602 sets forth the familiar rule requiring firsthand knowledge for the testimony of lay witnesses. Judges are not competent to testify in trials at which they preside under Rule 605, and jurors are not competent to testify in trials for which they sit as jurors under Rule 606(a) or to impeach their verdicts under Rule 606(b).

§ 601.5   The Role of the Judge and Jury

Rule 601 is the culmination of a historical process of restructuring the roles of the judge and jury in trial proceedings.[26] Except in cases where state law must be applied by federal courts, the jury has the prerogative of weighing the credibility of all testimony.[27] Testimonial defects that would

---

[23] *See, e.g.,* United States v. Hyson, 721 F.2d 856, 864 (1st Cir. 1983) (where a medical examination of a witness showed he was under the use of sedatives, the judge properly struck his testimony but permitted it two days later when examination showed him to be "clear and coherent"; United States v. Raineri, 670 F.2d 702 (7th Cir. 1981); United States v. Riley, 657 F.2d 1377 (8th Cir. 1982); United States v. Martino, 648 F.2d 367 (5th Cir. 1981).

[24] *See* United States v. Benn, 476 F.2d 1127 (D.C. Cir. 1972) (in sex offense prosecution, no error for trial judge to decline to order psychological examination of mentally retarded 18-year old victim, since he provided a comprehensible narrative that was substantially corroborated); *see also* 3 MUELLER & KIRKPATRICK, § 233.

[25] Rock v. Arkansas, 483 U.S. 44 (1987). *But see* Mersch v. City of Dallas, Texas, 207 F.3d 732 (5th Cir. 2000) (hypnotically-enhanced testimony by plaintiff was improperly admitted because she did not establish the training of the person conducting the sessions, the audiotapes of the sessions were not available, no corroborating evidence existed, and her pre- and post-hypnotic testimony were drastically different).

[26] *See* United States v. Jones, 482 F.2d 747 (D.C. Cir. 1973); *see also* 3 WEINSTEIN'S FEDERAL EVIDENCE § 601.03.

[27] United States v. Hyson, 721 F.2d 856 (1st Cir. 1983); *see also* United States v. Jones,

have rendered a witness incompetent under the ancient common law now must be brought to the jury's attention through impeachment of the witness.

The trial court retains some power to control the jury and analyze the credibility of a witness by directing a verdict for a civil party, commenting on the evidence, or setting aside a verdict because it is not supported by the weight of the evidence.[28]

§ 601.6   Application of State Law

The second sentence of Rule 601 states that "in a civil case, state law governs the witness's competency regarding a claim or defense for which state law supplies the rule of decision." This provision will be utilized when the *Erie* doctrine requires the federal courts to apply state law as a rule of decision to a particular issue or defense.[29] This provision will not be applied in cases where state law is used as a rule of decision but is not applicable by its own force, *e.g.,* when state law is incorporated by a judge in creating federal common law.[30]

---

482 F.2d 747 (D.C. Cir. 1973) (it has become the modern trend to limit even the trial court's power to exclude testimony because of incompetency and to make the pivotal question one of credibility, for the jury); United States v. Zeiler, 470 F.2d 717 (3d Cir. 1972) (the practice of disqualifying witnesses because of presumed bias has been abandoned; bias is examined through cross-examination and juries are free to disregard it).

[28] *See* 3 WEINSTEIN'S FEDERAL EVIDENCE § 601.03.

[29] *See generally,* Erie v. Tompkins, 304 U.S. 64 (1938); Hanna v. Plumer, 380 U.S. 460 (1965); Byrd v. Blue Ridge Rural Elec. Coop., 356 U.S. 525 (1958); *see also* Higgenbottom v. Noreen, 586 F.2d 719 (9th Cir. 1978).

[30] Seè the discussion of Rule 501 in the Conference Report; H.R. Rep. No. 93-1597, 93d Cong., 2d Sess. 7 (1974); *see also* 3 MUELLER & KIRKPATRICK, § 235.

Chapter 602

Rule 602. Need for Personal Knowledge

Rule 602. Need for Personal Knowledge

A witness may testify to a matter only if evidence is introduced sufficient to support a finding that the witness has personal knowledge of the matter. Evidence to prove personal knowledge may consist of the witness's own testimony. This rule does not apply to a witness's expert testimony under Rule 703.

---

§ 602.1   General Requirement of Personal Knowledge

Federal Evidence Rule 602 requires a witness to testify from firsthand, or personal, knowledge of the subject matter.[1] The subject of a witness's testimony must have been perceived through one or more of the senses of the witness. Traditionally, as well as under Rule 602, the firsthand knowledge requirement is treated as a matter of competency, *i.e.,* witnesses are "incompetent" to testify to any fact unless they possess firsthand knowledge (direct perception) of that fact. Accordingly, the requirement of the Rule exemplifies the common-law insistence upon the most reliable sources of information.[2] This philosophy is also evident in the treatment by the Rules

---

[1] *See generally,* 1 MCCORMICK, § 69; 3 WEINSTEIN'S FEDERAL EVIDENCE §§ 602.01–602.04; 3 MUELLER & KIRKPATRICK, §§ 236–237; 2 WIGMORE, §§ 650–670. *See also* Note, *Lay Opinion in Civil Cases—Speed of Motor Vehicles,* 4 VILL. L. REV. 245 (1959).

[2] *See* United States v. Hickey, 917 F.2d 901 (6th Cir. 1990) (witness who was shown to have a cocaine addiction, a lack of memory and uncertainty about details was still a competent witness because he had some personal knowledge); Elizarraras v. Bank of El Paso, 631 F.2d 366 (5th Cir. 1980) (reversible error to admit plaintiff's testimony where he had no personal knowledge and hearsay rule barred his relating what he had been told); United States v. Brown, 548 F.2d 1194 (5th Cir. 1977) (I.R.S. agent could not testify that over 90% of the returns that had been prepared by defendant contained overstated deductions where she was testifying on the basis of out-of-court statements made to her by taxpayers she had interviewed, rather than on the basis of her personal knowledge); *see also* United States v. Pastore, 537 F.2d 675 (2d Cir. 1976) (testimony unobjectionable where basis of witness's knowledge was made clear before he left the stand); United States v. Larry, 536 F.2d 1149 (6th Cir. 1976) (where testimony was not based on personal knowledge, proper to exclude testimony as to witness's belief about activities of another). *See generally*, 3 WEINSTEIN'S FEDERAL EVIDENCE § 602.02; 3 MUELLER & KIRKPATRICK, § 237; 1 MCCORMICK, § 10; 2 WIGMORE, §§ 650–670.

of opinion testimony, hearsay, and non-original documents.

§ 602.2   Foundation as to Personal Knowledge

The party offering the witness must establish the requisite personal knowledge through foundation evidence. Rule 602 expressly provides that extrinsic foundation evidence is not necessary; thus, the witness's own preliminary testimony may establish that the witness was in a position to see or otherwise perceive the matters to which he or she will testify. Also, this foundation for personal knowledge may be supplied by other witnesses or documentary evidence. This determination of competency is within the discretion of the trial court, and unless it is clearly apparent that the witness had no personal knowledge of the subject matter, a reviewing court will not disturb the finding.[3]

According to Rule 104(b) the proponent of the witness must establish a foundation "sufficient to support a finding" that the witness possesses firsthand knowledge of the facts to which the witness will testify. The standard, and the appropriate procedure, is discussed in conjunction with Rule 104(b) in Chapter 104, *supra.*

§ 602.3   Competency versus Weight

Assessment of the accuracy, as opposed to the existence, of a witness's perception is a question of credibility for the trier of fact. The fact-finder bears the responsibility of considering the adequacy of the witness's opportunity for knowing or observing the facts as to which testimony is provided. Accordingly, once the court determines that the foundation as to personal knowledge is sufficient to admit the testimony of the witness, any defects in testimony resulting from faulty perception should govern the weight to be accorded the offered testimony or the credibility of the witness.[4]

---

[3] *E.g.,* United States v. Thompson, 559 F.2d 552 (9th Cir. 1977) (bank robbery prosecution; where defendant claimed he had been at certain restaurant on day of robbery, restaurant manager could testify that receipt produced by defendant's father was not the type that was normally issued to customers, even though he did not become manager until three months after robbery; manager had ample personal knowledge to testify about normal company procedures); *cf.* Rabon v. Great Southwest Fire Ins. Co., 818 F.2d 306 (4th Cir. 1987) (district court committed reversible error in admitting evidence of nonprosecution for arson in civil suit against insurance company for nonpayment of claim; prosecutor's decision could be based on factors not relevant to the civil suit, and prosecutor's opinion as to whether insured started fire was inadmissible since outside prosecutor's personal knowledge); *see also* United States v. Larry, 536 F.2d 1149 (6th Cir. 1976). *See generally*, 3 WEINSTEIN'S FEDERAL EVIDENCE § 602.03; 3 MUELLER & KIRKPATRICK, § 237; 1 MCCORMICK, § 10; 2 WIGMORE, § 654.

[4] United States v. Evans, 484 F.2d 1178 (2d Cir. 1973) (in bank robbery three eyewitnesses properly permitted to testify over defendant's objection that identification rested not upon their personal familiarity with robber's appearance, but upon their recollection of surveillance film); Auerbach v. United States, 136 F.2d 882 (6th Cir. 1943) (criminal prosecution for concealing liquor; defendant's principal competitor permitted to testify that

§ 602.4   Rule 602 and Other Rules

Rule 602's personal knowledge requirement obviously intersects with the operation of Rule 802, the rule forbidding hearsay, when a witness testifies to something he learned from someone else. Because the distinction between the two objections is based only on the form of the testimony — depending on whether the witness claims to be quoting someone else — an objection invoking either rule should be sufficient to preserve the point for appeal.[5] But Rule 602 by itself does not always prevent an individual from relating statements made by others outside of the courtroom. A witness who has personal knowledge of the making of the statement is competent to testify that a particular statement was made, as long as that statement is admissible under the hearsay rules set forth in Article VIII of the Rules.[6] In similar fashion, Rule 602 is expressly made subject to the provisions of Article VII concerning the testimony of expert witnesses. Experts may render opinions that are not based upon firsthand observation or perception. Rule 703 specifically addresses the permissible bases of expert opinion.[7] Finally, Rule 602 reinforces Rule 701, which provides:

---

he overheard a conversation while he was in a telephone booth between two persons he never saw, and that one of them was the voice of defendant); *see also* Rule 104(b) and § 104.2, *supra.*

[5] United States v. Davis, 596 F.3d 852 (D.C. Cir. 2010).

[6] *E.g.,* United States v. Owens, 789 F.2d 750 (9th Cir. 1986) (the witness "must have personal knowledge as to the making of the out-of-court statement; he need not, however, have personal knowledge as to events that were the subject of his statement"); United States v. Stratton, 779 F.2d 820 (2d Cir. 1985) (the witness's testimony as to out-of-court statements by the defendant was properly admitted; the hearsay rules require only that the declarant (here, the defendant) have had personal knowledge of the events recounted, not the witness); United States v. Owens-El, 889 F.2d 913, 915–16 (9th Cir. 1989) ("personal knowledge requirement . . . applies at two levels: first, the witness who testifies must have personal knowledge of the making of the out-of-court statement, and second, the person who made the out-of-court statement must have had personal knowledge of the events on which he based his statement"; where a victim's injury caused memory loss so that he could not remember his assailant, yet he could remember telling the FBI that it was the defendant who attacked him, the victim's frontal wounds, the details in his deposition of the attack to the FBI and his vivid recall of talking to the FBI support a finding that the out-of-court statement was based on personal knowledge); United States v. Beasley, 545 F.2d 403 (5th Cir. 1977) (witness was asked whether he told IRS agents that two promoters had to pay off; witness affirmed statement); Cities Serv. Oil Co. v. Coleman Oil Co., 470 F.2d 925 (1st Cir. 1972) (witness could testify to the contents of records kept in the regular course of business without having personal knowledge of the facts therein reported).

[7] *See* § 703.1 *et seq., infra.* Rule 703, entitled "Bases of an Expert's Opinion Testimony," provides:

An expert may base an opinion on facts or data in the case that the expert has been made aware of or personally observed. If experts in the particular field would reasonably rely on those kinds of facts or data in forming an opinion on the subject, they need not be admissible for the opinion to be admitted. But if the facts or data would otherwise be inadmissible, the proponent of the opinion may disclose them to the jury only if their

If a witness is not testifying as an expert, testimony in the form of an opinion is limited to one that is:

(a)   rationally based on the witness's perception;

(b)   helpful to clearly understanding the witness's testimony or to determining a fact in issue; and

(c)   not based on scientific, technical, or other specialized knowledge within the scope of Rule 702.

---

probative value in helping the jury evaluate the opinion substantially outweighs their prejudicial effect.

Chapter 603

Rule 603. Oath or Affirmation to Testify Truthfully

Rule 603. Oath or Affirmation to Testify Truthfully

Before testifying, a witness must give an oath or affirmation to testify truthfully. It must be in a form designed to impress that duty on the witness's conscience.

---

§ 603.1   Oath or Affirmation

Rule 603 fundamentally requires that, before testifying, witnesses must declare their intention to relate the subject matter of their testimony truthfully.[1] The declaration of intent may be by oath or affirmation.

---

[1] For reasons that are impossible to guess, those involved in the stylistic revision of this rule (and Rule 604) earlier this year inexplicably phrased this requirement in terms of an obligation of the witness to *give* an oath or affirmation to testify truthfully. By extremely well-settled linguistic convention, witnesses and others who voluntarily undertake a solemn public obligation are always said to "*take* an oath," not to give one. This point is so clearly established that it is hard to imagine where the Revisers got any contrary impression. It was the view of William Shakespeare, *e.g.,* KING LEAR, III, vi ("I here take my oath before this honourable assembly, she kicked the poor King her father."), as well as Bryan Garner, who correctly notes that "A courtroom witness typically takes [an assertory] oath," and that a judicial oath is "an oath taken in the course of a judicial proceeding, esp. in open court." BLACK'S LAW DICTIONARY 1101 (8th ed. 2004). It is the usage that is consistently adopted by the Supreme Court of the United States, which invariably refers to an oath *taken* by a judge or a witness or a juror. *E.g.,* Smith v. Spisak, — U.S. —, 130 S. Ct. 676, 175 L. Ed. 2d 595, 605 (2010) (describing the oath that "the jurors had taken to uphold the law"); Caperton v. A.T. Massey Coal Co., Inc., — U.S. —, 129 S. Ct. 2252, 173 L. Ed 2d 1208, 1227 (2009) (all judges "take an oath" to uphold the Constitution) (Roberts, C.J., dissenting). It is the language consistently adopted in the Federal Rules of Criminal and Appellate Procedure, *e.g.,* Fed. R. Crim. P. 6(a)(2) (an alternate juror "*takes* the same oath" as other jurors); Fed. R. App. P. 45(a)(1) (the clerk of the court must "*take* the oath and post any bond required by law"); at no point in any of the other federal rules is any witness or juror said to give an oath. Finally, this is the usage that is most consistent with the equally well-settled convention that the official who places the witness under oath is said to "administer" — or to give — the oath. *E.g.,* Fed. R. Civ. P. 28(a)(1)(A) (depositions must be taken before an official who is authorized to "administer oaths"). It makes no sense to say that a court clerk *administers* an oath to a witness who at the same time *gives* the oath — unless perhaps the witnesses is giving it right back?

See generally, 1 MCCORMICK, §§ 62–63; 3 WEINSTEIN'S FEDERAL EVIDENCE

The oath or affirmation serves the dual purposes of arousing witnesses' conscience to speak the truth and exposing witnesses to punishment for perjury should they purposely testify falsely.[2] The Rule is consistent with the common law in authorizing any mode or declaration that witnesses subjectively believe to be binding on their conscience and in discarding the operative distinction between oaths and affirmations.

§ 603.2   Operation of the Oath or Affirmation Requirement

Regardless of the form of the oath or affirmation, it must be administered in the presence of an officer authorized to administer it, and it must be an unequivocal act by which the witness consciously undertakes the burden to testify truthfully.[3] The Rule clearly requires the court to focus on the witness's beliefs and to administer an oath or affirmation designed to affect whatever peculiarities or idiosyncrasies of conscience are presented.[4] Moreover, the Rule applies to all witnesses, including children, mentally

---

§§ 603.01–603.05; 3 MUELLER & KIRKPATRICK, §§ 238–239; 6 WIGMORE, §§ 1818–1829. *See also* Note, *A Reconsideration of the Sworn Testimony Requirement: Securing Trust in the Twentieth Century*, 75 MICH. L. REV. 1681 (1977).

[2] Wilcoxon v. United States, 231 F.2d 384 (10th Cir. 1956) (court stated the twofold purpose of the oath as binding the conscience of the witness and making him amenable to prosecution if he gives perjured testimony). Testimony taken in a foreign country can be admissible without an oath or affirmation in strict compliance with Rule 603 so long as "the manner of examination . . . is [not] so incompatible with our fundamental principles of fairness or so prone to accuracy or bias as to render the testimony inherently unreliable." United States v. Casamento, 887 F.2d 1141 (2d Cir. 1989) (quoting United States v. Salim, 855 F.2d 944 (2d Cir. 1988)) (depositions taken before Swiss judges without oath or affirmation were found to be sufficiently reliable). *See generally*, 3 WEINSTEIN'S FEDERAL EVIDENCE § 603.02; 3 MUELLER & KIRKPATRICK, § 238; 1 MCCORMICK, § 62; 6 WIGMORE, § 1827.

[3] *See, e.g.,* United States v. Saget, 991 F.2d 702 (11th Cir. 1993) (witness who swore an oath to God even though he was an atheist was competent to testify; testimony revealed that the witness took the oath seriously and understood his duty to tell the truth).

[4] *See, e.g.,* United States v. Zizzo, 120 F.3d 1338 (7th Cir. 1997) (stating that the fact that a witness admitted on cross-examination that the oath did not mean anything to him did not require the court to strike his entire testimony; witness had a history of perjuring himself and perjury convictions, and was well aware of the consequences of lying in court); United States v. Looper, 419 F.2d 1405 (4th Cir. 1969) (reversible error not to allow defendant to testify where he refused a form of affirmation that made a reference to God); United States v. Moore, 217 F.2d 428 (7th Cir. 1954), *rev'd*, 348 U.S. 966 (1955) (conscientious objector who had refused to submit to induction into armed forces because he refused to use the word "solemnly" on religious grounds; trial court refused to allow him to testify; court of appeals affirmed; Supreme Court reversed and remanded, finding *per curiam* that there was no requirement that the word "solemnly" be used); United States v. Ward, 973 F.2d 730 (9th Cir. 1992) (trial court abused its discretion in refusing to allow defendant to take an alternative oath that substituted the phrase "fully integrated honesty" for the word "truth" where the defendant offered to also take the traditional oath); *cf.* United States v. Kalaydjian, 784 F.2d 53 (2d Cir. 1986) (trial judge properly disallowed cross-examination of witness regarding why he chose to "affirm" rather than to swear; not only did the question violate Rule 610, but

impaired persons, and interpreters.[5] Witnesses who refuse to be sworn or to make an affirmation may be held in contempt.[6]

§ 603.3   Testimony in the Absence of Oath or Affirmation

The requirement of an oath may be waived by competent parties either expressly or impliedly, *e.g.,* when an adverse party goes forward without inquiry or objection.[7] Where no objection to unsworn testimony is interposed, and the party adversely affected is aware of the receipt of the unsworn testimony, the irregularity is waived. No constitutional provision is violated when unsworn testimony is received, and any objection to the sufficiency of the oath administered to a witness must be made prior to the rendition of a verdict.[8]

The failure to swear a witness may be cured by withdrawing the testimony of the witness, and then resubmitting the testimony after administering the oath or affirmation. Alternatively, the witness may, after oath or affirmation, adopt his or her prior unsworn testimony.

---

the right to affirm in Rule 603 would be meaningless if the decision to do so could be examined by the opposing party).

[5] *See* United States v. Allen J., 127 F.3d 1292 (10th Cir. 1997) (the oath requirement was satisfied where the court and prosecutor questioned juvenile witness with mild mental retardation about whether she knew to tell the truth in court and knew that she would be punished if she told a lie); United States v. Fowler, 605 F.2d 181 (5th Cir. 1979) (court properly refused to allow defendant to testify after he refused to swear or affirm to tell the truth); United States v. Fiore, 443 F.2d 112 (2d Cir. 1971) (error to question witness before grand jury who refused to take oath).

[6] United States v. Wilson, 421 U.S. 309 (1975); United States v. Brannon, 546 F.2d 1242 (5th Cir. 1977). *But see* Gordon v. Idaho, 778 F.2d 1397 (9th Cir. 1985) (trial judge abused discretion in dismissing suit because plaintiff refused either to "solemnly swear" or to "affirm upon pain and penalty of perjury"; plaintiff agreed to say, "I understand I must tell the truth" and agreed to testify under penalty of perjury). ·

[7] United States v. Odom, 736 F.2d 104 (4th Cir. 1984) (defendants could not raise objection on appeal to failure to swear witnesses at trial; the trial judge had concluded the witnesses should not be sworn and called this to the attention of the defense; the defense moved to strike the testimony, but withdrew the objections rather than have the witnesses recalled and sworn); United States v. Perez, 651 F.2d 268 (5th Cir. 1981).

[8] Jackson v. Garrity, 250 F. Supp. 1 (D. Md. 1965). *But see* United States v. Hawkins, 76 F.3d 545 (4th Cir. 1996) (defendant's conviction of criminal contempt was reversed due to trial court's error in permitting the prosecuting attorney, who had not taken an oath to testify truthfully, to identify the defendant as the individual who had been recalcitrant and uttered obscenities when called as a witness in a criminal case).

Chapter 604

Rule 604. Interpreter

Rule 604. Interpreter

An interpreter must be qualified and must give an oath or affirmation to make a true translation.

---

§ 604.1 Interpreter — In General

Federal Evidence Rule 604 subjects an interpreter to the qualifications and requirements of other expert witnesses under Article VII.[1] The purpose of Rule 604 is to identify the evidentiary function of an interpreter, and it does not provide authority governing the appropriateness or necessity of using an interpreter.

Where a witness is unable to speak or understand the English language, the court may in its discretion receive the witness's testimony through an interpreter, provided the interpreter takes an oath or affirmation declaring that he or she will render a true and literal translation.[2] The court's discretion, however, is more circumscribed in a criminal proceeding. If the accused or a witness on his or her behalf cannot adequately understand English, the court is required to determine if the defendant's lack of understanding made the proceedings unfair, and if so, to appoint an interpreter in order to protect the defendant's fundamental rights.[3]

---

[1] *See generally,* 3 WEINSTEIN'S FEDERAL EVIDENCE §§ 604.01–604.04; 3 MUELLER & KIRKPATRICK, §§ 240–241; 6 WIGMORE, § 1824. *See also* Chang and Araujo, *Interpreters for the Defense: Due Process for the Non-English-Speaking Defendant,* 63 CALIF. L. REV. 801 (1975); Note, *The Right to An Interpreter,* 25 RUTGERS L. REV. 145 (1970).

[2] Court Interpreters Act, 28 U.S.C. § 1827 (1978). *See generally,* 3 WEINSTEIN'S FEDERAL EVIDENCE § 604.02; 3 MUELLER & KIRKPATRICK, § 240; 3 WIGMORE, § 811.

[3] 3 WEINSTEIN'S FEDERAL EVIDENCE § 604.02; United States v. Carrion, 488 F.2d 12 (1st Cir. 1973) (indigent has right to interpreter when he or she has obvious difficulty with the language); United States v. Sanchez, 483 F.2d 1052 (2d Cir. 1973) (interpreter must be provided when necessary); United States ex rel. Negron v. New York, 434 F.2d 386 (2d Cir. 1970) (affirming issuance of writ of habeas corpus in connection with state murder conviction). *But see* Fairbanks v. Cowan, 551 F.2d 97 (6th Cir. 1977) (appointment of interpreter does not reach constitutional proportions); Cervantes v. Cox, 350 F.2d 855 (10th

The court also fixes the reasonable compensation of the interpreter in civil litigation[4] and criminal proceedings.[5] Additionally, the court determines who will pay for the interpreter's services.[6]

§ 604.2   Function of the Trial Judge

The determination of an interpreter's qualifications is an issue peculiarly within the discretion of the trial court as provided in Article VII of the Rules, and close relatives or friends of the witness are not precluded from serving as interpreters where such relatives qualify as experts.[7] Interpreters should be admonished by the court not to embellish or rearrange the words of the witness.[8]

The Rule permitting interpreters is itself a relaxation of the general proscription against testimony from sources lacking firsthand knowledge, and it remains within the discretion of the trial judge whether to apply strictly other Rules, such as those regarding leading questions, cross-examination, impeachment and the like.

§ 604.3   Credibility of the Interpreter; Function of the Trier of Fact

There are situations in which an interpreter's accuracy may become subject to attack. As in the case of other experts, interpreters possess varying degrees of ability and competence, and whether this ability will affect the accuracy of the translation becomes an issue for the trier of fact.[9] In such

---

Cir. 1965) (no constitutional right to court appointed interpreter).

[4] *See* Fed. R. Civ. P. 43(d), which provides:

The court may appoint an interpreter of its choosing; fix reasonable compensation to be paid from funds provided by law or by one or more parties; and tax the compensation as costs.

[5] *See* Fed. R. Crim. P. 28, which provides:

The court may select, appoint, and set the reasonable compensation for an interpreter. The compensation must be paid from funds provided by law or by the government, as the court may direct.

[6] *See* Fed. R. Civ. P. 43(d); Fed. R. Crim. P. 28.

[7] Fairbanks v. Cowan, 551 F.2d 97 (6th Cir. 1977) (judge appointed father of 31-year-old victim as interpreter where victim had mentality of six-year-old child); United States v. Addonizio, 451 F.2d 49 (3d Cir. 1971) (trial judge appointed wife of witness as interpreter); Chee v. United States, 449 F.2d 747 (9th Cir. 1971) (trial court had broad discretion in determining qualifications of interpreters).

[8] Court Interpreters Act, 28 U.S.C. § 1827 (1978).

[9] Rule 702, entitled "Testimony by Expert Witnesses," provides:

A witness who is qualified as an expert by knowledge, skill, experience, training, or education may testify in the form of an opinion or otherwise if:

   (a)   the expert's scientific, technical, or other specialized knowledge will help the trier of fact to understand the evidence or to determine a fact in issue;

   (b)   the testimony is based on sufficient facts or data;

   (c)   the testimony is the product of reliable principles and methods; and

cases, the credibility of the interpreter and his or her competence to translate become issues properly for the jury.

———————

(d)   the expert has reliably applied the principles and methods to the facts of the case.

See also United States v. Miller, 806 F.2d 223 (10th Cir. 1986) (in criminal prosecution, trial court properly appointed interpreter without qualifying her as an expert; government witness had good understanding of English and defendant had expressly consented).

Chapter 605

Rule 605. Judge's Competency as a Witness

Rule 605. Judge's Competency as a Witness

The presiding judge may not testify as a witness at the trial. A party need not object to preserve the issue.

---

§ 605.1 Competency of Trial Judge — In General

Federal Evidence Rule 605 provides simply and without reservation that the judge presiding at the trial may not testify in that trial as a witness, and, further, that no objection need be interposed at trial to preserve the error on appeal.[1]

The application of the Rule does not render the testimony incompetent because it is of an unreliable nature; rather, incompetency is based upon practical reasons for rejecting this type of evidence. For example, if the judge may testify at the trial, "Who rules on objections? Who compels him to answer? Can he rule impartially on the weight and admissibility of his own testimony?, etc."[2]

The entire point behind Rule 605 is to ensure that no judge will ever be allowed to serve as a witness and a judge at the same trial. The rule is largely unnecessary to achieve that objective, however, since the federal disqualification statute already requires judges to disqualify themselves from presiding over any case if they have "personal knowledge of disputed evidentiary facts concerning the proceeding."[3] In the rare case in which a

---

[1] *See generally*, 1 MCCORMICK, § 68; 3 WEINSTEIN'S FEDERAL EVIDENCE §§ 605.01–605.07; 3 MUELLER & KIRKPATRICK, §§ 242–244; 6 WIGMORE, § 1909. *See also* Saltzburg, *The Unnecessarily Expanding Role of the American Trial Judge,* 64 VA. L. REV. 39 (1978); Field, *Double Jeopardy in Federal Criminal Cases,* 3 CALIF. W.L. REV. 76 (1967); Hart, *Testimony By a Judge or Juror,* 44 MARQ. L. REV. 183 (1960); Field, *Disability of the Judge in Federal Criminal Procedure,* 6 ST. LOUIS U.L.J. 150 (1960).

[2] Advisory Committee Note, Rule 605.

[3] 28 U.S.C. § 455(b)(1). The statute also requires judges to disqualify (or recuse) themselves from a case if for any other reason "his impartiality might reasonably be questioned." 28 U.S.C. § 455(a).

judge who is randomly assigned to a case happens to have been an eyewitness to some disputed event in the case (most likely as a result of having presided over some related litigation), he or she is required to withdraw from the case so that it may be assigned to some other judge. The judge will then be free to testify like any other eyewitness, if need be, without posing any risk of violating Rule 605. In the rare case in which a party is able to make a successful objection under this rule, it often means that the judge neglected the obligation to disqualify himself or herself long before either party was tempted to call the judge to the stand as a witness.

The rule does not prevent judges from testifying at a trial about matters that they witnessed while presiding over another trial, provided of course that some other judge is assigned to preside over the trial where the testimony is presented. For example, a judge who presided over a criminal trial may be called as a witness in a later hearing on a petition for post-conviction relief that raises questions about the events that took place at the original trial.

§ 605.2   When a Judge Is Called on or Testifies in a Civil Proceeding

In a civil case, when a presiding judge is called to testify by a party, the judge may either excuse himself or herself, or continue the trial. On excusing himself or herself, the judge must declare a mistrial and enter an order for a new trial.[4] If, however, the judge continues the trial and testifies to a material fact, the appellate court should generally reverse the judgment if the verdict implicates the party against whom the judge testified. In this situation prejudice is presumed to be extremely likely.[5]

If the judge is called to testify and does not testify at the trial, the appellate court must determine if the failure to testify was prejudicial to the appellant. If it is found to be prejudicial, a new trial should be ordered.[6] It should be noted that a party need not object to a violation of Rule 605 in order to preserve review of the issue. However, a violation of Rule 605 may be waived by both parties and the judge's testimony admitted.[7]

§ 605.3   When a Judge Is Called on or Testifies in a Criminal Proceeding

As in a civil trial, a presiding judge in a criminal trial who is called to testify by a party may either excuse himself or herself, or continue the trial. If the judge disqualifies himself or herself, Rule 25(a) of the Federal Rules of Criminal Procedure allows for the substitution of a new judge in the event

---

[4] *See, e.g.,* Stoltzfus v. United States, 264 F. Supp. 824 (E.D. Pa. 1967); *In re* Schoenfield, 608 F.2d 930 (2d Cir. 1979). *Compare* United States v. Schipani, 293 F. Supp. 156 (E.D.N.Y. 1968), *aff'd,* 414 F.2d 1262 (2d Cir. 1969) (retrial on transcript of trial before another judge).

[5] *See* 3 WEINSTEIN'S FEDERAL EVIDENCE § 605.05.

[6] *Id.*

[7] *Id.*

of the disability of the original trial judge.[8] Doubt, however, has been cast on the constitutional applicability of this rule in the context of a judge who is disqualified under Rule 605.[9] If the substitution is consensual on the part of the defendant and the prosecution, a due process problem does not arise.[10] If, however, the defendant does not agree to the substitution, the due process question again becomes an issue. Consequently, wise practice would lead the trial judge to order a mistrial where Rule 605 requires disqualification.[11]

If the mistrial is ordered, the problem becomes whether the defendant may be retried consistent with protections against double jeopardy. Retrial is permissible in cases where the judge is disabled and must withdraw during a trial. In the present context, however, neither party has caused the disability; the disability envisioned by Rule 605 is caused because a party has called the judge as a witness.[12] Judge Weinstein suggests retrial is permissible unless the prosecution has deliberately sought to invite a mistrial by calling the presiding judge.[13] The reviewing court should also consider whether the trial judge knew he or she would be called as a witness or was attempting to help the prosecution[14] or whether the prosecution called the trial judge in response to an unanticipated defense that was raised by the accused.[15] Additionally, the court should consider whether the testimony sought to be admitted concerned a material issue.[16] If the defendant calls the judge as a witness, he or she should be presumed to know that a mistrial will result by applications of Rule 605 and consequently to have acquiesced to a retrial.[17]

If the judge is called to testify but does not, the appellate court will determine if a reversible error has occurred. If it has, a new trial will be

---

[8] *See* Fed. R. Crim. P. 25(a).

[9] 2 WRIGHT, FEDERAL PRACTICE AND PROCEDURE—CRIMINAL, § 392.

[10] 3 WEINSTEIN'S FEDERAL EVIDENCE § 605.06; *cf.* Randel v. Beto, 354 F.2d 496 (5th Cir. 1965) (habeas corpus attack on state court conviction where judge had been substituted at trial; court indicated that substitution might violate right to jury trial); Freeman v. United States, 227 F. 732 (2d Cir. 1915) (did not permit substitution of judges as violation of right to jury trial).

[11] Freeman v. United States, 237 F. 815 (2d Cir. 1916).

[12] 3 WEINSTEIN'S FEDERAL EVIDENCE § 605.06.

[13] Carsey v. United States, 392 F.2d 810 (D.C. Cir. 1967); *see also* 3 WEINSTEIN'S FEDERAL EVIDENCE § 605.06.

[14] *Cf.* Downum v. United States, 372 U.S. 734 (1963).

[15] Wright v. Boles, 275 F. Supp. 571 (N.D.W. Va. 1967) (defendant not placed in double jeopardy where court had declared mistrial on defendant's motion in first prosecution, since state had called defendant's wife as witness without defendant's consent).

[16] 3 WEINSTEIN'S FEDERAL EVIDENCE § 605.06.

[17] *Id.*

ordered.[18] No objection is necessary to preserve appellate review of this issue.[19]

§ 605.4   When the Judge Implicitly Testifies in Violation of Rule 605

The judge may implicitly testify in a trial without formally taking the stand. When this occurs, Rule 605 has been violated and the appellate court should examine the record for reversible error.[20] Because of the great weight that the judge's comments are likely to be given by the jurors, even a single statement by the judge may require reversal if the statement directly addresses an important issue in the case and the other evidence on that point is inconclusive.[21] A special problem may arise when the court makes an impermissible comment on the facts under the pretext of judicial notice.[22] The court may also consider taking judicial notice of prior proceedings that are not substantiated by the record.[23] The materiality of the judge's comments is a crucial element in determining whether a reversible error has occurred in these contexts.[24]

---

[18] *Id.*

[19] *See* Advisory Committee Note, Rule 605.

[20] *See* Kennon v. Slipstreamer, Inc., 794 F.2d 1067 (5th Cir. 1986) (trial court committed reversible error in products liability suit against manufacturer by telling jury that plaintiffs had settled claims against wholesaler, retailer, and maker of a material used in the product, for $ 10 each); *cf.* Jones v. Benefit Trust Life Ins. Co., 800 F.2d 1397 (5th Cir. 1986) (trial judge properly excluded as evidence pre-trial ruling denying plaintiff's motion for summary judgment); Price Bros. Co. v. Philadelphia Gear Corp., 629 F.2d 444 (6th Cir. 1980) (sending trial judge's law clerk to gather evidence in a non-jury trial would be destructive of the appearance of impartiality required).

[21] United States v. Nickl, 427 F.3d 1286, 1292–1295 (10th Cir. 2005) (reversing a conviction solely because the trial judge interrupted the defense cross-examination, answered a question on an ultimate issue, and did not let the witness answer; the judge improperly voiced his opinion that he accepted the guilty plea from defendant's alleged conspirator only because he was convinced that she was actually guilty).

[22] Fox v. City of West Palm Beach, 383 F.2d 189 (5th Cir. 1967) (judge's order denying an injunction regarding property drainage was reversed because judge "made frequent factual statements based upon his own expertise with respect to lands in the area"); *but see* United States v. Bari, 599 F.3d 176 (2d Cir. 2010) (although a judge presiding at a trial may not testify in that trial as a witness, he is not improperly "testifying" if he takes judicial notice of some fact within the bounds of Rule 201).

[23] *See* Tyler v. Swenson, 427 F.2d 412 (8th Cir. 1970) (judge's denial of habeas corpus violated constitutional due process standards where judge relied on own recollection of events from conviction hearing); Soley v. Star & Herald Co., 390 F.2d 364 (5th Cir. 1968) (litigants should have opportunity to challenge even a judge's recollections); 3 WEINSTEIN § 605.07.

[24] *See* 3 WEINSTEIN'S FEDERAL EVIDENCE § 605.07.

Chapter 606

Rule 606. Juror's Competency as a Witness

Rule 606. Juror's Competency as a Witness

(a) **At the Trial.** A juror may not testify as a witness before the other jurors at the trial. If a juror is called to testify, the court must give a party an opportunity to object outside the jury's presence.

(b) **During an Inquiry into the Validity of a Verdict or Indictment.**

    (1) *Prohibited Testimony or Other Evidence.* During an inquiry into the validity of a verdict or indictment, a juror may not testify about any statement made or incident that occurred during the jury's deliberations; the effect of anything on that juror's or another juror's vote; or any juror's mental processes concerning the verdict or indictment. The court may not receive a juror's affidavit or evidence of a juror's statement on these matters.

    (2) *Exceptions.* A juror may testify about whether:

        (A) extraneous prejudicial information was improperly brought to the jury's attention;

        (B) an outside influence was improperly brought to bear on any juror; or

        (C) a mistake was made in entering the verdict on the verdict form.

---

§ 606.1   Rule 606(a) — Juror's Competency at Trial as Witness — In General

Rule 606(a) declares incompetent any witness who is a member of the jury impaneled to hear the case in question.[1] The rationale for disqualifying a juror under Rule 606 is similar to that underlying the disqualification of

---

[1] *See generally,* 2 McCORMICK, § 605; 3 WEINSTEIN'S FEDERAL EVIDENCE §§ 606.01–606.07; 3 MUELLER & KIRKPATRICK, §§ 245–255; 6 WIGMORE, § 1910. *See also* Comment, *Juror Privilege: The Answer to the Impeachment Puzzle,* 3 W. NEW ENG. L. REV. 446 (1981); Broeder, *The Impact of the Vicinage Requirement: An Empirical Look,* 45 NEB. L. REV. 99 (1966); Carlson & Sunberg, *Attacking Jury Verdicts: Paradigms for Rule Revision,* 1977 ARIZ. ST. L.J. 247 (1977).

judges under Rule 605. First, counsel may be inhibited in cross-examining a juror, in fear of invoking an unfavorable reaction by the juror. Second, the juror may be unable to weigh objectively the credibility of his or her own testimony when it is contradicted by an adverse witness. Third, the juror may overidentify with one party and become biased. Fourth, the panel of jurors may more favorably weigh the testimony of a fellow juror.[2]

§ 606.2   Rule 606(b) — Juror's Competency to Testify at a Subsequent Proceeding Concerning Original Verdict or Indictment; Matters Internal to the Deliberative Process

Rule 606(b) reflects the common-law tradition of protecting and preserving the integrity of the jury room by declaring jurors generally incompetent to testify as to any matter purely internal to the jury's deliberations.[3] The Rule pertains to a jury's collective discussions and exchanges as well as individual jurors' mental and emotional deliberative processes. The Rule is designed to ensure the finality of verdicts and to protect jurors from being unceasingly harassed by defeated parties. In the absence of such protection, the confidentiality and candor of the jury room would become the constant subject of public investigation. Consequently, the Rule is designed to foster the time-honored and highly valued freedom of conference critical to the entire scheme of trial by jury,[4] and it erects a barrier to the introduction of

---

[2] 3 MUELLER & KIRKPATRICK, § 246.

[3] *E.g.,* United States v. Straach, 987 F.2d 232 (5th Cir. 1993) (affidavits by jurors concerning the validity of defendant's conviction were incompetent to impeach the verdict where the jurors claimed they voted with the other jurors only after they were pressured by the other members of the jury); United States v. Ayarza-Garcia, 819 F.2d 1043 (11th Cir. 1987) (article in which juror stated that he had gone along with verdict only to be practical indicated only juror's mental processes and did not suggest any reversible impropriety); United States v. Miller, 806 F.2d 223 (10th Cir. 1986) (trial judge properly denied inquiry into criminal conviction where juror expressed second thoughts and claimed undue influence by other jurors); Peveto v. Sears, 807 F.2d 486 (5th Cir. 1987) (trial court properly refused to order retrial where jurors thought that their "actual damages" were to be reported net of contributory negligence percentage rather than in gross); Sims' Crane Service, Inc. v. Ideal Steel Products, Inc., 800 F.2d 1553 (11th Cir. 1986) (although trial judge had instructed that gross negligence was a prerequisite to recovery, foreperson's explanation that the jury divided the damages sought in two because they did not find gross negligence on either side was not a basis for overturning the jury's verdict). *See generally,* 3 WEINSTEIN'S FEDERAL EVIDENCE § 606.04; 3 MUELLER & KIRKPATRICK, § 247; 1 MCCORMICK, § 68; 8 WIGMORE, § 2348. *See also* Comment, *Impeachment of Verdicts by Jurors—Rule of Evidence 606(b),* 4 WM. MITCH. L. REV. 417 (1978); Comment, *Judgment by Your Peers? The Impeachment of Jury Verdicts and the Case of the Insane Juror,* 21 N.Y.U.F. 57 (1975); Note, *Impeachment of Jury Verdicts,* 53 MARQ. L. REV. 258 (1970).

[4] *E.g.,* United States v. Ford, 840 F.2d 460 (7th Cir. 1988) (citing protection of jury from harassment by lawyers after verdict and protection of finality of verdict as reasons behind Rule 606(b)); Attridge v. Cencorp Div. of Dover Tech. Int'l, 836 F.2d 113 (2d Cir. 1987) (citing promotion of free discourse during jury deliberations, protection of jurors from harassment after trial and preservation of finality of verdicts as reasons behind Rule 606(b));

evidence from a juror concerning matters that are purely internal to the jury's deliberations.[5]

The restrictions of Rule 606(b) apply only to inquiry after the verdict or indictment has been reached and recorded.[6] Such restrictions, however, do not prevent a court from questioning members of a panel that returns with an ambiguous or internally inconsistent verdict.[7] The dangers of continual uncertainty and tampering with jurors, sought to be prevented by the Rule, are absent where the inquiry into the jury process is conducted by the court before the jurors are discharged and separated.[8]

Although the Rules of Evidence do not normally apply to sentencing hearings, the reasons underlying Rule 606(b) apply with equal force to jury deliberations regarding a defendant's sentence, and the principles behind the

---

see also Peveto v. Sears, Roebuck & Co., 807 F.2d 486 (5th Cir. 1987); Maldonado v. Missouri Pac. Ry. Co., 798 F.2d 764 (5th Cir. 1986).

[5] *See* Rule 606(b), Advisory Committee Note. *See also* United States v. Elder, 90 F.3d 1110 (6th Cir. 1996) (pursuant to Rule 606(b), the trial judge held a hearing to determine if the jurors who convicted the defendant of conspiracy to distribute cocaine had been influenced by an entry on the exhibit list referencing a newspaper article about an apartment fire the defendant allegedly started which killed several infants; on appeal, the court rejected the argument that counsel should have been allowed to review the jurors' notebooks as such review might reveal the jurors' thought process, comments, or calculations).

[6] This point is often missed by the courts. For example, one recent decision mistakenly held that Rule 606(b) precluded a judge from granting a party's motion during the *middle* of deliberations to investigate a complaint from one juror that another juror was improperly acting as an expert on a central issue in the case. Marquez v. City of Albuquerque, 399 F.3d 1216 (10th Cir. 2005) (reasoning that a "juror's personal experience" is not extraneous prejudicial information). That is false. Although other legal considerations counsel against interrupting juror deliberations lightly, Rule 606(b) does not limit jurors from revealing anything to anyone except "[d]uring an inquiry into the validity of a verdict or indictment," and so the rule imposes literally no constraints on the power of a judge to conduct otherwise appropriate investigation into possible juror misconduct or irregularities at any time before the verdict is returned.

[7] 3 WEINSTEIN'S FEDERAL EVIDENCE § 606.04; *see also* McCullough v. Conrail, 937 F.2d 1167 (6th Cir. 1991) (after final award was declared, jury was concerned that amount given was not what was intended; judge polled jury and re-announced award accordingly).

[8] "The reasons for the rule barring juror testimony, namely, the dangers of uncertainty and of tampering with the jurors to procure testimony, disappear in large part if such investigation as may be desired is made by the judge and takes place before the jurors' discharge and separation." Committee Note to the 2006 amendment to Rule 606 (citations omitted). Any errors that come to light when the jurors are polled "may be corrected on the spot, or the jury may be sent out to continue deliberations, or, if necessary, a new trial may be ordered." Committee Note to the 2006 amendment to Rule 606 (quoting Mueller & Kirkpatrick, EVIDENCE UNDER THE RULES 671 (2d ed. 1999)). *See also* Fed. R. Crim. P. 31(d) ("Jury Poll. After a verdict is returned but before the jury is discharged, the court must on a party's request, or may on its own, poll the jurors individually. If the poll reveals a lack of unanimity, the court may direct the jury to deliberate further or may declare a mistrial and discharge of the jury").

Rule may be relied upon to exclude evidence relating to jury deliberations regarding sentencing.[9]

By its express terms, Rule 606(b) includes within its proscription evidence tending to support as well as impeach verdicts. Likewise, it prohibits evidence from third parties concerning post-verdict statements by jurors.

§ 606.3 Juror's Competency as to Extraneous Prejudicial Information, Outside Influence, or Mistakes in Entering the Verdict on the Verdict Form

Rule 606(b)(2) recognizes limited situations in which a juror is competent to impeach a verdict or indictment after it has been rendered. A juror may testify as to whether any jurors were exposed to extraneous prejudicial information or improper outside influence, or whether a mistake was made in entering the verdict on the verdict form.

It will not always be apparent whether the testimony offered falls within this exception. While Rule 606(b)(2) does not explicitly define "extraneous prejudicial information" or improper "outside influence," admissibility should depend upon an initial finding that the substance of the juror's testimony is of a type concerning impermissible outside influence or information, and not merely evidence of the juror's individual or collective predisposition, mental state, or knowledge.[10] Moreover, the Rule only addresses the circumstances under which a juror is competent to provide evidence on the validity of a verdict, and it does not govern standards pertaining to the degree or substance of evidence necessary to set aside a verdict.[11]

Rule 606 will allow a juror to testify to misconduct such as acceptance of bribes,[12] or threats made against a juror.[13] Testimony may be admitted to

---

[9] *See* United States v. Jones, 132 F.3d 232 (5th Cir. 1998) ("[W]e are convinced that Rule 606(b) does not harm but helps guarantee the reliability of jury determinations in death penalty cases.").

[10] *See* United States v. Jones, 132 F.3d 232 (5th Cir. 1998) (evidence that jury instructions caused jury confusion was not evidence of extraneous forces impacting jury decision; an allegation of such jury confusion is not a matter about which a juror can competently testify); United States v. Swinton, 75 F.3d 374 (8th Cir. 1996) (court noted that the fact that one juror had informed the others that the defendant had a criminal record was extraneous prejudicial information, allowing another juror to testify to that fact, although ultimately the court found that the juror's statement was harmless).

[11] Rule 606, Advisory Committee Note.

[12] *E.g.,* Remmer v. United States, 347 U.S. 227, 229 (1954) ("any private communication, contact, or tampering, directly or indirectly" is presumptively prejudicial); Herring v. Blankenship, 662 F. Supp. 557 (W.D. Va. 1987) (juror received anonymous phone calls promising him favors if defendant were convicted; he was found competent to impeach verdict).

prove a juror was influenced by knowledge improperly obtained through extrinsic evidence such as books[14] or the news media.[15] Unauthorized views,[16] investigations,[17] or experiments[18] may be disclosed through juror testimony. Prejudicial conversations with parties,[19] witnesses,[20] or officers of the court[21] are also admissible.

---

[13] *E.g.,* Stimack v. Texas, 548 F.2d 588 (5th Cir. 1977) (jurors received phone calls from someone identifying himself as defense counsel and stating that jurors would be killed by Mafia if guilty verdict returned; grant of habeas corpus relief affirmed). *But cf.* Government of Virgin Islands v. Gereau, 523 F.2d 140 (3d Cir. 1975) (rumors of other killings and of FBI investigation would not constitute coercive force).

[14] United States v. Vasquez, 597 F.2d 192 (9th Cir. 1979).

[15] Marshall v. United States, 360 U.S. 310 (1959); United States v. Bruscino, 662 F.2d 450 (7th Cir. 1981), *rev'd on other grounds,* 687 F.2d 938 (7th Cir. 1982); Bulger v. McClay, 575 F.2d 407 (2d Cir. 1978) (where specific facts enter without appropriate safeguards, the constitutional role of jury is undermined).

[16] United States v. Simpson, 950 F.2d 1519 (10th Cir. 1991) (effect of jury of seeing coconspirator defendant in handcuffs held to be inconsequential); United States ex rel. De Lucia v. McMann, 373 F.2d 759 (2d Cir. 1967); Kilgore v. Greyhound Corp., Southern Greyhound Lines, 30 F.R.D. 385 (E.D. Tenn. 1962) (court held hearing to determine whether juror had visited scene of accident while trial was in progress; no prejudice since foreman stopped him from relating his experience to other jurors).

[17] Gafford v. Warden, U.S. Penitentiary, 434 F.2d 318 (10th Cir. 1970) (affidavit by one juror, to the effect that one or more others had checked the time a late show ended, and that a juror went to a gas station to determine whether it was open at a time stated by a witness, established grounds for a hearing to determine whether conviction of defendant violated Sixth Amendment rights to an impartial jury and to confront witnesses).

[18] *In re* Beverly Hills Fire Litigation, 695 F.2d 207 (6th Cir. 1982) (a new trial was required in action against aluminum wiring manufacturers in regard to a night club fire that killed 165 persons where a juror experimented with his own wiring and reported the results to the jury); United States v. Beach, 296 F.2d 153 (4th Cir. 1961) (appellate court remanded and ordered trial court to inquire whether jury had conducted experiments in jury room concerning conflict in testimony as to audibility of adding machines); *see also* United States v. Castello, 526 F. Supp. 847 (W.D. Tex. 1981); Simon v. Kuhlman, 488 F. Supp. 59 (S.D.N.Y. 1979).

[19] *See* United States v. Best, 939 F.2d 425 (7th Cir. 1991) (there was no prejudicial error in allowing the jury to use the government's evidence binders because they only contained copies of admissible evidence, and the jury did not rely on them to the exclusion of the other evidence); Leger v. Westinghouse Elec. Corp., 483 F.2d 428 (5th Cir. 1973) (where representative of defendant had deliberate conversations with juror, jury verdict set aside); Washington Gas Light Co. v. Connolly, 214 F.2d 254 (D.C. Cir. 1954) (appellate court ordered judge to decide issue of prejudice where juror called defendant gas company and sought advice as to functioning of furnace).

[20] *E.g.,* United States v. Pittman, 449 F.2d 1284 (9th Cir. 1971).

[21] United States v. United States Gypsum Co., 438 U.S. 422 (1978); United States v. Greer, 620 F.2d 1383 (10th Cir. 1980). *But see* Abatino v. United States, 750 F.2d 1442 (9th Cir. 1985) (juror's post-verdict statement that some jurors agreed to guilty verdict grudgingly because judge had indicated on Friday that he had another case to try on Monday was "incompetent"; the court noted that the jury poll showed unanimity).

But apart from those special and exceptional situations, the rule generally bars virtually all other kinds of post-judgment juror testimony on matters that were internal to the jury's deliberations. In the leading case of *Tanner v. United States,*[22] the Supreme Court held that this rule barred post-trial juror testimony that some of the jurors consumed alcohol and illegal substances during a criminal trial. The Court reasoned that such substances, even if they may have adversely affected the jurors' reasoning ability, were not an "external influence" like a bribe or a threat, but were more properly analogized to "allegations of a juror's inability to hear or comprehend at trial" or allegations of "physical or mental incompetence,"[23] which would also be inadmissible under this rule.[24] In keeping with that logic, the federal courts have applied Rule 606(b) to exclude evidence that one or more jurors misunderstood the consequences of the sentence they imposed upon the accused,[25] harbored racial prejudice toward the accused,[26] consulted a Bible during deliberations,[27] brought notes from home taken during the course of the trial,[28] improperly speculated as to why one codefendant suddenly

---

[22]   Tanner v. United States, 483 U.S. 107 (1987).

[23]   *Tanner,* 483 U.S. at 118 ("Courts wisely have treated allegations of a juror's inability to hear or comprehend at trial as an internal matter.")

[24]   In reaching this conclusion, the Court noted its approval of a number of lower court cases that had barred testimony offered to show that a juror was insane, failed to hear the instructions of the trial judge, suffered from a hearing impairment, or did not speak English. *Id.* (collecting cases). The Court also approvingly cited cases excluding evidence that "one or more jurors was inattentive during trial or deliberations, sleeping or thinking about other matters." *Tanner,* 483 U.S. at 121.

[25]   United States v. Jackson, 549 F.3d 963 (5th Cir. 2008) (jurors were not competent to testify that they mistakenly believed the accused would still be eligible for release after they sentenced him to life in prison); United States v. Johnson, 495 F.3d 951, 981 (8th Cir. 2007) (on motion for new trial by prisoner sentenced to death, district court could not consider admission by one juror that he was told by his son in prison, and explained to the other jurors, that the accused "would have three automatic appeals" and that the jury's verdict would merely "set the stage" for those appeals).

[26]   United States v. Benally, 546 F.3d 1230 (10th Cir. 2008) (trial court could not consider post-verdict juror affidavits reporting that some jurors harbored racial prejudice toward the accused and other Native Americans, and that they expressed a desire to "send a message" to others at the reservation).

[27]   Robinson v. Polk, 438 F.3d 350, 363–364 (4th Cir. 2006) ("Unlike [communications with outsiders], which impose pressure upon a juror apart from the juror himself, the reading of Bible passages invites the listener to examine his or her own conscience from within. In this way, the Bible is not an 'external' influence. In addition, reading the Bible is analogous to the situation where a juror quotes the Bible from memory, which assuredly would not be considered an improper influence.")

[28]   United States v. Connolly, 341 F.3d 16 (1st Cir. 2003) (the writing of notes by jurors at home about the day's testimony was not inconsistent with the court's instruction not to take notes during the testimony; If the notes actually made their way to the jury room during deliberation, they could not be considered an "extraneous" or "extrinsic" influence).

vanished from the trial,[29] drew an impermissible inference of guilt from the defendant's failure to testify,[30] slept through a trial,[31] developed a romantic interest in a witness,[32] disobeyed the judge's instructions during deliberations,[33] desired to reopen their deliberations,[34] felt intimidated by other jurors,[35] or began deliberating prematurely.[36] Also inadmissible is evidence that the jurors who sentenced a man to death had been very close to

---

[29] United States v. Bussell, 414 F.3d 1048, 1055 (9th Cir. 2005) (after one defendant fell to his death from hotel room in a possible suicide during the trial and judge instructed jurors to not speculate about the reasons for his sudden disappearance from the case, post-trial juror statements were not admissible to prove that some jurors erroneously speculated that he might have pled guilty).

[30] U.S. v. Wettstain, 618 F.3d 577 (6th Cir. 2010) (district judge properly refused to grant a new trial based on a letter from a juror who regretted voting to convict because he thought the decision of the defendants to not take the stand in their own defense "made them look guilty," and he later realized that he should not have assumed this, and because one of the two "was never found with anything").

[31] United States v. Sherrill, 388 F.3d 535 (6th Cir. 2004) (district court properly denied defendant's post-verdict request to interview members of the jury to verify a report that a member of the jury slept through the trial).

[32] United States v. Smith, 424 F.3d 992, 1013 (9th Cir. 2005) (even if a juror's "thought process was biased with his alleged 'infatuation' with Agent O'Keeffe, the court was not free to hear evidence in this regard" under Rule 606(b)).

[33] United States v. Rutherford, 371 F.3d 634 (9th Cir. 2004) (on a motion for a new trial, affidavits from jurors were not admissible to show that the jury ignored the court's instructions by discussing the defendant's failure to testify).

[34] United States v. Stover, 329 F.3d 859 (D.C. Cir. 2003) (after a jury returned a unanimous and final verdict as to one defendant and continued deliberating on charges against another, the court properly denied a request five days later from several jurors to reopen deliberations on charges against the first. Rule 606(b) precludes testimony from jurors "regarding their belated misgivings").

[35] Matthew v. Unum Life Ins. Co. of America, 639 F.3d 857 (8th Cir. 2011) (forbidding consideration of a post-trial communication to the court from a juror who expressed doubts about the accuracy of the jury's damages calculations "and reported feeling pressured by other jurors to accept [those] calculations"); U.S. v. Wettstain, 618 F.3d 577 (6th Cir. 2010) (on motion for a new trial, the judge properly refused to consider a statement from a juror who regretted their decision and who claimed the other jurors voted for a guilty verdict "simply [because they] wanted to hurry it up and get it over with"); United States v. McGhee, 532 F.3d 733 (8th Cir. 2008) (belated post-verdict complaints of intimidation by other jurors are not admissible); Estrada v. Scribner, 512 F.3d 1227 (9th Cir. 2008) (affidavits from two jurors claiming they were treated disrespectfully by other jurors and were pressured into issuing a guilty verdict were not admissible on defendant's motion for a new trial, and impermissibly presented the two jurors' subjective mental processes); United States v. Lakhani, 480 F.3d 171 (3d Cir. 2007) (a juror's claim that she acceded to a guilty verdict because of intimidation from other jurors is not a basis for inquiring into the validity of the verdict, because the juror had multiple opportunities to raise the issue with the judge);United States v. Briggs, 291 F.3d 958 (7th Cir. 2002) (this rule required trial judge to deny motion challenging guilty verdict on the basis of post-trial statement by a juror that she was "intimidated" by the others into voting guilty, where her statement confirmed that she had not been the subject of physical threats or influences by anyone outside the jury).

recommending life in prison.[37] Pre-rules case law declared jurors incompetent to show an improper compromise verdict[38] or a quotient verdict,[39] and the rule was intended to codify those cases.[40]

Under a recent amendment to Rule 606(b)(2), juror testimony is also permitted as to "whether there was a mistake in entering the verdict onto the verdict form."[41] It is still true, as one court stated years ago, that "cases to which this exception applies are few and far between."[42] The exception is narrowly limited to a clerical mistake in recording the jurors' agreement, and does not apply to the many cases in which jurors later claim that they were operating under some sort of mistake about what the law dictated as to the implications of their verdict. Thus, post-verdict jury testimony is allowed on "the verdict's accuracy in capturing what the jurors had agreed upon," such as whether, for example, the jury foreperson "wrote down, in response to an interrogatory, a number different from that agreed upon by the jury."[43] But such evidence would not be allowed as to whether "the jurors were operating under a misunderstanding about the consequences of the result that they agreed upon," because "an inquiry into whether the jury misunderstood or misapplied an instruction goes to the jurors' mental processes underlying the verdict."[44] This distinction should be easy for the courts to follow in most

---

[36] United States v. Logan, 250 F.3d 350 (6th Cir. 2001) (denial of defendants' motion for permission to interview jurors following allegations of juror misconduct was not erroneous; premature jury deliberations occurring during the course of a trial are internal influences on a jury that may not be challenged post-verdict).

[37] Beardslee v. Woodford, 327 F.3d 799 (9th Cir. 2003) (in federal habeas corpus proceeding brought by convicted murderer on death row, federal court could not consider affidavits signed by two jurors attesting that the jury was very close to recommending life in prison and would have done so if the accused could receive therapy in prison, even though the affidavits were "emotionally compelling").

[38] Hyde v. United States, 225 U.S. 347, 382 (1912) (after jurors were allegedly deadlocked between those who thought all defendants were guilty and those who thought they were all innocent, jurors were not competent to later testify that they agreed to break the deadlock by bartering votes and agreeing to convict some and acquit others).

[39] McDonald v. Pless, 238 U.S. 264 (1915) (although it would be "arbitrary and unjust" if twelve jurors agreed to simply add up the numbers each thought plaintiff should receive and divide the total by twelve, jurors were not competent to reveal the existence of such an arrangement after the verdict was returned).

[40] *See* Committee Note to Rule 606(b).

[41] This language was added to the Rule by an amendment in 2006, but the change largely codified the law as it stood in most circuits prior to the amendment.

[42] United States v. Dotson, 817 F.2d 1127, 1130, *amended on other grounds,* 821 F.2d 1034 (5th Cir. 1987).

[43] Advisory Committee Notes to the 2006 amendment to Rule 606 (citations omitted).

[44] Advisory Committee Notes to the 2006 amendment to Rule 606; Craig Outdoor Advertising, Inc. v. Viacom Outdoor, Inc., 528 F.3d 1001 (8th Cir. 2008) (where special verdict form asked jurors to award damages on different legal theories but did not ask jurors

cases, although there will be some close cases where the line between those two categories will be difficult to draw with confidence. It is most unclear, for example, how this exception will apply to juror testimony about an alleged mathematical error committed by the jury in calculating sums of numbers.[45]

There is also a regrettable ambiguity in a line from the Committee Notes stating that this new rules change will also apply to cases in which a jury foreperson "mistakenly stated that the defendant was 'guilty' when the jury had actually agreed that the defendant was not guilty."[46] That language could easily be interpreted as applying to the tragically frequent cases in which jurors claim they agreed that the defendant was *not* guilty beyond a reasonable doubt, but also agreed to report to the court that he *was* guilty (for example, to punish him for prior crimes), and only later realized that their verdict had been a terrible "mistake" that they wanted the court to correct.[47]

---

to report the total amounts awarded to each plaintiff, post-verdict affidavits obtained "from each juror" that "purport[ed] to explain what the jury meant by its verdict and how the jury determined what numbers to transcribe onto the verdict forms" could not be characterized as "clerical error" and were therefore not admissible).

[45] For example, one jury reportedly filled out its verdict form in a way that ordered a defendant to pay $1 million to each of his 1,800 alleged victims for a total of nearly $1.8 billion, although jurors reportedly later said that "the verdict was a mistake and that they actually meant to award $1 million total." Josh Grossberg, DAILY BREEZE, *Beach House Giveaway Figure Files Bankruptcy*, 2005 WLNR 17010514 (Oct. 20, 2005). In another case, the jurors admitted that the numbers on the verdict form accurately reflected the amounts to which they had agreed as to each individual line on the form, but claimed that they arrived at those numbers only through a mathematical miscalculation that (they later learned) added up to only 10% of what they had agreed to award the plaintiff. TeeVee Toons, Inc. v. MP3.Com, Inc., 148 F. Supp. 2d 276, 278 (S.D.N.Y. 2001) (tragically, the jurors agreed to reach a total verdict of about $3 million, but trusted the division of that total, into about 145 separate figures, to one juror who did so on her palm pilot calculator). It is not plain whether these kinds of "mathematical mistakes" would be admissible under the new rule. Reasonable minds will disagree as to whether these cases involve (in the words of the amended rule) a "mistake in entering the verdict onto the verdict form" and (in the words of the Committee Notes) a dispute as to whether the verdict form accurately captured "the *number . . .* agreed upon by the jury." Or do they merely involve what the Committee Notes call jurors "operating under a misunderstanding about the consequences of the *result* that they agreed upon," which would make them incompetent to testify to such things? It all depends, of course, on which "number" and which "agreement" you focus on: (1) the jurors' agreement as to the total amount the defendant should pay, or (2) their agreement as to what numbers the foreperson should write on each line of the verdict form? It is easy to find cases like these where jurors deny that the verdict form accurately reflected the former agreement but admit that it correctly captured the latter. Will such testimony now be admissible in federal court? Reasonable minds will disagree, but no honest observer can say that one answer is clearly dictated by the new rule or its Committee Notes.

[46] Committee Notes to the 2006 amendment to Rule 606 (citation omitted).

[47] *E.g.*, Bill Sizemore, *Ex-Seal Trainee Gets Boost in Bid for Pardon*, THE VIRGINIA PILOT, 2005 WLNR 7291753 (May 7, 2005) (after jury convicted a man of murder and sentenced him to 82 years in prison, the foreperson claimed that a majority of the jurors

If the new exception is read that broadly, as this line from the Committee Notes arguably suggests, it will take a huge and probably unintended bite out of Rule 606(b). It is much more likely that the Committee's unfortunate example was only intended to refer to the much less common situation of a foreperson who somehow made the clerical error of inaccurately recording that the jury found the defendant *guilty* even though the jurors had actually agreed and intended to tell the judge that the defendant was *not* guilty, and even though this amazing scrivener's error somehow went undetected when the verdict was read aloud by the judge in the presence of all the jurors and the defendant. Needless to say, that happens with extraordinary rarity, probably once every quarter of a century, and only in cases involving a fairly large number of counts in the indictment.[48]

§ 606.4   Procedure in Determining Juror Misconduct

Before investigating possible juror misconduct or attempting to gather affidavits that might be admissible under this rule, lawyers must take great care to comply with local rules governing such contact. A great number of federal district courts have now adopted local rules requiring court approval before trial lawyers may engage in or initiate post-trial contact with jurors for any reason. Any juror affidavits that are obtained in violation of those local rules may be excluded by the judge on that ground alone, regardless of whether they might have otherwise been admissible under an exception to this rule.[49]

While Rule 606(b) does not expressly establish a minimum showing of sufficiency that must be established before a judge will investigate a claim of jury misconduct, it is clear that the moving party must demonstrate that the tendered testimony is admissible under 606(b)(2).[50] Once this is

---

believed that he was innocent of the murder but should be somehow punished for his other criminal conduct); *Convictions of Florida Boys Tossed*, CHARLESTON GAZETTE, 2002 WLNR 1041687 (Oct. 18, 2002) (after convicting two young men of murdering their father, jury forewoman reported that "we never thought that these boys committed the crime," but decided to convict them so the children could be "taken somewhere where they could have a new life and learn to be productive citizens").

[48] *See, e.g.,* United States v. Dotson, 817 F.2d 1127, 1130, *amended on other grounds,* 821 F.2d 1034 (5th Cir. 1987) (court permitted to correct verdict where the announced verdict convicted defendant on ten counts but later telephone calls between jurors and judge revealed that the jury intended to acquit on the tenth count).

[49] Cuevas v. United States, 317 F.3d 751 (7th Cir. 2003) (on motion to set aside conviction based on allegations of juror misconduct uncovered during post-trial juror interviews, the district court did not abuse its discretion in refusing to consider the evidence as a sanction for defendant's violation of a local rule requiring court approval before post-trial contact with jurors, as required by most of the 94 federal district courts, thus rendering moot whether the evidence would have been admissible under Rule 606(b)).

[50] *See generally,* 3 WEINSTEIN'S FEDERAL EVIDENCE § 606.05; 3 MUELLER & KIRKPATRICK, §§ 251–253; United States v. Prosperi, 201 F.3d 1335 (11th Cir. 2000) (in a telephone call from a sitting juror to an excused alternate, the alternate advised the juror to withstand

established, the court should investigate the claim however insufficient this evidence may be standing alone.[51]

Even if juror testimony reveals that the jury was exposed to an improper outside influence or extraneous information, thus making such evidence admissible under Rule 606(b)(2), jurors may only disclose the nature of those factors and how many jurors were exposed to them. A juror may not testify as to "the effect of anything upon that juror's or another juror's vote; or any juror's mental processes concerning the verdict or indictment."[52] In cases of alleged jury tampering, some circuits will allow the jurors to disclose whether they felt "fear or anxiety" to help the judge decide whether the misconduct was objectively likely to have affected the verdict, but even those courts will not allow that juror to testify about her mental process in reaching the verdict or to directly disclose whether she thought the threats or her fear affected her vote or the verdict.[53] The judge is limited to determining whether the misconduct occurred and the number of jurors exposed to the misconduct.[54] Based on these facts, the court should apply an

---

the pressures from the other jurors to alter her vote and informed defense counsel about the call; the trial court properly investigated by talking to the alternate, but no hearing was held or necessary, in the absence of evidence of outside influences on the jury; the court did not abuse its discretion in failing to further investigate allegations of misconduct "entirely endemic to the deliberations").

[51] *See* Hard v. Burlington N. R.R., 812 F.2d 482 (9th Cir. 1987) (trial court erred in not holding evidentiary hearing where juror affidavit indicated he had lied on voir dire); Sullivan v. Fogg, 613 F.2d 465 (2d Cir. 1980); Tobias v. Smith, 468 F. Supp. 1287 (W.D.N.Y. 1979); United States v. Parker, 549 F.2d 998 (5th Cir. 1977); United States v. Doe, 513 F.2d 709 (1st Cir. 1975).

[52] Rule 606(b); *see* Fields v. Brown, 431 F.3d 1186, 1207 (9th Cir. 2005) ("Juror testimony about consideration of extrinsic evidence may be considered by a reviewing court, but juror testimony about the subjective effect of evidence on the particular juror or about the deliberative process may not"); Fullwood v. Lee, 290 F.3d 663 (4th Cir. 2002) (jurors may reveal that they were exposed to extraneous prejudicial information or any outside influence, but may not testify concerning the effect of the outside communication on the minds of the jurors. Thus, in habeas corpus action brought by convicted murderer, district court could consider evidence from a juror revealing that the jury had improperly learned from an outside source that the accused had already been sentenced to death for the same murder at an earlier trial; court could also consider juror's testimony that another juror was exposed to the influence of a husband who was "constantly telling her during the trial and during deliberations that she should convict him and sentence him to death," but could not consider the portion of the affidavit opining that the other juror "was strongly influenced" by her husband or that his pressure "caused her to vote" as she did).

[53] United States v. Elias, 269 F.3d 1003 (9th Cir. 2001) (testimony regarding a juror's "general fear or anxiety" following an incident of jury tampering is admissible to assist the court in determining whether outside influences were *objectively* likely to have improperly affected the verdict, although that juror may not testify to her opinion as to whether that fear affected her vote, nor on any other aspect of the jurors' mental process in reaching their verdict).

[54] 3 MUELLER & KIRKPATRICK, § 254; United States v. Greer, 620 F.2d 1383 (10th Cir.

objective evaluation to infer whether a prejudicial effect has occurred.[55]

§ 606.5   Affidavits and Other Evidence of Juror's Statements Competent Only to the Extent Testimony Is Competent

Where a juror's testimony would be inadmissible on an inquiry into a verdict, the juror's affidavit is likewise inadmissible even if it is offered by some other party. For example, where a party makes a motion for a new trial alleging juror misconduct, and attaches an affidavit of a juror in support of this motion, the court may not consider the affidavit unless the testimony of that same juror would be admissible under Rule 606(b)(2). Similarly, the affidavit or testimony of a third person, such as a friend or spouse, concerning a juror's out-of-court statements may not be considered, unless this third person has firsthand knowledge of the offending conduct.

1980); United States v. Howard, 506 F.2d 865 (5th Cir. 1975).

[55] 3 WEINSTEIN'S FEDERAL EVIDENCE § 606.05. *See, e.g.,* Sassounian v. Roe, 230 F.3d 1097 (9th Cir. 2000) (though the subjective effect of extrinsic evidence improperly introduced into jury deliberations could not be considered by the reviewing court, there was no doubt the improper evidence prejudiced the defendant when, after fifteen days of deliberation, the previously hung jury quickly came to agreement on the special circumstances surrounding a verdict). Wilson v. Vermont Castings, Inc., 170 F.3d 391 (3d Cir. 1999) (scope of court's inquiry into verdict is limited to existence of extraneous prejudicial information and the impact of such information on a reasonable juror, not the subjective effect on the actual jurors).

Chapter 607

Rule 607. Who May Impeach a Witness

Rule 607. Who May Impeach a Witness

Any party, including the party that called the witness, may attack the witness's credibility.

---

§ 607.1 Impeachment — In General

Rule 607 provides that any party may attack the credibility of a witness, including the party who called the witness to testify.[1] Rule 607 departs from the common-law tradition, sometimes known as the "voucher rule," that prevented a party from impeaching its own witness.[2]

Rule 607 does not limit or identify the techniques by which a party may impeach a witness. Its primary purpose, rather, is to abandon all pre-existing constraints imposed upon a party in regard to impeaching a witness that party has called to testify.[3] The voucher rule had previously been the subject of reform and erosion, and in certain recognized contexts, pre-Rule law permitted a party to impeach its own witness.[4] The most commonly encountered situation under pre-Rule practice where a party was permitted to attack the credibility of its own witness was under the so-called "surprise"

---

[1] *See generally,* 1 McCormick, §§ 43–50; 4 Weinstein's Federal Evidence §§ 607.01–607.10; 3 Mueller & Kirkpatrick, §§ 256–259; 3A Wigmore, §§ 896–918. *See also* Moss, *The Sweeping-Claims Exception to the Federal Rules of Evidence,* 1982 Duke L.J. 61 (1982); Note, *The Fifth Amendment and a Defendant's Pre-Arrest Failure to Come Forward: The Sounds of Silence,* 46 Alb. L. Rev. 546 (1982); Comment, *Impeachment of Cross-Examination Response with Suppressed Evidence: United States v. Havens,* 48 Tenn. L. Rev. 721 (1981); Diamond, *Inherent Problems in the Use of Pretrial Hypnosis on a Prospective Witness,* 68 Calif. L. Rev. 313 (1980).

[2] *See* Advisory Committee Note, Rule 607.

[3] *E.g.,* 3 Mueller & Kirkpatrick, § 257; *see also* United States v. DeLillo, 620 F.2d 939 (2d Cir. 1980) (government entitled to question and impeach witness when testimony conflicts with other prosecution witness's account); United States v. Dennis, 625 F.2d 782 (8th Cir. 1980) ("surprise is no longer a prerequisite").

[4] *See* Advisory Committee Note, Rule 607; *see also* 3 Wigmore, §§ 896–918.

principle.[5] Under the surprise exception, a party was permitted to impeach its own witness where the witness's testimony was authentically unanticipated and affirmatively damaging to the party's case.[6] Other exceptions to the voucher rule also developed.[7]

The Federal Rules of Evidence do not treat impeachment with a comprehensive constellation of rules, and much of the law governing impeachment in federal courts is in the nature of federal common law.[8] Rules governing certain aspects of impeachment include: Rule 608 and 609 pertaining to the character, acts, and criminal convictions of witnesses; Rule 610 pertaining to evidence relating to religious belief; and Rule 613 pertaining to prior inconsistent statement impeachment (also known as "self-contradiction"). Consequently, many impeachment principles, such as those governing the exposure of witnesses' bias or interest, are left uncodified.

Traditionally, the law of evidence has recognized several specific techniques that might be used to diminish the credibility of witnesses: prior inconsistent statement impeachment (self-contradiction); contradiction; specific acts of dishonesty; criminal convictions; character impeachment (propensity for lack of veracity); and exposing bias (interest in the outcome), perceptual incapacity, or mental incapacity.[9] Some additional techniques, such as encouraging a witness to recant on cross-examination, defy specific categorization but are unquestionably permissible. All means of impeachment are essentially designed to accomplish the same fundamental objective of diminishing the credibility or believability of the witness. Nevertheless, the diminution in credibility is not exclusively directed to suggesting or demonstrating that the witness is purposefully deceitful. Other defects in the testimony may diminish accuracy and devalue the credibility of the witness.

---

[5] *See, e.g.,* United States v. Jordano, 521 F.2d 695, 697 (2d Cir. 1975) ("surprise, if a necessary element for impeachment at the time of trial, was a very modest element and was not to be construed as synonymous with amazement"); Ewing v. United States, 386 F.2d 10 (9th Cir. 1967) (impeachment allowed for surprise testimony); *see also* United States v. Budge, 359 F.2d 732 (7th Cir. 1966) (impeachment allowed for surprise testimony); Goings v. United States, 377 F.2d 753 (8th Cir. 1967) (impeachment not allowed where witness's surprise testimony was not harmful to his side); United States v. Hicks, 420 F.2d 814 (5th Cir. 1970) (acknowledging use of impeachment where witness surprises party offering him).

[6] *See, e.g.,* United States v. Budge, 359 F.2d 732 (7th Cir. 1966); Goings v. United States, 377 F.2d 753 (8th Cir. 1967).

[7] *See, e.g.,* United States v. Browne, 313 F.2d 197 (2d Cir. 1963) (judge, not counsel, calls the witness); Stevens v. United States, 256 F.2d 619 (9th Cir. 1958) (impeachment of a compulsory witness); Gaines v. United States, 349 F.2d 190 (D.C. Cir. 1965) (impeachment under the guise of refreshing the recollection of the witness). For additional examples, *see* 4 WEINSTEIN'S FEDERAL EVIDENCE § 607.05; 3A WIGMORE, §§ 907–908.

[8] *See* 4 WEINSTEIN'S FEDERAL EVIDENCE § 607.03.

[9] *See* 1 McCORMICK, § 33.

Accordingly, the law of evidence has traditionally recognized that in addition to exposing the insincerity of a witness, impeachment may also operate to show less purposeful flaws in the testimony, *i.e.*, defects in narration (the witness misspoke), defects in perception (the witness misperceived), and defects in memory (the witness forgot).[10] In light of Rule 402 governing relevance, any technique not prohibited by the Rules that rationally operates to expose one of these testimonial defects (sincerity, narration, perception, and memory) may be used to impeach a witness.

Certain impeachment techniques are discussed in conjunction with the specific rules that pertain to them.[11] Others, in regard to which there is no codification, are discussed later in this chapter.

§ 607.2   Policy of Rule 607 in Rejecting the Voucher Rule

At common law, the voucher rule was predicated upon the theory that by offering a witness, a party would thereby guarantee his trustworthiness; consequently, such party logically could not be permitted to challenge the witness's testimony or credibility.[12] Even at common law, however, several exceptions to the blanket proscription against impeaching one's own witness had developed.[13] Courts generally came to recognize that the implacable impediment erected by the voucher rule too often served to frustrate the search for the truth rather than aid it.[14] Courts increasingly recognized that the voucher rule was based upon invalid assumptions concerning the relationships between parties and their witnesses. The fact that a party calls a witness does not mean that the party has exercised complete freedom in selecting the witness to testify.[15] Except in regard to such witnesses as experts or character witnesses, the party's choice of witnesses is dictated almost entirely by the particular facts in dispute, and the party usually has no choice but to call to the stand those witnesses with personal knowledge of the relevant facts.[16] Accordingly, Rule 607 is the culmination of a well-reasoned trend to jettison the voucher rule.[17]

---

[10] United States v. Lindstrom, 698 F.2d 1154 (11th Cir. 1983) (error to limit cross-examination when witness had history of mental infirmities and aggressively manipulative conduct); *see also* 1 McCORMICK, § 44.

[11] *See* Chapters 608, 609, 610, and 613, *infra.*

[12] *See generally,* 4 WEINSTEIN'S FEDERAL EVIDENCE § 607.02; 3 MUELLER & KIRKPATRICK, § 258; 3A WIGMORE, §§ 896–918. "[E]xcept in a few instances such as character witnesses or expert witnesses, the party has little or no choice of witnesses." 1 McCORMICK, § 38, at 126.

[13] *See* § 607.1, *supra.*

[14] 4 WEINSTEIN'S FEDERAL EVIDENCE § 607.02; 3 MUELLER & KIRKPATRICK, § 258; 1 McCORMICK, § 38; 3A WIGMORE, § 899.

[15] *See* 1 McCORMICK, § 38.

[16] *Id.*

[17] *See generally,* 4 WEINSTEIN'S FEDERAL EVIDENCE § 607.02; 3 MUELLER & KIRKPAT-

Some commentators have justifiably admonished, however, that abandonment of the voucher rule may have undesirable effects specifically in the context of prior inconsistent impeachment.[18] As the Federal Rules were originally proposed by the Supreme Court's Advisory Committee, all prior inconsistent statements of a witness were contemplated as admissible substantive evidence under Rule 801(d)(1)(A), a constituent rule of the hearsay scheme.[19] Nevertheless, Congress amended Rule 801(d)(1)(A) to provide that only prior inconsistent statements given under oath at a hearing, deposition, or formal proceeding could be considered as substantive evidence, *i.e.*, considered for the truth of their contents.[20] When Rule 607 was originally fashioned, it was contemplated that all prior inconsistent statements would be substantively admitted for their truth, and no abuse by a party impeaching its own witness could occur in the context of using a prior inconsistent statement to contradict the witness's testimony. Under the originally proposed version, all such statements would have been substantively admissible, and a party could not call a witness merely as a device for exposing to the jury a self-contradictory statement that was substantively inadmissible.[21] Under the adopted version of Rule 801(d)(1)(A), however,

---

RICK, § 258; 1 McCORMICK, § 38. *See also* Chambers v. Mississippi, 410 U.S. 284 (1973) (the voucher system as applied interfered with the defendant's constitutional rights under the confrontation clause; in that case, Chambers was the defendant in a murder case; another man had made several oral and one written confession to the crime that he repudiated in a preliminary hearing; Chambers' motion to cross-examine the witness as a hostile witness was denied; the court held that the voucher system interfered with his constitutional right to defend himself, because he was prevented from cross-examining the witness and was also restrained in his direct examination of the witness, because he would have been bound by any damaging statements made on direct examination).

[18] *See* 4 WEINSTEIN'S FEDERAL EVIDENCE § 607.02; 3 MUELLER & KIRKPATRICK, § 259. Most of the criticism is centered around the admission of prior inconsistent statements in cases similar to United States v. Morlang, 531 F.2d 183 (4th Cir. 1975). In that case, the defendant was indicted for bribery and attempted bribery. The government called as a witness a co-defendant who had entered a guilty plea to the charge. The government knew that the witness would not implicate the defendant with his direct testimony. On direct, the witness denied having had any conversations with a fellow prisoner that implicated the defendant in the crime charged. The government then called the prisoner to impeach the witness. The prisoner's testimony referred to statements of the witness that implicated the defendant. The appellate court reversed finding that the limiting instruction to use the prisoner's testimony only for the purpose of impeaching the witness was ineffective, and held that it was impermissible to call a witness a party knows will not testify to his advantage and then impeach the witness. Commentators generally agree with the appellate court's reversal of the conviction but not with its rationale. The question they raise is what is the outcome in cases where it is unclear if the party knew the witness would testify adversely. Judge Weinstein, for example, suggests Rule 403 be utilized to limit impeachment in this context. 4 WEINSTEIN'S FEDERAL EVIDENCE § 607.02.

[19] *See* the discussion of Rule 801, Chapter 801, *infra.*

[20] *See* Rule 801, Chapter 801, *infra.*

[21] *See* Advisory Committee Note, Rule 607.

this kind of abuse is conceivable if Rule 607 is applied indiscriminately. The abuse, to be fully understood, should be considered in conjunction with the description of prior inconsistent impeachment in the latter portion of this Treatise.[22] The problem specifically lies in the function of a limiting instruction that must accompany a witness's prior contradictory statement which, because it is otherwise inadmissible hearsay, must be limited to impeachment purposes.[23] In essence, the jury is instructed that it may not consider such a statement for its truth, but rather that it must consider the statement only for the purpose of evaluating the credibility of the witness who, because of conflicting versions of the same facts, cannot recount consistently.[24] For obvious reasons, the jury may decline to, or may not be able to, follow the instruction. Consequently, where some prior inconsistent statements may, and some may not, be considered substantively for their truth, impeaching one's own witness may be used as an artifice for exposing non-substantive prior inconsistent statements to the jury.

Control of this potential abuse is obviously placed in the trial judge. Most fundamentally, when a party seeks not to impeach, but rather to expose the jury to facts that it might misuse despite a limiting instruction, the latitude provided by Rule 607 is not apposite. Rule 607 pertains to "impeachment," and such misuse of prior inconsistent statements is not part of the process of "impeaching" one's own witness. The trial judge traditionally, as well as under the Rules, possesses inherent power to control any abuse of the principles of evidence. Such inherent authority is reflected in Rules 102, 403 and 611. In the section that follows, case law is analyzed that applies the inherent authority of the trial judge to avoid abuse of Rule 607 in the context of prior inconsistent statements.

§ 607.3 The Court's Power to Prohibit a Party from Impeaching Its Own Witness

Whenever an out-of-court inconsistent statement is offered solely for impeachment purposes and not as substantive evidence, there is a risk the jury will consider the statement for its truth even when it is accompanied by a limiting instruction from the trial judge. As discussed in the previous section, the problem is particularly acute in the context of a party impeaching its own witness. Reinforced by Rules 102 and 611, Rule 403 is properly applied in this situation to determine whether the use of the prior inconsistent statement to impeach the witness's credibility is substantially outweighed by the prejudicial impact that would result from the jury's potential improper use of the evidence.

When the court is asked to disallow a party's impeachment of a witness

---

[22] *See* Chapter 613, *infra.*

[23] *See* discussion of Rule 105, Chapter 105, *supra.*

[24] *See* Chapter 105, *supra,* and Chapter 613, *infra.*

under Rule 403, the court will consider the reliability and relevance of the offered evidence and to some degree the motivation of the party in impeaching its witness.[25] The reliability of the offered testimony will depend upon whether the witness has admitted making the prior inconsistent statement as well as the likelihood that the opponent of the witness will be able effectively to cross-examine the witness.[26]

The relevance of the impeachment evidence should be assessed in two ways: (1) the extent to which the evidence is probative of the witness's credibility, and (2) the danger of the evidence being used prejudicially as substantive evidence.[27] The court should also consider the effectiveness of a limiting instruction in avoiding improper use of the impeachment evidence.[28] If the relevance of the credibility evidence is low, and its potential prejudicial impact high, the court is justified in disallowing the impeachment of the witness.

Whether the party wishing to impeach its witness was surprised or damaged by the direct testimony may be considered in a Rule 403 balancing analysis.[29] Surprise is an indication that the impeachment request is not merely a device to allow the jury to consider a hearsay statement that is not substantively admissible under Rule 801. A finding by the court that the proponent of the impeachment has an improper motive may result in a denial

---

[25] *See, e.g.,* United States v. Grey Bear, 883 F.2d 1382 (8th Cir. 1989) (where a witness renounced prior to trial a statement he made to the FBI regarding a homicide, the government called the witness anyway, and the witness denied knowledge of the murder, impeachment of the witness's testimony with the statement made to the FBI was proper; the witness was not called for the purpose of circumventing the hearsay rule); Balogh's of Coral Gables, Inc. v. Getz, 798 F.2d 1356 (11th Cir. 1986) ("under Rule 607 a witness may not be called solely for the purpose of impeaching him and thereby obtaining otherwise inadmissible testimony"); United States v. Sebetich, 776 F.2d 412 (3d Cir. 1985) ("witnesses may not be called for the purposes of circumventing the hearsay rule by means of Rule 607").

[26] United States v. Rogers, 549 F.2d 490 (8th Cir. 1976) (proper to allow government to cross-examine its own witness concerning his prior statement that defendant had admitted guilt, even though witness denied that defendant had made any such admission and claimed memory lapse making cross-examination difficult); *see also* United States v. Robinson, 530 F.2d 1076 (D.C. Cir. 1976) (rebuttal testimony of witness shows that he was engaged in a criminal enterprise; must confront problem and weigh both prejudice and probative worth of impeachment in the spirit of balancing stressed in the Federal Rules).

[27] *See* United States v. Leslie, 542 F.2d 285 (5th Cir. 1976) (statement could be used even though it did not qualify as a prior inconsistent statement pursuant to Rule 801(d)(1), provided it satisfied the residual hearsay exception of Rule 803(24)).

[28] *See* United States v. DeLillo, 620 F.2d 939 (2d Cir. 1980). *Compare* Commonwealth v. Gee, 467 Pa. 123, 354 A.2d 875 (Pa. 1976).

[29] *See* Ordover, *Surprise! That Damaging Turncoat Witness Is Still With Us: An Analysis of Federal Rules of Evidence, 607, 801(d)(1)(A) and 403*, 5 HOFSTRA. L. REV. 65 (1976). *Compare* Parker v. United States, 363 A.2d 975 (D.C. App. 1976) (under D.C. Code surprise still required).

of the impeachment.[30]

§ 607.4   Impeachment by Exposure of Bias or Interest

The Federal Rules of Evidence do not specifically address when or how a party may impeach a witness by exposing a bias or interest of the witness. Consequently, case law continues to define the parameters of this type of impeachment.[31] When a party attempts to demonstrate a witness is biased or interested, it is relying on a theory of relevance premised on the fact that certain types of relationships may affect the witness's testimony, and consequently, the accuracy of the truthfinding process.[32] The exposure of potential bias or interest has always been considered highly relevant, and courts have been reluctant to hamper counsel's use of this impeachment technique.[33]

---

[30] *E.g.,* United States v. Miller, 664 F.2d 94 (5th Cir. 1981) (prosecutor's true purpose behind using inconsistent statement for impeachment was to present substantive evidence otherwise inadmissable); *see also* Whitehurst v. Wright, 592 F.2d 834 (5th Cir. 1979); United States v. Morlang, 531 F.2d 183 (4th Cir. 1975).

[31] *See* United States v. Lin, 101 F.3d 760 (D.C. Cir. 1996) (trial court did not err in precluding the defense attorney from questioning a witness about his involvement in a gambling business that was allegedly competing with the defendant's business; although the court recognized that the questioning might reveal bias, it found that the defendant had not provided an adequate foundation connecting the witness with the business to allow him to inquire into such a highly prejudicial matter).

[32] *See* 1 McCORMICK, § 39, at 130 ("Case law recognizes the slanting effect upon human testimony of the emotions or feelings of the witness toward the parties or the self-interest of the witness in the outcome of the case or in matters somehow related to the case"); *see also* 4 WEINSTEIN'S FEDERAL EVIDENCE § 607.04; Olden v. Kentucky, 488 U.S. 227 (1988) (after a prosecution witness testified that he heard the alleged rape victim cry out that she had been raped when she got out of the defendant's car, the accused was denied his rights under the Confrontation Clause when the trial judge precluded him from revealing that this seemingly "neutral" witness was the alleged victim's *lover,* which would have given her a possible motive to fabricate the crime to explain why she was getting out of another man's car late at night); United States v. Gorny, 732 F.2d 597 (7th Cir. 1984) (after defense tried to show innocent motives of government witness who had testified to dealings with the defendant, the government was permitted to impeach the witness's motives on redirect); Schledwitz v. United States, 169 F.3d 1003 (6th Cir. 1999) (where witness was presented at trial as a neutral, detached expert against a criminal defendant, the witness's involvement in the criminal investigation may be revealed to expose his potential bias).

[33] *See* United States v. Abel, 469 U.S. 45 (1984) (evidence revealing witness's and defendant's membership in organization having tenet to "commit perjury" admitted to show bias); *see also* United States v. Bratton, 875 F.2d 439 (5th Cir. 1989) (in a prosecution for aiding and abetting defendant's wife in the commission of wire fraud and for receiving stolen property, prosecution was permitted to impeach the wife's testimony that her husband was unaware of the crimes by introducing evidence that her testimony might have been motivated by fear of physical abuse from her husband; the 5th Circuit affirmed over objection that the evidence was unduly prejudicial under Rule 403, noting that bias is a highly relevant form of impeachment); United States v. Hankey, 203 F.3d 1160 (9th Cir. 2000) (trial court properly admitted gang expert's testimony that defense witness, who was member of defendant's gang,

Bias or interest may be proven by conduct or words of a witness.[34] Additionally, almost all types of relationships will facially establish some potential bias or interest. As Wigmore states, "The range of external circumstances from which probable bias may be inferred is infinite."[35]

The Rules of Evidence do not indicate whether there are foundation requirements that must be fulfilled before "extrinsic evidence" will be admitted to prove a witness's bias or interest. Extrinsic evidence is evidence offered to impeach the witness, offered after the witness sought to be impeached leaves the stand. For example, a party who wishes to prove a witness is the brother of the other party may choose to introduce other witnesses who will testify to the relationship. If instead the witness is on the stand, and counsel asks him about the relationship under question, and the witness concedes the relationship, the bias has been established by a means other than extrinsic proof. As the first example indicates, extrinsic proof uses substantial trial time to prove issues that may be objectively indisputable. Logic would dictate that some foundation should be required before allowing a party to impeach the witness through extrinsic evidence. Pre-Rule practice followed Wigmore's formula, that before a witness is impeached by extrinsic evidence of a prior statement indicating bias or interest, the witness should be asked the question and given the opportunity to confirm or deny

---

faced risk of beating or death if he testified against the defense); United States v. Manske, 186 F.3d 770 (7th Cir. 1999) (government witnesses' bias in favor of an accomplice who had pled guilty was a "quintessentially appropriate topic for cross-examination" by defense and should have been permitted because the bias of a witness is always probative). *But see* United States v. Williams, 875 F.2d 846 (11th Cir. 1989) (in a tax evasion prosecution, trial court did not abuse discretion in excluding evidence that a key prosecution witness had a longstanding love affair with a person engaged in litigation against the defendant); *see also* United States v. Weiss, 930 F.2d 185 (2d Cir. 1991) (trial judge properly exercised discretion in limiting defense cross-examination of prosecution witnesses to expose bias; once primary circumstances that produced bias were revealed, court had discretion to limit further questioning); United States v. Akitoye, 923 F.2d 221 (1st Cir. 1991) (prosecution asked defendant whether witness "had any reason to lie about" defendant; question was permissible to expose lack of bias).

[34] *See, e.g.,* United States v. Willis, 647 F.2d 54 (9th Cir. 1981); *see also* United States v. Nuccio, 373 F.2d 168 (2d Cir. 1967) (wrong to permit cross-examination on homosexuality merely to discredit, but not so as far as interrogation concerning repulsed homosexual advances to one of the defendants, since it went to witness's bias and motive); United States v. Diecidue, 603 F.2d 535 (5th Cir. 1979); United States v. Wright, 489 F.2d 1181 (D.C. Cir. 1973); Tinker v. United States, 417 F.2d 542 (D.C. Cir. 1969).

[35] 3A WIGMORE, § 949, at 784; *see, e.g.,* United States v. Abel, 469 U.S. 45 (1984) (evidence that rebuttal witness and defendant were in prison gang together was sufficient to show witness's bias towards defendant); United States v. Lawson, 683 F.2d 688 (2d Cir. 1982); United States v. Harris, 542 F.2d 1283 (7th Cir. 1977); 3A WIGMORE, § 949, at 784–786: ("Among the commoner sorts of circumstances [indicating bias] are all those involving some *intimate family relationship* to one of the parties . . . or some such relationship to a person, *other than a party*, who is involved on one . . . side of the litigation, or is otherwise prejudiced for or against one of the parties").

the statement.[36] Wigmore did not feel the same foundation was required if bias was to be proven by objective evidence of conduct.[37] Under the Wigmore formula a foundation was only necessary where impeachment was proven by a prior statement of the witness.

Rule 613(b) applies to the requirement of affording a witness the opportunity to explain or deny where "extrinsic evidence of a prior inconsistent statement by a witness's' is admitted.[38] The Rule by its terms does not extend to impeachment by bias or interest, but the policy of the Rule, however, is in agreement with the Wigmore model. Consequently, prior practice should be followed when impeachment is sought by showing bias or interest.[39] The Advisory Committee Note to Rule 613 indicates that when extrinsic evidence takes the form of biased conduct, the Rule is inapplicable.[40] This approach is consistent with the Wigmore rationale as well as prior practice.[41] The post-Rule practice should remain unchanged.

§ 607.5   Impeachment by Contradiction

An initial distinction must be made between impeachment by contradiction and impeachment through self-contradiction considered in conjunction with Rule 613. A simple illustration is helpful. A witness, X, testifies at trial that the truck that hit plaintiff was yellow. If opposing counsel wishes to establish X was wrong, he may proceed to contradict X in one of two ways. Counsel may either have another witness testify that he also saw the car and it was green or, alternately, counsel may choose to contradict X by introducing his deposition or statement (written or oral) in which he stated the car was green. When the second witness testifies the car was green, X has been "contradicted." When X's deposition or other statement is introduced, this is "self-contradiction" governed by Rule 613.

Impeachment by contradiction rests on a theory of relevance bottomed on

---

[36] 3A WIGMORE, § 953, at 801: ("the same reasons of fairness that require a witness to be given an opportunity of denying or explaining away a supposed self-contradictory utterance require him also to have a similar opportunity to deny or explain away a supposed utterance indicating bias"); *see* United States v. Hayutin, 398 F.2d 944 (2d Cir. 1968); Commer v. Pennsylvania R.R. Co., 323 F.2d 863 (2d Cir. 1963).

[37] 3A WIGMORE, § 953, at 802 n.2: It would be "erroneous to extend this rule to require prior inquiry as to an objective circumstance from which bias may be inferred."

[38] *See* Rule 613 and Chapter 613, *infra.*

[39] *See, e.g.,* United States v. DiNapoli, 557 F.2d 962 (2d Cir. 1977) (trial judge did not err in refusing to allow wife of government witness to testify about her husband's bias against defendant, where defense that had cross-examined husband for almost entire day failed to lay a foundation for the introduction of wife's evidence by bringing the alleged hostility to the witness's attention); United States v. Marzano, 537 F.2d 257 (7th Cir. 1976) (prejudice outweighed probative value of proffered impeaching testimony); *see also* 4 WEINSTEIN'S FEDERAL EVIDENCE § 607.04.

[40] *See* Advisory Committee Note, Rule 613.

[41] *See* 4 WEINSTEIN'S FEDERAL EVIDENCE § 607.04.

the inference that a witness whose testimony can be contradicted on specific issues is not to be believed as a whole.[42] The degree to which this impeachment technique will be effective depends upon the significance of the issue that is contradicted. Obviously, contradiction on a minor point will not have the same effect on the jury's presumption of the witness's credibility as would contradiction on a major issue.[43]

Impeachment by contradiction through extrinsic evidence can be time consuming or appear of exaggerated importance to the trier of fact.[44] Consequently, there has long been recognized a limitation on a party's right to contradict a witness by extrinsic evidence. Called the "collateral matter doctrine," this doctrine provides that a party may not present extrinsic evidence to contradict a witness on a so-called collateral matter.[45] This concept is sometimes expressed in the statement that where a witness testifies on cross-examination to a collateral matter, the questioner must "take the witness's answer," *i.e.,* the questioner may not disprove it by extrinsic evidence.[46] Substantive issues in the case are clear examples of issues that are not collateral; they are relevant to impeach a witness and are also admissible as substantive proof. Another category of non-collateral issues are facts that are offered to impeach the witness on an independent impeachment purpose that permits the use of extrinsic evidence, such as bias or interest, defective perception, or defective mental capacity.[47]

Judge Weinstein advocates the rejection of the collateral matter doctrine and suggests the trial courts should exclude extrinsic evidence where appropriate under Rule 403.[48] This change in analysis, however, should not frequently alter the ultimate admissibility or inadmissibility of evidence in a given situation. The avoidance of jury confusion and needless delay are both policies that underlie the collateral matter doctrine and issues to be considered in a balancing under Rule 403.

---

[42] *See* 1 McCORMICK, § 45.

[43] *See* United States v. Robinson, 544 F.2d 110 (2d Cir. 1976) (prosecution could properly attempt to impeach witness by proving that he had not received a check on the date that alibi witness claimed that he had picked up check while with defendant); United States v. Castillo, 181 F.3d 1129 (9th Cir. 1999) (after defendant in drug trafficking case took the stand and described himself as an anti-drug advocate who never used or touched drugs, the trial judge did not err in reversing his earlier decision and allowing the prosecution to call a rebuttal witness to tell about the defendant's 1997 arrest for possession of cocaine).

[44] *See, e.g.,* United States v. Harris, 542 F.2d 1283 (7th Cir. 1976) (no error to exclude evidence of prior sexual relationship where there was no indication how the witness's prior conduct would create bias); *see also* United States v. Jaqua, 485 F.2d 193 (5th Cir. 1973).

[45] Klein v. Keresey, 307 Mass. 51, 29 N.E.2d 703 (Mass. 1940).

[46] *See* 1 McCORMICK, § 45.

[47] 4 WEINSTEIN'S FEDERAL EVIDENCE § 607.06.

[48] *Id.*

§ 607.6   Impeachment by Demonstrating Defects in Mental Capacity or Perception

A witness may be mistaken in either perception or recollection of an event. In these situations, counsel may wish to impeach the witness by demonstrating a defect in the witness's narration or perception of the event. This type of impeachment is based upon the need to present accurate information to the jury,[49] and this same policy is reflected in Rule 602, which requires that every witness have firsthand knowledge of any event to which he or she testifies.[50]

When a party impeaches a witness and demonstrates a defect in the witness's ability to perceive or narrate an event, the party is not necessarily asserting the witness lacks firsthand knowledge of the event. The party is instead asserting that, for some reason, the witness testifying either did not correctly interpret what he or she saw, or is unable now to remember or testify accurately. Both Rules 602 and 607 attempt to ensure that only accurate information is presented to the jury.

Some types of perceptional defects may be demonstrated effectively through cross-examination or in-court experiment.[51] For example, the witness's memory may be tested by questions concerning circumstances connected or unconnected to the trial.[52] Additionally, in the trial judge's discretion, eyesight or hearing is easy to test by simple experiment in the courtroom. The extent to which extrinsic evidence will be admitted to prove a defect in narration or perception will be governed by the trial court's application of Rule 403.

When the testimonial defect arises because the witness was mentally incapable of perceiving the event, either because of mental disorder or through the use of drugs or alcohol, different problems arise. It has been suggested that the jury may not be able to assess accurately without the help of expert witnesses the effect a certain drug may have had on the ability of the witness to either accurately perceive the event in question or convey the information at trial.[53] Additionally, admitting evidence of drug or alcohol use by a witness may unfairly prejudice a party, particularly if the drug or

---

[49] United States v. Partin, 493 F.2d 750, 762 (5th Cir. 1974) ("It is just as reasonable that a jury be informed of a witness's mental incapacity at a time about which he proposes to testify as it would be for the jury to know that he then suffered an impairment of sight or hearing. It all goes to the ability to comprehend, know, and correctly relate the truth").

[50] *See* Rule 602 and Chapter 602, *supra.*

[51] *See, e.g.,* Battle v. United States, 345 F.2d 438 (D.C. Cir. 1955) (serious error in denying defense counsel the opportunity to cross-examine the witness respecting her eyesight, where identification of a man at night was the principal issue).

[52] *See* United States v. Hoffman, 415 F.2d 14 (7th Cir. 1969) (cross-examination permitted for testing witness's memory on solvency).

[53] 4 WEINSTEIN'S FEDERAL EVIDENCE § 607.05.

alcohol use could not in fact have influenced the witness's perception on the occasion in question.[54]

Most courts will admit evidence that the witness in question was intoxicated or drinking at the time the witness perceived the event.[55] While evidence of chronic alcoholism generally is not admitted,[56] Judge Weinstein believes that excluding evidence of chronic alcoholism is incorrect, because it ignores the long term physical effects the disease may have on the mental capacity of the alcoholic.[57]

There is no consistent rule under federal practice whether evidence of drug use will be admitted to impeach a witness. Some jurisdictions routinely allow evidence of drug use to be admitted without requiring a demonstration that the use of the drugs adversely affects the ability of the witness to testify.[58] The rationale of the court's following this practice is that drug use, like stealing, is indicative of dishonesty. Another group of cases requires the party wishing to admit the evidence to prove that the drug use impaired the witness's perception.[59] Some courts will admit the evidence assuming the jury can accurately assess the impact of the evidence of drug use as credibility.[60] This may, however, be a faulty conclusion given the fact that even experts cannot always agree on the impact of some drugs on the ability of the witness to perceive an event.[61]

When counsel wishes to introduce evidence of the use of a drug where there is no consensus on the impact of the drug on a witness's ability to perceive events, the court should take care to ascertain whether the conflicting expert testimony may be useful to the jury or result in a time-consuming digression. Rule 403 provides a vehicle to exclude evidence

---

[54] *Id.*

[55] *See* Rheaume v. Patterson, 289 F.2d 611 (2d Cir. 1961) (testimony that witness had been drinking during the morning and afternoon hours preceding the accident was relevant to witness's credibility); *see also* Dick v. Watonwan County, 562 F. Supp. 1083 (D. Minn. 1983), *rev'd on other grounds*, 738 F.2d 939 (8th Cir. 1984); Order of United Commercial Travelers v. Tripp, 63 F.2d 37 (10th Cir. 1933).

[56] Poppell v. United States, 418 F.2d 214 (5th Cir. 1969) (excluded testimony of a general reputation for intemperance was wholly unrelated to the ability of the witness to testify, and had no bearing on witness's veracity).

[57] 4 WEINSTEIN'S FEDERAL EVIDENCE § 607.05.

[58] United States v. Hoppe, 645 F.2d 630 (8th Cir. 1981); Guam v. Dela Rosa, 644 F.2d 1257 (9th Cir. 1980).

[59] *See, e.g.,* Kelly v. Maryland Casualty Co., 45 F.2d 782 (W.D. Va. 1938).

[60] *See, e.g.,* United States v. Jackson, 576 F.2d 46 (5th Cir. 1978) (court properly denied defense request for physical and mental examinations of witnesses, since it would infringe witness's privacy); *see also* United States v. Banks, 520 F.2d 627 (7th Cir. 1975); Gurleski v. United States, 405 F.2d 253 (5th Cir. 1968); United States v. Hicks, 389 F.2d 49 (3d Cir. 1968). *Compare* United States v. Cook, 608 F.2d 1175 (9th Cir. 1979).

[61] *See* 4 WEINSTEIN'S FEDERAL EVIDENCE § 607.05.

of questionable validity and possible prejudice to a party.[62] The proponent of such evidence should be able to demonstrate the relevance of the drug use on the witness's ability to perceive or narrate the event. The court should be advised of the dosage of drugs ingested, the impact of the drugs on the individual witness, the witness's past habit for ingesting drugs, and the time at which the witness took the drug in relation to the occurrence to which the witness is testifying.[63]

When a party wishes to establish the witness was mentally ill at the time he or she perceived the event, the question becomes whether psychiatric testimony may be admitted on the issue and whether a court can order the examination of the witness. Courts are reluctant to admit psychiatric evidence or order mental examinations because of the fear of testimony that is nonconclusive or confusing to the jury, and that results merely in a digression at trial.[64] Whether the evidence will be admitted or the examination ordered will depend upon the preliminary work of counsel in making a showing to the trial court. Counsel should demonstrate the type of mental illness suffered by the witness, the illnesses affecting the testimony or perception of the witness, and any prior history of mental illness, such as periods of prior commitment.[65] The court, of course, has discretion under Rule 403 to exclude the evidence if it is highly prejudicial, confusing or needlessly time consuming.[66]

---

[62] *See, e.g.,* United States v. Holman, 680 F.2d 1340 (11th Cir. 1982); *see also* United States v. Sampol, 636 F.2d 621 (D.C. Cir. 1980) (proffer that witness was under influence of drugs at time he witnessed events, but must be made outside hearing of jury where there was dubious basis for counsel's proffer). *Compare* United States v. James, 576 F.2d 1121 (5th Cir. 1978); United States v. Kizer, 569 F.2d 504 (9th Cir. 1978).

[63] *See* 4 WEINSTEIN'S FEDERAL EVIDENCE § 607.05.

[64] *See, e.g.,* United States v. Butt, 955 F.2d 77 (1st Cir. 1992) (absent a showing that a mental disorder affected credibility, no error would be found in disallowing impeachment from witness's mental hospital records); United States v. Provenzano, 688 F.2d 194 (3d Cir. 1982); United States v. Riley, 657 F.2d 1377 (8th Cir. 1981).

[65] *See* United States v. Lindstrom, 698 F.2d 1154 (11th Cir. 1983) (opposing counsel demonstrated witness's long history of mental disorder including periods of prior commitment to prevent witness from testifying); 4 WEINSTEIN'S FEDERAL EVIDENCE § 607.05.

[66] *See, e.g.,* United States v. Jackson, 576 F.2d 46 (5th Cir. 1978); United States v. Hughes, 411 F.2d 461 (2d Cir. 1969).

Chapter 608

Rule 608. A Witness's Character for Truthfulness or Untruthfulness

Rule 608. A Witness's Character for Truthfulness or Untruthfulness

(a) **Reputation or Opinion Evidence.** A witness's credibility may be attacked or supported by testimony about the witness's reputation for having a character for truthfulness or untruthfulness, or by testimony in the form of an opinion about that character. But evidence of truthful character is admissible only after the witness's character for truthfulness has been attacked.

(b) **Specific Instances of Conduct.** Except for a criminal conviction under Rule 609, extrinsic evidence is not admissible to prove specific instances of a witness's conduct in order to attack or support the witness's character for truthfulness. But the court may, on cross-examination, allow them to be inquired into if they are probative of the character for truthfulness or untruthfulness of:

   (1) the witness; or

   (2) another witness whose character the witness being cross-examined has testified about.

By testifying on another matter, a witness does not waive any privilege against self-incrimination for testimony that relates only to the witness's character for truthfulness.

---

§ 608.1 A Witness's Character for Truthfulness or Untruthfulness — In General

Rule 404(a), considered earlier in this Treatise, contains the general prohibition relating to the use of character evidence as a means of proving conforming conduct. Three exceptions, however, are set forth in Rule 404(a), which authorize the use of the character-conforming conduct inference in limited situations. Two of these exceptions are available in criminal cases; Rule 404(a)(2)(A) pertains to the character of the accused, and Rule 404(a)(2)(B) and Rule 404(a)(2)(C) pertain to the character of the victim. The third exception, Rule 404(a)(3), pertains to the character of a witness who takes the stand to testify, and this exception authorizes the use of the otherwise forbidden inferential pattern in regard to any witness who testifies in any suit, criminal or civil. Specifically, Rule 404(a)(3) authorizes the use of the character-conforming conduct inference as prescribed by Rules 607, 608 and 609.[1]

For reasons discussed in conjunction with Rule 404(a), character evidence has a tendency to arouse the emotions and prejudices of the trier of fact, and the use of character evidence is consequently attended by a substantial risk of a distortion of the fact-finding process. Accordingly, the use of character or propensity evidence as an inferential basis for establishing conduct consistent with the character trait or propensity is restricted to those situations delineated in the exceptions to Rule 404(a). Each exception reflects special policy considerations supporting the use of the otherwise prohibited inferential pattern.

The vast majority of evidence at most trials is admitted through the testimony of witnesses. Witnesses play a pivotal role in the fact-finding process of a trial, and, consequently, it is critical to the fact-finding process for litigants to be able to present impeachment or rehabilitation evidence regarding a witness's propensity to testify falsely or truthfully. In other words, there is a special need for evidence relating to a witness's character trait of veracity.

Rule 608 governs the use of character and conduct evidence for the purpose of impeaching the general character of a witness for honesty. The Rule applies to any witness, party or nonparty, and it applies in both civil and criminal cases. The Rule also governs the use of reputation and opinion evidence for rehabilitating a witness whose character for veracity has been impeached.

It must be emphasized that Evidence Rule 608 — just like Rules 609 and 610 — imposes certain limits upon the permissible method of cross-examination only when an attorney is attempting impeachment designed to show that the witness generally has a poor character for honesty or veracity.

---

[1] *See generally*, 1 McCORMICK, §§ 40–41; 4 WEINSTEIN'S FEDERAL EVIDENCE §§ 608.01–608.30; 3 MUELLER & KIRKPATRICK, §§ 260–272; 3 WIGMORE, §§ 977–988; 4 WIGMORE, §§ 1100–1144; 8 WIGMORE, § 2276. *See also* Hale, *Specific Acts and Related Matters as Affecting Credibility,* 1 HASTINGS L.J. 89 (1950); Ladd, *Techniques and Theory of Character Testimony,* 24 IOWA L. REV. 498 (1939); Noonan, *Inferences from the Invocation of the Privilege Against Self-Incrimination,* 41 VA. L. REV. 311 (1955); Note, *Expanding Double Jeopardy: Collateral Estoppel and the Evidentiary Use of Prior Crimes of Which the Defendant Has Been Acquitted,* 2 FLA. ST. U.L. REV. 511 (1974); Note, *Witnesses Under Rule VI of the Proposed Federal Rules of Evidence,* 15 WAYNE L. REV. 1236 (1969); Comment, *Procedural Protections of the Criminal Defendant—a Reevaluation of the Privilege Against Self-Incrimination and the Rule Excluding Evidence of Propensity to Commit Crime,* 78 HARV. L. REV. 426 (1964); Comment, *Use of Bad Character and Prior Convictions to Impeach a Defendant Witness,* 34 FORDHAM L. REV. 107 (1965).

As noted above, witnesses are often impeached through evidence that undermines the credibility of their testimony in ways that have nothing to do with their general propensity to tell the truth, such as evidence of bias, or defects in memory or perception.[2] Those other methods of impeachment are not restricted or regulated in any way by Rules 608 through 610, however. Those three rules only govern the admission of evidence about the general character of the witness for honesty or dishonesty, and not other matters that might tend to make the witness's testimony less credible in the particular case. This point is made plain enough by the repeated references in Rules 608(b) and 609(a) to the "character for truthfulness" of the witness being impeached under those rules.[3]

§ 608.2 Impeachment Through Opinion and Reputation Evidence of Character — In General

All witnesses who testify in any lawsuit are subject to impeachment by reputation and opinion evidence relating to their character for truthfulness.[4] This type of impeachment is presented through the testimony of character witnesses who have firsthand knowledge of the principal witness's reputation for truth and veracity in the community where they live or, in appropriate cases, in the business communities in which they operate.[5] Rule 608(a) also allows the character witness to testify in the form of personal opinion which, consistent with Rule 701, must be based on firsthand

---

[2] Chapter 607 of this Treatise, particularly § 607.1 (listing and distinguishing the most common traditional methods of impeaching the credibility of a witness).

[3] This pattern is the result of several recent amendments to those rules, which had previously referred to impeachment directed in any way to the "credibility" of the witness or her testimony. For a discussion of the background to these changes, *see* Duane, *The Proposed Amendments to FRE 608(b) and 804(b)(3): Two Great Ideas that Don't Go Far Enough*, 209 F.R.D. 235, 235–244 (2002).

[4] *E.g.,* United States v. Bruscino, 662 F.2d 450 (7th Cir. 1981); United States v. Rios, 611 F.2d 1335 (10th Cir. 1979); United States v. Mandel, 591 F.2d 1347 (4th Cir. 1979). *See generally,* 4 WEINSTEIN'S FEDERAL EVIDENCE §§ 608.20–608.22; 3 MUELLER & KIRKPAT-RICK, § 261; 3A WIGMORE, §§ 920–930.

[5] *E.g.,* United States v. Watson, 669 F.2d 1374 (11th Cir. 1982); *see also* United States v. Salazar, 425 F.2d 1284 (9th Cir. 1970) (where witness knew defendant "only through two months of occasional business dealings," this was insufficient foundation evidence to qualify him to testify to defendant's reputation for honesty and veracity); United States v. Augello, 452 F.2d 1135 (2d Cir. 1971) (where it was unclear that witness was a member of the communities in which defendant lived or worked, error to have admitted it as reputation testimony). *But see* United States v. Williams, 822 F.2d 512 (5th Cir. 1987) (in drug trafficking prosecution, court properly admitted testimony of government agents regarding defendant's reputation for truthfulness; prosecution was not required to establish extent of agents' knowledge where defendant failed to object to predicate that agents had investigated defendant thoroughly and worked in same neighborhood); United States v. Piccinonna, 885 F.2d 1529 (11th Cir. 1989) (trial court has discretion to admit polygraph evidence to impeach a witness's testimony if opposing party had adequate notice and a reasonable opportunity to conduct its own polygraph test).

knowledge.[6] The qualifications for an impeachment character witness are essentially the same as those for character witnesses under Rule 405.[7]

The character witness is called by the party seeking to impeach the primary witness, and the timing of the testimony of the character witness is determined by the impeaching party's next opportunity to call witnesses.[8] Consequently, a witness called by the plaintiff during its case-in-chief may be impeached by the defendant through a character witness called by the defendant during the case-in-defense. A witness called by defendant may be impeached by the plaintiff through a character witness called by the plaintiff during its case in rebuttal.

§ 608.3   Foundation as to Impeachment Character Witness's Knowledge

Prior to the character witness's testimony, a foundation must be elicited from the character witness that establishes the basis for the opinion or reputation testimony.[9] The foundation must demonstrate the character

---

[6] *See generally,* 4 WEINSTEIN'S FEDERAL EVIDENCE § 608.13; 3 MUELLER & KIRKPATRICK, § 261; 7 WIGMORE, §§ 1981–1986. *See also* Chapter 701, *infra.*

[7] *See, e.g.,* Michelson v. United States, 335 U.S. 469 (1948); United States v. Salazar, 425 F.2d 1284 (9th Cir. 1970); *see also* United States v. Augello, 452 F.2d 1135 (2d Cir. 1971) (witness's qualifications for knowing defendant had not been adequately established). *See also* United States v. Gonzalez-Maldonado, 115 F.3d 9 (1st Cir. 1997) (trial court erred in excluding a psychiatrist's testimony regarding the credibility of a conspirator whose conversations were tape-recorded and who was found incompetent to stand trial; the appellate court noted that, while there are limits on using expert testimony regarding credibility, there is no absolute bar to its use, and that such testimony was particularly relevant and important in a case such as this one where the jury cannot observe and evaluate the incompetent witness).

[8] United States v. Pacione, 950 F.2d 1348 (7th Cir. 1991) (the district court properly allowed opinion and reputation evidence of untruthfulness since it was given on direct examination); *see* United States v. Cylkouski, 556 F.2d 799 (6th Cir. 1977) (proper to rule that character witness could only testify after defendant testified and his truthfulness became an issue); *see also* United States v. Nace, 561 F.2d 763 (9th Cir. 1977) (where character witnesses lived in same community as principal witness for eight and 21 years respectively, both were adequate to testify as to reputation for truth and veracity of the principal witness).

[9] *E.g.,* United States v. Ruiz-Castro, 92 F.3d 1519 (10th Cir. 1996) (trial court did not err by not allowing the defendants to testify regarding the reputation of an undercover informant where they had "alleged no facts to suggest that they were personally acquainted or familiar with [the informant] or his alleged reputation for dishonesty"); United States v. Oliver, 492 F.2d 943 (8th Cir. 1974) (where character witnesses had been dormitory roommates of the complainant in rape case and had known her for seven weeks, error to exclude their testimony, since they were qualified to testify as to her truth and veracity); *see also* United States v. Salazar, 425 F.2d 1284 (9th Cir. 1970). *But see* United States v. Williams, 822 F.2d 512 (5th Cir. 1987) (in drug trafficking prosecution, court properly admitted testimony of government agents regarding defendant's reputation for truthfulness; prosecution was not required to establish extent of agents' knowledge where defendant failed to object to predicate that agents had investigated defendant thoroughly and worked in same neighborhood).

witness's familiarity with the primary witness's reputation, or in the alternative, where the character witness is to render an opinion as to the primary witness's veracity, the character witness's firsthand knowledge of the primary witness must be established. The familiarity with reputation, or knowledge of the person to be characterized, must pertain to a time period reasonably proximate to the trial testimony.[10]

§ 608.4 Substance of Impeachment Character Witness's Testimony

Rule 608 limits impeachment by character evidence to testimony regarding the principal witness's truth and veracity. The impeachment may not extend to an exploration of the primary witness's general character, and in this respect Rule 608 is generally consistent with pre-Rule law.[11] Rule 608 extends prior law, however, by permitting the use of opinion as well as reputation evidence in order to prove character, and consequently, Rule 608 is parallel to Rule 405.[12]

Rules 403 and 611 provide the trial judge with the inherent discretion to limit impeachment attacks through character evidence. Where the issue presented is whether the character witness is prepared to testify to the sufficiently distinct character trait of veracity, the trial court properly exercises its discretion when it excludes overly broad testimony as to general reputation for moral conduct.[13] The trial judge must ensure that the character witness is properly qualified to address the distinct character trait of veracity, *i.e.*, the propensity to tell the truth or to lie.

Under the Rule, character witnesses may not on direct examination testify to specific instances of conduct of the principal witness (the witness sought to be impeached). The testimony is restricted to the character witness's knowledge of the reputation, or opinion of the veracity, of the principal

---

[10] United States v. Watson, 669 F.2d 1374 (11th Cir. 1982) (noting that a long acquaintance with witness is not required for foundation for impeachment; merely recent but substantial familiarity is needed); United States v. Null, 415 F.2d 1178 (4th Cir. 1969).

[11] *E.g.,* United States v. Hedgcorth, 873 F.2d 1307 (9th Cir. 1989) (testimony excluded for attacking defendant's general character and not truthfulness); United States v. Greer, 643 F.2d 280 (5th Cir. 1981) (inquiry as to witness's general reputation not truth and veracity excluded); United States v. Walker, 313 F.2d 236 (6th Cir. 1963) (impeachment testimony must concern "truth and veracity," not general character); *see also* Salgado v. United States, 278 F.2d 830 (1st Cir. 1960).

[12] United States v. Lashmett, 965 F.2d 179 (7th Cir. 1992) (court declared that it was error for trial court to exclude opinion testimony concerning witness's truthfulness); United States v. Walker, 313 F.2d 236 (6th Cir. 1963); *see* United States v. Dotson, 799 F.2d 189 (5th Cir. 1986) (court states that Rule 608(a) makes clear that witnesses may state their opinions directly). *See generally.* 4 WEINSTEIN'S FEDERAL EVIDENCE § 608.13; 3 MUELLER & KIRKPATRICK, § 261. *See also* § 405.1, *supra*.

[13] *See* United States v. Herzberg, 558 F.2d 1219 (5th Cir. 1977) (trial court limited inquiry of defendant-witness to his reputation for "truthfulness" rather than "honesty and fair dealing").

witness.[14] Consistent with Rule 608(b)(2), however, the impeachment character witness may be cross-examined concerning specific instances of conduct of the primary witness.[15] Such specific instances must be probative of veracity.[16] While Rule 608(b)(2) is designed primarily to regulate the cross-examination of *rehabilitation* character witnesses, it simultaneously operates to authorize inquiry into acts reflective of truth-telling, *i.e.*, good acts probative of veracity where such acts are the subject of inquiry on cross-examination of an impeachment character witness. Accordingly, impeachment character witnesses may be asked on cross-examination whether they considered certain exemplary acts of the primary witness when formulating their direct examination testimony as to opinion or reputation.[17] From a tactical perspective, however, this inquiry should be undertaken with extreme caution because once the witness has been cross-examined about the basis of his direct examination testimony, further explanation may be authorized by the trial judge on redirect examination.

§ 608.5   Bolstering the Credibility of a Witness with Reputation and Opinion Evidence — When Authorized

Rule 608(a) provides that reputation and opinion evidence tending to establish the truthful propensity of any witness may be admitted only after the principal witness's *character* has in fact been attacked by opinion or reputation evidence or by other impeachment evidence that represents an attack on character.[18] The underlying theory provides that all witnesses under oath are presumed to be telling the truth and that the issue of a witness's truthfulness or credibility is collateral to the principal issues in the case.[19] While every witness's credibility is an issue for the trier of fact,[20] this does not, in the absence of an attack on character, authorize a party to bolster any witness through use of a character witness. The condition precedent for the use of a rehabilitation character witness is an attack on the *character* of the primary witness, and mere impeachment not involving the character of

---

[14] United States v. Nazarenus, 983 F.2d 1480 (8th Cir. 1993) (where defendant testified that he was driving fast to test adjustments to his car's alignment, admitting testimony from a witness that defendant frequently drove fast was a violation of Rule 608, but the resulting error was harmless); United States v. Mangiameli, 668 F.2d 1172 (10th Cir. 1982); United States v. Hoskins, 628 F.2d 295 (5th Cir. 1980) (no error to refuse to allow witness to give specific examples about why he doubted prosecution witness's honesty).

[15] *See generally,* 4 WEINSTEIN'S FEDERAL EVIDENCE § 608.23; 3 MUELLER & KIRKPATRICK, § 261.

[16] *See generally,* 4 WEINSTEIN'S FEDERAL EVIDENCE § 608.30; 3 MUELLER & KIRKPATRICK, § 266.

[17] 3 MUELLER & KIRKPATRICK, § 266.

[18] United States v. Mack, 643 F.2d 1119 (5th Cir. 1981); United States v. Solomon, 686 F.2d 863 (11th Cir. 1982); *see* Advisory Committee Note, Rule 608.

[19] 4 WEINSTEIN'S FEDERAL EVIDENCE §§ 608.11–608.12.

[20] *See, e.g.,* United States v. Angelini, 678 F.2d 380 (1st Cir. 1982).

the primary witness is insufficient to authorize the calling of a positive character witness.

A witness merely discredited by evidence of bias not involving corruption has not been subjected to *character* impeachment.[21] Also, where a prior inconsistent statement of a witness is introduced, where a witness is simply shown to be confused, or where a witness merely provides conflicting testimony, the witness's credibility may not be bolstered through a character witness attesting to the primary witness's good character for veracity.[22] By comparison, however, where impeachment is effected by a negative character witness pursuant to Rule 608(a), by interrogation as to acts probative of untruthful character under Rule 608(b), or by evidence of a criminal conviction under Rule 609, the *character* of the primary witness is, in fact, attacked and, therefore, may be rehabilitated with a positive character witness.[23] Beyond these presumptive attacks on character expressly addressed in the Rules, the careful discretion of the trial judge must be exercised on a case-by-case basis to determine whether the form of impeachment employed effectively operates as an attack on character.[24]

§ 608.6   Substance of Testimony from Rehabilitation Character Witness

Rehabilitation is accomplished by calling a character witness to testify to the truthful character of the impeached witness. The rehabilitation character witness is subject to the same rules governing impeachment character

---

[21] *See generally,* 4 WEINSTEIN'S FEDERAL EVIDENCE §§ 608.11–607.12; 3 MUELLER & KIRKPATRICK, § 269; 4 WIGMORE, § 1107.

[22] Stokes v. Delcambre, 710 F.2d 1120 (5th Cir. 1983); *see also* Homan v. United States, 279 F.2d 767 (8th Cir. 1960) (no right to introduce testimony in support of truthfulness unless it is an issue); Osborne v. United States, 542 F.2d 1015 (8th Cir. 1976).

[23] *See* United States v. Dotson, 799 F.2d 189 (5th Cir. 1986) (court states that "Rule 608(a) makes clear that witnesses may state their opinions directly"). *See generally,* 4 WEINSTEIN'S FEDERAL EVIDENCE §§ 608.11–608.12; 1 MCCORMICK, § 47.

[24] McCormick advocates a case-by-case evaluation of the trial court:

> Attempts to support the witness by showing his good character for truth have resulted in contradictory conclusions when the witness has been impeached by evidence of an inconsistent statement, or has been met by the adversary's evidence denying the facts to which the witness has so testified. If the witness has been impeached by the introduction of an inconsistent statement, the greater number of courts permit a showing of his good character for truth, but if the adversary has merely introduced evidence denying the facts to which the witness testified, the greater number of cases will not permit a showing of the witness's good character for truth. Convenient as automatic answers to these seemingly minor trial questions may be, surely it is unrealistic to handle them in this mechanical fashion. A more sensible view is the notion that the judge should consider in each case whether the particular impeachment for inconsistency or a conflict in testimony, or either of them, amounts in net effect to an attack on character for truth and should exercise his discretion accordingly to admit or exclude the character-support.

1 MCCORMICK, § 47, at 175–176.

witnesses. A foundation as to the basis for this testimony must be established, and the subject of testimony is limited to reputation and opinion. On cross-examination, the rehabilitation character witness may be interrogated concerning specific acts of conduct of the principal witness, and the procedure directly parallels that used in conjunction with Rule 405.[25] Whether a particular instance of conduct may be the subject of cross-examination is a matter treated in Rule 608(b) and discussed in § 608.9 of this Treatise.

§ 608.7   Rule 608(b) — Specific Instances of Conduct of the Principal Witness — In General

Rule 608(b) governs the use of specific acts of the primary witness where such instances of conduct are used to impeach the witness's credibility.[26] Procedurally, Rule 608(b) operates in two distinct contexts. Rule 608(b)(1) governs the procedure of cross-examining the primary witness concerning untruthful acts. Rule 608(b)(2) also governs the interrogation of a character witness concerning specific instances of untruthful conduct of the primary witness. As discussed previously in this Chapter, the latter procedure usually arises in the context of cross-examination of a rehabilitation character witness who is offered to bolster the credibility of an impeached principal witness.

In applying the Rule, it is important to recognize that Rule 608(b) governs specific acts of the principal witness that are not subject to, or that have not resulted in, conviction. Where impeachment is sought through exposing a conviction of the witness, Rule 609 is applicable.[27]

§ 608.8   Rule 608(b) — Restriction on Extrinsic Evidence; Exercise of Discretion by the Trial Judge

The exercise of discretion of Rule 608(b) contemplates that the trial judge must evaluate the probative value of the act before authorizing inquiry on cross-examination. The exercise of discretion entails balancing the probative value of the evidence against such counterweights as unfair prejudice, remoteness, and confusion.[28] Of course, prejudice is more likely in the case

---

[25] 4 WEINSTEIN'S FEDERAL EVIDENCE §§ 608.11–608.12; *see also* Chapter 405, *supra*.

[26] Evidence professors and judges almost invariably describe this form of impeachment as involving evidence of the "*prior acts*" by the witnesses, but "prior" is utterly redundant in this context. All acts used to impeach the witness, by necessity, are from some point in time prior to the testimony. *See* Duane, *Prior Convictions and Tuna Fish,* 7 SCRIBES J. OF LEGAL WRITING 160 (2000). It is no coincidence that "prior" does not even appear in the text of Rule 608.

[27] *See generally,* 4 WEINSTEIN'S FEDERAL EVIDENCE § 608.20; 3 MUELLER & KIRKPATRICK, §§ 267–268.

[28] United States v. Abel, 469 U.S. 45 (1984); United States v. Elliott, 89 F.3d 1360, 1368 (8th Cir. 1996) ("The reason for barring extrinsic evidence is to avoid holding mini-trials on peripherally related or irrelevant matters"); United States v. Fortes, 619 F.2d 108 (1st Cir.

of party witnesses.[29] Rule 608 is essentially a rule of limitation that prohibits proof of specific instances of conduct by evidence extrinsic to the cross-examination of the principal witness or of the character witness.[30] Such instances of conduct may be the subject of interrogation only on cross-examination of the principal witness, or on cross-examination of the character witness where the inquiry is probative of the principal witness's character for truthfulness.[31]

When the rule says that specific conduct may not be proved under this rule by "extrinsic evidence,"[32] it bars the use of any kind of evidence, including documents or the testimony of other witnesses, other than a direct admission by the witness being cross-examined that he committed the act. Documents used during the cross-examination of the witness may be shown to the witness without violating the rule, in the discretion of the court, but may not be admitted into evidence for that purpose.[33] Indeed, Rule 608(b) even bars

---

1980); United States v. Whitehead, 618 F.2d 523 (4th Cir. 1980); United States v. Cole, 617 F.2d 151 (5th Cir. 1980).

[29] *See, e.g.*, United States v. McMillon, 14 F.3d 948 (4th Cir. 1994) (trial court properly refused to allow defense counsel to cross-examine a prosecution witness concerning the witness's homosexual activities); United States v. Schwab, 886 F.2d 509 (2d Cir. 1989) (trial court erred by allowing the prosecution to impeach the defendant's credibility with questions regarding tax fraud and perjury charges of which the defendant had been acquitted); United States v. Pintar, 630 F.2d 1270 (8th Cir. 1980). *See generally*, 4 WEINSTEIN'S FEDERAL EVIDENCE § 608.20; 3 MUELLER & KIRKPATRICK, § 262.

[30] *See, e.g.,* Bonilla v. Yamaha Motors Corp., 955 F.2d 150 (1st Cir. 1992) (evidence of plaintiff's speeding tickets held inadmissible under Rule 608(b) as "extrinsic" evidence of misconduct to challenge the truthfulness of the witness); United States v. Ramos, 933 F.2d 968 (11th Cir. 1991) (Rule 608(b) prohibits the introduction of extrinsic evidence of a witness's conduct to attack the credibility of a witness); United States v. Peterson, 808 F.2d 969 (2d Cir. 1987) (in prosecution for possession of stolen check, court committed reversible error in admitting evidence that defendant had endorsed another check written to someone else).

[31] *Cf.* Boutros v. Canton Reg. Transit Auth., 997 F.2d 198 (6th Cir. 1993) (where plaintiff filed an action alleging wrongful termination based on his national origin, the introduction of evidence that plaintiff had behaved inappropriately towards a female passenger and was ultimately discharged as a result did not violate Rule 608(b); evidence was admitted to defend against plaintiff's allegations, not for impeachment purposes).

[32] The phrase "extrinsic evidence" also appears in Rule 613(b). *See* § 613.3 *infra*.

[33] *See* United States v. Jackson, 882 F.2d 1444 (9th Cir. 1989) (prosecution did not violate Rule 608(b) merely by showing defendant his sworn statement admitting misappropriation of funds 14 years earlier, without introducing the statement into evidence, in the hopes of eliciting an admission of the misconduct on cross-examination). Cross-examining attorneys attempting to "refresh the recollection" of the witness by showing him or her a document in this way, *see* Rule 612, must exercise great caution to see to it that the wording of any question posed to the witness while showing him the document does not effectively communicate to the jury the contents of that document, which would plainly violate Rule 608(b). *See also* Rule 103(d) (inadmissible evidence may not be "suggested to the jury by any means.")

"any reference to the consequences that a witness might have suffered as a result of an alleged bad act," including the fact that the witness "was disciplined or suspended for the conduct that is the subject of impeachment."[34] Such inquiries are just a roundabout way of asking a witness the obviously improper question: "Isn't it true that there are other people who believe that you committed this act, and who would presumably say that they thought you did it if I were allowed to call them, and aren't you lucky that I cannot?"[35]

In prohibiting extrinsic evidence of the specific acts of the principal witness, Rule 608(b) operates to curtail digressions. Parties conducting cross-examination are given broad latitude in pressing for an admission of an untruthful act as long as they proceed in good faith.[36] If, however, the witnesses deny the act, the cross-examiners have no other recourse in the matter. They are said to be "stuck with the answer," and the act may not be proven after the witness steps down. The prohibition of extrinsic evidence in such situations is designed to prevent the trier of fact from being sidetracked by collateral issues.[37]

Rule 608(b) only bans the use of extrinsic evidence when a witness is being impeached with questions about specific acts for the purpose of attacking the witness's "character for truthfulness."[38] There is no similar limitation when the specific acts of the witness are relevant to impeach the credibility of the witness in any other way, such as an attack on his bias or mental capacity, or through proof of contradiction or an inconsistent statement by the witness.[39] Thus, although witnesses may be asked to admit

---

[34] Committee Notes to the 2003 amendment to Rule 608(b).

[35] *See* United States v. Davis, 183 F.3d 231, 257 n.12 (3d Cir. 1999) (emphasizing that in attacking the defendant's character for truthfulness "the government cannot make reference to Davis's forty-four day suspension or that Internal Affairs found that he lied about" an incident because "[s]uch evidence would not only be hearsay to the extent it contains assertion of fact, it would be inadmissible extrinsic evidence under Rule 608(b)"); Saltzburg, *Impeaching the Witness: Prior Bad Acts and Extrinsic Evidence*, 7 CRIM. JUST. 28, 31 (Winter 1993) ("counsel should not be permitted to circumvent the no-extrinsic-evidence provision by tucking a third person's opinion about prior acts into a question asked of the witness who has denied the act").

[36] *See generally,* 4 WEINSTEIN'S FEDERAL EVIDENCE § 608.23; 3 MUELLER & KIRKPATRICK, § 262.

[37] *See generally,* 4 WEINSTEIN'S FEDERAL EVIDENCE § 608.20; 3 MUELLER & KIRKPATRICK, §§ 264–266; 3A WIGMORE, § 979; United States v. Matthews, 168 F.3d 1234 (11th Cir. 1999) (when a witness denies bad acts designed to impeach that witness's character for truthfulness, the questioning party must take the witness's answer and the acts may not be proved by extrinsic evidence unless the evidence would be material to another issue in the case).

[38] This language was changed in an amendment to the rule that took effect in 2003.

[39] United States v. Abel, 469 U.S. 45 (1984) (Rule 608(b) does not impose any limitations on lawyer's ability to impeach a witness through evidence showing a motive to lie in that

both that they once lied on a job application (to show their general lack of truthfulness) and that they took a bribe to lie in that very trial (to show their bias and motive to falsify), the cross-examiner may call other witnesses to prove only the latter accusation of dishonest misconduct if the witness denies them both. This is because the former method of impeachment, like any other circumstantial use of character to prove conduct on a particular occasion, has relatively much less probative value,[40] and so our legal tradition wisely forbids the waste of time that would be involved in proving such collateral matters if the witness is not willing to admit them.

§ 608.9   Rule 608(b) — Types of Specific Instances of Conduct Appropriate for Inquiry

In requiring the trial judge to weigh the probative value of impeachment evidence against its potential misuse by the jury, it is clear that Rule 608(b) contemplates inquiry into a limited class of acts committed by the principal witness. Only certain acts are rationally probative of truthfulness or untruthfulness, and all types of antisocial conduct will not qualify. Specific instances of conduct that might qualify include acts of cheating, embezzlement, fraud, and evidence destruction.[41] More violent acts, like force or intimidation, however, generally do not qualify, no matter how antisocial such acts might be.[42] Falling within the gray area is an act such as narcotics

---

particular case); *see also* Committee Notes to the 2003 amendment to Rule 608(b).

[40] That is, attacks on witnesses's "character for truthfulness" generally have much less probative value than other methods of impeachment because they give the jury at best a reason to question the honesty of the witnesses in general, but not a specific reason to doubt their testimony *in this very case*. A rational jury has little reason to doubt the testimony of disinterested nonparty witnesses to a vehicle accident just because they were once convicted of perjury in a totally unrelated case, if they have not been impeached or discredited in any other way. On the other hand, impeachment directed at the bias or mental capacity or prior inconsistent statements of the witnesses, by themselves, are all reasons to question their testimony in the very case before the jury. That gives them much greater probative value, and explains why our legal system is willing to allow much more time and leeway for the proof of such matters.

[41] *See* Carter v. Hewitt, 617 F.2d 961 (3d Cir. 1980) (quoting paragraph in Treatise); *see also* United States v. Studley, 892 F.2d 518 (7th Cir. 1989) (in a prosecution for defrauding the FHA, government could impeach the defendant with evidence he had renounced U.S. laws); United States v. Smith, 792 F.2d 441 (4th Cir. 1986) (government could seek to establish on cross-examination that defendant had procured the absence of a material witness); United States v. Leake, 642 F.2d 715 (4th Cir. 1981); Williams v. Warren Bros. Constr. Co., 412 A.2d 334 (Del. 1980). *See generally*, 4 WEINSTEIN'S FEDERAL EVIDENCE § 608.22; 3 MUELLER & KIRKPATRICK, § 262.

[42] United States v. Hill, 550 F. Supp. 983 (E.D. Pa. 1982), *aff'd*, 716 F.2d 893 (3d Cir. 1983) (excluding questioning concerning trespass and false imprisonment as not probative of truthfulness); United States v. Bynum, 566 F.2d 914 (5th Cir. 1978) (holding foster children against their will did not relate to truthfulness of witness); *see also* United States v. Dickens, 775 F.2d 1056 (9th Cir. 1985) (court committed reversible error in permitting government to cross-examine defendant about connection with "the mob"; association did not impugn

trafficking and certain crimes involving the theft of property.[43]

§ 608.10   Right of Witness to Foreclose Inquiry Unrelated to Credibility

The final sentence of Rule 608(b) provides that by taking the stand to testify, a witness does not waive the right against self-incrimination with respect to matters relating solely to the witness's character for honesty.[44] This provision, which applies to a criminal defendant as well as any other witness at any trial, is designed to encourage reluctant witnesses affording them protection against disclosure of past incriminating misconduct. The restriction on waiver applies as long as the inquiry into any misconduct is for the sole purpose of testing the witness's character for honesty and is not related to any other issue in the case.[45]

While this provision serves as notice that a witness does not waive the constitutional privilege against self-incrimination merely by taking the stand to testify, its practical effect is functionally limited. The Rule does not preclude interrogation about a conviction, since such inquiry is no longer incriminating. For the same reason, the Rule does not prevent inquiry into misconduct that can no longer be prosecuted due to the expiration of the statute of limitations. And, most notably, it does not curtail evidence of misconduct that is relevant to some issue other than the witness's general tendency toward dishonesty. Accordingly, the Rule provides a relatively

---

truthfulness); United States v. Davis, 183 F.3d 231 (3d Cir. 1999) (evidence that testifying police officer had stolen property and lied during an Internal Affairs investigation were properly admitted under Rule 608(b) as bearing on officer's truthfulness, but not evidence that the witness had assaulted a prostitute). *But see* United States v. Manske, 186 F.3d 770 (7th Cir. 1999) (abuse of discretion to prevent defendant from questioning government witnesses about threats made to them by an accomplice who had already pled guilty and was himself testifying against the defendant as part of his plea agreement; threatening to cause physical harm to a person who may testify against you is probative of truthfulness and of the witness's credibility in seeking to gain an advantage by providing false testimony against the defendant). *See generally,* 4 WEINSTEIN'S FEDERAL EVIDENCE § 608.22; 3 MUELLER & KIRKPATRICK, § 262; 3A WIGMORE, § 982.

[43] United States v. Mehrmanesh, 682 F.2d 1303 (9th Cir. 1982). *See generally,* 4 WEINSTEIN'S FEDERAL EVIDENCE § 608.22; 3 MUELLER & KIRKPATRICK, § 262; 1 MCCORMICK, § 42; 3A WIGMORE, §§ 981–987.

[44] *E.g.,* United States v. Burch, 490 F.2d 1300 (8th Cir. 1974) (proper to prevent defense cross-examination of prosecution witness in regard to past misconduct, since witness was facing state criminal charge and U.S. Attorney could not offer immunity).

[45] This point was obscured for many years by the original language of Rule 608(b), which formerly offered its protections to any witness being cross-examined about matters that affected in any way the "credibility" of the witness or his testimony. This language was narrowed in 2003 and now preserves the Fifth Amendment rights only of witnesses who are being cross-examined about matters that relate to nothing but their "character for truthfulness," following the written recommendation the Advisory Committee had received from one of the authors of this text. *See* Duane, *The Proposed Amendments to FRE 608(b) and 804(b)(3): Two Great Ideas that Don't Go Far Enough,* 209 F.R.D. 235, 238–239 (2002).

narrow exception to the general rule that all witnesses are subject to cross-examination for purposes of testing credibility.

Chapter 609

Rule 609. Impeachment by Evidence of a Criminal Conviction

Rule 609. Impeachment by Evidence of a Criminal Conviction

(a) **In General.** The following rules apply to attacking a witness's character for truthfulness by evidence of a criminal conviction:

    (1) for a crime that, in the convicting jurisdiction, was punishable by death or by imprisonment for more than one year, the evidence:

        (A) must be admitted, subject to Rule 403, in a civil case or in a criminal case in which the witness is not a defendant; and

        (B) must be admitted in a criminal case in which the witness is a defendant, if the probative value of the evidence outweighs its prejudicial effect to that defendant; and

    (2) for any crime regardless of the punishment, the evidence must be admitted if the court can readily determine that establishing the elements of the crime required proving — or the witness's admitting — a dishonest act or false statement.

(b) **Limit on Using the Evidence After 10 Years.** This subdivision (b) applies if more than 10 years have passed since the witness's conviction or release from confinement for it, whichever is later. Evidence of the conviction is admissible only if:

    (1) its probative value, supported by specific facts and circumstances, substantially outweighs its prejudicial effect; and

    (2) the proponent gives an adverse party reasonable written notice of the intent to use it so that the party has a fair opportunity to contest its use.

(c) **Effect of a Pardon, Annulment, or Certificate of Rehabilitation.** Evidence of a conviction is not admissible if:

    (1) the conviction has been the subject of a pardon, annulment, certificate of rehabilitation, or other equivalent procedure based on a finding that the person has been rehabilitated, and the person has not been convicted of a later crime punishable by death or by imprisonment for more than one year; or

    (2) the conviction has been the subject of a pardon, annulment, or other equivalent procedure based on a finding of innocence.

(d) Juvenile Adjudications. Evidence of a juvenile adjudication is admissible under this rule only if:

  (1) it is offered in a criminal case;

  (2) the adjudication was of a witness other than the defendant;

  (3) an adult's conviction for that offense would be admissible to attack the adult's credibility; and

  (4) admitting the evidence is necessary to fairly determine guilt or innocence.

(e) Pendency of an Appeal. A conviction that satisfies this rule is admissible even if an appeal is pending. Evidence of the pendency is also admissible.

---

§ 609.1   Rule 609(a) — Impeachment by Evidence of a Criminal Conviction — In General

Rule 609 governs the impeachment of a witness by evidence of criminal convictions of the witness.[1] Where a conviction is authorized by Rule 609 as appropriate for impeachment, it may be proven through an acknowledgment by the witness or by documentation from a public record.[2] It is critical to note that evidence admitted under Rule 609 is directed to the limited purpose of impeaching the witness's character for honesty, and the Rule does not contradict the general prohibition of certain forms of character evidence contained in Rule 404(b)(1).[3] This Rule does not apply to all methods of impeachment that might implicate the "credibility" of the witness. Rule 609, like Rule 608, only limits impeachment concerning the character of the witness for veracity, and has absolutely no bearing on other methods of impeachment, including evidence of criminal convictions, that might alter the jury's assessment of whether the witness is biased in a particular case.[4]

---

[1] *See generally,* 1 McCORMICK, § 42; 4 WEINSTEIN'S FEDERAL EVIDENCE §§ 609.01–609.25; 3 MUELLER & KIRKPATRICK, §§ 273–288; 3A WIGMORE, §§ 980–988; 4 WIGMORE, §§ 1106, 1116. Evidence professors and judges almost invariably describe this form of impeachment as involving evidence of the witness's "*prior* convictions," but "prior" is utterly redundant in this context. All convictions used to impeach the witness, by necessity, are from some point in time prior to his testimony. *See* Duane, *Prior Convictions and Tuna Fish,* 7 SCRIBES J. OF LEGAL WRITING 160 (2000). It is no coincidence that "prior" does not even appear in the text of Rule 609.

[2] The December 1, 1990, amendment to Rule 609(a) eliminated the requirement that a conviction may only be introduced on cross-examination. The Advisory Committee noted that it is a common practice for trial attorneys to "remove the sting" of impeachment on cross-examination by revealing convictions on direct examination. The extent to which convictions can be proved through testimony will be limited by Rule 403 and 611(a) to prevent "unfair or disruptive methods of proof." Rule 609(a), Advisory Committee Note.

[3] *See generally,* 4 WEINSTEIN'S FEDERAL EVIDENCE § 609.02; 3 MUELLER & KIRKPATRICK, §§ 279–281.

[4] This point was obscured for many years by the original language of Rule 609(a), which

Rule 609 has roots in traditional common-law practice that generally rendered incompetent as a witness any person who had been convicted of treason, a felony, or crimen falsi. Under modern practice, this blanket disqualification has been universally abandoned, and instead, the matter of convictions has been transformed to issues of credibility and impeachment. Modern practice rests upon the assumption that certain convictions of a witness are probative of lack of credibility, or as courts have suggested, that a witness's demonstrated willingness to engage in antisocial conduct in one instance is probative of willingness to give false testimony.[5]

Impeachment by evidence of a conviction frequently risks prejudice and confusion, and application of conviction impeachment may be particularly subject to misuse by the jury where, for example, an accused who takes the stand suffers revelations of past criminal conduct. Despite limiting instructions, impeachment through conviction evidence operates in this situation as an invitation to the jury to draw an inference from past conduct concerning the propensity of the accused to commit the crime charged rather than an inference regarding the witness's present propensity to tell the truth or lie on the witness stand.[6]

Rule 609(a) recognizes that in certain contexts evidence of a conviction of a witness may result in excessive prejudice when compared to the benefit obtained in assisting the jury to assess credibility. Consequently, a special exercise of discretion must be undertaken before certain types of convictions may be utilized by the prosecution in criminal cases. Also, consistent with the common law and pre-existing practice, certain convictions are rendered unavailable for impeachment because of minimal probative value as to credibility. Reading subsections (a)(1) and (a)(2) of Rule 609 together, convictions may not be used to attack a witness's character for truthfulness if they do not involve dishonesty or false statement and are not punishable by death or imprisonment for an excess of one year.

To summarize, for the purpose of affecting the credibility of a witness

---

formerly limited the ways in which convictions could be used for the purpose of attacking "the credibility of a witness." This language was narrowed in 2006 and now only places limits on the use of convictions to attack "the witness's character for truthfulness," based on a written recommendation the Advisory Committee had received several years earlier from one of the authors of this text. *See* Duane, *The Proposed Amendments to FRE 608(b) and 804(b)(3): Two Great Ideas that Don't Go Far Enough*, 209 F.R.D. 235, 240–242 (2002).

[5] *See, e.g.,* Blakney v. United States, 397 F.2d 648, 649–650 (D.C. Cir. 1968) ("as its language indicates, that law [D.C. Statute allowing impeachment by record of conviction] was put on the books almost 70 years ago for the primary purpose of removing the ancient common law disqualification of persons with criminal records from testifying in either civil or criminal cases. There is apparently no relevant legislative history, so we can only speculate as to why the attainder continued to some degree in the form of permissive employment of the past conviction to impeach credibility").

[6] *See* United States v. Lipscomb, 702 F.2d 1049 (D.C. Cir. 1983) (en banc); United States v. Bailey, 426 F.2d 1236 (D.C. Cir. 1970).

under Rule 609(a), convictions may be introduced pertaining to: (1) crimes punishable by death or imprisonment of more than one year, for most witnesses subject to Rule 403, or for the accused in criminal cases when the court in its special discretion allows the impeachment (subsection (a)(1)); or (2) crimes involving dishonesty or false statement regardless of the applicable sentence in all proceedings in regard to all witnesses (subsection (a)(2)).[7] The Rule authorizes the admission of evidence of convictions within these categories subject to the limitations expressed in subsections (b) through (d). In any case, the evidence so admitted is for the limited purpose of evaluating a witness's credibility, and because danger exists that the trier of fact may misuse the information, a limiting instruction from the court is appropriate.[8]

§ 609.2   Operation of Discretionary Balancing under Rule 609(a)(1) — Impeachment by Evidence of Capital Offenses and Crimes Punishable by Imprisonment in Excess of One Year

Rule 609(a)(1) regulates the use of convictions for impeachment where the crime underlying the conviction is punishable by death or imprisonment in excess of one year. Rule 609(a)(1) applies in both civil and criminal cases, and it applies to all witnesses, parties and non-parties.[9] Impeachment of a witness other than an accused with convictions designated in Rule 609(a)(1) is subject to the balancing test of Rule 403.[10] Before an accused can be impeached with evidence of a conviction identified in subsection (a)(1), the court must exercise special discretion.[11] Accordingly, the prosecution must show that the "probative value of [the] conviction[] as impeachment evidence outweighs . . . [its] prejudicial effect."[12] Accordingly, a special buffer of judicial discretion is provided for an accused in regard to the use of convictions identified in subsection (a)(1).

In rare instances, impeachment by a conviction of a defense witness other

---

[7] Rule 609(a), Advisory Committee Note.

[8] *See generally,* 3 MUELLER & KIRKPATRICK, § 274. United States v. Haslip, 160 F.3d 649 (10th Cir. 1998) (conviction may be admissible to impeach defendant even though evidence was not admissible under Rule 404; limiting instruction restricting use of evidence to evaluation of defendant's credibility was proper and necessary).

[9] *See generally,* 3 MUELLER & KIRKPATRICK, §§ 275–276.

[10] Rule 609(a), Advisory Committee Note.

[11] *Id.*

[12] Rule 609(a), Advisory Committee Note; *see also* Gee v. Pride, 992 F.2d 159 (8th Cir. 1993) (trial court permitted the admission of the record of defendant's conviction for possession of PCP after defendant testified on cross-examination that he had never used PCP); United States v. Pritchard, 973 F.2d 905 (11th Cir. 1992) (trial court admitted evidence of thirteen-year-old burglary conviction to impeach defendant in a bank robbery trial).

than the accused will impermissibly prejudice the accused.[13] For instance, if the crime committed by the defense witness is similar to the one with which the defendant is charged, the accused may be prejudiced. Likewise, where a close family member of the accused testifies for the defense, convictions of such a witness may arguably result in "spill-over" prejudice to the accused. These possibilities of prejudice to the accused resulting from impeachment of defense witnesses other than the accused are remote, and the general discretion under Rule 403 provides adequate protection to the defendant in regard to witnesses other than the accused himself or herself.[14] Rule 609(a)(1) expressly protects all parties from the prejudicial impeachment of their witnesses. When the witness is not the accused, the general discretion of Rule 403 is applicable.[15]

In applying the special balancing principle of Rule 609(a)(1) to the accused, a court must consider the type of prior crime.[16] Crimes that do not bear on credibility directly, such as murder or assault, are less probative of the witness's credibility than are crimes such as shoplifting or robbery that, by their elements, imply some dishonesty.[17] (Crimes directly involving dishonesty or false statement, such as perjury or fraud, will be admissible to impeach a witness under Rule 609(a)(2), discussed in § 609.4, *infra.*) However, under Rule 609(a)(1), even a crime with little bearing upon credibility may be admitted for impeachment purposes.[18]

In applying the special balancing principle of subsection (a)(1) to the

---

[13] *See* Rule 609(a), Advisory Committee Note; *see, e.g.,* United States v. Rosales, 680 F.2d 1304 (10th Cir. 1981); *cf.* United States v. Edwards, 549 F.2d 362 (5th Cir. 1977) (impeachment of codefendant by prior crimes not too prejudicial); *see also* United States v. Lewis, 626 F.2d 940 (D.C. Cir. 1980); United States v. Barnes, 622 F.2d 107 (5th Cir. 1980); United States v. Cohen, 544 F.2d 781 (5th Cir. 1977). *See generally,* 4 WEINSTEIN'S FEDERAL EVIDENCE §§ 609.04–609.05; 3 MUELLER & KIRKPATRICK, § 274.

[14] *See* Rule 609(a), Advisory Committee Note.

[15] Rule 609(a), Advisory Committee Note.

[16] Gordon v. United States, 383 F.2d 936, 939 (D.C. Cir. 1967) ("*[L]uck* also contemplated that it was for the defendant to present to the trial court sufficient reasons for withholding past convictions from the jury in the face of a statute which makes such convictions admissible. The underlying assumption was that prior convictions would ordinarily be admissible unless this burden is met"); *see also* United States v. Hayes, 553 F.2d 824 (2d Cir. 1977); United States v. Smith, 551 F.2d 348 (D.C. Cir. 1976); *cf.* United States v. Preston, 608 F.2d 626 (5th Cir. 1979); United States v. Vanderbosch, 610 F.2d 95 (2d Cir. 1979).

[17] *See, e.g.,* United States v. Cameron, 814 F.2d 403 (7th Cir. 1987) (trial court did not err in excluding conviction for possession of switchblade); United States v. Carroll, 663 F. Supp. 210 (D. Md. 1986) (trial court held conviction for felony theft not admissible without showing that it involved dishonesty or false statements); United States v. Halbert, 668 F.2d 489 (10th Cir. 1982) (mail fraud, false pretenses, aggravated robbery).

[18] United States v. Fountain, 642 F.2d 1083 (7th Cir. 1981) (premeditated murder; acknowledged general rule that a court should "err on the side of excluding a challenged prior

accused, the conviction history of the accused may be considered.[19] The length of time that has elapsed since the accused's conviction or release from prison is an objective manifestation of the witness's break with his or her criminal past.[20] A conviction that is excessively stale may also be rendered inadmissible to impeach a witness under Rule 609(b).

Whether the impeachment by the conviction will be allowed may also depend upon the importance of assessing the credibility of the accused as a witness.[21] The similarity between the prior crime committed by the accused and the crime with which he or she is charged will affect the likelihood of unfair prejudice to the accused if the conviction is admitted for impeachment.[22] If the prior crime and the charged crime are similar, it is more likely the jury will ignore the judge's limiting instruction to consider the conviction only on the issue of credibility, and it is likely in this situation that the jury will consider the conviction as evidence of the accused's propensity to commit the charged crime. Such an application of the conviction is an impermissible inference under Rule 404.

The tactical need for the accused to testify on his or her own behalf may militate against use of impeaching convictions. If it is apparent to the trial court that the accused must testify to refute strong prosecution evidence, then the court should consider whether, by permitting conviction impeachment, the court in effect prevents the accused from testifying.[23]

The court's ruling under Rule 609(a)(1) should be decided before trial[24]

---

conviction," but trial court could have concluded that the probative value of the conviction did outweigh its prejudicial effect).

[19] *E.g.,* United States v. Jones, 647 F.2d 696 (6th Cir. 1981).

[20] *E.g.,* United States v. Field, 625 F.2d 862 (9th Cir. 1980).

[21] United States v. Rosales, 680 F.2d 1304 (10th Cir. 1981) (probative value present, since witnesses were inmates whose testimony directly contradicted that of the guards; also inmates were serving substantial terms, giving them some motivation to testify falsely in a dispute with prison guards, diminishing prejudice); United States v. Bogers, 635 F.2d 749 (8th Cir. 1980) (cross-examination of defendant concerning state felony conviction permitted, because of the conflict in testimony between government and defense witnesses and the consequent importance of credibility issues); *see also* United States v. Jackson, 627 F.2d 1198 (D.C. Cir. 1980); United States v. Barnes, 622 F.2d 107 (5th Cir. 1980).

[22] *See* United States v. Hernandez, 106 F.3d 737 (7th Cir. 1997) (five-year-old conviction for possession of cocaine and marijuana was admissible to impeach the defendant who was being prosecuted for a kidnapping related to a drug transaction); United States v. Fay, 668 F.2d 375 (8th Cir. 1981); United States v. Beahm, 664 F.2d 414 (4th Cir. 1981).

[23] United States v. Williams, 939 F.2d 721 (9th Cir. 1991) (when the defense elicits impeaching conviction on direct, attempting to minimize the impact of such evidence, the defendant forfeits his right of appeal under Rule 609(a)(1)); United States v. Mehrmanesh, 682 F.2d 1303 (9th Cir. 1982); United States v. Jackson, 627 F.2d 1198 (D.C. Cir. 1980).

[24] *See* United States v. Burkhead, 646 F.2d 1283 (8th Cir. 1981); United States v. Cook, 608 F.2d 1175 (9th Cir. 1979); *see also* United States v. Oakes, 565 F.2d 170 (1st Cir. 1977) (explicit statements by District Court on the record revealing its knowledge of Rule 609(a)

and its rationale fully articulated on the record.[25] The prosecution has the burden of persuading the court that impeachment should be allowed under this subdivision.[26] The United States Supreme Court has ruled in *Luce v. United States*, however, that the trial court's *in limine* ruling under Rule 609(a)(1) is preserved and available for review only if the accused testifies at trial.[27] The precise nature of the defendant's testimony is necessary on review to weigh the conviction's probative value against its prejudicial effect as required under Rule 609(a)(1). The absence of the defendant's testimony would force a reviewing court to speculate whether the District Court would have actually allowed the conviction as impeachment evidence since initial *in limine* rulings are subject to change during the trial. Furthermore, the court would be forced to speculate whether the government would have actually used the convictions to impeach the defendant, especially where the defendant is subject to impeachment by other means. In addition, the reviewing court cannot assume that the trial court's adverse ruling was the sole reason for the defendant's decision not to testify. Finally, the Court reasoned that an *in limine* ruling under Rule 609(a), reviewable even when the defendant did not testify, would almost always result in an automatic reversal because the error that presumptively kept the defendant from testifying would not be considered "harmless." Consequently, the Court held that the defendant's testimony is necessary to determine the impact of any erroneous impeachment in light of the record as a whole. The testimony also discourages motions to exclude impeachment evidence made solely to "plant" reversible error in the event of a conviction. The Supreme Court's decision in *Luce* has been the subject of vigorous criticism, however, and has been rejected by many State courts, although the Supreme Court has recently reaffirmed its willingness to follow and extend the logic of that case.[28]

---

and basis for its resolution of the balancing problem "are most helpful to this court in carrying out our review").

[25] United States v. Preston, 608 F.2d 626 (5th Cir. 1979); United States v. Seamster, 568 F.2d 188 (10th Cir. 1978); United States v. Mahone, 537 F.2d 922 (7th Cir. 1976).

[26] *Cf.* Government of Virgin Islands v. Bedford, 671 F.2d 758 (3d Cir. 1982) (trial court's permitting impeachment of defendant by cross-examination concerning his conviction for possession of a switchblade knife was error, but harmless; felony conviction is not automatically admissible); United States v. Hendershot, 614 F.2d 648 (9th Cir. 1980) (ruling that bank robbery conviction would be usable to impeach defendant was reversible error; trial judge did not balance probative worth against prejudicial impact as he should have under Rule 609(a)(1)).

[27] Luce v. United States, 469 U.S. 38 (1984).

[28] For a vigorous criticism of *Luce* and a description of some of the reasons why many state courts have declined to follow it, see Duane, *Appellate Review of In Limine Rulings,* 182 F.R.D. 666, 679–90 (Jan. 1999) (urging Advisory Committee to refrain from codifying *Luce* in Rule 103(a); the Committee subsequently agreed that *Luce* should best remain uncodified). The United States Supreme Court has, however, more recently reaffirmed its adherence to the logic of that decision. *See* Ohler v. United States, 529 U.S. 753 (2000) (following and

§ 609.3   Rule 609(a)(1) — Convictions Appropriate for Impeachment under Subsection (a)(1) of Rule 609

Rule 609(a)(1) applies to those convictions that are punishable by death or imprisonment for more than one year under the relevant state or federal law. (Convictions for crimes involving dishonesty or false statement, regardless of punishment, are admissible under Rule 609(a)(2).) Accordingly, in regard to crimes that do not involve dishonesty or false statement, Rule 609(a) looks to the maximum possible punishment accompanying the conviction, and the Rule is cast in terms of the possible maximum sentence for a conviction in the jurisdiction in which the conviction was sustained.[29] Operation of the Rule does not depend upon the sentence that was actually imposed.[30] For example, a witness convicted of a drug-related offense punishable by imprisonment in excess of one year who received a suspended sentence may be impeached by evidence of the conviction. The crime was punishable by a term of incarceration within the scope of the Rule.

§ 609.4   Rule 609(a)(2) — Convictions Available for Impeachment Without Regard to Possible Penalty

Rule 609(a)(2) provides that convictions may also be used to impeach a witness's character for truthfulness, without regard to the punishment, if "the court can readily determine that establishing the elements of the crime required proving — or the witness's admitting — a dishonest act or false statement."[31] This clause applies to two different classes of offenses. First, it applies primarily to any conviction for a crime in the nature of *crimen falsi* — crimes such as perjury or subornation of perjury, forgery, false statement, criminal fraud, embezzlement, or false pretense, "in which the ultimate criminal act was itself an act of deceit."[32] To determine whether a conviction was for such an offense, it is necessary only to examine the statute defining the elements of the offense.

In addition, even in cases where an act of deceit is not an essential element

---

extending *Luce,* although in a case where neither party asked that *Luce* be overruled).

[29] *See* United States v. McLister, 608 F.2d 785 (9th Cir. 1979). *See generally,* 3 MUELLER & KIRKPATRICK, §§ 275–276.

[30] United States v. Hall, 588 F.2d 613 (8th Cir. 1978) (narcotics prosecution; no error to permit cross-examination of defendant concerning two felony convictions for distribution and possession of heroin, even though accused received suspended sentence for the conviction). *See generally,* 3 MUELLER & KIRKPATRICK, §§ 275–276.

[31] Rule 609(a)(2). Prior to its amendment in December 2006, this rule referred instead to convictions for offenses "involving" dishonesty or false statement, a somewhat ambiguous phrase that generated a fair amount of uncertainty and litigation.

[32] Committee Note to the 2006 amendment to Rule 609. *See* United States v. Brackeen, 969 F.2d 827 (9th Cir. 1992) (robbery is not a crime involving dishonesty or false statement); Cree v. Hatcher, 969 F.2d 34 (3d Cir. 1992) (willful failure to file federal tax return is not a crime of dishonesty or false statement)

of some criminal charge, this rule will apply if, under the facts of a particular case, "the conviction required proof (or in the case of a guilty plea, the admission of) an act of dishonesty or false statement."[33] For example, evidence that a witness was convicted is admissible under this subdivision even if the witness was prosecuted under a statute that does not expressly require proof of deceit, such as Obstruction of Justice, as long as the details of the case committed the prosecution to proving that the accused committed the crime by means of a false statement.[34] This limitation clarifies, for example, that a murder conviction is not admissible under this subdivision, even if the uncontradicted trial testimony showed that the killer apparently lied to gain entry to his victim's home, as long as the jury instructions did not require the jury find that the killer lied in order to convict. To determine whether a conviction qualifies under this provision, the proponent of the impeachment evidence will ordinarily be required to have ready proof of "information such as an indictment, a statement of admitted facts, or jury instructions to show that the factfinder had to find, or the defendant had to admit, an act of dishonesty or false statement in order for the witness to have been convicted."[35] Such a foundation will be sufficient only if these records permit the trial court to "readily" determine whether the conviction was of such a nature. The statute does not give the cross-examiner the right to "a 'mini-trial' in which the court plumbs the record of the previous proceeding to determine whether the crime was in the nature of *crimen falsi.*"[36]

If the cross-examiner can demonstrate that the witness has been convicted of a crime that "required the proof or admission of an act of dishonesty or false statement by the witness," Rule 609(a)(2) declares that evidence of the conviction is not merely admissible but "shall be admitted." This language, which does not appear in any other Federal Rule of Evidence, clarifies that the admission of such convictions is automatic without regard to its potential for unfair prejudice, and "is not within the discretion of the Court."[37]

---

[33] Committee Note to the 2006 amendment to Rule 609. *See* United States v. Foster, 227 F.3d 1096 (9th Cir. 2000) (defendant's misdemeanor conviction for receipt of stolen property was improperly admitted for impeachment when prosecution presented no details regarding the crime or the circumstances leading to conviction; "receipt of stolen property is not *per se* a crime of dishonesty" and may only be admitted under Rule 609(a)(2) to impeach a witness if the crime was committed by fraudulent or deceitful means).

[34] Committee Note to the 2006 amendment to Rule 609.

[35] *Id.*

[36] *Id.*; *see* United States v. Motley, 940 F.2d 1079 (7th Cir. 1991) (conviction for misdemeanor "Check Deception" properly excluded for lack of proof that it involved the commission of an act of dishonesty or false statement).

[37] Report of the House/Senate Conference Committee on Rule 609(a), found in Appendix A of this Treatise. The Report continues: "Such convictions are peculiarly probative of credibility and, under this rule, are always to be admitted. Thus, judicial discretion granted

§ 609.5   What Constitutes "Conviction" under Rule 609

By expressly providing that impeachment of witnesses may be effected through the introduction of certain convictions, Rule 609(a) does not authorize the use of arrests or indictments. The Rule, however, does not preclude use of a pending indictment against a witness for an impeachment purpose other than that regulated by Rule 609. For example, a pending indictment or arrest may be probative in showing bias, prejudice, interest or coercion.[38] Accordingly, where witnesses have been jointly indicted with the accused but awarded a separate trial, the witnesses' credibility may be impaired due to their interest in securing a favorable outcome at their own trial. For example, a witness indicted for receiving stolen property from the accused has an interest in the outcome of the action against the accused for theft. In this situation, the evidence of the witness's pending indictment may be admitted, not to impeach his or her general character for truthfulness under Rule 609, but to show that the witness's testimony may be biased or prejudiced.[39]

Generally, arrests or indictments not leading to convictions are inadmissible.[40] Similarly, convictions reversed on appeal prior to the witness's taking the stand are not available for impeachment use under the Rule, since the reversal vitiates the conviction.[41] This result obtains whether the reversal was occasioned by a finding that the guilty verdict was against the manifest weight of the evidence or that prejudicial procedural error attended the trial. In either event, whether the accused is discharged or the cause remanded for retrial, the conviction is erased as the fundament for Rule 609 impeachment.

It is an open question whether a conviction may be used for impeachment under this rule if that conviction was based upon a plea of nolo contendere. Prior to the adoption of the Federal Rules of Evidence, most federal courts had ruled that nolo convictions could not be used for that purpose, in keeping with the doctrine that such pleas were generally inadmissible for any

---

with respect to the admissibility of other prior convictions is not applicable to those involving dishonesty or false statement." *Id.*

[38] *See* 3 MUELLER & KIRKPATRICK, § 281.

[39] United States v. Martinez, 555 F.2d 1273 (5th Cir. 1977) (prosecution for conspiracy to distribute cocaine; reversible error to allow cross-examination of defendant concerning conviction for aiding and abetting in the commission of the same offense).

[40] *E.g.,* United States v. Werbrouck, 589 F.2d 273 (7th Cir. 1978) (police officer planting marijuana on certain person, which led to discharge of officer from police department, did not amount to conviction admissible to impeach under Rule 609); *see also* United States v. Ling, 581 F.2d 1118 (4th Cir. 1978). *But cf.* Wilson v. Attaway, 757 F.2d 1227 (11th Cir. 1985) (court properly used state conviction to impeach, despite "first offender" statute under which defendant pleaded guilty but was placed on probation without actual judgment of guilt or entry of conviction).

[41] United States v. Williams, 484 F.2d 428 (8th Cir. 1973). *See generally,* 3 MUELLER & KIRKPATRICK, § 287.

purpose against the one who entered the plea, and it is debatable whether those cases were overturned by the adoption of the federal rules. Rule 609 is silent on that question, although Rule 410 states without qualification that nolo pleas are "not, in any civil or criminal proceeding, admissible against the defendant who made the plea," which would seem to suggest that they may not be used for impeachment. Two federal circuit courts have held that convictions based upon "no contest" pleas may be used for impeachment under Rule 609, although the logic of those cases is open to serious question.[42] The obvious point behind Rule 410 is that "pleas of nolo contendere and convictions on the basis of such pleas are not admissible for purposes of proving that the defendant is guilty of the crime in question,"[43] which is precisely what a cross-examiner attempts to do when trying to impeach a witness by asking if the witness was convicted of a crime based on a plea of nolo contendere.[44] The most sensible conclusion is that Rule 410 excludes the use of convictions offered for impeachment at either a civil or a criminal trial, at least in cases where the witness being cross-examined is a party to the case,[45] and the two reported cases to the contrary should be viewed with considerable skepticism.

§ 609.6   Introduction of the Conviction

At one time, impeachment through convictions could only be effected through an acknowledgment of the conviction by the witness or by the introduction of a public record of the conviction during cross-examination.[46]

---

[42] For a more detailed discussion of those opinions and their failure to furnish a coherent account of Rule 410's language and purposes, *see* § 410.3, *supra.*

[43] United States v. Adedoyin, 369 F.3d 337, 345 (3d Cir. 2004). The court was not considering whether nolo pleas could be used for impeachment, although its sound reasoning would plainly compel a negative answer to that question.

[44] This is not to say that it is never proper to ask witnesses to admit that they suffered a conviction based upon a plea of nolo contendere, for such evidence is probably admissible in other contexts when it is offered to prove *merely* that witnesses were convicted, in those situations where the jury is not thereby being invited to infer anything as to whether the conviction was just or wrong. *See* § 410.3 *supra.* For example, Rule 410 does not forbid a prosecutor from proving that a man had been convicted based on a plea of nolo contendere, when offered to show that he later made a false statement in denying that he had any criminal record when applying for a visa to re-enter the country. United States v. Adedoyin, 369 F.3d 337, 345 (3d Cir. 2004). That makes sense, since the conviction in such a case is being offered to prove merely that he was a convicted felon and not to show, not even by implication, that he was guilty of that earlier offense. After all, even if he had been totally innocent and unjustly imprisoned in that earlier case, he was *still* a convicted felon and his denial of that fact was fraudulent. But that is not true when a conviction based upon a no contest plea is offered to impeach a witness under Rule 609; it makes no sense to ask the witness about his convictions as a method of impeaching his character unless one expects the jury to infer that he was convicted because he was *guilty* on the underlying charge.

[45] *See* § 410.3, *supra,* for a more thorough examination of all these points.

[46] *E.g.,* United States v. Bovain, 708 F.2d 606 (11th Cir. 1983).

Amended Rule 609(a) eliminates the restriction that convictions only be revealed on cross-examination and consequently conforms the Rule to the common practice whereby trial attorneys "remove the sting" of impeachment by revealing convictions on direct examination.

A direct examiner who elects that course, however, waives any claim of error in the admission of the conviction, even if the party first tried without success to have it excluded on a motion *in limine* and brought it out at trial only to make the best of a bad situation.[47]

The extent to which a conviction may be proved through extrinsic testimony is limited by Rules 403 and 611(a).[48] When impeachment is sought by introduction of a certified public record, no special foundation is necessary for the introduction of the certified public record because it is generally self-authenticating under Rule 902.[49]

When the cross-examination seeks to obtain an admission from the witness sought to be impeached that the witness has suffered a conviction, specific information about the conviction should be elicited. The date and place of the conviction should be established, but the specific details about the underlying crime are generally improper.[50]

Some courts have also approved questions about the sentence that was imposed on the witness following the conviction, but those holdings are open to extremely serious question. Rule 609 only authorizes the admission of evidence of a "conviction," a word that does not normally include the sentence imposed following a conviction. Moreover, information about the sentence imposed has no meaningful probative value in this context to the jurors, who lack enough information to make any intelligent assessment of what, if anything, the sentence tells them about the seriousness of the witness's offense, much less his or her propensity for dishonesty. If two witnesses were convicted of the same crime on different dates but given very different sentences, the disparity could be the product of one hundred variables having nothing to do with the seriousness of their offenses, including differences in their criminal records, their ability to work out a plea agreement, their willingness to testify against a codefendant, sentencing ranges in distinct jurisdictions, or the racial prejudices or idiosyncrasies of the sentencing judges. Sentencing details in isolation give a jury absolutely

---

[47] Ohler v. United States, 529 U.S. 753 (2000); *see* discussion at § 103.4, *supra.*

[48] Rule 609(a), Advisory Committee Note.

[49] *See* 5 WEINSTEIN'S FEDERAL EVIDENCE § 902.06; 5 MUELLER & KIRKPATRICK, § 542.

[50] United States v. Lopez-Medina, 596 F.3d 716 (10th Cir. 2010) (attorney cross-examining a witness about his criminal conviction is entitled to ask about the nature of the conviction — for example, that it was for possession of methamphetamines with intent to distribute — but has no right to inquire about the specific facts and circumstances involved in the commission of that offense).

no real assistance in assessing the honesty of the witness being impeached under Rule 609, and create a grave risk of unfair prejudice, especially when the witness is an accused or another party. Generally, in order to minimize the prejudicial effect, impeachment may not inquire into exact details concerning the crime underlying the conviction.[51]

Whenever a conviction is utilized to impeach a witness who is also a party, the party should request a limiting instruction under Rule 105 to minimize the prejudicial impact of the conviction and to ensure the jury will use the conviction only for the purpose of evaluating the credibility of the witness.

As a rehabilitative device, nothing in the Rule prohibits an "explanation" by the witness of extenuating circumstances of the conviction. Some courts permit "brief protestations" of innocence or testimony of extenuating circumstances to explain away the implications of a conviction. No collateral evidence of such extenuating circumstances, however, should be permitted in rehabilitation efforts.[52]

§ 609.7   Rule 609(b) — Time Limit

Under Rule 609(b), if more than ten years has elapsed since the date of conviction or the termination of confinement, whichever is later, the conviction is not admissible unless the court finds that the probative value of such evidence substantially outweighs its prejudicial effect.[53] The applicable period should be measured up to the date upon which the witness testifies, since the trier of fact must evaluate credibility at that moment.[54]

Where a party seeks to introduce evidence of a conviction that predates the ten-year limitation, the proponent must provide the adverse party with

---

[51] *E.g.,* United States v. Swanson, 9 F.3d 1354 (8th Cir. 1993) (where defendant testified on direct examination to a conviction for menacing, the prosecution was permitted to cross-examine defendant concerning facts in the police reports that were inconsistent with defendant's testimony; although generally the prosecution may not elicit specific details surrounding a conviction, in this case defendant attempted on direct examination to minimize his guilt; consequently, more extensive cross-examination was appropriate).

[52] United States v. Canniff, 521 F.2d 565 (2d Cir. 1975); Fagerstrom v. United States, 311 F.2d 717 (8th Cir. 1963); Thomas v. United States, 121 F.2d 905 (D.C. Cir. 1941).

[53] *See* Buziashvili v. Inman, 106 F.3d 709 (6th Cir. 1997) (in wrongful death action, admission of defendant's twenty-year-old grand larceny conviction for impeachment was harmless in light of the fact that the jury was already aware that the defendant had been convicted of assaulting, robbing and killing the deceased); United States v. Bensimon, 172 F.3d 1121 (9th Cir. 1999) (a criminal defendant prosecuted for drug offenses does not open himself to impeachment with a seventeen-year-old mail fraud conviction by testifying in passing that he observed religious holidays, served in the army, and was married with two children or by contradicting a government witness's testimony).

[54] United States v. Cathey, 591 F.2d 268 (5th Cir. 1979) (correct point from which to measure is the date one testified rather than the date when the trial commenced). *See generally,* 4 WEINSTEIN'S FEDERAL EVIDENCE § 609.06.

sufficient notice in writing of its intent to employ such evidence in order to provide ample opportunity to contest the use of the conviction. The burden is on the proponent to persuade the court that the probative value substantially outweighs its unfair prejudicial effect, and in ruling on such matters, the court should make an on-the-record finding supported by articulated facts and circumstances justifying the introduction.[55]

§ 609.8　　Rule 609(c) — Effect of Pardon, Annulment or Certification of Rehabilitation

Rule 609(c) provides that evidence of a conviction is not admissible for impeachment where a pardon, annulment, certificate of rehabilitation or other equivalent procedure is based either (i) upon a finding of innocence, or (ii) upon a required showing of rehabilitation and where the witness has not subsequently been convicted of a felony.

The Rule rests upon the theory that since a conviction is legally reflective of the witness's untrustworthiness, the effect on credibility may not be abated by a pardon based upon a finding other than that of innocence. Where the reasons for extending a pardon or annulment are not related to innocence, such as where a pardon is granted due to political influence or overcrowded jail conditions, the conviction is still probative of credibility.[56] By comparison, a pardon based upon a subsequent finding of innocence negates the presumption of untrustworthiness flowing from the conviction and, consequently, it abrogates the attendant negative effect on credibility.

While not negating the original damage to credibility, a finding of rehabilitation is believed to serve as sufficient evidence that the witness is now credible, *i.e.,* the witness should not suffer the stigma of untrustworthiness associated with a conviction.[57]

---

[55] United States v. Cavender, 578 F.2d 528 (4th Cir. 1978); *see also* Hunnicutt v. Wright, 986 F.2d 119 (5th Cir. 1993) (in medical malpractice case, trial court properly excluded evidence of plaintiff's felony convictions that were more than ten years old); United States v. Daniel, 957 F.2d 162 (5th Cir. 1992) (when calculating the ten-year period, the date of witness's release from confinement does not refer to a probation or parole period, but to the release from prison); United States v. Brown, 956 F.2d 782 (8th Cir. 1992) (in a drug trial the district court did not abuse its discretion in admitting a 1969 conviction for burglary since its probative value supported by facts and circumstances substantially outweighed its prejudicial effect).

[56] *See* 4 WEINSTEIN'S FEDERAL EVIDENCE § 609.03.

[57] United States v. Hamilton, 48 F.3d 149 (5th Cir. 1995) (trial court did not abuse its discretion in excluding evidence of the criminal acts and convictions of a prosecution witness; one conviction was twenty years old and the prosecution witness was later pardoned; another more recent criminal act by defendant did not result in a conviction because the court had deferred adjudication of the witness's guilt). *But see* Smith v. Tidewater Marine Towing, 927 F.2d 838 (5th Cir. 1991) (plaintiff's automatic pardon under a Louisiana statute after completion of probation in a prior criminal case simply restored plaintiff's civil rights and was not a showing of rehabilitation for purposes of 609(c); conviction was properly admitted

The burden of proving that a witness's conviction is inadmissible under Rule 609(c) rests with the party who opposes the use of the conviction, and it must be demonstrated that the pardon, annulment, or equivalent procedure bars introduction of an otherwise admissible conviction.[58]

§ 609.9   Rule 609(d) — Juvenile Adjudications

Rule 609(d) establishes a general principle that evidence of the juvenile adjudication of a witness is not admissible for the purpose of impeachment. The principle is predicated upon the dual concept that juvenile adjudications of delinquency are not probative of the witness's propensity to tell the truth as an adult and that since the purpose of the juvenile proceeding is not to punish the individual, it is undesirable to allow the juvenile offense to be treated as a criminal conviction that bears on the witness's credibility.[59]

Evidence of a juvenile adjudication is admissible under Rule 609(d) to impeach the witness in a limited situation, *i.e.,* when the judge determines in a criminal proceeding that admission of the evidence is necessary for a fair determination of the defendant's guilt or innocence. Where the trial judge is satisfied that such impeachment is necessary to protect the rights of the accused, Rule 609(d) allows a juvenile adjudication to be used to impeach the "credibility" of a prosecution witness in any way, and not merely through an attack on the character of the witness for truthfulness.[60] This exception to the general rule prohibiting impeachment by juvenile adjudication is inapplicable in civil proceedings or where the witness to be impeached is the criminal defendant.

The Rule does not preclude impeachment of a witness by inquiring into conduct for which the witness, although a juvenile at the time, was tried,

---

for impeachment purposes). *See generally,* 4 WEINSTEIN'S FEDERAL EVIDENCE § 609.03; 3 MUELLER & KIRKPATRICK, § 285.

[58] United States v. Wiggins, 566 F.2d 944 (5th Cir. 1978) (fact that defendant was released from a Halfway House, where he had been placed as a condition of his probation on a drug offense, did not make the conviction usable where neither the program and objectives of the institution nor the qualification required for release were demonstrated).

[59] *See* United States v. Ashley, 569 F.2d 975 (5th Cir. 1978); *see also* United States v. LeBlanc, 612 F.2d 1012 (6th Cir. 1980).

[60] This point is reflected in the fact that Rule 609(d) still refers broadly to offenses that might be admissible to attack the adult's "credibility." Even though the Advisory Committee has recently inserted the words "character for truthfulness" in almost every other place where Rule 608 and 609 formerly referred to the "credibility" of the witness, the Committee consciously chose to retain the word "credibility" in Rule 609(d) because "that subdivision is intended to govern the use of a juvenile adjudication for any type of impeachment." Committee Notes to the 2006 amendment to Rule 609. This was done precisely in accordance with a written recommendation that had been submitted to the Committee several years earlier by one of the authors of this treatise. *See* Duane, *The Proposed Amendments to FRE 608(b) and 804(b)(3): Two Great Ideas that Don't Go Far Enough,* 209 F.R.D. 235, 242–244 (2002).

convicted and sentenced as an adult where a distinct basis for admissibility is present.[61] The Rule also allows a party to use a juvenile record to impeach a witness by contradiction, since Rule 609 does not regulate contradiction as an impeachment device. Nor may the Rule operate so as to deny a constitutional right of a litigant, such as where an expunged juvenile record must be disclosed to enable the accused to present relevant evidence regarding a defense.[62]

§ 609.10 Rule 609(e) — Effect of Pendency of Appeal

The final provision of Rule 609 permits the introduction of convictions for impeachment despite the fact that an appeal is pending.[63] The Rule provides, however, that where a witness is questioned about a conviction that has since been appealed, the fact that the appeal is pending is admissible. Thus, the matter of the appeal is left to the trier of fact in weighing the conviction in regard to the issue of credibility, and the pendency of the appeal is appropriate for comment during closing argument.

---

[61] United States v. Canniff, 521 F.2d 565 (2d Cir. 1975).

[62] Davis v. Alaska, 415 U.S. 308 (1974) (despite state's interest in preserving privacy of juvenile records, defendant had constitutional right under confrontation clause to cross-examine prosecution witness about his juvenile adjudications, not as attack on his character for honesty but to show his motive to lie after stolen property was found near his home, because he knew that police would suspect him if he did not identify someone else as the thief).

[63] United States v. Klayer, 707 F.2d 892 (6th Cir. 1983); United States v. De La Torre, 639 F.2d 245 (5th Cir. 1981).

Chapter 610

Rule 610. Religious Beliefs or Opinions

Rule 610. Religious Beliefs or Opinions

Evidence of a witness's religious beliefs or opinions is not admissible to attack or support the witness's credibility.

---

§ 610.1 Religious Beliefs or Opinions as Affecting Credibility of Witness — In General

Rule 610 generally proscribes the introduction of evidence as to religious beliefs or opinions for the purpose of impeaching or bolstering a witness's credibility.[1] The Rule is in harmony with prior federal practice, which has long forbidden inquiry into the religious beliefs of a witness for the purpose of impeaching his or her character for truthfulness.[2]

The principle of inadmissibility contained in Rule 610 rests upon grounds of unfair prejudice and minimal probative value,[3] and it is likely derived, at least obliquely, from the federal constitutional guarantees of the free exercise of religion.[4] Accordingly, the Rule prohibits inquiries on cross-examination into the religious beliefs, or lack thereof, of a witness for the purpose of testing the witness's ability to tell the truth.

It should be noted that although Rule 603 still requires witnesses to swear or affirm before testifying that they will do so truthfully, the option of an

---

[1] *See generally,* 4 WEINSTEIN'S FEDERAL EVIDENCE §§ 610.01–610.03; 3 MUELLER & KIRKPATRICK, § 290; 1 MCCORMICK, § 46; 3A WIGMORE, § 936. *See also* Swancara, *Impeachment of Non-Religious Witness,* § 13 ROCKY MTN. L. REV. 336 (1941); *Non-Religious Witness,* 8 WIS. L. REV. 49 (1932); Note, *Evidence—Impeaching Witness by Showing Religious Belief,* 9 N.C.L. REV. 77 (1930).

[2] *See* 4 WEINSTEIN'S FEDERAL EVIDENCE § 610.02; 3 MUELLER & KIRKPATRICK, § 290.

[3] *See* Malek v. Federal Ins. Co., 994 F.2d 49 (2d Cir. 1993) (trial court erred in permitting cross-examination concerning a witness's and plaintiff's membership in a religious community); United States v. Sampol, 636 F.2d 621 (D.C. Cir. 1980); (noting that scope of prohibition includes unconventional religions); La Rocca v. Lane, 37 N.Y.2d 575, 376 N.Y.S.2d 93, 338 N.E.2d 606 (1975).

[4] *See generally,* 4 WEINSTEIN'S FEDERAL EVIDENCE § 610.02; 3 MUELLER & KIRKPATRICK, § 290; 1 MCCORMICK, § 46; 2 WIGMORE, § 518; 3A WIGMORE, § 936.

affirmation allows witnesses to avoid basing the declaration on any religious conviction.

§ 610.2   Admissible Evidence of Religious Beliefs

Since the impeachment process is limited by the concepts of relevance and unfair prejudice, the Rule restricts the introduction of evidence related to religious beliefs. The Rule does not, however, foreclose the admission of evidence of religious beliefs where such evidence is relevant in a manner other than to show that the witness's trustworthiness is enhanced or diminished by virtue of religious convictions.[5] Accordingly, the Rule does not exclude evidence tending to demonstrate bias or interest on the part of a witness, such as where the witness is affiliated with a church that is a party to the action. Under these circumstances, the probative value of the evidence is focused on a permissible target of inquiry, *e.g.*, bias or interest, rather than on the witness's credibility as indicated by the nature of his or her religious beliefs or opinions.[6]

---

[5] *See* United States v. Kalaydjian, 784 F.2d 53 (2d Cir. 1986) (trial judge properly disallowed cross-examination of witness asking why he chose to "affirm" rather than to swear).

[6] *See generally,* 4 WEINSTEIN'S FEDERAL EVIDENCE § 610.03; 3 MUELLER & KIRKPATRICK, § 290; 1 MCCORMICK, § 46; 3A WIGMORE, § 936.

Chapter 611

Rule 611. Mode and Order of Examining Witnesses and Presenting Evidence

Rule 611. Mode and Order of Examining Witnesses and Presenting Evidence

(a) **Control by the Court; Purposes.** The court should exercise reasonable control over the mode and order of examining witnesses and presenting evidence so as to:

   (1) make those procedures effective for determining the truth;

   (2) avoid wasting time; and

   (3) protect witnesses from harassment or undue embarrassment.

(b) **Scope of Cross-Examination.** Cross-examination should not go beyond the subject matter of the direct examination and matters affecting the witness's credibility. The court may allow inquiry into additional matters as if on direct examination.

(c) **Leading Questions.** Leading questions should not be used on direct examination except as necessary to develop the witness's testimony. Ordinarily, the court should allow leading questions:

   (1) on cross-examination; and

   (2) when a party calls a hostile witness, an adverse party, or a witness identified with an adverse party.

---

§ 611.1   Rule 611 — Background and Purpose

Rule 611 addresses the trial court's control over the mode and order of interrogating witnesses and presenting evidence, the scope of cross-examination, and the use of leading questions.[1] Essentially, the Rule

---

[1] *See generally,* 1 McCORMICK, §§ 4–8; 4 WEINSTEIN'S FEDERAL EVIDENCE §§ 611.01–611.06; 3 MUELLER & KIRKPATRICK, §§ 291–322; 3 WIGMORE, §§ 768–780; 5 WIGMORE, §§ 1390–1394; 6 WIGMORE, §§ 1884–1894; 8 WIGMORE, § 2276. *See also* Bergman, *A Practical Approach to Cross-Examination: Safety First,* 25 UCLA L. REV. 547 (1978); Carlson, *Scope of Cross-Examination and the Proposed Federal Rules,* 32 FED. B.J. 244 (1973); Carlson, *Cross-Examination of the Accused,* 52 CORNELL L.Q. 705 (1967); Cleary, *Evidence As a Problem in Communicating,* 5 VAND. L. REV. 277 (1952); Degnan,

embodies general principles enunciated elsewhere throughout the Rules, *e.g.,* Rules 102 and 403, and it specifically applies those principles to witnesses. It is designed to encourage flexibility in the reception of evidence by promoting the efficient determination of the truth without unnecessary abuse of the dignity of witnesses.[2]

Rule 611(a) gives the trial court authority to control the interrogation of witnesses and the presentation of evidence. In the exercise of its discretion, the trial court is guided by three principles, any or all of which may serve as the basis for the court's decision: (1) efficient determination of truth;[3] (2) avoidance of wasting time;[4] and (3) protection of witnesses from harassment or undue embarrassment.[5]

As submitted to Congress by the Supreme Court,[6] Rule 611(b) provided that a witness could be cross-examined on any relevant issue, including credibility, subject to the trial court's discretion to limit inquiry into matters

---

Non-Rules Evidence Law: Cross-Examination, 6 UTAH L. REV. 323 (1959); Denbeaux and Risinger, *Questioning Questions: Objections to Form in the Interrogation of Witnesses,* 33 ARK. L. REV. 439 (1980); Denroche, *Leading Questions,* 6 CRIM. L. Q. 21 (1963); Friendly, *The Fifth Amendment Tomorrow: The Case for Constitutional Change,* 37 U. CIN. L. REV. 671 (1968); Lawson, *Order of Presentation as a Factor in Jury Persuasion,* 56 KY. L.J. 523 (1968); Marshall, Marquis and Oskamp, *Effects of Kind of Questions and Atmosphere of Interrogation on Accuracy and Completeness of Testimony,* 84 HARV. L. REV. 1620 (1971); Westen, *Order of Proof: An Accused's Right to Control the Timing and Sequence of Evidence in His Defense,* 66 CALIF. L. REV. 935 (1978).

[2] *See, e.g.,* United States v. Kizer, 569 F.2d 504 (9th Cir. 1978) (defense counsel properly prevented from asking prosecution witness about prior drug use and hospitalization for drug addiction; Sixth Amendment interest outweighed by danger of harassing witness); *see also* Goings v. United States, 377 F.2d 753 (9th Cir. 1967), *later app.,* 393 F.2d 884 (8th Cir. 1967); Teti v. Firestone Tire and Rubber Co., 392 F.2d 294, 16 Ohio Misc. 80 (6th Cir. 1968).

[3] *E.g.,* United States v. Clark, 613 F.2d 391 (2d Cir. 1979); Beard v. Mitchell, 604 F.2d 485 (7th Cir. 1979); United States v. Cooper, 596 F.2d 327 (8th Cir. 1979).

[4] *See* United States v. O'Brien, 119 F.3d 523 (7th Cir. 1997) (trial court did not abuse its discretion by not allowing defendant to take the stand to offer surrebuttal evidence regarding an uncharged act offered to impeach the defendant's testimony where such evidence would only have been cumulative of testimony the defendant had already given); United States v. Coven, 662 F.2d 162 (2d Cir. 1981); *see also* United States v. Anthony, 565 F.2d 533 (8th Cir. 1977) (defendants allowed to cross-examine witnesses on both appearances, even though some witnesses were called twice); *see, e.g.,* Beard v. Mitchell, 604 F.2d 485 (7th Cir. 1979); United States v. Jackson, 549 F.2d 517 (8th Cir. 1977); United States v. Hathaway, 534 F.2d 386 (1st Cir. 1976).

[5] *See* United States v. Sampol, 636 F.2d 621 (D.C. Cir. 1980); *see also* United States v. Singh, 628 F.2d 758 (2d Cir. 1980) (in alleged exploitation of illegal aliens in violation of immigration laws, many government witnesses testified that they worked without pay at restaurant operated by defendants making only tips; no abuse by trial court in refusing to permit defense to establish that witness traveled to and from Bangladesh with another, since it was a collateral matter with little, if any, probative value).

[6] 3 MUELLER & KIRKPATRICK, § 291.

not the subject of testimony on direct examination.[7] Although the "wide open rule" received much favorable comment during congressional consideration, Congress ultimately chose to return to the traditional, more restrictive version of the rule on the grounds that it "facilitates orderly presentation by each party at trial"[8] and that "the factors of insuring an orderly and predictable development of the evidence weigh in favor of the narrower rule, especially when discretion is given to the trial judge to permit inquiry into additional matters."[9]

The first two sentences of Rule 611(c) provide that on direct examination leading questions generally should not be used except as necessary to develop the witness's testimony, but on cross-examination leading questions usually should be permitted.[10] This portion of the Rule remained unchanged by Congress. In the Advisory Committee's draft, as approved by the Supreme Court and submitted to Congress, the final sentence read, "In civil cases, a party is entitled to call an adverse party or witness identified with him and interrogate by leading questions."[11] Congress expanded the Rule to include criminal cases and specified that hostile witnesses could be interrogated by leading questions. The Senate Judiciary Committee noted "it may be difficult in criminal cases to determine when a witness is 'identified with an adverse party,' and thus the rule should be applied with caution."[12] The Committee also questioned whether the specific inclusion of hostile witnesses was necessary since the first sentence of Rule 611(c) already authorized the use of leading questions when necessary to develop the witness's testimony. Nevertheless, the Committee approved the amendment, finding "it was not intended to affect the meaning of the first sentence of the subsection and was intended solely to clarify the fact that leading questions are permissible in the interrogation of a witness, who is hostile in fact."[13]

§ 611.2 Rule 611(a) — Mode and Order of Proof Within Discretion of Court

Rather than attempt to formulate specific rules governing the mode and order of proof in all conceivable situations, Rule 611(a) leaves decisions on

---

[7] The Supreme Court's version of Rule 611(b) read: "A witness may be cross-examined on any matter relevant to any issue in the case, including credibility. In the interests of justice, the judge may limit cross-examination with respect to matters not testified to on direct examination." Draft of November, 1972, 56 F.R.D. 183, 273 (1972).

[8] H.R. REP. No. 93-650, 93d Cong., 1st Sess. 12 (1973).

[9] S. REP. No. 93-1277, 93d Cong., 2d Sess. 25 (1974).

[10] *See* Rule 611(c).

[11] Draft of November, 1972, 56 F.R.D. 183, 273 (1972).

[12] S. REP. No. 93-1277, 93d Cong., 2d Sess. 25–26 (1974).

[13] S. REP. No. 93-1277, 93d Cong., 2d Sess. 25–26 (1974).

these issues to the trial court's discretion.[14] In exercising its discretion, the trial court should seek to attain the objectives of effective ascertainment of the truth, avoidance of needless consumption of time, and prevention of undue embarrassment or harassment of witnesses. Since determinations on the mode and order of interrogating witnesses and presenting evidence depend on particular circumstances at trial that will not be apparent to the reviewing court from the record, the trial court's decision will not serve as the basis for reversal on appeal absent a clear showing of abuse of discretion and abridgment of a substantive right.[15]

Rule 611(a) seeks to effectuate goals similar to those underlying Rules 102 and 403 and recognizes that the manner in which evidence is presented may have a substantial impact on these objectives, independent of the substance of the evidence. Although the parties normally determine the order in which evidence is introduced and witnesses testify, Rule 611 empowers the trial court to make this decision.[16] At times the court's decision on the order of proof may affect admissibility of the evidence under Rule 104(a) or conditional relevance under Rule 104(b).[17] By setting the order of proof, the trial court also may be able to postpone its decision on whether to admit probative but prejudicial evidence until after the facts of the case have more fully developed.[18] The trial court has discretionary power over decisions such as whether and to what extent to allow redirect and re-cross-examination,[19] whether a witness can be recalled,[20] and whether a party may

---

[14] Rule 611(a), Advisory Committee Note.

[15] M.T. Bonk Co. v. Milton Bradley Co., 945 F.2d 1404 (7th Cir. 1991) (the district court did not abuse its discretion in terminating the direct examination of plaintiff's witness after ample time had been afforded); Johnson v. Ashby, 808 F.2d 676 (8th Cir. 1987) (while trial courts have discretion to place reasonable time limits on evidence presentation in order to prevent undue delay and avoid cumulative evidence, it is abuse of discretion for court to exclude non-cumulative, probative evidence simply because it would extend trial beyond allotted time); United States v. Leon, 679 F.2d 534 (5th Cir. 1982); Oberlin v. Marlin Am. Corp., 596 F.2d 1322 (7th Cir. 1979).

[16] Chamberlin v. Town of Stoughton, 601 F.3d 25 (1st Cir. 2010) (district judge has wide latitude in regulating the order in which the proof is developed; even though evidence may be relevant and admissible, the judge has the discretion to preclude a party from offering that evidence until after the jury first hears evidence about some other aspect of the case).

[17] 3 MUELLER & KIRKPATRICK, § 292.

[18] United States v. Brunson, 549 F.2d 348 (5th Cir. 1977) (robbery prosecution; proof of defendant's involvement in another robbery permitted to be introduced at end of government's case-in-chief on question of intent, since it was clear that intent would be an issue).

[19] United States v. Payne, 437 F.3d 540, 547 n.5 (6th Cir. 2006) (the right to recross-examination is usually within the discretion of the district judge and normally poses no constitutional issue, but if "new matters are elicited on redirect" of a prosecution witness, the Confrontation Clause gives the defense a constitutional right to recross-examination).

[20] Elgabri v. Lekas, 964 F.2d 1255 (1st Cir. 1992) (the court's discretionary power under Rule 611(a) takes precedence over Rule 611(c) and consequently, the district court did not err

reopen its case.[21] Where evidence could have been introduced during a party's case-in-chief but was not, it is within the court's discretion to allow or disallow its introduction on rebuttal.[22] Impeachment by cross-examination about bad acts under Rule 608(b) may be limited under Rule 611(a) where the questions are aimed solely at embarrassing or harassing the witness.[23] The trial court also can curtail cross-examination if it finds that the probative value of the witness's testimony is outweighed by the Rule 403 factors of prejudice, confusion of the issues, or time consumption.[24]

The trial court may prevent attempts by trial counsel to intimidate witnesses physically or psychologically. Since cross-examination necessarily entails confrontation of the witness, a certain degree of intimidation may be required to expose bias, untruthfulness, or uncertainty, but Rule 611(a) authorizes the trial court to disallow "*unnecessary* discomfort, caused by the excesses of over-zealous trial counsel."[25] The trial court's power over the mode of interrogation enables it to exclude abusive, misleading, or unfair questions, such as argumentative, repetitious, or ambiguous questions or questions that assume facts that are not in evidence. When a question is

---

in refusing to allow the calling of all defendants as adverse witnesses where the plaintiff had thoroughly cross-examined defendants during the defense case-in-chief); Price v. Seydel, 961 F.2d 1470 (9th Cir. 1992) (the district court erred in refusing to allow plaintiff to call the defendant as an adverse witness merely because defendant was not listed as a plaintiff's witness); United States v. Jensen, 608 F.2d 1349 (10th Cir. 1979); *see also* United States v. Heath, 580 F.2d 1011 (10th Cir. 1978) (no error to permit recall); United States v. Rucker, 557 F.2d 1046 (4th Cir. 1977) (recall properly allowed).

[21] United States v. Nunez, 432 F.3d 573, 579–582 (4th Cir. 2005) (although decision to reopen the case is normally committed to the discretion of the district judge, lower court committed reversible error in reopening the case, after jury deliberations had begun, to allow government to admit evidence that jurors had requested; the exhibit thereby gained distorted importance, prejudiced the defendants, and deprived them of an adequate opportunity to rebut the additional evidence).

[22] Page v. Barko Hydraulics, 673 F.2d 134 (5th Cir. 1982); United States v. Wilford, 710 F.2d 439 (8th Cir. 1983); United States v. Glass, 709 F.2d 669 (11th Cir. 1983); Smith v. Conley, 584 F.2d 844 (8th Cir. 1978).

[23] United States v. Singh, 628 F.2d 758 (2d Cir. 1980); United States v. Colyer, 571 F.2d 941 (5th Cir. 1978); United States v. Provoo, 215 F.2d 531 (2d Cir. 1954).

[24] United States v. 10.48 Acres of Land, 621 F.2d 338 (9th Cir. 1980); *see also* United States v. Gleason, 616 F.2d 2 (2d Cir. 1979) (cross-examination not permitted where it was beyond scope of direct and could have opened up a flood of evidence regarding a possibly confusing collateral issue); United States v. Walker, 613 F.2d 1349 (5th Cir. 1980) (where door opened by defense that witness was a prostitute, no error for government to bring out on re-direct that she was turning earnings over to defendant); *see, e.g.,* United States v. Summers, 598 F.2d 450 (5th Cir. 1979); United States v. Ellison, 557 F.2d 128 (7th Cir. 1977).

[25] 3 MUELLER & KIRKPATRICK, § 295; *see also* United States v. Maddox, 944 F.2d 1223 (6th Cir. 1991) (it was proper to admit evidence that defendant had mouthed a threat against the witness on the stand since this is probative of the defendant's consciousness of guilt).

objected to on one of these grounds, the court often will permit counsel to rephrase the question and continue.[26]

Rule 611(a) allows for innovative approaches to the reception of evidence, such as the "free narrative," where the witness is asked simply to relate his or her story without intermittent questions. As long as the manner of interrogation does not have a prejudicial effect on a witness or a party, the method chosen is within the court's discretion.[27]

The discretion of the trial judge to protect the witness from embarrassment or distress is subject to certain limits when the witness testifies for the prosecution in a criminal case. In *Coy v. Iowa,*[28] the United States Supreme Court held that the Confrontation Clause guaranteed a defendant a right to be within the view of prosecution witnesses testifying at the trial. In that case, the trial judge had allowed a screen to be placed between the accused and the two complaining witnesses so that they could not see the defendant while they were testifying. The Court held that this procedure violated the defendant's confrontation rights, as the "irreducible literal meaning" of the Confrontation Clause "guarantees the defendant a face-to-face meeting with witnesses."[29]

Although *Coy* was never overruled, it was severely limited in *Maryland v. Craig,*[30] which held that protective schemes may, in some circumstances, be devised to allow child abuse victims to testify without facing the defendant in open court. In *Craig,* the child victim testified through a one-way closed circuit television that allowed the prosecutor and the defense counsel to question the child while the defendant, the court, and the jury watched on a monitor, but the child was not even able (much less required) to see or confront the defendant. The Court remanded the case for further findings, holding that the state's interest in the physical and psychological well-being of child abuse victims may justify such measures. The Court stressed, however, that the need for such protective procedures must be shown on a case-by-case basis.

In order for such measures to be employed, *Craig* emphasized that the trial court must find that testifying against the defendant in open court would cause the child victim "emotional distress" that is "more than *de minimis*," which the court qualified as meaning something more than "mere nervous-

---

[26] 3 WIGMORE, §§ 780, 782; *see, e.g.,* United States v. Weiner, 578 F.2d 757 (9th Cir. 1978); United States v. Arlt, 567 F.2d 1295 (5th Cir. 1978); United States v. Cash, 499 F.2d 26 (9th Cir. 1974).

[27] 3 MUELLER & KIRKPATRICK, § 292.

[28] Coy v. Iowa, 487 U.S. 1012 (1988).

[29] *Coy,* 487 U.S. at 1016.

[30] Maryland v. Craig, 497 U.S. 836 (1990).

ness or excitement or some reluctance to testify."[31] In the *Craig* case, for example, prosecution experts testified that the children in that case, one of them only seven years old, "wouldn't be able to communicate effectively," "would probably stop talking and . . . withdraw and curl up," would "become highly agitated, that he may refuse to talk or if he did talk, that he would choose his subject regardless of the questions," and would "become extremely timid and unwilling to talk."[32] Nevertheless, lower courts have exhibited a remarkable willingness to extend the holding in *Craig* to witnesses in sex offense cases based upon much less evidence of emotional distress, including much older witnesses and witnesses who admitted they did not fear the accused.[33]

Even considering the normal deference owed to settled precedent under the doctrine of *stare decisis,* there is good reason to suspect that a majority of the Supreme Court might now be willing to narrow or overrule *Craig.* Of the five justices in the majority that decided *Craig,* only one of them is still on the Court. Justice Scalia, who authored the majority opinion in *Coy* and the dissent in *Craig,* has mounted a sustained campaign for its re-examination,[34] and has since authored three recent Court opinions that have explicitly overturned much of the foundation and reasoning upon which *Craig* was based.[35] In any future cases in which a prosecutor requests

---

[31] *Craig,* 497 U.S. at 856.

[32] *Id.* at 842 (internal quotation marks omitted).

[33] *E.g.,* Marx v. Texas, 528 U.S. 1034 (1999) (Scalia, J., dissenting from denial of certiorari) (six-year old witness allowed to testify against the accused via television even though she was not the victim, and even though her mother and examining doctor testified that she "want[ed] to" testify and was "ready for that"); Danner v. Kentucky, 525 U.S. 1010 (1998) (Scalia, J., dissenting from denial of certiorari) (fifteen-year old rape victim allowed to testify out of the presence of her father, the accused, even though she admitted she was not afraid of him and could not rule out the possibility of being able to testify in his presence with breaks in the testimony, merely because she "vaguely protested that she could not be near him").

[34] *See Marx* and *Danner,* supra.

[35] In *Crawford v. Washington,* 541 U.S. 36 (2004), Justice Scalia wrote the Court opinion overturning *Ohio v. Roberts,* upon which *Craig* had relied, in holding that "witnesses" covered by the Confrontation Clause must be produced for trial if available. *See* § 801.2 *infra.* In *Davis v. Washington,* 547 U.S. 813, 832–833 (2006), Justice Scalia explicitly rejected the suggestion that the Confrontation Clause may be interpreted with "greater flexibility" in domestic violence cases merely because those guilty of such offenses are notoriously prone "to intimidation or coercion of the victim." Then, in *United States v. Gonzalez-Lopez,* 548 U.S. 140, 145–146 (2006), Justice Scalia wrote a majority opinion that approvingly quoted his dissent in *Craig* for the proposition that it is not permissible to disregard the specific rights set forth in the Sixth Amendment merely because the purposes of those rights are arguably secured by other means that allegedly make the trial "on the whole, fair." In addition to the five justices making up the Court majority in *Gonzalez-Lopez,* Justice Thomas has also publicly joined Justice Scalia's statement that *Craig* was incorrectly decided, *see Marx* and *Danner, supra,* and so there are now several justices on the Court who did not join the

permission for a witness to testify outside the presence of the accused, cautious defense counsel should proceed on the assumption that *Maryland v. Craig* may not still be settled law by the time the defendant's appeal is heard, and should explicitly object for the record on the grounds that *Craig* was incorrectly decided.[36]

§ 611.3   Rule 611(b) — Scope of Cross-Examination

Rule 611(b) restricts the scope of cross-examination of a witness to matters bearing on credibility or that are within the subject matter of the direct examination. Inquiry into areas not authorized explicitly by the Rule is permissible only if authorized by the trial court in the exercise of its discretion.

Rule 611(b) as adopted is consistent with prior federal practice in the sense that the Rule rejects a "wide open" approach to cross-examination in favor of a narrower rule that limits the scope of cross-examination. Under the wide open rule, which is followed in England and a significant minority of states,[37] the witness may, subject to the court's control, be asked about any relevant fact on cross-examination, including matters not addressed on direct examination.[38] The wide-open rule is preferred by leading scholars, including McCormick and Wigmore, who contend that it advances the search for truth by providing an opportunity for witnesses to divulge all they know, in contrast to the scope-of-direct rule that permits the proponent of the witness to limit disclosure by carefully restricting the questions asked on direct.[39] As Dean McCormick stated:

> [I]n many instances a mere postponement of the questions will not necessarily be the result of a ruling excluding a cross-question as not in the scope of the direct. Unless the question is vital and he is fairly confident of a favorable answer, the cross-examiner will at the least take considerable risk if he calls the adversary's witness at a later

---

majority opinion in *Craig* and who have made it plain that they might be likely to give serious consideration to a request for its re-examination.

[36] It admittedly seems senseless for you to make an objection to a district judge's ruling when that ruling is clearly supported by existing precedents at the time of the trial, but if those precedents are overturned before your case is decided on appeal, your failure to object will limit the appeals court's review to a search for "plain error." Johnson v. United States, 520 U.S. 461 (1997); United States v. Hadley, 431 F.3d 484, 498 n.8 (6th Cir. 2005) (after *Johnson*, appellants must demonstrate plain error if they failed to make a "virtually useless" objection to district court ruling that was plainly supported by existing precedents at the time, even if those precedents were overturned by the time of appeal); United States v. Keys, 133 F.3d 1282 (9th Cir. 1998) (after *Johnson,* trial counsel must make objections even to actions supported at the time by a "solid wall of circuit authority," or they will be limited to plain error review if that wall crumbles before the appeal is decided).

[37] 1 McCormick, § 21.

[38] *See* 4 Weinstein's Federal Evidence § 611.03.

[39] 3 Mueller & Kirkpatrick, §§ 300–305.

stage as his own, and will often be motivated to abandon the inquiry. Getting concessions from the opponent's witness while his story is fresh is worth trying for. To call the perhaps unfriendly witness later when his first testimony is stale is usually a much less effective expedient.[40]

Dean Wigmore argued that in practice, the scope-of-direct rule is difficult to apply and it "increases the opportunities for securing a retrial on trifling errors of ruling which do not affect the merits of the cause or the truth of the facts."[41] An overabundance of technical appeals results from the imprecision in the definition of the scope-of-direct examination. Professor Degnan found the rule susceptible of six different interpretations:

[Cross-examination is limited] to (1) any issue properly a part of the case of the party who called the witness, as opposed to establishing the defenses or points of the cross-examiner, or (2) any issue properly a part of his case in chief, or (3) any issue or inference raised by testimony already received in the case, by whatever witness, or (4) any issue or inference raised by the testimony given by the witness presently being cross-examined, or (5) any transaction or occurrence testified to by that witness, even if those aspects of it were not mentioned by him, or (6) only those precise matters testified to by the witness upon direct examination.[42]

The better-reasoned cases find that cross-examination "may embrace any matter germane to the direct examination, qualifying or destroying it, or tending to elucidate, modify, explain, contradict, or rebut testimony given in chief by the witness."[43]

The rationale of restricted cross-examination is that the Rule preserves order in the presentation of evidence. The approach taken by Rule 611(b) allows each party to present its entire case without interruption from its opponent who, under the wide open approach, could present counter-evidence through the process of cross-examining the witness.[44] Other arguments in favor of a narrow scope of cross-examination generally have been rejected by the commentators.[45]

---

[40] 1 McCormick, § 23, at 87.

[41] 6 Wigmore, § 1888, at 710.

[42] Degnan, *Non-Rules Evidence Law: Cross-Examination*, 6 Utah L. Rev. 323, 330–31 (1959).

[43] Leeper v. United States, 446 F.2d 281 (10th Cir. 1971); *see also* Roberts v. Hollocher, 664 F.2d 200 (8th Cir. 1981); United States v. Dickens, 417 F.2d 958 (8th Cir. 1969).

[44] *See, e.g.*, Wills v. Russell, 100 U.S. (10 Otto) 621, 100 U.S. 621 (1879); United States v. Ellison, 557 F.2d 128 (7th Cir. 1977); United States v. Furr, 528 F.2d 578 (5th Cir. 1976).

[45] One argument supporting restricted cross-examination was that the calling party vouched for its witness only to the extent of direct examination and therefore should not be

Rule 611(b) alleviates to some degree the problem of excessive appeals contending that cross-examination went beyond the scope of direct, by granting the court discretion to allow inquiry on cross-examination in the manner that would be permitted on direct examination of the witness. In other words, if the court authorizes a broad cross-examination, in probing matters not addressed on direct, the examiner will be restricted from asking the witness leading questions, *i.e.*, a right counsel does not normally have on direct examination.[46] Leading questions also are disallowed on cross-examination in two other situations. If the party calling the witness is permitted to ask leading questions on direct examination because, for example, the witness is hostile to the calling party, on cross-examination leading questions usually will be disallowed.[47] Also, in a civil case where a party calls its opponent as a witness, leading questions are permitted on direct examination but not allowed on cross-examination, unless the same question could have been properly put to the same witness by that lawyer on direct examination (as would be true, for example, if the question involved some preliminary undisputed fact).[48]

---

bound by his testimony on cross-examination with no opportunity to impeach him. This argument is foreclosed by Rule 607's abandonment of the voucher principle. 4 WEINSTEIN'S FEDERAL EVIDENCE § 611.03. Another argument was that by permitting unrestricted cross-examination, a party could make his case by leading questions. Dean Wigmore rejected this argument on the following grounds:

> [T]he rule as to leading questions concerns the partisan disposition of the individual witness and depends on the supposed willingness of a partisan witness to assist his party . . . . Its criterion is solely the individual witness's state of mind—not the kind of fact that is to be asked, nor the stage of asking.

6 WIGMORE, § 1887, at 705.

[46] Lis v. Robert Packer Hosp., 579 F.2d 819 (3d Cir. 1978) (medical malpractice case; plaintiffs called physician to testify; after defense cross-examination was completed, trial judge permitted defendants to qualify the physician as its witness). *See generally*, 3 MUELLER & KIRKPATRICK, § 302.

[47] Morvant v. Construction Aggregates Corp., 570 F.2d 626 (6th Cir. 1978) (if witness is friendly to the cross-examiner, leading questions pose some danger of suggestiveness and in this situation a court is in its discretion to prohibit the use of leading questions on cross-examination); United States v. Bensinger Co., 430 F.2d 584 (8th Cir. 1970) (after permission secured to lead person as a hostile witness, proper thereafter to limit defense on cross-examination of witness to non-leading questions). Leading questions may be permitted on both direct and cross-examination if the witness is hostile to both parties or if leading questions are needed to develop the witness's testimony. 3 MUELLER & KIRKPATRICK, § 302. *But see* Ardoin v. J. Ray McDermott & Co., 684 F.2d 335 (5th Cir. 1982) (where defendant was allowed to ask leading questions of its own employees on cross-examination where the employees had originally been called as witnesses by the plaintiff, court held that it is the District Court's discretion whether to require non-leading questions when a party is cross-examining a friendly witness).

[48] Shultz v. Rice, 809 F.2d 643 (10th Cir. 1986) (in medical malpractice suit where plaintiff called defendant physician as an adverse witness, court held that defense counsel should not be allowed to use leading questions on cross-examination).

It is within the court's discretion to allow a broad or narrow cross-examination and the court may limit cross-examination of a witness normally allowed under Rule 611(b) by invoking Rule 403 or Rule 611(a). The court will be overruled on appeal only upon showing an abuse of discretion.[49] However, in a criminal case, excessively restrictive limits on the defendant's cross-examination of prosecution witnesses may amount to a violation of the constitutional right of confrontation.[50]

Cross-examination is seen as necessary to the truth-seeking function of a trial. Thus, where a witness refuses to submit to an appropriate cross-examination, the trial court may strike or exclude the witness's direct testimony, as there is a substantial danger of prejudice where the opposing party has not had the opportunity to test the truth of the direct testimony.[51] However, a witness may refuse to submit to cross-examination regarding a collateral issue without rendering his or her direct testimony inadmissible.

§ 611.4 Rule 611(b) — Cross-Examination Relating to the Credibility of the Witness

Rule 611(b) authorizes cross-examination as to matters affecting the credibility of the witness. Consequently, regardless of the factual substance

---

[49] *See* Losacco v. F.D. Rich Construction Co., 992 F.2d 382 (1st Cir. 1993) (trial court's ruling barring plaintiff's questioning of defendant's employee about the motivation behind the closing of defendant's plant where the employee had not testified about the subject on direct was within Rule 611(b)); United States v. Riggi, 951 F.2d 1368 (3d Cir. 1991) (where damaging new material came out on redirect, it was reversible error to forbid all recross-examination); *e.g.,* Alford v. United States, 282 U.S. 687 (1931); United States v. Diaz, 662 F.2d 713 (11th Cir. 1981); United States v. Young, 655 F.2d 624 (5th Cir. 1981); United States v. Praetorius, 622 F.2d 1054 (2d Cir. 1979); United States v. Lara, 181 F.3d 183 (1st Cir. 1999) (although defendant's direct examination was limited to ten questions about a carjacking, cross examination about the carjacking, a murder, two attempted murders, and a letter asking the gang to "muzzle" the defendant's former girlfriend was proper cross where the indictment charged the carjacking as one predicate act within the RICO conspiracy, and the defendant's direct testimony included a denial that the carjacking was related to the gang's activities).

[50] *See, e.g.,* Davis v. Alaska, 415 U.S. 308 (1974) (despite state's interest in preserving privacy of juvenile records, defendant had constitutional right under confrontation clause to cross-examine prosecution witness about his juvenile adjudications, not as attack on his character for honesty but to show his motive to lie after stolen property was found near his home, because he knew that police would suspect him if he did not identify someone else as the thief); Smith v. Illinois, 390 U.S. 129 (1968) (failure to permit defense to ask chief prosecution witness his correct name and address violated right of confrontation); United States v. Crumley, 565 F.2d 945 (5th Cir. 1978) (denial of right of confrontation resulted where defense was not permitted to ask prosecution witness if he had been charged with crime); *see also* § 611.5, *infra.*

[51] *See* Denham v. Deeds, 954 F.2d 1501 (9th Cir. 1992) (excluding testimony by witness who refused during cross-examination to answer questions regarding non-collateral matters); United States v. Esparsen, 930 F.2d 1461 (10th Cir. 1991) (trial court may exclude defense witness's testimony where witness refuses to submit to appropriate cross-examination).

of a witness's direct examination testimony, the witness's veracity may be the subject of inquiry on cross-examination. Accordingly, consistent with the specific rules regarding discrediting a witness, the impeachment of a witness is always appropriate on cross-examination regardless of the subject matter of his testimony.[52] It should be noted, however, that under Rule 608(b), a witness does not, by testifying, waive the privilege against self-incrimination as to matters that relate only to the witness's character for truthfulness.

§ 611.5   Rule 611(b) — Impact of Privilege Against Self-Incrimination

Rule 611(b) controls the scope of cross-examination to effectuate the orderly presentation of evidence at trial. Although it is true that witnesses who take the stand subject themselves to reasonable cross-examination, difficult issues may arise regarding constitutional privileges that may be invoked to limit the extent and subject matter of cross-examination. Individuals do not necessarily waive their constitutional rights merely by taking the stand.[53] To so hold would permit a principle of evidence, *i.e.,* a procedural device designed to govern the introduction of evidence at trial, to determine the scope of a witness's constitutional rights.[54]

§ 611.6   Rule 611(c) — Leading Questions

Rule 611(c) provides the court with discretion to control the use of leading questions. The authorized judicial control applies to both direct and cross-examination. The court's discretion is guided by the principle that leading questions generally are permissible on cross-examination but not on direct examination.[55] On direct examination where the witness favors the calling party's case, leading questions are disapproved because the witness may acquiesce in the version of events stated in the examiner's question rather than describe the occurrence as the witness actually remembers it.[56]

---

[52] *See* Olden v. Kentucky, 488 U.S. 227 (1988) (defendant's rights under the confrontation clause were violated when the trial court refused to allow him to impeach an alleged rape victim's testimony with evidence revealing a motive to fabricate the alleged crime).

[53] *See* Rule 611, Advisory Committee Note.

[54] In the case of criminal defendants who voluntarily testify in their own behalf but then on cross-examination seek to assert the privilege against self-incrimination, Rule 611(b) must give way to constitutional considerations in determining the scope of cross-examination. The extent to which the Rule must give way, however, has been subject to multiple interpretations and is a constantly changing area of evidence law. For a broader discussion on this topic, *see generally* 4 WEINSTEIN'S FEDERAL EVIDENCE § 611.04; 3 MUELLER & KIRKPATRICK, § 303; 8 WIGMORE, § 2276; 1 MCCORMICK, § 132.

[55] *E.g.,* United States v. Orand, 491 F.2d 1173 (9th Cir. 1973); United States v. Lewis, 406 F.2d 486 (7th Cir. 1969); Ewing v. United States, 135 F.2d 633 (D.C. Cir. 1942). *But see* Shultz v. Rice, 809 F.2d 643 (10th Cir. 1986) (court did not abuse discretion in permitting defense counsel to ask leading questions of defendant).

[56] 3 MUELLER & KIRKPATRICK, § 302.

Also, leading questions pose the dangers of providing a "false memory"[57] for the witness or of focusing the testimony solely on those aspects of the case favorable to the calling party.[58] On cross-examination where the witness is biased in favor of the opposing party, leading questions are permissible because the witness is less susceptible to their suggestiveness.[59]

A leading question is one that suggests the particular response desired by the examiner.[60] Many factors influence whether a question is leading. The form of a question may cause it to be leading. For example, a question that begins "Isn't it a fact . . ." is usually leading.[61] More often, however, whether a question is leading must be determined on a case-by-case basis. The examiner's tone of voice, gestures, or other non-verbal conduct may render an otherwise unobjectionable question leading.[62] Another factor is the context in which the question is asked.[63] Frequently, the degree of specificity determines whether a question is leading. Where the examiner describes an event in great detail and then asks the witness whether the event occurred, the question suggests that the correct response is "yes" and thus the question is leading.[64] Similarly, if the examiner phrases a question in the alternative, with one choice described in detail while the other is stated vaguely ("Did he say he would call you at six o'clock, or what?"), it is clear that the question seeks the detailed response.[65]

Where an objection that the questioner is leading the witness is sustained, the examiner generally is permitted to cure the objection by rephrasing the question or restating it without the objectionable gesture or tone of voice.[66] It is within the court's discretion to foreclose further inquiry on the subject,

---

[57] United States v. Cooper, 606 F.2d 96 (5th Cir. 1979); United States v. McGovern, 499 F.2d 1140 (1st Cir. 1974); United States v. Johnson, 495 F.2d 1097 (5th Cir. 1974); *see, e.g.,* United States v. Durham, 319 F.2d 590, 592 (4th Cir. 1963) ("[T]he essential test of a leading question is whether it so suggests to the witness the specific tenor of the reply desired by counsel that such a reply is likely to be given irrespective of an actual memory. The evil to be avoided is that of supplying a false memory for the witness's').

[58] *See* Denroche, *Leading Questions*, 6 CRIM. L.Q. 21 (1963).

[59] 1 MCCORMICK, § 6.

[60] 3 MUELLER & KIRKPATRICK, § 302; 1 MCCORMICK, § 6.

[61] 3 MUELLER & KIRKPATRICK, § 302.

[62] 4 WEINSTEIN'S FEDERAL EVIDENCE § 611.06.

[63] *See, e.g.,* 3 MUELLER & KIRKPATRICK, § 302.

[64] 1 MCCORMICK, § 6.

[65] *Id.*

[66] People v. Campbell, 43 Cal. Rptr. 237 (1965) (district attorney withdrew his question and properly reframed it after an objection for leading the witness); Georgetown v. Groff, 136 Ky. 662, 668 (Ky. 1910) (where questions were leading, the court "should have required counsel to so frame his questions as not to suggest the answers desired."); *see also* Allen v. Hartford Life Ins. Co., 72 Conn. 693 (Conn. 1900).

but this power is rarely exercised. As one commentator noted, "The harm done is usually not very significant, and continued use of leading questions in some circumstances will soon draw sharp criticism from the court and embarrass the examiner before the jury . . . . The jury soon realizes that it is the lawyer and not the witness who is testifying."[67]

Leading questions should be allowed on direct examination only when necessary to develop testimony or when used to elicit preliminary undisputed matters.[68] For example, exceptions may be made where the witness is a reticent child,[69] or where the witnesses have temporarily forgotten events on which they are being called to testify.[70]

Rule 611(c) expressly authorizes leading questions when a party calls a hostile witness, an adverse party, or a witness identified with an adverse party.[71] The court's discretion with regard to this use of leading questions appears limited to the determination of whether a witness is indeed hostile or identifiable with an adverse party.[72] A hostile witness is one who is so evasive or uncooperative on examination that the testimony is impeded. The Advisory Committee intended the term "witness identified with an adverse party" to be more expansive than former Rule 43(b) of the Federal Rules of Civil Procedure, which limited the witnesses automatically treated as hostile to "an adversary or an officer, director, or managing agent of a public or private corporation or of a partnership or association which is an adverse

---

[67] Enfield, *Direct Examination of Witnesses,* 15 ARK. L. REV. 32, 36 (1960).

[68] United States v. Fenner, 600 F.3d 1014 (8th Cir. 2010) (the use of leading questions on direct is generally discouraged but not automatically improper; the district court has wide latitude to permit their use when that is needed to develop the testimony of the witness); McClard v. United States, 386 F.2d 495 (8th Cir. 1967) ("ofttimes leading questions are asked on preliminary and collateral matters to expedite the trial. In any event, the control of leading questions is a matter left to the discretion of the trial judge").

[69] United States v. Iron Shell, 633 F.2d 77 (8th Cir. 1980); United States v. Littlewind, 551 F.2d 244 (8th Cir. 1977); Rotolo v. United States, 404 F.2d 316 (5th Cir. 1968); Antelope v. United States, 185 F.2d 174 (10th Cir. 1950); *see also* United States v. Demarrias, 876 F.2d 674 (8th Cir. 1989) (in a prosecution for sexual abuse of the defendant's 14 year-old stepdaughter, the court did not abuse its discretion in permitting the prosecutor to read the victim's statement and ask her if she wrote it).

[70] United States v. McGovern, 499 F.2d 1140 (1st Cir. 1974); Green v. United States, 348 F.2d 340 (D.C. Cir. 1965); Roberson v. United States, 249 F.2d 737 (5th Cir. 1957) (district attorney was permitted to ask leading questions to refresh the memory of the witness, based on statements from the transcript of the witness at the previous trial).

[71] United States v. Shursen, 649 F.2d 1250 (8th Cir. 1981); *see also* United States v. Brown, 603 F.2d 1022 (1st Cir. 1979) (no abuse of discretion in allowing witness to be examined by leading questions where witness had apparent lapses of memory and conveyed general confusion); *see, e.g.,* United States v. Karnes, 531 F.2d 214 (4th Cir. 1976).

[72] United States v. Diaz, 662 F.2d 713 (11th Cir. 1981); United States v. Tsui, 646 F.2d 365 (9th Cir. 1981); United States v. Brown, 603 F.2d 1022 (1st Cir. 1979).

party."[73] Under Rule 611(c), a witness may be "identified with an adverse party" due to employment by the party or mere sympathy with the party's cause.[74] For example, a party may examine an employee of his opponent by leading questions.[75] In a criminal case, the defense may put leading questions to a government informer called on direct examination.[76] Rule 611(c) embodies the general policy that leading questions in certain instances represent excessive intervention by trial counsel. Consequently, leading questions are appropriate only when necessary or when the adverse or hostile quality of the witness counterbalances counsel's effectiveness in leading the witness. The Rule is a more specific application of the court's general authority to control the mode and order of proof to ensure the orderly and efficient determination of the truth.[77] Since the use of leading questions generally lies within the discretion of the court, a determination as to the propriety of their use will not serve as the basis for reversal on appeal absent a clear showing that the adverse party has been unfairly prejudiced by an abuse of discretion.[78]

---

[73] Rule 611(c), Advisory Committee Note; *see also* 4 WEINSTEIN'S FEDERAL EVIDENCE § 611.06.

[74] 4 WEINSTEIN'S FEDERAL EVIDENCE § 611.06.

[75] *E.g.,* Perkins v. Volkswagen of Am., 596 F.2d 681 (5th Cir. 1979) (error in ruling that employee of defendant would be plaintiff's own witness if called by plaintiff).

[76] *E.g.,* United States v. Bryant, 461 F.2d 912 (6th Cir. 1972) (defense is permitted to ask leading questions of a Government witness such as an agent, who is closely identified with the interests of the Government, since such a witness will not be predisposed to accept suggestions offered by defense counsel's questions).

[77] *See* § 611.2, *supra.*

[78] *See* United States v. Ienco, 92 F.3d 564 (7th Cir. 1996) (trial judge erred in refusing to allow defense counsel to use leading questions when examining an adverse witness on an issue crucial to the defendant's defense); United States v. De Fiore, 720 F.2d 757 (2d Cir. 1983); Ellis v. City of Chicago, 667 F.2d 606 (7th Cir. 1981); United States v. Tsui, 646 F.2d 365 (9th Cir. 1981).

Chapter 612

Rule 612. Writing Used to Refresh a Witness's Memory

Rule 612. Writing Used to Refresh a Witness's Memory

    (a)   **Scope.** This rule gives an adverse party certain options when a witness uses a writing to refresh memory:

        (1)   while testifying; or

        (2)   before testifying, if the court decides that justice requires the party to have those options.

    (b)   **Adverse Party's Options; Deleting Unrelated Matter.** Unless 18 U.S.C. § 3500 provides otherwise in a criminal case, an adverse party is entitled to have the writing produced at the hearing, to inspect it, to cross-examine the witness about it, and to introduce in evidence any portion that relates to the witness's testimony. If the producing party claims that the writing includes unrelated matter, the court must examine the writing in camera, delete any unrelated portion, and order that the rest be delivered to the adverse party. Any portion deleted over objection must be preserved for the record.

    (c)   **Failure to Produce or Deliver the Writing.** If a writing is not produced or is not delivered as ordered, the court may issue any appropriate order. But if the prosecution does not comply in a criminal case, the court must strike the witness's testimony or — if justice so requires — declare a mistrial.

---

§ 612.1   Refreshing Recollection — In General

When a witness at a trial is unable or seems disinclined to relate the totality of facts within the witness's knowledge, a party is afforded the opportunity to prompt testimony or correct omissions by "refreshing" the witness's recollection through the use of an object or writing.[1] Rule 612

---

[1] *See generally,* 4 WEINSTEIN'S FEDERAL EVIDENCE §§ 612.01–612.09; 3 MUELLER & KIRKPATRICK, § 324; 1 MCCORMICK, § 9; 3 WIGMORE, §§ 758–765. *See, e.g.,* Bankers Trust Co. v. Publicker Indus., 641 F.2d 1361 (2d Cir. 1981); *see also* Carter, *Suppression of Evidence Favorable to an Accused,* 34 F.R.D. 87 (1964); Everett, *Discovery in Criminal Cases—In Search of a Standard,* 1964 DUKE L.J. 477; Kalo, *Refreshing Recollection: Problems with Laying a Foundation,* 10 RUTGERS-CAM. L.J. 233 (1979); Maguire & Quick,

pertains to one aspect of the process of refreshing a witness's recollection. Specifically, the Rule governs the production of writings used to revive a witness's memory either *at* trial or *before* trial.[2] Other aspects of the procedure are governed by case law and custom.

The process of refreshing a witness's recollection may involve any of a number of recognized techniques. It may assume the form of using a leading question where appropriate under the guidelines of Rule 611(c).[3] It may involve playing an audio or even a video recording for the witness.[4] Usually, however, the process involves showing the witness a writing, a picture, or a photograph in an effort to prompt the witness's recollection of a fact or event of which he or she has firsthand knowledge. After exposure to the memory jogging device, the witness then — at least in theory — testifies independently of the device as to the facts being offered into evidence. The device need not be admissible, and is usually neither admitted into evidence nor seen by the jury. After being used to revive the recollection, the device is devoid of evidentiary status,[5] and it effectively becomes inconsequential in the case unless the opposing party exercises the express options identified in Rule 612.[6] As stated in Rule 612, the memory-jogging device may be subject to production under certain circumstances, and if produced, may be inspected and used for cross-examination and introduced for consideration by the trier of fact.

It is obvious that the process of refreshing recollection invites a compliant witness to embrace as testimony anything the witness sees or reads in the document, picture, recording, etc. The risk has long been acknowledged but nevertheless accepted. Ultimately, control of the process is placed in the trial

---

Testimony: Memory and Memoranda, 3 How. L.J. 1 (1957); Orfield, *Discovery During Trial in Federal Criminal Cases: The Jencks Act,* 18 Sw. L.J. 212 (1964); Note, *Constitutionality of Conditional Mutual Discovery under Federal Rule 16,* 19 OKLA. L. REV. 417 (1969); Note, The P*rosecutor's Constitutional Duty to Reveal Evidence to the Defendant,* 74 YALE L.J. 136 (1964); Note, *The Constitutional Limits of Discovery,* 35 IND. L.J. 337 (1960); Comment, The *Aftermath of the Jencks Case,* 11 STAN. L. REV. 297 (1959).

[2] *See* Spivey v. Zant, 683 F.2d 881 (5th Cir. 1982); Marcus v. United States, 422 F.2d 752 (5th Cir. 1970).

[3] *See generally,* 3 MUELLER & KIRKPATRICK, § 324.

[4] *See generally,* 4 WEINSTEIN'S FEDERAL EVIDENCE § 612.02; *see also* United States v. Faulkner, 538 F.2d 724 (6th Cir. 1976) (tape recordings could be used to refresh recollection, even though they could not be introduced in evidence because they were partly unintelligible).

[5] *See* United States v. Scott, 701 F.2d 1340 (11th Cir. 1983); United States v. Davis, 551 F.2d 233 (8th Cir. 1977) (no reversal required where statement used to refresh recollection was not materially different from other evidence properly received); *see, e.g.,* United States v. Smith, 521 F.2d 957 (D.C. Cir. 1975).

[6] United States v. Smith, 521 F.2d 957 (D.C. Cir. 1975); *see also* Borel v. Fibreboard Paper Prod. Corp., 493 F.2d 1076 (5th Cir. 1973) (trial court may permit jury to inspect the writing on its own motion); *see, e.g.,* United States v. Booz, 451 F.2d 719 (3d Cir. 1971).

judge who must ensure that the technique is not used to introduce out-of-court statements in the memory jogging device.[7] Additionally, the adversary process, aided by the opposing party's rights identified in Rule 612, is presumed to expose such abuse through cross-examination.[8]

§ 612.2 Past Recollection Recorded Distinguished

The technique of refreshing a witness's recollection must be distinguished from the hearsay exception, "past recollection recorded," the subject of Rule 803(5). Under the technique of refreshing recollection, the witness reviews the writing to revive his or her memory of the material event and then proceeds to testify on the basis of present, personal knowledge. The writing itself is not offered as evidence. It merely serves as a memory jogging device, and compliance with the hearsay rule, the authentication rule, or the so-called "best evidence rule" is not required. In contrast, under the "past recollection recorded" exception to the general proscription against hearsay, the document itself is offered as the evidence.[9] Rule 803(5) may operate to admit written hearsay in certain instances where the witness's present recollection remains absent or incomplete and cannot be refreshed by the writing. Under Rule 803(5), the witness's trial testimony establishes the foundational fact that the witness's recollection was complete at the time of writing and that the facts were accurately recorded in the document. Obviously, where a writing is offered into evidence, it must comply with all the rules regarding the admissibility of documentary evidence, one of which is the hearsay rule. Where a writing is offered, one of the hearsay exceptions available to admit the out-of-court statement is Rule 803(5). Of course, other exceptions might be available as well.

§ 612.3 Prior Inconsistent Statement Distinguished

Refreshing a witness's recollection with a document must be distinguished from using a writing prepared by the witness for the purpose of "prior inconsistent statement" impeachment. Frequently, trial counsel will show a witness his prior statement in a mildly confrontational effort to encourage the witness to change some aspect of his testimony. Providing the usual practices attending "refreshing recollection" are followed, no real abuse occurs. In fact, the deviation from the written statement articulated in

---

[7] *See* 4 WEINSTEIN'S FEDERAL EVIDENCE § 612.02; 3 MUELLER & KIRKPATRICK, § 324; *see also* United States v. Socony-Vacuum Oil, 310 U.S. 150 (1940) (antitrust prosecution; grand jury testimony by government witnesses used to refresh their recollection); *see, e.g.,* United States v. Conley, 503 F.2d 520 (8th Cir. 1974); Esperti v. United States, 406 F.2d 148 (5th Cir. 1969).

[8] *See generally,* 4 WEINSTEIN'S FEDERAL EVIDENCE § 612.02.

[9] *See* United States v. Riccardi, 174 F.2d 883 (3d Cir. 1949); *see, e.g.,* Imperial Meat Co. v. United States, 316 F.2d 435 (10th Cir. 1963) (judge conducted extensive examination to determine whether witness needed to refresh memory); *see also* § 803.23, *infra,* for a discussion of Rule 803(5).

the testimony may be the product of a passing memory failure that is legitimately corrected by showing the witness his or her statement. As long as the statement is not read aloud to the witness, and merely shown to the witness, the process is legitimately an effort to refresh recollection.

Where the prior statement of a witness is exposed to the trier of fact in an effort to discredit the witness by demonstrating an inability to keep his or her story consistent, the process assumes the status of impeachment.[10] Self-contradiction or prior inconsistent impeachment is governed by principles that are distinguishable from those applicable to refreshing recollection, and these principles are discussed in conjunction with Rule 613.[11]

§ 612.4   Refreshing Recollection During the Course of Testimony

Before witnesses may be shown writings to refresh their recollection and aid their testimony, the court must be satisfied that the witness lacks a present recollection of the relevant events.[12] This lack of present recollection may be express, as where a witness cannot recall the events inquired into, or it may be apparent from the course of testimony, as where the witness's testimony is vague or incomplete.[13]

While the form of the questioning is largely within the discretion of the trial court,[14] the usual procedure is for trial counsel to elicit testimony first that the witness's unaided recollection is exhausted. The witness is then handed a writing and asked to read the document silently to refresh his or her recollection.[15] In order to avoid inviting the jury to accord the writing evidentiary status, the writing should not be read aloud. If after reading the document, the witness's recollection has been revived, he or she then proceeds to provide testimony as to the relevant facts.

---

[10] *See generally,* 3 MUELLER & KIRKPATRICK, § 324.

[11] 3 MUELLER & KIRKPATRICK, § 324; *see* Chapter 613, *infra.*

[12] *E.g.,* United States v. Morlang, 531 F.2d 183 (4th Cir. 1975); United States v. Lewis, 406 F.2d 486 (7th Cir. 1969).

[13] *See* United States v. Boyd, 606 F.2d 792 (8th Cir. 1979) (no abuse of discretion where witness assured court of need to refer to report summarizing his previous statements to FBI); Goings v. United States, 377 F.2d 753 (8th Cir. 1967) (discretion allows witness a chance to review statements given to a third person and then independently testify); *cf.* MORGAN, BASIC PROBLEMS OF EVIDENCE 62 (1962).

[14] *See* United States v. Rinke, 778 F.2d 581 (10th Cir. 1985) (government witness was properly allowed to testify on the basis of his notes, even though he occasionally read from his notes while testifying; court is empowered with broad discretion to determine whether witness is using writing to refresh memory or to give information on something he can no longer recall); *see also* United States v. Conley, 503 F.2d 520 (8th Cir. 1974); Esperti v. United States, 406 F.2d 148 (5th Cir. 1969).

[15] *E.g.,* United States v. Shoupe, 548 F.2d 636 (6th Cir. 1977); *see also* Johnston v. Earle, 313 F.2d 686 (9th Cir. 1962) (witness looked at copies of original notes prepared by another to refresh his memory); *cf.* Thompson v. United States, 342 F.2d 137 (5th Cir. 1965); Williams v. United States, 365 F.2d 21 (7th Cir. 1966).

It is well-established that the type of "writing" authorized under the refreshed recollection doctrine includes not only books, documents, or other papers, but recordings and photographs as well.[16] Since the object of the technique is to awaken the memory of a witness, any allusion to previous events that fulfills that purpose may be used. The "writing," further, need not be an original document or recording. Nor must it be a writing executed or previously adopted by the witness. Since the question is limited to whether the writing is calculated to refresh the witness's memory, the ultimate question of the writing's admissibility is inapposite.[17] Consequently, Articles VIII, IX and X of the Rules are inapplicable to the writing. In this regard, however, the witness's recollection must be genuinely revived after she inspects the writing so that her testimony is based upon present recollection and not a mere recitation of the contents of the writing.[18] Ultimately, it is incumbent upon the trial judge to ensure that the technique is not abused.

Where witnesses testify that a document fails to revive their memory of the material event or facts at issue, but testify that the writing was prepared or adopted by the witness when the subject matter was fresh in their memory, an adequate foundation may exist for the introduction of the writing itself under Rule 803(5). Alternatively, some other hearsay exception may be applicable. Accordingly, if the witness's memory is not revived, the writing itself may be admitted for the truth of its contents only if it meets the requirements of a hearsay exception.[19] Likewise, other considerations for the admissibility of documentary evidence, *e.g.,* authentication, "best evidence," etc., must be satisfied.

---

[16] *See* United States v. Faulkner, 538 F.2d 724 (6th Cir. 1976) (tape recordings); Williams v. United States, 365 F.2d 21 (7th Cir. 1966) (memorandum of conversation); United States v. Rappy, 157 F.2d 964 (2d Cir. 1946) (songs, photographs).

[17] *See* Twentieth Century Wear, Inc. v. Sanmark-Stardust, Inc., 747 F.2d 81 (2d Cir. 1984) (writing used to refresh recollection need not be admissible — and may even have been obtained illegally); United States v. Scott, 701 F.2d 1340 (11th Cir. 1983); *see also* United States v. Ricco, 566 F.2d 433 (2d Cir. 1977) (illegal wiretaps may be used before trial to refresh witness's recollection of his own conversations); *cf.* United States v. Baratta, 397 F.2d 215 (2d Cir. 1968).

[18] *See, e.g.,* United States v. Cheyenne, 558 F.2d 902 (8th Cir. 1977) (where FBI agent refreshed his recollection of defendant's confession by reading FBI report at suppression hearing and testified at trial without reference to the report, there was no error; no merit to defendant's argument that agent had no independent recollection, since defendant had a copy of the report and had full opportunity to probe agent on cross-examination); NLRB v. Federal Dairy Co., 297 F.2d 487, 488–89 (1st Cir. 1962) ("the witness, unless opposing counsel waives it, should not refresh his recollection until he has been examined without leading, if it is direct examination, and has testified that his recollection is exhausted"). *But cf.* United States v. Jimenez, 613 F.2d 1373 (5th Cir. 1980) (no showing of need necessary).

[19] *See* 4 WEINSTEIN'S FEDERAL EVIDENCE § 612.03; 3 MUELLER & KIRKPATRICK, § 324; 3 WIGMORE, §§ 762–764; *see also* cases cited in Chapter 804, *infra.*

§ 612.5 Production of the Writing Used to Refresh Recollection

The primary focus of Rule 612 is upon the production of a document used to revive the recollection of the witness. When a document is used *at trial* to refresh a witness's memory, the Rule provides that the adverse party is entitled, as of right, to inspect the writing, to cross-examine the witness concerning the document and to introduce those portions of the writing pertinent to the trial testimony.[20] When a document is used *before trial* to refresh the recollection of the witness, Rule 612(a)(2) provides the trial judge with discretion to order the production of the writing.[21] Accordingly, a writing used before the trial or hearing to prepare a witness's testimony is subject to production at the trial or hearing if the trial judge determines that "justice requires" such document to be inspected by the adverse party. A trial judge may refuse inspection when the documents contain sensitive material or contain information not closely related to the witness's testimony.[22]

The existence of a document used to refresh recollection frequently emerges during cross-examination, and a recess may be requested and granted where the document is not readily available for production. Once produced, the document may be used in conjunction with the cross-examination of the witness, and it may be submitted to the jury to the extent that it relates to the testimony, but only if offered by the cross-examiner.

It should be noted that when a document used to refresh a witness's recollection is submitted to the jury by the opposing party pursuant to Rule 612, the document is not being offered as substantive evidence. Rather, the document is offered as a basis for evaluating the testimony of the witness, and unless the document has an independent basis for admissibility as substantive evidence, the trial judge should instruct the jury to consider the document only for the limited purpose of assessing the credibility of the witness.[23]

---

[20] Pollard v. Commissioner of IRS, 786 F.2d 1063 (11th Cir. 1986) (court did not err in giving opponent only the writings actually used to refresh defendant's memory; government was not required to grant access to the administrative records); *see, e.g.,* Spivey v. Zant, 683 F.2d 881 (5th Cir. 1982); United States v. Howton, 688 F.2d 272 (5th Cir. 1982); United States v. Costner, 684 F.2d 370 (6th Cir. 1982).

[21] *See* United States v. Howton, 688 F.2d 272 (5th Cir. 1982); Tillman v. United States, 268 F.2d 422 (5th Cir. 1959); McGill v. United States, 270 F.2d 329 (D.C. Cir. 1959); 1 MCCORMICK, § 9; 3 WIGMORE, § 762.

[22] *See* United States v. Howton, 688 F.2d 272 (5th Cir. 1982). *See also* United States v. Muhammad, 120 F.3d 688 (7th Cir. 1997) (trial court did not abuse its discretion in allowing defendant access only to the summary of an FBI agent's notes taken during her interview with the defendant, and not the notes themselves, for the purpose of cross-examining the agent; the agent had relied only on the summary to refresh her recollection; moreover, the court found that the summary did not contradict the agent's notes).

[23] *See* Rule 105 and § 105.1 *et seq., supra.*

§ 612.6 Limitations on the Production of Writings Used to Refresh Recollection

By its express terms, Rule 612 is limited by Section 3500 of Title 18 of the United States Code, the so-called "Jencks Act." Accordingly, the discretion of the trial judge to order production of a writing used to refresh a witness's recollection must be understood in connection with the authority of the court to order production under this Act.[24]

The Jencks Act, now incorporated into Rule 26.2 of the Federal Rules of Criminal Procedure, provides that when any witness in a criminal case, other than the defendant, is called to the stand, the opposing attorney is entitled to see any statements made by that witness concerning the subject matter of the witness's trial testimony in the possession of the other attorneys. The rule effectively overrides any claims of attorney work product but not attorney-client privilege; that is why it applies to all testifying witnesses, even defense witnesses, except the defendant himself. This right is triggered only after the witness has testified on direct examination, and only if the party seeking disclosure makes such a request.[25]

Rule 612 and Criminal Rule 26.2 have one primary characteristic in common: they both identify situations in which a document — even one that might otherwise have been undiscoverable — may become subject to discovery in light of events at trial. Although the overlap between the two rules is great, they operate in distinct ways. Rule 612, which applies to all witnesses at all trials, both civil and criminal, authorizes discovery of writings only if they were used by the witnesses to refresh their memory, regardless of whether it was written by the witness or someone else. The *Jencks* doctrine codified in Criminal Rule 26.2, which applies only in criminal cases and only to witnesses other than the defendant, requires production of all statements that were written or dictated by witnesses concerning the subjects covered by their testimony on direct examination, regardless of whether they ever read them or used them to refresh their memory. Writings subject to disclosure under either rule are not always covered by the other. Both rules often come into play simultaneously, however, in the fairly common situation where government agents testifying in criminal cases are allowed to review their own investigative notes to assist their recollection.

---

[24] The Jencks Act, 18 U.S.C. § 3500, is so named because it was written as a Congressional response to, and to partially codify and partially limit, the holding in *Jencks v. United States,* 353 U.S. 657 (1957); *see also* Brady v. Maryland, 373 U.S. 83, 89 (1963) ("[S]uppression by the prosecution of evidence favorable to an accused upon request violates due process where the evidence is material either to guilt or to punishment irrespective of the good faith or bad faith of the prosecution." It should be noted that, in a criminal proceeding, the limitations of the Jencks Act may be superseded by the *Brady* doctrine).

[25] Fed. R. Crim. P. 26.2; *see also* 18 U.S.C. § 3500.

The two discovery rules differ in their operation in a way that coincides with their distinct underlying functions. Statements and other writings produced under Rule 612 are designed to assist the cross-examiner in demonstrating the extent to which the testimony of witnesses has been excessively influenced by the "script" that was shown to them before or during their testimony. *Jencks* material is made subject to discovery under Criminal Rule 26.2 primarily to permit the cross-examiner to determine whether the witnesses have changed or altered their testimony in any way, so that they may be more effectively impeached with their statements, if they are inconsistent with their trial testimony, under Rule 613.

Because Rule 612 expressly recites that its provisions are subject to the *Jencks* doctrine, the statute must prevail in the rare case where the two would yield inconsistent results. For example, if testifying witnesses admit at trial that they reviewed their case notes before testifying, disclosure of those notes to opposing counsel would ordinarily be discretionary with the court. But if the witness is a law enforcement agent who wrote the notes, the judge has no discretion in the matter because their production is mandatory under Criminal Rule 26.2.

An issue left unresolved by Rule 612 is the extent to which a witness may justifiably refuse to produce a writing used to revive recollection prior to trial under an assertion of privilege or under a work product doctrine. Rule 501 acknowledges the legitimacy of these doctrines, and should govern their application to Rule 612.[26]

The language of Rule 612 and its Advisory Committee Notes does not yield an unambiguous answer. According to the reported case law, the right

---

[26] *See* Fed. R. Civ. P. 26(b)(3). *See generally,* 4 WEINSTEIN'S FEDERAL EVIDENCE § 612.05; 3 MUELLER & KIRKPATRICK, 328. *See also* James Julian, Inc. v. Raytheon Co., 93 F.R.D. 138 (D. Del. 1982) (binder of documents prepared by plaintiff's counsel and reviewed by witnesses for plaintiff before their depositions was within work product doctrine, but court held that documents should be produced under Rule 612 because otherwise, defense counsel "cannot know or inquire into the extent to which the witnesses' testimony has been shaded by counsel's presentation of the factual background"); Wheeling Pittsburgh Steel Corp. v. Underwriters Lab. Inc., 81 F.R.D. 8 (N.D. Ill. 1978) (witness at deposition who was ex-employee of plaintiff, refreshed his recollection prior to deposition with file containing communications between representatives of the plaintiff; court granted defendant access to the files noting that access is limited only to those writings that may have fairly been said to have an impact upon the testimony of the witness); Sporck v. Peil, 759 F.2d 312 (3d Cir. 1985); Carter-Wallace, Inc. v. Hartz Mountain Indus., 553 F. Supp. 45 (S.D.N.Y. 1982); Al-Rowaishan Establishment Universal Trading & Agencies Ltd. v. Beatrice Foods Co., 92 F.R.D. 779 (S.C.N.Y. 1982) (principles precluding disclosure of work product revealing the attorney's thought processes outweighed the benefit to defendant of disclosure of digest prepared by plaintiff's attorney). *See generally,* Jos. Schlitz Brewing Co. v. Muller & Phipps, Ltd., 85 F.R.D. 118 (W.D. Mo. 1980) (hinting that even if witness had testified that he reviewed particular privileged documents before testifying, disclosure might have been denied).

to demand disclosure turns primarily on when the writing was consulted by witnesses to refresh their recollection. If the writing was consulted while the witness was being questioned, where Rule 612 seemingly makes disclosure mandatory, courts are in virtually complete agreement that any claims of attorney-client privilege or work product protection have been waived.[27] On the other hand, if the document was only reviewed before the witness began testifying, it is generally agreed that disclosure is discretionary with the court, based upon a balance between the need to protect the policies underlying the privilege or work-product protection and the cross-examiner's need for the document to examine the witness fully.[28]

§ 612.7 Failure to Produce a Writing Pursuant to Court Order Under Rule 612; Unrelated Matters in Document Used to Refresh Recollection

Under Rule 612(b), where a claim is made that the writing used to refresh recollection contains matters that are unrelated to the litigation and that have not affected the witness's testimony, the court has the duty to inspect the writing *in camera* to excise any unrelated portions. The remainder is delivered to the adverse party, preserving the portions excised in the record for purposes of appellate review.

Rule 612(c) provides that where a party fails to produce documents in compliance with the trial court's order, the court may make any further order necessitated by the ends of justice, including, in criminal cases, ordering a mistrial where the prosecution fails to comply.[29]

---

[27] *See* Mueller & Kirkpatrick, EVIDENCE § 6.69 (2d ed. 1999) ("There is little doubt that using documents to refresh memory on the stand waives or defeats claims of attorney-client privilege by the calling party or work product protection by the lawyer"); Epstein, THE ATTORNEY-CLIENT PRIVILEGE AND THE WORK-PRODUCT DOCTRINE 218, 415–416 (3d ed. 1997) (collecting cases).

[28] *See* Mueller & Kirkpatrick, EVIDENCE § 6.69, at 864–866 (2d ed. 1999); Epstein, THE ATTORNEY-CLIENT PRIVILEGE AND THE WORK-PRODUCT DOCTRINE 219, 416–422 (3d ed. 1997).

[29] The Advisory Committee Note to Rule 612 provides:

The consequences of nonproduction by the government in a criminal case are those of the Jencks statute, striking the testimony or in exceptional cases a mistrial. 18 U.S.C. § 3500(d). In other cases these alternatives are unduly limited, and such possibilities as contempt, dismissal, finding issues against the offender, and the like are available.

The Jencks Act is now incorporated into the Federal Rules of Criminal Procedure, Rule 26.2.

Chapter 613

Rule 613. Witness's Prior Statement

Rule 613. Witness's Prior Statement

(a) **Showing or Disclosing the Statement During Examination.** When examining a witness about the witness's prior statement, a party need not show it or disclose its contents to the witness. But the party must, on request, show it or disclose its contents to an adverse party's attorney.

(b) **Extrinsic Evidence of a Prior Inconsistent Statement.** Extrinsic evidence of a witness's prior inconsistent statement is admissible only if the witness is given an opportunity to explain or deny the statement and an adverse party is given an opportunity to examine the witness about it, or if justice so requires. This subdivision (b) does not apply to an opposing party's statement under Rule 801(d)(2).

---

§ 613.1   Witness's Prior Statement — In General

Rule 613 generally governs certain procedures that attend the process of impeaching a witness with a prior inconsistent statement.[1] Through the impeachment device of "self-contradiction," a witness may be interrogated about a statement made prior to trial which is inconsistent with his or her trial testimony.[2] The statement may be introduced during cross-examination, and in certain situations evidence of the contents of the prior statement may

---

[1] *See generally,* 4 WEINSTEIN'S FEDERAL EVIDENCE §§ 613.01–613.05; 3 MUELLER & KIRKPATRICK, §§ 329–333; 1 MCCORMICK, §§ 34–39; 3A WIGMORE, §§ 1017–1046. *See also* Hale, *Impeachment of Witnesses by Prior Inconsistent Statements,* 10 S. CAL. L. REV. 135 (1937); Ladd, *Some Observations on Credibility: Impeachment of Witnesses,* 52 CORNELL L.Q. 239 (1967); Slough, *Impeachment of Witnesses, Common Law Principles and Modern Trends,* 34 IND. L.J. 1 (1958); Note, *Modification of the Foundational Requirement for Impeaching Witnesses: California Evidence Code Section 770,* 18 HASTINGS L.J. 210 (1966); Comment, *Hearsay Under the Proposed Federal Rules: A Discretionary Approach,* 15 WAYNE L. REV. 1077 (1969); Comment, *Prior Inconsistent Statements as an Exception to the Hearsay Rule: An Analysis of People v. Johnson,* 6 SAN DIEGO L. REV. 92 (1969).

[2] It is most unfortunate that the title and text of Rule 613 refer to impeachment with the "*prior* statements" of a witness, because prior is always redundant in this context. All statements by witness used for impeachment, by necessity, are from some point in time prior to their testimony. *See* Duane, *Prior Convictions and Tuna Fish,* 7 SCRIBES J. OF LEGAL WRITING 160 (2000). But because the phrase "prior inconsistent statements" appears in the

be introduced after the witness has concluded his testimony.

The prior contradictory statement may be written or oral.[3] Where the statement is written, it may be used in conjunction with the cross-examination of the witness sought to be impeached. In certain cases, a written statement may be authenticated by a different witness and introduced after the primary witness (*i.e.*, the witness sought to be impeached) has concluded his or her testimony. Likewise, where the statement is oral, it may be the subject of inquiry or cross-examination, and, in certain instances, the statement may be the subject of testimony of a different witness who has firsthand knowledge of the primary witness's contradictory out-of-court statement. The purpose of self-contradiction is to demonstrate that the witness is the type of person who makes conflicting statements regarding the same set of facts. The suggestion to the trier of fact is that the witness is untrustworthy because of making intentional false statements or having a defect of memory.[4]

It should be noted that Rule 613 does not govern whether the prior statement may be considered by the trier of fact as substantive evidence, *i.e.*, for the truth of its contents. This issue, which involves hearsay considerations, is discussed at length in §§ 801.8 and 801.20 of this Treatise. Fundamentally, if the prior inconsistent statement is not admissible hearsay, its only function is to aid the trier of fact in assessing the credibility of the witness. In this situation, a limiting instruction from the trial judge should direct the jury to consider the prior statement not for its truth, but rather for the restricted purpose of assessing the trustworthiness of the witness. Where the prior statement is admissible hearsay, however, it serves a dual purpose. The statement operates to impeach the witness, and it may be considered as substantive evidence in the case. Generally, where the statement is substantively admissible pursuant to the hearsay system, no limiting instruction is necessary.

Rule 613 does not identify the circumstances under which self-contradiction impeachment is authorized. Rather, its primary function is to prescribe the procedure to be used in disclosing the statement to the witness and to his counsel. It also governs the procedure to be applied to "extrinsic evidence" of a prior inconsistent statement. Extrinsic evidence of an inconsistent statement is evidence that is offered after the witness sought to be impeached has finished testifying. Alternately stated, extrinsic evidence is evidence that is offered through the testimony of a different witness, or

---

rule and is now firmly lodged in the legal lexicon, the authors shall, with deep misgivings, adhere to that locution in this work.

[3] *See, e.g.,* United States v. Simmons, 567 F.2d 314 (7th Cir. 1977); United States v. Rogers, 549 F.2d 490 (8th Cir. 1976).

[4] *See* 3 MUELLER & KIRKPATRICK, § 329; 4 WEINSTEIN'S FEDERAL EVIDENCE § 613.02; 4 WIGMORE, § 1263.

written evidence authenticated by a distinct witness.

§ 613.2   Rule 613(a) — Interrogation on Prior Statement — In General

In essence, Rule 613(a) permits inquiry regarding a prior statement, whether written or oral, without requiring the witness to be apprised of its contents before questioning.[5] The prior practice in some federal courts was to follow the rule established in *Queen Caroline's* case.[6] Under this rule, the cross-examiner was required to reveal the statement to the witness prior to questioning. This procedure was founded on the interest of protecting the witness from unfair surprise.[7] Rule 613, however, dispenses with the *Queen's* Rule in favor of a procedure that is designed to enhance the effective use of cross-examination.[8]

To protect a party from any unfair advantage that might be gained by an adversary's inquiry concerning a prior statement, Rule 613(a) provides that on request the statement must be shown or disclosed to opposing counsel. Through this procedure, the party offering witnesses may protect them from unfair insinuations or misleading questions by making appropriate objections.[9] Moreover, redirect examination is available for the elicitation of an explanation as to the inconsistency.

The notable impact of Rule 613(a) is to give enhanced emphasis to the element of surprise, rather than disclosure, as a means of achieving accurate trial results.

---

[5] *E.g.,* Wood v. Stihl Inc., 705 F.2d 1101 (9th Cir. 1983); United States v. Williams, 668 F.2d 1064 (9th Cir. 1981). *But see* United States v. Marks, 816 F.2d 1207 (7th Cir. 1987) (where a statement taken from an FBI interview report was used to impeach witness, court properly allowed witness to look at the statement before being impeached by it; court held that the statement easily could have been garbled but appear authoritative to the jury because taken from FBI reports).

[6] 129 Eng. Rep. 976 (1820). *See generally,* 4 WIGMORE, § 1263.

[7] *See* Robertson v. M/S Sanyo Maru, 374 F.2d 463 (5th Cir. 1967) (error to have admitted statement that witness denied without proving authenticity or showing excuse for not producing original).

[8] *See* United States v. Gholston, 10 F.3d 384 (6th Cir. 1993) (prosecution properly cross-examined defense witness concerning a prior statement made to police; pursuant to Rule 613(a), prosecution was not required to produce extrinsic evidence of the statement before the impeachment attempt); Advisory Committee Note, Rule 613.

[9] United States v. Lawson, 683 F.2d 688 (2d Cir. 1982); *see also* United States v. Rogers, 549 F.2d 490 (8th Cir. 1976) (full discussion of evidentiary standards for use of extrinsic proof of prior inconsistent testimony for impeachment purposes); *see also* Nat'l Labor Relations Bd. v. Bakers of Paris, Inc., 929 F.2d 1427 (9th Cir. 1991) (though harmless, it was error to exclude a written, prior inconsistent statement to be used for the purpose of impeaching a witness or refreshing his or her recollection).

§ 613.3   Rule 613(b) — Extrinsic Evidence of Prior Inconsistent Statements

Rule 613(b) governs the admissibility of "extrinsic evidence" of a prior inconsistent statement of a witness where such statement is used pursuant to the impeachment device of self-contradiction. Extrinsic evidence includes any evidence other than an admission extracted on cross-examination from the witness being impeached, including a written or recorded version of the inconsistent statement, or the testimony of some other individual who claims to have heard an inconsistent oral statement made by that witness.[10] Consequently, extrinsic evidence may assume the form of testimony from another witness, or it may be a document containing the inconsistent statement. Accordingly, extrinsic evidence is evidence introduced other than through the testimony of the witness who is the subject of the impeachment.

Rule 613(b) requires only that the primary witness be given an opportunity at some point in the trial to explain or deny the inconsistent statement, and in contrast to the prior approach of federal courts, the explanation by the witness and interrogation by opposing counsel need not precede the introduction of extrinsic evidence.[11] This Rule, therefore, dispenses with the necessity of laying a foundation as a prerequisite to the introduction of extrinsic evidence. Prior practice generally required a foundation *prior to* the introduction of the inconsistent statement. The witness had to be interrogated concerning the substance of the statement, the time, place and circumstances of the making of the statement as well as an identification of persons present

---

[10] Such extrinsic evidence may not consist, however, of a written document that was not signed or written or dictated by the witness, but is rather an alleged summary of his oral statements prepared by someone else. United States v. De La Cruz Suarez, 601 F.3d 1202 (11th Cir. 2010) (on cross-examination of a government witness, the defense had no right to impeach that witness with an allegedly inconsistent statement prepared by an FBI agent concerning his interview with the witness; a witness may not be impeached by a non-verbatim statement, such as one described in a summary prepared by an investigator, which could not fairly be said to be the witness's own rather than the product of the investigator's selections, interpretations, and interpolations).

[11] United States v. Saget, 991 F.2d 702 (11th Cir. 1993) (trial court did not err in refusing to permit defense counsel to introduce evidence of a witness's prior inconsistent statement to federal agent without giving the witness an opportunity to explain or deny the statement); United States v. McLaughlin, 663 F.2d 949 (9th Cir. 1981); United States v. Hudson, 970 F.2d 948 (1st Cir. 1992) (trial court erred in excluding prior statements of a witness where the witness had already testified and gone back to jail by the time the defense tried to impeach his credibility); *see* Wammock v. Celotex Corp., 793 F.2d 1518 (11th Cir. 1986) (no sequence or timing is required as long as the witness has the opportunity to explain the statements); *see also* United States v. Praetorius, 622 F.2d 1054 (2d Cir. 1979) (trial court misinterpreted rule in requiring witness to be confronted with prior inconsistent statement immediately); United States v. Harvey, 547 F.2d 720 (2d Cir. 1976) (Rule 613 satisfied where witness was afforded an opportunity to explain or deny circumstances suggesting prejudice three times and reference was made to person with whom conversation was held so as to obviate any surprise).

to hear the statement if it was oral.[12] Rule 613 dispenses with this foundation requirement in favor of affording witnesses the opportunity to explain any inconsistency between their trial testimony and prior statement.

§ 613.4   Discretion to Dispense with the Explanation Requirement

Rule 613(b) affords the trial judge discretion to permit the introduction of extrinsic evidence in the absence of an opportunity for an explanation from the witness where "justice so requires." Occasion for the exercise of this discretion would arise, for example, where the witness has testified but has become unavailable before opposing counsel learns of a prior inconsistent statement.[13] In general, whether the trial judge will admit evidence under this rubric will depend upon several factors: the practicability of recalling the witness, the materiality of the issue to which the statement relates, the probable impact on the trial by not allowing introduction of the statement, and the effectiveness of a jury instruction in restricting the consideration of the statement by the jury.[14]

§ 613.5   Collateral Matter Doctrine

A basic common-law doctrine provides that a prior inconsistent statement relating to a "collateral matter" may not be proved by extrinsic evidence. It may, however, be the subject of inquiry while the witness is on the stand. The adoption of Rule 613 appears to leave this doctrine undisturbed.[15] On questioning a witness about a prior statement concerning a collateral matter, counsel must accept the witness's answer, because extrinsic evidence is not available to prove a prior statement embracing a collateral matter. Counsel may not produce other witnesses or documentary evidence to prove the factual nature of the statement as to the collateral matter.

The question of whether a matter is collateral is essentially a question of fact. McCormick defines a non-collateral matter as one involving "facts relevant to the issues in the cause."[16] A matter is not collateral if the fact inquired into could have been proved by either party as part of its

---

[12] *See* 1 McCormick, § 37.

[13] United States v. IBM, 432 F. Supp 138, 140 (S.D.N.Y. 1977) ("[T]he use of multi-page documents for impeachment purposes without providing specific references to the purported inconsistencies contained therein does not afford the witness an opportunity to explain or deny, or the opposing party an opportunity to interrogate him thereon. To the extent that the documents are also used as impeachment material, the witness and the adversary are entitled to specific notice of this intended use as well as the portions of the document and the witness's testimony which IBM alleges are contradictory or inconsistent"). *But see* United States v. McKinney, 954 F.2d 471 (7th Cir. 1992) (where defense counsel failed to give government witness an opportunity to explain or deny a prior inconsistent statement while on the stand, there was no abuse of discretion in refusing to allow counsel to recall the witness).

[14] *See* 4 Weinstein's Federal Evidence § 613.05.

[15] *See* Rule 102 and § 102.1, *supra*.

[16] *See* 1 McCormick, § 36, at 118.

case-in-chief, if it reveals a bias or interest on the part of the witness, or if it reveals a perceptual defect of the witness. Although not codified, the collateral matter doctrine appears to remain a part of federal law.[17]

§ 613.6 Rule 613 — The Degree of Inconsistency Required for Impeachment

When a prior statement is introduced to impeach a party, the impeaching party is relying upon an inference that the statement introduced will cast doubt on the credibility of the witness. The negative effect on the credibility of the witness will depend upon the degree of inconsistency between the prior statement and the witness's statement on the stand. McCormick suggests that a direct contradiction need not be found between the prior statement and the in-court testimony, and that "any material variance between the testimony and the previous statement will suffice."[18] Inconsistency will exist when a former statement does not mention a material fact to which the witness has presently testified that is so important that the witness would naturally have mentioned it in the prior statement.[19] Also, impeachment should be allowed when witnesses testify to facts at trial that in their prior statements they said they could not remember.[20]

Rule 613 does not contain a test that determines when a statement is inconsistent, so the degree of necessary inconsistency is governed by prior case law. A general test endorsed by McCormick is set forth in *United States v. Barrett*,[21] in which the court stated that, "It is enough if the proffered testimony, taken as a whole, either by what it says or by what it omits to say, affords some indication that the fact was different from the testimony of the witness whom it sought to contradict."[22]

§ 613.7 Statements of a Party-Opponent

The opportunity for explanation requirement of Rule 613(b) does not apply to out-of-court statements of a party-opponent admissible as substantive evidence under Rule 801(d)(2). Trial counsel, therefore, may prove that

---

[17] 1 MCCORMICK, § 36, at 118–19; *see* United States v. Nace, 561 F.2d 763 (9th Cir. 1977) (no error to refuse to allow defendant to use sworn statement by prosecution witness for impeachment on a collateral matter).

[18] 1 MCCORMICK, § 34, at 114; *see* United States v. McCrady, 774 F.2d 868 (8th Cir. 1985) (Rule 613 does not require diametrically opposed statements; inconsistency may be found in evasion, lack of recall, pretense or changes in position).

[19] United States v. McCrady, 774 F.2d 868 (8th Cir. 1985); *see also* United States v. Standard Oil Co., 316 F.2d 884 (7th Cir. 1963) (error to disallow defense cross-examination concerning prior statement by witness that omitted matters to which witness testified at trial); *see, e.g.,* Chicago, M. & St. P. R. Co. v. Harrelson, 14 F.2d 893 (8th Cir. 1926).

[20] *See* 1 MCCORMICK, § 34.

[21] United States v. Barrett, 539 F.2d 244 (1st Cir. 1976), *cited in* 1 MCCORMICK, § 34, at 115 n.19.

[22] United States v. Barrett, 539 F.2d 244, 254 (1st Cir. 1976).

a party-witness made an inconsistent statement without affording the party an opportunity to explain or deny the statement.

Out-of-court statements of a party, offered against the party, have an independent basis for admissibility under Rule 801(d)(2). Consistent with the estoppel theory supporting the admissibility of such statements under Rule 801(d)(2),[23] there is no requirement "for an opportunity for explanation requirement" for the introduction of extrinsic evidence of out-of-court statements of a party-witness. Providing they are offered against the party at trial, statements qualify for admission regardless of whether the party testifies as a witness.[24]

§ 613.8   Prior Inconsistent Statements — Constitutional Considerations

When a defendant exercises the right to testify at trial, statements ordinarily subject to the exclusionary rule and constitutionally inadmissible in the prosecution's case-in-chief are often admissible to impeach the defendant's inconsistent testimony. The exclusion of improperly obtained evidence is not an opportunity for the defendant to commit perjury. Further, the "speculative possibility" that this impeachment exception will encourage police misconduct is outweighed by the furtherance of the truth-seeking function of the court.[25]

---

[23] *See* United States v. Kenny, 645 F.2d 1323 (9th Cir. 1981); *see generally,* 4 WEINSTEIN'S FEDERAL EVIDENCE § 613.02; 3 MUELLER & KIRKPATRICK, § 332; 4 WIGMORE, § 1051.

[24] *See* § 801.23 *et seq., infra.*

[25] *See* Harris v. New York, 401 U.S. 222 (1971) (statement obtained in violation of Miranda v. Arizona, 384 U.S. 436 (1966) admissible to impeach defendant's testimony); Michigan v. Harvey, 494 U.S. 344 (1990) (statement taken in violation of defendant's Sixth Amendment right to counsel admissible to impeach defendant's testimony). *But see* James v. Illinois, 493 U.S. 307 (1990) (impeachment exception to exclusionary rule may not be extended beyond defendant's own testimony to include other defense witnesses).

Chapter 614

Rule 614. Court's Calling or Examining Witness

Rule 614. Court's Calling or Examining a Witness

(a) Calling. The court may call a witness on its own or at a party's request. Each party is entitled to cross-examine the witness.

(b) Examining. The court may examine a witness regardless of who calls the witness.

(c) Objections. A party may object to the court's calling or examining a witness either at that time or at the next opportunity when the jury is not present.

---

§ 614.1 Court's Calling or Examining a Witness — In General

Rule 614 permits trial judges to call and interrogate witnesses in civil and criminal cases.[1] The Rule is predicated on the theory that the trial judge bears the ultimate duty of ensuring that the truth emerges from the proceedings.[2] Since, as Wigmore explains, the power to adjudicate involves the power to uncover the truth, the authority to summon and question witnesses is an implied authority of judges.[3]

The power to call witnesses, however, may not be wielded indiscriminately by the trial judge, and where the trial court engages in excessive intervention, amounting to an abridgment of a party's right to an impartial

---

[1] *See generally,* 4 WEINSTEIN'S FEDERAL EVIDENCE §§ 614.01–614.05; 3 MUELLER & KIRKPATRICK, §§ 334–337; 1 McCORMICK, § 8; 3 WIGMORE, § 784; 9 WIGMORE, § 2484. *See also* Close, *The Right and Duty of a Trial Court to Call Witnesses in Civil Actions,* 25 INS. COUNS. J. 278 (1958); Gitelson & Gitelson, *A Trial Judge's Credo Must Include His Affirmative Duty to Be An Instrumentality of Justice,* 7 SANTA CLARA L. REV. 7 (1966); Newark & Samuels, *Let the Judge Call the Witness,* 1969 CRIM. L. REV. 399; Comment, *Evidence—Impeachment of Witness Called by Court,* 20 WAYNE L. REV. 1385 (1974); Note, *The Power of a Trial Judge to Call a Witness—A Tool to Mend Defects,* 21 S.C.L. REV. 224 (1969); Note, *The Trial Judge's Use of His Power to Call Witnesses—An Aid to Adversary Presentation,* 51 NW. U.L. REV. 761 (1957).

[2] *See, e.g.,* United States v. Leslie, 542 F.2d 285 (5th Cir. 1976); United States v. Wilson, 361 F.2d 134 (7th Cir. 1966).

[3] 9 WIGMORE, § 2484; 4 WEINSTEIN'S FEDERAL EVIDENCE § 614.02.

arbiter or the jury's obligation to determine the facts, the resulting prejudice to the affected party may be a reversible abuse of discretion.[4] There is often a fine line between helpful clarification and unwarranted intervention, and reviewing courts have cautioned that trial courts should exercise utmost care in calling witnesses.[5]

§ 614.2   Rule 614(a) — Calling by Court

Rule 614(a) follows prior federal practice in permitting the court to call witnesses on its own initiative or at the urging of counsel. Should the court elect to call a witness, all parties are allowed to cross-examine that witness. This procedure affords the trial judge flexibility in obtaining information he or she deems essential to a fair determination of the dispute but which the parties have failed to provide.[6]

As a practical matter, courts will approach the exercise of the right to call witnesses with some degree of circumspection, since merely presenting a person as the court's witness may clothe that witness with an enhanced measure of dignity and prestige. The result may be an unwarranted invasion of the adversarial system and the parties' interest in controlling the presentation of evidence in a dispute.[7]

§ 614.3   Rule 614(b) — Interrogation by Court

The power of the trial court to interrogate witnesses brought before it existed at common law and was recognized long before its codification in formal rules of evidence. This power, of course, is subject always to the restriction that the judge must maintain his or her status as an impartial

---

[4] *See* United States v. Herring, 602 F.2d 1220 (5th Cir. 1979) (no abuse of discretion, considering collateral nature of testimony, where court refused to call witness so that defendant could cross-examine him); *see also* United States v. Karnes, 531 F.2d 214 (4th Cir. 1976); *see, e.g.,* Smith v. United States, 331 F.2d 265 (8th Cir. 1964); United States v. Lutwak, 195 F.2d 748 (7th Cir. 1952), *aff'd,* 344 U.S. 604 (1953).

[5] *See, e.g.,* United States v. Barnhart, 599 F.3d 737 (7th Cir. 2010) (although district judges have broad discretion in questioning witnesses during direct or cross-examination to clarify testimony or assist the jury's understanding of the evidence, the judge may not assume the role of an advocate for either side by signaling through his questions that he thinks a witness is not credible or that he disbelieves a party's theory of the case; district judge erred in posing leading questions that "read like a cross-examination" and "served to emphasize uncontested facts that were highly unfavorable to the defense."); United States v. Cochran, 955 F.2d 1116 (7th Cir. 1992) (declining to reverse the district court's decision not to call witnesses under the rarely invoked Rule 614(a)).

[6] *See* Johnson v. United States, 333 U.S. 46 (1948) (dissenting opinion discusses right and duty of judge to call witnesses); United States v. Nelson, 570 F.2d 258, 262 (8th Cir. 1978) ("a federal district judge is more than a mere moderator and has an active duty to see that any trial, including a criminal one, is fairly conducted and the issues clearly presented").

[7] *See* Close, *The Right and Duty of a Trial Court to Call Witnesses in Civil Actions,* 25 INS. COUNS. J. 278, 287 (1958), *quoted in* 4 WEINSTEIN'S FEDERAL EVIDENCE § 614.03.

arbiter.[8] Accordingly, it would be an abuse of discretion for trial judges, through their interrogation, to convey to the jury their personal appraisal of the credibility of the witness or the merits of the case.[9] To do so would be to invade the province of the trier of fact in determining factual issues. However, the trial judge is permitted to comment on the evidence, provided, of course, that such commentary does not evince advocacy or bias.[10]

In reviewing any alleged prejudicial errors resulting from the court's independent interrogation of witnesses, a reviewing court will examine the questioning in light of the entire record and, based upon the totality of the circumstances, determine whether there has been a manifest abuse of discretion.[11]

§ 614.4 Rule 614(c) — Objections

The final provision of Rule 614 permits trial counsel to make objections to either the court's calling of its own witness or the court's manner of questioning of any witness. Moreover, Rule 614(c) provides that such objection is timely if it is made at the earliest opportunity out of the hearing of the jury.[12] The Rule seeks an accommodation between the attorney's

---

[8] *See, e.g.,* United States v. Moore, 627 F.2d 830 (7th Cir. 1980); Rogers v. United States, 609 F.2d 1315 (9th Cir. 1979).

[9] *See* Rivas v. Brattesani, 94 F.3d 802 (2d Cir. 1996) (reversing a judgment for the plaintiff because the trial judge's questioning of defense witness "conveyed to the jury the impression that [the Judge] held a fixed and unfavorable opinion of defendants, their counsel, and their position"); United States v. Welliver, 601 F.2d 203 (5th Cir. 1979); United States v. Hickman, 592 F.2d 931 (6th Cir. 1979); *see also* Advisory Committee Note, Rule 614.

[10] *See* United States v. Mizell, 88 F.3d 288 (5th Cir. 1996) (trial court did not err in asking questions of defendant's expert witness; questions were not a comment on the weight of the evidence, but rather served to clarify that the expert had no personal knowledge about certain matters and was relying on information supplied by the defendant); United States v. Holmes, 794 F.2d 345 (8th Cir. 1986) (trial court must avoid the appearance of advocacy); Union Carbide and Carbon Corp. v. Nisley, 300 F.2d 561 (10th Cir. 1961) ("a judge presiding over a federal court is not a mere umpire. He has both the responsibility of assuring the proper conduct of the trial and the power to bring out the facts of the case"); *see also* United States v. Guglielmini, 384 F.2d 602 (2d Cir. 1967); United States v. Barbour, 420 F.2d 1319 (D.C. Cir. 1969).

[11] *See* United States v. Evans, 994 F.2d 317 (7th Cir. 1993) (district court judge's questioning of defendant was not an abuse of discretion where lack of clarity of defendant's testimony justified judicial intervention); United States v. Gonzalez-Torres, 980 F.2d 788 (1st Cir. 1992) (trial judge's questioning of defendant was proper pursuant to Rule 614(b) where the questions clarified defendant's testimony on a confusing sequence of events); Ross v. Black & Decker, Inc., 977 F.2d 1178 (7th Cir. 1992) (trial judge's brief questioning of witness to clarify the witness's testimony was not an abuse of discretion); 4 WEINSTEIN'S FEDERAL EVIDENCE § 614.04; 3 MUELLER & KIRKPATRICK, § 336.

[12] *See* United States v. Barnhart, 599 F.3d 737 (7th Cir. 2010) (a party that is prejudiced by a judge's questioning of witnesses must make an objection to preserve a claim of judicial bias for appeal, despite the possible awkwardness of such steps, but is not required to make this objection in the jury's presence).

responsibility of timely objection to evidentiary matters and protection from the possible embarrassment or prejudice that would result from objecting to conduct from the bench in front of the jury. Under Rule 614(c), parties may assess the prejudice to their case before interposing an objection, since they do not forfeit the right to object by failing to object when the court first asks the question or calls the witness.

It must be noted that Rule 614(c) does not entirely relieve the litigant of its duty to object in order to preserve the exception on appeal. Where a party fails to object in timely fashion, *i.e.,* at the next available time when the jury is not present, objection to the alleged error will be forfeited and the court's action will not result in reversal unless it constitutes plain error.[13] The Rule implicitly recognizes the duty of counsel to preserve the objection to the improper introduction of any evidence, despite its solicitation by the bench.

---

[13] *See* United States v. Vega, 589 F.2d 1147 (2d Cir. 1978) (waiver); United States v. Hickman, 592 F.2d 931 (6th Cir. 1979) (plain error standard); *see also* Rule 103 and Chapter 103, *supra*; *see also* United States v. Kwiat, 817 F.2d 440 (7th Cir. 1987) (counsel may delay objecting but cannot fail to object at all); Stillman v. Norfolk & W.R. Co., 811 F.2d 834 (4th Cir. 1987) (claim of error not preserved for appeal where counsel failed to object).

Chapter 615

Rule 615. Excluding Witnesses

Rule 615. Excluding Witnesses

At a party's request, the court must order witnesses excluded so that they cannot hear other witnesses' testimony. Or the court may do so on its own. But this rule does not authorize excluding:

(a) a party who is a natural person;

(b) an officer or employee of a party that is not a natural person, after being designated as the party's representative by its attorney;

(c) a person whose presence a party shows to be essential to presenting the party's claim or defense; or

(d) a person authorized by statute to be present.

---

§ 615.1 Rule 615 — Excluding Witnesses — In General

Rule 615 provides that a party has a right to the separation of witnesses upon a timely request.[1] Where the request is made, the trial judge lacks the discretion to deny the request except in regard to certain necessary witnesses identified in the Rule. As the Advisory Committee Note reflects, the use of the term "must" in the Rule is intended to convey the absence of discretion of the trial judge in response to a separation request. The present rule adopts the position of Wigmore that:

> [The sequestration of a witness] seems properly to be demandable as of right, precisely as in cross-examination . . . . [Furthermore, to require counsel] to show some probable need to the judge, and to leave to the latter the estimation of the need, is to misunderstand the whole virtue of the expedient, and to deny it in perhaps that very situation of forlorn hope and desperate extreme when it is most

---

[1] *See generally,* 4 WEINSTEIN'S FEDERAL EVIDENCE §§ 615.01–615.06; 3 MUELLER & KIRKPATRICK, §§ 338–341; 6 WIGMORE, §§ 1837–1841. *See also* Comment, *Witnesses Under Article VI of the Proposed Federal Rules of Evidence,* 15 WAYNE L. REV. 1236; Note, *Witnesses—Enforcing a Sequestration Order to Exclude Witnesses—Barring the Witness from Testifying,* 11 KAN. L. REV. 410 (1963).

valuable and most demandable.[2]

The Rule is predicated upon the well-established practice of separating witnesses in order to facilitate the exposure of inconsistencies in their testimony. Likewise, the Rule is designed to prevent witnesses from shaping their testimony to conform with that of another.[3]

Rule 615 applies even at pretrial suppression and other evidentiary hearings, at least if witnesses will be testifying at those hearings.[4] But because the rule literally provides only that witnesses shall be excluded "so that they cannot hear other witnesses' testimony," the courts have generally agreed that the rule does not apply to proceedings where lawyers will be discussing the anticipated testimony of the witnesses in open court, such as a pretrial hearing concerning offers of proof,[5] or an opening statement at trial.[6] These cases are arguably based on an excessively narrow interpretation of the rule's purpose and language.[7] There is no dispute, however, that

---

[2] 6 WIGMORE, § 1839, at 467. However, courts have not required reversal due to failure to exclude, absent some showing of prejudice. *E.g.,* United States v. Greschner, 802 F.2d 373 (10th Cir. 1986); Hollman v. Dale Elec., 752 F.2d 311 (8th Cir. 1985); Marathon Pipe Line Co. v. Drilling Rig Rowan/Odessa, 699 F.2d 240 (5th Cir. 1983).

[3] United States v. Juarez, 573 F.2d 267 (5th Cir. 1978) (proper to exclude witnesses during closing arguments that often restate witnesses' testimony, since the trial judge could fear that if witnesses learned the testimony of other witnesses, the fairness of a second trial might be jeopardized); *see also* United States v. Leggett, 326 F.2d 613 (4th Cir. 1964); *but see* United States v. Collins, 340 F.3d 672 (8th Cir. 2003) (Rule 615 was not violated when two government witnesses were placed in the same holding cell before testifying; neither witness "could tell the other about the nature of his testimony because neither had testified prior to the time they were in the holding cell"); United States v. Rhynes, 218 F.3d 310 (4th Cir. 2000) (en banc) (because Rule 615 governs the conduct of witnesses, not the lawyers, and in light of the ethical and constitutional obligations of a defense lawyer to provide competent representation, Rule 615 does not limit the power and duty of defense counsel to conduct otherwise ethical interview of witnesses before calling them to the stand, even where thorough interview requires discussion of testimony given at the trial by others while witness was excluded from the courtroom).

[4] United States v. Brewer, 947 F.2d 404, 409–410 (9th Cir. 1991); United States v. Warren, 578 F.2d 1058, 1076 (5th Cir. 1978).

[5] United States v. West, 607 F.2d 300, 305–306 (9th Cir. 1979) (despite an admitted "danger of improper suggestion" during pretrial hearing over offers of proof, which "may have suggested testimony to those witnesses present in the courtroom, . . . such danger is not within the purview of Rule 615").

[6] United States v. Brown, 547 F.2d 36, 37 (3d Cir. 1976) ("Admittedly, there may exist a danger of improper suggestions to witnesses during counsel's opening statement, but that danger is not dealt with in Rule 615").

[7] After all, if the rule only forbids witnesses from staying in a courtroom when there is a danger that they might "hear other witnesses' testimony," but not when they might "hear *about* that testimony," one could argue that Rule 615 should not apply to a deaf witness who only wishes to sit in the courtroom to read lips, or to someone who only sat in the courtroom when a child witness was speaking through an interpreter (on the theory that "I could not hear

the judge has the inherent discretionary authority to order exclusion of witnesses from such proceedings,[8] even if Rule 615 does not require it, and such exclusion is always appropriate during opening statements and other pretrial hearings in open court when attorneys will be outlining the expected testimony of witnesses. Indeed, allowing a witness to remain in the courtroom during such proceedings may be worse than an actual violation of Rule 615 in its threat to the purposes underlying the rule.[9] Such situations present at least the same risk of improper suggestion, and the routine exclusion of witnesses during such matters is necessary to protect the spirit, if not the letter, of the rule.[10]

§ 615.2 Persons Not Subject to Exclusion

While the Rule mandates that witnesses must be separated at the request of a party, and further permits the court on its own motion to effect the same result, certain persons may not be excluded or separated under any circumstances.

Subsection (a) prohibits the separation of a party who is a natural

---

or understand one word of what the child was saying, and was only listening to the translator who had the microphone"). Good lawyers are just as effective as translators when it comes to using opening statements to communicate the important parts of the testimony they want out of their witnesses.

[8] *See West,* 607 F.2d at 305–306 ("The mandatory exclusion of witnesses exists only in an evidentiary hearing. Until that point, the exclusion of witnesses is within the discretion of the trial court"); *Brown,* 547 F.2d at 37 ("The decision as to whether witnesses should be excluded prior to counsel's opening statement is committed to the discretion of the district court"). This authority inheres in the judge's broad discretionary control over virtually all aspects of the courtroom and the trial that are not explicitly regulated in the rules, and is also reflected, for example, in the undisputed power of the judge to order that the witnesses be not merely excluded from the courtroom but also separated from each other and instructed to not discuss their testimony with each other during the trial, even though such an order is not provided for by Rule 615. United States v. Sepulveda, 15 F.3d 1161, 1175–1176 (1st Cir. 1993) (Rule 615 governs only exclusion of witnesses from the courtroom; it is within the discretion of the trial court to order additional restrictions such as prohibiting witnesses from discussing the case outside the courtroom).

[9] For example, plaintiff's witnesses who "merely" listen to opening statements will learn three things that they would not have heard if they only sat through some of the other testimony in the case in violation of Rule 615: (1) they will hear the plaintiff's lawyer describe what he or she hopes that plaintiff's witnesses will say, often with a higher level of accuracy and precision and eloquence than those witnesses will be capable of themselves; (2) they will get a vivid picture from the defense opening statement of what to watch out for on cross-examination and how to tailor their testimony accordingly; and (3) they will be exposed to the "big picture" of all the important details in the case that are expected from all witnesses for both sides, including those who will be testifying after them.

[10] Likewise, although Rule 615 does not routinely apply to pretrial depositions, *see* Fed. R. Civ. P. 30(c)(1) ("The examination and cross-examination of a deponent proceed as they would at trial under the provisions of the Federal Rules of Evidence, except Rules 103 and 615"), and the judge has the discretion to designate "the persons who may be present while the discovery is conducted" Fed. R. Civ. P. 26(c)(1)(E).

person.[11] Subsection (b) prohibits exclusion of the designated representative of a party that is not a natural person, *e.g.*, a corporate director, officer or employee, or a government agent or police officer responsible for the investigation of the case.[12] Subsection (c) prohibits separation or exclusion of a witness whose presence is shown by the party to be essential to the presentation of his cause.[13] For example, the court may allow expert witnesses to remain in the courtroom under this subsection if they will testify based upon facts or data revealed to them through the testimony of other witnesses at the trial.[14] The court may not separate expert witnesses who plan to testify at trial and will base their testimony on the facts or data contained in the testimony of other witnesses.[15] Under subsection (c), the

---

[11] *E.g.,* Varlack v. SWC Caribbean, Inc., 550 F.2d 171 (3d Cir. 1977) (it was reversible error to sequester person until he was formally made a party, where court refused to rule on whether it would permit complaint to be amended to add the additional party until some of the most important testimony in the case had been given).

[12] *See* United States v. Green, 324 F.3d 375. (5th Cir. 2003) ("[T]his Court has never decided whether the Government can designate more than one individual as its case agent, however we have permitted the exemption of more than one case agent from sequestration if their presence is essential to the presentation of the case. Although the government could not show any compelling reason why the presence in the courtroom of both testifying DEA agents was essential to its case, reversal was not required without a showing of specific prejudice to the defense); Roberts v. Galen of Virginia, Inc., 325 F.3d 776 (6th Cir. 2003) ("Corporations are allowed to choose any officer or employee as their designated representative" to remain at counsel table during the trial, not merely those with authority to bind the corporation. Furthermore, where corporation has ceased to operate and has no employees at time of trial, it may designate a former employee as its representative, who may therefore remain at trial despite general order sequestering witnesses); United States v. Sykes, 977 F.2d 1242 (8th Cir. 1992) (trial court did not err by permitting the government's agent to sit at the prosecution table throughout the trial and then to testify as an expert); United States v. Machor, 879 F.2d 945 (1st Cir. 1989) (trial court did not err by refusing to exclude the government's case agent in a trial for cocaine distribution); United States v. Jones, 687 F.2d 1265 (8th Cir. 1982) (trial judge did not err in exempting the government's case agent, a city police officer, from the exclusion order). *But see* United States v. Farnham, 791 F.2d 331 (4th Cir. 1986) (trial court committed reversible error in refusing defense request to exclude one of two FBI agents where the agents were testifying to the same conversation).

[13] United States v. Burgess, 691 F.2d 1146 (4th Cir. 1982); *see also* Morvant v. Constr. Aggregates Corp., 570 F.2d 626 (6th Cir. 1978) (not automatic basis for exemption from sequestration that expert witness may be assisted by being present in courtroom to hear testimony upon which he is expected to base his expert testimony; the decision whether to permit the expert witness to remain is within the discretion of the trial judge and should not normally be disturbed on appeal); *cf.* N.L.R.B. v. Pope Maintenance Corp., 573 F.2d 898 (5th Cir. 1978).

[14] *See* Rule 703 and Chapter 703, *infra.*

[15] *See* United States v. Seschillie, 310 F.3d 1208 (9th Cir. 2002) (in attempted murder case, district court abused its discretion in excluding from the courtroom the defendant's expert witness, who should have been allowed to remain in courtroom under Rule 615(3) to hear the testimony of the fact witnesses to assist him in forming an opinion as the possible explanations for an accidental shooting; exclusion is especially inappropriate where the

court has discretion in determining whether the witness's presence is essential, and the burden of demonstrating the necessity is upon the proponent of the witness.[16]

Subsection (d) was added to Rule 615 in 1998 to conform the Rule to relevant statutory provisions, most notably the Victim's Rights and Restitution Act of 1990 and the Victim Rights Clarification Act of 1997. These pieces of legislation were enacted in response to what was perceived as the routine exclusion of crime victims from criminal proceedings. Because this legislation supersedes the usual operation of Rule 615, subsection (d) was added to the Rule. Furthermore, by adding an exception of general applicability to Rule 615, future conforming amendments will be unnecessary.

The structure of Rule 615 appears to imply that the applicability of subsection (d) to a witness governed by a particular statutory provision will prevent the sequestration of that witness. However, specific legislation may merely alter the analysis as to whether the particular witness will be excluded from a proceeding, rather than guarantee the presence of that witness in the courtroom. For example, part of the legislation known as the "Victim of Crime Bill of Rights" that made the amendment to Rule 615 necessary, provides for a limited right of victims of certain crimes "to be present at all public court proceedings related to the offense, unless the court determines that testimony by the victim would be materially affected if the victim heard other testimony at trial." 42 U.S.C. § 10606(b)(4) (1999). The applicability of this provision thus neither ensures the presence of a crime victim at a proceeding nor automatically excludes the victim upon request of a party. Instead, the statute requires the court to determine whether the testimony of the victim will be "materially affected" by hearing other testimony.

---

witness will be testifying only as to his expert opinion, and not also as a fact witness, since there is no danger of his changing his recollections based on the testimony of the other witnesses); Malek v. Federal Ins. Co., 994 F.2d 49 (2d Cir. 1993) (in insurance claim where defendant claimed that a fire was the result of arson, trial court erred in excluding plaintiff's expert witness during the testimony of defendant's expert where plaintiff's expert was essential to the presentation of the case); Mayo v. Tri-Bell Indus., 787 F.2d 1007 (5th Cir. 1986) (expert witnesses were testifying based on the "facts or data in the case" and so were properly exempted from the exclusion of witnesses). *But see* Opus 3 Ltd. v. Heritage Park, Inc., 91 F.3d 625 (4th Cir. 1996) (trial court did not err in excluding general contractor hired by the defendant as an expert witness from the courtroom; in actuality, the contractor was both an expert witness and a fact witness, *and* the court found that the defendant did not establish that the contractor needed to hear the testimony of other witnesses in order to render an expert opinion).

[16] *See* Marathon Pipe Line Co. v. Drilling Rig Rowan/Odessa, 699 F.2d 240 (5th Cir. 1983); Government of Virgin Islands v. Edinborough, 625 F.2d 472 (3d Cir. 1980); United States v. Causey, 609 F.2d 777 (5th Cir. 1977); *see also* Curlee Clothing Corp. v. NLRB, 607 F.2d 1213 (8th Cir. 1979); Sturgis Newport Business Forms, Inc. v. N.L.R.B., 563 F.2d 1252 (5th Cir. 1977).

Furthermore, the Victim Rights Clarification Act of 1997 indicates that the court may not exclude a crime victim from a courtroom proceeding solely because the victim may eventually testify at a sentencing hearing. See 18 U.S.C. § 3510 (1999). This provision should be understood as restricting the court's "materially affected" determination under the Victim of Crime Bill of Rights, where applicable, to matters intrinsic to the fact-finding function of the court with respect to the guilt or innocence of the defendant, *i.e.*, matters other than the potential role of that witness in sentencing.

On first glance, the inclusion of a specific exception to Rule 615 is curious, as the general exception to the applicability of the Rules for "Act[s] of Congress" in Rule 402 appears to render subsection (4) unnecessary. However, closer investigation of Rule 402 reveals that the exceptions contained in that Rule apply only to the overarching precept that "[r]elevant evidence is admissible" and not to the Rules generally. This distinction supports the view of the concept of relevance as a central organizing principle embedded within the Rules of Evidence. The inclusion of a distinct exception to the procedure in Rule 615 for applicable statutory provisions reinforces the conception of the Rules as a codification of miscellaneous evidentiary doctrines as opposed to a comprehensive set of evidentiary regulation.

§ 615.3   Violation of a Separation Order

Where the exclusion or separation order is violated by a witness or party, the court possesses the customary discretion in taking corrective measures.[17] Remedial measures include citing the witness for contempt, preventing the witness from testifying, striking the witness's testimony, or permitting the transgression to reflect upon the witness's credibility.[18] Unfortunately, no remedy will fully rectify the damage. A contempt citation has the effect of

---

[17] *See, e.g.,* United States v. Ruiz Solorio, 337 F.3d 580 (6th Cir. 2003) (assuming without deciding that FRE 615 applies to communications between witnesses outside of the courtroom, the testimony is not excludable where the party offering the testimony did not knowingly violate the sequestration order, the district court limited the scope of the second witness's testimony, and there was no evidence that the second witness's testimony was tainted by the earlier testimony); Reeves v. International Tel. & Tel. Corp., 616 F.2d 1342 (5th Cir. 1980) (court refused to overturn district court's order prohibiting any testimony from witnesses with whom counsel for defendant met and discussed the case in preparation for testimony, in flagrant violation of previously entered sequestration and separation order).

[18] *See* 4 WEINSTEIN'S FEDERAL EVIDENCE § 615.07; *see also* United States v. McMahon, 104 F.3d 638 (4th Cir. 1997) (affirming a contempt conviction of a witness who, while under a sequestration order, paid his secretary to take notes during the trial and then reviewed those notes before testifying); United States v. Wilson, 103 F.3d 1402 (8th Cir. 1997) (trial court did not abuse its discretion in refusing to allow a defense witness to testify because that witness had been present in the courtroom during several days of testimony despite a sequestration order); Jerry Parks Equip. v. Southeast Equip. Co., 817 F.2d 340 (5th Cir. 1987) (testimony struck); United States v. Perry, 815 F.2d 1100 (7th Cir. 1987) (same).

punishing the witness involved and may deter others,[19] but it "does nothing to extinguish any false testimony which the witness may have fabricated by listening to other witnesses."[20] Commenting on the witness's noncompliance is undesirable because it may cause a jury to wrongfully diminish the weight of truthful testimony that was untainted by the witness's violation of the sequestration order.[21] Finally, forbidding the witness to testify at the trial is the severest sanction, and may have the effect of removing relevant evidence entirely from the jury's consideration.[22] Generally, the court may be reversed only for an abuse of discretion in taking such measures.[23]

---

[19] *See* 4 WEINSTEIN'S FEDERAL EVIDENCE § 615.07.

[20] Note, *Witnesses—Enforcing a Sequestration Order to Exclude Witnesses—Barring the Witness from Testifying*, 11 KAN. L. REV. 410, 411 (1963), *quoted in* 4 WEINSTEIN'S FEDERAL EVIDENCE § 615.07.

[21] *See* 4 WEINSTEIN'S FEDERAL EVIDENCE § 615.07.

[22] *See* United States v. Rhynes, 218 F.3d 310 (4th Cir. 2000) (en banc) (where a defendant is sanctioned for the misconduct of his lawyer in violation of Rule 615, "courts should impose the least severe sanction justified under the circumstances"; it would be an abuse of discretion to exclude testimony of defense witness as sanction for an inadvertent violation of Rule by defense counsel with no participation by the accused in the transgression); United States v. Nash, 649 F.2d 369 (5th Cir. 1981); Reeves v. I.T. & T. Corp., 616 F.2d 1342 (5th Cir. 1980); Holder v. United States, 150 U.S. 91 (1893) (a trial court may not routinely disqualify the testimony of a witness who violates a sequestration order without first finding that some particular factual issue exists that justifies such a drastic remedy).

[23] United States v. Tedder, 403 F.3d 836, 840 (7th Cir. 2005) (district court did not abuse its discretion in enforcing exclusion order by precluding the defense from calling a reputation witness on rebuttal, after that witness had been present during the trial. "If Tedder wanted this witness available for rebuttal, he should have kept him out of the courtroom"); Dutton v. Brown, 812 F.2d 593 (10th Cir. 1987) (in murder prosecution, it was abuse of discretion to strike testimony of defense witness where other means of enforcing the order were available); United States ex rel. Clark v. Fike, 538 F.2d 750 (7th Cir. 1976) (court was within discretion to allow witness who has disobeyed sequestration order to testify).

ARTICLE VII.

OPINIONS AND EXPERT TESTIMONY

Synopsis

Chapter 701

Rule 701. Opinion Testimony by Lay Witnesses

Rule 701. Opinion Testimony by Lay Witnesses

If a witness is not testifying as an expert, testimony in the form of an opinion is limited to one that is:

(a) rationally based on the witness's perception;

(b) helpful to clearly understanding the witness's testimony or to determining a fact in issue; and

(c) not based on scientific, technical, or other specialized knowledge within the scope of Rule 702.

---

§ 701.1 Lay Opinion Testimony — In General

Traditionally, courts have required lay witnesses to testify to facts rather than opinions. The line between fact and opinion often proved nearly impossible to draw, and Rule 701 obviates the necessity for such compartmentalization by permitting lay witnesses to render opinions when the criteria for admissibility contained in the Rule are satisfied.[1]

§ 701.2 History of the Rule Prohibiting Lay Opinion Testimony

Even before the adoption of the Federal Rules of Evidence, federal courts deviated from a strict interpretation of the general proposition that witnesses may testify only to facts and not to inferences or opinions predicated upon

---

[1] *See generally,* 1 MCCORMICK, § 11; 4 WEINSTEIN'S FEDERAL EVIDENCE, §§ 701.01–701.08; 3 MUELLER & KIRKPATRICK, §§ 342–347; 7 WIGMORE, §§ 1917–1929. *See also* Ladd, *Expert Testimony,* 5 VAND. L. REV. 414 (1952); Manning & Mewitt, *Psychiatric Evidence,* 18 CRIM. L.Q. 325 (1976); McCormick, *Opinion Evidence in Iowa,* 19 DRAKE L. REV. 245 (1970); Martin, *The Uncertain Rules of Certainty: An Analysis and Proposal for a Federal Evidence Rule,* 20 WAYNE L. REV. 781 (1974); Spector & Foster, *Admissibility of Hypnotic Statements: Is the Law of Evidence Susceptible?,* 38 OHIO L. REV. 567 (1977); Spies, *Opinion Evidence,* 15 ARK. L. REV. 105 (1960); Slovenko, *The Opinion Rule and Wittgenstein's Tractatus,* 14 MIAMI L. REV. 1 (1959); Tyree, *The Opinion Rule,* 10 RUTGERS L. REV. 601 (1956); Williams, *Law and Practice in the Identification of Controlled Drugs by Lay Testimony,* 11 CRIM. L. BULL. 814 (1975).

facts.[2] This general rule of exclusion was based largely on the misapprehension that opinions from witnesses would invade the province of the jury.[3] Exceptions to the general prohibition of opinion testimony developed, and at an early date, opinion testimony by experts was removed from the proscription of the general rule.[4] The "collective facts" or "shorthand rendition" exception developed after federal courts recognized that some lay testimony containing a composite of fact and opinion should be admitted when witnesses cannot adequately convey their point through strictly factual descriptions. For example, witnesses may testify to their conclusion or impression that someone was nervous rather than describing the various details that led them to reach this conclusion. On cross-examination, the opposing party can question the witnesses about the specific facts upon which they based their conclusion.[5]

The creation of the "collective facts" exception reveals a limited recognition of the invalidity of the fact/opinion dichotomy that underpins the general prohibition of opinion testimony. The now-obsolete exclusionary rule rested on the notion that a distinction always can be made between "fact" and "opinion." McCormick's condemnation of this concept is pertinent:

> There is no conceivable statement however specific, detailed and "factual," that is not in some measure the product of inference and reflection as well as observation and memory. The difference between the statement, "He was driving on the left-hand side of the

---

[2] *See, e.g.,* Panger v. Duluth, Winnipeg & Pac. Ry., 490 F.2d 1112 (8th Cir. 1974) (railway employees allowed to express opinions as to the safety of certain business practices); Fullerton v. Sauer, 337 F.2d 474 (8th Cir. 1964) (plaintiff allowed to express opinion on whether he could have avoided the auto accident when the car with which he collided suddenly came into view).

[3] 1 McCormick, § 12. The history of the rule against opinions by lay witnesses indicates that it may have developed due to a misunderstanding of the meaning of the word "opinion." Before the 1800's, "opinion" referred to a notion unsupported by definite knowledge. Therefore, the rule against opinions was another way of stating the requirement that witnesses must have personal knowledge of the facts. In reference to the firsthand knowledge rule, English text writers used the shorthand expression that witnesses must testify to facts, not opinions. In the American courts, "[t]his statement of the rule led to more than a hundred years of confusion." King & Pillinger, Opinion Evidence in Illinois 7 (1942).

[4] *See* 7 Wigmore, § 1917.

[5] 3 Mueller & Kirkpatrick, §§ 344–345; *see, e.g.,* Kerry Coal Co. v. United Mine Workers, 637 F.2d 957 (3d Cir. 1981) (witness's testimony that employees were nervous and afraid was a shorthand report of his observations); United States v. McClintic, 570 F.2d 685 (8th Cir. 1978) (prosecution witness permitted to testify that in his opinion defendant knew the goods were obtained by fraud); United States v. Freeman, 514 F.2d 1184 (10th Cir. 1975) (prosecution for interstate fraud scheme; bank officer properly permitted to testify that there was no doubt in his mind that appellant was selling all of his equipment; he was merely giving rendition of his knowledge).

road" which would be classed as "fact" under the rule, and "He was driving carelessly" which would be called "opinion" is merely a difference between a more concrete and specific form of descriptive statement and a less specific and concrete form. The difference between the so-called "fact," then, and "opinion," is not a difference between opposites or contrasting absolutes, but a mere difference in degree with no recognizable line to mark the boundary.[6]

In a particular case, the distinction between fact and opinion depends upon whether the lay witness's testimony relates to a critical issue or to a peripheral matter: "In the outer circle of collateral facts, near the rim of relevance, evidence in general terms will be received with relative freedom, but as we come closer to the hub of the issue, the courts have been more careful to call for details instead of inferences."[7]

§ 701.3 Standards of Admissibility — Opinions Rationally Based on the Perception of a Witness

Rule 701 permits the rendering of lay opinion testimony only when all three of the Rule's standards for admissibility are satisfied. The first standard articulated by the Rule, which requires that the opinion or inference of a lay witness be rationally based on the perceptions of the witness, is in actuality two distinct limitations. The first limitation is the principle prescribed by Rule 602, which requires that the witness have firsthand knowledge of the subject of the testimony.[8] The second limitation, termed the "rational connection" test, requires that the opinion or inference advanced by the witness must be one that a rational person would form on the basis of the observed facts.[9] Strained or contrived inferences do not satisfy the standard.

---

[6] 1 McCORMICK, § 11, at 42–43.

[7] 1 McCORMICK, § 12, at 47.

[8] Rushing v. Kansas City Southern. Ry., 185 F.3d 496 (5th Cir. 1999) (to counter defense expert's conclusions that sound levels from the rail switching yard near plaintiffs' residence were within federal limits, lay opinions by plaintiffs were admissible because they were based upon the plaintiffs' personal perceptions of the everyday noise and vibration levels as compared to the single night when the defense expert took his measurements).

[9] *See* United States v. Cournoyer, 118 F.3d 1279 (8th Cir. 1997) (in rape trial, defense opinion testimony that the rape charge was "another attempt [by the complainant] to get attention" was inadmissible; although defense had evidence that complainant had a history of suicide attempts, there was no rational basis for inferring that the rape accusation was false); Haun v. Ideal Industries, Inc., 81 F.3d 541 (5th Cir. 1996) (testimony by supervisor in age discrimination case that employer was phasing out older workers was admissible as opinion testimony based on perceptions where supervisor also stated that he had been told to "build a case" against an older worker and had heard remarks about his own age); Alexis v. McDonald's Restaurants of Mass., Inc., 67 F.3d 341 (1st Cir. 1995) (in racial discrimination case, trial court properly excluded lay opinion testimony from plaintiff's relatives that defendant's employees would have treated plaintiff differently if she were a "rich white woman"; court found no foundation for an inference that treatment toward plaintiff was based on racial discrimination); United States v. Yazzie, 976 F.2d 1252 (9th Cir. 1992) (in statutory

Likewise, mere speculations are not rendered admissible by the Rule.[10] However, the fact that the witness qualifies testimony with statements such as "I think" or "to the best of my recollection" does not transform the testimony into an inadmissible opinion under Rule 701.[11]

§ 701.4 Standards of Admissibility — Helpfulness to the Jury; Judicial Discretion

The second standard of admissibility articulated by Rule 701 is the requirement that the lay opinion testimony must be "helpful" to the trier of fact in understanding the testimony of the witness or in determining a fact in issue.[12] Under the "helpfulness" test, opinion evidence should be admitted in a wide range of situations. The witness should be able to testify in the form of opinion if necessary to avoid misleading the jury, *i.e.,* the witness cannot "accurately, adequately and with reasonable facility describe the fundamental facts upon which the opinion is erected."[13]

Witnesses should also be allowed to testify in the form of an opinion to conclusions or observations that they draw through their senses, such as "the appearance of persons or things, identity, the manner of conduct, competency of a person, degrees of light or darkness, sound, size, weight, distance and an endless number of things that cannot be described factually in words apart from inferences."[14] If the personal knowledge and helpfulness require-

---

rape trial, witnesses should have been permitted to testify that, at the time of the alleged sexual abuse, they believed the minor to be between sixteen and twenty years of age); *see, e.g.,* United States v. Paiva, 892 F.2d 148 (1st Cir. 1989) (in a trial for conspiracy to distribute cocaine, lay opinion testimony by a drug user that the substance she found in defendant's shoe was cocaine was admissible); 4 WEINSTEIN'S FEDERAL EVIDENCE §§ 701.03–701.04.

[10] Stagman v. Ryan, 176 F.3d 986 (7th Cir. 1999) (the opinion of a personnel officer that the plaintiff would not have been fired without the express approval of the defendant was based on mere speculation, not personal knowledge, and did not meet the first requirement of Rule 701).

[11] 4 WEINSTEIN'S FEDERAL EVIDENCE § 701.04.

[12] *See, e.g.,* United States v. Yazzie, 976 F.2d 1252 (9th Cir. 1992) (in statutory rape trial, witnesses should have been permitted to testify that, at the time of the alleged sexual abuse, they believed the minor to be between sixteen and twenty years of age); Mattison v. Dallas Carrier Corp., 947 F.2d 95 (4th Cir. 1991) (the district court did not abuse its discretion in admitting lay witness testimony because it was based on the witness's own observations and was probative of a fact in issue); United States v. Jackson, 569 F.2d 1003 (7th Cir. 1978) (trial judge properly refused to allow lay witness to testify why her husband was depressed); *see also* United States v. Thompson, 708 F.2d 1294 (8th Cir. 1983); Krueger v. State Farm Mut. Auto. Ins. Co., 707 F.2d 312 (8th Cir. 1983); United States v. Goodheim, 686 F.2d 776 (9th Cir. 1982).

[13] MORGAN, BASIC PROBLEMS OF EVIDENCE, § 217 (1962).

[14] Rule 701, Advisory Committee Note; *see, e.g.,* Singletary v. Secretary of Health, Educ. and Welfare, 623 F.2d 217 (2d Cir. 1980) (drunkenness); Young v. Illinois C.G.R. Co., 618 F.2d 332 (5th Cir. 1980) (poor condition of grade crossing); United States v. Arrasmith, 557 F.2d 1093 (5th Cir. 1977) (odor of marijuana); *see also* United States v. Murray, 523 F.2d 489

ments of Rule 701 are satisfied, lay witnesses should be permitted to testify to the "unspoken knowledge, intent, understanding or feelings of another."[15]

It is important to note that lay opinions are not "helpful" under the Rule whenever the jury can readily draw the necessary inferences and conclusions without the aid of the opinion. In this regard the true theory underlying the exclusion of lay opinion testimony is that such opinions are superfluous when the jury, unaided by opinion, can draw the necessary inferences as effectively as the witness.[16] Accordingly, the Rule vests considerable discretion in the trial court and mandates care in determining whether the jury will be aided by lay opinion testimony in reaching a just result.[17] Furthermore, in a proper case, lay opinion testimony otherwise admissible may be excluded by the trial court if the probative value of the testimony is sufficiently outweighed by the considerations set forth in Rule 403.

§ 701.5 Standards of Admissibility — Not Based on Specialized Knowledge; Distinguishing Lay and Expert Testimony

The 2000 Amendment to Rule 701 added a third standard of admissibility to lay opinion testimony. Rule 701(c) states that a lay witness who has not been identified and qualified as an expert may not offer an opinion that is "based on scientific, technical, or other specialized knowledge within the scope of Rule 702." In deciding whether a witness is offering lay or expert opinion, the court must evaluate not the qualifications of the witness, but rather the character of the testimony offered.[18] The admissibility of opinion testimony based on scientific, technical, or other specialized knowledge, regardless of who offers it, will turn on a Rule 702 analysis. Such an opinion cannot be admitted as lay opinion under Rule 701. The amendment that

---

(8th Cir. 1975); United States v. Mastberg, 503 F.2d 465 (9th Cir. 1974); Wood v. United States, 361 F.2d 802 (8th Cir. 1966). Several cases permit witnesses to identify the defendant as the subject of a surveillance photograph. *See, e.g.,* United States v. Allen, 787 F.2d 933 (4th Cir. 1986); United States v. Langford, 802 F.2d 1176 (9th Cir. 1986); United States v. Farnsworth, 729 F.2d 1158 (8th Cir. 1984).

[15] 3 MUELLER & KIRKPATRICK, §§ 344–345.

[16] *See* Cameron v. City of New York, 598 F.3d 50 (2d Cir. 2010) (in malicious prosecution action against two arresting officers, it was reversible error to allow two prosecutors and a police lieutenant to testify to their opinions on the credibility of the officers and whether there was probable cause to arrest or charge the plaintiffs; such testimony "violated bedrock principles of evidence law that prohibit witnesses (a) from vouching for other witnesses, (b) from testifying in the form of legal conclusions, and (c) from interpreting evidence that jurors can equally well analyze on their own").

[17] *See* 4 WEINSTEIN'S FEDERAL EVIDENCE § 701.02; 3 MUELLER & KIRKPATRICK, §§ 344–345.

[18] United States v. York, 600 F.3d 347 (5th Cir. 2010) (in criminal case, the defendant's father could not testify that his son suffered from organic brain damage as the result of his traumatic birth; the father's opinion was "speculative medical causation testimony," and not a proper topic for lay opinion because it was "not the type of opinion that one could reach as a process of everyday reasoning").

added Rule 701(c) was not designed to make any real change in the law, but merely to codify and clarify certain pre-existing legal standards, some of which had been widely misunderstood or downright ignored.

According to the Advisory Committee Note, this salutary amendment serves two functions. First, it ensures that any witness who offers the functional equivalent of expert opinion will be subjected to the rigorous standards for the admissibility of such evidence, thus "eliminat[ing] the risk that the reliability requirements set forth in Rule 702 will be evaded through the simple expedient of proffering an expert in lay witness clothing."[19] Second, the amendment makes it far more difficult for a party to circumvent the special expert witness disclosure requirements set forth in Federal Rule of Civil Procedure 26 and Federal Rule of Criminal Procedure 16, which require parties to disclose the names of all expert witnesses to be called at trial, as well as the experts' credentials and opinions. Again, Rule 701(c) is intended to prevent a party from evading those special rules for expert testimony "by simply calling an expert witness in the guise of a layperson."[20] By minimizing the risk of surprise expert testimony at trial, the Amendment is fully consistent with the Rules' stated purpose of securing fairness and efficiency in judicial administration.

The line between lay and expert opinion testimony is not always bright. Citing a 1992 Tennessee case, the Advisory Committee Note says the distinction is that lay testimony "results from a process of reasoning familiar in everyday life," while expert testimony "results from a process of reasoning which can be mastered only by specialists in the field."[21] However, the Note does not define how much particularized personal knowledge acquired by an individual may be relied upon before such knowledge becomes "specialized," thus making the resulting conclusions the equivalent of expert opinions.[22] As with any Rule 701 question, this is left to the court's discretion subject to Rule 403. When the same witness gives both lay and expert testimony, however, the court should take appropriate precautions to ensure that the jury is not influenced to give

---

[19] Rule 701, Advisory Committee Note.

[20] *Id.*

[21] *Id.* (citing State v. Brown, 836 S.W.2d 530, 549 (1992)).

[22] *Compare* United States v. Figueroa-Lopez, 125 F.3d 1241 (9th Cir. 1997) (law enforcement agents' opinion, that the accused was using code words to refer to drug quantities and prices, was based on their knowledge of the drug culture's vernacular and amounted to expert opinion), *with* United States v. Fenner. 600 F.3d 1014 (8th Cir. 2010) (in drug prosecution, government's confidential informants were properly permitted to explain slang terms and give their interpretations of what defendant and others said in recorded conversations, because the informants participated in the conversations and their explanations at trial were based on their perceptions), *and* United States v. Westbrook, 896 F.2d 330 (8th Cir. 1990) (two heavy amphetamine users properly allowed to testify that a substance was amphetamine).

undue weight to the lay opinion of that witness.[23]

---

[23] United States v. Baptiste, 596 F.3d 214 (4th Cir. 2010) (when a police officer testifies as both an expert and as a lay witness, the trial court should take steps to ensure that there is a clear demarcation in the jurors' minds between the witness's lay and expert roles, so they will not give his lay testimony additional weight because of his dual role as an expert; this should be accomplished by cautionary warnings or instructions, by requiring the witness to take separate trips to the stand in each capacity, or by ensuring that counsel makes clear when he is eliciting lay versus expert testimony).

Chapter 702

Rule 702. Testimony by Expert Witnesses

Rule 702. Testimony by Expert Witnesses

A witness who is qualified as an expert by knowledge, skill, experience, training, or education may testify in the form of an opinion or otherwise if:

(a) the expert's scientific, technical, or other specialized knowledge will help the trier of fact to understand the evidence or to determine a fact in issue;

(b) the testimony is based on sufficient facts or data;

(c) the testimony is the product of reliable principles and methods; and

(d) the expert has reliably applied the principles and methods to the facts of the case.

---

§ 702.1 Testimony by Expert Witnesses — In General

Rule 702, which governs the admissibility of expert testimony, performs four functions.[1] First, it serves as an authorization for the use of expert

---

[1] *See generally,* 1 McCormick, § 13; 4 Weinstein's Federal Evidence §§ 702.01–702.08; 3 Mueller & Kirkpatrick, §§ 348–353. *See also* Addison, *Expert Testimony on Eyewitness Perception,* 82 Dick. L. Rev. 465 (1978); Decker & Handler, *Voiceprint Identification—Out of the Frye Pan and Into Admissibility,* 26 Am. U. L. Rev. 314 (1977); Diamond & Louisell, *The Psychiatrist as an Expert Witness: Some Ruminations and Speculations,* 63 Mich. L. Rev. 1335 (1965); Donaher, Piehler, Twerski, & Weinstein, *The Technological Expert in Products Liability Litigation,* 52 Tex. L. Rev. 1303 (1974); Fassett, *The Third Circuit's Unique Response to Expert Testimony on Eyewitness Perception: Is What You See What You Get?,* 19 Seton Hall L. Rev. 697 (1989); Finkelstein, *A Statistical Analysis of Guilty Plea Practice in the Federal Court,* 89 Harv. L. Rev. 293 (1975); Frank, *Obscenity: Some Problems of Values and the Use of Experts,* 41 Wash. L. Rev. 631 (1966); Gianelli, *The Admissibility of Novel Scientific Evidence: Frye v. United States, a Half Century Later,* 80 Colum. L. Rev. 1197 (1980); *Golanski, Judicial Scrutiny of Expert Testimony in Environmental Tort Litigation,* 9 Pace Envtl. L. Rev. 349 (1992); Hale, *The Admissibility of Bite Mark Evidence,* 51 S. Cal. L. Rev. 309 (1978); Lewin, *Psychiatric Evidence in Criminal Cases for Purposes Other Than the Defense of Insanity,* 26 Syracuse L. Rev. 1051 (1975); Livingood, *Admissibility and Reliability of Expert Scientific Testimony After Daubert,* 61 Def. Couns. J. (1994); McLaughlin, *Discovery and Admissibility of Expert Testimony,* 63 Notre Dame L. Rev. 760 (1988); Myers, Bays, Becker, Berliner, Corwin & Saywitz, *Expert Testimony in Child Sexual Abuse Cases,* 68 Neb. L. Rev. (1989); O'Connor, *That's the Man:*

testimony. Second, the Rule articulates standards to be applied in determining whether expert testimony should be admitted in a particular case. Third, the Rule provides criteria to be applied in determining whether an individual tendered as an expert witness should be accorded expert status by the trial court. Finally, the Rule expands the form the expert testimony may assume.

§ 702.2   Rationale and Purpose of Rule 702

Expert testimony has traditionally been considered an exception to the general rule requiring witnesses to testify to facts rather than opinions.[2] The expert, by reason of his or her expertise in a particular area, is qualified to draw inferences from facts that a jury would be unable to draw. Because the expert's value to the litigation process lies in his or her special inferential skills, the expert is not required to have firsthand knowledge of the particular set of facts supporting his or her opinion or inference as is required of a lay witness under Rules 602 and 701.

Generally, expert testimony will be admissible if: (1) the expert's testimony will assist the trier of fact; and (2) the person giving the testimony is qualified as an expert concerning the matters upon which his or her testimony is based.

The following jury instruction, which has been approved for use in federal trials, aptly summarizes the role of expert witnesses in litigation:

> During the trial you heard the testimony of _____, who was described to us as an expert in _____. This witness was permitted to testify even though he did not actually witness any of the events involved in this trial. A person's training and experience may make him or her a true expert in a technical field. The law allows that person to state an opinion here about matters in that particular field. Merely because _____ has expressed an opinion does not mean, however, that you must accept this opinion. The same as with any other witness, it is up to you to decide whether you believe his testimony and choose to rely upon it. Part of that decision will depend on your judgment about whether his background of training and experience is sufficient for him to give the expert opinion that you heard. You must also decide whether his

---

A Sobering Study of Eyewitness Identification and the Polygraph, 49 St. John's L. Rev. 1 (1974); Poulter, *Daubert and Scientific Evidence: Assessing Evidentiary Reliability in Toxic Tort Litigation*, 1993 Utah L. Rev. 1307 (1993); Richards & Kidner, *Judicial Attitudes Towards Actuarial Evidence*, 124 New L.J. 105 (1974); Ringland, *Child Sex Abuse Evidence Problems—Update 1988*, 14 U. Dayton L. Rev. 147 (1988); Strong, *Language and Logic in Expert Testimony: Limiting Expert Testimony by Restrictions of Function, Reliability and Form*, 71 Or. L. Rev. 349 (1992); Weinstein, *Rule 702 of the Federal Rules of Evidence is Sound: It Should Not Be Amended*, 138 F.R.D. 631 (1991); Wolfgang, *The Social Scientist in Court*, 65 J. Crim. L. 239 (1974).

[2] *See* § 701.2, *supra.*

opinions were based on sound reasons, judgment, and information.[3]

§ 702.3   Subjects Regarding Which Expert Testimony Is Proper

The use of expert testimony enables the jury to draw the proper inferences from the facts introduced at trial. Under pre-Rule practice, the subject matter of the expertise of the witness had to relate to some area of specialization beyond the experience of laypersons.[4] Rule 702 is more expansive in providing that expert testimony may be admitted concerning all types of "specialized knowledge," including, specifically, scientific and technical matters.

While the test for the use of expert testimony requires that the trier of fact be aided by the expert's testimony,[5] this standard is both broad and relative, and often depends upon the particular subject or the particular witness. Wigmore articulated the test as, "[o]n *this subject* can a jury receive from *this person* appreciable help?"[6] Therefore, determinations concerning the admissibility of expert testimony must always be made on a case-by-case basis.

Two threshold inquiries that must be made when determining whether expert testimony will assist the trier of fact in a given circumstance are (1) whether the expert testimony is relevant; and (2) whether the expert testimony is reliable. Clearly, expert testimony must be relevant to the subject matter of the trial in order to assist the trier of fact.[7] Likewise, the

---

[3] Federal Judicial Center, Pattern Criminal Jury Instructions, No. 27, Reprinted in ** MODERN FEDERAL JURY INSTRUCTIONS—CRIMINAL ¶ FJC 27; *see also* 1MODERN FEDERAL JURY INSTRUCTIONS—CRIMINAL ¶ 7.01[5] (Matthew Bender); 4 WEINSTEIN'S FEDERAL EVIDENCE § 702.02.

[4] Bridger v. Union Ry. Co., 355 F.2d 382 (6th Cir. 1966); *see also* United States v. Scavo, 593 F.2d 837 (8th Cir. 1979); United States v. Johnson, 575 F.2d 1347 (5th Cir. 1978).

[5] *See* Advisory Committee Note, Rule 702; *see also* Marceaux v. Conoco, Inc., 124 F.3d 730 (5th Cir. 1997) (trial court did not commit plain error in admitting expert's testimony where expert provided the jury with specialized knowledge that would help the jurors determine a fact at issue); United States v. Rahm, 993 F.2d 1405 (9th Cir. 1993) (trial judge erred in excluding psychological testimony from an expert witness on the grounds that it was not conclusive; key concern is whether expert testimony will assist the trier of fact in determining a fact in issue); Kopf v. Skyrm, 993 F.2d 374 (4th Cir. 1993) (in a civil rights action involving the use of a police dog, trial court erred in excluding plaintiff's two experts on the handling of police dogs).

[6] 7 WIGMORE, § 1923, at 29 (emphasis in original).

[7] *See* Chapter 401, *supra,* for a discussion of relevance under the federal rules; *see, e.g.,* Daubert v. Merrell Dow Pharmaceutical, 509 U.S. 579 (1993) ("Rule 702's 'helpfulness' standard requires a valid scientific connection to the pertinent inquiry as a precondition to admissibility"); Quinones v. Pennsylvania Gen. Ins. Co., 804 F.2d 1167 (10th Cir. 1986) (expert's testimony concerning the average wages of "production workers in jewelry manufacturing" was irrelevant to the computation of the lost wages of a self-employed watch repairman, absent a proper foundation); United States v. Sorrentino, 726 F.2d 876 (1st Cir. 1984) (properly qualified expert's appraisal of antiques was irrelevant and thus did not assist

expert testimony must be based upon reliable theories or principles.[8]

Expert testimony concerning matters beyond the comprehension of laypersons will almost always assist the trier of fact, provided that such testimony is relevant.[9] In addition, federal courts may also admit expert

---

the trier of fact); United States v. Torniero, 735 F.2d 725 (2d Cir. 1984) (expert evidence is not immune from the general relevance requirement and irrelevant evidence must be excluded); United States v. Hawley, 592 F. Supp. 1186 (D.S.D. 1984), aff'd, 786 F.2d 249 (8th Cir. 1985) (proffered expert testimony was properly excluded where the expert was only "stating his opinions since such testimony was irrelevant and sought only for the purpose of eliciting legal conclusions"); Lanza v. Poretti, 537 F. Supp. 777 (E.D. Pa. 1982) (expert's testimony irrelevant where expert expressed two contradictory opinions, as expert's opinion was mere speculation); Leverette v. Louisville Ladder Co., 183 F.3d 339 (5th Cir. 1999) (in a products liability action where state law requires a particular showing, an otherwise qualified expert who failed to assess whether the product met the state law requirement would not be permitted to testify, because the testimony was not relevant to whether a defect existed under state law); Montgomery v. Noga, 168 F.3d 1282 (11th Cir. 1999) (in a copyright infringement action relating to shareware and shrink wrap licenses, an expert in the development, marketing, and licensing of commercial software used by individual banks was not qualified as an expert in matters pertinent to the case).

[8] See, e.g., Happel v. Walmart Stores, Inc., 602 F.3d 820 (7th Cir. 2010) (even though plaintiff's proposed expert was board certified in psychiatry and neurology, district court properly precluded him from testifying to an opinion that plaintiff's MS was aggravated by stress symptoms, because he had limited basis for that opinion, it was contradicted by some of the articles he cited, and his opinion amounted at best to little more than "an inspired hunch"); Fedorczyk v. Caribbean Cruise Lines, Ltd., 82 F.3d 69 (3d Cir. 1995) (expert opinion based on speculation or conjecture is inadmissible); In re Air Crash Disaster at New Orleans, 795 F.2d 1230, 1233–1234 (5th Cir. 1986) (trial court erred in admitting expert testimony concerning decedent's expected future earnings, as the proffered expert econo-mist's testimony was based on "assumptions . . . so abusive of the known facts, and so removed from any area of demonstrated expertise, as to provide no reasonable basis for calculating how much of Ted Eymard's income would have found its way into assets or savings to be inherited by his children"); United States v. Gonzales, 749 F.2d 1329, 1336 (9th Cir. 1984) (trial court did not err in refusing to admit expert testimony concerning a police officer's ability to converse in Spanish, as "the translation exercise proposed by appellant's counsel did not test basic informal conversational ability"); United States v. Esle, 743 F.2d 1465, 1473–1474 (11th Cir. 1984) (where the "basis of the expert's opinion has been thoroughly impeached" the trier of fact is "plainly authorized to reject the opinion entirely"); United States v. Sorrentino, 726 F.2d 876, 885 (1st Cir. 1984) (trial court did not err in excluding appraisal by expert who had made only an unofficial appraisal, as the unofficial appraisal "lacked a factual foundation, and could not 'assist the trier of fact' "); United States v. Van Wyk, 83 F. Supp. 2d 515 (D. N.J. 2000) (in a criminal prosecution for writing threatening letters, an FBI agent who is an expert in "forensic stylistics" could not testify as to his opinion that the defendant wrote the letters in question, because the field lacks scientific reliability; however, he could identify similarities in patterns in the writings that are significant in determining authorship, because such information could be helpful to the jury by facilitating its comparison of the writings); see also 3 MUELLER & KIRKPATRICK, § 350.

[9] See, e.g., Norton v. Caremark, Inc., 20 F.3d 330 (8th Cir. 1994) (expert testimony that plaintiff's lost pay damages resulted from being terminated was properly admitted because it was helpful to the jury and subject to cross-examination); United States v. Boney, 977 F.2d 624 (D.C. Cir. 1992) (expert testimony as to the likely roles of actors in a narcotics operation

testimony on subjects that are within the knowledge of the average juror in cases where the expert's testimony will add depth or precision to the trier of fact's existing knowledge.[10] However, where the subject matter upon which expert testimony is offered is wholly within the comprehension of the trier

---

based upon the facts of the case was admissible); United States v. Rivera, 971 F.2d 876 (2d Cir. 1992) (trial court properly admitted expert testimony describing the processes whereby heroin dealers purchase bulk "bricks" of heroin, "cut" the heroin, and then package and distribute the heroin); Dang Vang v. Toyed, 944 F.2d 476 (9th Cir. 1991) (expert's testimony that Hmong women are generally submissive to men and rely heavily on government officials held admissible to assist the trier of fact in understanding plaintiff's behavior and cultural norms); Wheeler v. John Deere Co., 935 F.2d 1090 (10th Cir. 1991) (mechanical engineer permitted to testify as an expert that a piece of farm machinery was "more dangerous than anticipated by ordinary consumers," as such testimony could help the jury in its understanding the case); Busby v. Orlando, 931 F.2d 764 (11th Cir. 1991) (trial court erred in excluding expert testimony concerning the interpretation of termination logs, since the expert's testimony "provided information that even the most competent jury could not have arrived at" by examining the logs on its own); United States v. Lundy, 809 F.2d 392 (7th Cir. 1987) (in trial for arson and mail fraud, expert testimony concerning highly technical evidence, such as burn rates and burn patterns, was admissible as such evidence is beyond the knowledge of average laypersons); Moeller v. Ionetics, Inc., 794 F.2d 653 (Fed. Cir. 1986) (in patent action involving a system of measuring positively charged ions, the trial court erred in concluding that the device in question was sufficiently simple to be understood by average laypersons without the aid of an expert). *See generally*, 4 WEINSTEIN'S FEDERAL EVIDENCE § 702.03; 3 MUELLER & KIRKPATRICK, § 350.

[10] *See* United States v. L.E. Cooke Co., 991 F.2d 336 (6th Cir. 1993) (trial court did not err in admitting expert witness's method of evaluating land even though the method may have been explained in a confusing manner where there was not comparable sales evidence); Quinones-Pacheco v. American Airlines, 979 F.2d 1 (1st Cir. 1992) (trial court did not err in barring expert testimony as to future earnings where the expert opinion rested on a medical assumption the record did not support); Dunn v. Hovic, 1 F.3d 1362 (3d Cir. 1992) (testimony by an expert witness who was a physician specializing in occupational medicine on the subject of a manufacturer's accountability for marketing an asbestos product was properly admitted); Carroll v. Otis Elevator Co., 896 F.2d 210 (7th Cir. 1990) (in a products liability action, plaintiff's expert in visual perception was properly allowed to testify regarding the attractiveness and accessibility to children of a bright red, uncovered, and easy-to-push elevator stop button despite defense objection that the testimony was within the knowledge of the average juror); Esler v. Safeway Stores, Inc., 585 F.2d 903 (8th Cir. 1978) (trial court did not err in admitting expert testimony by an expert in light illumination to testify as to how far away a crane could be seen where the expert's opinion was based on both reconstruction of the accident scene and an analysis of the light and visibility conditions that existed at the time of the accident); United States v Alexander, 816 F.2d 164 (5th Cir. 1987) (trial court erred in concluding that the jury would not be aided by the testimony of a photographic comparison expert and "orthodontist specializing in cephalometric," both of whom would have stated that the person pictured in certain photographs was not the defendant); United States v. Green, 525 F.2d 386, 390 (8th Cir. 1975) (expert testimony regarding "the unique and specific similarities between the clothes worn by one of the robbers, as shown by the surveillance photographs, and Green's clothes, worn by a model in the black and white photographs taken by the F.B.I."). *But see* United States v. Brewer, 783 F.2d 841, 842 (2d Cir. 1986) (trial court did not err in excluding expert testimony by a forensic anthropologist who would have testified that the defendant was not the same person pictured in surveillance photographs, as the lay jury "could compare the photographs of the robber with those of

of fact, expert testimony will not be helpful to the trier of fact and usually will be excluded.[11] The ultimate standard is always whether the expert brings a helpful quality to the litigation that otherwise would be lacking.[12]

Brewer without the special assistance of an expert").

[11] *See* United States v. Scheffer, 523 U.S. 303 (1998) (suggesting that polygraph experts should not be allowed to testify regarding whether an individual has lied as "[d]etermining the weight and credibility of witness testimony . . . has long been held to be 'the part of every case [that] belongs to the jury' "); United States v. Carr, 965 F.2d 408 (7th Cir. 1992) (trial court did not err in excluding the proffered expert testimony of a linguist regarding taped conversations, as the conversations were in English and were uncomplicated); United States v. Whalen, 940 F.2d 1027, 1033 (7th Cir. 1991) (in a trial where the defendant was an inmate who had slashed the throat of a cellmate with the AIDS virus who had suggested sex with the defendant, the trial court did not err in excluding expert testimony concerning psychological reactions of people facing extreme fear; the jury "did not require the insight of those possessing specialized knowledge in order to understand an individual's reaction to fear"); Persinger v. Norfolk & W.R. Co., 920 F.2d 1185, 1188 (4th Cir. 1990) (plaintiff's expert was improperly permitted to testify concerning the application of an "industrial safety formula," as the testimony "did no more than state the obvious," due to the fact that an average layperson knows that "it is more difficult to lift objects from a seated position, especially when the lift is away from the body rather than close"); Peters v. Five Star Marine Service, 898 F.2d 448 (5th Cir. 1990) (trial court erred in admitting expert testimony concerning whether an employer had acted reasonably while requiring seamen to move equipment in heavy seas on slippery decks, as "the jury could adeptly assess this situation using only their common experience and knowledge").

[12] *See* United States v. Posado, 57 F.3d 428 (5th Cir. 1995) (trial court erred in ruling that results of polygraph tests were *per se* inadmissible; court of appeals remanded the case to the trial court for a reconsideration of whether the polygraph evidence is admissible under Rule 702 and Rule 403); Maffei v. Northern Ins. Co., 12 F.3d 892 (9th Cir. 1993) (trial court erred in excluding expert testimony from a thermal engineering expert concerning whether there had been a "hostile fire" as defined in an insurance policy; issue was a proper subject for expert testimony); United States v. Whitted, 994 F.2d 444 (8th Cir. 1993) (in sexual abuse trial, trial court erred in admitting an expert's opinion that abuse had occurred where the witnesses' opinion rested on the truthfulness of the victim); United States v. Curry, 977 F.2d 1042 (7th Cir. 1992) (trial judge's ruling excluding an expert witness who planned to testify about some of the unreliability factors surrounding many witness identifications was not an abuse of the judge's discretion); Arcoren v. United States, 929 F.2d 1235 (8th Cir. 1991) (expert testimony on battered woman syndrome held admissible due to the fact that such testimony aided the jury); Mercado v. Ahmed, 974 F.2d 863 (7th Cir. 1992) (exclusion of expert testimony on damages owed to the victim because of the loss of his pleasure of living as a result of his injuries was not an abuse of discretion); United States v. Cross, 928 F.2d 1030 (11th Cir. 1991) (in a child pornography trial, FBI expert permitted to testify that certain photography would appeal to a pedophile; danger of unfair prejudice did not outweigh substantial probative value); Fox v. Dannenberg, 906 F.2d 1253 (8th Cir. 1990) (experts with training in physical science could properly testify as to whether defendant or deceased was driving at the time of a fatal accident); United States v. Sickles, 524 F. Supp. 506 (D. Del. 1981), *aff'd,* 688 F.2d 827 (3d Cir. 1982); *see also* Zenith Radio Corp. v. Matsushita Elec. Indus. Co., 505 F. Supp. 1313 (E.D. Pa. 1980) ("[a]s defined by the Advisory Committee, the helpfulness inquiry is whether the untrained layman would be qualified to determine intelligently and to the best possible degree the particular issue without enlightenment from those having a specialized understanding of the subject involved in the dispute").

By necessity, the trial court must be afforded a substantial degree of discretion in determining whether to permit expert testimony in a particular case. Expert testimony may be excluded when it is more prejudicial than probative,[13] confusing to the jury[14] or unduly time-consuming.[15] However, doubts as to the usefulness of an expert's opinion should be resolved in favor of admissibility unless the helpfulness of the opinion is outweighed by such dangers as misleading the jury with an aura of infallibility that surrounds the evidence, waste of time, or surprise.[16]

The parties to the trial are usually given discretion to determine whether

---

[13] Rogers v. Raymark Indus., Inc., 922 F.2d 1426 (9th Cir. 1991) (plaintiff's expert testimony concerning asbestos insulation in a suit brought by a welder had very low probative value and very high potential to confuse the jury, due to the fact that the proffered expert worked in different yards than the defendant; in addition the expert was an insulator, not welder); United States v. Portsmouth Paving Corp., 694 F.2d 312 (4th Cir. 1982) (trial court did not err in excluding expert testimony, as instead of aiding the trier of fact, the testimony "amounted to unnecessary, cumulative evidence [that] might well have confused or misled the jury"); United States v. Davis, 772 F.2d 1339 (7th Cir. 1985) (trial court properly excluded expert psychiatric testimony that the defendant was a compulsive gambler; as the expert did not link the defendant's compulsive gambling to a compulsion or need to illegally obtain money, the probative value of such testimony would be "substantially outweighed by the danger of misleading the jury or confusing the issues").

[14] United States v. Long, 917 F.2d 691 (2d Cir. 1990) (expert testimony describing the structure and jargon of an organized crime organization was "only marginally relevant" and "highly prejudicial" in a case where there was a very thin connection to organized crime); United States v. Rouco, 765 F.2d 983, 995–96 (11th Cir. 1985) (defense expert not permitted to testify that the manner in which the defendant was arrested "fell below all known standards of proper police conduct," as such testimony may mislead the jury by creating the impression that the criminal's guilt was contingent upon the manner in which the criminal was arrested); United States v. Green, 548 F.2d 1261 (6th Cir. 1977).

[15] *See* Advisory Committee Note, Rule 702; *see also* United States v. Didomenico, 985 F.2d 1159 (2d Cir. 1993) (proffered expert testimony concerning "dependent personality disorder" was properly excluded in a theft trial since the proffered testimony did not assist the jury in determining whether the defendant had the required knowledge that the goods in question were stolen); F.H. Krear & Co. v. Nineteen Named Trustees, 810 F.2d 1250 (2d Cir. 1987) (trial court did not err in excluding proffered expert testimony concerning defects in a computer program and excessive fees charged for the program as such testimony was irrelevant, misleading, and cumulative); United States v. Thevis, 665 F.2d 616 (5th Cir. 1982) (trial court did not err in excluding proffered expert testimony concerning the problems inherent in eyewitness identification, as where the admission of such testimony would "open the door" to a barrage of questionable psychological evidence).

[16] Joy v. Bell Helicopter Textron, 999 F.2d 549 (D.C. Cir. 1993) (in accident case, trial court erred in admitting expert testimony on the decedent's earning potential where the testimony was speculative and based upon assumptions that the decedent would have engaged in completely new fields of business); United States v. Cruz, 981 F.2d 659 (2d Cir. 1992) (government expert's testimony was improperly admitted where its primary purpose was to bolster the credibility of one of the government's fact witnesses); United States v. Boissoneault, 926 F.2d 230 (2d Cir. 1991) (DEA expert's opinion that accused engaged in cocaine distribution was inadmissible because it drew a conclusion that jury could draw on its own); *see also* 4 WEINSTEIN'S FEDERAL EVIDENCE § 702.02.

they wish to introduce expert testimony. However, in some cases, most notably medical malpractice actions, the substantive law may require the plaintiff to produce expert evidence.[17] Expert testimony on American law is generally inadmissible,[18] although experts may testify about ordinary legal practices, such as negotiating a contract or the process of registering a corporation.[19] However, experts are permitted to testify on issues of foreign law.[20]

In *United States v. Scheffer*,[21] the Supreme Court held that expert testimony regarding polygraph test results can be excluded from trial without violating a defendant's Sixth Amendment rights.[22] In the course of its opinion, the Court also implied that such expert testimony should in

---

[17] International Brotherhood of Teamsters v. United States, 431 U.S. 324 (1977); Randolph v. Collectramatic, Inc., 590 F.2d 844 (10th Cir. 1979); Huddell v. Levin, 537 F.2d 726, 736 (3d Cir. 1976) ("where the issue concerns a product's design . . . expert opinion is the only available method to establish defectiveness, at least where the design is not patently defective").

[18] United States v. Jungles, 903 F.2d 468 (7th Cir. 1990) (trial court did not err in excluding expert testimony that was to include "a recitation of legal principles" concerning whether the defendant was an independent contractor); Specht v. Jensen, 853 F.2d 805 (10th Cir. 1988) (trial court erred in permitting an attorney witness to answer hypothetical questions concerning the legality of a search and seizure, as "[b]y permitting the jury to hear [the expert's] array of legal conclusions touching upon nearly every element of the plaintiff's burden of proof . . . the trial court allowed the expert to supplant both the court's duty to set forth the law and the jury's ability to apply this law to the evidence" and the expert was "improperly allowed to instruct the jury on how it should decide the case"); United States v. Bronston, 658 F.2d 920 (2d Cir. 1981) (expert opinion concerning whether an attorney breached his fiduciary duty was inadmissible); Marx & Co. v. Diners' Club, Inc., 550 F.2d 505 (2d Cir. 1977) (trial court erred in permitting expert to testify concerning the legal standards that apply to the securities trading business, as it is the job of the judge, not the witnesses, to explain the applicable legal principles to the jury); *cf.* Heflin v. Stewart County, 958 F.2d 709 (6th Cir. 1992) (in civil rights trial court properly admitted expert testimony that officials at a jail were "deliberately indifferent" to plaintiff's decedent's need for emergency medical assistance, as the expert did not claim any expertise and merely testified concerning the "proper procedures" to be used in such situations); Phillips v. Calhoun, 956 F.2d 949 (10th Cir. 1992) (in a civil rights suit for wrongful discharge, court properly admitted personnel directors to "offer their understanding of the customary meaning and usage of the terms" in employment manuals and job classification plans used by the state, as this testimony was an acceptable way to assist the trier of fact to understand such documents).

[19] 4 WEINSTEIN'S FEDERAL EVIDENCE § 702.04; *see also* Marx & Co. v. Diners' Club, Inc., 550 F.2d 505 (2d Cir. 1977) (attorney who was an expert in securities law could testify concerning the usual practices of the securities business, as such testimony assisted the trier of fact in evaluating the conduct of the parties against the standards of ordinary practice in the industry); Loeb v. Hammond, 407 F.2d 779 (7th Cir. 1969).

[20] *See* Fed. R. Civ. P. 44.1 (requiring notice in the pleadings and permitting the trial court to seek the aid of "any relevant material or source, including testimony, whether or not submitted by a party or admissible under the Federal Rules of Evidence").

[21] United States v. Scheffer, 523 U.S. 303 (1998).

[22] *See Id.*

general be inadmissible. The Court was faced with the issue of whether Military Rule of Evidence 707, which excludes polygraph evidence in court-martial proceedings, violated a defendant's constitutional right to present a defense. The Court found that the restriction contained in Rule 707 was a reasonable restriction on the defendant's right to present his case, and did not in any way preclude the defendant from introducing factual evidence or providing the court members with his perspective on the relevant details of the charged offense. According to the majority, Rule 707 served the legitimate purpose of ensuring that only reliable evidence is admitted at trial, as "there is simply no consensus that polygraph evidence is reliable."[23]

The Court went on to explain that excluding expert testimony regarding polygraph results also preserves the jury's role as "the lie detector" of the criminal justice system.[24] Traditionally, the question of witness credibility has been a question for the jury, and expert testimony is only allowed when the expert testifies about matters outside the knowledge or competency of the jury.[25] Allowing polygraph experts to provide an opinion as to whether a witness was telling the truth, in the Court's view, would diminish the jury's role in making credibility determinations.[26] Finally, the Court also stated that the *per se* exclusion on the admission of polygraph evidence imposed by Military Rule 707 was a permissible and proportionate means to avoid the collateral litigation that would be involved in determining whether polygraph evidence was admissible in a particular case.[27]

§ 702.4   Reliability of Expert Testimony

Rule 702 lists three distinct reliability requirements for expert testimony

---

[23] *Id.* 523 U.S. at 309. The Court also explained that "state and federal courts continue to express doubt about whether such evidence is reliable." *Scheffer,* 523 U.S. at 311. United States v. Cordoba, 194 F.3d 1053 (9th Cir. 1999) (polygraph testing does not meet standard of admissibility under *Daubert,* because error rates vary widely, such tests have not achieved general acceptance, and no standards controlling the procedures used in conducting the tests).

[24] *See Scheffer,* 523 U.S. at 309. "Determining the weight and credibility of witness testimony . . . has long been held to be 'the part of every case [that] belongs to the jury.' " (quoting Aetna Life Ins. Co. v. Ward, 140 U.S. 76, 88 (1891)).

[25] "Unlike other expert witnesses who testify about factual matters outside the jurors' knowledge, such as the analysis of fingerprints, ballistics, or DNA found at a crime scene, a polygraph expert can supply the jury only with another opinion, in addition to its own, about whether the witness was telling the truth." *Scheffer,* 523 U.S. at 309. *See* United States v. Batton, 602 F.3d 1191 (10th Cir. 2010) (trial court did not abuse its discretion in permitting expert testimony concerning the methods used by sex offenders, including their use of "grooming" to prepare their victims, which was not necessarily common knowledge among jurors; the trial court properly limited the testimony to "the correction of possible juror misconceptions regarding how sex offenders behave and what they look like," did not allow the expert to express an opinion on the guilt of the accused or the credibility of his accuser).

[26] *See Scheffer,* 523 U.S. at 314 (explaining "that the aura of infallibility attending polygraph evidence can lead jurors to abandon their duty to assess credibility and guilt").

[27] *See id.* at 315.

to be admissible: The testimony must be sufficiently based upon reliable facts or data, it must be the product of reliable principles and methods, and the witness must have applied the principles and methods reliably to the facts of the case. These requirements were added to the Rule in 2000, codifying the Supreme Court's holdings in *Daubert v. Merrell Dow Pharmaceuticals, Inc.,*[28] and its progeny, including *Kumho Tire Co. v. Carmichael,*[29] and *General Electric Co. v. Joiner,*[30] and applying their holdings to all expert testimony, whether based on scientific, technical, or other specialized knowledge.

Before 1993, federal courts differed over what quantum of reliability should be required for the admission of novel scientific evidence. Many courts followed the highly influential decision of the Court of Appeals for the District of Columbia in *Frye v. United States,*[31] which held that expert testimony deduced from a scientific principle or discovery "must be sufficiently established to have gained general acceptance in the particular field to which it belongs."[32] The natural result was the exclusion of accurate and reliable scientific evidence, at least on occasion, since there is always a lag time between even valid scientific discoveries and their general acceptance in the field. Other courts, however, rejected the so-called "*Frye* test," and interpreted Rule 702 as permitting the admission of expert testimony

---

[28] Daubert v. Merrell Dow Pharms., 509 U.S. 579 (1993).

[29] Kumho Tire Co. v. Carmichael, 526 U.S. 137 (1999).

[30] General Electric Co. v. Joiner, 522 U.S. 136 (1997).

[31] Frye v. United States, 293 F. 1013 (D.C. Cir. 1923).

[32] *Frye,* 293 F. at 1014; *see, e.g.,* United States v. Gillespie, 852 F.2d 475 (8th Cir. 1987) (evidence that does not qualify under *Frye* must be excluded); United States v. St. Pierre, 812 F.2d 417 (8th Cir. 1987) (trial court properly denied defendant's request to have an expert examine him to determine whether the defendant's psychological profile was consistent with that of a sex offender, as the scientific community did not recognize the existence of any such identifiable traits); United States v. McBride, 786 F.2d 45 (2d Cir. 1986) (the trial court wrongfully excluded the expert testimony of a psychiatrist who would have testified as to defendant's mental status at the time of the crime, as psychiatry was generally accepted in the field of medicine); United States v. Clifford, 543 F. Supp. 424 (W.D. Pa. 1982), *rev'd on other grounds,* 704 F.2d 86 (3d Cir. 1983) (expert testimony concerning forensic linguistic analysis properly excluded as such analysis had not reached the level of general acceptance in the pertinent scientific community); United States v. Distler, 671 F.2d 954 (6th Cir. 1981) (expert testimony concerning gas chromatograph analysis is admissible as such analysis is generally accepted amongst experts in oil matching); United States v. Tranowski, 659 F.2d 750 (7th Cir. 1981) (testimony by expert astronomer who sought to date photographs by measuring shadows and plotting the position of the sun was properly excluded, while the court did not dispute the theoretical soundness of such method of dating photos, no controlled experiments had been done to establish the accuracy of such a technique); Unites States v. Hendershot, 614 F.2d 648 (9th Cir. 1980) (admission of a shoeprint that was lifted using a technique commonly used to lift fingerprints was proper as such technique enjoyed common usage and was taught at a crime scene investigation course). *See generally,* 4 WEINSTEIN'S FEDERAL EVIDENCE § 702.05.

concerning novel scientific evidence if it was both relevant and reliable.[33] Yet another line of cases applied a hybrid of the "relevance" test and the *Frye* test.[34]

Against this background of inconsistent standards, the *Daubert* Court held that the Federal Rules of Evidence, not the *Frye* test, provide the standard for admitting expert scientific evidence. The Court held that the rules place appropriate limits on the admissibility of purportedly scientific evidence by requiring the trial judge to ensure that an expert's testimony rests on a reliable foundation and is relevant.

The *Daubert* Court set out a non-exhaustive list of inquiries that courts may find helpful in determining whether to admit novel scientific evidence: (1) can the theory or technique in question be tested and, if so, has it been? (2) has the theory or technique been published and subjected to peer review? (3) what is the known or potential rate of error when using the theory or technique? (4) do standards exist that can serve as controls on a technique's operation and, if so, were such standards employed in the matter in dispute? and (5) has the theory or technique been generally accepted?[35] By including general acceptance as one of these variables, the Court left room for courts to consider the *Frye* standard as part of their analysis. However, the Court

---

[33] *See, e.g.,* DeLuca v. Merrell Dow Pharmaceuticals, Inc., 911 F.2d 941 (3d Cir. 1990), *rev'g,* 131 F.R.D. 71 (D.N.J. 1990) (the Rules "embody a strong and undeniable preference for admitting any evidence having some potential for assisting the trier of fact and for dealing with the risk of error through the adversary process"); United States v. Downing, 753 F.2d 1224 (3d Cir. 1985) (rejecting the *Frye* test, observing that "a particular degree of acceptance of a scientific technique within the scientific community is neither a necessary nor a sufficient condition for admissibility"; focusing instead on the reliability of the evidence, the possibility that the evidence will mislead or confuse the jury, and the application of the evidence to the specific matter in dispute); United States v. Baller, 519 F.2d 463 (4th Cir. 1975) (admitting expert testimony concerning voice spectrogram analysis, observing that "[u]nless an exaggerated popular opinion of the accuracy of a particular technique makes its use prejudicial or likely to mislead the jury, it is better to admit relevant scientific evidence in the same manner as other expert testimony and allow its weight to be attacked by cross-examination and refutation"); United States v. Williams, 583 F.2d 1194 (2d Cir. 1978) (the so-called "*Frye*" test was superseded by the enactment of the Federal Rules of Evidence and that the appropriate standard for admission of novel scientific evidence demanded consideration of reliability, helpfulness, and a Rule 403 balancing test); *see also* Livingood, *Admissibility and Reliability of Expert Scientific Testimony After Daubert,* 61 DEF. COUNS. J. 19 (1994).

[34] *See* Christophersen v. Allied-Signal Corp, 939 F.2d 1106 (5th Cir. 1991) (applying the Rules as the standard for the admission of expert testimony concerning novel scientific evidence but using the *Frye* standard to limit the admissibility of such testimony); United States v. Shorter, 809 F.2d 54 (D.C. Cir. 1987) (combining the relevance requirement of Rule 702, the balancing test of Rule 403, and the *Frye* standard). *See generally* Note, *The New Gatekeepers: Judging Scientific Evidence in a Post-Frye World,* U. N.C. L. REV. 1060 (1994).

[35] Daubert v. Merrell Dow Pharms., 509 U.S. 579, 593–594 (1993).

modified the traditional *Frye* standard by adding that "[a] reliability assessment does not require, although it does permit, explicit identification of a relevant scientific community and an express determination of a particular degree of acceptance within that community." The Court stressed that by listing these factors, it did not seek to set forth a definitive checklist or test, but rather envisioned a flexible evaluation of the admissibility of expert testimony concerning novel scientific evidence.[36] The Court further emphasized that the trial court's inquiry should center on the scientific validity of the "principles and methodology" underlying the expert's conclusions, not the conclusions themselves.[37]

The *Daubert* Court mentioned in dictum that, while *Frye* dealt solely with the admissibility of novel scientific evidence, Rule 702 does not apply exclusively to novel scientific evidence. *Kumho Tire* established this as law. In *Kumho Tire*, the Court held that trial courts may apply the *Daubert* factors to determine the reliability of nonscientific expert testimony, depending on "the particular circumstances of the particular case at issue."[38]

The *Daubert* decision confirmed the trial court's role as a "gatekeeper" in determining the admissibility of evidence.[39] This view was reaffirmed in *Joiner,* when the Court held that abuse of discretion is the proper standard of

---

[36] *Id.* The federal courts that have been called upon to determine the admission of novel scientific evidence under Rule 702 since the *Daubert* decision have indeed been flexible in their use of the criteria enunciated in *Daubert. See, e.g.,* Granfield v. CSX Transportation, Inc., 597 F.3d 474 (1st Cir. 2010) (differential diagnosis is a proper scientific technique for expert testimony from a medical doctor, even if the expert did not rely on peer-reviewed studies in his causation diagnosis; "The mere fact of publication, or lack thereof, in a peer-reviewed journal is not a determinative factor in assessing the scientific validity of a technique or methodology on which an opinion is premised"); United States v. Rincon, 28 F.3d 921 (9th Cir. 1994) (under *Daubert* trial court properly excluded expert testimony on the subject of eyewitness identification because defendant failed to show that it was sufficiently reliable or relevant); United States v. Bonds, 12 F.3d 540 (6th Cir. 1993) (DNA evidence admissible under all of the *Daubert* inquiries); Porter v. Whitehall Laboratories, 9 F.3d 607 (7th Cir. 1993) (affirming the trial court's exclusion of expert testimony mainly on the grounds that the plaintiff's expert's testimony was mostly unsubstantiated speculation, which did not rise to the level of "scientific knowledge" required by *Daubert*); DeLuca v. Merrell Dow Pharmaceuticals, Inc., 6 F.3d 778 (3d Cir. 1993) (the trial court had relied on United States v. Downing, 753 F.2d 1224 (3d Cir. 1985), which in turn was relied on by *Daubert*; therefore, the result in the trial court was not inconsistent with *Daubert*); *See generally* Woodbury & Kaplan, *Daubert and Junk Science: Using Daubert to Exclude Expert Testimony,* 497 PRAC. L. INST. 459 (1994).

[37] Daubert v. Merrell Dow Pharms., 509 U.S. 579 (1993). *See, e.g.,* United States v. John, 597 F.3d 263 (5th Cir. 2010) (in most cases, in the absence of novel challenges, expert testimony on fingerprint comparisons is sufficiently reliable to be admissible without a *Daubert* hearing; the reliability of the technique has been tested in the adversarial system for over a century, has been routinely subject to peer review, and has a low rate of error).

[38] Kumho Tire Co. v. Carmichael, 526 U.S. 137 (1999).

[39] Daubert v. Merrell Dow Pharms., 509 U.S. 579 (1993).

appellate review regarding trial court decisions on the admission of evidence, including expert scientific testimony.[40] The *Joiner* decision thus leaves to the trial court the task of screening all evidence before admission to ensure its relevance and reliability.

The 2000 Amendment to Rule 702 incorporates all of these holdings. The Advisory Committee Note to the Rule lists the five *Daubert* factors, but goes on to explain that courts may use other appropriate factors in determining whether expert testimony is "sufficiently reliable." By applying the same requirements to all expert testimony, whether in the form of scientific, technical, or other specialized knowledge, Rule 702 codifies that portion of the *Kumho Tire* holding. Judges are to evaluate all expert testimony on the same general basis of reliability. The type of testimony proffered may, of course, affect how a judge weighs the various factors, or even which factors the judge weighs at all.

The Advisory Committee Note makes clear that if expert testimony fails any of the three reliability requirements, the testimony is to be excluded. This makes sense, since, for example, a valid methodology applied to unreliable facts or data would produce an unreliable, and therefore unhelpful, conclusion. Concerning the second and third reliability requirement, the Note, in accordance with the *Joiner* opinion, states that while the trial court's focus is to be on the reliability of the principles and methods the expert relies on and applies, a conclusion by an expert that is at odds with those reached by others in the field is a reasonable indication that those principles and methods have not been faithfully applied. However, the Note explains, contradictory testimony by more than one expert is not *per se* inadmissible. In our adversarial system, courts may fairly rely on counsel to expose imperfections in experts' methods, and may rely on the jury to determine which, if any, of two or more minimally reliable experts has reached the correct conclusion. Because of this, exclusion of testimony by a qualified expert should be the exception, rather than the rule. Admissible expert testimony need only be reasonably reliable; there is no requirement that the court find that the testimony is correct. As one federal court explained, "*Daubert* and Rule 702 are safeguards against unreliable or irrelevant opinions, not guarantees of correctness."[41]

§ 702.5 Qualifications of Expert Witness; Function of Trial Judge

Rule 702 addresses the qualifications necessary to accord a witness expert status. Under the Rule, special education or certification is not required; a witness may qualify as an expert by reason of his or her "knowledge, skill, experience,[42] training, or education.[43]" It is important to note that any one

---

[40] General Electric Co. v. Joiner, 522 U.S. 136 (1997).

[41] i4i Ltd. Partnership v. Microsoft Corp., 598 F.3d 831 (Fed. Cir. 2010).

[42] *See* Fox v. Dannenberg, 906 F.2d 1253 (8th Cir. 1990) (trial court erred in excluding

of these characteristics may qualify an individual as an expert, although in the usual case more than one of these factors will be present. The individual offered as an expert need not have complete knowledge of the field in question as long as the knowledge that the expert possesses will aid the trier of fact in performing its function. For example, although a medical degree does not make a doctor qualified to opine on all medical subjects, a physician in general practice is competent to testify about many medical problems even if they are typically treated by a medical specialist.[44]

---

testimony by engineers who investigated wreckage of car and testified as to who was driving; Rule 702 does not prefer academic training over practical experience, and these engineers had 20 years of experience in accident reconstruction and related disciplines); United States v. Paiva, 892 F.2d 148 (1st Cir. 1989) (detective who had 15 years of experience in the police force and was currently a member of a police narcotic unit was properly allowed to testify as an expert identifying powder as cocaine); United States v. Johnson, 575 F.2d 1347 (5th Cir. 1978) (person who had smoked marijuana over a thousand times, dealt in marijuana more than twenty times, and who had correctly identified marijuana more than one hundred times using physical inspection was permitted to testify as an expert that the marijuana in question had come from Colombia).

[43] Garnac Grain Co. v. Blackley, 932 F.2d 1563 (8th Cir. 1991) (trial court erred in an accounting malpractice suit by excluding expert testimony from a retired business professor with over 40 years of teaching experience; although the proffered witness had only worked in a public accounting firm for four years, any weaknesses in the witness' expertise went to weight, not admissibility); Lavespere v. Niagara Mach. & Tool Works, Inc., 910 F.2d 167 (5th Cir. 1990) (in a product liability suit, the trial judge did not err in hearing testimony from an expert with a doctorate in mechanical engineering, a master's degree in production engineering who also taught college level courses; although the expert had never designed a press brake, the expert's "purely academic" qualifications were sufficient, and "absence of hands-on experience" was relevant but not determinative); American Technology Resources v. United States, 893 F.2d 651 (3d Cir. 1990) (business professor was qualified to testify as an expert concerning the value of commercial distributorships where the professor held a Ph.D. in finance and taught college courses in speculative markets, corporate finance, investments, and real estate finance and had published scholarly articles on corporate finance and investments).

[44] Gayton v. McCoy, 593 F.3d 610 (7th Cir. 2010) (a physician was unqualified to offer testimony that inmate's heart failure would have been prevented by congestive heart failure medication, because the witness lacked specific knowledge in cardiology and pharmacology, and provided no basis for his testimony except that inmate's medication treated heart disease — but the court erred in precluding the witness from offering expert opinion that the inmate's vomiting combined with her diuretic medication may have contributed to her heart failure, because that opinion was not based on specialized knowledge held only by cardiologists, but knowledge that any competent physician would possess). *See also* Holbrook v. Lykes Bros. Steamship Co., 80 F.3d 777 (3d Cir. 1996) (in civil action alleging asbestos exposure by defendant, the trial court erred by refusing to permit the decedent's treating physician to testify concerning the diagnosis decedent was given; trial court erroneously concluded that, because physician did not specialize in oncology or pathology, the physician was not sufficiently qualified to testify as to such a difficult diagnosis); Sullivan v. Rowan Cos., Inc., 952 F.2d 141 (5th Cir. 1992) (the district court did not err in refusing to allow plaintiff's witness to testify as an expert since, although he had extensive practical experience, he lacked the educational background in the field); Genty v. Resolution Trust Corp., 937 F.2d 899 (3d

Expert testimony is not rendered inadmissible because the witness is not absolutely certain[45] or is not unbiased.[46] Relative weaknesses in the expert's body of expertise may be exposed on cross-examination in order to affect the weight that will be given to the expert's testimony.[47]

The determination of whether an individual qualifies as an expert is for the court pursuant to Rule 104(a).[48] As with other preliminary questions of admissibility, the trial court functions as a "gatekeeper" to screen out evidence that is not relevant and reliable.[49] And as with other questions of admissibility,[50] the trial court's determination regarding the qualifications of an expert witness will not be overturned absent a showing of clear abuse of discretion.[51]

§ 702.6   Forms of Expert Testimony

Traditionally, the primary purpose for qualifying a witness as an expert has been to enable that individual to express his or her opinion on the matter at issue. Rule 702 authorizes expert testimony in the form of opinion "or otherwise." Allowing an expert to testify in other than opinion form

---

Cir. 1991) (while lack of a medical degree does not automatically disqualify a toxicologist from testifying under Rule 702 as to health effects of nearby toxic wastes, in the present case there was insufficient evidence of expertise, and the testimony was properly excluded).

[45] Orth v. Emerson Elec. Co., 980 F.2d 632 (10th Cir. 1992) (inferential testimony, rather than direct testimony, from an expert witness on the internal workings of a valve was admissible; "[a]bsolute certainty is not required" in expert testimony); United States v. Johnson, 575 F.2d 1347 (5th Cir. 1978) (witness qualified as an expert to testify about marijuana and where it had come from, since he had smoked it more than a thousand times, and correctly identified it more than one hundred times and knew more about it than was within the knowledge of an average juror); *see also* United States v. Oaxaca, 569 F.2d 518 (9th Cir. 1978).

[46] *Cf.* United States v. Masson, 582 F.2d 961 (5th Cir. 1978).

[47] The "honesty, proficiency, and methodology" employed by an expert witness are "the features that are commonly the focus in the cross-examination of experts." Melendez-Diaz v. Massachusetts, 174 L. Ed. 2d 314, 328 (2009).

[48] *See* Chapter 104, *supra*.

[49] *See* Daubert v. Merrell Dow Pharms., 509 U.S. 579 (1993).

[50] *See* General Electric Co. v. Joiner, 522 U.S. 136 (1997) ("abuse of discretion is the proper standard by which to review a district court's decision to admit or exclude scientific evidence"); Old Chief v. United States, 519 U.S. 172 (1997); United States v. Abel, 469 U.S. 45 (1984).

[51] Tokio Marine & Fire Ins. Co. v. Grove Mfg. Co., 958 F.2d 1169 (1st Cir. 1992) (the district court did not abuse its discretion in refusing to qualify a "professional witness" as an expert on hydraulic cranes); Graham v. Abduct Laboratories, Div. of American Home Products Corp., 906 F.2d 1399 (10th Cir. 1990) (trial court has broad discretion in determining which individuals are qualified to present expert testimony; however, the trial court "may not employ that discretion to restrict viable and relevant theories offered by a party"); *see also* Grindstaff v. Coleman, 681 F.2d 740 (11th Cir. 1982); Dunn v. Sears, Roebuck and Co., 639 F.2d 1171 (5th Cir. 1981), *modified on other grounds,* 645 F.2d 511 (5th Cir. 1981).

introduces a measure of flexibility into Federal Practice. The "or otherwise" language of Rule 702 is designed to permit an expert to provide an exposition of relevant scientific, professional, technical or other principles as a basis for the trier of fact to apply those principles to the relevant issues. Thus, if the jury can draw the needed inferences itself after a technical foundation has been laid by the expert, counsel is free to forgo asking the expert's opinion on the ultimate issue.[53]

---

[53] *See* Advisory Committee Note, Rule 702.

Chapter 703

Rule 703. Bases of an Expert's Opinion Testimony

Rule 703. Bases of an Expert's Opinion Testimony

An expert may base an opinion on facts or data in the case that the expert has been made aware of or personally observed. If experts in the particular field would reasonably rely on those kinds of facts or data in forming an opinion on the subject, they need not be admissible for the opinion to be admitted. But if the facts or data would otherwise be inadmissible, the proponent of the opinion may disclose them to the jury only if their probative value in helping the jury evaluate the opinion substantially outweighs their prejudicial effect.

---

§ 703.1　Bases of an Expert's Opinion Testimony — In General

Rule 703 identifies three permissible sources of facts or data upon which experts may base their opinions or inferences. Two of these sources of expert testimony traditionally have been recognized by the court: the expert may predicate testimony on firsthand perceptions, or in the alternative, the expert may draw upon facts or information admitted in the hearing at which he or she is called to testify. Rule 703 departs from prior practice by recognizing a third permissible source of facts or data, *i.e.,* information the expert has been "made aware of" before the hearing. The Rule further provides that if the facts or data are reasonably relied upon by experts in the same field in reaching conclusions, the facts and data constitute a permissible basis for the expert's opinion even if they are not admissible in evidence.

§ 703.2　Policy of Rule 703

Under Rule 703, the permissible bases for expert opinion include facts the expert has been "made aware of" before the hearing.[1] If of a kind reasonably

---

[1] *See generally,* 1 McCORMICK, § 15; 4 WEINSTEIN'S FEDERAL EVIDENCE §§ 703.01–703.06; 3 MUELLER & KIRKPATRICK, §§ 354–359; 3 WIGMORE, § 687. *See also* Dession, *Trial of Economic and Technical Issues of Fact: II,* 58 YALE L.J. 1242 (1949); Diamond & Louisell, *The Psychiatrist As An Expert Witness: Some Ruminations and Speculations,* 63 MICH. L. REV. 1335 (1965); Dieden and Gasparich, *Psychiatric Evidence and Full Disclosure in the Criminal Trial,* 52 CAL. L. REV. 543 (1964); Maguire & Hahesy, *Requisite Proof of Bases for Expert Opinion,* 5 VAND. L. REV. 432 (1952); Martin, *The Uncertain Rule of Certainty: An Analysis and Proposal for a Federal Evidence Rule,* 20

relied upon, the data itself need not be admissible in evidence. Under previous practice, expert opinions based on evidence not admitted at trial normally were disallowed due to the rule against hearsay, although exceptions were recognized for certain experts, such as physicians[2] and real estate appraisers.[3] In defense of this innovation in the Rule, the Advisory Committee conceded that most of the facts or data upon which an expert would rely in forming an opinion would be admissible in evidence, but only after the expenditure of substantial time in producing and examining various authenticating witnesses.[4] Rule 703 was designed to avoid this needless waste of trial time.

The Rule also seeks to bring judicial procedure in line with the custom and practice of most experts. The critical nature of experts' determinations, according to Federal theory, guarantees the trustworthiness of the information upon which they rely.[5] McCormick notes that under Rule 703, the jury is asked to accept the expert witness's inference where it is based upon a hearsay assertion of fact that is, presumably, unsupported by any evidence at trial.[6] He responds to this criticism by noting that, "an expert in a science is competent to judge the reliability of statements made to him by other

---

WAYNE L. REV. 781 (1974); Rheingold, *The Basis of Medical Testimony*, 15 VAND. L. REV. 473 (1962); Romero, *The Admissibility of Scientific Evidence Under the New Mexico and Federal Rules of Evidence*, 6 N.M. L. REV. 187 (1976); Note, *Hearsay Bases of Psychiatric Opinion Testimony: A Critique of Federal Rule of Evidence 703*, 51 S. CAL. L. REV. 129 (1977).

[2] 4 WEINSTEIN'S FEDERAL EVIDENCE § 703.02 ("The rationale for exempting a physician's opinion from strict application of the hearsay rule is that reliance on hearsay is often necessary, and the use to which the facts are put guarantees their reliability"); *see, e.g.,* Padgett v. Southern Ry. Co., 396 F.2d 303 (6th Cir. 1968) (statements made to a physician for treatment are reliable, but statements made to a physician to qualify him to testify are not; Rule 803(4) rejects this distinction, and statements made for purposes of diagnosis could be the basis for opinions); Birdsell v. United States, 346 F.2d 775 (5th Cir. 1965) (history given by patient, results of tests, recorded objective observations by others); *see also* Kibert v. Peyton, 383 F.2d 566 (4th Cir. 1967); Brown v. United States, 375 F.2d 310 (D.C. Cir. 1966); Peterson v. Gaughan, 285 F. Supp. 377 (D. Mass. 1968), *aff'd,* 404 F.2d 1375 (1st Cir. 1968).

[3] *See* 4 WEINSTEIN'S FEDERAL EVIDENCE § 703.02 (appraisers were exempted from hearsay rule due to necessity); *see, e.g.,* United States v. 1129.75 Acres of Land, 473 F.2d 996 (8th Cir. 1973); District of Columbia Redevelopment Land Agency v. 61 Parcels of Land, 235 F.2d 864 (D.C. Cir. 1956).

[4] *See* Advisory Committee Note, Rule 703.

[5] Advisory Committee Note, Rule 703. *See* Ward v. Dixie National Life Insurance Co., 595 F.3d 164 (4th Cir. 2010) (in calculating the total damages suffered by the members of an insured class seeking compensation for cancer treatment, plaintiffs' certified public accountant could rely on hearsay evidence consisting of six spreadsheets containing actual charges for each patient's treatment, because the expert testified that such data was the type that was reasonably relied on by experts in his particular field in forming such opinions, and the defendants offered no evidence to the contrary).

[6] 1 MCCORMICK, § 15.

investigators or technicians. He is just as competent indeed to do this as a judge and jury are to pass upon the credibility of an ordinary witness on the stand."[7] The Advisory Committee adopted this reasoning in drafting Rule 703.

§ 703.3 Bases of Expert Testimony — Firsthand Knowledge

The Rule provides that a basis for expert testimony may be facts or data perceived by the expert through personal observations, examinations, or tests. When experts have personal knowledge of the facts or data underlying their opinions, the personal knowledge is a permissible predicate for the testimony. For example, an attending physician who treated an injured plaintiff would have firsthand knowledge of the facts that could permissibly support her expert opinion testimony as to the permanence of plaintiff's disability. In this instance the expert is aware of the supporting data by reason of her firsthand experience.

Where an expert has firsthand knowledge, it is unnecessary for the expert to assume any particular state of facts.[8] The testimony of an expert with firsthand knowledge is likely to be credible and convincing, especially if not elicited by means of a protracted hypothetical question.[9] Under Rule 705, the experts need not disclose the facts or data underlying their opinions or inferences before giving that opinion or inference, and no hypothetical question is required.

The witnesses are, of course, subject to attacks on their ability to observe the events in question. The testimony must also be relevant under Rule 401.[10]

§ 703.4 Bases of Expert Testimony — Evidence Admitted at the Hearing

Experts who lack firsthand knowledge of the facts supporting their opinions may base their opinions on items of evidence if the items have been previously admitted. Of course, Rule 703 does not specify that experts cannot be informed of pertinent facts before trial to prepare their testimony. Unquestionably, proper use of the expert witness contemplates application of

---

[7] 1 McCORMICK, § 15, 64–65.

[8] *See* 2 WIGMORE, § 675; 1 McCORMICK, § 14.

[9] 4 WEINSTEIN'S FEDERAL EVIDENCE § 703.03; *see also* Rheingold, *The Basis of Medical Testimony*, 15 VAND. L. REV. 473 (1962).

[10] *See, e.g.,* United States v. Ellsworth, 738 F.2d 333 (8th Cir. 1984) (trial court properly excluded psychiatric testimony regarding good faith and genuineness of belief as not an appropriate subject for an expert); United States v. Busic, 592 F.2d 13 (2d Cir. 1978) (expert psychiatric testimony properly excluded where only a showing of general criminal intent was required; "questions of intent and motivation are for the jury and not expert witnesses"); *see also* Horton v. W.T. Grant Co., 537 F.2d 1215 (4th Cir. 1976); *cf.* Nolan v. Greene, 383 F.2d 814 (6th Cir. 1967).

the expert's special skill in planning the presentation of evidence that serves as a foundation for the expert's testimony.

Rule 705 does not require that experts designate the specific facts supporting their opinion "in response to a hypothetical question or otherwise" before rendering an opinion. Consequently, the experts may be apprised of the necessary data by means of hypothetical question; they may simply sit at trial and hear the testimony and view the exhibits introduced; or they may be advised by counsel of the facts that have been proven. As long as the data or facts have been admitted into evidence, they may serve as a basis for an expert opinion or inference under this provision of Rule 703.[11]

§ 703.5   Bases of Expert Testimony — Evidence Not Admitted at the Hearing

When the experts lack personal knowledge of the operative facts and they are not made known to them at trial, the experts may still, within the court's discretion, rely upon hearsay evidence in forming opinions. Rule 703 recognizes that the customary restrictions on hearsay do not apply to expert witnesses.[12] The expert who is capable of assessing the accuracy of a given set of data need not be protected from forming an opinion based on hearsay evidence; however, jurors who lack scientific expertise should be protected by the hearsay rules due to their inability to assess accurately the reliability of the evidence without the procedural safeguards of a trial. Thus, the breadth of admissibility under this provision of Rule 703 will depend upon the trial court's assessment of the expert witness's ability to filter hearsay evidence and present the trier of fact with accurate testimony from which it can render a verdict.

An expert, however, cannot be used as a means to introduce inadmissible evidence by merely summarizing or repeating the information in court.[13]

---

[11] *See* Engebretsen v. Fairchild Aircraft Corp., 21 F.3d 721 (6th Cir. 1994) (expert testimony based upon investigative reports that were admitted into evidence after closing arguments was properly admitted; although the reports were admitted late, error was harmless).

[12] *See* 4 WEINSTEIN'S FEDERAL EVIDENCE § 703.04. *See also* First Nat'l Bank v. Lustig, 96 F.3d 1554 (5th Cir. 1996) (testimony of expert investigator was properly admitted even though the investigator's testimony was based in part on information he learned from bank officials; "[e]xperts may rely on hearsay evidence in forming their opinions"); *but see* Cummins v. Lyle Industries, 93 F.3d 362 (7th Cir. 1996) (excluding expert testimony based on hearsay evidence in design defect case where expert could not recall the names of the individuals spoken to about the product or the dates of the conversations).

[13] United States v. Ayala, 601 F.3d 256 (4th Cir. 2010) (in gang prosecution, three Government experts were properly allowed to testify, even though they relied in part on interviews with unnamed declarants; the experts offered their independent judgments, most of which related to the gang's general nature as a violent organization and were not about the defendants in particular, these judgments resulted from many years of observing the gang and

Expert witnesses have long been allowed to formulate opinions from facts not admissible in evidence, based on the idea that experts were less likely than jurors to be distracted or confused by such facts, or to give them undue weight. An amendment to Rule 703 now makes explicit, however, that experts cannot serve as high-paid smugglers to get otherwise inadmissible data before the jury. When experts reasonably rely on inadmissible information to form opinions or inferences, they may not disclose the underlying data on direct examination merely because their opinions or inferences are admitted, unless the court determines that the prejudicial effect of the data is substantially outweighed by its value in assisting the jury's evaluation of the expert's opinion. Because Rule 103(c) prevents even suggestions of inadmissible evidence from wafting into the jury box, a judge should exclude expert testimony that cannot be offered without disclosing inadmissible underlying facts, unless the testimony itself has a probative value that substantially outweighs its prejudicial effect. Even when this test is met, and otherwise inadmissible data is disclosed to the jury, either as part of the expert's testimony or in its support, Rule 105 requires the judge, upon request, to give an appropriate limiting instruction. Nothing in the amendment, of course, limits the ability of the adverse party upon cross-examination to bring out details of inadmissible data relied upon by the expert, typically for the purpose of impeaching the witness by questioning the reliability or completeness of the data upon which she relied.

The degree to which the trial judge allows experts to rely upon hearsay evidence for their testimony will depend upon a finding under Rule 104(a) that it was reasonable for the expert witness to rely on the hearsay evidence in forming the opinion.[14] One factor the court will consider is the established nature of the source of the expert witness's data,[15] *e.g.,* appraisal of real estate is more highly established than accidentology. Intangible factors may also play key roles in the judge's decision to permit the testimony. The trial judge's belief in the professional stature and ethics of the group to which the expert witness belongs could bear heavily on the latitude given the testifying

---

studying its methods, and the experts "did not act as mere transmitters and in fact did not repeat statements of particular declarants to the jury"); Barrett v. Acevedo, 169 F.3d 1155 (8th Cir. 1999) (evidence relied upon by experts in forming their opinions, when admitted, is not admitted for its truth but simply to show the basis for expert's opinion, and therefore is not hearsay).

[14] *E.g.,* Kelsay v. Consolidated Rail Corp., 749 F.2d 437 (7th Cir. 1984) (police officer who investigated the scene of an accident had a reasonable factual basis although he took no measurements); Ealy v. Richardson-Merrell, Inc., 897 F.2d 1159, 1160 (D.C. Cir. 1990) ("an expert opinion that Bendectin is a human teratogen which caused the plaintiff's birth defects is without scientific foundation"); Lima v. United States, 708 F.2d 502 (10th Cir. 1983); United States v. Cox, 696 F.2d 1294 (11th Cir. 1983); Barris v. Bob's Drag Chutes and Safety Equip., Inc., 685 F.2d 94 (3d Cir. 1982).

[15] *See* 4 WEINSTEIN'S FEDERAL EVIDENCE § 703.04; *see also* Carlson, *Policing the Bases of Modern Expert Testimony*, 39 VAND. L. REV. 577 (1986).

witness in forming an opinion.[16] Because Rule 703 is concerned with the reliability of expert opinions, to show that it is reasonable for the expert witness to rely on hearsay evidence in forming an opinion, the proponent of the witness should present evidence that other experts in the same field rely on the same type of evidence in making decisions in their work.[17]

In a criminal case, the defendant's constitutional right to confront the prosecution witnesses may entitle him or her to an opportunity to cross-examine the persons who provided the information upon which the expert relied.[18] However, the Supreme Court ruled that the Confrontation Clause does not require that experts recall the basis for their opinions. In *Delaware v. Fensterer,*[19] the prosecution sought to prove that the defendant strangled the victim using a cat leash. The prosecution's expert testified that hair on the leash that was similar to the victim's had been forcibly removed, but could not remember which of three methods he had used in making his determination. The Court held that the admission of the expert's testimony did not violate the Confrontation Clause because the defendant had an opportunity

---

[16] *See* Christophersen v. Allied-Signal Corp., 939 F.2d 1106 (5th Cir. 1991) (noting the doubts raised by the expert's lack of special experience in the field, the court held that the data upon which the expert based his opinion were inherently unreliable and consequently an inappropriate basis for expert opinion under Rule 703); 4 WEINSTEIN'S FEDERAL EVIDENCE § 703.04.

[17] *See, e.g.,* United States v. Seale, 600 F.3d 473 (5th Cir. 2010) (district court did not abuse its discretion during kidnapping prosecution by admitting opinion of government expert, a forensic pathologist, that deaths of victims were caused by fresh-water drowning, even though expert derived his opinion in part from statements by a conspirator; government expert also relied on autopsy reports, video footage of recovery of body, interviews with divers conducting recovery effort, FBI reports, and photographs of physical evidence); Arkwright Mutual Ins. Co. v. Gwinner Oil, Inc., 125 F.3d 1176 (8th Cir. 1997) (expert testimony based on inadmissible hearsay was properly admitted; the trial record revealed that the court had satisfied itself, through inquiry of the expert, that the hearsay report was a type of data reasonably relied upon by an expert in the field); United States v. Gresham, 118 F.3d 258 (5th Cir. 1997) (testimony by ATF agents that components of a pipe bomb had traveled in interstate commerce was admissible where the agents' testimony was based on discussions with manufacturers, corporate literature, ATF files, and other data reasonably relied upon by experts in this field, even though the data sources themselves were not admissible); Indian Coffee Corp. v. Procter & Gamble Co., 752 F.2d 891 (3d Cir. 1985) (trial court erroneously excluded testimony where it did not make inquiry as to what data experts in the field routinely rely on); Wilson v. Merrell Dow Pharmaceuticals, Inc., 893 F.2d 1149 (10th Cir. 1990) (in a products liability action for birth defects allegedly caused by Bendectin, trial court did not abuse its discretion by allowing defense experts to present charts of distribution of Bendectin and new stats on Bendectin therapy versus birth defect rates as a basis for testimony that Bendectin does not cause birth defects; the charts were a type "reasonably relied upon by birth defect experts"); *In re* Air Crash in Bali, Indonesia, 684 F.2d 1301 (9th Cir. 1982); United States v. Arias, 678 F.2d 1202 (4th Cir. 1982); United States v. Jones, 687 F.2d 1265 (8th Cir. 1982).

[18] *See generally,* 4 WEINSTEIN'S FEDERAL EVIDENCE § 703.06.

[19] Delaware v. Fensterer, 474 U.S. 15 (1985).

to cross-examine the expert. However, the Court cautioned that there may be situations in which the witness's recollection was so weak that his testimony would violate the right to confrontation.

As discussed in regard to Rule 702, trial judges have extensive discretion to admit or exclude expert testimony under Rule 703. Their rulings will be overturned only upon a showing of an abuse of this discretion.[20]

---

[20] *See, e.g.,* Berry v. Armstrong Rubber Co., 989 F.2d 822 (5th Cir. 1993) (trial court properly granted summary judgment for defendants where plaintiff's sole evidence to overcome defendant's motion was five expert opinions that failed to satisfy the requirements of Rule 703); Mendes-Silva v. United States, 980 F.2d 1482 (D.C. Cir. 1993) (trial court erred in granting summary judgment for defendant where plaintiff presented two expert witnesses who based their opinions on tests performed on plaintiff and on medical studies and literature); South Cent. Petroleum, Inc. v. Long Bros. Oil Co., 974 F.2d 1015 (8th Cir. 1992) (trial court properly admitted expert testimony where the expert's opinion relied on information not admitted at trial); United States v. Tranowski, 659 F.2d 750 (7th Cir. 1981).

Chapter 704

Rule 704. Opinion on an Ultimate Issue

Rule 704. Opinion on an Ultimate Issue

(a) **In General — Not Automatically Objectionable.** An opinion is not objectionable just because it embraces an ultimate issue.

(b) **Exception.** In a criminal case, an expert witness must not state an opinion about whether the defendant did or did not have a mental state or condition that constitutes an element of the crime charged or of a defense. Those matters are for the trier of fact alone.

§ 704.1 Opinion on an Ultimate Issue — In General

Rule 704 provides that testimony in the form of an opinion generally is not excludable because it addresses the ultimate issue in the case.[1] In criminal cases, however, expert witnesses are precluded from giving their opinion on the ultimate issue of whether the accused possessed the requisite mental state or condition.[2]

Although subsection (b) of Rule 704 was added by amendment as part of the Insanity Defense Reform Act of 1984,[3] the legislative history shows that

---

[1] *See generally,* 1 MCCORMICK, § 12; 4 WEINSTEIN'S FEDERAL EVIDENCE §§ 704.01–704.06; 3 MUELLER & KIRKPATRICK, §§ 360–362; 7 WIGMORE, §§ 1920–1921. *See also* Ladd, *Expert Testimony,* 5 VAND. L. REV. 414 (1952); Norvell, *Invasion of the Province of the Jury,* 31 TEX. L. REV. 731 (1953); Slough, *Testimonial Capacity, Evidentiary Aspects,* 36 TEX. L. REV. 1 (1957); Stoebuck, *Opinions on Ultimate Facts: Status, Trends, and a Note of Caution,* 41 DEN. L.C.J. 226 (1964); Note, *Evidence—Expert Testimony—The Ultimate-Issue Rule,* 40 CHI.-KENT L. REV. 147 (1963); Note, *Opinion Testimony "Invading the Province of the Jury,"* 20 U. CIN. L. REV. 484 (1951); Note, *Expert Testimony as an Invasion of the Province of the Jury,* 26 IOWA L. REV. 819 (1941).

[2] United States v. Watson, 171 F.3d 695 (D.C. Cir 1999) (Rule 704 forbids an opinion implying specialized knowledge of the accused's mental processes; expert testimony reflecting on the general modus operandi of drug dealers is not prohibited). *But see* United States v. Gomez-Osorio, 957 F.2d 636 (9th Cir. 1992) (though the district court did err, it did not constitute plain error to allow government expert to testify as to defendant's criminal intent).

[3] 18 U.S.C. § 20 (1984). The Act provides that insanity is an affirmative defense that the defendant must prove by clear and convincing evidence:

the scope of subsection (b) reaches not only the insanity defense but also "all such 'ultimate' issues, *e.g.*, premeditation in a homicide case, or lack of predisposition in entrapment."[4] It should be noted that the Rule as amended does not totally bar expert testimony on the criminal defendant's mental state, but instead, merely prohibits an expert from expressing his views on the ultimate issue that the trier of fact is to determine. For example, an expert may testify as to the diagnosis of the accused's mental condition but may not state an opinion on whether the defendant was legally insane.[5] The amendment does not otherwise change previous practice under Rule 704.

§ 704.2 Rationale

Case law once provided that a question to any witness was objectionable if it called for an opinion on the precise issue the jury was sworn to determine.[6] Courts sustaining the basic prohibition reasoned that allowing the witness to testify to one of the ultimate issues in the case would invade the province of the jury. The jury, it was feared, would abdicate its duty to determine the facts and instead, merely adopt the opinion of the witness.[7] A

(a) **Affirmative Defense.** It is an affirmative defense to a prosecution under any Federal statute that, at the time of the commission of the acts constituting the offense, the defendant, as a result of a severe mental disease or defect, was unable to appreciate the nature and quality or the wrongfulness of his acts. Mental disease or defect does not otherwise constitute a defense.

(b) **Burden of Proof.** The defendant has the burden of proving the defense of insanity by clear and convincing evidence.

[4] H. REP. NO. 98-1030, 98th Cong., 2d Sess. 224, 233, U.S. CODE CONG. & AD. NEWS 1984, p.1. *See, e.g.,* United States v. Hofus, 598 F.3d 1171 (9th Cir. 2010) (where accused is charged with attempting to coerce and entice a minor to engage in sexual activity, 18 U.S.C. § 2422(b), the trial court properly excluded the opinion of a defense expert that the accused engaged in sexual texting with the minor "in fantasy alone" and was unlikely to actually engage in sex with the child; expert testimony is not admissible to prove that the accused "did not really intend to entice or persuade the young girls, which is precisely the question for the jury").

[5] *See, e.g.,* United States v. Kristiansen, 901 F.2d 1463 (8th Cir. 1990) (questions relating to the symptoms and qualities of a mental disease are permissible whereas questions regarding culpability are not); United States v. Prickett, 604 F. Supp. 407 (S.D. Ohio 1985), *aff'd,* 790 F.2d 35 (6th Cir. 1986).

[6] *See, e.g.,* United States v. Spaulding, 293 U.S. 498 (1935) (in an action on war risk insurance policy, the medical opinions were without weight, since it was the ultimate issue to be decided by the jury; the experts should not have been allowed to state their conclusions on the whole case); *see also* Stoebuck, *Opinions on Ultimate Facts: Status, Trends, and a Note of Caution,* 41 DEN. L.C.J. 226 (1964); Slough, *Testamentary Capacity—Evidentiary Aspects,* 36 TEX. L. REV. 1 (1957).

[7] *See* United States v. Zipkin, 729 F.2d 384 (6th Cir. 1984) (trial court erred in permitting witness who was a bankruptcy judge to testify about the status of the law; the jury would likely give "special credence" to his testimony, thereby allowing the witness to usurp the function of the jury); United States v. Ragano, 476 F.2d 410 (5th Cir. 1973) (court erred in refusing to strike testimony by government witness in prosecution for filing false return, since

witness could not testify to "ultimate facts," but could testify only to "evidentiary facts," *i.e.,* those subsidiary facts introduced to prove ultimate facts.[8] Later cases carved out an exception to the prohibition that allowed experts to render opinions on the ultimate issue.[9]

As originally adopted, Rule 704 reflected the modern trend to abolish the ultimate issue prohibition. In practice, the distinction between an ultimate fact and an evidentiary fact proved too tenuous to be consistently applied.[10] McCormick concluded that the prohibition was "unduly restrictive, with many possible close questions of application" and can "often unfairly obstruct the presentation of a party's case, to say nothing of the illogic of the notion that opinions on ultimate facts usurp the function of the jury."[11]

Despite these criticisms, Rule 704(b) partially reinstates the prohibition against ultimate issue testimony. The amendment to Rule 704 reflects a legislative judgment that expert opinions on the ultimate issue of a criminal defendant's mental state are more misleading than helpful to the jury. Rule 704 was amended as part of an effort to clarify and improve federal law concerning the insanity defense and the procedures applicable to other offenders with mental diseases or defects. To illustrate the problems raised by the insanity defense, the Department of Justice offered the following description of a typical trial where the defense is raised:

> Since the experts themselves are in disagreement about both the meaning of the terms used to define the defendant's mental state and the effect of a particular state on the defendant's actions—but still freely allowed to state their opinion to the jury on the ultimate question of the defendant's sanity—it is small wonder that trials involving an insanity defense are arduous, expensive, and worst of all, thoroughly confusing to the jury. Indeed the disagreement of the experts is so basic that it makes rational deliberation by the jury virtually impossible.[12]

The amendment to Rule 704 is designed:

> . . . to eliminate the confusing spectacle of competing expert witnesses testifying to directly contradictory conclusions as to the ultimate legal issue to be found by the trier of fact. Under this

---

the testimony invaded the province of the jury, despite the "modern trend" to abandon the ultimate issue objection); *see also* Kentucky Trust Co. v. Glenn, 217 F.2d 462 (6th Cir. 1954).

[8] *See generally,* Note, *Opinion Testimony and Ultimate Issues—Incompatible?* 51 KY. L.J. 540 (1963). *See also* Note, *Opinion Testimony "Invading the Province of the Jury"* 20 U. CIN. L. REV. 484 (1951).

[9] Transportation Line v. Hope, 95 U.S. 297 (1877).

[10] 4 WEINSTEIN'S FEDERAL EVIDENCE § 704App.100.

[11] 1 MCCORMICK, § 12, at 49.

[12] H. REP. NO. 98-1030, 98th Cong., 2d Sess. 224, 225.

proposal, expert psychiatric testimony would be limited to present-ing and explaining their diagnoses, such as whether the defendant had a severe mental disease or defect and what the characteristics of such a disease or defect, if any, may have been.[13]

§ 704.3   Admissibility of Ultimate Issue Opinions

Rule 704(a) provides that testimony is not objectionable "just because it embraces an ultimate issue." But of course such testimony may be excluded on the basis of some other related objection, and the argument for such exclusion (not by coincidence) often becomes strongest in the case of testimony that comes closest to an opinion on the ultimate issue in a case. For example, under Rule 701 the opinion or inference is not admissible if it is not helpful to the trier of fact in the determination of a factual issue, and that danger is often greatest when the witness's testimony amounts to little more than telling the jury what result to reach.[14] When the jury can easily draw the inference from a simple recitation of facts by the witness, the witness's opinion on the ultimate issue might be excludable under Rule 701.

Where proffered testimony does not fall within the prohibition of Rule 704(b), courts should be reluctant to exclude the ultimate issue testimony of an expert under the standards set forth in Rule 702. Under Rule 702, which governs the admissibility of expert testimony, the trial court must determine that the subject matter of the testimony presented is helpful to the jury. To confer expert status on the witness, the expert's specialized body of knowledge must assist the trier of fact in determining a fact in issue or in understanding the evidence. It is the inability of the unaided jury to reach the ultimate opinion that renders the expert's opinion valuable. For this reason, an ultimate issue opinion by a properly qualified expert should not be excluded except in the extreme case where the expert's opinion is inherently misleading or unfairly prejudicial.[15]

---

[13] H. Rep. No. 98-1030, 98th Cong., 2d Sess. 224, 232.

[14] *E.g.,* Mitroff v. Xomox Corp., 797 F.2d 271 (6th Cir. 1986) (while testimony that embraces an ultimate issue is not per se objectionable, it rarely meets the test of being helpful to the jury, because the jury's opinion is as good as that of the witness); Owen v. Kerr-McGee Corp., 698 F.2d 236 (5th Cir. 1983) (testimony that only tells the witness what result to reach is not appropriate under Rule 704); United States v. Baskes, 649 F.2d 471 (7th Cir. 1980); *see also* United States v. Kelley, 615 F.2d 378 (5th Cir. 1980) (bank officers permitted to testify that documents had the capacity to influence the bank in prosecution for conspiracy to make false statements on applications for credit cards, loans, etc.; statements were helpful to jury); Bauman v. Centex Corp., 611 F.2d 1115 (5th Cir. 1980) (test is not whether evidence invades province of jury, but whether it is helpful in complex case involving issues of corporate management).

[15] *E.g.,* United States v. Lipscomb, 14 F.3d 1236 (7th Cir. 1994) (in drug case, law enforcement experts were permitted to give their opinions regarding whether the drugs found on defendant were for distribution or personal consumption); Fiataruolo v. United States, 8 F.3d 930 (2d Cir. 1993) (tax expert's testimony concerning whether defendant violated tax

§ 704.4   Discretion of the Trial Court

Rule 704(a)'s relaxation of the ultimate issue prohibition necessarily implies that the trial court must be vested with substantial discretion in its rulings as to the admissibility of ultimate issue testimony. Primarily, the trial court should be concerned with whether the jury can itself reach a correct conclusion unaided by the opinion of the witness. The Advisory Committee Note to Rule 704 concludes that the trial court has a secondary vehicle for excluding ultimate issue opinion under Rule 403.

In applying Rule 704(b), the trial court must determine not only whether the expert's testimony constitutes fact or opinion but also, if it is found to be opinion, whether it embraces an ultimate issue. Testimony by psychiatric experts must be "limited to presenting and explaining their diagnoses, such as whether the defendant had a severe mental disease or defect and what the characteristics of such a disease or defect, if any, may have been."[16]

---

law was properly admitted); United States v. West, 962 F.2d 1243 (7th Cir. 1992) (the district court erred by not allowing a psychiatrist to testify about the nature and extent of defendant's schizophrenia, even though there is some risk that an unguided jury could draw the wrong legal conclusion from such evidence); Hygh v. Jacobs, 961 F.2d 359 (2d Cir. 1992) (though harmless, it was error to allow law enforcement expert to opine on what constituted "deadly force" as this was a legal standard upon which only the judge should instruct); Heflin v. Stewart County, 958 F.2d 709 (6th Cir. 1992) (the district court did not err in allowing a correctional expert to testify as to proper prison procedure involving an alleged suicide); Johnson Group, Inc. v. Beecham, Inc., 952 F.2d 1005 (8th Cir. 1991) (the district court did not abuse its discretion in allowing expert testimony even though it included legal conclusions as to ultimate issues of the case); United States v. Milton, 555 F.2d 1198 (5th Cir. 1977) (in prosecution for illegal gambling government experts permitted to testify that lay off bets were being placed and to give their opinions as to the role each defendant played; no invasion of province of jury); *see also* Shatkin v. McDonnell Douglas Corp., 565 F. Supp. 93 (S.D.N.Y. 1983).

[16] H. REP. NO. 98-1030, 98th Cong., 2d Sess. 224, 232; *see* United States v. Dubray, 854 F.2d 1099 (8th Cir. 1988) (trial court did not err in admitting expert's opinion that defendant had not experienced a transient psychotic episode; although the testimony refuted defendant's only basis for the insanity defense, the expert testified only to his medical diagnosis and not to whether the defendant met the legal definition of insanity); *see also* United States v. Reno, 992 F.2d 739 (7th Cir. 1993) (expert's testimony describing how a person suffering from the same illness as that suffered by defendant would act did not violate Rule 704(b)); United States v. Salamanca, 990 F.2d 629 (D.C. Cir. 1993) (expert was properly permitted to testify that defendant had alcoholic brain damage and to explain how seventeen beers would likely affect such a person); United States v. Blumberg, 961 F.2d 787 (8th Cir. 1992) (in insanity defense case, trial judge properly barred a psychiatrist from giving his opinion that defendant did not appreciate the wrongfulness of his acts); United States v. DiDomenico, 985 F.2d 1159 (2d Cir. 1993) (trial court's ruling excluding a psychiatric expert witness who planned to testify that defendant suffered from personality disorder was not an abuse of discretion).

Chapter 705

Rule 705. Disclosing the Facts or Data Underlying an Expert's Opinion

Rule 705. Disclosing the Facts or Data Underlying an Expert's Opinion

Unless the court orders otherwise, an expert may state an opinion — and give the reasons for it — without first testifying to the underlying facts or data. But the expert may be required to disclose those facts or data on cross-examination.

---

§ 705.1   Disclosing the Facts or Data Underlying an Expert's Opinion — In General

Rule 705 sets forth the procedure governing the disclosure of the facts or data used by an expert in formulating an opinion.[1] The Rule departs from previous practice by allowing a properly qualified expert to testify as to his or her conclusions or opinions straightaway, without first laying a foundation of the facts and data that support the expert's opinion. Rule 705 places upon counsel the burden of eliciting the factual basis of an opposing expert's opinion on cross-examination.

The rationale behind Rule 705 is three-fold: (1) requiring an expert to lay a factual foundation prior to rendering his or her opinion is inefficient; (2) competent counsel will be able to expose any flaws in the expert's reasoning or methods upon cross-examination; and (3) the trial process has faith in the common sense and critical abilities of the trier of fact.[2] Laying the factual

---

[1] *See generally,* 1 MCCORMICK, §§ 14–15; 4 WEINSTEIN'S FEDERAL EVIDENCE §§ 705.01–705.08; 3 MUELLER & KIRKPATRICK, §§ 363–365; 2 WIGMORE, §§ 672–686. *See also* Conason, *Medical Cross-Examination—Refusal to Recognize Medical Authorities,* 10 TRIAL LAW. Q. 29 (1974); Friedenthal, *Discovery and Use of Adverse Party's Expert Information,* 14 STAN. L. REV. 455 (1962); Ladd, *Expert Testimony,* 5 VAND. L. REV. 414 (1952); Moller, *Cross-Examining the Plaintiff's Medical Expert,* 42 INS. COUNSEL J. 198 (1975); Note, *A Reconsideration of the Admissibility of Computerized Evidence,* 126 U. PA. L. REV. 425 (1977); Comment, *The Physician's Testimony—Hearsay Evidence or Expert Opinion—A Question of Professional Competence,* 55 TEX. L. REV. 296 (1975); Note, *Expert Witness and Hypothetical Questions,* 13 CASE W. RES. L. REV. 755 (1962).

[2] *See* 3 MUELLER & KIRKPATRICK, § 363.

groundwork for expert opinion can be very time-consuming, often resulting in disruptive and quibbling objections. In addition, putting "one party, who takes issue with individual points in a broad position taken by the other party, the burden of bringing such points to light, even though the other party bears the burden of persuasion on the whole position, is a procedural device familiar in other contexts."[3] In the end, of course, the trier of fact must decide what weight to give to the expert's testimony, using the facts elicited by counsel at trial.[4]

Rule 705 grants the trial court the right to order the preliminary disclosure of facts underlying the expert witness's opinion. Common situations where the trial court may require such preliminary disclosure are instances where the facts or data underlying the expert's opinion are needed before deciding whether, and to what extent, an expert should be allowed to testify under Rule 702 and 703.[5] However, an order of advance disclosure is not limited to such situations, but rather is at the trial court's discretion.

Rule 705 dispenses with any remnant of the common-law requirement that expert witnesses render their opinions in response to hypothetical questions. Under Rule 705 counsel may still ask hypothetical questions, but the Rule no longer requires the use of technique.

Rule 705 was amended effective December 1, 1993 in order to avoid a perceived conflict with Federal Rules of Civil Procedure 26(a)(2)(B) and 26(e)(1) and Rule 16 of the Federal Rules of Criminal Procedure, all of which require disclosure prior to trial of the basis and rationale for an expert's opinion.[6] The amended Rule makes it clear that an expert need not *testify* regarding underlying facts or data, although the expert may well be required to *disclose* such information under one of the above Rules.

§ 705.2   Use of Hypothetical Questions under Rule 705

In making the use of hypothetical questions optional, Rule 705 bows to the weight of modern commentary that assails the hypothetical question as an anachronism. As Wigmore concluded:

---

[3] 3 MUELLER & KIRKPATRICK, § 363, at 704 (citing the fact that in contract suits, plaintiffs need only allege the occurrence of conditions precedent in general terms, even though the plaintiff has the burden of proving the occurrence of such conditions precedent; the plaintiff must only introduce evidence regarding those conditions which the defendant claims did not occur).

[4] *See generally*, § 702, *supra,* for a discussion of the role that expert testimony plays in assisting the trier of fact.

[5] *See* Advisory Committee Note, Rule 705 (December 1, 1994, Amendment); *see also* Hayes v. Douglas Dynamics, Inc., 8 F.3d 88 (1st Cir. 1993) (Rule 705 does not permit a party to defeat a motion for summary judgment by presenting the bare conclusions of experts without any underlying data; motion should have included at least the factual basis for the expert's opinions).

[6] Advisory Committee Note, Rule 705 (1994 Amendment).

The hypothetical question, misused by the clumsy and abused by the clever, has in practice led to intolerable obstruction of truth. In the first place, it has artificially clamped the mouth of the expert witness, so that his answer to a complex question may not express his actual opinion on the actual case. This is because the question may be so built up and contrived by counsel as to represent only a partisan conclusion. In the second place, it has tended to mislead the jury as to the purport of actual expert opinion. This is due to the same reason. In the third place, it has tended to confuse the jury, so that its employment becomes a mere waste of time and a futile obstruction.[7]

The Advisory Committee adopted Wigmore's position that the use of a hypothetical question be purely elective.[8] Consequently, under Rule 705, the trial judge lacks the pre-Rule discretion to order trial counsel to use a hypothetical question when examining an expert witness.

Liberating attorneys from the mandatory use of the hypothetical question marks a significant advance in federal practice. Nevertheless, attorneys comfortable with the use of hypothetical questions will undoubtedly continue to use them whenever a tactical advantage may be attained. An attorney may, for example, wish to enlighten the jury as to the relative absence of controverted facts in a case by asking the expert to assume as a hypothesis the facts advanced by the opposing party. Likewise, the significance of a controverted fact may be emphasized by the use of comparative hypothetical questions proposed to the expert. When an attorney asks a hypothetical question likely to be confusing to the jury, a court has the power to exclude such a question pursuant to Rule 403.[9]

Hypothetical questions may take one of two forms, depending on whether the expert has observed the proceedings in which he or she is testifying.[10] If the expert has observed the proceedings, an attorney may pose a hypothetical question asking the expert to assume the truth of previous testimony. If the expert has not observed the proceedings, the questioner must ask that the expert assume the truth of certain enumerated facts. In this second instance, however, there must exist sufficient evidence for a jury finding that such facts exist or the court will strike the testimony.[11] Only the basic facts need

---

[7] 2 WIGMORE, § 686, at 962.

[8] *See* Advisory Committee Note, Rule 705.

[9] 4 WEINSTEIN'S FEDERAL EVIDENCE § 705.02.

[10] 3 MUELLER & KIRKPATRICK, § 364.

[11] Logsdon v. Baker, 517 F.2d 174 (D.C. Cir. 1975) (an expert may give his or her opinion based upon hypothetical facts, but those facts must be established by independent and properly introduced evidence); Vermont Food Indus. v. Ralston Purina Co., 514 F.2d 456, 463 (2d Cir. 1975) ("In asking a hypothetical question, the examiner may seek the witness's opinion on 'any combination of the facts within the tendency of the evidence' "); Daleiden

to be supplied by the party posing a hypothetical question, as long and overly detailed hypothetical questions may be confusing to both the expert and the trier of fact.[12] However, both forms of hypothetical questions should contain or refer to enough information to ensure that the expert's answer will not be misleading or incomprehensible. Rule 611 gives the trial judge discretion to reject questions that do not meet either of these criteria.[13]

§ 705.3   Disclosure of Supporting Facts under Rule 705

Rule 705 abolishes the pre-Rule position that required counsel to lay a factual foundation for an expert witness's testimony before the expert testified. The present Rule does not require a testimonial foundation unless the court in its discretion orders it.

The pre-Rule position has some merit. It is both sensible and logical to require the expert witness to disclose the facts that underlie his or her position. If these facts are not disclosed to the jury, the expert's opinion might be irrelevant and misleading if grounded on facts ultimately discounted by the trier of fact.[14] The trier of fact could not adequately assess the validity of the expert testimony without knowing the particular facts that support the expert opinion. The pre-Rule position was designed to aid the trier of fact in its assessment of the validity of the expert's opinion.

The Advisory Committee rejected the orthodox position because of the ineffective nature of the usual means of informing the witness of the underlying basis for the expert witness's testimony, *i.e.,* the hypothetical question discussed, *supra* in § 705.2. Also, by allowing the trial judge the discretion to order the disclosure of the facts that underlie the expert's testimony, the Rule provides a mechanism by which the court can ensure the

---

v. Carborundum Co., 438 F.2d 1017 (8th Cir. 1971) (while hypothetical questions cannot contain extra facts not properly introduced into evidence, here all the facts in the hypothetical question had been testified to by others, and the question was therefore proper).

[12] Mears v. Olin, 527 F.2d 1100, 1104 (8th Cir. 1975) (proper foundation had been laid for the hypothetical question as the record showed "that the hypotheticals assumed all material facts necessary for the experts to draw rational conclusions"); Cunningham v. Gans, 507 F.2d 496 (2d Cir. 1974) (upon retrial, it would be better for plaintiff "to ask shorter, less detailed hypothetical questions"; the defense could then attempt to attack by showing that the expert's "conclusions would be different if certain facts were also assumed or if certain assumed facts were changed rather than by voicing picky objections to complicated hypothetical questions"); Norland v. Washington Gen. Hosp., 461 F.2d 694, 698 (8th Cir. 1972) (hypothetical questions "must state all the facts upon which an expert witness is entitled to rely").

[13] *See* Ch. 611, *supra,* for a discussion of Rule 611.

[14] *See, e.g.,* Daniels v. Mathews, 567 F.2d 845 (8th Cir. 1977) (administrative law judge erred in asking an expert a question about claimant's capacity to do certain jobs without informing the expert of the underlying factual premise); Grand Island Grain Co. v. Roush Mobile Home Sales, 391 F.2d 35 (8th Cir. 1968) (objections to hypothetical questions sustained on the basis of insufficient proof); *see also* 4 WEINSTEIN'S FEDERAL EVIDENCE §§ 705.06–705.07; cf. Kaufman v. Edelstein, 539 F.2d 811 (2d Cir. 1976).

jury is made aware of facts that are necessary to a clear understanding of the expert's testimony.[15] Under Rule 705, when the facts or data that underlie the witness's testimony are disputed, they may be disclosed to the jury through cross-examination of the expert's witness.[16] The approach of Rule 705 places a "premium not only upon cross-examination, but also upon the kind of pretrial discovery which may be necessary to prepare the cross-examiner for the attack."[17] Under Rule 705 opposing counsel should be allowed wide latitude in cross-examination as to the facts underlying the expert's opinion.[18] However, the trial judge may and should impose

---

[15] 2 WIGMORE, § 686.

[16] *See, e.g.,* Vermont Food Indus. v. Ralston Purina Co., 514 F.2d 456 (2d Cir. 1975) ("[i]n asking a hypothetical question, the examiner may seek the witness's opinion on any combination of the facts within the tendency of the evidence"); United States v. Taylor, 510 F.2d 1283 (D.C. Cir. 1975) (defense psychiatric testimony, based in part upon examination of paintings, indicated that the accused was schizophrenic; on retrial of the insanity issue, it was improper to permit prosecutor to exhibit reproductions of paintings by Picasso, El Greco, Braque, Gaugin, Nolde, and Klee, and to ask whether witness would say that those artists suffered from mental illness).

[17] 3 MUELLER & KIRKPATRICK, § 364; *see also* United States v. Lawson, 653 F.2d 299 (7th Cir. 1981) ("In addition to the reasonable reliance requirement of Rule 703, a criminal defendant must . . . also have access to the hearsay information relied upon by an expert witness. Without such access, effective cross-examination would be impossible. Rule 705 . . . recognizes this requirement. The Advisory Committee Note to that rule states that it 'assumes that the cross-examiner has the advance knowledge which is essential for effective cross-examination.' "); Smith v. Ford Motor Co., 626 F.2d 784 (10th Cir. 1980) (judgment for plaintiff reversed upon finding that plaintiff significantly misled defendant regarding the subject matter of a physician's testimony, which hindered the defendant's discovery efforts and prejudiced the defendant's case); Perma Research & Development v. Singer Co., 542 F.2d 111 (2d Cir. 1976) (trial court did not err in admitting the plaintiff's expert testimony based on the "results of computer simulation"; court observed that defense counsel should have arranged to receive the details of the testimony in advance in order to avoid "unnecessarily belabored discussion of highly technical, tangential issues at trial").

[18] *See, e.g.,* United States v. Whitetail, 956 F.2d 857 (8th Cir. 1992) (in a murder trial where the defendant claimed to suffer from battered woman's syndrome, prosecutor properly asked experts questions regarding other fights in which the defendant had been the aggressor as these inquiries "addressed the underlying facts or data upon which her experts had based their opinions"); United States v. A & S Council Oil Co., 947 F.2d 1128 (4th Cir. 1991) (although the data on which an expert bases his or her opinion may not be admissible, opposing counsel may require the expert to reveal otherwise inadmissible underlying information upon cross-examination); Wilson v. Merrell Dow Pharmaceuticals, 893 F.2d 1149 (10th Cir. 1990) (in drug product liability suit, trial court properly admitted chart comparing the rate of birth defects to the sales of the drug, as defendant's counsel had the opportunity to expose defects in this method of showing causation upon cross-examination); United States v. Gillis, 773 F.2d 549 (4th Cir. 1985); Polk v. Ford Motor Co., 529 F.2d 259, 271 (8th Cir. 1976) (Rule 705 "make[s] it clear that an expert may give his conclusions without prior disclosure of the underlying facts. The weaknesses in the underpinnings of such opinions may be developed upon cross-examination and such weakness goes to the weight and credibility of the testimony").

reasonable limits upon cross-examination.[19] Further, cross-examination aimed at supporting the cross-examiner's case by attempting to introduce inadmissible hearsay should not be permitted.[20]

Pragmatic trial concerns will in most cases result in disclosure of the facts that underlie an expert witness's testimony. For example, expert witnesses who have firsthand knowledge of the facts of a dispute may be asked to disclose the foundation of their testimony, because the facts themselves must appear in the record in order to satisfy the proponent's burden of proof.[21] Rule 702 may also require that the witness exhibit some acquaintance with the underlying facts of the case in order to qualify as an expert witness.[22]

Expert testimony in criminal cases based on evidence not presented in

---

[19] *See* United States v. 10.48 Acres of Land, 621 F.2d 338 (9th Cir. 1980) (the scope and extent of cross-examination of an expert witness is within the sound discretion of the trial court and is not subject to exception unless the trial court's actions are wholly arbitrary, unreasonable, or abusive; however, the trial court need not extend cross-examination to permit questioning about collateral, immaterial or irrelevant matters); Hall v. Gen. Motors Corp., 647 F.2d 175 (D.C. Cir. 1980) (defense counsel could only cross-examine plaintiff's expert witness "on the bases for opinions he ventured on direct, but not on his qualifications as an expert" where defense counsel had objected to the witness's qualifications as an expert only after cross-examination was well underway); Caisson Corp. v. Ingersoll-Rand Co., 622 F.2d 672 (3d Cir. 1980) (in an action resulting from the alleged failure of a drill, the vice-president of the plaintiff contractor, who had some experience in construction, was permitted to testify to his opinion that "the shank failure resulted from a bending condition caused when the bit was rotated on uneven rock which in time caused the shank to crack," whereupon the defense attempted to cross-examine the witness concerning technical matters such as energy transfer; trial court did not err in excluding this line of questioning, as the questions were unrelated to the witness's expertise and the witness's lack of such knowledge "was admitted and was remarked upon by the trial judge, and therefore did not need to be established through cross-examination).

[20] *See* 3 MUELLER & KIRKPATRICK, § 364; *see also* Bobb v. Modern Products, Inc., 648 F.2d 1051, 1055–1056 (5th Cir. 1981) (wide latitude is usually given to a cross-examiner in attempting to discredit the witness; however, "cross-examination which attempts to impeach by slipping hearsay evidence into the trial will not be permitted, particularly in a case such as this one where the cross-examiner had previously succeeded in keeping out closely related evidence"); Bryan v. John Bean Div. of FMC Corp., 566 F.2d 541 (5th Cir. 1978) (during cross-examination plaintiff's counsel paraphrased and read verbatim from reports that were hearsay and were not admissible under any hearsay exceptions; trial court erred in permitting this, as the defendant's expert had not relied upon the conclusions of the reports but only on the data contained in the reports, so that "under the guise of impeachment, plaintiff's counsel was permitted to argue substantively evidence that did not impeach").

[21] 4 WEINSTEIN'S FEDERAL EVIDENCE § 705.05; *see also* Hayes v. Douglas Dynamics, Inc., 8 F.3d 88 (1st Cir. 1993) (Rule 705 does not apply in a summary judgment hearing); M & M Medical Supplies and Serv., Inc. v. Pleasant Valley Hosp., 981 F.2d 160 (4th Cir. 1992) (Rule 705 does not alter the requirement of the summary judgment rule that affidavits submitted in summary judgment proceedings set forth specific facts).

[22] *See* Ch. 702, *supra,* for a discussion of Rule 702.

court may give rise to Confrontation Clause issues.[23] However, the Supreme Court has held that the Confrontation Clause is satisfied if the defendant is given full opportunity to cross-examine the witness.[24]

§ 705.4   Disclosure of Supporting Facts: Relation to Rule 703

Rule 705 interfaces with Rule 703, which requires that the facts or data underlying the expert's opinion be facts directly perceived by the expert, facts already "admitted into evidence," or, in the alternative, hearsay facts that were reasonably relied upon by the expert witness in forming his or her opinion.[25] Where the expert lacks firsthand knowledge of the pertinent facts, Rule 705 places no restriction on the way in which the witness learns of the specific facts admitted into evidence. If the expert has the time and patience, he or she may sit at trial and hear the evidence as it is adduced. If the expert does not have such a flexible schedule, the data that he or she needs to formulate an opinion may be related to him or her in the form of a hypothetical question, or the counsel may inform the expert of relevant data.[26]

§ 705.5   Explaining the Expert Opinion

Consistent with prior Federal Law, Rule 705 provides that after the opinion of the expert is elicited, the expert may "give the reasons for it." A trial court errs if it excludes the testimony of an expert that provides an explanation of his or her opinion. The ability of the expert to explain his or her answer is vital to the jury's appreciation of the weight to be accorded expert opinions, and such explanation should not be limited except under extraordinary circumstances.

---

[23] 4 WEINSTEIN'S FEDERAL EVIDENCE § 705.08; *see also* § 801.5, *infra*, for a further discussion of Confrontation Clause issues.

[24] Delaware v. Fensterer, 474 U.S. 15 (1985) (conviction reversed on other grounds) ("The Confrontation Clause includes no guarantee that every witness called by the prosecution will refrain from giving testimony that is marred by forgetfulness, confusion, or evasion. To the contrary, the Confrontation Clause is generally satisfied when the defense is given a full and fair opportunity to probe and expose these infirmities through cross-examination, thereby calling to the attention of the factfinder the reasons for giving scant weight to the witness' testimony").

[25] *See* § 703, *supra*, for a discussion of Rule 703.

[26] *See* § 705.2, *supra*.

Chapter 706

Rule 706. Court-Appointed Expert Witnesses

Rule 706. Court-Appointed Expert Witnesses

(a) **Appointment Process.** On a party's motion or on its own, the court may order the parties to show cause why expert witnesses should not be appointed and may ask the parties to submit nominations. The court may appoint any expert that the parties agree on and any of its own choosing. But the court may only appoint someone who consents to act.

(b) **Expert's Role.** The court must inform the expert of the expert's duties. The court may do so in writing and have a copy filed with the clerk or may do so orally at a conference in which the parties have an opportunity to participate. The expert:

    (1) must advise the parties of any findings the expert makes;

    (2) may be deposed by any party;

    (3) may be called to testify by the court or any party; and

    (4) may be cross-examined by any party, including the party that called the expert.

(c) **Compensation.** The expert is entitled to a reasonable compensation, as set by the court. The compensation is payable as follows:

    (1) in a criminal case or in a civil case involving just compensation under the Fifth Amendment, from any funds that are provided by law; and

    (2) in any other civil case, by the parties in the proportion and at the time that the court directs — and the compensation is then charged like other costs.

(d) **Disclosing the Appointment to the Jury.** The court may authorize disclosure to the jury that the court appointed the expert.

(e) **Parties' Choice of Their Own Experts.** This rule does not limit a party in calling its own experts.

---

§ 706.1 Court-Appointed Expert Witnesses — Scope and Rationale

Rule 706 empowers the court, on its own motion, to appoint and select an expert witness to testify in a given lawsuit.[1] Although federal judges had inherent authority to appoint experts prior to the enactment of Rule 706, the power rarely was exercised.[2] The Rule was enacted to cure a variety of problems that surround the use of expert testimony authorized under Rule 702. Under the liberal standards qualifying expert witnesses, it is not uncommon for the trier of fact to be expected to determine which of two diametrically opposing views is the more valid assessment of an issue in controversy. In this situation, the trier of fact may be forced to choose between two conflicting interpretations of an event based upon the knowledge of two opposing experts, who look to the fringes of their disciplines for intellectual support of their respective positions. Rule 706 authorizes the trial court to appoint an expert witness who will restore some impartiality to the litigation,[3] and who will present the jury with an interpretation of the event in controversy that is based upon theory more generally supported in the given field.[4]

The Advisory Committee also concluded that Rule 706 would deter trial counsel from presenting partisan experts who were capable of being discredited by a court-appointed expert.[5] This, it was hoped, would have the desired effect of forcing weak cases into settlement and increasing the

---

[1] *See generally,* 1 MCCORMICK, § 17; 4 WEINSTEIN'S FEDERAL EVIDENCE §§ 706.01–706.06; 3 MUELLER & KIRKPATRICK, §§ 366–367; 2 WIGMORE, § 563. *See also* DeParq, *Law, Science, and the Expert Witness,* 24 TENN. L. REV. 166 (1956); Diamond, *The Fallacy of the Impartial Expert,* 3 ARCHIVES OF CRIM. PSYCHODYNAMICS 221 (1959); Griffin, *Impartial Medical Testimony: A Trial Lawyer in Favor,* 34 TEMP. L.Q. 402 (1961); Levy, *Impartial Medical Testimony—Revisited,* 34 TEMP. L.Q. 416 (1961); Myers, *The Battle of the Experts: A New Approach to an Old Problem in Medical Testimony,* 44 NEB. L. REV. 539 (1965); Morgan, *Suggested Remedy for Obstruction to Expert Testimony by Rule of Evidence,* 10 U. CHI. L. REV. 285 (1943); Sink, *The Unused Power of a Federal Judge to Call His Own Expert Witness,* 29 S. CAL. L. REV. 195 (1956); Travis, *Impartial Expert Testimony Under the Federal Rules of Evidence: A French Perspective,* 8 INT'L LAW 492 (1974); Van Dusen, *The Impartial Medical Expert System: The Judicial Point of View,* 34 TEMP. L.Q. 386 (1961); Wick & Kightlinger, *Impartial Medical Testimony Under the Federal Civil Rules: A Tale of Three Doctors,* 34 INS. COUNSEL L.J. 115 (1967); Comment, *Compelling Experts to Testify: A Proposal,* 44 U. CHI. L. REV. 851 (1977); *In re* Joint E. & S. Dist. Asbestos Litig., 982 F.2d 721 (2d Cir. 1992) (in complex asbestos case, trial court's appointment of an expert to advise the court on the feasibility of providing accurate estimates of future claims and to aid the court in selecting a panel of experts was within the authority granted by Rule 706).

[2] 3 MUELLER & KIRKPATRICK, § 366.

[3] *See* United States v. Faison, 564 F. Supp. 514 (D.N.J. 1983), *aff'd,* 725 F.2d 671 (3d Cir. 1983).

[4] Sink, *The Unused Power of a Federal Judge to Call His Own Expert Witness,* 29 S. CAL. L. REV. 195 (1956); *see also* 4 WEINSTEIN'S FEDERAL EVIDENCE § 706.02.

[5] Eastern Air Lines, Inc. v. McDonnell Douglas Corp., 532 F.2d 957 (5th Cir. 1976) (experts differed by $ 24.5 million in their estimates of plaintiff's losses; court on retrial should consider calling an expert witness on its own who could provide an objective insight into the difference in the opinion of the experts); *see* Rule 706, Advisory Committee Note.

general caliber of the experts testifying under Rule 702.[6]

Several arguments were advanced against the use of court-appointed experts, including: (1) the appointment of experts interferes with the adversary system's tradition of placing responsibility for presenting evidence on the parties;[7] (2) the jury may be overly impressed by the fact that the expert was selected by the court to render an unbiased opinion and consequently may rely too heavily on his opinion in reaching its decision;[8] (3) where the experts called by the parties give conflicting opinions due to a division in theory or philosophy within their field, it may be impossible to find a neutral witness because the expert will indorse one viewpoint or the other;[9] and (4) the use of court-appointed experts raises procedural uncertainties, such as the method of compensation and the availability of discovery by the parties.[10] The flexible approach taken by Rule 706 resolves many of these problems.[11]

§ 706.2   Procedure for Applying Rule 706

Before appointing an expert witness, the trial court is required to allow the parties to show cause why an expert witness should not be appointed by the court. Despite this procedure, trial counsel is unlikely to prevail on this issue because the arguments that a party would present to dissuade the trial court of its intention to appoint an expert witness are largely based upon factors that the court is more capable of assessing. For example, a party may argue that the appointed expert's testimony will be repetitious, or alternatively, that it will be misleading and prejudicial because the jury may unfairly assign a greater weight to the testimony of an expert appointed by the judge than it will to the expert testimony for a given party.[12] The court will respond that it has the discretion under Rule 403 to determine the extent of any prejudice resulting to a party from admitting evidence. Further, by refusing to inform the jury that the court appointed the witness under Rule 706(d), the expert's testimony will not be misleading.[13] As under other Rules granting discretion to the court, the judge's decision to appoint an expert witness should be overturned only upon finding an abuse of discretion.[14]

---

[6] *See* Report of the New Jersey Supreme Court Committee on Evidence 116 (1963). *See generally,* 4 WEINSTEIN'S FEDERAL EVIDENCE § 706.02; 3 MUELLER & KIRKPATRICK, § 366; 2 WIGMORE, § 563; 1 MCCORMICK, § 17.

[7] De Parq, *Law, Science and the Expert Witness,* 24 TENN. L. REV. 166 (1956).

[8] Levy, *Impartial Medical Testimony—Revisited,* 34 TEMP. L.Q. 416 (1961).

[9] 4 WEINSTEIN'S FEDERAL EVIDENCE § 706.02.

[10] 3 MUELLER & KIRKPATRICK, § 366.

[11] *See* § 706.2, *infra.*

[12] Levy, *Impartial Medical Testimony—Revisited,* 34 TEMP. L.Q. 416 (1961).

[13] *See* 4 WEINSTEIN'S FEDERAL EVIDENCE § 706.03.

[14] *See* Students of Cal. Sch. for the Blind v. Honig, 736 F.2d 538 (9th Cir. 1984), *vacated*

The court is granted the option under Rule 706(a) of selecting the expert it wishes to appoint, or it may request that counsel submit nominations of potential expert witnesses. The court in its discretion may either appoint the expert upon whom the parties agree, or it may select someone of its own choosing. The potential expert witness must agree to submit to appointment under Rule 706. The witness's qualifications will then be assessed under Rule 702.

An appointed expert witness who has agreed to testify is to be informed of his or her duties in writing by the court. The court then files a copy of this report with the clerk or submits a copy to a conference in which the parties, the appointed expert, and the judge participate. As Wigmore suggests, this type of conference may help to limit the scope of the conflict between the experts who will testify, thus avoiding confusion or waste of time at trial.[15] The Advisory Committee, however, thought that to require this conference would be expensive and time consuming, and consequently, Rule 706 authorizes a discretionary, rather than a mandatory conference.[16]

Rule 706 grants the parties the right to be informed of the expert witness's findings. Such apprisal may take many forms, but the parties have a right to depose the expert witness. Trial counsel is also authorized by the Rule to call the expert witness in the party's own case and to cross-examine the appointed expert. Rule 706 does not establish the point in the trial at which the court may appoint an expert witness. However, because the court must have time to: (1) hear motions against appointing the expert witness; (2) receive consent to appointment by the expert; (3) notify counsel and the expert of his duties through writing or the discretionary conference; (4) allow the expert time to make findings of fact; and (5) present the findings to trial counsel within reasonable time to prepare a cross-examination at trial,[17] it would appear the court should determine whether it wishes to appoint an expert witness at the pretrial stage. Liberal discovery should enable the court to determine at an early stage whether it will need to appoint an expert witness.[18]

---

on other grounds, 471 U.S. 148 (1985) ("appointments under Rule 706 are reviewable only for abuse of discretion"). *But see* Philadelphia Mortgage Trust, Maurice Baehr v. Touche Ross & Co., 930 F.2d 306 (3d Cir. 1991) (where bankruptcy trustee retained accountants on behalf of the estate, trial court erred in granting trustee's request for the taxation against defendant of accountant's fees; accountants were not neutral expert witnesses but were hired to aid trustee; also Rule 706 procedures of advance notice were not followed).

[15] The Committee on Expert Testimony of the American Bar Association Section of Judicial Administration, Report (Jan. 1970).

[16] Rule 706, Advisory Committee Note.

[17] United States v. Weathers, 618 F.2d 663 (10th Cir. 1980) (doubtful whether post-trial employment of psychiatric expert comported with Rule, yet only harmless error).

[18] *See* 4 WEINSTEIN'S FEDERAL EVIDENCE § 706.03.

§ 706.3 Compensation of Appointed Expert Witnesses under Rule 706(c)

Rule 706(c) applies to both criminal and civil proceedings, and it requires that compensation of appointed experts be reasonable. The Rule also delineates the source of the payment to the expert witness. In general the Rule charges compensation from a source "provided by law." Consequently, in a criminal case the Department of Justice will pay for the cost of the expert witness.[19] The Justice Department will also pay for the cost of the expert witness in a civil condemnation case under the just compensation clause of the Fifth Amendment.[20]

In civil actions not involving just compensation, the trial judge may charge each party with the expert witness's costs, to an extent the judge determines is fair. In assessing the expert's costs, the court will consider such factors as the nature of the case, the reason the court had to appoint an expert witness, the financial status of the parties, and the outcome of the litigation.[21]

---

[19] Decision of the Comptroller General B-139703 (March 21, 1980).

[20] *Id.*

[21] *See* 4 WEINSTEIN'S FEDERAL EVIDENCE § 706.06.

ARTICLE VIII.

HEARSAY

Synopsis

Chapter 801

Rule 801. Definitions That Apply to This Article; Exclusions from Hearsay

Rule 801. Definitions That Apply to This Article; Exclusions from Hearsay

(a) **Statement.** "Statement" means a person's oral assertion, written assertion, or nonverbal conduct, if the person intended it as an assertion.

(b) **Declarant.** "Declarant" means the person who made the statement.

(c) **Hearsay.** "Hearsay" means a statement that:

> **(1)** the declarant does not make while testifying at the current trial or hearing; and

> **(2)** a party offers in evidence to prove the truth of the matter asserted in the statement.

(d) **Statements That Are Not Hearsay.** A statement that meets the following conditions is not hearsay:

> **(1)** *A Declarant-Witness's Prior Statement.* The declarant testifies and is subject to cross-examination about a prior statement, and the statement:

>> **(A)** is inconsistent with the declarant's testimony and was given under penalty of perjury at a trial, hearing, or other proceeding or in a deposition;

>> **(B)** is consistent with the declarant's testimony and is offered to rebut an express or implied charge that the declarant recently fabricated it or acted from a recent improper influence or motive in so testifying; or

>> **(C)** identifies a person as someone the declarant perceived earlier.

> **(2)** *An Opposing Party's Statement.* The statement is offered against an opposing party and:

>> **(A)** was made by the party in an individual or representative capacity;

>> **(B)** is one the party manifested that it adopted or believed to be true;

(C) was made by a person whom the party authorized to make a statement on the subject;

(D) was made by the party's agent or employee on a matter within the scope of that relationship and while it existed; or

(E) was made by the party's coconspirator during and in furtherance of the conspiracy.

The statement must be considered but does not by itself establish the declarant's authority under (C); the existence or scope of the relationship under (D); or the existence of the conspiracy or participation in it under (E).

§ 801.1 The Hearsay System — An Overview

The hearsay system governs the admissibility of "out-of-court statements," *i.e.,* statements made by a person other than while testifying at the trial at which the statement is offered.[1]

In understanding the structure of the hearsay system, it is important to appreciate that the trial of a lawsuit customarily relies on three fundamental devices to maximize the accuracy of testimony submitted to the trier of fact:

---

[1] *See generally,* Blakely, *You Can Say That If You Want—The Redefinition of Hearsay in Rule 801 of the Proposed Federal Rules of Evidence,* 35 OHIO ST. L.J. 601 (1974); Booker & Morton, *The Hearsay Rule, the St. George Plays and the Road to the Year Twenty-Fifty,* 44 NOTRE DAME L. REV. 7 (1968); Donnelly, *The Hearsay Rule and Its Exceptions,* 40 MINN. L. REV. 455 (1956); Falknor, *The "Hear-say" Rule as a "See-Do" Rule: Evidence of Conduct,* 33 ROCKY MTN. L. REV. 133 (1961); Falknor, *"Indirect" Hearsay,* 31 TUL. L. REV. 3 (1956); Falknor, *Silence as Hearsay,* 89 U. PA. L. REV. 192 (1940); Finman, *Implied Assertions as Hearsay: Some Criticism of the Uniform Rules of Evidence,* 14 STAN. L. REV. 682 (1962); Graham, *"Stickperson Hearsay": A Simplified Approach to Understanding the Rule Against Hearsay,* 4 U. ILL. L. REV. 887 (1982); Humphreys, *In Search of the Reliable Conspirator: A Proposal Amendment to Federal Rule of Evidence 801(d)(2)(E),* 30 AM. CRIM. L. REV. 337 (1993); McCormick, *The Borderland of Hearsay,* 39 YALE L.J. 489 (1930); Maguire, *The Hearsay System: Around and Through the Thicket,* 14 VAND. L. REV. 741 (1961); Milich, *Re-examining Hearsay Under the Federal Rules: Some Method of the Madness,* 39 KAN. L. REV. 893 (1991); Morgan, *Hearsay,* 25 MISS. L.J. 1 (1953); Morgan, *A Suggested System of Utterances Admissible as Res Gestae,* 31 YALE L.J. 229 (1922); Morgan, *Hearsay Dangers and the Application of the Hearsay Concept,* 62 HARV. L. REV. 177 (1948); Park, *McCormick and the Concept of Hearsay: A Critical Analysis Followed by Suggestions to Law Teachers,* 65 MINN. L. REV. 423 (1981); Rice, *Should Unintended Implications of Speech Be Considered Nonhearsay? The Assertive/Nonassertive Distinction Under Rule 801(a) of the Federal Rules of Evidence,* 65 TEMPLE L. REV. 529 (1992); Rucker, *The Twilight Zone of Hearsay,* 9 VAND. L. REV. 453 (1956); Seligman, *An Exception to the Hearsay Rule,* 26 HARV. L. REV. 146 (1912); Tribe, *Triangulating Hearsay,* 87 HARV. L. REV. 957 (1974); Wellborn, *The Definition of Hearsay in the Federal Rules of Evidence,* 61 TEX. L. REV. 49 (1982); Weissenberger, *Unintended Implications of Speech and the Definition of Hearsay,* 65 TEMPLE L. REV. 529 (1992).

1. Prompt (*i.e.,* "fresh") cross-examination of witnesses testifying at trial.[2] This first safeguard is the most important of the three.

2. The oath administered to witnesses before they take the stand to testify at trial.[3]

3. The opportunity of the trier of fact to observe the demeanor of witnesses while they are testifying.

The common law of evidence developed a system of exclusion that rejects the admission of much evidence that fails to satisfy these three safeguards.[4] Accordingly, many out-of-court statements are rendered inadmissible by the hearsay system due to their inherent unreliability.

The general hearsay rule of exclusion is codified in Rule 802. It is important to recognize that Rule 802, "The Rule Against Hearsay," operates to exclude much evidence that is relevant but is flawed due to the fact that the evidence is inherently untrustworthy in such a way that the trier of fact would be incapable of attributing appropriate weight to the evidence.[5]

The first step in applying the hearsay system is determining whether the evidence in question fits the definition of hearsay in Rule 801(c). If the evidence is not hearsay, the evidence will not be excluded by the hearsay rule. Nevertheless, if the evidence fits the Rule 801(c) definition of hearsay, the evidence is presumptively inadmissible.

If the statement is hearsay under Rule 801(c), the second step in applying the hearsay system is determining whether there exists an exception to the basic definition of hearsay that will allow the admission of the hearsay. All such exceptions are contained in Rule 801(d). Technically, these exceptions describe the identified out-of-court statements as "not hearsay" or "non-hearsay." Functionally, however, such exceptions to the hearsay definition operate identically to exceptions to the exclusionary rule, by circumscribing admissible classes of out-of-court statements that are offered for their truth. Rule 801(d)(1) identifies certain prior statements of a witness that are admissible despite the fact that these statements fall within the basic Rule 801(c) definition of hearsay, while Rule 801(d)(2) renders admissible certain statements of a party where the statements are encompassed by the Rule 801(c) definition of hearsay.

The third step in applying the hearsay system requires the consideration of whether a statement that fits the Rule 801(c) definition of hearsay and not

---

[2] California v. Green, 399 U.S. 149 (1970); Pointer v. Texas, 380 U.S. 400 (1965).

[3] Bridges v. Wixon, 326 U.S. 135 (1945) (written statement under oath and signed "would have afforded protection against mistakes in hearing, mistakes in memory, mistakes in transcription").

[4] California v. Green, 399 U.S. 149 (1970); Bridges v. Wixon, 326 U.S. 135 (1945).

[5] Ladd, *The Hearsay We Admit,* 5 OKLA. L. REV. 271 (1952).

otherwise admissible may nevertheless be admissible pursuant to an exception to the exclusionary rule. These exceptions are contained within Rules 803, 804, and 807. In applying Rule 803 the availability of the out-of-court declarant is immaterial. However, in order to invoke an exception codified in Rule 804, the out-of-court declarant must be unavailable to testify at trial as provided for in Rule 804(a). It is important to keep in mind that the hearsay system operates as a rule of preference regarding the exceptions set out in Rule 804. The system prefers the declarant's testimony if it is available. If the declarant is unavailable under Rule 804(a), a hearsay statement from the declarant may be admitted provided (1) such a hearsay declaration exists, and (2) the hearsay declaration satisfies one of the exceptions of Rule 804(b).

Where hearsay is admitted under a Rule 803, Rule 804, or Rule 807 exception to the exclusionary rule, the admission will be based upon the policy that the class of hearsay in question is more reliable than hearsay in general.[6] As a general principle, a class of hearsay evidence is identified as an exception because the risk of one of the recognized testimonial defects is diminished. Such testimonial defects, which are normally exposed through cross-examination, are: (1) the risk of insincerity; (2) the risk of impaired perception; (3) the risk of a defect in memory; and (4) the risk of a defect in narration.[7] Usually, cross-examination can be utilized to attempt to expose one of these risks where a defect may occur during a witness's testimony at trial. Because hearsay involves out-of-court statements, fresh cross-examination is not available to test the accuracy of the hearsay statement. In an attempt to balance the problems associated with hearsay against the probative value of such declarations, the hearsay system defines certain classes of admissible hearsay in regard to which at least one of the testimonial risks is minimized.

The fourth step in applying the hearsay system involves determining whether a statement meeting the Rule 801(c) definition of hearsay and not otherwise admissible is nevertheless admissible pursuant to a statute or a rule of procedure identified in Rule 802.[8]

Finally, a criminal defendant may have a constitutional right to the admission of certain evidence despite the fact that the evidence in question

---

[6] 5 WEINSTEIN'S FEDERAL EVIDENCE § 807.02.

[7] *See* Morgan, *Hearsay Dangers and the Application of the Hearsay Concept,* 62 HARV. L. REV. 177 (1948); Stewart, *Perception, Memory, and Hearsay: A Criticism of Present Law and The Proposed Federal Rules of Evidence,* 1970 UTAH L. REV. 1; *see also* United States v. Owens, 789 F.2d 750 (9th Cir. 1986), *rev'd on other grounds,* 484 U.S. 554 (1988) ("Live testimony is considered reliable because it is given under oath, the jurors can observe the witness' demeanor, and the witness is subject to cross-examination"). *See generally,* 4 MUELLER & KIRKPATRICK, § 370.

[8] *See* Rule 802 and Chapter 802, *infra.*

falls within the Rule 801 definition of hearsay and despite the fact that no recognized exceptions will admit the hearsay.[9] Similarly, hearsay evidence admissible through one of the recognized exceptions may be subject to exclusion on constitutional grounds where the evidence is offered by the prosecution against the accused in a criminal case, *i.e.,* where its admission would deprive the accused of a fundamental right.[10]

§ 801.2   Hearsay and the Confrontation Clause of the Sixth Amendment

The hearsay rules provide, subject to various exceptions, that a party may ordinarily object to evidence about oral or written statements that were made outside of the courtroom. When that objecting party is the accused in a criminal case, the exclusion of such evidence may also be required by the Confrontation Clause of the Sixth Amendment, which provides: "In all criminal prosecutions, the accused shall enjoy the right . . . to be confronted with the witnesses against him."[11]

For nearly a quarter of a century after its decision in *Ohio v. Roberts,*[12] the Supreme Court interpreted the Confrontation Clause as imposing only a minimal constraint on a prosecutor's use of hearsay that would otherwise be admissible under the hearsay rules. As interpreted in *Roberts,* the Sixth Amendment allowed the admission of any unavailable witness's out-of-court statement against a defendant, even though that would deny the defendant any opportunity to literally confront the witness, as long as the statement was determined by the court to bear "adequate indicia of reliability," a test that was routinely met if the evidence either fell within "a firmly rooted hearsay

---

[9] *See* Chambers v. Mississippi, 410 U.S. 284 (1973). At defendant's trial for the murder of a police officer, the *Chambers* trial court ruled that the testimony of three witnesses to another man's confession to the murder was inadmissible hearsay. The Supreme Court reversed, holding that the testimony was admissible, even though it did not fall within a recognized hearsay exception. Because the evidence bore sufficient indicia of reliability, and because its exclusion would deny defendant's right to due process by preventing him from presenting witnesses in his defense, the admission of the evidence was held to be constitutionally compelled.

[10] *See* § 402.3, *supra.* Constitutional limitations to the various hearsay exceptions, where applicable, are discussed more fully in § 801.2, *infra.*

[11] U.S. Const., Amend VI. This is not the only way in which the Confrontation Clause intersects with the ordinary operation of the rules of evidence. As we have seen, a criminal defendant's right to confront the prosecution witnesses also carries certain important implications for the examination of the witnesses who *are* brought to the courtroom, including the general right to insist that prosecution witnesses not be allowed to testify in a manner that would prevent them from seeing the defendant, *see* § 611.2, *supra,* and the right to pursue certain lines of cross-examination and impeachment that demonstrate the witness's bias or motive to testify falsely, *see* § 607.4, *supra.*

[12] Ohio v. Roberts, 448 U.S. 56 (1980).

exception" or had "particularized guarantees of trustworthiness."[13] As a practical matter, this test rendered the Confrontation Clause largely duplicative of the hearsay rules, and greatly minimized the incentive for criminal defense attorneys to object on constitutional grounds to the admission of hearsay.

A quarter century of constitutional law based on *Roberts* has now been completely overturned, however, with the Supreme Court's recent decisions in *Crawford v. Washington*[14] and its progeny.[15] In this line of landmark cases, the Court abrogated *Roberts*, created a new constitutional standard for the admission of hearsay against a criminal defendant, and established for the first time in decades that the Sixth Amendment requires the exclusion of many extrajudicial statements that would otherwise be admissible under the hearsay rules (for example, in a civil case).[16]

Under *Crawford,* the admission of hearsay statements at a criminal trial no longer turns on whether the trial judge believes the evidence to be reasonably reliable. In that case, the Supreme Court concluded that "[w]here testimonial statements are involved, we do not think the Framers meant to leave the Sixth Amendment's protection to the vagaries of the rules of evidence, much less to amorphous notions of 'reliability.' "[17] The Court emphatically rejected the suggestion that the Confrontation Clause would allow the admission of testimonial hearsay merely because a statement was "deemed reliable by a judge," a process that would be "fundamentally at odds with the right of confrontation,"[18] or because the trial court believed that confrontation "would be of little value."[19] As the Supreme Court stated in *Crawford* with obvious disdain: "Dispensing with confrontation because

---

[13] *Roberts,* 448 U.S. at 66.

[14] Crawford v. Washington, 541 U.S. 36 (2004).

[15] Bullcoming v. New Mexico, 564 U.S. —, 131 S. Ct. 2705, 180 L. Ed. 2d 610 (2011); Michigan v. Bryant, 562 U.S. —, 131 S. Ct. 1143, 179 L. Ed. 2d 93 (2011); Melendez-Diaz v. Massachusetts, 557 U.S. —, 129 S. Ct. 2527, 174 L. Ed. 2d 314 (2009); Giles v. California, 554 U.S. 353 (2008); Whorton v. Bockting, 549 U.S. 406 (2007); Davis v. Washington, 547 U.S. 813 (2006).

[16] The test established in *Crawford* so thoroughly displaced the law of *Roberts* that no careful litigant can place any reliance on any judicial opinion written between 1980 and 2004 with respect to the Sixth Amendment's implications for the admission of hearsay against an accused. Although these cases established a new rule of procedure that governs all future criminal trials, as well as those cases that were still pending on direct review at the time *Crawford* was decided, they do not apply retroactively to older cases that became final on direct appeal or were already under collateral review. *Whorton v. Bockting,* 549 U.S. 406 (2007).

[17] *Crawford,* 541 U.S. at 61.

[18] *Id.*

[19] Melendez-Diaz v. Massachusetts, 557 U.S. —, 129 S. Ct. 2527, 174 L. Ed. 2d 314, 325 (2009).

testimony is obviously reliable is akin to dispensing with jury trial because a defendant is obviously guilty."[20] Even more recently, the Court has reaffirmed that the Sixth Amendment is not satisfied simply because a trial judge believes that some other arrangement short of confrontation "provides a fair enough opportunity for cross-examination."[21]

Rather, the Court adopted a new standard under which the admission of hearsay against a criminal defendant depends almost entirely on whether the hearsay is *testimonial*. The Court concluded that the Confrontation Clause, construed in light of its history and text, applies only to statements by "witnesses," which would only be true of those who give the functional equivalent of "testimony" against the accused.[22] If an extrajudicial statement of a witness is testimonial, it may not be admitted against the accused to prove the truth of what that witness said unless that witness is unavailable to testify and the defendant had a prior opportunity to cross-examine that witness.[23] Unless those two requirements are satisfied, it no longer matters, as it did under *Roberts,* whether the statement is deemed to be reliable by the

---

[20] *Crawford,* 541 U.S. at 62. More recent cases have sounded this same theme. Bullcoming v. New Mexico, 564 U.S. —, 131 S. Ct. 2705, 180 L. Ed. 2d 610, 62 (2011) ("This Court settled in *Crawford* that the obvious reliability of a testimonial statement does not dispense with the Confrontation Clause.") (internal punctuation omitted); Melendez-Diaz v. Massachusetts, 557 U.S. —, 129 S. Ct. 2527, 174 L. Ed. 2d 314, 327 & n.6 (2009) (testimonial hearsay is subject to the right of confrontation even if the declarant who made the statement "possessed the scientific acumen of Mme. Curie and the veracity of Mother Theresa."); Whorton v. Bockting, 549 U.S. 406, 419–420 (2007) (asserting that *Crawford* was not based on any assumption that the holding in that case would "improve the accuracy of factfinding in criminal trials," and that it was "unclear whether *Crawford,* on the whole, decreased or increased the number of unreliable out-of-court statements that may be admitted in criminal trials.") Unfortunately, this clear and almost unbroken line of cases was thrown into some confusion, at least temporarily, by *Michigan v. Bryant,* 562 U.S. —, 131 S. Ct. 1143, 179 L. Ed. 2d 93 (2011), which inexplicably asserted that the determination of whether a statement is testimonial is informed by "standard rules of hearsay, designed to identify some statements as reliable," id. at 107, and by consideration of whether a statement was made under circumstances where "the prospect of fabrication . . . is presumably significantly diminished." Id. at 109. These lines are not easily reconciled with the Court's subsequent reaffirmation in *Bullcoming,* less than four months later, that the Confrontation Clause is not satisfied merely because the trial judge believes that some testimonial hearsay is "obviously reliable." It is not surprising that only one member of the Court, Justice Sotomayor, joined the majority opinions in both *Bryant* and *Bullcoming.*

[21] *Bullcoming,* 564 U.S. —, 131 S. Ct. 2705, 180 L. Ed. 2d 610, 622 (2011)

[22] The Court based this conclusion on the history behind the development of the Confrontation Clause, as well as dictionary definitions of *witnesses* as those who "bear testimony," and *testimony* as "[a] solemn declaration or affirmation made for the purpose of establishing or proving some fact." *Crawford,* 541 U.S. at 51 (quoting 2 N. Webster, AN AMERICAN DICTIONARY OF THE ENGLISH LANGUAGE (1828)).

[23] *Crawford,* 541 U.S. at 53–54. These two conditions will of course rarely be satisfied apart from the special case of hearsay statements that are admissible under the exception codified in Federal Rule of Evidence 804(b)(1) for "Former Testimony."

trial judge.[24]

For years, the Supreme Court has often spoken of confrontation and cross-examination as if they were synonymous,[25] which would literally imply that the defendant has the right to insist that the declarant of a testimonial statement, if available, be called to the stand by the prosecution. That would be the conclusion most consistent with the fact that the Sixth Amendment actually speaks of a right to "be confronted" with the witnesses, and not a right to "confront" them. Nevertheless, a number of state courts after *Crawford* reasoned that the Confrontation Clause may be satisfied, even if a court admits testimonial statements without calling the witness to the stand, as long as the state makes the witness available for the defendant to subpoena and "confront" as an adverse witness during the defense case-in-chief.[26] The Supreme Court has rejected the reasoning of those cases, however, and has held that the prosecution must produce the witnesses against the accused,[27] and that the ability of a defendant to subpoena a government witness "is no substitute for the right of confrontation."[28] The Court concluded, however, that a state may adopt "notice-and-demand statutes" that require the prosecution to give pretrial notice of its intent to use some document at trial and that require the defendant — if he wishes to confront the author of that document — to make a pretrial demand for the state to produce that witness at trial.[29] Such statutes do not impermissibly shift to the accused the burden of calling the witnesses against him, but merely govern the timing of the defendant's objection under the Confrontation Clause and compel him to exercise those rights before trial.[30]

But what if hearsay is *not* testimonial? In *Crawford,* the Court expressly declined to decide whether nontestimonial hearsay would continue to be regulated by *Roberts* or would instead be "exempted . . . from Confronta-

---

[24] *Id.* at 68–69 ("Where testimonial statements are at issue, the only indicium of reliability sufficient to satisfy constitutional demands is the one the Constitution actually prescribes: confrontation").

[25] *E.g., Davis,* 547 U.S. at 822 n.1; *Crawford,* 541 U.S. at 59 n.9.

[26] *E.g.,* State v. Campbell, 719 N.W.2d 374, 377–378 (N.D. 2006) (even assuming that state crime lab reports admitted against the defendants were testimonial, the Confrontation Clause was satisfied because state law allowed the defendants to subpoena the scientists who prepared those reports, and the defense "waived any potential Confrontation Clause violation" by not attempting to do so).

[27] Melendez-Diaz v. Massachusetts, 557 U.S. —, 129 S. Ct. 2527, 174 L. Ed. 2d 314, 323 (2009).

[28] *Id.* at 319. The Court added that the Confrontation Clause is not satisfied by "a system in which the prosecution presents its evidence via *ex parte* affidavits and waits for the defendant to subpoena the affiants if he chooses." *Id.* at 330.

[29] *Id.* at 331.

[30] *Id.*

tion Clause scrutiny altogether."[31] More recently, however, the Supreme Court resolved in *Davis v. Washington* that nontestimonial hearsay "is not subject to the Confrontation Clause."[32] The Court has since made the same point even more explicitly, when it stated that *Crawford* resulted in the "elimination of Confrontation Clause protection against the admission of unreliable out-of-court nontestimonial statements," and that "the Confrontation Clause has no application to such statements and therefore permits their admission even if they lack indicia of reliability."[33] Because the Court made these points with some subtlety in *Davis* and has only overruled *Roberts sub silentio,* one early commentator predicted that the point was likely to escape the attention of the courts.[34] That prediction turned out to be surprisingly accurate, for a considerable number of federal appellate opinions handed down after *Davis* mistakenly asserted that nontestimonial hearsay continues to be subject to the constitutional rule of *Roberts,*[35] or at least that the Supreme Court has yet to resolve the issue.[36] These lower court opinions are mistaken and are not to be followed.[37] Where a hearsay statement offered against the accused is not testimonial, its admission or

---

[31] *Id.* at 68. The Court added that "we need *not* definitively resolve" whether to limit the "Confrontation Clause only to testimonial statements, leaving the remainder to regulation by hearsay law." *Id.* at 61 (emphasis added).

[32] "It is the testimonial character of the statement that separates it from *other hearsay* that, while subject to traditional limitations upon hearsay evidence, *is not subject to the Confrontation Clause.*" Davis v. Washington, 547 U.S. 813, 821 (2006) (emphasis added). The Court made this same point, albeit rather obliquely, when it declared that the Confrontation Clause's focus upon testimonial hearsay is a limitation "so clearly reflected in the text of the constitutional provision [that it] must fairly be said to mark out not merely its 'core,' but its perimeter," *id.* at 824, meaning that nontestimonial statements lie outside the reach of the Clause. The Court thereby resolved, as it said it was required to do, "whether the Confrontation Clause applies only to testimonial hearsay." *Id.* at 823.

[33] Whorton v. Bockting, 549 U.S. 406, 420 (2007). In his opinion for a unanimous Court, however, Justice Alito mistakenly stated that *Crawford* had clarified that nontestimonial hearsay is "not governed by [the Confrontation] Clause," *id.* at 413–414 (citing *Crawford,* 541 U.S. at 60), when in fact the Court had not decided that issue until *Davis.*

[34] Duane, *The Cryptographic Coroner's Report on* Roberts v. Ohio, 21 CRIMINAL JUSTICE 37 (Fall 2006) ("It is safe to assume that we have not yet seen the last time some court makes this same mistake in attempting to unravel what *Davis* says about the continued viability of *Roberts* and the applicability of the Sixth Amendment Confrontation Clause to nontestimonial hearsay. Indeed, at the moment the haunting question appears to be how long we will have to wait until a majority of the lower courts manage to get the answer to that question *right.*").

[35] United States v. Jimenez, 513 F.3d 62, 77 (3d Cir. 2008); United States v. Ramirez, 479 F.3d 1229, 1247 (10th Cir. 2007); Albrecht v. Horn, 485 F.3d 103 (3d Cir. 2007); United States v. Mooneyham, 473 F.3d 280 (6th Cir. 2007); Middleton v. Roper, 455 F.3d 838, 857 & n.6 (8th Cir. 2008); United States v. Thomas, 453 F.3d 838, 844 (7th Cir. 2006). All of those cases were decided after *Davis,* and several of them after *Whorton.*

[36] United States v. Norwood, 555 F.3d 1061, 1065–1066 (9th Cir. 2009).

[37] Slowly, but surely, this conclusion is now coming to the attention of the appellate

exclusion is simply not governed by the Confrontation Clause of the Sixth Amendment, and the trial court's decision is regulated entirely by the traditional rules governing the admission of hearsay evidence.[38]

Since the constitutional test for admissibility under the Confrontation Clause now turns on whether a statement is testimonial, much more will be written by the courts on that topic, but a number of fundamentals have already been clarified.

Without announcing a comprehensive definition of what makes a statement testimonial, the Supreme Court has at least identified the quintessential form of such evidence: "Whatever else the term covers, it applies at a minimum to prior testimony at a preliminary hearing, before a grand jury, or at a former trial; and to police interrogations,"[39] as well as guilty pleas entered by the defendant's former co-defendants and alleged conspirators,[40] although this list is not exhaustive.[41] The apparent common ground in these examples is that they all involve circumstances that would lead an objective observer to believe that the statement was made for an evidentiary purpose in aid of a police investigation or with an eye toward possible use in a criminal prosecution.[42] The paradigmatic (although not necessarily the only)

---

courts, including many of those Circuits that had previously missed the point. *See, e.g.,* United States v. Spotted Elk, 548 F.3d 641, 662 (8th Cir. 2008); Doan v. Carter, 548 F.3d 449, 458 (6th Cir. 2008); United States v. Burgos, 539 F.3d 641, 643 (7th Cir. 2008); United States v. Udeozor, 515 F.3d 260, 268 (4th Cir. 2008); United States v. Williams, 506 F.3d 151, 156 (2d Cir. 2007); United States v. Proctor, 505 F.3d 366, 372 (5th Cir. 2007).

[38] In other words, if hearsay is *testimonial,* the Sixth Amendment will often require its exclusion at a criminal trial even if that evidence would be admissible at a civil trial on the same charges, but the admissibility of *nontestimonial* hearsay will almost never depend on whether it is offered at a civil or criminal trial (unless it is offered under one of the rare hearsay exceptions that are limited to civil cases, such as FRE 803(8)).

[39] *Crawford,* 541 U.S. at 68.

[40] As another example of "plainly testimonial statements," the Court cited the formerly common federal practice of admitting evidence of a "plea allocution" by the accused's codefendant for the purpose of "showing [the] existence of a conspiracy." *Crawford,* 541 U.S. at 64; *see also Davis,* 547 U.S. at 825 (citing "guilty pleas and jury conviction of others" as evidence arising out of "the testimonial context"). This may have been technically dictum, but the lower courts have shown no hesitation in concluding after *Crawford* that plea allocutions are testimonial, since they are made in open court, under oath, and in response to structured questioning by the trial judge or the prosecutor, and those cases are surely correct. United States v. Lopez-Medina, 596 F.3d 716 (10th Cir. 2010); United States v. Riggi, 541 F.3d 94 (2d Cir. 2008); United States v. Reifler, 446 F.3d 65, 86–87 (2d Cir. 2006); United States v. Al-Sadawi, 432 F.3d 419, 425–426 (2d Cir. 2005); United States v. Zhou, 428 F.3d 361, 374 (2d Cir. 2005).

[41] For example, a written confession given to a prosecutor under oath is not one of the examples of a testimonial statement listed by the Supreme Court, but it has been held that such evidence is testimonial, United States v. Rodriguez-Marrero, 390 F.3d 1, 17 (1st Cir. 2004), and that ruling seems to be certainly correct.

[42] United States v. Tolliver, 454 F.3d 660, 664–665 (7th Cir. 2006) ("statements that a

example of a testimonial statement is one made in a situation "in which state actors are involved in a formal, out-of-court interrogation of a witness to obtain evidence for trial."[43] Statements made under such circumstances are testimonial even where the police interrogation "is conducted with all good faith," for a Confrontation Clause violation is committed at trial, not at the police station.[44]

When a court is attempting to determine whether a statement is testimonial, should it decide the primary purpose of the statement from the perspective of the speaker or the individual who was listening to or questioning that speaker? For several years after *Crawford,* many lower courts concluded that the issue should be determined from the perspective of the declarant who made the statement.[45] In *Michigan v. Bryant,* however, the Supreme Court instead chose to require "a combined inquiry that accounts for both the declarant and the interrogator," and that "examin[es] the statements and actions of all participants" in the encounter.[46] This test is an objective one, which looks not to "the subjective or actual purpose of the individuals involved in a particular encounter, but rather the purpose that reasonable participants would have had" in such a setting, after looking at

---

declarant makes in anticipation of or with an eye toward a criminal prosecution" are testimonial); United States v. Pugh, 405 F.3d 390, 399 (6th Cir. 2005) (witness's identification of defendant was testimonial because it was during police interrogation, was made to a government officer, and because "any reasonable person would assume that a statement that positively identified possible suspects in a picture of the crime scene would be used against those suspects in either investigating or prosecuting the offense"). *See also* Bullcoming v. New Mexico, 564 U.S. —, 131 S. Ct. 2705, 180 L. Ed. 2d 610, 623 (2011) (a statement created solely for an evidentiary purpose "in aid of a police investigation" is testimonial).

[43] Michigan v. Bryant, 562 U.S. —, 131 S. Ct. 1143, 179 L. Ed. 2d 93, 107 (2011).

[44] *Bryant,* 179 L. Ed. 2d at 107 (noting that even when the police act with all good faith and with no improper motives, "introduction of the resulting statements at trial can be unfair to the accused if they are untested by cross-examination").

[45] United States v. Tolliver, 454 F.3d 660, 664–665 (7th Cir. 2006) ("statements that a declarant makes in anticipation of or with an eye toward a criminal prosecution" are testimonial); United States v. Underwood, 446 F.3d 1340, 1347 (11th Cir. 2006) (citing United States v. Saget, 377 F.3d 223, 229 (2d Cir. 2004)); *see also* United States v. Johnson, 440 F.3d 832, 843 (6th Cir. 2006); United States v. Summers, 414 F.3d 1287, 1302 (10th Cir. 2005) ("a statement is testimonial if a reasonable person in the position of the declarant would objectively foresee that his statement might be used in the investigation or prosecution of a crime"). This is the same view that was ultimately endorsed by Justice Scalia, the author of the Court's opinions in *Crawford* and *Davis.* Michigan v. Bryant, 562 U.S. —, 131 S. Ct. 1143, 179 L. Ed. 2d 93, 120–121 (2011) (Scalia, J. dissenting).

[46] Michigan v. Bryant, 562 U.S. —, 131 S. Ct. 1143, 179 L. Ed. 2d 93, 113–114 (2011). The majority had no direct response to what Justice Scalia accurately described as the "glaringly obvious problem" that this test generates no obvious answer "where the police and the declarant each have one motive, but those motives conflict." Id. at 123 (Scalia, J., dissenting). The majority opinion in *Bryant* contains no clues as to how lower courts should handle such a situation, other than the direction to ascertain the objective that seems to be the "primary purpose" in the encounter.

"the statements and actions of the parties to the encounter, in light of the circumstances in which the interrogation occurs."[47]

Statements made in response to police interrogation may or may not be testimonial, depending on the primary purpose in conducting the interrogation.[48] In *Davis,* the Court held that statements made in the course of police interrogation are nontestimonial, and therefore not governed by the Confrontation Clause, if the circumstances objectively indicate "that the primary purpose of the interrogation is to enable police assistance to meet an ongoing emergency."[49] Such a finding is most likely if the witness was describing events as they were actually happening; if the witness faced an ongoing emergency; or if the conversation was not tranquil but frantic, perhaps over the phone,[50] especially if the caller was unprotected by the police and apparently still in possible immediate danger,[51] or if the questioning took place "in an exposed, public area, prior to the arrival of emergency medical services, and in a disorganized fashion."[52] This is true even of questions designed to establish the identity of the perpetrator, if the questioning officers' primary purpose was to ensure that "the dispatched officers might know whether they would be encountering a violent felon."[53] The threat or emergency need not be one faced by the speaker; even if the initial victim appears to have been removed from danger, the court must consider whether the primary purpose of the interrogation may have been to address "a potential threat to the responding police and the public at large."[54] Such a

---

[47] Id. at 108–109, 114.

[48] In *Crawford,* the Court stated that "interrogations by law enforcement officers fall squarely within [the] class" of testimonial hearsay, 541 U.S. at 53, but the Court later disavowed that categorical statement, explaining that "we had immediately in mind (for that was the case before us) interrogations solely directed at establishing the facts of a past crime, in order to identify (or provide evidence to convict) the perpetrator." *Davis,* 547 U.S. at 826.

[49] *Davis,* 547 U.S. at 822. More recently, the Court stated in dictum that "there may be *other* circumstances, aside from ongoing emergencies, when a statement is not procured with a primary purpose of creating an out-of-court substitute for trial testimony." *Bryant,* 131 S. Ct. at 1155, 179 L. Ed. 2d at 107 (emphasis in original). But the Court gave no indication of what such other circumstances might be in the context of a statement procured by the police.

[50] *Davis,* 547 U.S. at 826–827. *See also* United States v. Thomas, 453 F.3d 838, 843–844 (7th Cir. 2006) (911 call was not testimonial when caller reported "a dude that just got shot" and when the caller ended the conversation immediately upon the arrival of the police).

[51] *Davis,* at 831. Of course this logic applies with even greater force to someone crying out in panic or pain but not being interrogated at all, even if in police custody. United States v. Gonzales, 436 F.3d 560, 576 (5th Cir. 2006) (crime victim crying out in pain about his injuries was not making testimonial statement even though he was in police custody; a testimonial statement is "one made during a governmental *interrogation* or something similar thereto, not merely screaming out in pain to those in the vicinity").

[52] Michigan v. Bryant, 562 U.S. —, 131 S. Ct. 1143, 1160, 179 L. Ed. 2d 93, 112 (2011).

[53] *Davis,* at 827.

[54] Michigan v. Bryant, 179 L. Ed. 2d 93, 108 (2011). *See also id.* at 110 ("An assessment

finding is of course most likely if the case involved the use of a gun or other deadly weapon, or if the police were collecting information about an assailant whose motive and location were not yet known.[55] The medical condition of the speaker is also "important" because a victim with especially severe injuries is less likely to "have any purpose at all in responding to police questions," and more likely to give the police reason to suspect the existence "of a continuing threat to the victim, themselves, and the public."[56]

On the other hand, statements made in the course of police interrogation are testimonial, and therefore ordinarily made inadmissible by the Confrontation Clause, if the circumstances objectively indicate "that there is no such ongoing emergency, and that the primary purpose of the interrogation is to establish or prove past events potentially relevant to later criminal prosecution."[57] This is true even if the statements by the witness were "volunteered" or made in the absence of any interrogation,[58] and even if the statements were made at the alleged crime scene in response to initial inquiries from the police.[59] Such a finding is most likely, for example, if the witness was describing events some time after they happened, especially if the witness was already separated from the assailant, speaking at the station house, or otherwise under police protection, or responding calmly to structured police questioning.[60] Even a conversation that began in the midst of a seeming emergency "may evolve into testimonial statements" if it becomes clear during the conversation "that what appeared to be an emergency is not or is no longer an emergency or that what appeared to be a public threat is actually a private dispute," or if the suspect "is disarmed, surrenders, is

---

of whether an emergency that threatens the police and public is ongoing cannot narrowly focus on whether the threat solely to the first victim has been neutralized because the threat to the first responders and public may continue.")

[55] *Id.* at 116–118.

[56] *Id.* at 111. This observation in *Bryant,* among others, led two dissenting justices to complain with some force that the Court may have created "an expansive exception to the Confrontation Clause for violent crimes." *Id.* at 126 (Scalia, J., dissenting); *see also id.* at 130 (Ginsburg, J., dissenting).

[57] *Davis,* at 822.

[58] *Id.* at 822 n. 1. *See also* United States v. Hinton, 423 F.3d 355, 360–361 (3d Cir. 2005) (witness made a testimonial statement in positively identifying the defendant as his assailant to two officers while riding in a police cruiser in pursuit of the suspect; the witness "made the statement with knowledge that the officers were acting in their official capacity and investigating the reported crime," and an objective witness would have believed that this identification served the purpose of incriminating the defendant and would be available for use at trial).

[59] *Davis,* 547 U.S. at 831 & n.6. The Court added, however, that "at least the initial interrogation conducted in connection with a 911 call" is "ordinarily" designed to describe current circumstances requiring police assistance, which would not be testimonial. *Id.* at 827.

[60] *Id.* at 831–832.

apprehended, or . . . flees with little prospect of posing a threat to the public."[61]

In identifying the line between testimonial and nontestimonial statements, the distinguishing criterion has much to do with the formality of the statement and the circumstances under which it was made. In *Davis,* the Court stated that formality is "essential to testimonial utterance,"[62] More recently, however, the Court appears to have qualified that statement, concluding that formality is merely one factor to be considered, and that it is "not the sole touchstone of our primary purpose inquiry because . . . informality does not necessarily indicate the presence of an emergency or the lack of testimonial intent."[63] But the level of formality in an encounter between a witness and the police remains relevant because "formality suggests the absence of an emergency and therefore an increased likelihood that the purpose of the interrogation is to establish or prove past events potentially relevant to later criminal prosecution."[64] The required level of formality need not involve the administration of an oath or an appearance in a judicial proceeding, and may be established, for example, by the fact that the statement was made under circumstances where a false statement would be punishable as a criminal offense.[65] The Court has not yet clarified, however, whether a testimonial statement must always be attended by criminal penalties if false, or whether the required level of solemnity can sometimes be established by other means, although some lower courts had assumed before *Davis* that it could be,[66] and that conclusion is probably

---

[61] *Bryant,* 179 L. Ed. 2d at 112.

[62] *Davis,* at 830 n. 5. *See also Crawford,* 541 U.S. at 51 (contrasting "[a]n accuser who makes a *formal* statement to government officers" with "one who makes a *casual* remark to an acquaintance") (emphasis added).

[63] *Bryant,* 179 L. Ed. 2d at 112. In *Bryant,* the Court stated for the first time that a testimonial statement may be either "formal or informal," *id.* at 107, and apparently regarded the "formality" variable as the least important part of the equation, turning to a consideration of that factor only after examining every other possible basis for determining whether the statement at issue was testimonial. *See id.* at 119 ("Finally, we consider the informality of the situation and the interrogation.")

[64] *Id.* at 112 (internal punctuation omitted).

[65] *Davis,* 547 U.S. at 830 ("It imports sufficient formality, in our view, that lies to police officers are criminal offenses").

[66] *See* United States v. Summers, 414 F.3d 1287, 1302–1303 (10th Cir. 2005) (suspect's incriminating question to the police, "How did you guys find us so fast?," was testimonial and inadmissible under *Crawford* when offered against his co-defendant, even though the suspect had not been read his *Miranda* rights and was not subject to formal interrogation, because he had been taken into physical custody by the police and his question to the police was "loosely akin to a confession" and a reasonable person in his position "would objectively foresee that an inculpatory statement implicating himself and others might be used in a subsequent investigation or prosecution").

correct.[67]

It is not yet clear whether testimonial statements are limited to those knowingly given to government officials. At its very core, the definition surely includes "[a]n accuser who makes a formal statement to government officers,"[68] and the doctrine reflects a special historical concern over "[t]he involvement of government officers in the production of testimonial evidence,"[69] although the Court has not yet decided "whether [or] when statements made to someone other than law enforcement personnel are 'testimonial.'"[70] At least in dictum, the Court has more recently declared that statements made by a crime victim "to friends and neighbors . . . [or] to physicians in the course of receiving treatment," even if those statements described crimes committed against that speaker, "would be excluded, if at all, only by hearsay rules,"[71] which would plainly seem to imply that such statements could never be testimonial. But it is clear that most, if not all, statements made to friends and acquaintances are not testimonial, even if only because they lack the requisite solemnity and formality of testimony knowingly given to the police or prosecutors.[72] Thus, statements made by a child abuse victim are testimonial if they were recorded in an interview by a "forensic interviewer" who was "collecting information for law enforcement,"[73] but not if they were recorded by a physician to whom the child was taken for medical treatment,[74] or if they were elicited through questioning by foster parents appointed by the state.[75]

As an example of evidence that would be "clearly nontestimonial," the Court has cited "statements made unwittingly to a government informant"

---

[67] In *Crawford,* the Court said without elaboration that at least some dying declarations are "clearly" testimonial. *Crawford,* 541 U.S. at 56 n.6. A statement by a person in the settled expectation of imminent death is made in a sober and solemn moment, but surely not because of fear that he or she will face any criminal penalties if the statement proves to be false and he or she unexpectedly survives.

[68] *Crawford,* 541 U.S. at 51.

[69] *Id.* at 53.

[70] *Davis,* 547 U.S. at 823 n.2. *See also* Michigan v. Bryant, 562 U.S. —, 131 S. Ct. 1143, 179 L. Ed. 2d 93 108 n.3 (2011) (noting once again that the question is still unsettled).

[71] Giles v. California, 554 U.S. 353, 376 (2008) (dictum).

[72] Horton v. Allen, 370 F.3d 75, 83–84 (1st Cir. 2004) (defendant's private conversation with friend was not testimonial; it was private, did not involve formalized documents, was not made under examination, and was not made "under circumstances in which an objective person would reasonably believe that the statement would be available for use at a later trial").

[73] United States v. Bordeaux, 400 F.3d 548, 555 (8th Cir. 2005).

[74] United States v. Peneaux, 432 F.3d 882, 896 (8th Cir. 2005).

[75] *Id.* at 896 (foster parents are not agents of the state for the purposes of *Crawford*).

by a defendant's conspirators.[76] For this reason, four members of the Court have more recently stated that the hearsay rule admitting statements by a conspirator "does not pertain to a constitutional right."[77] Although this was technically dictum, the courts of appeals have shown no hesitation in holding that statements by conspirators in furtherance of a conspiracy are not testimonial,[78] especially when, as is often true, the statements are not assertions of historical fact but are merely the means by which the crime is planned.[79]

The Court has indicated that the epitome of a nontestimonial statement would be "an offhand, overheard remark,"[80] "a casual remark to an acquaintance,"[81] or "statements from one prisoner to another."[82] Lower courts have followed these suggestions in a number of cases to uphold the admission of statements made by people who were talking with a friend in confidence, or at least thought that they were doing so.[83] Indeed, one appeals

---

[76] *Davis,* 547 U.S. at 825; *see also Crawford,* 541 U.S. at 56 (listing "statements in furtherance of a conspiracy" as an example of "statements that by their nature [are] not testimonial").

[77] Giles v. California, 554 U.S. 353, 374 n.6 (2008) (Scalia, J.; plurality opinion for four justices). Curiously, however, Justice Scalia also wrote, a bit tentatively, that "an incriminating statement in furtherance of the conspiracy would *probably* never be [] testimonial," *id.* (emphasis added), as if perhaps to leave open the possibility that there might be some rare case in which a different result would be recognized. It remains to be seen whether that qualification turns out to be an unnecessary understatement. In light of all the Court has written in *Crawford* and its progeny about the definition of "testimonial hearsay," which almost always requires a showing that the declarant was knowingly assisting the authorities in preparing a criminal prosecution, it would indeed be difficult to imagine a case in which such a statement could be offered against a member of the declarant's conspiracy and somehow intended to further the objectives of that same conspiracy.

[78] United States v. Underwood, 446 F.3d 1340, 1346–1347 (11th Cir. 2006); United States v. Bridgeforth, 441 F.3d 864, 869 (9th Cir. 2006); United States v. Hansen, 434 F.3d 92, 100 (1st Cir. 2006); United States v. Martinez, 430 F.3d 317, 329 (6th Cir. 2005); United States v. Allen, 425 F.3d 1231, 1235 (9th Cir. 2005); United States v. Sanchez-Berrios, 424 F.3d 65, 75 (1st Cir. 2005); United States v. Delgado, 401 F.3d 290 (5th Cir. 2005).

[79] United States v. Faulkner, 439 F.3d 1221, 1226–1227 (10th Cir. 2006).

[80] *Crawford,* 541 U.S. at 51.

[81] *Id.* ("An accuser who makes a formal statement to government officers bears testimony in a sense that one who makes a casual remark to an acquaintance does not").

[82] *Davis,* 547 U.S. at 825.

[83] United States v. Franklin, 415 F.3d 537, 543–545 (6th Cir. 2005) (statement by a man to his friend was not testimonial when later offered at trial against that declarant and his co-defendant even though the statement implicated both men); Ramirez v. Dretke, 398 F.3d 691, 695 n.3 (5th Cir. 2005) (conspirator's statements to a friend, implicating both himself and defendant, were admissible against defendant on trial for capital murder; testimonial evidence does not include "spontaneous out-of-court statements made outside any arguably judicial or investigatory context"); United States v. Manfre, 368 F.3d 832, 838 n.1 (8th Cir. 2004) (comments "made to loved ones or acquaintances . . . are not the kind of

courts has extended this logic even as far as supposedly informal conversations between law enforcement officers in the course of their investigative work,[84] although that reasoning seems questionable and it remains to be seen whether the Supreme Court will go that far in narrowing the reach of the Confrontation Clause.

In *Crawford,* the Supreme Court made a passing assertion that "business records" are not testimonial,[85] and the federal courts have taken that to mean that the records of private businesses and personal records are not testimonial evidence within the meaning of *Crawford,* at least if they were not prepared in anticipation of trial or a criminal prosecution,[86] and those cases are almost certainly correct.[87] But many lower courts extended that logic to justify the admission of documents that were prepared by law enforcement agents or other government officials,[88] including perhaps even affidavits and

---

memorialized, judicial-process-created evidence of which *Crawford* speaks"); United States v. Lee, 374 F.3d 637, 645 (8th Cir. 2004) ("Kehoe's statements to his mother do not implicate the core concerns of the confrontation clause"); United States v. Saget, 377 F.3d 223, 229 (2d Cir. 2004) ("statements to a confidential informant, whose true status is unknown to the declarant, do not constitute testimony within the meaning of *Crawford*").

[84] Middleton v. Roper, 455 F.3d 838, 856–857 (8th Cir. 2006) (prosecutor's alleged statement to sheriff, to the effect that the case against a prosecution witness was dropped because of the weakness of the case and not as a favor in exchange for his cooperation, was held to be not testimonial but was more akin to "a non-custodial conversation," even though it was between law enforcement officers).

[85] *Crawford,* 541 U.S. at 56 (listing "business records" as an example of "statements that by their nature [are] not testimonial"). The Court has more recently explained that business records are not testimonial because the were "created for the administration of an entity's affairs and not for the purpose of establishing or proving some fact at trial." Melendez-Diaz v. Massachusetts, 557 U.S. —, 129 S. Ct. 2527, 174 L. Ed. 2d 314, 329 (2009).

[86] United States v. Hagege, 437 F.3d 943, 958 (9th Cir. 2006) (business records of foreign banks are not testimonial); United States v. Gilbertson, 435 F.3d 790, 796 (7th Cir. 2006) (odometer statements by sellers of used cars, although arguably analogous to affidavits, were not testimonial evidence against the accused, a car dealer charged with later tampering with those odometers, because the statements were made before his alleged crime, were not initiated by the government, and "were not made with the respective declarants having an eye towards criminal prosecution"); United States v. Jamieson, 427 F.3d 394, 411 (6th Cir. 2005) (business records, including medical records and insurance applications and policies, are not testimonial); Parle v. Runnels, 387 F.3d 1030 (9th Cir. 2004) (entries in murder victim's diary were not testimonial).

[87] *See* Melendez-Diaz v. Massachusetts, 557 U.S. —, —, 129 S. Ct. 2527, 174 L. Ed. 2d 314, 322 n.1 (2009) ("Additionally, documents prepared in the regular course of equipment maintenance may well qualify as nontestimonial records"); *id.* at 322 n.2 ("[M]edical reports created for treatment purposes . . . would not be testimonial under our decision today.")

[88] United States v. Ballesteros-Selinger, 454 F.3d 973, 974–975 (9th Cir. 2006) *op. replaced, remanded,* 2007 U.S. App. LEXIS 11237 (9th Cir. 2007) (memorandum of oral decision by immigration judge at deportation hearing, offered to prove that the defendant had been deported, was not testimonial); United States v. Bahena-Cardenas, 411 F.3d 1067, 1075 (9th Cir. 2005) (immigration document that "was not made in anticipation of litigation and

other documents created in actual preparation for the criminal trial as long as those documents merely record "unambiguous factual matter."[89] All of those cases were thrown into serious question, however, and at least most of them were effectively overruled, by the Supreme Court's decision in *Melendez-Diaz v. Massachusetts,* which held that affidavits prepared by a state crime laboratory showing the results of a chemical analysis were testimonial, and therefore subject to the Confrontation Clause.[90] The Court based this conclusion on the fact that such reports provided "the precise testimony the analysts would be expected to provide if called at trial," and were made by analysts who must have been aware of their "evidentiary purpose."[91] This is true even if the report was neither sworn nor notarized, as long as it was otherwise formalized and prepared for an evidentiary purpose to prove some fact in a criminal proceeding or in aid of a police investigation.[92]

. . . is simply a routine, objective, cataloging of an unambiguous factual matter" is nontestimonial). Documents in an alien's INS file, such as a warrant of deportation signed by an INS official who witnessed the deportation of the defendant, have also been held to be admissible as nontestimonial business records. United States v. Caraballo, 595 F.3d 1214 (11th Cir. 2010) (routinely and mechanically kept INS records, such as warrants of deportation, are not "testimonial" hearsay subject to the Confrontation Clause, because they are routinely completed by Customs and Border Patrol agents in the course of their non-adversarial duties, not in the course of preparing for a criminal prosecution. In prosecution for illegally smuggling aliens into the country, the court did not err in admitting an INS form that contained only routine biographical information such as the entrant's name, date and place of birth, parents' names, height, weight, address, country of citizenship, and information concerning whether the entrant had an immigration visa); *see also* United States v. Garcia, 452 F.3d 36 (1st Cir. 2006); United States v. Valdez-Maltos, 443 F.3d 910, 911 (5th Cir. 2006); United States v. Bahena-Cardenas, 411 F.3d 1067, 1074–1075 (9th Cir. 2005); United States v. Cantellano, 430 F.3d 1142, 1145 (11th Cir. 2005); *see also* United States v. Rueda-Rivera, 396 F.3d 678, 680 (5th Cir. 2005).

[89] United States v. Weiland, 420 F.3d 1062, 1077 (9th Cir. 2005) (a routine certification by the custodian of a domestic public record, such as a record of a defendant's state court convictions, even if done in an affidavit prepared for the purposes of litigation, is merely the "routine cataloguing of an unambiguous factual matter" and is therefore not a testimonial statement subject to *Crawford,* especially in light of "the serious logistical challenge" of making such state and local officials available for cross-examination in the countless criminal cases heard each day).

[90] Melendez-Diaz v. Massachusetts, 557 U.S. —, 129 S. Ct. 2527, 174 L. Ed. 2d 314 (2009). The affidavit in that case was a "certificate of analysis" showing the results of a forensic analysis, reporting that a substance seized by the police was cocaine. The Court rejected any suggestion, however, that the Sixth Amendment required the production of "anyone whose testimony may be relevant in establishing the chain of custody, authenticity of the sample, or accuracy of the testing device." *Id.* at 322 n.1. The Court concluded that: "It is up to the prosecution to decide what steps in the chain of custody are so crucial as to require evidence; but what testimony is introduced must (if the defendant objects) be introduced live." *Id.*

[91] *Id.* at 318.

[92] Bullcoming v. New Mexico, 564 U.S. —, 131 S. Ct. 2705, 180 L. Ed. 2d 610, 623–624

Moreover, once a lab report or some other document is determined to be testimonial, it cannot be introduced through the "surrogate testimony" of a scientist from the same lab but "who did not sign the certification or observe the test reported in the certification."[93] The accused has the right "to be confronted with the analyst who made the certification," in keeping with the general rule that an out-of-court testimonial statement "may not be introduced against the accused at trial unless the witness who made the statement is unavailable and the accused has had a prior opportunity to confront that witness."[94] Indeed, the Court stated, in a bit of emphatic dictum, that even a police report containing "an objective fact" — such as the number above a house door or the read-out of a radar gun — could not be admitted through the testimony of some other police officer who was able to testify only about the technology used by the observing officer or the police department's general procedures.[95]

By refusing to recognize a "forensic evidence" exception to the Confron-

---

(2011). In effect, the Court appears to have decided that such "business records" prepared for trial by government officials are an example of what the Court had in mind when it referred to inadmissible testimonial statements that fall "within some broad, modern hearsay exception, even if that exception might be justifiable in other circumstances." *Crawford,* 541 U.S. at 56 n.7.

[93] *Bullcoming,* 564 U.S. —, 131 S. Ct. 2705, 180 L. Ed. 2d 610, 622 (2011).

[94] *Id.* at 613–614. Curiously, less than one week after deciding *Bullcoming,* the Court granted certiorari to decide the question: "Whether a state rule of evidence allowing an expert witness to testify about the results of DNA testing performed by non-testifying analysts, where the defendant has no opportunity to confront the actual analysts, violates the Confrontation Clause." Williams v. Illinois, No. 10-8505 (June 28, 2011). Judging from the opinion of the Illinois court, it appears that the court intends to use the case to resolve Justice Sotomayor's suggestion that a different result might obtain in a case where "an expert witness was asked for his independent opinion about underlying testimonial reports that were not themselves admitted into evidence." *Bullcoming,* 564 U.S. —, 131 S. Ct. 2705, 180 L. Ed. 2d 610, 629 (Sotomayor, J., concurring). *See, e.g.,* United States v. Turner, 591 F.3d 928 (7th Cir. 2010) (the Sixth Amendment Confrontation Clause does not demand that a chemist or other testifying expert must have done the lab work himself; trial court properly allowed the supervisor analyst at a laboratory to testify as an expert regarding his opinion that the substance sold by defendant was cocaine, even though he was not the analyst which conducted the testing; he reached the same conclusions as the testing analyst, whose work he was required to supervise and approve, and nothing from the testing analyst's notes, machine test results, or final report was introduced into evidence); United States v. Ayala, 601 F.3d 256 (4th Cir. 2010) (in gang prosecution, testimony of three Government experts did not violate the Confrontation Clause, even though the experts relied in part on interviews with unnamed declarants; the experts offered their independent judgments, most of which related to the gang's general nature as a violent organization and were not about the defendants in particular, these judgments resulted from many years of observing the gang and studying its methods, and experts "did not act as mere transmitters and in fact did not repeat statements of particular declarants to the jury")

[95] *Bullcoming,* 180 L. Ed. 2d at 621. But the Court's opinion in *Bullcoming* did not necessarily resolve whether, as some lower courts had held, the Confrontation Clause could be satisfied through the testimony of a supervising analyst.

tation Clause,[96] the Supreme Court's holding in *Melendez-Diaz* required a drastic change in the criminal trials of the many state courts that had previously admitted government lab and test reports without insisting on an opportunity for the accused to confront the agent who prepared the report. That case represented a relatively less significant change in federal court, however, because the federal version of the hearsay exception for public records and reports — unlike the similar versions in many state courts — does not apply "in a criminal case, [to] a matter observed by law-enforcement personnel."[97] But no similar restriction appears in Rule 803(10), the federal hearsay exception for "Absence of a Public Record," which authorizes the admission of a written certificate "that a diligent search failed to disclose a public record or statement," offered as evidence that no such record existed. Although many lower federal courts initially held in the wake of *Crawford* that such certificates were not subject to Confrontation,[98] that suggestion was drawn into very serious question by the reasoning of *Melendez-Diaz*, which specifically cited with approval certain authorities holding that the Confrontation Clause applied to "a clerk's certificate attesting to the fact that the clerk had searched for a particular relevant record and failed to find it."[99] In April 2011, the Advisory Committee on the Federal Rules of Evidence proposed an amendment to add a "notice and demand" provision to Rule 803(10); that proposed amendment, if adopted, will provide that a written certificate "that a diligent search failed to produce a public record or statement" is admissible in a criminal case "if the prosecutor in a criminal case intends to offer a certification, the prosecutor provides written notice of that intent at least 14 days before trial, and the defendant does not object in writing within 7 days of receiving the notice — unless the court sets a different time for the notice or the objection.

---

[96] *Id.* at 620 (noting that *Melendez-Diaz* had refused to create a "forensic evidence" exception to the rule of *Crawford*).

[97] Rule 803(8)(A)(ii).

[98] United States v. Cervantes-Flores, 421 F.3d 825, 830–834 (9th Cir. 2005) (a certificate of nonexistence of record, or CNR, submitted to prove that the defendant had not received the Attorney General's consent to reenter the United States, was not testimonial even though it was prepared for trial by a government official and at the request of the prosecutor, because the records that were reviewed to prepare that CNR had not been prepared for trial).

[99] *Melendez-Diaz*, 557 U.S. at —, 129 S. Ct. 2527, 174 L. Ed. 2d 314 at 329. The Court noted that certain common law authorities did allow the admission of affidavits by clerks to authenticate or provide a copy of an otherwise admissible record, but not to "create a record for the sole purpose of providing evidence against a defendant." *Id.* Lower federal courts since *Melendez-Diaz* have recognized that affidavits and certificates created in preparation for a criminal trial to verify the nonexistence of a record are still testimonial. United States v. Martinez-Rios, 595 F.3d 581 (5th Cir. 2010) (in a prosecution for illegal reentry into the United States, a certificate of nonexistence of record (CNR), which reflected that a deported defendant had not received consent for readmission into the United States, was testimonial, and its admission therefore violated his rights under the Confrontation Clause, because the field office director who created the CNR did not testify).

One of the most important unresolved questions is how *Crawford* applies to statements that were surreptitiously collected by the police from people who did not know they were being recorded. The courts have had little difficulty in rejecting constitutional challenges to the admission of wiretapped conversations, on the theory that the participants in such conversations obviously do not anticipate the use of such statements against them at trial.[100] In one case, the court of appeals extended that reasoning to recorded conversations between conspirators when the incriminating statements were then admitted against a third member of the group. The court reasoned that the recorded statement was not testimonial because people in the declarant's position would not have anticipated that their statements to a trusted acquaintance would ever be used at a criminal trial against their mutual friend.[101] That reasoning is plausible after *Davis* but open to question, especially since the FBI in that case "gave [the informant] a recording device, instructed him in its use, and told him the subject matter that they wanted him to record."[102] Even after *Davis,* it is debatable whether a prosecutor can so easily evade the requirements of the Sixth Amendment by so thoroughly and deliberately participating in the creation of incriminating evidence that would be indisputably testimonial if only the declarants knew their comments were being recorded by a government agent.[103]

Testimonial hearsay is barred by the Sixth Amendment only if the statement is offered as evidence of the truth of what was said by that witness, and only if that witness does not testify about the statement at trial. Regardless of whether a statement is testimonial, therefore, its exclusion is

---

[100] United States v. Hendricks, 395 F.3d 173, 181 (3d Cir. 2005) (wiretapped conversations are not testimonial; "the very purpose of Title III intercepts is to capture conversations that the participants believe are not being heard by the authorities and will not be available for use in a prosecution").

[101] United States v. Johnson, 440 F.3d 832, 843 (6th Cir. 2006).

[102] *Johnson,* 440 F.3d at 836. Even though the conversation was evidently between members of a conspiracy, there was no indication that it was in furtherance of the conspiracy, or the admissibility of those statements would have been a much simpler matter under *Crawford,* which specifically approved the hearsay exception for statements in furtherance of a conspiracy.

[103] The admission of such evidence is not easily reconciled with the Court's concern over the "unique potential for prosecutorial abuse" that is presented by the "[i]nvolvement of government officers in the production of testimony with an eye toward trial." *Crawford,* 541 U.S. at 56 n.7. For another recent case open to similar criticism in light of *Crawford, see United States v. Burden,* 600 F.3d 204 (2d Cir. 2010), which held that a confidential government informant did not make testimonial statements subject to the Confrontation Clause when he wore a wire to record a conversation he had with others, even though he knew the conversation was being recorded for use at a criminal trial. The Court of Appeals reasoned that nothing the informant said was spoken for the purpose of making an accusation, but rather to elicit inculpating statements by others present, and that such statements are not remotely equivalent to in-court testimony or its equivalent, and are even further from being formalized testimonial material.

not required by the Confrontation Clause if the one who made the statement "is present at trial to defend or explain it,"[104] even if the witness has only a very limited ability to answer questions about the statement.[105] The Confrontation Clause is also not implicated if a statement is admitted "for purposes other than establishing the truth of the matter asserted" in that statement.[106] Courts must take care, however, to ensure that *Crawford* is not circumvented by allowing police officers to relate incriminating reports about the accused for the supposed purpose of giving the jury so-called "background" evidence about the initiation of their investigation, especially when the reasons for the police activities can be explained without exposing the jury to the details of incriminating reports received by the police.[107]

Hearsay statements admitted as dying declarations apparently pose no difficulty under the Confrontation Clause, even if they would otherwise satisfy the test for testimonial statements, although the issue technically remains an open question.[108] The Court has stated that the Sixth Amendment

---

[104] *Crawford,* 541 U.S. at 59 n.9 ("when the declarant appears for cross-examination at trial, the Confrontation Clause places no constraints at all on the use of his prior testimonial statements"); *see also* United States v. Garcia, 447 F.3d 1327, 1335–1336 (11th Cir. 2006) (the Sixth Amendment does not prohibit the admission of statements if the declarant testifies at trial to the same statement and is available to be cross-examined about it).

[105] United States v. Kappell, 418 F.3d 550, 553–556 (6th Cir. 2005) (no Confrontation Clause violation from admission of statements made by two minor victims of alleged sexual abuse to a psychotherapist because the children both testified and were cross-examined about those statements, even though "they often answered without providing details and were unresponsive to some questions"). *See also* United States v. Owens, 484 U.S. 554 (1988) (right to confrontation satisfied where witness who made identification of defendant out of court appeared in court and willingly answered questions about the statement, even though he had been assaulted and had lost his memory of the event).

[106] *Crawford,* 541 U.S. at 59 n.9; *see also* United States v. Lore, 430 F.3d 190, 209 (3d Cir. 2005) (statements before grand jury by co-defendants of the accused containing "self-exculpatory statements denying all wrongdoing" were not offered for their truth but "were admitted because they were so obviously false"). For example, statements by a government informant in a recorded conversation with the accused are not hearsay or testimonial evidence subject to *Crawford* if they are admitted not to prove the truth of what that witness said but only to give the jury an intelligible context for the portions of the recording containing the defendant's statements. United States v. Tolliver, 454 F.3d 660, 665 (7th Cir. 2006); United States v. Hansen, 434 F.3d 92, 100 (1st Cir. 2006); United States v. Walter, 434 F.3d 30, 35 (1st Cir. 2006); United States v. Jimenez, 419 F.3d 34, 44 (1st Cir. 2005).

[107] United States v. Maher, 454 F.3d 13, 22–23 (1st Cir. 2006) (cautioning lower courts about the risk of reversal from the improper admission of hearsay on this theory, even if it is accompanied by an instruction to the jury that such evidence is not admitted for its truth). *See also* Duane, *Arresting Officers and Treating Physicians: When May a Witness Testify to What Others Told Him for the Purpose of Explaining His Conduct?*, 18 REGENT UNIV. L. REV. 229 (2005–2006).

[108] In federal court, this exception is codified as "statements under the belief of imminent death." *See* Rule 804(b)(2).

"is most naturally read as a reference to the right of confrontation at common law, admitting only those exceptions established at the time of the founding,"[109] and noted that the hearsay exception for dying declarations was established at common law beyond dispute.[110] But the Court has not yet decided "whether the Sixth Amendment incorporates an exception for testimonial dying declarations," noting only that "[i]f this exception must be accepted on historical grounds, it is *sui generis.*"[111] In many cases this difficult constitutional issue will fortunately be moot, either because the dying declaration was not testimonial[112] or because the defendant obtained "the absence of [the] witness by wrongdoing,"[113] which "extinguishes confrontation claims on essentially equitable grounds."[114]

Regardless of whether a hearsay statement is offered as a dying declaration or under some other hearsay exception, an accused may not assert the denial of the right to confront a witness if the unavailability of that witness was caused by the accused's own wrongdoing. In keeping with the venerable legal maxim that no man shall profit by his own wrong, the accused forfeits any constitutional objection to a hearsay statement under the doctrine of "forfeiture by wrongdoing"[115] if the trial judge concludes that the accused sought "to undermine the judicial process by procuring or coercing silence from witnesses" or otherwise obtained "the absence of the witness by

---

[109] *Crawford v. Washington,* 541 U.S. 36, 54 (2004).

[110] *Crawford,* 541 U.S. at 56 n.6.

[111] *Id. See also* Michigan v. Bryant, 562 U.S. —, 131 S. Ct. 1143, 179 L. Ed. 2d 93, 103 n.1 (2011) (again suggesting, without deciding, that "dying declarations, even if testimonial, might be admissible as a historical exception to the Confrontation Clause.")

[112] Without deciding the matter, the Court has stated that "many dying declarations may not be testimonial," *Crawford,* 541 U.S. at 56 n.6, and has held that nontestimonial hearsay statements are "not subject to the Confrontation Clause." *Davis,* 547 U.S. at 821. The Court did not say when a dying declaration would be nontestimonial, although the most likely case would presumably be a person who is describing the cause of his or her imminent death not to a police officer but in confidence to a friend, or a person who is blaming the imminent death on the accidental actions of a loved one (and who therefore would be less likely to wish or foresee that the statement would end up being used in a criminal prosecution).

[113] *Davis,* 547 U.S. at 833.

[114] *Id.* (quoting *Crawford,* 541 U.S. at 62). A dying declaration is admissible in a criminal case only if the prosecution is for homicide, the statement concerns the cause or circumstances of the declarant's imminent death, and the witness is deceased or otherwise unavailable by the time of trial. *See* Rule 804(b)(2). Any time all three of those conditions are true of hearsay offered against the accused by a prosecutor, it will always be the case that the defendant "wrongfully caused — or acquiesced in wrongfully causing — the declarant's unavailability as a witness, and did so intending that result" Rule 804(b)(6), as long as it can also be proved that the murder was committed for the purpose of preventing that witness from testifying. *See* Giles v. California, 554 U.S. 353 359 (2008). Rule 804(b)(6).

[115] *Crawford,* 541 U.S. at 62.

wrongdoing."[116] This is not technically an exception to the Confrontation Clause, but a doctrine that "extinguishes confrontation claims on essentially equitable grounds."[117] Consequently, when a hearsay statement is admitted against the accused under this doctrine, it makes no difference whether the statement is testimonial.[118] Before a statement can be admitted against the accused under this doctrine, however, the prosecution must be able to demonstrate by a preponderance of the evidence that the accused intentionally "engaged in conduct *designed* to prevent the witness from testifying."[119] This constitutional doctrine avoids the creation of "an intolerable incentive for defendants to bribe, intimidate, or even kill witnesses against them."[120] Such a finding may be supported, in appropriate cases, by evidence that the accused had committed "domestic violence," including "[e]arlier abuse, or threats of abuse, intended to dissuade the victim from resorting to outside help," or other conduct "designed to prevent testimony to police officers or cooperation in criminal prosecutions."[121] But without evidence of such an intent, testimonial hearsay is not admissible under the doctrine of "forfeiture by wrongdoing," even if the accused committed some wrongdoing that did in fact intentionally cause some individual to become unavailable, where the accused "had not done so to prevent the person from testifying — as in the

---

[116] *Davis,* 547 U.S. at 833.

[117] *Id.* (quoting *Crawford,* 541 U.S. at 62). In federal court, this requires a showing that the accused "wrongfully caused — or acquiesced in wrongfully causing — the declarant's unavailability as a witness, and did so intending that result." Rule 804(b)(6); *see* § 804.33, *infra.*

[118] Moreover, for the same reason, a defendant who causes a witness to become unavailable also forfeits the right to seek the admission of hearsay statements by that witness under any exception conditioned upon a showing that the witness is unavailable. *See* § 804.8, *infra.*

[119] Giles v. California, 554 U.S. 353, 359 (2008). This conclusion, the central holding in *Giles,* thereby overruled a number of earlier cases which had concluded that even testimonial statements can be admitted under the Sixth Amendment any time the accused intentionally killed the declarant, even if he had not done so for the purpose of preventing that victim from testifying against him. *E.g.,* United States v. Garcia-Meza, 403 F.3d 364, 370–371 (6th Cir. 2005).

[120] *Giles,* 554 U.S. at 365.

[121] *Id.,* 554 U.S. at 377. The Court in *Giles* held that such evidence of abuse could be sufficient to support a finding that the abuser had in fact acted with the requisite intent "to prevent the witness from testifying" when he later made her unavailable by killing her, thereby making her unable to testify about the abuse committed *before* her unavailability. The Court did not explicitly discuss whether domestic abuse can also support such a finding when the abuse victim is still *alive* at the time of his trial, perhaps on charges for that very abuse, but unwilling or afraid to testify because of his intimidation and abuse. That conclusion would seemingly follow, however, from the Court's desire to eliminate any incentive for criminals to "bribe, *intimidate,* or even kill witnesses against them." *Id.,* 554 U.S. at 365 (emphasis added); *cf.* Rule 804(a)(2) (a witness may be "unavailable" if he or she persists in refusing to testify despite a court order to do so).

typical murder case involving accusatorial statements by the victim."[122]

Which criminal cases will be most affected by the new constitutional standard established by *Crawford* and *Davis*? It may be too early to predict with certainty, but those cases will almost surely have the greatest impact on the admissibility of statements in three classes of cases: (1) testimonial reports to the police that were admitted under the exceptions for present sense impressions and excited utterances,[123] and (2) testimonial confessions, including guilty pleas, that formerly were admitted under the hearsay exception for statements against the interest of the declarant,[124] and (3) laboratory reports and other documents prepared for use at trial by forensic scientists or other government investigators, admitted under some version of the hearsay exception for public records and reports.[125] In almost every federal case decided since *Crawford* in which some statement was held to have been erroneously admitted in violation of the Confrontation Clause, the statement was admitted under one of these hearsay exceptions.[126] These are the cases in which defense counsel must now be especially vigilant to watch for a possible constitutional objection.

After *Crawford* and *Davis,* it is now more vital than ever for criminal defense attorneys to plainly state on the record that they object to the admission of hearsay under both the hearsay rules and the Sixth Amendment. To preserve a claim under *Crawford* for appeal, it is not sufficient for

---

[122] *Giles,* 554 U.S. at 365; *see also id.* 554 U.S. at 368 (noting the inapplicability of this exception to "the innumerable cases in which the defendant was on trial for killing the victim, but was not shown to have done so for the purpose of preventing testimony"). The reasons why this exception does not routinely apply to most typical murder prosecutions are discussed more fully in § 804.33, *infra.*

[123] *See* Rule 803(1) and (2). These are the two hearsay exceptions most frequently invoked to justify the admission of statements to the police by crime victims and witnesses, including *Michigan v. Bryant,* 562 U.S. —, 131 S. Ct. 1143, 179 L. Ed. 2d 93 (2011), and the two companion cases decided by the Court in *Davis v. Washington,* 547 U.S. 813 (2006).

[124] *See* Rule 804(b)(3). This is the hearsay exception most frequently invoked to justify the admission of incriminating statements and confessions made by the defendant's codefendants, conspirators, and other criminal suspects after their arrest, as the prosecutor did at trial in *Crawford.*

[125] *See* Rule 803(8) and (10). These are the hearsay exceptions that were used to justify the admission of lab reports against the defendants in *Bullcoming v. New Mexico,* 564 U.S. —, 131 S. Ct. 2705, 180 L. Ed. 2d 610 (2011), and *Melendez-Diaz v. Massachusetts,* 557 U.S. —, 129 S. Ct. 2527, 174 L. Ed. 2d 314 (2009).

[126] Of course, even before *Crawford,* many of the most plainly "testimonial" statements admitted in criminal cases were admitted under the exception for "former testimony," Rule 804(b)(1), but those cases will not be affected by *Crawford,* since that hearsay exception already requires a showing that the witness was unavailable and that the accused had an adequate opportunity for cross-examination. In the wake of *Crawford* and *Davis,* it is safe to assume that virtually all testimonial hearsay statements in federal court will now be admitted either under Rule 804(b)(1) or not at all.

defense counsel to object merely that the evidence is inadmissible as "hearsay"; such an objection is not sufficient to preserve a constitutional challenge to that evidence under the Confrontation Clause.[127] And in state court, the defense attorney who merely objects on hearsay grounds, or even on state constitutional grounds, has probably forfeited the right to federal review of any claim that the evidence was admitted in violation of the Confrontation Clause, either on direct appeal to the Supreme Court[128] or on a petition for habeas corpus.[129] These preservation of error rules were especially harsh before *Crawford,* because under *Roberts* a trial judge's ruling on a hearsay objection would virtually never change merely because the defendant also threw in an objection under the Confrontation Clause. But these rules make more sense after *Crawford,* because now, for the first time in decades, a statement will often be inadmissible in a criminal case under *Crawford* even if its admission would otherwise be perfectly proper under the hearsay rules.

Because the Confrontation Clause applies only to criminal prosecutions, federal appeals courts have been unanimous in holding that *Crawford* does not apply to supervised release revocation proceedings,[130] criminal sentencing proceedings,[131] or civil forfeiture proceedings brought by the Govern-

---

[127] United States v. Arbolaez, 450 F.3d 1283, 1291 n.8 (11th Cir. 2006); United States v. Baker, 432 F.3d 1189, 1206 n.12 (11th Cir. 2005); United States v. Hadley, 431 F.3d 484, 498 & n.8 (6th Cir. 2005); United States v. Chau, 426 F.3d 1318, 1321–1322 (11th Cir. 2005); United States v. Luciano, 414 F.3d 174, 178 (1st Cir. 2005); United States v. Dukagjini, 326 F.3d 45, 60 (2d Cir. 2003); United States v. LaHue, 261 F.3d 993, 1009 (10th Cir. 2001); Greer v. Mitchell, 264 F.3d 663, 689 (6th Cir. 2001); *but see* United States v. Summers, 414 F.3d 1287, 1297 n.7 (10th Cir. 2005) (even though most of the trial discussion over defense objection centered on the hearsay rules, defense counsel adequately preserved Sixth Amendment objection for appeal because he "repeatedly emphasiz[ed] his inability to cross-examine" the declarant).

[128] The Supreme Court will not consider a federal claim preserved for direct appeal on a petition for a writ of certiorari if the defendant in state court merely made a constitutional objection without specifying whether he was referring to the state or federal constitution. Howell v. Mississippi, 543 U.S. 440 (2005).

[129] A federal district court cannot grant a writ of habeas corpus under 28 U.S.C. § 2254 unless the federal nature of a constitutional claim was fairly presented to both the trial and appellate courts in the state court system. Baldwin v. Reese, 541 U.S. 27 (2004); Duncan v. Henry, 513 U.S. 364, 365–366 (1995) (defendant convicted in state court cannot obtain federal habeas corpus review of claim that evidence was admitted in violation of the United States Constitution where he only raised a "similar" claim of a violation of state evidence law; exhaustion of state remedies requirement means that state courts "surely must be alerted to the fact that prisoners are asserting claims under the United States Constitution.")

[130] United States v. Kelley, 446 F.3d 688, 690 (7th Cir. 2006); United States v. Williams, 443 F.3d 35, 45 (2d Cir. 2006); United States v. Rondeau, 430 F.3d 44, 47–48 (1st Cir. 2005); United States v. Hall, 419 F.3d 980, 985 (9th Cir. 2005); United States v. Kirby, 418 F.3d 621, 627 (6th Cir. 2005).

[131] United States v. Paull, 551 F.3d 516, 527–528 (6th Cir. 2009); United States v. Miller,

ment.[132]

§ 801.3   Definition of a Statement

Rule 801(a) provides the definition of a "statement." Because the definition of hearsay in Rule 801(c) comprehends out-of-court "statements," evidence that does not meet the definition of a statement cannot constitute hearsay. Rule 801(a) defines a statement for hearsay purposes as either an oral or written assertion, or conduct of a person that is intended to be an assertion.[133]

Any oral statement made outside of the courtroom that is reported by a witness on the stand is a statement under Rule 801(a). Likewise, documentary evidence contains out-of-court statements. It is important to remember, however, that not all oral or written out-of-court statements are hearsay. Whether an out-of-court statement is hearsay and presumptively inadmissible is determined by Rule 801(c). Also, where an out-of-court statement does fall within the definition of Rule 801(c), it may nevertheless be admissible pursuant to an exception to the basic definition or the exclusionary rule or pursuant to other bases identified in Rule 802.[134]

According to Rule 801(a), certain nonverbal conduct may be a statement. Many nonverbal signals are obviously the equivalent of words for the purposes of communication. Nodding, pointing, and the sign language of the hearing impaired are plainly assertive conduct that is the equivalent of spoken words. Such conduct may be hearsay if the requirements of Rule 801(c) are satisfied.[135] The same result would have been reached under

---

450 F.3d 270, 273–274 (7th Cir. 2006); United States v. Lizardo, 445 F.3d 73, 88 (1st Cir. 2006); United States v. Littlesun, 444 F.3d 1196, 1199–1200 (9th Cir. 2006); United States v. Cantellano, 430 F.3d 1142, 1146 (11th Cir. 2005); United States v. Martinez, 413 F.3d 239, 240 (2d Cir. 2005); United States v. Katzopoulos, 437 F.3d 569, 576 (6th Cir. 2006); United States v. Brown, 430 F.3d 942, 944 (8th Cir. 2005)

[132] United States v. $40,955 in U.S. Currency, 554 F.3d 752, 758 (9th Cir. 2009).

[133] *Cf.* United States v. Tokars, 95 F.3d 1520 (11th Cir. 1996) (trial court properly admitted testimony that defendant's murdered wife had given documents to a third person with instructions to turn those documents over to the police if something happened to her; wife's direction was not hearsay because it was not a statement of fact or assertion offered for its truth); United States v. Alvarez, 960 F.2d 830 (9th Cir. 1992) ("Garnika, Spain" inscription on a pistol was not an assertion subject to the hearsay rules although it was relied upon to show the foreign origin of the pistol); United States v. Lewis, 902 F.2d 1176, 1179 (5th Cir. 1990) (questions asked by an unknown caller were "not hearsay because they do not, and were not intended to assert anything").

[134] *See* Rule 802 and Chapter 802, *infra.*

[135] *See* 2 McCORMICK, § 250; *see also* United States v. Caro, 569 F.2d 411 (5th Cir. 1978) (pointing to car as the source of heroin is assertive conduct and constitutes inadmissible hearsay); United States ex rel. Carter Equipment Co. v. H.R. Morgan, Inc., 544 F.2d 1271 (5th Cir. 1977), *rev'd on other grounds,* 554 F.2d 164 (5th Cir. 1977) (initialing invoices is nonverbal assertion by person signing that signifies that the signor owes money).

federal case law prior to the adoption of the federal rules.[136]

Other types of cognitive nonverbal conduct are more difficult to characterize as statements. The conduct of a person may reflect his or her belief, and in certain situations a person's belief, circumstantially established by the conduct, might be relevant in a particular case. Early case law often found conduct, relevant in circumstantially reflecting belief, to be hearsay. The classic case of *Wright v. Doe d'Tatham*,[137] held that whenever conduct is relevant in reflecting belief, hearsay communications exist because the belief should be subjected to the safeguards of cross-examination, oath, and opportunity for observation of demeanor.[138] In *Tatham,* the proponent sought to establish the testator's competence by introducing into evidence several letters to the testator that were written by persons deceased at the time of the trial, under the theory that the matters discussed in the letters and their general tone demonstrated the writers' belief that the testator was sane.[139] The House of Lords found that the letters contained inadmissible hearsay because the writers' actions in sending such letters were implied assertions that the testator was mentally competent. Consequently, according

---

[136] United States v. Nakaladski, 481 F.2d 289 (5th Cir. 1973) (can be inferred from court's comments that defendant's smile coupled with silence amounted to an assertion; silence and smile were admissible as a party admission); United States v. Ross, 321 F.2d 61 (2d Cir. 1963) (pointing to a list of identifying numbers was a communication; error in admitting hearsay was not prejudicial in context of case).

[137] Wright v. Doe d'Tatham, 112 Eng. R. 488 (1837).

[138] *See* § 801.1, *supra. See generally,* 2 McCORMICK, § 250; Weissenberger, *Unintended Implications of Speech and the Definition of Hearsay,* 65 TEMPLE L. REV. 857 (1993); Weissenberger, *Hearsay Puzzles: An Essay on Federal Evidence Rule 803(3),* 64 TEMPLE L. REV. 145 (1991); *see also* United States v. Groce, 682 F.2d 1359 (11th Cir. 1982) (markings on map supposedly showing the course of a shrimping vessel allegedly used in conspiracy to smuggle marijuana into the United States were not intended as assertions and thus did not constitute inadmissible hearsay); United States v. Ariza-Ibarra, 605 F.2d 1216 (1st Cir. 1979) (in prosecution for conspiracy to possess and distribute cocaine, district court erred in admitting evidence that informant, whose tip led to the arrest of defendants, previously had provided information leading to successful prosecution of drug offenders; evidence of informant's past ability to identify drug offenders was tantamount to hearsay statement that he believed defendants were guilty); United States v. Zenni, 492 F. Supp. 464 (E.D. Ky. 1980) (in prosecution for illegal bookmaking activities, statement of unknown persons telephoning their bets to defendant's establishment were admissible as implied assertions of caller's belief that bets could be placed at the premise's telephone; statements were not admissible hearsay because callers did not intend to make an assertion about the fact sought to be proved). In the *Zenni* decision, Judge Bertelsman provides a particularly helpful analysis of the contemporary application of the *Wright v. Doe d'Tatham* doctrine. As illustrated by Judge Bertelsman's analysis, the definition of hearsay under Rule 801 renders all "implied assertions" to be non-hearsay even where such "implied assertions" are verbal. Accordingly, no statement is offered for its truth where the declarant does not intend to assert conclusions or beliefs merely implied by the declarant's out-of-court statement. *See* § 801.6, *infra,* for a discussion of *Zenni.*

[139] Wright v. Doe d'Tatham, 112 Eng. R. 488 (1837).

to the House of Lords, the sending of such letters should be treated the same as an express declaration of the testator's sanity.[140] In the course of the opinion, several other examples of implied assertions barred by the hearsay rule were given, including: (1) proof that underwriters paid the amount of the policy as evidence of the loss of a ship; (2) proof that a person was elected to office as evidence of his sanity; (3) proof that a wager was paid as evidence that the event that was the subject of the bet occurred; (4) proof that the deceased captain embarked in a ship with his family after conducting an inspection of the ship as evidence that the ship was seaworthy.[141]

Early cases generally followed the reasoning of the *Tatham* decision, providing that the court in question even recognized the hearsay issue.[142] The modern trend, however, in accord with the views of most commentators, is to find a statement in conduct only when the actor subjectively intended to make an assertion.[143] As McCormick observed, in the examples set forth in *Tatham* as well as the facts of the case itself, the actor did not intend to make an assertion by his or her conduct, and therefore the hearsay risk of insincerity is minimized.[144] Although the risks of errors in perception, memory, and narration still exist, the reduction of the insincerity risk justifies the admission of the evidence. The Advisory Committee endorsed this rationale in promulgating Rule 801(a), which treats nonverbal conduct as a statement only in those situations where the actor subjectively intends his or her conduct to be an assertion:

> Admittedly, evidence of this character is untested with respect to the perception, memory, and narration (or their equivalents) of the actor, but the Advisory Committee is of the view that these dangers are minimal in the absence of an intent to assert and do not justify the loss of the evidence on hearsay grounds. No class of evidence is free of the possibility of fabrication, but the likelihood is less with nonverbal than with assertive verbal conduct.[145]

Under Rule 801, whether conduct may be a statement depends upon

---

[140] *Id.*

[141] *Id.*

[142] *See, e.g.,* Hanson v. State, 254 S.W. 691 (Ark. 1923); Powell v. State, 88 Tex. Crim. 367, 227 S.W. 188 (Tex. Crim. App. 1921). *See generally,* Falknor, *The "Hear-Say" Rule as a "See-Do" Rule: Evidence of Conduct,* 33 ROCKY MTN. L. REV. 133 (1961).

[143] *See* United States v. May, 622 F.2d 1000 (9th Cir. 1980) (trial court's ruling that photographs were not hearsay affirmed, since they were not assertions); United States v. Moskowitz, 581 F.2d 14 (2d Cir. 1978) (police artist's sketch is not hearsay under Rule 801).

[144] 2 MCCORMICK § 250; *see also* Falknor, *The "Hear-Say" Rule as a "See-Do" Rule: Evidence of Conduct,* 33 ROCKY MTN. L. REV. 133, 136 (1961) ("[if] in doing what he does a man has no intention of asserting the existence or non-existence of a fact, it would appear that the trustworthiness of this conduct is the same whether he is an egregious liar or a paragon of veracity").

[145] Rule 801(a), Advisory Committee Note.

whether the actor subjectively intended to make a communicative assertion.[146] Where evidence of conduct is offered on the theory that it is not intended by the actor as an assertion, and consequently not excludable under the hearsay system, the burden of showing that an assertion is intended should logically fall on the party objecting to the admission of the evidence on hearsay grounds.

In certain situations, a person may make an utterance that is not intended as an assertion or may make a statement that is not relevant in a way that depends upon the truth of the substance of the words actually spoken. These types of verbal conduct are considered in §§ 801.5–801.10, *infra*.

§ 801.4   Definition of Declarant

Rule 801(b) defines "declarant" as a person who makes a statement. Accordingly, a declarant is a person who makes an oral or written statement or who engages in intentionally assertive conduct. Under the Rule 801(c) definition of hearsay, the declarant is the person who makes the out-of-court statement that is reported or otherwise introduced at trial through a witness or a document.[147]

The use of the word "person" is significant in the definition of a declarant. Under the hearsay system, only a person may make a statement. Accordingly, machine or animal "statements" cannot be hearsay. The trail of a bloodhound, consequently, cannot be hearsay, and likewise, the meter reading on a radar machine cannot be hearsay. As a result, such animal or machine statements are not subject to exclusion under the hearsay system.[148]

§ 801.5   Definition of Hearsay

Rule 801(c) codifies the generally accepted definition of hearsay. Hearsay is defined as a statement, other than one made by the declarant while testifying at the trial or hearing, offered in evidence to prove the truth of the matter asserted.[149] Two key components must be identified in order to apply the definition of hearsay. The first component of the hearsay definition relates to out-of-court statements. Hearsay potentially involves any statement made outside of the courtroom by any person, including a prior statement made by a witness who later testifies. In applying this element of the definition, it is necessary to determine when and where the statement was made. If the statement was made off of the witness stand prior to the

---

[146] *See* 2 MCCORMICK, § 250.

[147] Grimes v. Employers Mut. Liab. Ins. Co., 73 F.R.D. 607 (D. Alaska 1977).

[148] *See* Lempert & Saltzburg, A MODERN APPROACH TO EVIDENCE (1982).

[149] *See* United States v. Bagaric, 706 F.2d 42 (2d Cir. 1983) (in racketeering prosecution pursuant to RICO statute alleging international extortion scheme, defendant was not denied a chance to rebut the evidence linking him to planned attack on a certain victim where the defendant's testimony constituted excludable hearsay); *see also* Winans v. Rockwell Int'l. Corp., 705 F.2d 1449 (5th Cir. 1983).

testimony, then the statement qualifies as an "out-of-court statement."

The second element of the hearsay definition provides that the out-of-court statement must be one a party "offers in evidence to prove the truth of the matter asserted in the statement." The application of this element of the definition requires an examination of whether the statement is offered to prove the substance of its contents. If the statement is offered for its truth, then the second element of the hearsay definition is satisfied, *i.e.,* the out-of-court statement is hearsay.[150] Where an out-of-court statement is offered for its truth and determined to be hearsay, the evidence is presumptively inadmissible, and admissibility may only be achieved through the vehicle of an exception to the basic definition, an exception to the exclusionary rule, or some other basis identified in Rule 802.

Not all out-of-court statements are relevant in a lawsuit in a manner that relies upon their truthfulness. When an out-of-court statement is relevant in a manner that does not depend upon the truth of the statement, the out-of-court statement is not hearsay under the Rule 801(c) definition, and consequently, the exclusionary rule does not apply.[151]

---

[150] United States v. Davis, 596 F.3d 852 (D.C. Cir. 2010) (when man was accused of fraud by using fraternity funds for his personal purposes, the trial judge properly precluded him from offering bills that he had prepared to supposedly show the reason for the payments; a bill is hearsay if it is offered to prove the truth and the accuracy of the representation on its face as to what work was performed and for what purpose).

[151] Of course, the purpose in offering the evidence must be relevant according to the substantive law in the particular lawsuit. *See* § 401.1 *et seq., supra; see also* United States v. Aguwa, 123 F.3d 418 (6th Cir. 1997) (declarant's statements properly admitted as non-hearsay where they were offered to provide background information explaining how and why agents began their investigation of the defendant); United States v. Lis, 120 F.3d 28 (4th Cir. 1997) (in prosecution for embezzlement, the defendant attempted to rebut association that her expenses exceeded her income by introducing evidence of a briefcase that contained money she claimed her late husband had received as kickbacks from his clients; the trial court erred in excluding as hearsay columns of numbers totaling the amount of cash in the briefcase that were written in the husband's handwriting as the numbers were introduced not to show the accuracy of the husband's math skills, but to show "a link between [the] husband and the money in the briefcase"); Wallace v. Texas Tech. Univ., 80 F.3d 1042 (5th Cir. 1996) (statements made by the head basketball coach that an assistant coach refused to follow his directions were admissible as non-hearsay in a suit by the assistant coach alleging discrimination in not being rehired; the statements were not offered for their truth, but to show why the coach's contract was not renewed); United States v. Jaramillo-Suarez, 942 F.2d 1412 (9th Cir. 1991) (evidence of a "pay/owe sheet" held admissible as circumstantial physical evidence of drug transactions not offered for the truth of its contents); United States v. Blandina, 895 F.2d 293 (7th Cir. 1989) (in a tax evasion prosecution based on the net worth method, testimony by IRS agents that they had asked coin collectors whether they bought coins from the defendant and the collectors had answered in the negative was not hearsay because it was offered to show that the agents had pursued the defendant's explanation for his assets and not for the truth of the coin collectors' statements); United States v. Koskerides, 877 F.2d 1129 (2d Cir. 1989) (in a tax evasion prosecution based on the net worth method, IRS agents' conversations with the defendant's family were not admitted for their truth but

Sections 801.6–801.10, *infra*, contain analyses of traditionally recognized classes of non-hearsay out-of-court statements. There is no requirement that a particular out-of-court statement must fit within one of these classes in order to qualify as admissible non-hearsay. Nevertheless, these recognized categories are helpful in determining whether a statement should be classified as non-hearsay.

§ 801.6   Implied Assertions and the Assertion-Oriented Approach of the Federal Rules of Evidence

Rule 801(a) defines a "statement" as "a person's oral assertion, written assertion, or nonverbal conduct, if the person intended it as an assertion."[152] Consequently, under the Federal Rules, if conduct is not intended as an assertion, it cannot be hearsay.[153] Likewise, conduct and oral communications intended to be assertive, but offered to prove something distinct from the fact intended to be communicated, are not hearsay.[154] And, of course, where the evidence is not hearsay, it cannot be excluded by the hearsay proscription. This so-called "assertion-oriented" approach of the Federal Rules has usually been thought to be derived from the language in Advisory Committee Note to Rule 801(a).[155]

---

rather to show that agents had pursued defendant's claim of gifts); Gutierrez-Rodriguez v. Cartagena, 882 F.2d 553 (1st Cir. 1989) (in a personal injury action against a police officer and his superiors, plaintiff was permitted to introduce police case files containing at least 13 civilian complaints against the officer with regards to the issue of whether the officer's superiors failed to supervise him; the complaints were not hearsay because they were not introduced to show the truth of the allegations contained in them, but rather to show that the officer's supervisors had improperly ignored an "aberrational number of complaints against him"); Beech Aircraft Corp. v. Rainey, 488 U.S. 153 (1988) (a statement offered under the common-law rule of completeness to prove what the plaintiff had said about the accident six months after it occurred was not hearsay because it was not offered to prove the truth of the matter asserted); Tennessee v. Street, 471 U.S. 409 (1985) (a codefendant's confession was admitted to rebut the defendant's defense that his confession was a coerced imitation; codefendant's confession was not admitted to prove the truth of the matter asserted in the confession but to demonstrate the defendant's confession was not an imitation). *See also* United States v. Toney, 161 F.3d 404 (6th Cir. 1998) (prior consistent statements that are inadmissible hearsay if offered for their truth may nonetheless be admissible to rehabilitate an impeached witness).

[152] *See* § 801.2, *supra,* for a general discussion regarding assertions.

[153] *See generally,* 4 MUELLER & KIRKPATRICK, §§ 373–79; 2 MCCORMICK, § 246; 5 WEINSTEIN'S FEDERAL EVIDENCE § 801.10. *See also* § 801.3, *supra.*

[154] *See generally,* 4 MUELLER & KIRKPATRICK, §§ 485–490; 2 MCCORMICK, § 249; 5 WEINSTEIN'S FEDERAL EVIDENCE § 801.11. *But see* United States v. Palma-Ruedas, 121 F.3d 841 (3d Cir. 1997) (where the defendant offered his greeting "Nice to meet you" to rebut the allegation that he had previously met the person greeted, the trial court did not err in excluding the statement as hearsay because it was offered for the truth of the implied assertion).

[155] *See* Park, *McCormick and the Concept of Hearsay: A Critical Analysis Followed by Suggestions to Law Teachers,* 65 MINN. L. REV. 423 (1981) (assertion-oriented definition of

The contemporary approach to the admissibility of indirect or implied assertions of beliefs under the Federal Rules of Evidence is illustrated by the case of *United States v. Zenni*.[156] In *Zenni*, government agents answered the defendant's telephone on several occasions during the course of their search of defendant's premises.[157] Each caller requested the placing of bets on various sporting events. Charged with illegal bookmaking activities, the defendant objected to the introduction of this evidence on the grounds that the callers' bets constituted hearsay.[158] While the evidence is relevant because it inferentially reflects a belief of the callers that they were telephoning a betting establishment, the district court found that these statements were not inadmissible hearsay because the callers did not intend to make an assertion concerning the fact sought to be proven, that is, that the defendant was a bookmaker.[159] Recognizing that the Federal Rules of Evidence reject the *Tatham* doctrine, discussed *supra* in § 801.3, the *Zenni* court noted that the definition of hearsay under Rule 801 does not include unintended, "implied assertions" even when such implied assertions are verbal.[160]

The drafters of the Federal Rules of Evidence considered indirect or implied assertions to possess enhanced reliability because of the minimized possibility of conscious fabrication by the declarant. Intuitively, it is not difficult to appreciate that an indirect assertion, such as "Put fifty on Lucky Boy to win," is less susceptible to the dangers of deliberate deception than an out-of-court direct assertion, such as the declaration to a law enforcement agent, "Mr. Zenni is operating a book-making establishment." The latter statement is hearsay when offered to prove the fact that it asserts because the declarant is consciously seeking to express that fact. When such intentions are present, the motivations that might compromise accuracy come into play, for example: a desire to frame Zenni; a need to curry favor with the law enforcement officer, etc. When the assertion is indirect, and no reliance is induced or expected as to the accuracy of the belief, accuracy is thought to be more likely.[161]

The assertion-oriented approach of the Rules differs from the common-law approach to such unintended communications. Under the traditional

---

hearsay focuses on whether out-of-court statement will be used to prove truth of what it asserts).

[156] United States v. Zenni, 492 F. Supp. 464 (E.D. Ky. 1980).

[157] *Id.*

[158] *Id.*

[159] *Id.*

[160] *Id.*

[161] *See* Weissenberger, *Hearsay Puzzles: An Essay on Federal Evidence Rule 803(3)*, 64 TEMP. L. REV. 145 (1991); Weissenberger, *Unintended Implications of Speech and the Definition of Hearsay*, 65 TEMP. L. REV. 857 (1992).

common law, implied assertions, even though not intended, were hearsay when offered to prove the truth of the matter impliedly asserted.[162] The common-law hearsay proscription excluded such evidence because the value of the evidence depends upon the credibility of the out-of-court declarant.[163] Such an approach has traditionally been considered to be "declarant-oriented" because it focuses primarily upon the source of evidence in determining its value.[164] The difference between the assertion-oriented and declarant-oriented definitions of hearsay is illustrated by the following example involving a falsehood:

> Suppose that X is charged with committing a crime in Boston. The police talk to X's wife, who tells them that X was with her in Denver on the day in question. The wife's statement is demonstrably false, and the prosecution seeks to use it against X for the inference that X's wife lied because she knew him to be guilty. Under an assertion-oriented definition, the wife's statement is not hearsay because it is not offered to prove the truth of the matter asserted. Under a declarant-oriented definition, however, the statement would be hearsay because the trier's use of it requires reliance on the wife's power of memory, perception, and narration.[165]

Some commentators have argued against the Rules' assertion-oriented approach, proposing instead an analysis that focuses on the derivative quality of an implied assertion.[166] These critics argue that where an implied assertion is derived from a primary statement that is factually assertive, there may be conscious falsification in the primary assertion that in turn contaminates the derivative or implied assertion.[167] An example is the statement, "My Nephew, John, is the most attentive and caring member of the family."[168] If the statement was said satirically, then reliance on an

---

[162] Rice, *Should Unintended Implications of Speech Be Considered Nonhearsay? The Assertive/Nonassertive Distinction Under Rule 801(a) of the Federal Rules of Evidence*, 65 TEMP. L. REV. 529 (1992).

[163] *See* Bacigal, *Implied Hearsay: Defusing the Battle Line Between Pragmatism and Theory*, 11 S. ILL. U. L.J. 1127 (1987); Rice, *Should Unintended Implications of Speech Be Considered Nonhearsay? The Assertive/Nonassertive Distinction Under Rule 801(a) of the Federal Rules of Evidence*, 65 TEMP. L. REV. 529 (1992).

[164] Rice, *Should Unintended Implications of Speech Be Considered Nonhearsay? The Assertive/Nonassertive Distinction Under Rule 801(a) of the Federal Rules of Evidence*, 65 TEMP. L. REV. 529 (1992).

[165] Park, *McCormick and the Concept of Hearsay: A Critical Analysis Followed by Suggestions to Law Teachers*, 65 MINN. L. REV. 423 (1981).

[166] *See generally*, Rice, *Should Unintended Implications of Speech Be Considered Nonhearsay? The Assertive/Nonassertive Distinction Under Rule 801(a) of the Federal Rules of Evidence*, 65 TEMP. L. REV. 529 (1992).

[167] *Id.*

[168] *Id.*

implied assertion that the declarant was fond of John for use in a will contest would be misplaced.[169] In such situations, some commentators suggest, the assertion-oriented approach of the Rules is flawed due to the fact that, even though the declarant did not intend to assert the implied communication, and therefore could intend no falsehood concerning it, the declarant's intent to assert the primary communication can inject conscious fabrication into both the primary and the derivative messages.[170]

A common-sense approach to this problem is to recognize that where a statement that cannot be true or false is used as a basis for an implied assertion, the implied assertion is circumstantially more reliable than hearsay generally, and its admission is justified. Implied assertions are frequently derived from primary utterances[171] that do not primarily assert factual propositions.[172] Such utterances are intended as communications and, thus, are distinguishable from non-assertive conduct. Nevertheless, they are not designed to express or induce reliance on factual propositions of the type usually constituting testimony.[173] These statements are often instrumental in accomplishing some end, such as placing a bet: "Put two dollars to win on Paul Revere in the third at Pimlico." Intuitively, it appears that utterances in this category are not infected with defects of insincerity because the declarant intends to accomplish something other than making a factual assertion. Consequently, the notion of conscious or intentional insincerity has no meaning in the context of this class of utterances unless the analysis is strained to entertain the extremely rare possibility that it is the implied message that is sought to be misleading. After all, anything verbal can be used as a basis for deception or insincerity.[174] Nevertheless, certain

---

[169] *Id.*

[170] *Id. See generally,* Tribe, *Triangulating Hearsay,* 87 HARV. L. REV. 957 (1974) (discussion of the defects that may compromise the accuracy of hearsay).

[171] In this discussion, the term "primary utterance" or "primary communication" is used to denote the utterance from which the implied assertion is derived.

[172] *See* Park, *McCormick and the Concept of Hearsay: A Critical Analysis Followed by Suggestions to Law Teachers,* 65 MINN. L. REV. 423, 447 n.77 (discussing J. L. Austin, PHILOSOPHICAL PAPERS, 235–236 (2d ed. 1970): "Austin discussed what he calls 'performance utterances,' providing as examples 'I do [take this woman as my wife],' 'I apologize,' and 'I name this ship the Queen Elizabeth.' These utterances, he says, 'couldn't possibly be true or false,' and 'if a person makes an utterance of this sort we should say that he is doing something rather than merely saying something'").

[173] 6 WIGMORE § 1788 (it is the use of an out-of-court statement as a "testimonial" statement that makes it inherently untrustworthy).

[174] *See* Rice, *Should Unintended Implications of Speech Be Considered Nonhearsay? The Assertive/Nonassertive Distinction Under Rule 801(a) of the Federal Rules of Evidence,* 65 TEMP. L. REV. 529 (1992). There are, of course, many possible intricate deceptions in any statement intended to be communicative. For example, the declarant of the statement, "Put two dollars to win on Paul Revere in the third at Pimlico," could be aware that a law enforcement officer might intercept the communication, and therefore he might be intention-

types of statements are by their nature not designed to communicate messages that are factually true or false. Where the primary message cannot be consciously infected by a sincerity defect, the implied message possesses enhanced reliability. Alternatively stated, where the primary communication is itself not fact-assertive, the risk of insincerity in the implied message is extremely low.[175]

Using this common-sense approach, it is clear that utterances that cannot be true or false, consequently, provide inherently reliable predicates for implied assertions, because by their nature, the possibility of insincerity in the implied message is very low; the only possibility of insincerity in the implied assertion is where the declarant actually expects and induces reliance on the implied message. By comparison, if the primary message is a factual assertion capable of being false, then "[a]s a chain can be no stronger than its weakest link, implied assertions are no more reliable than the assertions from which they are being derived."[176] Applying this approach to the statement "My nephew, John, is the most attentive and caring member of the family,"[177] if the statement was said satirically, then an implied assertion that the declarant was fond of John would be inaccurate.[178] Consequently, the insincere primary statement, intentionally assertive, may lead to an unintended, yet insincere implied assertion. Any implied message derived from this example is no more reliable than the primary message. Such a primary message is intended to assert a factual proposition, and it is inherently distinguishable from primary communications that are incapable of being factually false.[179]

While scholarly debate concerning the merits of the Rules' assertion-oriented approach makes an interesting intellectual exercise and may impact

---

ally communicating an implied message that might falsely suggest that the place called is a betting establishment.

[175] Examples of such statements include the following:

(1) Primary Communication: "Put two dollars on Paul Revere in the third at Pimlico." The implied assertion is "I am calling a place where bets can be made.

(2) Primary Communication: "Is John at home?" The implied assertion is "I have called [or I am at the door of] the place where John lives.

(3) Primary Communication: "Don't stick your hand in the disposal." The implied assertion is "Disposals can harm your hand."

(4) Primary Communication: "Treat Ralph with penicillin" (statement by treating physician). The implied assertion is "Ralph has a bacterial infection.

[176] Rice, *Should Unintended Implications of Speech Be Considered Nonhearsay? The Assertive/Nonassertive Distinction Under Rule 801(a) of the Federal Rules of Evidence*, 65 TEMP. L. REV. 529 (1992).

[177] *Id.*

[178] *Id.*

[179] Such primary communications include instructions and questions.

the evolving interpretation of the Rules of Evidence, it is important to recognize that the assertion-oriented approach appears to be the predominant position in interpreting Rule 801(c).

§ 801.7   Non-Hearsay, Out-of-Court Statements; Statements Offered for Effect on a Particular Listener or Reader

If a witness testifies that D, an out-of-court declarant, made the statement "A murdered B," and the proponent of the witness is seeking to establish the relevant proposition that A did in fact murder B, the substance of the statement coincides with the matter sought to be proved. Consequently, the out-of-court statement is hearsay and would only be admissible pursuant to one of the exceptions noted in Rule 802. If the purpose for which the out-of-court statement is offered is altered, however, a non-hearsay use of the out-of-court statement may result. Accordingly, where a statement is relevant under the facts and circumstances of a case to show its impact or effect on a particular listener, the statement may be relevant without regard to its truth.[180]

To illustrate, where the relevant purpose for offering the out-of-court statement, "A murdered B," is to show emotional injury inflicted upon a particular listener, *e.g.,* B's spouse, the statement is not offered for its truth. A qualified witness may testify to the fact that the statement was made in the presence of B's spouse in order to substantiate the emotional trauma caused by the out-of-court declarant. Under these facts, the immediate emotional trauma inflicted upon B's spouse is identical regardless of whether the out-of-court declarant is truthful or deceitful in his assertion. All that matters is the fact that the statement was made in the presence of B's spouse. Accordingly, such an out-of-court statement is not hearsay and is not affected by the exclusionary rule.

Statements communicating warnings and notices,[181] and threats to the

---

[180] *See, e.g.,* Barrett v. Acevedo, 169 F.3d 1155 (8th Cir. 1999) (evidence relied upon by experts in forming their opinions, when admitted, is not admitted for its truth but simply to show the basis for expert's opinion, and therefore is not hearsay); *see also* United States v. Zizzo, 120 F.3d 1338 (7th Cir. 1997) (trial court did not err in admitting taped conversation between an undercover informant and unindicted conspirators; the out-of-court statements of the conspirators were admissible under Rule 801(d)(2)(E) and the statements of the informant were admissible to provide a context for the conspirators' statements and show the statements that prompted the declarants' admissible statements).

[181] *See, e.g.,* United States v. Freeman, 619 F.2d 1112 (5th Cir. 1980) (mail fraud prosecution stemming from sale of oil leases that defendant never owned; letter of complaint by investors was properly used to cross-examine a defendant concerning his good-faith defense; it was not hearsay since it was not offered to prove the truth of contents of the letter); *see also* United States v. De Vincent, 632 F.2d 147 (1st Cir. 1980) (in extortionate extension of credit case, evidence that the victim was told that the defendant had been in jail for loan sharking was offered for its effect on the hearer, not for its truth); United States v. Sheehan, 428 F.2d 67 (8th Cir. 1970); United States v. Press, 336 F.2d 1003 (2d Cir. 1964).

accused to show reasonable apprehension of danger, may fall within this category of non-hearsay, out-of-court statements.[182]

§ 801.8   Non-Hearsay, Out-of-Court Statements; Verbal Acts or Operative Facts

In cases in which words have independent legal consequences, the words are relevant without regard to their truth, and such statements are not hearsay.[183] These types of statements are customarily known as "verbal acts" or "operative facts." For example, if an out-of-court statement made by D, "A murdered B," is offered by A to establish that D slandered A by accusing him of a crime, relevance attaches to the making of the statement rather than the truth of the statement.[184] The out-of-court statement is not offered for its truth, and consequently, it is not hearsay. Another example of "verbal acts" or "operative facts" would be statements that are the terms of an oral or written contract or statements that show that an agreement was made.[185] The law imposes certain consequences in regard to such statements regardless of their truth, and accordingly, such out-of-court statements are not hearsay. Statements also may constitute operative facts in cases involving fraud,[186] entrapment,[187] conspiracy,[188] or extortion.[189] Likewise, statements forming

---

[182] *See* 2 McCORMICK, § 249; United States v. Herrera, 600 F.2d 502 (5th Cir. 1979); *see also* Park v. Huff, 493 F.2d 923 (5th Cir. 1974).

[183] *See, e.g.,* United States v. Southard, 700 F.2d 1 (1st Cir. 1983); Yarborough v. City of Warren, 383 F. Supp. 676 (E.D. Mich. 1974).

[184] If the truth of the statement in the illustration becomes relevant, it would be by virtue of the assertion of an affirmative defense presumably supportive of D's case. The proponent of the evidence discussed in the illustration would be merely seeking to establish that the operative words were spoken; the proponent does not seek to establish the truthfulness of the words.

[185] Mueller v. Abdnor, 972 F.2d 931 (8th Cir. 1992) (in contract dispute, admission of the terms of contract and the accompanying correspondence was not error because all of the documents were admitted to show the existence of contractual terms, not assertions of their truth); Ries Biologicals, Inc. v. Bank of Santa Fe, 780 F.2d 888 (10th Cir. 1986) (the relevance of statements guaranteeing payments was not their truth or falsity but the fact that they were made at all); NLRB v. H. Koch & Sons, 578 F.2d 1287 (9th Cir. 1978).

[186] Itel Capital Corp. v. Cups Coal Co., 707 F.2d 1253 (11th Cir. 1983); United States v. Gibson, 690 F.2d 697 (9th Cir. 1982).

[187] Crispo v. United States, 443 F.2d 13 (9th Cir. 1971) (statements of informer bearing on defendant's entrapment defense should have been admitted).

[188] United States v. Saavedra, 684 F.2d 1293 (9th Cir. 1982); *see* United States v. Alvarez-Porras, 643 F.2d 54 (2d Cir. 1981) (statements were admissible to show defendants' involvement in the conspiracy, where they indicated that she had brought stuff from Columbia and was going to accompany principal in narcotics ring the following morning, since it constituted significant verbal acts made regardless of their truth); United States v. Wolfson, 634 F.2d 1217, 1219 (9th Cir. 1980) ("[w]hen a witness is present at a meeting between a group of conspirators, and they orally, in his presence, agree upon the conspiracy, its objectives, and its modus operandi, the witness's testimony about what each of them said is

the basis for a claim of solicitation under a criminal statute fall within the category of verbal acts or operative facts.[190]

§ 801.9   Non-Hearsay, Out-of-Court Statements; Verbal Parts of Acts

Where the legal significance of an act, considered in isolation, is ambiguous, contemporaneous statements made by the actors may be admissible as verbal parts of the act to clarify the nature of the transaction. For example, the delivery of money may constitute a loan, gift, bribe, or some other transaction. Utterances by the parties that explain the character of their conduct are not barred by the hearsay rule where the substantive law is concerned only with the objective conduct rather than the state of mind or intent of the actors.[191] The statements are not hearsay because they are not offered for the truth of the matter asserted. The truth or falsity of such statements is inconsequential. For instance, a person who uses words indicating the intent to make a gift on delivering money cannot later demand repayment of the money as a loan even if that was his or her true intention at the time of the transfer.[192]

To qualify as non-hearsay, the statement must not be offered for its truth. If a contemporaneous statement regarding an act "makes an assertion about some previous act, condition, or event, it is hearsay to the extent that it tends to prove what it asserts."[193]

§ 801.10   Non-Hearsay, Out-of-Court Statements; State of Mind

Where the state of mind of the declarant is relevant in a lawsuit,

---

not hearsay; it is not offered to prove that what the conspirators said is true, but to prove their verbal acts in saying it"); United States v. Mazyak, 650 F.2d 788 (5th Cir. 1981).

[189] United States v. De Vincent, 632 F.2d 147 (1st Cir. 1980) (in prosecution for making extortionate extension of credit, statement that defendant had been jailed for loansharking and was "pretty bad" was admissible); *see* United States v. Lynn, 608 F.2d 132 (5th Cir. 1979).

[190] *See, e.g.,* United States v. Monaco, 700 F.2d 577 (10th Cir. 1983) (police testimony limited to describing the service that prostitutes had offered and the corresponding prices was not hearsay because it was offered only to show that the encounters between the undercover officer and the prostitutes took place); United States v. Jones, 663 F.2d 567 (5th Cir. 1981) (in prosecution for threats against judge and prosecutor, court properly permitted sections of transcripts to be read to jury because the statements contained "operative words of this criminal action"). *See generally,* 6 WIGMORE, § 1766.

[191] Bank v. Kennedy, 84 U.S. (17 Wall.) 19, 21 L. Ed. 554 (1873); *see* United States v. Romano, 684 F.2d 1057 (2d Cir. 1982) (requests to give money to the "boys in the union" was evidence admissible as utterances contemporaneous with independently admissible non-verbal act of picking up the money); United States v. Jackson, 588 F.2d 1046 (5th Cir. 1979) (witness permitted to testify, since court classified statements made as non-hearsay statements under Rule 801(c) — utterances made contemporaneously with a non-verbal act for the purpose of throwing light on it); *cf.* United States v. Abascal, 564 F.2d 821 (9th Cir. 1977).

[192] Morgan, *A Suggested Classification of Utterances Admissible as Res Gestae,* 31 YALE L.J. 229 (1922).

[193] 4 MUELLER & KIRKPATRICK, §§ 385–390.

out-of-court statements of the declarant that do not directly assert the state of mind are not offered for their truth.

To illustrate, if a child makes the out-of-court statement, "My father, A, murdered B," this out-of-court statement may be relevant in a particular case in a manner that does not rely upon the truth of the matter asserted, *i.e.*, the fact of the purported murder.[194] Rather it might be reported by a witness on the stand in order to demonstrate the state of mind of the child where this state of mind is relevant, *e.g.*, in a custody proceeding. Where such fear or antipathy is relevant, the proponent of the out-of-court statement may be seeking to establish antipathy to, or the fear of the father by the child, circumstantially reflected in the child's statement. Consequently, the out-of-court statement would not be offered for its truth, and it would be admissible as a non-hearsay out-of-court statement.[195]

Similarly, statements of an out-of-court declarant that manifest the declarant's insanity are not offered for their truth and are consequently not hearsay. Accordingly, in the classic example, if the out-of-court declarant states that he is Napoleon Bonaparte, such statement is not offered to establish the truth of the assertion, *i.e.*, that the declarant is Napoleon. Rather, the out-of-court, non-hearsay statement is offered as a manifestation of the declarant's deranged mental state.[196]

§ 801.11   Non-Hearsay, Out-of-Court Statements; Prior Inconsistent Statements Used for Impeachment Purposes

Prior inconsistent statements offered only for impeachment pursuant to the technique of self-contradiction are operatively not hearsay because of the limiting instructions that accompany such statements.[197] Such statements are admissible for the limited purpose of affecting the credibility of the witness sought to be impeached. Accordingly, a witness who testifies at trial that "X murdered B" may be impeached by his or her prior written or oral out-of-court contradictory statement, "A murdered B." Specific rules govern this impeachment procedure.[198]

When an inconsistent statement is used for impeachment, the contrived

---

[194] *See* Betts v. Betts, 3 Wn. App. 53, 473 P.2d 403 (Wash. Ct. App. 1970).

[195] *See* United States v. West, 666 F.2d 16 (2d Cir. 1981); *see also* Fun-Damental Too, Ltd. v. Gemmy Indus. Corp., 111 F.3d 993 (2d Cir. 1997) (in trademark infringement case, testimony that the plaintiff's dealers had complained that the infringing product was being sold at a lower price was offered to show the dealer's state of mind as a means of demonstrating consumer confusion, and was not offered to show that the infringing product was actually sold at a lower price).

[196] *See* 5 WEINSTEIN'S FEDERAL EVIDENCE § 801.11; 2 McCORMICK, § 249. It should be noted that where the out-of-court declarant directly asserts the emotion, *e.g.*, "I am afraid," the statement is usually admissible pursuant to Rule 803(3).

[197] *See* ROTHSTEIN, FEDERAL RULES OF EVIDENCE, 240 (2d ed. 1979).

[198] *See* Rule 613 and Chapter 613, *supra*.

but traditionally recognized theory is that the prior inconsistent statement of the witness is not offered to establish the truth of its substance, but rather only to show that the witness is the type of person who makes conflicting statements regarding the same set of facts. Where an out-of-court statement of a witness is offered solely for the purpose of impeachment, a limiting instruction from the trial judge must direct the trier of fact to consider the prior statement not for its truth, but rather only for the purpose of assessing the credibility of the witness.[199] This limiting instruction operates to afford the statement its non-hearsay character and function.

Prior statements of a witness that satisfy an exception for admissible hearsay may be considered for their substantive value, *i.e.*, they may be considered for their truth. Certain prior statements of a witness identified in Rule 801(d)(1)(A) are designated as admissible substantive evidence, and this exception particularly should be consulted.[200] Other hearsay exceptions may also be available to render the statement admissible as substantive evidence as well as for impeachment purposes. Of course, where the inconsistent statement is admissible for its substantive value as well as for impeachment, no limiting instruction is required or appropriate.

§ 801.12 Hearsay and Relevance

Whether an out-of-court statement is offered for its truth depends upon the statement's relevance in regard to the substantive issues of the particular case. Accordingly, the proponent of an out-of-court statement may not appropriately argue, for example, that the statement is offered to demonstrate effect on the listener where notice to the listener or impact on the listener is not a relevant issue in the case. Likewise, an out-of-court statement cannot be offered to demonstrate the state of mind of the declarant unless the declarant's state of mind is properly a relevant issue in the case.

§ 801.13 Rule 801(d)(1) Statements That Are Not Hearsay — A Declarant-Witness's Prior Statement

(d) **Statements That Are Not Hearsay.** A statement that meets the following conditions is not hearsay:

  (1) *A Declarant-Witness's Prior Statement.* The declarant testifies and is subject to cross-examination about a prior statement, and the statement:

---

[199] *See generally,* 2 MCCORMICK, § 251. *See also* United States v. Lipscomb, 425 F.2d 226 (6th Cir. 1970). The impeachment technique of self-contradiction is governed by Rule 613 and is discussed at § 613.1, *supra. But see* Sherman v. Burke Contracting, 891 F.2d 1527 (11th Cir. 1990) (where trial court admitted a tape recorded prior inconsistent statement to impeach a defense witness's credibility and defense counsel failed to request a limiting instruction, the court had no duty to give limiting instruction on its own initiative, and failure to give one did not constitute plain error).

[200] *See* § 801.19, *infra.*

(A)   is inconsistent with the declarant's testimony and was given under penalty of perjury at a trial, hearing, or other proceeding or in a deposition;

(B)   is consistent with the declarant's testimony and is offered to rebut an express or implied charge that the declarant recently fabricated it or acted from a recent improper influence or motive in so testifying; or

(C)   identifies a person as someone the declarant perceived earlier.

Under Rule 801(d) certain out-of-court statements of witnesses and parties are excepted from the definition of hearsay.[201] These designated out-of-court statements that are offered for their truth and fall within the basic definition of hearsay, are nevertheless considered to be "non-hearsay" by virtue of this exception to the basic definition. Because such statements are designated non-hearsay, they are not rendered inadmissible by the hearsay system. Under the more traditional approach, admissions of a party are designated as hearsay but admissible through an exception to the basic exclusionary rule. Also under the traditional approach, prior statements of a witness are admissible only under limited circumstances.[202]

---

[201] *See generally,* 2 MCCORMICK, § 251; 5 WEINSTEIN'S FEDERAL EVIDENCE §§ 801.20–801.21; 4 MUELLER & KIRKPATRICK, §§ 402–410; 5 WIGMORE, § 1361; 6 WIGMORE, § 1766. *See also* Bein, *Prior Inconsistent Statements: The Hearsay Rule, 801(d)(1)(A) and 803(24),* 26 UCLA L. REV. 967 (1979); Blakely, *Substantive Use of Prior Inconsistent Statements Under the Federal Rules of Evidence,* 64 KY. L.J. 3 (1976); Graham, *Prior Inconsistent Statements: Rule 801(d)(1)(B) of the Federal Rules of Evidence, Critique and Proposal,* 30 HASTINGS L.J. 575 (1979); Graham, *Employing Inconsistent Statements for Impeachment and as Substantive Evidence: A Critical Review and Proposed Amendment of Federal Rules of Evidence 801(d)(1)(A), 613 and 607,* 75 MICH. L. REV. 1565 (1977); Gooderson, *Previous Consistent Statements,* 26 CAMBRIDGE L.J. 64 (1968); Mavet, *Prior Identification in Criminal Cases: Hearsay and Confrontation Issues,* 24 ARIZ. L. REV. 29 (1982); McCormick, *The Turncoat Witness: Previous Statements as Substantive Evidence,* 25 TEX. L. REV. 573 (1947); Morgan, *Hearsay Dangers and the Application of the Hearsay Concept,* 62 HARV. L. REV. 177 (1948); Reutlinger, *Prior Inconsistent Statements: Presently Inconsistent Doctrine,* 26 HASTINGS L.J. 361 (1974); Silbert, *Federal Rule of Evidence 801(d)(1)(A),* 49 TEMP. L.Q. 880 (1976); Weinstein, *Book Review of Eyewitness Testimony by Elizabeth F. Lotus,* 81 COLUM. L. REV. 441 (1981); Amarin Plastics v. Maryland Cup Corp., 946 F.2d 147 (1st Cir. 1991) (the court decided that there was no hearsay problem in admitting letters of a witness into evidence under Rule 801(d)(1); the prior statements become a part of his or her "oath-supported, court-given testimony subject to cross-examination . . .").

[202] Pre-Rule federal law followed the traditional approach. A witness's own statements were considered hearsay and, unless they fell within one of the very few exceptions to the hearsay rule, were inadmissible. *See, e.g.,* United States v. Gregory, 472 F.2d 484 (5th Cir. 1973); United States v. Cunningham, 446 F.2d 194 (2d Cir. 1971); Mississippi v. Durham,

Rule 801(d)(1) contains vehicles for the admission of prior out-of-court statements of witnesses. The term "witness" indicates that out-of-court declarants must be present to testify at the trial at which their statements are offered such that the declarants are subject to delayed cross-examination concerning their out-of-court statements.

Rule 801(d)(2), considered in a subsequent section of this Treatise, contains vehicles for the admission of out-of-court statements that may fairly be attributed to the parties to the litigation.

§ 801.14   Statements That Are Not Hearsay — Prior Inconsistent Statements

Rule 801(d)(1)(A) pertains exclusively to prior inconsistent statements of a witness used in conjunction with the impeachment technique of self-contradiction.[203] Where the out-of-court statement is inconsistent with the declarant's trial testimony and was given under the penalty of perjury at a deposition, trial, hearing, or like proceeding, the prior statement may be received for its truth.[204] Although the Rule does not offer a definition of inconsistency, federal courts have found statements to be inconsistent where a "reasonable . . . person could infer on comparing the whole effect of the two statements that they had been produced by inconsistent beliefs."[205] The jurors may use the out-of-court statement as substantive evidence and base their verdict upon it. Such statements are admissible because of procedural guarantees of trustworthiness. The prior inconsistent statement was made under oath and the declarant is subject to *delayed* cross-examination and evaluation of demeanor at the trial at which the statement is offered for the purpose of impeachment. Also, since the prior statement was nearer in time to the event at issue, it is arguably more trustworthy than the declarant's trial testimony because "memory hinges on recency."[206]

It is important to note that the substantive use of statements under Rule 801(d)(1)(A) is not restricted to situations where the party against whom the statement is offered had an opportunity to cross-examine the witness at the

---

444 F.2d 152 (5th Cir. 1971); *cf.* United States v. Hill, 481 F.2d 929 (5th Cir. 1973).

[203] *See* Rule 613 and § 613.1 *et seq., supra.*

[204] *See* United States v. Knox, 124 F.3d 1360 (10th Cir. 1997) (prior statements made by participants in mail fraud scheme at their change of plea hearings would have been admissible as non-hearsay under Rule 801(d)(1)(A) if proponent could have shown that the statements were inconsistent with the declarants' trial testimony, both of whom had claimed to not remember if the defendant was involved in the scheme); McMillian v. Johnson, 101 F.3d 1363 (11th Cir. 1996) (affidavits of witnesses constituted inadmissible hearsay and do not qualify as non-hearsay under Rule 801(d)(1)(A)).

[205] 5 WEINSTEIN'S FEDERAL EVIDENCE § 801.21; *see, e.g.,* United States v. Morgan, 555 F.2d 238 (9th Cir. 1977) (there was inconsistency between trial testimony and grand jury testimony, making the latter permissible pursuant to Rule 801(d)(1)(A)).

[206] 2 McCORMICK, § 251.

proceeding at which the statement was originally made.[207] For example, the prosecutor in a criminal case may wish to offer into evidence the grand jury testimony as a prior inconsistent statement. Under Rule 801(d)(1)(A), such grand jury testimony might be available as substantive evidence where offered to impeach the witness who had earlier testified at the grand jury hearing.[208] Because the declarant is a witness at trial and subject to cross-examination, the use of his or her prior inconsistent statements as substantive evidence against the accused does not violate the Confrontation Clause of the Constitution.[209]

Under pre-Rule federal law, a prior inconsistent statement of a witness, whether or not rendered under oath, was admissible only for impeachment purposes.[210] It could not be considered for its substantive value. Accordingly, under pre-Rule practice, where an out-of-court statement was offered to impeach the credibility of a witness, the jury could only consider the prior statement as a basis for assessing the credibility of the witness. A limiting instruction was required to restrict the jury's consideration to the proper purpose.[211]

It should be noted that prior inconsistent statements not conforming to Rule 801(d)(1)(A) are available for impeachment use. Where prior inconsistent statements do not conform with Rule 801(d)(1)(A), such statements

---

[207] *See* Rule 801, Advisory Committee Note.

[208] *See, e.g.,* United States v. Coran, 589 F.2d 70 (1st Cir. 1978); United States v. Marchand, 564 F.2d 983 (2d Cir. 1977) (witness's grand jury testimony that defendant was marijuana supplier was admissible at trial as substantive evidence after witness claimed he could not identify defendant as supplier); United States v. Long Soldier, 562 F.2d 601 (8th Cir. 1977) (where witness made statement before grand jury relating statements made to him by defendant concerning a crime and then denied at trial that conversation took place, grand jury testimony was admissible as substantive evidence); *see also* United States v. Owens, 484 U.S. 554 (1988) (court properly admitted out-of-court statement by victim naming defendant as assailant although victim could not remember seeing assailant; because the victim recalled identifying the defendant, the victim/declarant could be subjected to cross-examination).

[209] As long as a statement is admissible as a prior inconsistent statement or under any of the other hearsay rules, its exclusion is not required by the Confrontation Clause if the one who made the statement "is present at trial to defend or explain it." Crawford v. Washington, 541 U.S. 36, 59 n.9 (2004) ("when the declarant appears for cross-examination at trial, the Confrontation Clause places no constraints at all on the use of his prior testimonial statements"); *see also* United States v. Garcia, 447 F.3d 1327, 1335–1336 (11th Cir. 2006) (the Sixth Amendment does not prohibit the admission of statements if the declarant testifies at trial to the same statement and is available to be cross-examined about it). *See also* § 801.2, *supra.* It must be emphasized, however, that such facts are not always sufficient to get the proponent around a hearsay objection; a statement made out of court is sometimes excluded by the hearsay rules even though the declarant is on the witness stand and available to be questioned about the statement.

[210] *See, e.g.,* United States v. Allsup, 485 F.2d 287 (8th Cir. 1973); United States v. Rainwater, 283 F.2d 386 (8th Cir. 1960).

[211] *See* Rule 105.

are available for contradiction purposes only and the jury must be so instructed.[212] Where the prior inconsistent statement conforms with the requirements of Rule 801(d)(1)(A), the prior statement serves a dual function. It serves to impeach the witness, and it operates as substantive evidence. Consequently, no limiting instruction is necessary.

§ 801.15   Statements That Are Not Hearsay — Prior Consistent Statements

Rule 801(d)(1)(B) applies to prior statements of a witness used to rehabilitate the witness where such statements are consistent with the trial testimony of the witness. Under pre-Rule federal law, such evidence was admissible to bolster the credibility of a witness whose credibility had been attacked, but it could not be used as substantive evidence.[213]

Under Rule 801(d)(1)(B), a prior consistent statement of a witness is admissible as substantive evidence without regard to whether an oath or cross-examination attended the prior statement.[214] However, the witness must be subject to cross-examination at the proceeding where the prior consistent statement is offered, regarding both the trial testimony and the earlier statement.[215]

This subdivision has a narrow application. The exception is only triggered where there has been an express or implied inference of recent fabrication, fraud or improper motive of such a nature that a prior consistent statement would be probative to negate such impeachment. In this respect, therefore, the admissibility of prior consistent statements of a witness is dependent upon whether the opponent opens the door by attempting to impeach the witness.[216] Even after the door is opened by a party who attempts to impeach

---

[212] *See* § 801.8, *supra.* Of course, where offered only for the purpose of impeachment, the statement is subject to a limiting instruction. *See* Rule 105; *see also* United States v. Tafollo-Cardenas, 897 F.2d 976 (9th Cir. 1990) (district court erred by allowing a prior inconsistent statement to be used as substantive evidence where the statement was not given under oath at a trial, hearing, or other proceeding, or in a deposition).

[213] *See* United States v. Scholle, 553 F.2d 1109 (8th Cir. 1977); Comment, *Hearsay Under the Proposed Federal Rules: A Discretionary Approach,* 15 WAYNE L. REV. 1077 (1969).

[214] *See* 5 WEINSTEIN'S FEDERAL EVIDENCE § 801.22. *Compare* Rule 801(d)(1)(A).

[215] *See* United States v. Bond, 87 F.3d 695 (5th Cir. 1996) (trial judge did not err in refusing to allow defendant to introduce prior consistent statement under Rule 801(d)(1)(B) where the defendant was not subject to cross-examination); United States v. West, 670 F.2d 675 (7th Cir. 1982) (error to permit government witness to adduce rebuttal testimony describing prior consistent statement by one of its witnesses, since defense never had an opportunity to cross-examine the witness regarding the statement).

[216] *See* Advisory Committee Note, Rule 801(d)(1)(B); *see, e.g.,* United States v. Williams, 128 F.3d 1128 (7th Cir. 1997) (trial court properly refused to admit prior consistent statement as non-hearsay under Rule 801(d)(1)(B) where court was not convinced that prosecution had expressly or impliedly charged the declarant with recent fabrication and

a witness by suggesting that the testimony may have been the result of some event that gave rise to a motive to falsify or color the testimony, prior consistent statements are not admissible to rehabilitate the witness under this rule unless those statements were made before the event that allegedly gave rise to that motive.[217] The wording of Rule 801(d)(1)(B) indicates that impeachment of the witness must suggest that the witness intentionally changed his or her version of the events before prior consistent statements become admissible as substantive evidence.[218] Attempts to impeach the witness by showing a flaw in memory or narration do not charge him with having "recently fabricated" a statement or acting "from a recent improper influence or motive," and therefore should not open the door to the substantive use of prior consistent statements. The trial court has discretion to exclude prior consistent statements that constitute essentially cumulative

---

doubt existed as to whether the prior statement was made prior to the existence of the motive to fabricate); United States v. Khan, 821 F.2d 90 (2d Cir. 1987) (defense cross-examination implied witness was inconsistent; therefore witness's prior consistent statements were relevant and admissible); United States v. Martin, 798 F.2d 308 (8th Cir. 1986) (where cross-examination strongly implied that government witness was lying, government was permitted to introduce consistent statement); United States v. Lozada-Rivera, 177 F.3d 98 (1st Cir. 1999) (questions to a key government witness about his having gone to school with the defendant's children were not sufficient indication of bias, improper motive, or recent fabrication, to justify admitting the witness's detailed typewritten notes as a prior consistent statement to repair the witness's credibility; convictions reversed and remanded for new trial).

[217] Tome v. United States, 513 U.S. 150 (1995); *see also* United States v. Williams, 128 F.3d 1128 (7th Cir. 1997) (trial court properly refused to admit prior consistent statement as non-hearsay under Rule 801(d)(1)(B) where court was not convinced that prosecution had expressly or impliedly charged the declarant with recent fabrication and doubt existed as to whether the prior statement was made prior to the existence of the motive to fabricate); United States v. Lozada-Rivera, 177 F.3d 98 (1st Cir. 1999) (questions to a key government witness about his having gone to school with the defendant's children were not sufficient indication of bias, improper motive, or recent fabrication, to justify admitting the witness's detailed typewritten notes as a prior consistent statement to repair the witness's credibility); United States v. Toney, 161 F.3d 404 (6th Cir. 1998) (to admit a prior consistent statement to rebut an express or implied charge against the declarant of recent fabrication or improper influence or motive, the declarant must have made the statement before the motive to fabricate or improper influence or motive arose).

[218] *See* United States v. Wilkinson, 754 F.2d 1427 (2d Cir. 1985) (trial court properly permitted government to adduce prior consistent statement where defense implied recent fabrication or improper motive); United States v. Duncan, 693 F.2d 971 (9th Cir. 1982) (where defense counsel implied that customs agent had lied about an admission made to him, trial court did not err in admitting three prior consistent statements by the agent); United States v. Rinn, 586 F.2d 113 (9th Cir. 1978) (defense question to police officer whether the officer had prepared a report indicating a government witness named Neuberger had said that he was able to obtain large quantities of cocaine paved the way for government to establish on cross-examination of the police officer that Neuberger had said he was able to purchase this cocaine from the defendants); *see also* United States v. Herring, 582 F.2d 535 (10th Cir. 1978); United States v. Consolidated Packaging Corp. 575 F.2d 117 (7th Cir. 1978); United States v. Navarro-Varelas, 541 F.2d 1331 (8th Cir. 1976).

evidence.[219]

§ 801.16 Statements That Are Not Hearsay — Statements of Identification

Rule 801(d)(1)(C) provides for the admissibility of an out-of-court statement of identification made by a declarant after perceiving the person identified, where the declarant is a witness at the trial at which the statement of identification is offered. Rule 801(d)(1)(C) does not operate in the context of impeachment or rehabilitation as do Rule 801(d)(1)(A) and (B). Rather, its application is limited to the situation in which a witness is present at trial, and a prior out-of-court identification made by that witness is offered into evidence. Rule 801(d)(1)(C) operates independently of subdivisions (d)(1)(A) and (d)(1)(B) and therefore a prior statement of identification may be admissible even though it does not meet the requirements for a prior inconsistent or prior consistent statement.

Rule 801(d)(1)(C) extends the pre-Rule trend of admitting as substantive proof a prior identification made by a witness who is subject to cross-examination at trial,[220] provided constitutional demands are satisfied.[221] Rule 801(d)(1)(C) will apply to an out-of-court statement identifying an individual in a line-up, a street identification, or even a photographic array.[222] The Rule reflects a recognition that identification in the courtroom is frequently more suggestive and less reliable than a prior identification that is more proximate in time to the operative facts of the case. Courtroom identification has low probative value in light of the inherent suggestibility of the process, and accordingly, where the person who made the prior identification is available as a witness to testify, his or her earlier identification is admissible as substantive evidence.[223]

---

[219] 5 WEINSTEIN'S FEDERAL EVIDENCE § 801.22; *see, e.g.,* United States v. Mock, 640 F.2d 629 (5th Cir. 1981).

[220] *See* Gilbert v. California, 388 U.S. 263 (1967); *see also* Clemons v. United States, 408 F.2d 1230 (D.C. Cir. 1968) (identification at preliminary hearings).

[221] *See* United States v. Owens, 484 U.S. 554 (1988) (discussed further at the end of this section); *see also* United States v. Crews, 445 U.S. 463 (1980); Manson v. Brathwaite, 432 U.S. 98 (1977); Styers v. Smith, 659 F.2d 293 (2d Cir. 1981). *See generally,* § 801.2, *supra* (further discussion of confrontation clause issues).

[222] *See* United States v. Cueto, 611 F.2d 1056 (5th Cir. 1980); United States v. Fosher, 568 F.2d 207 (1st Cir. 1978); United States v. Mills, 535 F.2d 1325 (D.C. Cir. 1976).

[223] *See* United States v. Barbati, 284 F. Supp. 409 (E.D.N.Y. 1968); *see also* 2 MCCORMICK, § 251, at 122–123 ("Admissibility of the prior identification [where the person who made the identification is in court and available for cross-examination] has the support of substantial authority in the cases . . . . Justification is found in the unsatisfactory nature of courtroom identification and the safeguards which now surround staged out-of-court identifications"); United States v. Anglin, 169 F.3d 154 (2d Cir. 1999) (a prior identification by a witness is admissible regardless of whether the witness confirms the identification in court, as long as the witness otherwise testifies and is subject to cross-examination).

Rule 801(d)(1)(C) addresses only whether the hearsay hurdle may be overcome regarding statements of prior identification. The Rule does not purport to address constitutional bases for exclusion that might result from an identification conducted in a manner that would jeopardize constitutional rights.[224]

In *United States v. Owens,*[225] the Supreme Court analyzed the extent of cross-examination required by the Confrontation Clause and by Rule 801(d)(1)(c). In that case, a prison guard was assaulted by an inmate, resulting in a loss of memory. The guard identified the defendant from the hospital three weeks after the attack, but at trial could not recall seeing his assailant. The Court upheld the inmate's conviction, holding that the victim's availability satisfied the cross-examination requirement since he willingly answered questions, despite his memory loss.

§ 801.17   Rule 801(d)(2) Statements That Are Not Hearsay — An Opposing Party's Statement

(d)   Statements That Are Not Hearsay. A statement that meets the following conditions is not hearsay:

***

(2)   *An Opposing Party's Statement.* The statement is offered against an opposing party and:

(A)   was made by the party in an individual or representative capacity;

(B)   is one the party manifested that it adopted or believed to be true;

(C)   was made by a person whom the party authorized to make a statement on the subject;

(D)   was made by the party's agent or employee on a matter within the scope of that relationship and while it existed; or

(E)   was made by the party's coconspirator during and in furtherance of the conspiracy.

The statement must be considered but does not by

---

[224] *See, e.g.,* Kirby v. Illinois, 406 U.S. 682 (1972) (petitioner did not have constitutional right to counsel at police station showup that took place after arrest but before formal charges were made, therefore robbery victim's testimony describing his prior identification of petitioner at showup was admissible); United States v. Wade, 388 U.S. 218 (1967) (where defendant was deprived of aid of counsel at post-indictment lineup, his conviction was vacated pending hearing to determine whether courtroom identification was tainted by earlier illegal identification, thereby necessitating a new trial).

[225] United States v. Owens, 484 U.S. 554 (1988).

itself establish the declarant's authority under (C); the existence or scope of the relationship under (D); or the existence of the conspiracy or participation in it under (E).

Rule 801(d)(2) governs out-of-court statements that may be legally attributed to a party to the lawsuit.[226] Pre-Rule federal law characterized a statement of a party as either an exception to the hearsay rule,[227] non-hearsay,[228] or as a statement not within the purpose of the hearsay rule.[229] While under the codification of the Federal Rules of Evidence, prior statements of a party and statements legally attributable to a party are considered to be exceptions to the basic definition of hearsay, this codification does not effect a substantive change in federal law even in courts that espoused a different pre-Rule rationale for admissibility. The functional result is the same: The out-of-court statement of the party offered for its truth will be admissible at trial providing it conforms to one of the stated exceptions in Rule 801(d)(2).

---

[226] *See generally,* 2 McCORMICK, §§ 254–265; 5 WEINSTEIN'S FEDERAL EVIDENCE §§ 801.30–801.34; 4 MUELLER & KIRKPATRICK, §§ 411–430; 4 WIGMORE, §§ 1048, 1063–1067, 1069–1075, 1078, 1079; 9 WIGMORE, §§ 2588–2594. *See also* Boyce, *Rule 63(9)(a) of Uniform Rules of Evidence—A Vector Analysis,* 5 UTAH L. REV. 311 (1957); Dow, *KLM v. Tuller: A New Approach to Admissibility of Prior Statements of a Witness,* 41 NEB. L. REV. 598 (1962); Falknor, *Hearsay,* 1969 LAW & SOC. ORD. 591; Falknor, *Vicarious Admissions and the Uniform Rules,* 14 VAND. L. REV. 855 (1961); Gamble, *The Tacit Admission Rule: Unreliable and Unconstitutional Doctrine Ripe for Abandonment,* 14 GA. L. REV. 27 (1979); Griffin, *Admissions: A Time for Change,* 20 HOW. L.J. 128 (1977); Heller, *Admission by Acquiescence,* 15 U. MIAMI L. REV. 161 (1960); Hetland, *Admissions in the Uniform Rules: Are They Necessary?,* 46 IOWA L. REV. 307 (1961); Lev, *The Law of Vicarious Admissions—An Estoppel,* 26 U. CIN. L. REV. 17 (1957); Morgan, *Admissions as an Exception to the Hearsay Rule,* 30 YALE L.J. 355 (1921); Morgan, *Rationale of Vicarious Admissions,* 42 HARV. L. REV. 461 (1929); Strahorn, *A Reconsideration of the Hearsay Rule and Admissions,* 85 U. PA. L. REV. 564 (1937).

[227] *See, e.g.,* Dutton v. Evans, 400 U.S. 74 (1970); Sablan v. Territory of Guam, 434 F.2d 837 (9th Cir. 1970); *see also* Morgan, *Admission as an Exception to the Hearsay Rule,* 30 YALE L.J. 355 (1921).

[228] *See, e.g.,* United States v. Rosenstein, 474 F.2d 705, 711 n.2 (2d Cir. 1973) ("[W]e note that the new Federal Rules of Evidence do not classify admissions or coconspirators' declarations as exceptions to the hearsay rule, but rather as statements which are not hearsay"); *see also* WIGMORE, § 1048.

[229] *See, e.g.,* United States v. United Shoe Mach. Corp., 89 F. Supp. 349 (D. Mass. 1950) ("an extrajudicial admission of a party is receivable against him not as an exception to the hearsay rule, but as not being within the purpose of the hearsay rule"); *see also* United States v. Puco, 475 F.2d 1099 (5th Cir. 1973).

§ 801.18   Statements That Are Not Hearsay — Party's Own Statement

Rule 801(d)(2)(A) provides for the admissibility of statements by a party in an individual or representative capacity. An out-of-court statement of a party, offered against the party by the opposing party, is admissible pursuant to Rule 801(d)(2)(A).[230]

Until its most recent amendment, Rule 801(d)(2) referred for many years to "admissions" by an opposing party, but that term was often misleading. While the term "admission" appeared to imply that the out-of-court statement must be a confession or statement against interest, in actuality, any statement by a party is admissible providing it is offered against the party at trial. The statement need not be against the party's interest when it was made as long as the opposing party is offering the out-of-court statement at trial for a purpose that is appropriate in the lawsuit pursuant to the rules of relevance.[231] When the rule went through its stylistic revision in 2011, the Advisory Committee sensibly replaced the word "admissions" with the broader term "statements," noting that "not all statements covered by the exclusion are admissions in the colloquial sense — a statement can be within the exclusion even if it 'admitted' nothing and was not against the party's interest when made."[232]

There is no requirement that the party had first-hand knowledge of the

---

[230] *See* United States v. GAF Corp., 928 F.2d 1253 (2d Cir. 1991) (on divided rationales, the court held that the government's prior Bill of Particulars was admissible as a governmental admission in the current trial); Savarese v. Agriss, 883 F.2d 1194 (3d Cir. 1989) (an admission by a party opponent is admissible even if the party opponent is deceased at the time of the trial). *Compare* Kassel v. Gannett Co., 875 F.2d 935 (1st Cir. 1989) (brief from another case was improperly excluded in its entirety under Rule 403 confusion grounds where the brief was drafted by the plaintiff rather than an attorney, the issues in the two cases were similar and plaintiff's claims in his brief did not purport to be other than his views of what the real world facts were) *with* Hardy v. Johns-Manville Sales Corp., 851 F.2d 742 (5th Cir. 1988) (in an asbestos case, trial court erred in admitting excerpts of the appellate briefs filed by two of the defendants in unrelated cases; appellate briefs refer to what the record reflects rather than what the "real world facts actually are" and therefore would result in prejudice and jury confusion) *and* Vincent v. Louis Marx & Co., 874 F.2d 36 (1st Cir. 1989) (in a product liability suit against a tricycle manufacturer arising out of a collision between the 7-year-old tricycle operator and an automobile, the trial court erred in admitting plaintiff's complaint from an action against the car driver alleging that the driver "did have, or should have had a clear view of the plaintiff" without balancing the probative and prejudicial effect under Rule 403); United States v. Ramirez, 710 F.2d 535 (9th Cir. 1983); *see also* Coughlin v. Capitol Cement Co., 571 F.2d 290 (5th Cir. 1978) (admissions must be offered against, not for, party); United States v. Porter, 544 F.2d 936 (8th Cir. 1976) (distinguishing between statements admissible as substantive and admissible only to impeach).

[231] *See* § 401.1 *et seq., supra.*

[232] Advisory Committee Note to the 2011 amendment to Fed. R. Evid. 801(d)(2). But because the case law interpreting this rule has used the word *admissions* for decades, and because that word still appears in the rules of many states that have modeled their evidence

subject of the statement.[233] The party's admission may be express, or it may be inferred from the party's conduct where he or she intended to make an assertion.[234]

As a general principle, a party may not introduce his or her own out-of-court statement under this rule.[235] While other exceptions might be utilized to admit a proponent's own hearsay statement, the admissions exception is not available because such evidence is not offered *against* the party who made the out-of-court statement.

Statements by a party are admissible not because they are inherently more reliable as a class than hearsay generally. Rather, they are admissible by virtue of the nature of the adversary process. When an out-of-court statement is offered against a party, that party will not be heard to object about inability to cross-examine the declarant, observe the declarant's demeanor, or put the declarant under oath. Obviously, the declarant is the party who would object to the admissibility of the statement; such party will not be heard to complain that the safeguards normally attendant to testimonial evidence are unavailable in regard to his or her own statement. In essence, this doctrine is predicated on an estoppel theory.[236]

When a statement is admitted under this rule, it is admissible only against the party who made the statement, and not against others who are parties to the same case (unless perhaps its admission against the others can be justified under some other hearsay rule).[237] At least in civil cases, this fact frequently gives rise to situations in which the jurors must be instructed that a statement made out of court may be considered by them only in deciding the claims against one defendant but not against the others.[238] But the use of

---

rules on the Federal Rules, this work shall continue to refer to statements admissible under this rule as "admissions."

[233] Mahlandt v. Wild Canid Survival & Research Ctr., 588 F.2d 626 (8th Cir. 1978); Ross v. Salminen, 191 F. 504 (1st Cir. 1911).

[234] United States v. Myers, 550 F.2d 1036 (5th Cir. 1977); Harrington v. Sharff, 305 F.2d 333 (2d Cir. 1962). Where the actor did not intend to make an assertion, his conduct does not qualify as a statement under Rule 801(a) and therefore is not barred by the hearsay rule; *see also* United States v. Barrington, 806 F.2d 529 (5th Cir. 1986) (court properly admitted a letter written by the defendant to the trial judge implying her guilt of the charges).

[235] *See* Rule 801(d)(2)(A).

[236] *See generally,* 2 MCCORMICK, § 254. *See also* Lev, *The Law of Vicarious Admissions—An Estoppel,* 26 U. CIN. L. REV. 17 (1957); United States v. Barrington, 806 F.2d 529 (5th Cir. 1986) (court properly admitted a letter written by the defendant to the trial judge implying her guilt of the charges).

[237] Agere Systems, Inc. v. Advanced Environmental Technology Corp., 602 F.3d 204 (3d Cir. 2010) (in action brought by several companies seeking to recover cleanup costs associated with environmental pollution, proposed stipulation signed by several of the companies was inadmissible hearsay against one company which had refused to sign it).

[238] This is an example of "limited admissibility," in which evidence is admissible against

such instructions is generally forbidden in criminal cases, and the situation therefore much more complicated, because of the Supreme Court's ruling in *Bruton v. United States.*[239] In that case, as in many criminal cases, the prosecution offered evidence of a confession made out of court by one of two defendants who were tried together at the same trial, although the statement tended to implicate both men in the commission of the offense. The statement was of course admissible against the defendant who made the statement under Rule 801(d)(2)(A), but its use against the other defendant (Bruton) was barred by both the hearsay rules and the Confrontation Clause, because the one who made the statement elected not to testify at their joint trial and therefore was not available to be cross-examined by his codefendant.[240] Under these circumstances, the Supreme Court held, the Constitution forbids a trial judge from relying on a limiting instruction to protect the rights of the objecting defendant, because it is too unrealistic to expect jurors to be able to observe a judge's instruction that directs them to not consider "the powerfully incriminating extrajudicial statements of a codefendant, who stands accused side-by-side with the defendant."[241] Consequently, when the prosecution wishes to use evidence of a statement made by one of two codefendants that directly implicates both of them, but which is not admissible against the other defendant under the hearsay rules,[242] *Bruton* requires that the prosecution must either (1) try the two defendants in separate trials,[243] or else (2) redact the confession so that it makes no

---

one party but not against another. *See* Rule 105.

[239] Bruton v. United States, 391 U.S. 123 (1968). Although *Bruton* involved a trial in federal court, the Court's reasoning rested on its interpretation of the Sixth Amendment and is therefore binding on state courts as well. *E.g.,* Gray v. Maryland, 523 U.S. 185 (1998).

[240] This is why *Bruton* cases always involve what is sometimes called the problem of the "nontestifying codefendant." When two men are tried jointly as codefendants and the prosecution attempts to use a statement made by one of them that incriminates both men, the Fifth Amendment right of the declarant to remain silent often comes into irreconcilable conflict with the Sixth Amendment right of the other defendant to confront and cross-examine the witnesses against him. In the relatively rare case in which the declarant chooses to take the stand and is therefore available to be cross-examined by his codefendant about the statement he made out of court, there is no violation of the Confrontation Clause, *see* § 801.2 *supra,* although the use of such evidence against the other defendant may still be barred by the hearsay rules.

[241] *Bruton,* 391 U.S. at 135–136.

[242] Of course, if the statement by one defendant is *admissible* against his codefendant under some other hearsay exception, there is no *Bruton* problem at all, because the statement may be admitted against them both at their joint trial without the need for any limiting instruction at all. *See, e.g.,* PATTERN CRIMINAL JURY INSTRUCTIONS (Federal Judicial Center 1988), commentary to Instruction 37 ("Confession of One Defendant in Multidefendant Trial"), which notes that the instruction is not needed when a statement is admissible against both defendants (for example) under Rule 801(d)(2)(E) as a statement in furtherance of a conspiracy involving both of them.

[243] Obviously there is no *Bruton* problem (or need for redaction) if the two codefendants

reference to, and does not directly implicate, the other defendant.[244] Either of those arrangements is of course desirable from the perspective of the defendant named in the statement, and preferable to the now-forbidden alternative of a limiting instruction to the jurors that they must try to ignore the statement.

§ 801.19　Statements That Are Not Hearsay — Adoptive Admissions

Rule 801(d)(2)(B) provides for adoptive admissions of a party. Pursuant to this subdivision, an out-of-court statement by a person who is not a party is attributable to a party through express or implied adoption.[245] For the

---

are tried separately, for the confession will then be admitted only at the trial of the defendant who made the statement; since the other jury will never learn about that confession, the defendant at that trial of course has no right to confront or to cross-examine the one who made it.

[244] *See* PATTERN CRIMINAL JURY INSTRUCTIONS (Federal Judicial Center 1988), commentary to Instruction 37 ("Confession of One Defendant in Multidefendant Trial"), which notes that the "standard codefendant confession instruction is likely not as important as it once was due to the *Bruton* rule," but that "it is important to have such an instruction for situations in which exceptions to the *Bruton* rule apply, such as with redacted statements." *See* Richardson v. Marsh, 481 U.S. 200 (1987) (the Confrontation Clause is not violated by the admission of a nontestifying codefendant's confession with a proper limiting instruction if the confession is redacted to eliminate not only that defendant's name, but any reference to his or her existence); *but see* Gray v. Maryland, 523 U.S. 185 (1998) (*Bruton* forbids the admission of a confession by a nontestifying codefendant if the only redaction is the replacement of the defendant's name with a blank space, the word "deleted," or similar symbol; *Bruton* does not permit the admission of "statements that, despite redaction, obviously refer directly to someone, often obviously the defendant, and which involve inferences that a jury ordinarily could make immediately, even were the confession the very first item introduced at trial").

[245] *See* United States v. Jinadu, 98 F.3d 239 (6th Cir. 1996) (accusations made by police officer when he was interrogating the defendant were admissible as adoptive admissions where the defendant responded affirmatively to the accusations); United States v. Young, 814 F.2d 392 (7th Cir. 1987) (trial judge properly admitted testimony that co-offender had told defendant about a fingerprint found and defendant had said, "Yeah, I guess it must be mine"); United States v. Champion, 813 F.2d 1154 (11th Cir. 1987) (in trial on drug charges, court properly admitted the defendant's reaction to discussion of an aircraft that crashed while loaded with marijuana; two individuals were discussing the crash, which one attributed to alcohol, when the defendant interjected by nudging the speaker in the ribs and stating that he didn't want to talk about the incident anymore; the court found that defendant's response manifested his adoption of, or belief in the truth of, the other's statement); United States v. Handy, 668 F.2d 407 (8th Cir. 1982) (conspirators were discussing an attempt at killing victim, which ended up resulting in their retreat when a dog attacked; appellant interjected, "Yes, we did"; held to be an adoptive admission); United States v. Murray, 618 F.2d 892 (2d Cir. 1980) (no violation of confrontation in admitting tape of conversation between defendant and unavailable informant; jury was instructed not to consider statements for their truth except to the extent that appellant adopted them); United States v. Giese, 569 F.2d 527 (9th Cir. 1978) ("[n]either due process, fundamental fairness, nor any more explicit right contained in the constitution is violated by the admission of the silence of a person, not in custody or under indictment, in the face of accusations of criminal behavior"); United States

exception to apply, the statement must be offered against the adopting party, and it must be shown that a declarant made an out-of-court statement of which the party was apprised or had knowledge.[246] The party must have comprehended the statement[247] and either expressly acknowledged the truth of the statement or remained silent where a reasonable person would have denied the statement.[248] Whether a reasonable person would deny a statement will vary greatly with the circumstances under which the statement is made.[249] Nevertheless, the federal courts have been reluctant to utilize their discretion to endorse the liberal use of a party's silence as an adoptive admission.[250] As McCormick writes: "[T]he courts have evolved a variety of safeguarding requirements against misuse [of a party's silence as an adoptive admission] of which the following are illustrative. (1) The statement must have been heard by the party claimed to have acquiesced. (2) It must have been understood by him. (3) The subject matter must have been

---

v. Di Giovanni, 544 F.2d 642 (2d Cir. 1976) (direct admissions and adoptive admissions were satisfied by the testimony of cellmate of two defendants in which he related a three-way conversation of defendants describing the bank robbery); Schering Corp. v. Pfizer, Inc., 189 F.3d 218 (2d Cir. 1999) (a survey ordered by the defendant and an analysis of that survey by an employee of defendant was about a matter within the scope of her employment and thus was admissible against the defendant employer under Rule 801(d)(2)(D); her reliance on the survey manifested her adoption or belief in its truth, making it also admissible under Rule 801(d)(2)(B)).

[246] Cedeck v. Hamiltonian Savings & Loan Assoc., 551 F.2d 1136 (8th Cir. 1977).

[247] United States v. Sears, 663 F.2d 896, 904 (9th Cir. 1981) ("[T]he District Court should not submit the evidence of an admission by silence to the jury unless it first finds that sufficient foundational facts have been introduced for the jury reasonably to conclude that the defendant did actually hear, understand, and accede to the statement"); *see also* 2 McCormick, § 261.

[248] New England Mutual Life Ins. Co. v. Anderson, 888 F.2d 646 (10th Cir. 1989) (a newspaper article allegedly based on an interview with the defendant that reported that the defendant conspired to kill her husband was not admissible as an adoptive admission; plaintiff offered no proof that the defendant acquiesced in the article or that it was unreasonable for the defendant to remain silent); Southern Stone Co. v. Singer, 665 F.2d 698 (5th Cir. 1982) (letter written by plaintiff's counsel to individual defendant that purported to relate several statements made by recipient to writer concerning activities of the defendants should not have been admitted, since the circumstances surrounding the letter do not support a reasonable expectation of a response); United States v. Shulman, 624 F.2d 384 (2d Cir. 1980) (in the case of silence courts will consider the incriminatory content of the statement in order to determine whether the defendant actually has adopted the statement by his silence); United States v. Agee, 597 F.2d 350 (3d Cir. 1979) (en banc) (defendant did not remain silent, but made statements to the police that he knew to be false and that he hoped would prevent them from discovering an ongoing crime).

[249] *See generally,* 2 McCormick, § 261 for a comparative discussion of statements made during judicial proceeding, statements made during custodial interrogation, and statements made in contexts totally devoid of state influence or authority.

[250] *See* Note, *Silence as Incrimination in Federal Courts,* 40 Minn. L. Rev. 598 (1956); *see also* Note, *Tacit Criminal Admission,* 112 U. Pa. L. Rev. 210 (1963).

within his knowledge."[251] Absent these determinations, a statement of a third party will not be admitted as an adoptive admission by a party. Of course, there are situations in which a person has a constitutional right to remain silent. Under these circumstances, silence is inadmissible for constitutional reasons, and the question of an adoptive admission is not reached.[252] In any situation in which an adoptive admission is advanced, the burden is on the proponent of such evidence to demonstrate that the adoption was intended.[253]

The admission by acquiescence or adoption is a restricted doctrine applicable only where the statement made by another is reasonably attributable to the party against whom the statement is offered. Foundational requirements should be strictly applied to assure the existence of conditions that establish that the statement of another person is unequivocally attributable to a party. In some jurisdictions this very limited principle has been misapplied and enlarged to create a specious doctrine that provides for the indiscriminate admission of any statement that is merely made in the presence of a party. Such application of the doctrine of admission by acquiescence is totally misplaced, and any misconception concerning adoptive admissions under pre-Rule practice is clarified and rectified by the express provisions of Rule 801(d)(2)(B).[254]

§ 801.20   Statements That Are Not Hearsay — Vicarious Admissions

Vicarious admissions are recognized under Rule 801(d)(2)(C) and Rule 801(d)(2)(D). Under Rule 801(d)(2)(C), a statement that is authorized by a party may be imputed to that party and considered to be an admission for the purpose of the hearsay system.[255] Foundational evidence must establish that the declarant who made the out-of-court statement had express or implied "speaking authority" to make the declarations on behalf of the party opponent.[256] The substantive law of agency governs whether the declarant

---

[251] 2 MCCORMICK, § 262.

[252] *See* Fuson v. Jago, 773 F.2d 55 (6th Cir. 1985) (not only did the defendant's silence not clearly indicate adoption, but defendant could not be expected to react to co-defendant's statements after twice being advised of his right to remain silent); Doyle v. Ohio, 426 U.S. 610 (1976) (the Supreme Court held unconstitutional the use of a criminal defendant's silence after receiving *Miranda* warnings for impeachment purposes); *see also* United States v. Hale, 422 U.S. 171 (1975); *cf.* Moore v. Cowan, 560 F.2d 1298 (6th Cir. 1977).

[253] *See* Rule 104(a) and (b) and Chapter 104, *supra.*

[254] *See* 5 WEINSTEIN'S FEDERAL EVIDENCE § 801.31.

[255] *See, e.g.,* Astra Pharmaceutical Products v. Occupational Safety and Health Review Comm'n, 681 F.2d 69 (1st Cir. 1982); B-W Acceptance Corp. v. Porter, 568 F.2d 1179 (5th Cir. 1978); Securities and Exchange Comm'n v. American Realty Trust, 429 F. Supp. 1148 (E.D. Va. 1977).

[256] *See* 5 WEINSTEIN'S FEDERAL EVIDENCE § 801.32.

had speaking authority.[257]

Rule 801(d)(2)(D) authorizes the admission of a statement by a party's agent or servant concerning a matter within the scope of the agency or employment where the statement is offered against the party-principal or the party-employer. The proponent of the vicarious admission must establish a foundation that demonstrates that the declarant at the time of the making of the statement was an employee or an agent of the party against whom the statement is offered. Statements made before or after the employment or agency has concluded do not qualify as vicarious admissions.[258] Also, under Rule 801(d)(2)(D) the statement of the agent or employee need only be made "on a matter" within the scope of the agency or employment. Unlike pre-Rule law, no express or implied speaking authority need be established on behalf of the agent or employee as is required under Rule 801(d)(2)(C).[259]

Rule 801(d)(2)(D) is the product of a conceptual refinement of older case law that treated the admissibility of an agent's statement under the principle of res gestae.[260] While the resulting admissibility may be essentially the same under pre-Rule and post-Rule practice, the conceptual underpinnings of the res gestae doctrine are totally different from those that support Rule

---

[257] *See* United States v. Saks, 964 F.2d 1514 (5th Cir. 1992) (member of a limited partnership qualified as the agent of another member of the partnership and the first member's statements were properly admitted pursuant to Rule 801(d)(2)(D)); United States v. Sanders, 979 F.2d 87 (7th Cir. 1992) (trial court did not abuse its discretion by admitting a statement by defendant's lawyer pursuant to Rule 801(d)(2)(D) where the court found an agency relationship existed); *see also* Zaken v. Boerer, 964 F.2d 1319 (2d Cir. 1992) (where an agency relationship is shown, it is proper to admit an employee's admission as to a prior pregnancy discharge against the chief executive officer of a corporation); Baughman v. Cooper-Jarrett, Inc., 530 F.2d 529 (3d Cir. 1976) (employee had express or implied authority to speak about why employer was rejecting plaintiff's job application); United States v. Iaconetti, 406 F. Supp. 554 (E.D.N.Y. 1976), *aff'd*, 540 F.2d 574 (2d Cir. 1976).

[258] Johnson v. Weld County, Colorado, 594 F.3d 1202 (10th Cir. 2010) (in sex discrimination action against county employer, the plaintiff could not testify about damaging statements that were made by another man who was hired for the job denied to her. Even though he later became an employee of the county defendant, his statements were not attributable to his employer as statements by a party-opponent because he was not involved in the decision-making process affecting the employment action at issue; he was merely another candidate for the position, not yet a County employee.).

[259] Nekolny v. Painter, 653 F.2d 1164 (7th Cir. 1981); Town of East Troy v. Soo Line R. Co., 653 F.2d 1123 (7th Cir. 1980); United States v. Summers, 598 F.2d 450 (5th Cir. 1979); City of Tuscaloosa v. Harcros Chemicals, Inc., 158 F.3d 548 (11th Cir. 1998) (the standards in agency law need not be applied to demonstrate that an employee possesses "speaking authority"; it is sufficient under Rule 801(d)(2)(D) that the employee's statement relates to a matter within the scope of his employment or agency).

[260] Fairlie v. Hastings, 10 Ves. Jr. 123, 32 Eng. Rep. 792 (Ch. 1804); Vicksburg & Meridian R.R. v. O'Brien, 119 U.S. 99 (1886) (agent's statements are admissible against principal if they are res gestae of agent's acts that would bind principal).

801(d)(2)(D). Where an agent's statement has been admitted on a res gestae theory, the agent's statement must be made at the time of some act then being performed in the scope of the agent's duty.[261] Moreover, the act must be the central, operative fact of the case. Rule 801(d)(2)(D) provides for the admissibility of an agent's statement regardless of whether the agent makes the statement in conjunction with an act he is obligated to perform on behalf of the principal. The statement need only concern a matter within the scope of the agency or employment, and as long as the statement is made while the agency or employment continues, the agent's statement is admissible against the principal.[262]

In 1997, Rule 801(d)(2) was amended, resolving an uncertainty about whether the out-of-court statement by the agent or employee could be utilized to establish the foundational fact of the agency or employment. Under the revised Rule, the contents of the offered statement can be used to help establish that the declarant was authorized to make the statement by the party against whom the statement is offered, pursuant to subdivision (C), or to establish that the declarant was the agent or employee of the party against whom the statement is offered, and that the statement concerned a matter within the scope of that agency or employment and was made within the duration of the relationship, as required under subdivision (D).[263] However, the Rule also makes clear that the contents of the statement alone will not be

---

[261] *See* discussion of Rule 803(1), (2), (3) and (4), Chapter 803, *infra.*

[262] Moore v. KUKA Welding Systems & Robot Corp., 171 F.3d 1073 (6th Cir. 1999) (in a race discrimination action, employee was permitted to testify that another employee told him that a supervisor had told the latter to pass along that some "bad stuff" was going to happen to the plaintiff and that the testifying employee should not get involved if he wanted to keep his job; in a double hearsay analysis, the supervisor's statement made in the course of his employment was not hearsay, as it was exempt under Rule 801(d)(2)(D); the statement of the intermediary employee to the testifying employee was exempt under the same rule, as the supervisor was using him as an agent to pass along a message to the testifying employee); Blackburn v. United Parcel Service, Inc., 179 F.3d 81 (3d Cir. 1999) (on the question of whether the defendant company consistently enforced the anti-nepotism policy under which it alleged plaintiff-employee had been fired, defendant Human Resources Manager's testimony about two sets of relatives employed by defendant company would be admissible against the company under Rule 801(d)(2)(D)). Moreover, the agent need not have personal knowledge of the facts underlying his statement. Brookover v. Mary Hitchcock Memorial Hosp., 893 F.2d 411 (1st Cir. 1990); Schering Corp. v. Pfizer, Inc., 189 F.3d 218 (2d Cir. 1999) (a survey ordered by the defendant and an analysis of that survey by an employee of defendant was about a matter within the scope of her employment and thus was admissible against the defendant employer under Rule 801(d)(2)(D); her reliance on the survey manifested her adoption or belief in its truth, making it also admissible under Rule 801(d)(2)(B)).

[263] The amended Rule thus sides against those courts and commentators who felt that independent proof of the existence of the agency or employment was necessary to establish a proper foundation. *See* 5 WEINSTEIN'S FEDERAL EVIDENCE § 801.33; 4 MUELLER & KIRKPATRICK, § 420; *see also* United States v. Portsmouth Paving Corp., 694 F.2d 312 (4th Cir 1982); City of New York v. Pullman, Inc., 662 F.2d 910 (2d Cir. 1981) (federal

sufficient to establish either authorization or an agency relationship; instead, the contents should be considered in connection with other evidence, including the circumstances surrounding the statement, in determining whether the particular exception applies. The amendment thus serves to extend the reasoning of *Bourjaily v. United States*[264] to subdivisions (C) and (D) of Rule 801(d)(2).

Rule 801(d)(2)(C) and (D) should be interpreted as treating as admissions statements made by the agent to the principal as well as statements made to third persons.[265]

§ 801.21   Statements That Are Not Hearsay — Conspirator's Statements — In General

Rule 801(d)(2)(E) provides that the statement of a conspirator of a party, often described as the "coconspirator,"[266] is admissible against that party if the statement was made during the course of and in furtherance of the conspiracy.[267] In *Bourjaily v. United States,*[268] the Court held that a trial

---

government's funding for subway cars through the Urban Mass Transportation Act was not sufficient to create an agency relationship); Lubbock Feed Lots v. Iowa Beef Processors, 630 F.2d 250 (5th Cir. 1980); Oberlin v. Marlin American Corp., 596 F.2d 1322 (7th Cir. 1979); Federal Deposit Ins. Co. v. Glickman, 450 F.2d 416 (9th Cir. 1971).

[264] Bourjaily v. United States, 483 U.S. 171 (1987). For a more detailed discussion of the *Bourjaily* opinion, *see* § 801.21, *infra.*

[265] *See, e.g.,* Reid Bros. Logging Co. v. Ketchikan Pulp Co., 699 F.2d 1292 (9th Cir. 1983) (anti-trust action; report prepared by employee of company that was shareholder of defendant's parent company, and at the request of defendant's chairman of the board, and presented at a meeting attended by defendant's executives and circulated to offices and mangers was properly admitted); B-W Acceptance Corp. v. Porter, 568 F.2d 1179 (5th Cir. 1978) (corporate plaintiff had authorized its branch manager to testify at first trial; when this testimony was introduced by defendant at second trial it constituted an admission); Kingsley v. Baker/Beech-Nut Corp., 546 F.2d 1136 (5th Cir. 1977) (statements by agent to his principal covered by Rule 801(d)(2)(C)).

[266] The rule actually speaks of a statement made by a party's "coconspirator" — a word almost never used by nonlawyers — and legal writers almost invariably refer to the rule as the "co-conspirator's exception" to the hearsay rule. One of the authors of this Treatise, however, has demonstrated that the rule ought to refer simply to a party's "conspirator," which means the same thing. Because you cannot conspire with yourself, the use of the prefix "co-" here is as redundant and nonsensical as it would be in "co-partner" or "co-brother." Duane, *Some Thoughts on How the Hearsay Exception for Statements by Conspirators Should—And Should Not—Be Amended,* 165 F.R.D. 299, 304–312 (June 1996); *accord,* Friedman, THE ELEMENTS OF EVIDENCE 238 n.22 (2d ed. 1998).

[267] United States v. Wilder, 597 F.3d 936 (8th Cir. 2010) (in drug conspiracy prosecution, defendant could not offer a recording of exculpatory statements he made to an alleged conspirator after the two were arrested and held in police car, because the hearsay exception for statements by conspirators only allows statements to be offered at trial against members of the conspiracy, not by them); United States v. Diaz, 597 F.3d 56 (1st Cir. 2010) (any alleged error in the admission of statements by a conspirator is not preserved for appeal, and is therefore subject to review only for plain error, unless the defendant both (1) asks the court

court may consider the offered hearsay statement itself in making the preliminary factual determinations of whether the conspiracy existed and whether the statement was made in the furtherance of the conspiracy. In reaching this conclusion, the Court discarded the so-called "boot-strapping rule" that had prevented the use of the statement itself to support its own admission.[269] The Court also confirmed that the offering party must establish foundational facts pertinent to Rule 801(d)(2)(E) by a preponderance of the evidence.[270]

Rule 801(d)(2) was amended in 1997. Under the amended Rule, a court can consider the contents of a conspirator's statement in making the preliminary determination as to whether a conspiracy exists between the declarant and the party against whom the statement is offered. This amendment thus reflects the holding of the Supreme Court in *Bourjaily*. However, the amendment also clarifies an issue left unresolved by the *Bourjaily* court, specifically that the statement "does not by itself" establish the conspiracy. The trial court should consider circumstances surrounding the statement, such as the identity of the speaker and evidence corroborating the contents of the statement, in addition to the contents of the statement itself, in determining whether the proponent has proven the existence of a conspiracy by a preponderance of the evidence, as required under Rule 104(a). The Advisory Committee Note explains that every court of appeals that has resolved this issue has also required evidence beyond the mere contents of the statement to establish the existence of the conspiracy.[271] The

---

to rule on whether the declarant and the defendant were members of a conspiracy and whether the challenged statement was in furtherance of that conspiracy, and (2) then makes an objection to the court's ruling).

[268] Bourjaily v. United States, 483 U.S. 171 (1987). *Accord,* United States v. Wilson, 168 F.3d 916 (6th Cir. 1999) (court may consider conspirators' statements themselves when determining the existence of a conspiracy and ruling on the admissibility of the statements under Rule 801(d)(2)(E)).

[269] Glasser v. United States, 315 U.S. 60 (1942), announced the now obsolete bootstrapping doctrine that was later revisited in United States v. Nixon, 418 U.S. 683 (1974). The *Bourjaily* Court held that these cases were superseded by the adoption of the Federal Rules of Evidence, particularly Rule 104(a), which provides that the trial judge determines preliminary issues of admissibility and that the judge in making such determination is not bound by the Rules of Evidence, except those relating to privilege. *See* § 104.1, *supra.*

[270] Bourjaily v. United States, 483 U.S. 171 (1987).

[271] *See* the Advisory Committee Note for the 1997 Amendment to Rule 801. Even before its adoption, it was correctly predicted that this amendment would be "a frivolous little trifle that will have no impact on the way any case is decided in the real world," because in every reported case to consider this question there has always been at least some independent evidence to support the existence of a conspiracy, apart from the statement itself. Duane, *Some Thoughts on How the Hearsay Exception for Statements by Conspirators Should—And Should Not—Be Amended,* 165 F.R.D. 299, 304 (June 1996). Every court to "decide" the bootstrapping issue has done so by way of pure dictum, because there has never been a reported case with no independent evidence of a conspiracy, and there never will be. *See*

requirement of corroboration of course applies only to statements made by a conspirator out of court and admitted under this exception; where the defendant's alleged conspirator testifies at trial and is therefore subject to cross-examination, that uncorroborated testimony by itself may be sufficient to support a conviction.[272]

§ 801.22   Statements That Are Not Hearsay — Conspirator's Statements — Foundation — Degree of Proof

While the Rule is silent as to the standard of proof necessary to satisfy this foundational requirement, the Supreme Court has recently held that the existence of the conspiracy is sufficiently established when, as a foundation for use of the exception, the proponent of the statement has made a case of conspiracy by a preponderance of the evidence.

§ 801.23   Statements That Are Not Hearsay — Conspirator's Statements — When Statement Is Made

Application of Rule 801(d)(2)(E) requires consideration of the status of conspirators' statements made before the party has joined the conspiracy or after he has severed his connection with the conspiracy. It has long been held that statements of conspirators made before a party joins a conspiracy are admissible against him.[273] Nevertheless, it has also been traditionally recognized that once the party terminates his relationship with the conspiracy, or the conspiracy ends, subsequent statements of conspirators are not admissible against the party.[274] At least one commentator sees no logic in the distinction and advocates that only statements made by conspirators while the party is a member of the conspiracy should be admissible against the party.[275]

Another issue frequently arising under this exception is whether concealment efforts exhibit the continuation of a conspiracy such that statements made during the concealment phase are within the scope of the exception. It can be argued that one of the self-evident goals of any conspiracy is to avoid detection, and that consequently, any statement made by a conspirator in the concealment context is admissible against a party who is a member of the

---

Duane, *The Trouble with* United States v. Tellier: *The Dangers of Hunting for Bootstrappers and Other Mythical Monsters*, 24 AM. J. OF CRIM. LAW 215, 221 nn. 17 & 18 (Spring 1997).

[272] United States v. Benson, 591 F.3d 491 (6th Cir. 2010) (the requirement of extrinsic corroboration of statements by the conspirators of the accused only applies to the admission of hearsay statements made by conspirators out of court; where the prosecution produces the live testimony of those conspirators at trial, such testimony is not even hearsay, and so there is no requirement that the defendant's involvement in the conspiracy be proved through "independent evidence" before those conspirators can testify against him at trial).

[273] United States v. Tombrello, 666 F.2d 485 (11th Cir. 1982); United States v. Heater, 689 F.2d 783 (8th Cir. 1982); United States v. Torres, 685 F.2d 921 (5th Cir. 1982).

[274] United States v. Smith, 578 F.2d 1227 (8th Cir. 1978).

[275] 5 WEINSTEIN'S FEDERAL EVIDENCE § 801.34.

conspiracy. In *Krulewitch v. United States*,[276] however, the Supreme Court rejected this argument and restricted the federal conspirator hearsay exception to the duration of the conspiracy's "main aim." The Court reasoned that otherwise the conspiracy would never end. Even if the conspirator's statement is not admissible under the restrictive approach adopted by Rule 801(d)(2)(E), other exceptions in Article VIII may be used as vehicles for admission of the statement.[277]

§ 801.24 Statements That Are Not Hearsay — Conspirator's Statements — In Furtherance Requirement

In addition to showing the existence of a conspiracy and the party's membership in that conspiracy, the proponent of a conspirator's statement must also show that the statement was made in furtherance of the objectives of the conspiracy in order to satisfy Rule 801(d)(2)(E).[278] This requirement reflects prior case law.[279] This aspect of the rule is actually worded a bit imprecisely, because it literally requires a showing that the statement was made "in furtherance of the conspiracy," which would seem to imply that the statement must have actually succeeded in furthering the objectives of the conspiracy. But if the rule were interpreted that way it would lose most of

---

[276] Krulewitch v. United States, 336 U.S. 440 (1949).

[277] *See* Rules 801(d)(2)(B), 801(c), 801(d)(1)(A) and 804(b)(3); *see also* 5 WEINSTEIN'S FEDERAL EVIDENCE § 801.34.

[278] *See* 5 WEINSTEIN'S FEDERAL EVIDENCE § 801.34; *see also* United States v. Howard, 115 F.3d 1151 (4th Cir. 1997) (upholding admission of statement as admissions by a conspirator even though statement was made while the declarant was in jail; "[u]nfortunately, a conspiracy's activities do not always end when some of its members go to jail"); United States v. Williams, 87 F.3d 249 (8th Cir. 1996) (statements made during the concealment phase of a conspiracy may fall within the conspirator rule if the statements were made to enable other conspirators to pursue their common objective); United States v. Alonzo, 991 F.2d 1422 (8th Cir. 1993) (conspirator's post-arrest statement incriminating himself and defendant was not in furtherance of the conspiracy); United States v. McConnell, 988 F.2d 530 (5th Cir. 1993) (trial court erred in admitting a conspirator's statement implicating defendant where the prosecution failed to present evidence concerning the statement's context and the court of appeals could not find that the statement was in furtherance of the conspiracy); United States v. Edwards, 994 F.2d 417 (8th Cir. 1993) (conspirator's statements were properly admitted as in furtherance of the conspiracy even though the conversation also dealt with other topics); *see, e.g.,* United States v. Smith, 893 F.2d 1573 (9th Cir. 1990) (a calendar/ledger, which nine witnesses testified was used by a conspirator to detail cocaine transactions, was made in furtherance of the conspiracy and was admissible against the defendant); United States v. Handy, 668 F.2d 407 (8th Cir. 1982) (court may consider not only the nature of the statements, but take into account the time and circumstances under which they were made in determining whether they were intended to further the scheme's ultimate objective); United States v. Regilio, 669 F.2d 1169 (7th Cir. 1981) (statements made in furtherance of inducing buyer of cocaine not to leave).

[279] *See* Dutton v. Evans, 400 U.S. 74 (1970); Wong v. United States, 371 U.S. 471 (1963); Krulewitch v. United States, 336 U.S. 440 Ed. 790 (1949); *see also* United States v. Harris, 546 F.2d 234 (8th Cir. 1976).

its value to the system of justice. Most of the evidence that is obtained by law enforcement agents and admitted under this rule involves statements made by conspirators who *thought* they were talking to another member of the conspiracy and that they were furthering their mutual objectives, when actually (as they later learn) they were talking to an undercover agent or informant, and making admissions and disclosures that ultimately assisted the police in breaking up the conspiracy and undoing all of its objectives.[280] But that is of no moment. It is universally agreed that for purposes of this rule, in keeping with its obvious purposes, "it is enough that the statements were made with the intent to further the conspiracy's purpose"; success or actual furtherance is not necessary.[281] This exception will never apply, however, to conspirators who *know* that they are talking to the police or to a government informant, because such statements are made with the intent of undoing rather than assisting the conspiracy and its objectives.[282] Nor will it usually apply to idle boasts or conversation between conspirators about past activities, because such remarks usually do nothing to advance the purposes of the conspiracy,[283] except in cases where such statements about past activities and accomplishments are intended to obtain the confidence, allay the suspicions, or work up the courage of the listener.[284] Although not satisfying the conspirator exception, a statement not made in furtherance of

---

[280] Statements between true conspirators that actually further the purposes of the conspiracy are plentiful, of course, but usually do not find their way into the hands of the government, unless either (1) the statement was being recorded by the Government without their knowledge, or (2) one of the conspirators later agrees to cooperate with the government and testify to statements made by other members of the conspiracy.

[281] United States v. Stewart, 433 F.3d 273, 293 n.4 (2d Cir. 2006). *See also* United States v. King, 351 F.3d 859 (8th Cir. 2003) (statements made to a conspirator who is under the direction and surveillance of government agents are admissible); United States v. Frazier, 280 F.3d 835 (8th Cir. 2002) (a government informant posing as a member of a conspiracy but actually working to undermine its objectives could still testify at trial as to what he heard the true conspirators say in his presence and in furtherance of their objectives; when statements are repeated live in court, it is irrelevant whether the witness on the stand was truly a member of the conspiracy or whether he was acting in furtherance of its aims when he *heard* the statements).

[282] United States v. Frazier, 280 F.3d 835 (8th Cir. 2002) (where a supposed "member" of a conspiracy was actually a government informant working to undermine the conspiracy, his statements to the police were not in furtherance of the conspiracy and therefore could not be repeated in court by the officer).

[283] United States v. Darwich, 337 F.3d 645 (6th Cir. 2003) (casual conversations between the defendant's conspirators as to the amount of drugs bagged in one evening are inadmissible because they were not made in the furtherance of the conspiracy); United States v. Castillo, 615 F.2d 878 (9th Cir. 1980) (casual admission by conspirator did not further the conspiracy).

[284] United States v. Newton, 326 F.3d 253 (1st Cir. 2003) (although an "after-the-fact description" of drug-related murders by a conspirator does not further the conspiracy to commit murder, the statement was admissible because it functioned as reassurance that the drug organization's external threats of security and profitability were being effectively addressed); United States v. Westmoreland, 312 F.3d 302 (7th Cir. 2002) (statement by

a conspiracy may be nevertheless admissible as non-hearsay or under another exception to the hearsay rule.[285]

To be admissible under this rule, a statement is admissible as long as it was made by a member of the conspiracy in furtherance of the purposes of that conspiracy; it does not matter whether the statement was made to a listener who was also a member of the conspiracy.[286] In addition, it is not necessary for the prosecution to be able to identify the declarant by name; unsigned statements and statements made by someone in a group conversation are admissible as long as the offering party can show that the unknown declarant was more likely than not a member of the defendant's conspiracy.[287]

The "in furtherance" requirement is designed "to strike a balance between the great need for conspirators' statements in combatting undesirable criminal activity which is inherently secretive and difficult of proof, and the need to protect the accused against idle chatter of criminal partners as well as inadvertently misreported and deliberately fabricated evidence,"[288] and the requirement should be applied accordingly.

§ 801.25 Statements That Are Not Hearsay — Conspirator's Statements — Other Considerations

Even if the statements of a conspirator are not admissible against a party under Rule 801(d)(2)(E) because one of the foundational requirements for admissibility is lacking, such statements may be admissible under another Rule. Accordingly, statements of conspirators not offered for their truth may

---

defendant's conspirator to his wife that he and defendant had killed a man who "talked too much" was admissible against the defendant; the statement was in furtherance of the conspiracy because it was intended to frighten the wife and to dissuade her from informing the authorities); United States v. Miles, 290 F.3d 1341 (11th Cir. 2002) (statement by conspirator identifying defendant as the potential source of drugs was admissible against accused; it was made in furtherance of a conspiracy because the declarant was trying to persuade the listener to participate in the conspiracy); United States v. Mulder, 273 F.3d 91 (2d Cir. 2001) (mere "idle chatter" between conspirators is not in furtherance of a conspiracy, but statements intended to inform a conspirator of the status of the conspiracy are in furtherance thereof); United States v. Green, 180 F.3d 216 (5th Cir. 1999) (the "in furtherance" requirement must not be applied too strictly, and includes statements, even puffing and boasting, designed to obtain the confidence of the listener); United States v. Miller, 664 F.2d 94, 98 (5th Cir. 1981) ("Puffing, boasts, and other conversations are admissible when used by the declarant to obtain the confidence of one involved in the conspiracy or to allay suspicions").

[285] *See* United States v. Hackett, 638 F.2d 1179 (9th Cir. 1980) (false statement of conspirator admissible as non-hearsay and could be admitted against other conspirators).

[286] United States v. Ayala, 601 F.3d 256 (4th Cir. 2010).

[287] *Id.*

[288] 5 WEINSTEIN'S FEDERAL EVIDENCE § 801.34.

be admissible as non-hearsay under Rule 801(c).[289] Failure to deny a statement made outside the conspiracy but in the party's presence may qualify for admission pursuant to Rule 801(d)(2)(B).[290] Or a post-conspiracy declaration against interest may meet the test of Rule 804(b)(3).[291]

The conspirator exception is applicable in both criminal and civil cases.[292] There is no need to show that the party has been indicted for conspiracy for the exception to apply,[293] and the conspiracy forming the basis for admission of a conspirator's statement need not be the same conspiracy for which the defendant is now on trial.[294] These general rules would appear to be preserved on the face of the Federal Rule, with Rule 801(d)(2)(E) using the term "party" as opposed to "accused." Throughout the Rules, the latter term is reserved only for the criminal defendant.

§ 801.26   Unique Doctrines Applicable to Admissions

Admissions are unique forms of hearsay evidence. Because the underlying theory of an admission is essentially an estoppel doctrine, peculiar rules apply to parties' out-of-court statements. For example, the first-hand knowledge requirement of Rule 602 is relaxed in regard to statements of a party.[295] Also, as a general rule, an admission of a party will not be excluded because it expresses an opinion or a conclusion.[296] While lay opinions are

---

[289] *See* § 801.4, *supra.*

[290] *See* § 801.17, *supra.*

[291] *See* § 804.1 *et seq., infra.* Because of the considerable overlap between the two rules, it is common for the admission of an alleged conspirator's statement under Rule 801(d)(2)(E) to be affirmed on the alternative ground that the statement was obviously admissible as an "admission against interest" under Rule 804(b)(3). *E.g.,* United States v. Gjerde, 110 F.3d 595 (8th Cir. 1997); United States v. Sandoval-Curiel, 50 F.3d 1389, 1392 (7th Cir. 1995); United States v. Nazemian, 948 F.2d 522, 530–532 (9th Cir. 1991); United States v. Cruz, 797 F.2d 90, 97 (2d Cir. 1986); United States v. Harrell, 788 F.2d 1524, 1526 (11th Cir. 1986). Conversely, courts often need not decide whether a statement was properly admitted under Rule 804(b)(3) because it is admissible under Rule 801(d)(2)(E). *E.g.,* United States v. Salerno, 868 F.2d 524, 537 (2d Cir. 1989); United States v. Blackmon, 839 F.2d 900, 913 n.15 (2d Cir. 1988). Likewise, it is not unusual for a statement to be admissible under both exceptions. *E.g.,* United States v. Dugan, 902 F.2d 585, 589 (7th Cir. 1990); United States v. Stratton, 779 F.2d 820, 828 (2d Cir. 1985). The overlap between the operation of these two hearsay exceptions is obviously vast.

[292] *See* 5 WEINSTEIN'S FEDERAL EVIDENCE § 801.34 (Rule 801(d)(2)(E) applies in both civil and criminal cases, though it is most frequently involved in criminal litigation).

[293] 5 WEINSTEIN'S FEDERAL EVIDENCE § 801.34; *see also* United States v. Monaco, 702 F.2d 860 (11th Cir. 1983); United States v. Kiefer, 694 F.2d 1109 (8th Cir. 1982); United States v. Scavo, 593 F.2d 837 (8th Cir. 1979).

[294] United States v. Delgado, 401 F.3d 290 (5th Cir. 2005).

[295] *See* Mahlandt v. Wild Canid Survival & Research Ctr., 588 F.2d 626 (8th Cir. 1978); Russell v. United Parcel Serv., 666 F.2d 1188 (8th Cir. 1981); *see also* 2 MCCORMICK, § 255.

[296] Russell v. United Parcel Serv., 666 F.2d 1188 (8th Cir. 1981); Cox v. Esso Shipping

generally admissible where Rule 701 is satisfied,[297] an even lower threshold will apply to opinions embraced by an admission of a party.

Because an admission is substantive evidence, its admissibility does not depend upon whether the party has testified as a witness. In this respect the exceptions contained in Rule 801(d)(2) are distinguishable from those set forth in 801(d)(1). Where a *party* has testified, a pre-trial admission may, however, be used for the purposes of impeachment as a prior inconsistent statement.[298] Where a prior statement of a *party* is used for impeachment, it serves a dual function. On one hand the evidence affects the credibility of the party-witness, and on the other hand, the pre-trial statement is admissible as substantive evidence pursuant to Rule 801(d)(2).

§ 801.27 Admissions and Statements Against Interest Distinguished

Admissions of a party are often confused with statements against interest, which are defined in Rule 804(b)(3).[299] The statement against interest exception is based upon a different theory than that supporting the admission of a party. The statement against interest exception depends upon the statement being against interest at the time the declarant utters the out-of-court statement. The statement is inherently more reliable than hearsay generally because, presumably, people do not carelessly make statements that are against their interest. Also, the statement against interest exception applies only when the out-of-court declarant is unavailable as defined in Rule 804(a). An admission of a party, by comparison, only applies to an out-of-court statement of a *party*, and it is immaterial whether the statement was against interest when the party made the statement. Moreover, unavailability is not a consideration in applying the party admission exceptions.

Co., 247 F.2d 629 (5th Cir. 1957); Pekelis v. Transcontinental & Western Air, 187 F.2d 122 (2d Cir. 1951); *see* 2 MCCORMICK, § 256.

[297] *See* § 701.1 *et seq., supra.*

[298] *See* § 613.1 *et seq., supra.*

[299] As the Advisory Committee correctly noted, the former reference in Rule 801(d)(2) to "admissions" often raised "confusion in comparison with the Rule 804(b)(3) exception for declarations against interest." Advisory Committee Note to the 2011 amendment to Fed. R. Evid. 801(d)(2). That is why Rule 801(d)(2) has now been amended to refer more generally to any "statement" by an opposing party.

Chapter 802

Rule 802. The Rule Against Hearsay

Rule 802. The Rule Against Hearsay

Hearsay is not admissible unless any of the following provides otherwise:

- a federal statute;
- these rules; or
- other rules prescribed by the Supreme Court.

---

§ 802.1   The Rule Against Hearsay — Function

Rule 802 is the general rule of exclusion for statements falling within the definition of hearsay codified in Rule 801(c). Rule 802 provides that evidence that is hearsay is presumptively inadmissible unless the proponent of the evidence can properly invoke an exception to the basic definition or an exception to the exclusionary rule contained in either Rule 803 or 804. The Rule also permits legislative regulation of hearsay by specific reference to statutes that may also provide for the admissibility of hearsay to the extent not otherwise provided or prescribed by the Rules of Evidence.[1]

The Advisory Committee Note refers to several examples of rules or statutes that operate to admit hearsay evidence.[2] Among these include several references to the Federal Rules of Civil Procedure: Rule 4(g)): proof of service by affidavit; Rule 43(e): concerning the admissibility of affidavits when a motion is based on facts that do not appear on the record; Rule 56: the use of affidavits in summary judgment proceeding; and Rule 65(b): use of affidavits to support a petition for a temporary rehearing order.[3]

---

[1] *See generally,* 5 WEINSTEIN'S FEDERAL EVIDENCE §§ 802.01–801.07; 4 MUELLER & KIRKPATRICK, 2d §§ 431–432. *See also Consideration, in Determining Facts, of Inadmissible Hearsay Evidence Introduced Without Objection,* 79 A.L.R.2d 890; *Written Recitals or Statements as Within Rule Excluding Hearsay,* 10 A.L.R.2d 1035.

[2] *See* Advisory Committee Note, Rule 802.

[3] Although this point has not been widely noted, the Advisory Committee on the Rules of Evidence actually made a serious error in citing the use of "affidavits in summary judgment proceedings" as a supposed example of a Rule of Civil Procedure authorizing the use of otherwise inadmissible "hearsay that would not qualify under these Evidence Rules."

References to the Federal Rules of Criminal Procedure include: Rule 4(a): which authorizes affidavits to be used to establish probable cause to issue a search warrant and Rule 12(b)(4): which allows affidavits to be used to determine issues of fact in connection with motions to the court.

Several acts of Congress also have the effect of authorizing the use of affidavits or depositions. For example, in a N.L.R.B. proceeding, proof of service may be established through the use of affidavits.[4] Depositions are used in extradition proceedings[5] and in proceedings before the Customs Court when the value of merchandise is to be established.[6]

Finally, there are also Congressional statutes that do not purport to admit hearsay evidence, but that by their operation have this effect. These include statutes that provide what documents are used to establish title to a res,[7] or statutes that make findings of government articles prima facie evidence of the facts found.[8]

Advisory Committee Note, Rule 802. On the contrary, supporting and opposing affidavits on a motion for summary judgment may not be considered by the judge as evidence of "the truth of the matter," Anderson v. Liberty Lobby, 477 U.S. 242, 249 (1986), but solely as evidence of what the witnesses will say at a trial if there is one. By definition, therefore, they cannot be hearsay, which is a statement used "to prove the truth of the matter asserted in the statement." Rule 801(c). *See* Duane, *The Four Greatest Myths About Summary Judgment*, 52 WASH. & LEE L. REV. 1523, 1524–1553 (1995).

[4] 29 U.S.C. § 161(4).

[5] 18 U.S.C. § 3190.

[6] 28 U.S.C. § 2635; *see* 5 WEINSTEIN'S FEDERAL EVIDENCE § 802.07, for a more exhaustive list of statutes that authorize the admissibility of hearsay evidence.

[7] *See, e.g.,* 26 U.S.C. § 6340(b) (record of tax sale is conclusive on facts asserted).

[8] *See, e.g.,* 18 U.S.C. § 4245 (director of mental treatment facility to which a prisoner has been committed shall file a certificate with the clerk of the court that ordered commitment when the prisoner is no longer in need of treatment); 7 U.S.C. § 499(g)(b) (the Secretary of Agriculture's order under the Perishable Agricultural Commodities Act is evidence of the facts found).

Chapter 803

Rule 803. Exceptions to the Rule Against Hearsay — Regardless of Whether the Declarant Is Available as a Witness

Rule 803. Exceptions to the Rule Against Hearsay — Regardless of Whether the Declarant Is Available as a Witness

The following are not excluded by the rule against hearsay, regardless of whether the declarant is available as a witness:

(1) *Present Sense Impression.* A statement describing or explaining an event or condition, made while or immediately after the declarant perceived it.

(2) *Excited Utterance.* A statement relating to a startling event or condition, made while the declarant was under the stress of excitement that it caused.

(3) *Then-Existing Mental, Emotional, or Physical Condition.* A statement of the declarant's then-existing state of mind (such as motive, intent, or plan) or emotional, sensory, or physical condition (such as mental feeling, pain, or bodily health), but not including a statement of memory or belief to prove the fact remembered or believed unless it relates to the validity or terms of the declarant's will.

(4) *Statement Made for Medical Diagnosis or Treatment.* A statement that:

   (A) is made for — and is reasonably pertinent to — medical diagnosis or treatment; and

   (B) describes medical history; past or present symptoms or sensations; their inception; or their general cause.

(5) *Recorded Recollection.* A record that:

   (A) is on a matter the witness once knew about but now cannot recall well enough to testify fully and accurately;

   (B) was made or adopted by the witness when the matter was fresh in the witness's memory; and

   (C) accurately reflects the witness's knowledge.

If admitted, the record may be read into evidence but may be received as an exhibit only if offered by an adverse party.

(6) *Records of a Regularly Conducted Activity.* A record of an act, event, condition, opinion, or diagnosis if:

(A)   the record was made at or near the time by — or from information transmitted by — someone with knowledge;

(B)   the record was kept in the course of a regularly conducted activity of a business, organization, occupation, or calling, whether or not for profit;

(C)   making the record was a regular practice of that activity;

(D)   all these conditions are shown by the testimony of the custodian or another qualified witness, or by a certification that complies with Rule 902(11) or (12) or with a statute permitting certification; and

(E)   neither the source of information nor the method or circumstances of preparation indicate a lack of trustworthiness.

(7)   ***Absence of a Record of a Regularly Conducted Activity.*** Evidence that a matter is not included in a record described in paragraph (6) if:

(A)   the evidence is admitted to prove that the matter did not occur or exist;

(B)   a record was regularly kept for a matter of that kind; and

(C)   neither the possible source of the information nor other circumstances indicate a lack of trustworthiness.

(8)   ***Public Records.*** A record or statement of a public office if:

(A)   it sets out:

   (i)   the office's activities;

   (ii)   a matter observed while under a legal duty to report, but not including, in a criminal case, a matter observed by law-enforcement personnel; or

   (iii)   in a civil case or against the government in a criminal case, factual findings from a legally authorized investigation; and

(B)   neither the source of information nor other circumstances indicate a lack of trustworthiness.

(9)   ***Public Records of Vital Statistics.*** A record of a birth, death, or marriage, if reported to a public office in accordance with a legal duty.

(10)   ***Absence of a Public Record.*** Testimony — or a certification under Rule 902 — that a diligent search failed to disclose a public record or statement if the testimony or certification is admitted to prove that:

(A)   the record or statement does not exist; or

(B)   a matter did not occur or exist, if a public office regularly kept a record or statement for a matter of that kind.

(11)   ***Records of Religious Organizations Concerning Personal or Family History.*** A statement of birth, legitimacy, ancestry, marriage, divorce, death, relationship by blood or marriage, or similar facts of personal or family history, contained in a regularly kept record of a religious organization.

(12) *Certificates of Marriage, Baptism, and Similar Ceremonies.* A statement of fact contained in a certificate:

    (A) made by a person who is authorized by a religious organization or by law to perform the act certified;

    (B) attesting that the person performed a marriage or similar ceremony or administered a sacrament; and

    (C) purporting to have been issued at the time of the act or within a reasonable time after it.

(13) *Family Records.* A statement of fact about personal or family history contained in a family record, such as a Bible, genealogy, chart, engraving on a ring, inscription on a portrait, or engraving on an urn or burial marker.

(14) *Records of Documents That Affect an Interest in Property.* The record of a document that purports to establish or affect an interest in property if:

    (A) the record is admitted to prove the content of the original recorded document, along with its signing and its delivery by each person who purports to have signed it;

    (B) the record is kept in a public office; and

    (C) a statute authorizes recording documents of that kind in that office.

(15) *Statements in Documents That Affect an Interest in Property.* A statement contained in a document that purports to establish or affect an interest in property if the matter stated was relevant to the document's purpose — unless later dealings with the property are inconsistent with the truth of the statement or the purport of the document.

(16) *Statements in Ancient Documents.* A statement in a document that is at least 20 years old and whose authenticity is established.

(17) *Market Reports and Similar Commercial Publications.* Market quotations, lists, directories, or other compilations that are generally relied on by the public or by persons in particular occupations.

(18) *Statements in Learned Treatises, Periodicals, or Pamphlets.* A statement contained in a treatise, periodical, or pamphlet if:

    (A) the statement is called to the attention of an expert witness on cross-examination or relied on by the expert on direct examination; and

    (B) the publication is established as a reliable authority by the expert's admission or testimony, by another expert's testimony, or by judicial notice.

If admitted, the statement may be read into evidence but not received as an exhibit.

(19) ***Reputation Concerning Personal or Family History.*** A reputation among a person's family by blood, adoption, or marriage — or among a person's associates or in the community — concerning the person's birth, adoption, legitimacy, ancestry, marriage, divorce, death, relationship by blood, adoption, or marriage, or similar facts of personal or family history.

(20) ***Reputation Concerning Boundaries or General History.*** A reputation in a community arising before the controversy — concerning boundaries of land in the community or customs that affect the land, or concerning general historical events important to that community, state, or nation.

(21) ***Reputation Concerning Character.*** A reputation among a person's associates or in the community concerning the person's character.

(22) ***Judgment of a Previous Conviction.*** Evidence of a final judgment of conviction if:

(A) the judgment was entered after a trial or guilty plea, but not a nolo contendere plea;

(B) the conviction was for a crime punishable by death or by imprisonment for more than a year;

(C) the evidence is admitted to prove any fact essential to the judgment; and

(D) when offered by the prosecutor in a criminal case for a purpose other than impeachment, the judgment was against the defendant.

The pendency of an appeal may be shown but does not affect admissibility.

(23) ***Judgments Involving Personal, Family, or General History, or a Boundary.*** A judgment that is admitted to prove a matter of personal, family, or general history, or boundaries, if the matter:

(A) was essential to the judgment; and

(B) could be proved by evidence of reputation.

(24) ***[Other Exceptions.]*** [Transferred to Rule 807.]

---

§ 803.1   Rule 803(1) Present Sense Impression

The following are not excluded by the rule against hearsay, regardless of whether the declarant is available as a witness:

(1) ***Present Sense Impression.*** A statement describing or explaining an event or condition, made while or immediately after the declarant perceived it.

Rule 803(1), which provides a hearsay exception for statements of present sense impressions, is relatively new to the law of evidence.[1] Prior to the enactment of Rule 803(1), few federal cases recognized an exception for "present sense impressions." The federal courts, largely influenced by Wigmore, emphasized the necessity of the excitement of some stimulus as ensuring the trustworthiness of a spontaneous declaration, *i.e.*, the basis for the excited utterance exception of Rule 803(2).[2] Consequently, most courts required the statement to be uttered under the stress of some nervous shock,[3] or, in the alternative, resorted to the historically ambiguous concept of res gestae as a basis for admission.[4] Nevertheless, while the present sense impression was not recognized as an exception in pre-Rule case law, the underlying principle was sometimes endorsed.[5]

Rule 803(1) provides a vehicle for the admission of out-of-court state-

---

[1] *See generally,* 2 McCORMICK, § 271; 5 WEINSTEIN'S FEDERAL EVIDENCE §§ 803.01–803.30; 4 MUELLER & KIRKPATRICK, §§ 433–434. *See also* Arnold, *Presenting Business Records as Evidence in Federal Court,* 32 PRAC. LAW. 19 (1986); Falknor, *The Hearsay Rule and Its Exceptions,* 2 UCLA L. REV. 43 (1954); Foster, *Present Sense Impressions: An Analysis and a Proposal,* 10 LOY. U. CHI. L.J. 299 (1979); Goldman, *Distorted Vision: Spontaneous Exclamations as a "Firmly Rooted" Exception to the Hearsay Rule,* 23 LOY. L.A. L. REV. 453 (1990); Hutchins & Slesinger, *Some Observations on the Law of Evidence: Spontaneous Exclamations,* 46 COLUM. L. REV. 432 (1946); McFarland, *Dead Men Tell Tales: Thirty Times Three Years of the Judicial Process After Hillmon,* 30 VILL. L. REV. 1 (1985); Imwinkelried, *The Importance of the Memory Factor in Analyzing the Reliability of Hearsay Testimony: A Lesson Slowly Learnt—and Quickly Forgotten,* 41 FLA. L. REV. 215 (1989); Morgan, *Res Gestae,* 12 WASH. L. REV. 91 (1937); Morgan, *A Suggested Classification of Utterances Admissible as Res Gestae,* 31 YALE L.J. 229 (1922); Mosteller, *Child Sexual Abuse and Statements for the Purpose of Medical Diagnosis or Treatment,* 67 N.C. L. REV. 257 (1989); Quick, *Hearsay, Excitement, Necessity, and the Uniform Rules: A Reappraisal of Rule 63(4),* 6 WAYNE L. REV. 204 (1960); Ringland, *Child Sexual Abuse Evidence Problems—Update 1988,* 14 U. DAYTON L. REV. 146 (1988); Slough, *Res Gestae,* 2 U. KAN. L. REV. 246 (1954); Slough, *Spontaneous Statements and State of Mind,* 46 IOWA L. REV. 224 (1961); Thayer, *Bedingfield's Case—Declarations as a Part of the Res Gestae,* 15 AM. L. REV. 71 (1881); Tuerkheimer, *Convictions Through Hearsay in Child Sexual Abuse Cases: A Logical Progression Back to Square One,* 72 MARQ. L. REV. 47 (1988); Turner, *Admissibility of Accident Reports Into Evidence Under Federal Rule of Evidence 803(c),* 35 TRIAL LAW. GUIDE 137 (1991); Waltz, *The Present Sense Impression Exception to the Rule Against Hearsay: Origins and Attitudes,* 66 IOWA L. REV. 869 (1981); Weissenberger, *Hearsay Puzzles: An Essay on Federal Evidence Rule 803(3),* 64 TEMP. L. REV. 145 (1991).

[2] *See generally,* 2 McCORMICK, § 271.

[3] *See, e.g.,* Giffin v. Ensign, 234 F.2d 307 (3d Cir. 1956); Roth v. Swanson, 145 F.2d 262 (8th Cir. 1944); Kornicki v. Calmar S.S. Corp., 460 F.2d 1134 (3d Cir. 1972). *See generally,* 6 WIGMORE, § 1747.

[4] *See* definition and discussion, § 803.2 note 7, *infra.*

[5] *E.g.,* Emens v. Lehigh Valley R. Co., 223 F. 810 (N.D.N.Y. 1915) (where witness testified that immediately prior to grade crossing accident his wife said, "Do you suppose the people in that automobile see the train?" and "Why don't the train whistle?," these statements were properly admitted; court noted that the remarks were spontaneous and voluntary); *see also* Picker X-Ray Corp. v. Frerker, 405 F.2d 916 (8th Cir. 1969).

ments concerning an event or condition where the statement describes or explains the event. The statement must be uttered contemporaneously with the event or condition or "immediately after the declarant perceived it."[6] The exception to the hearsay rule embodied in Rule 803(1) is distinguishable from that contained in Rule 803(2) concerning excited utterances in that Rule 803(1) does not require the presence of a startling event as a stimulus for the utterance. Rule 803(1) merely requires a contemporaneous report of sense impressions. For example, where X and Y are standing at an intersection and X blurts out to Y, "Look at that blue truck, it's running the red light," Y may testify at trial as to X's statement under Rule 803(1). The statement is inadmissible under Rule 803(2), however, since presumably the event is not sufficiently startling.

§ 803.2   Policy Supporting Rule 803(1)

The hearsay exception for present sense impressions can be traced to the traditional common-law concept of res gestae,[7] a term historically denoting words or statements that accompany the principal litigated fact. The phrase, literally and in practice, is so vague and imprecise that it has served as a convenient means of escaping the hearsay proscription. Moreover, it has often been indiscriminately applied to several evidentiary principles, al-

---

[6] *See, e.g.,* Cargill, Inc. v. Boag Cold Storage Warehouse, Inc., 71 F.3d 545 (6th Cir. 1995) (trial court did not err in admitting employee's typed copies of notes that were taken during the process of employee's inspection of stock; although the copies were typed over by employee, he testified that he originally took the notes during the inspection process); United States v. Kehoe, 562 F.2d 65 (1st Cir. 1977) (reporter's notation that defendant had been sworn in prosecution for perjury arising out of testimony given by defendant before grand jury, the notation was properly admitted since it was made shortly after the event); *see also* Wolfson v. Mutual Life Ins. Co. of New York, 455 F. Supp. 82 (M.D. Pa. 1978), *aff'd,* 588 F.2d 825 (3d Cir. 1978); Hilyer v. Howat Concrete Co., 578 F.2d 422 (D.C. Cir. 1978); Nuttall v. Reading Co., 235 F.2d 546 (3d Cir. 1956). *See generally,* 2 McCormick, § 273; 5 Weinstein's Federal Evidence § 803.03; 4 Mueller & Kirkpatrick, § 434; Note, *Spontaneous Exclamations in the Absence of a Startling Event,* 46 Colum. L. Rev. 430 (1946); Comment, *Hearsay Under the Proposed Federal Rules: A Discretionary Approach,* 15 Wayne L. Rev. 1077 (1969).

[7] Literally, Latin for "things done." At common law, the term was broadly defined and applied to include evidence of any matter incidental to the main fact and explicative of it, including words and acts so intertwined with it as to constitute part of the transaction or occurrence. In essence, while these matters are incident of the act and not the act itself, they were considered admissible for their illustrative or explanatory value. United States v. King, 34 F. 302 (1888) (principle of res gestae admits "declarations of an individual made at the moment of a particular occurrence, when the circumstances are such that we may assume that his mind is controlled by the event . . . ." It must have been "made at a time when it was forced out as an utterance of truth, forced out against his will or without his will, and at a period of time so closely connected with the transaction that there has been no opportunity for subsequent reflection or determination as to what it might or might not be wise for him to say").

though some are not related to the hearsay rule.[8] Under the Rules of Evidence, evidence traditionally admitted by resort to the res gestae doctrine is categorized into four distinct exceptions to the hearsay rule: (i) present sense impressions (Rule 803(1)); (ii) excited utterances (Rule 803(2)); (iii) statements describing mental or physical condition (Rule 803(3)); and (iv) statements for purposes of medical treatment or diagnosis (Rule 803(4)). In related fashion, statements constituting verbal acts or verbal parts of acts, traditionally honored as res gestae, have been excluded from the threshold definition of hearsay under Rule 801(c). Thus, while courts may still make reference to the res gestae concept as reason for admitting certain evidence, it is clear that the increased sophistication of the hearsay rule has largely rendered the term obsolete as an expression of an evidentiary doctrine.[9]

The principle underlying the hearsay exception contained in Rule 803(1) is the assumption that statements of perception, describing the event and

---

[8] *See, e.g.,* 6 WIGMORE, § 1767, at 255:

> The phrase res gestae has long been not only entirely useless, but even positively harmful. It is useless, because every rule of evidence to which it has ever been applied exists as a part of some other well-established principle and can be explained in the terms of that principle. It is harmful, because by its ambiguity it invites the confusion of one rule with another and thus creates uncertainty as to the limitations of both. It ought therefore wholly to be repudiated as a vicious element in our legal phraseology. No rule of evidence can be created or applied by the mere muttering of a shibboleth. There are words enough to describe the rules of evidence. Even if there were no accepted name for one or another doctrine, any name would be preferable to an empty phrase so encouraging to looseness of thinking and uncertainty of decision.

See also Thayer, *Bedingfield's Case—Declarations as Part of Res Gestae*, 15 AMER. L. REP. 1 (1881); Morgan, *A Suggestive Classification of Utterances Admissible as Res Gestae*, 31 YALE L.J. 229 (1923). While commentators have for some time attacked the res gestae doctrine as not founded upon reliable principles of law or as an unwieldly "catch-all" phrase of convenience, courts have been reluctant to discard the doctrine in favor of more detailed examinations of evidence. *See, e.g.,* United States v. Leonard, 494 F.2d 955 (D.C. Cir. 1974).

[9] McCormick explains the doctrine's obsolescence:

> Commentators and, less frequently, courts, have criticized use of the phrase res gestae. Its vagueness and imprecision are, of course, apparent. Moreover, traditional limitations on the doctrine, such as the requirement that it be used only in regard to the principal litigated fact and the frequent insistence of concurrence (or at least a close relationship in time) between the words and the act or situation, have restricted its usefulness as a tool for avoiding unjustified application of the hearsay rule. Historically, however, the phrase served its purpose well. Its very vagueness made it easier for courts to broaden it and thus provide for the admissibility of certain declarations in new fields. But it seems clear that the law has now reached a stage at which this desirable policy of widening admissibility will be best served by other means. The ancient phrase can well be jettisoned, with due acknowledgment that it has served well its era in the evolution of evidence law.

2 MCCORMICK, § 268, at 207–08; *see also* Wabisky v. D. C. Transit System, Inc., 309 F.2d 317 (D.C. Cir. 1962) (identifying these various categories of res gestae, although not mentioning those statements not defined as hearsay).

uttered in close temporal proximity to the event, bear a high degree of trustworthiness. Due to the statement's contemporaneous nature, there is little danger of a lapse in memory. Also, there is little time for calculated misstatement, and the usual circumstance of other persons being present at the time serves as a check on any misstatement.[10] Consequently, the testimonial defects in memory and sincerity, normally attendant to other forms of hearsay, are largely absent where spontaneity is present and where the declarant's statement is free from distortion often resulting from impending events. Further, where the declarant is available for cross-examination, his or her credibility and narration of the event will be subject to verification before the trier of fact.[11]

§ 803.3   Requirement of Temporal Proximity

Admissibility of a hearsay statement under Rule 803(1) is conditioned on the statement being uttered either while the event or condition is being perceived by the declarant or "immediately after." This time requirement should be strictly applied, because it is the element of contemporaneity that serves as the basis for trustworthiness of this hearsay exception.[12] Generally, the Rule will be employed to admit statements uttered during the course of the event or transaction or seconds after the event or transaction. The phrase "immediately after" is intended to accommodate the pragmatic realization that an event may be so fleeting in time as to preclude simultaneous comment, and it consequently permits flexibility in admitting statements made moments after the event where a slight lapse in time appears natural under the circumstances. The time elapsed between the statement and event must be sufficiently short to indicate a lack of reflection on the event perceived — a fact that would detract from the trustworthiness of the utterance.[13] Accordingly, the "immediately after" language of Rule 803(1)

---

[10] 5 WEINSTEIN'S FEDERAL EVIDENCE § 803.03. The notable exception to those scholars supporting the recognition and usefulness of the present sense impression is Wigmore, who prefers to include such statements under the excited utterance exception. 6 WIGMORE, §§ 1745–1756. Since Wigmore stresses that trustworthiness is predicated more upon the nervous excitement produced by the declarant's exposure to a startling event than upon the contemporaneity of the utterance with the event, Wigmore advocates the presence of a startling event as a condition precedent to admission. *Compare* 6 WIGMORE, § 1757, *with* Morgan, *Res Gestae*, 12 WASH. L. REV. 91 (1937), *and* Thayer, *Bedingfield's Case— Declarations as Part of Res Gestae*, 15 AMER. L. REP. 1 (1881). *See also* Hutchins & Slesinger, *Some Observations on the Law of Evidence: Spontaneous Exclamations*, 28 COLUM. L. REV. 432 (1928).

[11] *See* 2 MCCORMICK, § 271; 4 MUELLER & KIRKPATRICK, § 434.

[12] *See, e.g.*, Pau v. Yosemite Park and Curry Co., 928 F.2d 880 (9th Cir. 1991) (deceased victim's statement implicating defendant after coming out of a coma was not "immediately thereafter" accident).

[13] *See* Advisory Committee Note, Rule 803(1): "Exception (1) recognizes that in many, if not most, instances precise contemporaneity is not possible, and hence a slight lapse is allowable."

should be strictly construed and narrowly applied such that operation of the Rule does not result in the admission of statements that do not satisfy the underlying rationale.[14]

§ 803.4   Requirement of "Perception" by Declarant

Rule 803(1) further requires that the declarant actually perceive the transaction or event described in the hearsay statement.[15] While "perceiving" most assuredly means, in the greater number of instances, "seeing,"[16] it may also include any other type of sensory perception, including hearing.[17] The Rule does not require that the declarant actually participate in the event, but the more removed the declarant was from the relevant event, the more questionable it is that the declarant actually did perceive it.[18]

Although the Rule does not predicate admission of hearsay under this exception upon the declarant being available to testify, a greater suspicion of

---

[14] *See generally,* Quick, *Hearsay, Excitement, Necessity and the Uniform Rules: A Reappraisal of Rule 63(4),* 6 WAYNE L. REV. 204, 210 (1960) ("Even the argument that . . . spontaneity . . . is a reasonable guaranty of sincerity has been questioned because psychological studies indicate that the time interval required to assure lack of conscious or unconscious falsification is measured in stopwatch time intervals rather than in minutes"). *See also* United States v. Cain, 587 F.2d 678 (5th Cir. 1979); United States v. Narciso, 446 F. Supp. 252 (E.D. Mich. 1977).

[15] United States v. Blakey, 607 F.2d 779, 785–786 (7th Cir. 1979) ("[T]he underlying rationale of the present sense impression exception is that substantial contemporaneity of event and statement minimizes unreliability due to defective recollection or conscious fabrication").

[16] 4 MUELLER & KIRKPATRICK, § 434; *see* Houston Oxygen Co. v. Davis, 139 Tex. 1 (Tex. 1942) (as one car was being passed by another, comment of driver that "they must have been drunk; we could find them somewhere on the road wrecked if they kept up that rate of speed"); *see also* United States v. Andrews, 765 F.2d 1491 (11th Cir. 1985) (government agent's contemporaneous recording of what he saw as he looked through window was admissible); Anderson v. State, 454 S.W.2d 740 (Tex. Crim. App. 1970) (at the very time the event was occurring the comment was made, "Seems like there is a car being stripped down the street there").

[17] *E.g.,* Nuttall v. Reading Co., 235 F.2d 546 (3d Cir. 1956) (reversible error to exclude statements by decedent's widow that were characterizations made at the time the event was perceived, and free from the possibility of lapse of memory on the part of the declarant; this contemporaneousness lessens the likelihood of conscious misrepresentation); *see also* MCA, Inc. v. Wilson, 425 F. Supp. 443, 451 (S.D.N.Y. 1976) (court admitted spontaneous reactions of cast and audience to the playing of an allegedly copied copyrighted song without authorization, as "sense impressions of weight . . . [t]heir spontaneity provides their reliability and cures any hearsay infirmities.").

[18] *See* 5 WEINSTEIN'S FEDERAL EVIDENCE § 803.03; *see, e.g.,* McClure v. Price, 300 F.2d 538 (4th Cir. 1962); *see also* Advisory Committee Note, Rule 803(1) (suggesting that declarant's statement via CB radio was inadmissible since the event was not "perceived" by the witness); *cf.* United States v. Portsmouth Paving, 694 F.2d 312 (4th Cir. 1982) (finding that witness had "perceived" a telephone call where he had heard words and saw the declarant hang up; court noted that the declarant was not an unidentified bystander, so that his capacity to observe could be substantiated).

untrustworthiness arises where the declarant does not appear.[19] Absent some foundational evidence from the declarant or other witness showing that the declarant actually perceived the event or transaction, the trustworthiness attendant to such hearsay statements is not present, and application of Rule 803(1) is inappropriate.

§ 803.5   Subject Matter Requirement

The express language of Rule 803(1) requires that the hearsay statement be one "describing or explaining" the condition or event perceived. Accordingly, a statement prompted by an event, but not descriptive or explanatory of it, is inadmissible under this exception. Where a statement is contemporaneous with an event and asserts the existence of the condition or the occurrence of the event perceived, it is "descriptive" within the language of Rule 803(1). If the statement tends to interpret, assess or evaluate the condition perceived, it is "explanatory" under the Rule.[20] While the "describing or explaining" elements should not be so narrowly applied as to exclude statements that moderately expand upon the declarant's perceptions, Rule 803(1) should not be used to admit statements that embrace a risk of a defect in memory. For example, if the declarant makes the out-of-court statement, "Look at that blue truck run the light; I saw that truck at the service station yesterday getting its brakes repaired," the latter statement should not be admitted under Rule 803(1). The statement as to an occurrence on the previous day unavoidably involves a possible defect in memory, and it is not a contemporaneous report of present sense impressions.

§ 803.6   Rule 803(2) Excited Utterance

The following are not excluded by the rule against hearsay, regardless of whether the declarant is available as a witness:

***

> **(2)   *Excited Utterance.*** A statement relating to a startling event or condition, made while the declarant was under the stress of excitement that it caused.

It has long been the law in the federal system that statements provoked by, and uttered contemporaneously with, startling events are admissible pursu-

---

[19] *See generally,* 5 WEINSTEIN'S FEDERAL EVIDENCE § 803.03.

[20] *Compare* MCA, Inc. v. Wilson, 425 F. Supp. 443 (S.D.N.Y. 1976) (statement admitted as explanatory of event) *with* Elek v. Boyce, 308 F. Supp. 26 (D.S.C. 1970) (hearsay statement inadmissible since neither descriptive nor explanatory). *See generally,* 5 WEINSTEIN'S FEDERAL EVIDENCE § 803.03. *But cf.* Michaels v. Michaels, 767 F.2d 1185 (7th Cir. 1985) (telex sent immediately after conversation with defendant could qualify as a present sense impression).

ant to an exception to the hearsay rule. Rule 803(2) codifies the traditional federal practice.[21]

Under the Rule, a declarant's hearsay statement in reaction to a startling external stimulus is admissible for the truth of the substance contained in the statement where the statement relates to the external event and is uttered under the stress of excitement occasioned by the event.[22] While the exceptions identified in Rule 803(1) and Rule 803(2) are frequently confused, their respective applications are distinct. Rule 803(2) requires the declaration to be in response to some startling occurrence, whereas Rule 803(1) does not. Rule 803(2) also differs from Rule 803(1) in not restricting the subject matter of the declaration to descriptive or explanatory statements of the event perceived.[23] Under Rule 803(2) that statement need only "relate" to the startling event. Accordingly, where the statement is in response to a startling event in satisfaction of Rule 803(2), the scope of the subject matter standard is considerably broader than that under Rule 803(1). Like Rule 803(1), however, Rule 803(2) represents a condensed and more refined facet of the common-law doctrine of res gestae,[24] and like Rule 803(1), Rule 803(2) does not require that the declarant be a participant in the

---

[21] *E.g.,* Travelers' Ins. Co. v. Miller, 62 F.2d 910 (7th Cir. 1932), Wicker v. Scott, 29 F.2d 807 (6th Cir. 1928); Travelers' Protective Ass'n v. West, 102 F. 226 (7th Cir. 1900); National Masonic Accident Ass'n v. Shyrock, 73 F. 774 (8th Cir. 1896); Cross Lake Logging Co. v. Joyce, 83 F. 989 (8th Cir. 1897). *See generally,* 4 MUELLER & KIRKPATRICK, §§ 435–436; 5 WEINSTEIN'S FEDERAL EVIDENCE § 803.04; 2 McCORMICK § 272; 6 WIGMORE, §§ 1745–1764. *See also* Hutchins & Slesinger, *Some Observations on the Law of Evidence: Spontaneous Exclamations,* 28 COLUM. L. REV. 432 (1928); Quick, *Hearsay, Excitement, Necessity, and the Uniform Rules: A Reappraisal of Rule 63(4),* 6 WAYNE L. REV. 204 (1960); Slough, *Res Gestae,* 2 U. KAN. L. REV. 246 (1954); Slough, *Spontaneous Statements and State of Mind,* 46 IOWA L. REV. 224 (1961); Stewart, *Perception, Memory, and Hearsay: A Criticism of Present Law and the Proposed Federal Rules of Evidence,* 1970 UTAH L. REV. 1; Comment, *Hearsay Under the Proposed Federal Rules: A Discretionary Approach,* 15 WAYNE L. REV. 1077 (1969).

[22] *E.g.,* United States v. Bowdach, 414 F. Supp. 1346 (S.D. Fla. 1976), *aff'd,* 561 F.2d 1160 (5th Cir. 1977) (statement excluded as not sufficiently relevant to fact sought to be proven); Zibelman v. Gibbs, 252 F. Supp. 360 (E.D. Pa. 1966) (even though made "reasonably close" to time of accident the statement was excluded because a routine rear-end collision is not particularly violent); Kornicki v. Calmar S.S. Corp., 460 F.2d 1134, 1139 (3d Cir. 1972) (court excluded utterance on the ground that it lacked spontaneity but noted that the statement was also a "matter of opinion rather than sensory perception."). *See generally,* 5 WEINSTEIN'S FEDERAL EVIDENCE § 803.04; 2 McCORMICK, § 272.

[23] *See* § 803.1 *et seq., supra.*

[24] Courts have referred to this exception as well as to others related to it, by the generic term res gestae. *E.g.,* United States v. Brady, 579 F.2d 1121 (7th Cir. 1978); United States v. Gutierrez, 576 F.2d 269 (10th Cir. 1978); United States v. Smith, 520 F.2d 1245 (8th Cir. 1975), *aff'd,* 533 F.2d 1077 (1975); Wetherbee v. Safety Cas. Co., 219 F.2d 274 (5th Cir. 1955).

startling event or condition.[25]

§ 803.7   Theory Supporting Rule 803(2)

The admissibility of hearsay statements classified as "excited utterances" is predicated upon the theory that a spontaneous statement by the declarant in response to an external startling stimulus indicates a sufficient degree of trustworthiness to warrant admission of the hearsay.[26] As the Supreme Court recently observed, such statements "are considered reliable because the declarant, in the excitement, presumably cannot form a falsehood."[27] Statements made in reaction to a startling stimulus are considered more trustworthy than hearsay generally on the dual grounds that, first, the stimulus renders the declarant incapable of fabrication and, second, the impression on the declarant's memory at the time of the statement is still fresh and intense. Accordingly, Rule 803(2) assumes that excited utterances are less susceptible to lapses of memory or dangers of insincerity than ordinary hearsay.[28] Of course, this reasoning also lends itself to a contradictory conclusion as to reliability, namely, that spontaneous reaction to a startling event increases the possibility of problems in narration or perception.[29] Such arguable untrustworthiness, however, has not been considered

---

[25] *E.g.,* United States v. Boyd, 620 F.2d 129 (6th Cir. 1980); *see also* McLaughlin v. Vinzant, 522 F.2d 448 (1st Cir. 1975) (court found it permissible to draw an inference from the force of statement, even though declarant witness did not witness the event, since she was accompanying defendant, and was somewhere in the immediate vicinity of the fatal event, and therefore possessed firsthand knowledge).

[26] *See* United States v. Glenn, 473 F.2d 191, 194 (D.C. Cir. 1972) (declarations of victims of violent crime "are sometimes admitted in evidence as exceptions to the hearsay rule, upon the theory that the shock of the injury and the excitement of the moment have produced an utterance that is spontaneous and sincere as distinguished from one engendered by deliberation and design"); McCurdy v. Greyhound Corp., 346 F.2d 224 (3d Cir. 1965) (res gestae exception since participant was incapable of reasoned reflection about the occurrence). *See generally,* 6 WIGMORE, § 1747; 5 WEINSTEIN'S FEDERAL EVIDENCE § 803.04; 2 MCCORMICK, § 272.

[27] Michigan v. Bryant, 562 U.S. —, 131 S. Ct. 1143, 179 L. Ed. 2d 93, 109 (2011).

[28] *E.g.,* David v. Pueblo Supermarket of St. Thomas, 740 F.2d 230 (3d Cir. 1984) (statement of witness to accident in personal injury suit was admissible where witness made unsolicited statement immediately after seeing eight-months-pregnant plaintiff fall); Murphy Auto Parts Co. v. Ball, 249 F.2d 508, 510 (D.C. Cir. 1957) ("the prompt, spontaneous character of the utterance under the impact and stress of the exciting event which stills the reflective process provides the circumstances which, experience shows us, make for reliability"); *see also* United States v. Knife, 592 F.2d 472 (8th Cir. 1979); *cf.* United States v. Moss, 544 F.2d 954 (8th Cir. 1976) (time factor coupled with subject matter of statement demonstrated that statement was not excited utterance within the exception).

[29] *See generally,* Stewart, *Perception, Memory, and Hearsay: A Criticism of Present Law and The Proposed Federal Rules of Evidence,* 1970 UTAH L. REV. 1; Hutchins & Slessinger, *Some Observations on the Law of Evidence,* 28 COLUM. L. REV. 432 (1928); Gardner, *The Perception and Memory of Witnesses,* 18 CORNELL L.Q. 391, 395 (1933) ("[S]hock . . . draws attention to the causes of the emotion and thus divides the attention as to the incident

sufficient to set aside the time-honored exception codified in Rule 803(2), and it is assumed that the critical characteristic of the exception is that the startling occurrence draws the declarant's complete attention to the perceived event so that other counterweights become negligible.

§ 803.8   Elements for Application of Rule 803(2)

In general, qualification of any hearsay statement as an "excited utterance" under Rule 803(2) depends upon the proponent of such evidence demonstrating three essential elements to the trial court's satisfaction: (i) that the statement was in reaction to a truly startling event; (ii) that the statement was made under the stress of excitement caused by that event; and (iii) that the statement relates to the event. Where any of these elements is wanting in foundational proof, the statement must be viewed more as a reflective narrative of the past event, and it does not qualify as an excited utterance under Rule 803(2).[30]

In applying the foundational elements, the Rule contemplates that the foundation should be judged on a subjective, rather than objective, standard. The critical feature is that the declarant in question was excited by, and moved to comment on, the occasion. That another person similarly situated would not react as emotionally is not the critical issue in determining admissibility under Rule 803(2).[31]

§ 803.9   Nature of the Stimulus — Requirement That Event or Condition Be Startling

Rule 803(2) conditions admissibility of statements within its scope on the

---

itself and the details immediately following it." Memory before the startling event is keen while memory accompanying or following the event is less reliable) (relying on Stratton, *Retroactive Hyperamnesia*, 26 Psych. Rev. 474 (1919)); *cf.* McLaughlin v. Vinzant, 522 F.2d 448 (1st Cir. 1975).

[30] *See, e.g.,* United States v. Sewell, 90 F.3d 326 (8th Cir. 1996) (trial court appropriately granted government's motion *in limine* to exclude the defendant's statement that the gun found in the car he was driving belonged to his brother and that he was unaware it was in the car as this statement does not fall under the excited utterance exception to the hearsay rule as there was no evidence that the statement was prompted by uncontrolled excitement); United States v. Cain, 587 F.2d 678 (5th Cir. 1979); United States v. Phelps, 572 F. Supp. 262 (E.D. Ky. 1983); Zibelman v. Gibbs, 252 F. Supp. 360 (E.D. Pa. 1966) (utterance was not excited, since accident was a routine rear-end collision, which was by no means spectacular, bloody, violent, etc., which in itself would lead inescapably to the inference that the utterances were shock-induced).

[31] *See* United States v. Lawrence, 699 F.2d 697 (5th Cir. 1983) (at trial for assault on post office truck driver with intent to rob, no abuse of discretion for trial judge to view statement as spontaneous or excited, that immediately after defendant had been arrested, truck driver asked arresting officer if he had heard defendant tell him that the truck driver was a dead man); United States v. Golden, 671 F.2d 369 (10th Cir. 1982) (statement of victim made to his mother after he drove to her house from scene at approximately 120 miles per hour, was properly admitted; statement occurred within 15 minutes of startling event); United States v. Napier, 518 F.2d 316 (9th Cir. 1975) (courts look to the effect of the event upon declarant; if the event caused excitement to that person, courts are satisfied).

existence of a "startling event or condition." In this regard, such events as an automobile crash, an assault, a murder or other catastrophe might readily qualify as "startling" events. Other less traumatic experiences, however, do not so readily admit inclusion. Whether an event is sufficiently startling depends upon its impact upon the declarant, and the subjective standard necessarily dictates an *ad hoc* approach in the application of this element.[32] Factors critical to this determination may include the nature of the event, the appearance, behavior or condition of the declarant, the content of the statement, the declarant's age and profession, his or her physical proximity to, or psychological perspective of, the event, and whether the statement was unsolicited or in response to a question.

In the majority of cases, the occurrence of the startling event is established by evidence independent of the declarant's statement, such as the testimony of other witnesses or circumstantial evidence showing an unusual event occurred.[33] There is nothing in the Rule or its underlying rationale, however, which would prevent proof of the existence of the startling event by the declarant's statement itself.[34] Consequently, where an individual suffers injury from a solitary mishap, his or her excited utterance made shortly after

---

[32] *E.g.,* Brunsting v. Lutsen Mountains Corp., 601 F.3d 813 (8th Cir. 2010) (in skier's negligence action against ski resort, statement by resort employee that the skier had hit a tree stump before his accident was admissible as an excited utterance; witness saw skier's near-fatal traumatic accident from chairlift, immediately rushed to the scene where skier was unconscious and believed to be near dead, others were trying to stabilize the skier until medical assistance arrived, the witness described herself as "just frantic," and was so nervous, panicked, and anxious from what had just happened that she felt shaky); Wheeler v. United States, 211 F.2d 19 (D.C. Cir. 1953) (in prosecution for carnal abuse of 10-year-old, girl's statement to grandmother naming defendant was properly received, since her statement was made within one hour of the event and she was highly distraught and in tears at the time).

[33] *E.g.,* McCurdy v. Greyhound Corp., 346 F.2d 224 (3d Cir. 1965) ("[w]hen the police arrived, McCurdy was still noticeably 'nervous' and 'shooken up.' In view of this, there is little danger that he had either the time to reflect or sufficient use of his reason to fabricate and manufacture an account of the accident"); Cole v. United States, 327 F.2d 360 (9th Cir. 1964); Wetherbee v. Safety Cas. Co., 219 F.2d 274, 278 (5th Cir. 1955) (pain and suffering "prolonged the influence of the event itself").

[34] *See* Insurance Co. v. Mosley, 75 U.S. (8 Wall) 397 (1869) (insurance policy case that turned on whether deceased had died from injuries incurred in an accidental fall down stairs or from natural causes; widow testified that he left his bed during the night and upon his return reported that he had fallen and hit the back of his head; widow's testimony that his voice was trembling was some evidence other than his declaration that a startling event had occurred); *see, e.g.,* Stewart v. Baltimore & Ohio R.R., 137 F.2d 527 (2d Cir. 1943). *See generally,* 2 MCCORMICK, § 272; Slough, *Res Gestae,* 12 WASH. L. REV. 91 (1937). *But see* Comment, *A Study Relating to the Hearsay Evidence Article of the Uniform Rules of Evidence,* 4 CAL. L. REV. 468 (1962) ("The judge would reason in a circle if, being bound by the hearsay rule, he nevertheless considered the statement for the purpose of establishing the very fact which is the condition precedent to his original consideration of that statement. He would, to use the hackneyed but respected figure, permit X's declaration to lift itself into evidence by its own bootstraps").

the accident should be received as proof that the event occurred. While arguably circular, this approach is particularly sound in actions where a firsthand account of the startling occurrence from a source other than the declarant may be unavailable.[35] Nevertheless, in any case in which the court is satisfied that the declarant was under the stress of excitement when the statement was made, the indicium of reliability is present, and the statement should be received even absent extrinsic foundation. Rule 104(a) expressly provides that the court is not bound by the Rules of Evidence, except those respecting privileges, in considering preliminary, foundational questions as to admissibility.[36]

§ 803.10   Requirement That Declarant Be Under Stress of Excitement Caused by Startling Event When Statement Is Uttered

To qualify as an "excited utterance," the hearsay statement must have been made while the declarant was under the nervous stress occasioned by the startling incident. This element is critical because the Rule is predicated upon the theory that excited utterances are more trustworthy than hearsay generally because the declarant has little or no capability of fabricating while under extreme stress. This requirement is essentially one of time, *i.e.,* in order to qualify under the exception, the declarant must have made the statement while still under the nervous strain resulting from the event.[37]

There is no set rule as to how much time may pass after the startling event before a statement is no longer an excited utterance, because the exception is primarily founded upon the declarant's inability to fabricate and not on the lack of time to do so.[38] While each set of facts must receive individual

---

[35] Wetherbee v. Safety Cas. Co., 219 F.2d 274 (5th Cir. 1955); Stewart v. Baltimore & Ohio R.R. Co., 137 F.2d 527 (2d Cir. 1943).

[36] *See* Chapter 104, *supra.*

[37] *See, e.g.,* United States v. Rivera, 43 F.3d 1291 (9th Cir. 1995) (fifteen-year-old victim's statement accusing the defendant of raping her, though made more than thirty minutes after intercourse, was properly admitted as an excited utterance; statement was made while the victim was still in a "semi-hysterical" state); Pau v. Yosemite Park and Curry Co., 928 F.2d 880 (9th Cir. 1991) (victim's statement upon awakening from coma was not under stress of excitement); United States v. Iron Shell, 633 F.2d 77 (8th Cir. 1980) (no abuse of discretion to admit statement made to police officer by 9-year-old victim of assault with intent to rape 45 minutes after the event; court took into consideration age of victim, testimony that she had struggled, that defendant had pulled down her jeans, and that officer asked only "what happened" to which victim replied in short bursts rather than detailed narrative); United States v. Lawrence, 699 F.2d 697 (5th Cir. 1983) (no abuse of discretion for trial judge to view statement made by victim to arresting officer as spontaneous or excited, that defendant told victim he was a dead man); United States v. Golden, 671 F.2d 369 (10th Cir. 1982) (statement made 15 minutes after startling event immediately after a high-speed flight admitted as spontaneous or excited).

[38] *See generally,* 5 WEINSTEIN'S FEDERAL EVIDENCE § 803.04; 6 WIGMORE, §§ 1750; United States v. Napier, 518 F.2d 316 (9th Cir. 1975) (courts look at the effect of the event

treatment, the trial court must focus on the declarant's state of mind at the time the statement was made, and the shock of the event must be present at that time in order for the exception to apply.[39] Factors contributing to this determination include physical characteristics such as the presence of shock or trauma, the age and maturity of the declarant, and periods of unconsciousness or pain, as well as the circumstances surrounding the statement, such as the nature of the startling event.[40] The tenor of the statement itself may also be considered.

Accordingly, trustworthiness is not determined solely by the lapse of time between the event and the hearsay exclamation, although the time elapsed may be probative in determining whether the declarant was still under stress when the statement was uttered.

§ 803.11   Subject Matter of Excited Utterance — Requirement That Statement "Relate" to the Startling Event

In contrast to the requisite element of a present sense impression statement under Rule 803(1), where the substance of the hearsay statement must "describe or explain" the event or condition,[41] Rule 803(2) requires only that the hearsay statement "relate" to the startling event or condition. A statement embracing facts that are distinct from the startling event or

---

upon the declarant as primary, and are satisfied as long as the event caused excitement to that person); United States v. Barnes, 464 F.2d 828 (D.C. Cir. 1972) (spontaneous, excited utterance where victim was allegedly burned to death by a fire set by defendant in the kitchen by means of gasoline poured on the floor, upholding receipt of testimony that victim said to defendant, "you had no call to do that to me" as she was being removed from the house to the hospital); United States v. Kearney, 420 F.2d 170, 175 (D.C. Cir. 1969) ("what must be taken into account is not only the length of the intervening time period, but also an assessment of the declarant's activities and attitudes in the meanwhile.").

[39] McCormick provides this characteristically cogent analysis:

Probably the most important of the many factors entering into this determination is the temporal element. If the statement occurs while the exciting event is still in progress, courts have little difficulty finding that the excitement prompted the statement. But as the time between the event and the statement increases, courts become more reluctant to find the statement an excited utterance. . . . A useful rule of thumb is that where the time interval between the event and the statement is long enough to permit reflective thought, the statement will be excluded in the absence of some proof that the declarant did not in fact engage in a reflective thought process.

2 MCCORMICK, § 272; see United States v. Mountain State Fabricating Co., 282 F.2d 263 (4th Cir. 1960) (under all the circumstances, the statement was excluded although it related to a startling event and was made shortly thereafter); Chestnut v. Ford Motor Co., 445 F.2d 967 (4th Cir. 1971) (remanded to trial court to reconsider exclusion of plaintiff's statement to doctor 20 hours after the accident where the plaintiff may still have been in nervous shock).

[40] E.g., Haggins v. Warden, Fort Pillow State Farm, 715 F.2d 1050 (6th Cir. 1983); United States v. Iron Shell, 633 F.2d 77 (8th Cir. 1980); United States v. Nick, 604 F.2d 1199 (9th Cir. 1979); McCurdy v. Greyhound Corp., 346 F.2d 224 (3d Cir. 1965).

[41] See § 803.3, supra.

condition may be admissible under Rule 803(2) where the statement in some rational manner relates to the event.[42]

While the fact that the statement neither describes nor explains the exciting condition or event may be an indication that the utterance is not truly spontaneous, the Rule only requires that the statement relate to the startling event.[43] Consequently, statements containing beliefs about past facts may be admissible where such remembered facts relate to the startling event that provoked the out-of-court statement. Consequently, if a declarant makes an out-of-court statement in response to a sufficiently startling event, "Look at that blue truck smash into that car; I saw that truck at the service station yesterday getting its brakes serviced," the entire declaration may be admissible under Rule 803(2). The latter statement regarding a past event at a service station rationally *relates* to the startling event even though it does not actually describe it.[44]

§ 803.12   Rule 803(3) Then-Existing Mental, Emotional, or Physical Condition

The following are not excluded by the rule against hearsay, regardless of whether the declarant is available as a witness:

***

(3)   *Then-Existing Mental, Emotional, or Physical Condition.* A statement of the declarant's then-existing state of mind (such as motive, intent, or plan) or emotional, sensory, or physical condition (such as mental feeling, pain, or bodily health), but not including a statement of memory or belief to prove the fact remembered or believed unless it relates to the validity or terms of

---

[42] Rule 803(2) does not admit statements made during or immediately after the event that bear no relation to it, however. This analysis of the Rule is in accord with that of Wigmore, who provides this simple example as illustrative of an inadmissible statement:

Suppose, for example, an injured passenger in a railway collision, thinking of his family's condition, exclaims "I hope that my insurance premium, which I mailed yesterday, has reached the company," referring to premium-money alleged by the insurance-company not to have been received.

6 WIGMORE, § 1754, at 226; *see* Murphy Auto Parts Co. v. Ball, 249 F.2d 508 (D.C. Cir. 1957) ("[A] careful analysis of the entire subject demonstrates that the third element, mechanically and narrowly construed, is a spurious element, and that reliability of the utterance is not inflexible, dependent upon the subject matter of the utterance."). *See generally,* 5 WEINSTEIN'S FEDERAL EVIDENCE § 803.04; 2 McCORMICK, § 272.

[43] *E.g.,* United States v. Napier, 518 F.2d 316 (9th Cir. 1975); Harrison v. United States, 200 F. 662 (6th Cir. 1912); *see also* United States v. Flecha, 539 F.2d 874 (2d Cir. 1976) (in narcotics prosecution, error to admit evidence of statement by codefendant made after arrest, "why so much excitement? If we are caught, we are caught;" statement indicated a lack of excitement). *See generally,* 4 MUELLER & KIRKPATRICK, §§ 435–436.

[44] *Compare* discussion of Rule 803(1) at § 803.5, *supra.*

the declarant's will.

Rule 803(3) codifies[45] a hearsay exception traditionally comprehended in part by the common-law phrase res gestae,[46] and it operates to admit hearsay statements offered in the context of four different situations: (i) statements as to then existing physical condition; (ii) statements as to then existing mental or emotional condition; (iii) certain statements probative of subsequent conduct; and (iv) statements of beliefs and intent concerning the declarant's will.[47] The Rule combines two common-law exceptions, *i.e.*, the relatively simple and less troublesome exception pertaining to statements concerning then existing physical conditions and the complicated and more difficult exception pertaining to statements concerning mental or emotional conditions.[48]

The underlying rationale for this hearsay exception is that statements concerning the declarant's then existing physical or mental condition are trustworthy because their spontaneity makes them at least as, if not more, reliable than testimony at trial on the same subject. Subsequent testimony concerning a prior condition at the very least would present a risk as to a

---

[45] *See generally,* 2 McCORMICK, §§ 273–276; 5 WEINSTEIN'S FEDERAL EVIDENCE § 803.05–803.08; 4 MUELLER & KIRKPATRICK, §§ 437–441; 6 WIGMORE, §§ 1718–1740. *See also* Hinton, *States of Mind and the Hearsay Rule,* 1 U. CHI. L. REV. 394 (1934); Hutchins & Slesinger, *Some Observations on the Law of Evidence—State of Mind to Prove an Act,* 38 YALE L.J. 283 (1929); McBaine, *Admissibility in California of Declarations of Physical or Mental Condition,* 19 CALIF. L. REV. 231 (1931); Maguire, *The Hillmon Case—Thirty-Three Years After,* 38 HARV. L. REV. 709 (1925); Morgan, *Hearsay Dangers and the Application of the Hearsay Concept,* 62 HARV. L. REV. 177 (1948); Payne, *The Hillmon Case—An Old Problem Revisited,* 41 VA. L. REV. 1011 (1955); Rice, *The State of Mind Exception to the Hearsay Rule: A Response to "Secondary" Relevance,* 14 DUQ. L. REV. 219 (1975–1976); Seidelson, *State of Mind Exception to the Hearsay Rule,* 13 DUQ. L. REV. 251 (1974); Seligman, *An Exception to the Hearsay Rule,* 26 HARV. L. REV. 146 (1912); Slough, *Res Gestae,* 2 KAN. L. REV. 121 (1953); Slough, *Spontaneous Statements and State of Mind,* 46 IOWA L. REV. 224 (1961); Weissenberger, *Hearsay Puzzles: An Essay on Federal Evidence Rule 803(3),* 64 TEMP. L. REV. 145 (1991). Comment, *Hearsay Under the Proposed Federal Rules: A Discretionary Approach,* 15 WAYNE L. REV. 1077 (1969).

[46] The exception contained in Rule 803(3) springs from the dual common-law exceptions that permitted the admission of hearsay statements demonstrating bodily pain and hearsay statements asserting emotions. Both exceptions rely upon an identical justification, *i.e.,* enhanced trustworthiness due to spontaneity. *See generally,* Slough, *Res Gestae,* 2 KAN. L. REV. 121, 126–27 (1953) ("The basic policy justifying this hearsay exception [for state of mind] parallels the policy . . . in relation to declarations of physical condition. Except for the fact that the physical condition exception found acceptance at an earlier date, the general principles underlying both exceptions are identical."). *See also* Wabisky v. D.C. Transit Sys., 309 F.2d 317 (D.C. Cir. 1962).

[47] 4 MUELLER & KIRKPATRICK, § 437.

[48] *See generally,* 5 WEINSTEIN'S FEDERAL EVIDENCE § 803.05.

defect in memory.[49] Moreover, the element of spontaneity attending statements of then existing conditions renders the risk of fabrication almost negligible since, as one commentator has noted, every person is "the world's foremost authority" on his contemporaneous internal states.[50] Of course, statements comprehended by Rule 803(3) are not conclusively trustworthy, since such declarations, even though sincerely uttered, may nevertheless be misleading because the declarant may have miscalculated his or her own motives, feelings, or physical sensations. Nevertheless, these risks are thought to be insufficient to preclude introduction of statements embraced by Rule 803(3), especially where the risk of a memory defect is so minimal. In this sense, the Rule 803(3) exception is parallel to the present sense impression exception formulated in Rule 803(1).

Whether the statement concerns a physical condition or a mental or emotional state, Rule 803(3) requires that the declaration be directed at a present condition, *i.e.*, a "then-existing" condition. Only where the subject matter of the statement is a present condition are the testimonial defects in memory and sincerity reduced. Where the statement concerns a past condition, the potential defects in memory and sincerity are present and the hearsay statement is not within this exception. Where the statement does not pertain to a "then-existing" condition, it must be viewed as a narrative of a past event formulated after time for reflection, and it is not admissible under Rule 803(3).[51]

---

[49] This reduced chance of fabrication is reinforced by the genuine need for such evidence. *See generally,* 6 WIGMORE, § 1714. As McCormick explains:

> Special reliability is provided furnished by the spontaneous quality of the declarations, assured by the requirement that the declarations purport to describe a condition presently existing at the time of the declaration. This assurance of reliability is almost certainly not always effective, however, since some of these statements describing present symptoms or the like are probably not spontaneous but rather calculated misstatements. Nevertheless, a sufficiently large percentage are undoubtedly spontaneous to justify the exception. The strong likelihood of spontaneity is also the basis for the special need for receiving the declarations. Being spontaneous, the hearsay statements are considered of greater probative value than the present testimony of the declarant.

2 MCCORMICK, § 274, at 226.

[50] *See* Moss v. Feldmeyer, 979 F.2d 1454 (10th Cir. 1992) (in medical malpractice action, decedent's statements rejecting hospital treatment were held to be admissible to show decedent's mental state); Seidelson, *The State of Mind Exception to the Hearsay Rule,* 13 DUQ. L. REV. 251 (1974). *But see* 4 MUELLER & KIRKPATRICK, § 437 (even though statements admitted under this exception will often be uttered spontaneously in response to an external stimulus, the rule does not require it; hence, there is no assurance of candor).

[51] *Compare* Mabry v. Travelers Ins. Co., 193 F.2d 497 (5th Cir. 1952) (contemporaneous expression of pain and suffering admissible) *with* Huff v. White Motor Corp., 609 F.2d 286 (7th Cir. 1979) (in wrongful death action, decedent's description of how accident occurred given to friend in hospital room properly excluded). *See also* United States v. Feldman, 825 F.2d 124 (7th Cir. 1987) (letter written by defendant accused of being the ringleader in an insurance fraud scheme held to be inadmissible under Rule 803(3) because the court found

Finally, Rule 803(3) should be compared with Rule 803(4), which pertains to statements made in aid of medical treatment or diagnosis. Rule 803(3) does not require that the statement be directed to, or made in the presence of medical personnel. Any person who had an opportunity to hear it may testify to the declaration, including friends, family, and unrelated bystanders.[52] While the respective scopes of Rule 803(3) and Rule 803(4) overlap, the applications of these hearsay exceptions are distinct.

§ 803.13   Declarations of Bodily Feelings, Symptoms, Condition

Rule 803(3) authorizes the introduction of declarants' statements concerning their present internal physical condition. Accordingly, Rule 803(3) operates as a vehicle for the admission of such statements as "I am ill," "I am tired," "I have a pain in my chest," and "I feel dizzy." Self-diagnostic statements or statements as to the external source of an internal condition are not, however, admissible under Rule 803(3) although they may be admissible under Rule 803(4). Accordingly, Rule 803(3) does not authorize admission of such statements as "X broke my arm," "I am in pain because I swallowed poison," or "That food made me ill."

A requisite element for qualification under this exception is that the expression must be contemporaneous with the physical sensation or condition and consequently, descriptions of past conditions (*i.e.*, past sensations, pains or physical symptoms) or descriptions of a past event are not admissible under Rule 803(3).[53] Accordingly, the statement "I felt ill yesterday" would not be admissible pursuant to this exception.

While the Rule is predicated upon the characteristic element of the contemporaneousness of the statement and the physical condition,[54] there is no requirement that the statement be made contemporaneously with an

---

a time lag made the letter reflective of defendant's state of mind concerning a past event).

[52] *E.g.,* Insurance Co. v. Mosley, 75 U.S. (8 Wall) 397 (1869) (wife); Northern Pac. R. Co. v. Urlin, 158 U.S. 271 (1895) (made to "any other person," dictum, citing 1 GREENLEAF, EVIDENCE); *see also* Baltimore & Ohio R.R. Co. v. Rambo, 59 F. 75 (6th Cir. 1893). *See generally,* 6 WIGMORE, § 1719.

[53] *E.g.,* Hartford Accident & Indem. Co. v. Carter, 110 F.2d 355 (5th Cir. 1940) (statement to treating physician that claimant had received a blow to the head was improperly received; it was the relation of a past event, not an exclamation of present pain or suffering); *see also* Wolf v. Procter & Gamble Co., 555 F. Supp. 613 (D.N.J. 1982); D'Angelo v. United States, 456 F. Supp. 127 (D. Del. 1978), *aff'd,* 605 F.2d 1194 (3d Cir. 1978) (employee's statement that he expected a promotion when he completed his training and obtained his license could not be considered as evidence that declarant's employer planned such a promotion).

[54] *See generally,* 5 WEINSTEIN'S FEDERAL EVIDENCE § 803.05, citing Northern Pac. R. Co. v. Urlin, 158 U.S. 271 (1895) ("[E]veryone knows that when injuries are internal and not obvious to visual inspection, the surgeon has to largely depend upon the responses and exclamations of the patient when subjected to examination").

external stimulus that produced the condition.[55] For example, where an individual is injured on Monday and still feels pain on Wednesday, a declaration on Wednesday concerning the person's then existing pain is admissible under Rule 803(3).

§ 803.14   State of Mind in Issue

A certain state of mind of a person may be a relevant factual issue,[56] and, while circumstantial evidence may be admitted to prove mental state, the most probative evidence of a person's mental state is usually the contemporaneous declarations of the person whose state of mind is at issue. Where the statements are *indirect* assertions of the mental state, the out-of-court statements are not hearsay. This type of admissible evidence of state of mind is discussed in § 801.7 of this Treatise. Where, however, the statements are direct assertions of the then existing mental or emotional condition, the statements are hearsay but nevertheless admissible pursuant to Rule 803(3).

Accordingly, where relevant, Rule 803(3) would operate as a vehicle for the admission of such statements as "I am depressed," "I am happy," "I am fond of X," and "I am afraid of X." Rule 803(3) will frequently be applied in criminal cases concerning bribery, extortion, or intimidation where the hearsay is probative of the victim's mental state.[57] The exception also arises with some frequency in civil cases where the statement is offered to show

---

[55] *E.g.,* Casualty Ins. Co. v. Salinas, 160 Tex. 445 (Tex. 1960) (reversible error to exclude testimony that plaintiff complained of present pain various times after his injury).

[56] *E.g.,* United States v. Partyka, 561 F.2d 118 (8th Cir. 1977) (out-of-court declarations of defendant admissible in criminal action in support of entrapment defense); Monroe v. Board of Ed., 65 F.R.D. 641 (D. Conn. 1975) (in action by high school student for wrongful suspension, defense affidavits filed in opposition to motion for summary judgment admissible to show motive or reason for the suspension). McCormick explains the particular rationale for this exception:

> This special assurance of reliability for statements of present state of mind rests, as in the case statements of bodily condition, upon their spontaneity and probable sincerity. This has been assured by the requirement that the statements must relate to a condition of mind or emotion existing at the time of the statement.

2 MCCORMICK, § 274, at 228–29; *see also* Slough, *Spontaneous Statements of State of Mind,* 46 IOWA L. REV. 224 (1961). *See generally,* 5 WEINSTEIN'S FEDERAL EVIDENCE § 803.06.

[57] *E.g.,* Hydrolevel Corp. v. American Soc. of Mechanical Eng's, 635 F.2d 118 (2d Cir. 1980), *aff'd,* 456 U.S. 556 (1982); *see also* United States v. Liu, 960 F.2d 449 (5th Cir. 1992) (the district court ruled properly in admitting a statement expressing the declarant's fear and in disallowing a statement as to the cause of his fear); United States v. Kelly, 722 F.2d 873 (1st Cir. 1983) (testimony that victim of extortion was afraid of perpetrator was admissible under the state of mind exception); Morris v. General Electric Credit Corp., 714 F.2d 32 (5th Cir. 1983) (in action by jewelry store against collection agency alleging loss of goodwill, hearsay letters and statements of jewelry store customers admitted that indicated customers' anger about the way the collection agency was handling accounts).

mental suffering, ill will, or malice.[58] In any case, Rule 803(3) may be appropriately applied wherever the declarant's mental state is relevant.[59]

§ 803.15   State of Mind to Demonstrate Subsequent Acts

Rule 803(3) not only admits declarants' statements where their state of mind is relevant; it also operates to admit statements concerning mental or emotional conditions where such mental states are probative of subsequent conduct.[60] In 1892, the Supreme Court, in the landmark case of *Mutual Life Insurance Co. v. Hillmon,*[61] endorsed the use of statements of plan or intent to show that the planned or intended act was undertaken. In a widow's action to collect the proceeds of insurance policies on the life of her husband, the main factual issue was whether the body of a man found shot at Crooked Creek was that of the insured, Hillmon. The defense argued that the body belonged to a man named Walters and sought to introduce in evidence letters from Walters to his sister and fiancee in which he stated that he planned to leave Wichita in early March with Hillmon.[62] The Supreme Court found that the letters should have been admitted:

> The letters in question were competent, not as narratives of facts communicated to the writer by others, nor yet as proof that he actually went away from Wichita, but as evidence that, shortly before the time when other evidence tended to show that he went away, he had the intention of going, and of going with Hillmon, which made it more probable both that he did go and that he went with Hillmon, than if there had been no proof of such intention.[63]

In accord with *Hillmon,* Rule 803(3) embraces declarations of plan or

----

[58] 2 McCORMICK, § 274. *See generally,* 5 WEINSTEIN'S FEDERAL EVIDENCE § 803.06; 6 WIGMORE, § 1732.

[59] Callahan v. A.E.V., Inc., 182 F.3d 237 (3d Cir. 1999) (in antitrust action, statements by unnamed customers of the plaintiffs that they stopped patronizing the plaintiffs' establishments because the defendants offered better prices and more choices were admissible under Rule 803(3) as showing the then existing state of mind of the declarant customers, whose identities were not important).

[60] *See generally,* 5 WEINSTEIN'S FEDERAL EVIDENCE § 803.07; 2 McCORMICK, § 275.

[61] Mutual Life Insurance Co. v. Hillmon, 145 U.S. 285 (1892). Hillmon was tried six times and the litigation continued over twenty years. For commentaries on the Hillmon decision and the concepts engendered thereby, *see* Payne, *The Hillmon Case—An Old Problem Revisited,* 41 VA. L. REV. 1011 (1955); Hutchins & Slesinger, *Some Observations on the Law of Evidence—State of Mind to Prove an Act,* 38 YALE L.J. 283 (1929); Seligman, *An Exception to the Hearsay Rule,* 26 HARV. L. REV. 146 (1912); Weissenberger, *Unintended Implications of Speech and the Definition of Hearsay,* 64 TEMP. L. REV. 145 (1992).

[62] The man who claimed he had accidentally shot Hillmon identified the body, but the defense contended that as part of a scheme to defraud the insurance companies, Hillmon killed Walters and then had his companion attempt to pass the body off as Hillmon. Mutual Life Ins. Co. v. Hillmon, 145 U.S. 285 (1892).

[63] Mutual Life Ins. Co. v. Hillmon, 145 U.S. 285 (1892).

intent to show subsequent conforming conduct. For example, the declarant's statement, "I plan to go to work tomorrow" is admissible as relevant evidence of the proposition that the declarant went to work on the day after the out-of-court statement. Likewise, statements such as "I plan to murder X," and "I don't intend to fulfill my obligations under the contract," are admissible under Rule 803(3) as probative evidence of the occurrence of the subsequent relevant conduct. In sum, a plan or intent is a mental state expressly comprehended by Rule 803(3).[64]

Arguably, the special reliability usually attending Rule 803(3) hearsay statements is absent where declarations of intent are offered to prove subsequent conduct, since it is less likely that a declared intention will be executed than it is that a declared state of mind is actually held. Further, there would appear to be no special need for this type of evidence where the declarant's conduct is an objective fact capable of proof in other ways.[65] Nevertheless, out-of-court statements of a declarant's plan, design, or intention are admissible to prove that the plan, design, or intention was executed by the declarant. Such statements comprehend then existing mental states, and as such, they do not suffer from possible defects in memory. Moreover, as relating to purely internal conditions, statements of intent, plan, or design are free of risks of defects in perception. Finally, while not conclusive proof of subsequent actions, statements of intent, plan, or design unquestionably alter the probabilities of subsequent conduct and are, consequently, relevant under Rule 401 as to whether the subsequent conduct occurred.

Accordingly, Rule 803(3) admits statements of intent as evidence of the declarant's subsequent conduct since at least a modicum of relevance is presented. Because the issue is really one of relevance, admission of evidence of state of mind offered to prove subsequent conduct is peculiarly

---

[64] United States v. Hughes, 970 F.2d 227 (7th Cir. 1992) (where defendant was charged with cocaine distribution, harmless error resulted where trial court erroneously excluded statements by defendant to his girlfriend that he was going to buy drugs for his personal use); Grove Fresh Distrib. v. New England Apple Prod., 969 F.2d 552 (7th Cir. 1992) (plaintiff was permitted to testify to statements from customers that they had switched to plaintiff's brand because they believed it was cheaper).

[65] McCormick posits the peculiar problem as follows, placing special emphasis upon factors involving relevance:

Despite the failure until recently to recognize the potential value of declarations of state of mind to prove subsequent conduct, it is now clear that out-of-court statements which tend to prove a plan, design, or intention of the declarant are admissible, subject to the usual limitations as to remoteness in time and apparent sincerity common to all declarations of mental state, to prove the plan, design, or intention of the declarant was carried out by the declarant.

2 McCormick, § 275, at 234–235; *see also* 5 Weinstein's Federal Evidence § 803.07 (questioning relevance of such evidence on the basis that the theory that an intent to perform an act is generally carried out questionable on psychological grounds).

subject to the general exclusionary principles of Rule 403. Obviously where the statement of intent and the subsequent event are separated by substantial time, the probative value of the out-of-court declaration of intent is relatively low. Likewise, certain tentative assertions of intent have marginal probative value of subsequent conduct. In such situations the risk that the trier of fact may use this evidence improperly may substantially outweigh its probative value, and Rule 403 may operate to preclude admission of the evidence.[66]

The reliability of a declaration of intent as proof of subsequent conduct is further reduced where the cooperation of another person in addition to the declarant is necessary to successfully carry out the act.[67] Arguably, *Hillmon* itself presented this type of joint action issue, because Walters' expressed intention to leave Wichita with Hillmon depended upon Hillmon's continued willingness to travel with Walters. The post-Rules force of *Hillmon* with respect to joint action is unclear. While the Advisory Committee stated that Rule 803(3) was not intended to disturb *Hillmon*,[68] the House Judiciary Committee disagreed:

> [T]he Committee intends that the Rule be construed to limit the doctrine of [Hillmon], so as to render statements of intent by a declarant admissible only to prove his future conduct, not the future conduct of another person.[69]

Federal courts have been inconsistent in their approaches to *Hillmon*-type issues.[70] However, a common-sense result can be arrived at if one realizes

---

[66] *See* United States v. Hogan, 886 F.2d 1497 (7th Cir. 1989) (in a trial for racketeering and tax fraud, the trial court properly excluded witness testimony that his father intended to make a gift to the defendant, not a bribe. The court found the comments to be too "speculative" to be admissible under Rule 803(3).).

[67] *See* 4 MUELLER & KIRKPATRICK, §§ 439–440; 5 WEINSTEIN'S FEDERAL EVIDENCE § 803.07; 2 MCCORMICK, § 275.

[68] Advisory Committee Note, Rule 803(3).

[69] H.R. Rep. No. 93-650, 93d Cong., 1st Sess. 13–14 (1973).

[70] *See, e.g.*, Gual Morales v. Hernandez Vega, 579 F.2d 677 (1st Cir. 1978) (plaintiff sought to prove that defendant was part of conspiracy against him and wanted court to consider affidavit that claimed employer's lawyer sought to get to defendant; court concluded, "statements that this lawyer is claimed to have made concerning his intention of seeing defendant would not be admissible against [defendant]"); United States v. Mangan, 575 F.2d 32 (2d Cir. 1978) (in prosecution for fraud against the government and related conspiracy, court noted government's argument and concluded that defendant's statements "might be admissible"); *cf.* United States v. Astorga-Torres, 682 F.2d 1331 (9th Cir. 1982) (codefendant's statements properly admitted as evidence of his intent, from which jury could properly draw inferences); United States v. Cicale, 691 F.2d 95 (2d Cir. 1982) (statements by declarant to undercover agent that he was going to meet his source in order to make arrangements to obtain heroin were admissible to show defendant's participation in conspiracy, where on each occasion declarant was seen soon afterward with defendant or arriving at defendant's address, thus supported by a "ring of reliability"). *See generally,* Weissenberger, *Hearsay Puzzles: An Essay on Federal Evidence Rule 803(3)*, 64 TEMP. L. REV. 145 (1991).

that many *Hillmon*-type declarations actually have two components: (1) a declaration of intent; and (2) an implied assertion admissible as non-hearsay pursuant to the application of Rule 801(c).[71] Take, for example, a situation where a declarant states, "I intend to go out with Michelle tonight," and this statement is offered as proof that Michelle had the opportunity to murder the declarant on the night of the utterance. Such a declaration's probative value lies primarily in establishing the actions of a person other than the declarant, and only secondarily in establishing the declarant's intent to cooperate in meeting Michelle. Consequently, at the time it is uttered, the statement, "I intend to go out with Michelle tonight," is offered to show that there has been an express arrangement preceding the statement between Michelle and the declarant. As evidence of such an arrangement, the statement is an admissible implied assertion, *i.e.,* it is a statement not offered for its truth but rather for what may be implied from it. Accordingly, when offered to implicate the accused, the statement, "I intend to go with Michelle tonight," is in reality two assertions. One assertion is a direct, internal statement of intent admissible under the *Hillmon* doctrine as embodied in Rule 803(3). Simultaneously, the declarant is making an indirect, external assertion manifesting a belief about Michelle — that is, the declarant believes that an arrangement has been made with Michelle for dinner. Visualizing what might have transpired, the statement inferentially reflects a telephone conversation or prior meeting between the declarant and the accused at which the date for dinner was arranged. This second, implicit message in the victim's expression of the plan to meet the accused is a classic admissible implied assertion.[72] Some federal authority has approved statements of intent to show joint action of the declarant and other persons, particularly where other corroborating evidence of the conduct is presented.[73] The subject of implied assertions is discussed in § 801.6, *supra*.

---

[71] *See* § 801.6, *supra*, for further discussion of implied assertions and their place in the hearsay system.

[72] *See* § 801.6, *supra*.

[73] United States v. Sperling, 726 F.2d 69 (2d Cir. 1984) (trial court properly admitted testimony of a witness that a drug dealer said she was going to meet her source at a specified time, and that at that time she met only with defendant, in conjunction with testimony of a second witness who stated that defendant's father had said he was going to send defendant to a specified place for a heroin transaction with the drug dealer and defendant was later seen there with her; the court held that the testimony as to declarants' states of mind was admissible against non-declarant/defendant when corroborated by independent evidence); *see* United States v. Astorga-Torres, 682 F.2d 1331 (9th Cir. 1982) (co-defendant's statements properly admitted as evidence of his intent, from which jury could properly draw inferences); United States v. Cicale, 691 F.2d 95 (2d Cir. 1982) (statements by declarant to undercover agent that he was going to meet his source in order to make arrangements to obtain heroin were admissible to show defendant's participation in conspiracy, where on each occasion declarant was seen soon afterward with defendant or arriving at defendant's address, thus supported by a "ring of reliability"); United States v. Moore, 571 F.2d 76 (2d Cir. 1978).

§ 803.16   State of Mind to Demonstrate Beliefs

While Rule 803(3) permits introduction of hearsay statements tending to demonstrate subsequent conduct by the declarant, a statement of belief is not admissible for the purpose of proving an act or conduct alleged to have been performed prior to the making of the statement.[74] Accordingly, Rule 803(3) excludes from the exception mental state declarations that are "a statement of memory or belief to prove the fact remembered or believed." A "belief" is a factual proposition that refers to events or occurrences external to the declarant such as actions of other people or other observed matters. Obviously, if the exception for statements of then existing mental condition included the mental states of memory or belief offered to prove facts external to the declarant, this exception would swallow the entire hearsay rule.[75] In the absence of this disqualification of statements of memory or belief, all hearsay statements could be construed as admissible declarations of mental state, thereby emasculating the entire hearsay system.[76]

Any statement that looks back to a prior event external to the declarant inevitably presents risks of defects in sincerity, perception, narration, and memory, and as a consequence, there is no justification for the admission of such hearsay statements. Statements tending to prove past conduct or facts are more appropriately termed "present memory" of a past event and are not admissible pursuant to Rule 803(3), except in certain situations occurring in will cases discussed in the next section.

§ 803.17   State of Body or Mind to Demonstrate Past Conduct Concerning Declarant's Last Will and Testament

While Rule 803(3) does not generally operate to admit statements of memory or belief to prove the fact remembered or believed, such statements of memory or belief are admissible where they relate to the execution,

---

[74] *See, e.g.,* Shepard v. United States, 290 U.S. 96 (1933) (statement of deceased made to nurse two days after the incident that "Dr. Shepard has poisoned me" inadmissible to prove she was poisoned); Marshall v. Commonwealth Aquarium, 611 F.2d 1 (1st Cir. 1979) (testimony by witness of declarant's recollection of telephone conversation inadmissible to prove contents of conversation). *See generally,* Payne, *The Hillmon Case—An Old Problem Revisited,* 41 VA. L. REV. 1011 (1955). Facts external to the declarant occurring contemporaneously with the out-of-court statement may be admissible under Rule 803(1) or (2).

[75] *See* 2 McCORMICK, § 276; 5 WEINSTEIN'S FEDERAL EVIDENCE § 803.08; 4 MUELLER & KIRKPATRICK, §§ 439–440; *see, e.g.,* United States v. Murray, 297 F.2d 812 (2d Cir. 1962); United States v. Margiotta, 688 F.2d 108 (2d Cir. 1982); Prather v. Prather, 650 F.2d 88 (5th Cir. 1981). *See generally,* Seligman, *An Exception to the Hearsay Rule,* 26 HARV. L. REV. 146 (1912).

[76] The clearest expression against this type of evidence is contained in Shepard v. United States, 290 U.S. 96, 105–106 (1933) (Cardozo, J.) ("[D]eclarations of intention, casting light upon the future, have been sharply distinguished from declarations of memory, pointing backwards to the past. There would be an end, or nearly that, to the rule against hearsay if the distinction were ignored"); *see also* 2 McCORMICK, §§ 275–276.

revocation, identification or terms of the declarant's will. In this regard, Rule 803(3) is in accord with the prevailing view.[77]

The rationale for this exception to the general inadmissibility of statements of past events is grounded on the special need for such evidence. The testator, who is the person best in a position to know the facts, and sometimes the only person in possession of such facts, is obviously unavailable at the time the will is in need of interpretation.[78] In almost every dispute over a will, the state of mind of the testator assumes paramount importance, and the testator's own statements are likely to be the most probative evidence of the import of his or her own will. This need for the testator's statement is often coupled with the recognition that a testator's statements bear peculiar reliability due to the fact that a will is a serious matter. Consequently, it is reasonably assumed that in the absence of suspicious circumstances, the testator spoke from firsthand knowledge and with due regard for the seriousness and candor required of the occasion.[79]

Under Rule 803(3) statements offered for the purpose of proving that the testator was of sound mind, that he or she harbored certain emotions or feelings toward those whom he or she either included or failed to mention, or that he or she was or was not under the sort of personal pressure amounting to "undue influence" are all admissible. Also admissible are statements indicating his or her intent to execute, revoke, or modify a will when offered to prove subsequent conforming conduct. The Rule, however, does not permit the introduction of a testator's hearsay statements of believed past facts to prove any facts that do not relate to the execution, revocation, identification, or terms of the declarant's will.[80]

---

[77] *See generally,* 2 McCORMICK, § 276.

[78] *E.g.,* Savoy v. Savoy, 220 F.2d 364 (D.C. Cir. 1954) (reversible error to exclude evidence that several months after tearing up a will that had been torn in two pieces and then taped together, the testator had made statements indicating that he had disposed of his property in the manner that the torn will provided); *see also* Lingham v. Harmon, 502 F. Supp. 302 (D. Md. 1980). *See generally,* 6 WIGMORE, § 1736; 2 McCORMICK, § 276; Slough, *Res Gestae,* 2 KAN. L. REV. 121 (1953); Advisory Committee Note, Rule 803(3).

[79] Under the pre-Rules decision of Throckmorton v. Holt, 180 U.S. 552 (1901), declarations of this type were often inadmissible unless they were near enough in time to the execution of the will to be considered part of the res gestae, whether they were made before or after the execution of the will. Regarding the decision, Wigmore says that it "is only a quicksand for those who seek guidance on the subject." 6 WIGMORE § 1736. Under Rule 803(3) all relevant statements of the testator made either before or after execution of the will are admissible. *See* 5 WEINSTEIN'S FEDERAL EVIDENCE § 803.08.

[80] *Compare* Yarbrough v. Prudential Ins. Co., 100 F.2d 547 (5th Cir. 1938) (error to admit wife's testimony that deceased had handed over insurance policy assuring her that it was paid as part of res gestae) *with* Krimlofski v. United States, 190 F. Supp. 734 (N.D. Iowa 1961) (general rule of construction admitting statements of testator regarding will especially is applicable in cases where designated beneficiary is not clear).

§ 803.18　Rule 803(4) Statement Made for Medical Diagnosis or Treatment

The following are not excluded by the rule against hearsay, regardless of whether the declarant is available as a witness:

***

(4) *Statement Made for Medical Diagnosis or Treatment.* A statement that:

(A) is made for — and is reasonably pertinent to — medical diagnosis or treatment; and

(B) describes medical history; past or present symptoms or sensations; their inception; or their general cause.

Rule 803(4), which governs the standards for admissibility of hearsay declarations made for the purpose of securing medical treatment or diagnosis, represents both a continuance and an extension of prior federal law.[81] Rule 803(4) codifies the last of four hearsay exceptions known under the common law as res gestae. Along with present sense impressions (Rule 803(1)), excited utterances (Rule 803(2)), and then existing mental, emotional or physical conditions (Rule 803(3)), Rule 803(4) represents the modern application of the now obsolete res gestae concept.[82] Under Rule 803(4) hearsay statements made by a declarant regarding present and past physical conditions are admissible where they are made in subjective contemplation of obtaining treatment or diagnosis. Prior to the adoption of the Rule, many of the federal courts restricted the exception to allow only statements of present symptoms.[83] Likewise, pre-Rule cases frequently limited the exception to include statements made in contemplation of

---

[81] *See generally,* 2 McCormick, §§ 277–278; 5 Weinstein's Federal Evidence § 803.09; 4 Mueller & Kirkpatrick, § 442; 6 Wigmore, §§ 1719–1720. *See also* Seidel & Gingrich, *Hearsay Objections to Expert Psychiatric Opinion Testimony and the Proposed Federal Rules of Evidence,* 39 UMKC L. Rev. 141 (1970); Slough, *Res Gestae,* 2 Kan. L. Rev. 41 (1953); Slough, *Spontaneous Statements and State of Mind,* 46 Iowa L. Rev. 224 (1961); Comment, *Hearsay Under the Proposed Federal Rules: A Discretionary Approach,* 15 Wayne L. Rev. 1077, 1134–1135 (1969); Note, *Medical Testimony and the Hearsay Rule,* 1964 Wash U.L.Q. 192; Note, *Evidence—Admissibility of Expressions of Pain and Suffering,* 51 Mich. L. Rev. 902 (1953).

[82] *See* § 803.2, *supra,* for a discussion of the common-law res gestae concept.

[83] *Compare* Meaney v. United States, 112 F.2d 538 (2d Cir. 1940) (reversible error to exclude physician's testimony of patient's "declarations as to the time of the onset of his disease and its immediate severity") *with* Felice v. Long Island R.R., 426 F.2d 192 (2d Cir. 1970) (reversible error to permit plaintiff to introduce medical reports prepared by treating physician indicating patient's description of circumstances of the accident causing his injury).

treatment alone but not those merely seeking diagnosis or assessment.[84] Rule 803(4) admits declarations without regard to the purpose of the examination or the need for the patient's medical history. Statements made in anticipation of diagnosis that are in preparation of the expert trial testimony are admissible, and consequently, Rule 803(4) avoids the necessity of making artificial distinctions between diagnoses made for treatment and those made for purposes of trial preparation.[85] Finally, it should be noted that Rule 803(4) does not permit the introduction of out-of-court statements by physicians as to the treatment prescribed or the diagnosis reached.[86] The hearsay exception in Rule 803(4) reaches only statements of persons seeking the treatment or diagnosis.

One rationale underpinning the exception for statements made for purposes of obtaining treatment and diagnosis is that the declarant's subjective motive generally guarantees trustworthiness; declarants have a motive to tell the truth because their treatment or diagnosis will depend upon what they say.[87] Also, there is a special need for such evidence in light of the

---

[84] *E.g.,* Nutt v. Black Hills Stage Lines, Inc., 452 F.2d 480 (8th Cir. 1971); *see also* Chicago & N.W.R. Co. v. Garwood, 167 F.2d 848 (8th Cir. 1948) (medical history of claimant in FELA action, which was given to physician only to qualify him as a favorable witness, and not for purposes of "effecting a cure," was inadmissible); Nashville, C. & St. L. R.R. Co. v. York, 127 F.2d 606 (6th Cir. 1942) (statements made to physician in order to qualify him as an expert witness inadmissible). *But see* Atlantic C.L.R. Co. v. Dixon, 207 F.2d 899 (5th Cir. 1953); Chicago R.R. Co. v. Kramer, 234 F. 245 (7th Cir. 1916).

[85] McCormick explains:

> The dubious propriety of these restrictions is probably at least partially responsible for the restrictive view taken by the courts as to what constitutes consultation solely for purposes of obtaining testimony from the physician consulted. The ultimate issue is whether there was any significant treatment motive; if this existed, any additional motive of obtained testimony is ignored. For example, a physician's testimony is not within these restrictions despite the fact that he was consulted after the declarant retained an attorney or even at the attorney's recommendation. The fact that no treatment was actually given is not controlling, but subsequent reliance upon advice of a treatment nature given by the physician is strong evidence of a treatment motive for the final consultation.

2 McCormick, § 278. *But see* 4 Mueller & Kirkpatrick, § 442.

[86] *See, e.g.,* Bombard v. Fort Wayne Newspapers, Inc., 92 F.3d 560 (7th Cir. 1996) (trial court properly found that plaintiff's testimony that his physician had said he would be able to work half-time was incompetent evidence; although Rule 803(4) provides for the admission of statements made by a patient to his doctor, it does not provide for the admission of statements made by the treating physician).

[87] *See* Roberts v. Hollocher, 664 F.2d 200 (8th Cir. 1981); *see, e.g.,* United States v. Narciso, 446 F. Supp. 252, 289 (E.D. Mich. 1977) ("[T]he rationale of [FRE 803(4)] is that statements made to physicians for purposes of diagnosis and treatment are exceptionally trustworthy since the declarant has a strong motive to tell the truth in order to receive proper care. Moreover, no other way of determining subjective symptoms has yet been devised."); *see also* 2 McCormick, § 277 ("[A]lthough statements to physicians are not likely to be

scarcity of evidence concerning subjective symptoms.[88]

Where the out-of-court statement is made to a physician consulted as a prospective expert witness, however, the exception rests more upon considerations of practicality than enhanced trustworthiness. Under pre-Rule practice such statements were inadmissible as substantive evidence since it was thought the declarant had a motive to make self-serving statements to the prospective expert witness. Such out-of-court statements could be introduced not for the truth of the contents, but to disclose the underlying basis for a physician's in-court opinion testimony.[89] As a practical matter, however, juries tended not to accord the distinction much deference despite an appropriate limiting instruction.[90] Consequently, Rule 803(4) admits statements made for the purpose of obtaining a diagnosis where the statement reveals data upon which the physician as an expert witness would be justified in relying in rendering an opinion.

The pre-Rule distinction between physicians called upon to treat a patient and those called upon in anticipation of testifying at trial resulted in the exclusion of out-of-court statements of present pain or symptoms as substantive proof of their existence because the declarant's motive to falsify or exaggerate was thought to vitiate the reliability generally attending statements to treating physicians. Prior practice also limited the use of statements as to medical history to demonstrating the basis for the physi-

---

spontaneous, since they are usually made in response to questions, their reliability is assured by the likelihood that the patient believes that the effectiveness of the treatment he receives may depend largely upon the accuracy of the information he provides the physician."). *Cf.* United States v. Matta-Ballesteros, 71 F.3d 754 (9th Cir. 1995), *amended,* 98 F.3d 1100 (9th Cir. 1996) (trial court did not abuse its discretion in excluding report of a prison psychologist; the defendant had been ordered to see the psychologist but did not believe he had any special reason to do so, and thus had no special incentive to be truthful).

[88] 5 WEINSTEIN'S FEDERAL EVIDENCE § 803.09. This is in accord with a rationale supporting the exception contained in Rule 803(3) for present sense impressions because a patient's description of a present physical sensation may well be from the best source of information; *see also* § 803.13, *supra.*

[89] *See generally,* Aetna Life Ins. Co. v. Quinley, 87 F.2d 732 (8th Cir. 1937) (expressing concern that if such statements were admitted for their truth, an injured person could be examined by a physician, relate his version of the facts, and then call the physician as a witness to recite the patient's account of what occurred).

[90] The Advisory Committee Note to Rule 803(4) states:

Conventional doctrine has excluded from the hearsay exception, as not within its guarantee of truthfulness, statements to a physician consulted only for the purpose of enabling him to testify. While these statements were not admissible as substantive evidence, the expert was allowed to state the basis of his opinion, including statements of this kind. The distinction thus called for was one most unlikely to be made by juries. The rule accordingly rejects the limitation.

See also O'Gee v. Dobbs Houses, 570 F.2d 1084 (2d Cir. 1978) (recognizing the futility of asking the jury to perform the mental gymnastics required under the common-law doctrine). *See generally,* 5 WEINSTEIN'S FEDERAL EVIDENCE § 803.09; 2 MCCORMICK, § 278.

cian's diagnosis and treatment and they were not admitted for the truth of *past* illness, symptoms, or injury.[91] Since the underlying rationale for each of these restrictions has been superseded by modern medical and legal practices, Rule 803(4) casts aside these limitations.

§ 803.19 "Reasonably Pertinent" Requirement

Rule 803(4) bases admissibility of statements made for purposes of obtaining medical treatment or diagnosis upon the objective standard that such hearsay declarations must be "reasonably pertinent" to the treatment or diagnosis sought. The exception consequently may operate as a vehicle for the admission of statements of medical history, past and present symptoms and conditions, past and present pain or sensations, the inception or cause of the medical condition or illness, and the external causal source, if any, of the medical condition, injury or illness.

Although the "reasonably pertinent to medical diagnosis or treatment" standard imparts a degree of objectivity, it should be read broadly in order to give meaning to the policy supporting the exception. Generally, the physician's conclusion as to pertinency should be decisive, despite the fact that on a conceptual level it is the declarant's subjective motives that control whether he or she is truthful. In practice, the doctor's analysis assumes greater importance since the physician usually directs the course of the examination through the questions asked. Consequently, the physician's solicitation of certain information indicates that the statement is reasonably pertinent to diagnosis or treatment.[92]

While statements concerning past injuries or conditions may be admitted pursuant to Rule 803(4), the pertinency standard generally operates to preclude expansion of the Rule beyond its underlying rationale by excluding statements that are clearly self-serving narrations of past events.[93] Never-

---

[91] Padgett v. Southern Ry. Co. 396 F.2d 303 (6th Cir. 1968) (approving receipt of expert testimony by examining physician where plaintiff relied upon the advice in obtaining treatment); *see* 5 WEINSTEIN'S FEDERAL EVIDENCE § 803.09 (procedural rules ensure the reliability of medical testimony by giving the parties access to medical reports before trial and empowering the judge to compel a party to undergo a mental or physical examination).

[92] *See* 5 WEINSTEIN'S FEDERAL EVIDENCE § 803.09; 2 MCCORMICK, § 277.

[93] This facet of the Rule is an expansion of pre-Rule federal law. Under prior law, such statements were restricted to present sensations of pain and did not embrace statements concerning medical history. *E.g.,* Aetna Life Ins. Co. v. Quinley, 87 F.2d 732, 733–734 (8th Cir. 1937) (if statements to a physician relating the circumstances attending an accident were admissible, "then an injured person might have himself examined by a physician called for treatment, relate to him the alleged facts with reference to the circumstances under which he received his injuries, [and] might [then] place this physician on the witness stand to narrate his version of the facts and circumstances under which he received his injuries, and not himself take the witness stand at all, and by so doing deprive the defendant of the right to cross-examination, and if he perchance employed a number of physicians, his testimony might be multiplied with impunity as far as cross-examination is concerned"); *cf.* Petrocelli

theless, the Rule should not be read as excluding details that the declarants includes as they apprise the physician of the necessary data, such as statements describing the general nature of the physical injury, the object causing the injury,[94] and the time of its occurrence.[95] Where a physician is consulted about an illness, the reasonably pertinent standard usually is satisfied by declarations of the believed cause, such as exposure, consump-

---

v. Gallison, 679 F.2d 286 (1st Cir. 1982) (Rule 803(4) provides a basis for admitting patient statements regarding medical history or prior treatment). McCormick provides the basis for extension of the rationale supporting present physical condition to statements of past conditions:

> This strong assurance of reliability has caused some courts to expand the exception to include statements made by a patient to a physician concerning past symptoms. This seems appropriate, as patients are likely to recognize the importance to their treatment of accurate statements as to past, as well as, present symptoms. Wider acceptance of this expansion might well be expected, although at present more courts would probably admit the testimony for the limited purpose of explaining the basis for the physician's conclusion than would admit it to prove the fact of the prior symptoms.

2 MCCORMICK, § 277; *see also* Advisory Committee Note, Rule 803(4). ("The same guarantee of trustworthiness extends to statements of past conditions and medical history, made for purposes of diagnosis or treatment").

[94] United States v. Iron Thunder, 714 F.2d 765 (8th Cir. 1983); *see also* United States v. Iron Shell, 633 F.2d 77 (8th Cir. 1980) (statements made to physician who examined nine-year-old female victim of the alleged assault with intent to rape on the night of the assault, repeated by doctor at trial properly received because of the patient's strong motive to tell the truth); *cf.* Brown v. Seaboard A. R. Co., 434 F.2d 1101 (5th Cir. 1970) (directed verdict in favor of defendant affirmed in personal injury case where only indication of defendant's negligence was in portion of medical report recorded by intern indicating that plaintiff had told the doctor that he was walking beside the train when a projection from the train struck him, causing him to fall under the train).

[95] *See* Gaussen v. United Fruit Co., 412 F.2d 72 (2d Cir. 1969); *see also* Britt v. Corporacion Peruana de Vapores, 506 F.2d 927 (5th Cir. 1975) (in slip-and-fall accident, defendant introduced medical record in which plaintiff was said to have attributed his back problem to the fact that he had been pitching flour, and receipt of this record was proper; "statements made for purposes of medical diagnosis or treatment which describe medical history or the general cause of an ailment are not excluded by the hearsay rule"); Pagano v. Magic Chef, Inc., 181 F. Supp. 146 (E.D. Pa. 1960) (proper for doctor to testify that he took defendant's statement as to fainting into consideration in rendering opinion and diagnosis). McCormick provides the rationale for this extension:

> The exception might be taken one step further to encompass statements made to a physician concerning the cause or the external source of the condition to be treated. In some cases the special assurance of the reliability — the patient's belief that accuracy is essential to effective treatment — also applies to statements concerning the cause, and a physician who views this as related to diagnosis and treatment might reasonably be expected to communicate this to the patient and perhaps take other steps to assure a reliable response. . . . On the other hand, when statements as to causation enter the realm of fixing fault it is unlikely that the patient or the physician regarded them as related to diagnosis or treatment. In such cases, the statements lack any assurance of reliability and would properly be excluded.

2 MCCORMICK, § 277.

tion of certain foods or inhaling noxious fumes, and the type of symptoms, such as pain, aches, fever, nausea, or dizziness.[96] Permitting the jury to hear details that the declarant naturally recites in obtaining medical treatment or diagnosis does not violate the purpose of the hearsay rule by exposing them to unreliable evidence.

Rule 803(4) does not open the door to all statements made to a physician, however. As Justice Scalia recently observed, "Police, paramedics, and doctors do not need to know the address where a shooting took place, the name of the shooter, or the shooter's height and weight to provide proper medical care."[97] Statements concerning fault or guilt usually are not reasonably pertinent to diagnosis or treatment.[98] A declarant's statements that his injury resulted, for example, from the defendant's negligent driving, refusing to provide a safe work environment, or maintaining an unreasonably dangerous condition, are immaterial to the diagnosis and treatment of an injury, and consequently, fall outside the scope of the exception. Similarly, assertions charging that the injury was knowingly and maliciously perpetrated by the defendant are inadmissible under the Rule.[99] A statement by a patient identifying the person who caused the patient's injuries may be

---

[96] *See* 2 McCormick, § 277. *See generally,* 4 Mueller & Kirkpatrick, § 442.

[97] Michigan v. Bryant, 562 U.S. —, 131 S. Ct. 1143, 179 L. Ed. 2d 93, 124 (2011) (Scalia, J., dissenting on other grounds).

[98] *See* Roberts v. Hollocher, 664 F.2d 200 (8th Cir. 1981) (in civil rights action against police officers for damages arising out of incident that led to plaintiff's requiring hospital treatment after arrest, district court properly excluded entry in hospital record that read, "multiple contusions and hematoma, consistent with excessive force"; statement was conclusion going to fault rather than the cause of the condition); United States v. Narciso, 446 F. Supp. 252, 289 (E.D. Mich. 1977) ("[FRE 803(4)] has never been held to apply to accusations of personal fault either in a civil or criminal context. Thus . . . it is stated that a statement by a patient that he was shot would be admissible, but a statement that he was shot by a white man would not." [court cites example given in Advisory Committee's Note to Rule 803(04): "[A] patient's statements that he was struck by an automobile would qualify but not his statement that the car was driven through a red light."]); United States v. Balfany, 965 F.2d 575 (8th Cir. 1992) (statement by child in sex abuse case identifying defendant did not render the statement inadmissible under Rule 803(4)). *But see* United States v. George, 960 F.2d 97 (9th Cir. 1992) (in a child sex abuse case, statements of fault were held admissible since they were procured for the purpose of providing medical treatment); United States v. Renville, 779 F.2d 430 (8th Cir. 1985) (in sexual abuse prosecution, trial court did not abuse discretion in admitting statements made by the child-victim to a physician implicating the child's stepfather); United States v. Provost, 969 F.2d 617 (8th Cir. 1992) (a ten-year-old child's out-of-court statement to a clinical psychologist implicating a family member was relevant to her diagnosis).

[99] *Compare* United States v. Iron Shell, 633 F.2d 77 (8th Cir. 1980) (admitted statements of nine-year-old female victim of alleged assault with intent to rape made in response to physician's questions concerning the cause of her injuries) *with* Roberts v. Hollocher, 664 F.2d 200 (8th Cir. 1981) (trial court properly excluded physician's diagnosis in medical record indicating patient's injuries were "consistent with excessive force"; *Iron Shell* was distinguished because in that case, there was no improper motive behind the declarations, the

admissible, however, in the rare case where that information is relevant to the doctor's treatment of those injuries. The most well-known example of such a situation is where a victim of child abuse is related to or living with the perpetrator, for one of the first steps in treating such abuse must often be the removal of the child or the abuser from the home.[100]

§ 803.20   By and to Whom

Although a hearsay declaration offered under Rule 803(4) typically will have been made to the physician by the person seeking medical treatment or diagnosis, the Rule also encompasses statements made by persons who bring the patient to the hospital or doctor's office, as long as the third person's statements are made in subjective contemplation of treatment or diagnosis. This result obtains, for example, where a parent brings a child to a doctor for treatment. The admission of statements in such circumstances rests on the assumption that the declarant's action in seeking medical assistance for the patient shows concern, which in turn is evidence of the sincerity of any statements made to the physician where the physician is prepared to rely upon the word of another who speaks for a patient who, for whatever reason, does not speak personally, trustworthiness is indicated.[101] Rule 803(4) does

---

age of the declarant assured trustworthiness and the statements aided the doctor in limiting his examination).

[100] United States v. Peneaux, 432 F.3d 882, 893–894 (8th Cir. 2005) (while a declarant's statements identifying the party allegedly responsible for her injuries is not normally pertinent to treatment or diagnosis or admissible under Rule 803(4), a statement by a child abuse victim that the abuser is a member of the victim's immediate household is "reasonably pertinent" to treatment or diagnosis, and is of the type reasonably relied upon by a physician for treatment or diagnosis. "Due to the nature of child sexual abuse, a doctor must be able to identify and treat not only physical injury, but also the emotional and psychological problems that typically accompany sexual abuse by a family member. Moreover, such a statement may be relevant to prevent future occurrences of abuse and to the medical safety of the child"); United States v. George, 960 F.2d 97 (9th Cir. 1992) (in a child sex abuse case, statements of fault were held admissible since they were for the purpose of providing medical treatment); United States v. Renville, 779 F.2d 430 (8th Cir. 1985) (in sexual abuse prosecution, trial court did not err in admitting statements by the child-victim to a physician implicating the child's stepfather); United States v. Provost, 969 F.2d 617 (8th Cir. 1992) (a ten-year-old child's out-of-court statement to a clinical psychologist implicating a family member was relevant to her diagnosis).

[101] See Advisory Committee Note, Rule 803(4). See generally, 4 MUELLER & KIRKPAT-RICK, § 442. See also Lovejoy v. United States, 92 F.3d 628 (8th Cir. 1996) (trial court did not abuse its discretion in admitting statements made by the mother of a child victim of sexual abuse to a nurse examining the child; the child was unable to communicate on her own, and the mother's statements helped identify the area of the child's body to be examined). The Rule does not preclude admission of statements made by a child to a physician, particularly where the evidence demonstrates that the child understands the function of doctors and nurses and the need to tell them the truth. See United States v. Norman T., 129 F.3d 1099 (10th Cir. 1997) (upholding trial court's admission of statements made by child victim of sexual abuse to her doctor, noting that the child had previously been to the hospital with her brother who needed asthma treatments).

not support admission, however, where it appears that the declarant does not have firsthand knowledge of the facts surrounding the injury and is basing his or her statement on pure speculation. Generally, where the relationship between the declarant and the patient is remote, the trustworthiness is less probable, not only due to the diminished incentive to tell the truth but also because a stranger may not be able to identify a patient's subjective symptoms as reliably as one who has greater familiarity with the patient.

Much the same analysis attends statements made to persons other than the treating or diagnosing physician. Rule 803(4) requires that the declarant make the statement in subjective contemplation that the statement will ultimately be relayed to a physician who will provide diagnosis or treatment. Consequently, Rule 803(4) may operate to admit hearsay declarations made to such persons as nurses, nurses' aides, interns, administrative assistants, paramedics, and ambulance drivers.[102] Likewise, where there is contemplation of medical treatment or diagnosis, the statement may be made to family members and friends, firefighters, police officers, etc. Moreover, the Rule operates to admit declarations where information is passed along from one individual to another, thus raising multiple hearsay issues.[103] For example, where the patient is found at the scene of an automobile accident and states to the attending paramedic that his jaw is in pain as a result of colliding with the steering wheel, and where this fact is passed along to the intern at the entrance of the hospital by the paramedic and then to the attending physician in the emergency room by the intern, the physician may testify to the statement at trial since the statement by the patient was made in contemplation of obtaining medical treatment and each person in the chain possessed the same purpose. Since the Rule does not limit the scope of the exception by reference to either the speaker or the listener, each statement in the chain may satisfy the exception.[104]

§ 803.21   Psychiatrists

Difficult problems may emerge where the out-of-court statement is made in order to obtain medical aid for a mental problem. Since Rule 803(4) does not require that a statement be relevant to the declarant's physical condition, a statement directed to, for example, a psychiatrist may be within the scope of the exception. The exception is not limited to psychiatrists, however, and extends to patients who seek diagnosis or treatment of mental health conditions from psychologists, psychotherapists, and trained social work-

---

[102] *See generally,* 5 WEINSTEIN'S FEDERAL EVIDENCE § 803.09; Advisory Committee Note, Rule 803(4).

[103] *E.g.,* O'Gee v. Dobbs Houses, 570 F.2d 1084 (2d Cir. 1978) (treating physician permitted to testify about not only what patient told him about her injuries, but what other doctors had told her about her injuries); *see* Advisory Committee Note, Rule 803(4).

[104] *See* Rule 805 and § 805.1, *infra.*

ers.[105] The patient's narrative ability, memory, perception, or truthfulness may be impaired by his mental condition, however, and therefore considerable discretion is required.[106]

Where psychiatric treatment or diagnosis is sought, questions of relevance and reliability may overshadow other issues arising under Rule 803(4). The trial judge has inherent discretion under Rule 403 to admit such statements only as proof of the condition complained of and not as proof of the occurrence of the related events. For example, statements made to a physician that exhibit hallucination, detachment or incoherence may be admitted as proof of the condition but may be excluded as proof of facts actually asserted.

Additionally, the psychiatrist should not be permitted to become a "surrogate witness" by testifying to a party's out-of-court statements as evidence on substantive issues, particularly where the party is a criminal defendant and elects not to testify.[107] In any event, where the reliability of such a statement appears minimal, and its probative value is substantially outweighed by its unfair prejudicial impact, or its tendency to confuse or mislead the jury, the statement is subject to exclusion under Rule 403.

§ 803.22   Rule 803(5) Recorded Recollection

The following are not excluded by the rule against hearsay, regardless of whether the declarant is available as a witness:

***

    (5)   ***Recorded Recollection.*** A record that:

        (A)   is on a matter the witness once knew about but now cannot recall well enough to testify fully and accurately;

        (B)   was made or adopted by the witness when the matter was fresh in the witness's memory; and

        (C)   accurately reflects the witness's knowledge.

---

[105] United States v. Kappell, 418 F.3d 550, 555–556 (6th Cir. 2005) (Rule 803(4) applies to statements made to a psychotherapist, even one who merely diagnoses and does not actually treat the patient); United States v. Running Horse, 175 F.3d 635, 638 (8th Cir. 1999) (applying Rule 803(4) to a child victim's statements to a psychologist); United States v. Tome, 61 F.3d 1446, 1451 (10th Cir.1995) (the rule could apply to a child victim's statements to a state caseworker); United States v. Yellow, 18 F.3d 1438, 1442 (8th Cir. 1994) (the rule could apply to a child victim's statements to "psychologists or trained social workers"); Morgan v. Foretich, 846 F.2d 941, 949–950 (4th Cir. 1988) (psychologist).

[106] *See generally,* 5 WEINSTEIN'S FEDERAL EVIDENCE § 803.09; 2 MCCORMICK, § 277.

[107] 4 MUELLER & KIRKPATRICK, § 442; *see* Drayton v. Jiffee Chemical Corp., 591 F.2d 352 (6th Cir. 1978) (in modifying damage award to small child who was accidentally doused with and disfigured by liquid drain cleaner, court assigned a very minimal value to the psychiatric testimony, since psychiatrist was consulted for trial testimony and not treatment, but did not reject the testimony altogether).

If admitted, the record may be read into evidence but may be received as an exhibit only if offered by an adverse party.

Rule 803(5) authorizes the introduction of recorded hearsay statements where the witness at trial no longer adequately remembers the substance of the writing.[108] The Rule is a codification of pre-existing federal law.[109] The exception, commonly referred to as "past recollection recorded," has long been recognized under the common law,[110] and its development has been closely linked with the evolution of the related doctrine, "refreshing recollection," now codified in part in Rule 612.

The distinction between "past recollection recorded" and "present recollection refreshed" is critical. As discussed in Chapter 612 of this Treatise,[111] the technique of refreshing recollection permits a trial witness who is unable or unwilling to recall an event to be prompted by resort to extrinsic aids, including documents, which might revive the witness's memory. Where the

---

[108] United States v. Jones, 601 F.3d 1247 (11th Cir. 2010) (trial court did not err in allowing prosecution to play for the jury a videotape of an interview with a sixteen-year-old witness as a past recollection recorded, because the witness viewed the video, verified the accuracy of the statements she made on the video, and established that she was no longer able to recall all the details that she described in that interview, but was available for the defense to cross-examine). *See generally,* 2 MCCORMICK, §§ 279–283; 5 WEINSTEIN'S FEDERAL EVIDENCE § 803.10; 4 MUELLER & KIRKPATRICK, § 443; 3 WIGMORE, §§ 735–755. *See also* Hutchins & Slesinger, *Memory,* 41 HARV. L. REV. 860 (1928); Morgan, *The Relation Between Hearsay and Preserved Memory,* 40 HARV. L. REV. 712 (1927); Note, *Past Recollection Recorded: The "Forward Looking" Federal Rules of Evidence Lean Backwards,* 50 NOTRE DAME L. REV. 737 (1975); Comment, *Hearsay Under the Proposed Federal Rules: A Discretionary Approach,* 15 WAYNE L. REV. 1077 (1969); Note, *Past Recollection Recorded,* 28 IOWA L. REV. 530 (1943).

[109] *See* United States v. Kelly, 349 F.2d 720 (2d Cir. 1965).

[110] McCormick briefly outlines this development in the common law:

By the middle 1600's it had become customary to permit a witness to refresh his memory by looking at a written memorandum and to testify from this then-revived memory. It often happened, however, that, although examining the writing did not bring the facts recorded back to the witness's memory, he was able to recognize the writing as one prepared by him and was willing to testify on the basis of the writing that the facts recited in it were true. By the 1700's this also was accepted as proper, although the theoretical difficulty of justifying the result was often swept under the rug by referring to it by the old term of "refreshing recollection," which clearly did not fit it. Beginning with the early 1800's, the courts came to distinguish between the two situations, and to recognize that the use of past recollection recorded was a far different matter from permitting the witness to testify from a memory refreshed by examining a writing.

2 MCCORMICK, § 279. *See generally,* Morgan, *The Relation Between Hearsay and Preserved Memory,* 40 HARV. L. REV. 712 (1927); Note, *Past Recollection Recorded: The "Forward Looking" Federal Rules of Evidence Lean Backwards,* 50 NOTRE DAME L. REV., 737 (1975).

[111] *See* § 612.1 *et seq., supra.*

memory of the witness is thereby adequately jogged, the witness proceeds to testify. Because the evidence is the trial testimony, there is no hearsay problem, and the document is not accorded evidentiary status when used pursuant to the refreshing recollection technique. Under the hearsay exception for "recorded recollection," however, the writing itself assumes evidentiary status. Where the witness is unable or disinclined to testify in conformity with an earlier recording that was made while the event was fresh in his or her mind, the recording itself may be introduced into evidence for the truth of the matters asserted in the writing. Consequently, under Rule 803(5) it is not the testimony of the witness, but the recorded recollection itself, which is submitted as evidence to the trier of fact.

At common law, two alternate theories existed to support the admissibility of extrajudicial statements contained in recorded recollections. Some courts treated the evidence, when offered for its truth, as hearsay but nevertheless forged the instant exception because of inherent trustworthiness. Alternatively, some courts deemed the recording to be adopted and incorporated into the present testimony of the witness, thereby eliminating the hearsay issue.[112] With either approach, however, the underlying rationales for the admission of the recorded recollection are identical, and statements of past recorded recollection traditionally have been viewed as reasonably trustworthy for three reasons: (i) while the declarants may not be cross-examined and their memory may not be tested on the precise substance of the recording (*i.e.*, because their memory is exhausted on the subject), they are otherwise available for cross-examination and a limited opportunity to test their sincerity and to uncover factors bearing upon their perceptive or narrative ability; (ii) the requirement that the recording be made while the matter was "fresh" in the mind of the declarant reduces the danger of failed or faulty memory at the time the statement was recorded; and, to a lesser extent, (iii) the requirement that the recording "correctly" state the facts of the matter asserted reduces to some degree the risk of ambiguity. A more pragmatic theory rests in the recognition that a contemporary, accurate record of a relevant event is inherently more trustworthy than a present recollection offered through trial testimony because the recorded recollection is more proximate in time to the event.[113] In recognition of all of the foregoing

---

[112] Treating the statement as adopted by the witness and therefore not constituting hearsay received general acceptance in the federal system under pre-Rule practice. *See, e.g.,* Ettelson v. Metropolitan Life Ins. Co., 164 F.2d 660, 667 ("This record, which he verified and adopted, thus became . . . a present evidentiary statement"); Lueders v. United States, 210 F. 419 (9th Cir. 1914) ("The rule is that if the witness, at or about the time the memorandum was made, knew its contents and knew them to be true, this legalizes and lets in both the testimony of the witness and the memorandum").

[113] Ins. Cos. v. Weides, 81 U.S. (14 Wall.) 375, 379 (1872). *See generally,* 5 WEINSTEIN'S FEDERAL EVIDENCE § 803.10; 2 McCORMICK, § 279; 3 WIGMORE, §§ 735–755. *See also* Advisory Committee Note, Rule 803(5).

reliability factors, Rule 803(5) provides that a memorandum of recorded recollection is hearsay, but may be admissible under certain conditions stated in the Rule.

To qualify for admission under Rule 803(5), a memorandum or recorded recollection must satisfy four requirements, each of which shall be addressed separately in the following sections of this Chapter: (i) the witness-declarant must lack a present recollection of the matter recorded; (ii) the recording of the witness's recollection must "correctly" reflect the prior "knowledge" of the declarant; (iii) the recorded recollection must have been made or adopted by the witness; and (iv) the recorded recollection must have been prepared or adopted at a time when the matter in question was "fresh" in the memory of the declarant.[114] Where any of these requirements is wanting, the recording or memorandum may not be admitted under Rule 803(5), although depending upon the surrounding circumstances, the hearsay declaration may be admitted under other exceptions, *e.g.,* as a prior inconsistent statement under Rule 801(d)(1)(A), as an admission under Rule 801(d)(2), or as a business record under Rule 803(6).

§ 803.23 Requirement That Witness Lack a Present Recollection of Matter Contained in Memorandum

Under Rule 803(5), the witness must lack memory or present knowledge of the recorded matter at the time of trial. The requirement reflects a preference for live testimony over recorded evidence whenever the former is available. This requirement is particularly compelling where the prior statements are prepared in anticipation of litigation. Absent this requirement, lengthy argumentative documents could be prepared prior to trial that would be merely adopted by the witness as part of his or her testimony.[115]

Accordingly, Rule 803(5) envisions a preliminary attempt by the party presenting the evidence to refresh the witness's recollection pursuant to the provisions of Rule 612. Only if this attempt is unsuccessful may the party

---

[114] Wolcher v. United States, 200 F.2d 493 (9th Cir. 1952). *See generally,* 4 MUELLER & KIRKPATRICK, § 443.

[115] McCormick explains:

> The traditional formulation of the rule, still adhered to by most courts, requires that before a past recollection recorded could be received in evidence the witness who made or recognized it as correct must testify that he lacks present memory of the events and therefore is unable to testify concerning them.

2 MCCORMICK, § 282; *see also* United States v. Felix-Jerez, 667 F.2d 1297 (9th Cir. 1982) (defendant who could speak no English was interrogated by marshal, whose questions were translated by prison guard; marshal made notes of his questions and defendant's answers as translated by guard; marshal then wrote statement from his notes; error to admit statement since there was no showing that marshal had insufficient recollection to testify); United States v. Judon, 567 F.2d 1289 (5th Cir. 1978) (admission of memorandum as an exhibit was error); *see, e.g.,* Baker v. Elcona Homes Corp., 588 F.2d 551 (6th Cir. 1978).

resort to Rule 803(5). The requirement that the witness make some demonstration of impaired memory to show that he "now cannot recall well enough to testify fully and accurately" is in part designed to discourage the indiscriminate use of self-serving statements, and consistent with this policy, the trial court must make a careful factual determination that the witness's memory is genuinely incomplete or exhausted before admitting the writing.

Since the Rule is based, at least in part, upon the assumption that a contemporary, accurate recording is likely to be more trustworthy (or suffer from fewer risks of faulty memory) than a present recollection at trial, hearsay declarations constituting recorded recollections may be admitted even if the witness still retains some knowledge of the facts. Accordingly, where the witness recalls the event in general terms but cannot describe it in detail, the Rule is sufficiently satisfied. In such cases, these details may be admitted to establish specific points that "tie up" the witness's testimony. To impose a blanket proscription against the admission of any recorded recollection in the absence of a complete failure of memory would be supported by neither the theoretical nor the pragmatic underpinnings of the exception. It would make no sense to admit the recorded statement only when the witness has no memory of the matter in question, since the statement is at least as reliable when the witness has at least some recollection of that matter, even if only in fragmented or general terms.[116] Incomplete recollection should operate to affect the weight of the evidence, not its admissibility.

Where Rule 803(5) is invoked in the context of an adverse or hostile witness, special consideration should be accorded to the requirement of insufficient memory. Where the claimed lack of memory is thought to be disingenuous or evasive, application of Rule 803(5) is proper as long as the trial court in its discretion determines from the witness's demeanor and testimony that he or she is not testifying "fully and accurately."[117] Where the court is satisfied that the proponent has made a good-faith effort to secure live testimony and that the witness's recalcitrance is not the product of

---

[116] *E.g.,* Lang v. Callahan, 788 F.2d 1416 (9th Cir. 1986) (rape victim's statement to police immediately after incident was admissible where victim had difficulty remembering events even after refreshing her memory by reading the prior statement); United States v. Porter, 986 F.2d 1014 (6th Cir. 1993) (trial court properly allowed parts of a witness's police statement to be read into the record where the witness remembered making the statement but did not remember what she had said and where she tried to tell the truth but, because of her drug use, was not sure she had done so); United States v. Senak, 527 F.2d 129 (7th Cir. 1975) (requirement satisfied where witness recalls part of conversation but cannot remember the remainder); *see also* United States v. Riley, 657 F.2d 1377 (8th Cir. 1981); United States v. Marcantoni, 590 F.2d 1324 (5th Cir. 1979). *See generally,* 5 WEINSTEIN'S FEDERAL EVIDENCE § 803.10.

[117] *E.g.,* United States v. Williams, 571 F.2d 344 (6th Cir. 1978) (witness exercising "selective memory" and therefore court admitted portions of statement asserted as not within present recollection).

collusion with the proponent, receipt of the declaration under Rule 803(5) may be proper. Where the witness repudiates certain parts of the statement, but not others, the Rules do not direct exclusion of the entire memorandum, and the discrepancy should operate to affect credibility and weight.

§ 803.24　Requirement That Memorandum Correctly Reflect Prior Knowledge of Matter Contained Therein

The requirement of Rule 803(5)(C) that the writing "accurately reflects the witness's knowledge," actually embodies two requirements, *i.e.,* prior firsthand knowledge and accuracy. In essence, the firsthand knowledge requirement dictates that the individual must have had personal knowledge of the underlying events as required by Rule 602.[118] The firsthand knowledge requirement thus aids in establishing the reliability of the statement.

The complementary requirement of Rule 803(5) that the recorded recollection accurately state the prior knowledge of the witness is obviously satisfied where witnesses can currently remember making the statement (though not the underlying facts) and can testify that they carefully ensured the accuracy of the recorded statement. Problems may arise in establishing accuracy, however, where the witness fails to recall not only the underlying facts or events, but also the specific occasion of the recording. Where the preparation of the writing does not involve a unique occasion, but is prepared in the routine course of personal bookkeeping or in conjunction with a business or profession, and the witness can testify to the routine method of preparation, the accuracy requirement should be satisfied. A different situation is presented, however, where the witness cannot recall the preparation of the record and can testify only that he or she would not have signed or prepared the memorandum had he not believed it to be a true and accurate account of the event in question. In this situation, most commentators advocate admitting the statement, despite the fact that the foundation is nothing more than a general declaration of honesty that reveals little about the accuracy of the statement at issue.[119] Consequently, where the witness

---

[118] *See* Greger v. International Jensen, 820 F.2d 937 (8th Cir. 1987) (no abuse of discretion where trial judge permitted plaintiff to read portions of her diary to jury; plaintiff testified that document was accurate and prepared contemporaneously with events described, but that she could not describe its contents from memory). *See generally,* § 602.1 *et seq., supra.*

[119] *E.g.,* United States v. Patterson, 678 F.2d 774 (9th Cir. 1982); Washington v. Washington, Virginia & Maryland Coach Co., 250 F. Supp. 888 (D.D.C. 1966) (accident report admitted where supervisor of preparer, although having no present recollection, testified that he had read it and would have caused it to be corrected if it had misstated the facts); *see also* United States v. Lewis, 954 F.2d 1386 (7th Cir. 1992) (there was no abuse of discretion in allowing a government report under Rule 803(5) since no indication of inaccuracy existed and the substance was corroborated by other evidence); 2 McCormick, § 283. *See generally,* 3 Wigmore, § 747.

can attest to the statement's accuracy only by such a nominal endorsement, the trial court should approach such a statement with considerable caution in exercising its discretion.

Finally, contradiction of a declaration contained in a memorandum of recorded recollection by another witness does not preclude admission under Rule 803(5) as long as the court finds that the memorandum accurately sets forth prior personal knowledge. Such contradiction presents an issue of credibility or weight to be assessed by the trier of fact, and it does not affect the threshold question of admissibility.

§ 803.25   Requirement That Memorandum Be Made or Adopted by Witness

The third requirement under Rule 803(5), that the statement be made or adopted by the witness, is relatively uncomplicated. Where the witness has written and signed the memorandum, Rule 803(5) is unarguably satisfied. Nevertheless, this requirement mandates no specific or particular formality, since the requirement is intended only to implement the fundamental concern that accuracy be assured. More specifically, this requirement of Rule 803(5) in essence corroborates the witness's assertion at trial that the account is accurate. Consequently, where the witness signed a document prepared by another or recorded the event without signing it, the instant requirement of Rule 803(5) should be satisfied. Only where the witness did not participate in preparing the prior statement in any way should it be excluded.[120]

Special problems may arise where there is joint authorship of the memorandum, *i.e.*, where one person observes the event in question and relates it to another who, in turn, records what the observer reported to him or her. Under such circumstances, the resultant recording may nevertheless be admissible under Rule 803(5), where each person in the chain satisfies each requirement of the Rule. The person who observed the matter must testify that he or she perceived the matter and accurately related the information to another, while the person who actually prepared the writing must testify that he or she listened and understood the statement, and accurately recorded it.[121] Where, however, a person in the chain fails to testify, the issue becomes one of multiple hearsay under Rule 805, and each out-of-court statement must either be classified as non-hearsay or satisfy an exception to the hearsay exclusionary rule.[122]

---

[120] 2 MCCORMICK, § 283; *see also* Felice v. Long Island R.R., 426 F.2d 192, 196 (2d Cir. 1970) ("no adequate foundation was, or apparently could have been, laid for qualifying the note as a record of past recollection"); *see, e.g.,* Curtis v. Bradley, 65 Conn. 99, 31 A. 591 (Conn. 1894).

[121] *See* Rule 805 and § 805.1, *infra.*

[122] *See, e.g.,* United States v. Williams, 571 F.2d 344 (6th Cir. 1978) (rejecting contention that accused's statement prepared by government agent, then signed and sworn by accused,

§ 803.26 Requirement That Memorandum Be Prepared or Adopted When "Fresh" in Declarant's Memory

The final element in Rule 803(5) provides that the memorandum containing past recorded recollection must have been "made or adopted" when the matter contained in the writing "was fresh in the witness's memory".[123] The requirement of "freshness" is intended to be liberally construed, and it should be construed as less restrictive than either the "immediacy" requirement for present sense impressions under Rule 803(1) or the "spontaneity" requirement for excited utterances under Rule 803(2). The fact that the declarant has had time for reflection before recording the facts of the event does not disqualify the writing under Rule 803(5). While absolute contemporaneousness between the event recorded and the writing is not required, it may be said generally that the lesser the lapse of time between the event and the recording, the greater the degree of reliability.[124]

Courts should focus on the circumstances surrounding the event and the recording as well as the lapse of time between the two in an effort to ascertain whether the resultant memorandum is reasonably reliable. In considering "freshness" and "accuracy," a court may justifiably consider whether the event in question was so significant to the declarant that his or her memory probably is unaffected by the time lapse, whether the memorandum was prepared by the declarant personally or at the declarant's

---

was not the accused's statement under Federal Rule 803(5): "By signing and swearing to the statement [the witness] adopted it.").

[123] Fed. R. Evid. 803(5)(B). *Compare* Maxwell's Ex'rs v. Wilkinson, 113 U.S. 656 (1885) (rejecting memorandum prepared some twenty months after event where witness relied on his habit never to sign something false) *with* United States v. Williams, 571 F.2d 344 (6th Cir. 1978) (although statement was recorded six months after event, witness testified unequivocally that the event was still "fresh" in his memory). McCormick provides a succinct statement of the rationale underlying this requirement:

> The writing must have been prepared or recognized as correct at a time close to the event. Some opinions use the older strict formulation that requires the writing to have been made or recognized as correct "at or near the time" of the events recorded. This finds some support in psychological research suggesting that a rapid rate of forgetting occurs within the first two or three days following the observation of the event. But the tendency seems to be towards acceptance of the formulation favored by Wigmore which would require only that the writing be made or recognized at a time when the events were fairly fresh in the mind of the witness. No precise formula can be applied to determine whether this test has been met; perhaps the best rule of thumb is that the requirement is not met if the time lapse is such, under the circumstances, as to suggest that the writing is not likely to be accurate.

2 MCCORMICK, § 281.

[124] 3 WIGMORE, § 745; *see* Comment, *Hearsay Under the Proposed Federal Rules: A Discretionary Approach,* 15 WAYNE L. REV. 1077 (1969). *But see* Hutchins & Slesinger, *Some Observations on the Law of Evidence: Memory,* 41 HARV. L. REV. 860 (1928); Gardner, *Perception and Memory of Witnesses,* 18 CORNELL L.Q. 391 (1933) (suggesting passage of a few days seriously enhances risk of error).

personal direction, whether it was cursorily reviewed and casually signed, and whether the recording was prepared in anticipation of litigation.[125]

§ 803.27   Procedure for Admission

Rule 803(5) provides that a memorandum or recording of a past recollection may be read into evidence "but may be received as an exhibit only if offered by an adverse party." The purpose of this provision is presumably to prevent the trier of fact from granting excessive weight to the writing or recording, because it generally is inextricably interwoven with and dependent upon the testimony of witnesses.[126] If the record is an electronic recording, the tape may be played to the jury during trial and transcribed in the record at that time.

While the writing or recording should be marked as an exhibit and lodged with the clerk to maintain a full record for appellate review, the exhibit should not be permitted in the jury room unless the adverse party so requests. Nevertheless, the Rule does not preclude re-reading portions of the transcript containing the past recorded recollection upon proper request from the jury.

§ 803.28   Rule 803(6) Records of a Regularly Conducted Activity

The following are not excluded by the rule against hearsay, regardless of whether the declarant is available as a witness:

***

(6)   ***Records of a Regularly Conducted Activity.*** A record of an act, event, condition, opinion, or diagnosis if:

   (A)   the record was made at or near the time by — or from information transmitted by — someone with knowledge;

   (B)   the record was kept in the course of a regularly conducted activity of a business, organization, occupation, or calling, whether or not for profit;

   (C)   making the record was a regular practice of that activity;

   (D)   all these conditions are shown by the testimony of the custodian or another qualified witness, or by a certification that complies with Rule 902(11) or (12) or with a statute permitting certification; and

---

[125] *See* 2 McCORMICK, § 281.

[126] 5 WEINSTEIN'S FEDERAL EVIDENCE § 803.10; Advisory Committee Note, Rule 803(5); *see also* Baker v. Elcona Homes Corp., 588 F.2d 551 (6th Cir. 1978) (if accident report was admitted into evidence, it could not have been done so under Rule 803(5)); United States v. Judon, 567 F.2d 1289 (5th Cir. 1978). *See generally,* Comment, *Hearsay Under the Proposed Federal Rules: A Discretionary Approach,* 15 WAYNE L. REV. 1077 (1969). This procedure received considerable criticism as not being in conformity with the principles supporting the Rule. *See* 2 McCORMICK, § 279; 3 WIGMORE, § 754.

(E)   neither the source of information nor the method or circumstances of preparation indicate a lack of trustworthiness.

The hearsay exception embodied in Rule 803(6)[127] replaces a similar provision contained in the Federal Business Records Act.[128] The phrase of the Rule that allows an otherwise admissible record to be excluded if "the source of information [or] the method or circumstances of preparation indicate a lack of trustworthiness" codifies pre-Rule practice but is a departure from the actual wording of the Act.[129] The exception is based on the recognition that "businesses have a financial incentive to keep reliable records,"[130] although in its modern formulation it is broad enough to include any record "kept in the course of a regularly conducted activity of a business, organization, occupation, or calling, whether or not for profit."[131]

The so-called "business record" exception can be traced to the common-law doctrine known as the "shop-book" rule,[132] under which the books of

---

[127] *See generally,* 2 McCormick, §§ 284–294; 5 Weinstein's Federal Evidence § 803.11; 4 Mueller & Kirkpatrick, §§ 444–451; 3 Wigmore, §§ 735–755; 5 Wigmore, §§ 1517–1561. *See also* Arnold, *Presenting Business Records in Federal Court,* 32 Prac. Law. 19 (1986); Delroy, *Flight Recordings as Evidence in Civil Litigation,* 9 Val. U.L. Rev. 321 (1975); Green, *The Model and Uniform Statutes Relating to Business Entries as Evidence,* 31 Tul. L. Rev. 49 (1956); Hale, *Hospital Records as Evidence,* 14 S. Cal. L. Rev. 99 (1941); Laughlin, *Business Entries and the Like,* 46 Iowa L. Rev. 276 (1961); Powell, *Admissibility of Hospital Records Into Evidence,* 21 Md. L. Rev. 22 (1961); Ray, *Business Records—A Proposed Rule of Admissibility,* 5 Sw. L.J. 33 (1951); Comment, *A Reconsideration of the Admissibility of Computer-Generated Evidence,* 126 U. Pa. L. Rev. 425 (1977); Note, *Admissibility of Computer-Kept Records,* 55 Cornell L.Q. 1033 (1970); Note, *Business Records Rule, Repeated Target of Legal Reform,* 36 Brooklyn L. Rev. 250 (1970); Comment, *Computer Print-Outs of Business Records and Their Admissibility in New York,* 31 Alb. L. Rev. 61 (1967); Note, *Revised Business Entry Statutes: Theory and Practice,* 48 Colum. L. Rev. 920 (1948).

[128] 28 U.S.C. § 1732(a)(1936). This provision was repealed when the Rules were enacted. For discussions of Rule 803(6), see 4 Mueller & Kirkpatrick, §§ 444–451; 5 Weinstein's Federal Evidence § 803.11.

[129] *See, e.g.,* Palmer v. Hoffman, 318 U.S. 109 (1943) (accident report excluded even though meeting the technical requirements of the act where it was "dripping with motivations to misrepresent"); *cf.* Tupman Thurlow Co. v. S.S. Cap Castillo, 490 F.2d 302 (2d Cir. 1974) (report that was normally made by defendant business should have been received where there was no indication that it was prepared with litigation in mind); Diamond Shamrock Corp. v. Lumbermens Mutual Casualty Co., 466 F.2d 722 (7th Cir. 1972) (error to exclude report of defendant where such reports were routinely prepared and there was no indication it was made to protect the party in later litigation).

[130] Michigan v. Bryant, 562 U.S. —, 131 S. Ct. 1143, 179 L. Ed. 2d 93, 128 (2011) (Scalia, J., dissenting on other grounds).

[131] Rule 803(6)(B).

[132] The genesis of the "business records" exception to the hearsay rule and its evolution

account of merchants, retailers, professionals and other entrepreneurs were admissible in evidence in certain limited situations. Originally, the shop-book rule applied only to merchants who kept their own books and who could prove the existence of debts only by their ledgers. Under the now obsolete common-law competency rules, there was a special need for such evidence because parties were disqualified as witnesses.[133] A distinct branch of the shop-book doctrine subsequently evolved, however, which admitted entries in a ledger recorded by a clerk who was deceased at the time of trial.[134] This later doctrine, known as the "regular entries" rule, focused more on the regularity of the entries than on the recorder. Where the books of account represented ledgers of the routine recording of transactions, purchases, sales, services, or labor, and contained original entries recorded contemporaneously with the transactions in the usual course of business, the book was admissible for the truth of its contents. Subsequent developments provided that anyone who contributed to the preparation of the document had to be produced or that person's absence justified.[135]

Although the common-law "regular entries" exception was appropriate for the relatively simple bookkeeping methods prevailing in a small business economy, it became increasingly unwieldy and incompatible with the ever-expanding and changing circles of business and finance, and there emerged a host of petty rules and exceptions founded more upon expediency than upon any adherence to common-law foundational doctrines. In the context of the larger corporate forms with complex data gathering systems, it proved impracticable to account for all the persons who had participated in gathering, transmitting, and entering the information contained in the records as an evidentiary means for proving a business transaction. Consequently, several efforts were made to codify a business records exception that would accommodate the diverse nature of modern business enterprises while preserving the guarantees of trustworthiness underlying the old "shop-book" rule.[136] Some of these efforts, such as the Commonwealth Fund Act and the Uniform Act, concentrated primarily on relaxing common-law requirements that every participant in the gathering, transmitting, and recording processes be produced or accounted for.[137]

---

to modern times in Anglo-American jurisprudence is traced in 2 McCORMICK, § 285, and 5 WIGMORE, § 1518. *See* 5 WEINSTEIN'S FEDERAL EVIDENCE § 803.11.

[133] *See generally,* § 601.1 *et seq., supra.*

[134] 2 McCORMICK, § 285; 5 WIGMORE, § 1518.

[135] 5 WEINSTEIN'S FEDERAL EVIDENCE § 803.11.

[136] *E.g.,* The Commonwealth Fund Act, 28 U.S.C. § 1732 (1936); Uniform Business Records as Evidence Act, 9A U.L.A. 506 (1965); Model Code Rule 514. *See generally,* MORGAN, THE LAW OF EVIDENCE, SOME PROPOSALS FOR ITS REFORM, 63 (1927); Note, *Business Records Rule: Repeated Target of Legal Reform,* 36 BROOKLYN L. REV. 241 (1970).

[137] 5 WEINSTEIN'S FEDERAL EVIDENCE § 803.11; *see also* Advisory Committee Note, Rule 803(6).

Rule 803(6) represents the most recent effort to reformulate, modernize, and codify the old shop-book rule while retaining the advantages of the prior formulations. It differs from previous formulations in that it operates to admit records of businesses not conducted for profit.[138] It expands pre-Rule law in that it is not limited to any particular type or form of record or subject of information. Accordingly, the current exception has operated to admit a wide diversity of documents.[139]

To qualify for admission under Rule 803(6), a business record must satisfy four essential elements: (i) the record must be one regularly recorded in a regularly conducted activity; (ii) it must have been entered by a person with knowledge of the act, event, or condition; (iii) it must have been recorded at or near the time of the transaction; and (iv) a foundation must be laid by the testimony or certificate of the "custodian" of the record or some "other qualified witness." Reflected in these elements is the recognition that the Rule places less emphasis on the repetitiveness and routineness of the record keeping function, emphasizing instead the fact that the record was made in conjunction with a routine of established operation or activity.

§ 803.29 Rationale

While the original "shop-book" rule was predicated more upon necessity than upon accuracy, the later evolution of the "regular entries" exception was derived more from the policy of reliability. Under the earlier formulations of the exception, these two principles, necessity and reliability, evolved into the underlying rationale pertaining to the necessity of obtaining relevant and reliable information without the undue inconvenience of producing all the participants in the record's creation.[140] Throughout the later evolution of this

---

[138] *See* Pittsburgh Press Club v. United States, 536 F.2d 572 (3d Cir. 1976) (in suit by private club where issue was club's tax exempt status, court refers to club's articles of incorporation, by-laws and receipts, although making no mention of business records exception). *See generally,* 4 MUELLER & KIRKPATRICK, § 444.

[139] *See, e.g.,* Royal China, Inc. v. Travelers Indem. Co., 497 F.2d 989 (6th Cir. 1974) (ledger cards); United States v. Cincotta, 689 F.2d 238 (1st Cir. 1982) (truck driver's notebook in which he recorded deliveries); United States v. Sheppard, 688 F.2d 952 (5th Cir. 1982) (freight bills containing handwritten notations to the effect that some of the shipment was missing); In Re Aircrash in Bali, Indonesia, 684 F.2d 1301 (9th Cir. 1982) (flight training records, as proof that airline had notice of pilot's inadequacies). *See generally,* 5 WEIN-STEIN'S FEDERAL EVIDENCE § 803.11; Note, *Admissibility of Computer—Kept Records,* 55 CORNELL L.Q. 1033 (1970); *see also* United States v. Briscoe, 896 F.2d 1476 (7th Cir. 1990) (computerized telephone records were properly admitted where the keeper of the records testified that entries are made into the computer when a telephone call is made, it is the regular practice of the telephone company to keep records of subscriber's calls and the computer scans the records for errors every fifteen seconds).

[140] *See generally,* 5 WEINSTEIN'S FEDERAL EVIDENCE § 803.11. This concern with minimizing undue inconvenience to the participants in the creation of the records was carried to new lengths with the 2000 amendment to Rule 803(6), which now allows the foundational requirements of the rule to be satisfied by an affidavit or other suitable certification, thus

doctrine, the element essential to any exception to the hearsay rule — the guarantee of trustworthiness or reliability — was presumed to be present for a variety of reasons: (i) such records are regularly checked for accuracy; (ii) the regularity and continuity of such records instill habits of precision in the preparer and custodian of the records; (iii) businesses can function only if they have accurate records and consequently businesses promote environments that ensure accuracy; and (iv) employees are generally required to prepare and maintain accurate records as part of their jobs, and they face possible embarrassment, censure, or termination if they err.[141]

Accordingly, Rule 803(6), like the common-law doctrines from which it evolved, rests upon the dual rationales of necessity and reliability. The Rule implicitly recognizes that modern business transactions are frequently dependent upon recorded data. This information is usually in the form of written documents or ledgers, but increasingly it is found in the memory of computers and retrievable only by means of CDs, printouts, screen displays, and the like. The reliability element is especially reinforced by current commercial pressures for accuracy.

Additionally, since a business record often consists of information derived from a variety of sources, its admission pursuant to Rule 803(6) averts the need for calling all persons involved in preparing the record. As a practical matter, the Rule recognizes that if the participants in modern business transactions were called to testify, they often would be unable to do more than state matters that could be observed from the record itself due to their involvement in a large number of such transactions.

Despite the fact that some degree of "self-interest" necessarily and naturally affects any business record offered under Rule 803(6), this risk is not deemed substantial enough to disqualify it as evidence except in certain limited situations discussed in § 803.35 of this Chapter.

§ 803.30   Medical Opinions and Diagnoses

Under pre-Rule practice, the federal courts were often reluctant to admit opinions or diagnoses contained in business records. The admission of

---

relieving the proponent of the need to produce time-consuming foundational testimony in court through live witnesses. *See* § 803.34, *infra.*

[141] McCormick explains:

> The exception is justified on grounds analogous to those underlying other exceptions to the hearsay rule. Unusual reliability is regarded as furnished by the fact that in practice regular entries have a comparatively high degree of accuracy (as compared to other memoranda) because such books and records are customarily checked as to correctness by systematic balance-striking, because the very regularity and continuity of the records is calculated to train the record-keeper in habits of precision, and because in actual experience the entire business of the nation and many other activities constantly function in reliance upon entries of this kind.

2 McCormick, § 286.

business records was limited to those that represented an "act, transaction, occurrence, event or condition."[142] The more rigorous standard was based upon the historical suspicion of any record that might be prepared with an eye to litigation. Rule 803(6) specifically embraces opinions and diagnoses in order to make admissible those that are "incident to or part of factual reports of contemporaneous events or transactions."[143] Federal courts have remained reluctant to admit records containing opinions or diagnoses that concern unusual physical conditions or psychiatric disorders.[144] Due to the subjective nature of opinions and diagnoses in these cases, physicians may reach different conclusions and therefore the trustworthiness of the records may be reduced unless the physician is in court to explain his findings and to be cross-examined.

Reports that are prepared to state or support expert opinions may be admissible provided the requirements of Rules 701–706 regarding expert testimony are met. Although such reports will not be relied upon in treating patients and therefore lack one indication of reliability, the professional standards of the expert supply an alternative guarantee of trustworthiness.[145] Moreover, the trial court retains discretion to require the preparer of the record to appear in court to testify as to his or her qualifications as an expert and to be cross-examined on the substance of the proposed testimony.[146]

---

[142] The Model Act provided only for records of an "act, transaction, occurrence or event." 28 U.S.C. § 1732(a). The Uniform Act dropped "transaction and occurrence" and added "condition." 9A U.L.A. 506. *See* New York Life Insurance Co. v. Taylor, 147 F.2d 297 (D.C. Cir. 1944) (applying the Federal Business Records Act [Model Act]); Standard Oil Company v. Moore, 251 F.2d 188 (9th Cir. 1957) ("[T]he context of § 1732, read as a whole, also indicate[s] that a writing cannot ordinarily be considered a 'memorandum or record' of an 'act, transaction, occurrence or event,' unless the recitals in such writings are factual in nature").

[143] Forward Communications Corp. v. United States, 608 F.2d 485 (Ct. Cl. 1979) (action for recovery of federal taxes; plaintiff sought to prove valuation by proffering report by appraiser; court held that report could not be admitted where record failed to disclose qualifications or identity of appraiser, and the opinions were not incident to or part of factual reports of contemporaneous events or transactions); *see also* United States v. Licavoli, 604 F.2d 613 (9th Cir. 1979); Velsicol Chemical Corp. v. Monsanto Co., 579 F.2d 1038 (7th Cir. 1978).

[144] *E.g.,* Phillips v. Neil, 452 F.2d 337 (6th Cir. 1971) (receipt of hospital records offered by prosecution in rebuttal of insanity defense violated defendant's rights under the Confrontation Clause, since the records contained opinions and conclusions and the accused had no opportunity to confront the authors of the reports); United States v. Bohle, 445 F.2d 54 (7th Cir. 1971) (in criminal prosecution, proper for trial judge to admit hospital records offered by defendant in support of insanity defense, since he advised the jury that they could be used only as a basis for expert opinion testimony with respect to diagnosis of defendant's medical condition).

[145] *See, e.g.,* Terrasi v. South Atlantic Lines, 226 F.2d 823 (2d Cir. 1955); *see also* 5 WEINSTEIN'S FEDERAL EVIDENCE § 803.11.

[146] Richardson v. Perales, 402 U.S. 389 (1971) (routine, standard, unbiased medical

The express language of Rule 803(6) accords the trial court discretion to exclude business records that reflect untrustworthiness in preparation, a matter specifically addressed in § 803.35 of this Chapter.

§ 803.31   Necessity That Record Be Regularly Prepared and Maintained in Course of Regularly Conducted Business Activity — Scope of Business

The first element for application of Rule 803(6) amounts to a dual condition embodying the modern concepts of a regular business-type activity and the regularity of record keeping.

In the first instance, the term "regularly conducted activity of a business" includes all types of commercial operations, including profit as well as non-profit institutions, *e.g.,* health, charitable, religious, and educational institutions.[147] Also included within this term would be fraternal groups, political parties, lobbying organizations, labor unions, trade and professional associations, and every variety of club or organization, as long as the routine of such bodies is characterized by the type of formality that guarantees the requisite degree of reliability. Additionally, where all other elements of the Rule are satisfied, the records of illegal enterprises are equally admissible, since the mere fact of illegality lessens neither the necessity for, nor reliability of, such records.[148] Further, while reference to a "business activity" usually suggests a venture involving more than one person, the Rule does not so provide. The Rule extends to the records of a sole proprietorship and the records of an individual who operates as an independent contractor.[149]

---

reports by physician specialists constituted substantial evidence; claimant should have taken advantage of the opportunity afforded him under applicable regulations to request subpoenas for the physicians); *see also* Petrocelli v. Gallison, 679 F.2d 286 (1st Cir. 1982). *See generally,* § 803.35, *infra,* for a discussion of trial court's power to exclude otherwise admissible records due to untrustworthiness.

[147] *See, e.g.,* Malek v. Federal Ins. Co., 994 F.2d 49 (2d Cir. 1993) (in arson case, trial court erred in excluding testimony of a social worker who was in charge of the case file on the tenant's children; the social worker kept her records in the regular course of business); United States v. Reese, 568 F.2d 1246 (6th Cir. 1977) (hospital scrapbook of newspaper clippings introduced to prove visiting hours); United States v. Sackett, 598 F.2d 739 (2d Cir. 1979) (hospital records reflecting patient's history properly received); Stone v. Morris, 546 F.2d 730 (7th Cir. 1976) (state prison records). *See generally,* 5 WEINSTEIN'S FEDERAL EVIDENCE § 803.11; 2 McCORMICK, § 288.

[148] *E.g.,* United States v. Hedman, 630 F.2d 1184 (7th Cir. 1980) (notebook kept by employee of lumber company recording illegal payoffs to city building inspectors); United States v. McPartlin, 595 F.2d 1321 (7th Cir. 1979) (desk calendar appointment diaries kept in connection with illegal bribery scheme); United States v. Baxter, 492 F.2d 150 (9th Cir. 1973), *cert. dismissed,* 414 U.S. 801 (1973) (customer book, notebook, miscellaneous papers and notes kept in connection with alleged drug importing conspiracy admitted under Federal Business Records Act).

[149] *E.g.,* United States v. McPartlin, 595 F.2d 1321 (7th Cir. 1979) (rejecting argument

Records prepared and maintained by an individual concerning purely personal matters are not within the scope of the instant exception.[150] The rationale for Rule 803(6) is not satisfied in the absence of some special indicia of reliability, such as periodic checking, reliance on the records by others, or some cognizable duty to keep reliable records. Accordingly, memoranda such as those contained in diaries, shopping lists, reminder notes, phone messages, checking or savings accounts, mileage records regarding an automobile for personal use, or inventories for a hobby ordinarily do not qualify.[151] Where, however, business and personal purposes are combined in one record, receipt of the business entries under Rule 803(6) may be proper. Accordingly, a checking account containing the financial record of one self-employed is admissible to the extent those entries reflect the individual business. The same analysis would apply to cars, boats, or planes used for both personal and business purposes.

In order to be admissible under Rule 803(6), the record must be one that is regularly maintained in the business. In addition, it must be shown that the record is prepared and maintained as part of the regular practice of the business.[152] This requirement is supportive of trustworthiness, and its practical impact is to exclude records prepared solely in anticipation of potential or pending litigation. This issue is more fully discussed in § 803.35, *infra*.

§ 803.32   Necessity of Personal Knowledge — Multiple Hearsay Problems

The second element that must be satisfied under Rule 803(6) is that the

---

that records prepared by a person for his own benefit are for that reason outside Rule 803(6)); United States v. Goins, 593 F.2d 88 (8th Cir. 1979) (memorandum made by tavern operator listing payments made to "silent or concealed partner").

[150] *See, e.g.,* Clark v. City of Los Angeles, 650 F.2d 1033 (9th Cir. 1981) (properly excluded). *But see* United States v. Hedman, 630 F.2d 1184 (7th Cir. 1980) (diary of employee recording pay-offs made to city officials was properly admitted where such entries were made with regularity and recorder kept diary because he felt he might have to account for the payments); Aluminum Co. of America v. Sperry Prod., 285 F.2d 911 (6th Cir. 1960) (notebook of inventor admitted in patent infringement case). *See generally,* Green, *The Model and Uniform Statutes Relating to Business Entries as Evidence,* 31 TUL. L. REV. 49 (1956).

[151] 4 MUELLER & KIRKPATRICK, § 444.

[152] *See* United States v. Blackburn, 992 F.2d 666 (7th Cir. 1993) (computer printouts of eyeglass analysis requested by the FBI from a private company were not admissible as business records because they were not kept in the regular course of business; court found that the records were admissible under the residual hearsay exception); United States v. Davis, 571 F.2d 1354 (5th Cir. 1978) (reversible error to receive in federal evidence a federal form filled out by custodian of records of arms manufacturer Colt indicating that a certain gun had been made by Colt and shipped by it to Georgia, since there was no indication that it was the regular practice of Colt to make such a record); Hiram Ricker & Sons v. Students Int'l Meditation Soc'y, 501 F.2d 550 (1st Cir. 1974) (applying Federal Business Records Act to find that the room-check made by plaintiff's maintenance employees "was hardly the kind of regular, systematic, business activity which is encompassed by the exception").

information be provided by "someone with knowledge." This condition is rather easily satisfied; it is parallel to the firsthand knowledge requirement for testifying witnesses under Rule 602.[153] This requirement rests upon the obvious reasoning that no business record may be more reliable than its source of information.[154] The Rule's insistence that the record be "made . . . by — or from information transmitted by — someone with knowledge" should, however, be liberally construed and applied. Where the actual name of the source is unknown, the record is not barred by the Rule as long as it is the regular practice of the business activity to procure the information from such employee or agent.[155]

While the source of the information must have personal knowledge, others participating in the chain of transmission of that record, including the person who ultimately causes the record to be made, need not have such knowledge. Essentially, this is a question of multiple hearsay, and the requirement is satisfied where each participant in the chain of transmission is acting in the course of that person's regularly conducted activity.[156]

---

[153] *See* discussion at § 602.1, *supra.*

[154] *See, e.g.,* Chaffee & Co. v. United States, 85 U.S. (18 Wall.) 516 (1874); *see also* United States v. Reese, 568 F.2d 1246 (6th Cir. 1977) (upholding receipt of scrapbook prepared by public relations department of hospital and containing Xerox copies of newspaper articles purporting to show visiting hours of hospital). *But see* Ricciardi v. Children's Hosp. Medical Ctr., 811 F.2d 18 (1st Cir. 1987) (in malpractice action, hand-written note by doctor with no personal knowledge of operation was inadmissible for showing what occurred during operation).

[155] *E.g.,* United States v. Reese, 568 F.2d 1246 (6th Cir. 1977) (court rejected contention that authenticating witness was not the supervisor who oversaw the preparation of the scrapbook, since the rule embraces records made on the basis of information transmitted by a person with knowledge, and the hospital itself would qualify as such a person). *See generally,* 4 MUELLER & KIRKPATRICK, § 444.

[156] United States v. Ahrens, 530 F.2d 781 (8th Cir. 1976) (personal knowledge on the part of the maker of the record is not a condition precedent to its admission under Federal Rule 803(6)); Lewis v. Baker, 526 F.2d 470 (2d Cir. 1975) (fact that employee had prepared the report on basis of information given to him by fellow employee did not make report inadmissible under the Federal Business Records Act; although the language of this exception under the Act was different from that under Rule 803(6), the opinion makes it clear the same result would obtain under the Rule). McCormick explains the rationale:

> Thus a business record containing an assertion by someone other than the maker should be admitted to prove the truth of that assertion only if the assertion itself comes within an exception to the hearsay rule. In most cases this involves essentially a double application of the business records exception.

2 MCCORMICK, § 290; *see also* Tongil Co. v. The Vessel "Hyundai Innovator," 968 F.2d 999 (9th Cir. 1992) (district court erred in allowing party to use hearsay documents to lay the foundation for the admission for business record); Ramrattan v. Burger King Corp., 656 F. Supp. 522 (D. Md. 1987) (court excluded bystanders' testimony to police at site of auto accident because while police were acting in ordinary course of business, bystanders were not); 5 WEINSTEIN'S FEDERAL EVIDENCE § 803.11.

Consequently, where the initial source of the business data has personal knowledge and each person in the chain of transmission is performing his or her routine function for the business concern, the record is admissible. In essence, Rule 803(6) creates a hearsay exception for each person in the chain, and the Rule requires only that the first person have personal knowledge of the facts or data recorded. It is critical to note, however, that each person in the chain must be an employee or agent of the business that retains the records in the regular course of its activity, *i.e.,* each person in the chain must have a business duty to report accurately to the business keeping the record. A duty to some other entity or a "civic duty" will not qualify.

Where the supplier of the information is not acting within the course of the business that retains the record, such as where a non-employee volunteers information to an employee-investigator, the multiple hearsay analysis requires a different result. In this situation, the volunteer's statement either must be defined as non-hearsay under Rule 801, or it must meet the tests of some other hearsay exception in order to admit the entire record under Rule 803(6). Rule 805 specifically admits hearsay contained within hearsay only where each statement is independently admissible. For example, a business record qualifying under Rule 803(6) might contain a statement of a volunteer embraced by Rule 803(2), which authorizes the admission of excited utterances. Here the entire document would be admissible despite the fact that the declarant of the excited utterance has no business duty to report to the business that keeps the record. Obviously, where a record prepared by one business is transmitted to another business, both records may qualify under Rule 803(6). Similarly, where the outsider's statement is defined as nonhearsay, *e.g.,* where it is offered for its impact on the listener (Rule 801(c)) or as an admission (Rule 801(d)), the source's statement is admissible where the record containing the statement was prepared in the ordinary course of business under Rule 803(6). Where the outsider's statement is not independently admissible, however, it must be excised from the record, and it is not admissible under Rule 803(6). This analysis is further amplified in Chapter 805 of this Treatise.

§ 803.33   Necessity That Record Be Made Contemporaneously With Act, Event or Condition

Rule 803(6) further requires that the transaction in question be recorded "at or near the time" of its occurrence. This element of contemporaneity, or "freshness," was required at common law, and it is intended to enhance accuracy. Like the contemporaneity requirement for past recollection recorded under Rule 803(5), the contemporaneity required here is not as strict as the "immediacy" test for present sense impressions under Rule 803(1) or the "spontaneity" test for excited utterances under Rule 803(2). Thus, entries should be admitted if they are of the type that businesses would ordinarily regard as current entries, *i.e.,* those recorded while the matter is still fresh and reasonably verified by the memories of the participants.[157]

§ 803.34   Foundational Requirements: Custodian or Some Other Qualified Person — Rule 902(11) and (12)

The final requirement of Rule 803(6) is that where a business record is offered, a foundation must first be established, normally through the testimony of either the custodian or some other qualified person. This foundational provision requires not only that the record be identified and authenticated in accordance with Article IX of the Rules, but also that the requirements of regular business activity, personal knowledge, and contemporaneity be shown as well.[158] Generally, the essential testimony is that of the custodian or other qualified person who can explain the record keeping practices of the organization. The phrase "other qualified person" should be broadly construed. For example, a certified public accountant or a purchasing agent who is not an employee of the entity, but understands the system used by the entity, should be qualified to testify to the foundation if he or she possesses firsthand knowledge of the facts supporting the requirements of Rule 803(6).[159]

---

[157] McCormick states:

> Whether an entry made subsequent to the transaction has been made within a sufficient time to render it within the exception depends upon whether the time span between the transaction and the entry was so great as to suggest a danger of inaccuracy by lapse of memory. Only if such a danger appears from the circumstances of the case should the entry be held to have been made beyond the time limitation.

2 McCormick, § 289. *See, e.g.,* Gulf South Mach. v. Kearney & Trecker Corp., 756 F.2d 377 (5th Cir. 1985) (logbook of machine malfunctions was properly admitted where plaintiff kept similar books for most of its machines, and entries were made within 24 hours of trouble with machine); United States v. Kim, 595 F.2d 755 (D.C. Cir. 1979) (telex from a bank stating that defendant had deposited funds to his account was properly excluded as hearsay, since it reported deposits that took place in 1975 but was not prepared until 1977; timeliness requirement could not be waived); *see also* United States v. Davis, 571 F.2d 1354 (5th Cir. 1978).

[158] *See, e.g.,* Norwood v. Great American Indem. Co., 146 F.2d 797 (3d Cir. 1944) (hospital record admitted under Federal Business Records Act); *see also* Stengel v. Belcher, 522 F.2d 438 (6th Cir. 1975). *See generally,* 5 WEINSTEIN'S FEDERAL EVIDENCE § 803.11; 2 McCormick, § 292; 5 WIGMORE, § 1530.

[159] *E.g.,* Brawner v. Allstate Indemnity Co., 591 F.3d 984 (8th Cir. 2010) (the custodian or other qualified witness called to lay the foundation for the admission of a business record under Rule 803(6) is not required to have personal knowledge regarding its creation, or to have personally participated in its creation, or even to know who actually recorded the information. A record created by a third party and integrated into another entity's records is admissible as the record of the custodian entity, so long as the custodian entity relied upon the accuracy of the record and the other requirements of Rule 803(6) are satisfied. A record prepared by the Veterans' Administration was properly admitted based on the testimony of a bank employee who could establish that she received and integrated those VA documents into the bank's record, that the bank relied on the accuracy of the documents, and that the documents were kept in the course of the bank's regularly conducted business); United States

Witnesses providing the foundation need not have firsthand knowledge of the transaction. Rather, it must be demonstrated that the witnesses are sufficiently familiar with the operation of the business and with the circumstances of the record's preparation, maintenance, and retrieval, that they can reasonably testify on the basis of this knowledge that the record is what it purports to be, and that it was made in the ordinary course of business consistent with the elements of Rule 803(6).[160] Where the witness fails to demonstrate this elemental knowledge, the evidence should not be admitted under Rule 803(6).[161]

Live courtroom testimony is no longer required to lay the foundation for the admission of a business record under Rule 803(6). Under an amendment effective December, 2000, the foundational requirements of the rule may be demonstrated through an affidavit or similar written certification signed by anyone who would have been qualified to testify to these requirements in court. When the business record is accompanied by such a written certification, it becomes a self-authenticating document under Rule 902(11)

---

v. Hathaway, 798 F.2d 902, 906 (6th Cir. 1986) (foundation for admission of corporate records properly laid by FBI agent; it may be done by "a government agent or other person outside the organization" who is familiar with its record keeping system); Matador Drilling Co. v. Post, 662 F.2d 1190 (5th Cir. 1981); *see also* United States v. Grossman, 614 F.2d 295 (1st Cir. 1980) (retail catalogue properly received where purchasing agent testified as to "the preparation, uses, and issuance of the catalogue"); United States v. Veytia-Bravo, 603 F.2d 1187 (5th Cir. 1979) (records prepared by arms dealer in compliance with federal regulations properly received, where agent of Bureau of Alcohol, Tobacco, and Firearms testified that the dealer had prepared the records and that they were currently in custody of the ATF).

[160] *E.g.,* United States v. Hathaway, 798 F.2d 902, 906 (6th Cir. 1986) (foundation for admission of corporate records properly laid by FBI agent; it may be done by "a government agent or other person outside the organization" who is familiar with its record keeping system); Pacific Service Stations Co. v. Mobil Oil Corp., 689 F.2d 1055, 1058 (Temp. Em. Ct. App. 1982); *see also* United States v. Colyer, 571 F.2d 941 (5th Cir. 1978) (where the witness testified that records were made and kept in regular course of business and that he was custodian of records and knowledgeable as to how they were handled, the records were admissible, even though person who made record did not testify); United States v. Reese, 568 F.2d 1246 (6th Cir. 1977) (no requirement that custodian had personal knowledge of the particular evidence contained in the record).

[161] *E.g.,* United States CFTC v. Dizona, 594 F.3d 408 (5th Cir. 2010) (although the witness who lays the foundation need not be the author of the record or be able to personally attest to its accuracy, the witness must be one who can explain the record keeping system of the organization and verify that the requirements of Rule 803(6) are met; a summary witness could not properly lay such a foundation when she did not have any knowledge regarding the keeping of the records, whether they were made at or near the time of the trade, or whether they were made by a person with knowledge of the trade); Karme v. Commissioner, 673 F.2d 1062 (9th Cir. 1982) (records of bank introduced by IRS agent outside Rule 803(6) since agent was not custodian and could not testify as to preparation); Calhoun v. Baylor, 646 F.2d 1158 (6th Cir. 1981) (no error to exclude records where the authenticating witness was "in no position to attest to their reliability"); Campbell v. Nordco Prod., 629 F.2d 1258 (7th Cir. 1980) (accident report excluded where authenticating witness indicated that the preparer was not acting within the ordinary course of business).

or (12), and is admissible without the need for live testimony.[162] This amended procedure is designed to relieve the proponent of the need to produce time-consuming foundational testimony in court through live witnesses. It is a reflection of the fact that authenticating witnesses dragged into the courtroom solely to lay the foundation for admission of a business record do not often take much time or yield much information of significant benefit to the cross-examiner.

The certification may be in the form of an affidavit under oath or any comparable affirmation or declaration made under penalty of perjury.[163] The amendment does not change the substantive requirements for admission of the business records. The written certification must show that the business record (1) was made at or near the time of the occurrence of the matters set forth by, or from information transmitted by, a person with knowledge of those matters; (2) was kept in the course of the regularly conducted activity; and (3) was made by the regularly conducted activity as a regular practice. If these requirements are met, the business record is self-authenticating, and admissible over any hearsay objection.

A party who desires to use this method for admitting business records at trial is required to "give an adverse party reasonable written notice of the intent to offer the record — and must make the record and certification available for inspection — so that the party has a fair opportunity to challenge them."[164] The written notice requirement is designed to give the opposing party an opportunity to depose the custodian or other foundation witness before trial, to see if close questioning would create any reason to exclude the business record or to give it less weight. If not, as is often the case, the system of justice is better served by allowing such pointless inquiry to take place before trial. On the other hand, if pretrial discovery confirms that questioning of the witness would yield some important information for the court or the jury, the party opposing its admission can ask that the record not be admitted by challenging the completeness of the certification. It remains the law, of course, that the judge may decline to admit business records over a hearsay objection, whether they are authenticated by affidavit or live testimony, if "the source of information [or] the method or circumstances of preparation indicate a lack of trustworthiness."[165] Even if the hearsay objection is overruled and the records are admitted without a foundation laid in court by a live witness, the opposing party may call the certifying witness, if the person is available to testify, for cross-examination at trial under Rule 806.

---

[162] Rule 902(11) and (12), respectively, govern the admission of certified copies of domestic and foreign records.

[163] *See* Advisory Committee Note, Rule 902(11) (citing 28 U.S.C. § 1746).

[164] Rule 902(11). *See* the discussion of this Rule in Chapter 902, *infra*.

[165] Rule 803(6).

§ 803.35   Exclusion Where Lack of Trustworthiness Is Indicated

Where a business record facially satisfies all the requirements of Rule 803(6), it may nevertheless be excluded on objection from the opponent where the trial court, in its discretion, determines that the source of the information or the method of its preparation indicates that the resultant record is untrustworthy.[166]

Special principles attend the admissibility of business records prepared in anticipation of litigation,[167] and courts are especially careful to scrutinize such records as accident reports because these records have proven peculiarly subject to distortion and self-interest.[168] Employees preparing accident report to be kept by their own employer present the most vivid illustration. Where a document generally satisfies the elements of Rule 803(6), but nevertheless was prepared in anticipation of possible use in litigation, the underlying rationale of trustworthiness is undercut.[169] As the Supreme Court recently put the point, documents are not admissible under this exception "if the regularly conducted business activity is the production of evidence for

---

[166] *See, e.g.,* Schaps v. Bally's Park Place, 58 B.R. 581 (E.D. Pa. 1986), *aff'd,* 815 F.2d 693 (3d Cir. 1987) (books and records of debtor were inadmissible based on lack of trustworthiness; they were not submitted by the regular custodian, and party admitted they were not kept in a business-like manner); Meder v. Everest & Jennings, 637 F.2d 1182 (8th Cir. 1981); *see also* Pan-Islamic Trade Corp. v. Exxon Corp., 632 F.2d 539 (5th Cir. 1980) (court did not determine if memorandum satisfied requirements of Rule 803(6) but excluded the memorandum nonetheless "because the circumstances of its preparation indicate a lack of trustworthiness").

[167] *See, e.g.,* Scheerer v. Hardee's Food Sys., Inc., 92 F.3d 702 (8th Cir. 1996) (trial court erred in slip-and-fall case by admitting "incident report" authored by a non-witness employee of the defendant; appellate court found the report lacked reliability because it was made with the knowledge that the incident would likely result in litigation); Mitchell v. American Export Isbrandtsen Lines, 430 F.2d 1023 (2d Cir. 1970) (in personal injury suit, no error to admit illness report prepared by defendant's physician who examined plaintiff where there is no motive to falsify or where surrounding circumstances negate such a motive; here, the entries were made during the course of a physician-patient relationship, and the preparing physician was testifying in court and subject to cross-examination); Lindheimer v. United Fruit Co., 418 F.2d 606 (2d Cir. 1969) (no error to admit report prepared by defendant's Safety Committee; the test in such a case is not simply the presence of a motive to falsify, but whether the motive is checked by other factors such as purpose and practice). *See generally,* 4 MUELLER & KIRKPATRICK, § 450.

[168] *See, e.g.,* Koppinger v. Cullen-Schiltz & Associates, 513 F.2d 901 (8th Cir. 1975) (accident report excluded in wrongful death action); Bracey v. Herringa, 466 F.2d 702 (7th Cir. 1972) (in civil rights action by prisoner against prison guards, "conduct reports" prepared by defendants that contained self-serving statements by defendants should be excluded; legal accountability of the guards may have affected the reports); *see also* § 803.34, *supra.*

[169] The leading case that is the genesis of the doctrine is Hoffman v. Palmer, 129 F.2d 976 (2d Cir. 1942), *aff'd,* 318 U.S. 109 (1943). *See* 2 MCCORMICK, § 287; 5 WEINSTEIN'S FEDERAL EVIDENCE § 803.11; *see also* United States v. Smith, 521 F.2d 957 (D.C. Cir. 1975) (discretion exercised; constitutional issue as to Sixth Amendment avoided).

use at trial."[170] In this situation the business duty to report accurately, which predominates in supporting the admissibility of business records, is feared to be, and often is, supplanted by a natural motivation of the preparer to color facts in favor of the business entity. In any case in which a subjective motivation to make self-serving statements in a business record is evident, the trial court is expressly accorded discretion under Rule 803(6) to exclude the document despite the fact that all requirements for the business record exception have been otherwise satisfied. Specifically, the Rule provides that a record satisfying the requisites of the exception is nevertheless inadmissible where "the source of information or the method or circumstances of preparation indicate lack of trustworthiness." The burden is upon the opponent of the document to show that it is sufficiently untrustworthy to warrant its exclusion.[171]

§ 803.36   Exclusion in Criminal Cases Under the Constitutional Guarantee of Confrontation

The discretion vested in the trial court under Rule 803(6) to exclude evidence qualified as a business record that is nevertheless deemed to be "untrustworthy" in either its preparation or maintenance is particularly required in criminal proceedings. The Rules of Evidence merely provide a system for the orderly presentation of evidence at trial and, though generally applicable in criminal as well as civil proceedings, the Rules are not designed to delineate the constitutional rights of litigants. Rule 803(6) does not in itself determine the extent of the accused's right to exclude evidence based upon the right of confrontation. At least in dictum, however, the Supreme Court has asserted that the admission of "business records" does not implicate the Confrontation Clause,[172] and the federal courts have taken that to mean that the admission of regular business and personal records does not pose any problem under that clause, at least if they were not prepared in anticipation of trial or a criminal prosecution.[173]

---

[170] Melendez-Diaz v. Massachusetts, 557 U.S. —, —, 129 S. Ct. 2527, 174 L. Ed. 2d 314, 328 (2009).

[171] *See* Advisory Committee Note, Rule 803(6). *See generally,* 5 WEINSTEIN'S FEDERAL EVIDENCE § 803.11.

[172] Crawford v. Washington, 541 U.S. 36, 56 (2004) (listing "business records" as an example of "statements that by their nature [are] not testimonial"). The Court has more recently clarified that out-of-court statements do not implicate the Confrontation Clause unless they are testimonial. *See* § 801.2, *supra.*

[173] Indeed, lower federal courts since *Crawford* have even gone so far as to extend this reasoning to business records prepared by law enforcement and other government officials in preparation for the criminal trial as long as those documents merely record "unambiguous factual matter," but those cases are open to serious question and it remains to be seen whether the Supreme Court intended for this exception to the Confrontation Clause to be interpreted so broadly. *See* § 801.2, *supra,* for a more detailed discussion of these points.

§ 803.37   Rule 803(7) Absence of a Record of a Regularly Conducted Activity

The following are not excluded by the rule against hearsay, regardless of whether the declarant is available as a witness:

***

    (7)   ***Absence of a Record of a Regularly Conducted Activity.*** Evidence that a matter is not included in a record described in paragraph (6) if:

        (A)   the evidence is admitted to prove that the matter did not occur or exist;

        (B)   a record was regularly kept for a matter of that kind; and

        (C)   neither the possible source of the information nor other circumstances indicate a lack of trustworthiness.

Rule 803(7) admits evidence of the absence of an entry in a record of a regularly conducted business activity.[174] It serves the simple purpose of permitting a fact to be proved by the absence of an entry in the same manner and under the same conditions as Rule 803(6) permits a fact to be proved by the existence of an entry.[175] Of course, where an entry is absent, evidence to that effect may not represent hearsay at all, since the preparer of the record (*i.e.,* the declarant) may intend to make no assertion about matters not mentioned.[176] Where no assertion is subjectively intended, there can be no out-of-court statement as defined by Rule 801(a), and in the absence of a

---

[174] *See generally,* 2 McCormick, § 287; 5 Weinstein's Federal Evidence § 803.12; 4 Mueller & Kirkpatrick, § 452; 5 Wigmore, § 1531. *See also* 30 Am. Jur. 2d, *Evidence,* § 959; Uniform Rules of Evidence, Rule 63(14).

[175] *See, e.g.,* United States v. Lanier, 578 F.2d 1246 (8th Cir. 1978) (testimony by auditor of failure to find deposits in Federal Reserve Bank admitted); Veneri v. Draper, 22 F.2d 33 (4th Cir. 1927) (bank ledger sheets admitted to show checks in question had not been charged against the account). Commentators uniformly support the introduction of such evidence. Wigmore succinctly states the rationale:

> When a book purports to contain all items transacted within the scope of the book's subject, the absence of an entry of transaction of a specific purport is in plain implication, a statement by the maker of the book that no such transaction was had. The psychology of it is the same as that of testimony on the stand by a person who denies that a sound took place in his presence because he heard no such sound . . . . The practical reliability of it is shown by every day's practice in every business house. All industry and commerce is daily conducted on the negative as well as on the affirmative showings of the regular books of entry.

5 Wigmore, § 1531, at 463; *see also* 2 McCormick, § 287.

[176] *See* Advisory Committee Note, Rule 803(7).

statement, no hearsay is presented.[177] Nevertheless, the subject has been addressed as an exception to the hearsay rule in order to remove any doubt and to eliminate the possibility that such evidence may be excluded.[178]

The rationale for this exception obviously mirrors the rationale supporting Rule 803(6), and the probative value of such evidence derives from similar factors.[179] The habits of precision of employees that render positive statements in such a record reliable also make the failure to mention trustworthy. In a regularly conducted business activity where a person with personal knowledge systematically prepares and maintains records at a time proximate to the occurrence of the event or transaction recorded, comprehensiveness and accuracy may be assumed. Consequently, lack of a record concerning the event is persuasive evidence of its nonoccurrence or nonexistence.

The final sentence of Rule 803(7) is identical to the corresponding language of Rule 803(6) and should be interpreted and treated the same.[180] Where the motivation and qualification of the record keeper and the manner of recording indicate untrustworthiness, the evidence of the absence of an entry in such a record may be excluded.

§ 803.38   Foundational Requirements

The foundational requirements for Rule 803(7) parallel those for Rule 803(6). The proponent of evidence of the absence of an entry must demonstrate that the business regularly maintained records of events or transactions like the one that was not recorded. The proponent also must demonstrate that the event or transaction not recorded was of such a nature that, had it occurred, it would have alerted the record keeper and would have been recorded immediately.

The foundations under Rule 803(6) and Rule 803(7) may differ in two significant ways. First, where Rule 803(6) expressly requires that business records be introduced by the testimony of "the custodian or other qualified witness," such language is notably omitted from Rule 803(7). Nevertheless, the custodian or another qualified witness may need to testify to satisfy the requirements of the Rule.[181] The omission probably results from the fact

---

[177] See § 801.2, *supra.*

[178] 5 WEINSTEIN'S FEDERAL EVIDENCE § 803.12.

[179] United States v. De Georgia, 420 F.2d 889, 893 (9th Cir. 1969) ("Regularly maintained business records are admissible in evidence as an exception to the hearsay rule because the circumstance that they are regularly-maintained records upon which the company relies in conducting its business assures accuracy not likely to be enhanced by introducing into evidence the original documents upon which the records are based"). *See generally,* 5 WEINSTEIN'S FEDERAL EVIDENCE § 803.12; 5 WIGMORE, § 1531.

[180] See § 803.35, *supra.*

[181] *E.g.,* United States v. Rich, 580 F.2d 929, 938 (9th Cir. 1978) ("Rule 803(7), which

that, as a practical matter, the foundational requirements may be relaxed where proof of a transaction's nonoccurrence is by way of the absence of an entry in a record. Second, where proof under Rule 803(6) generally takes the form of real evidence (*e.g.*, ledgers, notebooks, etc.), proof under Rule 803(7) may take the form exclusively of testimony to the effect that an examination of the relevant records revealed no mention of the event or transaction in question. Despite this distinction, the proponent of such evidence should be prepared to produce the relevant record at trial, especially where the absence of a record is the sole means of proving the nonexistence or nonoccurrence of a fact or an event.[182]

§ 803.39 Rule 803(8) Public Records

The following are not excluded by the rule against hearsay, regardless of whether the declarant is available as a witness:

***

(8) *Public Records.* A record or statement of a public office if:

    (A) it sets out:

        (i) the office's activities;

        (ii) a matter observed while under a legal duty to report, but not including, in a criminal case, a matter observed by law-enforcement personnel; or

        (iii) in a civil case or against the government in a criminal case, factual findings from a legally authorized investigation; and

    (B) neither the source of information nor other circumstances indicate a lack of trustworthiness.

Rule 803(8) contains an exception to the hearsay rule applicable to records and reports prepared and maintained by public offices and agencies.[183] The Rule reflects well-settled common-law[184] and legislative efforts

---

governs admission of evidence of the absence of entries in business records, does not specifically require the testimony of a custodian or another qualified witness; for the purpose of our opinion here, we assume, without deciding, that such a foundation is a necessary predicate to the admission of evidence of the entries, and that this requirement was not met").

[182] *See generally,* 4 MUELLER & KIRKPATRICK, § 452.

[183] *See generally,* 2 MCCORMICK, §§ 295–297; 5 WEINSTEIN'S FEDERAL EVIDENCE § 803.13; 4 MUELLER & KIRKPATRICK, §§ 453–458; 5 WIGMORE, §§ 1630–1684. *See also* Alexander, *Hearsay Exception for Public Records in Federal Criminal Trials,* 47 ALB. L. REV. 699 (1983); McCormick, *Can the Courts Make Wider Use of Reports of Official Investigations?,* 42 IOWA L. REV. 256 (1961); Note, *The Trustworthiness of Government Evaluative Reports Under Federal Rule of Evidence 803(8)(C),* 96 HARV. L. REV. 492 (1982); Note, *Scope of Federal Rule of Evidence 803(8)(C),* 59 TEX. L. REV. 155 (1980);

to codify the exception,[185] although some of the Rule's provisions represent somewhat of an expansion of pre-Rule law and remain the subject of some dispute.[186] Under common law, investigative reports, prepared by government agencies now admitted under subdivision (A)(iii) were often rejected on the basis of the rule against opinions. Rule 803(8)(A)(iii) represents a determination by the Advisory Committee and Congress that such reports possess sufficient indicia of reliability to be presumptively admissible. Nevertheless, the Rule provides an escape provision that allows exclusion if the trial judge determines that "the source of information [or] other circumstances indicate a lack of trustworthiness."[187]

The admissibility of public records was governed by the Official Records Act[188] prior to the adoption of the federal rules, except where some other specific statute applied.[189] This codification proved inadequate for two reasons. First, the statute admitted only records and reports of federal departments or agencies, and therefore severely restricted the scope of the exception. Rule 803(8) makes no distinction between federal and non-federal agencies, but simply requires that the record is that of a public body.[190] Second, the statute was so narrowly worded that courts often resorted to the Federal Business Records Act exception to admit public records.[191] Consequently, even though public records are more reliable than

Comment, *Admissibility of Evaluative Reports Under Federal Rule of Evidence 803(8)*, 68 KY. L.J. 197 (1979); Comment, *The Admissibility of Police Reports Under the Federal Rules of Evidence*, 71NW. U.L. REV. 691 (1976); Comment, *Hearsay Under the Proposed Federal Rules: A Discretionary Approach*, 15 WAYNE L. REV. 1076, 1156–62 (1969); Comment, *Evaluative Reports By Public Officials—Admissible as Official Statements?*, 30 TEX. L. REV. 112 (1951).

[184] 5 WIGMORE, § 1638a; *see also* Chesapeake & Delaware Canal Co. v. United States, 240 F. 903 (3d Cir. 1917), *aff'd*, 250 U.S. 193 (1919) (records of Treasury offered to prove receipts and disbursements of that Department).

[185] *E.g.*, Model Code of Evidence, Rule 516 (1942); Unif. R. Evid. 63 (16) (1953); Official Records Act, 28 U.S.C. § 1733 (1949).

[186] *See* §§ 803.44 and 803.45, *infra*.

[187] *See* 5 WEINSTEIN'S FEDERAL EVIDENCE § 803.13; United States v. Garland, 991 F.2d 328 (6th Cir. 1993) (evidence of the Ghanian convictions of two Ghanian citizens for defrauding an American citizen was admissible at defendant's trial pursuant to either Rule 803(8) or 803(22)).

[188] 28 U.S.C. § 1733(a) (1949). The statute provides: "Books or records of account or minutes of proceedings of any department or agency of the United States shall be admissible to prove the act, transaction or occurrence as a memorandum of which the same were made or kept." This section, by its own amendment, has been superseded by the Rules of Evidence when they apply.

[189] By virtue of Rule 802, specific statutes will continue to apply. *See* discussion of Rule 802, Chapter 802, *supra*.

[190] *See* Advisory Committee Note, Rule 803(8).

[191] 28 U.S.C. § 1732 (1949); *see, e.g.,* Blanchard v. United States, 360 F.2d 318 (5th Cir.

business records, the proponent of the former had to satisfy most foundational requirements for business records.[192] Rule 803(8) recognizes the inherent reliability of public records and so omits most foundational requirements found in Rule 803(6).

At the outset, it should be emphasized that the Rule's use of the descriptive term "public" when referring to the records embraced by the exception is actually a misnomer. The term "public" can connote simply that a record is "open to all" or "capable of being known or observed by all," as well as "made or done by a[n] officer of the government." Although each of these definitions has different connotations, the third definition indicates the general import of the Rule. A more accurate term, and one that should be engrafted into the Rule's provisions, is "official records." This term should be applied in order to avoid the uncertainty of the Rule's confusing terminology and to ensure that only records of governmental instrumentalities or officers are admitted. Moreover, such a reading reflects the common-law genesis of the hearsay exception codified in Rule 803(8).[193]

§ 803.40   Rationale

The rationale underlying the exception for official reports contained in Rule 803(8) rests upon the dual grounds of necessity and reliability. The necessity principle is twofold. First, there is a high likelihood that public officials may not have independent memory respecting their action in regard to entries that are frequently little more than mechanical; consequently, proof of the fact through the record may be necessary.[194] Second, the exception avoids the inconvenience of calling to the witness stand officials who have made written hearsay statements concerning events or transactions occurring within their jurisdictions.[195] Accordingly, Rule 803(8) does not require the

---

1966) (certificate of Drugs Disposal Committee of Federal Bureau of Narcotics); La Porte v. United States, 300 F.2d 878 (9th Cir. 1962) (selective service file); Kay v. United States, 255 F.2d 476 (4th Cir. 1958) (certificate of blood alcohol test prepared by state medical examiner).

[192] *See* § 803.34, *supra.*

[193] *See* 5 WIGMORE, § 1631; *see also* 2 MCCORMICK, § 295.

[194] *See* Wong Wing Foo v. McGrath, 196 F.2d 120, 123 (9th Cir. 1952) ("The reasons for this codified exception to the hearsay rule are principally two: There is a practical necessity for the use of such records to which is attached the presumption of a proper performance of official duty; and there is a great likelihood that a public official would have no memory at all respecting his action in hundreds of entries that are little more than mechanical. A further necessity lies in the inconvenience of calling to the witness stand all over the county government officers who have made in the course of their duties thousands of similar written hearsay statements concerning events coming within their jurisdictions").

[195] McCormick explains:

> A special need for this category of hearsay is found in the inconvenience of requiring public officials to appear in court and testify concerning the subject matter of their statements.

testimony of the custodian of the official record to testify for foundational purposes.

The further basis for this exception lies in the circumstantial guarantee of trustworthiness accorded official records. This principle is twofold as well. In the first instance, the Rule presumes that public servants are impartial and free from corruption and that they perform their official tasks carefully and promptly. Further, the Rule is predicated on the theory that an official record is necessarily subject to public scrutiny, thus exposing error in such records to prompt correction. Public scrutiny arguably supplies a further measure of reliability, since it prospectively operates as a stimulus to care and accuracy on the part of officials.[196] Also, it is likely that the routine underlying the preparation and maintenance of most official records reduces the risk of error.[197] Unlike this feature's reflection with regard to Rule 803(6) concerning business records, the concept of routine preparation has never been a foundation requirement of the official records exception. The fact remains, however, that for the vast majority of records introduced under Rule 803(8), this feature is present.

§ 803.41   Foundational Requirements — In General

The foundational conditions for evidence introduced pursuant to Rule 803(8) are minimal. Unlike the business records exception of Rule 803(6), the official records exception does not require the testimony of the custodian

---

2 MCCORMICK, § 295; *see also* 5 WEINSTEIN'S FEDERAL EVIDENCE § 803.13. *See generally,* 5 WIGMORE, § 1631.

[196] The thought here is a composite one and is closely related to that which is recognized as a reason for the exception for regular entries. Where an official record is one necessarily subject to public inspection, the facility and certainty with which errors would be exposed and corrected furnishes a special and additional guarantee of accuracy. Not only would the periodic inspection by members of the public tend to produce correction of errors actually perpetrated but, chiefly, the knowledge that the record is to be open to public inspection would subjectively act in advance as a stimulus to care and sincerity on the part of the official. 5 WIGMORE, § 1632; *see* Evanston v. Gunn, 99 U.S. 660 (1879); United States v. Hardin, 710 F.2d 1231 (7th Cir. 1983); *see also* 2 MCCORMICK, § 295. Both commentators emphasize, however, that while this circumstance of "publicity" serves to ensure reliability in many official records, and finds support in the common law, particularly in England, it is neither the only nor the most important basis for this hearsay exception. Were the fact of publicity most critical, a great many public records could be excluded upon a party's demonstration that, although the statement in question was "officially" recorded, it was never adequately subjected to public scrutiny. 5 WIGMORE, § 1632; 2 MCCORMICK, § 295.

[197] Wigmore provides the most cogent statement of this element:

The fundamental circumstance is that an official duty exists to make an accurate statement, and that this special and weighty duty will usually suffice as a motive to incite the officer to its fulfillment.

5 WIGMORE, § 1632, at 618; *see also* 2 MCCORMICK, § 295; 4 MUELLER & KIRKPATRICK, § 453.

or other qualified witness as a pre-condition to admissibility.[198] Official records frequently are admissible without a foundation witness, because the self-authentication provisions of Rule 902 obviate the need for live foundational testimony.[199] Similarly, in contrast to the exception for business records, Rule 803(8) does not require that the record be created contemporaneously with the event or transaction in question. Also, subdivisions (A)(i) and (A)(iii) have no requirement that the record be routinely maintained. Subdivision (A)(ii) does not expressly require routine recordkeeping, but it is limited to matters observed and reported in accordance with a legal duty, and therefore it usually is successfully invoked only with respect to regularly kept records.

Under pre-Rule practice, the official, *i.e.,* the declarant, must have possessed firsthand knowledge of the underlying event or transaction, although it was generally deemed sufficient if the record was based upon information received from a subordinate with personal knowledge.[200] Rule 803(8) is conspicuously silent in this regard, although nothing in Rules 803 and 804 should be construed to dispense with the requirement of personal knowledge by the declarant absent an express contrary indication. Accordingly, courts should construe Rule 803(8) in accordance with the fundamental purpose of the hearsay rule in excluding untrustworthy evidence.[201]

---

[198] *See* § 803.28 *et seq., supra. But see* Givens v. Lederle, 556 F.2d 1341 (5th Cir. 1977) (where documents offered were of questionable reliability, editor identified reports and was subject to cross-examination).

[199] *See* § 902.1 *et seq., infra. See, e.g.,* United States v. Taxe, 540 F.2d 961 (9th Cir. 1976) (certificate by Registrar of Copyrights admissible to prove date when sound recordings were first "fixed" and when they first became copyrightable); *see also* United States v. Harris, 446 F.2d 129 (7th Cir. 1971); American Airlines v. United States, 418 F.2d 180 (5th Cir. 1969); United States v. Van Hook, 284 F.2d 489 (7th Cir. 1961), *rev'd on other grounds,* 365 U.S. 609 (1961).

[200] *See* Comment, *Hearsay Under the Proposed Federal Rules: A Discretionary Approach,* 15 WAYNE L. REV. 1076 (1969). At common law, the requirement of firsthand knowledge by public officers was generally applied by reference to the scope of the officer's duty. Where the circumstances under which an official recorded a statement fell outside the scope of his lawful duty, or that of his subordinates, it was excluded. Where, on the other hand, it was clearly an official's duty to investigate and record or report irrespective of personal knowledge, the resulting statement was admitted. *See* La Porte v. United States, 300 F.2d 878 (9th Cir. 1962) (in prosecution for failure to perform civilian duties required by Selective Service Act, form prepared by Department of Charities stating that defendant did not report for work was properly received under Official Records Act); Olender v. United States, 210 F.2d 795, 801 (9th Cir. 1954) ("the facts stated in the document must have been within the personal knowledge and observation of the recording official or his subordinates"). *See generally,* 5 WEINSTEIN'S FEDERAL EVIDENCE § 803.13; 5 WIGMORE, §§ 1635–1638.

[201] *See generally,* 4 MUELLER & KIRKPATRICK, §§ 454–457. Wigmore suggests that with respect to records of an agency's internal activities (Rule 803(8)(A)) and facts observed pursuant to a legal duty (Rule 803(8)(B)), personal knowledge of the official (or of his or her subordinate) should be required because the official cannot fulfill the duty to carry out or

With respect to subdivision (A)(iii), a more flexible requirement of personal knowledge may be warranted. Reports introduced under subdivision (A)(iii), such as police accident reports and investigative field reports, will, more often than under subdivisions (A)(i) and (A)(ii), contain conclusions based upon facts of which the investigating official has no firsthand knowledge. Investigative reports are often a necessity prepared partially on the basis of interviews after the transaction in question has occurred.[202] Although there is arguably some danger that such reports will be based in part upon unreliable or inaccurate statements made by outsiders to the government, it is assumed that the report will reflect the expertise of the agency and that the reporting officials will have based their findings upon the most trustworthy information available to them.[203] In addition, it should be noted that Rule 803(8) contains an express provision that allows the trial judge to exclude reports where lack of trustworthiness is indicated.[204]

§ 803.42   Activities of Office or Agency, Rule 803(8)(A)(i)

Subdivision (A)(i) of Federal Rule of Evidence 803(8) admits records of a public office or agency to prove its activities. Foundational requirements for this exception are minimal, and where the record is authenticated in accordance with Article IX, it is presumed that dependable employees, acting in the course of their official duties, prepared and maintained accurate records on the basis of trustworthy information. Further, records offered under this subdivision are not subject to any use restrictions, *i.e.,* they may

---

supervise the transaction except so far as it is done by or before him or her, and thus the correlative duty to record, certify, or return involves necessarily a personal knowledge of the transaction. 5 WIGMORE, § 1635.

[202] *See, e.g.,* Smith v. Ithaca Corp., 612 F.2d 215 (5th Cir. 1980) (investigative report of Coast Guard regarding marine disaster); Moran v. Pittsburgh-Des Moines Steel Co., 183 F.2d 467 (3d Cir. 1950) (Bureau of Mines Report on gas tank explosion); *see also* MUELLER & KIRKPATRICK, §§ 454–457; 2 McCORMICK, § 297.

[203] *E.g.,* Smith v. Ithaca Corp., 612 F.2d 215 (5th Cir. 1980) (court admitted investigative report as trustworthy relying on "experience and expertise" of Coast Guard in investigating accidents, the timeliness of the investigation, and the impartiality of the Coast Guard); Baker v. Elcona Homes Corp., 588 F.2d 551 (6th Cir. 1978) (police accident report of matters observed by the officer and his factual findings; report held admissible under 803(8)(C) even though it contained findings based upon "disputed evidence," including an interview with one of the drivers involved, since that fact "no doubt had a bearing" upon the officer's conclusion).

[204] *See, e.g.,* Lubanski v. Coleco Indus., 929 F.2d 42 (1st Cir. 1991) (in products liability case, accident investigation report of police officer was excluded on basis other than untrustworthiness; no error resulted because officer testified as to the physical facts of the scene of the accident); Dallas & Mavis Forwarding Co. v. Stegall, 659 F.2d 721 (6th Cir. 1981) (not error to exclude state trooper's accident report based solely on story of biased eyewitness); Denny v. Hutchinson Sales Corp., 649 F.2d 816 (10th Cir. 1981) (findings based upon ex parte hearing of Colorado Civil Rights Commission properly excluded as untrustworthy; "[t]he lack of formal procedures and an opportunity to cross-examine witnesses are proper factors in determining the trustworthiness of the finding").

be offered as proof of the matter stated in the record against either party, in both civil and criminal cases.[205]

The admission of records containing simple assertions of fact regarding the function of the official agency under subdivision (A)(i) is the most accepted application of the doctrine. Examples of evidence admissible as proof of the activities of official agencies include: accounting records of governmental agencies;[206] dockets and journal entries of courts, legislative bodies and administrative tribunals;[207] certificates of title,[208] registry, death, and birth; records of licensing agencies;[209] and records of deeds and conveyances.[210] Often, records of this sort are arguably also within the scope of subdivision (A)(ii). Nevertheless, because these records are uncomplicated and concern factual matters involving the *internal* function of the particular agency, they are likely to be accurate and thus they qualify for admission under subdivision (A)(i). This qualification avoids the restrictions of subdivision (A)(ii) that operate in criminal proceedings.

A caveat to this generalized description of records qualifying under subdivision (A)(i) must, however, be noted. Where the focus of the particular record is more *external* to the functioning of the agency, in that it largely concerns the activities and conduct of certain citizens, or events or transactions outside the operation of the agency or office, it should not be

---

[205] *E.g.,* United States v. Union Nacional de Trabajadores, 576 F.2d 388 (1st Cir. 1978) (in criminal contempt prosecution, certified copy of marshal's return admitted as proof of service pursuant to Rule 803(8)(B); However, it is clear that reliance upon (A)(i) would have been equally appropriate). In a criminal case where the prosecution offers official records under Rule 803(8)(A)(i) against the accused, the defendant's Sixth Amendment right to confrontation may be violated. *See* § 801.2, *supra*.

[206] *E.g.,* Bank of Lexington v. Vining-Sparks Securities, 959 F.2d 606 (6th Cir. 1992) (letters of caution from the National Association of Securities Dealers (NASD) to a member firm were admissible under the "public records" exception); Chesapeake & Delaware Canal Co. v. United States, 250 U.S. 123 (1919) (accounting records of Treasury Department); Howard v. Perrin, 200 U.S. 71 (1906) (records of General Land Office); Southern Glass and Builders Supply Co., 398 F.2d 109 (5th Cir. 1968) (records of Small Business Administration).

[207] *E.g.,* Debs v. United States, 249 U.S. 211 (1919) (records of convictions); Carver v. Jackson, 29 U.S. (4 Pet.) 1 (1830) (journals of legislature).

[208] *E.g.,* United States v. King, 590 F.2d 253 (8th Cir. 1978) (certificates of ownership of motor vehicle).

[209] *E.g.,* Seese v. Volkswagenwerk A.G., 648 F.2d 833 (3d Cir. 1981) (motor vehicle standard of federal safety agency admitted as a "public record"); Van Bokkelen Rohr, S.A. v. Grumman Aerospace Corp., 432 F. Supp. 329 (E.D.N.Y. 1977) (minutes of meeting at which licenses denied admitted under Rule 803(8) generally).

[210] *E.g.,* Coan v. Flagg, 123 U.S. 117 (1887) (land office records); Galt v. Galloway, 29 U.S. (4 Pet.) 332 (1830) (land office); Knaggs v. Cleveland-Cliffs Iron Co., 287 F. 3143 (6th Cir. 1923) (deed).

admitted under subsection (A)(i).[211] It is more properly to be regarded as a record reflecting a matter observed under a legal duty, and it is consequently subject to the limiting aspects of subsection (A)(ii) that obviate certain constitutional confrontation problems in criminal cases by making specified official records inadmissible against the accused.

A final caveat to the application of subdivision (A)(i) relates to the confrontation rights of the accused in criminal cases; it is conceivable that an official record that meets the express conditions of Rule 803(8)(A)(i) is nevertheless inadmissible under the constitutional guarantee of confrontation, although that possibility seems remote in light of recent Supreme Court decisions in this area. The application of the Confrontation Clause to hearsay issues is discussed in § 803.2, *supra*.

§ 803.43   Matters Observable Under Legal Duty, Rule 803(8)(A)(ii)

Records of events or transactions within the scope of subdivision (A)(ii), which concern matters observed under a legal duty, are admissible as proof of matters external to the agency or public office.

In general, subdivision (A)(ii) is designed to embrace primarily factual records in a variety of forms, and Rule 803(8)(A)(ii) may be used as a vehicle for the admission of records reflecting events, transactions, and conditions of almost any sort. For example, the Rule encompasses records of the United States agencies or armed forces,[212] and records of state agencies, bureaus and administrative bodies,[213] including police report and hospital records. Some of these records (or portions thereof) may qualify as well

---

[211] *E.g.,* Minnehaha County v. Kelley, 150 F.2d 356 (8th Cir. 1945) (records of Weather Bureau containing rainfall data); La Porte v. United States, 300 F.2d 878 (9th Cir. 1962) (in prosecution for failure to perform civilian duties required by the Selective Service Act, report prepared by federal agency stating that defendant failed to report to work received under Official Records Act); *see* 4 MUELLER & KIRKPATRICK, §§ 454–457.

[212] *E.g.,* Distaff, Inc., v. Springfield Contracting Corp., 984 F.2d 108 (4th Cir. 1993) (trial court erred in excluding investigative report of a Navy fire inspector simply because the inspector was unavailable to testify at trial); Evanston v. Gunn, 99 U.S. 660 (1879) (meteorological observations of United States Signal Service); Minnehaha County v. Kelley, 150 F.2d 356 (8th Cir. 1945) (United States Weather Bureau rainfall data); United States v. Van Hook, 284 F.2d 489 (7th Cir. 1960), *rev'd on other grounds,* 365 U.S. 609 (1961) (letter from induction officer to District Attorney, pursuant to army regulations stating refusal to be inducted); United States v. Meyer, 113 F.2d 387 (7th Cir. 1940) (map of government engineer based upon information supplied by those working under his supervision).

[213] *See* Hughes v. United States, 953 F.2d 531 (9th Cir. 1992) (IRS Form 4340 is admissible under Rule 803(8)(B)); United States v. Aikins, 912 F.2d 285 (9th Cir. 1990), *amended,* 946 F.2d 608 (9th Cir. 1990) (State Department certificate asserting the consent of the Panamanian government to search a vessel held admissible under the public documents exception); United States v. Enterline, 894 F.2d 287 (8th Cir. 1990) (computer report listing stolen vehicles admitted under Rule 803(8)(B)); De Pinto v. Provident Sec. Life Ins. Co., 374 F.2d 37 (9th Cir. 1967) (report of state insurance examiner of Arizona admitted under Federal Business Records).

under subdivision (A)(i). Where, however, the clear focus of the report is on facts and circumstances *external* to the agency, qualification under either Rule 803(8)(A)(ii) or Rule 803(8)(A)(iii) is required for its admission. Although Rule 803(8)(A)(ii) operates to admit factual information contained in an accident report, such as a description of the scene and the degree of damage, subdivision (A)(iii) controls to the extent that the report contains evaluations of causation or fault, or other statements requiring interpretation of data.[214]

Three foundational requirements are imposed for admission of official records pursuant to Rule 803(8)(A)(ii). First, the governmental employee or agent who supplies the information must have firsthand knowledge of the event or condition described in the report.[215] Second, the source must be under a legal duty to report the information.[216] And third, the official agency must have a legal obligation to prepare and maintain the record, as the term "duty" implies. The second and third requirements should not be construed so as to require that an express duty be imposed by statute or regulation, but only that the nature of the agency's responsibilities be such that the record in question is of the type routinely or regularly prepared.[217] On the other hand, the personal knowledge requirement should be more carefully applied, especially where persons from outside the agency may contribute critical information, a situation raising problems of multiple hearsay.[218] The admissibility of investigatory reports is addressed in detail in § 803.44,

---

[214] *See, e.g.,* Baker v. Elcona Homes Corp., 588 F.2d 551 (6th Cir. 1978) (automobile collision report by police officer); Fraley v. Rockwell Int'l Corp., 470 F. Supp. 1264 (S.D. Ohio 1979) (naval office's report on air crash); Colvin v. United States, 479 F.2d 998 (9th Cir. 1973) (report of criminal investigator of Bureau of Indian Affairs describing scene of accident admitted under Official Records Act).

[215] *Cf.* United States v. Perlmuter, 693 F.2d 1290 (9th Cir. 1982) (reversible error to admit exhibit listing alleged convictions where there was no indication that person who signed the exhibit had firsthand knowledge of conviction or was under any legal duty to record convictions). *But see* United States v. Hudson, 479 F.2d 251 (9th Cir. 1972) (rule requiring firsthand knowledge does not apply where subordinate with firsthand knowledge reports to the recorder).

[216] *Cf.* Wetherill v. University of Chicago, 518 F. Supp. 1387 (N.D. Ill. 1981) (government report excluded where it was based on several non-official sources who had "no duty imposed by law" to report). Under pre-Rule law, reports made by private persons pursuant to a statutory duty were sometimes admissible. *E.g.,* Sternberg Dredging Co. v. Moran Towing and Transp. Co., 196 F.2d 1002 (2d Cir. 1952). However, the status and scope of this "exception" to the requirement is unclear. *See* 5 WEINSTEIN'S FEDERAL EVIDENCE § 803.13.

[217] *See* White v. United States, 164 U.S. 100 (1896) (record of county jailer properly received to prove that certain prisoner was there on a particular day; court notes that the requirement that the agency be legally required to keep the record does not demand that the duty be required by statutes; it is sufficient if the duty was required of the maker by his superior officer if it is necessary to the proper functioning of the office).

[218] *See* Colvin v. United States, 479 F.2d 998 (9th Cir. 1973) (Official Records Act does

infra.

§ 803.44 Special Problem: Admissibility of Investigative Reports

Rule 803(8)(A)(iii) provides an exception for reports containing "factual findings resulting from an investigation made pursuant to authority granted by law." While subdivisions (A)(i) and (A)(ii) have ample support in pre-Rule law, subdivision (A)(iii) has been the subject of considerable controversy. Two problems have arisen regarding the admissibility of "evaluative" reports: (1) whether the preparer must have possessed personal knowledge of the underlying facts, and (2) what determinations constitute "factual findings." The former problem is discussed in connection with foundational requirements in § 803.41, *supra.* To re-emphasize an earlier point, the fact that the findings contained in the report are based in part on hearsay should not in itself render the findings so untrustworthy as to be inadmissible.[219] In interpreting subdivision (A)(iii), it should be recognized that the intent of the drafters was to assume admissibility in the first instance but provide an escape provision for cases in which the court determines that the report is not sufficiently reliable.[220] Judge Weinstein suggests that "[i]f the trial court finds that the particular official in question would not have relied upon facts not directly observed unless, in the light of experience, the official knew them to be trustworthy, the investigative report should not be rejected on the ground of lack of personal knowledge."[221]

While the conclusions of a report based on hearsay are generally admissible under Rule 803(8)(A)(iii), the hearsay statements themselves, to the extent they appear in the report, are not admissible pursuant to this exception.[222] This seemingly inconsistent treatment is explained by the

---

not embrace records containing statements that are not within the personal knowledge of the recording official or his subordinates).

[219] *See* Hodge v. Seiler, 558 F.2d 284 (5th Cir. 1977) (in housing discrimination suit, "Final Investigation Report" of HUD property received against defense contention that it was hearsay; court noted that Rule 803(8)(C) makes such reports admissible); United States v. Amer. Tel. & Tel. Co., 498 F. Supp. 353, 364 (D.D.C. 1980) ("[T]he multiple hearsay issue is reducible to one of the trustworthiness of the factual findings."); *see also* Moss v. Ole South Real Estate, 933 F.2d 1300 (5th Cir. 1991) (the Magistrate erred in excluding an Air Force report from evidence where the report was timely made, involved all parties, and the investigators had held a hearing; a HUD report was properly excluded, however, due to lapse of time and incomplete interviewing).

[220] *See* Advisory Committee Note, Rule 803(8).

[221] 5 WEINSTEIN'S FEDERAL EVIDENCE § 803.13.

[222] *See* McKinnon v. Skil Corp., 638 F.2d 270 (1st Cir. 1981); *see also* John McShain, Inc. v. Cessna Aircraft Co., 563 F.2d 632 (3d Cir. 1977) (accident reports submitted to the National Transportation Safety Board were properly excluded as hearsay because Rule 803(8) exempts from the rule only reports by officials, and the government investigator's reports often contained statements by witnesses "which would make such memoranda encompass double hearsay"; elimination of these hearsay statements from the reports would have led to unwarranted delay and waste of time).

reliance of subdivision (A)(iii) on the skill of agency officials in sorting reliable from unreliable statements as they prepare public reports. Of course, where the hearsay statements that form the basis of an official report independently satisfy a distinct hearsay exception, the statements are admissible for their truth under a multiple hearsay theory.[223]

Whether "factual findings" indicate only facts, rather than conclusions or opinions, caused a split in the Circuit Courts in interpreting Rule 803(8)(A)(iii). The House Judiciary Committee, in approving the Rule added the caveat that the phrase should be "strictly construed and that evaluations or opinions contained in public reports shall not be admissible under this Rule."[224] However, the Senate Judiciary Committee strongly dissented from this narrow interpretation for two reasons. First, several statutes, preserved by Rule 802, admit evaluative reports of various kinds, thus indicating congressional support for the admission of evaluative reports. Second, the Advisory Committee found "evaluative" reports sufficiently reliable to be included within the provision, providing ample safeguards if they appear unreliable.[225]

Most of the Circuit Courts adopted the Senate's broad interpretation and did not attempt to distinguish between facts and opinions. However, at least two circuits adopted a narrower view. The Supreme Court resolved this split in *Beech Aircraft Corp. v. Rainey*.[226] The Eleventh Circuit had held that certain portions of an investigative report prepared by the Navy after a fatal plane crash were inadmissible because Rule 803(8)(A)(iii) did not encompass evaluative conclusions or opinions.[227] The Supreme Court reversed, holding that the Rule does not create a distinction between fact and opinion.[228] The Court noted that "the language of the Rule does not state that 'factual findings' are admissible, but that '*reports* . . . setting forth . . . factual findings' (emphasis added) are admissible. On this reading, the language of the Rule does not create a distinction between 'fact' and 'opinion.' "[229]

Additionally, the Court noted that the "escape provision" found in the final clause of the Rule permits exclusion if "the sources of information or other

---

[223] Federal Aviation Admin. v. Landy, 705 F.2d 624 (2d Cir. 1983) (in action to impose civil penalties for violation of FAA regulations, telex by German government to FAA was properly admitted as incorporated in the FAA's factual findings resulting from an investigation made pursuant to authority granted by law); *see also* Baker v. Elcona Homes Corp., 588 F.2d 551 (6th Cir. 1978).

[224] H.R. REP. NO. 93–650, 93d Cong., 1st Sess. 14 (1973).

[225] S. REP. NO. 93-1277, 93d Cong., 2d Sess. 18 (1974).

[226] Beech Aircraft Corp. v. Rainey, 488 U.S. 153 (1988).

[227] *Beech Aircraft Corp.*, 488 U.S. at 160.

[228] *Id.* at 170.

[229] *Id.* at 164.

circumstances indicate lack of trustworthiness."[230] The Court indicated that this trustworthiness inquiry applies to all elements of the report, and gives the trial judge discretion "to exclude an entire report or portions thereof — whether narrow 'factual' statements or broader 'conclusions' — that she determines to be untrustworthy."[231]

§ 803.45   Use Restrictions on Public Records and Reports in Criminal Cases, Rule 803(8)(A)(ii) and Rule 803(8)(A)(iii)

Rule 803(8)(A)(ii), in contrast to Rule 803(8)(A)(i), imposes a restriction in criminal cases upon the use of records or reports from "law-enforcement personnel" containing matters observed pursuant to official duty. Although the wording of Rule 803(8)(A)(ii) suggests such reports cannot be used by either the prosecution or defense, it is clear from the legislative history of the clause that Congress was only concerned with protecting the right of the accused to confront and cross-examine witnesses.[232] Under a broad definition of "law-enforcement personnel," reports such as ballistics analyses, blood-alcohol tests, and analyses of purported illegal substances could be excluded under this restriction, and at least one court has so construed the provision.[233] In *United States v. Oates,* the court defined "law-enforcement personnel" to include "at the least, any officer or employee of a governmental agency which has law enforcement responsibilities."[234] In *Oates,* the Court concluded that the full-time chemists of the United States Customs Service clearly fall within that definition and therefore, the chemist's report and worksheet prepared in connection with the analysis of a substance alleged to be heroin could be excluded under the Rule 803(8)(A)(ii) restriction.[235]

Other courts, however, have concluded that the restrictive language of subsection (A)(ii) is not an absolute bar to all public records offered by the government against the accused in criminal cases. In one line of cases, the courts have found that the Rule's restriction pertaining to "law-enforcement personnel" does not encompass the entire group of public officials who perform investigatory work and who prepare and maintain official re-

---

[230] *Id.* at 165.

[231] *Id.* at 167; *see also* Cortes v. Maxus Exploration Co., 977 F.2d 195 (5th Cir. 1992) (in sexual harassment case, trial court excluded an EEOC report that was highly prejudicial); Figures v. Board of Pub. Utils., 967 F.2d 357 (10th Cir. 1992) (trial court did not err in excluding a letter from the Department of Labor to defendant where the letter was simply a draft and was not officially endorsed or authorized to be sent out).

[232] *See* discussion of legislative history contained in United States v. Oates, 560 F.2d 45 (2d Cir. 1977); *see also* 5 WEINSTEIN'S FEDERAL EVIDENCE § 803.03.

[233] *E.g.,* United States v. Oates, 560 F.2d 45 (2d Cir. 1977).

[234] United States v. Oates, 560 F.2d 45 (2d Cir. 1977)

[235] United States v. Oates, 560 F.2d 45 (2d Cir. 1977)

cords.[236] Even though many government employees may, to a limited extent, have some indirect law enforcement responsibilities, the restriction should not be construed so broadly as to include records only remotely concerned with police and law enforcement operations. This exception to the restriction of subdivision (A)(ii) rests upon the theory that, "[i]n adopting this exception, Congress was concerned about prosecutors attempting to prove their case in chief simply by putting into evidence police officers' reports of their contemporaneous observations of crime."[237]

A related "exception" to the restriction of 803(A)(ii) has operated to admit reports found to be of routine and non-adversarial nature.[238] In *United States v. Orozco*,[239] the court concluded that Congress intended the restriction to exclude such reports only where the circumstances surrounding the official's observation were of such an adversarial nature as to indicate unreliability. Although the court concluded that a customs inspector was an official within

---

[236] *E.g.,* United States v. Hansen, 583 F.2d 325 (7th Cir. 1978); *see also* United States v. Union Nacional de Trabajadores, 576 F.2d 388 (1st Cir. 1978) (United States marshal's return stating that he had served injunction was admissible under Rule 803(8), since sheriffs' returns were admissible at common law and there was no indication of Congressional intent to overrule the common-law rule); United States v. Arias, 575 F.2d 253 (9th Cir. 1978) (in perjury prosecution, transcript from proceedings in which defendant had allegedly perjured himself was admitted in evidence, through testimony by court reporter who prepared it). *But see* United States v. Ruffin, 575 F.2d 346 (2d Cir. 1978) (computer print-out of an IRS record is inadmissible against a criminal defendant).

[237] United States v. Grady, 544 F.2d 598 (2d Cir. 1976). *See generally,* 5 WEINSTEIN'S FEDERAL EVIDENCE § 803.03; 4 MUELLER & KIRKPATRICK, §§ 454–457.

[238] *E.g.,* United States v. Caraballo, 595 F.3d 1214 (11th Cir. 2010) (routinely and mechanically kept INS records, such as warrants of deportation, are admissible under Rule 803(8)(B) because they are routinely completed by Customs agents in the course of their non-adversarial duties, not in the course of preparing for a criminal prosecution. In prosecution for illegally smuggling aliens into the country, the court properly admitted an INS form that contained only routine biographical information such as the entrant's name, date and place of birth, parents' names, height, weight, address, country of citizenship, and information concerning whether the entrant had an immigration visa); United States v. Dowdell, 595 F.3d 50 (1st Cir. 2010) (although the plain language of the so-called "law enforcement exception," Rule 803(8)(A)(ii), seems to categorically bar the introduction of all documents prepared by the police against the accused in a criminal case, ministerial and non-adversarial police records such as a booking sheet are admissible under the Rule, because they are not created in the adversarial and confrontational setting with which that rule is concerned); United States v. Puente, 826 F.2d 1415 (5th Cir. 1987) (in perjury prosecution where defendant was accused of lying to grand jury regarding a trip to Mexico, there was no error in admitting computer printouts showing defendant's son's car crossed the border on the specified date; the system was part of routine, objective border observations); United States v. Hernandez-Rojas, 617 F.2d 533 (9th Cir. 1980) (no error in admitting warrant of deportation, which contained notation of previous deportation; "this court has looked to the purpose of the law enforcement exception in determining admissibility"); United States v. King, 590 F.2d 253 (8th Cir. 1978) (certified documents of Missouri Department of Revenue showing that defendant was owner of car were admissible).

[239] United States v. Orozco, 590 F.2d 789 (9th Cir. 1979).

the meaning of subdivision (A)(ii), the court found the "simple recordation of license numbers of all vehicles which pass his station is not of the adversarial confrontation nature which might cloud his perception."[240] When the matter observed, however, is non-routine or adversarial in nature, the record containing the matter may not be used against the accused at trial under the express terms of subdivision (A)(ii).

Subdivision (A)(iii) prohibits the use of evaluative reports against the accused under any circumstances. Unlike subdivision (A)(ii), the operation of subdivision (A)(iii) is not affected by who made the report, and it excludes even routine or non-adversarial reports. This exclusion was predicated on the concern that admission in such cases would almost necessarily involve a collision with the confrontation rights of the accused.[241] Conversely, subdivision (A)(iii) expressly allows the introduction of investigative reports in civil cases and against the government in criminal cases.

It should be noted that the exclusion pertaining to reports of police officers and law enforcement personnel under subdivision (A)(ii) does not contain language expressly permitting the introduction of such reports against the government by the accused. However, subdivision (A)(ii) has been read to authorize admission at the request of the defendant.[242]

The potential overlap between subdivisions (A)(ii) and (A)(iii) should be apparent. To the extent that a report offered against an accused is characterized as one containing "matters observed" under subdivision (A)(ii), it may nevertheless be admitted by some courts under the theory that either the preparer does not fall within the class of "law-enforcement personnel" or that the report was of a routine and non-adversarial nature. However, a report characterized as purely evaluative under subdivision (A)(iii) will be excluded pursuant to the absolute use restriction contained therein. This problem of classification becomes particularly acute in the case of official laboratory reports such as ballistics analyses, blood-alcohol tests and analyses of suspected drugs. While such reports have traditionally been admissible,[243] some authority interpreting Rule 803(8) has concluded that official laboratory reports fall within subdivision (A)(iii) and are, therefore, absolutely inadmissible against the accused in a criminal case.[244] This position of inadmissibility is arguably supported by the construction of the

---

[240] United States v. Orozco, 590 F.2d 789 (9th Cir. 1979).

[241] *See* Advisory Committee Note, Rule 803(8); *see also* § 801.2, *supra*.

[242] United States v. Smith, 521 F.2d 957, 968 (D.C. Cir. 1975) (Rule 803(8) "appears to overlap rather than diminish 803(6)").

[243] *See, e.g.,* United States v. Stern, 519 F.2d 521 (9th Cir. 1975); United States v. Frattini, 501 F.2d 1234 (2d Cir. 1974); *see also* Imwinkelried, *The Constitutionality of Introducing Evaluative Laboratory Reports Against Criminal Defendants*, 30 HAST. L.J. 621 (1979).

[244] *See* United States v. Oates, 560 F.2d 45 (2d Cir. 1977).

Rule as well as policy considerations. Laboratory reports will, in the great majority of cases, contain more information of an evaluative nature than information merely reflecting "matters observed." Furthermore, there is ample support for the proposition that laboratory reports are susceptible of considerable error that will often not be evident from the face of the document.[245]

Arguments in favor of admitting certain evaluative reports have stressed three points: first, the existence of an improper motive on the part of the preparers of such reports is unlikely since they will ordinarily be scientists and technicians unconcerned with the impact of the report in a particular case; second, obtaining live testimony would involve considerable cost; and third, little would be gained from live testimony since it would most likely rest upon the reports rather than present memory.[246]

As a caveat, it should be noted that concern over a party's rights under the Confrontation Clause of the United States Constitution limited the application of the exception in criminal cases. The application of the Confrontation Clause to hearsay issues is discussed in § 803.2, *supra*.

The limiting aspects of Rule 803(8) may not be circumvented by introducing a public record under Rule 803(6), which pertains to records of regularly conducted activity.[247] Such circumvention would obviously result in a perversion of the intent and policy of the Rules.

§ 803.46   Trustworthiness

Rule 803(8) contains a "trustworthiness" clause identical to that of the Rule 803(6), under which the trial court may exclude an official record or report that otherwise satisfies the requirements of the Rule on the ground that the circumstances surrounding the source of the information or the manner of its recording indicate an unusual degree of unreliability.[248] In any event, the opponent of such evidence bears the burden of proving the untrustworthiness of the record once its proponent meets the foundational requirements.[249]

---

[245] *See* Imwinkelried, *The Constitutionality of Introducing Evaluative Laboratory Reports Against Criminal Defendants*, 30 HAST. L.J. 621 (1979).

[246] 4 MUELLER & KIRKPATRICK, §§ 454–457.

[247] *See* United States v. Orozco, 590 F.2d 789, 793 (9th Cir. 1979) ("while governmental functions would be included within the broad definition of 'business' in Rule 803(6), such a result is obviated by Rule 803(8), which is the 'business records' exception for public records such as those in issue here").

[248] *See* 4 MUELLER & KIRKPATRICK, § 458; *see, e.g.,* United States v. Orozco, 590 F.2d 789 (9th Cir. 1979) (although admitting receipt of customs records under Rule 803(8)(A)(ii), court suggests that records could be excluded if circumstances indicate lack of trustworthiness).

[249] *See* Reynolds v. Green, 184 F.3d 589 (6th Cir. 1999) (no error to exclude a report by an employee of a prison ombudsman's office that contained self-serving statements by the

The Advisory Committee Note to Rule 803(8) sets forth four considerations that may be helpful in determining the trustworthiness of records
offered under the Rule: (1) the timeliness of the investigation,[250] (2) the
special skill or experience of the official,[251] (3) whether a hearing was held
and the level at which it was conducted,[252] and (4) possible motivational
problems such as those suggested by *Palmer v. Hoffman.*[253] As the Advisory
Committee Note suggests, the list is not exhaustive of the factors that may
bear upon the trustworthiness of a particular record and the courts have
appropriately undertaken a case-by-case analysis of trustworthiness.[254]
Accordingly, even where one or more of the above factors has suggested
inadmissibility in a particular case, the record has nevertheless been
admitted where special guarantees of trustworthiness have been present.[255]

As indicated by the discussion of subdivision (A)(iii) contained in
§§ 803.44 and 803.45, *supra,* special problems of admissibility may attend
evaluative reports offered under the Rule. In *Zenith Radio Corp. v.*

---

plaintiff-prisoner and his mother; Rule 803(8) places a burden on the opponent of the official
record to show that the sources or information contained within it showed a lack of
trustworthiness and that burden was met here); Melville v. American Home Assur. Co., 443
F. Supp. 1064 (E.D. Pa. 1978), *rev'd on other grounds,* 584 F.2d 1306 (3d Cir. 1978); United
States v. Taxe, 540 F.2d 961 (9th Cir. 1976); Securities & Exchange Comm. v. General
Refractories Co., 400 F. Supp. 1248 (D.D.C. 1975).

[250] *See, e.g.,* Smith v. Ithaca Corp., 612 F.2d 215 (5th Cir. 1980); Baker v. Elcona Homes
Corp., 588 F.2d 551 (6th Cir. 1978); *see also* McCormick, *Can the Courts Make Wider Use
of Reports of Official Investigations?,* 42 IOWA L. REV. 363 (1957).

[251] *See, e.g.,* Baker v. Elcona Homes Corp., 588 F.2d 551 (6th Cir. 1978); Walker v.
Fairchild Indus., 554 F. Supp. 650 (D. Nev. 1982); Fraley v. Rockwell Int'l Corp., 470 F.
Supp. 1264 (S.D. Ohio 1979); *cf.* Sage v. Rockwell Int'l Corp., 477 F. Supp. 1205 (D.N.H.
1979) (lack of experience of investigator goes only to weight, not admissibility).

[252] *See, e.g.,* United States v. Corr, 543 F.2d 1042 (2d Cir. 1976) (erroneously suggesting
that SEC document lies outside Rule 803(8)(C); court found document to have but "minimal"
relevance).

[253] *See* Palmer v. Hoffman, 318 U.S. 109 (1943); *see also* Abdel v. United States, 670
F.2d 73 (7th Cir. 1982); Dallas & Mavis Forwarding Co. v. Stegall, 659 F.2d 721 (6th Cir.
1981); Robbins v. Whelan, 653 F.2d 47 (1st Cir. 1981); United States v. Stone, 604 F.2d 922
(5th Cir. 1979).

[254] *In re* Complaint of Paducah Towing Co., 692 F.2d 412 (6th Cir. 1982) (findings
resting largely on hearsay could be excluded; court finds, however, that objecting party did
not show untrustworthiness); United States v. Orozco, 590 F.2d 789 (9th Cir. 1979) (receipt
of computer records showing license numbers of cars crossing Mexican-American border
proper where the recording procedure was simple and the recording officer had opportunity
to correct mistakes as the numbers were entered).

[255] *E.g.,* United States v. School Dist., 577 F.2d 1339 (6th Cir. 1978) (error to exclude
administrative findings of HEW in school desegregation suit despite contention that school
district lacked subpoena power at hearings and there was no evidence that hearing examiner
possessed any special expertise; court found these to be suitable considerations but found that
circumstances indicated overall trustworthiness of the proceedings).

Matsushita Electric Industrial Co.,[256] the district court examined three additional factors that may be particularly relevant to the trustworthiness of evaluative reports: (1) the finality of the findings, (2) the extent to which the report is based upon hearsay or confidential sources, and (3) the possibility that the report reflects the agency's desire to further preconceived policy objectives, thus tainting the objectivity of the findings.[257]

§ 803.47   Rule 803(9) Public Records of Vital Statistics

The following are not excluded by the rule against hearsay, regardless of whether the declarant is available as a witness:

***

    (9) *Public Records of Vital Statistics.* A record of a birth, death, or marriage, if reported to a public office in accordance with a legal duty.

Rule 803(9) creates a hearsay exception for public records relating to births, deaths, and marriages.[258] It allows the contents of such records to be introduced as substantive evidence, thereby facilitating the proof of a wide variety of information, such as the date, time, place of birth, and identity of parents; date, time, and cause of death; date and place of marriage and the parties thereto.

The proponent of the record must establish that the report was made to a public office pursuant to requirements of law, and in this respect, the Rule relies heavily on existing state statutory reporting requirements.[259] Accordingly, Rule 803(9) should be read in conjunction with the applicable state statute as well as with Rule 902(4) and Rule 1005. Such records are self-authenticating if the certification is in accordance with the requirements set forth in Rule 902(4).[260] Alternatively, such records may be authenticated by a method provided in Rule 901, for example, by a witness who has compared the copy with the original and testifies that the record is what it is claimed to be. The two methods of authentication are acknowledged by Rule

---

[256] Zenith Radio Corp. v. Matsushita Electric Industrial Co., 505 F. Supp. 1125 (E.D. Pa. 1980), *rev'd,* 723 F.2d 238, 264 (3d Cir. 1983), *rev'd on other grounds,* 475 U.S. 574 (1986).

[257] Zenith Radio Corp. v. Matsushita Electric Industrial Co., 505 F. Supp. 1125 (E.D. Pa. 1980).

[258] *See generally,* 2 McCORMICK, §§ 299–300; 5 WEINSTEIN'S FEDERAL EVIDENCE § 803.14; 4 MUELLER & KIRKPATRICK, § 459; 5 WIGMORE, §§ 1674–1684. *See also* Comment, *Hearsay Under the Proposed Federal Rules: A Discretionary Approach,* 15 WAYNE L. REV. 1077 (1969).

[259] State statutes relating to this requirement are collected in 5 WIGMORE, § 1644.

[260] Under Rule 902(4), copies of public records are certified in accordance with provisions (1), (2) or (3) of Rule 902 or "a federal statute or a rule prescribed by the Supreme Court." *See* Advisory Committee Note, Rule 902(4).

1005, which permits certified copies of public records to be introduced in lieu of the original in order to prove the contents.[261] By virtue of the foregoing provisions, the foundational requirement of Rule 803(9) (*i.e.,* that the report was made to a public office in accordance with a legal duty) may be met, for example, by introducing the copy of a record made pursuant to the provisions of a state statute and certified in compliance with Rule 902(4).

Two problems may arise in fulfilling the requirements that the report be made pursuant to requirements of law. First, a state law may not have a requirement that the matter be reported. Second, the pertinent statute may even require that the matter involved be excluded from the report or that certain reported matters be excluded from evidence at trial.[262]

If a report required by statute also includes additional details that did not need to be reported under that statute, the court should nevertheless admit those details if they are so closely related to the required matters that their admission would be consistent with the purpose of the exception, or if those facts would logically be mentioned in the kind of report that the legislature has required.[263]

Matters that the state statute requires to be excluded from the report or from evidence at trial are more problematic. Such matters may only involve a legislative judgment as to the proper scope of the hearsay exception, in which case, the judgment may be considered by the court in determining the matter's reliability, but should not be taken as binding on the court any more than any other state hearsay rule that differs from the pertinent Federal Rule.[264] However, the exclusion by the state statute may reflect a legislative judgment regarding some substantive policy. In this situation, exclusion of the matter in deference to the state statute and its limits may well be justified.

An example of a statutory provision reflecting a substantive legislative judgment is a statute that forbids the recording of information about the paternity of an illegitimate child.[265] Such a prohibition may represent a legislative judgment as to the reliability of the matter as well as reflecting a worthy social policy. In cases where the statute and the Rule appear to be at variance, the court should determine the purpose sought to be achieved by the law and, unless the law merely represents an attempt to regulate the

---

[261] *See* Rule 1005 and Advisory Committee Note, Rule 1005.

[262] *E.g.,* Woodward v. United States, 167 F.2d 774 (8th Cir. 1948) (under Missouri law physician had a duty *not* to record information regarding paternity if birth was illegitimate); Pollack v. Metropolitan Life Ins. Co., 138 F.2d 123 (3d Cir. 1943) (birth certificate admitted to show age of parents even though state law did not require this to be recorded).

[263] 4 MUELLER & KIRKPATRICK, § 459.

[264] *See* Pollack v. Metropolitan Life Ins. Co., 138 F.2d 123 (3d Cir. 1943).

[265] *E.g.,* Woodward v. United States, 167 F.2d 774 (8th Cir. 1948) (statute prohibited any information in birth certificate relating to paternity if the birth was illegitimate).

receipt of hearsay, the court should give the state statute considerable weight in determining admissibility.

§ 803.48   Rationale

The rationale underlying the exception for records of vital statistics rests upon the familiar factors of necessity and reliability. The necessity principle is twofold. First, vital statistics regarding events such as births and marriages may become significant only in litigation occurring long after the event, and locating those who witnessed the event may be difficult. Further, those witnesses who are found will not likely have even traces of memory. Second, requiring direct testimony about such events would significantly inconvenience those called as witnesses without any corresponding benefit to the integrity of the fact-finding process.[266]

The trustworthiness principle is satisfied for four reasons: First, vital statistics are recorded by professionals in the performance of both their public and professional duty. Second, such statistics normally involve relatively uncomplicated facts, and their recording is ordinarily substantially contemporaneous with the event, thus minimizing the risks of faulty perception and memory. Third, since these events are fairly important to those who report them, it may safely be assumed that those involved will make an effort to be truthful. Finally, vital statistics will often be prepared before litigation is contemplated, and therefore the prospect of intentional misstatement by the reporter is reduced.[267]

§ 803.49   Foundation

As previously discussed in § 803.47 of this Chapter, records of vital statistics will often be self-authenticating, and accordingly, Rule 803(9) requires no foundational testimony of the custodian or other qualified witness as a pre-condition to admissibility. The Rule requires only that the report be made to a public office pursuant to requirements of law.[268]

Likewise, Rule 803(9) should not be interpreted as requiring firsthand knowledge by the recording official on every point contained in the report.[269] In some instances, the certifying officer will have personal

---

[266] *See* 4 MUELLER & KIRKPATRICK, § 459. *See, e.g.,* Charleston Nat'l Bank v. Hennessy, 404 F.2d 539, 540 (5th Cir. 1968) ("use of the certificate is a convenience . . . to require the official to be called from his public duties to testify may be inconvenient to him, the court, and the public"). *See generally,* 5 WIGMORE, § 1631; 2 MCCORMICK, § 295; 5 WEINSTEIN'S FEDERAL EVIDENCE § 803.14.

[267] *See generally,* 4 MUELLER & KIRKPATRICK, § 459.

[268] *See* 5 WEINSTEIN'S FEDERAL EVIDENCE § 803.14.

[269] 5 WEINSTEIN'S FEDERAL EVIDENCE § 803.14. The author concludes that in accordance with pre-Rule federal case law, Rule 803(9) should not be limited to statements based on firsthand knowledge, even though the general notes to Rule 803 state that the Rule does not dispense with such a requirement.

knowledge of the event recorded or certified, such as where notaries acknowledge that the signatory has personally appeared before them, or where a certificate of marriage is prepared by the person performing the ceremony.[270] However, where certificates require information such as the age, identity, or address of the person involved, the certifying officer will ordinarily lack firsthand knowledge of those matters and should be allowed to rely on hearsay declarations of those present and concerned. As a practical consideration, requiring firsthand knowledge of the recording official on such matters would virtually destroy the utility of the exception.[271]

§ 803.50 Application

Federal case law illustrates the manner in which public records may be used to establish a variety of facts. For example, court records may be used to establish the date or place of marriage.[272] A birth certificate may be offered as proof of the fact of birth, the date of birth,[273] and the identity of the parents.[274] Likewise, a death certificate may be introduced to prove the fact, date, time, and place of death.[275] Death certificates may also be introduced to prove the cause of death or the duration of an illness.[276]

However, in the latter two instances, special consideration should be given to the character of the contents of the report and the qualifications of the

---

[270] Charleston Nat'l Bank v. Hennessy, 404 F.2d 539, 541 (5th Cir. 1968) ("written official statements, which include certificates officially required to be made, are to some extent recognized as exceptions to the rules prohibiting hearsay assertions. There is a tendency to trustworthiness because the certificate is made by a public officer while carrying out his required duty and because the document is available for public inspection").

[271] 5 WIGMORE, § 1646 ("If we are to insist with pedantic strictness upon the entrant's personal knowledge, it will be found that the registers [of birth, marriage and death] will cease to be of much practical service for any purpose").

[272] E.g., Williams v. Butterfield, 145 F. Supp. 567 (E.D. Mich. 1956), aff'd, 250 F.2d 127 (6th Cir. 1957) (court approved receipt of record of marriage of plaintiff, asserting that plaintiff had been born in Pennsylvania, to set aside deportation order).

[273] E.g., United States v. Austrew, 202 F. Supp. 816 (D. Md. 1962), aff'd, 317 F.2d 926 (4th Cir. 1963) (birth certificate used to prove that girl was under eighteen).

[274] E.g., Williams v. Butterfield, 145 F. Supp. 567 (E.D. Mich. 1956), aff'd, 250 F.2d 127 (6th Cir. 1957) (court approved receipt of marriage license indicating that plaintiff's parents were married in Great Britain).

[275] E.g., Aetna Life Ins. Co. v. Mitchell, 180 F. Supp. 674 (D. Pa. 1960) (court received certified copies of coroner's report indicating time that husband and wife were shot; certificate was admissible, even though it was open to contradiction and not binding upon the jury).

[276] E.g., Minyen v. American Home Assurance Co., 443 F.2d 788 (10th Cir. 1971) (court upheld the introduction of a death certificate, which stated that death was caused by a brain tumor); Meth v. United Ben. Life Ins. Co., 198 F.2d 446 (3d Cir. 1952) (no error to receive death certificate prepared by attending physician which stated that "the interval from the onset of illness to the date of death was two years"); Hunter v. Derby Foods, 110 F.2d 970 (2d Cir. 1940) (proper to receive death certificate prepared by coroner on basis of autopsy, listing as the cause of death "accident — eating canned meat — enteritis with an acute nephritis").

person making the report. For instance, where it is disputed whether the decedent died as the consequence of a fall or from a brain tumor, as listed on his death certificate, the certificate should be admitted only where the maker possessed the necessary expertise to make such a distinction.[277] Likewise, where the onset of the decedent's fatal illness is in dispute, statements contained in the certificate as to the probable duration of the illness should be admitted only if made by a qualified physician.[278]

Frequently, a death certificate will state not only the physical or medical cause of death but will also state facts that may be relevant to determinations of fault or criminal liability. For instance, statements that the decedent committed suicide, or that the death resulted from an accident or homicide, may be contained in the certificate. While coroners and physicians are ordinarily not qualified to draw such conclusions, this may be required as part of the official's duties. Most courts have approved receipt of statements of this nature in appropriate circumstances.[279]

Although death certificates containing statements regarding fault may be admitted under Rule 803(9), such a report may also come within Rule 803(8)(A)(iii).[280] Where the report is offered as evidence against the accused in a criminal prosecution, it will be inadmissible under 803(8)(A)(iii). In other contexts, a report falling within both exceptions should be excluded if "sources of information [or] other circumstances indicate a lack of trustworthiness." When the record sought to be admitted speaks in terms of legal conclusions of the sort described above, and it was not prepared by a public official to bring it within the purview of Rule 803(8), the terms of Rule 803(9) would appear to determine admissibility. While Rule 803(9) does not contain a provision for discretionary exclusion if lack of trustworthiness is indicated, as does 803(8)(A)(iii), there is authority for the proposition that in the latter situation, the court should nonetheless consider whether circumstantial guarantees of trustworthiness are lacking in ruling on admissibility.[281]

---

[277] *See* 4 MUELLER & KIRKPATRICK, § 459.

[278] *See* Meth v. United Ben. Life Ins. Co., 198 F.2d 446 (3d Cir. 1952) (death certificate as evidence of onset of illness); *see also* 5 WIGMORE, § 1671.

[279] *See, e.g.,* Shell v. Parrish, 448 F.2d 528 (6th Cir. 1971) (error for trial court to delete language in death certificate that "victim fell in open ditch"); Metropolitan Life Ins. Co. v. Butte, 333 F.2d 82 (10th Cir. 1964) (error to exclude city physician's statement in death certificate that decedent "died a suicide as the result of carbon monoxide poisoning"); Thomas v. Conemaugh & B.L.R. Co., 234 F.2d 429 (3d Cir. 1956) (no error to receive coroner's death certificate as proof of cause of death).

[280] *See* § 803.45, *supra.*

[281] *See* Charleston Nat'l. Bank v. Hennessy, 404 F.2d 539 (5th Cir. 1968) (in personal injury suit, dispute over whether decedent died of a heart attack prior to being injured in an automobile accident; no abuse of discretion for trial court to delete from death certificate the statement that decedent "apparently had a heart attack"; the coroner was a layman without

Finally, it should be emphasized that the Rules of Evidence cannot operate as determinants of constitutional rights, and in criminal matters, introduction of a record pursuant to Rule 803(9) could operate to deny rights of confrontation. The accused's confrontation rights are more fully discussed in this Treatise in conjunction with Rules 803(6) and 803(8).

§ 803.51   Rule 803(10) Absence of a Public Record

The following are not excluded by the rule against hearsay, regardless of whether the declarant is available as a witness:

***

    (10)   *Absence of a Public Record.* Testimony — or a certification under Rule 902 — that a diligent search failed to disclose a public record or statement if the testimony or certification is admitted to prove that:

        (A)   the record or statement does not exist; or

        (B)   a matter did not occur or exist, if a public office regularly kept a record or statement for a matter of that kind.

Rule 803(10) admits evidence of the absence of a public record or entry in order to prove either the absence of certain documents or the nonexistence or nonoccurrence of a matter regarding which there would normally be a public record.[282] The Rule is similar in effect to the provisions of Rule 803(7), which governs proof of the absence of an entry in the records of a

---

medical training and there was no evidence showing him to be qualified as an expert on causes of death); *see also* 4 MUELLER & KIRKPATRICK, § 459.

[282] *See generally,* 2 MCCORMICK, §§ 299–300; 5 WEINSTEIN'S FEDERAL EVIDENCE § 803.15; 4 MUELLER & KIRKPATRICK, § 460; 5 WIGMORE, § 1633. Wigmore explains the rationale underlying this exception:

> Since the assumption of the fulfillment of duty is the foundation of the exception, it would seem to follow that if a duty exists to record certain matters when they occur, and if no record of such matters is found, then the *absence of any entry* about them is evidence that they did not occur; or, to put it another way, the record, taken as a whole, is evidence that the matters recorded, and those only, occurred.

5 WIGMORE, § 1633, at 624 (emphasis in original); *see also* United States v. Rith, 164 F.3d 1323 (10th Cir. 1999) (defendant charged with possession of illegal weapons and stolen property challenged the admission of a document from an ATF specialist stating that after diligent search, the specialist found no evidence that the defendant's two weapons were lawfully acquired by him; the evidence was admitted under Rule 803(10), and defendant's conviction was affirmed, despite evidence that the error rate in the database searched was at one time as high as fifty percent, because other evidence indicated the error rate had been lowered to three percent and cross examination of the specialist would be of little utility); United States v. Hale, 978 F.2d 1016 (8th Cir. 1992) (in firearms prosecution, trial court properly admitted an affidavit from an ATF specialist stating that he made a diligent search but was unable to locate any application by defendant to register his weapons).

regularly conducted business activity. The discussion of Rule 803(7) at § 803.37 *et seq.* of this Treatise should be consulted for further pertinent analysis.

Under pre-Rule law, evidence to prove the absence of a public record,[283] the nonexistence,[284] or the nonoccurrence[285] of a matter normally recorded by a public official was similarly admissible. In continuation of this practice, Rule 803(10) operates, for example, to allow proof that a person claiming to be a personal envoy of the president was, in fact, never employed as a personal representative of the president.[286]

§ 803.52   Foundation and Authentication Requirements

Rule 803(10) requires that in order to utilize the negative inference arising from the absence of a public record, a proponent of the evidence must establish that a diligent search failed to disclose the public record or entry.[287]

---

[283] *See* United States v. Sussman, 37 F. Supp. 294 (D. Pa. 1941) (proof of the absence of registration certificate in SEC files).

[284] *See* United States v. Rich, 580 F.2d 929 (9th Cir. 1978) (in prosecution for bank robbery, defendant alleged that on the day in question, he had loaned his car, which had been seen at the bank, to a certain individual; court properly allowed testimony by FBI official that he had searched various official records and had found no trace of the alleged borrower; [although the trial court erred in admitting the testimony because of foundation inadequacy, court affirms, noting that the defendant failed to object to the foundation]).

[285] Jackson v. United States, 250 F.2d 897 (5th Cir. 1958) (in prosecution for filing false claim for benefits as serviceman's widow, FBI official permitted to testify that a search of public records of defendant's county revealed no record that defendant and deceased had ever been divorced).

[286] *See* T'Kach v. United States, 242 F.2d 937 (5th Cir. 1957) (in prosecution for falsely representing oneself to be an officer and employee of the United States, affidavit of personnel officer and custodian of records for White House admitted to prove defendant was never employed in such a capacity); *see also* Fed. R. Civ. P. 44(b), which provides that:

> **(b) Lack of a Record.** A written statement that a diligent search of designated records revealed no record or entry of a specified tenor is admissible as evidence that the records contain no such record or entry. For domestic records, the statement must be authenticated under Rule 44(a)(1). For foreign records, the statement must comply with (a)(2)(C)(ii).

Fed. R. Crim. P. 27 makes Rule 44(b) applicable to criminal proceedings.

[287] *See* 4 MUELLER & KIRKPATRICK, § 460, at 614:

> It is hard to imagine an excuse for not using the word "diligent" in any certificate or testimony proffered under Rule 803(10), but there should be no magic attached to the term, and failure to use it should not be fatal if in fact the proponent makes a showing that a diligent search was made. Conversely, use of the term should not be conclusive if it appears that in fact the search was sloppy or half-hearted.

See also United States v. Hale, 978 F.2d 1016 (8th Cir. 1992) (in firearms prosecution, trial court properly admitted an affidavit from an ATF specialist stating that he made a diligent search but has been unable to locate any application by defendant to register his weapons); United States v. Yakobov, 712 F.2d 20 (2d Cir. 1983) (despite the certificate's recitation that

This may be shown either by testimony or by introduction of a certification prepared in accordance with Rule 902.[288]

Under pre-Rule law, testimony of the custodian of the records,[289] as well as testimony of a private citizen,[290] was admissible. However, at common law proof of the absence of an entry in a record was not permitted by the introduction of the certification of the custodian.[291] Rule 803(10) admits evidence in the form of a certification, provided that the authentication requirements of Rule 902 are met.

§ 803.53   Rule 803(11) Records of Religious Organizations Concerning Personal or Family History

The following are not excluded by the rule against hearsay, regardless of whether the declarant is available as a witness:

***

    (11)   *Records of Religious Organizations Concerning Personal or Family History.* A statement of birth, legitimacy, ancestry, marriage, divorce, death, relationship by blood or marriage, or similar facts of personal or family history, contained in a regularly kept record of a religious organization.

Rule 803(11) creates a hearsay exception for statements of personal or family history contained in a regularly kept record of a religious organization.[292] The principle incorporated into Rule 803(11) is generally in accord with pre-Rule law.[293]

"a diligent search" had been undertaken, error to admit certificate to show that defendant had not been licensed to deal in firearms where officer had searched only under defendant's name as misspelled: "The diligence requirement is one of substance, not form. It is not satisfied merely by a ritual incantation that the certificate results from a 'diligent' search").

[288] *See* § 803.41, *supra.*

[289] *See, e.g.,* T'Kach v. United States, 242 F.2d 937 (5th Cir. 1957) (testimony of custodian of records).

[290] *See, e.g.,* Moerman v. Zipco, 302 F. Supp. 439 (E.D.N.Y. 1969), *aff'd,* 422 F.2d 871 (2d Cir. 1969), *adhered to,* 430 F.2d 362 (2d Cir. 1969) (testimony of attorney that search of records failed to reveal defendant's registration required by Connecticut Blue Sky Law properly admitted).

[291] Federal Rule of Civil Procedure 44(b), in contrast to the common law, permits proof in the form of a certification by the custodian to show the nonexistence of a record. *See generally,* 5 WEINSTEIN'S FEDERAL EVIDENCE § 803.15; 5 WIGMORE, § 1678; 2 McCORMICK, § 300.

[292] *See generally,* 5 WEINSTEIN'S FEDERAL EVIDENCE § 803.16; 4 MUELLER & KIRKPATRICK, § 461; 5 WIGMORE, § 1633(b). *See also* 4 AM. JUR., *Proof of Facts, Death, Proof 3* (church record); 29 AM. JUR. 2d, *Evidence,* §§ 508, 875; 30 AM. JUR. 2d, *Evidence,* § 928.

[293] *See* Lewis v. Marshall, 30 U.S. (1 Pet.) 470 (1831) (register of burials in church).

Traditionally, church records were admitted under the business records exception.[294] Such a categorization, however, required proof of the foundational facts necessary to invoke the business record exception, for example, through the testimony of the custodian of the records. Moreover, such records could be used only to prove the fact that an activity, such as a baptism, had occurred and not to prove underlying facts of personal history, such as age of the child, which would not be within the personal knowledge of the recorder.[295] Rule 803(11), by way of contrast, does not require firsthand knowledge of the person preparing the entry.[296] Consequently, information on the enumerated subjects, *i.e.,* statements of births, marriages, divorces, deaths, and the like, are admissible if they meet the criteria of the Rule, without any inquiry into the source of the information. The only criteria that must be established relate to proof that the statements are contained in the records of a religious organization and that such records are those that are regularly kept by that organization.

§ 803.54   Rationale for the Exception

The hearsay exception for familial or personal history statements contained in the records of religious organizations is based on the circumstantial guarantees of trustworthiness of such records. The statements are generally made in connection with ceremonies such as a baptism, wedding, or funeral where there exists a lack of motivation to fabricate in regard to the type of information required on such occasions.[297] Furthermore, there is an opportunity for scrutiny of the information contained in such records by persons who would be in a position to verify or dispute the recorded data. The requirement that the record be "regularly kept" is a further safeguard as to reliability.

§ 803.55   Practical Considerations

The foundational evidence necessary to invoke the religious record hearsay exception is directed to the court. Such evidence includes proof as to the record itself, the regularity with which it is kept, and the nature of the organization from which the record emanates. Questions as to the bona fide status of a group as a religious organization must be decided by the court as a preliminary determination under Rule 104(a).[298]

In order to admit records of the type described by Rule 803(11), the proponent must properly authenticate the records in accordance with Article

---

[294] 5 WIGMORE, § 1523.

[295] 5 WEINSTEIN'S FEDERAL EVIDENCE § 803.16.

[296] *See* Advisory Committee Note, Rule 803(1).

[297] 5 WEINSTEIN'S FEDERAL EVIDENCE § 803.16; *cf.* Ruberto v. Commissioner, 774 F.2d 61 (2d Cir. 1985) (church records exception was inapplicable to taxpayer receipts from church for contributions in tax deficiency suit).

[298] 5 WEINSTEIN'S FEDERAL EVIDENCE § 803.16.

IX.

§ 803.56   Rule 803(12) Certificates of Marriage, Baptism, and Similar Ceremonies

The following are not excluded by the rule against hearsay, regardless of whether the declarant is available as a witness:

***

(12)   *Certificates of Marriage, Baptism, and Similar Ceremonies.* A statement of fact contained in a certificate:

    (A)   made by a person who is authorized by a religious organization or by law to perform the act certified;

    (B)   attesting that the person performed a marriage or similar ceremony or administered a sacrament; and

    (C)   purporting to have been issued at the time of the act or within a reasonable time after it.

Rule 803(12) provides for the admission of factual statements contained in a certificate of marriage, baptism, or other ceremony or sacrament.[299] The type of information that may be proved by such certificates is similar to that which may be proved under Rule 803(11).[300] Nevertheless, the events for which a certificate is issued are fewer in number than events or statements that may be kept in the records of a religious organization.

In some situations the scope of Rule 803(12) also overlaps with that of Rule 803(9). Accordingly, if the information is contained in a report made to a public office pursuant to a requirement of law, the statement may be proved either by the report under Rule 803(9) or by a certificate that complies with Rule 803(12). The former Rule may not be utilized, however, in connection with acts that are not required or authorized by law to be recorded. For example, baptisms are not required or authorized to be recorded, and proof regarding this sacrament must consequently be made either by certificate or

---

[299] *E.g.,* Blackburn v. Crawford, 70 U.S. (3 Wall.) 175 (1866) (baptismal certificate required by church usage to be kept); Young Ti v. United States, 246 F. 110 (3d Cir. 1917) (birth certificates from Chicago vital statistics department). *See generally,* 2 McCORMICK, § 299; 5 WEINSTEIN'S FEDERAL EVIDENCE § 803.17; 4 MUELLER & KIRKPATRICK, § 462; 5 WIGMORE, § 1674. *See also* Comment, *Hearsay Under the Proposed Federal Rules: A Discretionary Approach,* 15 WAYNE L. REV. 1077 (1969).

[300] *But see* Martinez v. Ribicoff, 200 F. Supp. 191 (D.P.R. 1961) (baptismal certificate inadmissible to prove parentage); United States v. Bukis, 17 F. Supp. 77 (D. Pa. 1936) (baptismal certificate from Lithuanian church was excluded when offered to show alien was native of that country; "[the certificate] was merely a church record of baptism and it was not admissible to prove the date or place of birth, even though it contained recitals of those facts").

by a Rule 803(11) or a Rule 803(13) record.

The rationale of the exception for marriage, baptismal, and other similar certificates is identical to that underlying Rule 803(11), namely, that a guarantee as to trustworthiness exists due to the unlikelihood that anyone would fabricate the type of information contained in such certificates.[301]

§ 803.57 Methodology

In order to invoke the exception as to certificates, the proponent must establish as a preliminary matter that the maker of the certificate, that is, a member of the clergy, public official, or other such person, was authorized to perform the act certified, either by law or by the precepts or practices of a religious organization. There must additionally be proof to satisfy the second criterion of the Rule, *i.e.*, that the certificate purports to have been issued at the time of the act in question or within a reasonable time thereafter. The requirement is met by a showing that the certificate bears a date of issuance that coincides with, or bears a reasonable correspondence with, the date of the act certified.[302] Finally, it should be noted that the certificate must be authenticated in accordance with Article IX of the Rules.

§ 803.58 Rule 803(13) Family Records

The following are not excluded by the rule against hearsay, regardless of whether the declarant is available as a witness:

***

(13) *Family Records.* A statement of fact about personal or family history contained in a family record, such as a Bible, genealogy, chart, engraving on a ring, inscription on a portrait, or engraving on an urn or burial marker.

Rule 803(13) creates a hearsay exception for statements concerning personal or family history contained in family Bibles, genealogies, charts, engravings on rings, inscriptions on family portraits, engravings on urns, crypts or tombstones, and the like.[303] The types of facts contemplated by the Rule are those identified in Rule 803(11), namely, statements of births, marriages, divorces, deaths, legitimacy, ancestry, relationship by blood or marriage, or similar facts.[304] Rule 803(13) is consistent with pre-Rule

---

[301] *See generally,* 5 WIGMORE, § 1645; 4 MUELLER & KIRKPATRICK, § 462.

[302] *See* 5 WEINSTEIN'S FEDERAL EVIDENCE § 803.17.

[303] *See generally,* 2 MCCORMICK, § 322; 5 WEINSTEIN'S FEDERAL EVIDENCE § 803.18; 4 MUELLER & KIRKPATRICK, § 463; 5 WIGMORE, §§ 1495–1496. *See also* Hale, *Proof of Facts of Family History,* 2 HASTINGS L.J. (1950); Comment, *Admissibility of Hearsay Evidence on Matters of Family History,* 5 ARK. L. REV. 58 (1951).

[304] 5 WEINSTEIN'S FEDERAL EVIDENCE § 803.18, citing House Judiciary Committee Report approving the adoption of Rule 803(13).

practice.[305]

A common theme is apparent in Rule 803(11), (12), and (13), both as to types of information deemed admissible and as to rationale. The specific rationale of Rule 803(13) is "the unlikelihood that members of a family would allow an untruthful inscription or entry to be made, or to remain without protest."[306] This guarantee of trustworthiness obviates any need to show that the entry was made by a family member or by someone with personal knowledge. It should be noted that similar matters of personal or family history may be proved by reputation evidence pursuant to Rule 803(18).

The items enumerated in this Rule would generally be offered as proof of the contents of the writing contained therein or inscribed thereon. Accordingly, there must also be some consideration of the "best evidence rule" set forth in Article X in determining whether the inscribed object must be used to prove the contents of the writing. This matter is specifically addressed in Chapter 1002 of this Treatise. Also, any writing offered must be authenticated in accordance with Article IX.

§ 803.59   Rule 803(14) Records of Documents That Affect an Interest in Property

The following are not excluded by the rule against hearsay, regardless of whether the declarant is available as a witness:

***

(14)   ***Records of Documents That Affect an Interest in Property.*** The record of a document that purports to establish or affect an interest in property if:

    (A)   the record is admitted to prove the content of the original recorded document, along with its signing and its delivery by each person who purports to have signed it;

    (B)   the record is kept in a public office; and

    (C)   a statute authorizes recording documents of that kind in that office.

Rule 803(14) permits the record of a document purporting to establish or

---

[305] *E.g.,* Lewis v. Marshall, 30 U.S. (5 Pet.) 470 (1831) (entry in family Bible admitted to prove date of death); Miami County Nat'l. Bank v. Bancroft, 121 F.2d 921 (10th Cir. 1941) (evidence in the form of genealogy and history of family admitted); *see also* Comment, *Admissibility of Hearsay Evidence in Matters of Family History,* 5 ARK. L. REV. 58 (1951); Annot., 29 A.L.R. 372 (1924). *See generally,* 2 McCORMICK, § 322.

[306] 5 WEINSTEIN'S FEDERAL EVIDENCE § 803.18; *see* 4 MUELLER & KIRKPATRICK, § 463.

affect an interest in property, such as a deed, to be admitted as proof of the content of the original recorded document and as proof of its execution and delivery.[307]

In order to utilize Rule 803(14), the proponent of the record must first establish that the record is that of a public office and that an applicable state statute authorizes the recording of documents of that kind in that office. Upon such a foundation, the record of a deed may be used as proof, for example, that at the time of execution, the grantor was an unmarried person where such fact can be derived from the record. Based on the grantor's signature, the record would also be admissible to prove that the grantor executed and delivered the deed.[308]

Contents of a title record may be proved without resort to this Rule, for example, pursuant to the public record exception or possibly the business record exception.[309] These other Rules would not necessarily, however, provide an exception as to proof of proper execution and delivery of the title or document.

Rule 803(14) is in accordance with the common law[310] and it functions, in essence, to render the hearsay prohibition inapplicable to records of instruments relating to real property recorded as evidence of the facts set forth in the original.[311]

§ 803.60   Rationale

The hearsay exception for records of title documents is supported by two rationales. First, necessity justifies the exception where the recorded document is of such an age that witnesses and declarants would in all likelihood be unavailable. Even in cases where such parties might be

---

[307] *See generally,* 2 MCCORMICK, § 323; 5 WEINSTEIN'S FEDERAL EVIDENCE § 803.19; 4 MUELLER & KIRKPATRICK, § 464; 5 WIGMORE, §§ 1647–1651. *See also* Comment, *Hearsay Under the Proposed Federal Rules: A Discretionary Approach,* 15 WAYNE L. REV. 1077 (1969).

[308] *See* Collins v. Streitz, 95 F.2d 430, 434 (9th Cir. 1938) ("[I]f the acknowledgment is made by the officers of a corporation, the certificate shall show that such persons as such officers [naming the office of each person] acknowledged the execution of the instrument as the free act and deed of such corporation, by each of them voluntarily executed"). *See generally,* 5 WEINSTEIN'S FEDERAL EVIDENCE § 803.19; 5 WIGMORE, § 1651; 4 MUELLER & KIRKPATRICK, § 464.

[309] 5 WEINSTEIN'S FEDERAL EVIDENCE § 803.19.

[310] *See, e.g.,* Carpenter v. Dexter, 75 U.S. (8 Wall.) 513 (1869); M'Keen v. Delancy, 9 U.S. (5 Cranch) 22 (1809). *See generally,* 5 WIGMORE, § 1651.

[311] *See, e.g.,* Connecticut Light & Power Co. v. Federal Power Com., 557 F.2d 349 (2d Cir. 1977) (administrative law judge relied upon historical material to grant the right to use and benefit of the Housatonic River; "evidence contained . . . in recorded deeds affecting interest in real property . . . are exceptions to the hearsay rule"); *see also* Advisory Committee Note, Rule 803(14).

available, the exception dispenses with the inconvenience of locating and utilizing such witnesses. Second, the exception is justified by the circumstantial guarantees of trustworthiness that attend recorded documents of this nature.

§ 803.61   Relation to Other Rules and Statutes

Analysis of the practical application of the hearsay rule regarding recorded title documents should include a consideration of the principles relating to authentication. In order to be offered into evidence as a hearsay exception, the record must be authenticated under Article IX. For example, it might be authenticated as an ancient document under Rule 901(b)(8) or as a public record under Rule 902(2) (domestic documents not under seal), or Rule 902(4) (certified copies of public records).

In addition, note should be taken of Rule 1005, the provisions of which allow contents of an official record to be proved by a copy certified or attested to be correct. In concert with Rule 1005, Rule 803(14) applies to the official record of a document and not to the original itself, the rationale being the trustworthiness that attends the recording process.

§ 803.62   Rule 803(15) Statements in Documents That Affect an Interest in Property

The following are not excluded by the rule against hearsay, regardless of whether the declarant is available as a witness:

***

   (15)   *Statements in Documents That Affect an Interest in Property.* A statement contained in a document that purports to establish or affect an interest in property if the matter stated was relevant to the document's purpose — unless later dealings with the property are inconsistent with the truth of the statement or the purport of the document.

Rule 803(15) admits into evidence recitals of fact contained in a document purporting to establish or affect an interest in property, where the matter stated is relevant to the purpose of the document.[312] The document may be excluded, however, upon a showing that dealings with the property since the document was made have been inconsistent with the truth of the statement or the purport of the document.

The Rule does not require the document to have been recorded or to be

---

[312] *See generally,* 2 MCCORMICK, § 323; 5 WEINSTEIN'S FEDERAL EVIDENCE § 803.20; 4 MUELLER & KIRKPATRICK, § 465; 5 WIGMORE, §§ 1573–1574. *See also* Comment, *Hearsay Under the Proposed Federal Rules: A Discretionary Approach,* 15 WAYNE L. REV. 1077 (1969).

recordable. Also, documents affecting personalty as well as realty are within the scope of the Rule, *e.g.,* contracts, bills of sale, security agreements, wills, estate inventories, and other documents that establish or affect an interest in property.[313] Rule 803(15) is essentially consistent with pre-Rule law.[314]

It should be noted that when the existence or occurrence of a particular transaction is at issue or the terms of a particular dispositive agreement are sought to be proven, the out-of-court statements constituting the agreement or dispositive document are not offered for their truth. In such case the statements are "verbal acts" or "operative facts," and as discussed in § 801.8 of this Treatise, a hearsay exception is not needed to admit the document in such a situation because of the non-hearsay nature of the statements. By comparison, Rule 803(15) applies where a party seeks to offer evidence on a factual matter that is the subject of a recital or a description in a dispositive document. For example, Rule 803(15) might be invoked to offer probative evidence as to the existence of an improvement on certain land where such fact is recited in an unrecorded deed. Likewise, the exception might be utilized to offer evidence that certain parties to a transaction were married where the document designates the parties as husband and wife or as tenants by the entirety.

§ 803.63   Conditions and Rationale

Rule 803(15) imposes two conditions to admissibility. First, there must be a showing that the statement sought to be introduced is relevant to the dispositive purpose of the document. The requirement provides some guarantee as to trustworthiness because a protest would be expected concerning any false information that is intrinsic to the transaction.[315] Second, the Rule provides that the hearsay exception is not available if dealings subsequent to the making of the document in question have been inconsistent with the statement or the purport of the document. In practical terms, where authentication is satisfied, the document should be admissible upon proof satisfying the first element unless the opponent offers to the court sufficient evidence of subsequent inconsistent dealings.

In addition to the two criteria specified in the Rule, other indicia of trustworthiness justify this exception. These include the circumstances under which dispositive instruments are made and the financial interests at stake that promote reliability, as well as the fact that the risk of errors in the

---

[313] *See* 5 WEINSTEIN'S FEDERAL EVIDENCE § 803.20; 2 MCCORMICK, § 323; 5 WIG-MORE, §§ 1573–1574.

[314] Although pre-Rule codifications generally recognized a similar exception to the hearsay rule, pre-Rule common law often admitted only statements contained in "ancient" documents. *See* 4 MUELLER & KIRKPATRICK, § 465. Rule 803(15) makes the age of the document insignificant, although, as a practical matter, the document will often be an ancient one. *See* Advisory Committee Note, Rule 803(15).

[315] 5 WEINSTEIN'S FEDERAL EVIDENCE § 803.20; 4 MUELLER & KIRKPATRICK, § 465.

transmission of statements is minimized because the statements are in writing.[316]

The Rule also rests in many instances on the basis of necessity, especially where litigation arises at a time when declarants or witnesses to the transaction may not be available. In such a case, although there is no requirement that the document under Rule 803(15) be of any given age, the instrument in question may well qualify as an ancient document under Rule 803(16).

§ 803.64   Rule 803(16) Statements in Ancient Documents

The following are not excluded by the rule against hearsay, regardless of whether the declarant is available as a witness:

***

     (16)   *Statements in Ancient Documents.* A statement in a document that is at least 20 years old and whose authenticity is established.

Rule 803(16) permits written statements in a document to be offered for their truth upon a preliminary showing that the document is authentic and that it is at least twenty years old.[317]

Originally, the common-law doctrine of "ancient documents" pertained only to authenticity,[318] but many American courts admitted the authenticated

---

[316] 5 WEINSTEIN'S FEDERAL EVIDENCE § 803.20; *see* United States v. 478.34 Acres of Land, 578 F.2d 156 (6th Cir. 1978) (in condemnation proceeding "statistical survey" made by government engineer improperly admitted to prove the true prices paid for other land in the county; the survey was not relevant to prove the value of the defendant's land because the government failed to show that the other properties covered by the survey were comparable; moreover, the government made no effort to verify or authenticate the data and there was no way for the landowner to test the reliability or the accuracy of the data).

[317] *See generally,* 2 MCCORMICK, § 323; 5 WEINSTEIN'S FEDERAL EVIDENCE § 803.21; 4 MUELLER & KIRKPATRICK, § 466; 5 WIGMORE, §§ 1573–1574; 7 WIGMORE, § 2145. *See also* Wickes, *Ancient Documents and Hearsay,* 8 TEX. L. REV. 451 (1930); Note, *Recitals in Ancient Documents,* 46 IOWA L. REV. 448 (1961); Note, *The Effect of the Ancient Document Rule on the Hearsay Rule,* 83 U. PA. L. REV. 247 (1934); Comment, *Ancient Documents as an Exception to the Hearsay Rule,* 33 YALE L.J. 412 (1924).

[318] *See* 2 MCCORMICK, § 323; *see* Ninety Six v. Southern Railway Co., 267 F.2d 579 (4th Cir. 1959) (stating that the exception for ancient documents "deals only with the authentication of the document sought to be proved, and not with its competency or admissibility"); King v. Watkins, 98 F. 913, 917 (C.C.D. Va. 1899), *rev'd on other grounds,* 118 F. 524 (4th Cir. 1902) ("[T]he doctrine of admitting ancient documents in evidence, without proof of their genuineness, is based on the ground that they prove themselves, the witness being presumed to be dead. The doctrine goes no further than this. The questions of its relevance and admissibility as evidence cannot be affected by the fact that it is an ancient document. It is no more admissible on that ground than if it were a newly-executed instrument"). *See generally,* 5 WIGMORE, §§ 1573–1574; 5 WEINSTEIN'S FEDERAL EVIDENCE § 803.21; 4 MUELLER & KIRKPATRICK, § 466.

writing to prove the truth of statements made in the document.[319] The common-law tradition required the document in question to be in existence for at least *thirty years*, so in respect to age, Rule 803(16) represents a modification of pre-Rule law.[320]

§ 803.65 Application

The ancient document hearsay exception applies only to writings, but it contains no restriction as to the type of writing that may qualify under its terms. Thus, Rule 803(16) may be invoked in connection with documents of a formal nature, such as wills and deeds, as well as any other types of writing, such as letters, leases, powers of attorney, receipts, maps, and public surveys.[321]

The Rule contains an express requirement that the authenticity of the document must be established in order for the hearsay exception to apply. Inclusion of such a requirement within the hearsay rule is redundant inasmuch as establishment of authenticity of documents is always a prerequisite to the admissibility of a writing. Nevertheless, the provision serves to emphasize that the Rule must be read in conjunction with Rule 901(b)(8), "Ancient documents or data compilations." Under the latter Rule, authentication requires proof not only that the document is at least twenty years old, but also that the document's condition is such that it creates no suspicion as to authenticity, and that the document was found in a place where, if authentic, it would likely be.[322] Pre-Rule cases required a similar showing, with the exception of the longer age requirement.[323] Accordingly, compliance with the authentication requirements of Rule 901(b)(8) will simultaneously satisfy the hearsay requirements of Rule 803(16).

---

[319] *See, e.g.,* Stewart Oil Co. v. Sohio Petroleum Co., 202 F. Supp. 952 (E.D. Ill. 1962), *aff'd,* 315 F.2d 759 (7th Cir. 1963) (recognizing hearsay exception for ancient documents but finding particular document inadmissible on basis of untrustworthiness); Burns v. United States, 160 F. 631 (2d Cir. 1908) (maps); *cf.* Lee Pong Tai v. Acheson, 104 F. Supp. 503 (D. Pa. 1952).

[320] For a recital of common-law decisions, see Comment, *Ancient Documents as an Exception to the Hearsay Rule,* 33 YALE L.J. 412 (1924).

[321] *See* Advisory Committee Note, Rule 803(16); 5 WEINSTEIN'S FEDERAL EVIDENCE § 803.21; *see, e.g.,* Bell v. Combined Registry Co., 536 F.2d 164 (7th Cir. 1976) (letters and magazine articles); Dallas County v. Commercial Union Assurance Co., 286 F.2d 388 (5th Cir. 1961) (newspaper story); *see also* United States v. Koziy, 728 F.2d 1314 (11th Cir. 1984) (documents used by Ukranian police in World War II were properly admitted in denaturalization hearings since authenticated and more than 20 years old); United States v. Hajda, 135 F.3d 439 (7th Cir. 1998) (statement given during trial in 1945 was admissible as an ancient document).

[322] *See* Rule 901(b)(8) and related discussion, § 901.1 *et seq., infra,* in this Treatise as to conditions creating suspicion and the likely sources of authentic documents.

[323] *E.g.,* McGuire v. Blount, 199 U.S. 142 (1905); Fulkerson v. Holmes, 117 U.S. 389 (1886).

§ 803.66   Rationale

The hearsay exception for ancient documents has been criticized mainly on the basis that age alone does not assure reliability.[324] Nevertheless, proponents of the exception have pointed to the special necessity of admitting such evidence due to the passage of twenty or more years.[325] The Rule accepts the latter argument and attempts to infuse an element of trustworthiness through authentication procedures, namely, by requiring the absence of suspicious condition of the document and by requiring a showing that the document was found in a logical place for a document of its nature. Other guarantees of trustworthiness are supplied: (i) by the fact that the document is in writing, thereby minimizing any errors in transmission; (ii) by the age itself, which provides that the document was likely generated prior to the present controversy and consequently was not influenced by any partisanship or motive to falsify; and finally, (iii) by imposing the usual qualifications as to out-of-court declarants, *i.e.*, that the declarant be required to have firsthand knowledge of the facts asserted.[326] While strict compliance with the firsthand knowledge requirement may not be feasible with regard to ancient documents, courts may nonetheless require a showing that the declarant was in a position to have had the requisite knowledge.[327]

In sum, the need for the exception outweighs the possible risks of admitting unreliable evidence. If circumstances are shown that suggest unreliability, for example, where the document was written at a time when a motive for misrepresentation already existed, the judge may exclude the document pursuant to Rule 403 on the basis that the possibility of prejudice or confusion outweighs the probative value of such evidence.[328]

§ 803.67   Rule 803(17) Market Reports and Similar Commercial Publications

The following are not excluded by the rule against hearsay, regardless of whether the declarant is available as a witness:

***

(17)   *Market Reports and Similar Commercial Publications.* Market quotations, lists, directories, or other compilations that are

---

[324] *See* 5 WEINSTEIN'S FEDERAL EVIDENCE § 803.21; 2 MCCORMICK, § 323.

[325] 2 MCCORMICK, § 323; *see also* Wickes, *Ancient Documents and Hearsay*, 8 TEX. L. REV. 451 (1930); 4 MUELLER & KIRKPATRICK, § 466.

[326] *See* 5 WEINSTEIN'S FEDERAL EVIDENCE § 803.21; 2 MCCORMICK, § 323; *see also* Advisory Committee Note, Rule 803, which states: "In a hearsay situation, the declarant is, of course, a witness, and neither this rule nor Rule 804 dispenses with requirement of firsthand knowledge. It may appear from his statement or be inferable from the circumstances. See Rule 602."

[327] *Id.*

[328] 5 WEINSTEIN'S FEDERAL EVIDENCE § 803.21.

generally relied on by the public or by persons in particular occupations.

Rule 803(17) authorizes the admission of certain commercial publications and reports as substantive proof of the information contained in such sources, including market quotations, tabulations, lists, directories, and other published compilations.[329] These reports and publications are admissible where the proponent shows by way of foundation that the publication sought to be introduced is one that is both generally used and generally relied upon either by the public or by persons in particular occupations. Rule 803(17) is in accord with pre-Rule law.[330]

§ 803.68   Scope and Rationale of the Exception

Numerous types of publications are encompassed by the exception for market reports and commercial publications. In fact, as one commentator has noted, "The only difficulty with the exception is determining how narrowly it should be interpreted."[331] In determining the type of publication to which the exception properly applies, implementation of the rationale for the exception should be sought. While the exception is supported by necessity (*i.e.*, because of the near impossibility of obtaining testimony from each person who contributed to the publication), it is most fundamentally justified by the trustworthiness that attends reports prepared with the knowledge that the public and persons in particular trades will rely upon them and will continue to rely upon them only if they are in fact trustworthy.[332]

The exception is appropriately invoked for reports and publications that contain objective facts as opposed to statements of opinion. Accordingly, such items as stock market quotations,[333] reports of prices listed in trade

---

[329] *See generally,* 2 MCCORMICK, § 321; 5 WEINSTEIN'S FEDERAL EVIDENCE § 803.22; 4 MUELLER & KIRKPATRICK, § 467; 6 WIGMORE, §§ 1702–1706. *See also* McElroy, *Public Surveys—The Latest Exception to the Hearsay Rule,* 28 BAYLOR L. REV. 59 (1976); Sorenson & Sorenson, *The Admissibility and Use of Opinion Research Evidence,* 28 N.Y.U. L. REV. 1213 (1953); Note, *Commercial Lists,* 46 IOWA L. REV. 455 (1961); Note, *Mercantile Credit Reports as Evidence,* 44 MINN. L. REV. 719 (1960); Note, *Public Opinion Surveys as Evidence: The Pollsters Go to Court,* 66 HARV. L. REV. 498 (1953).

[330] *See* Advisory Committee Note, Rule 803(17).

[331] 5 WEINSTEIN'S FEDERAL EVIDENCE § 803.22.

[332] *Id*; *see also* 4 MUELLER & KIRKPATRICK, § 467; 2 MCCORMICK, § 321; 6 WIGMORE, §§ 1702–1706.

[333] *See* Virginia v. West Virginia, 238 U.S. 202, 212 (1915) ("[I]t is unquestioned that in proving the fact of market value, accredited price-current lists and market reports, including those published in trade journals or newspapers which are accepted as trustworthy, are admissible in evidence"); G.E. Employees Secur. Corp. v. Manning, 137 F.2d 637 (3d Cir. 1943) (since "a free and ready market existed" at the necessary times, "the value of the stock may be established by the market quotations"); *see also* United States v. Anderson, 532 F.2d

journals[334] and newspapers,[335] city directories,[336] and mortality and annuity tables[337] have been recognized as within the exception. In addition, the Rule has been found to embrace annual books published by a car manufacturer reflecting a car's estimated value[338] and "industrial statistics" reflecting annual or quarterly corporate income as published by the Internal Revenue Service or similar government agency.[339]

§ 803.69   Utilization of the Exception

Proper considerations in determining the admissibility of a publication under this exception may include the manner in which it was prepared and the extent to which it is consulted by members of a trade or by the public.[340] It has been suggested that courts should determine whether the publication in question meets the requisite standard of trustworthiness entitling it to hearsay exemption. If not, the court should exclude such a report or require

---

1218 (9th Cir. 1976); Coplin v. United States, 88 F.2d 652 (9th Cir. 1937).

[334] *See In re* Cliquot's Champagne, 70 U.S. (3 Wall.) 114 (1865) (trial court properly received Prices-Current prepared by Parisian wine dealer indicating wholesale prices of wine); Wolcher v. United States, 200 F.2d 493 (9th Cir. 1952) (error to exclude evidence of weekly issues of the "Billboard" for the year in question, since it was a national publication and a trade paper specializing in the sort of information in issue; conviction for tax evasion reversed).

[335] *See* Virginia v. West Virginia, 238 U.S. 202 (1915) (proper to accredit stock market quotations published in a newspaper of high reputation); United States v. Anderson, 532 F.2d 1218 (9th Cir. 1976) (value of stock proved by evidence of the over-the-counter price as published in the Wall Street Journal).

[336] *See* Williams v. Campbell Soup Co., 80 F. Supp. 865 (D. Mo. 1948) (proper to use city directory to find address of business in order to determine if business is doing business in the forum state; "the directory of a city is continually used for business purposes and experience has shown that the data contained therein is dependable").

[337] *See* Roberts v. United States, 316 F.2d 489 (3d Cir. 1963) (mortality tables); *see also* Kanelos v. Kettler, 406 F.2d 951 (D.C. Cir. 1968); Kershaw v. Sterling Drug, Inc., 415 F.2d 1009 (5th Cir. 1969).

[338] *See* United States v. Johnson, 515 F.2d 730 (7th Cir. 1975) (testimony as to "Red Book" value of stolen Cadillacs was properly received, since published by National Market Reports for more than 64 years).

[339] *See* Aero Spacelines, Inc. v. United States, 530 F.2d 324 (Ct. Cl. 1976) (statistics published by IRS and FTC with SEC).

[340] *See, e.g.,* United States v. Martin, 167 F. Supp. 301, 302–03 (D. Ill. 1958) (Dunn & Bradstreet credit reports not admissible since they "are not prepared or made under the supervision or control of any employer or officer of the creditor companies, and therefore are not records whose trustworthiness can be established by the testimony of any person who systematically kept or supervised the records of these companies"); *see also* United States v. Mount, 896 F.2d 612 (1st Cir. 1990) (in a trial for knowingly transporting in interstate commerce stolen, rare historical documents, publications relied upon by manuscript dealers to locate President Lincoln's original documents were admitted under Rule 803(17)); Phillip Van Heusen, Inc. v. Korn, 204 Kan. 172, 460 P.2d 549, 552 (Kan. 1969) ("[T]he general rule is that a credit report of a commercial or credit reporting company such as Dunn & Bradstreet is not admissible in evidence").

that the offer thereof be made pursuant to another exception, for example, as a business record, which requires a more extensive foundation as a prerequisite to admissibility.[341]

Reports or publications offered pursuant to Rule 803(17) must be authenticated and relevant. Many of the writings falling within this exception will be self-authenticating under Rule 902(5) (official publications), Rule 902(6) (newspapers and periodicals), or Rule 902(7) (trade inscriptions and the like). Others may be easily authenticated under Rule 901(b)(7) (public records or reports) or Rule 901(b)(8) (ancient documents or data compilation).

§ 803.70　Rule 803(18) Statements in Learned Treatises, Periodicals, or Pamphlets

The following are not excluded by the rule against hearsay, regardless of whether the declarant is available as a witness:

***

(18)　　*Statements in Learned Treatises, Periodicals, or Pamphlets.* A statement contained in a treatise, periodical, or pamphlet if:

　　(A)　the statement is called to the attention of an expert witness on cross-examination or relied on by the expert on direct examination; and

　　(B)　the publication is established as a reliable authority by the expert's admission or testimony, by another expert's testimony, or by judicial notice.

　　If admitted, the statement may be read into evidence but not received as an exhibit.

Rule 803(18) creates a hearsay exception for statements contained in published treatises, periodicals, or pamphlets on a subject of history, medicine, or other science or art established as a reliable authority to the extent that such statements are called to the attention of an expert witness upon cross-examination or relied upon by the witness in direct examination. The reliability of the authority may be established by the testimony or admission of the witness, by other expert testimony, or by judicial notice.

---

[341] 5 WEINSTEIN'S FEDERAL EVIDENCE § 803.22. Judge Weinstein argues that Rule 803(17) should not be utilized to admit mercantile credit reports, for example, which may not be based on firsthand knowledge and which may include "the kind of gossip against which the hearsay rule is designed to protect — opinions of neighbors, ex-spouses, and disgruntled former employees." The author suggests that such a report should be admitted, if at all, "only when the proponent can show that the information was obtained and compiled in a manner indicative of trustworthiness." 5 WEINSTEIN'S FEDERAL EVIDENCE § 803.22; *see also* 4 MUELLER & KIRKPATRICK, § 467.

Once the authority is established as reliable, statements contained in treatises and the like that are addressed on direct or cross-examination may be considered as substantive evidence.[342]

At common law, the only permissible use of learned treatises was to show the basis for the expert's opinion on direct examination, or for impeachment on cross-examination.[343] Courts differed on the proper use of treatises for impeachment purposes, however:

> Most courts have permitted this use where the expert has relied upon the specific material in forming the opinion to which he testified on direct, some of these courts have extended the rule to situations in which the witness admits to having relied upon some general authorities although not that particular material sought to be used to impeach him. Other courts have required only that the witness himself acknowledge that the material sought to be used to impeach him is a recognized authority in his field; if he does so, the material may be used although the witness himself may not have relied upon it. Finally, some courts have permitted this use without regard to the witness's having relied upon or acknowledged the authority of the source if the cross-examiner establishes the general authority of the material by any proof or judicial notice.[344]

In drafting Rule 803(18), the Advisory Committee extended the last approach described above by permitting statements contained in learned treatises to be offered to prove the truth of the matter asserted due to the inherent reliability of such works. To prevent the possibility of misuse of the evidence by the jury, however, statements contained in books and articles

---

[342] *See generally,* 2 MCCORMICK, § 321; 5 WEINSTEIN'S FEDERAL EVIDENCE § 803.23; 4 MUELLER & KIRKPATRICK, § 468; 6 WIGMORE, §§ 1690–1692. *See also* Goldman, *The Use of Learned Treatises in Canadian and United States Litigation,* 24 U. TORONTO L. REV. 423 (1974); Comment, *Learned Treatises in Illinois: Are We Witnessing the Birth of a New Hearsay Exception?,* 9 LOY. U. CHI. L.J. 193 (1977); Comment, *Substantive Admissibility of Learned Treatises and the Medical Malpractice Plaintiff,* 71 NW. U.L. REV. 678 (1976); Note, *Evidence—Products Liability—Federal Rule of Evidence 803(18)—Federal Rule of Admitting Evidence May Be of Significant Litigational Importance, Especially in Products Liability Suits,* 27 S.C. L. REV. 766 (1976); Note, *Learned Treatises and Rule 803(b)(18) of the Proposed Federal Rules of Evidence,* 5 VAL. U.L. REV. 126 (1970); Comment, *Learned Treatises as Direct Evidence: The Alabama Experience,* 1967 DUKE L.J. 1157; Comment, *Medical Malpractice—Expert Testimony,* 60 NW. U.L. REV. 834 (1966); Note, *Learned Treatises,* 46 IOWA L. REV. 463 (1961); Note, *Medical Treatises as Evidence—Helpful But Too Strictly Limited,* 29 U. CIN. L. REV. 255 (1960).

[343] *E.g.,* Brown v. United States, 419 F.2d 337, 341 (8th Cir. 1969) ("medical treatises, recognized by the expert witness as authoritative, may be used in cross-examination, but are not admissible to prove the probative facts or opinions in the treatises, since they are subject to the hearsay rule"). *See generally,* 6 WIGMORE, §§ 1690–1708; 5 WEINSTEIN'S FEDERAL EVIDENCE § 803.23; 4 MUELLER & KIRKPATRICK, § 468; 2 MCCORMICK, § 321.

[344] 2 MCCORMICK, § 321.

may not be offered as substantive evidence independent of expert testimony.[345]

§ 803.71   Rationale

The common law's failure to recognize a hearsay exception for learned treatises rested upon four principal objections: First, the trier of fact may be confused by scholarly works of a technical nature and may be misled into according material undue weight. A second concern is that there exists a potential for the proponent of the evidence to present it out of context or in a distorted form. Third, live testimony by an expert has been considered a better means to resolve technical issues than consulting written works. Finally, it is argued that information and skills in the fields of art, science, and history change so rapidly that learned treatises and the like become quickly outdated, thus presenting the opportunity for the proponent of the material to present obsolete information to the trier of fact.[346]

The drafters of Rule 803(18), in accord with the position advanced by most legal writers, found that the concerns underlying the hearsay objection are not significant.[347] The Rule's requirement that the admission of the treatise accompany the examination and cross-examination is believed to obviate the problems of misunderstanding and misapplication. Moreover, the prohibition against receiving the publication as an exhibit contained in the last sentence of the Rule provides an additional safeguard against the misuse of such evidence.[348]

The second argument that passages from publications may be presented out of context is clearly applicable as well to expert testimony by virtue of what the expert witness chooses to disclose or not disclose. The Rule recognizes that the adversarial process provides a sufficient safeguard to this type of abuse in the latter instance and should likewise be sufficient where learned treatises are presented.[349]

The objection that written material is inferior to live testimony is likewise without merit. There is no reason to assume that a testifying expert will possess a requisite degree of knowledge and experience and that authors of books and articles will lack it. Moreover, any deficiency presented by publications will largely be compensated by the testimony of the expert

---

[345] *See* 5 WEINSTEIN'S FEDERAL EVIDENCE § 803.23.

[346] *See* 6 WIGMORE, § 1690.

[347] *See* 5 WEINSTEIN'S FEDERAL EVIDENCE § 803.23; 2 MCCORMICK, § 321; Note, *Learned Treatises*, 46 IOWA L. REV. 463 (1961).

[348] *See* Advisory Committee Note, Rule 803(18); *see also* 4 MUELLER & KIRKPATRICK, § 468.

[349] *See* 5 WEINSTEIN'S FEDERAL EVIDENCE § 803.23; Comment, *Learned Treatises as Direct Evidence: The Alabama Experience*, 1967 DUKE L.J. 1157.

required under the Rule.[350] Finally, there is as much likelihood that the knowledge underlying the opinion of an expert witness will be outdated as there is that information contained in publications will be. Just as the proponent of expert testimony must demonstrate the qualifications of the expert before he or she is permitted to testify, the proponent of a learned publication must demonstrate that the material is reliable before it can be offered into evidence. Furthermore, the availability of cross-examination provides an additional safeguard against the danger that obsolete information will be presented.[351]

Learned treatises also satisfy the criteria of trustworthiness and necessity that traditionally underlie hearsay exceptions. Authors of publications have a strong incentive to be truthful and accurate since their works will be subject to the scrutiny of other professionals in their field. Related to this guarantee of trustworthiness is the fact that the authors of books and articles do not have a motive to misrepresent or distort information because such materials will not be prepared in anticipation of litigation.[352]

There is a special need for the exception since it is unlikely that the party seeking to prove a matter will be able "to produce all or even the best experts in any given case, and excluding written works by experts whose live testimony is beyond reach results only in depriving the trier of fact of useful information."[353]

§ 803.72   Foundation

Rule 803(18) provides that the party offering a publication must establish it as a "reliable authority." This requirement may be met by the testimony or admission of the expert witness or by other expert testimony that the expertise of the author is recognized in the field and that the particular publication is regarded as accurate by other professionals.[354] Alternatively,

---

[350] 4 MUELLER & KIRKPATRICK, § 468.

[351] See id.; see also 6 WIGMORE, § 1690.

[352] See Advisory Committee Note, Rule 803(18).

[353] 4 MUELLER & KIRKPATRICK, § 468; see, e.g., Cook v. Navistar Int'l Trans. Corp., 940 F.2d 207 (7th Cir. 1991) (though harmless, it was error to limit to impeachment purposes the admissibility of industry publications showing the defendant's awareness of accepted standards); Johnson v. William C. Ellis & Sons Iron Works, Inc., 609 F.2d 820 (5th Cir. 1979) (exclusion of safety codes was reversible error, since they are prepared by organizations for the chief purpose of promoting safety and are inherently trustworthy); Bair v. American Motors Corp., 473 F.2d 740 (3d Cir. 1973) (reversible error to exclude statistical surveys prepared by Automotive Crash Injury Research of Cornell University).

[354] See Burgess v. Premier Corp., 727 F.2d 826 (9th Cir. 1984); Weise v. United States, 724 F.2d 587 (7th Cir. 1984); see also Dawson v. Chrysler Corp., 630 F.2d 950 (3d Cir. 1980) (no error in admitting reports prepared for United States Department of Transportation, since authoritativeness of reports was inferentially conceded and defendant failed to object to use of the reports); Maggipinto v. Reichman, 481 F. Supp. 547 (E.D. Pa. 1979) (treatise was used solely for impeachment; court must decide whether authority is reliable before it can admit

the requirement may be satisfied by judicial notice of the reliability of the treatise. Widely accepted publications such as the Merck Index, The Encyclopedia Britannica and the Physician's Desk Reference are examples of the types of materials admissible through judicial notice.[355] It should be noted that judicial notice under Rule 803(18) does not assign probative value to the evidence. Rather, judicial notice under the Rule operates only to qualify the work as a reliable source, and, accordingly, the question of the material's weight should be left to the jury.[356]

In order to use a treatise as substantive evidence, the proponent also must demonstrate either that the expert relied upon the work on direct examination or that the work was called to the attention of the expert on cross-examination. This requirement is "designed to ensure that the materials are used only under the chaperonage of an expert to assist and explain in applying them."[357] To this end, admission of a treatise is proper only when an expert is given an opportunity to rebut or explain the material, to give a reaction to the work and the basis for this reaction.[358] Where the proponent's expert proves to be a hostile witness, the proponent should be permitted to call the witness's attention to the publication through the use of leading questions pursuant to Rule 611.[359]

---

treatise); *cf.* Dawsey v. Olin Corp., 782 F.2d 1254 (5th Cir. 1986) (where no experts testified that government manual was reliable, and one witness stated it was unreliable, trial court did not err in prohibiting plaintiffs from using manual to cross-examine that witness).

[355] *E.g.*, Baenitz v. Ladd, 363 F.2d 969 (D.C. Cir. 1966) (court approves judicial notice of facts contained in chemistry treatise where information was also published in the *Encyclopedia Britannica*); Application of Hartop, 311 F.2d 249 (C.C.P.A. 1962) (in patent litigation court approves judicial notice of information from "The Merck Index of Chemicals and Drugs"); *see also* Wise v. George C. Rothwell, Inc., 382 F. Supp. 563 (D. Del. 1974), *aff'd without op.*, 513 F.2d 627 (3d Cir. 1975) (judicial notice of average perception reaction and stopping distance for passenger vehicles traveling at 40 miles per hour); Azoplate Corp. v. Silverlith, Inc., 367 F. Supp. 711 (D. Del. 1973), *aff'd without op.*, 506 F.2d 1050 (3d Cir. 1974) (judicial notice of certain chemical dictionaries).

[356] *See* 5 WEINSTEIN'S FEDERAL EVIDENCE § 803.23.

[357] 2 McCORMICK, § 321; *see* Dartez v. Fibreboard Corp., 765 F.2d 456 (5th Cir. 1985) (admission of articles to establish relevant medical knowledge in asbestos liability suit was improper where plaintiff's expert did not testify regarding articles).

[358] *See* Tart v. McGann, 697 F.2d 75 (2d Cir. 1982); *see also* Generella v. Weinberger, 388 F. Supp. 1086 (E.D. Pa. 1974) (error for administrative law judge to rely upon four medical publications, since the cited publications are not recognized as standard authority by the medical field, and no experts were called); *see, e.g.*, Foster v. McKeesport Hosp., 260 Pa. Super. 485 (Pa. Ct. Super. 1978); Kansas City v. Dugan, 524 S.W.2d 194 (Mo. Ct. App. 1975).

[359] *See* Rule 611(c) and accompanying discussion, Chapter 611, *supra; cf.* Stottlemire v. Cawood, 215 F. Supp. 266 (D.D.C. 1963) (pre-Rules medical malpractice case; physician called by plaintiff did not answer questions as expected; plaintiff not permitted to contradict witness with treatise because such works were not admissible as substantive evidence and

§ 803.73   Scope of the Exception

Although Rule 803(18) expressly mentions statements contained in a "treatise, periodical, or pamphlet," the scope of the exception extends to any scholarly work, regardless of its form, where a proper foundation is laid For example, charts extracted from a learned treatise,[360] almanacs, interest tables, astronomical calculations,[361] authoritative videotapes,[362] and government publications[363] may be admitted under the Rule.

While publications offered under Rule 803(18) will often be of a medical nature, the Rule is not restricted to medical treatises. Rather, it operates to admit works "on the subject of history, medicine or other science or art."[364]

The final sentence of Rule 803(18) contains the restriction that evidence offered under the Rule may not be "received as an exhibit." As previously discussed in § 803.71, *supra,* this restriction is designed to prevent the trier of fact from misunderstanding or misapplying the evidence as a result of its examination in the jury room.[365] However, this restriction should not be read so broadly as to preclude the proponent from presenting the evidence to the jury in the form of a visual presentation where the presentation aids the trier of fact in evaluating and understanding the material.[366]

§ 803.74   Rule 803(19) Reputation Concerning Personal or Family History

The following are not excluded by the rule against hearsay, regardless of

---

party not permitted to impeach his own witness; this result would be different under Rule 607 and 803(18)).

[360] United States v. Mangan, 575 F.2d 32 (2d Cir. 1978) (proper to admit into evidence chart from a learned treatise, since its significance had been fully explored with the expert); *see also* Jamison v. Kline, 454 F.2d 1256 (3d Cir. 1972).

[361] Bair v. American Motors Corp., 473 F.2d 740 (3d Cir. 1973) (learned treatises include "annuity tables, weather reports, and tables of the rise and fall of the tide, all of which have been admitted in evidence").

[362] Costantino v. Herzog, 203 F.3d 164 (2d Cir. 2000) (an authoritative videotape can be a learned treatise despite the lack of specific mention of such a source in Rule 803(18); trial judge properly allowed jury to view such a videotape after an *in camera* review and an independent verification of the tape's authoritativeness).

[363] Dawson v. Chrysler Corp., 630 F.2d 950 (3d Cir. 1980); Garbincius v. Boston Edison Co., 621 F.2d 1171 (1st Cir. 1980).

[364] *E.g.,* Connecticut Light & Power Co. v. Federal Power Com. 557 F.2d 349 (2d Cir. 1977) (historical teatises); United States v. Erdos, 474 F.2d 157 (4th Cir. 1973) (psychiatric treatise); George v. Morgan Constr. Co., 389 F. Supp. 253 (E.D. Pa. 1975) (industry safety standard published by International Labour Organization).

[365] *See* Advisory Committee Note, Rule 803(18); 5 WEINSTEIN'S FEDERAL EVIDENCE § 803.23; *see, e.g.,* United States v. Mangan, 575 F.2d 32 (2d Cir. 1978) (court refuses to fault trial judge for not permitting handwriting charts to be taken to the jury room, although noting that it may be difficult to "read" charts into evidence).

[366] 4 MUELLER & KIRKPATRICK, § 468; *see, e.g.,* United States v. Mangan, 575 F.2d 32 (2d Cir. 1978), *cert. denied,* 439 U.S. 931 (1978).

whether the declarant is available as a witness:

***

(19) ***Reputation Concerning Personal or Family History.*** A reputation among a person's family by blood, adoption, or marriage — or among a person's associates or in the community — concerning the person's birth, adoption, legitimacy, ancestry, marriage, divorce, death, relationship by blood, adoption, or marriage, or similar facts of personal or family history.

Rule 803(19) authorizes the admission of reputation evidence when offered to prove a fact of personal or family history.[367] The reputation evidence may be drawn from three sources, namely: (i) from among members of a person's family; (ii) from the person's associates; or (iii) from someone in the community. The facts sought to be proven may include reputation as to those matters specified in the Rule, *i.e.*, a person's birth, adoption, marriage, divorce, death, legitimacy, relationship by blood, adoption or marriage, ancestry, or any other similar fact concerning personal or family history.

Several other hearsay exceptions pertain to related matters. The Rule covers the same subject matter as that which may be proved by records of religious organizations under Rule 803(11), by family records under Rule 803(13), or, where the declarant is unavailable, by statements of personal or family history under Rule 804(b)(5). Also, Rule 803(22) authorizes proof by judgments of personal or family history matters where they would be provable by reputation evidence.

The Rule is generally in accord with prior law.[368] Its justification lies in the special need for this type of evidence due to the difficulty in obtaining other evidence of family matters and in the circumstantial guarantee of trustworthiness afforded by the likelihood "that these matters have been sufficiently inquired about and discussed with persons having personal knowledge so that a trustworthy consensus has been reached."[369]

§ 803.75 Application of the Rule

Rule 803(19) is confined to reputation evidence as to personal or family

---

[367] *See generally,* 2 McCORMICK, § 322; 5 WEINSTEIN'S FEDERAL EVIDENCE § 803.24; 4 MUELLER & KIRKPATRICK, § 469; 5 WIGMORE, §§ 1580, 1602–1605. *See also* Hale, *Proof of Facts of Family History*, 2 HASTINGS L.J. 1 (1950); Comment, *Hearsay Under the Proposed Federal Rules: A Discretionary Approach*, 15 WAYNE L. REV. 1077 (1969); Note, *Reputation*, 46 IOWA L. REV. 426 (1961).

[368] *See generally,* 5 WIGMORE, §§ 1602–1606; 2 McCORMICK, § 322.

[369] 5 WEINSTEIN'S FEDERAL EVIDENCE § 803.24; *see also* 4 MUELLER & KIRKPATRICK, § 469; Advisory Committee Notes, Rules 803(19), (20) and (21).

history matters and not to direct statements of such matters. Reputation in this regard refers to the composite of a large number of out-of-court declarations evincing belief in a particular fact or set of facts. As a prerequisite to offering reputation testimony, the proponent must establish that the witness belongs to one of the three groups specified in the Rule and that he or she accordingly has sufficient familiarity with the subject matter, *i.e.,* the reputation as to personal or family history of the person in question. If it appears that sufficient familiarity is lacking, the judge may exclude the testimony.[370]

The Rule does not establish any preference among the three groups of witnesses, *i.e.,* family, associates, or community.[371] Nor is there any requirement as to when the reputation must have been formulated. While not affecting admissibility, these considerations may affect the weight to be accorded the evidence by the trier of fact. For example, the trier might well accord more weight to reputation testimony offered by a close family member than to that offered by a business associate. Likewise, more weight might be attributed to reputation evidence that appears to be long standing than to that which is shown to have developed after the instant controversy arose.[372] If, however, sufficient indications of unreliability exist that outweigh the probative value of the evidence, the testimony is subject to exclusion pursuant to Rule 403.

§ 803.76   Rule 803(20) Reputation Concerning Boundaries or General History

The following are not excluded by the rule against hearsay, regardless of whether the declarant is available as a witness:

***

(20)   *Reputation Concerning Boundaries or General History.* A reputation in a community — arising before the controversy — concerning boundaries of land in the community or customs that

---

[370] *See* Young Ah Chor v. Dulles, 270 F.2d 338 (9th Cir. 1959) (reversible error to receive testimony concerning genealogy where witness "was not in any sense an intimate acquaintance" of the family); Blackburn v. United Parcel Service, Inc., 179 F.3d 81 (3d Cir. 1999) (on his claim that UPS did not uniformly apply the anti-nepotism policy under which it allegedly fired him, plaintiff-employee could not use this hearsay exception to prove that other familial relationships were tolerated by UPS, as he was unable to establish the existence of any community, let alone any reputation within it, with his allegations that a single person had told him that someone had a relative of some type working somewhere within UPS).

[371] *Cf.* United States v. Mid-Continent Petroleum Corp. 67 F.2d 37 (10th Cir. 1933) (in general, proof of reputation and tradition should ordinarily be accepted only from the family in question; however, in exceptional circumstances, proof of reputation among friends, acquaintances or the neighborhood is admissible).

[372] *See* 5 WEINSTEIN'S FEDERAL EVIDENCE § 803.24; 4 MUELLER & KIRKPATRICK, § 469.

affect the land, or concerning general historical events important to that community, state, or nation.

Rule 803(20) creates a hearsay exception for two categories of reputation evidence: (i) that relating to boundaries of or customs affecting land; and (ii) that relating to important events of general history.[373]

The use of reputation evidence to prove the location of public and private boundaries and customs affecting land was well established at common law.[374] While the exception is justified by the general lack of other reliable sources of information, it is more fundamentally supported by the trustworthiness that attends general reputation concerning facts of community interest.[375] Traditionally, however, the reputation had to be "ancient," that is, it had to derive from a past generation.[376] The Rule eliminates any requirement concerning antiquity while retaining the common-law requirement that the reputation as to boundaries or customs must antedate the present controversy.[377] It should be noted that boundaries may also be proved by judgments under Rule 803(22).

§ 803.77   In General

Rule 803(20) also encompasses a hearsay exception for reputation concerning events of general history. While there is no requirement under this portion of the Rule that the reputation antedate the instant controversy, the event must be one that is important to the community, state or nation in which it occurred, "so that it can accurately be said that there is a high probability that the matter underwent general scrutiny as the community reputation was formed."[378] Here again, the Rule dispenses with any requirement that the matter in question be an ancient one, although some

---

[373] *See generally,* 2 MCCORMICK, § 324; 5 WEINSTEIN'S FEDERAL EVIDENCE § 803.25; 4 MUELLER & KIRKPATRICK, § 470; 5 WIGMORE, §§ 1582–1595. *See also* Note, *Reputation,* 46 IOWA L. REV. 426 (1961).

[374] 5 WIGMORE, §§ 1586–1587.

[375] *See* 5 WEINSTEIN'S FEDERAL EVIDENCE § 803.25, citing Wally v. United States, 148 Ct. Cl. 371 (Ct. Cl. 1960); *see also* 2 MCCORMICK, § 324, which explains the underpinnings of the reputation exceptions as follows:

> A general lack of other reliable sources of information provides the necessity. A high probability of reliability is provided by restricting the use of reputation to those subjects in regard to which persons with personal knowledge are likely to have disclosed facts which have been the subject of general inquiry; thus the community's conclusion is likely to be accurate.

See generally, 4 MUELLER & KIRKPATRICK, § 470.

[376] 5 WIGMORE, § 1582; 2 MCCORMICK, § 324.

[377] *See* Advisory Committee Note, Rule 803(20). *See generally,* 5 WIGMORE, § 1592.

[378] 2 MCCORMICK, § 324.

commentators suggest that use of the term "history" suggests some require-ment of age.[379] This suggestion may be an unnecessary concession to an outdated common-law requirement, however, since certain events of recent occurrence may well be of general historical value to a community or nation.

Reputation evidence utilized to prove events or facts of general history will often consist of a written record[380] which may also be admissible under the exception for ancient documents or business records, or be appropriate for judicial notice.[381]

§ 803.78   Rule 803(21) Reputation Concerning Character

The following are not excluded by the rule against hearsay, regardless of whether the declarant is available as a witness:

***

(21)   ***Reputation Concerning Character.*** A reputation among a per-son's associates or in the community concerning the person's character.

Rule 803(21) provides that evidence in the form of reputation is admissible for its truth.[382] The reputation may be that which a person enjoys "among [his] associates or in the community."

While reputation evidence was traditionally limited to that derived from the neighborhood in which a person lived,[383] Rule 803(21) expands the groups from which character evidence may be derived in acknowledgment of the highly mobile nature of modern society. The term "associates" may refer to a variety of settings such as business, church, or social groups, and the only prerequisite to utilization of the exception is a showing that the person characterized is sufficiently known in the group in question to have

---

[379] *Id*; *see also* 4 MUELLER & KIRKPATRICK, § 470; 5 WEINSTEIN'S FEDERAL EVIDENCE § 803.26; Pan American World Airways v. Aetna Casualty & Surety Co., 368 F. Supp. 1098 (S.D.N.Y. 1973), *aff'd*, 505 F.2d 989 (2d Cir. 1974) (membership of foreign paramilitary or terrorist groups, as well as the facts of even small battles or guerrilla attacks cannot be "reported" in court); *cf.* Morris v. Lessee of Harmer's Heirs, 32 U.S. (7 Pet.) 554 (1833) (no error in receipt of book of author who was within the reach of the process of the court, since the party objecting to the proof had himself called the author to testify, making the book admissible to explain or qualify his testimony).

[380] *See, e.g.,* Connecticut Light & Power Co. v. Federal Power Com., 557 F.2d 349 (2d Cir. 1977) (historical writing). *See generally,* 5 WEINSTEIN'S FEDERAL EVIDENCE § 803.26; 5 WIGMORE, § 1597.

[381] *See* 5 WIGMORE, § 1597.

[382] *See generally,* 2 MCCORMICK, § 324; 5 WEINSTEIN'S FEDERAL EVIDENCE § 803.27; 4 MUELLER & KIRKPATRICK, § 471; 5 WIGMORE, §§ 1608–1621. *See also* 82 A.L.R.3d 525, *Admissibility of Testimony as to General Reputation at Place of Employment.*

[383] 5 WIGMORE, § 1615.

permitted others to have become acquainted with the person such that a reputation has developed. These prerequisites are established through the qualification of a reputation witness who must have sufficient familiarity with the reputation of the person in question to offer probative testimony on the subject.

Rule 803(21) effects a result that is consistent with pre-Rule law.[384]

§ 803.79   Purpose and Extent of the Exception

Rule 803(21) serves to reinforce other Rules that allow the introduction of reputation testimony in specific situations. For example, under Rule 404(a)(2)(A), defendants in criminal trials may offer evidence of their character, and if they do so, the prosecution may offer character evidence to rebut that which the defendant has offered. Additionally, under Rule 404(a)(2)(B), the accused and the prosecution may under certain circumstances offer evidence relating to the character of the victim. In these instances, and also in situations where character itself is "in issue" in the case, Rule 405 permits proof of character to be established by testimony as to reputation. Reputation testimony as to the truthfulness of a witness may also be offered pursuant to Rule 608.[385] Rule 803(21) ensures that where reputation evidence is admissible, it may be received for the truth of the matter asserted. The exception is necessary because reputation "consists of a summary of uncross-examined views expressed outside the courtroom offered to prove the truth of the matter asserted."[386]

Rule 803(21) does not attempt to specify the situations in which character evidence is admissible. Nor does it address the specific type of character trait that may be proved by means of reputation evidence. The Rule merely provides that such evidence will not be excluded because of hearsay considerations. The admissibility of character evidence and the permissible focus of such evidence depend upon considerations of relevance as well as the criteria set forth in the Rules identified above. Moreover, such evidence, even though admissible, may be excluded pursuant to Rule 403 if the prejudicial effect is deemed substantially to outweigh its probative value.

---

[384] *See* Michelson v. United States, 335 U.S. 469 (1948) (the hearsay exception allows a witness "to summarize what he has heard in the community, although much of it may have been said by persons less qualified to judge than himself"). *See generally,* 2 MCCORMICK, § 324; 4 MUELLER & KIRKPATRICK, § 471.

[385] *See, e.g.,* United States v. Prevatt, 526 F.2d 400 (5th Cir. 1976) ("character witnesses may testify as to a defendant's reputation in the community under a common exception of the hearsay rule"); United States v. Oliver, 492 F.2d 943 (8th Cir. 1974) (Rule 803(21) admits evidence of reputation as to the truth and veracity of a witness).

[386] 5 WEINSTEIN'S FEDERAL EVIDENCE § 803.27; *see also* Moore v. United States, 123 F.2d 207, 210 (5th Cir. 1941) ("[m]ere rumors are not reputation but reputation involves a notion of the general estimate of a person by the community as a whole").

§ 803.80   Rule 803(22) Judgment of a Previous Conviction

The following are not excluded by the rule against hearsay, regardless of whether the declarant is available as a witness:

***

(22)   ***Judgment of a Previous Conviction.*** Evidence of a final judgment of conviction if:

    (A)   the judgment was entered after a trial or guilty plea, but not a nolo contendere plea;

    (B)   the conviction was for a crime punishable by death or by imprisonment for more than a year;

    (C)   the evidence is admitted to prove any fact essential to the judgment; and

    (D)   when offered by the prosecutor in a criminal case for a purpose other than impeachment, the judgment was against the defendant.

The pendency of an appeal may be shown but does not affect admissibility.

Subject to specified restrictions, Rule 803(22) authorizes the admission into evidence of felony convictions in subsequent civil and criminal actions to prove any fact essential to the previous criminal judgment.[387] The evidence offered pursuant to this exception must be that of a final judgment, entered after a trial or upon a guilty plea, but not upon a plea of nolo contendere. The conviction must relate to a crime punishable by death or imprisonment in excess of one year, and in criminal prosecutions, the Government may not utilize the conviction of persons other than the accused

---

[387] *See generally,* 2 MCCORMICK, § 298; 5 WEINSTEIN'S FEDERAL EVIDENCE § 803.28; 4 MUELLER & KIRKPATRICK, § 472; 4 WIGMORE, § 1346; 5 WIGMORE, § 1671. *See also* Bush, *Criminal Convictions as Evidence in Civil Proceedings,* 29 MISS. L.J. 276 (1959); Cowen, *The Admissibility of Criminal Convictions in Subsequent Civil Proceedings,* 40 CALIF. L. REV. 225 (1952); Hinton, *Judgment of Conviction—Effect on a Civil Case as Res Judicata or as Evidence,* 27 ILL. L. REV. 195 (1932); Comment, *Hearsay Under the Proposed Federal Rules: A Discretionary Approach,* 15 WAYNE L. REV. 1077 (1969); Note, *Use of Record of Criminal Conviction in Subsequent Civil Action Arising From the Same Facts as the Prosecution,* 64 MICH. L. REV. 702 (1966); Note, *Judgments as Evidence,* 46 IOWA L. REV. 400 (1961); Note, *Admissibility and Weight of a Criminal Conviction in a Subsequent Civil Action,* 39 VA. L. REV. 995 (1953); Note, *Evidence: Judgments: Admissibility in Evidence in a Civil Action of Party's Conviction of Traffic Infraction,* 35 CORNELL L.Q. 872 (1950); Note, *Admissibility of Traffic Conviction as Proof of Facts in Subsequent Civil Action,* 50 COLUM. L. REV. 529 (1950); Note, *Evidence—Traffic Infraction—Admissibility as Proof of Underlying Fact,* 16 BROOK. L. REV. 286 (1950); Note, *Effect of a Criminal Conviction in Subsequent Civil Suits,* 50 YALE L.J. 499 (1941).

for a purpose other than impeachment. Evidence offered pursuant to Rule 803(22) is merely probative, rather than conclusive, of the fact sought to be proved.

While Rule 803(22) is in conflict with the common-law practice of most state jurisdictions,[388] it is in accord with prior federal law and policy.[389]

§ 803.81　Rationale of the Rule

A hearsay exception is necessary to admit evidence of a conviction because, "[a]nalytically, such a judgment of conviction is hearsay, since it is based on the opinion of twelve persons who have not been cross-examined and have no personal knowledge of the underlying facts."[390]

The principal rationale for a hearsay exception for convictions is that of reliability.[391] The exception reflects faith in the criminal justice system and in the capacity of jurors to arrive at a just determination.[392] Reliability is also assured by the high burden of proof in criminal cases and by the defendant's motivation to defend fully in the face of a serious criminal charge.[393]

§ 803.82　Scope of the Rule

Rule 803(22) limits the use of previous judgments in several respects. Notably, the exception operates to admit criminal judgments only, and civil judgments are admissible only to the extent provided by other Rules or by the non-evidentiary doctrines of res judicata and collateral estoppel. Also, evidence of final criminal judgments is limited to convictions resulting from a trial or a guilty plea. These requirements assure reliability by providing either that a full trial will have preceded the conviction or that the defendant will have admitted guilt in accordance with procedures that assure the plea is made knowingly, voluntarily, and with full appreciation of the conse-

---

[388] *See* Comment, *Hearsay Under the Proposed Federal Rules: A Discretionary Approach*, 15 WAYNE L. REV. 1077 (1969); 5 WIGMORE, § 1671(a).

[389] *See, e.g.,* United States v. Fabric Garment Co., 366 F.2d 530, 534 (2d Cir. 1966) ("Under federal law, a criminal conviction will work an estoppel in favor of the government in a subsequent civil proceeding with respect to questions distinctly put in issue and directly determined in the criminal prosecution"); Connecticut Fire Ins. Co. v. Ferrara, 277 F.2d 388 (8th Cir. 1960) (arson conviction admitted in suit on fire insurance policy); United States Fidelity & Guar. Co. v. Moore, 306 F. Supp. 1088 (N.D. Miss. 1969) (prior criminal conviction given conclusive effect in subsequent civil action). *See generally,* 2 MCCORMICK, § 298.

[390] 5 WEINSTEIN'S FEDERAL EVIDENCE § 803.28.

[391] *Id.; see also* 4 MUELLER & KIRKPATRICK, § 472.

[392] *See* 5 WIGMORE, § 1671a. *But see* Hinton, *Judgment of Conviction—Effect in a Civil Case as Res Judicata or as Evidence*, 27 ILL. L. REV. 195 (1932).

[393] 2 MCCORMICK, § 298; United States v. Garland, 991 F.2d 328 (6th Cir. 1993) (evidence of the Ghanian convictions of two Ghanian citizens for defrauding an American citizen was admissible at defendant's trial pursuant to either Rule 803(8) or Rule 803(22)).

quences.[394] By way of contrast, a plea of nolo contendere is not admissible. The result is in accordance with Rule 410 and with previous practice.[395]

The Rule is limited by its terms to convictions, and it does not accord hearsay exemption to judgments of acquittal. The latter are excluded because they show, at most, that the prosecution did not prove each element of the case beyond a reasonable doubt. Since a judgment of acquittal does not prove innocence, it is excluded due to minimal or nonexistent relevance.[396] As a further limitation, the exception applies only to convictions for crimes punishable by death or imprisonment in excess of one year. Again, the rationale for the limitation is reliability, *i.e.*, the motivation to defend fully is significantly less where the charge involves a misdemeanor.[397]

Admissibility of convictions is further limited when evidence of the conviction is offered against the accused in a criminal trial. In this context the Government may not use the conviction of any person other than the accused for a purpose other than impeachment. Consequently, while the government may utilize a third person's conviction to impeach that person as a witness under Rule 609,[398] it may not use a conviction of a third person against the accused as proof of any fact essential to the prior determination. The limitation has a constitutional derivation, namely, that of the accused's

---

[394] *See* Fed. R. Crim. P. 11(c) and (d).

[395] *See* Advisory Committee Note, Rule 803(22); Chapter 410, *supra*; *see, e.g.,* Greenberg v. Cutler-Hammer, 403 F. Supp. 1231 (E.D. Wis. 1975) (citing Treatise to find that Rule 803(22) "makes clear that evidence of a final judgment based upon a plea of nolo contendere cannot be used to prove any fact essential to sustain the judgment").

[396] 5 WEINSTEIN'S FEDERAL EVIDENCE § 803.28; 2 McCORMICK, § 298. *But cf.* Bush, *Criminal Convictions as Evidence in Civil Proceedings*, 29 MISS. L.J. 276 (1959) (suggesting that judgments of acquittal should be admitted "since the failure of the state to prove guilt to the required degree may have some tendency to show that the accused was not in fact guilty"). *See* United States v. Irvin, 787 F.2d 1506 (11th Cir. 1986) (acquittals are hearsay, "unlike judgments of conviction").

[397] 5 WEINSTEIN'S FEDERAL EVIDENCE § 803.28; *see also* Rule 410, which provides, *inter alia*, that a plea of guilty in a violations bureau is not admissible in any civil or criminal proceeding against the person who made the plea. Judge Weinstein suggests that the policy of admitting only judgments of felonies should be extended such that guilty pleas in non-felony cases would not be allowed as admissions or as statements against interest, notwithstanding case law to the contrary. It might be argued in response that evidence of a guilty plea may not be as persuasive to a jury as a judgment, and that a party against whom a guilty plea has been admitted may always explain the circumstances surrounding the plea and advance reasons limiting its weight.

[398] Although a conviction utilized for impeachment purposes under Rule 609 presumably requires a hearsay exception, it may be more appropriate to invoke Rule 803(8) rather than Rule 803(22) in this context since the conviction itself is the focus of proof rather than the facts underlying the conviction. The point is academic, however, since convictions are an acknowledged method of impeachment and a hearsay objection would be frivolous.

right to "be confronted with the witnesses against him."[399] As discussed in the following section, the Government may, however, utilize the conviction of the accused as long as it is not prevented from doing so by the prohibition of Rule 404(b) or by constitutional considerations.[400]

§ 803.83 Application of the Rule

Subject to the limitations discussed in the foregoing section, the Rule admits evidence of previous convictions in criminal and civil actions as proof of any fact essential to sustain the conviction. Consequently, the proponent must establish not only the conviction itself through, for example, introduction of a certified record, but the party must also establish that the fact sought to be proved was essential to sustain the prior judgment. The judge must determine that issue as a preliminary matter, based, if necessary, upon "an examination of the record, including the pleadings, the evidence submitted, the instructions under which the jury arrived at its verdict, and any opinions of the court."[401]

Admissibility of a conviction to prove a fact essential to that determination also depends on its relevance to, and admissibility in, the action in which it is offered as evidence. In this regard, the proponent may not run afoul of the forbidden inference of Rule 404(b), that is, by utilizing the previously established fact as evidence of character in order to prove that a person acted in conformity therewith. The evidence may, on the other hand, be offered for other purposes such as those expressly authorized in Rule 404(b), that is, to prove motive, opportunity, intent, preparation, plan, knowledge, identity, or absence of mistake or accident.[402]

Evidence offered pursuant to Rule 803(22) is not conclusive of the fact

---

[399] *See* United States v. Diaz, 936 F.2d 786 (5th Cir. 1991) (Rule 803(22) prohibits the introduction into evidence of guilty pleas of third parties for the purpose of proving an element of the crime); Kirby v. United States, 174 U.S. 47 (1899) (in prosecution for possession of stolen postage stamps, conviction reversed where the only evidence that the stamps were stolen was the record of the conviction of the thieves); Advisory Committee Note, Rule 803(22); *cf.* Roe v. United States, 316 F.2d 617 (5th Cir. 1963) (record of conviction of third person admissible to show defendant's state of mind). Also distinguished should be the situation in which the conviction of a third person is an element of the crime.

[400] *See* § 404.21 *et seq.*, *supra*; *see also* § 801.2, *supra*.

[401] Emich Motors Corp. v. GMC, 340 U.S. 558, 569–571 (1951) (plaintiff auto dealer properly allowed to introduce evidence of a prior antitrust conviction of General Motors as "prima facie evidence of the general conspiracy for the purpose of monopolizing the financing of General Motors cars, and also of its effectuation by coercing General Motors dealers to use GMAC"); 5 WEINSTEIN'S FEDERAL EVIDENCE § 803.28.

[402] It should be noted that Rule 404(b) is broader than Rule 803(22) in that it covers any evidence of other crimes, wrongs or acts. Use of a prior conviction under 803(22) is, accordingly, an expedient method of proving the prior crime when evidence thereof is admissible under Rule 404(b). Where prior act evidence is admissible consistent with Rule 404(b), however, any admissible evidence may be used to prove the occurrence of the act. A conviction is but one means of proving the act.

sought to be proved, and the opponent may explain the conviction and may offer any evidence rebutting the fact sought to be proved by the proponent. Nevertheless, convictions may be excessively persuasive and, if such evidence would be unfairly prejudicial, exclusion pursuant to Rule 403 may be indicated.

Pendency of an appeal of the conviction does not affect admissibility, although it may be offered to affect weight. The opponent may accordingly show that an appeal is pending in order to limit the persuasiveness of the conviction evidence. The Rule is thus parallel to Rule 609(e).

§ 803.84   Rule 803(23) Judgments Involving Personal, Family, or General History, or a Boundary

The following are not excluded by the rule against hearsay, regardless of whether the declarant is available as a witness:

***

(23)   *Judgments Involving Personal, Family, or General History, or a Boundary.* A judgment that is admitted to prove a matter of personal, family, or general history, or boundaries, if the matter:

(A)   was essential to the judgment; and

(B)   could be proved by evidence of reputation.

Rule 803(23) authorizes admissibility of a judgment as substantive proof of certain matters in a subsequent action.[403] The matters that may be proved by this method are limited to those of personal, family, or general history, or boundaries. The exception is further circumscribed by the requirements that the fact sought to be proved must have been essential to the prior judgment and that the matter must be one that would be provable by reputation evidence. The exception is consequently of limited application.

The subject matter overlap between Rule 803(23) and the hearsay exceptions for reputation testimony, *i.e.,* Rule 803(19) and (20), is apparent, and the connection between the two concepts — judgments and reputation — is historically based. The hearsay exception as to judgments was justified at early common law because judgments were considered to be evidence of reputation, that is, a jury verdict was thought to be based upon the individual knowledge of the jurors. Consequently, it represented the reputation in the neighborhood.[404] Although the historical underpinnings no longer exist, a

---

[403] *See generally,* 2 McCORMICK, § 325; 5 WEINSTEIN'S FEDERAL EVIDENCE § 803.29; 4 MUELLER & KIRKPATRICK, § 473; 5 WIGMORE, § 1593. *See also* Comment, *Hearsay Under the Proposed Federal Rules: A Discretionary Approach,* 15 WAYNE L. REV. 1077 (1969).

[404] 5 WEINSTEIN'S FEDERAL EVIDENCE § 803.29; 5 WIGMORE, § 1593; Advisory Committee Note, Rule 803(23); *see, e.g.,* Patterson v. Gaines, 47 U.S. (6 How.) 550, 559

separate exception for the admissibility of judgments has persisted. The exception is justified by the assumed reliability of the judicial process reinforced by the belief that, at the least, judgments are as reliable as reputation.[405] The Rule, accordingly, maintains the link between the two concepts, and in what is perhaps a cautious approach, limits the use of judgments to those matters provable by reputation. Any restrictions on the use of reputation evidence are consequently applicable to the use of judgments under this Rule.[406]

§ 803.85   Res Judicata and Collateral Estoppel Distinguished

Two judicial doctrines, res judicata and collateral estoppel, must be distinguished from the concept reflected in Rule 803(23). Rule 803(23) permits the use of judgments as *evidence*. Such evidence is not conclusive, however, and may be rebutted in the same fashion as any other item of evidence.[407] This use of a judgment is distinct from the concept of res judicata in which a judgment operates as a bar to further litigation between the same parties concerning the same subject matter. It is also distinct from the concept of collateral estoppel which operates as a bar to relitigation of facts previously litigated between the same parties. A judgment offered under Rule 803(23), then, is merely probative of the fact to which it is relevant. It is not conclusive of the matter.

§ 803.86   Scope of the Exception

Unlike Rule 803(22), Rule 803(23) does not limit the types of judgments that may be utilized as evidence, *i.e.*, civil or criminal. It is unclear whether a civil judgment properly qualified may be utilized in a subsequent criminal action as proof of one of the specified topics, even though a higher burden of proof is required in criminal trials.[408] Arguably, although the prosecution

---

(1840) ("The general rule certainly is, that a person cannot be affected, much less concluded, by any evidence, decree, or judgment, to which he was not actually, or in consideration of law, privy. But the general rule has been departed from so far that wherever reputation would be admissible evidence, there a verdict between strangers, in a former action, is evidence also; such as in cases of manorial rights, public rights of way, immemorial custom, disputed boundaries, and pedigrees").

[405] 5 WEINSTEIN'S FEDERAL EVIDENCE § 803.29; *see also* 4 MUELLER & KIRKPATRICK, § 473.

[406] *See* 5 WEINSTEIN'S FEDERAL EVIDENCE § 803.29; *see also* § 803.81 *et seq.*, *supra*, and § 803.86 *et seq.*, *infra*.

[407] *See* Jung Yen Loy v. Cahill, 81 F.2d 809 (9th Cir. 1936) (evidence of prior determination by immigration officers affirming citizenship of appellant's father was admitted, but rebutted and overcome by appellant's positive testimony); United States v. Mid-Continent Petroleum Corp., 67 F.2d 37 (10th Cir. 1933) (findings by Dawes Commission as to age, sex, and alias were admissible, but not conclusive).

[408] *See* 5 WEINSTEIN'S FEDERAL EVIDENCE § 803.29, in which the author raises this question and notes that while such evidence is as reliable as reputation evidence that may be introduced in a criminal action, there is a risk that a jury may be far more impressed with a

must prove every element of the crime beyond a reasonable doubt but does not need to establish every piece of evidence to that standard in order to obtain admissibility of such evidence, a civil judgment offered pursuant to Rule 803(23) should be admitted in criminal cases with an understanding that such admission does not in any manner alter the prosecution's burden of proof on any element of the crime. The differential burdens of proof reflect on the weight to be accorded the evidence. Nevertheless, if any risk of undue prejudice is presented by the admission of such evidence, it may be excluded pursuant to Rule 403.

§ 803.87 Application of the Exception

The proponent who seeks to offer a judgment as proof of a matter specified in Rule 803(23) must first establish the judgment itself, for example, through the use of a certified copy of the court record. The proponent must further establish that the matter sought to be introduced was "essential" to the prior judgment. The court must determine as a preliminary matter whether a sufficient showing of "essentiality" has been made to justify admission of the judgment. The proponent must also show that the matter sought to be introduced through this vehicle would be provable by evidence of reputation, for example, facts of personal or family history such as those specified in Rule 803(19). If proof of a matter would require evidence other than reputation, Rule 803(23) may not be utilized.

§ 803.88 Former Rule 803(24)

In 1997, the text of Rule 803(24), containing a residual hearsay exception, was deleted and transferred to Rule 807. Refer to Chapter 807, *infra,* for a discussion of the residual exception.

---

judgment than with reputation testimony. The author suggests that a judge must consequently weigh the probative value of such evidence against the danger of prejudice in determining its admissibility. *See* Comment, *Hearsay Under the Proposed Federal Rule: A Discretionary Approach,* 15 WAYNE L. REV. 1077, 1200 (1969) ("The civil judgment is at least as trustworthy as the reputation evidence which may be introduced in the criminal action."). Pre-Rule law recognized the essence of this exception in Grant Brothers Construction Co. v. United States, 232 U.S. 647 (1914). In that case, the Supreme Court held that the finding of an administrative board that certain persons were aliens was properly admitted in a subsequent action by the government to recover penalties against a third party for violations of the Alien Contract Labor Act. Although the court commented that the action under the Act was technically civil in form, "it is in fact in the nature of a criminal proceeding in that it seeks to recover a penalty for the commission of a crime."

Chapter 804

Rule 804. Exceptions to the Rule Against Hearsay — When the Declarant Is Unavailable as a Witness

Rule 804. Exceptions to the Rule Against Hearsay — When the Declarant Is Unavailable as a Witness

    (a)   **Criteria for Being Unavailable.** A declarant is considered to be unavailable as a witness if the declarant:

        (1)   is exempted from testifying about the subject matter of the declarant's statement because the court rules that a privilege applies;

        (2)   refuses to testify about the subject matter despite a court order to do so;

        (3)   testifies to not remembering the subject matter;

        (4)   cannot be present or testify at the trial or hearing because of death or a then-existing infirmity, physical illness, or mental illness; or

        (5)   is absent from the trial or hearing and the statement's proponent has not been able, by process or other reasonable means, to procure:

            (A)   the declarant's attendance, in the case of a hearsay exception under Rule 804(b)(1) or (6); or

            (B)   the declarant's attendance or testimony, in the case of a hearsay exception under Rule 804(b)(2), (3), or (4).

    But this subdivision (a) does not apply if the statement's proponent procured or wrongfully caused the declarant's unavailability as a witness in order to prevent the declarant from attending or testifying.

    (b)   **The Exceptions.** The following are not excluded by the rule against hearsay if the declarant is unavailable as a witness:

        (1)   *Former Testimony.* Testimony that:

            (A)   was given as a witness at a trial, hearing, or lawful deposition, whether given during the current proceeding or a different one; and

            (B)   is now offered against a party who had — or, in a civil case, whose predecessor in interest had — an opportunity and similar motive to develop it by direct, cross-, or redirect examination.

(2) ***Statement Under the Belief of Imminent Death.*** In a prosecution for homicide or in a civil case, a statement that the declarant, while believing the declarant's death to be imminent, made about its cause or circumstances.

(3) ***Statement Against Interest.*** A statement that:

(A) a reasonable person in the declarant's position would have made only if the person believed it to be true because, when made, it was so contrary to the declarant's proprietary or pecuniary interest or had so great a tendency to invalidate the declarant's claim against someone else or to expose the declarant to civil or criminal liability; and

(B) is supported by corroborating circumstances that clearly indicate its trustworthiness, if it is offered in a criminal case as one that tends to expose the declarant to criminal liability.

(4) ***Statement of Personal or Family History.*** A statement about:

(A) the declarant's own birth, adoption, legitimacy, ancestry, marriage, divorce, relationship by blood, adoption, or marriage, or similar facts of personal or family history, even though the declarant had no way of acquiring personal knowledge about that fact; or

(B) another person concerning any of these facts, as well as death, if the declarant was related to the person by blood, adoption, or marriage or was so intimately associated with the person's family that the declarant's information is likely to be accurate.

(5) **[*Other Exceptions.*]** [Transferred to Rule 807.]

(6) ***Statement Offered Against a Party That Wrongfully Caused the Declarant's Unavailability.*** A statement offered against a party that wrongfully caused — or acquiesced in wrongfully causing — the declarant's unavailability as a witness, and did so intending that result.

---

§ 804.1   Admissible Hearsay When Declarant Unavailable

Rule 804 establishes a rule of preference for the admissibility of certain types of hearsay:[1] "The preference is for in-court testimony over hearsay,

---

[1] *See generally,* 2 McCORMICK, § 253; 5 WEINSTEIN'S FEDERAL EVIDENCE § 804.03; 4 MUELLER & KIRKPATRICK, §§ 480–87; 5 WIGMORE, §§ 1401–1414, 1456. *See also* Kirkpatrick, *Confrontation and Hearsay: Exemptions from the Constitutional Unavailability Requirement,* 70 MINN. L. REV. 665 (1986); Stewart, *Perception, Memory, and Hearsay: A*

and hearsay, if of a certain quality, over a complete loss of evidence."[2] In contrast to the Rule 803 exceptions to the hearsay rule, the admissibility of Rule 804(b) exceptions is dependent upon laying a foundation satisfactory to the court[3] that the declarant is unavailable as a witness.[4]

The availability-unavailability distinction of Rule 803 and 804 is a product of historical development, with the criterion of unavailability developing in conjunction with particular hearsay exceptions.[5] While there remains substantial dispute among commentators as to which exceptions should be conditioned upon the showing of the declarant's unavailability,[6] designated classes of hearsay are admitted under Rule 804 on the assumption that it is better to admit Rule 804 hearsay than receive no evidence at all.[7]

Subsection (a) of Rule 804 defines situations in which a declarant is considered unavailable, and subsection (b) sets forth five hearsay exceptions that are conditional on the unavailability of the declarant. One substantial change in pre-Rule law effected by Rule 804 is that the Rule makes the standard of unavailability uniform for each exception.[8]

§ 804.2   Unavailability — An Overview

Rule 804(a) identifies five types of situations in which a declarant is "unavailable as a witness" and in which the condition to the utilization of the Rule 804(b) exceptions is satisfied: (1) where the declarant's testimony is exempt due to privilege; (2) where the declarant refuses to testify; (3) where the declarant testifies to a lack of memory; (4) where the declarant is unable to testify due to death, illness or infirmity; and (5) where the declarant is absent and the proponent of the declarant's statement has been unable to obtain the testimony by process or reasonable means.[9]

Criticism of Present Laws and the Proposed Federal Rules of Evidence, 1970 UTAH L. REV. 1; Weissenberger, *The Former Testimony Hearsay Exception: A Study in Rulemaking, Judicial Revisionism, and the Separation of Powers*, 67 N.C. L. REV. 295 (1989); Comment, *Evidence—Hearsay Exception—Requirements for Unavailability of Witness in Criminal Case Under the Federal Law of Evidence*, 29 RUTGERS L. REV. 133 (1975); Comment, *Evidence: The Unavailability Requirement of Declaration Against Interest Hearsay*, 55 IOWA L. REV. 477 (1969); Comment, *Hearsay Under the Proposed Federal Rules: A Discretionary Approach*, 15 WAYNE L. REV. 1079 (1969).

[2] Comment, *Evidence: The Unavailability Requirement of Declaration Against Interest Hearsay*, 55 IOWA L. REV. 477 (1969); *see* Advisory Committee Note, Rule 804.

[3] *See* Advisory Committee Note, Rule 804; *see also* Rule 104(a) and § 104.1, *supra.*

[4] Advisory Committee Note, Rule 804.

[5] *Id.; see also* 5 WEINSTEIN'S FEDERAL EVIDENCE § 804.03.

[6] 5 WEINSTEIN'S FEDERAL EVIDENCE § 804.03.

[7] *Id.*

[8] Advisory Committee Note, Rule 804.

[9] *See id. See generally,* 4 MUELLER & KIRKPATRICK, §§ 480–487; 2 MCCORMICK, § 253; 5 WEINSTEIN'S FEDERAL EVIDENCE § 804.03; 5 WIGMORE, §§ 1401–1418.

Although the wording of Rule 804(a) emphasizes the unavailability of the declarant, the crucial issue is whether the declarant's *testimony* is unavailable. In each of the first three types of situations identified in Rule 804(a), the declarant may be present in the courtroom, but hearsay is admissible because his or her testimony is unavailable.[10] Rule 804(a) treats "unavailability" in a uniform fashion. Consequently, if any of the identified situations arise, the witness is unavailable regardless of which of the Rule 804(b) exceptions is invoked to admit the hearsay.

Rule 804(a) also provides that if the proponent of the hearsay statement procured the unavailability of the declarant, the declarant is not considered unavailable. Consequently, the hearsay statement would be inadmissible under Rule 804(b). The obvious justification for this principle is that a proponent of hearsay should not be permitted to evade the Rule or benefit from evidence made admissible by his or her own wrongdoing.[11]

Rule 804 continues the traditional practice of placing the burden of establishing the unavailability of a declarant on the proponent of the hearsay.[12] The court must determine whether the declarant is unavailable as

---

[10] *Cf.* 2 MCCORMICK, § 253 ("the critical factor is the unavailability of [the witness'] testimony."); 5 WEINSTEIN'S FEDERAL EVIDENCE § 804.03; *e.g.,* Walden v. Sears, Roebuck & Co., 654 F.2d 443 (5th Cir. 1981) (court erred in excluding testimony of minor who was present in the courtroom but could not recall what happened during the accident in question; "the crucial factor is not the unavailability of the witness but rather the unavailability of his testimony"); Mason v. United States, 408 F.2d 903 (10th Cir. 1969) ("the important element is whether the testimony of the witness is sought and is available, not whether the witness's body is available"). *See also* Rosenfeld v. Basquiat, 78 F.3d 84 (2d Cir. 1996) (in diversity action, where state Dead Man's Statute prevents an interested party from testifying, his testimony may not be introduced under Rule 804; the Dead Man's Statute is not a rule of privilege making the interested party's testimony unavailable, but a rule of competency, declaring that the interested party's testimony is inadmissible; "the hearsay exception in Rule 804 gives no license to bypass the [state] statute barring [the] testimony").

[11] *See, e.g.,* Reynolds v. United States, 98 U.S. 145 (1878) ("[T]he rule has its foundation in the maxim that no one shall be permitted to take advantage of his own wrong.").

[12] 4 MUELLER & KIRKPATRICK, § 480; *see, e.g.,* Nat'l Labor Relations Bd. v. Augusta Bakery Corp., 957 F.2d 1467 (7th Cir. 1992) (it was not error to exclude an affidavit on hearsay grounds where the proponent failed to demonstrate either why the declarant was absent or why it had been unable to procure his attendance); Burns v Clusen, 798 F.2d 931 (7th Cir. 1986) (trial court erred in admitting testimony of victim whose unavailability was based on mental illness where no express findings were made regarding the duration of the illness, symptoms of which included both an active and residual phase; however, the error was harmless); United States v. Draiman, 784 F.2d 248 (7th Cir. 1986) (declarant was not unavailable where neither party knew declarant's whereabouts at the time of the trial and the proponent did not make a showing that declarant was actually unavailable); United States v. Fernandez-Roque, 703 F.2d 808, 812–813 (5th Cir. 1983); United States v. Pelton, 578 F.2d 701, 709 (8th Cir. 1978) (unavailability not established where attorney simply stated that declarant would exercise her privilege against self-incrimination; the possibility that she "might decide to choose to exercise her privilege amounted to a wholly inadequate showing of unavailability under Rule 804(a)(1)").

a witness, and it has considerable discretion in making its determination.[13] Under Rule 104(a) the court is not bound by the Rules of Evidence, except in regard to privileges, in considering the foundational evidence as to unavailability.

Rule 804 not only treats all types of unavailability uniformly, it also treats civil and criminal cases alike.[14] Consistent with the Sixth Amendment, however, courts have required a more stringent application of the unavailability standard in criminal cases where the evidence is offered against the accused.[15]

§ 804.3   Rule 804(a)(1) Criteria for Being Unavailable — Privilege

  (a) **Criteria for Being Unavailable.** A declarant is considered to be unavailable as a witness if the declarant:

      (1) is exempted from testifying about the subject matter of the declarant's statement because the court rules that a privilege applies;

Rule 804(a)(1) provides that a witness's valid claim of privilege, exempting him or her from testifying, satisfies the unavailability requirement of Rule 804.[16] The witness's bare assertion of the privilege, however, is insufficient to make the witness unavailable. Instead, the court must rule that assertion of the privilege is justified.[17]

Unavailability due to a justified assertion of privilege occurs most frequently because of a claim of spousal privilege[18] or the privilege against

---

[13] 4 MUELLER & KIRKPATRICK, § 480; *see also* Bickel v. Korean Air Lines Co., 96 F.3d 151 (6th Cir. 1996) (in wrongful death actions, upholding the admission of videotaped expert testimony from a prior trial; experts were originally unavailable due to the fact that they were testifying elsewhere, and although the experts became available before the presentation of the videotaped testimony was completed, court did not err in continuing to use the videotape rather than calling the experts as live witnesses at that point).

[14] *See* 5 WEINSTEIN'S FEDERAL EVIDENCE § 804.03.

[15] *Id.*; *see also* 4 MUELLER & KIRKPATRICK, § 480; § 801.2, *supra,* and § 804.7, *infra.*

[16] The Rule is consistent with previous practice in the federal courts. *See, e.g.,* United States v. Elmore, 423 F.2d 775, 778 (4th Cir. 1970) ("[T]he requirement that the declarant be unavailable to testify is satisfied by the fact that West successfully asserted his fifth amendment privilege against self-incrimination and declined to answer any questions about the matter"); *see also* United States v. Allen, 409 F.2d 611 (10th Cir. 1969).

[17] 4 MUELLER & KIRKPATRICK, § 481; 5 WEINSTEIN'S FEDERAL EVIDENCE § 804.03. *See* United States v. Peterson, 100 F.3d 7 (2d Cir. 1996) (rejecting defendant's argument that his state grand jury testimony should have been admissible as prior testimony when he invoked his privilege against self-incrimination in a federal trial for possession of a firearm by a felon; court stated that "[w]hen the defendant invokes his Fifth Amendment privilege, he has made himself unavailable to any other party, but he is not unavailable to himself").

[18] United States v. Montague, 421 F.3d 1099, 1103 (10th Cir. 2005); United States v.

self-incrimination.[19] In criminal cases, witnesses who successfully assert the Fifth Amendment privilege are unavailable within the meaning of this rule, unless the prosecution agrees to give the witness "immunity" — that is, a guarantee that the testimony by the witness will not be used in any later criminal prosecution of that witness. The prosecution has some measure of discretion in deciding when it will extend immunity to a witness, and the courts will not generally force the prosecution to do so every time the defense makes such a request. An immunized witness is not "unavailable" under Rule 804(a)(1), because at that point the witness no longer has a valid Fifth Amendment privilege, so none of the Rule's exceptions would apply to hearsay statements by that witness. Moreover, the absence of a valid privilege means that the witness can be compelled to testify and held in contempt if he or she refuses to do so.[20]

§ 804.4   Rule 804(a)(2) Criteria for Being Unavailable — Refusal to Testify

(a)   **Criteria for Being Unavailable.** A declarant is considered to be unavailable as a witness if the declarant:

***

(2)   refuses to testify about the subject matter despite a court order to do so;

Rule 804(a)(2) conforms to the pre-existing majority practice that recognizes that "[i]f a witness simply refuses to testify, despite the bringing

---

Lilley, 581 F.2d 182 (8th Cir. 1978); *see also* United States v. Marchini, 797 F.2d 759 (9th Cir. 1986) (marriage of defendant to witness after the latter's grand jury testimony made the witness unavailable; the grand jury testimony was therefore properly received into evidence); United States v. Mathis, 559 F.2d 294 (5th Cir. 1977) (extra-judicial statements made by wife could not be admitted, since witness was not unavailable where trial judge found that marriage was a sham and witness would testify against her husband if ordered to do so); United States v. Trammel, 445 U.S. 40 (1980) (only the witness spouse holds a testimonial privilege, so that the defendant spouse cannot prevent the witness spouse from testifying).

[19] *E.g.,* United States v. Woolbright, 831 F.2d 1390 (8th Cir. 1987) (alleged co-offender who claimed Fifth Amendment privilege was unavailable); United States v. Salvador, 820 F.2d 558 (2d Cir. 1987) (witness who claimed Fifth Amendment privilege was unavailable); United States v. Harrell, 788 F.2d 1524 (11th Cir. 1986) (where defendant was declarant and was exercising Fifth Amendment privilege, he was unavailable); United States v. Rodriguez, 706 F.2d 31 (2d Cir. 1983); United States v. Gibbs, 703 F.2d 683 (3d Cir. 1983); United States v. Zappola, 646 F.2d 48 (2d Cir. 1981).

[20] *See, e.g.,* United States v. Gabriel, 715 F.2d 1447 (10th Cir. 1983) (where government offered to immunize declarant, declarant was not unavailable within the meaning of the Rule); (government's refusal to grant immunity to witness who claimed privilege against self-incrimination did not prevent the witness from testifying). *See generally,* Westen, *Confrontation And Compulsory Process: A Unified Theory Of Evidence For Criminal Cases,* 91 HARV. L. REV. 567 (1978).

to bear upon him [or her] of all appropriate judicial pressures, the conclusion that as a practical matter he is unavailable can scarcely be avoided."[21]

The Rule requires that the proponent of the hearsay show more than an indication by the potential witness of an unwillingness to testify. The witness must disobey a court order to testify,[22] and this disobedience by the witness in the face of a court order distinguishes a refusal to testify from an assertion of a privilege. Without the requirement of disobedience of a court order, the *mistaken* assertion of a privilege not to testify would satisfy the requirement of unavailability.[23]

§ 804.5   Rule 804(a)(3) Criteria for Being Unavailable — Lack of Memory

(a)   **Criteria for Being Unavailable.** A declarant is considered to be unavailable as a witness if the declarant:

       ***

       (3)   testifies to not remembering the subject matter;

Rule 804(a)(3) extends prior case law by providing that a hearsay declarant is unavailable if he or she testifies to a lack of memory as to the content of the out-of-court declaration.[24] Rule 804(a)(3) rejects the argument that an assertion of lack of memory in this context invites perjury from witnesses who seek to avoid being impeached or cross-examined as to the subject matter.[25] Instead, the Rule adopts the modern position that the value of admission of the hearsay statements outweighs the danger arising from the potential for perjury.[26] Moreover, the potential for perjury can be addressed in several ways. The court can determine that the testimony as to

---

[21] 2 McCormick, § 253.

[22] United States v. Bizzard, 674 F.2d 1382 (11th Cir. 1982); *see also* United States v. Bailey, 581 F.2d 341 (3d Cir. 1978) (declarant was brought before trial judge and stated that he would not testify; court then told him he was being ordered to testify, whereupon he still refused to testify); United States v. Garner, 574 F.2d 1141 (4th Cir. 1978) (grand jury witness refused to testify, persisting in his refusal even after court granted him immunity and threatened him with contempt); United States v. Gonzalez, 559 F.2d 1271 (5th Cir. 1977) (government witness refused to testify at trial, even though he had already been convicted, was granted immunity, and was ultimately found in contempt); *cf.* United States v. Pelton, 578 F.2d 701 (8th Cir. 1978) (witness's attorney's statement that witness would refuse to testify was inadequate foundation to establish unavailability of witness).

[23] *See* 5 WEINSTEIN'S FEDERAL EVIDENCE § 804.03 (arguing that silence due to an ill-founded claim of privilege may constitute unavailability due to refusal to testify).

[24] Advisory Committee Note, Rule 804.

[25] *See, e.g.,* Turner v. Missouri-Kansas-Texas Ry. Co., 346 Mo. 28 (Mo. 1940). *See generally,* Annot., 129 A.L.R. 843.

[26] 2 McCormick, § 253; 5 Wigmore, § 1408.

forgetfulness is made in bad faith and refuse to find that the unavailability condition is satisfied.[27] The hearsay, however, still might be admissible under Rule 804(a)(2) as a refusal to testify, unless the claim of forgetfulness was procured by the proponent of the hearsay.[28] Alternatively, if the hearsay statement is former testimony subject to cross-examination, the court can treat the in-court claim of lack of memory as a denial of the prior testimony that is then admissible for its truth as a prior inconsistent statement under Rule 801(d)(1)(A).[29] The declarant would still be subject "to cross-examination on his motives and memory" by the opposing party.[30] Finally, the prior testimony might be admissible under Rule 803(5) as recorded recollection,[31] particularly where the opponent of the witness seeks admission of the hearsay.[32]

§ 804.6   Rule 804(a)(4) Criteria for Being Unavailable — Death and Infirmity

(a)   **Criteria for Being Unavailable.** A declarant is considered to be unavailable as a witness if the declarant:

***

(4)   cannot be present or testify at the trial or hearing because of death or a then-existing infirmity, physical illness, or mental illness; or

---

Rule 804(a)(4) follows a long established tradition in treating a declarant of Rule 804(b) hearsay as unavailable when the declarant is determined to be dead.[33] Rule 804(a)(4) also incorporates traditional practice that a declarant is unavailable where he or she is subject to mental or physical infirmity.[34]

The infirmity condition was early viewed as an extension of the rule that

---

[27] *See* 5 WEINSTEIN'S FEDERAL EVIDENCE § 804.03 ("Cross-examination about the making of the statement [alleging lack of memory] and his present recollection gives the trial judge a good opportunity for assessing the witness's credibility").

[28] *See* § 804.8, *infra.*

[29] 4 MUELLER & KIRKPATRICK, § 483; 5 WEINSTEIN'S FEDERAL EVIDENCE § 804.03.

[30] *See* 2 MCCORMICK, § 253; *accord* 5 WIGMORE, § 1408 ("the witness must be called in order that [his lack of memory] may appear, so that in practical application there would be no dispensation of his presence").

[31] *See* 5 WIGMORE, § 1408.

[32] *See* § 803.10, *supra.*

[33] 2 MCCORMICK, § 253.

[34] Advisory Committee Note, Rule 804; *see* 5 WEINSTEIN'S FEDERAL EVIDENCE § 804.03 ("Unavailability exists if the trial judge finds that the declarant is suffering from a physical condition which is not expected to improve and which renders him unable to testify within a reasonable time").

death constituted unavailability.[35] One obvious difference is that infirmity, unlike death, may not be permanent. If an infirmity is temporary, the trial can be continued until the witness is available,[36] and continuance may be necessary to satisfy the criminal defendant's constitutional right to confrontation in certain situations.[37] Rather than continuing the trial, the court may make other arrangements because of an infirm witness, such as obtaining testimony at the bedside of the witness. The trial judge must be given discretion to decide what is most appropriate based upon the facts of each case.[38] One difficulty with temporary infirmity is that mental infirmity may not be clearly temporary, and consistent with the right of confrontation, a case of transitory incapacity may be of such uncertain duration as to constitute a "permanent" unavailability justifying admission of hearsay.[39]

In the case of mental infirmity, the judge must decide, based on the opinions of medical experts, whether the witness will sufficiently improve to sustain the rigors of a trial and to offer useful testimony. The judge may order a continuance if there is a strong probability of recovery.[40] The question before the judge is not one of legal insanity because, according to Rule 601, insanity need not disqualify a person from being a witness.[41] If a person is competent to testify, but will be traumatized by testifying at trial or will offer useless testimony, then the witness is effectively unavailable.[42] McCormick has suggested that the question of the unavailability of the witness should be decided by determining whether the prior hearsay is more reliable than the present testimony of the mentally infirm witness,[43] but the judge's determination can be further complicated by the fact that the witness may have been mentally or emotionally impaired at the time the prior statement was made.[44]

§ 804.7   Rule 804(a)(5) Criteria for Being Unavailable — Absence

     (a)   **Criteria for Being Unavailable.** A declarant is considered to be unavailable as a witness if the declarant:

        ***

---

[35] *See generally,* 2 McCormick, § 253.

[36] *E.g.,* Parrott v. Wilson, 707 F.2d 1262 (11th Cir. 1983); United States v. Faison, 679 F.2d 292 (3d Cir. 1982).

[37] *See generally,* § 801.2, *supra,* for a discussion of Confrontation Clause issues.

[38] 4 Mueller & Kirkpatrick, § 484; 5 Weinstein's Federal Evidence § 804.03.

[39] 5 Weinstein's Federal Evidence § 804.03; *e.g.,* Parrott v. Wilson, 707 F.2d 1262 (11th Cir. 1983).

[40] *See* 4 Mueller & Kirkpatrick, § 484.

[41] Advisory Committee Note, Rule 804.

[42] 4 Mueller & Kirkpatrick, § 484.

[43] 2 McCormick, § 253.

[44] 5 Weinstein's Federal Evidence § 804.03.

(5) is absent from the trial or hearing and the statement's proponent has not been able, by process or other reasonable means, to procure:

(A) the declarant's attendance, in the case of a hearsay exception under Rule 804(b)(1) or (6); or

(B) the declarant's attendance or testimony, in the case of a hearsay exception under Rule 804(b)(2), (3), or (4).

Rule 804(a)(5) provides that if a person and his testimony cannot be procured, the witness is unavailable. The Rule requires that not only must the declarant be unavailable, but his or her *testimony*, which in many cases includes a deposition, must be unavailable. Congress included the requirement in the Rule that an attempt be made to depose the witness before the witness is found unavailable and his hearsay statements are admitted under Rule 804(b)(2), (3), or (4).[45]

Although the question of whether absence makes a person unavailable may seem obvious,[46] several issues may be presented. First, the position that the permanent or indefinite absence of a person from a jurisdiction is a sufficient basis for finding the person unavailable as a witness has been limited in criminal cases.[47] In federal criminal trials the government must subpoena the witness,[48] as well as search for the witness or attempt in other ways to enforce the subpoena.[49] Additionally, the government must use "reasonable means" to secure the witness's appearance, such as keeping track of or restraining the witness.[50] According to the United States Supreme

---

[45] Advisory Committee Note, Rule 804.

[46] 2 McCormick, § 253.

[47] 5 Weinstein's Federal Evidence § 804.03. *See generally,* 2 McCormick, § 253; 5 Wigmore, § 1404. For a discussion of Confrontation Clause issues involving absent declarants, *see* § 801.2, *supra.*

[48] 4 Mueller & Kirkpatrick, § 485.

[49] *See* Ohio v. Roberts, 448 U.S. 56 (1980) (Confrontation Clause was not violated by admission of preliminary hearing testimony of witness who was unavailable at trial where prosecution unsuccessfully tried to serve subpoenas five times at witness's last known residence and questioned witness's mother, who stated she did not know her daughter's whereabouts); *see also* United States v. Lynch, 499 F.2d 1011 (D.C. Cir. 1974). *But see* United States v. Johnson, 108 F.3d 919 (8th Cir. 1997) (no error in admitting K-9 officer's testimony from original trial under Rule 804(b)(1) in retrial of a drug-trafficking case; officer was on vacation in Florida during retrial and court found both that his testimony was relatively unimportant to the case and that the defendant had failed to show any specific need for cross-examination beyond what occurred at the first trial).

[50] *See* United States v. Harbin, 112 F.3d 974 (8th Cir. 1997) (error, although harmless in the instant case, to admit grand jury testimony of defendant's sister under Rule 801(b)(1); the prosecution had learned that the sister was working at a hotel in Mississippi and made no

Court decision in *Ohio v. Roberts*,[51] the "reasonable means" principle does not require the government to engage in futile acts in an attempt to procure the testimony of a witness.

Second, in civil cases the proponent's obtaining the issuance of a subpoena for the witness generally suffices as a reasonable effort to procure the witness.[52]

Third, at least for purposes of Rule 804(b)(2), (3) and (4), using "reasonable means" to secure a witness's availability includes attempting to take the witness's deposition when the witness cannot appear at the trial.[53]

§ 804.8   Hearsay Proponent Procurement of Unavailability of Declarant

According to the last sentence of Rule 804(a), a party who causes some declarant to be unavailable may not rely on that unavailability to admit any hearsay statements by that declarant under any of the exceptions set forth under Rule 804(b). This restriction applies only to a party who intentionally caused the declarant to be unavailable for the purpose of preventing that person from attending or testifying; mere negligence in allowing a person to become unavailable will not preclude the responsible party from the use of the exceptions set forth in Rule 804 to admit a statement by that missing witness.[54] This is of course in keeping with the venerable doctrine of equity

---

effort to serve her there or to serve her when she visited her mother every three weeks); United States v. Casamento, 887 F.2d 1141 (2d Cir. 1989) (in an international narcotics ring prosecution, the government used "reasonable means" to secure the declarant's appearance when the Asst. U.S. Attorney spoke to the Director of Italy's Office of Extradition and was informed that Italy would not extradite the declarant); United States v. Thomas, 705 F.2d 709 (4th Cir. 1983); United States v. Puckett, 692 F.2d 663 (10th Cir. 1982); Perricone v. Kansas City S. Ry., 630 F.2d 317 (5th Cir. 1980); Creamer v. Gen'l Teamsters Local Union 326, 560 F. Supp. 495 (D. Del. 1983). *See generally,* 4 MUELLER & KIRKPATRICK, § 485 (discussing reasonableness standard).

[51] Ohio v. Roberts, 448 U.S. 56 (1980); *see also* § 801.2, *supra,* for a discussion of issues arising under the Confrontation Clause.

[52] 2 MCCORMICK, § 253; United States v. Squella-Avendano, 478 F.2d 433 (5th Cir. 1973) (deponent's unavailability was sufficiently established by virtue of the absence of an extradition treaty with Chile); *cf.* Azalea Fleet v. Dreyfus Supply & Machinery Corp., 782 F.2d 1455 (8th Cir. 1986) (declarant was unavailable who had moved out of the jurisdiction before the trial); McIntyre v. Reynolds Metals Co., 468 F.2d 1092 (5th Cir. 1972); Trade Development Bank v. Continental Ins. Co., 469 F.2d 35 (2d Cir. 1972). *But see* Kirk v. Raymark Indus., Inc., 61 F.3d 147 (3d Cir. 1995) (trial court erred in asbestos case by admitting testimony given by an "unavailable" expert witness in a prior, unrelated asbestos trial; although the expert was beyond the subpoena power of the court, the plaintiff had made no effort to contact the expert and offer him his usual expert witness fee and hence had not used "reasonable means" to produce the witness).

[53] 5 WEINSTEIN'S FEDERAL EVIDENCE § 804.03.

[54] *See* United States v. Seijo, 595 F.2d 116 (2d Cir. 1979) (in illegal harboring case government had procured absence of declarants for the purpose of preventing them from

that no man shall be allowed to profit from his own wrong, for any action that intentionally causes a witness to become unavailable — whether by bribery, threats, intimidation, or physical injury — will almost always amount to witness tampering, obstruction of justice, or some other criminal misconduct. To allow a party to take advantage of Rule 804 to arrange the admission of otherwise inadmissible hearsay through such means would be illogical, and might create an intolerable incentive for parties to engage in such misconduct.[55] Moreover, Rule 804 furnishes an additional disincentive and sanction against any attempt to make a witness unavailable, for such conduct permits the opposing party to then insist upon the admission of any relevant statements made by the unavailable witness under any circumstances, including even those statements that would have been inadmissible if the witness were still available to testify.[56]

By contrast, it should be remembered that no similar limitation is imposed on the admissibility of hearsay statements under Rule 803, because those statements are admissible without regard to the availability of the declarant, and thus create no incentive for anyone to make such witnesses unavailable. Consequently, even if there is evidence that a party has caused some declarant to become unavailable to testify, there is no unfairness in allowing that party to offer evidence of out-of-court statements by that witness that are admissible under the exceptions in Rule 803 — for example, an "excited utterance" under Rule 803(2) — because such statements could have been admitted even if the witness were present in the courtroom. Even in that case, however, the opposing party would be allowed to make use of Rule 804(b)(6) to seek the admission of any other hearsay statements made by that witness under any circumstances.

§ 804.9   Rule 804(b)(1) The Exceptions — Former Testimony

(b)   **The Exceptions.** The following are not excluded by the rule

---

testifying, since Rule 804(a) requires a "purpose" to prevent witnesses from attending or testifying); United States v. Mathis, 550 F.2d 180 (4th Cir. 1976) (trial court properly admitted testimony by prosecution witness given at prior trial on same charge, since the disappearance of the witness was due to inadvertence, not reckless disregard of an obligation by prison officials to produce her).

[55] This provision — which essentially dictates that "you cannot take advantage of or profit from the absence of a witness if *you* intentionally caused that person to be unavailable" — obviously bears a close parallel to the rule that admits second-hand copies of documents when the original has been lost or destroyed "not by the *proponent* acting in bad faith." Rule 1004(a) (emphasis added); *see* Chapter 1004, *infra.*

[56] *See* Rule 804(b)(6) ("Statement Offered Against a Party That Wrongfully Caused the Declarant's Unavailability"), discussed in § 804.33, *infra.* Of course, like any other hearsay rule, Rule 804(b)(6) will require the court to overrule a *hearsay* objection to the admission of statements by the unavailable declarant, but will not justify (much less require) the admission of hearsay evidence that is subject to some other possible objection (for example, Rule 408, or some privilege held by the objecting party), because that objection would have been sustained even if the witness had been available.

against hearsay if the declarant is unavailable as a witness:

(1)   *Former Testimony.* Testimony that:

    (A)   was given as a witness at a trial, hearing, or lawful deposition, whether given during the current proceeding or a different one; and

    (B)   is now offered against a party who had — or, in a civil case, whose predecessor in interest had — an opportunity and similar motive to develop it by direct, cross-, or redirect examination.

Rule 804(b)(1) creates a hearsay exception[57] for former testimony[58] by an unavailable declarant[59] where the declarant made the statement under oath while testifying "as a witness" in a "proceeding" and the party against whom the statement is offered (or in civil cases "a predecessor in interest") had an "opportunity" and "similar motive" to "develop" the declarant's testimony by direct, redirect or cross-examination at the former proceeding. In *United*

---

[57] *See generally,* 2 McCORMICK, §§ 301–308; 5 WEINSTEIN'S FEDERAL EVIDENCE § 804.04; 4 MUELLER & KIRKPATRICK, §§ 488–494; 5 WIGMORE, §§ 1370, 1371, 1386–1389, 1402–1415, 1660–1669; 7 WIGMORE, §§ 2098–2099, 2103. *See also* Falknor, *Former Testimony and the Uniform Rules: A Comment,* 38 N.Y.U. L. REV. 651 (1963); Comment, *Hearsay Under the Proposed Federal Rules: A Discretionary Approach,* 15 WAYNE L. REV. 1077 (1969); Note, *Affidavits, Depositions, and Prior Testimony,* 46 IOWA L. REV. 356 (1961).

[58] Wigmore classified such statements contained in former testimony as nonhearsay, in light of the fact that they are, by definition, given under oath with adequate opportunity for cross-examination:

> When, therefore, a statement has already been subjected to cross-examination and is hence admitted—as in the case of a deposition or testimony at a former trial—it comes in because the rule is satisfied, not because an exception to the rule is allowed. The statement may have been made before the present trial, but if it has already been subjected to proper cross-examination, it has satisfied the rule and needs no exception in its favor.

5 WIGMORE, § 1370, at 55. This position reflects Wigmore's characteristic emphasis upon the value of cross-examination in ensuring reliability. Most courts and commentators, however, adopt the position taken by Rule 804(b)(1) that such statements are hearsay and thus require a specific exception for their introduction as substantive evidence at trial. *See, e.g.,* United States v. Maturo, 536 F.2d 427 (D.C. Cir. 1976) (deposition in civil case admitted in criminal trial as a recognized exception to the hearsay rule); Morgan, BASIC PROBLEMS OF EVIDENCE 255 (1962). For a discussion of the former testimony exception *see* 4 MUELLER & KIRKPATRICK, §§ 488–494; 2 McCORMICK, §§ 301–308; 5 WEINSTEIN'S FEDERAL EVIDENCE § 804.04; 5 WIGMORE, §§ 1370, 1371, 1386–1389 (requirements of adequate opportunity to cross-examine); §§ 1402–1415 (unavailability of witness); §§ 1660–1669 (proof by official notes, records, reports, etc.); 7 WIGMORE §§ 2098, 2099, 2103 (proof of entire testimony).

[59] For a discussion of the requirement of unavailability, *see* § 804.1 *et seq., supra.*

States v. Salerno,[60] the Supreme Court held that former testimony may not be admitted under Rule 804(B)(1) without a showing of satisfaction of the "similar motive" requirement. The Court stated that nothing in Rule 804(B)(1) suggests that a court may admit former testimony absent satisfaction of each of the Rule's express elements.[61]

Since Rule 804(b)(1) is concerned solely with the hearsay issue, it does not affect an objection to the prior testimony evidence predicated upon some other basis that would render in person testimony with the same content objectionable.[62] Accordingly, although the prior testimony may qualify under Rule 804(b)(1), it may nevertheless be excluded because it is irrelevant or, if relevant, because of the operation of any other exclusionary rule or doctrine.

It should be noted that Rule 804(b)(1) is not the only vehicle for the admission of former testimony. For example, a transcript may be used for impeachment purposes under Rule 801(d)(1)(A).[63] Also, its receipt into evidence may be justified by resort to some other exception to the hearsay doctrine, such as a statement against interest under Rule 804(b)(3) or an admission under Rule 801(d)(2).[64] Alternately, testimony of a witness at a former hearing may be used at trial, not as proof of the matter asserted therein, but instead to refresh the witness's present recollection under Rule 612. The fact that a statement is contained in former testimony does not preclude application of other Rules for its use or admission at subsequent trials.

While official transcripts generally are used to prove former testimony, Rule 804(b)(1) does not mandate this type of proof. Admission of former

---

[60] United States v. Salerno, 505 U.S. 317 (1992).

[61] United States v. Salerno, 505 U.S. 317 (1992).

[62] United States v. Ricks, 882 F.2d 885 (4th Cir. 1989) (defense may admit a redacted version of prior testimony on cross-examination; Rule 106 does not mandate that former testimony must be admitted in its entirety); United States v. Cervantes, 542 F.2d 773 (9th Cir. 1976) (no abuse of discretion where trial judge excluded prior testimony of informant in unrelated case, since there had been extensive testimony as to informant's activities and criminal past); Hackley v. Roudebush, 520 F.2d 108 (D.C. Cir. 1975) (since testimony before hearing examiner in VA case is admissible in administrative proceedings it may pose a double hearsay problem, thus the parties should be able to object to the admissibility of particular portions of the administrative record on specific grounds).

[63] *See* discussion of Rule 801(d)(1)(A) in § 801.14, *supra.*

[64] *See, e.g.,* B-W Acceptance Corp. v. Porter, 568 F.2d 1179 (5th Cir. 1978) (defendant properly permitted to elicit from witness the substance of testimony given at prior trial by plaintiff's branch manager); United States v. Vecchiarello, 569 F.2d 656 (D.C. Cir. 1977) (previous depositions of defendants for prosecution for wire and mail fraud in civil action properly admitted in instant criminal action); Rule v. International Ass'n of Bridge, 568 F.2d 558 (8th Cir. 1977) (depositions taken in previous government action admissible in instant class action regardless whether deponents were available to testify).

testimony through a recorded transcript involves, by necessity, two levels of hearsay — the declarant and the reporter. In this context, the official transcript is usually admissible through the public records' exception of Rule 803(8), thus resolving the double hearsay problem.[65] But neither Rule 804(b)(1) nor the best evidence doctrine requires use of an official transcript, and, consequently, the proponent of former testimony may offer proof of the testimony in several other ways:[66] (i) through the testimony of a person who has firsthand knowledge of the former proceedings who remembers the general thrust of the testimony though perhaps not the exact language;[67] (ii) through the testimony of a firsthand observer whose recollection was refreshed by resort to a memorandum, such as a recording or stenographer's notes;[68] or (iii) through the notes of a firsthand observer if this evidence satisfies the requirements under Rule 803(5) for recorded recollection or under Rule 803(8) for public records.[69] Since it is arguable that at least one modern rationale for this exception is the unusual degree of reliability provided by official transcripts, where any other form of proof is offered, courts should be especially cautious in receiving evidence of former testimony.

Finally, where the proponent offers only part of the former testimony or deposition, the adverse party is entitled under Rule 106 to require the proponent to introduce any other part that should in fairness be considered by the trier of fact.[70]

§ 804.10 Former Testimony — Rationale

The common-law exception to the hearsay rule codified in Rule 804(b)(1)

---

[65] Mattox v. United States, 156 U.S. 237 (1895) (copy of stenographic report of former testimony supported by oath of stenographer and testimony of deceased witness is competent evidence); United States v. Arias, 575 F.2d 253 (9th Cir. 1975) (transcript of allegedly perjured testimony introduced against defendant); Hackley v. Roudebush, 520 F.2d 108 (D.C. Cir. 1975) (transcript of hearing forming basis of arbitrator's decision in discrimination proceedings admissible).

[66] 5 WEINSTEIN'S FEDERAL EVIDENCE § 804.04.

[67] *See* Meyers v. United States, 171 F.2d 800 (D.C. Cir. 1948) (former testimony could be proved by oral testimony of one present at former trial, even though transcript was available).

[68] 5 WEINSTEIN'S FEDERAL EVIDENCE § 804.04; *see* § 612.1 *et seq., supra*; 2 MCCORMICK, § 307.

[69] 5 WEINSTEIN'S FEDERAL EVIDENCE § 804.04; *see* § 803.22 *et seq.* and § 803.39 *et seq., supra*; 2 MCCORMICK, § 307; *see also* United States v. Arias, 575 F.2d 253 (9th Cir. 1978).

[70] *See* § 106.1, *supra*; *see also* 2 MCCORMICK, § 307 ("When only a portion of the former testimony of a witness is introduced by the proponent, the result may be a distorted and inaccurate impression. Hence the adversary is entitled to the introduction of such other parts as fairness requires, and to have them introduced at that time, rather than waiting until the presentation of his own case"); 5 WEINSTEIN'S FEDERAL EVIDENCE § 804.04.

is justified by the traditional policies of necessity and trustworthiness.[71] The necessity lies in the simple fact that the declarant, once available as a witness in a former proceeding, is unavailable at trial in accordance with Rule 804(a). Trustworthiness is present because, by definition, the declarant was under oath and subject to examination and cross-examination as a means of developing the testimonial evidence at the former proceeding. Where the declarant served as a witness under penalty of perjury, there exists a high degree of reliability that the substance of his or her prior testimony is accurate and complete, thus justifying its admission.[72]

It is somewhat anomalous, however, that hearsay statements taken under oath and subject to cross-examination do not qualify for admission absent an affirmative demonstration of unavailability of the declarant. The only explanation for this requirement seems to be traceable to the historical treatment of such evidence, coupled with the traditional suspicion of deciding cases without the benefit of live testimony. Where a transcript is presented to the trier of fact, an opportunity to evaluate a witness's demeanor is lacking.[73] In deference to this common-law approach, the exception for former testimony requires as a condition precedent the unavailability of the declarant.[74]

§ 804.11   "Testimony" Adduced in a "Proceeding"

Rule 804(b)(1) restricts use of a declarant's testimonial statements to those made in a duly authorized deposition or hearing of a "proceeding." The term "proceeding" should, absent any statutory definition, be broadly interpreted to encompass any form of official inquiry conducted in accordance with law, including judicial, administrative, and legislative forums.[75] Conversely, however, the term "testimony" should be restricted to only recorded statements that are made under oath and subject to prosecution for

---

[71]   *See* 4 MUELLER & KIRKPATRICK, § 488.

[72]   *See* Ohio v. Roberts, 448 U.S. 56 (1980) (upheld receipt of testimony by witness who had been subjected to what the court considered the functional equivalent of cross-examination); Mancusi v. Stubbs, 408 U.S. 204 (1972) (upheld receipt of testimony given in prior trial, since it was reliable and provided an adequate basis for evaluating its truth).

[73]   Broadcast Music v. Havana Madrid Restaurant Corp., 175 F.2d 77, 80 (2d Cir. 1949) ("[T]he liar's story may seem uncontradicted to one who merely reads it, yet it may be 'contradicted' in the trial court by his manner, his intonations, his grimaces, his gestures and the like — all matters which 'cold print does not preserve' and which constitute 'lost evidence' so far as an upper court is concerned.").

[74]   *See* Advisory Committee Note, Rule 804:

   However, opportunity to observe demeanor is what in large measure confers depth and meaning upon oath and cross-examination. Thus in cases under Rule 803 demeanor lacks the significance which it possesses with respect to testimony. In any event, the tradition, founded in experience, uniformly favors production of the witness if he is available. The exception indicates continuation of the policy.

[75]   *See* 4 MUELLER & KIRKPATRICK, § 489; 2 MCCORMICK, §§ 258, 305.

perjury.[76] Accordingly, Rule 804(b)(1) clearly encompasses testimony adduced at a former trial, a deposition, a grand jury proceeding, and an administrative hearing. Equally clear, the Rule does not include statements contained in affidavits, statements made to police during investigations, or other witness statements. Essentially, if the general requirements of an oath, adequate opportunity to examine or cross-examine, and present unavailability are satisfied, then the character of the tribunal and the precise form of the proceedings should not be determinative.

§ 804.12   Opportunity to Develop Testimony — Cross-Examination

Historically, the cross-examination attending prior testimony has been considered the foremost guarantee of reliability justifying this hearsay exception.[77] Where the opportunity for cross-examination was lacking in the prior tribunal, the formal testimony traditionally has been excluded. Even where the prior tribunal lacked jurisdiction to compel the testimony, the admission of testimonial evidence at a subsequent trial has been considered justified where the sworn statements of the witness, now dead or unavailable, about the facts of which the witness had knowledge, were made under such circumstances of opportunity and motive for cross-examination as to make them sufficiently trustworthy to be received into evidence.[78]

Under the Rule, *actual* cross-examination is not a condition precedent to admission of former testimony, but merely, as Wigmore has asserted, "an *opportunity to exercise the right to cross-examine if desired.*"[79] (Moreover, as discussed in the next section of this Chapter, an opportunity to develop testimony at the former proceeding by direct or redirect examination may also satisfy the Rule.) The rationale for this aspect of the Rule rests primarily upon estoppel principles. Wherever a party (or the party's predecessor in a civil case) fails or refuses to take the opportunity to test the testimony of a witness, it is presumed to have been because the party believed that the testimony could not or need not be disputed.[80] It is not unfair to make a party who forgoes cross-examination suffer the consequences.[81] Of course, in

---

[76] *See* United States v. Callahan, 442 F. Supp. 1213 (D.C. Minn. 1978), *later proceeding,* 455 F. Supp. 524 (D.C. Minn. 1978), *rev'd on other grounds,* 596 F.2d 759 (8th Cir. 1978) (transcript of the plea bargain made by a third person, who was unavailable not admissible, since declarant had not been sworn in and cross-examined).

[77] *See, e.g.,* Ohio v. Roberts, 448 U.S. 56 (1980); *see also* 5 WEINSTEIN'S FEDERAL EVIDENCE § 804.04.

[78] 2 McCORMICK, § 305; *see also* 5 WEINSTEIN'S FEDERAL EVIDENCE § 804.04.

[79] 5 WIGMORE, § 1371, at 55 (emphasis in original); *see also* Ohio v. Roberts, 448 U.S. 56 (1980).

[80] 2 McCORMICK, § 303; 5 WIGMORE, § 1371. *See generally,* 5 WEINSTEIN'S FEDERAL EVIDENCE § 804.04.

[81] 5 WEINSTEIN'S FEDERAL EVIDENCE § 804.04; *In re* Related Asbestos Cases, 543 F. Supp. 1142 (N.D. Cal. 1982).

some cases an opportunity for cross-examination is presented, but special circumstances hamper efforts to test the credibility of the witness or the reliability of the testimony. Accordingly, in order to satisfy the opportunity requirement of Rule 804(b)(1), "[t]he opportunity must have been such as to render the conduct of the cross-examination or the decision not to cross-examine meaningful in the light of the circumstances which prevail when the former testimony is offered."[82]

Factors affecting the opportunity requirement with regard to testimonial evidence include: (i) the nature of the former tribunal or hearing, *i.e.,* whether the rules of the forum or the scope of the inquiry furnished adequate opportunity to cross-examine; (ii) notice to the opponent as affecting the opportunity to prepare for any cross-examination; and (iii) the course of the cross-examination itself, and whether it furnished only an incomplete opportunity to test the witness's sincerity, narrative ability, perceptive ability, and memory.[83] This analysis obtains whether the evidence is in the form of trial or deposition testimony.

§ 804.13   Former Testimony — Direct or Indirect Examination

Rule 804(b)(1) permits testimony offered by parties at prior proceedings to be used against them where the parties or, in civil cases, their predecessors in interest, had an opportunity to develop the testimony by direct or cross-examination. While this practice is in consonance with the historical common-law, it creates different issues that do not arise where the evidence is offered *against the same party* in both proceedings. Where testimony adduced on direct examination by a party at a former proceeding is offered against that party at a subsequent proceeding, questions may fairly arise as to whether the direct examination at the former trial is the functional equivalent of adequate cross-examination. Commentators generally assert

---

[82] 2 MCCORMICK, § 302; *see* United States v. Ciak, 102 F.3d 38 (2d Cir. 1996) (affirming trial court's decision to allow testimony of witness who testified at first trial and who had since become unavailable to be read into the record of the defendant's retrial; although the retrial had been granted on the ground that the defendant's attorney had a fatal conflict of interest, the court did not hold that the cross-examination at the first trial was inadequate *per se,* particularly since the conflict had nothing to do with the unavailable witness; the court reviewed the substance of the record and found that trial counsel had made a serious effort to undermine and discredit the witness, pointing out inconsistencies in the witness's testimony, and found the testimony to be sufficiently reliable for admission under Rule 804(b)(1)); United States v. Monaco, 702 F.2d 860 (11th Cir. 1983); United States v. Franklin, 235 F. Supp. 338 (D.D.C. 1964). Courts have excluded prior testimony when the opportunity requirement of Rule 804(b)(1) has not been met. *See, e.g.,* Wetherill v. University of Chicago, 565 F. Supp. 1553 (N.D. Ill. 1983); *In re* Shangri-La Nursing Ctr., 31 B.R. 367 (E.D.N.Y. 1983); Matter of Sterling Navigation Co., 444 F. Supp. 1043 (S.D.N.Y. 1977).

[83] 2 MCCORMICK, § 302; United States v. DiNapoli 8 F.3d 909 (2d Cir. 1993) (en banc) (on remand from the Supreme Court, the Second Circuit determined the government did not have a motive to examine a witness during the grand jury testimony similar to what it would have had if the witness had testified at trial).

that direct examination should be considered the equivalent of cross-examination for the purposes of satisfying the prior testimony exception.[84] Because the opportunity for cross-examination is intended to protect a party against the evidence of an *adverse* witness, the party has no particular need to use such a device for a witness the party had offered at the prior trial. This common-law concept, coupled with the right to impeach a party's own witness under Rule 607, diminishes the problem to a significant degree. Accordingly, where the testimony of a witness at a prior trial is offered against the party who called the witness at the prior proceeding (or a successor in interest in a civil case), the "opportunity" requirements of Rule 804(b) may be satisfied.

The question may arise as to whether the opportunity requirement is satisfied where cross-examination testimony from a former proceeding is offered against the party who called the witness at the prior trial, hearing or deposition. In this context the issue focuses upon whether the party had an adequate opportunity to conduct a meaningful *redirect* examination of the witness as to the pertinent factual matter. As to the opportunity to conduct a redirect examination, the issues are essentially the same as those presented in the context of the opportunity to conduct a cross-examination, and the immediately preceding section of this Chapter sets forth the applicable analysis.

§ 804.14 "Identity of Issues" and "Identity of Parties" — Successor in Interest in Civil Cases

The former testimony exception at common law focused on whether the examination of the witness at the prior proceeding was substantially similar to what would have occurred at the current proceeding if the witness had testified.[85] Consequently, the common-law exception developed two related — though distinct — requirements: identity of parties and identity of issues.[86] These now obsolete requirements essentially represent an overly formalistic approach to fulfilling the goal of ensuring adequate development

---

[84] *See, e.g.,* 2 McCORMICK, § 303; 5 WEINSTEIN'S FEDERAL EVIDENCE § 804.04; Falknor, *Former Testimony and the Uniform Rules: A Comment*, 38 N.Y.U. L. REV. 651 (1963). Wigmore aptly explains:

> [T]he whole notion of cross-examination refers to one's right to probe the statements of an opponent's witness, not one's own witness; thus, if A has taken X's deposition or called X to the stand, and B has cross-examined, it is not for A to object that he has not had the benefit of cross-examination: that benefit was not intended for him nor needed by him; it was intended only to protect against an opponent's witness, who would be otherwise unexamined by A; and if A has had the benefit of examining a witness called on his own behalf, he has had all that he needs, and the right to probe by cross-examination is B's, not A's.

5 WIGMORE, § 1389, at 121.

[85] 5 WEINSTEIN'S FEDERAL EVIDENCE § 804.04.

[86] *Id.*

of the appropriate facts by the party against whom the testimony is now offered.[87] Rule 804(b)(1) abandons the strict common-law approach as to identity of issues in favor of the more critical consideration of ensuring that similar interests in developing facts are at stake in both proceedings. Consequently, Rule 804(b)(1) provides that former testimony may be admitted that ". . . is now offered against a party who had — or, in a civil case, whose predecessor in interest had — an opportunity and similar motive to develop it by direct, cross-, or redirect examination." As such, the Rule expands the common-law restrictions without abandoning the essential fairness policy supporting the common-law approach by focusing on the party against whom the hearsay is offered.

Rule 804(b)(1) reflects the historical concern "that it is generally unfair to impose upon the party against whom the hearsay evidence is being offered responsibility for the manner in which the witness was previously handled by another party"[88] except where, in a civil case, that other party was a predecessor in interest with a similar motive for interrogation. Consistent with this policy grounded in fairness, the relationship between the proponent of the prior testimony and any party in the prior proceeding is not significant in applying the Rule. Rather, it is the hearsay opponent's connection with the prior proceeding that is critical. The party against whom the hearsay is offered must have had an opportunity and similar motive to develop the testimony at the former proceeding, or in a civil case, his or her predecessor in interest must have had an opportunity and similar motive to develop the testimony.

The exact purport of the "predecessor in interest" language in the Rule is less than clear. The phrase could be narrowly construed as requiring privity between the opponent of the evidence and the party who had an opportunity to develop the testimony at the prior proceeding, as in the relationships of donor and donee, executor and testator, or principal and surety.[89] Conversely, the phrase could be read to require simply that the party to the prior proceeding, *i.e.* the predecessor, had a similar motive and "interest" as the present opponent. While such an expansive reading of this language would appear to reduce the opportunity requirement to a nullity, some federal courts interpreting the Rule, nevertheless, have read the language broadly to include virtually anyone who would satisfy the similar motive require-

---

[87] *See generally,* 5 WEINSTEIN'S FEDERAL EVIDENCE § 804.04; Advisory Committee Note, Rule 804(b)(1).

[88] Report of Committee on the Judiciary, House of Representatives, 93d Cong., 1st Sess., Federal Rules of Evidence, No. 93-650, p. 15 (1973).

[89] *See, e.g.,* Federal Deposit Ins. Corp. v. Glickman, 450 F.2d 416 (9th Cir. 1971) (in action by FDIC as bank receiver against obligor on promissory notes in favor of bank, proper to exclude testimony offered by government in prior criminal prosecution of bank president and another agent, offered in instant case by defendant to prove that another was agent); *see also* Metropolitan St. Ry. Co. v. Gumby, 99 F. 192 (2d Cir. 1900).

ment.[90] While perhaps reliability and fairness are not sacrificed by the broader interpretation of the predecessor in interest requirement, the stricter reading more logically comports with the customary meaning of the term "predecessor in interest," and moreover, it preserves the obvious intent of the Rule to require more than simply a similarity in motive as between the party developing the testimony at the prior proceeding and the party against whom it is offered in the instant proceeding.[91]

It should be noted that the flexibility in the Rule with respect to predecessors in interest expressly applies only in civil proceedings. Where the former testimony is offered against the accused in a criminal case, identity of parties is a strict requirement, a topic further discussed in § 804.16 of this Chapter.

§ 804.15 Similar Motive Requirement

The "similar motive" element of Rule 804(b)(1) is more expansive than the common-law identity of issues doctrine.[92] Different causes of action, additional issues, or a shift in theory are of no substantive consequence under the Rule and should not defeat admissibility.[93] At most what is required under Rule 804(b)(1) is that the *factual* issue upon which the testimony was offered in the prior proceeding must be the same as the *factual* issue upon which it is offered in the instant cause. Even this statement of the requirement of the Rule may be too restrictive in certain cases, and the similar motive requirement may be satisfied even in the absence of precise identity of *factual* issues. The Rule requires only a *similar* motive, not an *identical* motive, to develop or limit the testimony. The intent of the Rule is not to bind anyone to a position formerly adopted, as may be the theory in res judicata or collateral estoppel, but rather to salvage the testimonial evidence of a person now unavailable for its apparent worth. Consequently, the common-law identity of issue requirement is relaxed to provide that the issue in the prior proceeding (hence, the purpose for which the testimony was offered) must have been such that the present opponent had an adequate motive to test and further develop the prior testimony now

---

[90] Lloyd v. American Export Lines, 580 F.2d 1179 (3d Cir. 1978) (error in exclusion of testimony, preferring a "realistically generous" interpretation of the term "predecessor in interest" over "one that is formalistically grudging"); *see also* Clay v. Johns-Manville Sales Corp., 722 F.2d 1289 (6th Cir. 1983); *In re* Johns-Manville Asbestosis Cases, 93 F.R.D. 853 (N.D. Ill. 1982); *In re* Master Key Antitrust Litig., 72 F.R.D. 108 (D. Conn. 1976).

[91] *See* IBM Peripheral EDP Devices Antitrust Litig. v. IBM Corp., 444 F. Supp. 110 (N.D. Cal. 1978) (refusing to find parties in other cases predecessors in interest of party in instant case).

[92] 5 WEINSTEIN'S FEDERAL EVIDENCE § 804.04.

[93] *Id.* ("A shift in the theory of the case does not defeat admissibility when the underlying liability remains the same thereby guaranteeing cross-examination with the same purpose").

offered.[94] The Rule seeks to achieve fairness by imposing factual testimony on a party only where the party (or its predecessor in a civil case) had a motive to develop or, alternatively, to limit the weight of the testimony at the former proceeding.[95] Accordingly, the similar motive requirement should be read to mean "motive to develop *facts*" or "motive to *limit* the weight to be accorded the prior testimony."

The Rule treats former testimony and depositions equally,[96] despite the fact that a party may have a lessened or different motive to interrogate a deponent as opposed to a witness at trial. It is at least arguable that since the deposition is essentially a discovery technique, the motive to interrogate at a deposition is sufficiently distinct to preclude admissibility of statements of declarants taken during depositions. This argument, however, is grounded on faulty or obsolete premises and should not, *in itself*, lead to different treatment for depositions. Deponents may not be, and often are not expected to be, present at the trial or subsequent proceeding. Consequently, a party can rarely afford to forgo an opportunity to cross-examine and impeach the deponent, and any decision to defer interrogation should be seen as assuming the risk.[97] Even where the deposition is offered in a different proceeding than the one for which it was taken, if the opportunity and the similar motive requirements are satisfied, the hearsay generally should be admissible. The critical issue raised by Rule 804(b)(1) is whether to admit the evidence or completely sacrifice the testimony of the deponent, and, consequently, only genuinely dissimilar motives should result in exclusion.[98]

§ 804.16   Similar Motive — Criminal Proceedings — Constitutional Considerations

Rule 804(b)(1) is expressly applicable in criminal as well as civil proceedings. As is true with any hearsay offered in criminal cases, however, special problems may be presented by the accused's Sixth Amendment right to confront "the witnesses against him."[99]

---

[94] *See* 2 McCormick, § 304; 5 Weinstein's Federal Evidence § 804.04.

[95] Some courts have recognized the fairness policy of Rule 804(b)(1) when interpreting the rule. *See, e.g.,* DeLuryea v. Winthrop, 697 F.2d 222 (8th Cir. 1983); Complaint of Paducah Towing Co., 692 F.2d 412 (6th Cir. 1982); Lloyd v. American Export Lines, 580 F.2d 1179 (3d Cir. 1978); *In re* Johns-Manville Asbestosis Cases, 93 F.R.D. 853 (N.D. Ill. 1982); *In re* Master Key Antitrust Litig., 72 F.R.D. 108 (D. Conn. 1976).

[96] *See* Oberlin v. Marlin American Corp., 596 F.2d 1322 (7th Cir. 1979); Rutledge v. Electric Hose & Rubber Co., 327 F. Supp. 1267 (C.D. Cal. 1971), *aff'd,* 511 F.2d 668 (9th Cir. 1971).

[97] *Cf.* Wright Root Beer Co. v. Dr. Pepper Co., 414 F.2d 887 (5th Cir. 1969) (discovery depositions should be "fully admissible").

[98] 5 Weinstein's Federal Evidence § 804.04.

[99] *Id.*; § 804.1 *et seq., supra*; *see also* § 801.2, *supra*, for further discussion of Confrontation Clause issues. *See generally,* 4 Mueller & Kirkpatrick, § 491.

Where the government is unable through diligent efforts to produce the declarant at trial, however, the testimony of the declarant may be introduced against the accused under the former testimony exception where the testimony was adduced at a distinct trial of the accused and the earlier trial did not suffer from prejudicial constitutional infirmities.

More difficult problems, however, surround the use of testimony adduced at an accused's preliminary hearing on the charged offense. In this situation, it is at least arguable that, while an opportunity to cross-examine adverse witnesses at the preliminary hearing was presented, the "similar motive" to develop testimony does not exist. The interrogation at the preliminary hearing generally represents a "less searching exploration into the merits" of the government's case, because the issue under consideration is not the ultimate guilt or innocence of the accused but merely the existence of probable cause to believe that the accused committed the charged offense.[100] However, the United States Supreme Court in *Ohio v. Roberts,* has upheld the use against the accused of preliminary hearing testimony by a prosecution witness who was unavailable at trial.[101]

Finally, it should be noted that where the accused wishes to introduce former testimony qualifying under Rule 804(b)(1), the special constitutional problems under the confrontation clause are, of course, inapplicable, and in fact, due process may require admission of the testimony against the United States even though a state may have prosecuted the prior case.[102]

§ 804.17   Rule 804(b)(2) The Exceptions — Statement Under the Belief of Imminent Death

(b)   **The Exceptions.** The following are not excluded by the rule against hearsay if the declarant is unavailable as a witness:

***

(2)   *Statement Under the Belief of Imminent Death.* In a prosecution for homicide or in a civil case, a statement that the declarant, while believing the declarant's death to be

---

[100] Barber v. Page, 390 U.S. 719 (1968).

[101] Ohio v. Roberts, 448 U.S. 56 (1980). Although this case has been overruled in many other crucial respects, this aspect of the Court's holding in *Roberts* is surely still good law today, for the Court has reaffirmed that statements are never excluded by the Confrontation Clause as long as the witness is unavailable at the time of trial and the accused had a meaningful opportunity to cross-examine the witness at the time the statement was made. Crawford v. Washington, 541 U.S. 36 (2004); *see also* Giles v. California, 554 U.S. 353, 373 (2008) (dictum) ("Prior confronted statements by witnesses who are unavailable are admissible whether or not the defendant was responsible for their unavailability").

[102] *See* Chambers v. Mississippi, 410 U.S. 284 (1973); *cf.* United States v. Lanci, 669 F.2d 391 (6th Cir. 1982) (defendant's request to introduce testimony given in state criminal trial denied because state did not have "similar motive to develop facts concerning the bribery of an FBI employee").

imminent, made about its cause or circumstances.

The exception to the hearsay rule contained in Rule 804(b)(2) for statements traditionally known as "dying declarations" is a modern codification of the common-law doctrine.[103] It has been described by McCormick as ". . . the most mystical in its theory and traditionally the most arbitrary in its limitations."[104] The exception for deathbed statements, which developed in the common law well before the development of the general rule prohibiting hearsay, originally derived its assumed guarantee of trustworthiness from the religious belief that no person would want to "meet his maker with a lie on his lips."[105] In the more secular world, however, this rationale for the exception has largely been supplanted by the theory that the powerful psychological forces bearing on the declarant at the moment of death engender a compulsion to speak truthfully.[106] In any case, dying declarations are considered trustworthy because, given the restrictions on their use at trial, they are unlikely to be affected by problems in memory, although psychological stress and physical pain may as readily cause flaws in

---

[103] *See generally,* 2 McCORMICK, §§ 309–315; 5 WEINSTEIN'S FEDERAL EVIDENCE § 804.05; 4 MUELLER & KIRKPATRICK, § 495; 5 WIGMORE, §§ 1430–1452. *See also* Quick, *Some Reflections on Dying Declarations,* 6 HOW. L.J. 109 (1960); Comment, *The Admissibility of Dying Declarations,* 38 FORDHAM L. REV. 509 (1970); Note, *Dying Declarations,* 46 IOWA L. REV. 375 (1961).

[104] 2 McCORMICK, § 309; *see also* Quick, *Some Reflections on Dying Declarations,* 6 HOW. L.J. 109 (1960). *See generally,* 5 WIGMORE, § 1430. Notably, special reverence for the sincerity and veracity of deathbed statements was not lost upon the Bard, who expressed the doctrine long before it was accepted by judicial process. *E.g., Hamlet,* V, ii, 328–331 (1601) (Laertes: "[T]he foul practice / Hath turn'd itself on me; lo, here I lie, / Never to rise again: thy mother's poison'd: / I can no more: the king, the king's to blame"); *Henry IV, Part II,* IV, v, 182–188 (1598) (King Henry: "Come Hither, Harry, sit thou by my bed; / And hear, I think, the very latest counsel / That ever I shall breathe. God knows, my son, / By what by-paths and indirect crook'd ways / I met this crown; and I myself know well / How troublesome it sat upon my head"); *King John,* V, iv, 22–29 (1596) (Melun: "Have I not hideous death within my view, / Retaining but a quantity of life, / Which bleeds away, even as a form of wax / Resolveth from his figure 'gainst the fire? / What in the world should make me now deceive, / Since I must lose the use of all deceit? / Why should I then be false, since it is true / That I must die here and live hence by truth?").

[105] *See generally,* 4 MUELLER & KIRKPATRICK, § 495; 2 McCORMICK, § 309; 5 WEINSTEIN'S FEDERAL EVIDENCE § 804.05; 5 WIGMORE, § 1438.

[106] Advisory Committee Note, Rule 804(b)(2). Some commentators have looked askance at this exception's reliance upon modern psychological concepts for its primary justification. *See, e.g.,* Quick, *Some Reflections on Dying Declarations,* 6 HOW. L.J. 109, 112 (1960) ("Indeed, in many instances the declarant is either suffering from an appreciable amount of pain or anxiety which may itself cloud his perception and ability to communicate, or his perception and consciousness have been dulled by pain-depressant drugs"); Note, *Dying Declarations,* 46 IOWA L. REV. 357 (1961) (experience indicates that desires for revenge or self-exoneration or to protect one's loved ones may continue until the moment of death).

perception and narration.[107] It is for this reason that courts are, and should be, especially cautious in scrutinizing the admissibility of statements offered under this exception. The exception contained in Rule 804(b)(2) also rests in part upon the necessity principle.[108] The Rule does not require that the declarant be dead, but only unavailable as defined in Rule 804(a).[109] In the usual case, the words of the declarant are offered to prove that the accused was the murderer, and, in this situation, necessity assumes special importance in justifying the exception.

Rule 804(b)(2) admits hearsay statements of declarants who are under the belief that death is imminent, where the statement concerns the cause or circumstances of what the declarant believed to be impending death. Under the Rule the exception may be used in homicide cases, against or on behalf of the accused, as well as in any civil case. Accordingly, the Rule adopts the position of commentators that the reliability of the statement and its admissibility should not depend upon the character of the litigation in which it is offered.[110] If such statements are reliable against the accused in a

---

[107] One of the most notable and vociferous attacks against the dying declaration exception to the hearsay rule may be found in Kidd v. State, 258 S.2d 423, 429–430 (Miss. 1972) (Smith, J., concurring):

> [C]an it be said that a man who has been wounded and feels that he is dying, is by those circumstances alone, automatically stripped of all human malice, anger, and desire for revenge and is transformed *ipso facto* into a devout believer in life after death and in divine punishment? I cannot think so. Certainly the accused should not be deprived of his constitutional right to confrontation by the witnesses against him on a theory that meets neither the test of reason nor the facts of common knowledge and human experience. This harmful effect of the admission of this type of hearsay is enhanced by a recital of dramatic circumstances under which the statement is alleged to have been made, and the law having in effect declared this type of hearsay sacrosanct, there is no effective way to challenge its truth and it is more than just likely that the jury will attach undue importance to it and give it undue weight in arriving at a verdict.

See generally, 2 McCormick, § 314; 5 Weinstein's Federal Evidence § 804.05.

[108] *See* Carver v. United States, 164 U.S. 694 (1897) (dying declarations "are received from the necessitations of the case and to prevent an entire failure of justice, as it frequently happens that no other witnesses to the homicide are present."); Mattox v. United States, 146 U.S. 140 (1892) (mentioning "necessity" as reason for dying declaration exception and resolving the confrontation issue); United Services Auto. Asso. v. Wharton, 237 F. Supp. 255 (W.D.N.C. 1965) (in this case untested testimony held better than no testimony at all). *See generally,* 5 Wigmore, § 1436.

[109] *See* Advisory Committee Note, Rule 804(b)(2) ("unavailability is not limited to death"). Accordingly, where the subjective contemplation of death is present, an out-of-court statement may satisfy the exception where an unexpected recovery occurs and the declarant becomes unavailable for a reason identified in Rule 804(a) other than death.

[110] Wigmore condemned the limitation of the use of this Rule to certain types of cases:

> [I]t is as much consequence to the cause of justice that robberies and rapes be punished and torts and breaches of trust be redressed as that murders be detected; the notion that a crime is more worthy the attention of Courts than a civil wrong is a traditional relic of

homicide case, their reliability should not be diminished in, for example, a wrongful death action. Dying declarations remain, however, inadmissible in any criminal cases other than homicides.[111]

Additionally, Rule 804(b)(2) discards the common-law requirement that dying declarations be "voluntary" and uttered "in good faith." Commonly, these requirements were imposed to exclude statements made in response to questioning by bystanders, relatives, police officers, or investigators, and these requirements were especially designed to address questionable techniques of prodding answers out of a dying person.[112] In discarding these arbitrary restrictions, the Rule tacitly recognizes that the "good faith" element is satisfied by the declarant's belief in the imminence of death. Moreover, the "voluntariness" of any statement, as determined by the circumstances surrounding its making may be evaluated by the trial court under Rule 403.

Although Rule 804(b)(2) does not expressly so provide, the firsthand knowledge requirement of Rule 602 is applicable to the out-of-court statement of the declarant. Foundational evidence must be presented to permit the inference "that there was knowledge or the opportunity for knowledge as to the acts that are declared."[113]

§ 804.18   Requirement That Declarant Possess Subjective Belief in Certainty of Death — Spontaneity

Rule 804(b)(2) expressly provides that before a dying declaration may be admitted, foundational evidence must establish that the declarant possessed a subjective belief in the certainty of his or her death. In theory, it is subjective consciousness of the death that critically reduces the motivation for fabrication. There is no standard rule of thumb here, and the requisite

---

the days when civil justice was administered in the royal courts as a purchased favor, and criminal prosecutions in the King's name were zealously encouraged because of the fines which they added to the royal revenues . . . . The sanction of a dying declaration is equally efficacious whether it speaks of a murder or a robbery or a fraudulent will; and the necessity being the same, the admissibility should be the same . . . [The] limitations are heresies of the last century, which have not even the sanction of antiquity.

5 WIGMORE, § 1436; *see also* 2 MCCORMICK, § 311 ("The subsequent history of the rule is an object lesson in the dangers of the use by the judges of our system of precedents to preserve and fossilize judicial mistakes of an earlier generation."). *See generally,* 5 WEINSTEIN'S FEDERAL EVIDENCE § 804.05; Quick, *Some Reflections on Dying Declarations,* 6 HOW. L.J. 109 (1960).

[111] 5 WEINSTEIN'S FEDERAL EVIDENCE § 804.05.

[112] *See* discussion in § 804.18, *infra.*

[113] *See* Shepard v. United States, 290 U.S. 96 (1933); *see also* 2 MCCORMICK, § 313 ("If it appears that the declarant did not have adequate opportunity to observe the facts recounted, the declaration will be rejected for want of the knowledge qualification") (citing Mattox v. United States, 146 U.S. 140 (1892)). *See generally,* 5 WIGMORE, § 1445(2) and cases cited therein.

consciousness may be gleaned from many sources, including: the declarant's own words, the opinions of the attending physicians, the nature and extent of the wounds or illness, the fact that last rites were given, the statements made to the declarant about his or her condition, and similar circumstantial facts.[114] Moreover, the standard is subjective, and not what a "reasonable person" under similar conditions would believe regarding the imminence of his demise.[115] As long as the declarant subjectively believes in the certainty of the impending death, or as Justice Cardozo cogently notes, "a settled hopeless expectation that death is near at hand,"[116] the statement concerning its cause or surrounding circumstances satisfies the instant requirement.

It must be noted that the exception for dying declarations presumes that the declarant's statements possess a degree of spontaneity, thus resembling the underlying characteristics of the exceptions for present sense impressions under Rule 803(1) and excited utterances under Rule 803(2). This element is reflected in the Rule's use of the word "imminent." This spontaneity element, however, should not be viewed as imposing a particular time limit on the amount of time that may elapse between the making of the statement and the expected moment of death of the declarant. No doubt, since the Rule requires the expectancy of death to be *imminent*, knowledge of a terminally ill or fatally wounded declarant that death is likely to arrive in a matter of years, months, weeks or, in some cases, days should not suffice. Although it may generally be said that as more time passes between the utterance of the statement and the death of the declarant, it becomes less probable that the declarant believed death to be imminent,[117] the primary focus of the trial court should be on the presence of physical and psychological forces tending to ensure reliability in the substance of the statement.[118]

---

[114] *See, e.g.,* United States v. Barnes, 464 F.2d 828 (D.C. Cir. 1972) (belief in imminent death proved by declarant's statements and extent of injuries); United States v. Mobley, 421 F.2d 345 (5th Cir. 1970) (by what declarant has been told about illness or injuries and by physicians' opinions).

[115] *See* 4 MUELLER & KIRKPATRICK, § 495.

[116] Shepard v. United States, 290 U.S. 96 (1933); *see also* 5 WIGMORE, § 1440, at 292–293 ("It follows from the general principle that the belief must be, not merely of the possibility of death, nor even of its probability, but of its *certainty*. A less stringent rule might with safety have been adopted; but this is the accepted one") (emphasis in original).

[117] *See, e.g.,* Pfeil v. Rogers, 757 F.2d 850 (7th Cir. 1985) (declarant's statements preceding suicide were not admissible because they were not made immediately before suicide and so were not in contemplation of death); United States v. Tovar, 687 F.2d 1210 (8th Cir. 1982); United States v. Etheridge, 424 F.2d 951 (6th Cir. 1970) (approving receipt of statement by victim for dying declaration where he had been shot five times in the head and his own statements indicated that he contemplated death, notwithstanding the fact that declarant asked for an ambulance, since he did die shortly after making the declaration of naming his assailant).

[118] 4 MUELLER & KIRKPATRICK, § 495; 5 WEINSTEIN'S FEDERAL EVIDENCE § 804.05;

In this regard the fact that the statement was solicited does not, *per se*, preclude use of the instant exception. Often, a person in the throes of death may quite understandably be disposed "more toward silence than conversation, and the stimulus of a question may be essential" in eliciting information.[119] In fact, rational answers to pertinent inquiries may demonstrate the unlikelihood of misperception or a mistake in narration, thereby enhancing trustworthiness. Where it appears, however, that the interrogative technique was unduly burdensome or leading, so as to raise reasonable suspicions about the statement's accuracy, the trial court should exclude the statement under Rule 403.

§ 804.19　Requirement That Subject Pertain to "Cause or Circumstances" of Death

In conformity with the traditional common-law requirements, Rule 804(b)(2) requires that the statement concern "the cause or circumstances" while "believing the declarant's death to be imminent."[120] Some commentators have criticized the rule as too vague or too susceptible of narrow application.[121]

The limitation presents little problem in its application where a victim identifies the murderer and characterizes the attack as unprovoked. Similarly, the statement qualifies if it describes the accident or occurrence causing the declarant mortal injury.[122] More difficult problems, however,

---

see, e.g., Shepard v. United States, 290 U.S. 96, 99 (1933) ("[W]hat is decisive is the state of mind. Even so, the state of mind must be exhibited in the evidence, and not left to conjecture. The patient must have spoken with the consciousness of a swift and certain doom").

[119] 4 MUELLER & KIRKPATRICK, § 495. Statements made under the belief of imminent death may be solicited. *See* United States v. Barnes, 464 F.2d 828 (D.C. Cir. 1972); United States v. Etheridge, 424 F.2d 951 (6th Cir. 1970).

[120] 5 WIGMORE, § 1434, at 282 ("It must concern the facts leading up to or causing or attending the injurious act which has resulted in the declarant's death; for it is only to such facts that the supposed necessity for the statements can exist"). *See generally,* 4 MUELLER & KIRKPATRICK, § 495; 5 WEINSTEIN'S FEDERAL EVIDENCE § 804.05.

[121] *See* 5 WIGMORE, § 1434 (doctrine provides "opportunity for prolific quibbling"); 2 MCCORMICK, § 311; Quick, *Some Reflections on Dying Declarations,* 6 HOW. L.J. 109 (1960).

[122] United States v. Barnes, 464 F.2d 828 (D.C. Cir. 1972); United States v. Etheridge, 424 F.2d 951 (6th Cir. 1970); *see also* United States v. Mobley, 421 F.2d 345 (5th Cir. 1970) (statement by bank president, who had been beaten and shot in course of robbery, was a dying declaration, since declarant knew he was dying and had been told "that he would be able to see his family, his minister, and bank officials"); United Services Auto. Asso. v. Wharton, 237 F. Supp. 255 (W.D.N.C. 1965) (statement made by driver just prior to accident to the passenger [his wife] that "we will go to eternity together" as he put the accelerator on the floorboard and turned the car deliberately head-on into the tractor trailer, and further that he "did it on purpose" clearly qualifies as a dying declaration, even though the end anticipated by the declarant did not befall him).

arise where the statement relates not to direct causes, but to "circumstances" spatially or temporally removed from the declarant's expected death. Assertions concerning a previous threat or an earlier argument between the parties, or even those describing past physical pain or substances ingested or injected are illustrative. While a broad reading of the Rule would permit introduction of such statements, the trial court must nevertheless focus on the nexus between the time and circumstances of the event and the expected death in an effort to determine whether the declarant's subjective purpose is to describe the cause or circumstances of the expected death.[123] The determinant of admissibility here is, simply, whether the evidence will aid the trier of fact in ascertaining the truth, *i.e.*, whether it is sufficiently trustworthy and relevant to withstand the exclusionary provision of Rule 403.[124]

Rule 701's test of "helpfulness" should also resolve objections to the form of the statement where the declaration is phrased in terms of an opinion.[125] Where the requirements of firsthand knowledge and belief of imminent death are satisfied, a statement in opinion form should be admitted if it will help the fact-finding process, a contingency generally satisfied in light of the declarant's unavailability.

§ 804.20   Rule 804(b)(3) The Exceptions — Statement Against Interest

   (b)   **The Exceptions.** The following are not excluded by the rule against hearsay if the declarant is unavailable as a witness:

   ***

   (3)   ***Statement Against Interest.*** A statement that:

   (A)   a reasonable person in the declarant's position would have made only if the person believed it to be true because, when made, it was so contrary to the de-

---

[123] *See, e.g.,* Carver v. United States, 160 U.S. 553 (1896), *later appeal,* 164 U.S. 69 (1896) (endorses receipt of statement by murder victim as dying declaration; victim was shot on March 25, her statement was made on March 27, and she died on May 19); Mattox v. United States, 146 U.S. 140, 151–152 (1892), *later appeal,* 156 U.S. 237 (1895) ("[T]he length of time elapsing between the making of the declaration and the death is one of the elements to be considered, although . . . it is the impression of almost immediate dissolution, and not the rapid succession of death, in point of fact, that renders the testimony admissible").

[124] *See generally,* 5 WEINSTEIN'S FEDERAL EVIDENCE § 804.05.

[125] *See* 5 WIGMORE, § 1447, at 308:

   The theory of [the opinion rule] is that, wherever the witness can state specifically the detailed facts observed by him, the inferences to be drawn from them can equally well be drawn by the jury, so that the witness' inferences become superfluous. Now, since the declarant is here deceased, it is no longer possible to obtain from him by questions any more detailed data than his statement may contain, and hence his inferences are not in this instance superfluous.

clarant's proprietary or pecuniary interest or had so great a tendency to invalidate the declarant's claim against someone else or to expose the declarant to civil or criminal liability; and

(B) is supported by corroborating circumstances that clearly indicate its trustworthiness, if it is offered in a criminal case as one that tends to expose the declarant to criminal liability.

Rule 804(b)(3) codifies the common-law exception to the hearsay rule for statements against interest.[126] The Rule embraces the traditional exception for statements against the financial or proprietary interests of the declarant and statements that tend to subject the declarant to civil liability.[127] It significantly expands the traditional pre-Rule doctrine, however, to include statements that tend to subject the declarant to criminal punishment — statements against "penal" interest.[128] Insofar as the statement is against the

---

[126] *See generally,* 2 MCCORMICK, §§ 316–320; 5 WEINSTEIN'S FEDERAL EVIDENCE § 804.06; 4 MUELLER & KIRKPATRICK, §§ 496–503; 5 WIGMORE, §§ 1455–1477. *See also* Donelan, *An Increase in Interest,* FBI Law Enforcement Bulletin, May-July, 1974, 27; Fine, *Declarations Against Penal Interest in New York: Carte Blanche?,* 21 SYR. L. REV. 1095 (1970); Jefferson, *Declarations Against Interest: An Exception to the Hearsay Rule,* 58 HARV. L. REV. 1 (1944); Morgan, *Declarations Against Interest,* 5 VAND. L. REV. 451 (1952); Reimer, *Admissibility of Third Party Declarations Against a Surety Under Fidelity Covers,* INSURANCE COUNCIL JOURNAL, April, 1973, 306; Note, *Declaration Against Penal Interest Recognized as an Exception to the Hearsay Rule,* 1977 WASH. U. L.Q. 349; Note, *Declaration Against Penal Interest: What Must be Corroborated Under the Newly Enacted Federal Rules of Evidence,* Rule 804(b)(3)?, 9 VAL. U.L. REV. 421 (1975); Comment, *Evidence—The Unavailability Requirement of Declaration Against Interest Hearsay,* 55 IOWA L. REV. 477 (1969); Note, *Declarations Against Interest: A Critical Review of the Unavailability Requirement,* 52 CORNELL L.Q. 301 (1967).

[127] *See generally,* 2 MCCORMICK, § 316; 5 WIGMORE, §§ 1458–1467.

[128] Wigmore, as well as other eminent scholars, long assailed the limitation against statements tending to subject the declarant to criminal liability, characterizing it as a "barbarous doctrine," noting:

> [I]t cannot be justified on grounds of policy. The only plausible reason of policy that has ever been advanced for such a limitation is the policy of procuring fabricated testimony to such an admission if oral. This is the ancient rusty weapon that has always been brandished to oppose any reform in the rules of evidence, *viz.,* the argument of danger of abuse. This would be a good argument against admitting any witnesses at all, for it is notorious that some witnesses will lie and that it is difficult to avoid being deceived by their lies. The truth is that any rule which hampers an honest man in exonerating himself is a bad rule, even if it also hampers a villain in falsely passing for an innocent.

5 WIGMORE, § 1477, at 358–59; *see also* 2 MCCORMICK, § 318 ("[T]he argument of the danger of perjury is a dubious one since the danger is one that attends all human testimony"); Jefferson, *Declarations Against Interest: An Exception to the Hearsay Rule,* 58 HARV. L. REV. 1, 39 (1944) ("[P]enal interest is certainly as important to a person as pecuniary or

declarant's penal interest, the Rule imposes the safeguard that the statement, if offered under this exception at a criminal trial, must be "supported by corroborating circumstances that clearly indicate its trustworthiness."[129]

While Rule 804(b)(3) generally allows the trier of fact to consider statements against interest, Rule 403 nevertheless enables the trial judge to exclude statements otherwise qualifying under the exception where surrounding circumstances indicate that the probative value is substantially outweighed by the danger of its unfair prejudicial effect or tendency to confuse or mislead the trier of fact.[130]

Rule 804(b)(3) does not include within its scope statements that would be against the "social" interest of the declarant, *i.e.,* those tending to make the declarant "an object of hatred, ridicule, or disgrace" in his community.[131] Where only "social" interests are concerned, the requisite guarantees of

---

proprietary interest"); Morgan, *Declarations Against Interest*, 5 VAND. L. REV. 451, 475 (1952) ("settled foolish rule"). Justice Holmes, dissenting in Donnelly v. United States, 228 U.S. 243, 277 (1913), was no less vehement in his protest of the historical restriction:

> [T]he exception to the hearsay rule in the case of declarations against interest is well known; no other statement is so much against interest as a confession of murder; it is far more calculated to convince than dying declarations, which would be let in to hang a man; and when we surround the accused with so many safeguards, some of which seem to me excessive, I think we ought to give him the benefit of a fact that, if proved, commonly would have such weight.

Rule 804(b)(3) recognizes this criticism and expands the common law to include statements against penal interest, if corroborated.

[129] Rule 804(b)(3)(B). This corroboration requirement was advanced by Justice Holmes, dissenting in Donnelly v. United States, 228 U.S. 243 (1913), who argued for admission of a declaration against penal interest, when "coupled with circumstances pointing to its truth," and noted that one such factor would be that there existed no connection between the declarant and the accused. *See also* 2 MCCORMICK, § 318; 5 WEINSTEIN'S FEDERAL EVIDENCE § 804.06.

[130] 5 WEINSTEIN'S FEDERAL EVIDENCE § 804.06; *e.g.,* United States v. Love, 592 F.2d 1022 (8th Cir. 1979) (prior grand jury testimony offered by government properly excluded, since witness had formally been granted immunity prior to her grand jury testimony).

[131] As proposed by the Supreme Court, Rule 804(b)(3) included statements against these social interests, but Congress deleted the provision. *See* H.R. Rep. No. 93-650, 93d Cong., 1st Sess., pp. 15–16 (1973). The restriction against statements contrary to so-called "social interest," although in conformity with the common law, has been attacked by a number of commentators. *See, e.g.,* 2 MCCORMICK, § 318 ("Declarations against social interests, such as acknowledgements of facts which would subject the declarant to ridicule or disgrace, or facts calculated to arouse in the declarant a sense of shame or remorse, seem adequately buttressed in trustworthiness and should be received under the present principle"); Jefferson, *Declarations Against Interest: An Exception to the Hearsay Rule*, 58 HARV. L. REV. 1, 39 (1944) ("[O]ne [is not] likely to concede the existence of facts which would make him an object of social disapproval in the community unless the facts are true"); Morgan, *Declarations Against Interest*, 5 VAND. L. REV. 451, 475 (1952) ("[I]t requires no argument to convince that the realization of such a consequence is generally a much more powerful influence upon conduct, than the realization of legal responsibility for a sum of money").

trustworthiness are not thought sufficiently high to outweigh the danger that, in a world of rapidly changing moral attitudes, the statement may not have been against the declarant's interest as perceived by the declarant.

The foundational requirements for statements against interest under Rule 804(b)(3) are: (i) the declarant must be unavailable as defined in Rule 804(a); (ii) the declarant must have firsthand knowledge as contemplated by Rule 602; (iii) the nature of the statement must be such that a reasonable person would not have uttered it unless believing it to be true; and (iv) the statement must be contrary to a pecuniary, proprietary or penal interest of the declarant at the time of its utterance.[132] In addition, if the statement is offered in a criminal case and is one that tends to expose the declarant to criminal liability, there must be corroboration tending to guarantee the statement's trustworthiness.[133] The trial court must determine whether these foundational requirements are met pursuant to Rule 104(a). Since the requirements are derived from the rationale underlying the Rule, where any one is wanting, the statement may not be admitted under Rule 804(b)(3). Nothing, however, would preclude the statement's admission pursuant to some other hearsay exception, such as that for business records, Rule 803(6),[134] or public records, Rule 803(8).[135]

Until recently, this hearsay exception was very widely used by prosecutors as a vehicle for admitting statements that were made to law enforcement authorities by the accused's codefendants or alleged conspirators or partners in crime at some time after their arrest, perhaps even during plea negotiations or at the entry of a guilty plea.[136] Indeed, for many years such cases

---

[132] *See generally,* 2 McCORMICK, § 316; 5 WEINSTEIN'S FEDERAL EVIDENCE § 804.06; 5 WIGMORE, § 1471.

[133] *See, e.g.,* United States v. Toney, 599 F.2d 787 (6th Cir. 1979) (reversible error to exclude statement that was against interest because it "revealed his illicit gambling activities" and disclosed that he had "been gambling with a large sum of money a few hours after the bank robbery"); *see also* 5 WEINSTEIN'S FEDERAL EVIDENCE § 804.06; *cf.* United States v. Salvador, 820 F.2d 558 (2d Cir. 1987) (in drug prosecution, trial court properly excluded conspirator's statements exculpating the accused where there was no corroborating evidence). A court may look for corroboration even in a civil case. *See, e.g.,* American Automotive Accessories, Inc. v. Fishman, 175 F.3d 534 (7th Cir. 1999) (in civil action, employee caught in a check-cashing scheme made statements implicating defendant and then invoked Fifth Amendment; the statements were inadmissible because they lacked requisite corroborating circumstances and had been made for self-serving purposes).

[134] *See* § 803.28 *et seq., supra.*

[135] *See* § 803.39 *et seq., supra.*

[136] *See, e.g.,* Williamson v. United States, 512 U.S. 594 (1994), discussed more fully *infra,* § 804.23. These statements frequently fit the requirements of Rule 804(b)(3), because a statement is always against the penal interest of the declarant if it implicates both men in some common criminal activity, and the declarants of such statements are often unavailable by the time of their friend's trial because they have had a change of heart about co-operating with the government (typically because they have not received the plea deal they had hoped

accounted for a very large percentage of all evidence admitted under this exception. That once-common practice is now forbidden by the Supreme Court's recent decision in *Crawford v. Washington,*[137] which held that the Confrontation Clause absolutely precludes the admission of such testimonial statements against any defendant who did not make the statement, whether the statement implicates the declarant or the accused or both, where the defendant did not have the opportunity to cross-examine the declarant with respect to the statement.[138] That ruling will take an enormous bite out of the operation of this hearsay exception in criminal cases, and judges and lawyers must now proceed with great caution in placing any reliance on the extensive case law decided before 2004 involving the admission of evidence against the accused in a criminal case under this exception to the hearsay rule. As a practical matter, *Crawford* now dictates that this exception will be of no value to prosecutors at all, except for self-incriminating statements that were made by the defendant's alleged partners in crime to people other than the police (such as, for example, statements to their spouses and friends) and therefore were not testimonial.

§ 804.21 Statements of a Party-Opponent Distinguished

It is critical to appreciate the distinction between declarations constituting statements against interest, as identified in Rule 804(b)(3), and statements of a party-opponent, as defined in Rule 801(d)(2). The two are easily confused, because both involve kinds of statements that are adverse to the interest of the individual who made the statement at some point in time. When a statement is made by a *party* to some case and is offered against that party by an opposing party, it is admissible as "An Opposing Party's Statement" under Rule 801(d)(2); under such circumstances, the statement is typically

---

for), and so have decided instead to claim their Fifth Amendment privilege at his trial. Remember that this exception is usually not needed for the admission of statements made by the defendant's conspirators and accessories *before* they are arrested or learn that they are talking to the police, because such statements are often admissible under 801(d)(2)(E) as statements in furtherance of the conspiracy.

[137] Crawford v. Washington, 541 U.S. 36 (2004).

[138] As one example of "plainly testimonial statements" that may never be admitted against a defendant who did not have the chance to cross-examine the declarant, the Court cited the formerly common federal practice of admitting evidence of a "plea allocution" by the accused's codefendant for the purpose of "showing [the] existence of a conspiracy." *Crawford,* 541 U.S. at 64. After *Crawford,* it is clear that plea allocutions are testimonial, since they are made in open court, under oath, and in response to structured questioning by the trial judge or the prosecutor, and those cases are surely correct. United States v. Reifler, 446 F.3d 65, 86–87 (2d Cir. 2006); United States v. Al-Sadawi, 432 F.3d 419, 425–426 (2d Cir. 2005); United States v. Zhou, 428 F.3d 361, 374 (2d Cir. 2005). *See* § 801.2, *supra,* for a more detailed discussion of these issues. Likewise, self-incriminating statements made to police officers by criminal suspects are also certainly testimonial in this sense, and just as clearly forbidden by the Confrontation Clause if offered against other suspects who did not make those statements.

against the interest of the speaker at the time it is used against him at trial — that is, after all, what makes the evidence relevant as part of his opponent's case. Under Rule 801(d)(2), statements offered at trial against the person who made the statement are admissible without regard to whether the declarant is unavailable, whether the statement was against any particular interest when made, whether the party had any firsthand knowledge of the underlying events, or whether any sort of "reasonable person" test is satisfied. Since the underlying theory of admissions by a party-opponent essentially rests upon principles of estoppel, rather than upon circumstantial guarantees of trustworthiness, the prerequisites to the introduction of statements against interest are not applicable to statements by a party-opponent. A statement admitted under Rule 804(b)(3), on the other hand, must have had apparent adverse consequences for the declarant *at the time of its utterance*. When the requirements of Rule 804(b)(3) are met, the statement is admissible even though the speaker is typically not a party and has no relationship with any party to the case.

§ 804.22   Rationale

Like the other hearsay exceptions contained in Rules 803 and 804, the exception for statements against interest is predicated upon the dual grounds of necessity and trustworthiness. The necessity principle is reflected by the requirement that the declarant be unavailable. Where unavailability is demonstrated, there exists a genuine need to accept the declarant's out-of-court statement, since obtaining evidence from the same source is otherwise impossible.[139]

The guarantee of trustworthiness is traditionally presumed to be present for statements against interest because human experience indicates that a statement asserting a fact distinctly against the declarant's interest is unlikely to be deliberately false or heedlessly incorrect. Consequently, statements conforming to Rule 804(b)(3) are admissible despite the fact that oath and cross-examination are wanting.[140] Accordingly, assertions adverse to a declarant's proprietary (*i.e.,* concerning interests in real or personal property), pecuniary (*i.e.,* concerning financial interests or acquisitions), or penal (*i.e.,* concerning one's liberty) interests are admitted on the theory that the sanctions of a judicial oath and cross-examination are justifiably

---

[139] *See* 5 WIGMORE, § 1456, at 326. ("The necessity principle, . . . as here applied, signifies the impossibility of obtaining other evidence from the same source, the declarant being unavailable in person on the stand. Whenever the witness is practically unavailable, his statements should be received") A discussion of the principles and requirements of unavailability is contained in § 804.1 *et seq., supra.*

[140] *See generally,* 5 WEINSTEIN'S FEDERAL EVIDENCE § 804.06; 4 MUELLER & KIRKPATRICK, § 496; 5 WIGMORE, §§ 1457–1464; 2 McCORMICK, § 316; Jefferson, *Declarations Against Interest: An Exception to the Hearsay Rule,* 58 HARV. L. REV. 1 (1944); Morgan, *Declarations Against Interest,* 5 VAND. L. REV. 451 (1952); Comment, *Hearsay Under the Proposed Federal Rules: A Discretionary Approach,* 15 WAYNE L. REV. 1079 (1969).

supplanted by the powerful sanction of self-interest, a human characteristic that accounts for the fact that people so very rarely say anything that could get themselves into financial or legal trouble that they know or believe they do *not* deserve. Although people are notoriously dishonest and unreliable when making statements about themselves, such dishonesty and exaggeration is virtually always of the sort that puts the speaker in a *better* light than the facts would warrant, not worse.

The generalized psychological theory supporting the admissibility of statements against interest may be superficially appealing, but the fact remains that common experience also teaches that individuals will fabricate or tell half-truths despite the personal consequences in order to protect friends or family members, to incriminate enemies or for other reasons.[141] Moreover, a person may inadvertently make a statement adverse to his or her personal interest, or may make an ambiguous statement that can be construed in different ways.[142] It is judicial cognizance of these facets of human nature that underlies the time-honored requirement that the need for the statement be supported by the unavailability of the declarant.[143]

§ 804.23   Admission of "Statement" of "Fact Asserted" Therein — "Reasonable Person" Test

The underlying rationale of Rule 804(b)(3) implicitly raises the problem of whether the statement itself or only the fact asserted in the statement must be adverse to the declarant's interest. While Rule 804(b)(3) provides that any "*statement* . . . contrary to . . . interest" is admissible, commentators like

---

[141] 5 WEINSTEIN'S FEDERAL EVIDENCE § 804.06; *cf.* United States v. Beydler, 120 F.3d 985 (9th Cir. 1997) (trial court erred in allowing detective to testify as to statements made by individual who implicated both himself and defendant in armed robbery where the declarant's statements were made in an isolated location in response to an undisguised threat couched in an invitation to make a deal); United States v. Paguio, 114 F.3d 928 (9th Cir. 1997) ("[a] motive of love might . . . induce a reasonable father to make a false self-inculpatory statement in order to save his son"); Lee v. Illinois, 476 U.S. 530 (1986) (declining to characterize a co-defendant's confession as a statement against penal interest because of a "codefendant's desire to shift or spread blame, curry favor, avenge himself, or divert attention to another").

[142] United States v. Guzman, 603 F.3d 99 (1st Cir. 2010) (statement by a person admitting his role in commission of arson was admissible at the request of the defense as a "statement against interest," even though the witness who heard the statement described it as "joking"; that allegation went to the weight of the evidence and not its admissibility).

[143] *See, e.g.,* United States v. Matlock, 415 U.S. 164 (1974) (statements by woman co-habitating with defendant were against her penal interest and carried their own indicia of reliability; statements would be admissible only if declarant were unavailable); Dutton v. Evans, 400 U.S. 74 (1970) (receipt of statement did not violate defense confrontation rights; making the statement was "against his penal interest"); Donnelly v. United States, 228 U.S. 243 (1913) (Holmes' dissenting opinion noting that "no other statement is so much against interest as a confession of murder").

Wigmore,[144] Morgan,[145] and to a more circumspect degree, McCormick,[146] have maintained that the *fact* must be contrary to a declarant's interest. These commentators have asserted generally that it is only because the fact is against interest that the overt and purposeful mention of it is likely to be true.

For the most part, this distinction will prove to be little more than academic quibbling because both the fact and the statement are likely to be against the declarant's interest. However, in some situations the distinction may be important. For example, in some cases the fact may be against the declarant's interest but the statement is not because it is made to the declarant's attorney or spouse and therefore is subject to a privilege. In this situation, if one focuses on the *fact asserted*, the historical guarantee of trustworthiness is present; but, if one focuses on the *statement* and the situation in which the declarant communicated, the indicia of reliability are not present. Under these facts, a restrictive application of the Rule would preclude admission of the statement if the privilege should be waived or avoided after the making of the statement.

A related issue pertains to whether the scope of the exception applies only to statements that are individually contrary to the declarant's interest, or whether the exception also applies to collateral statements made as part of the same declaration. The Supreme Court addressed this issue in *Williamson v. United States,*[147] In *Williamson,* a man named Harris was stopped for weaving on the highway, and a search of his vehicle revealed 19 kilograms of cocaine. Shortly after Harris's arrest, he was interviewed two times by a DEA officer. During these interviews, Harris identified Williamson as the cocaine's owner. After Harris refused to testify at Williamson's trial, the district court ruled that the DEA agent could recount the content of his interviews with Harris under the Rule 804(b)(3) exception for statements against penal interest, due to the fact that Harris had freely admitted to

---

[144] *See* 5 WIGMORE, § 1462, at 337:

It must be remembered that it is not merely the statement that must be against interest, but the fact *stated*. It is because the fact is against interest that the open and deliberate mention of it is likely to be true. Hence the question whether the *statement* of the fact could create liability is beside the mark.

(emphasis in original).

[145] Morgan, BASIC PROBLEMS OF EVIDENCE, 291–92 (1963) (a ". . . declarant's subjective stimulus to tell the truth lies in the disserving quality of the fact declared").

[146] *See* 2 MCCORMICK, § 316 ("[T]he declaration must state facts which are against the pecuniary or proprietary interest of the declarant, or the making of the declaration itself must create evidence which would endanger his pocketbook if the statement were true"); *see also* Jefferson, *Declarations Against Interest: An Exception to the Hearsay Rule*, 58 HARV. L. REV. 1, 60 (1944) ("The probability of trustworthiness comes from the facts asserted being disserving in character"). *See generally,* 5 WEINSTEIN'S FEDERAL EVIDENCE § 804.06; 4 MUELLER & KIRKPATRICK, § 496.

[147] Williamson v. United States, 512 U.S. 594 (1994).

receiving the cocaine and, in doing so, had identified Williamson as the cocaine's owner.

The Supreme Court reversed the district court's ruling on the interpretation of the term "statement" as used in Rule 804(b)(3). While agreeing that the district court's ruling would have been correct under an expansive reading of the statutory term "statement" that would encompass extended declarations, the Court held that "the most faithful reading of Rule 804(b)(3) is that it does not allow admission of non-self-inculpatory statements, even if they are made within a broader narrative that is generally self-inculpatory."[148] The Court reasoned that, although the term "statement" could mean either an extended declaration or a single remark, the principles behind the Rule point toward the narrower reading.[149] Rule 804 "is founded on the commonsense notion that reasonable people, even reasonable people who are not especially honest, tend not to make self-inculpatory statements unless they believe them to be true."[150] This rationale does not extend to the more expansive interpretation of "statement," as the safeguards usually associated with self-inculpatory statements do not enhance the credibility of the non-self-inculpatory parts of a generally self-inculpatory statement.[151] As the Court observed, "[o]ne of the most effective ways to lie is to mix falsehood with truth, especially truth that seems particularly persuasive because of its self-inculpatory nature."[152]

Where a statement includes self-serving and disserving facts, the trial court should attempt to sever the statement, admitting only that portion which is supported by the underlying rationale, *i.e.,* that against interest.[153]

---

[148] *Williamson,* 512 U.S. at 600–601.

[149] *Id.* at 599.

[150] *Id.*

[151] *Id.*

[152] *Id.* at 599–600.

[153] Most commentators support the concept of severance. *E.g.,* 2 MCCORMICK, § 319:

When a declaration contains statements of facts in favor of interest, and in addition statements of facts against interest, three methods of handling the evidence under this exception have been advocated. First, admit the entire declaration because part is disserving and hence by a kind of contagion of truthfulness, all will be trustworthy. Second, compare the strength of the self-serving interest and the disserving interest in making the statement as a whole, and admit it all if the disserving interest preponderates, and exclude it all if the self-serving interest is greater. Third, admit the disserving parts of the declaration, and exclude the self-serving parts. The third solution seems the most realistic method of adjusting admissibility to trustworthiness, where the serving and disserving parts can be severed.

See generally, 4 MUELLER & KIRKPATRICK, § 496; 5 WEINSTEIN'S FEDERAL EVIDENCE § 804.06; 5 WIGMORE, § 1464; Morgan, *Declarations Against Interest,* 5 VAND. L. REV. 451 (1952). A more cautious approach is advocated by Professor Jefferson. *See* Jefferson, *Declarations Against Interest: An Exception to the Hearsay Rule,* 58 HARV. L. REV. 1, 60

It cannot be emphasized strongly enough that the once-important statutory issue decided by the Court in *Williamson* will arise much less frequently after the Court's recent decision in *Crawford v. Washington*,[154] which held that the Confrontation Clause absolutely precludes the admission of testimonial statements by a criminal suspect to the police, when those statements are offered against any defendant who did not make the statement, regardless of whether the statement directly implicates the declarant or the accused or both.[155] Indeed, if another case arose today involving the facts that were present in *Williamson*, there is no doubt that exclusion of the entire statement would now be required by the Confrontation Clause, thus giving the accused even more protection than the ruling of that case.[156]

A determination of whether a statement is "against interest" will depend upon the context of the statement and the circumstances under which it is made. The appropriateness of focusing on the circumstances surrounding the making of the statement in determining satisfaction of the "against interest" requirement is further reinforced by, and not entirely distinct from, the "reasonable person" test of the Rule. In determining whether a statement is self-serving or disserving under the traditional statement against interest exception, the declarant must have been apparently *aware* that his or her statement was contrary to some personal interest. Since the exception may

---

(1944) ("[I]t would seem, therefore, that the courts are not justified in admitting self-serving statements merely because they accompany disserving statements, and a neutral collateral statement should serve no better"); Lee v. Illinois, 476 U.S. 530 (1986) (rejecting the state's theory that the interlocking nature of defendant's and co-defendant's confessions made co-defendant's confession reliable and therefore admissible; the discrepancies between the two confessions were not insignificant. Co-defendant's confession is inherently unreliable because of his "desire to shift or spread blame, curry favor, avenge himself, or divert attention to another").

[154] Crawford v. Washington, 541 U.S. 36 (2004).

[155] In *Williamson*, the Court explicitly avoided decision on the admissibility of such evidence under the Confrontation Clause. *See Williamson*, 512 U.S. at 605 (because the disputed statements in that case were deemed inadmissible under Rule 804(b)(3), the Court added that "we need not address Williamson's claim that the statements were also made inadmissible by the Confrontation Clause"). Ironically, the statutory issue presented in *Williamson* was easier than the constitutional objection, given the nebulous nature of the Court's Confrontation Clause jurisprudence at that time. After *Crawford*, the constitutional objection by a defendant in that kind of a case is now easier and more decisive than the challenge of deciding precisely which parts of the codefendant's statement might be inadmissible under Rule 804(b)(3) and the holding in *Williamson*.

[156] After *Williamson*, for example, courts frequently allowed a prosecutor to use as evidence only the parts of the declarant's confession that were self-inculpatory ("I was part of a conspiracy to rob the bank") after redacting the parts that directly inculpated the accused ("And Tony was part of the plan too"), but that was still a net gain for the prosecutor, who would then be able to tie that admission to Tony through other evidence that he and the declarant were together on the day of the robbery. After *Crawford*, however, the entire statement would now be inadmissible if it was knowingly given to the police, even the parts that only indirectly incriminate the accused.

only be invoked where the declarant is unavailable, however, the question of personal awareness usually may be resolved only by resort to objective circumstantial evidence.[157] Since it is impossible to read a person's mind, Rule 804(b)(3) states the requirement that the declarant knew and understood the ramifications of his statement as an *objective* test: Would a "reasonable person *in the declarant's position*" have made the statement if it were untrue?[158] The "in declarant's position" language clearly reflects an intent to include the surrounding circumstances and factual context of the statement in the evaluation of whether the statement is contrary to the declarant's interest.

The trial court may consider surrounding circumstances in determining whether the declarant knew his or her statement was against interest. Since the Rule is cast in terms of an objective standard, however, the trial court generally should assume that the declarant acted as a reasonable person would in similar circumstances.[159] Subjective psychological factors indicating a lack of trustworthiness and detracting from reliability may be addressed by the trial court under Rule 403.

§ 804.24 Foundational Requirements — Unavailability and Personal Knowledge

The traditional requirement that the declarant be unavailable has been retained as a prerequisite to the admission of a statement against interest, although, consistent with pre-Rule authority, the definition of "unavailability" has been expanded beyond the common-law limitation of death.[160]

Consistent with Rule 602, Rule 804(b)(3) maintains the common-law

---

[157] *See* Jefferson, *Declarations Against Interest: An Exception to the Hearsay Rule*, 58 HARV. L. REV. 1 (1944); *see also* 5 WIGMORE, § 1456.

[158] *E.g.,* 2 MCCORMICK, § 316 ("[T]he declarant, as in the case of hearsay exceptions generally, must, so far as appears, have had the opportunity to observe the facts, as witnesses must have."); 5 WIGMORE, § 1471, at 346–47:

> The qualifications of the declarant . . . with reference to testimonial *knowledge of the fact* stated are those of the ordinary witness . . . It has once or twice loosely been said that the declarant must have "peculiar knowledge"; but so far as this may mean a knowledge better than that ordinarily required of witnesses, *i.e.*, the usual knowledge by personal observation, . . . it is not the law.

(emphasis in original).

[159] 5 WEINSTEIN'S FEDERAL EVIDENCE § 804.06; *see, e.g.,* United States v. MacDonald, 688 F.2d 224 (4th Cir. 1982).

[160] *See, e.g.,* Oscar Gruss & Son v. Lumbermens Mut. Casualty Co., 422 F.2d 1278 (2d Cir. 1970) (declarant apparently outside reach of process); Gichner v. Antonio Troiano Tile & Marble Co., 410 F.2d 238, 242–243 (D.C. Cir. 1969) (in finding that statement made to police was against the interest of the declarant, court stated: "it is not necessary for the statement to include every aspect of negligence; it is enough if the statement could reasonably provide an important link in a chain of evidence which is the basis for civil liability;" case was remanded to determine whether declarant was unavailable).

requirement that the declarant have personal knowledge.[161] Though un-stated, this requirement is implicit in the concept of statements against interest.[162]

§ 804.25　Foundational Requirements — Contrary to Interest — "Pecuniary or Proprietary" Interest — "Penal" Interest

Traditionally, the statement against interest exception admitted only those declarations that, *at the time of their making*, could be characterized as contrary to the pecuniary or proprietary interest of the declarant. Common examples of statements affecting proprietary interests are acknowledgments that the declarant does not own particular property, or that the declarant has conveyed or encumbered it in some manner.[163] Similarly, statements concerning boundary lines and easements, or acknowledgments that one's ownership is something less than fee simple, have traditionally been embraced within the exception for proprietary interest.[164]

The traditional exception for pecuniary interest is best illustrated by such statements as acknowledgments of a debt on the theory that to owe a debt is contrary to one's financial interest.[165] Somewhat less obvious, but also included, are statements acknowledging the receipt of money in payment of a debt owing to the declarant or statements that certain money is being held in trust.[166] These traditional limitations to the subjects of money and property have been expanded to include adverse statements concerning liability for unliquidated damages for a tort claim or a seeming breach of contract, or, conversely, waiver of a defense to any such action.[167] Rule 804(b)(3) is sufficiently broad to encompass all the traditionally admitted subjects, and it should be construed even more expansively in a contempo-rary age when the majority of people are aware of the possibility and consequences of civil litigation.

Under the Rule, however, a statement of an employee of a business entity is not within the scope of the exception simply because it tends to subject the

---

[161] *E.g.,* United States v. Lanci, 669 F.2d 391 (6th Cir. 1982); *see also* United States v. Toney, 599 F.2d 787 (6th Cir. 1979) (reversible error to exclude statement made by individual after he was arrested for robbery that both he and defendant had won a great deal of money, since this statement was against his interest, both because it revealed his illicit gambling activities and because it disclosed that he had been gambling with a large sum of money a few hours after the bank robbery).

[162] Comment, *Declarations Against Interest—Rules of Admissibility*, 62 Nw. U. L. Rev. 934 (1968).

[163] 2 McCormick, § 317.

[164] *Id. See generally,* Morgan, Basic Problems of Evidence (1963); 5 Weinstein's Federal Evidence § 804.06; 4 Mueller & Kirkpatrick, § 497.

[165] 2 McCormick, § 317.

[166] *Id.*

[167] *Id.*

entity to some obligation, although the declaration may nevertheless qualify as an admission in an action where the entity is a party.[168] The statement may be adverse to the declarant's interest in the sense that his employer may disapprove and reprimand him, but this is more analogous to the social interests, discussed earlier, that are not embraced by Rule 804(b)(3). To satisfy the against interest requirement, the statement must *directly* affect the pecuniary interest of the declarant, as where the declarant is a partner with a personal stake in the earnings of the entity, or where the declarant faces demotion or termination due to the statement. Here, the pecuniary interest is patent, and the statement satisfies the condition of being contrary to an interest within the scope of Rule 804(b)(3).

A major expansion of the historical common-law limitations on hearsay statements against interest is effected by the inclusion in Rule 804(b)(3) of statements adversely affecting the declarant's "penal" interest, or in the language of the Rule, those which tend to "expose [him] to criminal liability." This expansion of the Rule, supported by most commentators,[169] is a recognition that restriction of the exception to material interests ignores other equally compelling human motives. A statement against penal interest, however, must be carefully scrutinized to ensure that the declaration was contrary to the declarant's interest at the time of its utterance. Where the statement is offered to incriminate the accused, the against interest requirement is strictly construed because "the consequent denial or diminution of so essential and fundamental a confrontation value as the opportunity to cross-examine demands that the competing interest to which that value yields be 'closely examined.' "[170] Moreover, in certain situations discussed in the following section of this Chapter, corroboration is a condition to the admissibility of statements against penal interests.

As to third party confessions exculpating the accused that qualify under the Rule, the "against interest" requirement should ordinarily be satisfied where the substance of the declaration admits culpability for the crime of which the accused stands charged or incriminates both the declarant and the accused in some other crime, thus presenting an alibi or similar affirmative defense to the charged offense.[171] In these situations, corroboration is expressly required.

---

[168] *See generally,* Morgan, BASIC PROBLEMS OF EVIDENCE (1963); Jones, *Evidence* § 9:10 (rev. ed. 1972); 4 MUELLER & KIRKPATRICK, § 497.

[169] *Cf.* United States v. Gabay, 923 F.2d 1536 (11th Cir. 1991) (defendant's accomplice gave testimony at earlier trial and died; transcript of accomplice's testimony held admissible as statement against interest because even though part of plea bargain, statement did not tend to shift blame to defendant).

[170] United States v. Sarmiento-Perez, 633 F.2d 1092 (5th Cir. 1980) (citing Chambers v. Mississippi, 410 U.S. 284 (1973)).

[171] 5 WEINSTEIN'S FEDERAL EVIDENCE § 804.06; 4 MUELLER & KIRKPATRICK, § 500.

§ 804.26   Statements Against Penal Interest — Requirement of "Corroborating Circumstances" — In General

Under Rule 804(b)(3), statements against the declarant's penal interest offered to exculpate the accused must be "corroborated" prior to their admission. At the outset, it should be noted that this corroboration requirement should not be confused with the corroboration rule for substantive crimes such as treason.[172] The Rule pertains to the introduction of discrete items of evidence, not the substantive elements of an offense.

To the extent that an out-of-court statement exculpates the accused by embodying an admission to the perpetration of the crime with which the accused is charged, the corroboration requirement is derived from a long-standing recognition that third-party out-of-court confessions are inherently subject to fabrication and abuse. A variety of factors, such as a grant of immunity by the prosecution or personal ties with the accused, may motivate the declarant to concoct a third-party confession or to make an out-of-court statement that is beneficial to the accused by creating a reasonable doubt as to the accused's guilt.[173] Moreover, the unavailability of the declarant, required by Rule 804, hinders attempts to attack the credibility of the witness and protects the witness from possible prosecution for perjury. Third-party confessions may possess a high degree of probative value,[174] however, and the accused's need for such evidence is obvious. Consequently, the Rule reaches a compromise by enabling the accused to offer the exculpatory statement of an unavailable third party but gives the prosecution the opportunity to exclude such evidence where corroboration is lacking.

Just what constitutes sufficient "corroborating circumstances" must be determined on a case-by-case basis. Where the facts contained in the declarant's statement are supported by proof outside of the statement itself, the corroboration requirement should be satisfied. For example, if a third party confesses to committing the crime charged against the accused, the declarant's revelation of facts about the crime that only the perpetrator could know should be sufficient corroboration. However, the defense should not be required to produce independent evidence confirming the substance of the declarant's statement. Rather, evidence amounting to corroborating circum-

---

[172] 5 WEINSTEIN'S FEDERAL EVIDENCE § 804.06.

[173] Williamson v. United States, 512 U.S. 594 (1994) ("One of the most effective ways to lie is to mix falsehood with truth, especially truth that seems particularly persuasive because of its self-inculpatory nature"); United States v. Paguio, 114 F.3d 928 (9th Cir. 1997) ("[a] motive of love might . . . induce a reasonable father to make a false self-inculpatory statement in order to save his son" and possibility that the father's statement might be fabricated to protect the son cuts in favor of exclusion of the statement).

[174] Williamson v. United States, 512 U.S. 594 (1994) ("reasonable people, even reasonable people who are not especially honest, tend not to make self-inculpatory statements unless they believe them to be true").

stances clearly indicating trustworthiness is satisfactory, such as proof that the statement was made to a law enforcement officer who would respond officially.[175] In general, the corroboration requirement should be satisfied if the evidence allows "a reasonable [person] to believe that the statement might have been made in good faith and that it could be true."[176] The trial court should consider the entire context in which the declaration was made in an effort to determine whether sufficient corroboration as to the trustworthiness of the statement has been established.[177]

Although the express language of the Rule requires that corroboration be directed toward the trustworthiness, *i.e.,* the accuracy, of the out-of-court statement, some courts have excluded evidence as not meeting the corroboration requirement where the credibility of the witness recounting the out-of-court statement was questionable.[178] However, the witness's credibility can be evaluated by the trier of fact because this testimony is given under

---

[175] United States v. Hatfield, 591 F.3d 945 (7th Cir. 2010) (the trial court erred in refusing to admit out-of-court statements recorded in a police report by a man who admitted that he and three other persons, rather than either of the defendants, had committed one of the burglaries that the defendants were accused of. The statement was against the speaker's penal interest, and the circumstances sufficiently confirmed its trustworthiness, even though he changed his story twice before admitting his involvement in the burglary, because there was no suggestion that he knew the defendants; in none of his versions of the burglary did he implicate them; and his ultimate version was corroborated by the fact that he had dialed 911 while the burglary was in progress and by the accuracy of certain information in his initial statement to the police).

[176] 5 WEINSTEIN'S FEDERAL EVIDENCE § 804.06; *see, e.g.,* United States v. Paguio, 114 F.3d 928 (9th Cir. 1997) (trial court was acting within its discretion in admitting father's statements that he, and not son, had made false statements to a bank where the evidence showed that the father had initiated the transaction, where the father's business had generated the false 1099 forms to support the false statements, and where his role was so dominant that the bank officials were somewhat confused as to whether they were dealing with the father or son); United States v. Zirpolo, 704 F.2d 23 (1st Cir. 1983); United States v. Rodriguez, 706 F.2d 31 (2d Cir. 1983).

[177] 5 WEINSTEIN'S FEDERAL EVIDENCE § 804.06; *see, e.g.,* United States v. Barone, 114 F.3d 1284 (1st Cir. 1997) ("the corroboration that is required by Rule 804(b)(3) is not independent evidence supporting the truth of the matters asserted by the hearsay statement, but evidence that clearly indicated that the statements are worthy of belief, based on the circumstances in which the statements were made"); United States v. MacDonald, 688 F.2d 224 (4th Cir. 1982); *see also* United States v. Garris, 616 F.2d 626 (2d Cir. 1979) ("it suffices . . . that a remark which is itself neutral as to the declarant's interest be integral to a larger statement which is against the declarant's interest;" here the sister's repetition of defendant's admission, even putting aside its weight against her as an accessory after the fact in the Banker's Trust robbery, was integral to her admission of complicity in the Manufacturers Hanover Trust robbery, since it explained her motive to aid her brother's escape after the Bankers Trust robbery).

[178] United States v. Rodriguez, 706 F.2d 31 (2d Cir. 1983); United States v. Poland, 659 F.2d 884 (9th Cir. 1981); United States v. Annese, 631 F.2d 1041 (1st Cir. 1980); United States v. Bagley, 537 F.2d 162 (5th Cir. 1976).

oath and is subject to cross-examination and observation of demeanor. Consequently, it is the out-of-court *declarant's* veracity, not the *witness's* veracity, that must be corroborated.[179] As the Advisory Committee has correctly observed, "In assessing whether corroborating circumstances exist, some courts have focused on the credibility of the witness who relates the hearsay statement in court. But the credibility of the witness who relates the statement is not a proper factor for the court to consider in assessing corroborating circumstances. To base admission or exclusion of a hearsay statement on the witness's credibility would usurp the jury's role of determining the credibility of testifying witnesses."[180] Nevertheless, in many, if not in most cases, corroboration of the declarant's trustworthiness will functionally coincide with corroboration of the veracity of the witness on the stand who transmits the out-of-court statement against interest.

§ 804.27   Corroboration — Standards Applicable to Declarations Tending to Exculpate the Accused

In regard to statements against penal interest tending to exculpate the accused, a strict standard for corroboration has been particularly discouraged by the United States Supreme Court in *Chambers v. Mississippi*.[181] In *Chambers*, the Court reversed the conviction of the accused on due process grounds where the state court prevented extensive cross-examination of a witness who had admitted on a number of occasions that he had committed the crime with which the accused stood charged. The witness later repudiated these statements and offered an alibi, but the accused proved the alibi to be concocted and showed that the witness was near the scene. The accused was denied the opportunity to cross-examine the witness due to the jurisdiction's "voucher rule." Likewise, he was prevented from calling witnesses who overheard the repeated out-of-court statements admitting to the crime. While Rule 804(b)(3) would probably be inapplicable in light of the witness's presence in court, the *Chambers* court, in *dicta*, indicated that

---

[179] *See* United States v. Salvador, 820 F.2d 558 (2d Cir. 1987) (where there was no corroborating evidence and declarant had reason to lie, statement made to prosecutor was not admissible in favor of defendant); United States v. Katsougrakis, 715 F.2d 769 (2d Cir. 1983); United States v. Brainard, 690 F.2d 1117 (4th Cir. 1982); *see also* United States v. Satterfield, 572 F.2d 687 (9th Cir. 1978) (defendant sought to offer statement by codefendant, who was unavailable because he refused to testify, exculpating defendant, which was allegedly made during course of an argument while both were inmates in penitentiary two years after bank robbery in question; court found that even assuming declarant made the statement, there were insufficient corroborating circumstances as to trustworthiness of statement because it was not really against penal interest, a substantial length of time had elapsed between statement and robbery, and because a substantial portion of the statement that lent it credibility was not integral part of statement and not against interest; corroborating circumstances "must clearly" indicate the trustworthiness of the statement).

[180] Advisory Committee Note to the 2010 amendment to Fed. R. Evid. 804(b)(3).

[181] Chambers v. Mississippi, 410 U.S. 284 (1973). *See generally,* 5 WEINSTEIN'S FEDERAL EVIDENCE § 804.06.

due process requires the trial court to permit proof that the hearsay statements in question represented admissible declarations against penal interest:

> Few rights are more fundamental than that of an accused to present witnesses in his own defense . . . . In the exercise of this right, the accused, as is required of the State, must comply with established rules of procedure and evidence designed to assure both fairness and reliability in the ascertainment of guilt and innocence. Although perhaps no rule of evidence has been more respected or more frequently applied in jury trials than that applicable to the exclusion of hearsay, exceptions tailored to allow the introduction of evidence which in fact is likely to be trustworthy have long existed. The testimony rejected by the trial court here bore persuasive assurances of trustworthiness and thus was well within the basic rationale of the exception for declarations against interest. That testimony also was critical to Chambers' defense. In these circumstances, where constitutional rights directly affecting the ascertainment of guilt are implicated, the hearsay rule may not be applied mechanistically to defeat the ends of justice . . . .
>
> . . . [We] hold quite simply that under the facts and circumstances of this case the rulings of the trial court deprived Chambers of a fair trial.[182]

The pertinence of *Chambers* to the developing law of "corroboration" under Rule 804(b)(3) is unclear in light of unique facts of the case, *i.e.*, the witness's availability, the application of the state's "voucher" rule, and the fact that error was found in the truncated cross-examination after damaging evidence had already been admitted. Still, the emphasis of the *Chambers* court upon the reliability factor of the third-party confession, finding support for trustworthiness in scant attendant circumstances, lends weight to the assertion that where the third-party confession tends to exculpate the accused, an overly restrictive construction of the corroboration requirement may raise questions of constitutional significance.[183]

---

[182] Chambers v. Mississippi, 410 U.S. 284 (1973).

[183] 5 WEINSTEIN'S FEDERAL EVIDENCE § 804.06; *see also* Green v. Georgia, 442 U.S. 95 (1979) (citing *Chambers*; death sentence vacated where accused was prohibited from introducing at sentencing trial the confession of the codefendant for the actual murderous act upon victim; holding grounded in due process since Georgia law does not recognize statements against penal interest as exception to hearsay rule); *see, e.g.*, United States v. MacDonald, 688 F.2d 224 (4th Cir. 1982); *see also* United States v. Benveniste, 564 F.2d 335 (9th Cir. 1977) (reversible error to exclude statements by co-offender, since defendant did not "play a significant role" and statements had been offered in support of entrapment defense).

§ 804.28   Corroboration — Standards Applicable to Declarations Tending to Inculpate the Accused

Until very recently, Rule 804 did not expressly require corroboration of statements inculpating the accused as a precondition to admissibility of the statement on behalf of the prosecution, although many courts had nevertheless imposed such a requirement.[184] The rule was amended last year to provide that the requirement of corroborating circumstances applies to all declarations against penal interest offered in criminal cases, because the Advisory Committee reasoned that "[a] unitary approach to declarations against penal interest assures both the prosecution and the accused that the Rule will not be abused and that only reliable hearsay statements will be admitted under the exception."[185] The admissibility of statements against interest inculpating the accused will almost inevitably raise issues under the Sixth Amendment;[186] it is clear that this rule is subject to severe constitutional limits in criminal cases. In *Lee v. Illinois*,[187] the Supreme Court rejected the state's theory that the interlocking nature of defendant's and co-defendant's confessions made co-defendant's confession reliable and therefore admissible where the discrepancies between the two confessions were significant. The Court held that the co-defendant's confession was inherently unreliable because of his "desire to shift or spread blame, curry favor, avenge himself, or divert attention to another."[188]

§ 804.29   Rule 804(b)(4) The Exceptions — Statement of Personal or Family History

(b)   **The Exceptions.** The following are not excluded by the rule against hearsay if the declarant is unavailable as a witness:

***

(4)   *Statement of Personal or Family History.* A statement about:

(A)   the declarant's own birth, adoption, legitimacy, ancestry, marriage, divorce, relationship by blood, adoption,

---

[184] As the Advisory Committee noted last year, "A number of courts have applied the corroborating circumstances requirement to declarations against penal interest offered by the prosecution, even though the text of the Rule did not so provide." Advisory Committee Note to 2010 Amendment to FED. R. EVID. 804(b)(3). *See, e.g.,* United States v. Shukri, 207 F.3d 412 (7th Cir. 2000); United States v. Katsougrakis, 715 F.2d 769 (2d Cir. 1983); United States v. Riley, 657 F.2d 1377 (8th Cir. 1981); United States v. Sarmiento-Perez, 633 F.2d 1092 (5th Cir. 1980); United States v. Alvarez, 584 F.2d 694 (5th Cir. 1978) (corroboration required for statements against penal interest implicating the accused).

[185] Advisory Committee Note to 2010 Amendment to Fed. R. Evid. 804(b)(3).

[186] *See* §§ 801.2 and 804.20, *supra.*

[187] Lee v. Illinois, 476 U.S. 530 (1986).

[188] *Id.* 476 U.S. at 545.

or marriage, or similar facts of personal or family history, even though the declarant had no way of acquiring personal knowledge about that fact; or

(B)   another person concerning any of these facts, as well as death, if the declarant was related to the person by blood, adoption, or marriage or was so intimately associated with the person's family that the declarant's information is likely to be accurate.

Rule 804(b)(4) codifies one of the oldest exceptions to the hearsay rule and, in several ways, significantly expands its scope. Rule 804(b)(4)(A) admits statements concerning an unavailable declarant's own personal or family history, embracing such topics as "birth, adoption, legitimacy, ancestry, marriage, relationship by blood." Rule 804(b)(4)(B) admits declarations concerning these subjects pertaining to another person if the declarant was related by blood, adoption, or marriage, or ". . . was so intimately associated with the person's family that the declarant's information is likely to be accurate."[189] The exception was originally termed at common law the "pedigree exception," since it generally applied only to matters of genealogy, *i.e.,* questions of lineage, descent and succession, and it usually operated only in inheritance cases where pedigree was an issue.[190] The Rule, in accordance with the modern trend, has expanded the historical exception to encompass the whole area of family history — an enlargement designated by the Rule's title.

The Rule departs from the common-law restriction against declarations concerning the family history of another person. Traditionally, it was believed that only members of the family could be presumed to have accurate knowledge of pedigree facts that are acquired by the normal interest in family affairs.[191] Rule 804(b)(4)(B), in conformity with the view espoused by Wigmore,[192] extends the common-law restriction to include

---

[189] *See generally,* 2 McCORMICK, § 322; 5 WEINSTEIN'S FEDERAL EVIDENCE § 804.07; 4 MUELLER & KIRKPATRICK, § 504; 5 WIGMORE, §§ 1480–1503. *See also* Hale, *Proof of Facts of Family History,* 2 HASTINGS L.J. 1 (1950); Note, *Pedigree,* 46 IOWA L. REV. 414 (1962); Comment, *Admissibility of Hearsay Evidence on Matters of Family History,* 5 ARK. L. REV. 58 (1951).

[190] *E.g.,* Flora v. Anderson, 75 F. 217 (6th Cir. 1896). *See generally,* 5 WEINSTEIN'S FEDERAL EVIDENCE § 804.07; 2 McCORMICK, § 322; 5 WIGMORE, § 1480; 4 MUELLER & KIRKPATRICK, § 504.

[191] *See generally,* 5 WEINSTEIN'S FEDERAL EVIDENCE § 804.07; Note, *Pedigree,* 46 IOWA L. REV. 414 (1961); Comment, *Hearsay Under the Proposed Federal Rules: A Discretionary Approach,* 15 WAYNE L. REV. 1077 (1969); Comment, *Admissibility of Hearsay Evidence on Matters of Family History,* 5 ARK. L. REV. 58 (1951).

[192] "[I]t seems too much to say that only those who have this immediate property-interest

declarants "intimately associated" with the family, *e.g.*, family physicians, lawyers, clergy, nurses, and domestic servants, or intimate friends and neighbors, where circumstances indicate trustworthiness in an extended, close relationship with the family in question.[193] Even where this degree of intimacy cannot be sufficiently demonstrated, however, such facts may nevertheless be admissible under Rule 803(19) as the general reputation in the community, whether or not the declarant is available.[194]

Similarly, if the hearsay facts are contained in a writing, they may be admissible, regardless of the declarant's availability, under such exceptions as those governing regularly conducted activity (Rule 803(6)), public records or reports (Rule 803(8)), records of vital statistics (Rule 803(9)), records of marriage, baptismal or similar certificates (Rule 803(12)), family records (Rule 803(13)), or ancient documents (Rule 803(16)).

§ 804.30   Foundational Requirements

The conditions precedent to the admission of statements of personal or family history are threefold: (i) unavailability of the declarant as defined in Rule 804(a) must be established,[195] (ii) the statement must be restricted to the subject matters described in the Rule; and (iii) an appropriate relation to, or association with, the family in question must be shown. Each of these foundational requirements represents the modern expansion of the common-law tradition, and the Rule presents little complexity or difficulty in construction or application.

What is notable about Rule 804(b)(4), as it relates to other hearsay rules and its antecedent common-law restrictions, is what is *not* required as a condition to admissibility under the exception contained therein. In the first instance, the Rule continues in force the common-law requirement that, in lieu of personal knowledge as that term is defined in Rule 602, the declarant must appear to have familiarity, or fair opportunity for acquiring familiarity, with the subject matter asserted in the declaration. Strict adherence to the

---

in learning the family history [because of the possibility of inheritance] can possibly have adequate information; for family physicians and chaplains, old servants, and intimate friends may in cases be equally and sufficiently informed." 5 WIGMORE, § 1487, at 382; *see also* 2 McCORMICK, § 322.

[193] *See* Advisory Committee Note, Rule 804(b); *see also* 5 WIGMORE, § 1487, at 382 ("[I]t is not necessary to maintain that the statements of *any friend* are always admissible; but it is desirable to disavow any limitation which would exclude the statements of one whose intimacy with the family could leave no doubt as to his sufficient knowledge, equally with the family members, of the facts of family history."). *See generally,* 5 WEINSTEIN'S FEDERAL EVIDENCE § 804.07; 4 MUELLER & KIRKPATRICK, § 504.

[194] *See* § 803.10 *et seq., supra; see also* 5 WEINSTEIN'S FEDERAL EVIDENCE § 804.07; 2 McCORMICK, § 322; 5 WIGMORE, § 1605.

[195] In so providing, the Rule expands the concept of "unavailability" beyond the common-law requirement of death, and thus supersedes decisional law to the contrary. *See, e.g.,* Flora v. Anderson, 75 F. 217 (6th Cir. 1896) (declarant must be dead).

general rule of personal observation, however, was not required at common law and is not required under the Rule.[196] Consequently, while statements about other persons must be predicated upon some familiarity with the family, statements concerning the declarant's *own* age, descent, or similar family history are admissible despite the fact that the declarant could not possibly have personally perceived and remembered the event. The personal knowledge requirement, therefore, applies only to statements about others, and moreover, it is not as strict as that imposed by Rule 602.

Second, and most significant, the Rule does not restrict admissibility to declarations made *ante litem motam, i.e.,* prior in time to the commencement of the controversy. This restriction was imposed at common law in light of the historical reliance upon the rationale that prior to the controversy, the declarant would have no apparent motive, bias, or interest in giving false information concerning his or her pedigree,[197] but might well have a motive to falsify such information once the controversy had begun. Elimination of this restriction is justified on the grounds that it is increasingly difficult to establish with any reasonable certainty the point at which a controversy arises. Moreover, the applicability of the exclusionary provisions of Rule 403 to the instant Rule enables the trial court to exclude untrustworthy or misleading evidence.[198] Thus, the exception for statements concerning family history no longer requires a demonstration that the statement was uttered at a time when no bias or interest could affect its content.

§ 804.31 Rationale

At common law, the exception for declarations concerning personal or

---

[196] *E.g.,* 5 WIGMORE, § 1486, at 378:

> It is of course *not* to be expected that *personal observation* shall be demanded, *i.e.,* that only from those who were present at birth, wedding, or death, shall hearsay statements be received; this would be to misconceive the theory of the exception. That theory is that the constant (though casual) mention and discussion of important family affairs, whether of the present or of past generations, puts it in the power of members of the family circle to be fully acquainted with the original personal knowledge and the consequent tradition on the subject, and that those members will therefore know, as well as anyone can be expected to know, the facts of the matter. It is not that they have, each and all, a knowledge by personal observation, but that they at least know the fact as accepted by family understanding and tradition, and that this understanding, based as it was originally on observation, is prima facie trustworthy.

See also Pollack v. Metropolitan Life Ins. Co., 138 F.2d 123 (3d Cir. 1943) (reversible error to exclude evidence offered by defendant that statement made by decedent indicating his age was within the family history exception in beneficiary's action against life insurance company).

[197] *See* 2 McCORMICK, § 322; 5 WIGMORE, § 1483.

[198] 5 WIGMORE, § 1484; *cf.* United States v. Carvalho, 742 F.2d 146 (4th Cir. 1984) (statements regarding reasons for marrying are not statements of facts and are not admissible under Rule 804(b)(4)).

family history rested upon the usual principles of necessity and trustworthiness. The necessity principle was derived from the general difficulty of obtaining any other evidence in matters of family history.[199] As enunciated by Justice Story, "In cases of pedigree, [hearsay] is admitted upon the ground of necessity, or the great difficulty and sometimes the impossibility of proving remote facts of this sort by living witnesses, . . . there being no 'lis mota' or other interest to affect the credit of the statement."[200]

The circumstantial guarantee of trustworthiness was supplied at common law by the notion that the declarations of family affairs are trustworthy and deserving of consideration by judges and juries in the same fashion as they are in the ordinary affairs of life.[201] This rationale presumes that in common human experience pronouncements of this sort are likely to rest upon accurate knowledge with due regard for the truth of the matter asserted, at least in the absence of circumstantial indicia to the contrary.

Application of the common-law rule, however, was expressly conditioned upon a showing that the declarant had no motive to fabricate or distort the facts, and, accordingly, it imposed the requirement that the statement must have been made *ante litem motam, i.e.,* before the controversy that led to the litigation in which the declaration is offered. Rule 804(b)(4) eliminates this historical condition. Consequently, while the common-law rationale holds true for statements that qualify as *ante litem motam,* those declarations made after the controversy arises must rest upon an alternate rationale, namely, that a statement concerning a fact within the Rule will not be uttered unless it is reliable, regardless of the presence of bias, interest, or passion. In this regard, the Rule is peculiarly subject to the exclusionary provisions of Rule 403, and where the court in its discretion finds that the statement was made under suspicious circumstances, indicating low probative value, it may exclude it totally. Alternately, the court may admit the statement and permit the fact that the statement was made after the controversy to affect the

---

[199] *See generally,* 5 WIGMORE, §§ 1480–1482; Note, *Pedigree,* 46 IOWA L. REV. 414 (1961); Comment, *Admissibility of Hearsay on Matters of Family History,* 5 ARK. L. REV. 58 (1951).

[200] Ellicott v. Pearl, 35 U.S. (10 Pet.) 412 (1836); *see also* Fulkerson v. Holmes, 117 U.S. 389, 393 (1886) ("[T]his exception has been recognized on the ground of necessity; for as, in inquiries respecting relationship or descent, facts must often be proved which occurred many years before the trial and were known to but few persons, it is obvious that the strict enforcement in such cases of the rule against hearsay evidence would frequently occasion failure of justice.").

[201] *See generally,* 2 MCCORMICK, § 322; 5 WIGMORE, § 1482; *see, e.g.,* Rassano v. Immigration and Naturalization Serv., 377 F.2d 971, 973 (7th Cir. 1966) ("[T]he family history exception is based in part upon the inherent trustworthiness of declarations by a family member regarding matters of family history and the usual unavailability of other evidence on these matters").

weight of the evidence.[202]

§ 804.32   Former Rule 804(b)(5)

In 1997, the text of Rule 804(b)(5), containing a residual hearsay exception, was deleted and transferred to Rule 807. Refer to Chapter 807 for a discussion of the residual exception.

§ 804.33   Rule 804(b)(6) The Exceptions — Statement Offered Against a Party That Wrongfully Caused the Declarant's Unavailability

(b)   **The Exceptions.** The following are not excluded by the rule against hearsay if the declarant is unavailable as a witness:

   ***

 (6)   *Statement Offered Against a Party That Wrongfully Caused the Declarant's Unavailability.* A statement offered against a party that wrongfully caused — or acquiesced in wrongfully causing — the declarant's unavailability as a witness, and did so intending that result.

Under Rule 804(b)(6), a party cannot object to, as hearsay, the admission of statements made by a declarant whose unavailability for trial resulted when that party "wrongfully caused — or acquiesced in wrongfully causing — the declarant's unavailability." All parties are subject to this Rule. For example, if a criminal defendant were to kill or threaten a witness to prevent him or her from testifying, the defendant would have forfeited the right to object to the admission of the victim's statements on hearsay grounds.[203] A prosecutor who intimidates a defense witness to the extent that the witness refuses to testify also loses the right to raise a hearsay objection to statements by that defense witness.

Similarly, if a civil party were to cause or allow a wrong resulting in an adverse witness not testifying, that party would not be heard to object to the witness's testimony on hearsay grounds. The rule was designed to thwart those who wrongly attempt to keep an adverse witness from testifying at trial.[204]

---

[202] *See* Rassano v. Immigration and Naturalization Serv., 377 F.2d 971 (7th Cir. 1966); McClaskey v. Barr, 54 F. 781 (6th Cir. 1893); *see also* 5 WEINSTEIN'S FEDERAL EVIDENCE § 804.07.

[203] *See, e.g.,* United States v. Montague, 421 F.3d 1099, 1103 (10th Cir. 2005) (defendant procured the unavailability of his wife, who asserted her marital privilege at trial, based on evidence of domestic abuse and his contact with her during her visits to him in jail); United States v. White, 116 F.3d 903 (D.C. Cir. 1997) (defendants who murdered a witness thereby forfeited their confrontation clause and hearsay objections to the statement of that witness).

[204] The Advisory Committee Note to the 1997 Amendments states that the rule

In order to overcome a hearsay objection using this Rule, the party offering the declarant's statement(s) must establish, by a preponderance of the evidence, both that the declarant is unavailable, as defined in Rule 804(a), and that the declarant's unavailability was brought about either by some deliberate wrongdoing or acquiescence therein by the objecting party that intentionally procured the declarant's unavailability "as a witness." This last limitation confirms that the statutory hearsay exception does not reach every murder case, for example, unless the trial judge is persuaded that the defendant's motive was to prevent the murder victim from being able to testify at some sort of proceeding.[205] Of course, no murder is ever committed merely for the purpose of preventing the victim from testifying at the trial for her murder; that would be a logical absurdity. The accused could accomplish that result so much more simply, and avoid a murder trial altogether, by not killing anyone in the first place. In murder prosecutions where hearsay statements by the victim are arguably admissible against the accused under the doctrine of "forfeiture by wrongdoing," there will always be evidence that the accused feared or suspected the victim otherwise would have testified against him or his friends because of some misconduct committed *before* the murder.

As long as the defendant intended to cause the victim to be unavailable to testify at some trial, it does not matter whether the defendant was anticipating the same trial where the evidence is eventually admitted; "[a] defendant who wrongfully and intentionally renders a declarant unavailable as a witness in any proceeding forfeits the right to exclude, on hearsay grounds, the declarant's statements at that proceeding and any subsequent proceeding."[206] The rule applies to a defendant whose conspirators take steps to make a witness unavailable, as long as those acts were foreseeable to the defendant and in furtherance of their common aims, even if there was no explicit agreement to kill adverse witnesses.[207] Although the rule does not literally require that the wrongdoing consist of a criminal act, any wrongdoing that successfully and intentionally makes a witness unavailable

---

"recognizes the need for a prophylactic rule to deal with abhorrent behavior 'which strikes at the heart of the system of justice itself." Rule 804, Advisory Committee Note to 1997 Amendment, quoting United States v. Mastrangelo, 693 F.2d 269, 273 (2d Cir. 1982).

[205] As the Supreme Court recently noted with approval, scholarly commentators are unanimous in concluding that Federal Rule 804(b)(6) "applies only if the defendant has in mind the particular purpose of making the witness unavailable." Giles v. California, 554 U.S. 353, 367 (2008) (quoting 5 MUELLER & KIRKPATRICK, FEDERAL EVIDENCE § 8:134 (3d ed. 2007)).

[206] United States v. Gray, 405 F.3d 227, 242 (4th Cir. 2005).

[207] United States v. Carson, 455 F.3d 336, 361–362 (D.C. Cir. 2006) ("the reasons why a defendant forfeits his confrontation rights apply with equal force to a defendant whose coconspirators render the witness unavailable, so long as their misconduct was within the scope of the conspiracy and reasonably foreseeable to the defendant," even if there is "no direct evidence of an explicit agreement to kill adverse witnesses").

or unwilling to testify would almost certainly amount to witness tampering, obstruction of justice, or some other criminal offense.

The amendment reflects the decisions of every circuit that has resolved this question, which have all accepted the principle of forfeiture by misconduct.[208] Although the circuits had not applied a uniform evidence standard,[209] the amended rule has adopted the Rule 104(a) preponderance of the evidence standard "in light of the behavior the new Rule 804(b)(6) seeks to discourage."[210]

When a statement is admissible against a criminal defendant under this exception, there will be no impediment to its admission under the Confrontation Clause. Just as this rule extinguishes the defendant's rights to object to hearsay under Rule 802, any constitutional objections are also forfeited by a defendant who obtained "the absence of [the] witness by wrongdoing,"[211] which "extinguishes confrontation claims on essentially equitable grounds."[212] Just like Federal Rule 804(b)(6), however, the Confrontation Clause allows the admission of hearsay evidence against the accused under the doctrine of "forfeiture by wrongdoing" only if the actions of the accused were intentionally calculated to make the witness unavailable to testify.[213]

---

[208] *See, e.g.,* United States v. Aguiar, 975 F.2d 45, 47 (2d Cir. 1992); United States v. Potamitis, 739 F.2d 784, 789 (2d Cir. 1984); Steele v. Taylor, 684 F.2d 1193, 1199 (6th Cir. 1982); United States v. Balano, 618 F.2d 624, 629 (10th Cir. 1979); United States v. Carlson, 547 F.2d 1346, 1358–59 (8th Cir. 1977).

[209] Most reported cases have applied a preponderance of the evidence standard, while *United States v. Thevis,* 665 F.2d 616, 631 (5th Cir. 1982), applied a clear and convincing evidence standard.

[210] Rule 804, Advisory Committee Note to 1997 Amendment. This is the standard that the courts have continued to apply since the codification of this doctrine in Rule 804(b)(6). *E.g.,* United States v. Carson, 455 F.3d 336, 361–362 (D.C. Cir. 2006); United States v. Rivera, 405 F.3d 227, 242 (4th Cir. 2005); *see also* Davis v. Washington, 547 U.S. 813, 833 (2006), *on remand, remanded,* 853 N.E.2d 477 (noting, without deciding the issue, that federal courts applying this rule have generally applied the preponderance-of-the-evidence standard).

[211] Davis v. Washington, 547 U.S. 813, 833 (2006), *on remand, remanded,* 853 N.E.2d 477 (Ind. 2006).

[212] *Davis,* 457 U.S. at 833 (quoting Crawford v. Washington, 541 U.S. 36 (2004)). *See* § 801.2, *supra.*

[213] Giles v. California, 554 U.S. 353 (2008). This point is discussed more fully at § 801.2, *supra.*

Chapter 805

Rule 805. Hearsay Within Hearsay

Rule 805. Hearsay Within Hearsay

Hearsay within hearsay is not excluded by the rule against hearsay if each part of the combined statements conforms with an exception to the rule.

---

§ 805.1   Hearsay Within Hearsay

Rule 805 expressly authorizes the admission of multiple hearsay where each element or level of hearsay conforms to an exception to the hearsay rule.[1] While not explicitly set forth in the express language of the Rule, Rule 805 *implicitly* authorizes the admission of multiple levels of out-of-court statements offered for their truth where each level conforms to *either* a hearsay exception (*i.e.,* the exceptions set forth in Rule 803 and 804) or an exception to the *definition* of hearsay. These latter exceptions are set forth in Rule 801(d)(1) and Rule 801(d)(2). For example, where an admission of a party admissible under Rule 801(d)(2) is contained within a business record admissible under Rule 803(6), the entire document is admissible. Likewise, where an out-of-court statement, not offered for its truth, is contained within an admissible hearsay statement, Rule 805 implicitly provides that both levels of out-of-court statements are admissible. For example, where a witness's prior inconsistent statement, not under oath, offered only for its impeachment value is contained within a public record admissible under Rule 803(8), both levels of out-of-court statements may be received.[2] The converse of the latter example, however, does not obtain, and where a hearsay statement, admissible under an exception, is embraced within an out-of-court statement not offered for its truth, neither level is rendered admissible by Rule 805. The first level of hearsay must be admissible for its

---

[1] *See generally,* 5 WEINSTEIN'S FEDERAL EVIDENCE §§ 805.01–805.06; 4 MUELLER & KIRKPATRICK, §§ 508–509; 5 WIGMORE, § 1361–1363. *See also* Jelsema, Murphy, Nichols, & Tannenbaum, *Hearsay Under the Proposed Federal Rules: A Discretionary Approach*, 15 WAYNE L. REV. 1077 (1969); §§ 801.8 through 801.20, *supra.*

[2] *E.g.,* United States v. Smith, 521 F.2d 957 (D.C. Cir. 1975) (hearsay recorded by police officer in Form 251 is admissible if it was an admission, spontaneous exclamation, dying declaration, or declaration against interest).

truth (*i.e.*, via an exception to the definition or the exclusionary rule) in order to establish that the embraced hearsay statement was actually uttered or otherwise made. All of the foregoing analysis, while not explicit on the face of Rule 805, is implicitly indicated by the Rule and the theory of the hearsay system.[3]

Many examples of multiple hearsay exist in federal law. A witness's testimony concerning an out-of-court statement that the witness made to an FBI agent constitutes hearsay where the statement is offered for its truth; the testimony constitutes double hearsay where the statement of the witness describes statements made to the witness by others that are also offered for their truth.[4] A document offered for the truth of its contents is hearsay because it was prepared out-of-court; where the document is based upon data derived from other sources that are also offered for their truth, it is double hearsay.[5] When a witness testifies that an informer has made an out-of-court statement to him, it is hearsay when the testimony is offered for its truth; where the substance of the informer's statement is offered for its truth to prove what the conspirator told the informer, it is double hearsay.[6] A plaintiff may call a witness to testify that he heard a statement made by the opposing party, but a newspaper article quoting a *reporter* who claims to have heard such a statement is inadmissible hearsay.[7]

Rule 805 provides that hearsay within hearsay is not excluded under the hearsay rule where each component of the multiple hearsay is admissible under an exception to the hearsay rule.[8] For example, when a medical record

---

[3] *See* 5 WEINSTEIN'S FEDERAL EVIDENCE § 805.02 ("The . . . result [of Rule 805] could be achieved in the absence of a rule").

[4] United States v. Beasley, 545 F.2d 403 (5th Cir. 1977); *see also* United States v. Melia, 691 F.2d 672 (4th Cir. 1982) (FBI agent statement that witness had told him information that others had told witness about sale of stolen jewelry to defendant).

[5] Hunters Int'l. Mftg. Corp. v. Christiana Metals Corp., 561 F. Supp. 614 (E.D. Mich. 1982) (invoices and testimony of non-expert layperson introduced en masse by plaintiff are without foundation); *see also* Williams v. Tri-County Growers, 747 F.2d 121 (3d Cir. 1984) (trial court erred in excluding report compiled by U.S. Dept. of Labor containing a statement by defendant's agent indicating defendant had violated Farm Labor Contractor Registration Act).

[6] *See, e.g.,* T. Harris Young & Assoc. v. Marquette Electronics, 931 F.2d 816 (11th Cir. 1991) (in tortious interference case, appeals court extensively discussed issue of multiple hearsay).

[7] Nooner v. Norris, 594 F.3d 592 (8th Cir. 2010) (in civil action against Arkansas Department of Corrections, a statement by the Department's spokeswoman would be admissible against it as a statement by a party-opponent, but that would not allow a plaintiff to offer a newspaper article written by a reporter who quoted one of the defendant's spokeswomen; newspaper articles are "rank hearsay").

[8] *See* Cook v. Arrowsmith Shelburne, Inc., 69 F.3d 1235 (2d Cir. 1995) (in gender discrimination case, trial court did not err in admitting testimony from the plaintiff that her supervisors had told her that the general manager wanted a man to have her job; both the

containing a patient's statement of the manner in which the injury occurred is offered to prove the cause of the injury, Rule 805 would require that both the record and the patient's statement qualify for admission under an exception to the hearsay rule. The record might be admissible if it satisfies Rule 803(6), "Records of regularly conducted activity." The statement made by the patient might be admissible as a statement against interest under Rule 804(b)(3) if the patient is unavailable, or as a statement made for the purpose of medical diagnosis under Rule 803(4). In such a situation, the report would be admissible without any deletion of the patient's statement.[9]

A special problem of double hearsay lies in establishing a proper foundation to show that the internal hearsay actually satisfies an exception to the hearsay rule.[10] Failure to lay a proper foundation may require exclusion of the evidence or excision of the internal hearsay statements from the otherwise admissible hearsay evidence.[11]

§ 805.2 Multiple Hearsay Exceeding Two Levels

Rule 805 does not limit admissibility to double, *i.e.,* two-level, hearsay; rather, multiple hearsay exceeding two levels of out-of-court statements is admissible as long as each level of out-of-court statement possesses a basis for admission. One difficulty with multiple hearsay is that the reliability of the evidence is diminished by each additional layer of hearsay.[12] Rule 403

---

supervisors' and general manager's comments were admissible as admissions under Rule 801(d)(2)(D)). *But see* Jacklyn v. Schering-Plough Healthcare Prods. Sales Corp., 176 F.3d 921 (6th Cir. 1999) (it was proper to exclude gender discrimination; plaintiff's allegation that her former supervisor told her that he heard the supervisor who ultimately fired plaintiff say that he did not want females working for him; even though the underlying statement might demonstrate the declarant's state of mind, the former supervisor's statement was not made in the course of his employment); United States v. Mackey, 117 F.3d 24 (1st Cir. 1997) (statement made by defendant's bookmaker that the defendant, who was charged with bank robbery, had won $60, 000 on bets was found inadmissible; although the FBI report that contained the statement was arguably a public record, thus qualifying the report for admission, the bookmaker's statement was neither a statement against interest nor did it fall within any other exception and hence was inadmissible).

[9] *See* Wilson v. Zapata Off-Shore Co., 939 F.2d 260 (5th Cir. 1991) (it was not reversible error to admit the statement of plaintiff's sister in hospital records that plaintiff is a "habitual liar" where the sister disclaimed the statement at trial and ample other evidence cast doubt on plaintiff's credibility).

[10] Gross v. Burggraf Constr. Co., 53 F.3d 1531 (10th Cir. 1995) (ruling in gender discrimination suit that a witness's testimony that he had heard from a coworker that the plaintiff's supervisor had made derogatory remarks about plaintiff's gender was inadmissible because the plaintiff failed to produce testimony from a witness with firsthand knowledge or other evidence showing that the supervisor actually made the statements).

[11] *See* Tongil v. The Vessel "Hyundai Innovator," 968 F.2d 999 (9th Cir. 1992) (district court erred in allowing party to use hearsay documents to lay the foundation for the admission for business records); United States v. Lang, 589 F.2d 92 (2d Cir. 1978).

[12] Comment, *Hearsay Under the Proposed Federal Rules: A Discretionary Approach*, 15 WAYNE L. REV. 1077 (1969).

authorizes the court to exclude multiple hearsay when it determines that the reliability of the evidence has been diminished to an unacceptable degree.[13] Undoubtedly, in a particular case where reliability has been excessively undermined, Rule 403 might justify exclusion of double hearsay as well.[14] The principal question is whether the reliability arising from satisfaction of exceptions to the hearsay rule is counterbalanced by the increased unreliability inherent in each additional tier of hearsay.[15]

---

[13] Comment, *Hearsay Under the Proposed Federal Rules: A Discretionary Approach*, 15 WAYNE L. REV. 1077 (1969) (suggesting that after a number of repetitions the evidence is merely rumor).

[14] *See* § 403.1 *et seq., supra.*

[15] *See* 5 WEINSTEIN'S FEDERAL EVIDENCE § 805.06, citing Naples v. United States, 344 F.2d 508 (D.C. Cir. 1964).

Chapter 806

Rule 806. Attacking and Supporting the Declarant's Credibility

Rule 806. Attacking and Supporting the Declarant's Credibility

When a hearsay statement — or a statement described in Rule 801(d)(2)(C), (D), or (E) — has been admitted in evidence, the declarant's credibility may be attacked, and then supported, by any evidence that would be admissible for those purposes if the declarant had testified as a witness. The court may admit evidence of the declarant's inconsistent statement or conduct, regardless of when it occurred or whether the declarant had an opportunity to explain or deny it. If the party against whom the statement was admitted calls the declarant as a witness, the party may examine the declarant on the statement as if on cross-examination.

---

§ 806.1   Attacking and Supporting the Credibility of Hearsay Declarant — An Overview

Rule 806 delineates the procedure for attacking and, if attacked, supporting the credibility of declarants of hearsay statements admitted at trial.[1] Acknowledging that admissions by authorized spokespersons, agents or conspirators are technically not hearsay under Rule 801(d)(2)(C), (D), and (E),[2] Rule 806 treats such admissions as hearsay for the purpose of impeaching or rehabilitating the declarant.[3] Rule 806 authorizes the admissibility of any evidence that would be admissible to impeach or rehabilitate a declarant of hearsay if the declarant had testified as a witness,[4] and in so doing, the Rule reflects the position that justice is best served by presentation

---

[1] *See generally,* 1 McCormick, § 37; 5 Weinstein's Federal Evidence §§ 806.01–806.07; 4 Mueller & Kirkpatrick, §§ 510–511; 3A Wigmore, § 1025–1039. *See also* Hale, *Inconsistent Statements,* 10 S. Cal. L. Rev. 135 (1937).

[2] *See* § 801.19, *supra.*

[3] *See also* United States v. Shay, 57 F.3d 126 (1st Cir. 1995) (a statement admitted under Rule 801(d)(2)(A) could be impeached despite the fact that Rule 806 does not specifically refer to such statements; the drafters of the Rules felt that it was unnecessary to include statements admissible under Rule 801(d)(2)(A) and (B) because the credibility of a party-opponent is always subject to attack).

[4] *See* Advisory Committee Note, Rule 806.

of all evidence relevant to the reliability of statements made out-of-court.[5]

Rule 806 has three principal effects. First, Rule 806 provides that the credibility of a hearsay declarant may be attacked by any evidence that would be admissible to attack the credibility of the declarant if the declarant had testified as a witness.[6] The most frequently encountered practical effect of the Rule is to permit a hearsay declarant to be impeached by inconsistent statements.[7] Of course, other means of impeachment provided by Article VI may also be used. Additionally, the credibility of a hearsay declarant may be rehabilitated once it has been attacked.[8] Second, Rule 806 eliminates, with respect to hearsay declarants, the Rule 613 requirement that the declarant must be afforded an opportunity to explain or deny the statements.[9] Third, Rule 806 allows a party to call as a witness the declarant of hearsay offered against that party and to question the declarant concerning the hearsay as if under cross-examination.[10]

§ 806.2   The Procedure

Rule 806 provides that a party may attack or support the credibility of a hearsay declarant by any evidence that would be admissible if the declarant had testified in court.[11] For example, just as a party pursuant to Rule 608 may attack a *witness's* credibility by opinion or reputation evidence, so also may a party attack or support a hearsay *declarant's* credibility by opinion or reputation evidence concerning the declarant's character for truthfulness or untruthfulness.[12] Rule 806 continues the policy of Rule 608 that rehabilitative evidence of truthfulness is inadmissible until the declarant's character for truthfulness is attacked.

Pursuant to Rule 609, the credibility of the declarant may be attacked by

---

[5] *See* 1 MCCORMICK, § 37; United States v. Becerra, 992 F.2d 960 (9th Cir. 1993) (trial court erred in denying defendant the opportunity to impeach a hearsay declarant's credibility with evidence of her criminal convictions); *cf.* 3A WIGMORE, § 1033.

[6] *See* § 806.2, *infra. See also* Rules 608 and 609. Credibility also may be attacked in other ways, *e.g.,* by showing the bias of a hearsay declarant. *Cf.* United States v. Check, 582 F.2d 668 (2d Cir. 1978) (impeachment technique employed by defense counsel of use of witness to get at complete testimony of confidential undercover informant without calling him was entirely proper).

[7] *See* Advisory Committee Note, Rule 806.

[8] *Cf.* Rule 608(a)(2).

[9] *See* § 806.3, *infra.*

[10] *See* § 806.4, *infra.*

[11] Similarly, evidence that could not be used to impeach a declarant were he or she to serve as a witness at trial cannot be used to impeach the declarant. *See* United States v. Trzaska, 111 F.3d 1019 (2d Cir. 1997) (a second statement made by the declarant could not be used to impeach his credibility because the statement was not necessarily inconsistent with his hearsay statement).

[12] United States v. Lechoco, 542 F.2d 84 (D.C. Cir. 1976) (government's closing argument evidences the extent to which defendant's honesty was in issue).

evidence of conviction of specified crimes.[13] Additionally, the credibility of a declarant may be attacked by demonstrating the declarant's biases and prejudices.[14] Finally, Rule 806 provides that the credibility of a hearsay declarant may be attacked by an inconsistent statement in the manner analyzed in the next section.[15]

§ 806.3   Inconsistent Statements Attacking the Hearsay Declarant's Credibility

Rule 806 adopts the majority position that impeachment of a hearsay statement may be effected by introduction of inconsistent statements without the requirement of affording the declarant an opportunity to explain or deny the inconsistent statement.[16] Rule 806 does not, however, adopt Wigmore's suggestion that a foundation should be required where the declarant *could* have been afforded an opportunity to explain or deny the inconsistency, *i.e.,* as in the case of prior testimony at a hearing or deposition. Wigmore would dispense with the foundation only where the declarant could not reasonably be afforded the opportunity to explain or deny the contradictory statement.[17] Contrary to Wigmore's position, Rule 806 applies broadly and uniformly and does not distinguish, for example, dying declarations from prior testimony.[18]

Because hearsay, by its nature, occurs prior to trial, Rule 806 does not limit, as does Rule 613, attack of a hearsay declarant to impeachment by *prior* inconsistent statements.[19] Instead, evidence of an inconsistent statement made at any time either before or after the hearsay declaration is admissible to impeach the hearsay declarant.[20]

---

[13] *See* United States v. Noble, 754 F.2d 1324 (7th Cir. 1985) (trial court did not err in admitting evidence of defendant's conviction for counterfeiting after he introduced taped conversation in which he denied knowledge of counterfeiting operations. Admission of the statement permitted declarant/defendant to be impeached as if he had testified); United States v. Lawson, 608 F.2d 1129 (6th Cir. 1979) (by putting hearsay statements before jury, his counsel made Lawson's credibility an issue the same as if Lawson had made the statements from the witness stand).

[14] *See* United States v. Check, 582 F.2d 668 (2d Cir. 1978).

[15] *See* § 806.3, *infra.*

[16] *See* Carver v. United States, 164 U.S. 694 (1897); Trade Dev. Bank v. Continental Ins. Co., 469 F.2d 35 (2d Cir. 1972); McConney v. United States, 421 F.2d 248 (9th Cir. 1969). *But see* Mattox v. United States, 156 U.S. 237 (1895); *see also* 1 MCCORMICK, § 37; 3A WIGMORE, § 1033; 4 MUELLER & KIRKPATRICK, § 511.

[17] 3A WIGMORE, §§ 1030–1035.

[18] *See* 1 MCCORMICK, § 37.

[19] *See* Advisory Committee Note, Rule 806.

[20] *See* United States v. Wuagneux, 683 F.2d 1343 (11th Cir. 1982) (after defense introduced statement against interest by accountant, government was permitted to introduce for impeachment purposes another statement by the accountant that was inconsistent with the first).

Where an inconsistent statement is introduced to contradict and impeach a hearsay declarant, the inconsistent statement should be introduced during the case of the party who is offering the impeaching statement. The case of the proponent of the hearsay statement should not be interrupted for the purpose of receiving the inconsistent statement offered for impeachment.

§ 806.4   Cross-Examination of a Hearsay Declarant

Where a party calls as a witness the declarant of hearsay that was admitted against the party, Rule 806 provides that the party may examine the declarant on the hearsay as if on cross-examination.[21] In so providing, Rule 806 complements Rule 611(c), which provides for cross-examination of hostile and adverse witnesses by the proponent of the witness,[22] and Rule 607, which, subject to certain express limitations, allows a party to impeach its own witness.[23]

---

[21] *But see* United States v. Paris, 827 F.2d 395 (9th Cir. 1987) (statements properly admitted under Rule 801(d)(2)(E) were not rendered inadmissible by declarant's unavailability to take the witness stand and be cross-examined).

[22] *See* § 611.1 *et seq., supra.*

[23] *See* § 607.1 *et seq., supra.*

Chapter 807

Rule 807. Residual Exception

Rule 807. Residual Exception

(a) **In General.** Under the following circumstances, a hearsay statement is not excluded by the rule against hearsay even if the statement is not specifically covered by a hearsay exception in Rule 803 or 804:

  (1) the statement has equivalent circumstantial guarantees of trustworthiness;

  (2) it is offered as evidence of a material fact;

  (3) it is more probative on the point for which it is offered than any other evidence that the proponent can obtain through reasonable efforts; and

  (4) admitting it will best serve the purposes of these rules and the interests of justice.

(b) **Notice.** The statement is admissible only if, before the trial or hearing, the proponent gives an adverse party reasonable notice of the intent to offer the statement and its particulars, including the declarant's name and address, so that the party has a fair opportunity to meet it.

---

§ 807.1 History and Rationale

Rule 807 provides for the admission of hearsay statements that do not fall within a specific exception under Rule 803 or 804, but have "equivalent circumstantial guarantees of trustworthiness," provided the statements satisfy certain additional requirements.[1] This residual exception provides a vehicle for admitting hearsay "in situations unanticipated by other exceptions, but involving equal guarantees of trustworthiness."[2]

---

[1] *See generally,* 2 MCCORMICK §§ 325–327, 5 WEINSTEIN'S FEDERAL EVIDENCE §§ 807.01–807.04; 4 MUELLER & KIRKPATRICK, § 512. *See also* Weinstein, *Probative Force of Hearsay,* 46 IOWA L. REV. 331 (1961); Chadbourn, *Bentham and the Hearsay Rule—A Benthamite View of Rule 63(4)(c) of the Uniform Rules of Evidence,* 75 HARV. L. REV. 932 (1962); Quick, *Hearsay, Excitement, Necessity and the Uniform Rules: A Reappraisal of Rule 63(4),* 6 WAYNE L. REV. 204 (1960).

[2] Weissenberger, *The Admissibility of Grand Jury Transcripts: Avoiding the Constitu-*

Adopted in 1997, Rule 807 is essentially a restatement of former Rules 803(24) and 804(b)(5), provisions containing residual exceptions to the hearsay rule that were deleted in 1997 to facilitate future amendments to those rules.[3] The history and rationale behind the residual exceptions contained in the former rules are relevant to an understanding of Rule 807.

The legislative history of former Rules 803(24) and 804(b)(5) illustrates that the exceptions contained therein represented a compromise between the competing goals of allowing flexibility in the development of the hearsay system on one hand and ensuring some degree of certainty for trial preparation on the other. Although the Supreme Court approved the Advisory Committee's draft, the House Judiciary Committee deleted the residual exceptions from Rules 803 and 804 as "injecting too much uncertainty into the law of evidence and impairing the ability of practitioners to prepare for trial."[4] The Committee believed that "if additional hearsay exceptions are to be created, they should be by amendments to the Rules, not on a case-by-case basis."[5]

The Senate Judiciary Committee reinstated the residual exceptions, but added several restrictions to narrow their scope. While the Senate's draft was intended to provide room for growth in the hearsay rules, the Committee nevertheless cautioned that "[i]t is intended that the residual hearsay exceptions will be used very rarely, and only in exceptional circumstances."[6] The Conference Committee approved the Senate's version of the Rules, but added a requirement that the proponent of the evidence offered under one of the residual exceptions must give his opponent sufficient notice before trial to enable him to prepare to meet the evidence.[7] As enacted, Rules 803(24) and 804(b)(5) adopted the approach taken by some pre-Rules decisions that evaluated the trustworthiness of and need for a particular hearsay statement

---

tional Issue, 59 TUL. L. REV. 335 (1984). *See* Advisory Committee Note, Rule 803(24); *see also* United States v. Ismoila, 100 F.3d 380 (5th Cir. 1996) (affirming trial court's admission of bank customer reports of missing or stolen credit cards in prosecution for credit card fraud; although the reports were not admissible under the business records exception of Rule 803(6) because they were not prepared in the regular course of the customer's business, the reports were admissible under the residual hearsay exception); United States v. Blackburn, 992 F.2d 666 (7th Cir. 1993) (construing former Rule 803(24); computer printouts of eyeglass analysis requested by the FBI from a private company were not admissible as business records because they were not kept in the regular course of business; court found that the records were admissible under the residual hearsay exception); United States v. Ellis, 935 F.2d 385 (1st Cir. 1991) (statements of three-year-old sex complainant relating to her demonstration of events with anatomically correct dolls held to satisfy residual exception requirements).

[3] *See* the Advisory Committee Note to Rule 807.

[4] H. R. Rep. No. 93-650, 93d Cong., 1st Sess., at 5–6 (1973).

[5] *Id.*

[6] S. Rep. No. 93-1277, 93d Cong., 2d Sess., at 18–20 (1974).

[7] H. R. Conf. Rep. No. 93-1597, 93d Cong., 2d Sess., at 3 (1974).

rather than the strict applicability of a specific exception.[8] The residual exception now embodied in Rule 807 continues to allow courts to follow this approach to the admission of hearsay.

§ 807.2 Basic Application

Hearsay offered under Rule 807 must satisfy five requirements to be admissible. First, the statements must possess "circumstantial guarantees of trustworthiness" that are "equivalent" to those supporting the specific hearsay exceptions.[9] In assessing reliability, courts should consider a variety of factors.[10] Some courts infer reliability from the absence of the traditional hearsay dangers, *i.e.*, problems in perception, narration, memory, and sincerity.[11] Other decisions find that the factors that support the specific hearsay exceptions, such as spontaneous statements or dying declarations,

---

[8] *See, e.g.*, Chestnut v. Ford Motor Co., 445 F.2d 967 (4th Cir. 1971) (noting modern trend to consider need and trustworthiness rather than formal labels); United States v. Kearney, 420 F.2d 170 (D.C. Cir. 1969) (admitting statement made by police officer one day prior to his death as "in the penumbra of both the spontaneous utterance and dying declaration exceptions to the hearsay rule"); Dallas County v. Commercial Union Assur. Co., 286 F.2d 388 (5th Cir. 1961) (in action to determine insurance coverage where plaintiffs claimed courthouse tower had been struck by lightning, court permitted defendant to introduce 1901 newspaper article that reported a fire in the tower while the courthouse was being built; the court declined to categorize the hearsay in one of the recognized exceptions, finding it was admissible "because it is necessary and trustworthy, relevant and material").

[9] Starter Corp. v. Converse, Inc., 170 F.3d 286 (2d Cir. 1999) (court may rely on survey evidence to establish the likelihood of confusion in a trademark dispute if the survey contains sufficient circumstantial guarantees of trustworthiness).

[10] *See, e.g.*, United States v. Smith, 591 F.3d 974 (8th Cir. 2010) (to determine whether the recorded interview of a child victim is admissible under the residual hearsay exception of Rule 807, the district court must consider the training and experience of the interviewer; whether the child was interviewed using open-ended questions; the age of the child and whether the child used age-appropriate language in discussing the abuse; the length of time between the incident of abuse and the making of the hearsay statement; and whether the child repeated the same facts consistently to adults); United States v. Sanchez-Lima, 161 F.3d 545 (9th Cir. 1998) (sworn videotaped statements of witnesses offered by the accused met requirements for admission under residual exception to the rule excluding hearsay; circumstantial guarantees of trustworthiness include: (1) statements were made voluntarily; (2) statements were made under oath; (3) statements were subject to penalty of perjury; (4) statements were based on facts within the declarants' personal knowledge; (5) statements were not contradictory; (6) jurors had the opportunity to view witnesses' demeanor; (7) government had the opportunity to develop witnesses' testimony before they became unavailable; (8) government had notice and option to participate in taking videotaped statements; (9) and statements constituted evidence of material fact regarding defendant's self-defense theory and honest mistake of fact as to agents' identity).

[11] *See, e.g.*, United States v. White, 611 F.2d 531 (5th Cir. 1980) (evidence of claim form properly received as trustworthy because it was executed only three months after the check should have arrived, and "length of time between an event and the declarant's statement concerning it is a significant indicator of reliability"); *see also* United States v. Smith, 571 F.2d 370 (7th Cir. 1978); Grimes v. Employers Mut. Liab. Ins. Co., 73 F.R.D. 607 (D. Alaska 1977).

are indicative of reliability.[12] The existence of corroborating evidence and the declarant's availability to testify may also be important considerations.[13]

Second, the evidence must be "offered as evidence of a material fact." In essence, this amounts to a restatement of the requirement of relevance already imposed by Rule 401 and 402.[14]

Third, the hearsay statement must be "more probative on the point for which it is offered than any other evidence that the proponent can obtain through reasonable efforts." This requirement imposes a duty of diligence on the proponent in seeking better evidence than the proffered hearsay. In determining what constitutes "reasonable efforts," the court should weigh the importance of the evidence, the financial resources available to the proponent and the amount at stake in the action.[15] Taking these factors into consideration, the court must find that the hearsay statement is more probative than other available evidence in order to render the statement admissible.[16]

---

[12] *See, e.g.,* United States v. Sinclair, 74 F.3d 753 (7th Cir. 1996) (trial court did not abuse its discretion in excluding hearsay statement offered under the residual exception; although the statement was against the declarant's interest, the lapse of time between the statement and the event it described meant that it did not have the same characteristic of trustworthiness as statements offered under the categorical exceptions); Herdman v. Smith, 707 F.2d 839 (5th Cir. 1983); *see also* United States v. McPartlin, 595 F.2d 1321 (7th Cir. 1979) (entries made in desk calendar appointment diary kept by government witness were admissible within Rule 803(24) since they were regularly made, and in light of the entries).

[13] *See* United States v. Spotted War Bonnet, 933 F.2d 1471 (8th Cir. 1991) (in a child sex abuse case, actual testimony by declarants plus an opportunity for cross-examination satisfies the requirements of the Confrontation Clause); United States v. Vretta, 790 F.2d 651 (7th Cir. 1986) (in prosecution for kidnapping resulting in death, victim's claims that the defendant was threatening him were sufficiently corroborated by the fact that the victim had told several persons and that the victim's wife had heard the threat); United States v. Hitsman, 604 F.2d 443 (5th Cir. 1979) (college transcript properly received as reliable since corroborated by government witness); United States v. Barnes, 586 F.2d 1052 (5th Cir. 1978) (previous confession by defense witness); United States v. Williams, 573 F.2d 284 (5th Cir. 1978) (pre-trial affidavit by prosecution witness); *see also* Sherrell Perfumers, Inc. v. Revlon, Inc., 524 F. Supp. 302 (S.D.N.Y. 1980).

[14] *See* United States v. Boulahanis, 677 F.2d 586 (7th Cir. 1982); *see also* DeMars v. Equitable Life Assur. Soc., 610 F.2d 55 (1st Cir. 1979) (error to permit plaintiff to introduce letter from deceased physician, since plaintiff did not satisfy the dilligence/probativity requirement; any other physician could have been obtained to render an opinion on fairly short notice); Huff v. White Motor Corp., 609 F.2d 286 (7th Cir. 1979) (statement made by plaintiff satisfied the materiality requirement of the catchall exception); United States v. Friedman, 593 F.2d 109 (9th Cir. 1979) (receipt of Chilean travel documents satisfied materiality requirement, since they showed appellant's entrance into and exit from Chile at relevant times).

[15] *See* Byrd v. Hunt Tool Shipyards, Inc., 650 F.2d 44 (5th Cir. 1981); United States v. American Cyanamid Co., 427 F. Supp. 859 (S.D.N.Y. 1977).

[16] *See* United States v. Howard, 774 F.2d 838 (7th Cir. 1985) (deceased declarant's

Fourth, the proponent must show that its admission would serve "the purposes of these rules and the interests of justice." This requirement is based on the same principles as Rule 102 and in practice has not engendered much discussion.[17]

Finally, the statement is not admissible unless the proponent notifies the opponent of the intention to offer it "before trial or hearing." The proponent of the statement must also inform the adversary of "[the statement's] particulars, including the declarant's name and address, so that the party has a fair opportunity to meet it." While notice generally should be given at the pre-trial conference or earlier, in some cases courts have excused the proponent's failure to give advance notice where the party's conduct was reasonable in light of the circumstances.[18] In such cases the court may grant a continuance in order to enable the adversary to prepare to meet the statement. Other courts, however, have construed this requirement inflexibly and have found that failure to give notice prior to trial acts as a complete bar to the admission of the statement.[19]

The proponent of evidence offered under the residual exception bears the burden of proving that the five requirements have been satisfied. Admissibility of the statement is determined by the trial court pursuant to Rule 104(a). Even where all the requirements are met, however, the court retains discretion to exclude the statement pursuant to Rule 403 to prevent unfair prejudice, confusion of the issues, or undue delay.[20]

---

statements were admissible where they were by a seemingly disinterested party and were the only available direct proof on point); United States v. Welsh, 774 F.2d 670 (4th Cir. 1985) (where other material evidence was available but involved a witness lacking credibility, trial court did not err in excluding deceased declarant's statements; in affirming, the appellate court noted that the proponent confused the probative element with a credibility element); Huff v. White Motor Corp., 609 F.2d 286 (7th Cir. 1979) (court had "little choice except to attempt to replicate the exercise of discretion that would be made by a trial judge in making the ruling").

[17] *See* United States v. Friedman, 593 F.2d 109 (9th Cir. 1979) (upholding receipt of Chilean travel documents, noting that appellants received sufficient advance notice); United States v. Mathis, 559 F.2d 294 (5th Cir. 1977) ("tight reins must be held to insure that this provision does not emasculate our well developed body of law and the notions underlying our evidentiary rules").

[18] *See* United States v. Coney, 51 F.3d 164 (8th Cir. 1995) (trial court did not abuse its discretion in refusing to admit a report under the residual hearsay exception where the defendant disclosed the report to opposing counsel only forty-five minutes before she wanted to introduce it at trial); *see also* Piva v. Xerox Corp., 654 F.2d 591 (9th Cir. 1981); United States v. Bailey, 581 F.2d 341 (3d Cir. 1978) (reversible error to receive statement by alleged co-offender, because of its questionable reliability and devastating impact); State Farm Mut. Auto Ins. Co. v. Gudmunson, 495 F. Supp. 794 (D. Mont. 1980).

[19] *See* United States v. Cowley, 720 F.2d 1037 (9th Cir. 1983); Elizarraras v. Bank of El Paso, 631 F.2d 366 (5th Cir. 1980); United States v. Ruffin, 575 F.2d 346 (2d Cir. 1978); United States v. Oates, 560 F.2d 45 (2d Cir. 1977).

[20] *See, e.g.,* United States v. Kim, 595 F.2d 755 (1979) (telex summarizing banking

§ 807.3   Application: Admissibility of Grand Jury Transcripts

There has been a conflict in the circuits over whether the testimony of a witness before the grand jury may be admitted against the accused under the residual exception now contained in Rule 807, when the witness is unavailable to testify at trial.[21] Since grand jury transcripts fail to satisfy the requirements of any of the specific hearsay exceptions, this issue "may have wide ramifications in the criminal justice system."[22] The former testimony exception contained in Rule 804(b)(1) is inapplicable because grand jury proceedings are essentially *ex parte* and do not afford the defendant an opportunity to "develop [the testimony] by direct, cross-, or redirect examination."[23]

While some decisions justified the admission of grand jury transcripts on the basis of enhanced reliability, a careful examination of the legislative history of the residual exception and the former testimony exception shows that the use of the residual exception for this purpose may be improper. The residual exception was intended to cover situations unanticipated when the specific hearsay exceptions were drafted where the proffered hearsay possessed equivalent indications of reliability.[24] In many cases, the residual exception may properly be used to admit hearsay statements that are reliable but fail to satisfy the precise requirements of one of the specific exceptions. However, the residual exception should not be used to circumvent the

---

transactions properly excluded, since it did not have circumstantial guarantees of trustworthiness, because it was not sent for business purposes and was not relied upon by the business). *See generally,* 5 WEINSTEIN'S FEDERAL EVIDENCE § 807.02.

[21] *See* United States v. Dent, 984 F.2d 1453 (7th Cir. 1993) (harmless error resulted where the court admitted the grand jury transcript of a witness who was abroad during the trial); United States v. Snyder, 872 F.2d 1351 (7th Cir. 1989) (although the trial court had improperly admitted the jury testimony of a witness who had since died, the error did not require reversal because the defendant corroborated substantial facts of the testimony when he took the stand); United States v. West, 574 F.2d 1131 (4th Cir. 1978) (witness who testified before the grand jury was murdered before he could testify at trial. The court found the required indicia of reliability in the fact that the witness was debriefed after each encounter with the defendant and signed a statement of what transpired at the meeting; additionally, the witness's grand jury testimony was corroborated by evidence of tapes from a body transmitter the witness wore and surveillance photographs of the defendant making the heroin buys. The court noted that though the witness was unavailable for cross-examination, the FBI agents who corroborated the witness's testimony were subject to cross-examination); United States v. West, 574 F.2d 1131 (4th Cir. 1978) (court admitted testimony of a witness who testified before the grand jury and who later denied the truth of his grand jury testimony at trial; the court found the required indicia of reliability in the fact that an unindicted conspirator confirmed the testimony of the reluctant witness).

[22] United States v. Carlson, 547 F.2d 1346 (8th Cir. 1976) (prior grand jury testimony by unavailable government witness implicating defendant in previous transaction satisfied diligence/probativity requirement).

[23] *See* Rule 804(b)(1).

[24] *See* § 804.32, *supra.*

policies underlying the hearsay rule or the specific exceptions: "[I]f the admission of the hearsay under the residual exception runs afoul of some other Federal Rule, the other rule should control to exclude the hearsay. Where Congress has specifically addressed an issue in another rule, the more general language of the residual exceptions must give way."[25]

The admission of grand jury transcripts pursuant to Rule 807 is contrary to the policy underlying the former testimony exception of Rule 804(b)(1) and therefore should not be permitted. In addition to the bases of trustworthiness and need that traditionally support hearsay exceptions, Rule 804(b)(1) is also based on a policy of fairness to the party against whom the evidence is offered. The legislative history of the exception shows that Congress found it "generally unfair" to admit former testimony against a party who did not have an "opportunity and similar motive to develop [the testimony] by direct, cross-, or redirect examination."[26] Since the accused does not have the opportunity to develop the testimony of a witness before the grand jury, such testimony is clearly inadmissible under the former testimony exception because its use would be unfair. Grand jury testimony is equally inadmissible under Rule 807, regardless of its enhanced reliability, because its admission would circumvent the fairness policy underlying Rule 804(b)(1).

Because the Federal Rules of Evidence render grand jury testimony inadmissible where the witness does not testify at trial, courts do not need to reach the constitutional issue of whether the use of this evidence violates the accused's right of confrontation unless the hearsay objection is waived.[27] In light of recent developments that have done much to clarify and simplify the constitutional question presented, however, it is now plain that the admission of grand jury testimony is always forbidden under the Sixth Amendment,

---

[25] Sonenshein, *The Residual Exceptions to the Federal Hearsay Rule: Two Exceptions in Search of a Rule*, 57 N.Y.U. L. REV. 867 (1982); *see, e.g.,* United States v. Metz, 608 F.2d 147 (5th Cir. 1979) (statement inadmissible under Rule 804(b)(3) also inadmissible under Rule 804(b)(5)); United States v. Kim, 595 F.2d 755 (D.C. Cir. 1979) (telex inadmissible under Rule 803(6) inadmissible under Rule 803(24)).

[26] H. R. Rep. No. 650, 93d Cong., 1st Sess. (1973), *reprinted in* 1974 U.S. Code Cong. & Ad. News 7075. In civil cases, former testimony is admissible if a party or his predecessor in interest had an opportunity to develop the witness's testimony. In criminal cases, however, the accused himself must have had this opportunity at the former proceeding; the "predecessor in interest" provision does not apply.

[27] Weissenberger, *The Admissibility of Grand Jury Transcripts: Avoiding the Constitutional Issue*, 59 TUL. L. REV. 335 (1984). *See generally,* Spector Motor Co. v. McLaughlin, 323 U.S. 101 (1944) ("[I]f there is one doctrine more deeply rooted than any other in the process of constitutional adjudication, it is that we ought not to pass on questions of constitutionality . . . unless such adjudication is unavoidable"); United States v. Gonzalez, 559 F.2d 1271 (5th Cir. 1977) (court declined to address Sixth Amendment issue because it found grand jury transcripts inadmissible under Rules of Evidence).

even if the declarant is unavailable by the time of trial, if that testimony is offered against an accused.[28]

---

[28] Crawford v. Washington, 541 U.S. 36, 68 (2004). Such testimonial statements are never admissible under *Crawford* against someone who did not have the chance to cross-examine the witness at the time the statement was made, and nobody is allowed to cross-examine witnesses at an *ex parte* grand jury proceeding. For a much more detailed discussion of this issue, *see* § 801.2, *supra*.

ARTICLE IX.

AUTHENTICATION AND IDENTIFICATION

Synopsis

753

Chapter 901

Rule 901. Authenticating or Identifying Evidence

Rule 901. Authenticating or Identifying Evidence

(a) **In General.** To satisfy the requirement of authenticating or identifying an item of evidence, the proponent must produce evidence sufficient to support a finding that the item is what the proponent claims it is.

(b) **Examples.** The following are examples only — not a complete list — of evidence that satisfies the requirement:

(1) *Testimony of a Witness with Knowledge.* Testimony that an item is what it is claimed to be.

(2) *Nonexpert Opinion About Handwriting.* A nonexpert's opinion that handwriting is genuine, based on a familiarity with it that was not acquired for the current litigation.

(3) *Comparison by an Expert Witness or the Trier of Fact.* A comparison with an authenticated specimen by an expert witness or the trier of fact.

(4) *Distinctive Characteristics and the Like.* The appearance, contents, substance, internal patterns, or other distinctive characteristics of the item, taken together with all the circumstances.

(5) *Opinion About a Voice.* An opinion identifying a person's voice — whether heard firsthand or through mechanical or electronic transmission or recording — based on hearing the voice at any time under circumstances that connect it with the alleged speaker.

(6) *Evidence About a Telephone Conversation.* For a telephone conversation, evidence that a call was made to the number assigned at the time to:

(A) a particular person, if circumstances, including self-identification, show that the person answering was the one called; or

(B) a particular business, if the call was made to a business and the call related to business reasonably transacted over the telephone.

(7) *Evidence About Public Records.* Evidence that:

(A) a document was recorded or filed in a public office as authorized by law; or

757

      (B)   a purported public record or statement is from the office where items of this kind are kept.

    (8)   ***Evidence About Ancient Documents or Data Compilations.*** For a document or data compilation, evidence that it:

      (A)   is in a condition that creates no suspicion about its authenticity;

      (B)   was in a place where, if authentic, it would likely be; and

      (C)   is at least 20 years old when offered.

    (9)   ***Evidence About a Process or System.*** Evidence describing a process or system and showing that it produces an accurate result.

    (10)   ***Methods Provided by a Statute or Rule.*** Any method of authentication or identification allowed by a federal statute or a rule prescribed by the Supreme Court.

---

§ 901.1   Rule 901(a) Authenticating or Identifying Evidence

    (a)   **In General.** To satisfy the requirement of authenticating or identifying an item of evidence, the proponent must produce evidence sufficient to support a finding that the item is what the proponent claims it is.

Authentication and identification are terms that apply to the process of laying a foundation for the admission of such nontestimonial evidence as documents and objects.[1] These terms may also refer to the foundational evidence that identifies a person's voice on a tape recording or in a telephone conversation.[2] Conceptually, the function of authentication or identification is to establish, by way of preliminary evidence, a connection between the evidence offered and the relevant facts of the case. The connection is necessary in order to establish the relevance of the particular object or item, since an object or item is of no relevance if it is not attributed to, or connected with, a particular person, place, or issue in a case. For example,

---

[1] *See generally,* 2 MCCORMICK, § 218; 5 WEINSTEIN'S FEDERAL EVIDENCE § 901.02; 5 MUELLER & KIRKPATRICK §§ 512–513; 7 WIGMORE, §§ 2128–2135. *See also* Alexander and Bickel, *The Authentication of Documents Requirements: Barrier to Falsehood or to Truth,* 10 SAN DIEGO L. REV. 266 (1973); Broun, *Authentication and Contents of Writings,* 1969 LAW AND THE SOCIAL ORDER 611 (1969); Eisenberg and Fenstel, *Pretrial Identification,* 58 MARQ. L. REV. 659 (1975); Michael and Adler, *Real Proof:* I, 5 VAND. L. REV. 344 (1952); Strong, *Liberalizing the Authentication of Private Writings,* 52 CORNELL L. REV. 284 (1967); Levin, *Authentication and the Content of Writings,* 10 RUTGERS L. REV. 632 (1956).

[2] The examples set forth in Rule 901(b) for establishing authenticity also demonstrate the type of evidence subject to this requirement. The illustrations cover documentary evidence, other tangible real proof, *i.e.,* objects of any sort, as well as conversations and processes or systems.

a writing purportedly signed by a party to an action is of no relevance and hence of no significance to the case unless evidence is offered that it was actually authored or signed by that person.[3] The Rules pertinent to authentication may consequently be viewed as specialized rules of relevance.[4] Article IX provides the methodology by which to establish "connective relevance," and it defines the standard by which the determination as to admissibility will be made.

Accordingly, Rule 901(a) provides that authentication or identification is a prerequisite to admissibility. Additionally, it sets forth the standard by which the initial determination of admissibility shall be governed, *i.e.,* the "sufficient to support a finding" standard. Rule 901(b) sets forth various methodologies, in a non-exhaustive listing of ten examples, by which items of evidence may be authenticated or identified in order to meet the threshold standard of Rule 901(a). Rule 902, governing self-authentication, provides that certain types of written evidence are deemed authenticated without the necessity of any foundational testimony.

In addition to establishing authenticity pursuant to Rule 901 or 902, parties may utilize a variety of pretrial procedures that obviate the necessity of authenticating or identifying evidence at trial.[5] For example, a party may submit to the opponent a request for an admission as to the genuineness of any document. Alternatively, a party may seek to establish authenticity of certain evidence through pleadings, interrogatories, or depositions. Likewise, a party may elicit a stipulation as to authenticity during a pretrial conference.[6]

It should be kept in mind that authentication is merely one prerequisite to

---

[3] As theorized by Wigmore, authentication or identification is "an inherent logical necessity." 7 WIGMORE, § 2129, at 704. Dean Wigmore explains that, "[i]n short, when a claim or offer involves impliedly or expressly any element of personal connection with a corporal object, that connection must be made to appear, like the other elements, or else the whole fails in effort." 7 WIGMORE, § 2129, at 704. *See* Advisory Committee Note, Rule 901(a); *see, e.g.,* United States v. Ladd, 885 F.2d 954 (1st Cir. 1989) (testimony by a state chemist regarding laboratory procedures was sufficient to authenticate the defendant's lab results, despite evidence of sloppy procedures within the lab. However, where the identification number on a blood sample received by a private laboratory differed from the defendant's identification number, but was later changed to look like the defendant's number without explanation, connective relevance was not established).

[4] 5 WEINSTEIN'S FEDERAL EVIDENCE § 901.02. Judge Weinstein notes that in a theoretical sense, the rules as to authentication are redundant of relevance requirements implicit in Rules 401 and 402. He concludes, however, that the traditional justifications for erecting a preliminary condition of fact for admission of writings — possibility of fraud, mistaken attribution, and jury credulity — still militate in favor of explicitly recognizing the special problems of authentication and identification; *see also* 5 MUELLER & KIRKPATRICK, § 513.

[5] 5 MUELLER & KIRKPATRICK, § 513; *see also* Advisory Committee Note, Rule 901.

[6] For a more detailed discussion as to alternative methods of establishing authenticity, *see* Rules 901(b)(10) and § 901.1 *et seq., supra.*

the admissibility of certain types of evidence. In addition to establishing connective relevance through authentication, a proponent of evidence may need to satisfy requirements as to hearsay, best evidence, and general relevance principles in order to achieve admissibility of the evidence in question.

§ 901.2   Threshold Standard of Authenticating Evidence

Rule 901(a) sets forth a standard of authentication that effectively operates to screen out certain evidence that cannot meet a minimal threshold test of connective relevance. The Rule accordingly provides that "[t]o satisfy the requirement of authenticating or identifying an item of evidence, the proponent must produce evidence sufficient to support a finding that the item is what the proponent claims it is." The "sufficient to support a finding" standard merely means that foundational evidence must be sufficient to constitute a rational basis for a jury decision that the primary evidence is what its proponent claims it to be.[7] The proponent need not offer conclusive evidence as a foundation but must merely offer sufficient evidence to allow the question as to authenticity or genuineness to reach the jury. The threshold that is to be met — that is, the quantity and nature of the authentication evidence that must be introduced — may vary depending upon the purpose for which the substantive evidence is offered.[8] The threshold standard consequently reflects the principle that both the judge and the jury participate in the determination as to authenticity, as discussed in § 901.3, *infra*. The standard itself is not rigorous, and its low threshold reflects an orientation of the Rules toward favoring the admission of evidence.[9]

§ 901.3   Function of the Court and the Jury in Authentication

While both the judge and the jury participate in determinations as to authenticity, only the judge makes determinations as to admissibility. The judge must make an initial determination that the foundational evidence has met the threshold standard of admissibility, *i.e.,* that the foundational

---

[7] *See* United States v. Holmquist, 36 F.3d 154, 168 (1st Cir. 1994) ("the burden of authentication does not require the proponent of the evidence to rule out all possibilities inconsistent with authenticity, or to prove beyond any doubt that the evidence is what it purports to be. Rather, the standard for authentication, and hence for admissibility, is one of reasonable likelihood"); United States v. Inserra, 34 F.3d 83, 90 (2d Cir. 1994) (to properly authenticate evidence, all that a party need provide is "a rational basis from which the jury may conclude" that the evidence is what the proponent claims it is).

[8] *See* United States v. Alicea-Cardoza, 132 F.3d 1 (1st Cir. 1997) (because the government introduced a pen register summary of beeper messages only to show that the defendant had received certain messages, the government only needed to establish that the register recorded the messages the defendant received; the government did not have to introduce evidence sufficient to authenticate the identity of the person who sent them).

[9] *See* United States v. Van Wyhe, 965 F.2d 528 (7th Cir. 1992) (defendant failed to present a witness with personal knowledge of a book, resulting in the book's inadmissibility); 5 WEINSTEIN'S FEDERAL EVIDENCE § 901.02; 5 MUELLER & KIRKPATRICK, § 513.

testimony is sufficient to support a rational jury finding as to authenticity.[10] In this regard, the judge is governed by Rule 104(b), which defines the court's role in making decisions as to admissibility when the relevance of evidence depends upon the fulfillment of a condition of fact. When the issue is one of authentication or identification, the condition of fact relates to the genuineness of the item in question. Inasmuch as the ultimate determination as to genuineness is a jury question, the court must, under Rule 104(b), admit the evidence upon the introduction of foundational evidence sufficient to support a finding as to authenticity.[11]

If a proper foundation is offered, the judge may not exclude the evidence merely because he or she does not believe it to be genuine.[12] The ultimate question of authenticity is within the province of the jury.[13] The preliminary determination as to whether a party has met the threshold standard of Rule 901(a) is, however, within the court's discretion. Additionally, a judge may exclude evidence pursuant to Rule 403 if there exists a danger of unfair prejudice, confusion of the issues, or misleading the jury. Exclusion pursuant to Rule 403 may occur more frequently in connection with real proof than with testimonial proof due to the impact that such evidence is likely to have upon jurors.[14]

If the judge admits evidence upon a sufficient showing as to authenticity, the jury considers the evidence. In this regard, it should be noted that an

---

[10] *See* United States v. Paulino, 13 F.3d 20, 23 (1st Cir. 1994) ("In respect to matters of authentication, the trial court serves a gatekeeping function. If the court discerns enough support in the record to warrant a reasonable person in determining that the evidence is what it purports to be, then Rule 901(a) is satisfied").

[11] *See* Rule 104(a) and (b), and Chapter 104, *supra,* for a discussion as to the limitation on the court's role in making preliminary admissibility determinations; *see also* Rule 1008, which similarly limits the court's role in determining the admissibility of other evidence of contents of writings and the like, and hence excusal of using an original, when certain questions are raised in connection with the writing.

[12] *See* Ricketts v. City of Hartford, 74 F.3d 1397, 1410–1411 (2d Cir. 1996) (the role of the trial judge is not to determine the authenticity of evidence, but to decide whether sufficient evidence has been put forward to support a jury finding of authenticity).

[13] *See* 2 McCormick, § 227, at 555:

> It must be noticed, however, that authenticity is not to be classed as one of those preliminary questions of fact conditioning admissibility under technical evidentiary rules of competency or privilege. As to these latter, the trial judge will permit the adversary to introduce controverting proof on the preliminary issue in support of his objection, and the judge will decide this issue, without submission to the jury, as a basis for his ruling on admissibility. On the other hand, the authenticity of a writing or statement is not a question of the application of a technical rule of evidence. It goes to genuineness and conditional relevance, as the jury can readily understand. Thus, if a prima facie showing is made, the writing or statement comes in, and the ultimate question of authenticity is left to the jury.

[14] 5 Weinstein's Federal Evidence § 901.02.

opponent of evidence is never precluded from contesting the genuineness of any item, even after it has been admitted upon a preliminary showing as to authenticity.[15] Even in the absence of contradictory testimony, however, the jury need not accept the foundational evidence as truthful. It need not believe that the evidence is in any way connected to the facts of the case. The jury may, accordingly, reject the authenticity of the evidence and accord it no weight.[16]

In view of the jury's role with regard to authentication, the proponent of evidence requiring authentication may offer foundational evidence that exceeds that which is required to satisfy the threshold standard of Rule 901(a). The proponent may offer evidence under any one or more of the ten examples listed in Rule 901(b) not only to establish admissibility of the particular item of proof but also to persuade the trier of fact, consistent with the proponent's burden of proof, as to the genuineness of such item. It must be emphasized that the standard as to admissibility for authenticating evidence is the low threshold, "sufficient to support a finding." This standard is considerably less demanding than such burdens of proof as "a preponderance of the evidence" or "beyond a reasonable doubt."

§ 901.4   Rule 901(b)(1) Example — Testimony of a Witness with Knowledge

(b)   Examples. The following are examples only — not a complete list — of evidence that satisfies the requirement:

(1)   *Testimony of a Witness with Knowledge.* Testimony that an item is what it is claimed to be.

Rule 901(b) provides illustrations of authentication and identification that may be used to meet the threshold standard provided in Rule 901(a). As specified in the introduction of Rule 901(b), the ten examples are presented by way of illustration only and not by way of limitation. Moreover, the illustrative methods are not mutually exclusive, and two or more may be utilized in combination in order to authenticate or identify a particular item of evidence.[17]

---

[15] *Id.*; 5 MUELLER & KIRKPATRICK, § 513.

[16] 5 WEINSTEIN'S FEDERAL EVIDENCE § 901.02. Once the evidence is admitted the question becomes one of credibility and probative force and the trier may ultimately disbelieve the proponent's proof and entirely disregard or substantially discount the persuasive impact of the evidence admitted. *See also* 5 MUELLER & KIRKPATRICK, § 513.

[17] *See* United States v. Jimenez Lopez, 873 F.2d 769 (5th Cir. 1989) (record of conviction that was not admissible under Rule 902 because it was not under seal was admissible under Rule 901 because the examples in Rule 901(b)(1) to (b)(10) are illustrative rather than exhaustive). *See generally,* 2 MCCORMICK, § 220; 5 WEINSTEIN'S FEDERAL EVIDENCE § 901.03; 5 MUELLER & KIRKPATRICK,, § 514; 2 WIGMORE, § 666; *see also* Evans, *The*

Rule 901(b)(1) provides that any competent witness who has knowledge that a matter is what its proponent claims may testify to such pertinent facts, thereby establishing, in whole or in part, the foundation for authentication.[18] The witness may be either a lay or expert witness, whose knowledge may be either direct or circumstantial.[19] Moreover, the witness is not required to provide conclusive evidence as to authenticity. Rather, the testimony must merely be relevant to the issue of authenticity or identification, and it must be, either of itself or in combination with other testimony or evidence, sufficient to support a jury finding that the matter is what its proponent claims.[20]

Testimony of a witness with knowledge may be utilized to authenticate documentary evidence of all types. It may also be used in connection with other types of evidence, such as tangible objects, photographs, films, recordings and the like. It should be noted that in many instances, Rule 901(b)(1) may be used in conjunction with one or more of the other examples listed in the Rule. For example, a witness might identify an object as being the same as that involved in a crime, based on the fact that the witness recovered the item from the scene of the crime and on the fact that the item possesses distinctive characteristics sufficient to authenticate it pursuant to Rule 901(b)(4).

The knowledge of a witness testifying pursuant to Rule 901(b)(1) may be derived from a variety of sources. For example, a witness may have participated in or observed an event or transaction, or he or she may have heard a pertinent conversation.[21] Knowledge may also be acquired through a person's position or experience. For example, the manager of a bookkeeping department should have sufficient firsthand knowledge to authenticate

---

Competency of Testamentary Witnesses, 25 MICH. L. REV. 238 (1927).

[18] *See* Rule 602, providing that a witness may not testify to a matter unless evidence is introduced sufficient to support a finding that he has personal knowledge of the matter.

[19] *See* 5 WEINSTEIN'S FEDERAL EVIDENCE, § 901.03: "Any witness may, of course, present relevant testimony concerning events that transpired outside the witness' own presence, where there are other circumstances which give the witness some circumstantial knowledge of the events through or based upon the witness' own perceptions"; *see also* United States v. Whittington, 783 F.2d 1210 (5th Cir. 1986) (persons who signed as witnesses may identify a document by identifying their own signatures and that of one of the principals; they need not identify every page and need not have been present at time of signature of principal so long as they were familiar with the person's signature; once the document is admitted, the opposing party may attempt to discredit the document); United States v. McNair, 439 F. Supp. 103 (E.D. Pa. 1977), *aff'd*, 571 F.2d 573 (3d Cir. 1978).

[20] 5 WEINSTEIN'S FEDERAL EVIDENCE § 901.03; *see also* 5 MUELLER & KIRKPATRICK, § 514. It should be noted, however, that the less precisely one testifies, the more likely the proponent will fail in an attempt to admit the evidence.

[21] 5 WEINSTEIN'S FEDERAL EVIDENCE § 901.03 ("Relevant testimony concerning knowledge obtained by way of the five senses is ordinarily admissible"); *see* Fox v. Order of United Commercial Travelers of America, 192 F.2d 844 (5th Cir. 1951).

bookkeeping entries made under his or her supervision.[22] An expert witness, who has knowledge of the nature of the evidence in question based on his or her skill or experience, may offer testimony that circumstantially authenticates the item.[23]

Authentication of evidence is merely one prerequisite to admissibility for certain types of evidence, and satisfaction of Article IX does not guarantee that an item will be admitted. Other evidentiary doctrines, such as hearsay, best evidence, and general relevance must be considered and satisfied if pertinent to admissibility in a given case. Additionally, admission of an authenticated item of evidence is not conclusive proof: the trier of fact is free to accord it whatever weight it deems appropriate. In this regard, the opponent of any evidence authenticated by testimony of a witness with knowledge may attack the issue of genuineness by cross-examination of the authenticating witness or by offering conflicting rebuttal evidence.[24]

§ 901.5   Authentication of Documentary Evidence

A writing may be authenticated under Rule 901(b)(1) by testimony of a witness who has firsthand knowledge of the execution, preparation or custody of the writing. For example, where connective relevance involves attributing authorship or execution to a particular individual, persons who were present at the signing of the document may testify that the document offered at trial is the same one they saw executed by a particular individual.[25] Additionally, witnesses may authenticate a writing based on their familiarity with the writing, acquired by having read, typed, or prepared it,[26] or by having supervised its preparation or having had custody of the document.[27] With regard to business records, for example, authenticating

---

[22] 5 WEINSTEIN'S FEDERAL EVIDENCE § 901.03; *see also* 5 MUELLER & KIRKPATRICK, § 514.

[23] *See* 5 WEINSTEIN'S FEDERAL EVIDENCE § 901.03.

[24] United States v. Whittington, 783 F.2d 1210 (5th Cir. 1986) (once the disputed evidence is admitted, the opposing party may attempt to discredit it in the eyes of the trier of fact).

[25] *See* 5 WEINSTEIN'S FEDERAL EVIDENCE § 901.03; 2 McCORMICK, § 219.

[26] 5 WEINSTEIN'S FEDERAL EVIDENCE § 901.03; 5 MUELLER & KIRKPATRICK, § 514; *see also* United States v. Durham, 868 F.2d 1010 (8th Cir. 1989) (copy of a threatening letter sent to murder victim allegedly authored by the defendant was authenticated by victim's mother and sister, both of whom had seen and read the original letter); United States v. Moskowitz, 581 F.2d 14 (2d Cir. 1978) (bank robbery prosecution; sketch by police artist was properly received on basis of testimony by eyewitness "that they had previously said the sketch looked like the robber," this satisfied the authentication requirements of Rule 901, and testimony by the artist was unnecessary).

[27] *See* United States v. Harrington, 923 F.2d 1371 (9th Cir. 1991) (police officer required to establish chain of custody of cigarette pack seized from defendant at time of arrest; once presumption of proper chain of custody was raised, defendant could rebut with evidence of tampering); United States v. Porter, 821 F.2d 968 (4th Cir. 1987) (photographs of defendant

testimony might be offered by a witness who prepared the record, or by one who supervised the preparation of such record.[28] Any firsthand knowledge of a writing, however acquired, is an appropriate basis for testimony on the issue of authentication where the testimony logically connects the document with the issues of the case.[29]

§ 901.6   Identification of Real Proof

The testimony of a witness with knowledge will often be used to authenticate or identify items of real proof. Foundational testimony must establish a connection between the physical evidence offered at trial and the relevant transaction, incident, person, or place. In other words, the witness must identify the item in a way that ties it to an element in the case.[30]

Authentication of real proof under Rule 901(b)(1) involves offering testimony of a witness with firsthand knowledge that is sufficient to support a finding that the object offered at trial is the same object as that connected to the operative relevant facts of the case, and that the condition of the object is substantially unchanged.[31] In order to establish this foundation, testimony may be offered as to unique characteristics, such as a serial number, an identification tag, or a distinct appearance.[32] Where the item does not possess unique characteristics, it may be identified by the person or persons who had custody of the item from the time it was found in connection with the relevant fact of the case until the time it is offered into evidence. If more than one person has had custody, identification may involve establishing a "chain of custody." Pursuant to this technique, testimony is provided by each

---

with conspirators, used to show that the persons photographed knew one another before the pictures were seized, were sufficiently authenticated where chain of custody was established by officer who received the photographs and a witness identified the persons and places pictured); United States v. Whittington, 783 F.2d 1210 (5th Cir. 1986) (persons who signed as witnesses may identify a document by identifying their own signatures and that of one of the principals; they need not identify every page and need not have been present at time of signature of principal so long as they were familiar with the person's signature; once the document is admitted, the opposing party may attempt to discredit the document); 2 MCCORMICK, § 219.

[28] United States v. Atchley, 699 F.2d 1055 (11th Cir. 1983) (not essential that authenticating witness be the one who actually prepared the records).

[29] Clifford v. Transouth Financial Corp., 566 F.2d 1023 (5th Cir. 1978) (security deed without notarial seal admissible in light of notary's testimony as to its execution); *see In re Bobby Boggs*, 819 F.2d 574 (5th Cir. 1987) (bankruptcy court did not abuse discretion in admitting copies of payment and performance bonds offered into evidence pursuant to a state statute, where the statute was analogous to the "testimony of a witness with knowledge" example of Rule 901(b)(1)).

[30] *See* United States v. Fortes, 619 F.2d 108 (1st Cir. 1980).

[31] 2 MCCORMICK, § 212; *see* United States v. S. B. Penick & Co., 136 F.2d 413 (2d Cir. 1943) (evidence must remain unchanged in important respects); *see also* Rule 901(a), which establishes the threshold standard for authentication and identification.

[32] Walker v. Firestone Tire & Rubber Co., 412 F.2d 60 (2d Cir. 1969).

person who had custody of the item from the time it was taken from its relevant setting in the operative facts of the case until the time it is offered at trial. The "chain of custody" procedure for identifying real proof was utilized prior to the adoption of the Rules and is illustrated by the pre-Rule cases.[33] In applying the "chain of custody" technique at trial, a possible break in the chain of custody does not render the evidence inadmissible, but raises a question of weight of the evidence for the jury.[34] Establishing such a chain of custody authenticates an item by showing the improbability "that the original item has either been exchanged with another or been contaminated or tampered with."[35]

In a criminal prosecution, the government is not required to call every witness who handled an exhibit before that exhibit may be admitted into evidence; the proponent of the evidence need only make a showing that the physical exhibit is in substantially the same condition as when the crime was committed. In making this determination, there is a "presumption of regularity," presuming that the government officials who had custody of the exhibits discharged their duties properly. The chain of custody need not be perfect, and gaps in the chain go to the weight of the evidence, not its admissibility. In addition, the government does not have to exclude all possibilities of tampering with the evidence, as long as it took reasonable precautions to preserve the original condition of the evidence.[36]

---

[33] *See* Gallego v. United States, 276 F.2d 914 (9th Cir. 1960) (tracing chain of custody sufficient in narcotics case); *see also* United States v. S. B. Penick & Co., 136 F.2d 413 (2d Cir. 1943).

[34] *See* United States v. Boykins, 9 F.3d 1278, 1285 (7th Cir. 1993) (absent evidence of tampering, there is "a presumption that a system of regularity accompanied the handling of evidence" in official custody and that "[g]aps in the chain of custody go to the weight of the evidence rather than its admissibility"); United States v. Brown, 136 F.3d 1176 (7th Cir. 1998) (recollection of eyewitness to events was sufficient to authenticate an audiotape of the events; when chain of custody is in question but there is no evidence of any tampering, there is a presumption that a system of regularity accompanied handling of the evidence if exhibits are at all times within official custody; possibility of break in chain of custody of evidence goes to weight of evidence, not its admissibility); United States v. Jardina, 747 F.2d 945 (5th Cir. 1984); United States v. White, 569 F.2d 263 (5th Cir. 1978).

[35] 2 McCORMICK, § 212. "It should, however, always be borne in mind that foundational requirements are essentially requirements of logic, and not rules of art. Thus, *e.g.,* even a radically altered item of real evidence may be admissible if its pertinent features remain unaltered." 2 McCORMICK, § 212 at 8–9.

[36] United States v. Turner, 591 F.3d 928 (7th Cir. 2010) (cocaine samples allegedly taken from the accused were admissible even though the Government did not present any witness who had personal knowledge of how they were handled by the lab analyst after she received them from the police, because the Government was able to verify that it took reasonable precautions to preserve the evidence in its original condition); United States v. Mejia, 597 F.3d 1329 (D.C. Cir. 2010) (although a break in the chain of custody may sometimes require exclusion of the evidence, exclusion was not required of a note found by a DEA agent in the defendant's wallet about ten minutes after the wallet was seized, apparently by Salvadoran

Change that occurs in an item of real proof between the time it was connected with the operative facts of the case and the time of trial does not necessarily render the item inadmissible. It may still be properly authenticated as long as the proponent offers testimony that describes or explains the change.[37] Any change in evidence, however, must not be so great as to render the evidence irrelevant or misleading, and, in this regard, the judge may reject any evidence where its changed condition warrants application of the exclusionary provision of Rule 403. Change may be manifested, for example, whenever the evidence offered at trial is a sample drawn from a larger mass. Such evidence should be admissible where the authenticating evidence indicates that the sample is accurately representative of the mass and that it has undergone no changes that would affect its relevance.[38]

The adoption of the Rules of Evidence emphasizes through the express language of Rule 901(a) and Rule 901(b) that there is no singularly prescribed method of authentication for a particular item of real proof. Any foundational evidence satisfying the threshold standard set forth in Rule 901(a) is sufficient to meet the authentication requirement. It must be remembered, however, that because the trier of fact is required to ascribe weight to the genuineness of any item of real proof, the foundation of preference in a given case may often involve more than an effort to satisfy the minimal test of Rule 901(a). Accordingly, in an effort to convince the trier of fact of a particular element of its case beyond a reasonable doubt, the prosecution might establish a meticulous foundation under the chain of custody technique where a less exacting foundation would satisfy Rule 901(a).

§ 901.7   Authentication of Other Types of Demonstrative Evidence

Identification or authentication is also required with other types of demonstrative evidence such as photographs, x-rays, video films, and the like.[39] Identification of photographs, for example, under Rule 901(b)(1) requires testimony that the authenticating witness has firsthand knowledge of the person, place, or object depicted.[40] It is not necessary that the witness

---

police; the brief ten-minute gap between defendant's arrest and the agent's taking possession of the list made it implausible that the list was planted, tampered with or misidentified).

[37] *See* United States v. Lambert, 580 F.2d 740 (5th Cir. 1978) (physical condition of vehicle identification number plates altered substantially by time of trial admissible because officers who seized plates were thoroughly cross-examined about original condition).

[38] *See* 2 McCormick, § 212.

[39] *See* United States v. Blackwell, 694 F.2d 1325 (D.C. Cir. 1982) (tangible evidence such as photographs must be authenticated or identified); United States v. Pageau, 526 F. Supp. 1221 (N.D.N.Y. 1981) (videotape depicting alleged crime must be authenticated, but no separate authentication required for sound portion of the same videotape).

[40] *See* United States v. Brannon, 616 F.2d 413 (9th Cir. 1980) (testimony by bank tellers that defendant was the person depicted in surveillance photo was approved by the court); *see*

was the actual photographer or even that the witness saw the photograph being taken.[41] The witness must testify that the photograph fairly and accurately represents the person, place, or object that it purports to portray,[42] or, alternatively, the witness must testify as to any differences between the portrayal and the item sought to be portrayed.[43]

§ 901.8   Rule 901(b)(2) Example — Nonexpert Opinion About Handwriting

(b) **Examples.** The following are examples only — not a complete list — of evidence that satisfies the requirement:

***

(2) *Nonexpert Opinion About Handwriting.* A nonexpert's opinion that handwriting is genuine, based on a familiarity with it that was not acquired for the current litigation.

Rule 901(b)(2) governs the authentication of documentary evidence by testimony of a nonexpert who is familiar with the handwriting of the author or signatory of a document that is handwritten or signed. Consistent with the conceptual basis of authentication, this type of authentication is probative of the attribution of authorship or execution where these issues are relevant in the case.

Conceptually and mechanically, the method of authentication provided by this provision is among the simplest of the Rule 901(b) techniques. Essentially, the authenticating witness is asked whether he or she is familiar with the handwriting of the author or signatory and, if so, whether the document or signature in question is in the handwriting of that person. An affirmative response to the latter question provides sufficient authentication to warrant admission of the document into evidence.[44] As discussed in the following section, there may be additional inquiry, either on direct or cross-examination, concerning the basis of the witness's familiarity with the handwriting in question. The latter inquiry, however, is directed more to the

---

also United States v. Porter, 821 F.2d 968 (4th Cir. 1987) (photographs of defendant with conspirators, used to show that the persons photographed knew one another before the pictures were seized, were sufficiently authenticated where chain of custody was established by officer who received the photographs and a witness identified the persons and places pictured).

[41] *See* United States v. Clayton, 643 F.2d 1071 (5th Cir. 1981).

[42] *See* United States v. Richardson, 562 F.2d 476 (7th Cir. 1977) (bank surveillance photographs authenticated by testimony that they fairly and accurately depicted the robbery).

[43] Photographs, movies, x-rays and similar evidence may, of course, be authenticated by other means. *See, e.g.,* Rule 901(b)(9), "Process or System," and § 901.38 *et seq., infra.*

[44] *See generally,* 2 McCORMICK, § 221; 5 WEINSTEIN'S FEDERAL EVIDENCE § 901.04; 5 MUELLER & KIRKPATRICK, § 516; 2 WIGMORE, § 570; 3 WIGMORE, §§ 694–697.

weight to be accorded such lay testimony than to the admissibility of the document.[45]

§ 901.9   Bases of Familiarity

A witness may be familiar with the handwriting of another person through any one of a number of means.[46] The only explicit limitation imposed by the Rule is that the witness's familiarity must not have been acquired for purposes of the litigation in which he or she is testifying. Sufficient familiarity may be acquired through a special relationship with the author, *e.g.*, a familial or business relationship, that allows the witness to testify concerning the genuineness of a document. For example, a husband may testify that a document bears his wife's signature, or an employee may testify similarly as to a document written or signed by his or her superior.[47] In these examples familiarity is acquired by virtue of a relationship with repeated exposure to the person's handwriting rather than by a single instance of viewing the handwriting. Pre-Rule law has held, however, that a witness who has merely seen the person write on one or more occasions may offer testimony sufficient to authenticate a document.[48] Additionally, it has been held that testimony may be offered by one who has "seen writings purporting to be those of the person in question under circumstances indicating their genuineness,"[49] even though the witness has never actually seen the person write anything or sign his or her name. For example, requisite familiarity may be acquired through an exchange of correspondence with the person in question.[50] Notably, then, the standard for assessing the qualification of a witness under this Rule is quite liberal, and the personal knowledge

---

[45] *See* Holmes v. Goldsmith, 147 U.S. 150 (1893) (questions on cross-examination permitted to show the strength and value of witness's opinion).

[46] United States v. Carriger, 592 F.2d 312 (6th Cir. 1979) (general familiarity by observing signers write their names); Throckmorton v. Holt, 180 U.S. 552 (1901) (familiarity acquired by having engaged in correspondence for several years); United States v. Dreitzler, 577 F.2d 539 (9th Cir. 1978) (former secretary permitted to testify as to handwriting of employer).

[47] 5 WEINSTEIN'S FEDERAL EVIDENCE § 901.04; 5 MUELLER & KIRKPATRICK, § 515; *see also* United States v. Dreitzler, 577 F.2d 539 (9th Cir. 1978) (former secretary of defendant was qualified as nonexpert to testify as to whether certain handwriting was that of defendant).

[48] Rogers v. Ritter, 79 U.S. 317 (1871) (clerk in recorder's office, custodian of archives, and secretary for Board of Land Commissioners all permitted to testify because the circumstances of observing signatures in question enabled them to judge genuineness with a degree of certainty).

[49] 2 MCCORMICK, § 221.

[50] *Id.* McCormick provides further illustration of this type of familiarity, such as where the witness "has seen writings which the person has asserted are his own, or has been present in an office or other place where genuine writings of a particular person in the ordinary course of business would naturally be seen." 2 MCCORMICK, § 221.

requirement of Rule 602 is satisfied by a minimal showing.[51]

§ 901.10   Admissibility versus Weight of Nonexpert Opinion

As noted in the previous section, a document may be authenticated under this Rule on rather scant testimony pertaining to the issue of familiarity with a person's handwriting. Inquiry into the extent of familiarity goes to the weight to be accorded nonexpert testimony.[52] Accordingly, a jury may be persuaded to accord little weight to the testimony of a witness who has viewed the handwriting of a person on one or two occasions as compared with a witness who has been in a position to view the handwriting on numerous occasions. Likewise, the testimony of a nonexpert on the issue of genuineness may be outweighed by other factors, such as the witness's "lack of credibility, by the contradictory testimony of an expert, or by the jury's own comparison [Rule 901(b)(3)], or by inconsistency with other evidence."[53]

§ 901.11   Utility of Nonexpert Testimony

Opinion testimony of a nonexpert on the issue of genuineness of handwriting is admissible by virtue of Rule 701. Rule 701 authorizes testimony in the form of opinion by a lay witness where the opinion is rationally based on the perception of the witness and where it is helpful to the determination of a fact in issue, *i.e.,* in this case, genuineness.[54] The permissive standard of Rule 901(b)(2) as to a witness's qualification to testify on this issue, however, has compelled McCormick to question the utility of such testimony.[55] He notes that nonexpert testimony on the issue of genuineness is "essentially meaningless in cases where the authenticity is actually disputed," inasmuch as "[i]f a writing is in fact questioned no person not trained in the science and art of document examination is truly competent to distinguish a skilled forgery from a genuine writing."[56] The author similarly questions the utility of this methodology in cases of undisputed authenticity where courts might just as easily establish a

---

[51] 2 McCORMICK, § 221; *see also* Strong, *Liberalizing the Authentication of Private Writings*, 52 CORNELL L.Q. 284 (1967).

[52] *See* Holmes v. Goldsmith, 147 U.S. 150 (1893); *see also* Throckmorton v. Holt, 180 U.S. 552 (1901).

[53] 5 WEINSTEIN'S FEDERAL EVIDENCE § 901.04. The author suggests that witnesses may also be tested by asking them to identify a genuine specimen among false copies, or by asking the witnesses whether they would rely on the signatures they identified in an ordinary business transaction; *see also* 5 MUELLER & KIRKPATRICK, § 515.

[54] *See* Throckmorton v. Holt, 180 U.S. 552 (1901); *cf.* United States v. Johnson, 805 F.2d 753 (7th Cir. 1986) (bank assistant cashier could testify to the lack of similarity between signature on check and that on bank's signature card).

[55] 2 McCORMICK, § 221.

[56] *Id.*

presumption as to authenticity in the absence of challenge.[57] In response it might be noted that the Rule provides a measure of reliability by requiring the testimony of a witness who has acquired at least passing familiarity with the handwriting of the author or signatory of a document being offered into evidence.

§ 901.12   Rule 901(b)(3) Example — Comparison by an Expert Witness or the Trier of Fact

(b)   **Examples.** The following are examples only — not a complete list — of evidence that satisfies the requirement:

***

(3)   *Comparison by an Expert Witness or the Trier of Fact.* A comparison with an authenticated specimen by an expert witness or the trier of fact.

Rule 901(b)(3) provides for authentication or identification by comparison of the item in question with a specimen. The comparison may be made either by the trier of fact in situations in which a layperson would be competent to make such a comparison, or by a witness who has been qualified as an expert pursuant to Article VII of the Rules. If the item is authenticated by expert testimony sufficient to support a finding that the matter in question is what its proponent claims it to be, it will be admitted. However, as in the case of all forms of authentication, the ultimate question as to authenticity or genuineness remains a question of fact for the jury. Where Rule 901(b)(3) is utilized and expert testimony is not offered, the trier of fact makes both the initial and ultimate decision as to authenticity, subject to control by the court as discussed in § 901.3, *supra.*[58]

The technique of comparison with a specimen may be utilized in a variety of situations to authenticate or identify such items as handwriting, typewriting, bullets, tire tread marks, shoe prints, fingerprints, voiceprints, hair, blood, fabric fibers, and the like.[59] In each instance, the goal of the comparison is to establish relevance by connecting the item in question with an incident, person, or place where, for example, authorship, use of a gun by

---

[57] *Id.*

[58] *See generally,* 2 MCCORMICK, § 221; 5 WEINSTEIN'S FEDERAL EVIDENCE § 901.05; 5 MUELLER & KIRKPATRICK, § 516; 2 WIGMORE, § 570; 7 WIGMORE, §§ 1997–2015. *See also* Hilton, *The Detection of Forgery,* 30 J. CRIM. L. & CRIMINOLOGY, 568 (1939); Inbau, *Toy Witness Identification of Handwriting (an Experiment),* 34 ILL. L. REV. 433 (1939); Strong, *Liberalizing the Authentication of Private Writings,* 52 CORNELL L.Q. 284 (1967); Note, 41 OR. L. REV. 154 (1962); *Modern Educational Aids for Simplified Explanations of Handwriting Comparisons,* 13 J. OF FORENSIC SCI. 509 (1968).

[59] *See* 5 WEINSTEIN'S FEDERAL EVIDENCE § 901.05; 5 MUELLER & KIRKPATRICK, § 516.

an individual, or presence at a particular location is a relevant fact of the case. Establishment of authenticity by means of this technique "depends upon a statistical demonstration or assumption that the markings or other identifying characteristics are so rare (alone or in combination) that it is likely that they had the same source."[60] The comparison of an unidentified writing with a genuine specimen has long been recognized as a valid authentication technique,[61] although as discussed in the next section, the Rule is less restrictive than prior law with respect to the evidence necessary to authenticate a specimen.[62]

§ 901.13   Authentication of the Specimen

Use of the comparison technique to establish authenticity actually involves two levels of authentication, *i.e.*, authentication of the specimen and authentication of the offered exhibit. In order to establish the requisite connective relevance, the item or document in question must be compared with an item the authenticity of which has been demonstrated. Authenticity of the specimen, then, is a logical prerequisite to the procedure. With regard to the specimen, the Rule requires only that it be authenticated to the same degree of proof as any other item, that is, by evidence sufficient to support a finding that the specimen is genuine. In theory, then, if not in practice, the Rule modifies prior law at least with respect to writings. Courts previously required that genuineness of the specimen be established by clear and convincing proof or, in some cases, by proof beyond a reasonable doubt.[63] Despite the apparently less rigorous standard required by the Rule, there is a logical justification for requiring a more compelling showing of the specimen's genuineness where the authenticity of the item in question depends entirely upon the authenticity of the specimen. Where appropriate, the trial judge is justified in excluding the specimen pursuant to Rule 403 in order to avoid unnecessary confusion.[64]

---

[60] 5 WEINSTEIN'S FEDERAL EVIDENCE § 901.05.

[61] *See* Advisory Committee Note, Rule 901; *see also* Brandon v. Collins, 267 F.2d 731 (2d Cir. 1959) (comparing signature with "concededly authentic signature"); United States v. Ortiz, 176 U.S. 422 (1900).

[62] 5 WEINSTEIN'S FEDERAL EVIDENCE § 901.05; *see also* United States v. Stembridge, 477 F.2d 874 (5th Cir. 1973) (on basis of exemplars and job application form, government expert testified that the accused wrote a certain note used in the alleged bank robbery; during "rigorous cross-examination" by defense counsel, the expert admitted that he could not identify the note as being defendant's handwriting on the basis of the exemplars alone; on redirect, government was properly permitted to bring out the opinion of the expert that the accused had disguised or distorted the exemplars, but that the printing on the exemplars and the application form were produced by the same person; "it is not improper for the prosecution to show that the defendant attempted to avoid providing a valid handwriting sample by intentionally distorting his handwriting").

[63] *See* Advisory Committee Note, Rule 901(b)(3).

[64] 5 WEINSTEIN'S FEDERAL EVIDENCE § 901.05; 5 MUELLER & KIRKPATRICK, § 516.

Establishing authenticity of a specimen should ideally be accomplished by means of a stipulation obtained prior to trial. It may also be established through pretrial discovery procedures such as a request for admission.[65] Otherwise, the proponent may demonstrate that the specimen is self-authenticating under Rule 902, or, alternately, establish its authenticity by a technique provided by Rule 901(b).[66] A specimen or exemplar may be received into evidence as such even though its substance is not itself relevant to any issue in the case.[67]

Appropriate specimens may be obtained from a variety of sources including writings already in evidence for some other purpose, documents contained in the official case file, business records, or private writings.[68] A handwriting specimen, for example, might be obtained in a civil case through interrogatories or a pretrial request for production, or by an in-court request made during cross-examination.[69] A handwriting or voice specimen of a defendant in a criminal case, or other type of specimen, may also be obtained by compulsion without violating the defendant's Fifth or Sixth Amendment rights.[70]

§ 901.14   Comparison by Expert or by Trier of Fact

Given an authenticated specimen, Rule 901(b)(3) requires that a comparison of the item in question be made by the trier of fact or by an expert witness. In either case, unlike Rule 901(b)(2), there need be no prior familiarity with the specimen or the handwriting.

Comparison by the trier of fact is appropriate in those instances where a layperson's knowledge is sufficient to compare the specimen and the item sought to be authenticated. In other instances, where meaningful comparison requires some specialized skill or knowledge, an expert witness should provide the authentication testimony.

---

[65] Fuston v. United States, 22 F.2d 66 (9th Cir. 1927) (defendant's signature on answer in attorney's office and testimony of attorney identifying client is sufficient).

[66] *See* United States v. Minker, 197 F. Supp. 295 (E.D. Pa. 1961), *aff'd,* 312 F.2d 632 (3d Cir. 1962) (an example of using Rule 901(b)(2)).

[67] 5 WEINSTEIN'S FEDERAL EVIDENCE § 901.05 *et seq.*

[68] 5 WEINSTEIN'S FEDERAL EVIDENCE § 901.05; 5 MUELLER & KIRKPATRICK, § 516; *see also* Reining v. United States, 167 F.2d 362 (5th Cir. 1948) (allowing comparison to signature on pleading filed in a state court action); Moore v. United States, 91 U.S. 270 (1875) (use of paper giving power of attorney as specimen).

[69] *See* United States v. Wylie, 919 F.2d 969 (9th Cir. 1990) (jury was properly permitted to evaluate a drug dealer's bookkeeping records).

[70] *See, e.g.,* Gilbert v. California, 388 U.S. 263 (1967) (handwriting exemplars obtained from defendant by compulsion held to be non-testimonial and consequently not violative of defendant's Fifth Amendment right against self-incrimination); *see also* Schmerber v. California, 384 U.S. 757 (1965) (blood samples); United States v. Williams, 704 F.2d 315 (6th Cir. 1983) (defendant required to read a neutral passage from *Time* magazine for the purpose of voice identification).

Where an expert is used to establish authenticity under Rule 901(b)(2), the expert witness preliminarily must be qualified under the provisions of Rule 702, and the proponent must lay a sufficient foundation demonstrating that the witness possesses the requisite knowledge, skill, experience, training, or education to be qualified as an expert in the area of, *e.g.*, handwriting or ballistics analysis. An expert need not be such by profession in order to testify on a particular subject; rather, he or she must "possess skill or knowledge in the identification of handwriting which makes [him or her] more capable of comparing handwriting samples than the jury."[71]

An explanation of the expert's conclusion is desirable in order to persuade the trier of fact to accord significant weight to the testimony.[72] Explication of the underlying reasons is furthermore appropriate since the jury must ultimately reach its own conclusion as to authenticity, utilizing the expert's testimony only as an aid.[73] Accordingly, an unsupported conclusion will be of little probative value on the issue of authenticity.

Experts are subject to cross-examination both as to their qualifications as experts and as to the basis of their opinion on authenticity.[74] With regard to the latter, it is permissible to test the expert's skill by an in-court demonstration. For example, a handwriting expert may be tested by having the expert attempt to identify genuine signatures from among a group of genuine and false signatures.[75] While any reasonable test of skill should be allowed, the court should exclude as unreasonable or unfair tests of skill that would properly require specialized equipment or chemicals unavailable to the expert in a courtroom setting.[76]

§ 901.15   Comparison with Specimen — Application

The most common application of the comparison technique of authentication traditionally has been in the area of expert testimony on handwriting.[77] More recently, the technique has been used increasingly to identify a

---

[71] 5 WEINSTEIN'S FEDERAL EVIDENCE § 901.05; 5 MUELLER & KIRKPATRICK, § 516; 7 WIGMORE, § 2004.

[72] *See* Rules 703 and 705, § 703.1 *et seq.* and § 705.1 *et seq., supra.*

[73] 5 WEINSTEIN'S FEDERAL EVIDENCE § 901.05; 5 MUELLER & KIRKPATRICK, § 516. The jury is free to accept or reject the opinions and comparison results of an expert. *See, e.g.,* Strauss v. United States, 311 F.2d 926 (5th Cir. 1963).

[74] 5 WEINSTEIN'S FEDERAL EVIDENCE § 901.05.

[75] 5 WEINSTEIN'S FEDERAL EVIDENCE § 901.05; 5 MUELLER & KIRKPATRICK, § 516.

[76] *Id.*

[77] *See, e.g.,* United States v. McGlory, 968 F.2d 309 (3d Cir. 1992) (testimony of a handwriting expert held to be sufficient under Rule 901(b)(3) to show the authenticity of handwritten notes); United States v. Stembridge, 477 F.2d 874 (5th Cir. 1973) (job application form used for comparison; such proof was expressly stated to be an "illustration of evidence sufficient to support a finding that the matter in question was what its proponent claimed").

person's voice and thus to authenticate conversations.[78] As noted previously, however, the technique provides a means for authenticating a wide variety of items.[79] For example, an experiment might identify a typewritten sheet by analyzing marks peculiar to a given typewriter and also by noting any unique characteristics of the typist where the specimen and the offered document have allegedly been typed by the same person.[80] Another frequent use of the comparison technique is in the science of ballistics where the proponent seeks to establish, for example, that a victim was killed by a bullet from the accused's gun.[81] In such a case, the prosecution may seek to establish through expert testimony that bullets found in the possession of the defendant bear markings similar to those of identified bullets taken from the victim or from the scene of the killing.[82] In each case of authentication by comparison, the proponent is establishing connective relevance in a some-what indirect manner as compared with the other Rule 901(b) illustrations, *i.e.,* by using an identified specimen to complete the connection.

§ 901.16   Role of Judge, Witness, and Jury

As discussed in the foregoing sections, the comparison required by Rule 901(b)(3) may be made either by the trier of fact or by an expert witness. In the former case, the jury is presented with the item in question in order to compare it with the authenticated specimen. Both the offered exhibit and the specimen for comparison are taken into the jury room for examination. To be admitted to the jury for consideration, however, the specimen must meet the threshold "sufficient to support a finding" standard for authentication. If expert testimony is utilized, the preliminary decision as to admissibility is made by the court; that is, the judge determines first whether the specimen,

---

[78] *See, e.g.,* United States v. Baynes, 687 F.2d 659 (3d Cir. 1982); United States v. Williams, 583 F.2d 1194 (2d Cir. 1978) (voice analysis held to have reached a level of reliability sufficient to warrant its use in a courtroom for identification purposes); *see also* Cederbaums, *Voiceprint Identification: A Scientific and Legal Dilemma,* 5 CRIM. L. BULL. 323 (1969); Jones, *Danger—Voiceprints Ahead,* 11 AM. CRIM. L. REV. 549 (1973). The process involves spectrographic analysis in which a voice exemplar is run through a spectrograph. The expert then determines whether the sound wave patterns from the exemplar match those produced by the voice on the tape recording sought to be authenticated. Weinstein discusses this method of authentication and identification under Federal Rule 901(b)(5). *See generally,* 5 WEINSTEIN'S FEDERAL EVIDENCE § 901.07, *et seq.* In this sense, voice identification by an expert through spectrographic analysis and comparison, rather than by the opinion of a lay person who is familiar with the voice of the person sought to be identified, may be seen as a specialized application of Rule 901(b)(3). It should be noted in this regard that the illustrations provided in Rule 901(b) are not necessarily mutually exclusive, and, in some situations, the terms of two or more illustrations may be pertinent to the authentication of a particular item.

[79] *See* Pyle and Mockbee, *Authentication and Identification,* 49 MISS. L.J. 151 (1978).

[80] *See* 5 WEINSTEIN'S FEDERAL EVIDENCE § 901.05; 5 MUELLER & KIRKPATRICK, § 516.

[81] *Id.*

[82] *See* Medley v. United States, 155 F.2d 857 (D.C. Cir. 1946).

and then whether the exhibit, satisfies the minimal finding as to authenticity. Ultimately, however, authenticity or genuineness, both of the specimen and of the item to be identified, is a question for the jury in attributing weight.[83] Accordingly, any demonstrative evidence utilized by the expert witness to explain his or her opinion, such as photographs, diagrams and the like, should be available to the jury for their consideration.[84]

Whether the comparison as to authenticity is made by the trier of fact or by an expert, the judge retains control over the procedure. In either case, the judge must make a preliminary determination as to authenticity of the specimen and, if necessary to avoid confusion, may exclude it under Rule 403 if there is a substantial risk of misleading the trier of fact. Where expert testimony is utilized, the judge must also determine whether the expert witness has been sufficiently qualified and, as previously noted, must determine whether the expert's testimony constitutes evidence sufficient to support a finding as to authenticity of the item in question. The court must also determine the admissibility of any evidence utilized by the expert to justify or explain the expert's conclusion.

§ 901.17   Rule 901(b)(4) Example — Distinctive Characteristics and the Like

(b)   **Examples.** The following are examples only — not a complete list — of evidence that satisfies the requirement:

***

(4)   **Distinctive Characteristics and the Like.** The appearance, contents, substance, internal patterns, or other distinctive characteristics of the item, taken together with all the circumstances.

Rule 901(b)(4) provides for authentication by reference to distinctive identifying characteristics of an item. Such characteristics may relate to appearance, contents, substance, internal patterns or the like, and, when taken in conjunction with surrounding circumstances, proof of unique qualities may provide foundational evidence sufficient to authenticate an item. Authentication in this situation is used to connect the item in question with a particular person or place where that connection is relevant to an issue in the case.

---

[83] 5 WEINSTEIN'S FEDERAL EVIDENCE § 901.05; 5 MUELLER & KIRKPATRICK, § 516.

[84] *See, e.g.,* 5 WEINSTEIN'S FEDERAL EVIDENCE § 901.05, where Judge Weinstein recommends that the jury should be allowed to take handwriting specimen into the jury room to compare it with the writing to be identified. *See also id.,* where the issue concerns identification of bullets: "The jury should be allowed to make its own comparison of the bullets, and it should be allowed to use the expert's photographs or microscope for the comparison if these aids are offered.").

The methodology of Rule 901(b)(4) establishes connective relevance by means of circumstantial evidence rather than by direct proof.[85] Unique characteristics, as discussed in the following sections, may be utilized to authenticate items such as letters, other written documents, telegrams, and voices over the telephone. Rule 901(b)(4) represents no significant departure from prior law.[86]

§ 901.18   Authentication by Proof of Contents or Substance — In General

Foundational evidence as to distinctive contents or substances of an item may operate as a basis for authentication. One mode of circumstantial proof illustrative of this application of the Rule is a showing of the unlikelihood that anyone but the purported writer or speaker would be familiar with the contents of the document or statements in question.[87] The probative value of such evidence depends upon the relative obscurity of the subject matter, since familiarity with a topic of common knowledge would not advance the task of identifying the author or speaker. Accordingly, a proponent seeking to establish authenticity of an item pursuant to this method must offer foundational evidence as to the subject matter of the item in question, the degree to which such subject matter is known, and the purported author or speaker's familiarity with the unique subject matter. Where the subject matter is not generally known and the purported author or speaker is shown to have had knowledge of its substance, there exists foundational evidence sufficient to support a finding that that person is the source of the item.[88]

The inference may be strengthened by proof of consistent surrounding circumstances such as, for example, evidence that a document was one of a series of consistent transactions in which the purported author was a known participant.[89] Of course, even though a preliminary finding of authenticity is

---

[85] *See generally*, 2 McCormick, § 225; 5 Weinstein's Federal Evidence § 901.06; 5 Mueller & Kirkpatrick, §§ 517–522; 7 Wigmore, §§ 2148–2154. *See also* Annots.: *Proof of Authenticity or Genuineness of Letter Other than byProof of Handwriting or Typewriting*, 9 A.L.R. 984 (1920); *Proof of Authorship or Identity of Sender of Telegram as Prerequisite of itsAdmission in Evidence*, 5 A.L.R.3d 1018 (1966).

[86] *See* Advisory Committee Note, Rule 901(b)(4).

[87] 2 McCormick, § 225; 5 Weinstein's Federal Evidence § 901.06; 5 Mueller & Kirkpatrick, § 518.

[88] It need not be shown that the purported author was the only person who could have known the pertinent details contained in a document. This idea, espoused by Wigmore, at 7 Wigmore, § 2148, is not carried over into the Rules. *See* 5 Weinstein's Federal Evidence § 901.06. Weinstein recognizes that the force of the inference decreases as the number of people who know of the details and who might have written the document increases. *See also* 5 Mueller & Kirkpatrick, § 518; *see, e.g.,* United States v. Wilson, 532 F.2d 641 (8th Cir. 1976) (provides a helpful discussion of other circumstantial evidence, along with the contents, that may be probative on the issue of authenticity).

[89] *See* 5 Weinstein's Federal Evidence § 901.06; *see e.g.,* United States v. Hoag, 823

made sufficient to admit the evidence, an opponent may seek to diminish its weight by offering evidence to the contrary.[90] As with all forms of authentication, authenticity may be challenged by the opponent and disbelieved by the trier of fact.

§ 901.19   Authentication by Proof of Contents — Reply Technique

One specific application of authentication by proof of contents is known as the reply technique or the reply doctrine.[91] If it can be shown, for example, that a letter was written to a particular person, and that the letter being offered into evidence is purported to be written by another person in timely response to the communication of the first person, the second letter's authenticity may be established by virtue of its unique contents.[92] Authentication in this instance rests upon the theory that the reply document reflects the respondent's knowledge of details derived from the first communication that are not generally known.[93]

F.2d 1123 (7th Cir. 1987) (court properly admitted letters bearing defendant's company's letterhead that referred to specific transactions that occurred around the date of the letter); United States v. Reyes, 798 F.2d 380 (10th Cir. 1986) (court did not abuse discretion in admitting names from handwritten notes seized from defendant's residence; source and contents of the notes and the correspondence of the information in the notes to members of the conspiracy under prosecution provided sufficient foundation for admission); United States v. Luschen, 614 F.2d 1164 (8th Cir. 1980) (drug prosecution; notebook found in defendant's bedroom in the handwriting of a single person apparently describing drug transactions and interpreted for the trier of fact by an expert was properly received; contents of a writing may be used in determining identity of author: "who wrote the notebook was established by the correspondence of the dates and prices to those involved in the case;" extrinsic evidence linked defendant to various drug transactions at least circumstantially).

[90] *See* 5 WEINSTEIN'S FEDERAL EVIDENCE § 901.06, in which the author notes, for example, that:

> the hypothesis based on knowledge may be rebutted by evidence raising a serious question of forgery, since it becomes possible that the identifying details were added by someone to give an air of verity to the document rather than by the purported author who obtained the information in the usual way.

See also United States v. Wilson, 532 F.2d 641 (8th Cir. 1976) (court admitted contents of two notebooks found in house, which according to informer were being used in narcotics operation; informer further testified that drug transactions were recorded in these notebooks; author of notebooks was unknown, but court found that contents, containing nicknames of defendants and code terms referring to heroin, were sufficient to make a prima facie showing of authenticity, which had not been countered by any evidence from the defendants).

[91] 2 MCCORMICK, § 225; 5 WEINSTEIN'S FEDERAL EVIDENCE § 901.06; 5 MUELLER & KIRKPATRICK, § 518.

[92] *See* 2 MCCORMICK, § 225; *see also* Winel v. United States, 365 F.2d 646 (8th Cir. 1966) (authenticity of letter established where it can be shown that the letter was sent in reply to a previous communication).

[93] In 2 MCCORMICK, § 225, at 50, the author notes other corroborating inferences as follows:

> In view of the regularity of the mails the first letter would almost invariably come

In order to utilize the reply technique, the proponent of the purported reply must establish that the first letter was actually sent to the person whose reply communication is sought to be authenticated. This may be established by testimony by the first letter itself or by a copy.[94] Proof of other corroborating circumstances may also be made, such as the fact that the reply letter bears the address of the purported writer on a letterhead or personalized stationery.[95]

The reply or knowledge technique may be utilized to authenticate evidence such as a telegram[96] or a telephone conversation.[97] For example, a speaker in a telephone conversation may be identified circumstantially where he or she subsequently took some action that was prompted by the discussion held during the telephone call in question.[98]

§ 901.20 Authentication by Proof of Distinctive Characteristics of Appearance

In addition to proof relating to a unique knowledge of contents, authenticity may be established by proof concerning distinctive characteristics of appearance or physical attributes of an item. For example, a letter's "physical appearance, postmark, return address, contents, and letterhead

---

exclusively into the hands of X, or those authorized to act for him, who would alone know of the terms of the letter. It is supported also by the fact that in common experience we know that reply letters do come from the person addressed in the first letter.

[94] As noted by McCormick, the requirements of Article X may have to be satisfied where the reply letter merely refers to or responds to the terms of the first letter. If the first letter is in the hands of the party opponent, a notice to produce may be required prior to any attempt to prove the contents by means of a copy; *see* Rule 1004; 2 MCCORMICK, § 225; *see also* Levinson v. United States, 5 F.2d 567 (6th Cir. 1925) (certain letters were properly authenticated; as to one, court notes that it "was a response to a request addressed to the furniture company at Cincinnati only two days before;" letters in question were on company letterhead and seemingly sent from its place of business in Cincinnati).

[95] 5 WEINSTEIN'S FEDERAL EVIDENCE § 901.06; *see also* National Acci. Soc. v. Spiro, 78 F. 774 (6th Cir. 1897) (letter was properly identified, despite fact that signature was affixed by rubber stamp, and seal was lacking, because it was one received in reply to one addressed to defendant at its home office in New York; it came from New York and was a communication from defendant, and was accepted since it was written on the business letterhead of the corporation).

[96] *See* 2 MCCORMICK, § 225, noting that some courts are reluctant to authenticate telegrams pursuant to this theory.

[97] Van Riper v. United States, 13 F.2d 961 (2d Cir. 1926) (Judge Learned Hand applied the reply letter doctrine to telephone conversation).

[98] *See* 5 WEINSTEIN'S FEDERAL EVIDENCE § 901.08; 5 MUELLER & KIRKPATRICK, § 518. Authentication of telephone conversations under Rule 901(b)(4) may be indicated where the witness cannot identify the caller or recipient's voice so as to satisfy Rule 901(b)(5), or where the requirements of Rule 901(b)(6), relating particularly to authentication of outgoing telephone calls, cannot be met.

may in combination sufficiently authenticate the writing."[99] Another example of unique physical appearance is that of a signature affixed by a rubber stamp, where it can be shown that it was the purported writer's custom to use such a stamp.[100]

§ 901.21   Authentication by Proof of Internal Patterns

A writing may be authenticated pursuant to Rule 901(b)(4) by internal linguistic patterns or characteristics that connect a particular person to the writing in question.[101] The formalized science dealing with this area is known as psycholinguistics, that is, "the study of the relationship between messages and characteristics of the persons sending messages."[102] Proof of pertinent linguistic traits may be offered by a psycholinguist, although expert testimony is not necessarily required.

Expert testimony may be utilized, of course, to bolster such an argument, although such supporting evidence would go to weight rather than admissibility.[103] It should be noted that where an expert testifies by comparing the linguistic patterns of a document sought to be authenticated with a writing specimen, there exists a theoretical and functional overlap with the authentication technique provided by Rule 901(b)(3). The duplication, however, poses no practical problems in authenticating the document.

§ 901.22   Authentication by Proof of External Circumstances

Circumstantial proof relating to external circumstances, such as custody

---

[99] *See* United States v. Bello-Perez, 977 F.2d 664 (1st Cir. 1992) (anonymous letter was sufficiently authenticated where there was substantial indicia of defendant's authorship); 5 WEINSTEIN'S FEDERAL EVIDENCE § 901.06. Judge Weinstein concludes that by such proof, the appearance of the letter, in essence, "speaks for itself and makes the document self-authenticating." Technically, Judge Weinstein's statements may be overly broad if taken literally because prior foundational evidence must generally establish the connection between such indicia of authenticity and the facts of the case. For example, if a postmark is probative of authenticity, some evidence must establish the connective relevance of the mark, *e.g.,* that the writer resided in the location indicated by the postmark. *See also* 5 MUELLER & KIRKPATRICK, § 517.

[100] 5 WEINSTEIN'S FEDERAL EVIDENCE § 901.06; 5 MUELLER & KIRKPATRICK, § 517.

[101] *See* Advisory Committee Note, Rule 901(b)(4); 5 WEINSTEIN'S FEDERAL EVIDENCE § 901.06 *et seq.*

[102] 5 WEINSTEIN'S FEDERAL EVIDENCE § 901.06; 5 MUELLER & KIRKPATRICK, § 522. A comprehensive treatment of this topic is provided in Arens and Meadows, *Psycholinguistics and the Confession Dilemma*, 56 COLUM. L. REV. 19 (1956). More explicitly, the psycholinguist explores such things as the "length, type, and distribution of sentences, relative frequency of imagery, word length and extent of vocabulary" to provide "some evidence of idiosyncratic characteristics of writers." Arens and Meadows, *Psycholinguistics and the Confession Dilemma*, 56 COLUM. L. REV. 25 (1956); *see also* Comment, *Stylistics Evidence in the Trial of Patricia Hearst*, 1977 ARIZ. ST. L. J. 387 (1977) (useful general discussion of evidence of stylistics and psycholinguistics).

[103] 5 WEINSTEIN'S FEDERAL EVIDENCE § 901.06; 5 MUELLER & KIRKPATRICK, § 522.

of an item, for example, may be utilized in conjunction with appearance, contents, substance, and the like, to authenticate an item. In this regard, proof that a document was found in the possession of the purported writer, or that it came from a corporate defendant's files, is strong circumstantial evidence of authenticity.[104] While testimony by one who has had custody of an item may be offered pursuant to Rule 901(b)(1), witnesses who have not actually had custody might testify pursuant to this Rule that they recognizes the document offered at trial as one which was removed from the business's files by virtue of its distinctive characteristics or contents.

Other external circumstances that may support a finding of authenticity include the integration of the document in question within a continuum of correspondence or a series of consistent transactions.[105] It may also be shown that the document contains references to an independently established event or to particular relationships or places with which the purported writer was integrally connected.[106]

§ 901.23   Rule 901(b)(5) Example — Opinion About a Voice

   (b)   **Examples.** The following are examples only — not a complete list — of evidence that satisfies the requirement:

   ***

   (5)   ***Opinion About a Voice.*** An opinion identifying a person's voice — whether heard firsthand or through mechanical or electronic transmission or recording — based on hearing the voice at any time under circumstances that connect it with the alleged speaker.

Rule 901(b)(5) governs the identification of a particular voice by anyone who has familiarity with the alleged speaker's voice. Such testimony provides the requisite connection between a voice, heard either directly or otherwise, and the alleged speaker where the speaker's identity is relevant to an issue in the case.

Voice identification is established by opinion evidence, that is, by testimony of witnesses that, based upon their familiarity with a speaker's voice, they believe that the voice sought to be identified or authenticated is that of the specific speaker. The technique may be utilized to authenticate, for example, a telephone call received by the witness, or a tape recording that is being offered into evidence. The opinion may be offered by a lay

---

[104] *See* 2 McCormick, § 224. *Compare* Rule 901(b)(7) (concerning custodial evidence pertaining to public records or reports).

[105] 5 Weinstein's Federal Evidence § 901.06; 5 Mueller & Kirkpatrick, § 519.

[106] *Id.*

person or by an expert witness.

§ 901.24 Subject Matter of the Identification

The voice that is the subject of the identification may have been heard by the witness either directly or indirectly.[107] Direct, firsthand exposure to a voice might occur where the witness heard someone talking in the next room but did not see the speaker. Similarly, the witness may have heard a conversation in the dark, or may have been exposed to a conversation while otherwise unable to see the speaker.[108] In these cases, identification of the speaker by means of voice familiarity is required inasmuch as a visual identification of the speaker's person is not possible.

Indirect exposure to a voice may, according to the Rule, be through mechanical or electronic transmission or by means of a recording. Accordingly, voice identification may be pertinent to authenticating a voice heard over a telephone, a public address system, a radio broadcast, or an audio recording.[109] Regardless of the manner in which a witness has experienced a particular voice, he may identify that voice if he has the requisite familiarity with the alleged speaker's voice.

§ 901.25 Voice Identification by Lay or Expert Witness

It is clear from the provisions of Rule 901(b)(5) that anyone who has heard the voice of the alleged speaker, at any time, may offer opinion

---

[107] *See generally*, 2 McCORMICK, § 226; 5 WEINSTEIN'S FEDERAL EVIDENCE § 901.07; 5 MUELLER & KIRKPATRICK, § 523; 2 WIGMORE, §§ 658. *See also* Decker & Handler, *Voiceprint Identification Evidence—Out of the Frye Pan and into Admissibility*, 26 AM. U. L. REV. 314 (1977); Greene, *Voiceprint Identification: The Case in Favor of Admissibility*, 13 AM. CRIM. L. REV. 171 (1975); Kamine, *The Voiceprint Technique: Its Structure and Reliability*, 6 SAN DIEGO L. REV. 213 (1969); Kersta, *Speaker Recognition and Identification by Voiceprints*, 40 CONN. B.J. 586 (1966); O'Neill, *The Reliability of the Identification of the Human Voice*, 33 J. OF AMER. INST. OF CRIM. LAW AND CRIMINOLOGY 487 (1943); Thomas, *Voiceprint—Myth or Miracle (The Eyes Have It)*, 3 U. OF SAN FERNANDO L. REV. 15 (1974); Weintraub, *Voice Identification, Writing Exemplars and the Privilege Against Self-Incrimination*, 10 VAND. L. REV. 485 (1967); Weissman, *Voiceprints and the Defense*, 10 N. ENG. L. REV. 25 (1974); Symposium, Trial Magazine, Jan. Feb. 1973, p. 44; Note, *A Foundational Standard for the Admission of Sound Recordings into Evidence in Criminal Trials*, 4 S. CAL. L. REV. 1273 (1979); Comment, *Voiceprints: The Determination of Admissibility*, 2 U. DAYTON L. REV. 73 (1977).

[108] *See* United States v. Wilkes, 451 F.2d 938 (2d Cir. 1971) (narcotics agent overheard conversation while outside defendant's apartment); Auerbach v. United States, 136 F.2d 882 (6th Cir. 1943) (witness overheard conversation while in a phone booth).

[109] *See* United States v. Thomas, 586 F.2d 123 (9th Cir. 1978) (identification of tape conversation); *see also* United States v. Carrasco, 887 F.2d 794 (7th Cir. 1989) (in a trial for counterfeiting alien registration and social security cards, court properly admitted tape recordings where the defendant's voice was identified by an informant who had met with the defendant); United States v. Louis, 814 F.2d 852 (2d Cir. 1987) (court properly admitted tape recordings of defendant's conversations with drug dealer where tapes authenticated by conspirator who identified defendant's voice).

testimony sufficient to identify the voice. Such a witness need not offer conclusive proof on the issue of identity but must merely offer testimony sufficient to establish a rational jury finding of identity.[110] Accordingly, a lay witness who has heard the alleged speaker on but one occasion may, within the court's discretion, give an opinion as to the identity of the voice in question.[111] Although such testimony may be sufficient to support admissibility, the circumstances surrounding the identification may be considered by the jury in assessing the weight to be accorded such an identification. Consequently, the jury may consider information, elicited on direct or cross-examination concerning, for example:

> [t]he opportunity a witness had to become familiar with the speaker's voice, its peculiarities, the time between hearing and identification, acuteness of the witness' hearing and the witness' state of awareness and proximity to the speaker at the time the voice was heard.[112]

Rule 901(b)(5) contemplates that voice identification by a lay witness will be in the form of an opinion, apparently in recognition of the obvious fact that testimony of this nature cannot be conclusive. In this regard, the Rule is analogous to Rule 901(b)(2), which provides for authentication of handwriting by opinion testimony of a lay witness who is familiar with the alleged author's handwriting. The two provisions differ, however, with respect to the foundation required for such testimony. In order to testify as to the genuineness of handwriting, familiarity of the authenticating witness with

---

[110] 5 WEINSTEIN'S FEDERAL EVIDENCE § 901.07; *see also* Auerbach v. United States, 136 F.2d 882 (6th Cir. 1943) (testimony was properly received despite the fact that witness did not even see the two men, one of whom he identified by the conversation he overheard while he was in a telephone booth in the lobby of a hotel; although it was possible that the witness could be mistaken, and despite the lack of certainty involved, this testimony was used to identify the defendant's voice).

[111] United States v. Cook, 600 F.3d 847 (7th Cir. 2010) (a police officer could identify the defendant as one of several people whose voice could be heard on a wiretapped phone conversation, even if his familiarity was only based on having heard the defendant speaking several sentences totaling 62 words at a few pretrial hearings; a witness may identify a voice even if he has only "minimal familiarity" with the speaker's voice, and questions about the basis for the identification generally go to the weight of the testimony rather than its admissibility); United States v. Axselle, 604 F.2d 1330 (10th Cir. 1979) (witness heard defendant's voice once at a hearing 30 days after telephone conversation to be identified; this exposure to defendant's voice sufficed); *see, e.g.,* United States v. Santana, 898 F.2d 821 (1st Cir. 1990) (DEA undercover agent permitted to testify as to the identity of defendant's voice that he had heard on tape even though he had never seen defendant); United States v. Cooke, 795 F.2d 527 (6th Cir. 1986) (district court properly permitted FBI agent to identify defendant's voice on wiretap recordings where agent had heard defendant speak in court on two occasions).

[112] *See, e.g.,* United States v. Moia, 251 F.2d 255 (2d Cir. 1958) (a government agent had twelve telephone conversations with an unidentified person whose voice he recognized during a face-to-face conversation the day after the last call).

the alleged author's handwriting must pre-exist the litigation. Rule 901(b)(5) contains no similar time requirement regarding the witness's familiarity with the alleged speaker's voice. As discussed in the following section, the familiarity as to voice may be acquired at any time and presumably may be acquired specifically for purposes of the litigation in which the voice identification is offered.

Rule 901(b)(5) does not specify the type of witness who may give opinion testimony as to voice identification, and such testimony may be given by a lay or expert witness.[113] Expert testimony may involve the use of voice prints and the spectrographic comparison of, for example, the tape recorded voice of a known speaker with that of a speaker whose identity is sought to be established.[114] Voice identification by an expert witness may be viewed as a specialized application of Rule 901(b)(3), because the expert testifies on the basis of comparing a given voice with a specimen of known origin. Familiarity based upon "hearing" the voice of the alleged speaker as provided by Rule 901(b)(5) should be construed broadly enough to include familiarity based upon voice print analysis.[115] In view of studies that indicate the relative unreliability of voice recognition by most laypersons, voice print authentication is particularly warranted.[116]

§ 901.26   Foundational Requirements for Voice Identification Testimony

The proponent of voice identification testimony must establish by way of foundation that the witness has some familiarity with the alleged speaker's voice. According to the Rule, this may be established by showing that the witness has heard the voice sought to be identified "at any time under circumstances that connect it with the alleged speaker." Consequently, the requisite familiarity may arise from exposure to the alleged speaker's voice prior to or subsequent to the conversation or communication in question.

---

[113] *Cf.* Advisory Committee Note, Rule 901(b)(5) (noting that aural voice identification is not a subject of expert testimony). For an implicit rejection of this view, see 5 WEINSTEIN'S FEDERAL EVIDENCE § 901.07; 5 MUELLER & KIRKPATRICK, § 523. *See also* United States v. Hughes, 658 F.2d 317 (5th Cir. 1981) (past conversations); United States v. Cuesta, 597 F.2d 903 (5th Cir. 1979) ("[R]ule 901(b)(5) merely requires that the witness have some familiarity with the voice he identifies"); United States v. Vitale, 549 F.2d 71 (8th Cir. 1977) (testimony of witness that he had spoken twice to defendant and recognized his voice on telephone as sufficient foundation); United States v. McCartney, 264 F.2d 628 (7th Cir. 1959) (agent heard three calls by putting his ear near receiver and recognized voice as defendant's when he met him a few hours later).

[114] *See* 5 WEINSTEIN'S FEDERAL EVIDENCE § 901.07; 5 MUELLER & KIRKPATRICK, § 523.

[115] *See id.*; 5 MUELLER & KIRKPATRICK, § 523; *see also* Kamine, *The Voiceprint Technique: Its Structure and Reliability*, 6 SAN DIEGO L. REV. 213 (1969).

[116] *See* O'Neill, *The Reliability of the Identification of the Human Voice*, 3 J. CRIM. L. AND CRIMINOLOGY 487 (1942).

In the typical situation, witnesses offering opinions on voice identification will do so based on their *prior* familiarity with the voice in question. For example, witnesses may authenticate a telephone conversation by testifying that they received a telephone call from a person whom they were able to identify because they were familiar with that person's voice from previous communications.[117]

The pertinent identification to which the witness is testifying need not, however, occur simultaneously with the witness's exposure to the voice the identity of which is in question. Thus, for example, witnesses might have been exposed to an unfamiliar voice that they are able to identify at a later point in time based on subsequently acquired familiarity.[118] It should be pointed out that in this situation the witnesses are not so much identifying or remembering the prior voice as they are identifying the present voice, of known origin, as being the same as that which they previously experienced. Subsequent identification might occur, for example, where the witnesses were victims of a robber who, although masked, had spoken several sentences in the victim's (witness's) presence. Assuming the robber was previously unknown to the victim, voice identification would occur, if at all, based on the witness's subsequent exposure to a known suspect's voice. The foundation in this instance would consist of testimony by the witnesses that they became familiar with the accused's voice through subsequent encounters during which the accused spoke. Such subsequent exposure might be voluntary on the part of the accused, or it might involve a compulsory elicitation of the accused's voice on a recording or during a line-up.[119] In this latter regard, courts have held that the prosecution may compel an accused to give a voice exemplar without violating the accused's constitu-

---

[117] *See* Advisory Committee Note, Rule 901(b)(5) ("The requisite familiarity may be acquired either before or after the particular speaking which is the subject of the identification").

[118] Advisory Committee Note, Rule 901(b)(5); *see* United States v. Cook, 600 F.3d 847 (7th Cir. 2010) (police officer could identify the defendant's voice on a wiretapped phone conversation based on having heard the defendant speaking at later pretrial hearings); United States v. DiMuro, 540 F.2d 503 (1st Cir. 1976) (agent properly allowed to identify defendant's voice in June telephone conversations on basis of "a personal confrontation" in August).

[119] *See* 5 WEINSTEIN'S FEDERAL EVIDENCE § 901.07; 5 MUELLER & KIRKPATRICK, § 523; *see also* United States v. Chibbaro, 361 F.2d 365 (3d Cir. 1966) (defendant and other suspects were observed and listened to from behind a one-way mirror); United States v. Wade, 388 U.S. 218 (1967) (compelled voice exemplar does not infringe Fifth Amendment right against self-incrimination); Meggs v. Fair, 621 F.2d 460 (1st Cir. 1980) (voice identification testimony based upon hearing defendant speak did not violate Fifth Amendment privilege against self-incrimination, despite fact that defendant did not know he was being listened to at the police station, where there was no showing that his statements were used for any other purpose than to identify him).

tional rights.[120]

A voice exemplar might also consist of a tape recording of a person whose identity is known. Conversely, the voice sought to be identified may be a recorded voice. In either case, the proponent should offer foundational testimony to the effect that the recording is an accurate reproduction of the voice in question or that the recording equipment is of such a quality as to assure accurate reproduction.[121]

§ 901.27   Evidence Establishing Voice Identification

Voice identification pursuant to Rule 901(b)(5) may be offered into evidence in one of several forms. Witnesses may testify as to their opinion that a voice they heard on a particular occasion was that of a given person. Alternatively, the evidence may consist of a tape recording that is played in the courtroom, accompanied by testimony of a witness who identifies the voice on the recording.[122] In some cases, a transcript of a tape may be admissible where a transcript would aid authentication in, *e.g.,* revealing

---

[120] Compulsory voice exemplars are categorized, along with blood samples, visual display of one's person and the like, as real or physical evidence rather than testimonial communication, and as such they do not violate the accused's privilege against self-incrimination. *See, e.g.,* United States v. Williams, 704 F.2d 315 (6th Cir. 1983) (defendant compelled to read a neutral passage from *Time* magazine for purposes of voice identification); *see* 5 WEINSTEIN'S FEDERAL EVIDENCE § 901.07; 5 MUELLER & KIRKPATRICK, § 523; *cf.* Weintraub, *Voice Identification, Writing Exemplars and the Privilege Against Self-Incrimination,* 10 VAND. L. REV. 485 (1967). Judge Weinstein points out, however, that the constitutional propriety of obtaining a voice exemplar may depend upon the manner in which a voice identification is conducted and the words a suspect is asked to repeat. 5 WEINSTEIN'S FEDERAL EVIDENCE § 901.07.

[121] *See* 5 WEINSTEIN'S FEDERAL EVIDENCE § 901.07; 5 MUELLER & KIRKPATRICK, § 524; *see also* 58 A.L.R.2d 1024 (1958).

[122] The easiest way to lay such a foundation is through the testimony of a witness who participated in the conversation, United States v. Smith, 591 F.3d 974 (8th Cir. 2010) (a witness can authenticate a DVD or an audio recording, even if the recording was not marked, if the witness can verify that she participated in the conversation that is shown or heard on the recording), but the witness who identifies the voice need not have participated in the conversation. United States v. Shukitis, 877 F.2d 1322 (7th Cir. 1989) (in a drug prosecution, an agent who was present during a recorded conversation was permitted to identify the voices on the tape although he did not take part in the conversations). *See* 5 WEINSTEIN'S FEDERAL EVIDENCE § 901.07; 5 MUELLER & KIRKPATRICK, § 524. Where the evidence itself consists of sound recordings, Judge Herlands, of the Southern District of New York, suggests several elements that should be established by foundation testimony. These include the following:

That the recording device was capable of taking the conversation now offered in evidence.
That the operator of the device was competent to operate the device.
That the recording is authentic and correct.
That changes, additions or deletions have not been made in the recording.
That the recording has been preserved in a manner that is shown to the court.
That the speakers are identified.
That the conversation elicited was made voluntarily and in good faith, without any kind of inducement.

speech patterns.[123] It should be noted that evidence of this type, as well as any testimony as to contents, is being offered to prove identity of a speaker and not as proof of the contents of what was said.[124] It should also be kept in mind that admissibility of a tape recording or transcript thereof is within the discretion of the trial judge. The former might be rejected, for example, where the recordings were of poor quality or where, for some other reason, it would not be helpful to the jury.[125]

Evidence concerning voice identification may be buttressed by circumstantial evidence, some of which may properly fall within one of the other Rule 901(b) illustrations. For example, the witness's identification of a voice may be based partially on distinctive characteristics of a speaker's voice, such as a speech impediment. In such a case, the identification is based on Rule 901(b)(4) as well as Rule 901(b)(5). Other circumstantial evidence may affect the weight of the identification testimony. For example, a witness's voice identification may be reinforced by evidence that the alleged speaker was present at the particular place and at the time where the witness claims to have heard that person's voice.

§ 901.28 Rule 901(b)(6) Example — Evidence About a Telephone Conversation

(b) **Examples.** The following are examples only — not a complete list — of evidence that satisfies the requirement:

***

(6) *Evidence About a Telephone Conversation.* For a telephone conversation, evidence that a call was made to the number assigned at the time to:

(A) a particular person, if circumstances, including self-identification, show that the person answering was the one called; or

---

The elements are derived from the pre-Rule case of United States v. McKeever, 169 F. Supp. 426 (S.D.N.Y. 1958), *rev'd on other grounds,* 271 F.2d 669 (2d Cir. 1959). Since the enactment of Rule 901, the *McKeever* test is no longer rigidly followed but serves only as a guideline.

[123] 5 WEINSTEIN'S FEDERAL EVIDENCE § 901.07; 5 MUELLER & KIRKPATRICK, § 524; *see* United States v. McMillan, 508 F.2d 101 (8th Cir. 1974) (found to be appropriate, in the sound discretion of the trial judge, to furnish the jurors with copies of a transcript to assist them in listening to the tapes).

[124] The same evidence may be utilized to prove contents if the same are not rendered inadmissible because of the hearsay exclusionary rules or because of noncompliance with the best evidence provisions of Article X.

[125] *See* 5 WEINSTEIN'S FEDERAL EVIDENCE § 901.07; 5 MUELLER & KIRKPATRICK, § 524; *see also* United States v. Watson, 594 F.2d 1330 (10th Cir. 1979) (upholding use of transcripts of taped conversations since proponent offered proof of the accuracy of the transcripts at a pretrial hearing).

> **(B)**   a particular business, if the call was made to a business
> and the call related to business reasonably transacted
> over the telephone.

Rule 901(b)(6) provides for the authentication of telephone conversations.[126] More particularly, the Rule is designed to apply specifically to calls initiated by the person who offers the foundational testimony, *i.e.,* the person initiating an outgoing call.[127] The Rule is applicable in the case of telephone calls both to individuals and business establishments, with a slightly different foundational requirement indicated for each. The Rule provides a method for attributing oral statements to a particular speaker or to a person who speaks for a particular business establishment where the identity of the speaker is relevant to an issue in the case. Establishing identity by means of Rule 901(b)(6) largely involves the use of circumstantial rather than direct proof.

The standard for authenticating telephone calls is liberal.[128] Initially, there must be evidence that a call was placed to a number assigned at the time by the telephone company to a particular person or business. Such evidence may consist of testimony or other proof such as, for example, telephone company records.[129] The additional specific requirements for authenticating calls to individuals and to business establishments are discussed in the following sections. It should be noted that if a sufficient foundation is

---

[126] *See generally,* 2 McCormick, § 226; 5 Weinstein's Federal Evidence § 901.08; 5 Mueller & Kirkpatrick, §§ 525–527; 7 Wigmore, § 2155. *See also* Comment, *Authentication and the Best Evidence Rule Under the Federal Rules of Evidence,* 16 Wayne L. Rev. 195 (1969); Annot., *Admissibility of Telephone Conversations in Evidence,* 71 A.L.R. 5 (1927), 105 A.L.R. 326 (1936).

[127] *See* Advisory Committee Note, Rule 901(b)(6). For a discussion as to authentication of incoming telephone calls, see Rule 901(b)(4) and Rule 901(b)(5) and accompanying discussion at § 901.53 *et seq., infra.* As to analogous authentication of amateur radio transmissions, see the discussion in 5 Weinstein's Federal Evidence § 901.08. Judge Weinstein also discusses authentication of telephone calls, both incoming and outgoing, by a variety of techniques other than specified by Rule 901(b)(6), in a discussion that is perhaps more pertinent to Rules 901(b)(4) and 901(b)(5). *See* 5 Weinstein's Federal Evidence § 901.08.

[128] *See* 5 Weinstein's Federal Evidence § 901.08; 5 Mueller & Kirkpatrick, § 525.

[129] *See* 5 Weinstein's Federal Evidence § 901.08; 5 Mueller & Kirkpatrick, § 525; *see also* United States v. Sawyer, 607 F.2d 1190 (7th Cir. 1980) (call to defendant Sawyer placed by Revenue Agent was properly authenticated because it was "undisputed that the number listed in the agent's report was Sawyer's business number"); Palos v. United States, 416 F.2d 438, 440 (5th Cir. 1969) (narcotics prosecution; government agent Villar properly authenticated phone call that he placed: "Villar dialed a number registered to the appellant. When the phone was answered, Villar asked 'Palitos?', a name under which appellant was known, and received a response 'Yes, this is he.' ").

established, testimony as to the contents of the telephone conversation is admissible as long as it is not otherwise excludable on such bases as general relevance or hearsay. The Rule is premised upon factors that are indicative of trustworthiness. These include the presumed accuracy of the telephone system, the probable absence of a motive to falsify on the part of the answering party, and the lack of opportunity for premeditated misrepresentation of fraud.[130] The Rule codifies the majority rule in the United States as to both personal and business telephone calls.[131]

Rule 901(b)(6) is not an exclusive method for authenticating outgoing telephone calls. As discussed in the Advisory Committee's Note to Rule 901(b)(6), the testifying witness may also identify the recipient of the call on the basis of voice recognition pursuant to Rule 901(b)(5) or on the basis that contents of the recipient's statements related to matters known only by the alleged speaker, as provided in Rule 901(b)(4).[132]

§ 901.29   Authenticating Telephone Calls to an Individual

In order to authenticate a telephone call to an individual under Rule 901(b)(6), there must be testimony that a call was made to an assigned number. Additionally, there must be circumstantial evidence that identifies the person who answered the call as the one who was intended to be called.[133] This element may be satisfied by testimony that the recipient identified himself, or by other circumstances that are probative of identity. Self-identification is recognized as a reliable indicium of identity in the case of outgoing calls, because in such situations there is a probable absence of motive and opportunity to falsify.[134] The same guarantees are not necessarily present in connection with incoming calls, where self-identification is insufficient in itself to establish authenticity.[135]

---

[130] *See* 2 McCormick, § 226. The Rule reflects what Wigmore calls "mercantile custom," which assumes in ordinary circumstances that: "the numbers in the telephone directory do correspond to the stated names and addresses, and the operators do call up the correct number, and the person does in fact answer." 7 Wigmore, § 2155, *cited in* 5 Weinstein's Federal Evidence § 901.08; *see also* O'Neal v. Esty, 637 F.2d 846, 850 (2d Cir. 1980) ("[I]n this circuit, self-identification of the person called at a place where he reasonably could be expected to be has long been regarded as sufficient.").

[131] *See* Advisory Committee Note, Rule 901(b).

[132] Advisory Committee Note, Rule 901(b)(5),

[133] *See* United States v. Benjamin, 328 F.2d 854 (2d Cir. 1964) (self-identification and proper dialing establishes prima facie case for authenticity). Self-identification alone, without evidence that a number assigned in a telephone directory was called, is insufficient to authenticate a telephone conversation. *See* United States v. Ross, 321 F.2d 61 (2d Cir. 1963) (fact that man who telephoned customer identified himself with defendant's name was not sufficient to permit jury to infer that defendant was caller).

[134] 2 McCormick, § 226.

[135] Incoming telephone calls must be authenticated pursuant to Rule 901(b)(4) or Rule 901(b)(5). These Rules may also provide the methodology for authenticating outgoing

In addition to self-identification, identity may be proved by a variety of circumstances. For example, a telephone call may produce results that are unlikely to have occurred in the absence of the call, such as where an action is requested of the recipient and that action is subsequently taken by the individual in question.[136] Alternatively, there might be testimony that a conversation played an intermediate and significant role in ongoing negotiations, or that the recipient's statements reflected familiarity with matters known only by the one to whom the call was made.[137]

§ 901.30   Authenticating Telephone Calls to a Business

Authentication of telephone calls to a business establishment requires, in addition to evidence that a call was made to a number assigned by the telephone company, evidence that the call was made to a place of business and that the conversation related to business reasonably transacted over the telephone. In such a case, where the witness has spoken with someone purporting to speak for the business with respect to business matters, "it is presumed that the speaker was authorized to speak for the employer."[138] The Rule should apply to all types of business concerns, including public offices.[139]

If the answering person has purported to speak for the business, it is not necessary that his individual identity be established, as long as the conversation is circumstantially probative of the identity of the place of business.[140] In this regard, the Rule requires that the conversation relate to business "reasonably transacted" over the telephone. The requirement is

---

telephone calls to a person at a number other than that assigned to him in a telephone directory. For example, in accordance with the provisions of Rule 901(b)(4), there might be testimony that a person told the witness to call him at a given number, and that the witness subsequently called that number. Self-identification in such an instance would operate as the distinctive contents required by Rule 901(b)(4), which, taken in conjunction with the alleged speaker's having given the witness a number to call, should be sufficient to authenticate the telephone conversation.

[136] *See* 5 WEINSTEIN'S FEDERAL EVIDENCE § 901.08; 5 MUELLER & KIRKPATRICK, § 526.

[137] *Id.*

[138] 2 MCCORMICK, § 226; 5 WEINSTEIN'S FEDERAL EVIDENCE § 901.08; 7 WIGMORE, § 2156. Judge Weinstein notes that a business must accept the consequences of having invited the public, by listing a business telephone number in a directory, to transact business with the company by calling that number. In such a case, the business "cannot prevent the admission of testimony concerning a call placed to his business office by claiming that the person answering was not authorized to do so." 5 WEINSTEIN'S FEDERAL EVIDENCE § 901.08.

[139] 5 WEINSTEIN'S FEDERAL EVIDENCE § 901.08; *see* Zurich General Accident & Liability Co. v. Baum, 159 Va. 404, 165 S.E. 518 (Va. 1932) (listing a business telephone number in a directory is assumed to be an invitation to the public to transact business with the company by calling that number; presumption is that they authorize communications made over the telephone in ordinary business transactions).

[140] 5 WEINSTEIN'S FEDERAL EVIDENCE § 901.08; 5 MUELLER & KIRKPATRICK, § 526.

somewhat nebulous, but should be interpreted liberally in view of the Rules' policy toward favoring the admissibility of evidence. In this regard, the recipient of the call "need only speak with apparent understanding of the matter put to him."[141]

§ 901.31 Witnesses Who May Testify as to Telephone Conversations

In most situations, testimony pursuant to Rule 901(b)(6) will be offered by the person who made the telephone call that is sought to be authenticated. Under pre-Rule Federal law, and under the Rule, the witnesses competent to authenticate a telephone conversation are not limited to the participants.[142] People who eavesdrop or otherwise overhear telephone conversations may testify to the conversation they heard by satisfying the same requirements of authentication that apply to the participants.[143] The role that witnesses played in a call to which they testify is not determinative of the admissibility of their testimony.[144]

§ 901.32 Rule 901(b)(7) Example — Evidence About Public Records

    (b)   **Examples.** The following are examples only — not a complete list — of evidence that satisfies the requirement:

        ***

        (7)   ***Evidence About Public Records.*** Evidence that:

            (A)   a document was recorded or filed in a public office as authorized by law; or

            (B)   a purported public record or statement is from the office where items of this kind are kept.

---

[141] *See* United States v. Kingston, 971 F.2d 481 (10th Cir. 1992) (voices on telephone calls were properly authenticated where the agents called the number given to them, the voice identified itself as defendant and it relayed information about the property that only defendant possessed); 5 WEINSTEIN'S FEDERAL EVIDENCE § 901.08; 5 MUELLER & KIRKPATRICK, § 526; *see also* Rice v. Fidelity & Casualty Co. of New York, 250 Mich. 398, 230 N.W. 181 (Mich. 1930) ("the call for Mr. Upington at his business telephone number, together with the claimed relevant reply . . . furnished prima facie proof of identity").

[142] *See* United States v. Bucur, 194 F.2d 297 (7th Cir. 1952) (same rules of authentication apply to bystander or non-participant); *see also* 5 WEINSTEIN'S FEDERAL EVIDENCE § 901.08; *see, e.g.,* United States v. Scully, 546 F.2d 255 (9th Cir. 1976), *vacated and remanded on other grounds sub. nom.,* United States v. Cabral, 430 U.S. 902 (1977) (authentication by circumstantial evidence).

[143] 5 WEINSTEIN'S FEDERAL EVIDENCE § 901.08; 5 MUELLER & KIRKPATRICK, § 527; *see* United States v. Savage, 564 F.2d 728 (5th Cir. 1977); *see, e.g.,* Rathbun v. United States, 236 F.2d 514 (10th Cir. 1956) (wiretapper).

[144] 5 WEINSTEIN'S FEDERAL EVIDENCE § 901.08; 5 MUELLER & KIRKPATRICK, § 527. Questions as to whether a person actually heard the conversation, as well as the accuracy of his interpretation, are questions of fact that affect weight.

Rule 901(b)(7) provides for authentication of public records based upon a prima facie showing that the records are from a public office where records of that type are kept.[145] Accordingly, a party may authenticate public records by foundational evidence that, prior to the trial, such records were in the custody of an appropriate public office. By its terms, the Rule applies to writings that are authorized by law to be recorded or filed in a public office and that are in fact so recorded or filed.[146] Additionally, the Rule applies to any purported public record, report, statement, or data compilation, in any form, that is kept in a public office.[147]

The policy justification for such a rule is based upon the circumstantial guarantees of trustworthiness that attend recorded or filed documents. Such guarantees arise from the duty imposed upon public officials to accept only purportedly genuine writings for recording or filing.[148]

Authentication of public records pursuant to Rule 901(b)(7) contemplates that the record itself will be offered into evidence. Frequently, however, due to the inconvenience or impossibility of producing the original public record in court, the proponent will seek to introduce a copy of the record. If the

---

[145] *See generally*, 2 McCORMICK, § 224; 5 WEINSTEIN'S FEDERAL EVIDENCE § 901.09; 5 MUELLER & KIRKPATRICK, § 528; 7 WIGMORE, §§ 2158–2159. *See also* Annots., *Federal Civil Procedure Rule 44 and Federal Criminal Procedure Rule 27, Relating to Proof of Official Records*, 70 A.L.R.2d 1227 (1960); *What are Official Records within the Purview of 28 U.S.C. § 1733,Making Such Records or Books Admissible in Evidence*, 50 A.L.R.2d 1197 (1956); *Mutilations, Alterations, and Deletions as Affecting Admissibility in Evidence of Public Records*, 28 A.L.R.2d 1143 (1953); *Authentication or Verification of Photograph as Basis for Introduction in Evidence* (§ 11 "Photographs of or Constituting Part of, Public Record") (1950); *Compelling Production or Authentication for use as Evidence of Court Records or Writings or Object in Custody of Court or Officer Thereof,* 170 A.L.R. 334 (1947).

[146] *See* Advisory Committee Note, Rule 901(b)(7); 5 WEINSTEIN'S FEDERAL EVIDENCE § 901.09; 5 MUELLER & KIRKPATRICK, § 528; Rule 901(a) (as to the standard for authentication).

[147] Rule 901(b)(7) refers to a purported public "record," a term of art which "includes a memorandum, report, or data compilation." Rule 101(b)(4).

[148] *See* 2 McCORMICK, § 224:

If a writing purports to be an official report or record and is proved to have come from the proper public office where such official papers are kept, it is generally agreed that this authenticates the offered document as genuine. This result is founded on the probability that the officers in custody of such records will carry out their public duty to receive or record only genuine official papers and reports. Accordingly, it is the official duty to record and maintain the document, rather than the duty to prepare it, which constitutes the document a public record. Similarly, where a public office is the depository for private papers, such as wills, conveyances, or income tax returns, the proof that such a purporting deed, bill of sale, tax return or the like has come from the proper custody is usually accepted as sufficient authentication. This again can be sustained on the same principle if it appears that the official custodian had a public duty to verify the genuineness of the papers offered for record or deposit and to accept only the genuine.

copy is certified, it may be authenticated pursuant to Civil Rule 44 or Criminal Rule 27,[149] or pursuant to Rule 902(5).[150] If the copy is uncertified, it may also be offered into evidence and authenticated pursuant to Rule 901(b)(7). In such a case, however, the proponent must also satisfy the best evidence requirements set forth in Rule 1005, which governs the admissibility of copies as proof of the contents of public records. A copy may be utilized if it is certified or, alternatively, if it is authenticated by a witness who has compared it with the original. Accordingly, a proponent who offers an uncertified copy of a public record must elicit testimony from a witness that satisfies the requirements of Rule 1004 or Rule 1005 and must establish, through testimony of that witness or otherwise, the foundational requirements of Rule 901(b)(7). The latter requirements are discussed in § 901.34, *infra*.

Authenticity of public records is merely one prerequisite to admissibility. In addition to establishing genuineness, the proponent must consider any other pertinent evidentiary requirements such as those relating to the best evidence rules, as discussed above, or to general relevance and hearsay rules.[151]

§ 901.33   Types of Evidence Admissible as a Public Record or Report

Rule 901(b)(7) applies expressly to two categories of evidence. The first includes any writing that is authorized by law to be recorded or filed and in fact recorded or filed in a public office. The definition includes writings of both a public and private nature, as long as they are authorized to be recorded or filed in a public office and are so recorded or filed. The range of pertinent writings may include, for example, judicial records,[152] legislative records,[153] records of administrative agencies,[154] records of correctional

---

[149] Federal Rule of Civil Procedure 44 and Federal Rule of Criminal Procedure 27 provide that foreign or domestic records, or entries therein, if otherwise admissible, may be evidenced by an official publication of the record or by a certified copy. *See* 5 MUELLER & KIRKPATRICK, § 528.

[150] Rule 902(4) provides that certified copies of certain public records are self-authenticating. *See* Rule 902(4) and § 902.9 *et seq., supra.*

[151] *See* 2 MCCORMICK, § 224, at 51:

> As is true with ancient documents, the question of the authenticity of official records should not be confused with the ultimate admissibility of such records. It is quite possible for a public record to be perfectly genuine, and yet remain inadmissible for some distinguishable reason, *e.g.,* that it is excludable hearsay.

See also Rule 803(8) and accompanying discussion at § 803.39 *et seq., supra.*

[152] United States v. Jimenez Lopez, 873 F.2d 769 (5th Cir. 1989) (concerning a record of the proceedings in the U.S. Magistrate's court).

[153] United States v. Aluminum Co. of America, 1 F.R.D. 71 (S.D.N.Y. 1939) (Senate document containing letter by Special Assistant to the Attorney General, two memoranda by

institutions and law enforcement agencies,[155] coroner's records and reports,[156] tax returns,[157] selective service files, weather reports, patent office records, military records, and any other official records from an office of any level of government, domestic as well as foreign.[158]

The second category of evidence included within Rule 901(b)(7) is composed of any purported public record, report, statement, or data compilation, in any form that is kept in a public office. The category includes, for example, reports of investigations by public officials, such as a geology and water resources report published by a water conservation board.[159] The Rule refers to data compilations in any form. Consequently, public records or reports may consist of writings, as well as videotapes, public recordings, computer printouts, and the like.[160]

§ 901.34   Foundation as to Custody of Public Records and Reports

In addition to establishing that an exhibit is a public record or report within the limit of Rule 901(b)(7), the proponent must show that the exhibit

---

Special Assistant to the Attorney General, and a report, all concerning alleged violations of court decree by Alcoa).

[154] Wausau Sulphate Fibre Co. v. Commissioner, 61 F.2d 879 (7th Cir. 1932) (testimony of counsel that certain waivers were from the files of the Bureau of Internal Revenue); *cf.* Concrete Engineering Co. v. Commissioner, 58 F.2d 566 (8th Cir. 1932) (containing signature of Commissioner).

[155] United States v. Locke, 425 F.2d 313 (5th Cir. 1970) (statement signed by prisoner).

[156] Manocchio v. Moran, 919 F.2d 770 (1st Cir. 1990) (autopsy report admitted without medical examiner's presence was properly authenticated at trial, and thus did not violate the confrontation clause).

[157] Desimone v. United States, 227 F.2d 864 (9th Cir. 1955) (tax returns produced from file in offices of the federal government were official records).

[158] Lowe v. United States, 389 F.2d 51 (5th Cir. 1968) (Sec. 1606.35(a) of the Code of Federal Regulations provides that "any officer or employee of the Selective Service System who produces the records of a registrant in court shall be considered the custodian"); Pardo v. United States, 369 F.2d 922 (5th Cir. 1966) (selective service files); United States v. Ward, 173 F.2d 628 (2d Cir. 1949) (selective service files); Morgan v. United States, 149 F.2d 185 (5th Cir. 1945) (price memorandum apparently filed with local War Price and Rationing Board by Company operated by defendant; document was properly authenticated, in part by the showing that it was taken from the official file of the Board); *see* 5 WEINSTEIN'S FEDERAL EVIDENCE § 901.09.

[159] 5 WEINSTEIN'S FEDERAL EVIDENCE § 901.09.

[160] *See id.*; 5 MUELLER & KIRKPATRICK, § 528; *see also* Halloran, *Judicial Data Centers,* 52 JUDICATURE 156 (1958) (computerized data compilations are presently maintained by several judicial districts, and the use of computers is likely to increase as more public offices seek to reduce the paperwork involved in keeping records of such matters as traffic violations, jury management, docketing, calendaring accounting, criminal records, and post-trial treatment of convicts); *cf.* Sunset Motor Lines, Inc. v. Lu-Tex Packing Co., 256 F.2d 495 (5th Cir. 1958) (punch card for an IBM machine kept by the United States Department of Agriculture excluded as hearsay and because it was not certified as required by Fed. R. Civ. P. 44(a)).

is from the public office where items of its type are kept. The requisite foundation of appropriate custody may be established in one of several ways. Accordingly, custody may be shown by pertinent testimony of a person from the office where the particular record was kept, by a certification from the appropriate office, by testimony of any person with knowledge, or by judicial notice.[161] It must appear from the foundational evidence that the custodial public office was an appropriate, *i.e.*, authorized, depository for the record or report in question.[162] The foundational witness, however, need not be the actual custodian of the record, nor need the witness have any particular knowledge of the contents of the record.[163] The witness must merely be able to satisfy the threshold requirement of showing that the record was in the custody of the appropriate public office.[164]

§ 901.35   Rule 901(b)(8) Example — Evidence About Ancient Documents or Data Compilations

(b)   **Examples.** The following are examples only — not a complete list — of evidence that satisfies the requirement:

      ***

(8)   ***Evidence About Ancient Documents or Data Compilations.*** For a document or data compilation, evidence that it:

    (A)   is in a condition that creates no suspicion about its authenticity;

    (B)   was in a place where, if authentic, it would likely be; and

    (C)   is at least 20 years old when offered.

Rule 901(b)(8) provides a method for authenticating any document or data compilation on the combined bases of age and corroborating circumstances

---

[161] 5 WEINSTEIN'S FEDERAL EVIDENCE § 901.09; *see* United States v. Blackwood, 878 F.2d 1200 (9th Cir. 1989) (in a prosecution for filing false tax returns, IRS agent testimony that the forms were in the custody of the IRS combined with testimony that the IRS customarily affixes locator numbers to filed returns, was sufficient to make a prima facie showing that the returns were authentic); United States v. Locke, 425 F.2d 313 (5th Cir. 1970) (statement signed by prisoner); Pardo v. United States, 369 F.2d 922 (5th Cir. 1966); Maroon v. Immigration & Naturalization Serv., 364 F.2d 982 (8th Cir. 1966).

[162] *See, e.g.,* Bank of United States v. White, 33 U.S. 262 (1834) (clerk of court certifying matters outside of his duties and powers).

[163] *See* 5 WEINSTEIN'S FEDERAL EVIDENCE § 901.09; 5 MUELLER & KIRKPATRICK, § 528.

[164] *See id.* Proof of proper custody does not depend so much on the familiarity of office personnel with the material in question as with the authority of the office in which the material is found. Persons who keep records in a public office need not be able to authenticate the material by their personal knowledge if proper custody is shown.

as to genuineness.[165] The threshold standard of admissibility may be satisfied by showing that a document is at least twenty years old, that its condition creates no suspicion as to its authenticity, and that it was kept or found in a place where, if authentic, it would likely be.

Rule 901(b)(8) represents a modification of prior law in two respects. First, the Rule includes data compilations as well as documents in recognition of modern methods of recording information.[166] Second, the Rule reduces to twenty years the common-law age requirement of thirty years.[167] The age reduction from thirty years is justified because a twenty-year period sufficiently guarantees that the document or data compilation was prepared prior to the inception of the controversy that forms the basis for the litigation.[168]

The rationale underlying the authentication of ancient documents focuses upon necessity and trustworthiness. First, the age of such evidence makes authentication by direct testimony difficult where the author, maker, or other witnesses with knowledge of the document have become unavailable due to the passage of time.[169] Second, the Rule admits evidence where the age requirements and the specified circumstantial evidence of authenticity indicate little likelihood of any motivation for false or fraudulent attribution.[170]

---

[165] *See generally,* 2 McCormick, § 223; 5 Weinstein's Federal Evidence § 901.10; 5 Mueller & Kirkpatrick, § 529; 7 Wigmore, §§ 2138–2146. *See also* Annots., *Dispensing with Proof of Proper Custody as Condition of Admission of Ancient Document,* 29 A.L.R. 630 (1924); *Questions of Evidence Involved in the Inspection and Examination of Typewritten Documents and Typewriting Machines,* 406 A.L.R. 721 (1937); *Admissibility in Evidence of Ancient Maps and the Like,* 46 A.L.R.2d 1320 (1956).

[166] *See* 5 Weinstein's Federal Evidence § 901.10; 5 Mueller & Kirkpatrick, § 529.

[167] See Advisory Committee Note, Rule 902(b)(8), for a thorough discussion of the reasons for the reduction.

[168] 5 Weinstein's Federal Evidence § 901.10; 5 Mueller & Kirkpatrick, § 529.

[169] 2 McCormick, § 223; *see* Wilson v. Snow, 228 U.S. 217 (1913) (deed more than thirty years old proved itself; court notes underlying theory that witnesses are dead and that it is impossible in such cases to produce testimony as to signing, sealing, and delivery by grantor); In Re Estate of Hall, 328 F. Supp. 1305 (D.D.C. 1971), *aff'd,* 466 F.2d 340 (D.C. Cir. 1971) (reason for ancient documents rule is the practical unavailability of testimony from those who actually witness the execution).

[170] 5 Weinstein's Federal Evidence § 901.10. Judge Weinstein contends that the Rule is based upon the improbability of fraud rather than upon the unavailability of attesting witnesses. *See* 5 Mueller & Kirkpatrick, § 529; *see, e.g.,* McGuire v. Blount, 199 U.S. 142 (1905) (in approving receipt of records of certain proceedings conducted during Spanish control of Florida, there was no evidence that the originals were lost, nor "any evidence of a fraudulent substitution of a made-up record in the interest of parties to be benefited thereby"); Fulmer v. Connors, 665 F. Supp. 1472 (N.D. Ala. 1987) (court admitted a 1941 payroll book of a defunct coal company; documents of requisite age and derived from proper

Authentication of an ancient document or data compilation under Rule 901(b)(8) simultaneously satisfies the hearsay requirements of Rule 803(16).[171] Nevertheless, the proponent may need to address best evidence considerations and must address general relevance principles in order to ensure admissibility of the document or data compilation.[172] As with all evidence, the court may exclude an ancient document pursuant to Rule 403 under appropriate circumstances.

§ 901.36 Types of Evidence to which the Ancient Document Rule Applies

Rule 901(b)(8) may be utilized to authenticate a variety of documentary evidence. By its terms the Rule applies to any "document or data compilation." "Data compilation" should be broadly interpreted, and according to at least one commentator, this term should include the items and processes listed in Rule 1001(1) and Rule 1001(2),[173] *i.e.,* photostating, photography, magnetic impulse, mechanical or electronic recording, X-ray films, video tapes, motion pictures, and the like. In any event, the Rule may be interpreted broadly in view of the illustrative rather than restrictive nature of Rule 901(b).[174]

Pre-Rule cases illustrate the types of documents that may be authenticated pursuant to the ancient document authentication doctrine. The technique has been utilized to establish the authenticity of such documents as letters,[175]

---

custody are admissible without direct proof of their execution where free from suspicious appearance); *see also* United States v. Kairys, 782 F.2d 1374 (7th Cir. 1986) (in denaturalization proceedings against defendant for alleged Nazi activity during World War II, court properly admitted defendant's Nazi SS personnel card obtained from archives of U.S.S.R. Defendant's claim that card was inaccurate and that U.S.S.R. routinely forged such items went to weight, not admissibility; card matched other authenticated Nazi personnel cards, was found where authentic cards are routinely found).

[171] *See* Rule 803(16) and accompanying analysis at § 803.64 *et seq., supra.*

[172] *See, e.g.,* 2 MCCORMICK, § 223:

It should be borne in mind that, despite the utility of the rule here discussed, it is merely a rule of authentication, the satisfaction of which does not necessarily guarantee the admission of the writing authenticated. Thus, it is sometimes forgotten that a writing may be proved perfectly genuine and yet remain inadmissible as being, *e.g.,* hearsay or secondary evidence. This source of confusion is compounded by a partial overlap between the requirements of the present rule and those of the distinct doctrine which holds that recitals in certain types of ancient instruments may be received as evidence of the facts recited. The latter doctrine, however, constitutes an exception to the rule against hearsay and is quite distinct from the present rule concerning authentication.

2 MCCORMICK, § 223 at 46–47.

[173] 5 WEINSTEIN'S FEDERAL EVIDENCE § 901.10.

[174] *Id.; see* 5 MUELLER & KIRKPATRICK, § 529.

[175] Bell v. Combined Registry Co., 397 F. Supp. 1241 (N.D. Ill. 1975), *aff'd,* 536 F.2d 164 (7th Cir. 1975) (letters and newspaper articles from the 1930's and 1940's were

wills,[176] deeds,[177] and maps.[178] Other examples might include newspapers or other periodicals.[179] It should be noted, however, that resort to Rule 901(b)(8) may be unnecessary with regard to certain of these documents, inasmuch as they may be self-authenticating under Rule 902.[180]

§ 901.37   Requisite Foundation for Authenticating Ancient Documents

The authentication of ancient documents is dependent upon foundational testimony relating to three considerations: age, condition, and custody. Accordingly, there must be foundational evidence that the document or data compilation is at least twenty years old. Age may be established "by the testimony of a witness with knowledge, by expert testimony, by the physical appearance of the proffered evidence, or even by the contents of the material itself together with surrounding circumstances."[181] A witness who was familiar with the signature of a person deceased for twenty years or more, for example, might identify the signature on a document as being that of the decedent, thereby establishing circumstantially the age of the document.[182] An expert witness might be utilized to establish age by comparison testimony as to handwriting, or by identifying the age of the paper, ink, or

---

admissible under "ancient documents" exception to hearsay rule).

[176] *In re* Estate of Hall, 328 F. Supp. 1305 (D.D.C. 1971), *aff'd,* 466 F.2d 34 (D.C. Cir. 1971); *see also* Smythe v. New Orleans Canal & Banking Co., 93 F. 899 (5th Cir. 1899) (considering the ancient character of the will, and the long line of possession of the property in question under it, it was properly admitted in evidence, having stood as a muniment of title to lands of great value for at least 100 years).

[177] Fulkerson v. Holmes, 117 U.S. 389 (1886) (deed offered as proof that grantor was son of patentee of land in question was properly received under ancient documents rule; in discussing propriety of admitting deed, court noted that grantee had claimed title under the deed for more than sixty years); *see* Wilson v. Snow, 228 U.S. 217 (1913) (deed more than thirty years old proved itself where possession of the land in question had been consistent with its terms for more than forty years).

[178] Burns v. United States, 160 F. 631 (2d Cir. 1909) (approving receipt of maps under ancient documents rule).

[179] Dallas County v. Commercial Union Assurance Co. 286 F.2d 388, 396–397 (5th Cir. 1961) (a newspaper article almost sixty years old was admitted to show that a fire had taken place; "it is inconceivable to us that a newspaper reporter in a small town would report there was a fire in the dome of the new courthouse — if there had been no fire; he is without motive to falsify"); *see* 5 MUELLER & KIRKPATRICK, § 529.

[180] For example, under Rule 902(6), newspapers and periodicals are self-authenticating, as are acknowledged documents under Rule 902(8).

[181] 5 WEINSTEIN'S FEDERAL EVIDENCE § 901.10. Judge Weinstein notes that these elements are not exclusive and that any facts supporting the inference that the document or data compilation has been in existence for twenty years or more should satisfy the age requirements for admission under the Rule. 5 WEINSTEIN'S FEDERAL EVIDENCE § 901.10; *see also* 5 MUELLER & KIRKPATRICK, § 529.

[182] 5 WEINSTEIN'S FEDERAL EVIDENCE § 901.10.

typewriting.[183] Information in the document itself may establish age, such as a written date, a postmark, certificate of recording, or the like.[184] As illustrated by the foregoing examples, any reliable evidence may be utilized as long as it is probative of the age of the document in question.[185]

Consistent with the second express requirement of Rule 901(b)(8), the condition of an ancient document must be such that it raises no suspicion as to authenticity.[186] This requirement relates to the appearance or the contents of the document. Accordingly, questions of authenticity may be raised by evidence that the document has been altered or tampered with, such as by erasures or other changes. Suspicion may also be raised where statements in the document are inconsistent with historical fact.[187] Conversely, genuineness may be corroborated by proof of acts or transactions that are consistent with the contents of the documents or by attestation or recording.[188]

The third requirement of Rule 901(b)(8) provides that the proponent must show, through testimony or otherwise, that the document or data compilation was taken from a place where, if genuine, it would likely be. In other words, it must be shown that the evidence was in an appropriate custodial place or possession prior to its use at trial.[189] Appropriateness of custody will depend primarily on the nature of the evidence. For example, a data compilation would likely be in the possession of the grantee named therein.[190] Conversely, for example, a deed would not normally be in the possession of the

---

[183] 5 WEINSTEIN'S FEDERAL EVIDENCE § 901.10; 5 MUELLER & KIRKPATRICK, § 529.

[184] *Id.*

[185] Judge Weinstein argues that the twenty-year figure should not be regarded as an absolute necessity, as long as the document appears to be authentic. 5 WEINSTEIN'S FEDERAL EVIDENCE § 901.10; *see also* Smythe v. New Orleans Canal & Banking Co., 93 F. 899 (5th Cir. 1899) (papers offered in evidence that bore signs of great age and of having been partially burned and doused with water admitted as ancient documents after court received evidence that office in which they were found had suffered a fire more than twenty years before trial).

[186] *See, e.g.,* McGuire v. Blount, 199 U.S. 142 (1905) (referring to the "ancient appearance" of the record offered, noted with respect to matters admitted under the ancient documents rule the necessity to "show that they are of the age of thirty years").

[187] 5 WEINSTEIN'S FEDERAL EVIDENCE § 901.10; 5 MUELLER & KIRKPATRICK, § 529.

[188] *See* Rule 902(8) as to self-authentication of acknowledged documents.

[189] 5 WEINSTEIN'S FEDERAL EVIDENCE § 901.10. Judge Weinstein notes that a chain of custody for the twenty year period need not be established in order to prove this element. Rather, the element will be satisfied "as long as all custodians or places of custody accounted for are consistent with the nature of the material." 5 WEINSTEIN'S FEDERAL EVIDENCE § 901.10; *see, e.g.,* Fulkerson v. Holmes, 117 U.S. 389 (1886).

[190] 5 WEINSTEIN'S FEDERAL EVIDENCE § 901.10; 5 MUELLER & KIRKPATRICK, § 529; *see, e.g.,* McGuire v. Blount, 199 U.S. 142 (1905) ("While the testimony tends to show that these documents were subjected to various changes of possession during the transition of the government of Florida from Spain to the United States, and upon the evacuation of Pensacola during the Civil War, there is nothing to establish that they were ever out of the hands of a proper custodian.").

grantor or some third party to the instrument. Where the custodial requirement cannot be satisfied, authenticity must be established, if at all, through
a means other than Rule 901(b)(8).

§ 901.38   Rule 901(b)(9) Example — Evidence About a Process or System

(b)   **Examples.** The following are examples only — not a complete list
— of evidence that satisfies the requirement:

***

(9)   *Evidence About a Process or System.* Evidence describing a
process or system and showing that it produces an accurate
result.

Rule 901(b)(9) provides a method for authenticating the resulting product
of a process or system. Authentication under Rule 901(b)(9) is established by
foundational evidence that describes the process or system and that shows
that the process or system produces an accurate result.[191] It should be kept
in mind that a preliminary showing of accuracy is merely one prerequisite to
the admissibility of such results. As with all authenticated evidence, the
exhibit must be relevant to an issue in the case and must satisfy any pertinent
hearsay or best evidence requirements.

Rule 901(b)(9) may be utilized in a wide variety of situations that are
discussed in the following section. Establishing authenticity pursuant to the
method provided by this Rule is not new to federal law.[192]

§ 901.39   Illustrative Applications of Authentication of a Process or System

The method of establishing authenticity provided by Rule 901(b)(9) may

---

[191] *See generally,* 2 MCCORMICK, § 228; 5 WEINSTEIN'S FEDERAL EVIDENCE § 901.11;
5 MUELLER & KIRKPATRICK, § 530; 7 WIGMORE, §§ 2158–2160. *See also* Bigelow,
Counseling the Computer User, 52 A.B.A.J. 461 (1966); Brown, *Electronic Brains and the
Legal Mind: Computing the Data Computer's Collision with the Law,* 71 YALE L.J. 239
(1961); Dessin, *The Trial of Economic and Technological Issues of Fact: II,* 58 YALE L.J.
1242 (1949); Freed, *The Effect of Computer Technology on Legal Liability,* Proceedings of
the Corporate Lawyers' Institute, Univ. of Wisc. 49 (1962); Freed, *A Lawyer's Guide
Through the Computer Maze,* 6 PRAC. LAWYER 15 (1960); McCoid, *The Admissibility of
Sample Data into a Court of Law: Some Further Thoughts,* 4 UCLA L. REV. 233 (1956);
Roberts, *A Practitioner's Primer on Computer-Generated Evidence,* 41 U. CHI. L. REV. 254
(1974); Scott, *X-Ray Pictures as Evidence,* 44 MICH. L. REV. 173 (1946); Sherman &
Kinnard, *The Development, Discovery, and Use of Computer Support Systems in Achieving
Efficiency in Litigation,* 79 COLUM. L. REV. 267 (1979); Sigmon, *Rules of Evidence Before
the I.C.C.* 31 GEO. WASH. L. REV. 258 (1962); Tapper, *Evidence From Computers,* 8 GA. L.
REV. 562 (1974).

[192] Symposium, *Law and Computers in the Mid-Sixties,* ALI-ABA (1966); Scott,
Roentgenograms and their Chronological Legal Recognition, 27 ILL. L. REV. 674 (1930).

be utilized in connection with any process or system that produces results that a party desires to introduce into evidence. For example, Rule 901(b)(9) will frequently be used to authenticate computer results.[193] In view of the ever-increasing utilization of computers in all aspects of society, this application of the Rule will undoubtedly increase substantially.[194] There is no requirement under Rule 901(b)(9) that printouts have been produced in the regular course of business although this factor may be significant if Rule 803(6), "Records of regularly conducted activity," is used as a basis for satisfying the hearsay issue. Consequently, printouts produced either in the course of business or expressly for use at trial may be authenticated under Rule 901(b)(9).[195] Use of computer printouts is especially valuable in cases in which analyses and syntheses of massive data are involved.[196]

Rule 901(b)(9) may be utilized to authenticate results from processes or systems other than computer systems. Such processes and systems may include, for example, x-ray films,[197] motion pictures, audio recordings,[198] medical tests such as electrocardiograms and electroencephalograms,[199] and

---

[193] *See generally,* 5 WEINSTEIN'S FEDERAL EVIDENCE § 901.11; 5 MUELLER & KIRKPATRICK, § 530. *See also* Rule 901(b)(9), Advisory Committee Note; *see, e.g.,* United States v. Scholle, 553 F.2d 1109 (8th Cir. 1977) (computer analysis of physical characteristics of drugs seized and tested throughout the country); United States v. Liebert, 519 F.2d 542 (3d Cir. 1975) (computer-prepared list of nonfilers of income tax returns discoverable by defense in prosecution for failure to file return: computer output is admissible in criminal case under certain circumstances). For further discussion of the use of Rule 901(b)(9) to authenticate computer-generated evidence, *see* § 901.41, *infra.*

[194] For an early but leading case in the area of authenticating computer printouts, see Transport Indemnity Co. v. Seib, 132 N.W.2d 871 (Neb. 1965). In this case, the Nebraska Supreme Court held that computer printouts produced from data stored on and retrieved from magnetic tapes were admissible in evidence under the Nebraska Business Records Act.

[195] *See* 5 WEINSTEIN'S FEDERAL EVIDENCE § 901.11.

[196] *Id.* Some possible computer outputs that can be authenticated by the accuracy of the process or system involved include translations, quality control or inspection systems, analyses of census data in reapportionment cases, and other instances where the mass of data involved is so great that use of an electronic computer is the only practical manner of gathering evidence. *See, e.g.,* Butterworth v. Dempsey, 237 F. Supp. 302 (D. Conn. 1965); Bush v. Martin, 251 F. Supp. 484 (S.D. Tex. 1966); *see also* Rule 1006 and § 1006.1 *et seq., infra,* (pertaining to "Summaries").

[197] 5 WEINSTEIN'S FEDERAL EVIDENCE § 909.11; 5 MUELLER & KIRKPATRICK, § 530; *see also* Scott, *X-ray Pictures as Evidence,* 44 MICH. L. REV. 773 (1946); Annot., *X-Ray Reports—Admissibility,* 6 A.L.R.2d 406 (1949).

[198] 5 WEINSTEIN'S FEDERAL EVIDENCE § 909.11; *see* LeRoy v. Sabena Belgian World Airlines, 344 F.2d 266 (2d Cir. 1965) (transcript of inflight radio conversation between plane that ultimately crashed and ground control).

[199] 5 WEINSTEIN'S FEDERAL EVIDENCE § 901.11; 5 MUELLER & KIRKPATRICK, § 530; *see* Croll v. John Hancock Mut. Life Ins. Co., 198 F.2d 562 (3d Cir. 1952). *See generally,* Annot., *Admissibility in Civil Action of Electroencephalogram, Electrocardiogram, or Other*

certain out-of-court experiments,[200] polls, and surveys.[201]

§ 901.40   Establishing Admissibility of Evidence as to Process or System Results — Foundation

Rule 901(b)(9) sets forth two foundational requirements that govern the admissibility of results from a process or system. First, the process or system must be described. Second, there must be evidence that the process or system produces an accurate result. The requisite foundation may be established by testimony from a person with knowledge of the process or system in question. Description of computer functions may be provided either by the person who had control and direction of the computer system, or by someone who is familiar with the operation of the equipment that was used.[202]

The type of process or system involved dictates the type of foundation that should be established, and the admissibility of process or system results contemplated by Rule 901(b)(9) may frequently involve judicial notice, stipulations, or expert testimony. For example, a court might judicially notice the manner in which a computer performs mathematical operations.[203] Likewise, admissibility of survey results or opinion polls may require expert testimony that the poll or survey was conducted according to recognized scientific polling methods and that the persons polled represent an accurate sampling of the universe under consideration.[204]

Record Made by Instrument Used in Medical Test, or of Report Based upon Such a Test, 66 A.L.R.2d 536 (1959).

[200] *See, e.g.*, State v. Sheppard, 100 Ohio App. 399, 128 N.E.2d 504 (Ohio Ct. App. 1955) (experiments must be performed with identical or substantially similar equipment and under conditions closely approximating those existing at the time of the occurrence in order for the result to be admissible).

[201] 5 WEINSTEIN'S FEDERAL EVIDENCE § 901.11; 5 MUELLER & KIRKPATRICK, § 530; *see also* Union Carbide Corp. v. Ever-Ready, Inc., 531 F.2d 366 (7th Cir. 1976) (public opinion surveys offered on issue of public confusion); President & Trustees of Colby College v. Colby College-New Hampshire, 508 F.2d 804 (1st Cir. 1975) (expert testimony based on survey); Stix Products, Inc. v. United Merchants & Mfgrs., 295 F. Supp. 479 (S.D.N.Y. 1968) (survey evidence received to determine consumer understanding of word "contact"); Zippo Mfg. Co. v. Rogers Imports, 216 F. Supp. 670 (S.D.N.Y. 1963) (survey evidence received to determine whether shape and design of cigarette lighters had acquired secondary meaning).

[202] *See* Advisory Committee Note, Rule 901(b)(9); 5 WEINSTEIN'S FEDERAL EVIDENCE § 901.11: "The witness should describe the computer's operation with enough detail to support a finding that the result is accurate and reliable"; *see also* 5 MUELLER & KIRKPATRICK, § 530. For further discussion of the use of Rule 901(b)(9) to authenticate computer-generated evidence, *see* § 901.41, *infra*.

[203] *See* 5 WEINSTEIN'S FEDERAL EVIDENCE § 901.11; 5 MUELLER & KIRKPATRICK, § 530; *see also* Advisory Committee Note, Rule 901(b)(9) (it is pointed out that the instant provision "does not, of course, foreclose taking judicial notice of the accuracy of the process or system").

[204] 5 WEINSTEIN'S FEDERAL EVIDENCE § 901.11; 5 MUELLER & KIRKPATRICK, § 530;

In addition to determining whether the requisite foundation has been established under Rule 901(b)(9), the court may properly employ other judicial controls with regard to such evidence. In view of the complexity that is frequently involved in this area, the court may impose pretrial procedures to ensure that the opposing party will have an adequate opportunity to review and rebut the evidence in question and to prepare a competent cross-examination of any authenticating witnesses.[205] Accordingly, a party intending to offer such evidence may be required in advance of trial to submit to opposing counsel the underlying data, the program method or other method of interpretation employed, and the conclusions or results that were reached.[206] The court may impose such conditions to admissibility in its discretion in order to ensure fairness and economy.[207] The court may exercise further control with regard to admitting such evidence during the trial, pursuant to Rule 403, when considerations of undue delay, confusion, and the like emerge.

§ 901.41   Computer-Generated Evidence

Rule 901(b)(9) is also likely to serve as the basis for the authentication of various types of computer-generated evidence [CGE], not only for computer-generated printouts of data, but also for other, more recently-developed types of CGE, including digital reproductions of static images or still two- or three-dimensional illustrations, digital animation, simulations and recreations, and computerized models.[208] In today's courtroom, CGE

> is indeed extraordinarily versatile. For example, it has been prof-
> fered to re-create airplane accidents, to re-enact automobile acci-
> dents, to assess the fair market value of land based on projected
> present values of royalty interests in gas and oil wells . . . and to
> construct hypothetical markets in an antitrust claim for purposes of
> illustrating anticompetitive behavior.[209]

---

see Pyle and Mockbee, *Authentication and Identification*, 49 MISS. L.J. 151 (1978).

[205] 5 WEINSTEIN'S FEDERAL EVIDENCE § 901.11; 5 MUELLER & KIRKPATRICK, § 530; *see* United States v. Scholle, 553 F.2d 1109 (8th Cir. 1977) (defense counsel should be advised before trial of the nature of computer evidence and the likelihood that it will be offered in evidence so that defense can prepare for cross-examination or rebuttal; if such warning has not been given, district court would be well advised, upon motion, to allow a continuance); *cf.* United States v. Liebert, 519 F.2d 542 (3d Cir. 1975) (government's offer of services of expert in connection with computerized I.R.S. data, along with relevant handbooks, procedures, and additional data, was enough to protect defense right to cross-examine the computer testimony confronting him by analyzing the reliability of the computer system in theory and checking the accuracy of the system in fact).

[206] 5 WEINSTEIN'S FEDERAL EVIDENCE § 901.11; 5 MUELLER & KIRKPATRICK, § 530.

[207] *See* Rule 102 and Chapter 102, *supra*.

[208] *See* Edward A. Hannan, *Computer Generated Evidence: Testing the Envelope*, 63 DEF. COUNS. J. 353 (1996).

[209] Edward A. Hannan, *Computer Generated Evidence: Testing the Envelope*, 63 DEF.

Other types of CGE that may be introduced at trial include evidence of computer-related crimes, such as the creation of a computer virus, and evidence of electronic contracts.[210]

The impact that a computer-generated video recreation could have upon a trial was demonstrated in litigation stemming from the 1985 Delta crash at the Dallas/Fort Worth Airport. In that case, the government created a video re-enactment of the last fifteen minutes of the flight, using data from the flight recorder, radar facilities, and the assistance of a weather reconstruction expert to produce "a [computer-generated] depiction of the weather as it would have been viewed from the cockpit."[211] To increase the dramatic impact of the recreation, the computer animation was synchronized with a tape of the cockpit voice recorder, helping to provide the jury with the feeling that they were seeing the final moments of the flight as it happened.

The use of CGE in a trial is not without dangers of its own. Primary among these is the fact that most CGE reconstructions or models are based on incomplete data. Computer reconstruction involves a process by which the operator supplies the known data and lets the computer fill in the blanks by applying certain algorithms and other scientific processes. The question of whether the reconstruction accurately represents the event in question, however, is not one of authentication, but one that goes to the weight and credibility of the evidence. Thus it is ultimately a question for the jury.[212] For the evidence to be admitted, all that must be shown is that a reasonable juror could conclude that the recreation is what the proponent claims it to be.

COUNS. J. 354 (1996) (citing United States v. 1, 606.00 Acres of Land, 698 F.2d 402 (10th Cir. 1983); Perma Research and Dev. v. Singer Co., 542 F.2d 111 (2d Cir. 1976); Pearl Brewing Co. v. Joseph Schlitz Brewing Co., 415 F. Supp. 1122 (S.D. Tex. 1976); People v. McHugh, 124 Misc. 2d 559, 476 N.Y.S.2d 721 (N.Y. Sup. Ct. 1984); Kathlynn G. Fadely, *Use of Computer-Generated Evidence in Aviation Litigation: Interactive Video Comes to Court*, 55 AIR L. & COM. 839 (1990). *See also* Timothy W. Cerniglia, *Computer-Generated Exhibits—Demonstrative, Substantive or Pedagogical—Their Place in Evidence*, 18 AM. J. TRIAL ADVOC. 1 (1994); Michael J. Henke, *Admissibility of Computer-Generated Animated Reconstructions and Simulations*, 35 TRIAL LAW. GUIDE 434 (1991); Edward J. Bardelli, Note, *The Use of Computer Simulations in Criminal Prosecutions*, 40 WAYNE L. REV. 1357 (1994); Marc A. Ellenbrogen, Comment, *Lights, Camera, Action: Computer-Animated Evidence Gets its Day in Court*, 34 B.C. L. REV. 1087 (1993); Vicki S. Menard, Comment, *Admission of Computer-Generated Visual Evidence: Should There Be Clear Standards?*, 6 SOFTWARE L.J. 325 (1993).

[210] *See* Stanley A. Kurzban, *Authentication of Computer-Generated Evidence in the United States Federal Courts*, 35 IDEA: J. L. & TECH. 437 (1995).

[211] Kathlynn G. Fadely, *Use of Computer-Generated Evidence in Aviation Litigation: Interactive Video Comes to Court*, 55 AIR L. & COM. 839, 898–899 (1990).

[212] *See* Kathlynn G. Fadely, *Use of Computer-Generated Evidence in Aviation Litigation: Interactive Video Comes to Court*, 55 AIR L. & COM. 839, 891 (1990) ("The accuracy of conclusions drawn from processing the data goes to the weight of the evidence . . . . Whether or not evidence presented is accurate is a question for the trier of fact . . . . Determination of adequacy of the foundation is within the discretion of the trial judge.").

A second danger inherent in the use of CGE is the possibility that the trier of fact will be unduly prejudiced by, or give undue weight to, the CGE. Where the court perceives such a danger, however, it can exclude the evidence under Rule 403.[213]

Despite the versatility of and dangers involved with CGE, authentication can still be accomplished according to the jurisprudence developed under Rule 901(b)(9). CGE, whatever its form, serves essentially the same function as other types of evidence, including documentary and demonstrative evidence, authenticated under the Federal Rules, albeit often "on a grander and more dramatic scale."[214] In the absence of any special rules governing the introduction of CGE, courts have looked to and should continue to be guided by traditional evidentiary principles to determine the authenticity of CGE.[215]

The two essential requirements of authentication remain that the proponent must both describe the process or system for generating the CGE, and produce evidence that the process or system produces an accurate result. Factors that may affect whether a party has met these requirements include such concerns as the accuracy, reliability, and trustworthiness of the input data; the reasonableness of the assumptions used to quantify non-measured items (*i.e.*, to fill in the blanks); the training of the technicians who input, processed and retrieved the data; whether the hardware and software employed are commercially recognized and used in a capacity they were intended to perform, and whether any relevant data has been overlooked.[216]

---

[213] *See* Van Houten-Maynard v. ANR Pipeline, Inc., 1995 U.S. Dist. LEXIS 7046, *37–*38 (N.D. Ill. May 23, 1995) ("[T]his type of evidence can be highly influential upon a jury, well beyond its reliability and materiality, due to its documentary-type format presented in a 'television' like medium. Additionally, we believe that computer animation evidence . . . may well have an undue detrimental effect on other more reliable . . . evidence").

[214] Kathlynn G. Fadely, *Use of Computer-Generated Evidence in Aviation Litigation: Interactive Video Comes to Court*, 55 AIR L. & COM. 839, 882 (1990).

[215] *See* Hannan, *Computer Generated Evidence: Testing the Envelope*, 63 DEF. COUNS. J. 354, 357–358 (1996). *See also* Kathlynn G. Fadely, *Use of Computer-Generated Evidence in Aviation Litigation: Interactive Video Comes to Court*, 55 AIR L. & COM. 839, 882 (1990) ("In discussing admissibility of computer-generated documentary materials, courts and commentators cite traditional evidentiary principles"); Carole E. Powell, Comment, *Computer Generated Visual Evidence: Does* Daubert *Make a Difference?* 12 GA. ST. U. L. REV. 577 (1996) (explaining that CGE can be authenticated as a process or system by establishing the accuracy and reliability of both the computer, including hardware and software, and the system's output).

[216] *See* Hannan, *Computer Generated Evidence: Testing the Envelope*, 63 DEF. COUNS. J. 354, 357–358 (1996); Kathlynn G. Fadely, *Use of Computer-Generated Evidence in Aviation Litigation: Interactive Video Comes to Court*, 55 AIR L. & COM. 839, 890–891 (1990). *See also* Monarch Federal Savings & Loan Ass'n v. Genser, 156 N.J. Super. 107, 383 A.2d 475, 487–88 (N.J. Super. 1977) (identifying the following factors as relevant to the admissibility of CGE: (1) the competency of the computer operators, (2) the type of computer

In any event, the quantity and nature of foundational proof required to admit CGE may depend on how the evidence is to be used. For example, CGE simulations and recreations will likely require a stronger foundation than CGE illustrations of general principles.[217]

§ 901.42   Presentation at Trial of Evidence as to Results

The manner of presenting evidence as to results from processes or systems will vary according to the type of evidence involved and the complexity of such results. In some instances, where the results are simple and straight-forward, testimony alone may be presented. For example, a police officer may testify that his radar system indicated the defendant's speed. In other instances, presentation of results may involve the use of tangible proof, such as x-ray film, computer printouts, or electrocardiogram tapes. Additionally, a party may wish to clarify or simplify results by the use of charts, graphs, or written summaries, especially when the underlying data is voluminous. Because it is within the province of the trier of fact to assess the weight of any authenticated evidence, the proponent may well present foundational evidence that goes beyond that which is required to satisfy the threshold admissibility standard in order to convince the trier of fact of the accuracy and probative force of the results in question. For example, a person testifying as to the accuracy of computer printouts may, in addition to describing the system and its output, describe the controls utilized to detect human and machine errors.[218] The trier of fact may, of course, also consider any evidence either elicited on cross-examination of the proponent's own witnesses, which militates against the accuracy of the admitted results.

As previously emphasized, authentication is not tantamount to admissibility, and the proponent of process or system results must consider principles of hearsay, relevance, and best evidence in addition to authentication in attempting to introduce such evidence.

§ 901.43   Rule 901(b)(10) Example — Methods Provided by a Statute or Rule

(b)   **Examples.** The following are examples only — not a complete list — of evidence that satisfies the requirement:

***

(10)   *Methods Provided by a Statute or Rule.* Any method of authentication or identification allowed by a federal statute or a rule prescribed by the Supreme Court.

---

used and its acceptance as standard equipment, and (3) the procedure for input and output of information, including controls and checks for reliability).

[217] *See* Hannan, *Computer Generated Evidence: Testing the Envelope*, 63 DEF. COUNS. J. 354, 357–358 (1996).

[218] 5 WEINSTEIN'S FEDERAL EVIDENCE § 901.11; 5 MUELLER & KIRKPATRICK, § 530.

Rule 901(b)(10) is in effect a clarifying provision.[219] The Rule preserves methodologies of authentication or identification provided by certain legislative provisions and by other rules promulgated by the Supreme Court. Rule 901(b)(10) reinforces the caveat expressed in the introductory sentence of the Rule, *i.e.,* that the provisions of Rule 901(b) are by way of illustration only and not by way of limitation.[220]

§ 901.44   Illustrative Authentication Statutes and Rules

Alternative means of authentication or identification may be derived, for example, from federal statutes, state statutes, and the Federal Rules of Civil Procedure and Criminal Procedure. For example, the Federal Business Records Act[221] provides a simplified method for authentication of numerous types of documents. The Act exempts certain public documents and private writings that were made in the regular course of business if the keeping of such records was in fact a regular procedure of that business.[222]

The Rules of Civil and Criminal Procedure contain several provisions pertinent to authentication or identification. For example, Civil Rule 10(c) permits a party to attach a written instrument to a pleading, thereby making it a part of the pleading for all purposes. Authenticity of the attached instrument may be established unless its genuineness is denied.[223] Of similar effect is Rule 56(e) pertaining to evidence in support of, or in opposition to a motion for summary judgment. The Rule requires that a party submitting affidavits attach sworn or certified copies of all papers or parts thereof referred to in the affidavit. Unless objection is made concerning such documentation, the court will consider it in making its determination as to whether there exists a genuine issue for trial.

Civil Rule 44(a) provides a method for authenticating foreign or domestic official records either by an official publication thereof or by a copy attested

---

[219] *See generally,* 2 MCCORMICK, § 228; 5 WEINSTEIN'S FEDERAL EVIDENCE § 901.12; 5 MUELLER & KIRKPATRICK, § 531; 5 WIGMORE, §§ 1638(a), 1651, 1672, 1674, 1675, 1676, 1677, 1678, 1679, 1680, 1680(b), 1681, 1684; 7 WIGMORE, §§ 2162, 2164, 2167. *See also* Cohn, *The NewFederal Rules of Civil Procedure,* 54 GEO. L.J. 1204 (1966); Kaplan, *Continuing Work of the Civil Committee: 1966 Amendments of the Federal Rules of Civil Procedure(II),* 81 HARV. L. REV. 591 (1968); Smit, *International Aspects of Federal Civil Procedure,* 61 COLUM. L. REV. 1031 (1961); *International Litigation Under the United States Code,* 65 COLUM. L. REV. 1015 (1965).

[220] *See* 5 WEINSTEIN'S FEDERAL EVIDENCE § 901.12; 5 MUELLER & KIRKPATRICK, § 531; *see also* Pyle and Mockbee, *Authentication and Identification,* 49 MISS. L.J. 151 (1978).

[221] 28 U.S.C. § 1732.

[222] 5 WEINSTEIN'S FEDERAL EVIDENCE § 901.12; 5 MUELLER & KIRKPATRICK, § 531; *see also* 18 U.S.C. § 3190.

[223] *See* 5 WEINSTEIN'S FEDERAL EVIDENCE § 901.12; 5 MUELLER & KIRKPATRICK, § 531.

by a person designated in the Rules and certified in the manner specified. Such procedures also may be utilized in criminal proceedings by virtue of Criminal Rule 27. Depositions may be authenticated for use at trial by the procedure provided by Civil Rule 30(f) and 31(b).

The Rules of Civil Procedure contain other provisions that may be utilized in order to dispense with offering proof at trial as to authenticity. For example, a party may utilize Civil Rule 36, Requests for Admission, in order to elicit an admission as to the genuineness of any document described in the request. Unless the opposing party responds within the designated time period, the matter is admitted. Pursuant to Civil Rule 36(b), any matter admitted is conclusively established unless the court permits withdrawal or amendment of the admission. Such a procedure might also be utilized to identify objects of real evidence other than documents.[224] Authentication or identification might also be established through the vehicle of interrogatories (Civil Rule 33) or depositions (Civil Rule 30 or 31), although in somewhat less effective fashion, since responses to interrogatories or deposition questions are subject to equivocation and are not necessarily conclusive on the issue of authenticity.[225]

Questions of authenticity may also be resolved through determinations at pretrial conferences in both civil and criminal cases. Accordingly, Civil Rule 16 provides that a court may adopt pretrial procedural rules in order to accomplish various objectives, including "the possibility of obtaining admissions of fact and of documents which will avoid unnecessary proof."[226] Moreover, parties may, of course, stipulate to the genuineness or authenticity of any document or other object.

---

[224] *Id. See generally,* 8 WRIGHT & MILLER, FEDERAL PRACTICE AND PROCEDURE (CIVIL), §§ 2151–2265 (1970) (discussing this provision).

[225] 5 WEINSTEIN'S FEDERAL EVIDENCE § 901.12. Judge Weinstein points out that authentication issues in criminal cases are less likely to be resolved through the use of pretrial or discovery procedures, inasmuch as depositions in criminal cases are granted only in exceptional circumstances, discovery is limited, and there is no provision analogous to the civil rules' request for admissions. *See* 5 MUELLER & KIRKPATRICK, § 531. *See* 28 U.S.C. § 1733(a), which provides that some writings of federal governmental agencies can be self-authenticated:

> Books or records of account or minutes of proceedings of any department or agency of the United States shall be admissible to prove the act, transaction, or occurrence as a memorandum of which the same were made or kept.

[226] Fed. R. Civ. P. 16(c)(2)(C).

Chapter 902

Rule 902. Evidence That Is Self-Authenticating

Rule 902. Evidence That Is Self-Authenticating

The following items of evidence are self-authenticating; they require no extrinsic evidence of authenticity in order to be admitted:

(1) ***Domestic Public Documents That Are Sealed and Signed.*** A document that bears:

    (A) a seal purporting to be that of the United States; any state, district, commonwealth, territory, or insular possession of the United States; the former Panama Canal Zone; the Trust Territory of the Pacific Islands; a political subdivision of any of these entities; or a department, agency, or officer of any entity named above; and

    (B) a signature purporting to be an execution or attestation.

(2) ***Domestic Public Documents That Are Not Sealed but Are Signed and Certified.*** A document that bears no seal if:

    (A) it bears the signature of an officer or employee of an entity named in Rule 902(1)(A); and

    (B) another public officer who has a seal and official duties within that same entity certifies under seal — or its equivalent — that the signer has the official capacity and that the signature is genuine.

(3) ***Foreign Public Documents.*** A document that purports to be signed or attested by a person who is authorized by a foreign country's law to do so. The document must be accompanied by a final certification that certifies the genuineness of the signature and official position of the signer or attester — or of any foreign official whose certificate of genuineness relates to the signature or attestation or is in a chain of certificates of genuineness relating to the signature or attestation. The certification may be made by a secretary of a United States embassy or legation; by a consul general, vice consul, or consular agent of the United States; or by a diplomatic or consular official of the foreign country assigned or accredited to the United States. If all parties have been given a reasonable opportunity to investigate the document's authenticity and accuracy, the court may, for good cause, either:

    (A) order that it be treated as presumptively authentic without final certification; or

(B)   allow it to be evidenced by an attested summary with or without final certification.

(4)   *Certified Copies of Public Records.* A copy of an official record — or a copy of a document that was recorded or filed in a public office as authorized by law — if the copy is certified as correct by:

(A)   the custodian or another person authorized to make the certification; or

(B)   a certificate that complies with Rule 902(1), (2), or (3), a federal statute, or a rule prescribed by the Supreme Court.

(5)   *Official Publications.* A book, pamphlet, or other publication purporting to be issued by a public authority.

(6)   *Newspapers and Periodicals.* Printed material purporting to be a newspaper or periodical.

(7)   *Trade Inscriptions and the Like.* An inscription, sign, tag, or label purporting to have been affixed in the course of business and indicating origin, ownership, or control.

(8)   *Acknowledged Documents.* A document accompanied by a certificate of acknowledgment that is lawfully executed by a notary public or another officer who is authorized to take acknowledgments.

(9)   *Commercial Paper and Related Documents.* Commercial paper, a signature on it, and related documents, to the extent allowed by general commercial law.

(10)   *Presumptions Under a Federal Statute.* A signature, document, or anything else that a federal statute declares to be presumptively or prima facie genuine or authentic.

(11)   *Certified Domestic Records of a Regularly Conducted Activity.* The original or a copy of a domestic record that meets the requirements of Rule 803(6)(A)-(C), as shown by a certification of the custodian or another qualified person that complies with a federal statute or a rule prescribed by the Supreme Court. Before the trial or hearing, the proponent must give an adverse party reasonable written notice of the intent to offer the record — and must make the record and certification available for inspection — so that the party has a fair opportunity to challenge them.

(12)   *Certified Foreign Records of a Regularly Conducted Activity.* In a civil case, the original or a copy of a foreign record that meets the requirements of Rule 902(11), modified as follows: the certification, rather than complying with a federal statute or Supreme Court rule, must be signed in a manner that, if falsely made, would subject the maker to a criminal penalty in the country where the certification is signed. The proponent must also meet the notice requirements of Rule 902(11).

§ 902.1   Evidence That Is Self-Authenticating — In General

In contrast to Rule 901, which requires foundational evidence on the issue of authentication, Rule 902 eliminates the requirement of an extrinsic foundation for certain specified types of documents. Documents that fall within one of the twelve categories identified within Rule 902 are considered self-authenticating. Consequently, the proponent of such a document need not offer any foundational evidence as to authenticity. If the document is otherwise admissible, it will be admitted without any testimony or other extrinsic evidence on the issue of genuineness.

§ 902.2   Theory of Self-Authentication

The theory of self-authentication is that certain documents, by their very nature, are self-evidently genuine on their face.[1] Documents such as those under seal or those which bear a certification or acknowledgment contain sufficient indicia of genuineness to justify their admissibility without further extrinsic evidence on the issue. In such cases, where the risk of forgery is slight,[2] practical considerations of time, expense, and necessity dictate that foundational evidence be regarded as inessential.[3] Accordingly, the proponent of the document is relieved of the obligation of meeting the threshold test that the document is what the party claims it to be. Rule 902 is applicable to various documents that experience has proved are generally reliable in showing their own authenticity.[4]

---

[1] *See generally*, 2 MCCORMICK, § 218; 5 WEINSTEIN'S FEDERAL EVIDENCE § 902.02; 5 MUELLER & KIRKPATRICK, § 538; 7 WIGMORE, §§ 2130–2169. *See also* Bigham, *Presumption, Burden of Proof, and the Uniform Commercial Code*, 21 VAND. L. REV. 184 (1968); Smit, *International Aspects of Federal Civil Procedure*, 61 COLUM. L. REV. 1031 (1961); Comment, *Judicial Notice and Presumptions Under the Proposed Federal Rules of Evidence*, 16 WAYNE L. REV. 209 (1969); Note, *The Law of Evidence in the Uniform Commercial Code*, 1 GA. L. REV. 44 (1966); *Evidence-Authentication-Necessity of Proof of Genuineness of Documents*, 29 TEMP. L.Q. 109 (1955); Note, *Evidence—Authentication of Documents-Proof of Publication*, 15 S. CAL. L. REV. 115 (1941); Comment, *Evidence-Authentication of Advertisement by Contents-Name Appearing in the Document*, 26 IOWA L. REV. 134 (1940).

[2] "Fortifying circumstances—difficulty, ease of detection and criminal sanctions— generally make the danger of forgery very slight in connection with this limited class of self-authenticating documents." 5 WEINSTEIN'S FEDERAL EVIDENCE § 902.02; *see also* 7 WIGMORE, § 2161.

[3] *See* 5 WEINSTEIN'S FEDERAL EVIDENCE § 902.02:

"In the case of innumerable writings which almost invariably correctly show their origins on their face, the slight obstacle to fraud presented by authentication requirements is far outweighed by the time and expense of proving authenticity. The danger of injustice and delay is greater than the danger of forgery."

See also 2 MCCORMICK, § 228; 7 WIGMORE, § 2161; *see, e.g., In re* The Atlanta, 82 F. Supp. 218 (S.D. Ga. 1948) (purportedly photostatic copy of official publication of Statutes of Republic of Panama held sufficiently authenticated; book was in Library of the New York Lawyer's Association and attorneys are "familiar with its high standing as a law library").

[4] 5 WEINSTEIN'S FEDERAL EVIDENCE § 902.02; *see* 5 MUELLER & KIRKPATRICK, § 538.

§ 902.3   Practical Significance of Self-Authentication

The doctrine of self-authentication relieves the proponent of a document from establishing, by way of testimony or other evidence, that the document is what the proponent claims it to be. The document is not, however, by virtue of this doctrine, deemed to be conclusively genuine. Although the preliminary barrier to admissibility is removed, the jury may still determine that the document is not genuine and accord it no weight in its deliberations. Similarly, the opponent of the evidence may dispute its authenticity and offer evidence that seeks to undermine a finding of genuineness.[5] In cases where authenticity is questioned or rebutted, the court may explain to the jury the background and theory of self-authentication.[6]

It must be kept in mind that the doctrine of self-authentication addresses only one of the preliminary questions as to admissibility of a document. In order to establish the admissibility of a self-authenticating document, the proponent must satisfy any pertinent evidentiary doctrines relating, *e.g.,* to hearsay, best evidence and general relevance. A self-authenticating document may also, under circumstances such as those set forth in Rule 403, be excluded by the trial judge for reasons entirely apart from the genuineness of the document.

§ 902.4   Rule 902(1) Domestic Public Documents That Are Sealed and Signed

The following items of evidence are self-authenticating; they require no extrinsic evidence of authenticity in order to be admitted:

(1)   *Domestic Public Documents That Are Sealed and Signed.* A document that bears:

> (A)   a seal purporting to be that of the United States; any state, district, commonwealth, territory, or insular possession of the United States; the former Panama Canal Zone; the Trust Territory of the Pacific Islands; a political subdivision of any of these entities; or a department, agency, or officer of any

---

[5] *See* Advisory Committee Note, Rule 902; *see also* 5 WEINSTEIN'S FEDERAL EVIDENCE § 902.02; 2 MCCORMICK, § 228; 5 MUELLER & KIRKPATRICK, § 538; *see, e.g.,* United States v. Giacalone, 408 F. Supp. 251 (E.D. Mich. 1975), *rev'd on other grounds,* 541 F.2d 508 (6th Cir. 1976) (defendant moved to dismiss indictment on ground that special United States attorney had no authority to conduct grand jury proceedings; certified copy of oath of office established authority where defendant "neither contradicted nor challenged the authenticity of this document"); Hedger v. Reynolds, 216 F.2d 202 (2d Cir. 1954) (notary's certificate of acknowledgment admitted but held to be rebuttable evidence); *cf.* United States v. Kaufman, 453 F.2d 306 (2d Cir. 1971) (defendant convicted of falsely making affidavits, although evidence indicated the various notary publics never took his signature under oath).

[6] 5 WEINSTEIN'S FEDERAL EVIDENCE, § 902.02: "Should authenticity become an issue, the court may explain to the jury the background of reliability such as, for example, the sanctions against forgery of documents having government seals."

entity named above; and

(B)   a signature purporting to be an execution or attestation.

Rule 902(1) applies the doctrine of self-authentication to domestic public documents that contain two indicia of genuineness.[7] The document must bear a seal that purports to be that of the United States, a State, or other domestic political entity, subdivision, officer or agency. Additionally, the document must bear a signature that purports to be an attestation or execution.

Rule 902(1) is justified by the practical consideration that forgery is a crime and that detection is fairly easy and certain.[8] The Rule is derived from various common-law doctrines and statutory provisions that governed the admissibility of documents under seal.[9] Prior to the adoption of the Rules, state and federal statutes enacted in furtherance of the full faith and credit clause of the United States Constitution provided for the authentication and admissibility of the statutes, judicial records, public records, and the like of other states and their political subdivisions.[10] Such statutes were generally more restrictive and more problematic than the provisions of Rule 902(1).[11]

§ 902.5   Documents Cognizable under the Rule

Rule 902(1) applies to any document bearing the purported seal of the United States, or of any state, district, Commonwealth, territory, or insular possession thereof.[12] It also includes possessions of the United States, specifically the Panama Canal Zone[13] and the Trust Territory of the Pacific

---

[7] *See generally,* 2 McCORMICK, § 218; 5 WEINSTEIN'S FEDERAL EVIDENCE § 902.03; 5 MUELLER & KIRKPATRICK, § 539; 7 WIGMORE, §§ 2161–2165. *See also* Hunter, FEDERAL TRIAL HANDBOOK, § 58.6, "Authentication of domestic public documents under seal;" 30 AM. JUR. 2D, §§ 963, 966, 988, 991, 996.

[8] Advisory Committee Note, Rule 902(1). The Rule may be theoretically based, in whole or in part, upon the doctrine of judicial notice. *See id.; see also* 5 WEINSTEIN'S FEDERAL EVIDENCE § 902.03; 5 MUELLER & KIRKPATRICK, § 539.

[9] 5 WEINSTEIN'S FEDERAL EVIDENCE § 902.03.

[10] 5 WEINSTEIN'S FEDERAL EVIDENCE § 902.03; 5 MUELLER & KIRKPATRICK, § 539; *see also* United States v. Amedy, 24 U.S. (11 Wheat) 392 (1826); United States v. Johns, 4 U.S. (4 Dall.) 412 (C.C.D. Pa. 1806).

[11] *See* 5 WEINSTEIN'S FEDERAL EVIDENCE § 902.03; 5 MUELLER & KIRKPATRICK, § 539; *see also* United States v. Trotter, 538 F.2d 217 (8th Cir. 1976) (certificates by Commissioner of Bureau of Motor Vehicles and Governor of State of Indiana, duly signed and sealed, satisfied Federal Rule of Evidence 902(1)).

[12] *See* Hughes v. United States, 953 F.2d 531 (9th Cir. 1992) (IRS Form 4343 is self-authenticating).

[13] Inasmuch as the Panama Canal is no longer under the control of the United States government, the references to documents under seal of the Panama Canal Zone appear to have no further pertinence.

Islands. The Rule further obviates problems that arose at common law by extending the doctrine to documents under the seal of any political subdivision, department, officer, or agency of the entities named above. There is accordingly no limitation on the level of public authority to which the Rule applies. The Rule, however, retains the common-law exclusion of documents under private seal.[14]

Rule 902(1) may be utilized as the basis for admitting a broad spectrum of documents including, for example, original documents bearing the seal of an executing officer or certified copies of public documents bearing the seal of a custodian on a certificate authenticating the copies.[15] The Rule may also be used in connection with a document that attests to the absence of specified documents within the records of the office the seal of which the document bears.[16]

§ 902.6   Rule 902(2) Domestic Public Documents That Are Not Sealed but Are Signed and Certified

The following items of evidence are self-authenticating; they require no extrinsic evidence of authenticity in order to be admitted:

***

    (2) *Domestic Public Documents That Are Not Sealed but Are Signed and Certified.* A document that bears no seal if:

        (A) it bears the signature of an officer or employee of an entity named in Rule 902(1)(A); and

        (B) another public officer who has a seal and official duties within that same entity certifies under seal — or its equivalent — that the signer has the official capacity and that the signature is genuine.

Rule 902(2) provides for self-authentication of domestic public documents that do not bear a seal.[17] In view of the fact that a signed public

---

[14] 5 WEINSTEIN'S FEDERAL EVIDENCE § 902.03; *see* 7 WIGMORE, § 2169.

[15] 5 WEINSTEIN'S FEDERAL EVIDENCE § 902.03; *see* United States v. Wingard, 522 F.2d 796 (4th Cir. 1975) (holding FDIC certificate admissible without authentication by custodian; cites Rule 902, not then yet in effect, as indicative of rule generally followed in federal courts); United States v. Mackenzie, 601 F.2d 221 (5th Cir. 1979) (order of Texas Board of Medical Examiners cancelling license to practice medicine); United States v. Moore, 555 F.2d 658 (8th Cir. 1977) (certificate of United States Postal Service).

[16] *See* Pyle and Mockbee, *Authentication and Identification*, 49 Miss. L.J. 151 (1978); Rule 803(10); United States v. Farris, 517 F.2d 226 (7th Cir. 1975) (computer data compilations officially certified under seal were self-authenticating and properly admitted in evidence for the purpose of showing that income tax returns had not been filed).

[17] *See generally*, 2 MCCORMICK, § 218; 5 WEINSTEIN'S FEDERAL EVIDENCE § 902.04; 5

document not under seal poses a greater risk of forgery than that of a document under seal,[18] the Rule requires that two levels of authenticating indicia appear on the document. First, the document in question must purport to bear the signature, in an official capacity, of an officer or employee of any entity specified in Rule 902(1). This signature need not be under seal, and in most situations in which Rule 902(2) is utilized, the signing officer will lack an official seal. Second, the document must bear a certification, under seal, of a public officer having a seal, who has official duties in the political subdivision of the officer or employee. The certification must attest that the signing officer or employee has the requisite official capacity and that the signature is genuine.

The requirements of Rule 902(2) as to the certifying officer serve two purposes. First, the requirement that the certifying officer have official duties in the same governmental entity as the signing officer ensures that he or she will have sufficient knowledge of the other officer to be familiar with the signing officer's signature and official capacity.[19] Second, the requirement that the certifying officer have a seal and make the requisite certification under seal ensures that the document will bear the same guarantees against forgery, and hence of authenticity, as those documents admissible under Rule 902(1).

Where a document is offered pursuant to Rule 902(2), the signatures of both officers, accompanied by the seal of the certifying officer, are indicative in themselves that the requirements of the Rule have been satisfied.[20] Consequently, the document will be admitted without any preliminary showing of the underlying premises, for example, that the officer signing the document had no seal or that the officer signed in his or her official capacity.[21] The court may assume such facts by virtue of the theory of self-authentication, that is, that the document on its face is evidence of its genuineness.

MUELLER & KIRKPATRICK, § 540; 7 WIGMORE, § 2167. *See also* 30 AM. JUR. 2D, §§ 963, 966, 988, 991, 996.

[18] *See* Advisory Committee Note, Rule 902(2).

[19] 5 WEINSTEIN'S FEDERAL EVIDENCE § 902.04; 5 MUELLER & KIRKPATRICK, § 540; *see also* United States v. Wilson, 732 F.2d 404 (5th Cir. 1984) (court properly admitted affidavit of Executive Director of CIA to counter defendant's claim that he was involved with CIA where Director's duties included overall management, and affidavit was attested to by the custodian of the CIA seal); Morgan v. Curtenius, 17 F. Cas. 747, 4 McLean 366 (C.C.D. Ill. 1848), *aff'd*, 61 U.S. (20 How) 1 (1857) (signature of probate judge accepted without his seal since certificate of judge indicated his court, formerly one of record, no longer had a seal); Hagen v. Porter, 156 F.2d 362 (9th Cir. 1946) (relying on California statute permitting judicial notice of government officers).

[20] 5 WEINSTEIN'S FEDERAL EVIDENCE § 902.04; *see* 5 MUELLER & KIRKPATRICK, § 540.

[21] 5 WEINSTEIN'S FEDERAL EVIDENCE § 902.04; 5 MUELLER & KIRKPATRICK, § 540; *see also* Willink v. Miles, 30 F. Cas. 62, F. Cas. No. 17768, Pet. C.C. 429 (C.C.D. Pa. 1817) (justice of peace assumed to have office he claims).

Rule 902(2) rejects the notion that a document bearing an official signature and nothing more is self-evidently authentic.[22]

§ 902.7   Rule 902(3) Foreign Public Documents

The following items of evidence are self-authenticating; they require no extrinsic evidence of authenticity in order to be admitted:

***

(3) *Foreign Public Documents.* A document that purports to be signed or attested by a person who is authorized by a foreign country's law to do so. The document must be accompanied by a final certification that certifies the genuineness of the signature and official position of the signer or attester — or of any foreign official whose certificate of genuineness relates to the signature or attestation or is in a chain of certificates of genuineness relating to the signature or attestation. The certification may be made by a secretary of a United States embassy or legation; by a consul general, vice consul, or consular agent of the United States; or by a diplomatic or consular official of the foreign country assigned or accredited to the United States. If all parties have been given a reasonable opportunity to investigate the document's authenticity and accuracy, the court may, for good cause, either:

(A)   order that it be treated as presumptively authentic without final certification; or

(B)   allow it to be evidenced by an attested summary with or without final certification.

Rule 902(3) applies the concepts of self-authentication to foreign public documents that bear two indicia of genuineness.[23] First, the document must purport to be executed or attested by a person, in an official capacity, who is authorized by the laws of a foreign country to make the execution or attestation. Second, there must be a certification that attests, directly or indirectly, to the genuineness of the signature and the official position of the executing or attesting person. In this regard, Rule 902(3) requires a final certification on foreign documents made by a United States official (a secretary of an embassy or legation, consul general, consul, vice consul, or consular agent) or by a foreign official (a diplomatic or consular official)

---

[22] *See generally*, 7 WIGMORE, § 2167.

[23] *See generally*, 2 MCCORMICK, § 218; 5 WEINSTEIN'S FEDERAL EVIDENCE § 902.05; 5 MUELLER & KIRKPATRICK, § 541; 7 WIGMORE, §§ 2161–2162. *See also* Hunter, FEDERAL TRIAL HANDBOOK, § 58.8, "Authentication of Foreign Public Documents"; 30 AM. JUR. 2D, §§ 966–968, 970, 990; Smit, *International Aspects of Federal Civil Procedure*, 61 COLUM. L. REV. 1062 (1961).

assigned or accredited to the United States.

Where the United States or foreign official is familiar with the person who has executed or attested the document in question, the final certification must attest to the genuineness of the signature and the official position of the executing or attesting person. Where there is no direct familiarity, the procedure of Rule 902(3) involves a chain of authentication, the last link of which consists of a certification by the appropriate United States or foreign official. In such a case, the final certification must attest to the genuineness of the signature and official position of any foreign official whose certificate of genuineness of signature and official position in turn corroborates the execution or attestation. Alternately, the final certification may result from a chain of certificates of genuineness that begins with a certificate corroborating the execution or attestation. The Rule, in essence, provides a procedure whereby the signature of a foreign official, certified as genuine, either directly or through a chain of certificates, by an appropriate United States or foreign official, is sufficient to render the document self-authenticating.

§ 902.8   Scope and Effect of Rule 902(3)

Rule 902(3), which is derived from Civil Procedure Rule 44(a)(2), represents a far more liberal view toward the admissibility of foreign documents than that of the common law, which accorded self-authenticating status only to foreign documents under seal of state.[24] Civil Rule 44(a)(2) and the correlative Criminal Rule 27 provide an authentication procedure for copies of foreign official records based upon an attestation and certification.[25] Rule 902(3) adopts the procedure set forth in the Civil Rule with

---

[24] 5 WEINSTEIN'S FEDERAL EVIDENCE § 902.05; *see* 7 WIGMORE, § 2162; *see, e.g.,* United States v. Regner, 677 F.2d 754 (9th Cir. 1982) (court admitted certified records of state-run Hungarian taxicab company); United States v. Klissas, 218 F. Supp. 880 (D.C. Md. 1963) (Greek birth certificate); New York Life Insurance Co. v. Aronson, 38 F. Supp. 687 (D.C. Pa. 1941) (Polish birth certificate).

[25] *See* Advisory Committee Note, Rule 902(3). Federal Rule of Civil Procedure 44(a)(2) which, by the terms of Federal Rule of Criminal Procedure 27, is also applicable to criminal cases, provides as follows:

A foreign official record, or an entry therein, when admissible for any purpose, may be evidenced by an official publication thereof; or a copy thereof, attested by a person authorized to make the attestation, and accompanied by a final certification as to the genuineness of the signature and official position (i) of the attesting person, or (ii) of any foreign official whose certificate of genuineness of signature and official position relates to the attestation or is in a chain of certificates of genuineness of signature and official position relating to the attestation. A final certification may be made by a secretary of embassy or legation, consul general, consul, vice consul, or consular agent of the United States, or a diplomatic or consular official of the foreign country assigned or accredited to the United States. If reasonable opportunity has been given to all parties to investigate the authenticity and accuracy of the documents, the court may, for good cause shown, (i) admit an attested copy without final certification or (ii) permit the foreign official

slight modifications. Rule 902(3) applies to originals as well as copies and also expands the concept to embrace foreign public *documents* rather than the more limiting category of public *records*.[26] The structure of the Rule recognizes the practical problems associated with the authentication of foreign documents.[27]

Rule 902(3) follows Civil Rule 44(a)(2) in setting forth two other provisions that derive from practical considerations relating to litigation and the adversary system. Accordingly, if all parties have been given a reasonable opportunity to investigate the authenticity and accuracy of official documents, the court may upon a showing of good cause dispense with the requirement of final certification. The court must dispense with the final certification requirement if the United States and the foreign country where the official document is located are parties to a treaty or convention that abolishes or displaces the requirement, such as the Hague Convention Abolishing the Requirement of Legalization for Foreign Public Documents. Alternatively, the court may permit the documents to be evidenced by an attested summary, with or without a final certification.[28]

§ 902.9   Rule 902(4) Certified Copies of Public Records

The following items of evidence are self-authenticating; they require no extrinsic evidence of authenticity in order to be admitted:

***

(4)   *Certified Copies of Public Records.* A copy of an official record — or a copy of a document that was recorded or filed in a public office as authorized by law — if the copy is certified as correct by:

    (A)   the custodian or another person authorized to make the certification; or

---

record to be evidenced by an attested summary with or without a final certification. The final certification is unnecessary if the record and the attestation are certified as provided in a treaty or convention to which the United States and the foreign country in which the official record is located are parties.

[26] *See* Advisory Committee Note, Rule 902(3); *see also* 5 MUELLER & KIRKPATRICK, § 541; *see, e.g.,* United States v. Pena-Jessie, 763 F.2d 618 (4th Cir. 1985) (court properly admitted diplomatic note showing Panama's grant of permission to board a vessel that was then seized); United States v. Perlmuter, 693 F.2d 1290 (9th Cir. 1982) (allegedly official documents from Israel that purported to show criminal convictions and fingerprints of appellant admissible where there was neither evidence of attestation by authorized Israeli acting in official capacity nor final certification or good cause for lack of certification; "aura of authenticity" found by district court insufficient).

[27] Pyle & Mockbee, *Authentication and Identification*, 49 MISS. L.J. 151 (1978).

[28] *See* Raphaely Int'l v. Waterman S.S. Corp., 972 F.2d 498 (2d Cir. 1992) (where opponent had nine years before the trial to challenge the authenticity of foreign public documents and failed to present any evidence casting doubt on their authenticity, the court found good cause to dispense with the requirement of final certification); 5 WEINSTEIN'S FEDERAL EVIDENCE § 902.05.

(B)   a certificate that complies with Rule 902(1), (2), or (3), a
federal statute, or a rule prescribed by the Supreme Court.

Rule 902(4) sets forth requirements under which copies of certain public
records are admissible as self-authenticating documents.[29] The Rule applies
to copies of official entries, records, or reports. It also applies to any
document authorized by law to be recorded or filed and actually recorded or
filed in a public office, including data compilations in any form. The Rule
does not apply to unrecorded documents.[30]

Rule 902(4) is premised upon necessity and convenience in view of the
problems associated with producing original public documents at trial.[31] The
Rule is further justified by the guarantees of trustworthiness that attend the
certification process. The concept of utilizing certified copies as proof of
public documents is not new to federal law,[32] although prior law generally
required proof of additional facts and circumstances in order to authenticate
the copy.

§ 902.10   Certification Requirements

Rule 902(4) requires that a copy of a document offered pursuant to this
Rule bear a certification by the custodian or other person authorized to make
copies of such documents. The certification must attest to the correctness of
the copy. Additionally, it must be made in compliance with the provisions of
paragraph (1), (2), or (3) of Rule 902, or in compliance with any federal law
or rule of the Supreme Court. The required content of the certificate
consequently depends upon the type of document in question.[33] Accord-

---

[29] *See generally*, 2 McCORMICK, § 218; 5 WEINSTEIN'S FEDERAL EVIDENCE § 902.06; 5
MUELLER & KIRKPATRICK, § 542; 5 WIGMORE, §§ 1677, 1680. *See also* Smit, *International
Aspects of Federal Civil Procedure*, 61 COLUM. L. REV. 1062 (1961); Hunter, FEDERAL
TRIAL HANDBOOK, § 58.9; *Authentication of Certified Copies of Public Records*, 30 AM. JUR.
2d, §§ 963, 988, 991, 996, 1006, 1011–1013, 1041.

[30] Advisory Committee Note, Rule 902(4).

[31] *See* 5 WEINSTEIN'S FEDERAL EVIDENCE § 902.06; 5 MUELLER & KIRKPATRICK, § 542;
see also United States v. Wilson, 690 F.2d 1267 (9th Cir. 1982) (copy of Judgment and
Commitment Order, certified on both sides, adequately authenticated under Rule 902(4));
United States v. Simmons, 476 F.2d 33 (9th Cir. 1973) (certified Selective Service file "prime
example of self-authentication").

[32] *See, e.g.,* United States v. Percheman, 32 U.S. (7 Pet.) 51 (1833); United States v.
Johns, 4 U.S. (4 Dall.) 412 (1806).

[33] *See* 5 WEINSTEIN'S FEDERAL EVIDENCE § 902.06; *see also* United States v. Beason,
690 F.2d 439 (5th Cir. 1982) (Rule 902 does not require that actual custodian of official
records secure certification of delegation of custodial authority from head of agency entrusted
with custody of document; certification by actual custodian satisfies Rule so that certificate by
custodian of National Firearms Registration and Transfer Record that no registration in
defendant's name existed sufficed without requiring certificate from Secretary of Treasury

ingly, a foreign public document may be evidenced by a certified copy, the certification of which is made in compliance with Rule 902(3). Similarly, a copy of an official domestic or foreign record may be authenticated by the procedure set forth in Civil Rule 44 or Criminal Rule 27.[34] There are several federal statutes under which a certified copy will be admissible under Rule 902(4).[35] Additionally, copies may be admitted pursuant to rules that in effect dispense with authentication requirements. For example, parties may stipulate to the genuineness of a document or copy thereof pursuant to Civil Rule 16(c)(3), or the proponent may elicit an admission of genuineness pursuant to Civil Rule 36(a).

Compliance with the certification requirements of Rule 902(4) simultaneously satisfied the best evidence requirements set forth in Rule 1005. Under the latter provision, contents of an official record or recorded document may be proved by a copy certified as correct in accordance with Rule 902, as long as the document is otherwise admissible.

§ 902.11   Rule 902(5) Official Publications

The following items of evidence are self-authenticating; they require no extrinsic evidence of authenticity in order to be admitted:

***

    (5)   ***Official Publications.*** A book, pamphlet, or other publication purporting to be issued by a public authority.

Rule 902(5) applies the doctrine of self-authentication to books, pam-

---

that custodian had been given custody); United States v. Stone, 604 F.2d 922 (5th Cir. 1979) (photographic copy of "progress sheet" prepared by Regional Disbursing Center of Treasury was properly authenticated under 902(4) by attached affidavit of officer with legal custody and direct supervision of the progress sheets); United States v. Moore, 555 F.2d 658 (8th Cir. 1977) (approving receipt of certified copy of certification of mailing; this exhibit bore a certification under formal seal of the United States Postal Service that said document constituted a true copy of the record retained in the official custody of the United States Postal Service).

[34] Advisory Committee Note, Rule 902(4).

[35] *See* 5 WEINSTEIN'S FEDERAL EVIDENCE § 902.06; 5 MUELLER & KIRKPATRICK, § 542; *see, e.g.,* 28 U.S.C. § 1745 (copies of Patent Office documents can be authenticated); 25 U.S.C. § 6 (copies of public documents, records, maps, or papers kept by the office of the Commissioner of Indian Affairs can be authenticated); 31 U.S.C. § 46 (copies of any books, records, or other documents, and transcripts from the books and proceedings of the General Accounting Office can be certified by the Comptroller General or the Assistant Comptroller under its seal); 28 U.S.C. § 1740 (copies of all documents and papers and official entries can be authenticated by a consul or vice-consul); 38 U.S.C. § 202 (copies of public documents in files of Veteran's Administration can be authenticated by seal and certificate of Administrator or his delegate); 28 U.S.C. § 1736 (extracts from the Journals of the Senate and the House of Representatives and from the Executive Journal of the Senate can be authenticated by certification by the Secretary of the Senate or the clerk of the House of Representatives).

phlets and other publications that purport to be issued by public authority.[36] The Rule relieves the proponent from establishing by way of foundation that the publication was actually printed or issued by public authority. Documents purporting to be so issued are accordingly self-authenticating, although their admissibility may depend upon other considerations as well. Specifically, documents covered by Rule 902(5) are admissible as long as the proponent also satisfies any other pertinent requirements relating to such principles as hearsay, best evidence and general relevance.

Rule 902(5) is most commonly applied in connection with statutes, court reports, rules and regulations,[37] although by its terms the Rule may apply to any publication that purports to be issued by public authority.[38] The Rule specifies no limitations as to the level of governmental authority that must authorize the publication, and accordingly, the Rule should be accorded a broad interpretation.[39]

The doctrine set forth in Rule 902(5) is generally in accordance with prior practice relating to the authentication of official publications.[40] Civil Rule 44 and Criminal Rule 27, which form the basis of Rule 902(5), provide that domestic[41] or foreign official records[42] may be evidenced by an official

---

[36] *See generally,* 2 McCORMICK, § 218; 5 WEINSTEIN'S FEDERAL EVIDENCE § 902.07; 5 MUELLER & KIRKPATRICK, § 543; 5 WIGMORE, § 1684. *See also* Hunter, FEDERAL TRIAL HANDBOOK, § 58.10, "Authentication of Official Publications;" Smit, *International Aspects of Federal Civil Procedure,* 6 COLUM. L. REV. 1031 (1961); 30 AM. JUR. 2d §§ 969, 971, 991, 1110.

[37] Advisory Committee Note, Rule 902(5).

[38] *See* 5 WEINSTEIN'S FEDERAL EVIDENCE § 902.07; 5 MUELLER & KIRKPATRICK, § 543; *see, e.g.,* California Asso. of Bioanalysts v. Rank, 577 F. Supp. 1342 (C.D. Cal. 1983) (report of USDHHS, bearing official seal of the agency, was self-authenticating); Watkins v. Holman, 41 U.S. (16 Pet.) 25 (1842) (American State Papers); Gregg v. Forsyth, 65 U.S. (24 How.) 179 (1860) (American State Papers); Stewart v. United States, 211 F. 41 (9th Cir. 1914) (map); United States v. Shafer, 132 F. Supp. 659 (D. Md. 1955) (unsigned document in Federal Register).

[39] *See* 5 WEINSTEIN'S FEDERAL EVIDENCE § 902.07; 5 MUELLER & KIRKPATRICK, § 543. Recognition of locally published documents may theoretically be premised upon judicial notice of such publications. *See* Funk v. Commissioner, 163 F.2d 796 (3d Cir. 1947); *see, e.g.,* Stewart v. United States, 211 F. 41 (9th Cir. 1914) (territorial map showing boundaries of White Mountain Indian Reservation properly received without independent proof of authenticity, where recitals on its face sufficiently evidence its character as a public document, indicating that it was issued from the General Land Office under the authority of the Secretary of the Interior); United States v. Shafer, 132 F. Supp. 659 (D.C. Md. 1955), *aff'd,* 229 F.2d 124 (4th Cir. 1955) (regulations, proclamation, notice published in Federal Register are presumptively valid and correctly reproduced).

[40] *See* Advisory Committee Note, Rule 902(5); *see also* 5 WEINSTEIN'S FEDERAL EVIDENCE § 902.07.

[41] Federal, state, or local official publications can be self-authenticating. *See* Frates v. Eastman, 57 F.2d 522 (10th Cir. 1932) (official publication of city ordinances self-authenticating).

publication thereof.

§ 902.12   Rule 902(6) Newspapers and Periodicals

The following items of evidence are self-authenticating; they require no extrinsic evidence of authenticity in order to be admitted:

***

> **(6)** *Newspapers and Periodicals.* Printed material purporting to be a newspaper or periodical.

Rule 902(6) makes the doctrine of self-authentication applicable to non-official printed materials purporting to be newspapers or periodicals.[43] The status of self-authentication is justified by the unlikelihood of forgery with regard to such documents.[44] Consequently, the documents identified in the Rule require no foundational evidence as to authenticity, although there may remain disputed issues regarding the authority and responsibility for items contained in such documents.[45]

Rule 902(6) makes no specific reference to notices and advertisements contained within newspapers and periodicals. The Rule merely states that there need be no extrinsic authentication evidence with regard to "[p]rinted material purporting to be a newspaper or periodicals." The Advisory Committee's Note to the Rule suggests that advertisements and notices are included within the grant of self-authenticating status.[46]

---

[42] *See* Advisory Committee Note, Rule 902(5); 5 WEINSTEIN'S FEDERAL EVIDENCE § 902.07; 5 MUELLER & KIRKPATRICK, § 543; *see also* Smit, *International Aspects of Federal Civil Procedure*, 62 COLUM. L. REV. 1031 (1961).

[43] *See generally*, 2 MCCORMICK, § 218; 5 WEINSTEIN'S FEDERAL EVIDENCE § 902.08; 5 MUELLER & KIRKPATRICK, § 544; 4 WIGMORE, § 1234; 7 WIGMORE, § 2150. *See also* Note, *Evidence-Authentication of Documents-Proof of Publication*, 15 S. CAL. L. REV. 115 (1941); Strong, *Liberalizing the Authentication of Private Writings*, 52 CORNELL L.Q. 284 (1967); 29 AM. JUR. 2d § 885.

[44] Advisory Committee Note, Rule 902(6); 5 WEINSTEIN'S FEDERAL EVIDENCE § 902.08; 5 MUELLER & KIRKPATRICK, § 543.

[45] *See* 7 WIGMORE, § 2150; Advisory Committee Note, Rule 902(6).

[46] *See* 5 WEINSTEIN'S FEDERAL EVIDENCE § 902.08; *see also* Mancari v. Frank P. Smith, Inc., 114 F.2d 834 (D.C. Cir. 1902) (Rutledge, J., dissenting); Canada Uniform Acts: Draft Act, § 42 (1938) ("the production of a printed copy of a newspaper shall be prima facie evidence that any notice or advertisement contained therein was inserted, advertised, and published in that newspaper by the person, by whom, or in whose behalf, the notice or advertisement purports or appears to be inserted, advertised, or published"); *cf.* 39 U.S.C., § 4005(b) (1964) ("public advertisement . . . is prima facie evidence that the latter is the agent or representative of the advertisers"); *see, e.g.,* Comment, *Evidence-Authentication of Advertisement by Contents-Name Appearing in the Document*, 26 IOWA L. REV. 115 (1940); Note, *Evidence-Authentication-Necessity of Proof of Genuineness of Documents*, 29 TEMP. L.Q. 109 (1955).

§ 902.13   Scope and Utility of Rule 902(6)

Rule 902(6) relaxes the common-law requirements relating to the authentication of newspapers and periodicals.[47] Pursuant to the Rule, the types of printed material that are self-authenticating may range from newspapers of general circulation to specialized periodicals having a limited readership.[48]

Newspapers or periodicals may be utilized as proof of a variety of matters. For example, in a libel action, the publication containing the allegedly libelous material may be offered as evidence against the party whose authorship is claimed.[49] If authorization is disputed, the opponent may seek to convince the trier of fact that the advertisement was not properly authorized even though the publication and the advertisement have been admitted pursuant to the principle of self-authentication. Periodicals and newspapers may also be utilized as proof of collateral matters such as date and place of publication.[50]

§ 902.14   Rule 902(7) Trade Inscriptions and the Like

The following items of evidence are self-authenticating; they require no extrinsic evidence of authenticity in order to be admitted:

***

    (7)   *Trade Inscriptions and the Like.* An inscription, sign, tag, or label purporting to have been affixed in the course of business and indicating origin, ownership, or control.

Rule 902(7) accords self-authenticating status to trade inscriptions, signs, tags, or labels, as long as they purport to have been affixed in the course of business and are indicative of ownership, control, or origin.[51] Such evidence will generally be introduced to prove ownership or control. For example, in a products liability action, the plaintiff may offer into evidence an item of

---

[47] *See* 5 WEINSTEIN'S FEDERAL EVIDENCE § 902.08; 5 MUELLER & KIRKPATRICK, § 544.

[48] 5 MUELLER & KIRKPATRICK, § 544.

[49] 5 MUELLER & KIRKPATRICK, § 544.

[50] *See* 5 WEINSTEIN'S FEDERAL EVIDENCE § 902.08; 5 MUELLER & KIRKPATRICK, § 544; Ellis v. Lyford, 270 Mass. 96, 169 N.E. 800 (Mass. 1930) (newspaper that by its title page purports to be printed or published in such city, town, or county, and which has a circulation therein, shall be deemed to have been published therein).

[51] *See generally,* 5 WEINSTEIN'S FEDERAL EVIDENCE § 902.09; 5 MUELLER & KIRKPATRICK, § 545; 7 WIGMORE, §§ 2129, 2150, 2152. *See also* Note, *Evidence—Authentication— Necessity of Proof of Genuineness of Documents,* 39 TEMP. L.Q. 109 (1955); Hunter, FEDERAL TRIAL HANDBOOK, § 58.12, "Authentication of Trade Inscriptions and the Like"; Mueller, *Instructing the Jury Upon Presumptions in Civil Cases: Comparing Federal Rule 301 with Uniform Rule 301,* 12 AM. JUR. 2d § 477; *Owning, Leasing, or Otherwise Engaging in Business of Furnishing Services for Taxicabs as Basis of Tort Liability for Acts of Taxi Driver Under Respondeat Superior Doctrine,* 8 A.L.R.3d § 818.

real proof, such as a container for food, that is alleged to have caused injury. The defendant's distinctive label on the container is self-authenticating and consequently admissible as proof, for example, that the defendant processed the items in question. As with all authenticated evidence, the opponent is free to rebut the issue of authenticity.[52]

Rule 902(7) applies generally to commercial and mercantile tags or labels, and includes also such items as inscriptions on containers or vehicles, and signs of various types such as billboards. The Rule is justified because there is only a slight risk of forgery of such items, due both to the difficulty of reproduction and because trademark infringement involves serious penalties. "Great efforts are devoted to inducing the public to buy in reliance on brand names, and substantial protection is given them. Hence, the fairness of this treatment finds recognition in the cases."[53]

The Rule requires that the inscription, label, or the like purport to have been affixed in the course of business. This phrase should be interpreted broadly to include any on-going enterprise or institution regardless of its commercial or non-commercial nature, including, for example, a private university or social organization that uses an identifying inscription or symbol.[54]

§ 902.15   Rule 902(8) Acknowledged Documents

The following items of evidence are self-authenticating; they require no

---

[52] *See* 5 WEINSTEIN'S FEDERAL EVIDENCE § 902.09; 5 MUELLER & KIRKPATRICK, § 545. Rule 902(7) is especially helpful in the area of products liability where plaintiffs have sometimes encountered difficulty in attempting to link defendants to defective products. *See, e.g.,* Weiner v. Mager & Throne, Inc., 167 Misc. 338, 3 N.Y.S. 2d 918 (N.Y. Ct. App. 1938) (plaintiff purchased an unwrapped loaf of bread from defendant B, to which was affixed the "trade label" of defendant M & T; finding worms embedded in a slice of bread from which he had eaten, and in the rest of the loaf, plaintiff allegedly became ill and nauseated; in the absence of counterproof that M & T did not manufacture the bread, court drew inference from trade label that M & T was the manufacturer); Swift & Co. v. Hawkins, 174 Miss. 253, 164 So. 231 (Miss. 1935) (on basis of tradename "Brookfield" appearing on cheese wrappers, which name is exclusively used by Swift & Co., evidence sufficiently identified defendant as the manufacturer); Curtiss Candy Co. v. Johnson, 163 Miss. 426, 141 So. 762 (Miss. 1932) (plaintiff purchased candy bar in package bearing label "Baby Ruth Candy, The Curtiss Candy Company"; candy bar allegedly contained ground glass, from the ingestion of which plaintiff suffered injuries; jury was warranted in finding that this bar came from defendant's factory containing glass).

[53] Advisory Committee Note, Rule 902(7).

[54] *See* 5 WEINSTEIN'S FEDERAL EVIDENCE § 902.09; 5 MUELLER & KIRKPATRICK, § 545. In the absence of strong contrary proof, the court should assume that the mark was placed in the regular course of business if it is in a form that would ordinarily be used. *See* United States v. Hitsman, 604 F.2d 443 (5th Cir. 1979) (court found college transcript of defendant to be a self-authenticating document under Rule 901 and 902; court took judicial notice of the existence of the college and found it was normal for a college to make such a record in the course of its operations, and that the exhibit had the indicia of being an authentic copy since it bore a seal above the registrar's signature).

extrinsic evidence of authenticity in order to be admitted:

***

> **(8)**   *Acknowledged Documents.* A document accompanied by a certificate of acknowledgment that is lawfully executed by a notary public or another officer who is authorized to take acknowledgments.

Rule 902(8) provides that documents accompanied by a certificate of acknowledgment are self-authenticating.[55] In such cases, the certificate of acknowledgment serves as sufficient evidence that the document is what it purports to be.[56] The Rule constitutes a significant expansion of the common-law approach to the authentication of acknowledged documents.[57] The Rule does not specify the form that the acknowledgment must take. Nor, for example, does it require that the certificate be under seal unless the applicable acknowledgment law so requires.[58] The general rule with respect to acknowledgments requires a standard of only substantial compliance rather than strict compliance with the procedures of an acknowledgment statute.[59]

As long as the basic requirements of the pertinent acknowledgment statute are met, the document should be admitted without any foundational evidence as to authenticity.[60] Where foreign acknowledgments are at issue, the provisions of Rule 902(3) may supersede those of Rule 902(8), thus requiring additional certifications in order for the document to be deemed

---

[55] *See generally*, 2 McCORMICK, § 218; 5 WEINSTEIN'S FEDERAL EVIDENCE § 902.10; 5 MUELLER & KIRKPATRICK, § 546; 7 WIGMORE, § 2165. *See also* Hunter, FEDERAL TRIAL HANDBOOK, § 58.13, "Authentication of Acknowledged Documents"; 29 AM. JUR. 2d §§ 853, 863; Annots., *Admissibility, in Action Against Notary Public, of Evidence as to Usual Business Practice of Notary Public of Identifying Person Seeking Certificate of Acknowledgement*, 59 A.L.R.3d 1327 (1974); *Liability of Notary Public or his Bond for Negligence in Performance of Duties*, 44 A.L.R.3d 555 (1972); Liability of Notary Public or his Bond for Willful or Deliberate Misconduct in Performance of Duties, 44 A.L.R.3d 1243 (1972).

[56] *See* Advisory Committee Note, Rule 902(8); *see also* 7 WIGMORE, § 2165.

[57] 5 WEINSTEIN'S FEDERAL EVIDENCE § 902.10; 5 MUELLER & KIRKPATRICK, § 546; 7 WIGMORE, § 2165.

[58] Compare the Report of House Committee on the Judiciary Note to Rule 902(8):

> Rule 902(8)as submitted by the Court referred to certificates of acknowledgment "under the hand and seal of" a notary public or other officer authorized by law to take acknowledgments. The Committee amended the Rule to eliminate the requirement, believed to be inconsistent with the law in some States, that a notary public must affix a seal to a document acknowledged before him.

[59] 5 WEINSTEIN'S FEDERAL EVIDENCE § 902.10; 5 MUELLER & KIRKPATRICK, § 546.

[60] 5 MUELLER & KIRKPATRICK, § 546.

self-authenticating.[61]

Rule 902(8) is justified by the guarantees of trustworthiness provided by acknowledgments:

> The duties of his office obligate a notary public to take reasonable steps to ascertain the true identity of a person who appears before him for the purpose of acknowledging execution of an instrument or swearing to a statement; those duties also include truthfully certifying to the underlying fact that the person acknowledged execution of the instrument or swore to the statement; and the certificate of the notary, usually sealed and bearing a stamped indication of commission and its expiration date, is easily recognized and likely itself to be genuine because forgery would be somewhat difficult and subject to stiff penalty.[62]

The risk of a false acknowledgment is slight in view of various statutory penalties that attend unauthorized acknowledgments.[63]

As with all self-authenticating documents, the principle is that an acknowledged document is admissible into evidence, as long as it is not otherwise excludable, in the absence of an extrinsic foundation. Self-authentication, however, is not conclusively determinative of the issue of authenticity. The opponent may offer rebuttal testimony in support of a contention that the document is not authentic. Such evidence goes to the weight to be given the acknowledged document rather than to the question of admissibility.[64]

§ 902.16   Rule 902(9) Commercial Paper and Related Documents

The following items of evidence are self-authenticating; they require no extrinsic evidence of authenticity in order to be admitted:

***

   (9)   *Commercial Paper and Related Documents.* Commercial paper, a signature on it, and related documents, to the extent allowed by general commercial law.

---

[61] 5 WEINSTEIN'S FEDERAL EVIDENCE § 902.10. The last sentence of Rule 902(8) allows the court to admit foreign documents under some circumstances even if the formalities have not been followed.

[62] 5 MUELLER & KIRKPATRICK, § 546; *see* 5 WEINSTEIN'S FEDERAL EVIDENCE § 902.10.

[63] 5 MUELLER & KIRKPATRICK, § 546.

[64] 5 MUELLER & KIRKPATRICK, § 546; *see also* Hedger v. Reynolds, 216 F.2d 202 (2d Cir. 1954) (notary's certificate upon the document authorizing insured to change beneficiary in life insurance policy was rebuttable); *cf.* United States v. Kaufman, 453 F.2d 306 (2d Cir. 1971) (defendant claimed documents purporting to be affidavits were not, because notary had not taken his sworn statement before affixing signature; rejected).

Rule 902(9) expressly adopts the tenets of general commercial law in applying the doctrine of self-authentication to commercial paper, signatures thereon, and documents relating thereto.[65] Reference must accordingly be made to the Uniform Commercial Code, which has been adopted in all states[66] in order to determine the extent to which such documents are self-authenticating.

While four provisions of the Uniform Commercial Code are pertinent to the issue of self-authentication, only one of these specifically addresses the issue of authenticity.[67] Section 1-202 expressly provides that certain commercial documents issued by a third party to a contract "shall be prima facie evidence of [their] own authenticity and genuineness and of the facts stated in the document by the third party." Such documents include those purporting to be a bill of lading, a policy or certificate of insurance, an official weigher's or inspector's certificate, a consular invoice or any other document authorized or required by the contract to be issued by a third party. As long as the document is "in due form" it is self-authenticating pursuant to Rule 902(9).[68]

Three other provisions of the Code that relate to the admissibility of commercial documents contain implied provisions as to self-authentication. Section 3-307 accords a presumption of genuineness to signatures on negotiable instruments and, by implication, allows the introduction of signed instruments without any proof as to authenticity. Specifically, the statute provides that a signature on an instrument is admitted unless it is specifically denied in the pleadings.[69] If a denial is made, the burden is then upon the person claiming under the signature to establish its genuineness. However, the proponent is expressly aided in most circumstances by a statutorily

---

[65] *See generally*, 2 McCORMICK, § 218; 5 WEINSTEIN'S FEDERAL EVIDENCE § 902.11; 5 MUELLER & KIRKPATRICK, § 547; 7 WIGMORE, § 2130. *See also* Bigham, *Presumptions, Burden of Proof and the Uniform Commercial Code*, 21 VAND. L. REV. 177 (1968); Louisell, *Constructing Rule 301: Instructing the Jury on Presumptions in Civil Actions and Proceedings*, 63 VA. L. REV. 281; Note, *Judicial Notice and Presumptions Under the Proposed Federal Rules of Evidence*, 16 WAYNE L. REV. 215 (1969); Note, *The Law of Evidence in the Uniform Commercial Code*, 1 GA. L. REV. 44 (1966).

[66] Louisiana adopted only Articles 1, 3, 4 and 5. LA. REV. STAT. §§ 10:1-101 to 10:5-117 (1975).

[67] *See* 5 WEINSTEIN'S FEDERAL EVIDENCE § 902.11; 5 MUELLER & KIRKPATRICK, 2d § 547.

[68] U.C.C. § 1-202 (1977); *see* 5 WEINSTEIN'S FEDERAL EVIDENCE § 901.11; 5 MUELLER & KIRKPATRICK, § 547; *see also* United States v. Carriger, 592 F.2d 312 (6th Cir. 1979) (in tax evasion prosecution, trial court erred in excluding promissory notes offered by defendant as evidence of his opening net worth on the ground that they had been insufficiently authenticated; mere production of a note is prima facie evidence of its validity, citing U.C.C. § 3-307 and Rule 902).

[69] U.C.C. § 3-307 (1977).

imposed presumption that the signature is genuine or authorized, and consequently, the signature is admissible and is presumed authentic unless the opponent offers sufficient rebuttal evidence to support a finding that the signature is forged or unauthorized.[70] To the extent that the statute accords a *presumption* of authenticity to signed negotiable instruments, it goes beyond the doctrine of self-authentication.[71] In any event, the concept of self-authentication is inherent in the codified presumption of genuineness. Admissibility pursuant to Rule 902(9) is accordingly consistent with the effect of the code and with its apparent intent.[72]

Section 8-105(2) of the Uniform Commercial Code provides a similar format for the introduction and effect of signatures on securities. The code provides that securities are negotiable instruments, and consequently, that in an action on a security, a signature thereon is admitted unless specifically denied. Also, it is presumed genuine or authorized. The foregoing discussion concerning Section 3-307 is equally applicable to this section.

The fourth applicable Section is 3-510, which addresses the issue of evidence of dishonor and notice of dishonor. The code provides that certain documents are admissible in evidence, and it further creates a presumption of dishonor and of any notice of dishonor specified on the document.[73] The types of evidence specified include a formal certificate of protest, the purported stamp by a drawee that payment was refused, or bank records that indicate dishonor.[74] The foregoing types of evidence are consequently self-authenticating, and, in the absence of contrary evidence sufficient to support a finding, the introduction of such evidence creates a presumption of dishonor and of notice of dishonor if the latter is indicated on the face of the document. If the opponent introduces sufficient evidence contrary to the presumption, the question of authenticity is left to the trier of fact.

§ 902.17   Rationale of Rule 902(9)

Self-authentication of commercial paper and related documents under Rule 902(9) is prompted by considerations of necessity and convenience. The Rule is further justified by guarantees of trustworthiness that are reflected by the reliance upon such documents by the business community and by society in general.[75] For example, the third-party documents have

---

[70] *See* Rule 301 and accompanying discussion, Chapter 301, *supra*, relating to the effect of presumptions.

[71] In most instances of self-authentication, the document is admitted without foundational evidence but it is not *presumed* to be authentic, *i.e.*, it is merely *prima facie* authentic.

[72] *See* 5 WEINSTEIN'S FEDERAL EVIDENCE § 901.11; 5 MUELLER & KIRKPATRICK, § 547.

[73] 5 MUELLER & KIRKPATRICK, § 547.

[74] U.C.C. § 3-510 (1976); *see* 5 WEINSTEIN'S FEDERAL EVIDENCE § 901.11; 5 MUELLER & KIRKPATRICK, § 547.

[75] *See* 5 WEINSTEIN'S FEDERAL EVIDENCE § 901.11.

traditionally been relied upon as trustworthy in commerce.[76] The Uniform Commercial Code, in recognition of this fact, eliminates the common-law practice that required authentication of such documents by foundational evidence relating to the execution or preparation of the document.[77]

The status accorded to evidence of dishonor is also justified by the indicia of trustworthiness attending the modes of proof specific in Section 3-510. Accordingly, self-authentication of a formal certificate of protest is justified by the duties under which a notary operates.[78] As to the other modes of proof, "[i]t is improbable that bank records will show a dishonor that did not exist or that a holder will attempt to proceed on the basis of dishonor if he could have obtained payment."[79] Accordingly, stamps of the drawee bank and bank records are also allowed into evidence and carry a presumption of authenticity.[80]

The rationale underlying self-authentication of signatures on commercial instruments is based mainly upon necessity. Negotiable instruments by their nature frequently pass through many hands, and accordingly, a recipient of such an instrument would likely have no knowledge of the circumstances surrounding its execution.[81] The lack of accessibility to evidence on this issue, combined with the general reliance upon negotiable instruments by the business community, justifies the application of the doctrine of self-authentication to such instruments.

§ 902.18   Rule 902(10) Presumptions Under a Federal Statute

The following items of evidence are self-authenticating; they require no extrinsic evidence of authenticity in order to be admitted:

***

   (10)   *Presumptions Under a Federal Statute.* A signature, document, or anything else that a federal statute declares to be presumptively or prima facie genuine or authentic.

Rule 902(10) confers self-authenticating status to any signature, document or other matter that is declared to be authentic by any Act of

---

[76] *See* 5 WEINSTEIN'S FEDERAL EVIDENCE § 902.11. Such documents are thought to be trustworthy, especially when introduced against one of the parties to the contract because they were given a preferred status by the parties when they required them, and because they are made by a third party who normally has no connection with any of the parties other than as the maker of one of these documents.

[77] 5 WEINSTEIN'S FEDERAL EVIDENCE § 902.11.

[78] *Id.*

[79] *Id.*

[80] *Id.*

[81] *Id.*

Congress.[82] Specifically, the Rule incorporates any federal law that declares a matter to be "presumptively or prima facie genuine or authentic." The effect is twofold. First, the provisions of Rule 902(10) indicate that the examples of self-authentication set forth in Rule 902 are not exclusive.[83] Second, the Rule expressly acknowledges the continuing applicability of statutes that address the issue of self-authentication.

Rule 902(10) refers to statutes that declare a matter to be presumptively genuine as well as those that declare a matter to be prima facie genuine. Statutes that grant presumptive authenticity to a matter go beyond the doctrine of self-authentication in the sense that the trier of fact is bounded by the presumption in the absence of evidence sufficient to support a finding to the contrary.[84]

Rule 902(10) incorporates federal statutes pertinent to the issue of self-authentication.[85] Many of the applicable statutes deal with other evidentiary considerations as well as authentications.[86] The subject matter of such statutes includes the admissibility of, for example, notarized documents,[87] or documents bearing particular signatures, such as a tax return, S.E.C. registration, or negotiable instrument,[88] as well as official publications[89] and certain records and reports filed with government agencies.[90] There may frequently be an overlap between the statutes incorporated in Rule 902(10) and other illustrations regarding authentication and self-authentication. Rule 902(9), for example, which incorporates the self-authentication provisions of general commercial law, is actually redundant with reference to Rule 902(10) in that it represents a particularization of the latter Rule.

---

[82] *See generally,* 2 MCCORMICK, § 218; 5 WEINSTEIN'S FEDERAL EVIDENCE § 902.12; 5 MUELLER & KIRKPATRICK, § 548. *See also* Hunter, FEDERAL TRIAL HANDBOOK, § 58.15, "Authentication of Documents, Presumed Under Acts of Congress to be Authentic."

[83] *See* Advisory Committee Note, Rule 902.

[84] *See* Rule 902(9) and accompanying discussion, Chapter 902, *supra,* regarding the distinction between presumptive and prima facie authenticity.

[85] For an example of pertinent federal statutes that address self-authentication, *see* Advisory Committee Note, Rule 902(10). *See* 5 WEINSTEIN'S FEDERAL EVIDENCE § 902.12; *see also* 5 MUELLER & KIRKPATRICK, § 548.

[86] 5 WEINSTEIN'S FEDERAL EVIDENCE § 902.12; 5 MUELLER & KIRKPATRICK, § 548.

[87] *Id.*; 5 MUELLER & KIRKPATRICK, § 548; *see* 22 U.S.C. § 4221; 22 U.S.C. § 4215; 33 U.S.C. §§ 875, 876.

[88] *See, e.g.,* 26 U.S.C. §§ 6062, 6064; *see also* 5 WEINSTEIN'S FEDERAL EVIDENCE § 902.12; 5 MUELLER & KIRKPATRICK, § 548; United States v. Mangan, 575 F.2d 32 (2d Cir. 1978) (in prosecution of IRS Agent for fraud, tax return and material from personnel file, all purporting to have been prepared and signed by defendant, were properly used as exemplars; presumption of genuineness of signature on tax return).

[89] *See, e.g.,* 44 U.S.C. §§ 1507, 1510(a) (Federal Register).

[90] *See, e.g.,* 47 U.S.C. § 412 (F.C.C.).

§ 902.19 Judicial Precedent Regarding Self-Authentication

Although Rule 902(10) incorporates only legislative enactments, courts should arguably be open to setting judicial precedent on the subject of self-authentication. In view of the liberal standard of admissibility reflected by the authentication Rules, courts might adopt judicial rules to facilitate litigation and to obviate technical requirements in situations that do not warrant the time and expense associated with requirements of establishing authenticity of certain documents. For example, courts might well extend the doctrine of self-authentication to all documents produced during discovery or that have a connection with the party against whom they are offered unless there is a specific disclaimer of genuineness.[91]

§ 902.20 Rule 902(11) and (12) Certified Domestic and Foreign Records of a Regularly Conducted Activity

The following items of evidence are self-authenticating; they require no extrinsic evidence of authenticity in order to be admitted:

***

(11) *Certified Domestic Records of a Regularly Conducted Activity.* The original or a copy of a domestic record that meets the requirements of Rule 803(6)(A)-(C), as shown by a certification of the custodian or another qualified person that complies with a federal statute or a rule prescribed by the Supreme Court. Before the trial or hearing, the proponent must give an adverse party reasonable written notice of the intent to offer the record — and must make the record and certification available for inspection — so that the party has a fair opportunity to challenge them.

(12) *Certified Foreign Records of a Regularly Conducted Activity.* In a civil case, the original or a copy of a foreign record that meets the requirements of Rule 902(11), modified as follows: the certification, rather than complying with a federal statute or Supreme Court rule, must be signed in a manner that, if falsely made, would subject the maker to a criminal penalty in the country where the certification is signed. The proponent must also meet the notice requirements of Rule 902(11).

---

[91] *See* 2 MCCORMICK, § 228, at 57: "The concept of self-authentication was subsequently extended dramatically in federal criminal proceedings by enactment of a statute which confers self-authenticating effect on foreign records of regularly conducted activity which are certified by the custodian in accordance with the statute. This development in turn motivated the Conference of Commissioners on Uniform State Laws to amend Uniform Rule 902 to provide for self-authentication of 'certified' business records, domestic as well as foreign." *See generally* WEINSTEIN'S FEDERAL EVIDENCE § 902.02 (in some cases, foundational facts as to authenticity are within the knowledge of the opponent of the evidence, thereby "making it unfair to require the proponent to present this evidence").

Added in December 2000, Rule 902(11) and (12) complement Rule 803(6), the "business records" exception to the hearsay rule. As amended in 2000, Rule 803(6) permits a party to lay a foundation for the admission of business records by certification, rather than live courtroom testimony, to substantially reduce the time and expense of producing usually uncontroversial testimony about the general methods of creating such records. Rule 902(11) provides that business records, certified by one with knowledge of the system that produces such records, will be self-authenticating, provided the certification states that the evidence meets each of the three requirements found in Rule 803(6). The Advisory Committee Note to the Rule explains that a "declaration that satisfies 28 U.S.C. § 1746 [an unsworn statement made under penalty of perjury] would satisfy the declaration requirement of Rule 902(11), as would any comparable certification under oath."[92]

Rule 902(12) makes the same procedure available for self-authentication of foreign business records. It is virtually identical in language and effect to Rule 902(11). This Rule is limited in its application to civil cases, because a similar provision is already made for self-authentication of foreign business records in criminal cases by statute, 18 U.S.C. § 3505. Since the declaration originates outside of the United States, it must be signed in a manner that would, if falsely made, subject the signer to criminal penalty under the laws of the country where it is signed.[93]

---

[92] *See* Advisory Committee Note, Rule 902(11) (citing 28 U.S.C. § 1746).

[93] Rule 902(12). For additional discussion of the operation of these two new forms of self-authentication, *see* § 803.34, *supra.*

Chapter 903

Rule 903. Subscribing Witness's Testimony

Rule 903. Subscribing Witness's Testimony

A subscribing witness's testimony is necessary to authenticate a writing only if required by the law of the jurisdiction that governs its validity.

---

§ 903.1 Subscribing Witness's Testimony — In General

A subscribing witness is a person who witnesses or attests another individual's signature on an instrument and signs or subscribes his or her own name as testimony to the authenticity of that signature. Rule 903 provides that authentication of a writing need involve the testimony of a subscribing witness only if such testimony is ". . . required by the law of the jurisdiction that governs its validity." Accordingly, where there is no applicable statutory or common-law provision requiring testimony of a subscribing witness, authentication of a document may be established, in some jurisdictions, pursuant to any of the provisions of Rule 901 or 902.[1] For example, there are pertinent statutory provisions concerning authentication of a will sought to be entered in probate.[2] Where the validity of a writing is governed by the laws of another jurisdiction, the laws of that jurisdiction must be consulted regarding authentication requirements. Wills are generally the only documents that states require to be authenticated by subscribing witnesses, and even this requirement is beginning to erode.[3] However, since wills are not probated in federal court, the state requirement of a subscribing witness will rarely affect Rule 903.[4]

---

[1] *See generally,* 2 MCCORMICK, § 220; 5 WEINSTEIN'S FEDERAL EVIDENCE §§ 903.01–903.02; 5 MUELLER & KIRKPATRICK, §§ 549–550; 4 WIGMORE, §§ 1287–1321. *See also* Comment, *Judicial Notice and Presumptions Under the Proposed Federal Rules of Evidence,* 16 WAYNE L. REV. 217 (1969); 20 AM. JUR. 2d §§ 851–853, 923–929 (1967); Annots.: *Abrogation of Common Law Rule,* 65 A.L.R. 324 (1930); Proof of Due Execution, 79 A.L.R. 389 (1931).

[2] *See* Advisory Committee Note, Rule 903; *see also* § 903.3, *infra.*

[3] 5 WEINSTEIN'S FEDERAL EVIDENCE § 903.02.

[4] 5 MUELLER & KIRKPATRICK, § 550.

§ 903.2   Common-Law Practice as to Testimony of Subscribing Witnesses

Traditionally at common law, when a document signed by subscribing witnesses was sought to be introduced into evidence, the proponent was required to first call an attesting witness, or, alternatively, to show that all attesters were unavailable before the proponent could call any other witness to authenticate the document.[5] The rule applied even where the document was not required by law to be attested.[6] The origin of the common-law rule was apparently rooted in early legal practices regarding the types of witnesses who could testify in court. It was also supported by questionable theories concerning an implicit agreement by the parties to the document to make the attester their witness to prove execution, as well as the attester's alleged preferential position to testify as to any fraud, duress or the like.[7] As the rule became more removed from its historical basis, the requirement of calling or accounting for particular persons was recognized by some courts as a burdensome and largely unjustifiable task. Consequently, various exceptions were formulated pertaining to ancient documents, writings collateral to the suit, and certified copies of recorded conveyances.[8] At an early date, federal courts modified the common-law rule to permit authentication of a document by the party who executed it, without the necessity of first calling a subscribing witness.[9]

§ 903.3   Scope and Application of Rule 903

Rule 903 dispenses with the requirement of testimony by subscribing witnesses unless the laws of the jurisdiction governing the validity of the writing require such testimony in order to authenticate the particular writing. As discussed in § 903.1 of this Chapter, wills are the most common subject for legislation in this area.

Testimony by subscribing witnesses, where mandated by applicable law,

---

[5] 2 McCORMICK, § 220; *see* 5 WEINSTEIN'S FEDERAL EVIDENCE § 903.02; 4 WIGMORE, § 1287, *et seq.; see, e.g.,* Jones v. Underwood, 28 Barb. 481 (Sup. Ct. 1858) (setting forth the traditional common-law requirements); Hollenback v. Fleming, 6 Hill 303 (N.Y. Sup. Ct. 1844) (even proof of confession or acknowledgment of the party not permitted to be received as a substitute for the testimony of the subscribing witness).

[6] *See* Advisory Committee Note, Rule 903.

[7] *See* 5 WEINSTEIN'S FEDERAL EVIDENCE § 903.02; 4 WIGMORE § 1288 (discussing the faulty premises upon which the common-law rule was apparently based).

[8] *See* 2 McCORMICK, § 220.

[9] *See, e.g.,* Drew v. Wadleigh, 7 Me. 94 (1930) (in action on promissory note, plaintiff was properly permitted to impeach defense witness by introducing a contract between plaintiff and the witness; contract tended to show that witness had acknowledged to be true certain facts in conflict with his testimony; since purpose of plaintiff was not to advance a claim on the contract, court here rejected defense contention that receipt of the contract was error because attesting witness was not called).

applies only where the validity of the document is in question, that is, where the party introducing it is seeking to prove "execution of the document by the person making it, *i.e.,* to authenticate its genuineness."[10] Such is the case, for example, where a will is offered into probate for the purpose of transferring property according to its terms. If, however, the proponent of the document is seeking to prove something other than the document's execution and validity, *e.g.,* delivery, proof of family history, or the like, the requirement for subscribing witness testimony does not operate.[11]

---

[10] 4 WIGMORE, § 1293; *see* 5 WEINSTEIN'S FEDERAL EVIDENCE § 903.02.

[11] 4 WIGMORE, § 1293.

ARTICLE X.

CONTENTS OF WRITINGS, RECORDINGS, AND PHOTOGRAPHS

Synopsis

Chapter 1001

Rule 1001. Definitions That Apply to This Article

Rule 1001. Definitions That Apply to This Article

In this article:

(a) A "writing" consists of letters, words, numbers, or their equivalent set down in any form.

(b) A "recording" consists of letters, words, numbers, or their equivalent recorded in any manner.

(c) A "photograph" means a photographic image or its equivalent stored in any form.

(d) An "original" of a writing or recording means the writing or recording itself or any counterpart intended to have the same effect by the person who executed or issued it. For electronically stored information, "original" means any printout — or other output readable by sight — if it accurately reflects the information. An "original" of a photograph includes the negative or a print from it.

(e) A "duplicate" means a counterpart produced by a mechanical, photographic, chemical, electronic, or other equivalent process or technique that accurately reproduces the original.

---

§ 1001.1 The Best Evidence Rule — An Overview

The so-called "best evidence" rule is an ancillary rule of evidence having only a limited application. The essence of the best evidence rule is that in proving the contents of a writing, recording, or photograph, the original is preferentially required; but if the original is unavailable through no fault of the proponent of the evidence, secondary evidence may be admitted.[1]

---

[1] *See generally,* 2 MCCORMICK, §§ 214, 229–231, 235; 6 WEINSTEIN'S FEDERAL EVIDENCE §§ 1001.01–1001.11; 5 MUELLER & KIRKPATRICK, §§ 551–590; 3 MCCORMICK, §§ 790, 792–798; 4 WIGMORE §§ 1173–1180, 1230, 1232–1241. *See also* Broun, *Authentication and the Contents of Writings,* 4 ARIZ. ST. L.J. 611 (1969); Byers, *Microfilming of Business Records,* 6 DRAKE L. REV. 74 (1957); Cleary & Strong, *The Best Evidence Rule: An Evaluation in Context,* 51 IOWA L. REV. 383 (1952); Cleary, *Evidence—Best Evidence Rule-Admissibility of a Carbon Copy as Primary Evidence,* 3 VILL. L. REV. 217 (1958); Gardner, *The Camera Goes to Court,* 24 N.C. L. REV. 233 (1946); Gray, *Motion Pictures in*

The best evidence rule does not apply to proving the contents of physical objects or things other than writings, recordings, or photographs.[2] Accordingly, there is no general requirement that the most probative evidence be used to prove a fact in every instance, and evidence need only be relevant under Rule 401 to satisfy the threshold qualification for admissibility. Nevertheless, there may be statutory requirements, independent of the Rules of Evidence, which require a certain type of evidence as the "best evidence," *e.g.,* postmark on petition to I.R.S. must be proven to establish timely filing.[3]

Because the application of the rule is limited to situations in which the contents of a writing, recording, or photograph are to be proven,[4] the name, "best evidence rule," is a misnomer. More accurate would be "the original writing or document rule."[5] Even this name is misleading because Rule 1003

Evidence, 15 IND. L.J. 408 (1940); Jones, *Authentication and Contents of Writings*, 5 OKLA. L. REV. 383 (1952); Levin, *Authentication and the Contents of Writings*, 10 RUTGERS L. REV. 632 (1956); McMorrow, *Authentication and the Best Evidence Rule Under the Federal Rules of Evidence*, 16 WAYNE L. REV. 195 (1969); Mouser & Philbin, *Photographic Evidence—Is There a Recognized Basis for Admissibility?*, 8 HASTINGS L.J. 310 (1957); Parodis, *The Celluloid Witness*, 37 U. COLO. L. REV. 235 (1965); Portman, *Mechanical Testimony*, 17 CLEV.-MAR. L. REV. 519 (1968); Scott, *X-Ray Pictures as Evidence*, 44 MICH. L. REV. 773 (1946); Tracy, *The Introduction of Documentary Evidence*, 24 IOWA L. REV. 436 (1939); Wallace, *Computer Printouts of Business Records and Their Admissibility in New York*, 31 ALB. L. REV. 61 (1967); Wharton, *Duplicate Originals and the Best Evidence Rule*, 19 OHIO ST. L.J. 520 (1958).

[2] *See, e.g.,* Burney v. United States, 339 F.2d 91 (5th Cir. 1964) (prosecution for possession of non-tax-paid distilled spirits; government agents testified that they tasted and smelled the contents of the containers; court implicitly approved the position that the best evidence doctrine applies only to writings); Chandler v. United States, 318 F.2d 356 (10th Cir. 1963) (alleged unlawful removal and transportation of non-tax-paid spirits; court here rejected defense best evidence objection to testimony by government agents that they seized containers of whiskey that did not bear revenue stamps; court held that best evidence Rule does not apply to situations like this, but is limited to cases where the question relates to the contents of written documents); Francis v. United States, 239 F.2d 560 (10th Cir. 1956) (prosecution for possession of marijuana seeds, where government had to show that the seeds were capable of germinating; court here rejected defense best evidence objection to testimony by government chemist that he determined the seeds to be marijuana, and that he planted some and obtained sprouts within three and a half days).

[3] Shipley v. Commissioner, 572 F.2d 212 (9th Cir. 1979) (tax court dismissed petition for redetermination of tax liability for lack of jurisdiction, holding that taxpayers had not met jurisdictional requirements for timely filing; court rejected argument of taxpayers that they should be allowed to show that they sent the petition by certified mail and that the postmark date on the receipt was within the time allowed; statute made the actual postmark critical; postmarked receipt had not been introduced into evidence, so secondary evidence of its existence and date stamped on it was prohibited; no indication given that receipt could not be readily produced).

[4] *See, e.g.,* Sayen v. Rydzewski, 387 F.2d 815 (7th Cir. 1967); Driggers v. United States, 384 F.2d 158 (5th Cir. 1967).

[5] *See* 2 MCCORMICK, § 229, at 61. McCormick notes that "[t]he only actual role that the 'best evidence' phrase denotes today is the rule requiring the production of the original

provides that a duplicate, as defined in Rule 1001(4), is admissible to the same extent as an original except where a question exists as to the authenticity of the original or where admission of the duplicate instead of the original would be unfair.[6]

While the best evidence rule generally requires use of the original to prove the contents of a writing, recording, or photograph, Article X in Rules 1004, 1005, 1006, and 1007 sets forth exceptions in accordance with which secondary evidence may be admissible. Consequently, the best evidence rule is a rule of preference under which the original is preferred to secondary evidence. Secondary evidence may be admitted, however, where one of a number of conditions is shown to obtain.[7]

While Article X contains no express definition of "secondary evidence," it is clear that secondary evidence is any evidence that is probative of contents other than the original itself. For example, secondary evidence of the contents of a document could be testimony of a person with firsthand knowledge of the contents (*i.e.*, a person who saw the document and remembers its substance), or it could be a hand transcribed copy. It should be noted that, except in Rule 1005 regarding public records, Article X does *not* erect a hierarchy of secondary evidence such that, for example, a hand transcribed copy is preferred to oral testimony. Once an exception to the requirement for the original is satisfied, any secondary evidence may be used to prove contents. As stated in the Advisory Committee Note to Federal Rule 1004:

> The rule recognizes no "degrees" of secondary evidence. While strict logic might call for extending the principle of preference beyond simply preferring the original, the formulation of a hierarchy of preferences and a procedure for making it effective is believed to involve unwarranted complexities. Most, if not all, that would be accomplished by an extended scheme of preferences will, in any event, be achieved through the normal motivation of a party to present the most convincing evidence possible and the arguments and procedures available to his opponent if he does not. . . .

Finally, it should be noted that the best evidence rule is triggered only when the *contents* of a writing, recording, or photograph is the object of

---

writing." 2 MCCORMICK, § 229, at 61; *see, e.g.,* Edwards v. Swilley, 118 S.W.2d 584 (Ark. 1938).

[6] *See* Rule 1003; §§ 1003.2–100.3, *infra*.

[7] *See* Rules 1004, 1005, 1006 and 1007 and discussion of Rules in accompanying Chapters, *infra*; *see also* 5 MUELLER & KIRKPATRICK,d § 552; *cf.* United States v. Alexander, 326 F.2d 736 (4th Cir. 1964) (reproduction of check failed to pick up the name and address of the payee, and these had been typed on the copy; absent an objection that the indictment was misleading, any testimony that the item in question was a treasury check payable to someone other than the accused should have sufficed to identify it).

proof. Any other consequential fact sought to be proven will not invoke application of the rule.

§ 1001.2   Scope of Application of Best Evidence Rule

As noted previously, Article X creates a preference for the "original evidence" only where a party seeks to prove the contents of writings, recordings and photographs.[8] By defining key terms, Rule 1001 effectively delineates the scope of the best evidence rule. Accordingly, Rule 1001(a) defines a "writing." Rule 1001(b) defines a "recording." Rule 1001(c) defines a "photograph." Rule 1001(d) defines an "original," providing separate definitions for "writings and recordings," for "photographs" and for "computer printouts." Rule 1001(e) defines a "duplicate" and implicitly distinguishes a duplicate from a copy.

§ 1001.3   Definition of Writings and Recordings

Rule 1001(a) and Rule 1001(b) define a "writing" and "recording" in their broadest sense. Any setting down of "letters, words, or numbers, or their equivalent" by virtually any means constitutes a writing or recording.[9] A writing or recording is not only a setting down of inscriptions of letters and numbers, but also any compilation or recording of data such as might be produced by a computer, electronic device, or other newly developed machine or technique.[10] Thus, Rule 1001(a) and Rule 1001(b) allow the application of the best evidence rule to accommodate technological developments. These rules are also sufficiently broad to include within their purview the setting down of any symbols that have a verbal or numerical translation.

---

[8] *E.g.,* Can-Am Eng'g Co. v. Henderson Glass, Inc., 814 F.2d 253 (6th Cir. 1987) (defendant's objection to testimony of plaintiff's witness as to certain sales figures was appropriate where the records were neither present in court, nor offered into evidence); White Indus. v. Cessna Aircraft Co., 611 F. Supp. 1049 (W.D. Mo. 1985) (plaintiff's testimony of his examination of documents in Federal Aviation Administration offices in Oklahoma City was inadmissible under best evidence rule; neither records nor copies were in the record and plaintiff made no showing that they were unobtainable); *see* Rule 1002, Advisory Committee Note.

[9] *E.g.,* Seiler v. Lucasfilm, Ltd., 797 F.2d 1504 (9th Cir. 1986) (plaintiff's drawings were "writings" within the meaning of Rule 1001(1), noting that although the drawings did not consist of "letters, words, or numbers," they could be regarded as "their equivalent"); United States v. Truglio, 731 F.2d 1123 (4th Cir. 1984) (in seizure of certain audiotapes pursuant to search warrant authorizing seizure of records, warrant's failure to make specific mention of "written or electronic records" did not render the warrant defective because Advisory Committee Note to Rule 1001(1) dictates expansion of definition of writings and recordings to include modern developments); *see* Rule 1001, Advisory Committee Note (including computers, photographic systems, and other modern developments).

[10] Rule 1001, Advisory Committee Note; *e.g.,* United States v. Truglio, 731 F.2d 1123 (4th Cir. 1984).

§ 1001.4   Application of Rule 1001(a) and Rule 1001(b)

The scope of the definition of terms "writing" and "recording" is not a question entirely free from dispute. A traditional problem involves the determination of whether an inscribed object, *e.g.*, a policeman's badge or a tombstone, is always a writing or recording subject to the best evidence rule.[11] Clearly, where the verbal or numerical contents of the inscribed object are not being proven, the best evidence rule is not triggered.[12] Commentators generally have maintained, however, that even where the contents of the inscribed object are to be proven, the object itself need not be produced, unless in the discretion of the court, factors are present that would justify requiring use of the original object.[13] There is little federal authority from which to predict whether a given court will require the production of an object simply because it is inscribed.[14] Factors that should be considered by the trial judge in deciding whether to require proof by the original inscribed object include: (i) whether precise information is required; (ii) whether the original is feasibly subject to production; (iii) whether a view of the object is practical or appropriate; (iv) whether the inscribed data is central or peripheral to the litigation; and (v) whether secondary evidence (*e.g.*, a photograph) is equally as probative as the original.

Where contents are the object of proof, federal courts have clearly held that writings within the scope of the best evidence rule include written contracts,[15] written statements or letters,[16] corporate records,[17] and public records.[18]

§ 1001.5   Definition of a Photograph — In General

Rule 1002 extends the traditional best evidence rule by including photographs within its scope.[19] Rule 1001(c) defines photograph to include

---

[11] *See generally,* 2 McCormick, § 232; 6 Weinstein's Federal Evidence § 1001.03; 5 Mueller & Kirkpatrick, § 552; 4 Wigmore, § 1182.

[12] *See* § 1002.1 *et seq., infra.*

[13] *See generally,* 2 McCormick, § 232; 6 Weinstein's Federal Evidence § 1001.03; 5 Mueller & Kirkpatrick, § 552; 4 Wigmore, § 1182.

[14] *See* Watson v. United States, 224 F.2d 910 (5th Cir. 1955) (conviction reversed where oral testimony was admitted to prove that whiskey bottles did not contain labels or tax stamps, instead of producing the bottles themselves). *Contra* Burney v. United States, 339 F.2d 91 (5th Cir. 1964) (implicitly held that best evidence doctrine applies only to writings).

[15] Vigano v. Wylain, Inc., 633 F.2d 522 (8th Cir. 1980); *e.g.,* Time Share Vacation Club v. Atlantic Resorts, 735 F.2d 61 (3d Cir. 1984) (in contract suit plaintiff "would bear the burden of producing copy of entire contract, or at least, proffer an explanation for its absence" on remand).

[16] Weeks v. Latter Day Saints Hosp., 418 F.2d 1035 (10th Cir. 1969).

[17] Farber v. Servan Land Co., 662 F.2d 371 (5th Cir. 1981).

[18] *See* §§ 1005.1–1005.2, *infra.*

[19] 4 Wigmore, § 1183; 5 Kirkpatrick, § 554; *see also* 2 McCormick, § 232, at 65:

"a photographic image or its equivalent stored in any form."

Offering photographs at trial will only invoke the best evidence rule when the contents of the photograph itself are at issue. For example, in the case of an allegedly obscene film, the film's contents must be proved in order to establish the alleged obscenity.[20] The best evidence rule would consequently operate to prefer use of the original film, and secondary evidence would only be appropriate where an exception to the best evidence rule could be satisfied. Where, however, a photograph of an item, itself not a writing, recording, or photograph, is available to prove the appearance of the item, the best evidence rule does not operate to prefer the photograph over other evidence. Proof of the appearance of the object of the photograph is not subject to the best evidence rule.[21] For example, where the appearance of a person is sought to be proven, the best evidence rule is not involved. A photograph of the person in question is probative evidence of the person's appearance, but it is not preferred over any other method of proof. Other probative evidence of the person's appearance, *e.g.*, testimony of a person with first-hand knowledge, would be equally admissible. This result is more fully discussed in Chapter 1002, *infra*.

§ 1001.6   Still Photographs

Still photographs do not invoke the best evidence rule unless a party is trying to prove the contents of the photographs.[22] For example, the contents of the photograph may be at issue where the photograph contains or reveals evidence to be derived uniquely from the photograph, such as a photograph produced by an automatically activated surveillance camera at a bank.[23] This

---

"while it is difficult to accept that photographs of objects exhibit more intricacy of detail than do the objects photographed, concentrating attention upon content does provide a rationale for bringing photographs within it where their contents are sought to be proved."

[20] *See* United States v. Levine, 546 F.2d 658 (5th Cir. 1977) (obscenity prosecution; court rejected defense Best Evidence objection to use in evidence of "release print" of allegedly obscene motion picture, finding that under Rule 1001(2), the workprint or cut negative as well as the answer prints and release prints were originals of the filmmaking process); *see also* Rule 1002, Advisory Committee Note.

[21] HUGHES & CANTOR, PHOTOGRAPHS IN CIVIL LITIGATION, 61–69 (1973); 2 SCOTT, PHOTOGRAPHIC EVIDENCE, § 1003 (1969); *e.g.*, Guam v. Ojeda, 758 F.2d 403 (9th Cir. 1985) (court held pictures of stolen jewelry were properly admitted in a burglary case, because the best evidence rule applied only to writings and recordings, not to other physical evidence).

[22] *See* McMorrow, *Authentication and the Best Evidence Rule Under the Federal Rules of Evidence*, 16 WAYNE L. REV. 195 (1969).

[23] *See, e.g.,* Hill v. State, 221 Ga. 65, 142 S.E.2d 909 (Ga. 1965) (defendant tried for robbery; state introduced evidence of photographs of art objects taken by defendant rather than the art works themselves; court rejected Best Evidence objection by defense since the Best Evidence rule applies only to the contents of a writing; trial court did not err in admitting the photographs of the art objects over the objection that they were not the best evidence); *see also* United States v. Taylor, 530 F.2d 639 (5th Cir. 1976) (bank surveillance camera; film properly received even though no teller saw the events).

use of a photograph to prove contents is relatively rare, because usually a photograph is introduced merely to illustrate the testimony of a witness based on firsthand perceptions.[24] Accordingly, where a photograph is used to illustrate the testimony of a witness with firsthand knowledge of the subject of the photograph, the best evidence rule is inapplicable because the object of proof is not the contents of the photograph itself, but the existence or nature of the subject of the photograph.

A photograph of a document that is itself subject to the best evidence rule may be inadmissible because the photograph of the documentary evidence is secondary evidence of the contents of the document. Thus, a photograph of a medical record cannot be admitted to prove the contents of the record unless one of the exceptions to Rule 1002 is shown to obtain, or a statute so provides.

§ 1001.7   Videotapes and Motion Pictures

Videotapes and motion pictures have generally been admitted at trial without best evidence issues arising, because usually when offered, videotapes and films are used to illustrate the testimony of a witness who has firsthand knowledge of the subject depicted.[25] Nevertheless, situations involving libel, copyright infringement, or invasion of privacy may raise best evidence questions because in these types of cases, the contents of the tape or film may be at issue.

The principal type of case involving best evidence questions has concerned obscenity.[26] Federal courts have readily admitted duplicates of films to prove that a particular film is obscene.[27] Frames of films have been admitted as still photographs, even though the whole film is excluded for reasons of prejudice, delay, repetition, or confusion.[28] Nevertheless, there is the possibility of distortion where a film is edited prior to admission, either due to the absence of relevant or counterbalancing passages or due to the

---

[24] 6 WEINSTEIN'S FEDERAL EVIDENCE § 1001.04; 5 MUELLER & KIRKPATRICK, § 554.

[25] *Id.; see also* Barham v. Nowell, 243 Miss. 441, 138 So.2d 493 (Miss. 1962) (plaintiff walking normally, and walking up and down stairs); Lambert v. Wolf's, Inc., 132 So.2d 522 (La. Ct. App. 1961) (plaintiff bending over and lifting heavy objects); Wren v. St. Louis Pub. Serv. Co., 333 S.W.2d 92 (Mo. 1960) (plaintiff working, lifting).

[26] *See, e.g.,* United States v. Levine, 546 F.2d 658 (5th Cir. 1977); *see also* Paradis, *The Celluloid Witness,* 37 U. COLO. L. REV. 235 (1965).

[27] 3 SCOTT, *Photographic Evidence,* § 1291 (1969); *see, e.g.,* United States v. One Reel of 35mm Color Motion Picture, 491 F.2d 956 (2d Cir. 1974) (government need produce no more than film itself to show obscenity); People v. Byrnes, 33 N.Y.2d 343, 352 N.Y.S.2d 913, 308 N.E.2d 435 (N.Y. 1974) (photograph sufficiently corroborated fact of rape, sodomy, and incest).

[28] 3 SCOTT, *Photographic Evidence,* § 1295 (1969); *Motion Pictures as Evidence,* AM. JUR. 2d, 8 PROOF OF FACTS, 153, 155 (1960); *see* Rule 403 and § 403.1 *et seq., supra; see also Motion Pictures as Evidence,* AM. JUR. 2d, 8 PROOF OF FACTS, 153 (1960).

emphasis given particular items.[29]

§ 1001.8   X-rays

X-rays and X-ray films may invoke the operation of the best evidence rule when offered at trial.[30] X-rays are frequently used at trial to corroborate or illustrate the testimony of a medical expert regarding the physical condition of the person X-rayed. Where the object of proof is the physical condition of the person X-rayed (*e.g.*, a broken bone), the best evidence rule does not operate to prefer the X-ray over the testimony of the medical expert. The physical condition of the person in question is not a writing, recording, or photograph, and, consequently, the best evidence rule is not triggered.[31] The X-ray and the testimony are equally admissible to prove facts that are not within the scope of the rule, and the testimony based on firsthand knowledge of the injury or condition is admissible in the absence of the X-ray. Where, however, the X-ray is offered to establish a fact that may be derived only from the contents of the X-ray (*e.g.*, a hairline bone fracture), the best evidence rule is invoked. While the ultimate fact to be proven is the physical condition of the person X-rayed, the only source of the information is the X-ray itself, and consequently its contents are sought to be proven.[32] The

---

[29] The spirit, although not the letter, of Rule 106 would appear to apply. Rule 106 provides: "If a party introduces all or part of a writing or recorded statement, an adverse party may require the introduction, at that time, or any part — or any other writing or recorded statement — that in fairness ought to be considered at the same time." In any event, Rule 403 is available as a basis for excluding misleading evidence.

[30] *See generally,* HUGHES & CANTOR, PHOTOGRAPHS IN CIVIL LITIGATION, 68–69 (1973); 3 SCOTT, *Photographic Evidence,* § 1273 (1969). *See also* Chicago, R.I. & P.R. Co. v. Howell, 401 F.2d 752 (10th Cir. 1968) (in dictum agreeing that testimony based on an X-ray should not be received without the X-ray "because testimony alone would not be the best evidence"); Gay v. United States, 118 F.2d 160 (7th Cir. 1941) (in suit on war risk insurance policy, it was error to admit testimony by physician interpreting chest X-ray without producing the X-ray plate, for the testimony was not the best evidence); Cellamare v. Third Ave. Transit Corp., 77 N.Y.S.2d 91 (N.Y. Ct. App. 1948) (in personal injury action, prejudicial error to permit plaintiff's expert medical witness to testify over objection to matters shown on X-rays without producing the X-ray pictures and introducing them in evidence).

[31] *See* § 1002.1, *infra.*

[32] Rules 602 and 703 reinforce the analysis. Testimony based on firsthand knowledge is impossible where the condition is only apparent through use of the X-ray. Thus, testimony as to the condition would be incompetent; testimony as to the contents of the X-ray would be secondary evidence. *See* Sirico v. Cotto, 67 Misc. 2d 636, 324 N.Y.S.2d 483 (N.Y. Ct. App. 1971) (testimony by physician based upon examination of X-ray excluded on account of best evidence doctrine, where proponent did not offer the X-ray or account for its nonproduction; court acknowledged that physician was an expert in radiology and that the opinion of such a person is admissible in evidence to the extent that it will appreciably help the jury to analyze the proof, find the facts, and render a verdict); Patrick & Tillman v. Matkin, 1932 OK 59, 154 Okla. 232, 7 P.2d 414 (Okla. 1932) (in employee's suit to recover disability benefits, it was error to admit plaintiff's expert testimony as to what X-ray showed; court held X-rays to be

foregoing distinction is frequently overlooked, however, and, consequently, many courts have applied the best evidence rule in virtually any case in which X-rays are introduced into evidence.[33] Of course, the best evidence rule is unquestionably applicable where the contents of the X-rays are at issue, *e.g.,* where in proving malpractice it is claimed that the physician misread an X-ray.

§ 1001.9   Originals — An Overview

Rule 1001(d) provides distinct definitions of "originals" for writings or recordings, photographs, and computer or electronic output. The definitions are not necessarily parallel, *e.g.,* although intent is essential to determining whether a writing is an original, intent is irrelevant to determining whether a photograph is an original.

"Original" as used in Chapter X is a term of art. What a layperson would treat as an original may be treated as a duplicate or copy in court.[34] Moreover, what is an original for one action, may be a duplicate or copy for another action arising from the same operative facts.[35]

§ 1001.10   Original Writings or Recordings

Rule 1001(d) provides that an original "writing or recording" is the

---

within Best Evidence Doctrine, but also emphasized importance of expert testimony; Dr. Shaw as an expert was a competent witness to testify as to what the X-ray disclosed, but at the same time the petitioners were entitled to see and examine the picture for the purpose of cross-examination, and submit the same to other experts for interpretation); *cf.* United States v. Leight, 818 F.2d 1297 (7th Cir. 1987) (district court properly admitted diagnostic-quality copies of X-ray after government accidentally destroyed original X-ray, on basis that X-ray is a "photograph" for evidentiary purposes and original of a photograph includes any print made therefrom).

[33] 29 AM. JUR. 2d, *Evidence,* § 485 (1967); *see* Fuller v. Lemmons, 1967 OK 106, 434 P.2d 145 (Okla. 1967) (court applied Best Evidence Rule to exclude expert testimony where the X-ray was in court but was not formally introduced into evidence); Neill v. Fidelity Mutual Life Ins. Co., 119 W. Va. 694, 195 S.E. 860 (W. Va. 1938) (opposing party had opportunity to examine the X-rays outside of court, through the discovery process).

[34] *See* the discussion of Rule 1001(4), § 1001.13 *et seq., infra; see also* 4 WIGMORE, § 1232; Jones, Notes & Comments, *Authentication and Contents of Writings,* 5 OKLA. L. REV. 383 (1952); *see, e.g.,* United States v. Rangel, 585 F.2d 344 (8th Cir. 1978) (since defendant used altered photocopy of receipt in demanding unlawful payment, contents of photocopy and not of original receipt had to be proved).

[35] *See generally,* United States v. Taylor, 648 F.2d 565 (9th Cir. 1981) (where letter was telecopied from San Diego to Houston, either telecopied letter or photocopy thereof may have been the document on which Texas bank relied, making it the legally operative original); 2 MCCORMICK, § 235; 6 WEINSTEIN'S FEDERAL EVIDENCE § 1001.08; 5 MUELLER & KIRK-PATRICK, § 556; 4 WIGMORE, § 1232. *See also* Cartier v. Jackson, 59 F.3d 1046, 1048 (10th Cir. 1995) (in copyright infringement action where the plaintiff was trying to prove that the defendant had copied her song, the "best evidence" was not the original master tape, but the demo tape that she claimed the defendant had heard and copied; thus, to introduce secondary evidence of the song's contents, the plaintiff must establish that the demo tapes were lost or destroyed).

writing or recording itself or any counterpart *intended* by the person executing or issuing it to be an original.[36] Thus, a contract that is signed by the parties is an original even though the parties may not have initially distinguished that writing for execution.[37]

Rule 1001(d) provides that the definition of an original includes a counterpart intended by the person issuing or executing it to be an original. It may be an original whether or not it was written before or after another, was copied from another, or was itself used to make a copy.[38] Accordingly, a "duplicate original," *i.e.*, a counterpart of an original instrument intended by the parties to have the effect of an original,[39] is to be treated as an original.[40] Focusing upon the issuer's or executor's intention to determine whether a counterpart of a writing is an original is far simpler than tests proposed by McCormick[41] and Wigmore.[42]

Finally, it should be noted that a "duplicate original" is a distinguishable concept from that of a "duplicate." Duplicates are discussed in § 1001.13 *et seq., infra*. The concept of a "duplicate original" or "multiple original" arises in the situation where, by virtue of intent, there is more than one original, *e.g.*, where parties to a bilateral contract intend that each should have an executed original. The concept of a "duplicate" arises in the situation where, under Rules 1001(e) and 1003, an accurate copy is introduced and treated as an original for purposes of the best evidence rule, *e.g.*, where a party offers a carbon copy or a photographic copy of a document where the contents of the document are at issue.

§ 1001.11   Original Photographs

Rule 1001(d) provides that an original of a photograph is either "the negative or a print from it." Accordingly, either the negative or the print made from the negative is equally admissible in evidence as an original.[43]

---

[36] Jones, C.R., Notes & Comments, *Authentication and Contents of Writings*, 5 OKLA. L. REV. 383 (1952).

[37] 4 WIGMORE, § 1233.

[38] 6 WEINSTEIN'S FEDERAL EVIDENCE § 1001.08; *see also* 4 WIGMORE, § 1232; Jones, Notes & Comments, *Authentication and Contents of Writings*, 5 OKLA. L. REV. 383 (1952); *see, e.g.*, United States v. Rangel, 585 F.2d 344 (8th Cir. 1978) (since defendant used altered photocopy of receipt in demanding unlawful payment, contents of photocopy and not of original receipt had to be proved, citing Treatise).

[39] 2 McCORMICK, § 236.

[40] *See* Rule 1001, Advisory Committee Note.

[41] 2 McCORMICK, § 235, at 71 ("The question to be asked, then, is whether, under the substantive law, the creation, publication or other use of Y may be viewed as affecting the rights of the parties in a way material to the litigation")

[42] 4 WIGMORE, § 1232, at 548 ("Is this the very document whose contents are desired to be, and in the now state of the issues by the substantive law may be, proved?").

[43] *See, e.g.*, United States v. Leight, 818 F.2d 1297 (7th Cir. 1987) (diagnostic-quality

The value of a print is that it is easily understandable and readable.[44] Negatives, however, are not only the ultimate source from which prints are made; they often indicate variations in shades or hues not reproduced in the prints.[45]

Rule 1001(e) makes clear that enlargements or reductions made from a particular negative are not originals but duplicates. Treating enlargements and reductions as duplicates instead of originals provides the court with an element of discretion under Rule 1003 to determine whether admission of an enlargement or reduction instead of an original would be unfair to the adverse party.[46]

§ 1001.12   Original Computer Data

Rule 1001(d) provides that "any printout — or other output readable by sight" from a computer or electronic device is an original if the printout accurately reproduces the data that is stored. In addition to the printout, the computer data cards and magnetic tape should also be admissible as originals.[47] Two theories would justify such a view: (i) the data cards and

---

copy of x-ray film may constitute an "original" for purposes of evidence law); *cf.* Rule 1001(3), Advisory Committee Note (construing federal rule as including as originals prints as well as negatives, due to practicality and common usage).

[44] 6 WEINSTEIN'S FEDERAL EVIDENCE § 1001.08; 5 MUELLER & KIRKPATRICK, § 558; *see, e.g.,* United States v. Jacobs, 513 F.2d 564 (9th Cir. 1974), *rev'd on other grounds*, 430 U.S. 188 (1977) (in connection with defense attack upon search warrant, court rejected contention that the allegedly obscene film that was seized was inadmissible absent a showing that it was the actual print received from interstate commerce on the date alleged in the indictment; government is permitted to establish that a print of the same film was received from interstate commerce as alleged, and may use any copy of the film to establish the obscenity of the film; question whether prints are identical must be a collateral subject for the jury's determination); International Union, United Auto., Aircraft & Agric. Implement Workers v. Russell, 88 So.2d 175 (Ala. 1956), *aff'd,* 356 U.S. 634 (1956) (in litigation arising out of labor dispute, motion picture of behavior at picket line was properly received, despite fact that film was a copy and not the original film).

[45] 3 SCOTT, PHOTOGRAPHIC EVIDENCE, § 1476 (1969); *see also* Beach v. Chollett, 31 Ohio App. 8, 166 N.E. 145 (Ohio Ct. App. 1928) (where X-ray plates were introduced, no error to exclude two photographs or prints taken from two of these plates; proponent's witness testified that the prints were correct reproductions from the plates, but he further stated that they were not nearly so accurate as the plates, and did not show as much as the plates themselves, and that the prints were not reliable).

[46] *See* Chapter 1003, *infra.*

[47] *E.g.,* United States v. Catabran, 836 F.2d 453 (9th Cir. 1988) (computer printouts of a business ledger stored by computer were the actual records of the company and admissible); *cf.* United States v. Foley, 598 F.2d 1323 (4th Cir. 1979) (alleged conspiracy on the part of certain realtors to fix real estate prices in violation of antitrust laws; defense objected to the receipt of a chart summarizing the percentage of houses sold by each defendant on the basis of purchase loans guaranteed by V.A. or F.H.A.; chart was made from data contained in machine-readable diskettes; while diskettes were not made available, defendants did obtain a computer printout of the information they contained, and therefore the printouts qualified as

magnetic tape are analogous to the negatives of a photograph, and (ii) the data cards and magnetic tape are recordings themselves that are originals. Of course, because magnetic tape generally is not readable by a juror, the tape itself may not possess probative value under Rule 401.

§ 1001.13   Duplicates — In General

Rule 1001(e) provides a general definition of a duplicate: any counterpart that accurately reproduces the original. Accurate reproduction may be achieved by any of a variety of ways designated in the Rule: by the same impression, as in the case of a carbon copy; from the same matrix, as in the case of a published book; by means of photography, as in the case of photostats, enlargements, or reductions; by mechanical or electronic recordings as in the case of a tape recording; by chemical reproduction, as in the case of a thermofax copy; or by equivalent techniques. The last phrase of the Rule allows the definition of a duplicate to accommodate developments of new technology for recording and reproducing data and information, such as CDs, DVDs, and flash drives. Consistent with the policy underlying the best evidence rule that seeks to ensure the accurate presentation of the contents of the original, duplicates are generally admissible to prove contents to the same extent as originals.[48] Because an additional policy of the best evidence rule is the prevention of fraud, Rule 1003 provides the court with the discretion to require use of an original where introduction of a duplicate would be unfair or misleading.[49]

§ 1001.14   Carbon Copies

Rule 1001 allows carbon copy duplicates of originals to be admissible to the same extent as originals unless special circumstances dictate otherwise.[50]

---

duplicates of the diskettes within the meaning of Rule 1001(4)); *see also* United States v. Russo, 480 F.2d 1228 (6th Cir. 1973) (assuming that properly functioning computer equipment is used, once the reliability and trustworthiness of the information put into the computer has been established, the computer printouts should be received as evidence of the transactions covered by the input).

[48] United States v. Perry, 925 F.2d 1077 (8th Cir. 1991) (still photographic image taken from a videotape is a duplicate for the purposes of Rule 1001(4) and admissible to same extent as an original); United States v. Wagoner, 713 F.2d 1371 (8th Cir. 1983) (telephone billing records showing calls between conspirators were properly admitted because records were shown to be accurate reproductions of originals and therefore constituted duplicate originals under Rule 1001(4) and were admissible to same extent as originals under Rule 1003); Cardona Tirado v. Shearson Lehman American Exp., 634 F. Supp. 158 (D.P.R. 1986) (court rejected plaintiff's argument that photocopy of agreement clause was inadmissible due to his illegible signature as more formalistic than substantive, noting that plaintiff did not deny the existence of the agreement); *see* 2 McCORMICK, § 236; *see also* United States v. Gerhart, 538 F.2d 807 (8th Cir. 1976) (photocopy could have been admitted as a duplicate instead of secondary evidence where the original was lost).

[49] *See* Rule 1003, Advisory Committee Note; *see also* § 1003.3, *infra*; *see, e.g.,* Broun, *Authentication and Contents of Writings*, 4 ARIZ. ST. L.J. 613 (1969).

[50] *E.g.,* Greater Kansas Laborers Pension Fund v. Thummel, 738 F.2d 926 (8th Cir. 1984)

Rule 1001(e) clearly provides that carbon copies are duplicates, regardless of the intention of their maker, *i.e.,* carbon copies are "produced by the same impression as the original," and consequently, are defined as duplicates.[51]

§ 1001.15   Duplicates from the Same Matrix by Means of Photography

Consistent with Rules 1001(e) and 1003, courts have generally permitted the use of copies of books or newspapers to prove contents. Courts have viewed such evidence as highly reliable due to an assumption that fixed type or common plates are employed.[52]

Rule 1001(e) generally extends federal law, however, in providing that photographically produced copies are duplicates, and it should be noted that photographic copies that reduce or enlarge the original are considered to be duplicates under Rule 1001(e). Pre-Rule federal law treated such evidence as secondary.[53]

Additional methods of reproduction that satisfy Rule 1001(e) include digital reproduction, facsimile, and photocopy technology. Copies produced by modern means should be treated as duplicates under the Rule, despite Wigmore's concern that copies were historically not much better than secondary evidence due to their poor quality of reproduction.[54] Photocopies have been widely accepted as duplicates so long as there is no genuine question as to their authenticity.[55] The better view under Rule 1001(e) is that they are duplicates that can be excluded under Rule 1003 if the quality of reproduction is inadequate.

(carbon copy of a contract was properly admitted as an original, notwithstanding the fact that defendant's signature appeared on the carbon in a somewhat obscured fashion and someone had written the owner's name over the signature); *see* Rule 1001, Advisory Committee Note; *see also* Rule 1003; *see, e.g.,* Stern Equipment Co. v. Portell, 116 A.2d 601 (D.C. Mun. App. 1955) (although the contract in evidence was a carbon copy, it was a signed copy, and therefore a duplicate original rather than a mere copy).

[51] *See, e.g.,* CTS Corp. v. Piher Int'l Corp., 527 F.2d 95 (7th Cir. 1975) (although there is no direct testimony describing the document as a carbon copy, in the absence of any evidence to the contrary, we draw this inference from the copy of the document that was offered for examination in light of the testimony of the witness); Liberty Chair v. Crawford, 193 N.C. 531, 137 S.E. 577 (N.C. 1927) (no evidence that carbons were made at same time held not admissible).

[52] *See* 2 McCORMICK, § 236, at 73: "[T]here is warrant for believing that the courts would accept as primary evidence of the contents of a given book or a given issue of a newspaper any other book or newspaper printed from the same sets of fixed type, or the same plates or mats. A like result should be reached as to all copies run off from the same mat by the multigraph, lithoprint, or other duplicating process."

[53] *E.g.,* Toho Bussan Kaisha, Ltd. v. American President Lines, Ltd., 265 F.2d 418 (2d Cir. 1959).

[54] 4 WIGMORE, § 1234.

[55] *E.g.,* United States v. Haddock, 956 F.2d 1534 (10th Cir. 1992).

§ 1001.16 Electronic or Mechanical Re-recording

Rule 1001(e) adopts a rule treating re-recordings as duplicates; subject to the limits set out in Rule 1003, they are as admissible as the original. This approach is contrary to the traditional general rule that such re-recordings are only secondary evidence.[56] Re-recordings of tapes or discs generally are used to provide a more durable copy than the original recording. Likewise, re-recording may produce a copy that is easier to hear or interpret. In the latter case, Rule 1003 provides the court with the discretion to require introduction of the original if the re-recording distorts the original recording in an unfair or misleading way.[57] Finally, it should be clear that a transcript of a recording produced by hand or type is not a duplicate because it would not be an electronic or mechanical re-recording that meets the accuracy requirements of Rule 1001(e).[58]

---

[56] *See* Rule 1001, Advisory Committee Note.

[57] *E.g.,* United States v. Carrasco, 887 F.2d 794 (7th Cir. 1989) (duplicate tape recordings were admissible where an informant who was a participant in the recorded conversations testified that the tapes were true and accurate); United States v. Rengifo, 789 F.2d 975 (1st Cir. 1986) (court has long upheld the use of composite as evidence); United States v. Devous, 764 F.2d 1349 (10th Cir. 1985) (when proper foundation is laid, tapes copied from other tapes are admissible as "duplicates" under Rules 1001(4) and 1003); United States v. DiMatteo, 716 F.2d 1361 (11th Cir. 1983) (copies of recordings of telephone conversations were properly admitted despite defense objection that copies were not originals), *vacated on other grounds,* 469 U.S. 1101 (1985); *see* Rule 1003, Advisory Committee Note; *cf.* United States v. Denton, 556 F.2d 811 (6th Cir. 1977) (composite tape made from re-recording of original tape was properly received; use of composite tape saved the court much time and inconvenience); People v. Albert, 6 Cal. Rptr. 473 (Cal. Ct. App. 1960) (re-recording of a recorded conversation and a transcript of the recording were submitted in evidence along with a police officer's testimony that the transcript and re-recording were accurate reproductions; the original wire recording was not produced due to its unavailability).

[58] *See* Rule 1003, Advisory Committee Note.

Chapter 1002

Rule 1002. Requirement of the Original

Rule 1002. Requirement of the Original

An original writing, recording, or photograph is required in order to prove its content unless these rules or a federal statute provides otherwise.

---

§ 1002.1 The Best Evidence Rule Defined

Rule 1002 restates the traditional best evidence rule in modern and liberal terms.[1] The best evidence rule requires that in proving the contents of a writing, recording, or photograph, the original must be offered as evidence unless a foundation is laid to account for its nonproduction.[2] Additionally, Rule 1002 expressly provides that the Rule's application may be limited by statute and by other rules of evidence.[3]

The general scope of Rule 1002 is in part determined by Rule 1001, which defines the terms used in Rule 1002.[4] Rules 1001 and 1002 expand the traditional best evidence rule by making the rule applicable not only to writings but also to recordings, photographs, and electronically recorded data.[5]

Article X, including Rule 1002, refrains from use of the term "best

---

[1] *See generally,* 1 MCCORMICK, §§ 229–233; 6 WEINSTEIN'S FEDERAL EVIDENCE §§ 1002.01–1002.05; 5 MUELLER & KIRKPATRICK, §§ 567–571; 4 WIGMORE, §§ 1171–1183. *See also* Broun, *Authentication and Contents of Writings,* 4 ARIZ. ST. L.J. 611 (1969); Cleary & Strong, *The Best Evidence Rule: An Evaluation in Context,* 51 IOWA L. REV. 825 (1966); Levin, *Authentication and Content of Writings,* 10 RUTGERS L. REV. 632 (1956); Comment, *Authentication and the Best Evidence Rule Under the Federal Rules of Evidence,* 16 WAYNE L. REV. 195 (1969); Note, *A Critical Appraisal of the Application of the Best Evidence Rule,* 21 RUTGERS L. REV. 526 (1967).

[2] *See* 2 MCCORMICK, § 230; 4 WIGMORE, §§ 1173–1174; *see also* United States v. Alexander, 326 F.2d 736, 739 (4th Cir. 1964) ("it is now generally recognized that the 'best evidence' phrase denotes only the rule of evidence which requires that the contents of an available written document be proved by introduction of the document itself").

[3] *See* Rule 1002, Advisory Committee Note.

[4] *See* §§ 1001.3, 1001.14, *supra.*

[5] *See generally,* 4 WIGMORE, § 1183.

evidence rule," as does the Advisory Committee Note to Rule 1002.[6] The reluctance of the drafters to use such a rubric is undoubtedly due to the recognition that the term is really a misnomer. The term "best evidence rule" is misleading because the rule has only a limited horizon, *i.e.*, there simply is no general requirement to produce the best evidence available to prove consequential facts.[7] Instead, the rule is applicable only when proving the contents of a writing, recording, or photograph. As McCormick has noted, a better name would be "the original document rule."[8] Even this name may be misleading because Rule 1003 makes duplicates admissible in nearly all situations in which Rule 1002 requires that originals be offered.[9]

§ 1002.2　Purpose of the Best Evidence Rule

Five related policies supporting the best evidence rule have been identified.[10] First, because words are so easily misunderstood and slight differences in words or terms have such a substantial effect on meaning, and ultimately on rights, the best evidence rule is said to be necessary to guarantee the accuracy of evidence introduced to prove the contents of writings, recordings, and some photographs.[11] Second, because secondary evidence is frequently a reproduction of the original, the possibility of error in reproduction necessitates production of the original.[12] Because a "duplicate" as defined in Rule 1001(e) provides such a high degree of accuracy in reproduction, Rule 1003 provides a sensible approach that avoids the harshness of a technical reading of the best evidence rule. Rule 1003 authorizes the use of duplicates unless exceptional conditions exist.[13] Third, requiring use of the original may provide information that copies cannot, *e.g.*, watermarks or indications of the ink type that may aid in the

---

[6] *See* Rule 1002, Advisory Committee Note.

[7] *See, e.g.*, Herring v. Administrator, Federal Aviation Admin., 532 F.2d 1003 (5th Cir. 1976) (in connection with license suspension proceedings, rejected pilot's contention that judge should have looked at plane itself or its records to determine its condition, court found that there is no such requirement; best evidence has no meaning in the present context and applies only to the requirement that the terms of a writing be shown by production of the original document, unless the document is shown to be unavailable for reasons other than the serious fault of the proponent); *see also* Rice v. United States, 411 F.2d 485 (8th Cir. 1969); Wallin v. Greyhound Corp., 341 F.2d 521 (6th Cir. 1965).

[8] *See* 2 McCORMICK, § 230.

[9] *See* Rule 1003, Advisory Committee Note.

[10] *See generally,* 2 McCORMICK, § 231; 4 WIGMORE, §§ 1179–1180; Broun, *Authentication and Content of Writings*, 4 ARIZ. ST. L.J. 611 (1969); Cleary & Strong, *The Best Evidence Rule: An Evaluation in Context*, 51 IOWA L. REV. 825 (1966); Levin, *Authentication and Content of Writings*, 10 RUTGERS L. REV. 632 (1956).

[11] *See, e.g.*, MORGAN, BASIC PROBLEMS OF EVIDENCE, 385–87 (1962).

[12] *See* 2 McCORMICK, § 231; Broun, *Authentication and Content of Writings*, 4 ARIZ. ST. L.J. 611 (1969).

[13] *See* § 1003.1, *infra.*

identification of a writing.[14] Rule 1003, which generally allows duplicates to be admitted instead of originals, is not inconsistent with this policy. Rule 1003 provides that the original may be required in lieu of a duplicate where a "genuine question is raised about the original's authenticity." Fourth, the prevention of fraud is fostered by the requirement of the original.[15] Although Wigmore contends that fraud is not always prevented by the application of the rule,[16] McCormick notes that prevention of fraud remains a significant justification:

It has long been observed that the opportunity to inspect original writings may be of substantial importance in the detection of fraud. At least a few modern courts and commentators appear to regard the prevention of fraud as an ancillary justification of the rule. Unless this view is accepted it is difficult to explain the rule's frequent application to copies produced by modern techniques that virtually eliminate the possibility of unintentional mistransmission.[17]

Clearly then, prevention of fraud is at least an ancillary justification for the rule. The final reason suggests that the best evidence rule, in addition to guarding against the mistransmission of the contents of a writing, should also assure that portions of a text, though accurately transmitted, are not selectively removed from a document or a series of documents for use at trial. The best evidence rule, under this rationale, would assure that the jury receives a complete picture of the evidence before rendering its verdict.[18]

§ 1002.3 Application of the Best Evidence Rule; Proving the Contents of Writings, Recordings, and Photographs

Rule 1002 is applicable only when two conditions concur: (1) the evidence involves a writing, recording, or photograph, and (2) the object of proof is the contents of that writing, recording, or photograph.

The first condition indicates that Rule 1002 is inapplicable in proving the nature of uninscribed physical objects or a fact that is subsequently memorialized in a writing. Accordingly, the best evidence rule as codified in Rule 1002 does not require that a confiscated substance be introduced into evidence to prove the nature, identity, or status of the substance.[19] Whether

---

[14] *See* 4 WIGMORE, § 1179, at 417 ("Moreover, the original may contain, and the copy will lack, such features of handwriting, paper, and the like, as may afford the opponent valuable means of learning legitimate objections to the significance of the document").

[15] United States v. Manton, 107 F.2d 834 (2d Cir. 1938); Rogers, *The Best Evidence Rule*, 20 WIS. L. REV. 278 (1945).

[16] 4 WIGMORE, § 1180.

[17] 2 MCCORMICK, § 231, at 62–63.

[18] Toho Bussan Kaisha, Ltd. v. American President Lines, Ltd., 265 F.2d 418 (2d Cir. 1959); *see also* 2 MCCORMICK, § 231.

[19] *E.g.*, Guam v. Ojeda, 758 F.2d 403 (9th Cir. 1985) (pictures of stolen jewelry were

a writing is the object of proof may be unclear in particular relatively unusual cases, *e.g.,* where the writing on an inscribed chattel such as a tombstone is sought to be proven.[20] Nevertheless, when the fact to be proven is independent of the contents of a writing, even though some writing may contain evidence of the fact, it is clear that the best evidence rule is inapplicable. Accordingly, the best evidence rule does not require exclusion, for example, of workers' testimony as to their salary even though payroll records containing the same information are available.[21] Likewise, in the classic illustration, the best evidence rule does not require use of a receipt that memorializes a transaction where the fact of the transaction is the object of proof. In this illustration the transaction exists and is binding in the absence of the receipt. The receipt is merely one means of proof available to establish the transaction, and oral testimony to prove the transaction is equally admissible. In sum, the best evidence rule is not triggered simply because some act or transaction is subsequently recorded in a writing.[22]

The second condition for invocation of the best evidence rule provides that the rule is applicable only where a party offering evidence seeks to prove the *contents* of the writing, recording, or photograph. A party seeks to prove the contents of a writing, recording, or photograph only where the issue is what the writing or recording says or what the photograph depicts. Generally, if the testifying witness only knows of the contents of a writing, recording, or photograph due to having read, heard, or viewed the writing, recording, or photograph, then the original or a duplicate is required to satisfy the best evidence rule. However, where the issue is the status, nature, or identity of the thing described in a writing or recording, or depicted in the photograph, the best evidence rule is inapplicable.[23] Several examples may

---

properly admitted in burglary case, because best evidence rule applied only to writings and recordings, not to other physical evidence); *see, e.g.,* United States v. Marcantoni, 590 F.2d 1324 (5th Cir. 1979); Burney v. United States, 339 F.2d 91 (5th Cir. 1964).

[20] *See* § 1001.4, *supra.*

[21] Sayen v. Rydzewski, 387 F.2d 815 (7th Cir. 1967) (negligence action; plaintiff allowed to testify respecting his income; courts do not bar oral proof of a matter merely because it is also provable by a writing; question is one of admissibility, not weight); *e.g.,* R & R Assoc. v. Visual Scene, Inc., 726 F.2d 36 (1st Cir. 1984) (testimony of company president as to cost of procuring allegedly defective sunglasses did not violate Rule 1002; he was not attempting to prove the contents of a writing, but rather "by his own direct testimony to prove a particular fact"); *see also In re* Ko-Ed Tavern, 129 F.2d 806 (3d Cir. 1942) (testimony by witness as to who owned capital stock in corporation admitted over objection that books of corporation were best evidence); Herzig v. Swift & Co., 146 F.2d 444 (2d Cir. 1945).

[22] *See* Allstate Ins. Co. v. Swann, 27 F.3d 1539, 1542–1543 (11th Cir. 1994) (the best evidence rule does not "require production of a document simply because the document contains facts that are also testified to by a witness" provided the proponent of the evidence is not seeking to prove the content of the document).

[23] *E.g.,* United States v. Sliker, 751 F.2d 477 (2d Cir. 1984) (affirming defendants' convictions arising out of scheme to defraud a bank, court held that the government could

clarify the distinction.

Where the issue is whether a written contract obligates a party to perform in a certain way, the best evidence rule is applicable because the contract, being embodied in the writing, is established by proving the content of the writing.[24] Where the issue is whether a person committed perjury at a hearing, however, a transcript of the hearing is not the best evidence of what the person said. Other evidence such as the testimony of a witness who heard the alleged perjury is equally admissible.[25] The best evidence rule is not triggered, because the object of the proof is what was said at the hearing — not what is recorded in the transcript. The transcript is merely one means of proving the testimony at the hearing. Here, the spoken words form a basis for the perjury, and the perjury would exist even absent the preparation of the transcript. It should be noted, however, that a different analysis would obtain where, in order to prove the oral perjury, a witness is offered who bases his or her testimony entirely on a reading of the contents of the transcript. Here the witness lacks firsthand knowledge of the oral perjury. He or she possesses firsthand knowledge only of the contents of the transcript, and she is consequently offering testimony as to the contents of a writing. Under these facts Rule 602 and Rule 1002 intersect to provide that the original transcript is preferred to the secondary evidence, *i.e.*, the oral testimony offered to prove the contents of the transcript. Nevertheless, as between the transcript and a witness with firsthand knowledge of the oral perjury, there is no preference under Rule 1002, and each is equally appropriate. By

---

prove that the bank was federally insured through testimony, without producing a writing documenting the insurance, because the fact sought to be proved was the existence of insurance not the contents of the writing); *see* Rule 1002, Advisory Committee Note.

[24] Harrington v. United States, 504 F.2d 1306 (1st Cir. 1974) (in tax refund suit, plaintiff sought to prove an alteration in a contract by evidence in the form of a copy of an agreement purporting to be a modification of the contract; court upheld exclusion of the copy); *e.g.,* Time Share Vacation Club v. Atlantic Resorts, 735 F.2d 61 (3d Cir. 1984) (once defendant raised in personam jurisdictional defense, plaintiff must produce a copy of entire contract or an explanation for its absence where it relies wholly upon the contract to establish contacts); *see also* Weeks v. Latter-Day Saints Hosp., 418 F.2d 1035 (10th Cir. 1969) (suit for body burns sustained by two-year-old infant as a result of contact with a temperature-controlled mattress in hospital; evidence of hospital rules properly excluded; Best Evidence Doctrine barred oral testimony as to their contents).

[25] Meyers v. United States, 171 F.2d 800 (D.C. Cir. 1948) (businessman charged with perjury before a Senate Subcommittee looking into suspected waste and profiteering; Subcommittee's lawyer permitted to testify as to substance of testimony given by business-man during hearings; thereafter transcript of that testimony was also introduced; court upheld convictions, but Judge Prettyman wrote a strenuous and now-famous dissent, arguing that receipt of this testimony called for reversal). *See also* United States v. Branham, 97 F.3d 835, 853 (6th Cir. 1996) (the best evidence rule was not violated when a witness provided a summary of the inaudible portions of a videotaped conversation he had with the defendants because he was present during the original conversation; the fact that the conversation was recorded did not require the use of the tape as the best evidence of the conversation).

comparison, however, if the alleged perjury occurred because of a purposeful misrepresentation of a fact set forth in a signed, sworn affidavit, the best evidence rule would apply to prefer the original affidavit. Here the perjury does not exist apart from the words embodied in the writing.

Where a motion picture is offered to prove an external fact, such as the mobility of the plaintiff, the best evidence rule is not implicated because the contents of the film are not at issue, only the mobility of the plaintiff.[26] The best evidence rule is applicable, however, in an obscenity trial at which the film is claimed to be obscene. In such a case the best evidence rule is applicable because the object of proof is the content of the film, *i.e.*, the issue to be resolved is the content of the film.[27]

When proving the confession of a person, a taped recording of the confession would be the best evidence of the confession, only if the tape is itself viewed as the confession, much as a signed, written confession is the confession itself. Otherwise, the tape recording is merely a recording of the oral confession and the best evidence rule is not involved.[28]

§ 1002.4 Exceptions to Rule 1002 in Statutes and Rules

Rule 1002 provides that the originals must be used to prove the contents of writings, recordings, or photographs *except* as provided in the Federal Rules of Evidence or by Acts of Congress. Article X contains a number of such exceptions. Rule 1003 provides that duplicates are admissible to the same extent as originals unless there is a genuine question as to authenticity or where admission of the duplicate would be unfair. Rule 1004 provides four exceptions to the rule: (1) original is lost or destroyed; (2) original is not obtainable by judicial process; (3) original is in possession of adverse party; or (4) original pertains to collateral matter. Rule 1005 provides that copies of public records are admissible as originals if properly certified. Upon

---

[26] Kortz v. Guardian Life Ins. Co. of America, 144 F.2d 676 (10th Cir. 1944); Maryland Cas. Co. v. Coker, 118 F.2d 43 (5th Cir. 1941).

[27] United States v. Levine, 546 F.2d 658 (5th Cir. 1977) (alleged interstate shipment of obscene films; court quoted Rule 1002, and noted that motion pictures are within the ambit of the definition of "photograph" under Rule 1002).

[28] *E.g.*, United States v. Fagan, 821 F.2d 1002 (5th Cir. 1987) (in prosecution for mail fraud, trial court properly admitted testimony by deputy sheriff describing conversation he had with defendant about scheme even though deputy had tape recorded conversation; best evidence rule did not apply because prosecution was not trying to prove contents of tape, but rather contents of conversation); United States v. Rose, 590 F.2d 232 (7th Cir. 1978) (where government sought to prove contents of conversation, not contents of tape recording, best evidence rule was inapplicable). *But cf.* Daniels v. United States, 393 F.2d 359 (D.C. Cir. 1968) (issue whether police had reasonable cause to arrest defendant because they heard police broadcast describing him in connection with robbery; court stated that although point had not been raised, the government in this kind of case should be required to produce tape or log entry of the broadcast as only the best evidence of the information contained in the broadcast).

proper notice, Rule 1006 allows admission of charts, calculations, or summaries based on originals if the originals are voluminous and cannot be conveniently introduced. Finally, Rule 1007 authorizes the use of certain admissions by adverse parties in order to prove the contents of writings. Although various foundations must be laid before the exceptions of these Rules may be invoked, each provides for the nonapplication of Rule 1002.

The Advisory Committee Note to Rule 1002 cites two examples of Acts of Congress that have statutorily created situations in which a copy of a document is to be treated as an original under Rule 1002, *i.e.,* 26 U.S.C. § 7513 allows for the photographic reproduction of tax returns and documents and 44 U.S.C. § 399(a) provides for the photographic copying of documents in the National Archives.[29] These two examples are in no sense the only situations in which Congress has acted in a manner affecting the application of Rule 1002.[30]

Rule 1002 is not superseded by statutes that treat copies as originals. Instead, Rule 1002 merely requires that originals be admitted, including copies statutorily declared to be originals.[31]

---

[29] *See* Rule 1002, Advisory Committee Note.

[30] *See* discussion in 6 WEINSTEIN'S FEDERAL EVIDENCE § 1002.04; *see also* 5 MUELLER & KIRKPATRICK, § 571.

[31] *See* Rule 1002, Advisory Committee Note.

Chapter 1003

Rule 1003. Admissibility of Duplicates

Rule 1003. Admissibility of Duplicates

A duplicate is admissible to the same extent as the original unless a genuine question is raised about the original's authenticity or the circumstances make it unfair to admit the duplicate.

---

§ 1003.1   Duplicates — Admissible as Originals

The Federal Rules provide both a broad definition of duplicates[1] and a wide authorization for their admission.[2] While, inapplicable with respect to certified copies of public records,[3] Rule 1003 provides that duplicates are generally admissible as originals in all cases except where there is a genuine question of the authenticity of the original or where admission of the duplicate instead of the original would be unfair.[4]

---

[1] *See generally,* 2 McCORMICK, §§ 229, 231, 235, 236; 6 WEINSTEIN'S FEDERAL EVIDENCE §§ 1003.01–1003.05; 5 MUELLER & KIRKPATRICK, §§ 572–574; 4 WIGMORE, §§ 1177–1180, 1190, 1198, 1229, 1232–1241, 1249. *See also* Broun, *Authentication and the Contents of Writings,* 4 ARIZ. ST. L.J. 611 (1969); Cleary & Strong, *The Best Evidence Rule: An Evaluation in Context,* 51 IOWA L. REV. 825 (1966); Cleary, *Evidence—Best Evidence Rule—Admissibility of a Carbon Copy as Primary Evidence,* 3 VILL. L. REV. 217 (1958); Note, *Authentication and the Best Evidence Rule Under the Federal Rules of Evidence,* 16 WAYNE L. REV. 195 (1969); Comment, *The Best Evidence Rule—A Criticism,* 3 NEWARK L. REV. 200 (1938).

[2] *See* Rule 1001(4); *see also* § 1001.13, *supra.*

[3] Rule 1003; *see* § 1005.1, *infra.*

[4] Rule 1003; *e.g.,* Tyson v. Jones & Laughlin Steel Corp., 958 F.2d 756 (7th Cir. 1992) (the defendant did not meet his burden of showing that a genuine issue of authenticity existed under Rule 1003); United States v. Patten, 826 F.2d 198 (2d Cir. 1987) (lower court properly admitted duplicates of stolen checks because defendant did not raise a colorable issue as to authenticity of the original checks or the accuracy of the photographs admitted at trial); *In re* Bobby Boggs, Inc., 819 F.2d 574 (5th Cir. 1987) (no abuse of discretion arose from the admission of photo-mechanical duplicates of a subcontractor's performance and payment bonds in a bankruptcy dispute, where no showing was made that admission of copies in lieu of original bonds was unfair or that duplicates did not fairly reproduce originals, and no evidence was offered to dispute affidavit attesting to accuracy of duplicates); United States v. Leight, 818 F.2d 1297 (7th Cir. 1987) (trial judge did not err in admitting diagnostic copies

The scope and theory of the admissibility of duplicates has been discussed in §§ 1001.13–1001.16, *supra*. As noted, duplicates are generally reliable copies or reproductions of originals produced by methods that tend to ensure accuracy.[5] Duplicates are distinguishable from copies intended by the parties to be originals, *i.e.,* "duplicate originals." As discussed in § 1001.13 of this Treatise, duplicate originals are admissible without regard to the Rule 1003 consideration of authenticity and fairness.[6]

Although Federal law is not completely devoid of authority treating duplicates as admissible in place of originals,[7] Rule 1003 does expand the previously accepted position in some courts that duplicates of originals are only secondary evidence.[8] Rule 1003 provides that a duplicate is admissible without requiring the proponent to make a showing that he cannot produce the original.[9] Instead, the only questions concerning admissibility to be considered by the court pursuant to Rule 1003[10] are (i) whether there is a genuine question of authenticity,[11] and (ii) whether admission of the

---

of an x-ray because defendant did not raise a genuine question concerning the authenticity of the copies by merely speculating that there might be some difference between them and the original); *see also* United States v. Tombrello, 666 F.2d 485 (11th Cir. 1982) (even if exemplified copies of state docket entries were not originals but duplicates, they were admissible because no genuine issue was raised as to authenticity of original, and under circumstances it was not unfair to admit them).

[5] *See* Rule 1003, Advisory Committee Note; Wharton, *Duplicate Originals and the Best Evidence Rule*, 19 OHIO ST. L.J. 520 (1958).

[6] Wharton, *Duplicate Originals and the Best Evidence Rule*, 19 OHIO ST. L.J. 520 (1958).

[7] *See, e.g.,* United States v. Wolf, 455 F.2d 984 (9th Cir. 1972) (alleged refusal to be inducted into armed forces; court summarily dismissed as "nonsense" the defense objection to a "certified copy" of the selective service file, and the claim that the original file should have been offered; court suggested that if defendant had any reason to question the accuracy of the copy, he could have subpoenaed the original); Myrick v. United States, 332 F.2d 279 (5th Cir. 1963) (alleged fraud; bank photostatic copies of checks properly received); Johns v. United States, 323 F.2d 421 (5th Cir. 1963) (rejected defense best evidence objection to introduction of re-recording, where counsel conceded openly that the tape was an accurate re-recording of the wire); Sauget v. Johnston, 315 F.2d 816 (9th Cir. 1963) (suit for dissolution of joint venture and accounting; court rejected Best Evidence objection to receipt in evidence of a copy of the agreement).

[8] *See, e.g.,* Tampa Shipbuilding & Eng'g Co. v. General Constr. Co., 43 F.2d 309 (5th Cir. 1930) (criticized receipt of "office copy" in form of carbon duplicate that was not a duplicate original because not so used by the parties; court noted that the original may have been corrected or altered before sending, but found that error was cured by testimony that original order was in fact received).

[9] United States v. Enstam, 622 F.2d 857 (5th Cir. 1980) (Xerox copy of blank letterhead stationery properly received despite defense objection based in part upon fact that there was no explanation for the disappearance of the original, which had been given to government agents).

[10] *See* § 1008.3, *infra*.

[11] *E.g.,* United States v. Moore, 710 F.2d 157 (4th Cir. 1983) (trial court did not err in

duplicate in the circumstances would be unfair.[12]

Functionally, Rule 1003 provides that duplicates are presumptively the equivalent of originals. Accordingly, the burden is on the opponent of the duplicate to establish conditions requiring the use of the original.

§ 1003.2   Duplicates and Questions of Authenticity

Duplicates are not admissible as originals where there is a genuine question as to the authenticity of the original. Prevention of fraud is one of the justifications for the best evidence rule,[13] and where there is some question that the original is not authentic, a duplicate may lack its usual degree of reliability. Consequently, admission of the duplicate may be contrary to the resolution of the issue of authenticity. Of course, where the question of the authenticity of the original is so substantial that even the original would be inadmissible, a duplicate would be inadmissible.[14]

At least two types of situations raise questions of authenticity requiring production of the original under Rule 1003. Where there is a question as to whether the original has been altered after the reproduction has been made, whether accidentally, negligently, or fraudulently, production of the original should be required.[15] Alternatively, where there is a genuine issue of whether the original is what its proponent claims it to be, a duplicate is inadmissible.[16] A principal reason for inadmissibility of a duplicate in this

---

admitting photocopies of both sides of an incriminating piece of paper found in the wallet of an alleged participant in an armed robbery where the original had been returned to the alleged participant, the copies were identified by him as accurate, and defendant offered no evidence that placed their authenticity in doubt); *see* § 1003.2, *infra*; *see also* United States v. Gipson, 609 F.2d 893 (8th Cir. 1979) (alleged theft of barbed wire belonging to government; court rejected defense contention of error in receipt of copies of documents acknowledging receipt by the Government of the barbed wire in question; since defendant raised no objection as to the authenticity of the original, and did not claim any unfairness, receipt of the duplicates was proper under Rule 1003).

[12] *See* § 1003.3, *infra*.

[13] *See* § 1002.2, *supra*. *See generally,* 2 McCormick, § 231; 6 Weinstein's Federal Evidence § 1003.02; 5 Mueller & Kirkpatrick, § 573; 4 Wigmore, §§ 1179–1180.

[14] 6 Weinstein's Federal Evidence § 1001.03; 5 Mueller & Kirkpatrick, § 574; *see* Toho Bussan Kaisha, Ltd. v. American President Lines, Ltd., 265 F.2d 418 (2d Cir. 1959) (court feared that photocopies prepared specifically for trial were subject to possibility of fraud); *see, e.g.,* Cleary, *Evidence—Best Evidence Rule—Admissibility of a Carbon Copy as Primary Evidence,* 3 Vill. L. Rev. 219 (1958).

[15] 4 Wigmore, § 1190; *see* Blade v. Noland, 12 Wend. (N.Y.) 173, 176 (1834) ("no case is to be found, where if a party has deliberately destroyed the higher evidence without explanation, showing affirmatively that the act was done with pure motives, and repelling every suspicion of a fraudulent design, that he had the benefit of it; there is no honest purpose for which a party without any mistake would deliberately destroy the evidence of an existing debt").

[16] *See* United States v. Georgalis, 631 F.2d 1199 (5th Cir. 1980); *see also* CTS Corp. v. Piher Int'l Corp., 527 F.2d 95 (7th Cir. 1975) (in bench-tried patent infringement action, trial

situation is that it may lack indicia of authenticity that may have derived only from the original, *e.g.,* the watermark of paper used in a letter.[17]

Whether a genuine question of authenticity exists is for the court to decide.[18] Presumably, an unsupported objection by opposing counsel is insufficient to raise a genuine question.[19] Instead, some evidence should be introduced into the record to raise the issue.[20]

§ 1003.3   Duplicates and Questions of Unfairness

Duplicates are not admissible as originals where admission of the duplicate in lieu of the original would be unfair. The determination of unfairness is for the court.[21]

Although the Rule does not define the concept of unfairness, there are common situations that arise when duplicates of documents should not be

---

court excluded evidence of a purchase order in the form of a carbon copy rather than a ribbon copy on basis of plaintiff's Best Evidence objection).

[17] 4 WIGMORE, § 1180.

[18] Federal Deposit Ins. Corp. v. Rodenberg, 571 F. Supp. 455 (D. Md. 1983) (photocopies of relevant documents were admissible despite the fact that minor portions were deleted in photocopies; relevant terms were clear and subject to only one reasonable interpretation); *cf.* United States v. Webster, 750 F.2d 307 (5th Cir. 1984) (photocopies of fuel ticket allegedly received by defendant were properly received into evidence after unavailability of original was established, and defendant himself introduced copy of receipt with alterations of which he now complained); *see* § 1008.3, *infra.*

[19] *See* United States v. Bakhtiar, 994 F.2d 970 (2d Cir. 1993) (trial court did not err in admitting duplicates of counterfeit checks into evidence where defendant failed to challenge their authenticity or the fairness in admitting them); United States v. Georgalis, 631 F.2d 1199 (5th Cir. 1980) (duplicate may be admitted unless opposing counsel meets the burden of showing that there is a genuine issue as to the authenticity of the unintroduced original); *e.g.,* Tyson v. Jones & Laughlin Steel Corp., 958 F.2d 756 (7th Cir. 1992) (the defendant did not meet his burden of showing that a genuine issue of authenticity existed under Rule 1003); United States v. Patten, 826 F.2d 198 (2d Cir. 1987) (duplicates properly admitted because defendant did not raise colorable issue as to authenticity of original or the accuracy of photographs admitted at trial).

[20] *Cf.* United States v. Morgan, 555 F.2d 238 (9th Cir. 1977) (duplicate presumptively admissible without evidence in record raising question of authenticity); *see also* Pahl v. Commissioner of Internal Revenue, 150 F.3d 1124 (9th Cir. 1998) (court admitted duplicate of an original document where it did not find a genuine question raised concerning its authenticity, despite denials from a signatory of the document).

[21] *See* § 1008.3, *infra; see also* United States v. Alexander, 326 F.2d 736 (4th Cir. 1964) (defendant accused of stealing check from mail; court refused to admit thermofax reproduction of check, which because of mechanical error had failed to reproduce the name and address of the payee; the original was not produced nor its absence explained); Hi Hat Elkhorn Coal Co. v. Kelly, 205 F. Supp. 764 (1962) (dispute between Elkhorn, as successor in interest to grantor, and defendants as heirs to grantees, in which Elkhorn claimed that the official record of the deed omitted certain terms found in the actual deed, and offered a purported office carbon copy as proof; in this bench-tried equity action, court concluded that Elkhorn did not show that the proffer was a copy of the final deed actually conveyed).

admitted into evidence. For example, where a duplicating process fails to reproduce some of the most essential parts of an original, *e.g.,* where reservation clauses are omitted from the photostat of a deed, fairness may require production of the original.[22] Where a re-recording is made highlighting a particular conversation by eliminating background noises, fairness may dictate production of the original.[23] Also, where the duplicate is illegible or unintelligible,[24] the original may justify a court's determination that admission of a duplicate would be unfair.[25]

It should be noted that a situation may arise in which an original has become illegible but the duplicate has not. Rule 1003 fails to be illuminative. Wigmore suggests that in such a case the duplicate can be required.[26] Nevertheless, where the original is illegible and thus effectively destroyed, Rule 1004(a) rejects Wigmore's suggestion and admits any secondary evidence.[27] In such a situation the proponent would likely elect to use the duplicate because of its high probative value, but he is permitted to prove the contents with any available secondary evidence.

---

[22] *Cf.* Amoco Prod. Co. v. United States, 619 F.2d 1383 (10th Cir. 1980) (duplicate copy of a deed excluded where reservation clauses omitted).

[23] Fountain v. United States, 384 F.2d 624 (5th Cir. 1967) (court refused to admit re-recording where confused mixture of three or four voices and mechanical interference in the original recording made it impossible to accurately determine whether the re-recording accurately reproduced the conversations transcribed on the original); *see also* United States v. Stephenson, 121 F. Supp. 274 (D.D.C. 1954) (court refused to admit transcript of re-recordings that differed with each other and whose accuracy could not be determined due to hearing difficulties with the recording).

[24] *Cf.* Evans v. Holsinger, 242 Iowa 990, 48 N.W.2d 250 (Iowa 1951) (where birth certificate duplicate lacked complete information due to deletion, original required); *see also* Liberty Chair Co. v. Crawford, 193 N.C. 531, 137 S.E. 577 (N.C. 1927) (court rejected carbon copies of letters because of a lack of proper foundation); Mitchell v. United States, 214 Ga. 473, 105 S.E. 2d 337 (Ga. 1958) (alleged carbon copy rejected, since no proof of any original and copy contained signature only in type).

[25] *Cf.* Von Brimer v. Whirlpool Corp., 536 F.2d 838 (9th Cir. 1976) (duplicate excluded where discovery orders violated).

[26] 4 WIGMORE, § 1229.

[27] *See* § 1004.11, *infra.*

Chapter 1004

Rule 1004. Admissibility of Other Evidence of Content

Rule 1004. Admissibility of Other Evidence of Content

An original is not required and other evidence of the content of a writing, recording, or photograph is admissible if:

(a) all the originals are lost or destroyed, and not by the proponent acting in bad faith;

(b) an original cannot be obtained by any available judicial process;

(c) the party against whom the original would be offered had control of the original; was at that time put on notice, by pleadings or otherwise, that the original would be a subject of proof at the trial or hearing; and fails to produce it at the trial or hearing; or

(d) the writing, recording, or photograph is not closely related to a controlling issue.

---

§ 1004.1 Exceptions to Production of the Original — An Overview

Rule 1004 lists four general situations in which originals are excused and in which secondary evidence may be used to prove the contents of a writing, recording or photograph.[1] The Rule codifies exceptions traditionally accepted by federal courts.[2]

If one of the Rule 1004 exceptions applies, a party may prove the contents

---

[1] *See generally,* 2 McCormick, §§ 234–241; 6 Weinstein's Federal Evidence §§ 1004.01–1004.41; 5 Mueller & Kirkpatrick, §§ 575–580; 4 Wigmore, §§ 1188, 1189, 1192–1217, 1252–1254, 1264–1275. *See also* Levin, *Authentication and Contents of Writings,* 10 Rutgers L. Rev. 632 (1956); Note, *Symposium—The Proposed Federal Rules of Evidence: Part II—Authentication and the Best Evidence Rule Under the Federal Rules of Evidence,* 16 Wayne L. Rev. 195 (1969); Note, *Function of Judge and Jury,* 43 Harv. L. Rev. 165 (1929); Comment, *Evidence—Degrees of Secondary Evidence—Problems in Application of the So-Called "American Rule",* 38 Mich. L. Rev. 864 (1940); Note, *Evidence—What is Required to Establish a Lost Instrument,* 15 U. Det. L.J. 192 (1952); Note, *Evidence—Documents—"Best Evidence" Rule Applied to Prevent Introduction of a Recording of a Destroyed Recording,* 64 Harv. L. Rev. 1369 (1951); Note, *Charred Documents,* 16 Am. Jur., Proof of Facts, 665 (1965).

[2] Renner v. Bank of Columbia, 22 U.S. (9 Wheat.) 581 (1824); 2 McCormick, § 237; 4 Wigmore, §§ 1188, 1189, 1192–1198.

of a writing, recording or photograph with any secondary evidence.[3] Rule 1004 rejects the concept of degrees of secondary evidence and allows any form of secondary evidence to be used to prove the contents of the original where an exception is satisfied. Accordingly, duplicates need not be produced instead of other secondary evidence where the original is not required.[4]

The broad applicability of Rule 1004 is superseded in certain situations by Rule 1005, and in effect, Rule 1005 does erect a hierarchy of secondary evidence for the proof of contents of public records.[5] Where original public records are unavailable, certified copies are required if available. Rule 1005 also provides for the admission of other secondary evidence where neither original nor certified copies of public records are available.[6] The Rule 1005 exception provision generally parallels Rule 1004.[7]

Rule 1004 reflects the theory that total exclusion of relevant evidence is less desirable than admission of relevant secondary evidence,[8] and functionally, Rule 1004 requires the party offering the secondary evidence to lay a foundation justifying the nonproduction of the original. Accordingly, the party offering the secondary evidence bears the burden of showing either that the original is unavailable for one of the reasons listed in Rule 1004(a) through (c) or that the original need not be produced because it concerns only a collateral matter pursuant to Rule 1004(d). Where the court accepts the adequacy of the foundation, the secondary evidence may be used.[9]

---

[3] United States v. Shoels, 685 F.2d 379 (10th Cir. 1982) (prosecution could introduce photographs of checks taken by FBI when original checks were stolen and no bad faith shown); United States v. Cambindo Valencia, 609 F.2d 603 (2d Cir. 1979) (citing Rule 1004); Diplomat Homes, Inc. v. Commercial Standard Ins. Co., 394 F. Supp. 558 (W.D. Mo. 1975) (citing Rule 1004).

[4] *Cf.* 4 WIGMORE, § 1229 (allowing secondary evidence on the basis of discretion; noting value of duplicate); *see also* Neville Constr. Co. v. Cook Paint and Varnish Co., 671 F.2d 1107 (8th Cir. 1982) (in breach of warranty action by buyer of insulation for losses suffered as a result of fire, no error in permitting buyer to testify concerning contents of defendant's brochure describing fire retardant characteristics of insulation when fire destroyed brochure; plaintiff did not have to produce similar brochure distributed by defendant since no degrees of secondary evidence are recognized); United States v. Standing Soldier, 538 F.2d 196 (8th Cir. 1976) (oral testimony of contents of note could be given, since Rule 1004 recognizes no degrees of secondary evidence).

[5] *See* § 1005.4, *infra.*

[6] *See* Rule 1005.

[7] *See* § 1005.4, *infra* (noting generally parallel treatment but raising question of dissimilarity where the public record is relevant to a collateral matter only).

[8] *See generally,* 2 MCCORMICK, § 237.

[9] *E.g.,* United States v. Shoels, 685 F.2d 379 (10th Cir. 1982) (after government authenticated photographs and laid a proper foundation, "admission of such secondary evidence lies within the discretion of the trial court"); *see* § 1008.3, *infra* (determination of preliminary question of law for court to decide).

§ 1004.2   Originals Lost or Destroyed — An Overview

Rule 1004(a) codifies the principle long accepted in the federal system that where an original is lost or destroyed, secondary evidence of the contents of the original is admissible[10] providing the party offering the secondary evidence has not lost or destroyed the original in bad faith.[11] The Rule, however, allows admission of secondary evidence offered by a party who lost or destroyed the original as long as the action was not taken in bad faith.[12]

Rule 1004(a) reflects the policy of Article X by requiring the best *available* evidence.[13] Because the best evidence, *i.e.* the original, is not being offered, Rule 1004(a) places the burden on the party offering secondary evidence to establish as a foundation that the original has been lost or destroyed.

Although it may be impossible in a particular case to prove directly that all originals have been lost or destroyed, the court may be satisfied by circumstantial evidence that the original has been lost or destroyed.[14] The court has substantial discretion in its determination of the adequacy of the foundation establishing the unavailability of the original.[15]

---

[10] *See* Rule 1005, Advisory Committee Note. *See also* United States v. Workinger, 90 F.3d 1409, 1415–16 (9th Cir. 1996) (because the tape recording of a witness's deposition was destroyed during the ordinary course of business and not at the behest of the proponent of the evidence, a transcript of the tape was admissible to prove the contents of the deposition).

[11] *E.g.,* Seiler v. Lucasfilm, Ltd., 808 F.2d 1316 (9th Cir. 1986) (plaintiff's claim that drawings were destroyed by flood was inherently contradictory and unsupported by neutral witnesses; record supported finding that plaintiff's originals were lost or destroyed in bad faith); *see* 2 WIGMORE, § 291, at 221.

[12] *E.g.,* Estate of Gryder v. Commissioner, 705 F.2d 336 (8th Cir. 1982) (in deficiency assessment proceedings, Commissioner was properly permitted to prove contents of business records by secondary evidence; originals had been negligently, but not in bad faith, destroyed by the IRS following criminal trial); *see* United States v. Balzano, 687 F.2d 6 (1st Cir. 1982) (duplicate of tape admissible where tape was knowingly erased by government in order to transfer tape to cassette capable of audio replay; no bad faith and extensive showing of mechanics of original recording); United States v. Conry, 631 F.2d 599 (9th Cir. 1980) (proof of contents of waiver through circumstantial evidence was appropriate).

[13] *See* 2 McCORMICK, § 237 at 76 ("The production-of-documents rule is principally aimed, not at securing a writing at all hazards and in every instance, but at securing the best *obtainable* evidence of its contents").

[14] *E.g.,* United States v. Shoels, 685 F.2d 379 (10th Cir. 1982) ("admission of such secondary evidence lies within the discretion of the trial court"); White Indus. v. Cessna Aircraft Co., 611 F. Supp. 1049 (W.D. Mo. 1985) (circumstances surrounding destruction of original did not indicate that plaintiffs were responsible for loss or destruction of files or that they had acted in bad faith; use of secondary evidence was permitted with respect to contents of original records); *see* § 1008.3, *infra*.

[15] Probst v. Trustees of Board of Domestic Missions, 129 U.S. 182 (1889) (conceded that large amount of discretion must be used in trial court to determine whether original was

Finally, it should be noted that an original that has been mutilated or has become illegible is treated as one that has been destroyed.[16]

§ 1004.3   Proof of Loss or Destruction

Courts have traditionally placed the burden for proof of loss or destruction on the party offering secondary evidence.[17] The party offering the secondary evidence has the obligation to lay a foundation satisfactory to the court to show that the original cannot be produced.[18]

Rule 1004(a) does not expressly require parties offering secondary evidence to show that they undertook a reasonable or diligent search where they predicate nonproduction of the original on loss.[19] Nevertheless, Federal courts have traditionally required such a foundation where loss of the original is offered to justify use of secondary evidence.[20] The traditional requirement of a search will logically have continued applicability because in most situations the only way to prove loss is to show that the original could not be found following a reasonable and diligent search.[21] Of course, in particular circumstances, a showing of a reasonable or diligent search may

---

shown to have been lost); *see also* Wright v. Farmers Co-op of Arkansas and Oklahoma, 681 F.2d 549 (8th Cir. 1982); United States v. Covello, 410 F.2d 536 (2d Cir. 1969); United States v. Ross, 321 F.2d 61 (2d Cir. 1963); Willhoit v. Commissioner, 308 F.2d 259 (9th Cir. 1962).

[16] 6 WEINSTEIN'S FEDERAL EVIDENCE § 1004.11.

[17] Hacker v. Price, 166 Pa. Super. 404, 71 A.2d 851 (Pa. Super. Ct. 1950); *see also* Woicicky v. Anderson, 95 Conn. 534, 111 A. 896 (Conn. 1920); *cf.* Time Share Vacation Club v. Atlantic Resorts, Ltd., 735 F.2d 61 (3d Cir. 1984) (plaintiff corporation appealed dismissal of breach of contract suit for lack of in personam jurisdiction; because plaintiff had burden of proving defendant's minimum contacts with the forum for purpose of establishing jurisdiction and was relying solely on contract with defendant, plaintiff had burden of producing a copy of contract or proffering an explanation for its absence).

[18] *See* § 1008.3, *infra*. Trial courts will require varying degrees of certainty in establishing the loss or destruction of a document. The proponent, however, will not have to establish the loss or destruction of a document beyond a reasonable doubt. *See* United States v. Sutter, 62 U.S. (21 How.) 170 (1858); Western, Inc. v. United States, 234 F.2d 211 (8th Cir. 1956).

[19] *See* United States v. McGaughey, 977 F.2d 1067 (7th Cir. 1992) (government did not have to produce proof that the IRS agent had conducted a thorough search before presenting secondary evidence of the form); 4 WIGMORE, § 1195 (outlining tests for loss or destruction).

[20] *See, e.g.,* Colvin v. United States, 479 F.2d 998 (9th Cir. 1973) (wrongful death action brought by surviving spouse; error to permit plaintiff to testify as to decedent's probable income on the basis of daily diary that decedent kept); Nager Elec. Co. v. United States, 442 F.2d 936 (Ct. Cl. 1971); Kenner v. Commissioner, 445 F.2d 19 (7th Cir. 1971) (tax court sua sponte rejected testimony by physician taxpayer as to amounts he advanced to and obtained by way of reimbursements from a charitable hospital that he operated).

[21] 2 MCCORMICK, § 237; *e.g.,* Burroughs Wellcome Co. v. Commercial Union Ins. Co., 632 F. Supp. 1213 (S.D.N.Y. 1986) (court was satisfied that plaintiff met initial burden of proving loss or destruction of documents, because a diligent but unsuccessful search was made).

be inadequate to prove loss or destruction.[22]

Only where loss can be proven directly, or where the adverse party admits the loss, will the proponent of the secondary evidence be free of the obligation to show that he or she has undertaken a reasonable and diligent search.[23]

§ 1004.4   Bad Faith Loss or Destruction

Rule 1004(a) does not absolutely bar a proponent from introducing secondary evidence to prove the contents of the original where that party has itself lost or destroyed the original. Rule 1004(a) only prohibits a party from introducing secondary evidence where the party has lost or destroyed the original in bad faith.[24]

Whether bad faith destruction is involved is a question to be decided by the court prior to admission of the secondary evidence.[25] It should be noted that the adequacy of a foundation accounting for nonproduction of an original due to loss or destruction may depend on a party's showing of the absence of bad faith in the loss or destruction of the original.[26]

While Rule 1004(a) does not define "bad faith," it is clear that the term applies to the destruction of an original with the intent of preventing its use as evidence or with the intent of perpetrating a fraud.[27]

§ 1004.5   Unobtainability of an Original

Rule 1004(b) codifies the traditional federal practice of relieving the proponent from using the original to prove contents where the original is not obtainable by available judicial process.[28] Rule 1004(b) is an acknowledgment that the unobtainability of an original is tantamount to the original's loss or destruction.

---

[22] *See* DeAddio v. Darling & Co., 112 F. Supp. 166 (N.D. Ohio 1952).

[23] 2 MCCORMICK, § 237.

[24] Seiler v. Lucasfilm, Ltd., 808 F.2d 1316 (9th Cir. 1986) (in action of copyright infringement, district court properly excluded reconstructions of original drawings; record amply supported finding that plaintiff's originals were lost or destroyed in bad faith); *see* 4 WIGMORE, § 1198; Consolidated Coke Co. v. Commissioner, 25 B.T.A. 345 (1932), *aff'd,* 70 F.2d 446 (3d Cir. 1934) (in Tax Court proceedings, corporate taxpayer offered purported copy of minutes; secondary evidence disregarded since to permit a party to litigation to deliberately destroy evidence and then in his own behalf introduce a copy made by himself and his attorney would subvert the basic principles of the best evidence rule and promote chicanery).

[25] United States v. Bueno-Risquet, 799 F.2d 804 (2d Cir. 1986) (no error to admit evidence of Request Forms describing markings on lost bags of heroin, in absence of proof "that the government lost or destroyed the original evidence in bad faith"); *see* § 1008.3, *infra*.

[26] United States v. Balzano, 687 F.2d 6 (1st Cir. 1982).

[27] 2 MCCORMICK, § 237.

[28] United States v. Benedict, 647 F.2d 928 (9th Cir. 1981) (testimony by DEA agents as to business records in Thailand).

Although the Rule does not define the circumstances under which an original is unobtainable, case law provides that an original is unavailable when it is merely shown that the original is outside the court's jurisdiction.[29]

Nothing in Rule 1004(b) alters pre-Rule federal law that admits secondary evidence without any showing of an effort to obtain the original once it has been established that the original is outside the court's jurisdiction.[30] However, Rule 1004(2) requires that the proponent convince the court that no available practicable judicial process or procedure will bring forth the original.

Judge Weinstein suggests, however, that courts should require a party who wishes to obtain a document from a non-party outside of the court's jurisdiction under Rule 45(e) of the Federal Rules of Civil Procedure, to first attempt to depose the non-party possessing the document. Under Rule 28(a) of the Rules of Civil Procedure, depositions can be taken anywhere in the United States. Additionally, a subpoena duces tecum can then be ordered under Rule 45(d) to require the witness to bring the document to the deposition. If the witness fails to bring the document to the deposition, a sufficient showing has been made under Rule 1004(b). If the witness appears with the document, and will not give up possession of the document, then the party should make a copy and have it admitted in lieu of the original under Rule 1003.[31]

Where, the original at issue is a public record of a foreign jurisdiction, Rule 1004(b) is preempted by Rule 1005, which requires a certified copy to be used where the original cannot be produced.[32]

Unavailability as a basis for justifying use of secondary evidence may arise in a number of diverse situations. Rule 1004(b) is applicable where a third party within the jurisdiction refuses to produce a document.[33] Rule 1004(b) might also be the basis for the admission of secondary evidence of the contents of writings inscribed on objects where the objects cannot be readily produced in court. Accordingly, inscriptions on gravestones could be proven by secondary evidence where the court determines that gravestones are writings.[34] Another basis for nonobtainability of the original is presented

---

[29] *See, e.g.,* Hartzell v. United States, 72 F.2d 569 (8th Cir. 1934) (since cablegrams were sent from London, England, and the original was out of the jurisdiction of the court, such secondary evidence became admissible).

[30] United States v. Ratliff, 623 F.2d 1293 (8th Cir. 1980) (trial court assumed it had no subpoena power over documents in Germany; in absence of demonstration, appellate court did not find court's finding to be clearly erroneous).

[31] 6 WEINSTEIN'S FEDERAL EVIDENCE § 1004.20.

[32] Rule 1005.

[33] *See* 2 MCCORMICK, § 238.

[34] *See* 4 WIGMORE, § 1214 and § 1005.4, *infra; see also* 1001.4, *supra.*

where disclosure of the original is prevented by privilege.[35]

Whether a party has adequately shown that the original is not obtainable is a question for the court.[36] Clearly, the court has considerable discretion in making its determination.[37]

§ 1004.6   Unobtainability and Use of Subpoenas

Although generally no showing of an effort to produce the original is required where the original is determined to be outside the court's jurisdiction,[38] such an effort must be shown where the original is within the jurisdiction.[39] Essentially, the effort required is that of serving a writ of subpoena duces tecum on the party possessing the original.[40] Rule 45(d)(1) of the Federal Rules of Civil Procedure provides for service of such a writ. Secondary evidence should be admitted where the possessor of the original refuses to obey the subpoena.[41] Of course, failure to obey the subpoena may be deemed contempt of court.[42]

§ 1004.7   Original Possessed by Opponent

Rule 1004(c) provides that where an adverse party (i) possesses or controls an original, (ii) has received notice that the contents of the original will be an issue at a hearing, and (iii) fails to produce the original, secondary evidence of the original's contents will be admissible if offered by the opponent of the party in possession of the original.[43] Rule 1004(c) codifies the traditional common-law rule and effects no change in pre-Rule practice.[44]

It has been suggested that Rule 1004(c) is supported in part by the theory that an original that an adverse party refuses to produce is not more accessible than originals lost, destroyed, or unobtainable.[45] Rule 1004(c)

---

[35] *See* United States v. Haugen, 58 F. Supp. 436 (E.D. Wash. 1944), *aff'd,* 153 F.2d 850 (9th Cir. 1946) (where original confidential, secondary evidence admitted).

[36] *See* § 1008.3, *infra.*

[37] *See* § 1008.3, *infra.*

[38] *See* § 1004.1, *supra.*

[39] United States v. Taylor, 648 F.2d 565 (9th Cir. 1981) (trial court did not err in admitting photocopy of crucial letter where government represented that subpoenas requesting the original letter had been served on the parties and the original was not produced, and defendant's counsel failed to object to admission of copy).

[40] United States v. Taylor, 648 F.2d 565 (9th Cir. 1981).

[41] 2 McCormick, § 238.

[42] Fed. R. Civ. P. 45(e).

[43] *See generally,* 2 McCormick, § 239; 6 Weinstein's Federal Evidence § 1004.30; 5 Mueller & Kirkpatrick, § 579; 4 Wigmore, § 1199.

[44] *See generally,* Hodgson v. Humphries, 454 F.2d 1279 (10th Cir. 1972); Jones v. Atl. Ref. Co., 55 F. Supp. 17 (E.D. Pa. 1941).

[45] 2 McCormick, § 239.

differs from Rule 1004(b), however, in that a party who has provided adequate notice is permitted to offer secondary evidence even though the original could be, but has not been, subpoenaed or otherwise produced in discovery.[46] Accordingly, the more impressive justification of Rule 1004(c) is that it is compelled by the nature of the adversary process, *i.e.*, opponents to the introduction of secondary evidence will not be heard to object where they have possession of the original and have received notice that the contents will be proven at trial.

The question of whether the conditions have been met for admission of secondary evidence is one for the court to decide within a wide range of discretion.[47] The burden for laying the foundation is on the party offering the secondary evidence.[48]

§ 1004.8   Possession or Control

In its applicability to originals in the possession of the opponent, Rule 1004(c) accepts Wigmore's analysis that an original need not be in the actual personal custody of an adverse party for secondary evidence to be admissible after appropriate notice.[49] Instead, control of the original will suffice.[50]

The burden of proving control of the original by an adverse party is on the party offering the secondary evidence,[51] and the proof must be sufficient to satisfy the trial court.[52]

§ 1004.9   Notice to Opponent

As a condition precedent to the admission of secondary evidence, Rule 1004(c) requires that the party in possession of the original be given appropriate notice.[53] The notice required, however, need only indicate that proof of the contents of the original will be at issue at the trial or hearing,[54] and Rule 1004(c) does not require notice demanding production of the original.[55] The notice, as McCormick notes, lacks "compulsive force," and

---

[46] *See* § 1004.2, *supra.*

[47] *See* § 1008.3, *infra.*

[48] 2 McCORMICK, § 239.

[49] 4 WIGMORE, § 1200.

[50] *E.g.,* Consolidation Coal Co. v. Chubb, 741 F.2d 968, 972 (7th Cir. 1984) (appellate court rejected Consolidation Coal's objection to receipt of medical report quoting another physician's reading of X-ray; production of other physician's report or X-ray itself "would not be required as best evidence since access to such X-ray and reading was under the control of Consolidation Coal").

[51] 4 WIGMORE, § 1201.

[52] *See* § 1008.3, *infra.*

[53] *See* 6 WEINSTEIN'S FEDERAL EVIDENCE § 1004.32.

[54] *See* 2 McCORMICK, § 239.

[55] *Id*; *see also* Comment, *Authentication and the Best Evidence Rule under the Federal*

it merely provides the party possessing the original with the opportunity to prevent the admission of secondary evidence by production of the original at the trial.[56]

Rule 1004(c) continues the traditional rule that provides that satisfactory notice may be effected through the pleading or through other means.[57] Rule 1004(c) does not require any formal notice. Consequently, where the nature of the action indicates that the adverse party will be charged with possession of a written instrument, formal notice is unnecessary as a condition for the admission of secondary evidence.[58]

Rule 1004(c) does not discard the traditional position that notice must be reasonable. Accordingly, notice usually is not reasonable unless given prior to commencement of trial.[59] Only if it is apparent that the original is present in the courtroom in the personal custody of an adverse party will notice at trial be adequate.[60]

The burden of establishing the adequacy of notice is on the party offering the secondary evidence, and the proof must be sufficient to satisfy the discretion of the court.[61]

§ 1004.10   Failure to Produce the Original

Simple failure by the adverse party to bring the original to the trial or hearing satisfies the non-production condition of Rule 1004(c). Additionally, the offering by the adverse party of a document denied by the proponent of the secondary evidence to be the original constitutes failure to produce the original.[62]

If an adverse party fails to produce the original when secondary evidence is offered, traditionally that party has been barred from subsequent introduction of the original later in the trial or hearing.[63] Rule 403 provides a similar basis, *viz.,* unfair prejudice, for excluding the original.[64]

Rules of Evidence, 16 WAYNE L. REV. 195 (1969).

[56] 2 MCCORMICK, § 239; *see also* TransAmerica Ins. Co. v. Bloomfield, 401 F.2d 357 (6th Cir. 1968).

[57] *See* 6 WEINSTEIN'S FEDERAL EVIDENCE § 1004.32; 2 MCCORMICK, § 239; 4 WIGMORE, § 1205.

[58] *See* United States v. Marcantoni, 590 F.2d 1324 (5th Cir. 1979) (court suggested that defendants were "put on notice" that serial numbers of two $10 bills "would be subject of proof").

[59] *See* 6 WEINSTEIN'S FEDERAL EVIDENCE § 1004.32; 4 WIGMORE § 1208.

[60] 4 WIGMORE, § 1208.

[61] *See* § 1008.3, *infra.*

[62] 4 WIGMORE, § 1209.

[63] 4 WIGMORE, § 1210.

[64] *See* § 403.1 *et seq., supra.*

§ 1004.11   Secondary Evidence and Collateral Matters

Rule 1004(d) restates the common-law rule that proof of the contents of writings, recordings, or photographs may be proven by secondary evidence where the contents are not closely related to a controlling issue in the litigation.[65] As Wigmore has noted, when the terms of a document are not the basis of the dispute, considerations of convenience support admission of secondary evidence.[66] The court has discretion in determining whether proof of the contents is collateral to the matter at issue, and it can require production of the original if a genuine question arises as to the original's contents.[67]

§ 1004.12   When Originals Are Collateral

Rule 1004(d) does not provide criteria for determining when the contents of an original are merely collateral to the question at issue. McCormick, however, has suggested that three principal factors should be weighed by the court:

> . . . the centrality of the writing to the principal issues of the litigation; the complexity of the relevant features of the writing; and the existence of genuine dispute as to the contents of the writing.[68] The respective weight to be accorded these factors is left to the discretion of the court.

Pre-Rule case law provides some indication of standards to be applied in determining when a matter is collateral. For example, one case held that the contents of a patent assignment may be proven by secondary evidence where the issue is the validity of title.[69] Because the patent was issued on the assignment and the title was perfected, the assignment was held to be merely a collateral paper affecting the title.[70]

In the case of *Blachly v. United States*,[71] the court excused the production of the originals of promissory notes that the defendants had acquired from the targets of a fraudulent scheme to sell water softeners. The court held the

---

[65] *See generally,* 6 WEINSTEIN'S FEDERAL EVIDENCE § 1004.40. *See also* Bituminous Casualty Corp. v. Vacuum Tanks, Inc., 975 F.2d 1130 (5th Cir. 1992) (where insurance company could not find the policy, it should have produced secondary evidence of the policy's terms, not just the possible different policies available); United States v. Duffy, 454 F.2d 809 (5th Cir. 1972); Reistroffer v. United States, 258 F.2d 379 (8th Cir. 1968); Scullin v. Harper, 78 F. 460 (2d Cir. 1897).

[66] 4 WIGMORE, § 1253; *see also* Bouldin v. Massie's Heirs, 20 U.S. (7 Wheat.) 122 (1822).

[67] *See* § 1008.3, *infra.*

[68] 2 MCCORMICK, § 234, at 70; *see also* 4 WIGMORE, § 1253.

[69] *Id.*

[70] Bouldin v. Massie's Heirs, 20 U.S. (7 Wheat.) 122 (1822).

[71] Blachly v. United States, 380 F.2d 665 (5th Cir. 1967).

notes were not introduced to prove their exact terms, but instead were introduced to show the scheme by which the fraud was perpetrated.[72]

The Advisory Committee Note to Rule 1004 provides two additional examples: it is not necessary to produce the original of "a newspaper in an action for the price of publishing [the] defendant's advertisements,"[73] nor is it necessary to produce the original of the "street car transfer of [a] plaintiff claiming status as a passenger."[74]

---

[72] *Id.*

[73] *See* Rule 1004, Advisory Committee Note.

[74] Rule 1004, Advisory Committee Note.

Chapter 1005

Rule 1005. Copies of Public Records to Prove Content

Rule 1005. Copies of Public Records to Prove Content

The proponent may use a copy to prove the content of an official record — or of a document that was recorded or filed in a public office as authorized by law — if these conditions are met: the record or document is otherwise admissible; and the copy is certified as correct in accordance with Rule 902(4) or is testified to be correct by a witness who has compared it with the original. If no such copy can be obtained by reasonable diligence, then the proponent may use other evidence to prove the content.

---

§ 1005.1　Copies of Public Records to Prove Content — In General

Rule 1005 provides that a copy of the public record may be used to prove contents of the original record where the copy is certified as correct in accordance with Rule 902 or authenticated as correct by testimony from a witness who has compared the copy with the original.[1] The Rule also provides that if such a copy cannot be obtained by the exercise of reasonable diligence, "the proponent may use other evidence to prove the content."[2]

By establishing a preference for certified copies of official records and filed or recorded documents, Rule 1005 introduces into the Rules the concept of degrees of secondary evidence for public records.[3] Copies of official records that are authenticated by the stipulated requirements are preferred to any other secondary evidence that might be offered to prove the

---

[1] *See generally,* 2 MCCORMICK, § 240, 6 WEINSTEIN'S FEDERAL EVIDENCE §§ 1005.01–1005.06; 5 MUELLER & KIRKPATRICK, §§ 581–582; 4 WIGMORE, §§ 1215–1218. *See also* Broun, *Authentication and Contents of Writings,* 4 ARIZ. ST. L.J. 611 (1969); Cleary & Strong, *The Best Evidence Rule: An Evaluation in Context,* 51 IOWA L. REV. 825 (Summer 1966); Levin, *Authentication and the Content of Writings,* 10 RUTGERS L. REV. 632 (1956); Orfield, *Proof of Official Records in Federal Cases,* 22 MONT. L. REV. 137 (1961); Tracey, *The Introduction of Documentary Evidence,* 24 IOWA L. REV. 436 (1939); Comment, *Authentication and the Best Evidence Rule Under the Federal Rules of Evidence,* WAYNE L. REV. (1969).

[2] United States v. Rodriguez, 524 F.2d 485 (5th Cir. 1975) (Xerox copy of vehicle certificate of title satisfied Rule 1005).

[3] *See* 4 WIGMORE, § 1269.

contents of a public record. Accordingly, Rule 1005 preempts Rule 1003's general provision that duplicates are admissible as originals.[4] Additionally, Rule 1005 supersedes Rule 1004 insofar as Rule 1005 allows the use of a copy certified or testified to be correct without any showing that the original is lost, destroyed, unobtainable, or pertinent to a collateral matter. It further supersedes Rule 1004 by creating a mandatory preference for the use of certified copies over other types of secondary evidence. Rule 1004 creates no such preference once a prerequisite for dispensing with the original has been shown. Rule 1005 does not, however, supersede or conflict with Rule 1004 or other Rules in Article X when the object of proof is an unfiled original where a copy of the original has been filed or recorded with a public agency.[5] Rule 1005 comes into play only when the contents of the document actually on file are sought to be proved.

The underlying policies of Rule 1005 are convenience and protection of the public. The public would be inconvenienced by the absence of official records from the offices in which they are regularly kept. Additionally, the risk of loss or damage of such records would be present if the originals were required to be offered into evidence.[6] Accordingly, the certification requirement both protects the public and ensures a high degree of reliability of the evidence. Rule 1005 does not require, however, that copies of public records be offered in lieu of originals. Logically, an original is admissible if it is properly authenticated.[7]

§ 1005.2   Official Records and Filed or Recorded Documents

Rule 1005 applies when the contents of public records or filed or recorded documents are sought to be proven. Public records include "official records" as well as documents "recorded or filed in a public office as authorized by law."

---

[4] 6 WEINSTEIN'S FEDERAL EVIDENCE § 1005.02; 5 MUELLER & KIRKPATRICK, § 582; *see, e.g.,* Amoco Prod. Co. v. United States, 619 F.2d 1383 (10th Cir. 1980) (photocopy of what was purportedly a conformed copy of deed found in case file of the Bureau of Land Management would not necessarily qualify as a "public record" for purposes of authentication or hearsay; court therefore rejected defense contention that the records were authenticated under Federal Rules).

[5] 6 WEINSTEIN'S FEDERAL EVIDENCE § 1005.02. The example is given of a deed, the original of which is returned to the owner after a photostat is made for the public record. Under this analysis, "[t]he contents of the original in the hands of the owner may be proved in any way permitted by Article X." *See also* Amoco Prod. Co. v. United States, 619 F.2d 1383 (10th Cir. 1980) (original deed is not a public record and Rule 1004 rather than Rule 1005 applies to it).

[6] *See, e.g.,* Seese v. Volkswagenwerk A.G., 648 F.2d 833 (3d Cir. 1981) (computer printouts of the Fatal Accident Reporting System consisting of statistical information pertaining to fatal accidents maintained by National Highway Traffic and Safety Administration admissible as public records); *see also* 2 McCORMICK, § 240; 4 WIGMORE, § 1218.

[7] *See* Rule 901.

While not expressly defined, the term "official record" should apply to any document prepared and retained by any agency of government, state or federal, foreign or domestic. Such a broad reading of "official record" is indicated by the policy supporting the Rule discussed in § 1005.3, *infra.* Additional guidance as to the scope of the term "official record" is only marginally provided by the Federal Rules of Civil Procedures. FRCP 44, which also applies to "official records," and which might provide an indication of the interpretation of that term, has not been treated by the courts as a term of art.[8] In practice, however, the absence of a definition should not be problematic, and the horizon of the term "public record" should be broadly interpreted. The courts have treated the following as public records: court records,[9] weather reports,[10] summaries of foreign census records,[11] selective service records,[12] copies of foreign marriage records,[13] and tax returns.[14]

Rule 1005 also applies to documents "authorized to be recorded or filed and actually recorded or filed," thereby authorizing the proof of the contents of such recorded documents as deeds, leases, or mortgages[15] by a copy that meets the requisites of the Rule. The Rule pertains to *filed* documents as well as to *recorded* documents.[16] Whether a document is authorized to be filed or

---

[8] *See* 6 WEINSTEIN'S FEDERAL EVIDENCE § 1005.03; 5 MUELLER & KIRKPATRICK, § 581; *see also* Yaich v. United States, 283 F.2d 613 (9th Cir. 1960) (interdepartmental memo found to be a "public document"); Cohn v. United States, 258 F. 355 (2d Cir. 1919) (paper kept on file in a designated office that cannot be removed became "official").

[9] United States v. Locke, 425 F.2d 313 (5th Cir. 1970) (jailbreak prosecution; photostatic copy of record of judgment and commitment was properly admitted); Maroon v. Immigration and Naturalization Serv., 364 F.2d 982 (8th Cir. 1966) (petition for review of deportation orders; copies of records of indictment, judgment, sentence, and commitment properly admitted).

[10] Celanese Corp. of America v. Vandalia Warehouse Corp., 424 F.2d 1176 (7th Cir. 1970) (copy of a weather report was not admitted because it lacked the proper certification); H.R. Anderson v. Swift & Co., 380 F.2d 988 (6th Cir. 1967) (weather report admitted); Minnehaha County, S.D. v. Kelley, 150 F.2d 356 (8th Cir. 1945) (wrongful death action; summaries of weather records were admitted because the actual records were voluminous and intricate, and were of doubtful intelligibility to the jury without these explanatory summaries).

[11] United States v. Ghaloub, 385 F.2d 567 (2d Cir. 1966) (Syrian census records were official records).

[12] Pardo v. United States, 369 F.2d 922 (5th Cir. 1966) (authenticated by direct testimony of custodian).

[13] United States v. D'Agostino, 338 F.2d 490 (2d Cir. 1964).

[14] United States v. Farris, 517 F.2d 226 (7th Cir. 1975) (printouts of computerized tax records).

[15] Amoco Prod. Co. v. United States, 619 F.2d 1383 (10th Cir. 1980) (trial court properly applied Rule 1005 in admitting certified copy of recorded deed).

[16] Cohn v. United States, 258 F. 355 (2d Cir. 1919) (filed document in designated office

recorded will be of little significance if the document is actually filed or recorded, because the filing or recording constitutes prima facie evidence of authorization.[17] The requirement that documents be authorized for filing or recording encompasses both permissive and mandatory filing or recording.[18]

§ 1005.3   Certification of Copies

Rule 1005 provides that a copy of a public record may be authenticated by a certification as to its correctness made in compliance with Rule 902 or by testimony that it is correct from a witness who has compared the copy with the original. It should be noted that the required authentication concerns the accuracy of the copy, *i.e.,* the authentication testimony must show that the copy is an accurate reproduction of the original, and the accuracy of the actual contents of the original is not the pertinent issue.[19] Rule 902 provides that certified copies of public records are self-authenticating when the custodian or other person authorized to make a certification respecting a copy of an official report, record or recorded or filed document certifies the copy as correct.[20]

Federal law has long accepted an appropriate witness's testimony as proof of the correctness of a copy of a public record.[21] Nevertheless, the significance of this method of authenticating a copy is diminished by its excessive costs in comparison with the use of a certified copy.[22]

§ 1005.4   Reasonable Diligence and Other Evidence of Contents

Rule 1005 provides that if, by the exercise of reasonable diligence, a copy that satisfies Rule 1005 cannot be obtained, other evidence of the contents of the public record may be admitted. If a public record is accessible to the public, a copy of that record should ordinarily be obtained by the exercise of reasonable diligence. Nevertheless, failure to obtain a satisfactory copy might occur, for example, in regard to a foreign record where no official publication can be located or where the official transmitting the record fails to do so in a manner that complies with Rule 902. In such a case, if the court

---

is official); *e.g.,* United States v. Tombrello, 666 F.2d 485 (11th Cir. 1982) (Rule 1005 embraces "certified exemplified copies" of docket entries, properly received here as proof that defendant had been "under indictment" at the time when he allegedly received a firearm).

[17] 6 WEINSTEIN'S FEDERAL EVIDENCE § 1005.03; 5 MUELLER & KIRKPATRICK, § 582; *see, e.g.,* Amoco Prod. Co. v. United States, 619 F.2d 1383 (10th Cir. 1980).

[18] Cohn v. United States, 258 F. 355 (2d Cir. 1919).

[19] 6 WEINSTEIN'S FEDERAL EVIDENCE § 1005.04; 5 MUELLER & KIRKPATRICK, § 582.

[20] United States v. Farris, 517 F.2d 226 (7th Cir. 1975); *e.g.,* United States v. Torres, 733 F.2d 449 (7th Cir. 1984) (certificates of enrollment, prepared by the Menominee enrollment clerk and certified by her at trial to be accurate representations of the information contained in the original Tribal Roll, were admissible under Rule 902(4) as certified copies of original public record).

[21] Block's Case, 7 Ct. Cl. 406 (1871).

[22] 6 WEINSTEIN'S FEDERAL EVIDENCE § 1005.04; 5 MUELLER & KIRKPATRICK, § 582.

finds that the failure has occurred despite the exercise of reasonable diligence, any otherwise admissible secondary evidence may be offered to prove the contents of the document.[23] Secondary evidence might include, for example, an uncertified copy of a document, testimony by someone familiar with the contents of the document, or other documentary evidence, *e.g.,* a written summary of the contents of the official record.

Rule 1005 provides an exception to the requirement of production of a certified or authenticated copy that largely parallels Rule 1004's exception to the requirement of production of the original. In this regard, it might be questioned whether the standards for excusing production of the original set forth in Rule 1004 are incorporated into Rule 1005. The latter, for example, does not explicitly provide for the use of secondary evidence to prove the contents of public records relating to collateral matters as does Rule 1004(4). The possible justification for the differing treatment is the customary ease with which copies of public records can be obtained coupled with the persuasive nature of such records. Of course, it would be appropriate to construe the requirement of reasonable diligence as not requiring great exertion for a collateral matter, and a court would be justified in admitting secondary evidence in such instance.

---

[23] *But see* 4 WIGMORE, § 1268, at 649 (a party "must offer a copy, if he has one in his control, in preference to recollection testimony") (italics omitted).

Chapter 1006

Rule 1006. Summaries to Prove Content

Rule 1006. Summaries to Prove Content

The proponent may use a summary, chart, or calculation to prove the content of voluminous writings, recordings, or photographs that cannot be conveniently examined in court. The proponent must make the originals or duplicates available for examination or copying, or both, by other parties at a reasonable time and place. And the court may order the proponent to produce them in court.

---

§ 1006.1   Summaries, Charts, and Calculations — In General

Rule 1006 codifies the traditional best evidence rule exception,[1] which provides that where writings are voluminous or multifarious, summaries, abstracts or schedules may be admitted in evidence.[2] Just as the best

---

[1] *See generally*, 6 WEINSTEIN'S FEDERAL EVIDENCE §§ 1006.01–1006.08; 5 MUELLER & KIRKPATRICK, §§ 583–585; 4 WIGMORE, § 1230. *See also* Broun, *Authentication and Contents of Writings*, 4 ARIZ. ST. L.J. 611 (1969); *Symposium on the Proposed Federal Rules of Evidence: Part II*, 16 WAYNE L. REV. 195 (1969); Dewey, *Best Evidence Rule—Use of Summaries of Voluminous Originals*, 37 MICH. L. REV. 499 (1939); Comment, *Evidence: Best Evidence Rule: Admissibility of Secondary Evidence in Oklahoma*, 20 OKLA. L. REV. 56 (1967).

[2] Burton v. Driggs, 87 U.S. (20 Wall.) 125 (1873) (summary may be used to prove the contents of voluminous books and documents); *e.g.,* Goldberg v. United States, 789 F.2d 1341 (9th Cir. 1986) (IRS agent was permitted to summarize voluminous tax records); United States v. Schuster, 777 F.2d 264 (5th Cir. 1985), *vacated on other grounds*, 778 F.2d 1132 (5th Cir. 1985) (district court did not err in admitting into evidence government exhibits that summarized voluminous documentary evidence); United States v. Robinson, 774 F.2d 261 (8th Cir. 1985) (underlying documents were sufficiently voluminous to warrant summarization); *see also* Hodgson v. Humphries, 454 F.2d 1279 (10th Cir. 1972) (Fair Labor Standards Act; summaries used to speed up trial and avoid unnecessary detailed documentation); Braunstein v. Massachusetts Bank & Trust Co., 443 F.2d 1281 (1st Cir. 1971) (audit used as summary); Boston Sec., Inc. v. United Bonding Ins. Co., 441 F.2d 1302 (8th Cir. 1971) (accountant's summary); McGuire v. Davis, 437 F.2d 570 (5th Cir. 1971) (medical expenses); Miami Nat'l Bank v. Pennsylvania Ins. Co., 314 F. Supp. 858 (D.C. Fla. 1970) (summaries of bank's records). Where a party shows time lines and organizational charts to a jury but does not seek to admit them into evidence, their use at trial is not governed by Rule 1006, and is subject only to judge's discretionary control under Rule 611(a). United States v. Posada-Rios, 158 F.3d 832 (5th Cir. 1998).

evidence rule has been expanded by the Federal Rules to apply to recordings and photographs,[3] this exception has been extended to apply to voluminous recordings or photographs. Rule 1006 provides that charts or calculations as well as summaries may be used to prove the contents of voluminous documents.[4]

For a summary, calculation, or chart to be admissible under Rule 1006, three conditions must be satisfied. First, the writings, recordings, or photographs must be voluminous.[5] In keeping with Rule 1008, this is a question to be determined by the court.[6] The requirement that writings, recordings, or photographs be voluminous satisfies the general objective of this Rule, *i.e.,* maximizing the convenience of the presentation of evidence at trial.[7] Additionally, an issue of fairness, undue delay, or redundancy under Rule 403 may be involved where the writings, recordings, or photographs are not voluminous.[8] Second, a proper foundation must be laid for the introduction of the summary.[9] As a part of this requirement, the originals must be admissible for the summaries, calculations, or charts based on those

---

[3] *See* Rule 1001(a), (b).

[4] *See* United States v. Tannehill, 49 F.3d 1049, 1056–1057 (5th Cir. 1995) (trial court did not err in admitting summary of the contents of 28, 000 documents as the writings were clearly voluminous, making in-court examination of the documents "more than inconvenient"). *Cf.* United States v. Baker, 10 F.3d 1374 (9th Cir. 1993) (trial court violated Rule 1006 when it admitted into evidence a computer printout summarizing the proceeds from narcotics sales based upon notes taken by an FBI agent during the trial; Rule 1006 does not explicitly permit the introduction of a summary of oral testimony).

[5] Nichols v. Upjohn Co., 610 F.2d 293 (5th Cir. 1980) (the court admitted a summary of an FDA investigative report of a document of 94,000 pages); *e.g.,* United States v. Sutton, 795 F.2d 1040 (1986) (district court did not err in admitting summary exhibits under Rule 1006 to avoid unnecessary introduction of voluminous paper materials and where documents supporting the summary exhibits had been given to defendants during pretrial discovery); *see also* Javelin Investment, S.A. v. Ponce, 645 F.2d 92 (1st Cir. 1981) (reviewing court doubted the need for a summary, since material involved was simple, short, and straight forward, and not the type of voluminous writings that could not conveniently be examined in court).

[6] *See* § 1008.3, *infra.*

[7] R.R. Assoc. v. Visual Scene, Inc., 726 F.2d 36 (1st Cir. 1984) (in contract action, court properly admitted summary of allegedly defective merchandise, where defendant had ample opportunity to inspect goods and records summarized and the summary was "the only practical means of making their content available to judge and jury"); *see* § 1006.2, *infra.*

[8] *See* Rule 403 and Chapter 403, *supra.*

[9] United States v. Stephens, 779 F.2d 232 (5th Cir. 1985) (flow charts tracing use of loan proceeds were properly admitted under Rule 1006; appellate court noted that one proper method of laying foundation for such charts would be to admit "the documentation on which the summary is based"); United States v. Robinson, 774 F.2d 261 (8th Cir. 1985) (no error in receiving summary prepared by FBI agent; "sufficient foundation was laid" where trial court held voir dire examination outside presence of jury); United States v. Massachusetts Maritime Academy, 762 F.2d 142 (1st Cir. 1985) (in sex discrimination suit against Maritime Academy, lower court properly admitted exhibits summarizing Academy's applicant files;

originals to be admissible.[10] Also, charts, summaries and calculations may not include information not contained or computed from the originals.[11] Third, the originals or duplicates must be made available to all litigants for examination or copying at a reasonable time and place.[12] This requirement provides all litigants with the opportunity to determine the accuracy, completeness, and fairness of the charts, summaries, or calculations.

Charts, summaries, and calculations may be admissible under other Rules without satisfying the foregoing requirements. For example, where the originals on which a summary, chart, or calculation is based are unavailable and one of the exceptions of Rule 1004 is satisfied, the summary, chart, or calculation may be admissible as secondary evidence.[13] Alternatively, data

---

proper foundation for the exhibits was laid by testimony of two witnesses who testified as to method used in preparing summaries).

[10] State Office Sys. v. Olivetti Corp. of America, 762 F.2d 843 (10th Cir. 1985) (Rule 1006 permitted the use of summary of voluminous records but "only if all the records from which it is drawn are otherwise admissible"); Ford Motor Co. v. Auto Supply Co., 661 F.2d 1171 (8th Cir. 1981) (trademark infringement action; exhibit of summary of figures admissible, since the underlying figures would have been admissible); United States v. Seelig, 622 F.2d 207 (6th Cir. 1980) (admission of chart purporting to summarize sales activities at other drug stores was reversible error since there was no showing that other stores were the same size, covered same marketing area, charged same prices, etc.; chart therefore irrelevant). *See also* Bristol Steel & Iron Works v. Bethlehem Steel Corp., 41 F.3d 182, 189–90 (4th Cir. 1994) (noting that when a summary of voluminous writings is provided to the jury such summary is introduced as evidence, thus obviating the need to admit the originals as evidence and make them available to the jury during deliberations).

[11] Pritchard v. Liggett & Myers Tobacco Co., 295 F.2d 292 (3d Cir. 1961) (bibliography of original articles was not admissible as summary, since no showing was made that the materials were accurately summarized); *e.g.,* United States v. Dorta, 783 F.2d 1179 (4th Cir. 1986) (charges summarizing telephone toll records were properly received because they accurately summarized evidence already before jury); United States v. North Am. Reporting, 740 F.2d 50 (D.C. Cir. 1984) (no error to exclude summary charts, where they were derived from diverse and unreliable sources and included undocumented recollection and questionable assumptions).

[12] *E.g.,* United States v. Isaacs, 593 F.3d 517 (7th Cir. 2010). Rule 1006 requires a party seeking to introduce a summary of voluminous records to provide copies of those records to the opposing party at a reasonable time and place, which means that the opposing party must be given adequate time to examine the records to check the accuracy of the summary); United States v. Miller, 771 F.2d 1219 (9th Cir. 1985) (summaries may not be admitted unless the underlying documents are provided to opposing party prior to their being offered); Coates v. Johnson & Johnson, 756 F.2d 524 (7th Cir. 1985) (in employment discrimination summaries of suit, employer's disciplinary records were properly admitted; records were business records and the underlying records were made available prior to trial); Davis & Cox v. Summa Corp., 751 F.2d 1507 (9th Cir. 1985) (trial court properly excluded summaries, where the party offering them did not make the summaries or the underlying documents available until just prior to trial and one of the summaries did not "fairly represent" the underlying documents).

[13] John Irving Shoe Co. v. Dugan, 93 F.2d 711 (1st Cir. 1937) (secondary evidence of missing records not admissible without proof that they are lost, destroyed, or unavailable);

compilations based on public records may be admissible under Rule 1005.

One apparent difference between Rule 1006 and prior case law is that an expert is no longer required to prepare the chart, summary, or calculation.[14] Under Rule 1006, the fact that an expert did or did not prepare the chart, summary, or calculation would be a matter affecting the weight of the evidence, not its admissibility. In practice, however, attorneys usually will use experts, such as accountants, when preparing a chart, summary, or calculation. Note that attorneys trying a case cannot prepare summaries of other evidence that they plan to introduce pursuant to Rule 1006 themselves.[15]

§ 1006.2   Conceptual Basis for Rule 1006

Unlike the general justification for the best evidence rule,[16] the conceptual basis for Rule 1006 is rooted both in the convenience and the practicability[17] of introducing into evidence the contents of voluminous writings, recordings, or photographs. Although courts have been quite willing to admit charts, summaries, or calculations into evidence where such vehicles represent the only practical means of introducing the evidence, Rule 1006 provides that even where introduction of the originals is feasible, summaries may be introduced in any situation where convenience would be served.[18] The only limitation on this doctrine of convenience is imposed by Rule 403's prohibition of undue prejudice, delay, and redundancy.[19]

Equitable Life Assur. Soc. v. Sieg, 53 F.2d 318 (6th Cir. 1931) (summary of lost account books admissible as best evidence of their contents); *see also* Burton v. Driggs, 87 U.S. (20 Wall.) 125 (1873) (summary of unavailable bank books acceptable secondary evidence of their contents).

[14] *E.g.,* United States v. Jennings, 724 F.2d 436 (5th Cir. 1984) (charts summarizing and comparing data were properly received despite the absence of expert witness); *see* Needham v. White Lab., 639 F.2d 394 (7th Cir. 1981) (but the chart cannot be used as a foundation to admit articles upon which the chart was based, when the expert has not read all the articles).

[15] *See* United States v. Grajales-Montoya, 117 F.3d 356, 361 (8th Cir. 1997) (stating that Rule 1006 does not enable "the admission of a summary . . . prepared by a lawyer trying the case . . . that restates and distills other properly admitted exhibits").

[16] *See* § 1002.2, *supra*.

[17] 4 WIGMORE, § 1230.

[18] *E.g.,* United States v. Stephens, 779 F.2d 232 (5th Cir. 1985) (in prosecution for mail fraud, district court did not abuse its discretion in admitting charts summarizing evidence already received in prosecutions; the evidence was indisputably complex, involved hundreds of exhibits and examination of underlying material would have been inconvenient without summary charts); *see* United States v. Denton, 556 F.2d 811 (6th Cir. 1977) (court approved admission of "composite tape" made from duplicate copies of taped telephone conversations).

[19] *E.g.,* United States v. Porter, 821 F.2d 968 (4th Cir. 1987) (trial court did not err in admitting charts of telephone toll records that summarized evidence previously introduced; any prejudice attributable to highlighting of names was cured by cautionary instruction); United States v. North Am. Reporting, 740 F.2d 50 (D.C. Cir. 1984) (no error to exclude summary charts where these were derived from "diverse sources of various shades of

§ 1006.3   Requirement of Availability of Originals or Duplicates

Rule 1006 requires that either the original or a duplicate be made available to opposing parties for examination or copying at a reasonable time and place. Rule 1006 codifies the modern trend in that it requires only that documents be made available for inspection and copying, and the introduction of summaries is not conditional on the concomitant introduction of the originals or the delivery of the originals to the court for retention.[20] Rule 1006, however, provides for discretionary power in the court to order production of originals or duplicates.

Although Rule 1006 seems to impose an absolute requirement that the charts, summaries and exhibits be made available to all litigants, in light of Rules 102 and 103, it is not illogical to conclude that a party can effectively waive the requirements of Rule 1006 by a failure to object.

The development of liberal discovery and pre-trial conferences provides a framework within which Rule 1006 can effectively operate. Proponents of charts, summaries, and calculations can determine their admissibility by a motion in limine submitted prior to trial. Additionally, Federal Rule of Civil Procedure 34 provides for discovery of documents in the possession of a party without court order.[21] Nevertheless, the availability requirement embodied in Rule 1006 is independent of the discovery procedure of Federal Rule of Civil Procedure 34.[22]

§ 1006.4   Laying the Proper Foundation

In order for charts, summaries, or calculations to be admitted, either the proponent must lay a proper foundation for their admission or their admissibility must be the subject of a stipulation. Federal courts traditionally have required that where charts, summaries, or calculations are to be introduced into evidence, the person who prepared the summaries, supervised the originals, or controlled the originals must testify to the foundation.[23]

---

unreliability, including mere surmise, undocumented recollection and questionable assumptions"; appellate court invoked Rule 403); *see* Rule 403.

[20] United States v. Clements, 588 F.2d 1030 (5th Cir. 1979) (alleged gambling operation; government witness was properly permitted to testify); *cf.* Solari Furs v. United States, 436 F.2d 683 (8th Cir. 1971) (no error in consideration of summaries of original and genuine business records and papers); *see also* United States v. Atchley, 699 F.2d 1055 (11th Cir. 1983) (summary was properly received under Rule 1006, where duplicates of original records had already been admitted into court and therefore were available for examination by other parties).

[21] *See* Fed. R. Civ. P. 34.

[22] *See* 6 WEINSTEIN'S FEDERAL EVIDENCE § 1006.06; 5 MUELLER & KIRKPATRICK, § 585.

[23] McDaniel v. United States, 343 F.2d 785 (5th Cir. 1965) (government offered summaries of defendant's records prepared by a Certified Public Accountant who was a

The foundation must show that the charts, summaries, or calculations accurately reflect the information included in, or computed from the originals. Accordingly, inadmissible hearsay evidence may not be included in the summary,[24] except in the situation under Rule 703 in which expert witnesses are authorized to base their testimony on hearsay evidence.[25]

---

member of SEC and expert; he was allowed to state his conclusions); *e.g.,* Frank Music Corp. v. Metro-Goldwyn-Mayer, 772 F.2d 505 (9th Cir. 1985) (summary showing allocation of productions was properly received, where plaintiffs had ample opportunity to cross-examine vice-president for finance, under whose direction the summary was prepared).

[24] United States v. Goss, 650 F.2d 1336 (5th Cir. 1981) (admission of summaries of testimony of out-of-court witness should not have been received over hearsay objection); *e.g.,* AMPAT/Midwest, Inc. v. Illinois Tool Works, 896 F.2d 1035 (7th Cir. 1990) (summarized data admitted into evidence even though the data was summarized for litigation purposes and therefore outside the business records exception; the original figures were taken from plaintiff's regular business records and were within the "spirit if not the letter of" business records exception); Hackett v. Housing Auth. of San Antonio, 750 F.2d 1308 (5th Cir. 1985) (trial court erred in admitting summary of studies because underlying determinations were made on basis of conversations that constituted inadmissible hearsay and can form no part of Rule 1006 summary); Paddack v. Dave Christensen, Inc., 745 F.2d 1254 (9th Cir. 1984) (summary reports were not admissible under Rule 1006 because the reports relied not only upon employer's business records, but also upon information provided by union sources that constituted inadmissible hearsay and could not form basis for a summary).

[25] *See* Rule 703. *See generally,* §§ 703.1–703.5, *supra.*

Chapter 1007

Rule 1007. Testimony or Statement of a Party to Prove Content

Rule 1007. Testimony or Statement of a Party to Prove Content

The proponent may prove the content of a writing, recording, or photograph by the testimony, deposition, or written statement of the party against whom the evidence is offered. The proponent need not account for the original.

§ 1007.1   Testimony or Statement of a Party to Prove Content — An Overview

Rule 1007 sets forth an exception to the best evidence rule in providing for a method proving contents of a writing, recording, or photograph other than through the use of the original.[1] Rule 1007 authorizes proof of contents through the written admission by the party against whom offered or through admissions by such party made in testimony or deposition. Under Rule 1007 there is no necessity of accounting for the nonproduction of the original.

Pre-Rule federal law provided that any oral admission by the party against whom offered, under oath or not, could be used to prove the contents of a writing or record, without accounting for nonproduction of the original. This rule was established firmly in the leading English case, *Slatterie v. Pooley*,[2] which held that the defendant's out-of-court admission of an existing debt was admissible as original evidence, even though a schedule listing the debt ordinarily would have been the best evidence of the debt. Rule 1007 limits *Slatterie* by requiring the admission of the adverse party to be written or

---

[1] *See generally,* 2 McCORMICK, § 242; 6 WEINSTEIN'S FEDERAL EVIDENCE §§ 1007.01–1007.07; 5 MUELLER & KIRKPATRICK, §§ 586–587; 4 WIGMORE, § 1255. *See also* Comment, *Symposium on the Proposed Federal Rules of Evidence: Part II, Authentication and the Best Evidence Rule Under the Proposed Rules of Evidence,* 16 WAYNE L. REV. 195 (1969); Comment, *Evidence—Best Evidence Rule—Admissions of a Party as an Exception,* 17 TEX. L. REV. 371 (1939).

[2] 151 Eng. Rep. 579 (1840); *accord* Metropolitan Life Ins. Co. v. Hogan, 63 F.2d 654 (7th Cir. 1933); City of Cleveland v. Cleveland C.C. & St. L. Ry., 93 F. 113 (Cir. Ct. N.D. Ohio 1899), *rev'd on other grounds,* 147 F. 171 (6th Cir. 1906); *see also* 4 WIGMORE, § 1256.

made while under oath in testimony or deposition.[3] Unsworn oral out-of-court admissions occurring outside of hearings or depositions are not admissible to prove the contents of a writing.[4]

Rule 1007 should be interpreted to authorize admissions of the contents of originals made in testimony at grand jury proceedings and at unrelated actions, because such admissions being under oath at a formal proceeding satisfy the policies underlying the Rule. Additionally, Civil Procedure Rule 33 provides that answers to interrogatories be made in writing under oath. An admission of the contents of a writing, recording or photograph in response to interrogatories is consequently admissible under Rule 1007 as proof of the contents of a writing.[5]

Civil Procedure Rule 36, which authorizes requests for admissions, may generally be used by a party to require opposing parties to admit to the authenticity and contents of a writing.[6] The value of this method of proof is diminished by Civil Procedure Rule 36's requirement that a copy of the pertinent document be served on opposing parties with the request, unless it was previously made available.[7] An issue left unresolved by Rule 1007 and Procedure Rule 36 is whether a failure to reply to a Procedure Rule 36 request for admission constitutes an admission satisfying Rule 1007. The policy underlying Rule 1007 would seem to require an actual, express admission rather than one arising by implication.[8]

It should be emphasized that contents of the writing, recording, or photograph sought to be proven through Rule 1007 need not have been prepared by the party whose admission is offered as a vehicle of proof.

---

[3] *See* Rule 1007, Advisory Committee Note.

[4] 2 McCormick, § 242.

[5] *See* § 1007.2, *infra*. Basically, whenever an admission as to the content of a writing is made under oath and the admission is recorded, there will be little doubt either with respect to the sincerity of the speaker or mistransmission of the evidence.

[6] 6 Weinstein's Federal Evidence § 1007.07.

[7] Generally, such a copy will be a duplicate, itself admissible in most circumstances (Rule 1003). Of course, inability to obtain the original or copies may trigger the Rule 1004 exceptions. Thus, only convenience is at stake, not the ability to prove the contents. *E.g.,* Seiler v. Lucasfilm, Ltd., 797 F.2d 1504 (9th Cir. 1986) (in copyright infringement suit, trial court properly excluded plaintiff's drawings reconstructed from originals after determining that originals had been lost or destroyed in bad faith; Rule 1008 states that when admissibility of evidence depends upon fulfillment of condition of fact, the trial judge makes the determination of that condition of fact. If Seiler had shown that the originals had not been lost or destroyed in bad faith, his reconstructions would have been admissible and their accuracy determined by the jury).

[8] *See* § 1007.2, *infra*. Where reliability and accuracy are essential, admissions by silence are disfavored. Lumpkin v. Meskill, 64 F.R.D. 673 (D. Conn. 1974) (without considering question of best evidence, treating failure to admit data on accuracy of statistics in report under Federal Civil Rule 36 as equivalent to admission).

Accordingly, this exception to the best evidence rule may be used to prove the contents of, *e.g.*, a writing originally prepared by a person other than the party whose written or testimonial admission is used to prove contents.

Rule 1007 must be read as a limitation on Rule 801(d)(2), and a party's oral, out-of-court admission is generally admissible under Rule 801 unless it concerns the contents of a writing, recording, or photograph.[9] In that case, Rule 1007 would exclude the oral admission from evidence.[10] Additionally, the parol evidence rule frequently operates to complement Rule 1007 by limiting oral statements relating to writings.

Finally, it should be noted that Rule 1007 does not operate to preclude the introduction of oral, unsworn admissions by a party as secondary evidence to prove contents where justification for the nonproduction of the document falls under one of the exceptions contained in Rules 1004, 1005, and 1006.[11]

§ 1007.2   Theory of Rule 1007

The principle of Rule 1007 has been justified as a rule of convenience generally based on the theory that the admissions of an adverse party are reliable because such admissions are presumptively accurate and reliable.[12] Beyond accuracy, the original common-law rule was predicated on the same policy underlying the admission by a party exception to the hearsay rule, *viz.*, estoppel from denial at trial of the truth of admissions made out of court.[13] Not only was the policy of the common-law rule identical to the admission exception to the hearsay rule, but the common-law rule treated the admission of the contents of a writing as original evidence just like any other admission of a party.[14]

While Rule 1007 recognizes the convenience afforded by this exception to the best evidence rule, it places greater emphasis on accuracy and reliability than did the traditional exception by requiring the adverse party's admission

---

[9] *See* § 801.23, *supra.*

[10] The best evidence rule is a condition to admissibility independent of and in addition to hearsay considerations.

[11] *See* Rule 1007, Advisory Committee Note (the Note refers only to Rule 1004, but clearly other exceptions are equally available).

[12] Slatterie v. Pooley, 151 Eng. Rep. 579, 581 (1840) ("what a party himself admits to be true may reasonably be presumed to be so."); *see also* 4 WIGMORE, § 1255.

[13] *See* § 801.23, *supra.*

[14] *E.g.*, Greater Kansas City Laborers Pension Fund v. Thummel, 738 F.2d 926 (8th Cir. 1984) (carbon copy of contract properly admitted against defendant despite fact that apparent carbon image of defendant's signature had been overwritten in blue ink; this alteration would go to weight attached to document not to its admissibility); *see* Metropolitan Life Ins. Co. v. Hogan, 63 F.2d 654 (7th Cir. 1933) (admissions of defendant insurance company's agent admissible to prove contents); York Blouse Corp. v. Kaplowitz Bros., 97 A.2d 465 (D.C. 1957) (testimony of officer of defendant corporation admissible against corporation to prove contents); *see also* 4 WIGMORE, § 1255 *et seq.*

to be in writing or in testimony or deposition.[15] The traditional rule admitted evidence twice removed from the writing itself and, consequently, was subject to the dangers both of mistransmission by the witness[16] and of insincerity by the party.[17] A written admission eliminates the possibility of mistransmission, and an admission in testimony or deposition will meet an adequate standard of care on the part of the speaker due to the safeguards and solemnity accompanying the oath and proceedings.

§ 1007.3   Admissions by Party's Representatives

An issue not expressly resolved in Rule 1007 is whether the Rule applies only to admissions made personally by the adverse party or whether it also applies to admissions by that party's representative. Under Pre-Rule practice, courts have held corporations and partnerships bound by their representatives.[18]

The best reading of Rule 1007 can be obtained by equating the scope of the admission of a party of Rule 1007 with that of Rule 801(d)(2). Such a reading would authorize the admissibility of admissions even though made by persons other than the adverse party, where such admissions can be attributed to representatives of that party.[19] Additionally, the safeguard of requiring that the admission by a representative of a party be contained in a writing, testimony, or deposition supports a presumption of reliability with respect to representatives to the same extent as to parties.

---

[15] 2 McCormick, § 242.

[16] Mistransmission could arise due to fraud, faulty memorization or quotation out of context. *E.g.,* United States v. Kaatz, 705 F.2d 1237 (10th Cir. 1983) (tax evasion and filing false tax returns; summary based upon admissible business records was properly received where such summaries were put before the jury with limiting instructions).

[17] *See* 6 Weinstein's Federal Evidence § 1007.04; 5 Mueller & Kirkpatrick, § 587; 4 Wigmore, § 1255; *see also* Lawless v. Queale, 8 Ir. L. R., 382 (1845) (testimony of witness concerning adverse party's oral, extrajudicial admission of contents held inadmissible because of danger of fraud).

[18] Metropolitan Life Ins. Co. v. Hogan, 63 F.2d 654 (7th Cir. 1933).

[19] *See* § 801.25, *supra.*

Chapter 1008

Rule 1008. Functions of the Court and Jury

Rule 1008. Functions of the Court and Jury

Ordinarily, the court determines whether the proponent has fulfilled the factual conditions for admitting other evidence of the content of a writing, recording, or photograph under Rule 1004 or 1005. But in a jury trial, the jury determines — in accordance with Rule 104(b) — any issue about whether:

    (a)   an asserted writing, recording, or photograph ever existed;

    (b)   another one produced at the trial or hearing is the original; or

    (c)   other evidence of content accurately reflects the content.

---

§ 1008.1   Functions of the Court and Jury — In General

Rule 1008 allocates responsibility for deciding preliminary questions of fact involving the admissibility of evidence other than originals to prove the contents of writings, recordings, or photographs. Factual questions otherwise respecting admissibility, which in reality are determinative issues in the case and which generally turn on questions of credibility or the weight to be accorded certain evidence, are allocated to the trier of fact. Other preliminary questions of fact that relate to the admissibility of secondary evidence are within the province of the court.[1] Rule 1008's allocation of determinations as to admissibility is a specialized application of the court's power to determine preliminary matters under Rule 104.[2]

---

[1] *See generally,* 1 McCormick, § 53; 6 Weinstein's Federal Evidence §§ 1008.01–1008.05; 5 Mueller & Kirkpatrick, §§ 588–590; 4 Wigmore, Evidence in Trials at Common Law § 1192. *See also* Levin, *Authentication and Contents of Writings,* 10 Rutgers L. Rev. 632 (1956); Maguire and Epstein, *Preliminary Questions of Fact in Determining the Admissibility of Evidence,* 40 Harv. L. Rev. 392 (1927); Morgan, *The Law of Evidence, 1941–1945,* 59 Harv. L. Rev. 481 (1946); Morgan, *Functions of Judge and Jury in Determination of Preliminary Questions of Fact,* 43 Harv. L. Rev. 165 (1929); Morgan and Maguire, *Looking Backward and Forward at Evidence,* 50 Harv. L. Rev. 909 (1937); Comment, *Authentication and the Best Evidence Rule Under the Federal Rules of Evidence,* 16 Wayne L. Rev. 195 (1969); Comment, *A Critical Appraisal of the Application of the Best Evidence Rule,* 21 Rutgers L. Rev. 526 (1967).

[2] *See* Rule 1008, Advisory Committee Note; *see also* § 104.3, *supra.*

Because the distinction between preliminary factual questions and questions properly left to the jury may not be immediately apparent, Rule 1008 provides that the trier of fact, and not the court, must resolve questions as to (i) whether the original writings asserted to exist ever existed, (ii) which of writings claimed to be an original is such, and (iii) whether the secondary evidence accurately reproduces the contents of the original. The purpose of the allocation is similar to the policy underlying Rule 104(b),[3] *i.e.,* to ensure that issues are not determined prematurely due to the court's negative ruling on the admissibility of secondary evidence as to any one of the three issues enumerated.[4] The court, of course, retains its traditional control over jury determinations of these issues.[5] For example, if the opponent of secondary evidence objects on one of the grounds specified in Rule 1008 but then fails to offer evidence sufficient to support a finding that the challenge is valid, the determination as to the admissibility of secondary evidence remains exclusively within the province of the court. If, on the other hand, an objection is raised and evidence offered as to one of the issues identified in Rule 1008, and a reasonable juror could determine the issue on evidence offered, the court must leave the determination to the jury pursuant to proper instructions.[6] In sum, under Rule 1008 the trial judge is not permitted to make a preliminary determination as to the appropriateness of secondary evidence and exclude the secondary evidence based on a finding that embraces the conclusion that the original never existed, that some other writing, recording, or photograph is the original, or that the offered secondary evidence is not a faithful reproduction of the original. Such issues may not be taken from the trier of fact.

Under the Rule, the court decides all other preliminary questions of admissibility that depend upon the fulfillment of a condition of fact, and the court may exclude secondary evidence on such bases. The primary examples of questions properly determined by the court are the threshold showings required by Rule 1004 as a prerequisite to the admission of secondary evidence to prove the contents of a writing, recording or photograph, *e.g.,* that the original was lost or destroyed or otherwise was not obtainable.[7] Additionally, the court must decide preliminary questions raised by other

---

[3] *See* the discussion of Rule 104 at § 104.1, *supra.*

[4] *See* Rule 1008, Advisory Committee Note.

[5] *Cf.* Rule 1008, Advisory Committee Note (decision is not left to the uncontrolled decision of the jury because the jury is subject to traditional controls exercised by the judge); *see, e.g.,* Transamerica Ins. Co. v. Bloomfield, 401 F.2d 357 (6th Cir. 1968).

[6] *See* Lewis v. Kepple, 185 F. Supp. 884 (W.D. Pa. 1960), *aff'd,* 287 F.2d 409 (3d Cir. 1961); *see also* Nu Car Carriers, Inc. v. Traynor, 125 F.2d 47 (D.C. Cir. 1942) (nonexistence of written release asserted; properly authenticated secondary evidence must therefore be submitted to the jury over the best evidence objection, with the jury deciding the existence issue).

[7] *See* Chapter 1004, *supra; see also* United States v. Gerhart, 538 F.2d 807 (8th Cir. 1976)

Rules as to admissibility of secondary evidence, and must decide any question of privilege, for example, that might arise in connection with the offer of secondary evidence.[8]

§ 1008.2   Questions for the Trier of Fact

Rule 1008 provides that a question as to whether an original ever existed is left to the trier of fact.[9] The issue will usually arise as a question of credibility where witnesses have contradicted one another with respect to the existence of the original.[10] In such instances, the court should admit the secondary evidence and allow the jury to hear the evidence and determine its weight.[11] It should be noted that Rule 1008 comes into play only where a party seeks to prove the *contents* of a writing, recording, or photograph by evidence other than the original; the Rule does not apply where the issue is merely whether a writing, recording, or photograph exists.[12]

Rule 1008 also accords to the jury the decision as to which of two or more documents is the original.[13] Once a proper showing of authenticity pursuant to Article IX has been made, the competing documents should be admitted.[14] Again, the issue arises under this Rule only where the contents of the original document are at issue.[15]

Finally, Rule 1008 provides that a question as to whether secondary evidence accurately reproduces the original is a question for the trier of fact.[16] Once the court has determined that nonproduction of the original is justified, the accuracy of the offered secondary evidence is an issue for the trier of fact. Recognizing that this question goes to the weight of the evidence, the Rule does not insist on a particular type of secondary evidence in order to prove the contents of the original. Although Rule 1008 allocates this issue to the trier of fact, the court retains its general power over the

---

(photocopy of copy of check properly admitted; government was merely required to demonstrate that the original copy was lost).

[8] *See* United States v. Collins, 596 F.2d 166 (6th Cir. 1979) (alleged mail fraud; court rejected defense claim of error in receipt of summary and charts to aid jury's understanding of financial data).

[9] Dunbar v. United States, 156 U.S. 185 (1895); Nu Car Carriers, Inc. v. Traynor, 125 F.2d 47 (D.C. Cir. 1942).

[10] *E.g.,* Equitable Life Assurance Soc. v. Sieg, 53 F.2d 318 (6th Cir. 1931).

[11] *See* §§ 104.1–104.5, *supra.*

[12] *See* § 1002.3, *supra.*

[13] 6 WEINSTEIN'S FEDERAL EVIDENCE, § 1008.05; 5 MUELLER & KIRKPATRICK, § 590.

[14] 6 WEINSTEIN'S FEDERAL EVIDENCE, § 1008.05.

[15] *See* Rule 1008, Advisory Committee Note.

[16] *See* Cooper v. Brown, 126 F.2d 874 (3d Cir. 1942) (action for accounting of partnership assets; plaintiff claimed that a waiver of interest on a mortgage held by defendant had been executed; testimony of contents should have been excluded, since there had been no showing of personal knowledge; issue of existence and contents were properly kept from the jury).

determination of factual issues and may, for example, bar the admission of evidence that is prejudicial, confusing or misleading.[17] Additionally, the court has discretion to require the availability or production of originals where the admitted secondary evidence consists of charts, summaries or calculations.[18]

§ 1008.3 Preliminary Decisions for the Court

Rule 1002 sets forth a general preference for use of the original to prove the contents of a writing, recording, or photograph. Use of the original is excused where the proponent shows satisfaction of another Rule or statute that authorizes proof of contents by alternative means. In each case, the admissibility of secondary evidence (*i.e.*, evidence other than the original) depends upon the fulfillment of a preliminary factual condition. Determinations as to whether a party has made the requisite factual showing justifying nonproduction of the original are for the court under Rule 1008.

Rule 1004 specifies four alternative conditions of fact that will satisfy the foundational requirement for use of secondary evidence in order to prove the contents of a writing, recording or photograph. Accordingly, in Rule 1004(a), the preliminary questions for the court concern the adequacy of the foundation for the admission of secondary evidence upon a claim that the original has been lost or destroyed.[19] The court must determine that all originals have suffered either of these fates.[20] The court must also decide that a diligent search has been made for the original by the proponent where there is no foundational proof as to destruction.[21] Additionally, if a challenge

---

[17] *See* Rule 403 and § 403.3, *supra.*

[18] *See* § 1006.3, *supra.*

[19] Sylvania Elec. Prod. v. Flanagan, 352 F.2d 1005 (1st Cir. 1965) (contract suit; error to permit plaintiff to testify to content of bills and invoices; burden was on plaintiff to show that he had used all reasonable means to obtain the original); *e.g.,* United States v. Feldman, 788 F.2d 544 (9th Cir. 1986) (trial court denied admission of secondary evidence on ground of insufficient authentication; appellate court upheld this determination on ground that defendant's foundation for this evidence was too tenuous and well within discretion of trial court to exclude it).

[20] Willhoit v. Commissioner, 308 F.2d 259 (9th Cir. 1962) (when secondary evidence is offered and the proponent seeks to excuse nonproduction of the original, sufficiency of the preliminary proof of diligence in searching for the original is addressed to the sound discretion of the trial judge); Sellmayer Packaging Co. v. Commissioner, 146 F.2d 707 (4th Cir. 1944) (no error to exclude testimony by taxpayer's accountant as to certain transactions, where tax court ruled that the taxpayer had not borne the burden of showing that the sales slips had ceased to exist).

[21] United States v. Gerhart, 538 F.2d 807 (8th Cir. 1976) (in prosecution for knowingly making a false statement on a loan application, a photocopy of a photocopy of a check was properly admitted against defendant, since government demonstrated that the photocopy was what it purported to be and accurately reflected the contents of the original photocopy); *e.g.,* Burroughs Wellcome Co. v. Commercial Union Ins. Co., 632 F. Supp. 1213 (S.D.N.Y. 1986) (court was satisfied that plaintiff met initial burden of proving loss or destruction of original

is raised on the issue that the proponent of the secondary evidence actually lost or destroyed the originals in bad faith, the court must determine the validity of the challenge and the concomitant question of admissibility of the secondary evidence. Determination of these preliminary factual questions is within the court's discretion, although, of course, such decisions cannot be arbitrary.[22]

Admission of secondary evidence under Rule 1004(b) requires the court to determine preliminarily whether all originals are beyond the court's jurisdiction and whether any available judicial process or procedure, for example, issuance of a subpoena duces tecum, could produce an original.[23] Again, the determination is within the court's discretion, and where the foundation is inadequate, the court may exclude the secondary evidence.

Under Rule 1004(c), preliminary questions for the court include whether the original is under the control of a party at the time an adverse party seeks to prove its contents, whether adequate notice has been furnished to the adverse party that the contents of the original would be the subject of proof at the hearing, and whether the party in possession of the original has failed to make the original available.[24] In connection with the question of whether the opponent failed to produce an original, the court may have to decide whether the document in question is admissible in view of an opponent's claim that it is protected by constitutional or testimonial privilege.[25] Of course, if the opponent intends to assert a privilege claim, she should nonetheless have the original at the hearing in order for the judge to examine it if necessary, or for use by the proponent if the claim of privilege is rejected.

Rule 1004(d) pertaining to collateral matters raises two preliminary questions for the court: (i) a determination of the controlling issues of a case,

---

because a diligent but unsuccessful search was made).

[22] United States v. Jacobs, 475 F.2d 270 (2d Cir. 1973) (alleged dealing in stolen government securities; photocopy of alleged agreement among conspirators was properly received); United States v. Covello, 410 F.2d 536 (2d Cir. 1969) (alleged interstate gambling and criminal fraud; copies of telephone toll records were properly admitted; diligent search had not uncovered the originals). *E.g.,* United States v. Bueno-Risquet, 799 F.2d 804 (2d Cir. 1986) (trial court properly exercised its discretion to admit secondary evidence where there was no indication that government lost or destroyed original evidence in bad faith).

[23] Western, Inc. v. United States, 234 F.2d 211 (8th Cir. 1956) (bankruptcy proceedings, deposition sufficed to establish that debtor corporation assumed the obligations of a partnership; sufficiency of foundation was laid for admission of secondary evidence).

[24] Transamerica Ins. Co. v. Bloomfield, 401 F.2d 357 (6th Cir. 1968); *e.g.,* Consolidation Coal Co. v. Chubb, 741 F.2d 968 (7th Cir. 1984) (court rejected Consolidation Coal's objection to receipt of medical report quoting another physician's reading of X-ray; production of other physician's report or X-ray itself was not required as best evidence because access to such X-ray and reading was under the control of Consolidation Coal).

[25] *See* Chapter 501, *supra.*

and (ii) a determination of whether the contents of the original are closely related to one of those issues.[26] Although the standards for determination of these questions are discretionary with the court, Rule 1004(d) requires a greater connective showing to controlling issues than mere relevance in order to justify an insistence on use of the original.

In addition to Rule 1004, other Rules involve the court in admissibility determinations regarding proof of contents by means other than the original. For example, in determining the admissibility of duplicates under Rule 1002, it is for the court to decide whether there is a genuine issue as to the authenticity of the original or whether unfairness would result by use of the duplicate in lieu of the original.[27]

Rule 1005 allows proof of contents of official records under certain circumstances, thereby requiring the court to determine whether a copy of a public record is properly certified or adequately authenticated by a witness who has compared the original with the copy.[28] Alternatively, the court must determine whether a copy conforming to those requirements cannot be obtained by the exercise of reasonable diligence prior to admitting other evidence of the contents of public records.[29] Of course, if an issue is raised as to whether an original public record ever existed, the question is ultimately left to the trier of fact.

Rule 1006, allowing use of charts, summaries, or calculations to prove contents, raises several preliminary questions for the court: (i) whether the contents of documentary evidence can be conveniently examined in court; (ii) whether the originals or duplicates have been made available to all parties as required by the Rule; and (iii) whether there are special reasons for requiring the actual production of the originals or duplicates in court.[30] In making a determination as to the admissibility of summaries, charts, or

---

[26] *See* 2 McCormick, § 234.

[27] *E.g.,* United States v. Patten, 826 F.2d 198 (2d Cir. 1987) (no error to admit duplicates of stolen checks where defense did not raise colorable issue about authenticity of original checks or accuracy of photographs); United States v. Moore, 710 F.2d 157 (4th Cir. 1983) (photocopies properly received where no genuine question of authenticity or unfairness has been raised); *see* § 1003.3, *supra.*

[28] *See* Chapter 1005, *supra.*

[29] *Id.*

[30] United States v. Collins, 596 F.2d 166 (6th Cir. 1979) (alleged mail fraud; court rejected defense claim of error in receipt of summaries and charts to aid jury's understanding of financial data); United States v. Bartone, 400 F.2d 459 (6th Cir. 1968) (if summaries are offered, trial judge must carefully examine them in order to determine that everything is supported by proof); *e.g.,* United States v. Stephens, 779 F.2d 232 (5th Cir. 1985) (summary flow charts tracing use of proceeds were properly admitted under Rule 1006, which "requires [that] (1) the underlying writings be voluminous and (2) in-court examination not be convenient"; decision of trial judge to admit charts is subject only to an abuse of discretion standard of review).

calculations, the court must necessarily also decide upon the admissibility of the underlying documents.

Rule 1007 also involves preliminary questions to be decided by the court. The Rule supersedes Rule 1004 and allows proof of contents by the testimony, deposition, or written admission of the party against whom the evidence is offered, without accounting for nonproduction of the original. The court must consequently decide whether a particular sworn statement is part of the testimony or deposition of a party, or whether a written document is an admission of a party.[31]

---

[31] *See* Development Corp. of America v. United Bonding Ins. Co., 413 F.2d 823 (5th Cir. 1969) (performance bond suit; no error in receipt into evidence of photographic copy of bond; court decided that defendant admitted the genuineness of the copy of the bond by formal answer to interrogatories).

ARTICLE XI.
MISCELLANEOUS RULES

Synopsis

Chapter 1101

Rule 1101. Applicability of the Rules

Rule 1101. Applicability of the Rules

(a) **To Courts and Judges.** These rules apply to proceedings before:

- United States district courts;
- United States bankruptcy and magistrate judges;
- United States courts of appeals;
- the United States Court of Federal Claims; and
- the district courts of Guam, the Virgin Islands, and the Northern Mariana Islands.

(b) **To Cases and Proceedings.** These rules apply in:

- civil cases and proceedings, including bankruptcy, admiralty, and maritime cases;
- criminal cases and proceedings; and
- contempt proceedings, except those in which the court may act summarily.

(c) **Rules on Privilege.** The rules on privilege apply to all stages of a case or proceeding.

(d) **Exceptions.** These rules — except for those on privilege — do not apply to the following:

(1) the court's determination, under Rule 104(a), on a preliminary question of fact governing admissibility;

(2) grand-jury proceedings; and

(3) miscellaneous proceedings such as:

- extradition or rendition;
- issuing an arrest warrant, criminal summons, or search warrant;
- a preliminary examination in a criminal case;
- sentencing;
- granting or revoking probation or supervised release; and
- considering whether to release on bail or otherwise.

(e)   **Other Statutes and Rules.** A federal statute or a rule prescribed by the Supreme Court may provide for admitting or excluding evidence independently from these rules.

---

§ 1101.1   Rule 1101(a) and Rule 1101(b) — Scope

Rule 1101(a) initially lists the various courts that are within the Supreme Court's rule-making power and then applies the Federal Rules of Evidence to proceedings within these courts.[1] The Advisory Committee compiled the list of courts contained in Rule 1101(a) from the various enabling acts creating the courts and from Congressional statutes that applied future enacted rules or procedures for specified federal courts.[2] Noticeably, administrative and agency hearings are not subject to the Rules of Evidence under Rule 1101(a).[3]

The Rules of Evidence apply in proceedings before a magistrate or bankruptcy judge,[4] and to judges of the courts listed except in the situations or proceedings identified under Rule 1101(d). Arbitrators may be bound by the Rules of Evidence.[5]

Rule 1101(b) contemplates a unitary system of evidence. Thus, the Rule applies to all proceedings, civil and criminal, regardless of whether the issue is tried to the court or to a jury.[6] In certain instances, other Rules draw distinctions between certain types of cases, *i.e.,* civil and criminal cases. For

---

[1] *See generally,* 6 WEINSTEIN'S FEDERAL EVIDENCE §§ 1101.01–1101.04; 5 MUELLER & KIRKPATRICK, §§ 591–96; 1 WIGMORE, § 4. *See also* Albert, *Application of Rules of Evidence to Administrative Proceedings: The Case of the Occupational Safety and Health Review Commission,* 47 AD. L. REV. 135 (1975); Friendly, *Some Kind of Hearing,* 123 U. PA. L. REV. 1267 (1975); Russell, *Federal Rules of Evidence With Special Emphasis on Bankruptcy Proceedings,* 49 AM. BANKR. L.J. 231 (1975); Smith, *Evidence Admissible During the Punishment Stage of a Criminal Trial,* 7 ST. MARY'S L.J. 38 (1975); Note, *The Constitutionality of Statutes Permitting Increased Sentences for Habitual or Dangerous Criminals,* 89 HARV. L. REV. 356 (1975).

[2] *See* Rule 1101, Advisory Committee Note.

[3] *See* American Coal v. Benefits Review Bd., 738 F.2d 387 (10th Cir. 1984) (appellate court noted that Federal Rules of Evidence apply to federal courts and U.S. magistrates only, and so are wholly inapplicable to administrative hearings); Calhoun v. Bailar, 626 F.2d 145 (9th Cir. 1980) (court rejected any per se rule that holds that hearsay can never constitute substantial evidence); E.E.O.C. v. University of Notre Dame du Lac, 551 F. Supp. 737 (N.D. Ind. 1982) (actions to enforce an administrative subpoena are encompassed within the phrase "civil actions and proceedings" making Rule 501 applicable), *reversed on other grounds,* 715 F.2d 331 (7th Cir. 1983).

[4] *In re* Clifford, 566 F.2d 1023 (5th Cir. 1978) (authentication pursuant to Rule 901 in bankruptcy); *In re* Sheehan, 350 F. Supp. 907 (W.D. Mo. 1972) (best evidence in bankruptcy proceeding).

[5] *See* Drayer v. Krasner, 572 F.2d 348 (2d Cir. 1978).

[6] 5 MUELLER & KIRKPATRICK, § 593.

example, under Rule 404 certain applications of character evidence are available only to the criminal accused.[7] Other examples may be found in Rule 104(c) and Rule 608. Where the Rules make a distinction between civil and criminal cases, the difference in treatment is usually supported by long-standing doctrines that seek to foster fundamental protections with a minimal suppression of helpful proof.

Whether a specific rule of evidence will apply in a given case cannot be determined solely from the face of Rule 1101. In some instances a court governed by the Federal Rules of Evidence under Rule 1101(a) will be required by other Rules[8] or constitutional principles[9] to apply state evidentiary rules in the determinations of a specific issue arising in a proceeding.

§ 1101.2 Proceedings in Contempt of Court

Rule 1101(b) excepts from the operation of the Rules contempt proceedings in which the court may act "summarily." The Rules are inapplicable only when the contempt is committed within the view or presence of the court or so near to the court as to disturb its proceedings and impair due respect for its authority.[10] Only in such a contempt situation may a court act summarily. In this sense, the only contempt proceedings exempted from the Rules are those involving charges for "direct" contempt, *i.e.,* obstreperous or disrespectful conduct that occurs in the presence of the court.[11]

In determining what is meant by the limiting phrase, "the presence of the court," it has been held that "the court" consists not simply of the judge, the courtroom, the jury, or jury room individually, but of all of these combined. In short, the court is present wherever any one of its constituent parts is engaged in the activity of the judiciary.[12]

To maintain a summary proceeding for contempt, the alleged misbehavior must require immediate punishment or deterrence in order to preserve the court's authority. The contempt must occur in the presence of the court or before any of its constituent parts, and it must obstruct the administration of justice by impeding or influencing a pending case. In such circumstances, the judge is the "evidence," since he or she has witnessed the contemptuous conduct. Accordingly, relaxation of the formal Rules of Evidence in summary contempt proceedings is appropriate. In all other contempt proceedings the Rules are fully operative.

---

[7] *See* Rule 404(a) and Chapter 404, *supra*; *see also* Michelson v. United States, 335 U.S. 469 (1948).

[8] *See* Rules 302, 501, 601 and 902(9).

[9] *See* Erie R.R. Co. v. Tompkins, 304 U.S. 64 (1938).

[10] *See generally,* discussion of Federal Rule of Criminal Procedure 42 in 27 MOORE'S FEDERAL PRACTICE CRIMINAL PROCEDURE § 642.03.

[11] *See* 5 MUELLER & KIRKPATRICK, § 593.

[12] *See* WRIGHT & MILLER, FEDERAL PRACTICE AND PROCEDURE (CIVIL), § 2960 (1973).

§ 1101.3 Privileges

Federal Evidence Rule 1101(c) is direct in its instruction that the law of privileges applies in any proceeding, including, as noted in Rule 1101(c), those proceedings specifically exempted from the application of the Rules. Thus, a person may assert a privilege at any stage of any proceeding.[13]

The preservation of privileges is, of course, at tension with a system designed to reveal the truth.[14] Nevertheless, time-honored, societal values are fostered by the continuation of privileges. Privileges, however characterized, are not lightly conferred and are not, therefore, expansively construed. The law of privileges is comprehensively treated in Article V of the Rules of Evidence and in Chapter 501, *supra.*

§ 1101.4 Admissibility Determinations

Despite the fact that the Rules are, as a whole, designed to elicit the truth by providing an orderly system for the introduction and reception of relevant evidence, their application in some situations would be either overly burdensome or entirely contrary to the nature of the proceeding. Accordingly, Rule 1101(d) excepts certain proceedings from the operation of the Rules where the application of the Rules would be counterproductive or inappropriate.

The first of these exceptions concerns determinations by the court on the admissibility of evidence. Rule 1101(d)(1) excepts such admissibility determinations by reference to Rule 104(a), and Rule 104(a) provides that the court is not bound by the Rules, except with respect to privileges, when ruling on questions of admissibility, qualifications of witnesses, or the existence of a privilege. For example, where the admissibility of particular evidence necessarily rests upon the existence of some condition such as the qualification of an expert, responsibility for this threshold determination has traditionally resided with the court. The Rule incorporates this practice.[15] Where the determination is factual, the court may decide the question on the basis of otherwise inadmissible facts.[16]

In addition, the nonprivilege Rules of Evidence do not apply to preliminary hearings in criminal cases where the purpose is to determine whether there exists "probable cause" to hold the accused for further proceedings.[17] The reasoning for this provision is that the nonprivilege Rules of Evidence

---

[13] *But cf.* United States v. Bein, 728 F.2d 107 (2d Cir. 1984) (presentation to a grand jury of matters subject to the attorney-client privilege "is not per se prohibited").

[14] *See* United States v. Nixon, 418 U.S. 683 (1974). *But see* United States v. Ocanas, 628 F.2d 353 (5th Cir. 1980).

[15] *See* 1 McCORMICK, § 53 (5th ed. 1999).

[16] 1 McCORMICK, § 53 (5th ed. 1999).

[17] *See* Fed. R. Crim. P. 5.1(a).

do not govern grand jury proceedings, and also because it is feared that making the rules applicable to preliminary hearings would increase the number of preliminary motions.[18]

The inapplicability of the Rules to admissibility determinations is in part predicated on the principle that any evidence, once admitted, is thereafter subject to attack by the opposing party. Where, for example, expert opinion testimony is admitted over objection, the opposing party retains the right to demonstrate that the expertise of the witness is faulty or that the information relied upon by the expert is inadequate or inaccurate.

§ 1101.5 Grand Juries and Miscellaneous Criminal Proceedings

Except with respect to privileges, Rule 1101(d)(2) specifically exempts proceedings before grand juries from the operation of the Rules.[19] The purpose of the grand jury is to make a preliminary determination of whether there exists reasonable cause to believe that the accused engaged in the conduct complained of, and whether such conduct constitutes a crime under the laws of the United States.[20] These determinations are to be made regardless of the evidence that may eventually be admitted at trial. The duty of the grand jury is to approve or disapprove the government's cause of action in a criminal case, and the issue before the grand jury is whether the government has in its possession certain facts demonstrating the substantive requirements essential to a criminal conviction.[21] Since the determination of ultimate truth of factual allegations is not the province of the grand jury, the system of evidence embodied in the Rules is not essential to the integrity of its proceedings. Accordingly, grand jury proceedings are exempted from the evidentiary dictates of the Rules.[22]

For much the same reasons, Rule 1101(d)(3) excepts from the Rules

---

[18] *See* Notes of the Advisory Committee on the Criminal Rules, 48 F.R.D. 553, 569–573 (1970).

[19] *See* United States v. Bein, 728 F.2d 107 (2d Cir. 1984) (presentation to a grand jury of matters subject to the attorney-client privilege "is not per se prohibited").

[20] *See* Kamisar, LaFave, Israel, *Modern Criminal Procedure*, 5th Ed., 1980, at 1025; *see also* Dong Haw v. Superior Court, 81 Cal. App. 2d 153, 183 P.2d 724 (1947).

[21] Hammond v. Brown, 323 F. Supp. 326 (D.C. Cir. 1971), *aff'd,* 450 F.2d 480 (6th Cir. 1971).

[22] *See* United States v. Calandra, 414 U.S. 338 (1974) (while grand jury may consider incompetent evidence, it may not violate a valid privilege, whether established by the constitution, statutes, or the common law); United States v. Costello, 350 U.S. 359 (1956) (indictment sufficient even though based entirely on hearsay); United States v. Ocanas, 628 F.2d 353 (1980) (even if information obtained in violation of appellants' Sixth Amendment right to counsel, that would not be grounds to challenge the indictment); *see also* United States v. McKenzie, 678 F.2d 629 (5th Cir. 1982) (grand juror can visit place mentioned in testimony and discuss findings with fellow jurors); United States v. Mackey, 405 F. Supp. 854 (E.D.N.Y. 1975) (violation of an evidentiary privilege in grand jury proceedings does not justify dismissing indictment).

certain unique criminal proceedings that need not be attended by the usual evidentiary safeguards. Proceedings in extradition or rendition are essentially administrative in nature.[23] The process involves the surrender of an individual to the jurisdiction where the alleged crime was committed. The proceeding merely seeks to determine the fact of an outstanding warrant and not the facts of the charges levied in the warrant by the petitioning jurisdiction. Consequently, the Rules are inapplicable.[24]

The Rules do not apply to sentencing proceedings. The entire theoretical foundation for sentencing is inconsistent with the system of evidence that seeks to ensure a correct and fair determination of guilt or innocence. Once guilt has been determined, the court is under a duty to pass sentence upon the convicted individual by resorting to information that is essentially irrelevant to the adjudication of culpability.[25] Accordingly, pre-sentence investigation and reports containing, among other things, information about the accused's past activities are normally prepared with an eye toward placing before the court the life and personality of the accused. Evidence such as hearsay and prior acts are contained in pre-sentence reports. While the Rules might preclude the use of such evidence in determining guilt, the relevant consideration in sentencing is not related to such a determination. Rather, the issue is one of personalized sanctions. Accordingly, evidence concerning prior acts, hearsay evidence, and character evidence are highly probative to the sentencing function.[26] Subjection of this proceeding to the Rules would serve no purpose consistent with prevailing theories of sentencing, and, consequently, sentencing hearings are exempted from the Rules.

The granting of probation is subsumed within the sentencing process discussed above. For the same reasons set forth above, the granting of parole by an executive board is likewise excepted from the Rules of Evidence. As a matter of policy, the prisoner has no legitimate expectation of liberty during the term of his or her sentence. This policy is extended to apply equally to the continuing incarceration and the conditions imposed upon the

---

[23] *See* Melia v. United States, 667 F.2d 300 (2d Cir. 1981); Simmons v. Braun, 627 F.2d 635 (2d Cir. 1980).

[24] *See* Messina v. United States, 728 F.2d 77 (2d Cir. 1984) (appellant's motion for discovery of information used against him in extradition proceedings was properly denied because Rules of Evidence are not applicable to extradition hearing; court analogized to grand jury hearing); Eain v. Wilkes, 641 F.2d 504 (7th Cir. 1981).

[25] Morrissey v. Brewer, 408 U.S. 471 (1972); United States v. McCallum, 677 F.2d 1024 (4th Cir. 1982).

[26] *See* United States v. Davis, 170 F.3d 617 (6th Cir. 1999) (hearsay is admissible in sentencing hearings); United States v. Ruminer, 786 F.2d 381 (10th Cir. 1986) (sentencing judge properly considered defendant's failure to cooperate during plea bargaining); United States v. Ray, 683 F.2d 1116 (7th Cir. 1982) (trial court entitled to consider broad range of information, largely unlimited as to kind or source in sentencing); United States v. Torrez-Flores, 624 F.2d 776 (7th Cir. 1980) (only privilege rules apply).

parolee if released.[27] Consequently, parole hearings are not governed by the usual system of proof.

Where either probation or parole is sought to be revoked, however, the government attempts to deprive an individual of a freedom that has once been granted. With respect to parole revocation, significant constitutional guarantees are applicable.[28] The same constitutional protections do not apply with equal force to the revocation of probation proceedings,[29] although Criminal Rule 32.3 does grant the accused the right to counsel prior to the revocation of probation. In regard to both parole and probation revocation, the court is guided by principles of fundamental fairness and not by the formal Rules of Evidence.[30]

The same theories underpinning the exemption from formal Rules of Evidence for grand juries apply with enhanced force to the issuance of criminal summons, arrest warrants, and search warrants. Here, the ultimate duty of the court is not to determine the truth of the underlying allegations, but only to determine whether reasonable or probable cause exists to believe that a certain person has committed a crime[31] or that certain contraband is located in a certain place.[32] Accordingly, the evidentiary safeguards contained in the Rules must give way to the overriding consideration of efficient and effective law enforcement.[33] To subject these investigatory proceedings

---

[27] United States v. Jarrett, 705 F.2d 198 (7th Cir. 1983); *see* United States v. Francischine, 512 F.2d 827 (5th Cir. 1975) (rules other than with respect to privileges do not apply in proceedings for revoking probation); United States v. Dozier, 543 F. Supp. 880 (M.D. La. 1982) (Rules of Evidence not applicable to probation revocation hearing); *see, e.g.,* U. S. ex rel. Lombardino v. Heyd, 318 F. Supp. 648 (E.D. La. 1970), *aff'd,* 438 F.2d 1027 (5th Cir. 1970) (exclusionary rule does not apply); McArthur v. United States, 434 F. Supp. 163 (S.D. Ind. 1976), *aff'd,* 559 F.2d 1226 (7th Cir. 1977) (Rules of Evidence do not apply to parole board proceedings).

[28] Morrissey v. Brewer, 408 U.S. 471 (1972); United States ex rel. Vitoratos v. Campbell, 410 F. Supp. 1208 (D.C. Ohio 1976).

[29] *See* United States v. Bell, 785 F.2d 640 (8th Cir. 1986) (Federal Rules of Evidence are not applicable to probation revocation proceedings); United States v. Francischine, 512 F.2d 827 (5th Cir. 1975); Arciniega v. Freeman, 439 F.2d 776 (9th Cir. 1971), *rev'd on other grounds,* 404 U.S. 4 (1971); McArthur v. United States Bd. of Parole, 434 F. Supp. 163 (S.D. Ind. 1976), *aff'd,* 559 F.2d 1226 (7th Cir. 1977); U. S. ex rel. Lombardino v. Heyd, 318 F. Supp. 648 (E.D. La. 1970), *aff'd,* 438 F.2d 1027 (5th Cir. 1970).

[30] United States v. Bari, 599 F.3d 176 (2d Cir. 2010) (although the Federal Rules of Evidence do not apply with their normal force in supervised release revocation hearings, they nevertheless provide some useful guidelines to ensure that any findings made at such hearings are based on "verified facts" and "accurate knowledge"; evidentiary constraints in such proceedings are loosened but not altogether absent).

[31] *See* Fed. R. Crim. P. 4(a) and 4(c); *see also* Eain v. Wilkes, 641 F.2d 504 (7th Cir. 1981) (extradition proceeding).

[32] *See, e.g.,* United States v. Gosser, 339 F.2d 102 (6th Cir. 1965).

[33] *See, e.g.,* Coury v. United States, 426 F.2d 1354 (6th Cir. 1970).

to the formal principles of proof would needlessly impede the paramount process of detection and arrest. If evidence seized pursuant to a defective warrant is tainted, there remains ample time to challenge the admission of such evidence, and it is thought to be more advantageous to society's interests that such errors be raised prior to or during trial than prior to the initial issuance of the arrest or search warrant.

The granting and setting of bail, like sentencing, is a task peculiarly within the province of the court. The overriding policy is that of assuring the accused's appearance at trial.[34] As in sentencing, the facts pertinent to a bail hearing are not probative of the guilt or innocence of the accused. The primary concern is the balancing of the accused's likelihood to appear when properly summoned against the accused's freedom and opportunity to prepare a defense. Given the nature and purpose of the proceeding, in which the court must address the character of the accused and the severity of the charged offense, the Rules of Evidence would do little to aid the court in this highly personalized function. Therefore, bail hearings are excepted from the operation of the Rules.[35]

§ 1101.6   Rule 1101(e) — Scope

Rule 1101(e) is self-explanatory. It provides that an Act of Congress or a rule promulgated by the Supreme Court may identify grounds for admission or exclusion of evidence independently of the Federal Rules of Evidence. Such statutory evidence rules are typically contained in the context of a particular piece of legislation with respect to special sorts of proceedings, most of them conducted by a court or an administrative tribunal without a jury.

---

[34] *See generally,* Stack v. Boyle, 342 U.S. 1 (1951).

[35] United States v. Montemayor, 666 F.2d 235 (5th Cir. 1982).

Chapter 1102

Rule 1102. Amendments

Rule 1102. Amendments

These rules may be amended as provided in 28 U.S.C. § 2072.

---

§ 1102.1   Rule 1102 in General — The Procedure Established in 28 U.S.C. §§ 2072 and 2074

Section 2072 of title 28 of the United States Code reads as follows:

(a)   The Supreme Court shall have the power to prescribe general rules of practice and procedure and rules of evidence for cases in the United States district courts (including proceedings before magistrates thereof) and courts of appeals.

(b)   Such rules shall not abridge, enlarge or modify any substantive right. All laws in conflict with such rules shall be of no further force or effect after such rules have taken effect.

(c)   Such rules may define when a ruling of a district court is final for the purposes of appeal under section 1291 of this title.

Section 2074 of title 28 of the United States Code reads as follows:

(a)   The Supreme Court shall transmit to the Congress not later than May 1 of the year in which a rule prescribed under section 2072 [28 USCS § 2072] is to become effective a copy of the proposed rule. Such rule shall take effect no earlier than December 1 of the year in which such rule is so transmitted unless otherwise provided by law. The Supreme Court may fix the extent such rule shall apply to proceedings then pending, except that the Supreme Court shall not require the application of such rule to further proceedings then pending to the extent that, in the opinion of the court in which such proceedings are pending, the application of such rule in such proceedings would not be feasible or would work injustice, in which event the former rule applies.

(b)   Any such rule creating, abolishing, or modifying an evidentiary privilege shall have no force or effect unless approved by Act of Congress.

Rule 1102 establishes that the procedure by which the Federal Rules of Evidence are to be amended is to be found in 28 U.S.C. §§ 2072 and 2074.[1] Section 2072 generally provides that the Supreme Court has the power to prescribe amendments to the Federal Rules of Evidence subject to Congressional action, while § 2074 establishes the submission of proposed rules to Congress. Rule 1102 was amended in 1991 to belatedly conform Rule 1102 to the Judicial Improvements and Access to Justice Act, enacted in 1988.[2] The 1991 amendment effectively substituted § 2072 of title 28 for § 2076 of title 28, which previously described the amendment procedure. The amendment was technical in nature, and no substantive changes were intended.[3]

Under § 2074, a proposed amendment to the Rules of Evidence must be submitted to Congress by May 1, with an effective date of no earlier than December 1 of the same year. This leaves a balance of seven months in which Congress may take action to block an amendment, increasing the waiting period by one month. Previously, either House of Congress had 180 days in which to pass a resolution blocking an amendment, an arrangement specifically described in former § 2076. The inclusion of the phrase "unless otherwise provided by law" in the second sentence of § 2074(a) should be interpreted as connoting a similar procedure. Unless either House of Congress takes such action, the rule is enacted into law and takes effect on the prescribed date, but no earlier than December 1 in the year it was submitted to Congress.

Section 2074 permits the Supreme Court to determine the extent to which new rules of evidence or amendments apply to proceedings already in progress. However, if the lower court in which a proceeding is pending makes a determination that application of the new rule or amendment would not be feasible or would work injustice, then the new rule or amendment will not apply in that proceeding. The statute requires the former rule of evidence to apply in those situations.

Section 2074, like former § 2076, mandates Congressional action on any

---

[1] *See generally,* 6 WEINSTEIN'S FEDERAL EVIDENCE §§ 1102.01–1102.03; Siegal, *Changes in Federal Jurisdiction and Practice Under the New (Dec. 1, 1990) Judicial Improvements Act,* 133 F.R.D. 61 (1991); Carrington, *"Substance" and "Procedure" in the Rules Enabling Act,* 1989 DUKE L.J. 281.

[2] Pub. L. No. 100-702, 102 Stat. 4642 (1988).

[3] *See* Rule 1102, Advisory Committee Note (on amendment effective Dec. 1, 1990).

rule "creating, abolishing, or modifying an evidentiary privilege." Unlike other rules that take effect automatically, barring Congressional action, any rule involving an evidentiary privilege shall not take effect unless specifically approved by an Act of Congress.

§ 1102.2   Rationale

Rule 1102 was enacted in a form that refers to a statute for its substantive provision, apparently as an effort to reinforce Congress's jurisdictional role in framing the Rules of Procedure for the federal court system.[4]

Although it originally pertained to former § 2076, the report by the House Judiciary Committee and the Senate Judiciary Committee provides some insight into the rationale underlying the substance of the current procedural scheme. The Committees were concerned that Congress continue to play an appropriate role in the rule-making process.[5] This theme is embodied in the lengthy time period required before a rule automatically becomes law in the absence of congressional action and in Congress' power to initiate the amendment process.[6]

Another concern of the House Judiciary Committee was the source of the Supreme Court's power to promulgate and amend the Rules of Evidence.[7] Prior Rules Enabling Acts provided that the Supreme Court may prescribe rules of "practice and procedure," which are then submitted to Congress. Congress did not share the Supreme Court's confidence that this language authorized the Supreme Court to promulgate rules of evidence for the federal courts.[8] The express language of § 2072(a) resolves any doubt on this issue.

Under the original Rules Enabling Acts, Congressional approval was required for any amendment proposed by the Supreme Court. However, the Senate Committee determined that such specific approval "was not needed with respect to subsequent amendments which would likely be of more modest dimension."[9] The Committee believed that a requirement of affir-

---

[4] *See* House Judiciary Committee Report on 28 U.S.C. § 2076; Senate Judiciary Committee Report on 28 U.S.C. § 2076.

[5] House Judiciary Committee Report on 28 U.S.C. § 2076; Senate Judiciary Committee Report on 28 U.S.C. § 2076.

[6] Former § 2076 provided that "[a]ny rule whether proposed or in force may be amended by Act of Congress." The Senate Judiciary Committee felt that while the power of Congress to initiate the amendment process "has been generally understood, the committee feels it should be made clear." Although the current statutory scheme contains no similar clarifying provision, it cannot be seriously contended that the absence of such provision implies that Congress intended to take away their own power to amend a current rule of evidence or initiate the rule-making process. Still, the inclusion of a clarifying provision would resolve any doubt, especially considering the existence of the provision in former § 2076.

[7] House Judiciary Committee Report, § 2076.

[8] *See* Rule 1101, Advisory Committee Note.

[9] Senate Judiciary Committee Report, § 2076.

mative Congressional action might result in "worthwhile amendments not being approved because of other pressing demands on the Congress."[10] The current scheme "strikes a sound balance between the proper role of Congress in the amendatory process and the dictates of convenience and legislative priorities."[11]

Despite agreeing with the Senate Committee on this last point, the House Committee was troubled by the prospect of the Supreme Court exercising legislative power over matters bearing heavily on important social policies, especially in the areas governing privileges.[12] Thus, § 2074(b) implements a policy that, with respect to evidentiary privileges, Congress shall play the key role in formulating changes in the law by requiring affirmative Congressional action on the matter rather than the exercise of the veto power it holds with respect to other amendments.[13] The legitimacy of this position is based on the assumption that Congress will make changes in the area of privileges only after a careful examination of the social policies underlying the existence of the privilege.

---

[10] *Id.*

[11] *Id.*

[12] *Id.*

[13] *Id.*

Chapter 1103

Rule 1103. Title

Rule 1103. Title

These rules may be cited as the Federal Rules of Evidence.

Rule 1103 is self-explanatory. Throughout this Treatise, the authors have cited the Federal Rules of Evidence in the form mandated by Rule 1103 or as simply, the Rules of Evidence.

Appendix A

Advisory Committee Notes to The Federal Rules of Evidence

ARTICLE I.
GENERAL PROVISIONS
Rule 101. Scope; Definitions

ADVISORY COMMITTEE NOTE TO THE 2011 AMENDMENT.

The language of Rule 101 has been amended, and definitions have been added, as part of the general restyling of the Evidence Rules to make them more easily understood and to make style and terminology consistent throughout the rules. These changes are intended to be stylistic only. There is no intent to change any result in any ruling on evidence admissibility.

The reference to electronically stored information is intended to track the language of Fed. R. Civ. P. 34.

The Style Project

The Evidence Rules are the fourth set of national procedural rules to be restyled. The restyled Rules of Appellate Procedure took effect in 1998. The restyled Rules of Criminal Procedure took effect in 2002. The restyled Rules of Civil Procedure took effect in 2007. The restyled Rules of Evidence apply the same general drafting guidelines and principles used in restyling the Appellate, Criminal, and Civil Rules.

1. General Guidelines

Guidance in drafting, usage, and style was provided by Bryan Garner, *Guidelines for Drafting and Editing Court Rules,* Administrative Office of the United States Courts (1969) and Bryan Garner, *Dictionary of Modern Legal Usage* (2d ed. 1995). *See also* Joseph Kimble, *Guiding Principles for Restyling the Civil Rules, in Preliminary Draft of Proposed Style Revision of the Federal Rules of Civil Procedure,* at page x (Feb. 2005) (available at http://www.uscourts.gov/uscourts/ RulesAndPolicies/rules/Prelim_draft_proposed_pt1.pdf); Joseph Kimble, *Lessons in Drafting from the New Federal Rules of Civil Procedure,* 12 Scribes J. Legal Writing 25 (2008–2009). For specific commentary on the Evidence restyling project, see Joseph Kimble, *Drafting Examples from the Proposed New Federal Rules of Evidence,* 88 Mich. B.J. 52 (Aug. 2009); 88 Mich. B.J. 46 (Sept. 2009); 88 Mich. B.J. 54 (Oct. 2009); 88 Mich. B.J. 50 (Nov. 2009).

2. Formatting Changes

Many of the changes in the restyled Evidence Rules result from using format to achieve clearer presentations. The rules are broken down into constituent parts, using progressively indented subparagraphs with headings and substituting vertical for horizontal lists. "Hanging indents" are used throughout. These formatting changes make the structure of the rules graphic and make the restyled rules easier to read and understand even when the words are not changed. Rules 103, 404(b), 606(b), and 612 illustrate the benefits of formatting changes.

3. Changes to Reduce Inconsistent, Ambiguous, Redundant, Repetitive, or Archaic Words

The restyled rules reduce the use of inconsistent terms that say the same thing in different ways. Because different words are presumed to have different meanings, such inconsistencies can result in confusion. The restyled rules reduce inconsistencies by using the same words to express the same meaning. For example, consistent expression is achieved by not switching between "accused" and "defendant" or between "party opponent" and "opposing party" or between the various formulations of civil and criminal action/case/proceeding.

The restyled rules minimize the use of inherently ambiguous words. For example, the word "shall" can mean "must," "may," or something else, depending on context. The potential for confusion is exacerbated by the fact the word "shall" is no longer generally used in spoken or clearly written English. The restyled rules replace "shall" with "must," "may," or "should," depending on which one the context and established interpretation make correct in each rule.

The restyled rules minimize the use of redundant "intensifiers." These are expressions that attempt to add emphasis, but instead state the obvious and create negative implications for other rules. The absence of intensifiers in the restyled rules does not change their substantive meaning. *See, e.g.,* Rule 104(c) (omitting "in all cases"); Rule 602 (omitting "but need not"); Rule 611(b) (omitting "in the exercise of discretion").

The restyled rules also remove words and concepts that are outdated or redundant.

4. Rule Numbers

The restyled rules keep the same numbers to minimize the effect on research. Subdivisions have been rearranged within some rules to achieve greater clarity and simplicity.

5. No Substantive Change

The Committee made special efforts to reject any purported style improvement that might result in a substantive change in the application of a rule. The Committee considered a change to be "substantive" if any of the following conditions were met:

a. Under the existing practice in any circuit, the change could lead to a different result on a question of admissibility (e.g., a change that requires a court to provide either a less or more stringent standard in evaluating the admissibility of particular evidence);

b. Under the existing practice in any circuit, it could lead to a change in the procedure by which an admissibility decision is made (e.g., a change in the time in which an objection must be made, or a change in whether a court must hold a hearing on an admissibility question);

c. The change would restructure a rule in a way that would alter the approach that courts and litigants have used to think about, and argue about, questions of admissibility (e.g., merging Rules 104(a) and 104(b) into a single subdivision); or

d. The amendment would change a "sacred phrase"—one that has become so familiar in practice that to alter it would be unduly disruptive to practice and expectations. Examples in the Evidence Rules include "unfair prejudice" and "truth of the matter asserted."

ADVISORY COMMITTEE NOTE.

Rule 1101 specifies in detail the courts, proceedings, questions, and stages of proceedings to which the rules apply in whole or in part.

ADVISORY COMMITTEE NOTE TO 1993 AMENDMENT.

This revision is made to conform the rule to changes made by the Judicial Improvements Act of 1990.

Rule 102. Purpose

ADVISORY COMMITTEE NOTE TO THE 2011 AMENDMENT.

The language of Rule 102 has been amended as part of the restyling of the Evidence Rules to make them more easily understood and to make style and terminology consistent throughout the rules. These changes are intended to be stylistic only. There is no intent to change

any result in any ruling on evidence admissibility.

ADVISORY COMMITTEE NOTE.

For similar provisions *see* Rule 2 of the Federal Rules of Criminal Procedure, Rule 1 of the Federal Rules of Civil Procedure, California Evidence Code § 2, and New Jersey Evidence Rule 5. (Neither the Report of the Senate Judiciary Committee, nor the Report of the House/Senate Conferees made comments directed separately toward Rule 102.)

Rule 103. Rulings on Evidence

ADVISORY COMMITTEE NOTE TO THE 2011 AMENDMENT.

The language of Rule 103 has been amended as part of the restyling of the Evidence Rules to make them more easily understood and to make style and terminology consistent throughout the rules. These changes are intended to be stylistic only. There is no intent to change any result in any ruling on evidence admissibility.

ADVISORY COMMITTEE NOTE.

Subdivision (a) states the law as generally accepted today. Rulings on evidence cannot be assigned as error unless (1) a substantial right is affected, and (2) the nature of the error was called to the attention of the judge, so as to alert him to the proper course of action and enable opposing counsel to take proper corrective measures. The objection and the offer of proof are the techniques for accomplishing these objectives. For similar provisions *see* Uniform Rules 4 and 5; California Evidence Code §§ 353 and 354; Kansas Code of Civil Procedure §§ 60-404 and 60-405. The rule does not purport to change the law with respect to harmless error. *See* 28 U.S.C. § 2111, F.R. Civ.P. 61, F.R. Crim.P. 52, and decisions construing them. The status of constitutional error as harmless or not is treated in Chapman v. California, 386 U.S. 18, 87 S.Ct. 824, 17 L.Ed.2d 705 (1967), reh. denied id. 937, 87 S.Ct. 1283, 18 L.Ed.2d 241.

Subdivision (b). The first sentence is the third sentence of Rule 43(c) of the Federal Rules of Civil Procedure virtually verbatim. Its purpose is to reproduce for an appellate court, insofar as possible, a true reflection of what occurred in the trial court. The second sentence is in part derived from the final sentence of Rule 43(c). It is designed to resolve doubts as to what testimony the witness would have in fact given, and, in nonjury cases, to provide the appellate court with material for a possible final disposition of the case in the event of reversal of a ruling which excluded evidence. See 5 Moore's Federal Practice § 43.11 (2d ed. 1968). Application is made discretionary in view of the practical impossibility of formulating a satisfactory rule in mandatory terms.

Subdivision (c). This subdivision proceeds on the supposition that a ruling which excludes evidence in a jury case is likely to be a pointless procedure if the excluded evidence nevertheless comes to the attention of the jury. Bruton v. United States, 389 U.S. 818, 88 S.Ct. 126, L.Ed.2d 70 (1968). Rule 43(c) of the Federal Rules of Civil Procedure provides: "The court may require the offer to be made out of the hearing of the jury." In re McConnell, 370 U.S. 230, 82 S.Ct. 1288, 8 L.Ed.2d 434 (1962), left some doubt whether questions on which an offer is based must first be asked in the presence of the jury. The subdivision answers in the negative. The judge can foreclose a particular line of testimony and counsel can protect his record without a series of questions before the jury, designed at best to waste time and at worst "to waft into the jury box" the very matter sought to be excluded.

Subdivision (d). This wording of the plain error principle is from Rule 52(b) of the Federal Rules of Criminal Procedure. While judicial unwillingness to be constricted by mechanical breakdowns of the adversary system has been more pronounced in criminal cases, there is no scarcity of decisions to the same effect in civil cases. In general, see Campbell, Extent to Which Courts of Review Will Consider Questions Not Properly Raised and Preserved, 7 Wis.L.Rev. 91, 160 (1932); Vestal, Sua Sponte Consideration in Appellate Review, 27 Fordham L.Rev. 477 (1958–59); 64 Harv.L.Rev. 652 (1951). In the nature of things the application of the plain error rule will be more likely with respect to the admission of evidence than to exclusion, since failure to comply with normal requirements of offers of proof is likely to produce a record which simply does not disclose the error.

ADVISORY COMMITTEE NOTES TO THE 2000 AMENDMENTS.

The amendment applies to all rulings on evidence whether they occur at or before trial, including so-called "in limine" rulings. One of the most difficult questions arising from in limine and other evidentiary rulings is whether a losing party must renew an objection or offer of proof when the evidence is or would be offered at trial, in order to preserve a claim of error on appeal. Courts have taken differing approaches to this question. Some courts have held that a renewal at the time the evidence is to be offered at trial is always required. *See, e.g.,* Collins v. Wayne Corp., 621 F.2d 777 (5th Cir. 1980). Some courts have taken a more flexible approach, holding that renewal is not required if the issue decided is one that (1) was fairly presented to the trial court for an initial ruling, (2) may be decided as a final matter before the evidence is actually offered, and (3) was ruled on definitively by the trial judge. *See, e.g.,* Rosenfeld v. Basquiat, 78 F.3d 84 (2d Cir. 1996) (admissibility of former testimony under the Dead Man's Statute; renewal not required). Other courts have distinguished between objections to evidence, which must be renewed when evidence is offered, and offers of proof, which need not be reviewed after a definitive determination is made that the evidence is inadmissible. *See, e.g.*, Fusco v. General Motors Corp., 11 F.3d 259 (1st Cir. 1993). Another court, aware of this Committee's proposed amendment, has adopted its approach. Wilson v. Williams, 182 F.3d 562 (7th Cir. 1999) (en banc). Differing views on this question create uncertainty for litigants and unnecessary work for the appellate courts. The amendment provides that a claim of error with respect to a definitive ruling is preserved for review when the party has otherwise satisfied the objection or offer of proof requirements of Rule 103(a). When the ruling is definitive, a renewed objection or offer of proof at the time the evidence is to be offered is more a formalism than a necessity. *See* Fed.R.Civ.P. 46 (formal exceptions unnecessary); Fed.R.Cr.P. 51 (same); United States v. Mejia-Alarcon, 995 F.2d 982, 986 (10th Cir. 1993) ("Requiring a party to renew an objection when the district court has issued a definitive ruling on a matter that can be fairly decided before trial would be in the nature of a formal exception and therefore unnecessary."). On the other hand, when the trial court appears to have reserved its ruling or to have indicated that the ruling is provisional, it makes sense to require the party to bring the issue to the court's attention subsequently. *See, e.g.*, United States v. Vest, 116 F.3d 1179, 1188 (7th Cir. 1997) (where the trial court ruled in limine that testimony from defense witnesses could not be admitted, but allowed the defendant to seek leave at trial to call the witnesses should their testimony turn out to be relevant, the defendant's failure to seek such leave at trial meant that it was "too late to reopen the issue now on appeal"); United States v. Valenti, 60 F.3d 941 (2d Cir. 1995) (failure to proffer evidence at trial waives any claim of error where the trial judge had stated that he would reserve judgment on the in limine motion until he had heard the trial evidence).

The amendment imposes the obligation on counsel to clarify whether an in limine or other evidentiary ruling is definitive when there is doubt on that point. *See, e.g.*, Walden v. Georgia-Pacific Corp., 126 F.3d 506, 520 (3d Cir. 1997) (although "the district court told plaintiffs' counsel not to reargue every ruling, it did not countermand its clear opening statement that all of its rulings were tentative, and counsel never requested clarification, as he might have done.").

Even where the court's ruling is definitive, nothing in the amendment prohibits the court from revisiting its decision when the evidence is to be offered. If the court changes its initial ruling, or if the opposing party violates the terms of the initial ruling, objection must be made when the evidence is offered to preserve the claim of error for appeal. The error, if any in such a situation occurs only when the evidence is offered and admitted. United States Aviation Underwriters, Inc. v. Olympia Wings, Inc., 896 F.2d 949, 956 (5th Cir. 1990) ("objection is required to preserve error when an opponent, or the court itself violates a motion in limine that was granted"); United States v. Roenigk, 810 F.2d 809 (8th Cir. 1987) (claim of error was not preserved where the defendant failed to object at trial to secure the benefit of a favorable advance ruling).

A definitive advance ruling is reviewed in light of the facts and circumstances before the trial court at the time of the ruling. If the relevant facts and circumstances change materially after the advance ruling has been made, those facts and circumstances cannot be relied upon on appeal unless they have been brought to the attention of the trial court by way of a renewed, and timely, objection, offer of proof, or motion to strike. *See* Old Chief v. United States, 519 U.S. 172, 182, n. 6 (1997) ("It is important that a reviewing court evaluate the trial court's decision from its perspective when it had to rule and not indulge in review by hindsight."). Similarly, if the court decides in an advance ruling that proffered evidence is admissible subject to the eventual introduction by the proponent of a foundation for the evidence, and that foundation is never provided, the opponent cannot claim error based on the failure to establish the foundation unless the opponent calls that failure to the court's attention by a timely motion to strike or other suitable motion. *See* Huddleston v. United States, 485 U.S. 681, 690, n. 7 (1988) ("It is, of course, not the responsibility of the judge sua sponte to ensure that the foundation evidence is offered; the objector must move to strike the evidence if at the close of the trial the offeror has failed to satisfy the condition.").

Nothing in the amendment is intended to affect the provisions of Fed.R.Civ.P. 72(a) or 28 U.S.C. § 636(b)(1) pertaining to nondispositive pretrial rulings by magistrate judges in proceedings that are not before a magistrate judge by consent of the parties. Fed.R.Civ.P. 72(a) provides that a party who fails to file a written objection to a magistrate judge's nondispositive order within ten days of receiving a copy "may not thereafter assign as error a defect" in the order. 28 U.S.C. § 36(b)(1) provides that any party "may serve and file written objections to such proposed findings and recommendations as provided by rules of court" within ten days of receiving a copy of the order. Several courts have held that a party must comply with this statutory provision in order to preserve a claim of error. *See, e.g.,* Wells v. Shriners Hospital, 109 F.3d 198, 200 (4th Cir. 1997) ("[i]n this circuit, as in others, a party 'may' file objections within ten days or he may not, as he chooses, but he 'shall' do so if he wishes further consideration."). When Fed.R.Civ.P. 72(a) or 28 U.S.C. § 636(b)(1) is operative, its requirement must be satisfied in order for a party to preserve a claim of error on appeal, even where Evidence Rule 103(a) would not require a subsequent objection or offer of proof.

Nothing in the amendment is intended to affect the rule set forth in Luce v. United States, 469 U.S. 38 (1984), and its progeny. The amendment provides that an objection or offer of proof need not be renewed to preserve a claim of error with respect to a definitive pretrial ruling. *Luce* answers affirmatively a separate question: whether a criminal defendant must testify at trial in order to preserve a claim of error predicated upon a trial court's decision to admit the defendant's prior convictions for impeachment. The *Luce* principle has been extended by many lower courts to other situations. *See* United States v. DiMatteo, 759 F.2d 831 (11th Cir. 1985) (applying *Luce* where the defendant's witness would be impeached with evidence offered under Rule 608). *See also* United States v. Goldman, 41 F.3d 785, 788 (1st Cir. 1994) ("Although *Luce* involved impeachment by conviction under Rule 609, the reasons given by the Supreme Court for requiring the defendant to testify apply with full force to the kind of Rule 403 and 404 objections that are advanced by Goldman in this case."); Palmieri v. DeFaria, 88 F.3d 136 (2d Cir. 1996) (where the plaintiff decided to take an adverse judgment rather than challenge an advance ruling by putting on evidence at trial, the in limine ruling would not be reviewed on appeal); United States v. Ortiz, 857 F.2d 900 (2d Cir. 1988) (where uncharged misconduct is ruled admissible if the defendant pursues a certain defense, the defendant must actually pursue that defense at trial in order to preserve a claim of error on appeal); United States v. Bond, 87 F.3d 695 (5th Cir. 1996) (where the trial court rules in limine that the defendant would waive his fifth amendment privilege were he to testify, the defendant must take the stand and testify in order to challenge that ruling on appeal).

The amendment does not purport to answer whether a party who objects to evidence that the court finds admissible in a definitive ruling, and who then offers the evidence to "remove the sting" of its anticipated prejudicial effect, thereby waives the right to appeal the trial court's ruling. *See, e.g.*, United States v. Fisher, 106 F.3d 622 (5th Cir. 1997) (where the trial judge ruled in limine that the government could use a prior conviction to impeach the defendant if he testified, the defendant did not waive his right to appeal by introducing the conviction on direct examination); Judd v. Rodman, 105 F.3d 1339 (11th Cir. 1997) (an objection made in limine is sufficient to preserve a claim of error when the movant, as a matter of trial strategy, presents the objectionable evidence herself on direct examination to minimize its prejudicial effect); Gill v. Thomas, 83 F.3d 537, 540 (1st Cir. 1996) ("by offering the misdemeanor evidence himself, Gill waived his opportunity to object and thus did not preserve the issue for appeal"); United States v. Williams, 939 F.2d 721 (9th Cir. 1991) (objection to impeachment evidence was waived where the defendant was impeached on direct examination).

NOTE BY FEDERAL JUDICIAL CENTER.

The House bill contains the word "judge." The Senate amendment substitutes the word "court" in order to conform with usage elsewhere in the House bill. The conference adopts the Senate amendment.

Rule 104. Preliminary Questions

ADVISORY COMMITTEE NOTE TO THE 2011 AMENDMENT.

The language of Rule 104 has been amended as part of the restyling of the Evidence Rules to make them more easily understood and to make style and terminology consistent throughout the rules. These changes are intended to be stylistic only. There is no intent to change any result in any ruling on evidence admissibility.

ADVISORY COMMITTEE NOTE.

Subdivision (a). The applicability of a particular rule of evidence often depends upon the existence of a condition. Is the alleged expert a qualified physician? Is a witness whose former testimony is offered unavailable? Was a stranger present during a conversation between attorney and client? In each instance the admissibility of evidence will turn upon the answer to the question of the existence of the condition. Accepted practice, incorporated in the rule, places on the judge the responsibility for these determinations. McCormick § 53; Morgan, Basic Problems of Evidence 45–50 (1962).

To the extent that these inquiries are factual, the judge acts as a trier of fact. Often, however, rulings on evidence call for an evaluation in terms of a legally set standard. Thus when a hearsay statement is offered as a declaration against interest, a decision must be made whether it possesses the required against-interest characteristics. These decisions, too, are made by the judge.

In view of these considerations, this subdivision refers to preliminary requirements generally by the broad term "questions," without attempt at specification.

This subdivision is of general application. It must, however, be read as subject to the special provisions for "conditional relevancy" in subdivision (b) and those for confessions in subdivision (c).

If the question is factual in nature, the judge will of necessity receive evidence pro and con on the issue. The rule provides that the rules of evidence in general do not apply to this process. McCormick § 53, p. 123, n. 8, points out that the authorities are "scattered and inconclusive," and observes:

"Should the exclusionary law of evidence, 'the child of the jury system' in Thayer's phrase, be applied to this hearing before the judge? Sound sense backs the view that it should not, and that the judge should be empowered to hear any relevant evidence, such as affidavits or other reliable hearsay."

This view is reinforced by practical necessity in certain situations. An item, offered and objected to, may itself be considered in ruling on admissibility, though not yet admitted in evidence. Thus the content of an asserted declaration against interest must be considered in ruling whether it is against interest. Again common practice calls for considering the testimony of a witness, particularly a child, in determining competency. Another example is the requirement of Rule 602 dealing with personal knowledge. In the case of hearsay, it is enough, if the declarant "so far as appears [has] had an opportunity to observe the fact declared." McCormick, § 10, p. 19.

If concern is felt over the use of affidavits, by the judge in preliminary hearings on admissibility, attention is directed to the many important judicial determinations made on the basis of affidavits. Rule 47 of the Federal Rules of Criminal Procedure provides:

"An application to the court for an order shall be by motion . . . . It may be supported by affidavit."

The Rules of Civil Procedure are more detailed. Rule 43(c), dealing with motions generally, provides:

"When a motion is based on facts not appearing of record the court may hear the matter on affidavits presented by the respective parties, but the court may direct that the matter be heard wholly or partly on oral testimony or depositions."

Rule 4(g) provides for proof of service by affidavit. Rule 56 provides in detail for the entry of summary judgment based on affidavits. Affidavits may supply the foundation for temporary restraining orders under Rule 65(b).

The study made for the California Law Revision Commission recommended an amendment to Uniform Rule 2 as follows:

"In the determination of the issue aforesaid [preliminary determination], exclusionary rules shall not apply, subject, however, to Rule 45 and any valid claim of privilege." Tentative Recommendation and a Study Relating to the Uniform Rules of Evidence (Article VIII, Hearsay), Cal. Law Revision Comm'n, Rep., Rec. & Studies, 470 (1962). The proposal was not adopted in the California Evidence Code.

The Uniform Rules are likewise silent on the subject. However, New Jersey Evidence Rule 8(1), dealing with preliminary inquiry by the judge, provides:

"In his determination the rules of evidence shall not apply except for

Rule 4 [exclusion on grounds of confusion, etc.] or a valid claim of privilege."

Subdivision (b). In some situations, the relevancy of an item of evidence, in the large sense, depends upon the existence of a particular preliminary fact. Thus when a spoken statement is relied upon to prove notice to X, it is without probative value unless X heard it. Or if a letter purporting to be from Y is relied upon to establish an admission by him, it has no probative value unless Y wrote or authorized it. Relevance in this sense has been labelled "conditional relevancy." Morgan, Basic Problems of Evidence 45, 46 (1962). Problems arising in connection with it are to be distinguished from problems of logical relevancy, e.g. evidence in a murder case that accused on the day before purchased a weapon of the kind used in the killing, treated in Rule 401.

If preliminary questions of conditional relevancy were determined solely by the judge, as provided in subdivision (a), the functioning of the jury as a trier of fact would be greatly restricted and in some cases virtually destroyed. These are appropriate questions for juries. Accepted treatment, as provided in the rule, is consistent with that given fact questions generally. The judge makes a preliminary determination whether the foundation evidence is sufficient to support a finding of fulfillment of the condition. If so, the item is admitted. If after all the evidence on the issue is in, pro and con, the jury could reasonably conclude that fulfillment of the condition is not established, the issue is for them. If the evidence is not such as to allow a finding, the judge withdraws the matter from their consideration. Morgan, *supra*; California Evidence Code § 403; New Jersey Rule 8(2). *See also* Uniform Rules 19 and 67.

The order of proof here, as generally, is subject to the control of the judge.

Subdivision (c). Preliminary hearings on the admissibility of confessions must be conducted outside the hearing of the jury. *See* Jackson v. Denno, 378 U.S. 368, 84 S.Ct. 1774, 12 L.Ed.2d 908 (1964). Otherwise, detailed treatment of when preliminary matters should be heard outside the hearing of the jury is not feasible. The procedure is time consuming. Not infrequently the same evidence which is relevant to the issue of establishment of fulfillment of a condition precedent to admissibility is also relevant to weight or credibility, and time is saved by taking foundation proof in the presence of the jury. Much evidence on preliminary questions, though not relevant to jury issues, may be heard by the jury with no adverse effect. A great deal must be left to the discretion of the judge who will act as the interests of justice require.

NOTE BY FEDERAL JUDICIAL CENTER.

The Rule enacted by the Congress is the Rule prescribed by the

Supreme Court, amended by substituting "court" in place of "judge," with appropriate pronominal change, and by adding to subdivision (c) the concluding phrase, "or when an accused is a witness, if he so requests."

REPORT OF THE HOUSE COMMITTEE ON THE JUDICIARY. *Rule 104(c)*

Rule 104(c) as submitted to the Congress provided that hearings on the admissibility of confessions shall be conducted outside the presence of the jury and hearings on all other preliminary matters should be so conducted when the interests of justice require. The Committee amended the Rule to provide that where an accused is a witness as to a preliminary matter, he has the right, upon his request, to be heard outside the jury's presence. Although recognizing that in some cases duplication of evidence would occur and that the procedure could be subject to abuse, the Committee believed that a proper regard for the right of an accused not to testify generally in the case dictates that he be given an option to testify out of the presence of the jury on preliminary matters.

The Committee construes the second sentence of subdivision (c) as applying to civil actions and proceedings as well as to criminal cases, and on this assumption has left the sentence unamended.

ADVISORY COMMITTEE NOTE.

Subdivision (d). The limitation upon cross-examination is designed to encourage participation by the accused in the determination of preliminary matters. He may testify concerning them without exposing himself to cross-examination generally. The provision is necessary because of the breadth of cross-examination under Rule 611(b).

The rule does not address itself to questions of the subsequent use of testimony given by an accused at a hearing on a preliminary matter. *See* Walder v. United States, 347 U.S. 62 (1954); Simmons v. United States, 390 U.S. 377 (1968); Harris v. New York, 401 U.S. 222 (1971).

REPORT OF THE SENATE COMMITTEE ON THE JUDICIARY.

Rule 104(d) Preliminary Questions: Testimony by accused

Under Rule 104(c) the hearing on a preliminary matter may at times be conducted in front of the jury. Should an accused testify in such a hearing, waiving his privilege against self-incrimination as to the preliminary issue, Rule 104(d) provides that he will not generally be subject to cross-examination as to any other issue. This rule is not, however, intended to immunize the accused from cross-examination where, in testifying about a preliminary issue, he injects other issues into the hearing. If he could not be cross-examined about any issues gratuitously raised by him beyond the scope of the preliminary matters, injustice might result. Accordingly, in order to prevent any such unjust result, the committee intends the rule to be construed to provide that the accused may subject himself to cross-examination as to issues raised by his own testimony upon a preliminary matter before a jury.

ADVISORY COMMITTEE NOTE.

Subdivision (e). For similar provisions *see* Uniform Rule 8; California Evidence Code § 406; Kansas Code of Civil Procedure § 60-408; New Jersey Evidence Rule 8(1).

Rule 105. Limiting Evidence That Is Not Admissible Against Other Parties or for Other Purposes

ADVISORY COMMITTEE NOTE TO THE 2011 AMENDMENT.

The language of Rule 105 has been amended as part of the restyling of the Evidence Rules to make them more easily understood and to make style and terminology consistent throughout the rules. These changes are intended to be stylistic only. There is no intent to change any result in any ruling on evidence admissibility.

ADVISORY COMMITTEE NOTE.

A close relationship exists between this rule and Rule 403 which . . . [provides for] exclusion when "probative value is substantially outweighed by the danger of unfair prejudice, confusion of the issues, or misleading the jury." The present rule recognizes the practice of admitting evidence for a limited purpose and instructing the jury accordingly. The availability and effectiveness of this practice must be taken into consideration in reaching a decision whether to exclude for unfair prejudice under Rule 403. In Bruton v. United States, 389 U.S. 818, 88 S.Ct. 126, 19 L.Ed.2d 70 (1968), the Court ruled that a limiting instruction did not effectively protect the accused against the prejudicial effect of admitting in evidence the confession of a codefendant which implicated him. The decision does not, however, bar the use of limited admissibility with an instruction where the risk of prejudice is less serious.

Similar provisions are found in Uniform Rule 6; California Evidence Code § 355; Kansas Code of Civil Procedure § 61-406; New Jersey Evidence Rule 6. The wording of the present rule differs, however, in repelling any implication that limiting or curative instructions are sufficient in all situations.

REPORT OF HOUSE COMMITTEE ON THE JUDICIARY.

Rule 106 as submitted by the Supreme Court (now Rule 105 in the bill) dealt with the subject of evidence which is admissible as to one party or for one purpose but is not admissible against another party or for another purpose. The Committee adopted this Rule without change on the understanding that it does not affect the authority of a court to order a severance in a multi-defendant case.

NOTE BY FEDERAL JUDICIAL CENTER.

Because Rule 105 as proposed by the Supreme Court was eliminated by Congress, the number of the Rule was changed from 106, as promulgated by the Supreme Court, to 105. The Rule enacted by the Congress is the Rule prescribed by the Supreme Court as Rule 106, amended by substituting "court" in place of "judge."

Rule 106. Remainder of or Related Writings or Recorded Statements

ADVISORY COMMITTEE NOTE TO THE 2011 AMENDMENT.

The language of Rule 106 has been amended as part of the restyling of the Evidence Rules to make them more easily understood and to make style and terminology consistent throughout the rules. These changes are intended to be stylistic only. There is no intent to change any result in any ruling on evidence admissibility.

ADVISORY COMMITTEE NOTE.

The rule is an expression of the rule of completeness. McCormick § 56. It is manifested as to depositions in Rule 32(a)(1) of the Federal Rules of Civil Procedure, of which the proposed rule is substantially a restatement.

The rule is based on two considerations. The first is the misleading impression created by taking matters out of context. The second is the inadequacy of repair work when delayed to a point later in the trial. *See* McCormick § 56; California Evidence Code § 356. The rule does not in any way circumscribe the right of the adversary to develop the matter on cross-examination or as part of his own case.

For practical reasons, the rule is limited to writings and recorded statements and does not apply to conversations.

NOTE BY FEDERAL JUDICIAL CENTER.

The Rule enacted by the Congress is the Rule prescribed by the Supreme Court as Rule 107 without change.

ARTICLE II.
JUDICIAL NOTICE

Rule 201. Judicial Notice of Adjudicative Facts

ADVISORY COMMITTEE NOTE TO THE 2011 AMENDMENT.

The language of Rule 201 has been amended as part of the restyling of the Evidence Rules to make them more easily understood and to make style and terminology consistent throughout the rules. These changes are intended to be stylistic only. There is no intent to change

any result in any ruling on evidence admissibility.

ADVISORY COMMITTEE NOTE.

Subdivision (a). This is the only evidence rule on the subject of judicial notice. It deals only with judicial notice of "adjudicative" facts. No rule deals with judicial notice of "legislative" facts. Judicial notice of matters of foreign law is treated in Rule 44.1 of the Federal Rules of Civil Procedure and Rule 26.1 of the Federal Rules of Criminal Procedure.

The omission of any treatment of legislative facts results from fundamental differences between adjudicative facts and legislative facts. Adjudicative facts are simply the facts of the particular case. Legislative facts, on the other hand, are those which have relevance to legal reasoning and the lawmaking process, whether in the formulation of a legal principle or ruling by a judge or court or in the enactment of a legislative body. The terminology was coined by Professor Kenneth Davis in his article An Approach to Problems of Evidence in the Administrative Process, 55 Harv L Rev 364, 404–407 (1942). The following discussion draws extensively upon his writings. In addition, *see* the same author's Judicial Notice, 55 Colum L Rev 945 (1955); Administrative Law Treatise, ch. 15 (1958); A System of Judicial Notice Based on Fairness and Convenience, in Perspectives of Law 69 (1964).

The usual method of establishing adjudicative facts is through the introduction of evidence, ordinarily consisting of the testimony of witnesses. If particular facts are outside the area of reasonable controversy, this process is dispensed with as unnecessary. A high degree of indisputability is the essential prerequisite.

Legislative facts are quite different. As Professor Davis says:

"My opinion is that judge-made law would stop growing if judges, in thinking about questions of law and policy, were forbidden to take into account the facts they believe, as distinguished from facts which are 'clearly . . . within the domain of the indisputable.' Facts most needed in thinking about difficult problems of law and policy have a way of being outside the domain of the clearly indisputable." A System of Judicial Notice Based on Fairness and Convenience, *supra*, at 82.

An illustration is Hawkins v. United States, 358 U.S. 74, 79 S.Ct. 136, 3 L.Ed.2d 125 (1958), in which the Court refused to discard the common law rule that one spouse could not testify against the other, saying, "Adverse testimony given in criminal proceedings would, we think, be likely to destroy almost any marriage." This conclusion has a large intermixture of fact, but the factual aspect is scarcely "indisputable." *See* Hutchins and Slesinger, Some Observations on the Law of

Evidence—Family Relations, 13 Minn. L. Rev. 675 (1929). If the destructive effect of the giving of adverse testimony by a spouse is not indisputable, should the Court have refrained from considering it in the absence of supporting evidence?

"If the Model Code or the Uniform Rules had been applicable, the Court would have been barred from thinking about the essential factual ingredient of the problems before it, and such a result would be obviously intolerable. What the law needs at its growing points is more, not less, judicial thinking about the factual ingredients of problems of what the law ought to be, and the needed facts are seldom 'clearly' indisputable." Davis, *supra*, at 83.

Professor Morgan gave the following description of the methodology of determining domestic law:

"In determining the content or applicability of a rule of domestic law, the judge is unrestricted in his investigation and conclusion. He may reject the propositions of either party or of both parties. He may consult the sources of pertinent data to which they refer, or he may refuse to do so. He may make an independent search for persuasive data or rest content with what he has or what the parties present . . . . [T]he parties do no more than to assist; they control no part of the process." Morgan, Judicial Notice, 57 Harv.L.Rev. 269, 270–271 (1944).

This is the view which should govern judicial access to legislative facts. It renders inappropriate any limitation in the form of indisputability, any formal requirements of notice other than those already inherent in affording opportunity to hear and be heard and exchanging briefs, and any requirement of formal findings at any level. It should, however, leave open the possibility of introducing evidence through regular channels in appropriate situations. *See* Borden's Farm Products Co. v. Baldwin, 293 US 194, 55 S.Ct. 187, 79 L.Ed 281 (1934), where the cause was remanded for the taking of evidence as to the economic conditions and trade practices underlying the New York Milk Control Law.

Similar considerations govern the judicial use of non-adjudicative facts in ways other than formulating laws and rules. Thayer described them as a part of the judicial reasoning process.

"In conducting a process of judicial reasoning, as of other reasoning, not a step can be taken without assuming something which has not been proved; and the capacity to do this with competent judgment and efficiency, is imputed to judges and juries as part of their necessary mental outfit." Thayer, Preliminary Treatise on Evidence 279–280 (1898).

As Professor Davis points out, A System of Judicial Notice Based on Fairness and Convenience, in Perspectives of Law 69, 73 (1964), every case involves the use of hundreds or thousands of non-evidence facts. When a witness in an automobile accident case says "car," everyone, judge and jury included, furnishes, from non-evidence sources within himself, the supplementing information that the "car" is an automobile, not a railroad car, that it is self-propelled, probably by an internal combustion engine, that it may be assumed to have four wheels with pneumatic rubber tires, and so on. The judicial process cannot construct every case from scratch, like Descartes creating a world based on the postulate *Cogito, ergo sum*. These items could not possibly be introduced into evidence, and no one suggests that they be. Nor are they appropriate subjects for any formalized treatment of judicial notice of facts. *See* Levin and Levy, Persuading the Jury with Facts Not in Evidence: The Fiction-Science Spectrum, 105 U.Pa.L.Rev. 139 (1956).

Another aspect of what Thayer had in mind is the use of non-evidence facts to appraise or assess the adjudicative facts of the case. Pairs of cases from two jurisdictions illustrate this use and also the difference between non-evidence facts thus used and adjudicative facts. In People v. Strook, 347 Ill. 460, 179 NE 821 (1932), venue in Cook County had been held not established by testimony that the crime was committed at 7956 South Chicago Avenue, since judicial notice would not be taken that the address was in Chicago. However, the same court subsequently ruled that venue in Cook County was established by testimony that a crime occurred at 8900 South Anthony Avenue, since notice would be taken of the common practice of omitting the name of the city when speaking of local addresses, and the witness was testifying in Chicago. People v. Pride, 16 Ill.2d 82, 156 N.E.2d 551 (1951). And in Hughes v. Vestal, 264 N.C. 500, 142 S.E.2d 361 (1965), the Supreme Court of North Carolina disapproved the trial judge's admission in evidence of a state-published table of automobile stopping distances on the basis of judicial notice, though the court itself had referred to the same table in an earlier case in a "rhetorical and illustrative" way in determining that the defendant could not have stopped her car in time to avoid striking a child who suddenly appeared in the highway and that a nonsuit was properly granted. Ennis v. Dupree, 262 N.C. 224, 136 S.E.2d 702 (1964). *See also* Brown v. Hale, 263 NC 176, 139 S.E.2d 210 (1964); Clayton v. Rimmer, 262 N.C. 302, 136 S.E.2d 562 (1964). It is apparent that this use of non-evidence facts in evaluating the adjudicative facts of the case is not an appropriate subject for a formalized judicial notice treatment.

In view of these considerations, the regulation of judicial notice of facts by the present rule extends only to adjudicative facts.

What, then, are "adjudicative" facts? Davis refers to them as those "which relate to the parties," or more fully:

"When a court or an agency finds facts concerning the immediate parties—who did what, where, when, how, and with what motive or intent—the court or agency is performing an adjudicative function, and the facts are conveniently called adjudicative facts . . . .

"Stated in other terms, the adjudicative facts are those to which the law is applied in the process of adjudication. They are the facts that normally go to the jury in a jury case. They relate to the parties, their activities, their properties, their businesses." 2 Administrative Law Treatise 353.

Subdivision (b). With respect to judicial notice of adjudicative facts, the tradition has been one of caution in requiring that the matter be beyond reasonable controversy. This tradition of circumspection appears to be soundly based, and no reason to depart from it is apparent. As Professor Davis says:

"The reason we use trial-type procedure, I think, is that we make the practical judgment, on the basis of experience, that taking evidence, subject to cross-examination and rebuttal, is the best way to resolve controversies involving disputes of adjudicative facts, that is, facts pertaining to the parties. The reason we require a determination on the record is that we think fair procedure in resolving disputes of adjudicative facts calls for giving each party a chance to meet in the appropriate fashion the facts that come to the tribunal's attention, and the appropriate fashion for meeting disputed adjudicative facts includes rebuttal evidence, cross-examination, usually confrontation, and argument (either written or oral or both). The key to a fair trial is opportunity to use the appropriate weapons (rebuttal evidence, cross-examination, and argument) to meet adverse materials that come to the tribunal's attention." A System of Judicial Notice Based on Fairness and Convenience, in Perspectives of Law 69, 93 (1964).

The rule proceeds upon the theory that these considerations call for dispensing with traditional methods of proof only in clear cases. Compare Professor Davis' conclusion that judicial notice should be a matter of convenience, subject to requirements of procedural fairness. Id., 94.

This rule is consistent with Uniform Rule 9(1) and (2) which limit judicial notice of facts to those "so universally known that they cannot reasonably be the subject of dispute," those "so generally known or of such common notoriety within the territorial jurisdiction of the court that they cannot reasonably be the subject of dispute," those "capable of immediate and accurate determination by resort to easily accessible sources of indisputable accuracy." The traditional textbook treatment has included these general categories (matters of common knowledge, facts capable of verification), McCormick §§ 324, 325, and then has passed on into detailed treatment of such specific topics as facts relating to the personnel and records of the court, id. § 327, and other governmental facts, id. § 328. The California draftsmen, with a background of detailed statutory regulation of judicial notice, followed a somewhat similar pattern. California Evidence Code §§ 451, 452. The Uniform Rules, however, were drafted on the theory that these particular matters are included within the general categories and need no specific mention. This approach is followed in the present rule.

The phrase "propositions of generalized knowledge," found in Uniform Rule 9(1) and (2) is not included in the present rule. It was, it is believed, originally included in Model Code Rules 801 and 802 primarily in order to afford some minimum recognition to the right of the judge in his "legislative" capacity (not acting as the trier of fact) to take judicial notice of very limited categories of generalized knowledge. The limitations thus imposed have been discarded herein as undesirable, unworkable, and contrary to existing practice. What is left, then, to be considered, is the status of a "proposition of generalized knowledge" as an "adjudicative" fact to be noticed judicially and communicated by the judge to the jury. Thus viewed, it is considered to be lacking practical significance. While judges used judicial notice of "propositions of generalized knowledge" in a variety of situations: determining the validity and meaning of statutes, formulating common law rules, deciding whether evidence should be admitted, assessing the sufficiency and effect of evidence, all are essentially nonadjudicative in nature. When judicial notice is seen as a significant vehicle for progress in the law, these are the areas involved, particularly in developing fields of scientific knowledge. *See* McCormick 712. It is not believed that judges now instruct juries as to "propositions of generalized knowledge" derived from encyclopedias or other sources, or that they are likely to do so, or, indeed, that it is desirable that they do so. There is a vast difference between ruling on the basis of judicial notice that radar evidence of speed is admissible and explaining to the jury its principles and degree of accuracy, or between using a table of stopping distances of automobiles at various speeds in a judicial evaluation of testimony and telling the jury its precise application in the case. For cases raising doubt as to the propriety of the use of medical texts by lay triers of fact in passing on disability claims in administrative proceedings, *see* Sayers v. Gardner, 380 F2d 940 (6th Cir. 1967): Ross v. Gardner, 365 F2d 554 (6th Cir. 1966); Sosna v. Celebrezze, 234 F. Supp. 289 (ED Pa. 1964); Glendenning v. Ribicoff, 213 F Supp 301 (WD Mo. 1962).

Subdivisions (c) and (d). Under subdivision (c) the judge has a discretionary authority to take judicial notice, regardless of whether he is so requested by a party. The taking of judicial notice is mandatory, under subdivision (d), only when a party requests it and the necessary information is supplied. This scheme is believed to reflect existing practice. It is simple and workable. It avoids troublesome distinctions in the many situations in which the process of taking judicial notice is not recognized as such.

Compare Uniform Rule 9 making judicial notice of facts universally known mandatory without request, and making judicial notice of facts generally known in the jurisdiction or capable of determination by resort to accurate sources discretionary in the absence of request but mandatory if request is made and the information furnished. *But see Uniform* Rule 10(3), which directs the judge to decline to take judicial notice if available information fails to convince him that the matter falls clearly within Uniform Rule 9 or is insufficient to enable him to notice it judicially. Substantially the same approach is found in California Evidence Code §§ 451–453 and in New Jersey Evidence Rule 9. In contrast, the present rule treats alike all adjudicative facts which are subject to judicial notice.

Subdivision (e). Basic considerations of procedural fairness demand an opportunity to be heard on the propriety of taking judicial notice and the tenor of the matter noticed. The rule requires the granting of that opportunity upon request. No formal scheme of giving notice is provided. An adversely affected party may learn in advance that judicial notice is in contemplation, either by virtue of being served with a copy of a request by another party under subdivision (d) that judicial notice be taken, or through an advance indication by the judge. Or he may have no advance notice at all. The likelihood of the latter is enhanced by the frequent failure to recognize judicial notice as such. And in the absence of advance notice, a request made after the fact could not in fairness be considered untimely. See the provision for hearing on timely request in the Administrative Procedure Act, 5 USC § 556(e). *See also* Revised Model State Administrative Procedure Act (1961), 9C ULA § 10(4) (Supp 1967).

Subdivision (f). In accord with the usual view, judicial notice may be taken at any stage of the proceedings, whether in the trial court or on appeal. Uniform Rule 12; California Evidence Code § 459; Kansas Rules of Evidence § 60-412; New Jersey Evidence Rule 12; McCormick § 330, p. 712.

Subdivision (g). Much of the controversy about judicial notice has centered upon the question whether evidence should be admitted in disproof of facts of which judicial notice is taken.

The writers have been divided. Favoring admissibility are Thayer, Preliminary Treatise on Evidence 308 (1898); 9 Wigmore § 2567; Davis, A System of Judicial Notice Based on Fairness and Convenience, in Perspectives of Law, 69, 76–77 (1964). Opposing admissibility are Keeffe, Landis and Shaad, Sense and Nonsense about Judicial Notice, 2 Stan L Rev 664, 668 (1950); McNaughton, Judicial Notice—Excerpts Relating to the Morgan-Whitmore Controversy, 14 Vand L Rev 779 (1961); Morgan, Judicial Notice, 57 Harv L Rev 269, 279 (1944); McCormick 710–714. The Model Code and the Uniform Rules are predicated upon indisputability of judicially noticed facts.

The proponents of admitting evidence in disproof have concentrated largely upon legislative facts. Since the present rule deals only with judicial notice of adjudicative facts, arguments directed to legislative facts lose their relevancy.

Within its relatively narrow area of adjudicative facts, the rule contemplates there is to be no evidence before the jury in disproof. The judge instructs the jury to take judicially noticed facts as established. This position is justified by the undesirable effects of the opposite rule in limiting the rebutting party, though not his opponent, to admissible evidence, in defeating the reasons for judicial notice, and in affecting the substantive law to an extent and in ways largely unforeseeable. Ample protection and flexibility are afforded by the broad provision for opportunity to be heard on request, set forth in subdivision (e).

[The following paragraph accompanied only the March, 1969 Draft of Rule 201. *See* 46 FRD 161, 205 (1969). A different version of this paragraph accompanied the March, 1971 Draft, 51 FRD 315, 335 (1971) and the November, 1972 Draft, 56 FRD 183, 207 (1972). We set forth the 1969 version because the Congress restored essentially the 1969 draft of the provisions to which this paragraph of Notes refers.]

Criminal cases are treated somewhat differently in the rule. While matters falling within the common fund of information supposed to be possessed by jurors need not be proved, State v. Dunn, 221 Mo 530, 120 SW 1179 (1909), these are not, properly speaking, adjudicative facts but an aspect of legal reasoning. The considerations which underlie the general rule that a verdict cannot be directed against the accused in a criminal case seems to foreclose the judge's directing the jury on the basis of judicial notice to accept as conclusive any adjudicative facts in the case. State v. Main, 94 R.I. 338, 180 A.2d 814 (1962); State v. Lawrence, 120 Utah 323, 234 P2d 600 (1951). *Cf.* People v. Mayes, 113 Cal 618, 45 P 860 (1896); Ross v. United States, 374 F2d 97 (8th Cir. 1967). However, this view presents no obstacle to the judge's advising the jury as to a matter judicially noticed, if he instructs them that it need not be taken as conclusive.

REPORT OF THE HOUSE COMMITTEE ON THE JUDICIARY.

Rule 201(g) as received from the Supreme Court provided that when judicial notice of a fact is taken, the court shall instruct the jury to accept that fact as established. Being of the view that mandatory instruction to a jury in a criminal case to accept as conclusive any fact judicially noticed is inappropriate because contrary to the spirit of the Sixth Amendment right to a jury trial, the Committee adopted the 1969 Advisory Committee draft of this subsection, allowing a mandatory instruction in civil actions and proceedings and a discretionary instruction in criminal cases.

NOTE BY ADVISORY COMMITTEE ON JUDICIAL NOTICE OF LAW.

By rules effective July 1, 1966, the method of invoking the law of a foreign country is covered elsewhere. Rule 44.1 of the Federal Rules of Civil Procedure; Rule 26.1 of the Federal Rules of Criminal Procedure. These two new admirably designed rules are founded upon the assumption that the manner in which law is fed into the judicial process is never a proper concern of the rules of evidence but rather of the rules of procedure. The Advisory Committee on Evidence, believing that this assumption is entirely correct, proposes no evidence rule with respect to judicial notice of law, and suggests that those matters of law which, in addition to foreign-country law, have traditionally been treated as requiring pleading and proof and more recently as the subject of judicial notice be left to the Rules of Civil and Criminal Procedure.

NOTE BY FEDERAL JUDICIAL CENTER.

The Rule enacted by the Congress is the rule prescribed by the Supreme Court with the following changes: (1) In subdivisions (c) and (d) the words "judge or" before "court" were deleted. (2) Subdivision (g) as it is shown was substituted in place of, "The judge shall instruct the jury to accept as established any facts judicially noticed." The substituted language is from the 1969 Preliminary Draft, 46 F.R.D. 161, 195.

ARTICLE III.
PRESUMPTIONS IN CIVIL CASES

Rule 301. Presumptions in Civil Cases Generally

ADVISORY COMMITTEE NOTE TO THE 2011 AMENDMENT.

The language of Rule 301 has been amended as part of the restyling of the Evidence Rules to make them more easily understood and to make style and terminology consistent throughout the rules. These changes are intended to be stylistic only. There is no intent to change any result in any ruling on evidence admissibility.

ADVISORY COMMITTEE NOTE.

This rule governs presumptions generally. *See* Rule 302 for presumptions controlled by state law and Rule 303 for those against an accused in a criminal case.

Presumptions governed by this rule are given the effect of placing upon the opposing party the burden of establishing the nonexistence of the presumed fact, once the party invoking the presumption establishes the basic facts giving rise to it. The same considerations of fairness, policy, and probability which dictate the allocation of the burden of the various elements of a case as between the prima facie case of a plaintiff and affirmative defenses also underlie the creation of presumptions. These considerations are not satisfied by giving a lesser effect to presumptions. Morgan and Maguire, Looking Backward and Forward at Evidence, 50 Harv L Rev 909, 913 (1937); Morgan, Instructing the Jury upon Presumptions and Burden of Proof, 47 Harv L Rev 59, 82 (1933); Cleary, Presuming and Pleading: An Essay on Juristic Immaturity, 12 Stan L Rev 5 (1959).

The so-called "bursting bubble" theory, under which a presumption vanishes upon the introduction of evidence which would support a finding of the nonexistence of the presumed fact, even though not believed, is rejected as according presumptions too "slight and evanescent" an effect. Morgan and Maguire, *supra*, at p. 913.

In the opinion of the Advisory Committee, no constitutional infirmity attends this view of presumptions. In Mobile, J. & K. C. R. Co. v. Turnipseed, 219 US 35, 31 S Ct 136, 55 L Ed 78 (1910), the Court upheld a Mississippi statute which provided that in actions against railroads proof of injury inflicted by the running of trains should be prima facie evidence of negligence by the railroad. The injury in the case had resulted from a derailment. The opinion made the points (1) that the only effect of the statute was to impose on the railroad the duty of producing some evidence to the contrary, (2) that an inference may be supplied by law if there is a rational connection between the fact proved and the fact presumed, as long as the opposite party is not precluded from presenting his evidence to the contrary, and (3) that considerations of public policy arising from the character of the business justified the application in question. Nineteen years later, in Western & Atlantic R. Co. v. Henderson, 279 US 639, 49 S Ct 445, 73 L Ed 884 (1929), the Court overturned a Georgia statute making railroads liable for damages done by trains, unless the railroad made it appear that reasonable care had been used, the presumption being against the railroad. The declaration alleged the death of plaintiff's husband from a grade crossing collision, due to specified acts of negligence by defendant. The jury were instructed that proof of the injury raised a presumption of negligence; the burden shifted to the railroad to prove ordinary care; and unless it did so, they should find for plaintiff. The instruction was held erroneous in an opinion stating (1) that there was no rational connection between the mere fact of collision and negligence on the part of anyone, and (2) that the statute was different from that in *Turnipseed* in imposing a burden upon the railroad. The reader is left in a state of some confusion. Is the difference between a derailment and a grade crossing collision of no significance? Would the *Turnipseed* presumption have been bad if it had imposed a burden of persuasion on defendant, although that would in nowise have impaired its "rational connection"? If *Henderson* forbids imposing a burden of persuasion on defendants, what happens to affirmative defenses?

Two factors serve to explain *Henderson*. The first was that it was common ground that negligence was indispensable to liability. Plaintiff thought so, drafted her complaint accordingly, and relied upon the presumption. But how in logic could the same presumption establish her alternative grounds of negligence that the engineer was so blind he could not see decedent's truck and that he failed to stop after he saw it? Second, take away the basic assumption of no liability without fault, as *Turnipseed* intimated might be done ("considerations of public policy arising out of the character of the business"), and the structure of the decision in *Henderson* fails. No question of logic would have arisen if the statute had simply said: a prima facie case of liability is made by proof of injury by a train; lack of negligence is an affirmative defense, to be pleaded and proved as other affirmative defenses. The problem would be one of economic due process only. While it seems likely that the Supreme Court of 1929 would have voted that due process was denied, that result today would be unlikely. *See*, for example, the shift in the direction of absolute liability in the consumer cases. Prosser, The Assault upon the Citadel (Strict Liability to the Consumer), 69 Yale LJ 1099 (1960).

Any doubt as to the constitutional permissibility of a presumption imposing a burden of persuasion of the nonexistence of the presumed fact in civil cases is laid at rest by Dick v. New York Life Ins. Co., 359 US 437, 79 S Ct 921, 3 L Ed 2d 935 (1959). The Court unhesitatingly applied the North Dakota rule that the presumption against suicide imposed on defendant the burden of proving that the death of insured, under an accidental death clause, was due to suicide.

"Proof of coverage and of death by gunshot wound shifts the burden to the insurer to establish that the death of the insured was due to his suicide." 359 US at 443, 79 S Ct at 925.

"In a case like this one, North Dakota presumes that death was accidental and places on the insurer the burden of proving that death resulted from suicide." *Id.* at 446, 79 S Ct at 927.

The rational connection requirement survives in criminal cases, Tot v. United States, 319 US 463, 63 S Ct 1241, 87 L Ed 1519 (1943), because the Court has been unwilling to extend into that area the greater-includes-the-lesser theory of Ferry v. Ramsey, 277 US 88, 48 S Ct 443, 72 L Ed 796 (1928). In that case the Court sustained a Kansas statute under which bank directors were personally liable for deposits made with their assent and with knowledge of insolvency, and the fact of insolvency was prima facie evidence of assent and knowledge of insolvency. Mr. Justice Holmes pointed out that the state legislature could have made the directors personally liable to depositors in every case. Since the statute imposed a less stringent liability, "the thing to be considered is the result reached, not the possibly inartificial or clumsy way of reaching it." *Id.* at 94, 48 S Ct at 444. Mr. Justice Sutherland dissented: though the state could have created an absolute liability, it did not purport to do so; a rational connection was necessary, but lacking, between the liability created and the prima facie evidence of it: the result might be different if the basis of the presumption were being open for business.

The Sutherland view has prevailed in criminal cases by virtue of the higher standard of notice there required. The fiction that everyone is presumed to know the law is applied to the substantive law of crimes as an alternative to complete unenforceability. But the need does not extend to criminal evidence and procedure, and the fiction does not encompass them. "Rational connection" is not fictional or artificial, and so it is reasonable to suppose that Gainey should have known that his presence at the site of an illicit still could convict him of being connected with (carrying on) the business, United States v. Gainey, 380 U.S. 63, 85 S. Ct. 754, 13 L. Ed. 2d 658 (1965), but not that Romano should have known that his presence at a still could convict him of possessing it, United States v. Romano, 382 US 136, 86 S Ct 279, 15 L Ed 2d 210 (1965).

In his dissent in Gainey, Mr. Justice Black put it more artistically:

"It might be argued, although the Court does not so argue or hold, that Congress if it wished could make presence at a still a crime in itself, and so Congress should be free to create crimes which are called 'possession' and 'carrying on an illegal distillery business' but which are defined in such a way that unexplained presence is sufficient and indisputable evidence in all cases to support conviction for those offenses. *See* Ferry v. Ramsey, 277 US 88, 48 S Ct 443, 72 L Ed 796. Assuming for the sake of argument that Congress could make unexplained presence a criminal act, and ignoring also the refusal of this Court in other cases to uphold a statutory presumption on such a theory, *see* Heiner v. Donnan, 285 US 312, 52 S Ct 358, 76 L Ed 772, there is no indication here that Congress intended to adopt such a misleading method of draftsmanship, nor in my judgment could the statutory provisions if so construed escape condemnation for vagueness, under the principles applied in Lanzetta v. New Jersey, 306 US

451, 59 S Ct 618, 83 L Ed 888, and many other cases." 380 US at 84, n 12, 85 S Ct at 766.

And the majority opinion in *Romano* agreed with him:

"It may be, of course, that Congress has the power to make presence at an illegal still a punishable crime, but we find no clear indication that it intended to so exercise this power. The crime remains possession, not presence, and with all due deference to the judgment of Congress, the former may not constitutionally be inferred from the latter." 382 US at 144, 86 S Ct at 284.

The rule does not spell out the procedural aspects of its application. Questions as to when the evidence warrants submission of a presumption and what instructions are proper under varying states of fact are believed to present no particular difficulties.

REPORT OF THE HOUSE COMMITTEE ON THE JUDICIARY.

[The following Report refers to the version of Rule 301 originally passed by the House of Representatives. The enacted version of Rule 301, set forth prior to the Advisory Committee's Note above, differs significantly.]

Rule 301 as submitted by the Supreme Court provided that in all cases a presumption imposes on the party against whom it is directed the burden of proving that the nonexistence of the presumed fact is more probable than its existence. The Committee limited the scope of Rule 301 to "civil actions and proceedings" to effectuate its decision not to deal with the question of presumptions in criminal cases. (*See* note on Rule 303 in discussion of Rules deleted.) With respect to the weight to be given a presumption in a civil case, the Committee agreed with the judgment implicit in the Court's version that the so-called "bursting bubble" theory of presumptions, whereby a presumption vanishes upon the appearance of any contradicting evidence by the other party, gives to presumptions too slight an effect. On the other hand, the Committee believed that the Rule proposed by the Court, whereby a presumption permanently alters the burden of persuasion, no matter how much contradicting evidence is introduced—a view shared by only a few courts—lends too great a force to presumptions. Accordingly, the Committee amended the Rule to adopt an intermediate position under which a presumption does not vanish upon the introduction of contradicting evidence, and does not change the burden of persuasion; instead it is merely deemed sufficient evidence of the fact presumed, to be considered by the jury or other finder of fact.

REPORT OF THE SENATE COMMITTEE ON THE JUDICIARY.

[The following Report refers to the version of Rule 301 which the Congress ultimately enacted.]

This rule governs presumptions in civil cases generally. Rule 302 provides for presumptions in cases controlled by State law.

As submitted by the Supreme Court, presumptions governed by this rule were given the effect of placing upon the opposing party the burden of establishing the nonexistence of the presumed fact, once the party invoking the presumption established the basic facts giving rise to it.

Instead of imposing a burden of persuasion on the party against whom the presumption is directed, the House adopted a provision which shifted the burden of going forward with the evidence. They further provided that "even though met with contradicting evidence, a presumption is sufficient evidence of the fact presumed, to be considered by the trier of fact." The effect of the amendment is that presumptions are to be treated as evidence.

The committee feels the House amendment is ill-advised. As the joint committees (the Standing Committee on Practice and Procedure of the Judicial Conference and the Advisory Committee on the Rules of Evidence) stated: "Presumptions are not evidence, but ways of dealing with evidence." This treatment requires juries to perform the task of considering "as evidence" facts upon which they have no direct evidence and which may confuse them in performance of their duties. California had a rule much like that contained in the House amendment. It was sharply criticized by Justice Traynor in Speck v. Sarcer and was repealed after 93 troublesome years.

Professor McCormick gives a concise and compelling critique of the presumption as evidence rule:

*   *   *   *   *

Another solution, formerly more popular than now, is to instruct the jury that the presumption is 'evidence', to be weighed and considered with the testimony in the case. This avoids the danger that the jury may infer that the presumption is conclusive, but it probably means little to the jury, and certainly runs counter to accepted theories of the nature of evidence.

For these reasons the committee has deleted that provision of the House-passed rule that treats presumptions as evidence. The effect of the rule as adopted by the committee is to make clear that while evidence of facts giving rise to a presumption shifts the burden of coming forward with evidence to rebut or meet the presumption, it does not shift the burden of persuasion on the existence of the presumed facts. The burden of persuasion remains on the party to whom it is allocated under the rules governing the allocation in the first instance.

The court may instruct the jury that they may infer the existence of the presumed fact from proof of the basic facts giving rise to the presumption. However, it would be inappropriate under this rule to instruct the jury that the inference they are to draw is conclusive.

REPORT OF THE HOUSE/SENATE CONFERENCE COMMITTEE.

[*The "senate amendment" to which the following Report refers, embodies Rule 301 in the form which Congress ultimately enacted.*]

The House bill provides that a presumption in civil actions and proceedings shifts to the party against whom it is directed the burden of going forward with evidence to meet or rebut it. Even though evidence contradicting the presumption is offered, a presumption is considered sufficient evidence of the presumed fact to be considered by the jury. The Senate amendment provides that a presumption shifts to the party against whom it is directed the burden of going forward with evidence to meet or rebut the presumption, but it does not shift to that party the burden of persuasion on the existence of the presumed fact.

Under the Senate amendment, a presumption is sufficient to get a party past an adverse party's motion to dismiss made at the end of his case-in-chief. If the adverse party offers no evidence contradicting the presumed fact, the court will instruct the jury that if it finds the basic facts, it may presume the existence of the presumed fact. If the adverse party does offer evidence contradicting the presumed fact, the court cannot instruct the jury that it may *presume* the existence of the presumed fact from proof of the basic facts. The court may, however, instruct the jury that it may infer the existence of the presumed fact from proof of the basic facts.

The Conference adopts the Senate amendment.

NOTE BY FEDERAL JUDICIAL CENTER.

The bill passed by the House substituted a substantially different Rule in place of that prescribed by the Supreme Court. The Senate bill substituted yet a further version, which was accepted by the House, was enacted by the Congress, and is the current Rule.

Rule 302. Applying State Law to Presumptions in Civil Cases

ADVISORY COMMITTEE NOTE TO THE 2011 AMENDMENT.

The language of Rule 302 has been amended as part of the restyling of the Evidence Rules to make them more easily understood and to make style and terminology consistent throughout the rules. These changes are intended to be stylistic only. There is no intent to change any result in any ruling on evidence admissibility.

ADVISORY COMMITTEE NOTE.

A series of Supreme Court decisions in diversity cases leaves no doubt of the relevance of Erie Railroad Co. v. Tompkins, 304 US 64, 58 S Ct 817, 82 L Ed 1188 (1938), to questions of burden of proof. These decisions are Cities Service Oil Co. v. Dunlap, 308 US 208, 60 S Ct 201, 84 L Ed 196 (1939), Palmer v. Hoffman, 318 US 109, 63 S Ct 477, 87 L Ed 645 (1943), and Dick v. New York Life Ins. Co., 359 US 437, 79 S Ct 921, 3 L Ed 2d 935 (1959). They involved burden of proof, respectively, as to status as bona fide purchaser, contributory negligence, and nonaccidental death (suicide) of an insured. In each instance the state rule was held to be applicable. It does not follow, however, that all presumptions in diversity cases are governed by state law. In each case cited, the burden of proof questioned had to do with a substantive element of the claim or defense. Application of the state law is called for only when the presumption operates upon such an element. Accordingly the rule does not apply state law when the presumption operates upon a lesser aspect of the case, i.e. "tactical" presumptions.

The situations in which the state law is applied have been tagged for convenience in the preceding discussion as "diversity cases." The designation is not a completely accurate one since Erie applies to any claim or issue having its source in state law, regardless of the basis of federal jurisdiction, and does not apply to a federal claim or issue, even though jurisdiction is based on diversity. Vestal, Erie R. R. v. Tompkins: A Projection, 48 Iowa L Rev 248, 257 (1963); Hart and Wechsler, The Federal Courts and the Federal System, 697 (1953); 1A Moore, Federal Practice 0.305[3] (2d ed., 1965); Wright, Federal Courts, 217–218 (1963). Hence the rule employs, as appropriately descriptive, the phrase "as to which state law supplies the rule of decision." *See* ALI Study of the Division of Jurisdiction Between State and Federal Courts, § 2344(c), p. 40, PFD No. 1 (1965).

NOTE BY FEDERAL JUDICIAL CENTER.

Congress merely added the phrase "and proceedings" after "civil actions." No substantive change was involved. The Rule enacted by the Congress is the Rule prescribed by the Supreme Court, as amended.

ARTICLE IV.
RELEVANCE AND ITS LIMITS

Rule 401. Test for Relevant Evidence

ADVISORY COMMITTEE NOTE TO THE 2011 AMENDMENT.

The language of Rule 401 has been amended as part of the restyling of the Evidence Rules to make them more easily understood and to make style and terminology consistent throughout the rules. These changes are intended to be stylistic only. There is no intent to change any result in any ruling on evidence admissibility.

ADVISORY COMMITTEE NOTE.

Problems of relevancy call for an answer to the question whether an item of evidence, when tested by the processes of legal reasoning, possesses sufficient probative value to justify receiving it in evidence. Thus, assessment of the probative value of evidence that a person purchased a revolver shortly prior to a fatal shooting with which he is charged is a matter of analysis and reasoning.

The variety of relevancy problems is coextensive with the ingenuity of counsel in using circumstantial evidence as a means of proof. An enormous number of cases fall in no set pattern, and this rule is designed as a guide for handling them. On the other hand, some situations recur with sufficient frequency to create patterns susceptible of treatment by specific rules. Rule 404 and those following it are of that variety; they also serve as illustrations of the application of the present rule as limited by the exclusionary principles of Rule 403.

Passing mention should be made of so-called "conditional" relevancy. Morgan, Basic Problems of Evidence 45–46 (1962). In this situation, probative value depends not only upon satisfying the basic requirement of relevancy as described above but also upon the existence of some matter of fact. For example, if evidence of a spoken statement is relied upon to prove notice, probative value is lacking unless the person sought to be charged heard the statement. The problem is one of fact, and the only rules needed are for the purpose of determining the respective functions of judge and jury. *See* Rules 101(b) and 901. The discussion which follows in the present note is concerned with relevancy generally, not with any particular problem of conditional relevancy.

Relevancy is not an inherent characteristic of any item of evidence but exists only as a relation between an item of evidence and a matter properly provable in the case. Does the item of evidence tend to prove the matter sought to be proved? Whether the relationship exists depends upon principles evolved by experience or science, applied logically to the situation at hand. James, Relevancy, Probability and the Law, 29 Calif.L.Rev. 689, 696, n. 15 (1911), in Selected Writings on Evidence and Trial 610, 615, n. 15 (Fryer ed. 1957). The rule summarizes this relationship as a "tendency to make the existence" of the fact to be proved "more probable or less probable." Compare Uniform Rule 1(2) which states the crux of relevancy as "a tendency in reason," thus perhaps emphasizing unduly the logical process and ignoring the need to draw upon experience or science to validate the general principle upon which relevancy in a particular situation depends.

The standard of probability under the rule is "more . . . probable than it would be without the evidence." Any more stringent requirement is unworkable and unrealistic. As McCormick § 152, p. 317, says, "A brick is not a wall," or, as Falknor, Extrinsic Policies Affecting Admissibility, 10 Rutgers L. Rev. 574, 576 (1956), quotes Professor

McBaine, ". . . [I]t is not to be supposed that every witness can make a home run." Dealing with probability in the language of the rule has the added virtue of avoiding confusion between questions of admissibility and questions of the sufficiency of the evidence.

The rule uses the phrase "fact that is of consequence to the determination of the action" to describe the kind of fact to which proof may properly be directed. The language is that of California Evidence Code § 210, it has the advantage of avoiding the loosely used and ambiguous word "material." Tentative Recommendation and a Study Relating to the Uniform Rules of Evidence (Art. I, General Provisions), Cal. Law Revision Comm'n, Rep., Rec. & Studies, 10–11 (1964). The fact to be proved may be ultimate, intermediate, or evidentiary; it matters not, so long as it is of consequence in the determination of the action. *Cf.* Uniform Rule 1(2) which requires that the evidence relate to a "material" fact.

The fact to which the evidence is directed need not be in dispute. While situations will arise which call for the exclusion of evidence offered to prove a point conceded by the opponent, the ruling should be made on the basis of such considerations as waste of time and undue prejudice (*see* Rule 403), rather than under any general requirement that evidence is admissible only if directed to matters in dispute. Evidence which is essentially background in nature can scarcely be said to involve disputed matter, yet it is universally offered and admitted as an aid to understanding. Charts, photographs, views of real estate, murder weapons, and many other items of evidence fall in this category. A rule limiting admissibility to evidence directed to a controversial point would invite the exclusion of this helpful evidence, or at least the raising of endless questions over its admission. *Cf.* California Evidence Code § 210, defining relevant evidence in terms of tendency to prove a disputed fact.

NOTE BY FEDERAL JUDICIAL CENTER.

The Rule enacted by the Congress is the Rule prescribed by the Supreme Court without change. Congress made no change in Rule 401; it was not the subject of floor debate. No witnesses at the Hearings before the Special Subcommittee on Criminal Justice of the Committee on the Judiciary expressed any dissatisfaction with the Rule. The Senate Hearings were also free of criticism.

Rule 402. General Admissibility of Relevant Evidence

ADVISORY COMMITTEE NOTE TO THE 2011 AMENDMENT.

The language of Rule 402 has been amended as part of the restyling of the Evidence Rules to make them more easily understood and to make style and terminology consistent throughout the rules. These changes are intended to be stylistic only. There is no intent to change

any result in any ruling on evidence admissibility.

ADVISORY COMMITTEE NOTE.

The provisions that all relevant evidence is admissible, with certain exceptions, and that evidence which is not relevant is not admissible are "a presupposition involved in the very conception of a rational system of evidence." Thayer, Preliminary Treatise on Evidence 264 (1898). They constitute the foundation upon which the structure of admission and exclusion rests. For similar provisions *see* California Evidence Code §§ 350, 351. Provisions that all relevant evidence is admissible are found in Uniform Rule 7(f); Kansas Code of Civil Procedure § 60-407(f); and New Jersey Evidence Rule 7(f); but the exclusion of evidence which is not relevant is left to implication.

Not all relevant evidence is admissible. The exclusion of relevant evidence occurs in a variety of situations and may be called for by these rules, by the Rules of Civil and Criminal Procedure, by Bankruptcy Rules, by Act of Congress, or by constitutional considerations.

Succeeding rules in the present article, in response to the demands of particular policies, require the exclusion of evidence despite its relevancy. In addition, Article V recognizes a number of privileges; Article VI imposes limitations upon witnesses and the manner of dealing with them; Article VII specifies requirements with respect to opinions and expert testimony; Article VIII excludes hearsay not falling within an exception; Article IX spells out the handling of authentication and identification; and Article X restricts the manner of proving the contents of writings and recordings.

The Rules of Civil and Criminal Procedure in some instances require the exclusion of relevant evidence. For example, Rules 30(b) and 32(a)(3) of the Rules of Civil Procedure, by imposing requirements of notice and unavailability of the deponent, place limits on the use of relevant depositions. Similarly, Rule 15 of the Rules of Criminal Procedure restricts the use of depositions in criminal cases, even though relevant. And the effective enforcement of the command, originally statutory and now found in Rule 5(a) of the Rules of Criminal Procedure, that an arrested person be taken without unnecessary delay before a commissioner or other similar officer is held to require the exclusion of statements elicited during detention in violation thereof. Mallory v. United States, 354 US 449, 77 S Ct 1356, 1 L Ed 2d 1479 (1957); 18 U.S.C. § 3501(c).

While congressional enactments in the field of evidence have generally tended to expand admissibility beyond the scope of the common law rules, in some particular situations they have restricted the admissibility of relevant evidence. Most of this legislation has consisted of the formulation of a privilege or of a prohibition against disclosure.

8 U.S.C. § 1202(f), records of refusal of visas or permits to enter United States confidential, subject to discretion of Secretary of State to make available to court upon certification of need; 10 U.S.C. § 3693, replacement certificate of honorable discharge from Army not admissible in evidence; 10 U.S.C. § 8693, same as to Air Force; 11 U.S.C. § 25(a) (10), testimony given by bankrupt on his examination not admissible in criminal proceedings against him, except that given in hearing upon objection to discharge; 11 U.S.C. § 205(a), railroad reorganization petition, if dismissed, not admissible in evidence; 11 U.S.C. § 403(a), list of creditors filed with municipal composition plan not an admission; 13 U.S.C. § 9 (a), census information confidential, retained copies of reports privileged; 47 U.S.C. § 605, interception and divulgence of wire or radio communications prohibited unless authorized by sender. These statutory provisions would remain undisturbed by the rules.

The rule recognizes but makes no attempt to spell out the constitutional considerations which impose basic limitations upon the admissibility of relevant evidence. Examples are evidence obtained by unlawful search and seizure, Weeks v. United States, 232 US 383, 34 S Ct 341, 58 L Ed 652 (1914); Katz v. United States, 389 US 347, 88 S Ct 507, 19 L Ed 2d 576 (1967); incriminating statement elicited from an accused in violation of right to counsel, Massiah v. United States, 377 US 201, 84 S Ct 1199, 12 L Ed 2d 246 (1964).

REPORT OF THE HOUSE COMMITTEE ON THE JUDICIARY.

Rule 402 as submitted to the Congress contained the phrase "or by other rules adopted by the Supreme Court." To accommodate the view that the Congress should not appear to acquiesce in the Court's judgment that it has authority under the existing Rules Enabling Acts to promulgate Rules of Evidence, the Committee amended the above phrase to read "or by other rules prescribed by the Supreme Court pursuant to statutory authority" in this and other Rules where the reference appears.

NOTE BY FEDERAL JUDICIAL CENTER.

The Rule enacted by the Congress is the Rule prescribed by the Supreme Court, with the first sentence amended by substituting "prescribed" in place of "adopted," and by adding at the end thereof the phrase "pursuant to statutory authority."

Rule 403. Excluding Relevant Evidence for Prejudice, Confusion, Waste of Time, or Other Reasons

ADVISORY COMMITTEE NOTE TO THE 2011 AMENDMENT.

The language of Rule 403 has been amended as part of the restyling of the Evidence Rules to make them more easily understood and to

make style and terminology consistent throughout the rules. These changes are intended to be stylistic only. There is no intent to change any result in any ruling on evidence admissibility.

ADVISORY COMMITTEE NOTE.

The case law recognizes that certain circumstances call for the exclusion of evidence which is of unquestioned relevance. These circumstances entail risks which range all the way from inducing decision on a purely emotional basis, at one extreme, to nothing more harmful than merely wasting time, at the other extreme. Situations in this area call for balancing the probative value of and need for the evidence against the harm likely to result from its admission. Slough, Relevancy Unraveled, 5 Kan.L.Rev. 1, 12–15 (1956); Trautman, Logical or Legal Relevancy—A Conflict in Theory, 5 Van.L.Rev. 385, 392 (1952); McCormick § 152, pp. 319–321. The rules which follow in this Article are concrete applications evolved for particular situations. However, they reflect the policies underlying the present rule, which is designed as a guide for the handling of situations for which no specific rules have been formulated.

Exclusion for risk of unfair prejudice, confusion of issues, misleading the jury, or waste of time, all find ample support in the authorities. "Unfair prejudice" within its context means an undue tendency to suggest decision on an improper basis, commonly, though not necessarily, an emotional one.

The rule does not enumerate surprise as a ground for exclusion, in this respect following Wigmore's view of the common law. 6 Wigmore § 1849. *Cf.* McCormick § 152, p. 320, n. 29, listing unfair surprise as a ground for exclusion but stating that it is usually "coupled with the danger of prejudice and confusion of issues." While Uniform Rule 45 incorporates surprise as a ground and is followed in Kansas Code of Civil Procedure § 60-445, surprise is not included in California Evidence Code § 352 or New Jersey Rule 4, though both the latter otherwise substantially embody Uniform Rule 45. While it can scarcely be doubted that claims of unfair surprise may still be justified despite procedural requirements of notice and instrumentalities of discovery, the granting of a continuance is a more appropriate remedy than exclusion of the evidence. Tentative Recommendation and a Study Relating to the Uniform Rules of Evidence (Art. VI, Extrinsic Policies Affecting Admissibility), Cal. Law Revision Comm'n, Rep., Rec. & Studies, 612 (1964). Moreover, the impact of a rule excluding evidence on the ground of surprise would be difficult to estimate.

In reaching a decision whether to exclude on grounds of unfair prejudice, consideration should be given to the probable effectiveness or lack of effectiveness of a limiting instruction. *See* Rule 106 and

Advisory Committee Note thereunder. The availability of other means of proof may also be an appropriate factor.

NOTE BY FEDERAL JUDICIAL CENTER.

The Rule enacted by the Congress is the Rule prescribed by the Supreme Court without change.

Rule 404. Character Evidence; Crimes or Other Acts

ADVISORY COMMITTEE NOTE TO THE 2011 AMENDMENT.

The language of Rule 404 has been amended as part of the restyling of the Evidence Rules to make them more easily understood and to make style and terminology consistent throughout the rules. These changes are intended to be stylistic only. There is no intent to change any result in any ruling on evidence admissibility.

ADVISORY COMMITTEE NOTE.

Subdivision (a). This subdivision deals with the basic question whether character evidence should be admitted. Once the admissibility of character evidence in some form is established under this rule, reference must then be made to Rule 405, which follows, in order to determine the appropriate method of proof. If the character is that of a witness, *see* Rules 608 and 609 for methods of proof.

Character questions arise in two fundamentally different ways. (1) Character may itself be an element of a crime, claim, or defense. A situation of this kind is commonly referred to as "character in issue." Illustrations are: the chastity of the victim under a statute specifying her chastity as an element of the crime of seduction, or the competency of the driver in an action for negligently entrusting a motor vehicle to an incompetent driver. No problem of the general relevancy of character evidence is involved, and the present rule therefore has no provision on the subject. The only question relates to allowable methods of proof, as to which *see* Rule 405, immediately following. (2) Character evidence is susceptible of being used for the purpose of suggesting an inference that the person acted on the occasion in question consistently with his character. This use of character is often described as "circumstantial." Illustrations are: evidence of a violent disposition to prove that the person was the aggressor in an affray, or evidence of honesty in disproof of a charge of theft. This circumstantial use of character evidence raises questions of relevancy as well as questions of allowable methods of proof.

In most jurisdictions today, the circumstantial use of character is rejected but with important exceptions: (1) an accused may introduce pertinent evidence of good character (often misleadingly described as "putting his character in issue"), in which event the prosecution may rebut with evidence of bad character; (2) an accused may introduce pertinent evidence of the character of the victim, as in support of a claim of self-defense to a charge of homicide or consent in a case of rape, and the prosecution may introduce similar evidence in rebuttal of the character evidence, or, in a homicide case, to rebut a claim that deceased was the first aggressor, however proved; and (3) the character of a witness may be gone into as bearing on his credibility. McCormick §§ 155–161. This pattern is incorporated in the rule. While its basis lies more in history and experience than in logic an underlying justification can fairly be found in terms of the relative presence and absence of prejudice in the various situations. Falknor, Extrinsic Policies Affecting Admissibility, 10 Rutgers L. Rev. 574, 584 (1956); McCormick § 157. In any event, the criminal rule is so deeply imbedded in our jurisprudence as to assume almost constitutional proportions and to override doubts of the basic relevancy of the evidence.

The limitation to pertinent traits of character, rather than character generally, in paragraphs (1) and (2) is in accordance with the prevailing view. McCormick § 158, p. 334. A similar provision in Rule 608, to which reference is made in paragraph (3), limits character evidence respecting witnesses to the trait of truthfulness or untruthfulness.

The argument is made that circumstantial use of character ought to be allowed in civil cases to the same extent as in criminal cases, i.e. evidence of good (nonprejudicial) character would be admissible in the first instance, subject to rebuttal by evidence of bad character. Falknor, Extrinsic Policies Affecting Admissibility, 10 Rutgers L. Rev. 574, 581–583 (1956); Tentative Recommendation and a Study Relating to the Uniform Rules of Evidence (Art. VI. Extrinsic Policies Affecting Admissibility), Cal. Law Revision Comm'n, Rep., Rec. & Studies, 657–658 (1964). Uniform Rule 47 goes farther, in that it assumes that character evidence in general satisfies the conditions of relevancy, except as provided in Uniform Rule 48. The difficulty with expanding the use of character evidence in civil cases is set forth by the California Law Revision Commission in its ultimate rejection of Uniform Rule 47, id., 615:

"Character evidence is of slight probative value and may be very prejudicial. It tends to distract the trier of fact from the main question of what actually happened on the particular occasion. It subtly permits the trier of fact to reward the good man and to punish the bad man because of their respective characters despite what the evidence in the case shows actually happened."

Much of the force of the position of those favoring greater use of character evidence in civil cases is dissipated by their support of Uniform Rule 48 which excludes the evidence in negligence cases, where it could be expected to achieve its maximum usefulness.

Moreover, expanding concepts of "character," which seem of necessity to extend into such areas as psychiatric evaluation and psychological testing, coupled with expanded admissibility, would open up such vistas of mental examinations as caused the Court concern in Schlagenhauf v. Holder, 379 U.S. 104, 85 S.Ct. 234, 13 L.Ed.2d 152 (1964). It is believed that those espousing change have not met the burden of persuasion.

Notes of Advisory Committee on 2000 amendments. Rule 404(a)(1) has been amended to provide that when the accused attacks the character of an alleged victim under subdivision (a)(2) of this Rule, the door is opened to an attack on the same character trait of the accused. Current law does not allow the government to introduce negative character evidence as to the accused unless the accused introduces evidence of good character. *See, e.g.,* United States v. Fountain, 768 F.2d 790 (7th Cir. 1985) (when the accused offers proof of self-defense, this permits proof of the alleged victim's character trait for peacefulness, but it does not permit proof of the accused's character trait for violence).

The amendment makes clear that the accused cannot attack the alleged victim's character and yet remain shielded from the disclosure of equally relevant evidence concerning the same character trait of the accused. For example, in a murder case with a claim of self-defense, the accused, to bolster this defense, might offer evidence of the alleged victim's violent disposition. If the government has evidence that the accused has a violent character, but is not allowed to offer this evidence as part of its rebuttal, the jury has only part of the information it needs for an informed assessment of the probabilities as to who was the initial aggressor. This may be the case even if evidence of the accused's prior violent acts is admitted under Rule 404(b), because such evidence can be admitted only for limited purposes and not to show action in conformity with the accused's character on a specific occasion. Thus, the amendment is designed to permit a more balanced presentation of character evidence when an accused chooses to attack the character of the alleged victim.

The amendment does not affect the admissibility of evidence of specific acts of uncharged misconduct offered for a purpose other than proving character under Rule 404(b). Nor does it affect the standards for proof of character by evidence of other sexual behavior or sexual offenses under Rules 412–415. By its placement in Rule 404(a)(1), the amendment covers only proof of character by way of reputation or opinion.

The amendment does not permit proof of the accused's character if the accused merely uses character evidence for a purpose other than to prove the alleged victim's propensity to act in a certain way. *See* United States v. Burks, 470 F.2d 432, 434–5 (D.C. Cir. 1972) (evidence of the alleged victim's violent character, when known by the accused, was admissible "on the issue of whether or not the defendant reasonably feared he was in danger of imminent great bodily harm"). Finally, the amendment does not permit proof of the accused's character when the accused attacks the alleged victim's character as a witness under Rule 608 or 609.

The term "alleged" is inserted before each reference to "victim" in the Rule, in order to provide consistency with Evidence Rule 412.

Subdivision (b) deals with a specialized but important application of the general rule excluding circumstantial use of character evidence. Consistently with that rule, evidence of other crimes, wrongs, or acts is not admissible to prove character as a basis for suggesting the inference that conduct on a particular occasion was in conformity with it. However, the evidence may be offered for another purpose, such as proof of motive, opportunity, and so on, which does not fall within the prohibition. In this situation the rule does not require that the evidence be excluded. No mechanical solution is offered. The determination must be made whether the danger of undue prejudice outweighs the probative value of the evidence in view of the availability of other means of proof and other factors appropriate for making decisions of this kind under Rule 403. Slough and Knightly, Other Vices, Other Crimes, 41 Iowa L. Rev. 325 (1956).

REPORT OF THE HOUSE COMMITTEE ON THE JUDICIARY.

Rule 404(b)

The second sentence of Rule 404(b) as submitted to the Congress began with the words "This subdivision does not exclude the evidence when offered." The Committee amended this language to read "It may, however, be admissible," the words used in the 1971 Advisory Committee draft, on the ground that this formulation properly placed greater emphasis on admissibility than did the final Court version.

REPORT OF THE SENATE COMMITTEE ON THE JUDICIARY.

Rule 404(b). Character Evidence Not Admissible To Prove Conduct: Other crimes, wrongs, or acts

This rule provides that evidence of other crimes, wrongs, or acts is not admissible to prove character but may be admissible for other specified purposes such as proof of motive.

Although your committee sees no necessity in amending the rule itself, it anticipates that the use of the discretionary word "may" with respect to the admissibility of evidence of crimes, wrongs, or acts is not intended to confer any arbitrary discretion on the trial judge. Rather, it is anticipated that with respect to permissible uses for such evidence, the trial judge may exclude it only on the basis of those considerations set forth in Rule 403, i.e. prejudice, confusion or waste of time.

NOTE BY FEDERAL JUDICIAL CENTER.

The Rule enacted by the Congress is the Rule prescribed by the Supreme Court, with the second sentence of subdivision (b) amended by substituting "It may, however, be admissible" in place of "This subdivision does not exclude the evidence when offered."

ADVISORY COMMITTEE NOTE TO 1991 AMENDMENT.

Rule 404(b) has emerged as one of the most cited Rules in the Rules of Evidence. And in many criminal cases evidence of an accused's extrinsic acts is viewed as an important asset in the prosecution's case against an accused. Although there are a few reported decisions on use of such evidence by the defense, *see, e.g.*, United States v. McClure, 546 F.2d 670 (5th Cir. 1990) (acts of informant offered in entrapment defense), the overwhelming number of cases involve introduction of that evidence by the prosecution.

The amendment to Rule 404(b) adds a pretrial notice requirement in criminal cases and is intended to reduce surprise and promote early resolution on the issue of admissibility. The notice requirement thus places Rule 404(b) in the mainstream with notice and disclosure provisions in other rules of evidence. *See, e.g.*, Rule 412 (written motion of intent to offer conviction older than 10 years), Rule 803(24) and 804(b)(5) (notice of intent to use residual hearsay exceptions).

The Rule expects that counsel for both the defense and the prosecution will submit the necessary request and information in a reasonable and timely fashion. Other than requiring pretrial notice, no specific time limits are stated in recognition that what constitutes a reasonable request or disclosure will depend largely on the circumstances of each case. *Compare* Fla. Stat. Ann. § 90.404(2)(b) (notice must be given at least 10 days before trial) *with* Tex. R. Evid. 404(b) (no time limit).

Likewise, no specific form of notice is required. The Committee considered and rejected a requirement that the notice satisfy the particularity requirements normally required of language used in a charging instrument. *Cf.* Fla. Stat. Ann. § 90.404(2)(b) (written disclosure must describe uncharged misconduct with particularity required of an indictment or information). Instead, the Committee opted for a generalized notice provision which requires the prosecution to apprise the defense of the general nature of the evidence of extrinsic acts. The Committee does not intend that the amendment will supersede other rules of admissibility or disclosure, such as the Jencks Act, 18 U.S.C. § 3500, *et seq.* nor require the prosecution to disclose directly or indirectly the names and addresses of its witnesses, something it is currently not required to do under Federal Rule of Criminal Procedure 16.

The amendment requires the prosecution to provide notice, regardless of how it intends to use the extrinsic act evidence at trial, i.e., during its case-in-chief, for impeachment, or for possible rebuttal. The court in its discretion may, under the facts, decide that the particular request or notice was not reasonable, either because of the lack of timeliness or completeness. Because the notice requirement serves as condition precedent to admissibility of 404(b) evidence, the offered evidence is inadmissible if the court decides that the notice requirement has not been met.

Nothing in the amendment precludes the court from requiring the government to provide it with an opportunity to rule *in limine* on 404(b) evidence before it is offered or even mentioned during trial. When ruling *in limine*, the court may require the government to disclose to it the specifics of such evidence which the court must consider in determining admissibility.

The amendment does not extend to evidence of acts which are "intrinsic" to the charged offense, *see* United States v. Williams, 900 F.2d 823 (5th Cir. 1990) (noting distinction between 404(b) evidence and intrinsic offense evidence). Nor is the amendment intended to redefine what evidence would otherwise be admissible under Rule 404(b). Finally, the Committee does not intend through the amendment to affect the role of the court and the jury in considering such evidence. *See* Huddleston v. United States, 485 U.S. 681, 108 S.Ct. 1496 (1988).

ADVISORY COMMITTEE NOTE TO PROPOSED 1995 AMENDMENT.

The Committee has redrafted Rules 413, 414 and 415 which the Violent Crime Control and Law Enforcement Act of 1994 conditionally added to the Federal Rules of Evidence.* These modifications do not change the substance of the congressional enactment. The changes were made in order to integrate the provisions both substantively and stylistically with the existing Rules of Evidence; to illuminate the intent expressed by the principal drafters of the measure; to clarify drafting ambiguities that might necessitate considerable judicial attention if they remained unresolved; and to eliminate possible constitutional infirmities.

The Committee placed the new provisions in Rule 404 because this rule governs the admissibility of character evidence. The congressional enactment constitutes a new exception to the general rule stated in

---

* Congress provided that the rules would take effect unless within a specified time period the Judicial Conference made recommendations to amend the rules that Congress enacted.

subdivision (a). The Committee also combined the three separate rules proposed by Congress into one subdivision (a)(4) in accordance with the rules' customary practice of treating criminal and civil issues jointly. An amendment to Rule 405 has been added because the authorization of a new form of character evidence in this rule has an impact on methods of proving character that were not explicitly addressed by Congress. The stylistic changes are self-evident. They are particularly noticeable in the definition section in subdivision (a)(4)(C) in which the Committee eliminated, without any change in meaning, graphic details of sexual acts.

The Committee added language that explicitly provides that evidence under this subdivision must satisfy other rules of evidence such as the hearsay rules in Article VIII and the expert testimony rules in Article VII. Although principal sponsors of the legislation had stated that they intended other evidentiary rules to apply, the Committee believes that the opening phrase of the new subdivision "if otherwise admissible under these rules" is needed to clarify the relationship between subdivision (a)(4) and other evidentiary provisions.

The Committee also expressly made subdivision (a)(4) subject to Rule 403 balancing in accordance with the repeatedly stated objectives of the legislation's sponsors with which representatives of the Justice Department expressed agreement. Many commentators on Rules 413–415 had objected that Rule 403's applicability was obscured by the actual language employed.

In addition to clarifying the drafter's intent, an explicit reference to Rule 403 may be essential to insulate the rule against constitutional challenge. Constitutional concerns also led the Committee to acknowledge specifically the opposing party's right to offer in rebuttal character evidence that the rules would otherwise bar, including evidence of a third person's prior acts of sexual misconduct offered to prove that the third person rather than the party committed the acts in issue.

In order to minimize the need for extensive and time-consuming judicial interpretation, the Committee listed factors that a court may consider in discharging Rule 403 balancing. Proximity in time is taken into account in a related rule. *See* Rule 609(b). Similarity, frequency and surrounding circumstances have long been considered by courts in handling other crimes evidence pursuant to Rule 404(b). Relevant intervening events, such as extensive medical treatment of the accused between the time of the prior proffered act and the charged act, may affect the strength of the propensity inference for which the evidence is offered. The final factor—"other relevant similarities or differences"—is added in recognition of the endless variety of circumstances that confront a trial court in rulings on admissibility. Although subdivision (4)(A) explicitly refers to factors that bear on probative value, this enumeration does not eliminate a judge's responsibility to take into account the other factors mentioned in Rule 403 itself—"the danger of unfair prejudice, confusion of the issues, . . . misleading the jury, . . . undue delay, waste of time, or needless presentation of cumulative evidence." In addition, the Advisory Committee Note to Rule 403 reminds judges that "The availability of other means of proof may also be an appropriate factor."

The Committee altered slightly the notice provision in criminal cases. Providing the trial court with some discretion to excuse pretrial notice was thought preferable to the inflexible 15-day rule provided in Rules 414 and 415. Furthermore, the formulation is identical to that contained in the 1991 amendment to Rule 404(b) so that no confusion will result from having two somewhat different notice provisions in the same rule. The Committee eliminated the notice provision for civil cases stated in Rule 415 because it did not believe that Congress intended to alter the usual time table for disclosure and discovery provided by the Federal Rules of Civil Procedure.

The definition section was simplified with no change in meaning. The reference to "the law of a State" was eliminated as unnecessarily confusing and restrictive. Conduct committed outside the United States ought equally to be eligible for admission. Evidence offered pursuant to subdivision (a)(4) must relate to a form of conduct proscribed by either chapter 109A or 110 of title 18, United States Code, regardless of whether the actor was subject to federal jurisdiction.

COMMITTEE NOTE TO 2006 AMENDMENT.

The Rule has been amended to clarify that in a civil case evidence of a person's character is never admissible to prove that the person acted in conformity with the character trait. The amendment resolves the dispute in the case law over whether the exceptions in subdivisions (a)(1) and (2) permit the circumstantial use of character evidence in civil cases. *Compare Carson v. Polley*, 689 F.2d 562, 576 (5th Cir. 1982) ("when a central issue in a case is close to one of a criminal nature, the exceptions to the Rule 404(a) ban on character evidence may be invoked"), *with SEC v. Towers Financial Corp.*, 966 F.Supp. 203 (S.D.N.Y. 1997) (relying on the terms "accused" and "prosecution" in Rule 404(a) to conclude that the exceptions in subdivisions (a)(1) and (2) are inapplicable in civil cases). The amendment is consistent with the original intent of the Rule, which was to prohibit the circumstantial use of character evidence in civil cases, even where closely related to criminal charges. *See Ginter v. Northwestern Mut. Life Ins. Co.*, 576 F.Supp. 627, 629–30 (D. Ky. 1984) ("It seems beyond peradventure of doubt that the drafters of F.R.Evi. 404(a) explicitly intended that all character evidence, except where 'character is at issue' was to be excluded" in civil cases).

The circumstantial use of character evidence is generally discouraged because it carries serious risks of prejudice, confusion and delay. *See Michelson v. United States,* 335 U.S. 469, 476 (1948) ("The overriding policy of excluding such evidence, despite its admitted probative value, is the practical experience that its disallowance tends to prevent confusion of issues, unfair surprise and undue prejudice."). In criminal cases, the so-called "mercy rule" permits a criminal defendant to introduce evidence of pertinent character traits of the defendant and the victim. But that is because the accused, whose liberty is at stake, may need "a counterweight against the strong investigative and prosecutorial resources of the government." C. Mueller & L. Kirkpatrick, *Evidence: Practice Under the Rules*, pp. 264–5 (2d ed. 1999). See also Richard Uviller, *Evidence of Character to Prove Conduct: Illusion, Illogic, and Injustice in the Courtroom*, 130 U.Pa.L.Rev. 845, 855 (1982) (the rule prohibiting circumstantial use of character evidence "was relaxed to allow the criminal defendant with so much at stake and so little available in the way of conventional proof to have special dispensation to tell the factfinder just what sort of person he really is"). Those concerns do not apply to parties in civil cases.

The amendment also clarifies that evidence otherwise admissible under Rule 404(a)(2) may nonetheless be excluded in a criminal case involving sexual misconduct. In such a case, the admissibility of evidence of the victim's sexual behavior and predisposition is governed by the more stringent provisions of Rule 412.

Nothing in the amendment is intended to affect the scope of Rule 404(b). While Rule 404(b) refers to the "accused," the "prosecution," and a "criminal case," it does so only in the context of a notice requirement. The admissibility standards of Rule 404(b) remain fully applicable to both civil and criminal cases.

Rule 405. Methods of Proving Character

ADVISORY COMMITTEE NOTE TO THE 2011 AMENDMENT.

The language of Rule 405 has been amended as part of the restyling of the Evidence Rules to make them more easily understood and to make style and terminology consistent throughout the rules. These changes are intended to be stylistic only. There is no intent to change any result in any ruling on evidence admissibility.

ADVISORY COMMITTEE NOTE.

The rule deals only with allowable methods of proving character, not with the admissibility of character evidence, which is covered in Rule 404.

Of the three methods of proving character provided by the rule, evidence of specific instances of conduct is the most convincing. At the same time it possesses the greatest capacity to arouse prejudice, to confuse, to surprise, and to consume time. Consequently the rule confines the use of evidence of this kind to cases in which character is, in the strict sense, in issue and hence deserving of a searching inquiry. When character is used circumstantially and hence occupies a lesser status in the case, proof may be only by reputation and opinion. These latter methods are also available when character is in issue. This treatment is, with respect to specific instances of conduct and reputation, conventional contemporary common law doctrine. McCormick § 153.

In recognizing opinion as a means of proving character, the rule departs from usual contemporary practice in favor of that of an earlier day. *See* 7 Wigmore § 1986, pointing out that the earlier practice permitted opinion and arguing strongly for evidence based on personal knowledge and belief as contrasted with "the secondhand, irresponsible product of multiplied guesses and gossip which we term 'reputation'." It seems likely that the persistence of reputation evidence is due to its largely being opinion in disguise. Traditionally character has been regarded primarily in moral overtones of good and bad: chaste, peaceable, truthful, honest. Nevertheless, on occasion nonmoral considerations crop up, as in the case of the incompetent driver, and this seems bound to happen increasingly. If character is defined as the kind of person one is, then account must be taken of varying ways of arriving at the estimate. These may range from the opinion of the employer who has found the man honest to the opinion of the psychiatrist based upon examination and testing. No effective dividing line exists between character and mental capacity, and the latter traditionally has been provable by opinion.

According to the great majority of cases, on cross-examination inquiry is allowable as to whether the reputation witness has heard of particular instances of conduct pertinent to the trait in question. Michelson v. United States, 335 U.S. 469, 69 S.Ct. 213, 93 L. Ed. 168 (1948): Annot., 47 A.L.R.2d 1258. The theory is that, since the reputation witness relates what he has heard, the inquiry tends to shed light on the accuracy of his hearing and reporting. Accordingly, the opinion witness would be asked whether he knew, as well as whether he had heard. The fact is, of course, that these distinctions are of slight if any practical significance, and the second sentence of subdivision (a) eliminates them as a factor in formulating questions. This recognition of the propriety of inquiring into specific instances of conduct does not circumscribe inquiry otherwise into the bases of opinion and reputation testimony.

The express allowance of inquiry into specific instances of conduct on cross-examination in subdivision (a) and the express allowance of it as part of a case in chief when character is actually in issue in subdivision (b) contemplate that testimony of specific instances is not generally permissible on the direct examination of an ordinary opinion witness to character. Similarly as to witnesses to the character of witnesses under Rule 608(b). Opinion testimony on direct in these situations ought in general to correspond to reputation testimony as now given, i.e., be confined to the nature and extent of observation and acquaintance upon which the opinion is based. *See* Rule 701.

NOTE BY FEDERAL JUDICIAL CENTER.

The Rule enacted by the Congress is the Rule prescribed by the Supreme Court without change. The bill reported by the House Committee on the Judiciary deleted the provision in subdivision (a) for making proof by testimony in the form of an opinion, but the provision was reinstated on the floor of the House. [120 Cong. Rec. 2370–73 (1974).]

ADVISORY COMMITTEE NOTE TO PROPOSED 1995 AMENDMENT.

The addition of a new subdivision (a)(4) to Rule 404 necessitates adding a new subdivision (c) to Rule 405 to govern methods of proof. Congress clearly intended no change in the preexisting law that precludes the prosecution or a claimant from offering reputation or opinion testimony in its case in chief to prove that the opposing party acted in conformity with character. When evidence is admissible pursuant to Rule 404(a)(4), the proponents proof must consist of specific instances of conduct. The opposing party, however, is free to respond with reputation or opinion testimony (including expert testimony if otherwise admissible) as well as evidence of specific instances. In a criminal case, the admissibility of reputation or opinion testimony would, in any event, be authorized by Rule 404(a)(1). The extension to civil cases is essential in order to provide the opponent with an adequate opportunity to refute allegations about a character for sexual misconduct. Once the opposing party offers reputation or opinion testimony, however, the prosecution or claimant may counter using such methods of proof.

Rule 406. Habit; Routine Practice

ADVISORY COMMITTEE NOTE TO THE 2011 AMENDMENT.

The language of Rule 406 has been amended as part of the restyling of the Evidence Rules to make them more easily understood and to make style and terminology consistent throughout the rules. These changes are intended to be stylistic only. There is no intent to change

any result in any ruling on evidence admissibility.

ADVISORY COMMITTEE NOTE.

Subdivision (a). An oft-quoted paragraph, McCormick, § 162, p. 340, describes habit in terms effectively contrasting it with character:

"Character and habit are close akin. Character is a generalized description of one's disposition, or of one's disposition in respect to a general trait, such as honesty, temperance, or peacefulness. 'Habit,' in modern usage, both lay and psychological, is more specific. It describes one's regular response to a repeated specific situation. If we speak of character for care, we think of the person's tendency to act prudently in all the varying situations of life, in business, family life, in handling automobiles and in walking across the street. A habit, on the other hand, is the person's regular practice of meeting a particular kind of situation with a specific type of conduct, such as the habit of going down a particular stairway two stairs at a time, or of giving the hand-signal for a left turn, or of alighting from railway cars while they are moving. The doing of the habitual acts may become semi-automatic."

Equivalent behavior on the part of a group is designated "routine practice of an organization" in the rule.

Agreement is general that habit evidence is highly persuasive as proof of conduct on a particular occasion. Again quoting McCormick § 162, p. 341:

"Character may be thought of as the sum of one's habits though doubtless it is more than this. But unquestionably the uniformity of one's response to habit is far greater than the consistency with which one's conduct conforms to character or disposition. Even though character comes in only exceptionally as evidence of an act, surely any sensible man in investigating whether X did a particular act would be greatly helped in his inquiry by evidence as to whether he was in the habit of doing it."

When disagreement has appeared, its focus has been upon the question what constitutes habit, and the reason for this is readily apparent. The extent to which instances must be multiplied and consistency of behavior maintained in order to rise to the status of habit inevitably gives rise to differences of opinion. Lewan, Rationale of Habit Evidence, 16 Syracuse L. Rev. 39, 49 (1964). While adequacy of sampling and uniformity of response are key factors, precise standards for measuring their sufficiency for evidence purposes cannot be formulated.

The rule is consistent with prevailing views. Much evidence is excluded simply because of failure to achieve the status of habit. Thus, evidence of intemperate "habits" is generally excluded when offered as proof of drunkenness in accident cases, Annot., 46 A.L.R.2d 103, and evidence of other assaults is inadmissible to prove the instant one in a civil assault action, Annot., 66 A.L.R.2d 806. In Levin v. United States, 338 F.2d 265, 119 U.S.App.D.C. 156 (1964), testimony as to the religious "habits" of the accused, offered as tending to prove that he was at home observing the Sabbath rather than out obtaining money through larceny by trick, was held properly excluded:

> "It seems apparent to us that an individual's religious practices would not be the type of activities which would lend themselves to the characterization of 'invariable regularity.' [1 Wigmore 520.] Certainly the very volitional basis of the activity raises serious questions as to its invariable nature, and hence its probative value." Id. at 272.

These rulings are not inconsistent with the trend towards admitting evidence of business transactions between one of the parties and a third person as tending to prove that he made the same bargain or proposal in the litigated situation. Slough, Relevancy Unraveled, 6 Kan.L.Rev. 38–41 (1957). Nor are they inconsistent with such cases as Whittemore v. Lockheed Aircraft Corp., 65 Cal.App.2d 737, 151 P.2d 670 (1944), upholding the admission of evidence that plaintiff's intestate had on four other occasions flown planes from defendant's factory for delivery to his employer airline, offered to prove that he was piloting rather than a guest on a plane which crashed and killed all on board while en route for delivery.

A considerable body of authority has required that evidence of the routine practice of an organization be corroborated as a condition precedent to its admission in evidence. Slough, Relevancy Unraveled, 5 Kan.L.Rev. 404, 449 (1957). This requirement is specifically rejected by the rule on the ground that it relates to the sufficiency of the evidence rather than admissibility. A similar position is taken in New Jersey Rule 49. The rule also rejects the requirement of the absence of eyewitnesses, sometimes encountered with respect to admitting habit evidence to prove freedom from contributory negligence in wrongful death cases. For comment critical of the requirements *see* Frank, J., in Cereste v. New York, N. H. & H. R. Co., 231 F.2d 50 (2d Cir. 1956), *cert. denied,* 351 U.S. 951, 76 S.Ct. 848, 100 L. Ed. 1475, 10 Vand.L.Rev. 447 (1957); McCormick § 162, p. 342. The omission of the requirement from the California Evidence Code is said to have effected its elimination. Comment, Cal.Ev.Code § 1105.

Subdivision (b).[*] Permissible methods of proving habit or routine conduct include opinion and specific instances sufficient in number to

---

[*] Note that Congress deleted subdivision (b) in enacting Rule 406.

warrant a finding that the habit or routine practice in fact existed. Opinion evidence must be "rationally based on the perception of the witness" and helpful, under the provisions of Rule 701. Proof by specific instances may be controlled by the overriding provisions of Rule 403 for exclusion on grounds of prejudice, confusion, misleading the jury, or waste of time. Thus the illustrations following A.L.I. Model Code of Evidence Rule 307 suggests the possibility of admitting testimony by W that on numerous occasions he had been with X when X crossed a railroad track and that on each occasion X had first stopped and looked in both directions, but discretion to exclude offers of 10 witnesses, each testifying to a different occasion.

Similar provisions for proof by opinion or specific instances are found in Uniform Rule 50 and Kansas Code of Civil Procedure § 60-450. New Jersey Rule 50 provides for proof by specific instances but is silent as to opinion. The California Evidence Code is silent as to methods of proving habit, presumably proceeding on the theory that any method is relevant and all relevant evidence is admissible unless otherwise provided. Tentative Recommendation and a Study Relating to the Uniform Rules of Evidence (Art. VI. Extrinsic Policies Affecting Admissibility), Rep., Rec. & Study, Cal. Law Rev. Comm'n, 620 (1964).

REPORT OF THE HOUSE COMMITTEE ON THE JUDICIARY: PROPOSED RULE.

Rule 406(b)

Rule 406 as submitted to Congress contained a subdivision (b) providing that the method of proof of habit or routine practice could be "in the form of an opinion or by specific instances of conduct sufficient in number to warrant a finding that the habit existed or that the practice was routine." The Committee deleted this subdivision believing that the method of proof of habit and routine practice should be left to the courts to deal with on a case-by-case basis. At the same time, the Committee does not intend that its action be construed as sanctioning a general authorization of opinion evidence in this area.

NOTE BY FEDERAL JUDICIAL CENTER.

The Rule enacted by the Congress is subdivision (a) of the Rule prescribed by the Supreme Court. Subdivision (b) of the Court's Rule was deleted for reasons stated in the Report of the House Committee on the Judiciary set forth above.

Rule 407. Subsequent Remedial Measures

ADVISORY COMMITTEE NOTE TO THE 2011 AMENDMENT.

The language of Rule 407 has been amended as part of the restyling of the Evidence Rules to make them more easily understood and to

make style and terminology consistent throughout the rules. These changes are intended to be stylistic only. There is no intent to change any result in any ruling on evidence admissibility.

Rule 407 previously provided that evidence was not excluded if offered for a purpose not explicitly prohibited by the Rule. To improve the language of the Rule, it now provides that the court may admit evidence if offered for a permissible purpose. There is no intent to change the process for admitting evidence covered by the Rule. It remains the case that if offered for an impermissible purpose, it must be excluded, and if offered for a purpose not barred by the Rule, its admissibility remains governed by the general principles of Rules 402, 403, 801, etc.

ADVISORY COMMITTEE NOTE.

The rule incorporates conventional doctrine which excludes evidence of subsequent remedial measures as proof of an admission of fault. The rule rests on two grounds. (1) The conduct is not in fact an admission, since the conduct is equally consistent with injury by mere accident or through contributory negligence. Or, as Baron Bramwell put it, the rule rejects the notion that "because the world gets wiser as it gets older, therefore it was foolish before." Hart v. Lancashire & Yorkshire Ry. Co., 21 L.T.R. N.S. 261, 263 (1869). Under a liberal theory of relevancy this ground alone would not support exclusion as the inference is still a possible one. (2) The other, and more impressive, ground for exclusion rests on a social policy of encouraging people to take, or at least not discouraging them from taking, steps in furtherance of added safety. The courts have applied this principle to exclude evidence of subsequent repairs, installation of safety devices, changes in company rules, and discharge of employees, and the language of the present rule is broad enough to encompass all of them. *See* Falknor, Extrinsic Policies Affecting Admissibility, 10 Rutgers L.Rev. 574, 590 (1956).

The second sentence of the rule directs attention to the limitations of the rule. Exclusion is called for only when the evidence of subsequent remedial measures is offered as proof of negligence or culpable conduct. In effect it rejects the suggested inference that fault is admitted. Other purposes are, however, allowable, including ownership or control, existence of duty, and feasibility of precautionary measures, if controverted, and impeachment. 2 Wigmore § 283; Annot., 64 A.L.R.2d 1296. Two recent federal cases are illustrative. Boeing Airplane Co. v. Brown, 291 F.2d 310 (9th Cir. 1961), an action against an airplane manufacturer for using an allegedly defectively designed alternator shaft which caused a plane crash, upheld the admission of evidence of subsequent design modification for the purpose of showing that design changes and safeguards were feasible. And Powers v. J. B. Michael & Co., 329 F.2d

674 (6th Cir. 1964), an action against a road contractor for negligent failure to put out warning signs, sustained the admission of evidence that defendant subsequently put out signs to show that the portion of the road in question was under defendant's control. The requirement that the other purpose be controverted calls for automatic exclusion unless a genuine issue be present and allows the opposing party to lay the groundwork for exclusion by making an admission. Otherwise the factors of undue prejudice, confusion of issues, misleading the jury, and waste of time remain for consideration under Rule 403.

For comparable rules, *see* Uniform Rule 51; California Evidence Code § 1151; Kansas Code of Civil Procedure § 60-451; New Jersey Evidence Rule 51.

NOTE BY FEDERAL JUDICIAL CENTER.

Congress made no change in Rule 407, and it was neither the subject of floor debate, nor the subject of discussion during the course of committee hearings on the Rules in the House of Representatives. Therefore, the Rule enacted by the Congress is the Rule prescribed by the Supreme Court without change.

ADVISORY COMMITTEE NOTE TO 1997 AMENDMENT.

The amendment to Rule 407 makes two changes in the rule. First, the words "an injury or harm allegedly caused by" were added to clarify that the rule applies only to changes made after the occurrence that produced the damages giving rise to the action. Evidence of measures taken by the defendant prior to the "event" causing "injury or harm" do not fall within the exclusionary scope of Rule 407 even if they occurred after the manufacture or design of the product. *See* Chase v. General Motors Corp., 856 F.2d 17, 21–22 (4th Cir. 1988).

Second, Rule 407 has been amended to provide that evidence of subsequent remedial measures may not be used to prove "a defect in a product or its design, or that a warning or instruction should have accompanied a product." This amendment adopts the view of a majority of the circuits that have interpreted Rule 407 to apply to products liability actions. *See* Raymond v. Raymond Corp., 938 F.2d 1518, 1522 (1st Cir. 1991); In re Joint Eastern District and Southern District Asbestos Litigation v. Armstrong World Industries, Inc., 995 F.2d 343 (2d Cir. 1993); Cann v. Ford Motor Co., 658 F.2d 54, 60 (2d Cir. 1981), *cert. denied*, 456 U.S. 960 (1982); Kelly v. Crown Equipment Co., 970 F.2d 1273, 1275 (3d Cir. 1992); Werner v. Upjohn, Inc., 628 F.2d 848 (4th Cir. 1980), *cert. denied*, 449 U.S. 1080 (1981); Grenada Steel Industries, Inc. v. Alabama Oxygen Co., Inc., 695 F.2d 883 (5th Cir. 1983); Bauman v. Volkswagenwerk Aktiengesellschaft, 621 F.2d 230, 232 (6th Cir. 1980); Flaminio v. Honda Motor Company, Ltd., 733 F.2d

463, 469 (7th Cir. 1984); Gauthier v. AMF, Inc., 788 F.2d 634, 636–37 (9th Cir. 1986).

Although the amendment adopts a uniform federal rule, it should be noted that evidence of subsequent remedial measures may be admissible pursuant to the second sentence of Rule 407. Evidence of subsequent remedial measures that is not barred by Rule 407 may still be subject to exclusion on Rule 403 grounds when the dangers of prejudice or confusion substantially outweigh the probative value of the evidence.

Rule 408. Compromise Offers and Negotiations

ADVISORY COMMITTEE NOTE TO THE 2011 AMENDMENT.

The language of Rule 408 has been amended as part of the restyling of the Evidence Rules to make them more easily understood and to make style and terminology consistent throughout the rules. These changes are intended to be stylistic only. There is no intent to change any result in any ruling on evidence admissibility.

Rule 408 previously provided that evidence was not excluded if offered for a purpose not explicitly prohibited by the Rule. To improve the language of the Rule, it now provides that the court may admit evidence if offered for a permissible purpose. There is no intent to change the process for admitting evidence covered by the Rule. It remains the case that if offered for an impermissible purpose, it must be excluded, and if offered for a purpose not barred by the Rule, its admissibility remains governed by the general principles of Rules 402, 403, 801, etc.

The Committee deleted the reference to "liability" on the ground that the deletion makes the Rule flow better and easier to read, and because "liability" is covered by the broader term "validity." Courts have not made substantive decisions on the basis of any distinction between validity and liability. No change in current practice or in the coverage of the Rule is intended.

ADVISORY COMMITTEE NOTE.

As a matter of general agreement, evidence of an offer to compromise a claim is not receivable in evidence as an admission of, as the case may be, the validity or invalidity of the claim. As with evidence of subsequent remedial measures, dealt with in Rule 407, exclusion may be based on two grounds. (1) The evidence is irrelevant, since the offer may be motivated by a desire for peace rather than from any concession of weakness of position. The validity of this position will vary as the amount of the offer varies in relation to the size of the claim and may also be influenced by other circumstances. (2) A more consistently impressive ground is promotion of the public policy favoring the compromise and settlement of disputes. McCormick §§ 76, 251. While the rule is ordinarily phrased in terms of offers of compromise, it is apparent that a similar attitude must be taken with respect to completed compromises when offered against a party thereto. This latter situation will not, of course, ordinarily occur except when a party to the present litigation has compromised with a third person.

The same policy underlies the provision of Rule 68 of the Federal Rules of Civil Procedure that evidence of an unaccepted offer of judgment is not admissible except in a proceeding to determine costs.

The practical value of the common law rule has been greatly diminished by its inapplicability to admissions of fact, even though made in the course of compromise negotiations, unless hypothetical, stated to be "without prejudice," or so connected with the offer as to be inseparable from it. McCormick § 251, pp. 540–541. An inevitable effect is to inhibit freedom of communication with respect to compromise, even among lawyers. Another effect is the generation of controversy over whether a given statement falls within or without the protected area. These considerations account for the expansion of the rule herewith to include evidence of conduct or statements made in compromise negotiations, as well as the offer or completed compromise itself. For similar provisions *see* California Evidence Code §§ 1152, 1154.

The policy considerations which underlie the rule do not come into play when the effort is to induce a creditor to settle an admittedly due amount for a lessor sum. McCormick § 251, p. 540. Hence the rule requires that the claim be disputed as to either validity or amount.

The final sentence of the rule serves to point out some limitations upon its applicability. Since the rule excludes only when the purpose is proving the validity or invalidity of the claim or its amount, an offer for another purpose is not within the rule. The illustrative situations mentioned in the rule are supported by the authorities. As to proving bias or prejudice of a witness, *see* Annot., 161 A.L.R. 395, contra, Fenberg v. Rosenthal, 348 Ill.App. 510, 109 N.E.2d 402 (1952), and negativing a contention of lack of due diligence in presenting a claim, 4 Wigmore § 1061. An effort to "buy off" the prosecution or a prosecuting witness in a criminal case is not within the policy of the rule of exclusion. McCormick § 251, p. 542.

For other rules of similar import, *see* Uniform Rules 52 and 53; California Evidence Code §§ 1152, 1154; Kansas Code of Civil Procedure §§ 60-452, 60-453; New Jersey Evidence Rules 52 and 53.

REPORT OF THE HOUSE COMMITTEE ON THE JUDICIARY.

[Note, that the form of the Rule referred to herein was revised by the Senate (see the Senate Committee Report, infra), and the version of the

Rule which was enacted is substantially different from the House version herein described.]

Under existing federal law evidence of conduct and statements made in compromise negotiations is admissible in subsequent litigation between the parties. The second sentence of Rule 408 as submitted by the Supreme Court proposed to reverse that doctrine in the interest of further promoting non-judicial settlement of disputes. Some agencies of government expressed the view that the Court formulation was likely to impede rather than assist efforts to achieve settlement of disputes. For one thing, it is not always easy to tell when compromise negotiations begin, and informal dealings end. Also, parties dealing with government agencies would be reluctant to furnish factual information at preliminary meetings; they would wait until "compromise negotiations" began and thus hopefully effect an immunity for themselves with respect to the evidence supplied. In light of these considerations, the Committee recast the Rule so that admissions of liability or opinions given during compromise negotiations continue inadmissible, but evidence of unqualified factual assertions is admissible. The latter aspect of the Rule is drafted, however, so as to preserve other possible objections to the introduction of such evidence. The Committee intends no modification of current law whereby a party may protect himself from future use of his statements by couching them in hypothetical conditional form.

REPORT OF THE SENATE COMMITTEE ON THE JUDICIARY.

This rule as reported makes evidence of settlement or attempted settlement of a disputed claim inadmissible when offered as an admission of liability or the amount of liability. The purpose of this rule is to encourage settlements which would be discouraged if such evidence were admissible.

Under present law, in most jurisdictions, statements of fact made during settlement negotiations, however, are excepted from this ban and are admissible. The only escape from admissibility of statements of fact made in a settlement negotiation is if the declarant or his representative expressly states that the statement is hypothetical in nature or i[s] made without prejudice. Rule 408 as submitted by the Court reversed the traditional rule. It would have brought statements of fact within the ban and made them, as well as an offer of settlement, inadmissible.

The House amended the rule and would continue to make evidence of facts disclosed during compromise negotiations admissible. It thus reverted to the traditional rule. The House Committee report states that the Committee intends to preserve current law under which a party may protect himself by couching his statements in hypothetical form.[1] The

---

[1] *See* Report No. 93-650, dated November 15, 1973.

real impact of this amendment, however, is to deprive the rule of much of its salutary effect. The exception for factual admissions was believed by the Advisory Committee to hamper free communication between parties and thus to constitute an unjustifiable restraint upon efforts to negotiate settlements—the encouragement of which is the purpose of the rule. Further, by protecting hypothetically phrased statements, it constituted a preference for the sophisticated, and a trap for the unwary.

Three States which had adopted rules of evidence patterned after the proposed rules prescribed by the Supreme Court opted for versions of rule 408 identical with the Supreme Court draft with respect to the inadmissibility of conduct or statements made in compromise negotiations.[2]

For these reasons, the committee has deleted the House amendment and restored the Rule to the version submitted by the Supreme Court with one additional amendment. This amendment adds a sentence to insure that evidence, such as documents, is not rendered inadmissible merely because it is presented in the course of compromise negotiations, if the evidence is otherwise discoverable. A party should not be able to immunize from admissibility documents otherwise discoverable merely by offering them in a compromise negotiation.

REPORT OF THE HOUSE/SENATE CONFERENCE COMMITTEE.

The House bill provides that evidence of admissions of liability or opinions given during compromise negotiations is not admissible, but that evidence of facts disclosed during compromise negotiations is not inadmissible by virtue of having been first disclosed in the compromise negotiations. The Senate amendment provides that evidence of conduct or statements made in compromise negotiations is not admissible. The Senate amendment also provides that the rule does not require the exclusion of any evidence otherwise discoverable merely because it is presented in the course of compromise negotiations.

The House bill was drafted to meet the objection of executive agencies that under the rule as proposed by the Supreme Court, a party could present a fact during compromise negotiations and thereby prevent an opposing party from offering evidence of that fact at trial even though such evidence was obtained from independent sources. The Senate amendment expressly precludes this result.

The Conference adopts the Senate amendment.

NOTE BY FEDERAL JUDICIAL CENTER.

As finally enacted by Congress, Rule 408 is identical to the version

---

[2] Nev. Rev. Stats., §§ 48, 105; N. Mex. Stats. Anno. (1973 Supp.) § 20-4-408; West's Wis. Stats. Anno. (1973 Supp.) §§ 904.08.

promulgated by the Supreme Court with a minor addition (the word "also" in the final sentence between "rule" and "does"), and the insertion of a new third sentence, which provides: "The rule does not require the exclusion of any evidence otherwise discoverable merely because it is presented in the course of compromise negotiations." Other amendments, proposed by the House bill, were not enacted, for reasons set forth in the Report of the Senate Committee of the Judiciary and in the Report of the House/Senate Conference Committee set forth above.

COMMITTEE NOTE TO 2006 AMENDMENT.

Rule 408 has been amended to settle some questions in the courts about the scope of the Rule, and to make it easier to read. First, the amendment provides that Rule 408 does not prohibit the introduction in a criminal case of statements or conduct during compromise negotiations regarding a civil dispute by a government regulatory, investigative, or enforcement agency. See, e.g., United States v. Prewitt, 34 F.3d 436, 439 (7th Cir. 1994) (admissions of fault made in compromise of a civil securities enforcement action were admissible against the accused in a subsequent criminal action for mail fraud). Where an individual makes a statement in the presence of government agents, its subsequent admission in a criminal case should not be unexpected. The individual can seek to protect against subsequent disclosure through negotiation and agreement with the civil regulator or an attorney for the government.

Statements made in compromise negotiations of a claim by a government agency may be excluded in criminal cases where the circumstances so warrant under Rule 403. For example, if an individual was unrepresented at the time the statement was made in a civil enforcement proceeding, its probative value in a subsequent criminal case may be minimal. But there is no absolute exclusion imposed by Rule 408.

In contrast, statements made during compromise negotiations of other disputed claims are not admissible in subsequent criminal litigation, when offered to prove liability for, invalidity of, or amount of those claims. When private parties enter into compromise negotiations they cannot protect against the subsequent use of statements in criminal cases by way of private ordering. The inability to guarantee protection against subsequent use could lead to parties refusing to admit fault, even if by doing so they could favorably settle the private matter. Such a chill on settlement negotiations would be contrary to the policy of Rule 408.

The amendment distinguishes statements and conduct (such as a direct admission of fault) made in compromise negotiations of a civil claim by a government agency from an offer or acceptance of a compromise of such a claim. An offer or acceptance of a compromise of any civil claim is excluded under the Rule if offered against the defendant as an admission of fault. In that case, the predicate for the evidence would be that the defendant, by compromising with the government agency, has admitted the validity and amount of the civil claim, and that this admission has sufficient probative value to be considered as evidence of guilt. But unlike a direct statement of fault, an offer or acceptance of a compromise is not very probative of the defendant's guilt. Moreover, admitting such an offer or acceptance could deter a defendant from settling a civil regulatory action, for fear of evidentiary use in a subsequent criminal action. See, e.g., Fishman, Jones on Evidence, Civil and Criminal, § 22:16 at 199, n.83 (7th ed. 2000) ("A target of a potential criminal investigation may be unwilling to settle civil claims against him if by doing so he increases the risk of prosecution and conviction.").

The amendment retains the language of the original rule that bars compromise evidence only when offered as evidence of the "validity", "invalidity", or "amount" of the disputed claim. The intent is to retain the extensive case law finding Rule 408 inapplicable when compromise evidence is offered for a purpose other than to prove the validity, invalidity, or amount of a disputed claim. See, e.g., Athey v. Farmers Ins. Exchange, 234 F.3d 357 (8th Cir. 2000) (evidence of settlement offer by insurer was properly admitted to prove insurer's bad faith); Coakley & Williams v. Structural Concrete Equip., 973 F.2d 349 (4th Cir. 1992) (evidence of settlement is not precluded by Rule 408 where offered to prove a party's intent with respect to the scope of a release); Cates v. Morgan Portable Bldg. Corp., 780 F.2d 683 (7th Cir. 1985) (Rule 408 does not bar evidence of a settlement when offered to prove a breach of the settlement agreement, as the purpose of the evidence is to prove the fact of settlement as opposed to the validity or amount of the underlying claim); Uforma/Shelby Bus. Forms, Inc. v. NLRB, 111 F.3d 1284 (6th Cir. 1997) (threats made in settlement negotiations were admissible; Rule 408 is inapplicable when the claim is based upon a wrong that is committed during the course of settlement negotiations). So for example, Rule 408 is inapplicable if offered to show that a party made fraudulent statements in order to settle a litigation.

The amendment does not affect the case law providing that Rule 408 is inapplicable when evidence of the compromise is offered to prove notice. See, e.g., United States v. Austin, 54 F.3d 394 (7th Cir. 1995) (no error to admit evidence of the defendant's settlement with the FTC, because it was offered to prove that the defendant was on notice that subsequent similar conduct was wrongful); Spell v. McDaniel, 824 F.2d 1380 (4th Cir. 1987) (in a civil rights action alleging that an officer used excessive force, a prior settlement by the City of another brutality claim was properly admitted to prove that the City was on notice of aggressive behavior by police officers).

The amendment prohibits the use of statements made in settlement negotiations when offered to impeach by prior inconsistent statement or through contradiction. Such broad impeachment would tend to swallow the exclusionary rule and would impair the public policy of promoting settlements. See McCormick on Evidence at 186 (5th ed. 1999) ("Use of statements made in compromise negotiations to impeach the testimony of a party, which is not specifically treated in Rule 408, is fraught with danger of misuse of the statements to prove liability, threatens frank interchange of information during negotiations, and generally should not be permitted."). See also EEOC v. Gear Petroleum, Inc., 948 F.2d 1542 (10th Cir.1991) (letter sent as part of settlement negotiation cannot be used to impeach defense witnesses by way of contradiction or prior inconsistent statement; such broad impeachment would undermine the policy of encouraging uninhibited settlement negotiations).

The amendment makes clear that Rule 408 excludes compromise evidence even when a party seeks to admit its own settlement offer or statements made in settlement negotiations. If a party were to reveal its own statement or offer, this could itself reveal the fact that the adversary entered into settlement negotiations. The protections of Rule 408 cannot be waived unilaterally because the Rule, by definition, protects both parties from having the fact of negotiation disclosed to the jury. Moreover, proof of statements and offers made in settlement would often have to be made through the testimony of attorneys, leading to the risks and costs of disqualification. See generally Pierce v. F.R. Tripler & Co., 955 F.2d 820, 828 (2d Cir. 1992) (settlement offers are excluded under Rule 408 even if it is the offeror who seeks to admit them; noting that the "widespread admissibility of the substance of settlement offers could bring with it a rash of motions for disqualification of a party's chosen counsel who would likely become a witness at trial").

The sentence of the Rule referring to evidence "otherwise discoverable" has been deleted as superfluous. See, e.g., Advisory Committee Note to Maine Rule of Evidence 408 (refusing to include the sentence in the Maine version of Rule 408 and noting that the sentence "seems to state what the law would be if it were omitted"); Advisory Committee Note to Wyoming Rule of Evidence 408 (refusing to include the sentence in Wyoming Rule 408 on the ground that it was "superfluous"). The intent of the sentence was to prevent a party from trying to immunize admissible information, such as a pre-existing document, through the pretense of disclosing it during compromise negotiations. See Ramada Development Co. v. Rauch, 644 F.2d 1097 (5th Cir. 1981). But even without the sentence, the Rule cannot be read to protect pre-existing information simply because it was presented to the adversary in compromise negotiations.

Rule 409. Offers to Pay Medical and Similar Expenses

ADVISORY COMMITTEE NOTE TO THE 2011 AMENDMENT.

The language of Rule 409 has been amended as part of the restyling of the Evidence Rules to make them more easily understood and to make style and terminology consistent throughout the rules. These changes are intended to be stylistic only. There is no intent to change any result in any ruling on evidence admissibility.

ADVISORY COMMITTEE NOTE.

The considerations underlying this rule parallel those underlying Rules 407 and 408, which deal respectively with subsequent remedial measures and offers of compromise. As stated in Annot., 20 A.L.R.2d 291, 293.

> "[G]enerally, evidence of payment of medical, hospital, or similar expenses of an injured party by the opposing party, is not admissible, the reason often given being that such payment or offer is usually made from humane impulses and not from an admission of liability, and that to hold otherwise would tend to discourage assistance to the injured person."

Contrary to Rule 408, dealing with offers of compromise, the present rule does not extend to conduct or statements not a part of the act of furnishing or offering or promising to pay. This difference in treatment arises from fundamental differences in nature. Communication is essential if compromises are to be effected, and consequently broad protection of statements is needed. This is not so in cases of payments or offers or promises to pay medical expenses, where factual statements may be expected to be incidental in nature.

For rules on the same subject, but phrased in terms of "humanitarian motives," *see* Uniform Rule 52; California Evidence Code § 1152; Kansas Code of Civil Procedure § 60-452; New Jersey Evidence Rule 52.

NOTE BY FEDERAL JUDICIAL CENTER.

Congress made no change in Rule 409, and it was neither the subject of floor debate, nor a topic of discussion at the committee hearings; the Rule enacted by Congress is the Rule prescribed by the Supreme Court without change.

Rule 410. Pleas, Plea Discussions, and Related Statements

ADVISORY COMMITTEE NOTE TO THE 2011 AMENDMENT.

The language of Rule 410 has been amended as part of the restyling of the Evidence Rules to make them more easily understood and to

make style and terminology consistent throughout the rules. These changes are intended to be stylistic only. There is no intent to change any result in any ruling on evidence admissibility.

ADVISORY COMMITTEE NOTE.

Withdrawn pleas of guilty were held inadmissible in federal prosecutions in Kercheval v. United States, 274 U.S. 220, 47 S.Ct. 582, 71 L. Ed. 1009 (1927). The Court pointed out that to admit the withdrawn plea would effectively set at naught the allowance of withdrawal and place the accused in a dilemma utterly inconsistent with the decision to award him a trial. The New York Court of Appeals, in People v. Spitaleri, 9 N.Y.2d 168, 212 N.Y.S.2d 53, 173 N.E.2d 35 (1961), reexamined and overturned its earlier decisions which had allowed admission. In addition to the reasons set forth in Kercheval, which was quoted at length, the court pointed out that the effect of admitting the plea was to compel defendant to take the stand by way of explanation and to open the way for the prosecution to call the lawyer who had represented him at the time of entering the plea. State court decisions for and against admissibility are collected in Annot., 86 A.L.R.2d 326.

Pleas of *nolo contendere* are recognized by Rule 11 of the Rules of Criminal Procedure, although the law of numerous States is to the contrary. The present rule gives effect to the principal traditional characteristic of the *nolo* plea, i.e. avoiding the admission of guilt which is inherent in pleas of guilty. This position is consistent with the construction of Section 5 of the Clayton Act, 15 U.S.C. § 16(a), recognizing the inconclusive and compromise nature of judgments based on *nolo* pleas. General Electric Co. v. City of San Antonio, 334 F.2d 480 (5th Cir. 1964); Commonwealth Edison Co. v. Allis-Chalmers Mfg. Co., 323 F.2d 412 (7th Cir. 1963), cert. denied 376 U.S. 939, 84 S.Ct. 794, 11 L.Ed.2d 659; Armco Steel Corp. v. North Dakota, 376 F.2d 206 (8th Cir. 1967); City of Burbank v. General Electric Co., 329 F.2d 825 (9th Cir. 1964). *See also* state court decisions in Annot., 18 A.L.R.2d 1287, 1314.

Exclusion of offers to plead guilty or *nolo* has as its purpose the promotion of disposition of criminal cases by compromise. As pointed out in McCormick § 251, p. 543.

"Effective criminal law administration in many localities would hardly be possible if a large proportion of the charges were not disposed of by such compromises."

See also People v. Hamilton, 60 Cal.2d 105, 32 Cal.Rptr. 4, 383 P.2d 412 (1963), discussing legislation designed to achieve this result. As with compromise offers generally, rule 408, free communication is needed, and security against having an offer of compromise or related statement admitted in evidence effectively encourages it.

Limiting the exclusionary rule to use against the accused is consistent with the purpose of the rule, since the possibility of use for or against other persons will not impair the effectiveness of withdrawing pleas or the freedom of discussion which the rule is designed to foster. *See* A.B.A. Standards Relating to Pleas of Guilty § 2.2 (1968). *See also* the narrower provisions of New Jersey Evidence Rule 52(2) and the unlimited exclusion provided in California Evidence Code § 1153.

REPORT OF THE HOUSE COMMITTEE ON THE JUDICIARY.

[Note, that the phrase referred to in the following note was enacted with the original version of the Rule, but was deleted from the present version of the Rule, without comment.]

The Committee added the phrase "Except as otherwise provided by Act of Congress" to Rule 410 as submitted by the Court in order to preserve particular congressional policy judgments as to the effect of a plea of guilty or of nolo contendere. *See* 15 U.S.C. 16(a). The Committee intends that its amendment refers to both present statutes and statutes subsequently enacted.

REPORT OF THE SENATE COMMITTEE ON THE JUDICIARY.

[Note, that the present version of Rule 410 differs markedly from the original version, to which the following note refers, and it is clear today that under Rule 410 a plea bargaining statement by the defendant cannot be introduced against him for impeachment purposes if he takes the stand on his own behalf.]

As adopted by the House, rule 410 would make inadmissible pleas of guilty or nolo contendere subsequently withdrawn as well as offers to make such pleas. Such a rule is clearly justified as a means of encouraging pleading. However, the House rule would then go on to render inadmissible for any purpose statements made in connection with these pleas or offers as well.

The committee finds this aspect of the House rule unjustified. Of course, in certain circumstances such statements should be excluded. If, for example, a plea is vitiated because of coercion, statements made in connection with the plea may also have been coerced and should be inadmissible on that basis. In other cases, however, voluntary statements of an accused made in court on the record, in connection with a plea, and determined by a court to be reliable should be admissible even though the plea is subsequently withdrawn. This is particularly true in those cases where, if the House rule were in effect, a defendant would be able to contradict his previous statements and thereby lie with impunity.[3] To prevent such an injustice, the rule has been modified to

---

[3] *See* Harris v. New York, 401 U.S. 222 (1971). [Senate Judiciary Committee's footnote.]

permit the use of such statements for the limited purposes of impeachment and in subsequent perjury or false statement prosecutions.

REPORT OF THE HOUSE/SENATE CONFERENCE COMMITTEE.

[Note, that the version of Rule 410 presently in effect is not the version referred to in the following note.]

The House bill provides that evidence of a guilty or nolo contendere plea, of an offer of either plea, or of statements made in connection with such pleas or offers of such pleas, is inadmissible in any civil or criminal action, case or proceeding against the person making such plea or offer. The Senate amendment makes the rule inapplicable to a voluntary and reliable statement made in court on the record where the statement is offered in a subsequent prosecution of the declarant for perjury or false statement.

The issues raised by Rule 410 are also raised by proposed Rule 11(e)(6) of the Federal Rules of Criminal Procedure presently pending before Congress. This proposed rule, which deals with the admissibility of pleas of guilty or nolo contendere, offers to make such pleas, and statements made in connection with such pleas, was promulgated by the Supreme Court on April 22, 1974, and in the absence of congressional action will become effective on August 1, 1975. The conferees intend to make no change in the presently-existing case law until that date, leaving the courts free to develop rules in this area on a case-by-case basis.

The Conferees further determined that the issues presented by the use of guilty and nolo contendere pleas, offers of such pleas, and statements made in connection with such pleas or offers, can be explored in greater detail during Congressional consideration of Rule 11(c)(6) of the Federal Rules of Criminal Procedure. The Conferees believe, therefore, that it is best to defer its effective date until August 1, 1975. The Conferees intend that Rule 410 would be superseded by any subsequent Federal Rule of Criminal Procedure or Act of Congress with which it is inconsistent, if the Federal Rule of Criminal Procedure or Act of Congress takes effect or becomes law after the date of the enactment of the act establishing the rules of evidence.

The conference adopts the Senate amendment with an amendment that expresses the above intentions.

Rule 411. Liability Insurance

ADVISORY COMMITTEE NOTE TO THE 2011 AMENDMENT.

The language of Rule 411 has been amended as part of the restyling of the Evidence Rules to make them more easily understood and to make style and terminology consistent throughout the rules. These changes are intended to be stylistic only. There is no intent to change

any result in any ruling on evidence admissibility.

Rule 411 previously provided that evidence was not excluded if offered for a purpose not explicitly prohibited by the Rule. To improve the language of the Rule, it now provides that the court may admit evidence if offered for a permissible purpose. There is no intent to change the process for admitting evidence covered by the Rule. It remains the case that if offered for an impermissible purpose, it must be excluded, and if offered for a purpose not barred by the Rule, its admissibility remains governed by the general principles of Rules 402, 403, 801, etc.

ADVISORY COMMITTEE NOTE.

The courts have with substantial unanimity rejected evidence of liability insurance for the purpose of proving fault, and absence of liability insurance as proof of lack of fault. At best the inference of fault from the fact of insurance coverage is a tenuous one, as is its converse. More important, no doubt, has been the feeling that knowledge of the presence or absence of liability insurance would induce juries to decide cases on improper grounds. McCormick § 168; Annot., 4 A.L.R.2d 761. The rule is drafted in broad terms so as to include contributory negligence or other fault of a plaintiff as well as fault of a defendant.

The second sentence points out the limits of the rule, using well established illustrations. *Id.* For similar rules *see* Uniform Rule 54; California Evidence Code § 1155; Kansas Code of Civil Procedure § 60-454; New Jersey Evidence Rule 54.

NOTE BY FEDERAL JUDICIAL CENTER.

Congress made no change in Rule 411, and it was neither the subject of floor debate, nor a topic of discussion at the committee hearings. Therefore, the Rule enacted by Congress is the Rule prescribed by the Supreme Court without change.

Rule 412. Sex-Offense Cases: The Victim's Sexual Behavior or Predisposition

ADVISORY COMMITTEE NOTE TO THE 2011 AMENDMENT.

The language of Rule 412 has been amended as part of the restyling of the Evidence Rules to make them more easily understood and to make style and terminology consistent throughout the rules. These changes are intended to be stylistic only. There is no intent to change any result in any ruling on evidence admissibility.

CONGRESSIONAL ACTION.

Public Law 95-540, the Privacy Protection for Rape Victims Act of 1978, adds Rule 412 to the Federal Rules of Evidence. Public Law 95-540 was approved by the House of Representatives on October 10,

1978 and by the Senate on October 12, 1978. It was signed by President Carter on October 28, 1978 and accordingly became effective with respect to trials begun after November 28, 1978 since section 3 of Public Law 95-540 provides that:

> The amendments made by this Act shall apply to trials which begin more than thirty days after the date of the enactment of this Act.

In case of a retrial begun after this date, the new rule would apply so that evidence admitted at an earlier trial might not be admitted on the retrial. *See* discussion of "Effective Date" under Rule 1103.

In the House of Representatives, Representatives Holtzman, Mann and Wiggins discussed the bill at length. The following excerpts from their remarks suggests the tenor of the discussion:

Mr. MANN. Mr. Speaker, for many years in this country, evidentiary rules have permitted the introduction of evidence about a rape victim's prior sexual conduct. Defense lawyers were permitted great latitude in bringing out intimate details about a rape victim's life. Such evidence quite often serves no real purpose and only results in embarrassment to the rape victim and unwarranted public intrusion into her private life.

The evidentiary rules that permit such inquiry have in recent years come under question: and the States have taken the lead to change and modernize their evidentiary rules about evidence of a rape victim's prior sexual behavior. The bill before us similarly seeks to modernize the Federal Evidentiary rules.

The present Federal Rules of Evidence reflect the traditional approach. If a defendant in a rape case raises the defense of consent, that defendant may then offer evidence about the victim's prior sexual behavior. Such evidence may be in the form of opinion evidence, evidence of reputation, or evidence of specific instances of behavior. Rule 404(a)(2) of the Federal Rules of Evidence permits the introduction of evidence of a "pertinent character trait." The Advisory Committee note to that rule cites, as an example of what the rule covers, the character of a rape victim when the issue is consent. Rule 405 of the Federal Rules of Evidence permits the use of opinion or reputation evidence or the use of evidence of specific behavior to show a character trait."

Thus, Federal evidentiary rules permit a wide ranging inquiry into the private conduct of a rape victim, even though that conduct may have at best a tenuous connection to the offense for which the defendant is being tried. H.R. 4727 amends the Federal Rules of Evidence to add a new rule, applicable only in criminal cases, to spell out when, and under what conditions, evidence of a rape victim's prior sexual behavior can be admitted. The new rule provides that reputation or opinion evidence about a rape victim's prior sexual behavior is not admissible. The new rule also provides that a court cannot admit evidence of specific instances of a rape victim's prior sexual conduct except in three circumstances.

The first circumstance is where the Constitution requires that the evidence be admitted. This exception is intended to cover those infrequent instances where, because of an unusual chain of circumstances, the general rule of inadmissibility, if followed, would result in denying the defendant a constitutional right.

The second circumstance in which the defendant can offer evidence of specific instances of a rape victim's prior sexual behavior is where the defendant raises the issue of consent and the evidence is of sexual behavior with the defendant. To admit such evidence, however, the court must find that the evidence is relevant and that its probative value outweighs the danger of unfair prejudice.

The third circumstance in which a court can admit evidence of specific instances of a rape victim's prior sexual behavior is where the evidence is of behavior with someone other than the defendant and is offered by the defendant on the issue of whether or not he was the source of semen or injury. Again, such evidence will be admitted only if the court finds that the evidence is relevant and that its probative value outweighs the danger of unfair prejudice.

The new rule further provides that before evidence is admitted under any of these exceptions, there must be an in camera hearing—that is, a proceeding that takes place in the judge's chambers out of the presence of the jury and the general public. At this hearing, the defendant will present the evidence he intends to offer and be able to argue why it should be admitted. The prosecution, of course, will be able to argue against that evidence being admitted.

The purpose of the in camera hearing is twofold. It gives the defendant an opportunity to demonstrate to the court why certain evidence is admissible and ought to be presented to the jury. At the same time, it protects the privacy of the rape victim in those instances when the court finds that evidence is inadmissible. Of course, if the court finds the evidence to be admissible, the evidence will be presented to the jury in open court.

The effect of this legislation, therefore, is to preclude the routine use of evidence of specific instances of a rape victim's prior sexual behavior. Such evidence will be admitted only in clearly and narrowly defined circumstances and only after an in camera hearing. In determining the admissibility of such evidence, the court will consider all of the facts and circumstances surrounding the evidence, such as the amount of time that lapsed between the alleged prior act and the rape charged in the prosecution. The greater the lapse of time, of course, the less likely it is that such evidence will be admitted.

Mr. Speaker, the principal purpose of this legislation is to protect rape victims from the degrading and embarrassing disclosure of intimate details about their private lives. It does so by narrowly circumscribing when such evidence may be admitted. It does not do so, however, by sacrificing any constitutional right possessed by the defendant. The bill before us fairly balances the interests involved—the rape victim's interest in protecting her private life from unwarranted public exposure; the defendant's interest in being able adequately to present a defense by offering relevant and probative evidence; and society's interst in a fair trial, one where unduly prejudicial evidence is not permitted to becloud the issues before the jury.

Mr. WIGGINS. Mr. Speaker, this legislation addresses itself to a subject that is certainly a proper one for our consideration. Many of us have been troubled for years about the indiscriminate and prejudicial use of testimony with respect to a victim's prior sexual behavior in rape and similar cases. This bill deals with that problem. It is not, in my opinion, Mr. Speaker, a perfect bill in the manner in which it deals with the problem, but my objections are not so fundamental as would lead me to oppose the bill.

I think, Mr. Speaker, that it is unwise to adopt a per se rule absolutely excluding evidence of reputation and opinion with respect to the victim—and this bill does that—but it is difficult for me to foresee the specific case in which such evidence might be admissible. The trouble is this, Mr. Speaker: None of us can foresee perfectly all of the various circumstances under which the propriety of evidence might be before the court. If this bill has a defect, in my view it is because it adopts a per se rule with respect to opinion and reputation evidence. Alternatively we might have permitted that evidence to be considered in camera as we do other evidence under the bill.

I should note, however, in fairness, having expressed minor reservations, that the bill before the House at this time does improve significantly upon the bill which was presented to our committee.

I will not detail all of those improvements but simply observe that the bill upon which we shall soon vote is a superior product to that which was initially considered by our subcommittee.

Ms. HOLTZMAN. Too often in this country victims of rape are humiliated and harassed when they report and prosecute the rape. Bullied and cross-examined about their prior sexual experiences, many find the trial almost as degrading as the rape itself. Since rape trials become inquisitions into the victim's morality, not trials of the defendant's innocence or guilt, it is not surprising that it is the least reported crime. It is estimated that as few as one in ten rapes is ever reported.

Mr. Speaker, over 30 States have taken some action to limit the vulnerability of rape victims to such humiliating cross-examination of their past sexual experiences and intimate personal histories. In federal courts, however, it is permissible still to subject rape victims to brutal cross-examination about their past sexual histories. H.R. 4727 would rectify this problem in Federal Courts and I hope, also serve as a model to suggest to the remaining states that reform of existing rape laws is important to the equity of our criminal justice system.

H.R. 4727 applies only to criminal rape cases in Federal courts. The bill provides that neither the prosecution nor the defense can introduce any reputation or opinion evidence about the victim's past sexual conduct. It does permit, however, the introduction of specific evidence about the victim's past sexual conduct in three very limited circumstances.

First, this evidence can be introduced if it deals with the victim's past sexual relations with the defendant and is relevant to the issue of whether she consented. Second, when the defendant claims he had no relations with the victim, he can use evidence of the victim's past sexual relations with others if the evidence rebuts the victim's claim that the rape caused certain physical consequences, such as semen or injury. Finally, the evidence can be introduced if it is constitutionally required. This last exception, added in subcommittee, will insure that the defendant's constitutional rights are protected.

Before any such evidence can be introduced, however, the court must determine at a hearing in chambers that the evidence falls within one of the exceptions.

Furthermore, unless constitutionally required, the evidence of specific instances of prior sexual conduct cannot be introduced at all if it would be more prejudicial and inflammatory than probative.

Congressional Record, October 10, 1978, H11944–11945

In the Senate, further explanatory remarks were offered by Senators Thurmond, Bayh and Biden.

Mr. THURMOND . . . .

H.R. 4727, as passed by the House, essentially does the following:

First. Prohibits any use of reputation or opinion evidence of the past sexual behavior of the victim in a criminal prosecution for rape or assault with intent to commit rape.

Second. Restricts the use of direct evidence of the past sexual behavior of the victim of rape and assault with intent to commit rape to three situations:

(a) Where the judge finds after a hearing that admission of the evidence is required under the Constitution;

(b) The judge finds after a hearing that the past sexual behavior was with a person other than the accused and is being offered to show that someone other than the accused was the source of semen or injury; and

(c) The judge finds after a hearing that the past sexual behavior was with the accused and is offered by the accused solely on the issue of consent.

Third. Creates notice and hearing procedures on the evidentiary issues delineated by the bill.

. . .

Mr. BAYH . . . .

. . . Under the provisions of H.R. 4727, a new rule of evidence applicable only in criminal cases would make evidence of prior sexual history inadmissible except under three circumstances.

First, in order to make sure that we are [not] infringing upon a defendant's civil liberties, such evidence may be admissible where it is required under the constitution. Thus exception is intended to cover those instances where, because of an unusual set of circumstances, if the general rule of inadmissibility were to be followed, it might deprive a defendant of his Constitutional rights.

The second circumstance in which the defendant can offer evidence of a rape victim's prior sexual history is where the defendant raises the issue of consent and the evidence is of sexual behavior with the defendant.

The third circumstance in which a court can admit evidence of prior sexual history is where the evidence may show that sexual relations occurred between the victim and someone other than the defendant.

Evidence which might fall under these exceptions is not automatically admissible however. If the defendant proposed to offer evidence in either category, he must first make a written offer of proof which is submitted to the presiding judge. If the judge then decides after an in camera hearing that such evidence is admissible, he must make a written order specifically identifying the evidence to be admitted and describing exactly the areas of cross-examination to be permitted. This procedure is designed to afford the victim maximum notice of the questioning that may occur.

Mr. BIDEN . . . .

. . . [It] is important that we keep in mind the constitutional rights of the defendant to a fair trial. Therefore this bill has been carefully drafted to keep the reform within constitutional limits.

The bill clearly permits the defendant to offer evidence where it is constitutionally required. Indeed, the bill specifically recognizes two circumstances where the evidence may be admitted. However, the bill also would establish a special in camera procedure whereby the question of admissibility could be litigated without harm to the privacy rights of the victim or the constitutional rights of the defendant.

Congressional Record, October 12, 1978, S18579-S18581.

ADVISORY COMMITTEE NOTE TO 1994 AMENDMENT.

Rule 412 has been revised to diminish some of the confusion engendered by the original rule and to expand the protection afforded alleged victims of sexual misconduct. Rule 412 applies to both civil and criminal proceedings. The rule aims to safeguard the alleged victim against the invasion of privacy, potential embarrassment and sexual stereotyping that is associated with public disclosure of intimate sexual details and the infusion of sexual innuendo into the factfinding process. By affording victims protection in most instances, the rule also encourages victims of sexual misconduct to institute and to participate in legal proceedings against alleged offenders.

Rule 412 seeks to achieve these objectives by barring evidence relating to the alleged victim's sexual behavior or alleged sexual predisposition, whether offered as substantive evidence or for impeachment, except in designated circumstances in which the probative value of the evidence significantly outweighs possible harm to the victim.

The revised rule applies in all cases involving sexual misconduct without regard to whether the alleged victim or person accused is a party to the litigation. Rule 412 extends to "pattern" witnesses in both criminal and civil cases whose testimony about other instances of sexual misconduct by the person accused is otherwise admissible. When the case does not involve alleged sexual misconduct, evidence relating to a third-party witness' alleged sexual activities is not within the ambit of Rule 412. The witness will, however, be protected by other rules such as Rules 404 and 608, as well as Rule 403.

The terminology "alleged victim" is used because there will frequently be a factual dispute as to whether sexual misconduct occurred. It does not connote any requirement that the misconduct be alleged in the pleadings. Rule 412 does not, however, apply unless the person against whom the evidence is offered can reasonably be characterized as a "victim of alleged sexual misconduct." When this is not the case, as for instance in a defamation action involving statements concerning sexual misconduct in which the evidence is offered to show that the alleged defamatory statements were true or did not damage the plaintiff's reputation, neither Rule 404 nor this rule will operate to bar the evidence; Rule 401 and 403 will continue to control. Rule 412 will, however, apply in a Title VII action in which the plaintiff has alleged sexual harassment.

The reference to a person "accused" is also used in a non-technical sense. There is no requirement that there be a criminal charge pending against the person or even that the misconduct would constitute a criminal offense. Evidence offered to prove allegedly false prior claims by the victim is not barred by Rule 412. However, this evidence is subject to the requirements of Rule 404.

Subdivision (a). As amended, Rule 412 bars evidence offered to prove the victim's sexual behavior and alleged sexual predisposition. Evidence, which might otherwise be admissible under Rules 402, 404(b), 405, 607, 608, 609, or some other evidence rule, must be excluded if Rule 412(a) requires. The word "other" is used to suggest some flexibility in admitting evidence "intrinsic" to the alleged sexual misconduct. *Cf.* Committee Note to 1991 amendment to Rule 404(b).

Past sexual behavior connotes all activities that involve actual physical conduct, i.e. sexual intercourse and sexual contact, or that imply sexual intercourse or sexual contact. *See, e.g.,* United States v. Galloway, 937 F.2d 542 (10th Cir. 1991), *cert. denied,* 113 S.Ct. 418 (1992) (use of contraceptives inadmissible since use implies sexual activity); United States v. One Feather, 702 F.2d 736 (8th Cir. 1983) (birth of an illegitimate child inadmissible); State v. Carmichael, 727 P.2d 918, 925 (Ran. 1986) (evidence of venereal disease inadmissible). In addition, the word "behavior" should be construed to include activities of the mind, such as fantasies or dreams. *See* 23 C. Wright & R. Graham, Jr., *Federal Practice and Procedure,* § 5384 at p. 548 (1980) ("While there may be some doubt under statutes that require 'conduct,' it would seem that the language of Rule 412 is broad enough to encompass the behavior of the mind.").

The rule has been amended to also exclude all other evidence relating to an alleged victim of sexual misconduct that is offered to prove a sexual predisposition. This amendment is designed to exclude evidence that does not directly refer to sexual activities or thoughts but that the proponent believes may have a sexual connotation for the factfinder. Admission of such evidence would contravene Rule 412's objectives of shielding the alleged victim from potential embarrassment and safeguarding the victim against stereotypical thinking. Consequently, unless the (b)(2) exception is satisfied, evidence such as that relating to the alleged victim's mode of dress, speech, or lifestyle will not be admissible.

The introductory phrase in subdivision (a) was deleted because it lacked clarity and contained no explicit reference to the other provisions of law that were intended to be overridden. The conditional clause, "except as provided in subdivisions (b) and (c)" is intended to make clear that evidence of the types described in subdivision (a) is admissible only under the strictures of those sections.

The reason for extending the rule to all criminal cases is obvious. The strong social policy of protecting a victim's privacy and encouraging victims to come forward to report criminal acts is not confined to cases that involve a charge of sexual assault. The need to protect the victim is equally great when a defendant is charged with kidnapping, and evidence is offered, either to prove motive or as background, that the defendant sexually assaulted the victim.

The reason for extending Rule 412 to civil cases is equally obvious. The need to protect alleged victims against invasions of privacy, potential embarrassment, and unwarranted sexual stereotyping, and the wish to encourage victims to come forward when they have been sexually molested do not disappear because the context has shifted from a criminal prosecution to a claim for damages or injunctive relief. There is a strong social policy in not only punishing those who engage in sexual misconduct, but in also providing relief to the victim. Thus, Rule 412 applies in any civil case in which a person claims to be the victim of sexual misconduct, such as actions for sexual battery or sexual harassment.

Subdivision (b). Subdivision (b) spells out the specific circumstances in which some evidence may be admissible that would otherwise be barred by the general rule expressed in subdivision (a). As amended, Rule 412 will be virtually unchanged in criminal cases, but will provide protection to any person alleged to be a victim of sexual misconduct regardless of the charge actually brought against an accused. A new exception has been added for civil cases.

In a criminal case, evidence may be admitted under subdivision (b)(1) pursuant to three possible exceptions, provided the evidence also satisfies other requirements for admissibility specified in the Federal Rules of Evidence, including Rule 403. Subdivisions (b)(1)(A) and (b)(1)(B) require proof in the form of specific instances of sexual behavior in recognition of the limited probative value and dubious reliability of evidence of reputation or evidence in the form of an opinion.

Under subdivision (b)(1)(A), evidence of specific instances of sexual behavior with persons other than the person whose sexual misconduct is alleged may be admissible if it is offered to prove that another person was the source of semen, injury or other physical evidence. Where the prosecution has directly or indirectly asserted that the physical evidence originated with the accused, the defendant must be afforded an opportunity to prove that another person was responsible. *See* United

States v. Begay, 937 F.2d 515, 523 n. 10 (10th Cir. 1991). Evidence offered for the specific purpose identified in this subdivision may still be excluded if it does not satisfy Rules 401 or 403. *See, e.g.*, United States v. Azure, 845 F.2d 1503, 1505–06 (8th Cir. 1988) (10 year old victim's injuries indicated recent use of force; court excluded evidence of consensual sexual activities with witness who testified at in camera hearing that he had never hurt victim and failed to establish recent activities).

Under the exception in subdivision (b)(1)(B), evidence of specific instances of sexual behavior with respect to the person whose sexual misconduct is alleged is admissible if offered to prove consent, or offered by the prosecution. Admissible pursuant to this exception might be evidence of prior instances of sexual activities between the alleged victim and the accused, as well as statements in which the alleged victim expressed an intent to engage in sexual intercourse with the accused, or voiced sexual fantasies involving the specific accused. In a prosecution for child sexual abuse, for example, evidence of uncharged sexual activity between the accused and the alleged victim offered by the prosecution may be admissible pursuant to Rule 404(b) to show a pattern of behavior. Evidence relating to the victim's alleged sexual predisposition is not admissible pursuant to this exception.

Under subdivision (b)(1)(C), evidence of specific instances of conduct may not be excluded if the result would be to deny a criminal defendant the protections afforded by the Constitution. For example, statements in which the victim has expressed an intent to have sex with the first person encountered on a particular occasion might not be excluded without violating the due process right of a rape defendant seeking to prove consent. Recognition of this basic principle was expressed in subdivision (b)(1) of the original rule. The United States Supreme Court has recognized that in various circumstances a defendant may have a right to introduce evidence otherwise precluded by an evidence rule under the Confrontation Clause. *See, e.g.*, Olden v. Kentucky, 488 U.S. 227 (1988) (defendant in rape cases had right to inquire into alleged victim's cohabitation with another man to show bias).

Subdivision (b)(2) governs the admissibility of otherwise proscribed evidence in civil cases. It employs a balancing test rather than the specific exceptions stated in subdivision (b)(1) in recognition of the difficulty of foreseeing future developments in the law. Greater flexibility is needed to accommodate evolving causes of action such as claims for sexual harassment.

The balancing test requires the proponent of the evidence, whether plaintiff or defendant, to convince the court that the probative value of the proffered evidence "substantially outweighs the danger of harm to any victim and of unfair prejudice to any party." This test for admitting evidence offered to prove sexual behavior or sexual propensity in civil cases differs in three respects from the general rule governing admissibility set forth in Rule 403. First, it reverses the usual procedure spelled out in Rule 403 by shifting the burden to the proponent to demonstrate admissibility rather than making the opponent justify exclusion of the evidence. Second, the standard expressed in subdivision (b)(2) is more stringent than in the original rule; it raises the threshold for admission by requiring that the probative value of the evidence substantially outweigh the specified dangers. Finally, the Rule 412 test puts "harm to the victim" on the scale in addition to prejudice to the parties.

Evidence of reputation may be received in a civil case only if the alleged victim has put his or her reputation into controversy. The victim may do so without making a specific allegation in a pleading. *Cf.* Fed.R.Civ.P. 35(a).

Subdivision (c). Amended subdivision (c) is more concise and understandable than the subdivision it replaces. The requirement of a motion before trial is continued in the amended rule, as is the provision that a late motion may be permitted for good cause shown. In deciding whether to permit late filing, the court may take into account the conditions previously included in the rule: namely whether the evidence is newly discovered and could not have been obtained earlier through the existence of due diligence, and whether the issue to which such evidence relates has newly arisen in the case. The rule recognizes that in some instances the circumstances that justify an application to introduce evidence otherwise barred by Rule 412 will not become apparent until trial.

The amended rule provides that before admitting evidence that falls within the prohibition of Rule 412(a), the court must hold a hearing in camera at which the alleged victim and any party must be afforded the right to be present and an opportunity to be heard. All papers connected with the motion and any record of a hearing on the motion must be kept and remain under seal during the course of trial and appellate proceedings unless otherwise ordered. This is to assure that the privacy of the alleged victim is preserved in all cases in which the court rules that proffered evidence is not admissible, and in which the hearing refers to matters that are not received, or are received in another form.

The procedures set forth in subdivision (c) do not apply to discovery of a victim's past sexual conduct or predisposition in civil cases, which will be continued to be governed by Fed. R. Civ. P. 26. In order not to undermine the rationale of Rule 412, however, courts should enter appropriate orders pursuant to Fed. R. Civ. P. 26(c) to protect the victim against unwarranted inquiries and to ensure confidentiality. Courts should presumptively issue protective orders barring discovery unless the party seeking discovery makes a showing that the evidence sought to be discovered would be relevant under the facts and theories of the particular case, and cannot be obtained except through discovery. In an action for sexual harassment, for instance, while some evidence of the alleged victim's sexual behavior and/or predisposition in the workplace may perhaps be relevant, non-work place conduct will usually be irrelevant. *Cf.* Burns v. McGregor Electronic Industries Inc., 989 F.2d 959, 962–63 (8th Cir. 1993) (posing for a nude magazine outside work hours is irrelevant to issue of unwelcomeness of sexual advances at work). Confidentiality orders should be presumptively granted as well.

One substantive change made in subdivision (c) is the elimination of the following sentence: "Notwithstanding subdivision (b) of Rule 104, if the relevancy of the evidence which the accused seeks to offer in the trial depends upon the fulfillment of a condition of fact, the court, at the hearing in chambers or at a subsequent hearing in chambers scheduled for such purpose, shall accept evidence on the issue of whether such condition of fact is fulfilled and shall determine such issue." On its face, this language would appear to authorize a trial judge to exclude evidence of past sexual conduct between an alleged victim and defendant in a civil case based upon the judge's belief that such past acts did not occur. Such an authorization raises questions of invasion of the right to a jury trial under the Sixth and Seventh Amendments. *See* 1 S. Saltzburg & M. Martin, *Federal Rules Of Evidence Manual*, 396–97 (5th ed. 1990).

The Advisory Committee concluded that the amended rule provided adequate protection for all persons claiming to be the victims of sexual misconduct, and that it was inadvisable to continue to include a provision in the rule that has been confusing and that raises substantial constitutional issues.

Rule 413. Similar Crimes in Sexual-Assault Cases

ADVISORY COMMITTEE NOTE TO THE 2011 AMENDMENT.

The language of Rule 413 has been amended as part of the restyling of the Evidence Rules to make them more easily understood and to make style and terminology consistent throughout the rules. These changes are intended to be stylistic only. There is no intent to change any result in any ruling on evidence admissibility.

Rule 413 is not a product of the usual procedure by which Federal Rules of Evidence are crafted. It was added to the Federal Rules of Evidence by Public Law 103-322, the Violent Crime Control and Law Enforcement Act of 1994. Public Law 103-322 was adopted September 13, 1994, and became effective July 9, 1995. The implementation procedure of the rule was set forth in section 320935 of Public Law 103-322 as follows:

(b) Implementation.—The amendments made by subsection (a) [enacting Rules 413, 414, and 415] shall become effective pursuant to subsection (d).

(c) Recommendations by Judicial Conference.—Not later than 150 days after the date of enactment of this Act [Sept. 13, 1994], the Judicial Conference of the United States shall transmit to Congress a report containing recommendations for amending the Federal Rules of Evidence as they affect the admission of evidence of a defendant's prior sexual assault or child molestation crimes in cases involving sexual assault and child molestation. The Rules Enabling Act shall not apply to the recommendations made by the Judicial Conference pursuant to this section.

(d) Congressional action.—

(1) If the recommendations described in subsection (c) are the same as the amendment made by subsection (a) [enacting Rules 413, 414, and 415], then the amendments made by subsection (a) shall become effective 30 days after the transmittal of the recommendations.

(2) If the recommendations described in subsection (c) are different than the amendments made by subsection (a) [enacting Rules 413, 414, and 415], the amendments made by subsection (a) shall become effective 150 days after the transmittal of the recommendations unless otherwise provided by law.

(3) If the Judicial Conference fails to comply with subsection (c), the amendments made by subsection (a) [enacting Rules 413, 414, and 415] shall become effective 150 days after the date the recommendations were due under subsection (c) unless otherwise provided by law.

(e) Application.—The amendments made by subsection (a) [enacting Rules 413, 414, and 415] shall apply to proceedings commenced on or after the effective date of such amendments.

In accordance with subsection (c), the Judicial Conference submitted its report concerning the proposed rules on February 9, 1995; its recommendations differed from the proposed rules. Congress neither followed the Conference's recommendations nor otherwise altered the proposed rules. As a result, according to subsection (d), the proposed rules became effective on July 9, 1995.

CONGRESSIONAL DISCUSSION.

Floor Statement of the Principal House Sponsor, Representative Susan Molinari, Concerning the Prior Crimes Evidence Rules for

Sexual Assault and Child Molestation Cases (Congressional Record, August 21, 1994, H8991-H8992):

Mr. Speaker, the revised conference bill contains a critical reform that I have long sought to protect the public from crimes of sexual violence—general rules of admissibility in sexual assault and child molestation cases for evidence that the defendant has committed offenses of the same type on other occasions. The enactment of this reform is first and foremost a triumph for the public—for the women who will not be raped and the children who will not be molested because we have strengthened the legal system's tools for bringing the perpetrators of these atrocious crimes to justice.

Senator Dole and I initially proposed this reform in February of 1991 in the Women's Equal Opportunity Act bill, and we later re-introduced it in the Sexual Assault Prevention Act bills of the 102d and 103d Congresses. The proposal also enjoyed the strong support of the Administration in the 102d Congress, and was included in President Bush's violent crime bill of that Congress, S. 635. The Senate passed the proposed rules on Nov. 5, 1993, by a vote of 75 to 19, in a crime bill amendment offered by Senator Dole. This Chamber endorsed the same rules on June 29, 1994, by a vote of 348 to 62, through a motion to instruct conferees that I offered.

The rules in the revised conference bill are substantially identical to our earlier proposals. We have agreed to a temporary deferral of the effective date of the new rules, pending a report by the Judicial Conference, in order to accommodate procedural objections raised by opponents of the reform. However, regardless of what the Judicial Conference may recommend, the new rules will take effect within at most 300 days of the enactment of this legislation, unless repealed or modified by subsequent legislation.

The need for these rules, their precedential support, their interpretation, and the issues and policy questions they raise have been analyzed at length in the legislative history of this proposal. I would direct the Members' attention particularly to two earlier statements:

The first is the portion of the section-by-section analysis accompanying these rules in section 801 of S. 635, which President Bush transmitted to Congress in 1991. That statement appears on pages S 3238 [to] S 3242 of the daily edition of the Congressional Record for March 13, 1991.

The second is the prepared text of an address—entitled "Evidence of Propensity and Probability in Sex Offense Cases and Other Cases" by Senior Counsel David J. Karp of the Office of Policy Development of the U.S. Department of Justice. Mr. Karp, who is the author of the new evidence rules, presented this statement on behalf of the Justice

Department to the Evidence Section of the Association of American Law Schools on January 9, 1993. The statement provided a detailed account of the views of the legislative sponsors and the Administration concerning the proposed reform, and should also be considered an authoritative part of its legislative history.

These earlier statements address the issues raised by this reform in considerable detail. In my present remarks, I will simply emphasize the following essential points:

> The new rules will supersede in sex offense cases the restrictive aspects of Federal Rule of Evidence 404(b). In contrast to Rule 404(b)'s general prohibition of evidence of character or propensity, the new rules for sex offense cases authorize admission and consideration of evidence of an uncharged offense for its bearing "on any matter to which it is relevant." This includes the defendant's propensity to commit sexual assault or child molestation offenses, and assessment of the probability or improbability that the defendant has been falsely or mistakenly accused of such an offense.

In other respects, the general standards of the rules of evidence will continue to apply, including the restrictions on hearsay evidence and the court's authority under Evidence Rule 403 to exclude evidence whose probative value is substantially outweighed by its prejudicial effect. Also, the government (or the plaintiff in a civil case) will generally have to disclose to the defendant any evidence that is to be offered under the new rules at least 15 days before trial.

The proposed reform is critical to the protection of the public from rapists and child molesters, and is justified by the distinctive characteristics of the cases it will affect. In child molestation cases, for example, a history of similar acts tends to be exceptionally probative because it shows an unusual disposition of the defendant—a sexual or sadosexual interest in children that simply does not exist in ordinary people.

Moreover, such cases require reliance on child victims whose credibility can readily be attacked in the absence of substantial corroboration. In such cases, there is a compelling public interest in admitting all significant evidence that will illumine the credibility of the charge and any denial by the defense.

Similarly, adult-victim sexual assault cases are distinctive, and often turn on difficult credibility determinations. Alleged consent by the victim is rarely an issue in prosecutions for other violent crimes—the accused mugger does not claim that the victim freely handed over [his] wallet as a gift but the defendant in a rape case often contends that the victim engaged in consensual sex and then falsely accused him. Knowledge that the defendant has committed rapes on other occasions is frequently critical in assessing the relative plausibility of these claims and accurately deciding cases that would otherwise become unresolvable swearing matches.

The practical effect of the new rules is to put evidence of uncharged offenses in sexual assault and child molestation cases on the same footing as other types of relevant evidence that are not subject to a special exclusionary rule. The presumption is in favor of admission. The underlying legislative judgment is that the evidence admissible pursuant to the proposed rules is typically relevant and probative, and that its probative value is normally not outweighed by any risk of prejudice or other adverse effects.

In line with this judgment, the rules do not impose arbitrary or artificial restrictions on the admissibility of evidence. Evidence of offenses for which the defendant has not previously been prosecuted or convicted will be admissible, as well as evidence of prior convictions. No time limit is imposed on the uncharged offenses for which evidence may be admitted; as a practical matter, evidence of other sex offenses by the defendant is often probative and properly admitted, notwithstanding very substantial lapses of time in relation to the charged offense or offenses. *See, e.g.*, United States v. Hadley, 918 F.2d 848, 850–51 (9th Cir. 1990), cert. dismissed, 113 S.Ct. 486 (1992) (evidence of offenses occurring up to 15 years earlier admitted); State v. Plymate, 345 N.W.2d 327 (Neb.1984) (evidence of defendant's commission of other child molestations more than 20 years earlier admitted).

Finally, the practical efficacy of these rules will depend on faithful execution by judges of the will of Congress in adopting this critical reform. To implement the legislative intent, the courts must liberally construe these rules to provide the basis for a fully informed decision of sexual assault and child molestation cases, including assessment of the defendant's propensities and questions of probability in light of the defendant's past conduct.

REPORT OF THE JUDICIAL CONFERENCE OF THE UNITED STATES.

Report of the Judicial Conference of the United States on the Admission of Character Evidence in Certain Sexual Misconduct Cases

I. INTRODUCTION.

This report is transmitted to Congress in accordance with the Violent Crime Control and Law Enforcement Act of 1994, Pub.L. No. 103-322 (September 13, 1994). Section 320935 of the Act invited the Judicial Conference of the United States within 150 days (February 10, 1995) to submit "a report containing recommendations for amending the Federal Rules of Evidence as they affect the admission of evidence of a defendant's prior sexual assault or child molestation crimes in cases involving sexual assault or child molestation."

Under the Act, new Rules 413, 414, and 415 would be added to the Federal Rules of Evidence. These Rules would admit evidence of a defendant's past similar acts in criminal and civil cases involving a sexual assault or child molestation offense for its bearing on any matter to which it is relevant. The effective date of new Rules 413–415 is contingent in part upon the nature of the recommendations submitted by the Judicial Conference.

After careful study, the Judicial Conference urges Congress to reconsider its decision on the policy questions underlying the new rules for reasons set out in Part III below.

If Congress does not reconsider its decision on the underlying policy questions, the Judicial Conference recommends incorporation of the provisions of new Rules 413–415 as amendments to Rules 404 and 405 of the Federal Rules of Evidence. The amendments would not change the substance of the congressional enactment but would clarify drafting ambiguities and eliminate possible constitutional infirmities.

II. BACKGROUND.

Under the Act, the Judicial Conference was provided 150 days within which to make and submit to Congress alternative recommendations to new Evidence Rules 413–415. Consideration of Rules 413–415 by the Judicial Conference was specifically excepted from the exacting review procedures set forth in the Rules Enabling Act (codified at 28 U.S.C. §§ 2071–2077). Although the Conference acted on these new rules on an expedited basis to meet the Act's deadlines, the review process was thorough.

The new rules would apply to both civil and criminal cases. Accordingly, the Judicial Conference's Advisory Committee on Criminal Rules and the Advisory Committee on Civil Rules reviewed the rules at separate meetings in October 1994. At the same time and in preparation for its consideration of the new rules, the Advisory Committee on Evidence Rules sent out a notice soliciting comment on new Evidence Rules 413, 414, and 415. The notice was sent to the courts, including all federal judges, about 900 evidence law professors, 40 women's rights organizations, and 1, 000 other individuals and interested organizations.

III. DISCUSSION.

On October 17–18, 1994, the Advisory Committee on Evidence Rules met in Washington, D.C. It considered the public responses, which included 84 written comments, representing 112 individuals, 8 local and 8 national legal organizations. The overwhelming majority of judges, lawyers, law professors, and legal organizations who responded opposed new Evidence Rules 413, 414, and 415. The principal objections expressed were that the rules would permit the admission of unfairly prejudicial evidence and contained numerous drafting problems not intended by their authors.

The Advisory Committee on Evidence Rules submitted its report to the Judicial Conference Committee on Rules of Practice and Procedure (Standing Committee) for review at its January 11–13, 1995 meeting. The committee's report was unanimous except for a dissenting vote by the representative of the Department of Justice. The advisory committee believed that the concerns expressed by Congress and embodied in new Evidence Rules 413, 414, and 415 are already adequately addressed in the existing Federal Rules of Evidence. In particular, Evidence Rule 404(b) now allows the admission of evidence against a criminal defendant of the commission of prior crimes, wrongs, or acts for specified purposes, including to show intent, plan, motive, preparation, identity, knowledge, or absence of mistake or accident.

Furthermore, the new rules, which are not supported by empirical evidence, could diminish significantly the protections that have safeguarded persons accused in criminal cases and parties in civil cases against undue prejudice. These protections form a fundamental part of American jurisprudence and have evolved under long-standing rules and case law. A significant concern identified by the committee was the danger of convicting a criminal defendant for past, as opposed to charged, behavior or for being a bad person.

In addition, the advisory committee concluded that, because prior bad acts would be admissible even though not the subject of a conviction, mini-trials within trials concerning those acts would result when a defendant seeks to rebut such evidence. The committee also noticed that many of the comments received had concluded that the Rules, as drafted, were mandatory—that is, such evidence had to be admitted regardless of other rules of evidence such as the hearsay rule or the Rule 403 balancing test. The committee believed that this position was arguable because Rules 413–415 declare without qualification that such evidence "is admissible." In contrast, the new Rule 412, passed as part of the same legislation, provided that certain evidence "is admissible if it is otherwise admissible under these Rules." Fed.R.Evid. 412(b)(2). If the critics are right, Rules 413–415 free the prosecution from rules that apply to the defendant including the hearsay rule and Rule 403. If so, serious constitutional questions would arise.

The Advisory Committees on Criminal and Civil Rules unanimously, except for representatives of the Department of Justice, also opposed the new rules. Those committees also concluded that the new rules would permit the introduction of unreliable but highly prejudicial evidence and would complicate trials by causing mini-trials of other alleged wrongs.

After the advisory committees reported, the Standing Committee unanimously, again except for the representative of the Department of Justice, agreed with the view of the advisory committees.

It is important to note the highly unusual unanimity of the members of the Standing and Advisory Committees, composed of over 40 judges, practicing lawyers, and academicians, in taking the view that Rules 413–415 are undesirable. Indeed, the only supporters of the Rules were representatives of the Department of Justice.

For these reasons, the Standing Committee recommended that Congress reconsider its decision on the policy questions embodied in new Evidence Rules 413, 414, and 415.

However, if Congress will not reconsider its decision on the policy questions, the Standing Committee recommended that Congress consider an alternative draft recommended by the Advisory Committee on Evidence Rules. That Committee drafted proposed amendments to existing Evidence Rules 404 and 405 that would both correct ambiguities and possible constitutional infirmities identified in new Evidence Rules 413, 414, and 415 yet still effectuate Congressional intent. In particular, the proposed amendments:

(1) expressly apply the other rules of evidence to evidence offered under the new rules;

(2) expressly allow the party against whom such evidence is offered to use similar evidence in rebuttal;

(3) expressly enumerate the factors to be weighed by a court in making its Rule 403 determination;

(4) render the notice provisions consistent with the provisions in existing Rule 404 regarding criminal cases;

(5) eliminate the special notice provisions of Rules 413–415 in civil cases so that notice will be required as provided in the Federal Rules of Civil Procedure; and

(6) permit reputation or opinion evidence after such evidence is offered by the accused or defendant.

The Standing Committee reviewed the new rules and the alternative recommendations. It concurred with the views of the Evidence Rules Committee and recommended that the Judicial Conference adopt them.

IV. RECOMMENDATIONS.

The Judicial Conference concurs with the views of the Standing Committee and urges that Congress reconsider its policy determinations underlying Evidence Rules 413–415. In the alternative, the attached amendments to Evidence Rules 404 and 405 are recommended, in lieu of new Evidence Rules 413, 414, and 415. The alternative amendments to Evidence Rules 404 and 405 are accompanied by the Advisory Committee Notes, which explain them in detail.

Rule 404. Character Evidence Not Admissible to Prove Conduct; Exceptions; Other Crimes

* * *

(4) Character in sexual misconduct cases. Evidence of another act of sexual assault or child molestation, or evidence to rebut such proof or an inference therefrom, if that evidence is otherwise admissible under these rules, in a criminal case in which the accused is charged with sexual assault or child molestation, or in a civil case in which a claim is predicated on a party's alleged commission of sexual assault or child molestation.

(A)   In weighing the probative value of such evidence, the court may, as part of its rule 403 determination, consider:

   (i)   proximity in time to the charged or predicate misconduct;

   (ii)   similarity to the charged or predicate misconduct;

   (iii) frequency of the other acts;

   (iv)   surrounding circumstances;

   (v)   relevant intervening events; and

   (vi)   other relevant similarities or differences.

(B)   In a criminal case in which the prosecution intends to offer evidence under this subdivision, it must disclose the evidence, including statements of witnesses or a summary of the substance of any testimony, at a reasonable time in advance of trial, or during trial if the court excuses pretrial notice on good cause shown.

(C)   For purposes of this subdivision,

   (i)   "sexual assault" means conduct—or an attempt or conspiracy to engage in conduct of the type proscribed by chapter 109A of title 18, United States Code, or conduct that involved deriving sexual pleasure or gratification from inflicting death, bodily injury, or physical pain on another person irrespective of the age of the victim—regardless of whether that conduct would have subjected the actor to federal jurisdiction.

   (ii)   "child molestation" means conduct—or an attempt or conspiracy to engage in conduct of the type proscribed by chapter 110 of title 18, United States Code, or conduct, committed in relation to a child below the age of 14 years, either of the type proscribed by chapter 109A of title 18, United States Code, or that involved deriving sexual pleasure or gratification from inflicting death, bodily injury, or physical pain on another person—regardless of whether that conduct would have subjected the actor to federal jurisdiction.

(b) Other crimes, wrongs, or acts. Evidence of other crimes, wrongs, or acts is not admissible to prove the character of a person in order to show action in conformity therewith except as provided in subdivision (a) . . . .

Note to Rule 404(a)(4).

The Committee has redrafted Rules 413, 414 and 415 which the Violent Crime Control and Law Enforcement Act of 1994 conditionally added to the Federal Rules of Evidence. These modifications do not change the substance of the congressional enactment. The changes were made in order to integrate the provisions both substantively and stylistically with the existing Rules of Evidence; to illuminate the intent expressed by the principal drafters of the measure; to clarify drafting ambiguities that might necessitate considerable judicial attention if they remained unresolved; and to eliminate possible constitutional infirmities.

The Committee placed the new provisions in Rule 404 because this rule governs the admissibility of character evidence. The congressional enactment constitutes a new exception to the general rule stated in subdivision (a). The Committee also combined the three separate rules proposed by Congress into one subdivision (a)(4) in accordance with the rules' customary practice of treating criminal and civil issues jointly. An amendment to Rule 405 has been added because the authorization of a new form of character evidence in this rule has an impact on methods of proving character that were not explicitly addressed by Congress. The stylistic changes are self-evident. They are particularly noticeable in the definition section in subdivision (a)(4)(C) in which the Committee eliminated, without any change in meaning, graphic details of sexual acts.

The Committee added language that explicitly provides that evidence under this subdivision must satisfy other rules of evidence such as the hearsay rules in Article VIII and the expert testimony rules in Article VII. Although principal sponsors of the legislation had stated that they intended other evidentiary rules to apply, the Committee believes that the opening phrase of the new subdivision 'if otherwise admissible under these rules' is needed to clarify the relationship between subdivision (a)(4) and other evidentiary provisions.

The Committee also expressly made subdivision (a)(4) subject to Rule 403 balancing in accordance with the repeatedly stated objectives of the legislation's sponsors with which representatives of the Justice Department expressed agreement. Many commentators on Rules 413–415 had objected that Rule 403's applicability was obscured by the actual language employed.

In addition to clarifying the drafters' intent, an explicit reference to Rule 403 may be essential to insulate the rule against constitutional challenge. Constitutional concerns also led the Committee to acknowledge specifically the opposing party's right to offer in rebuttal character evidence that the rules would otherwise bar, including evidence of a third person's prior acts of sexual misconduct offered to prove that the third person rather than the party committed the acts in issue.

In order to minimize the need for extensive and time-consuming judicial interpretation, the Committee listed factors that a court may consider in discharging Rule 403 balancing. Proximity in time is taken into account in a related rule. *See* Rule 609(b). Similarity, frequency and surrounding circumstances have long been considered by courts in handling other crimes evidence pursuant to Rule 404(b). Relevant intervening events, such as extensive medical treatment of the accused between the time of the prior proffered act and the charged act, may affect the strength of the propensity inference for which the evidence is offered. The final factor—"other relevant similarities or differences" is added in recognition of the endless variety of circumstances that confront a trial court in rulings on admissibility. Although subdivision (4)(A) explicitly refers to factors that bear on probative value, this enumeration does not eliminate a judge's responsibility to take into account the other factors mentioned in Rule 403 itself—"the danger of unfair prejudice, confusion of the issues, . . . misleading the jury, . . . undue delay, waste of time, or needless presentation of cumulative evidence." In addition, the Advisory Committee Note to Rule 403 reminds judges that "availability of other means of proof may also be an appropriate factor."

The Committee altered slightly the notice provision in criminal cases. Providing the trial court with some discretion to excuse pretrial notice was thought preferable to the inflexible 15-day rule provided in Rules 414 and 415. Furthermore, the formulation is identical to that contained in the 1991 amendment to Rule 404(b) so that no confusion will result from having two somewhat different notice provisions in the same rule. The Committee eliminated the notice provision for civil cases stated in Rule 415 because it did not believe that Congress intended to alter the usual time table for disclosure and discovery provided by the Federal Rules of Civil Procedure. The definition section was simplified with no change in meaning. The reference to 'the law of a State' was eliminated as unnecessarily confusing and restrictive. Conduct committed outside the United States ought equally to be eligible for admission. Evidence offered pursuant to subdivision (a)(4) must relate to a form of conduct proscribed by either chapter 109A or 110 of title 18, United States Code, regardless of whether the actor was subject to federal jurisdiction.

Rule 405. Methods of Proving Character.

(a) Reputation or opinion. In all cases in which evidence of character or a trait of character of a person is admissible, proof may be made by testimony as to reputation or by testimony in the form of an opinion except as provided in subdivision (c) of this rule. On cross-examination, inquiry is allowable into relevant specific instances of conduct.

* * *

(c) Proof in sexual misconduct cases. In a case in which evidence is offered under rule 404(a)(4), proof may be made by specific instances of conduct, testimony as to reputation, or testimony in the form of an opinion, except that the prosecution or claimant may offer reputation or opinion testimony only after the opposing party has offered such testimony.

Note to Rule 405(c).

The addition of a new subdivision (a)(4) to Rule 404 necessitates adding a new subdivision (c) to Rule 405 to govern methods of proof. Congress clearly intended no change in the preexisting law that precludes the prosecution or a claimant from offering reputation or opinion testimony in its case in chief to prove that the opposing party acted in conformity with character. When evidence is admissible pursuant to Rule 404(a)(4), the proponents proof must consist of specific instances of conduct. The opposing party, however, is free to respond with reputation or opinion testimony (including expert testimony if otherwise admissible) as well as evidence of specific instances. In a criminal case, the admissibility of reputation or opinion testimony would, in any event, be authorized by Rule 404(a)(1). The extension to civil cases is essential in order to provide the opponent with an adequate opportunity to refute allegations about a character for sexual misconduct. Once the opposing party offers reputation or opinion testimony, however, the prosecution or claimant may counter using such methods of proof.

Rule 414. Similar Crimes in Child-Molestation Cases

ADVISORY COMMITTEE NOTE TO THE 2011 AMENDMENT.

The language of Rule 414 has been amended as part of the restyling of the Evidence Rules to make them more easily understood and to make style and terminology consistent throughout the rules. These changes are intended to be stylistic only. There is no intent to change any result in any ruling on evidence admissibility.

Rule 414 is not a product of the usual procedure by which Federal Rules of Evidence are crafted. It was added to the Federal Rules of Evidence by Public Law 103-322, the Violent Crime Control and Law Enforcement Act of 1994. Public Law 103-322 was adopted September 13, 1994, and became effective July 9, 1995. For full discussion of the implementation of this rule, as well as Congressional Discussion and the Report of the Judicial Conference of the United States on this rule, see the legislative history of Rule 413.

Rule 415. Similar Acts in Civil Cases Involving Sexual Assault or Child Molestation

ADVISORY COMMITTEE NOTE TO THE 2011 AMENDMENT.

The language of Rule 415 has been amended as part of the restyling of the Evidence Rules to make them more easily understood and to make style and terminology consistent throughout the rules. These changes are intended to be stylistic only. There is no intent to change any result in any ruling on evidence admissibility.

Rule 415 is not a product of the usual procedure by which Federal Rules of Evidence are crafted. It was added to the Federal Rules of Evidence by Public Law 103-322, the Violent Crime Control and Law Enforcement Act of 1994. Public Law 103-322 was adopted September 13, 1994, and became effective July 9, 1995. For full discussion of the implementation of this rule, as well as Congressional Discussion and the Report of the Judicial Conference of the United States on this rule, see the legislative history of Rule 413.

ARTICLE V.
PRIVILEGES

Rule 501. Privilege in General

ADVISORY COMMITTEE NOTE TO THE 2011 AMENDMENT.

The language of Rule 501 has been amended as part of the restyling of the Evidence Rules to make them more easily understood and to make style and terminology consistent throughout the rules. These changes are intended to be stylistic only. There is no intent to change any result in any ruling on evidence admissibility.

[Note that there is no Advisory Committee Note to this Rule. The Committee's version of this Rule differed substantially from the Rule enacted. The Rules enacted by Congress substituted the single Rule 501 in place of the thirteen Rules dealing with privilege prescribed by the Supreme Court as Article V. The reasons given in support of the congressional action

are stated in the Report of the House Committee on the Judiciary, the Report of the Senate Committee on the Judiciary, and Report of the House/Senate Conference Committee, set forth below.]

REPORT OF THE HOUSE COMMITTEE ON THE JUDICIARY.

Article V as submitted to Congress contained thirteen Rules. Nine of those Rules defined specific non-constitutional privileges which the federal courts must recognize (i.e. required reports, lawyer-client, psychotherapist-patient, husband-wife, communications to clergymen, political vote, trade secrets, secrets of state and other official information, and identity of informer). Another Rule provided that only those privileges set forth in Article V or in some other Act of Congress could be recognized by the federal courts. The three remaining Rules addressed collateral problems as to waiver of privilege by voluntary disclosure, privileged matter disclosed under compulsion or without opportunity to claim privilege, comment upon or inference from a claim of privilege, and jury instruction with regard thereto.

The Committee amended Article V to eliminate all of the Court's specific Rules on privileges. Instead, the Committee, through a single Rule, 501, left the law of privileges in its present state and further provided that privileges shall continue to be developed by the courts of the United States under a uniform standard applicable both in civil and criminal cases. That standard, derived from Rule 26 of the Federal Rules of Criminal Procedure, mandates the application of the principles of the common law as interpreted by the courts of the United States in the light of reason and experience. The words "person, government, State, or political subdivision thereof" were added by the Committee to the lone term "witnesses" used in Rule 26 to make clear that, as under present law, not only witnesses may have privileges. The Committee also included in its amendment a proviso modeled after Rule 302 and similar to language added by the Committee to Rule 601 relating to the competency of witnesses. The proviso is designed to require the application of State privilege law in civil actions and proceedings governed by Erie R. Co. v. Tompkins, 304 U.S. 64 (1938), a result in accord with current federal court decisions. *See* Republic Gear Co. v. Borg-Warner Corp., 381 F2d 551, 555–556 n.2 (2nd Cir. 1967). The Committee deemed the proviso to be necessary in the light of the Advisory Committee's view (*see* its note to Court Rule 501) that this result is not mandated under *Erie*.

The rationale underlying the proviso is that federal law should not supersede that of the States in substantive areas such as privilege absent a compelling reason. The Committee believes that in civil cases in the federal courts where an element of a claim or defense is not grounded upon a federal question, there is no federal interest strong enough to justify departure from State policy. In addition, the Committee considered that the Court's proposed Article V would have promoted forum shopping in some civil actions, depending upon differences in the privilege law applied as among the State and federal courts. The Committee's proviso, on the other hand, under which the federal courts are bound to apply the State's privilege law in actions founded upon a State-created right or defense, removes the incentive to "shop."

REPORT OF THE SENATE COMMITTEE ON THE JUDICIARY.

[The version of Rule 501 recommended in this Report differs in the second sentence from the enacted Rule set forth above.]

Article V as submitted to Congress contained 13 rules. Nine of those rules defined specific nonconstitutional privileges which the Federal courts must recognize (i.e., required reports, lawyer-client, psychotherapist-patient, husband-wife, communications to clergymen, political vote, trade secrets, secrets of state and other official information, and identity of informer.) Many of these rules contained controversial modifications or restrictions upon common law privileges. As noted *supra*, the House amended article V to eliminate all of the Court's specific rules on privileges. Through a single rule, 501, the House provided that privileges shall be governed by the principles of the common law as interpreted by the courts of the United States in the light of reason and experience (a standard derived from rule 26 of the Federal Rules of Criminal Procedure) except in the case of an element of a civil claim or defense as to which State law supplies the rules of decision, in which event state privilege law was to govern.

The committee agrees with the main thrust of the House amendment: that a federally developed common law based on modern reason and experience shall apply except where the State nature of the issues renders deference to State privilege law the wiser course, as in the usual diversity case. The committee understands that thrust of the House amendment to require that State privilege law be applied in "diversity" cases (actions on questions of State law between citizens of different States arising under 28 U.S.C. § 1332). The language of the House amendment, however, goes beyond this in some respects, and falls short of it in others: State privilege law applies even in nondiversity, Federal question civil cases, where an issue governed by State substantive law is the object of the evidence (such issues do sometimes arise in such cases); and, in all instances where State privilege law is to be applied, e.g., on proof of a State issue in a diversity case, a close reading reveals that State privilege law is not to be applied unless the matter to be proved is an element of that state claim or defense, as distinguished from a step along the way in the proof of it.

The committee is concerned that the language used in the House amendment could be difficult to apply. It provides that "in civil actions . . . with respect to an element of a claim or defense as to which State law supplies the rule of decision," State law on privilege applies. The question of what is an element of a claim or defense is likely to engender considerable litigation. If the matter in question constitutes an element of a claim, State law supplies the privilege rule; whereas if it is a mere item of proof with respect to a claim, then, even though State law might supply the rule of decision, Federal law on the privilege would apply. Further, disputes will arise as to how the rule should be applied in an antitrust action or in a tax case where the Federal statute is silent as to a particular aspect of the substantive law in question, but Federal cases had incorporated State law by reference to State law.[4] Is a claim (or defense) based on such a reference a claim or defense as to which federal or State law supplies the rule of decision?

Another problem not entirely avoidable is the complexity or difficulty the rule introduces into the trial of a Federal case containing a combination of Federal and State claims and defenses, e.g. an action involving Federal antitrust and State unfair competition claims. Two different bodies of privilege law would need to be consulted. It may even develop that the same witness-testimony might be relevant on both counts and privileged as to one but not the other.[5]

The formulation adopted by the House is pregnant with litigious mischief. The committee has, therefore, adopted what we believe will be a clearer and more practical guideline for determining when courts should respect State rules of privilege. Basically, it provides that in criminal and Federal question civil cases, federally evolved rules on privilege should apply since it is Federal policy which is being enforced.[6] Conversely, in diversity cases where the litigation in question turns on a substantive question of State law, and is brought in the Federal courts because the parties reside in different States, the committee believes it is clear that State rules of privilege should apply unless the proof is directed at a claim or defense for which Federal law supplies the rule of decision (a situation which would not commonly arise.)[7] It is intended that the State rules of privilege should apply

---

[4] For a discussion of reference to State substantive law, *see* note on Federal Incorporation by Reference of State Law, Hart & Wechster, *The Federal Courts and the Federal System*, pp. 491–94 (2d Ed. 1973).

[5] The problems with the House formulation are discussed in Rothstein, "The Proposed Amendments to the Federal Rules of Evidence," 62 Georgetown University Law Journal 125 (1973) at notes 25, 26 and 70–74, and accompanying text.

[6] It is also intended that the Federal law of privileges should be applied with respect to pendant state law claims when they arise in a Federal question case.

[7] While such a situation might require use of two bodies of privilege law, federal and state,

equally in original diversity actions and diversity actions removed under 28 U.S.C. § 1441 (b).

Two other comments on the privilege rule should be made. The committee has received a considerable volume of correspondence from psychiatric organizations and psychiatrists concerning the deletion of rule 504 of the rule submitted by the Supreme Court. It should be clearly understood that, in approving this general rule as to privileges, the action of Congress should not be understood as disapproving any recognition of a psychiatrist-patient, or husband-wife, or any other of the enumerated privileges contained in the Supreme Court rules. Rather, our action should be understood as reflecting the view that the recognition of a privilege based on a confidential relationship and other privileges should be determined on a case-by-case basis.

Further, we would understand that the prohibition against spouses testifying against each other is considered a rule of privilege and covered by this rule and not by rule 601 of the competency of witnesses.

REPORT OF HOUSE/SENATE CONFERENCE COMMITTEE.

Rule 501 deals with the privilege of a witness not to testify. Both the House and Senate bills provide that federal privilege law applies in criminal cases. In civil actions and proceedings, the House bill provides that state privilege law applies "to an element of a claim or defense as to which State law supplies the rule of decision." The Senate bill provides that "in civil actions and proceedings arising under 28 U.S.C. § 1332 or 28 U.S.C. § 1335, or between citizens of different States and removed under 28 U.S.C. § 1441(b) the privilege of a witness, person, government, State or political subdivision thereof is determined in accordance with State law, unless with respect to the particular claim or defense, Federal law supplies the rule of decision."

The wording of the House and Senate bills differs in the treatment of civil actions and proceedings. The rule in the House bill applies to evidence that relates to "an element of a claim or defense." If an item of proof tends to support or defeat a claim or defense, or an element of a claim or defense, and if state privilege law applies to that item of proof.

---

in the same case, nevertheless the occasions on which this would be required are considerably reduced as compared with the House version, and confined to situations where the Federal and State interests are such as to justify application of neither privilege law to the case as a whole. If the rule proposed here results in two conflicting bodies of privilege law applying to the same piece of evidence in the same case, it is contemplated that the rule favoring reception of the evidence should be applied. This policy is based on the present rule 43(a) of the Federal Rules of Civil Procedure which provides: In any case, the statute or rule which favors the reception of the evidence governs and the evidence shall be presented according to the most convenient method prescribed in any of the statutes or rules to which reference is herein made.

Under the provision in the House bill, therefore, state privilege law will usually apply in diversity cases. There may be diversity cases, however, where a claim or defense is based upon federal law. In such instances, federal privilege law will apply to evidence relevant to the federal claim or defense. *See* Sola Electric Co. v. Jefferson Electric Co., 317 U.S. 173 (1942).

In nondiversity jurisdiction civil cases, federal privilege law will generally apply. In those situations where a federal court adopts or incorporates state law to fill interstices or gaps in federal statutory phrases, the court generally will apply federal privilege law. As Justice Jackson has said:

A federal court sitting in a non-diversity case such as this does not sit as a local tribunal. In some cases it may see fit for special reasons to give the law of a particular state highly persuasive or even controlling effect, but in the last analysis its decision turns upon the law of the United States, not that of any state.

D'Oench, Duhme & Co. v. Federal Deposit Insurance Corp., 315 U.S. 447, 471 (1942) (Jackson, J., concurring). When a federal court chooses to absorb state law, it is applying the state law as a matter of federal common law. Thus, state law does not supply the rule of decision (even though the federal court may apply a rule derived from the decisions), and state privilege law would not apply. *See* C. A. Wright, *Federal Courts* 251–252 (2d ed. 1970); Holmberg v. Armbrecht, 327 U.S. 392 (1946); DeSylva v. Ballentine, 351 U.S. 570, 581 (1956); 9 Wright & Miller, *Federal Rules and Procedure* § 2408.

In civil actions and proceedings, where the rule of decision as to a claim or defense or as to an element of a claim or defense is supplied by state law, the House provision requires that state privilege law apply.

The Conference adopts the House provision.

Rule 502. Attorney-Client Privilege and Work Product; Limitations on Waiver

ADVISORY COMMITTEE NOTE TO THE 2011 AMENDMENT.

The language of Rule 502 has been amended as part of the restyling of the Evidence Rules to make them more easily understood and to make style and terminology consistent throughout the rules. These changes are intended to be stylistic only. There is no intent to change any result in any ruling on evidence admissibility.

ADVISORY COMMITTEE NOTE

Explanatory Note (Revised 11/28/2007)

This new rule has two major purposes:

1) It resolves some longstanding disputes in the courts about the

effect of certain disclosures of communications or information protected by the attorney-client privilege or as work product—specifically those disputes involving inadvertent disclosure and subject matter waiver.

2) It responds to the widespread complaint that litigation costs necessary to protect against waiver of attorney-client privilege or work product have become prohibitive due to the concern that any disclosure (however innocent or minimal) will operate as a subject matter waiver of all protected communications or information. This concern is especially troubling in cases involving electronic discovery. See, e.g., Hopson v. City of Baltimore, 232 F.R.D. 228, 244 (D.Md. 2005) (electronic discovery may encompass "millions of documents" and to insist upon "record-by-record pre-production privilege review, on pain of subject matter waiver, would impose upon parties costs of production that bear no proportionality to what is at stake in the litigation").

The rule seeks to provide a predictable, uniform set of standards under which parties can determine the consequences of a disclosure of a communication or information covered by the attorney-client privilege or work-product protection. Parties to litigation need to know, for example, that if they exchange privileged information pursuant to a confidentiality order, the court's order will be enforceable. Moreover, if a federal court's confidentiality order is not enforceable in a state court then the burdensome costs of privilege review and retention are unlikely to be reduced.

The rule makes no attempt to alter federal or state law on whether a communication or information is protected under the attorney-client privilege or work-product immunity as an initial matter. Moreover, while establishing some exceptions to waiver, the rule does not purport to supplant applicable waiver doctrine generally.

The rule governs only certain waivers by disclosure. Other common-law waiver doctrines may result in a finding of waiver even where there is no disclosure of privileged information or work product. See, e.g., Nguyen v. Excel Corp., 197 F.3d 200 (5th Cir. 1999) (reliance on an advice of counsel defense waives the privilege with respect to attorney-client communications pertinent to that defense); Byers v. Burleson, 100 F.R.D. 436 (D.D.C. 1983) (allegation of lawyer malpractice constituted a waiver of confidential communications under the circumstances). The rule is not intended to displace or modify federal common law concerning waiver of privilege or work product where no disclosure has been made.

Subdivision (a). The rule provides that a voluntary disclosure in a federal proceeding or to a federal office or agency, if a waiver, generally results in a waiver only of the communication or information disclosed; a subject matter waiver (of either privilege or work product) is reserved for those unusual situations in which fairness requires a further disclosure of related, protected information, in order to prevent a selective and misleading presentation of evidence to the disadvantage of the adversary. See, e.g., In re United Mine Workers of America Employee Benefit Plans Litig., 159 F.R.D. 307, 312 (D.D.C. 1994) (waiver of work product limited to materials actually disclosed, because the party did not deliberately disclose documents in an attempt to gain a tactical advantage). Thus, subject matter waiver is limited to situations in which a party intentionally puts protected information into the litigation in a selective, misleading and unfair manner. It follows that an inadvertent disclosure of protected information can never result in a subject matter waiver. See Rule 502(b). The rule rejects the result in In re Sealed Case, 877 F.2d 976 (D.C. Cir. 1989), which held that inadvertent disclosure of documents during discovery automatically constituted a subject matter waiver.

The language concerning subject matter waiver—"ought in fairness"—is taken from Rule 106, because the animating principle is the same. Under both Rules, a party that makes a selective, misleading presentation that is unfair to the adversary opens itself to a more complete and accurate presentation.

To assure protection and predictability, the rule provides that if a disclosure is made at the federal level, the federal rule on subject matter waiver governs subsequent state court determinations on the scope of the waiver by that disclosure.

Subdivision (b). Courts are in conflict over whether an inadvertent disclosure of a communication or information protected as privileged or work product constitutes a waiver. A few courts find that a disclosure must be intentional to be a waiver. Most courts find a waiver only if the disclosing party acted carelessly in disclosing the communication or information and failed to request its return in a timely manner. And a few courts hold that any inadvertent disclosure of a communication or information protected under the attorney-client privilege or as work product constitutes a waiver without regard to the protections taken to avoid such a disclosure. See generally Hopson v. City of Baltimore, 232 F.R.D. 228 (D.Md. 2005), for a discussion of this case law.

The rule opts for the middle ground: inadvertent disclosure of protected communications or information in connection with a federal proceeding or to a federal office or agency does not constitute a waiver if the holder took reasonable steps to prevent disclosure and also promptly took reasonable steps to rectify the error. This position is in accord with the majority view on whether inadvertent disclosure is a waiver.

Cases such as Lois Sportswear, U.S.A., Inc. v. Levi Strauss & Co.,

104 F.R.D. 103, 105 (S.D.N.Y. 1985) and Hartford Fire Ins. Co. v. Garvey, 109 F.R.D. 323, 332 (N.D.Cal. 1985), set out a multi-factor test for determining whether inadvertent disclosure is a waiver. The stated factors (none of which is dispositive) are the reasonableness of precautions taken, the time taken to rectify the error, the scope of discovery, the extent of disclosure and the overriding issue of fairness. The rule does not explicitly codify that test, because it is really a set of non-determinative guidelines that vary from case to case. The rule is flexible enough to accommodate any of those listed factors. Other considerations bearing on the reasonableness of a producing party's efforts include the number of documents to be reviewed and the time constraints for production. Depending on the circumstances, a party that uses advanced analytical software applications and linguistic tools in screening for privilege and work product may be found to have taken "reasonable steps" to prevent inadvertent disclosure. The implementation of an efficient system of records management before litigation may also be relevant.

The rule does not require the producing party to engage in a post-production review to determine whether any protected communication or information has been produced by mistake. But the rule does require the producing party to follow up on any obvious indications that a protected communication or information has been produced inadvertently.

The rule applies to inadvertent disclosures made to a federal office or agency, including but not limited to an office or agency that is acting in the course of its regulatory, investigative or enforcement authority. The consequences of waiver, and the concomitant costs of pre-production privilege review, can be as great with respect to disclosures to offices and agencies as they are in litigation.

Subdivision (c). Difficult questions can arise when 1) a disclosure of a communication or information protected by the attorney-client privilege or as work product is made in a state proceeding, 2) the communication or information is offered in a subsequent federal proceeding on the ground that the disclosure waived the privilege or protection, and 3) the state and federal laws are in conflict on the question of waiver. The Committee determined that the proper solution for the federal court is to apply the law that is most protective of privilege and work product. If the state law is more protective (such as where the state law is that an inadvertent disclosure can never be a waiver), the holder of the privilege or protection may well have relied on that law when making the disclosure in the state proceeding. Moreover, applying a more restrictive federal law of waiver could impair the state objective of preserving the privilege or work-product protection for disclosures made in state proceedings. On the other hand, if the federal law is more protective, applying the state law of waiver to determine admissibility in federal court is likely to undermine the federal objective of limiting the costs of production.

The rule does not address the enforceability of a state court confidentiality order in a federal proceeding, as that question is covered both by statutory law and principles of federalism and comity. See 28 U.S.C. § 1738 (providing that state judicial proceedings "shall have the same full faith and credit in every court within the United States . . . as they have by law or usage in the courts of such State . . . from which they are taken"). See also Tucker v. Ohtsu Tire & Rubber Co., 191 F.R.D. 495, 499 (D.Md. 2000) (noting that a federal court considering the enforceability of a state confidentiality order is "constrained by principles of comity, courtesy, and . . . federalism"). Thus, a state court order finding no waiver in connection with a disclosure made in a state court proceeding is enforceable under existing law in subsequent federal proceedings

Subdivision (d). Confidentiality orders are becoming increasingly important in limiting the costs of privilege review and retention, especially in cases involving electronic discovery. But the utility of a confidentiality order in reducing discovery costs is substantially diminished if it provides no protection outside the particular litigation in which the order is entered. Parties are unlikely to be able to reduce the costs of pre-production review for privilege and work product if the consequence of disclosure is that the communications or information could be used by non-parties to the litigation.

There is some dispute on whether a confidentiality order entered in one case is enforceable in other proceedings. See generally Hopson v. City of Baltimore, 232 F.R.D. 228 (D.Md. 2005), for a discussion of this case law. The rule provides that when a confidentiality order governing the consequences of disclosure in that case is entered in a federal proceeding, its terms are enforceable against non-parties in any federal or state proceeding. For example, the court order may provide for return of documents without waiver irrespective of the care taken by the disclosing party; the rule contemplates enforcement of "claw-back" and "quick peek" arrangements as a way to avoid the excessive costs of pre-production review for privilege and work product. See Zubulake v. UBS Warburg LLC, 216 F.R.D. 280, 290 (S.D.N.Y. 2003) (noting that parties may enter into "so-called 'claw-back' agreements that allow the parties to forego privilege review altogether in favor of an agreement to return inadvertently produced privileged documents"). The rule provides a party with a predictable protection from a court order—predictability that is needed to allow the party to plan in advance to limit the prohibitive costs of privilege and work product review and retention.

Under the rule, a confidentiality order is enforceable whether or not it memorializes an agreement among the parties to the litigation. Party agreement should not be a condition of enforceability of a federal court's order.

Under subdivision (d), a federal court may order that disclosure of privileged or protected information "in connection with" a federal proceeding does not result in waiver. But subdivision (d) does not allow the federal court to enter an order determining the waiver effects of a separate disclosure of the same information in other proceedings, state or federal. If a disclosure has been made in a state proceeding (and is not the subject of a state-court order on waiver), then subdivision (d) is inapplicable. Subdivision (c) would govern the federal court's determination whether the state-court disclosure waived the privilege or protection in the federal proceeding.

Subdivision (e). Subdivision (e) codifies the well-established proposition that parties can enter an agreement to limit the effect of waiver by disclosure between or among them. Of course such an agreement can bind only the parties to the agreement. The rule makes clear that if parties want protection against non-parties from a finding of waiver by disclosure, the agreement must be made part of a court order.

Subdivision (f). The protections against waiver provided by Rule 502 must be applicable when protected communications or information disclosed in federal proceedings are subsequently offered in state proceedings. Otherwise the holders of protected communications and information, and their lawyers, could not rely on the protections provided by the Rule, and the goal of limiting costs in discovery would be substantially undermined. Rule 502(f) is intended to resolve any potential tension between the provisions of Rule 502 that apply to state proceedings and the possible limitations on the applicability of the Federal Rules of Evidence otherwise provided by Rules 101 and 1101.

The rule is intended to apply in all federal court proceedings, including court-annexed and court-ordered arbitrations, without regard to any possible limitations of Rules 101 and 1101. This provision is not intended to raise an inference about the applicability of any other rule of evidence in arbitration proceedings more generally.

The costs of discovery can be equally high for state and federal causes of action, and the rule seeks to limit those costs in all federal proceedings, regardless of whether the claim arises under state or federal law. Accordingly, the rule applies to state law causes of action brought in federal court.

Subdivision (g). The rule's coverage is limited to attorney-client privilege and work product. The operation of waiver by disclosure, as applied to other evidentiary privileges, remains a question of federal common law. Nor does the rule purport to apply to the Fifth Amendment privilege against compelled self-incrimination.

The definition of work product "materials" is intended to include both tangible and intangible information. See In re Cendant Corp. Sec. Litig., 343 F.3d 658, 662 (3d Cir. 2003) ("work product protection extends to both tangible and intangible work product").

COMMITTEE LETTER

The letter from the Committee on Rules of Practice and Procedure of the Judicial Conference of the United States to the Committee on the Judiciary of the U.S. Senate and House of Representatives, dated September 26, 2007, provided:

> On behalf of the Judicial Conference of the United States, I respectfully submit a proposed addition to the Federal Rules of Evidence. The Conference recommends that Congress adopt this proposed rule as Federal Rule of Evidence 502.

> The Rule provides for protections against waiver of the attorney-client privilege or work product immunity. The Conference submits this proposal directly to Congress because of the limitations on the rulemaking function of the federal courts in matters dealing with evidentiary privilege. Unlike all other federal rules of procedure prescribed under the Rules Enabling Act, those rules governing evidentiary privilege must by approved by an Act of Congress, 28 U.S.C. § 2074(b).

Description of the Process Leading to the Proposed Rule

> The Judicial Conference Rules Committees have long been concerned about the rising costs of litigation, much of which has been caused by the review, required under current law, of every document produced in discovery, in order to determine whether the document contains privileged information. In 2006, the House Judiciary Committee Chair suggested that the Judicial Conference consider proposing a rule dealing with waiver of attorney-client privilege and work product, in order to limit these rising costs. The Judicial Conference was urged to proceed with rulemaking that would:

> • protect against the forfeiture of privilege when a disclosure in discovery is the result of an innocent mistake; and

> • permit parties, and courts, to protect against the consequences of waiver by permitting disclosures of privileged information between the parties to litigation.

> The task of drafting a proposed rule was referred to the Advisory Committee on Evidence Rules (the "Advisory Committee"). The Advisory Committee prepared a draft Rule 502 and invited a select group of judges, lawyers, and academics to testify before the Advisory Committee about the need for the rule, and to suggest any improve-

ments. The Advisory Committee considered all the testimony presented by these experts and redrafted the rule accordingly. At its Spring 2006 meeting, the Advisory Committee approved for release for public comment a proposed Rule 502 that would provide certain exceptions to the federal common law on waiver of privileges and work product. That rule was approved for release for public comment by the Committee on Rules of Practice and Procedure ("the Standing Committee"). The public comment period began in August 2006 and ended February 15, 2007. The Advisory Committee received more that [sic] 70 public comments, and also heard the testimony of more than 20 witnesses at two public hearings. The rule released for public comment was also carefully reviewed by the Standing Committee's Subcommittee on Style. In April 2007, the Advisory Committee issued a revised proposed Rule 502 taking into account the public comment, the views of the Subcommittee on Style, and its own judgment. The revised rule was approved by the Standing Committee and the Judicial Conference. It is enclosed with this letter.

In order to inform Congress of the legal issues involved in this rule, the proposed Rule 502 also includes a proposed Committee Note of the kind that accompanies all rules adopted through the Rules Enabling Act. This Committee Note may be incorporated as all or part of the legislative history of the rule if it is adopted by Congress. See, e.g., House Conference Report 103-711 (stating that the "Conferees intend that the Advisory Committee Note on [Evidence] Rule 412, as transmitted by the Judicial Conference of the United States to the Supreme Court on October 25, 1993, applies to Rule 412 as enacted by this section" of the Violent Crime Control and Law Enforcement Act of 1994).

Problems Addressed by the Proposed Rule

In drafting the proposed Rule, the Advisory Committee concluded that the current law on waiver of privilege and work product is responsible in large part for the rising costs of discovery, especially discovery of electronic information. In complex litigation the lawyers spend significant amounts of time and effort to preserve the privilege and work product. The reason is that if a protected document is produced, there is a risk that a court will find a subject matter waiver that will apply not only to the instant case and document but to other cases and documents as well. Moreover, an enormous amount of expense is put into document production in order to protect against inadvertent disclosure of privileged information, because the producing party risks a ruling that even a mistaken disclosure can result in a subject matter waiver. Advisory Committee members also expressed the view that the fear of waiver leads to extravagant claims of privilege.

Members concluded that if there were a way to produce documents in discovery without risking subject matter waiver, the discovery process could be made much less expensive. The Advisory Committee noted that the existing law on the effect of inadvertent disclosures and on the scope of waiver is far from consistent or certain. It also noted that agreements between parties with regard to the effect of disclosure on privilege are common, but are unlikely to decrease the costs of discovery due to the ineffectiveness of such agreements as to persons not party to them.

Proposed Rule 502 does not attempt to deal comprehensively with either attorney-client privilege or work-product protection. It also does not purport to cover all issues concerning waiver or forfeiture of either the attorney-client privilege or work-product protection. Rather, it deals primarily with issues involved in the disclosure of protected information in federal court proceedings or to a federal public office or agency. The rule binds state courts only with regard to disclosures made in federal proceedings. It deals with disclosures made in state proceedings only to the extent that the effect of those disclosures becomes an issue in federal litigation. The Rule covers issues of scope of waiver, inadvertent disclosure, and the controlling effect of court orders and agreements.

Rule 502 provides the following protections against waiver of privilege or work product:

• Limitations on Scope of Waiver. Subdivision (a) provides that if a waiver is found, it applies only to the information disclosed, unless a broader waiver is made necessary by the holder's intentional and misleading use of privileged or protected communications or information.

• Protections Against Inadvertent Disclosure. Subdivision (b) provides that an inadvertent disclosure of privileged or protected communications or information, when made at the federal level, does not operate as a waiver if the holder took reasonable steps to prevent such a disclosure and employed reasonably prompt measures to retrieve the mistakenly disclosed communications or information.

• Effect on State Proceedings and Disclosures Made in State Courts. Subdivision (c) provides that 1) if there is a disclosure of privileged or protected communications or information at the federal level, then state courts must honor Rule 502 in subsequent state proceedings; and 2) if there is a disclosure of privileged or protected communications or information in a state proceeding, then admissibility in a subsequent federal proceeding is determined by the law that is most protective against waiver.

• Orders Protecting Privileged Communications Binding on Non-Parties. Subdivision (d) provides that if a federal court enters an order providing that a disclosure of privileged or protected communications or information does not constitute a waiver, that order is enforceable against all persons and entities in any federal or state proceeding. This provision allows parties in an action in which such an order is entered to limit their costs of pre-production privilege review.

• Agreements Protecting Privileged Communications Binding on Parties. Subdivision (e) provides that parties in a federal proceeding can enter into a confidentiality agreement providing for mutual protection against waiver in that proceeding. While those agreements bind the signatory parties, they are not binding on non-parties unless incorporated into a court order.

Drafting Choices Made by the Advisory Committee

The Advisory Committee made a number of important drafting choices in Rule 502. This section explains those choices.

1) The effect in state proceedings of disclosures initially made in state proceedings. Rule 502 does not apply to a disclosure made in a state proceeding when the disclosed communication or information is subsequently offered in another state proceeding. The first draft of Rule 502 provided for uniform waiver rules in federal and state proceedings, regardless of where the initial disclosure was made. This draft raised the objections of the Conference of State Chief Justices. State judges argued that the Rule as drafted offended principles of federalism and comity, by superseding state law of privilege waiver, even for disclosures that are made initially in state proceedings—and even when the disclosed material is then offered in a state proceeding (the so-called "state-to-state" problem). In response to these objections, the Advisory Committee voted unanimously to scale back the Rule, so that it would not cover the "state-to-state" problem. Under the current proposal state courts are bound by the Federal Rule only when a disclosure is made at the federal level and the disclosed communication or information is later offered in a state proceeding (the so-called "federal-to-state" problem).

During the public comment period on the scaled-back rule, the Advisory Committee received many requests from lawyers and lawyer groups to return to the original draft and provide a uniform rule of privilege waiver that would bind both state and federal courts, for disclosures made in either state or federal proceedings. These comments expressed the concern that if states were not bound by a uniform federal rule on privilege waiver, the protections afforded by Rule 502 would be undermined; parties and their lawyers might not be able to rely on the protections of the Rule, for fear that a state law would find a waiver even though the Federal Rule would not.

The Advisory Committee determined that these comments raised a legitimate concern, but decided not to extend Rule 502 to govern a state court's determination of waiver with respect to disclosures made in state proceedings. The Committee relied on the following considerations:

• Rule 502 is located in the Federal Rules of Evidence, a body of rules determining the admissibility of evidence in federal proceedings. Parties in a state proceeding determining the effect of a disclosure made in that proceeding or in other state courts would be unlikely to look to the Federal Rules of Evidence for the answer.

• In the Advisory Committee's view, Rule 502, as proposed herein, does fulfill its primary goal of reducing the costs of discovery in federal proceedings. Rule 502 by its terms governs state courts with regard to the effect of disclosures initially made in federal proceedings or to federal offices or agencies. Parties and their lawyers in federal proceedings can therefore predict the consequences of disclosure by referring to Rule 502; there is no possibility that a state court could find a waiver when Rule 502 would not, when the disclosure is initially made at the federal level.

The Judicial Conference has no position on the merits of separate legislation to cover the problem of waiver of privilege and work product when the disclosure is made at the state level and the consequence is to be determined in a state court.

2) Other applications of Rule 502 to state court proceedings. Although disclosures made in state court proceedings and later offered in state proceedings would not be covered, Rule 502 would have an effect on state court proceedings where the disclosure is initially made in a federal proceeding or to a federal office or agency. Most importantly, state courts in such circumstances would be bound by federal protection orders. The other protections against waiver in Rule 502—against mistaken disclosure and subject matter waiver—would also bind state courts as to disclosures initially made at the federal level. The Rule, as submitted, specifically provides that it applies to state proceedings under the circumstances set out in the Rule. This protection is needed, otherwise parties could not rely on Rule 502 even as to federal disclosures, for fear that a state court would find waiver even when a federal court would not.

3) Disclosures made in state proceedings and offered in a subsequent federal proceeding. Earlier drafts of proposed Rule 502 did not determine the question of what rule would apply when a disclosure is made in state court and the waiver determination is to be made in a subsequent federal proceeding. Proposed Rule 502 as submitted herein provides that all of the provisions of Rule 502 apply unless the state law of privilege is more protective (less likely to find waiver) than the federal law. The Advisory Committee determined that this solution best

preserved federal interests in protecting against waiver, and also provided appropriate respect for state attempts to give greater protection to communications and information covered by the attorney-client privilege or work-product doctrine.

4) Selective waiver. At the suggestion of the House Judiciary Committee Chair, the Advisory Committee considered a rule that would allow persons and entities to cooperate with government agencies without waiving all privileges as to other parties in subsequent litigation. Such a rule is known as a "selective waiver" rule, meaning that disclosure of protected communications or information to the government waives the protection only selectively—to the government—and not to any other person or entity.

The selective waiver provision proved to be very controversial. The Advisory Committee determined that it would not propose adoption of a selective waiver provision; but in light of the request from the House Judiciary Committee, the Advisory Committee did prepare language for a selective waiver provision should Congress decide to proceed. The draft language for a selective waiver provision is available on request.

Conclusion

Proposed Rule 502 is respectfully submitted for consideration by Congress as a rule that will effectively limit the skyrocketing costs of discovery. Members of the Standing Committee, the Advisory Committee, as well as their reporters and consultants, are ready to assist Congress in any way it sees fit.

Sincerely,
Lee H. Rosenthal
Chair, Committee on Rules of Practice and Procedure

HISTORICAL NOTES

Revision Notes and Legislative Reports
2008 Acts. Senate Report No. 110-264, see 2008 U.S. Code Cong. and Adm. News, p. 1305

Effective and Applicability Provisions

2008 Acts. Pub.L. 110-322, § 1(c), Sept. 19, 2008, 122 Stat. 3538, provided that: "The amendments made by this Act [enacting this rule] shall apply in all proceedings commenced after the date of enactment of this Act [Sept. 19, 2008] and, insofar as is just and practicable, in all proceedings pending on such date of enactment [Sept. 19, 2008]."

ARTICLE VI.
WITNESSES

Rule 601. Competency to Testify in General

ADVISORY COMMITTEE NOTE TO THE 2011 AMENDMENT.

The language of Rule 601 has been amended as part of the restyling of the Evidence Rules to make them more easily understood and to make style and terminology consistent throughout the rules. These changes are intended to be stylistic only. There is no intent to change any result in any ruling on evidence admissibility.

ADVISORY COMMITTEE NOTE.

[*Note, that this Advisory Committee Note was written before the Congressional changes.*]

This general ground-clearing eliminates all grounds of incompetency not specifically recognized in the succeeding rules of this Article. Included among the grounds thus abolished are religious belief, conviction of crime, and connection with the litigation as a party or interested person or spouse of a party or interested person. With the exception of the so-called Dead Man's Acts, American jurisdictions generally have ceased to recognize these grounds.

The Dead Man's Acts are surviving traces of the common law disqualification of parties and interested persons. They exist in variety too great to convey conviction of their wisdom and effectiveness. These rules contain no provision of this kind. * * *

No mental or moral qualifications for testifying as a witness are specified. Standards of mental capacity have proved elusive in actual application. A leading commentator observes that few witnesses are disqualified on that ground. Weihofen, Testimonial Competence and Credibility, 34 Geo.Wash.L.Rev. 53 (1965). Discretion is regularly exercised in favor of allowing the testimony. A witness wholly without capacity is difficult to imagine. The question is one particularly suited to the jury as one of weight and credibility, subject to judicial authority to review the sufficiency of the evidence. 2 Wigmore §§ 501, 509. Standards of moral qualification in practice consist essentially of evaluating a person's truthfulness in terms of his own answers about it. Their principal utility is in affording an opportunity on voir dire examination to impress upon the witness his moral duty. This result may, however, be accomplished more directly, and without haggling in terms of legal standards, by the manner of administering the oath or affirmation under Rule 603.

Admissibility of religious belief as a ground of impeachment is treated in Rule 610. Conviction of crime as a ground of impeachment is the subject of Rule 609. Marital relationship is the basis for privilege under Rule 505. Interest in the outcome of litigation and mental capacity are, of course, highly relevant to credibility and require no special treatment to render them admissible along with other matters bearing upon the perception, memory, and narration of witnesses.

REPORT OF THE HOUSE COMMITTEE ON THE JUDICIARY.

Rule 601 as submitted to the Congress provided that "Every person is competent to be a witness except as otherwise provided in these rules." One effect of the Rule as proposed would have been to abolish age, mental capacity, and other grounds recognized in some State jurisdictions as making a person incompetent as a witness. The greatest controversy centered around the Rule's rendering inapplicable in the federal courts the so-called Dead Man's Statutes which exist in some States. Acknowledging that there is substantial disagreement as to the merit of Dead Man's Statutes, the Committee nevertheless believed that where such statutes have been enacted they represent State policy which should not be overturned in the absence of a compelling federal interest. The Committee therefore amended the Rule to make competency in civil actions determinable in accordance with State law with respect to elements of claims or defenses as to which State law supplies the rule of decision. *Cf.* Courtland v. Walston & Co., Inc., 340 F. Supp. 1076, 1087–1092 (S.D.N.Y. 1972).

REPORT OF THE SENATE COMMITTEE ON THE JUDICIARY.

The amendment to Rule 601 parallels the treatment accorded Rule 501 discussed immediately above.

REPORT OF THE HOUSE/SENATE CONFERENCE COMMITTEE.

Rule 601 deals with competency of witnesses. Both the House and Senate bills provide that federal competency law applies in criminal cases. In civil actions and proceedings, the House bill provides that state competency law applies "to an element of a claim or defense as to which State law supplies the rule of decision." The Senate bill provides that "in civil actions and proceedings arising under 28 U.S.C. § 1332 or 28 U.S.C. § 1335, or between citizens of different States and removed under 28 U.S.C. § 1441(b) the competency of a witness, person, government, State or political subdivision thereof is determined in accordance with State law, unless with respect to the particular claim or defense, Federal law supplies the rule of decision."

The wording of the House and Senate bills differs in the treatment of civil actions and proceedings. The rule in the House bill applies to evidence that relates to "an element of a claim or defense." If an item of proof tends to support or defeat a claim or defense, or an element of a claim or defense, and if state law supplies the rule of decision for that claim or defense, then state competency law applies to that item of proof.

For reasons similar to those underlying its action on Rule 501, the Conference adopts the House provision.

Rule 602. Need for Personal Knowledge

ADVISORY COMMITTEE NOTE TO THE 2011 AMENDMENT.

The language of Rule 602 has been amended as part of the restyling of the Evidence Rules to make them more easily understood and to make style and terminology consistent throughout the rules. These changes are intended to be stylistic only. There is no intent to change any result in any ruling on evidence admissibility.

ADVISORY COMMITTEE NOTE.

". . . [T]he rule requiring that a witness who testifies to a fact which can be perceived by the senses must have had an opportunity to observe, and must have actually observed the fact" is a "most pervasive manifestation" of the common law insistence upon "the most reliable sources of information." McCormick § 10, p. 19. These foundation requirements may, of course, be furnished by the testimony of the witness himself; hence personal knowledge is not an absolute but may consist of what the witness thinks he knows from personal perception. 2 Wigmore § 650. It will be observed that the rule is in fact a specialized application of the provisions of Rule 104(b) on conditional relevancy.

This rule does not govern the situation of a witness who testifies to a hearsay statement as such, if he has personal knowledge of the making of the statement. Rules 801 and 805 would be applicable. This rule would, however, prevent him from testifying to the subject matter of the hearsay statement, as he has no personal knowledge of it.

The reference to Rule 703 is designed to avoid any question of conflict between the present rule and the provisions of that rule allowing an expert to express opinions based on facts of which he does not have personal knowledge.

NOTE BY FEDERAL JUDICIAL CENTER.

The Rule enacted by Congress is the Rule prescribed by the Supreme Court without change; the Rule was not the subject of floor debate.

Rule 603. Oath or Affirmation to Testify Truthfully

ADVISORY COMMITTEE NOTE TO THE 2011 AMENDMENT.

The language of Rule 603 has been amended as part of the restyling of the Evidence Rules to make them more easily understood and to make style and terminology consistent throughout the rules. These changes are intended to be stylistic only. There is no intent to change

any result in any ruling on evidence admissibility.

ADVISORY COMMITTEE NOTE.

The rule is designed to afford the flexibility required in dealing with religious adults, atheists, conscientious objectors, mental defectives, and children. Affirmation is simply a solemn undertaking to tell the truth; no special verbal formula is required. As is true generally, affirmation is recognized by federal law. "Oath" includes affirmation, 1 U.S.C. § 1; judges and clerks may administer oaths and affirmations, 28 U.S.C. §§ 459, 953; and affirmations are acceptable in lieu of oaths under Rule 43(d) of the Federal Rules of Civil Procedure. Perjury by a witness is a crime, 18 U.S.C. § 1621.

NOTE BY FEDERAL JUDICIAL CENTER.

The Rule enacted by Congress is the Rule prescribed by the Supreme Court without change; the Rule was not the subject of floor debate.

Rule 604. Interpreter

ADVISORY COMMITTEE NOTE TO THE 2011 AMENDMENT.

The language of Rule 604 has been amended as part of the restyling of the Evidence Rules to make them more easily understood and to make style and terminology consistent throughout the rules. These changes are intended to be stylistic only. There is no intent to change any result in any ruling on evidence admissibility.

ADVISORY COMMITTEE NOTE.

The rule implements Rule 13(f) of the Federal Rules of Civil Procedure and Rule 28(b) of the Federal Rules of Criminal Procedure, both of which contain provisions for the appointment and compensation of interpreters.

NOTE BY FEDERAL JUDICIAL CENTER.

The Rule enacted by Congress is the Rule prescribed by the Supreme Court without change; the Rule was not the subject of floor debate.

Rule 605. Judge's Competency as a Witness

ADVISORY COMMITTEE NOTE TO THE 2011 AMENDMENT.

The language of Rule 605 has been amended as part of the restyling of the Evidence Rules to make them more easily understood and to make style and terminology consistent throughout the rules. These changes are intended to be stylistic only. There is no intent to change any result in any ruling on evidence admissibility.

ADVISORY COMMITTEE NOTE.

In view of the mandate of 28 U.S.C. § 455 that a judge disqualify himself in "any case in which he . . . is or has been a material witness," the likelihood that the presiding judge in a federal court might be called to testify in the trial over which he is presiding is slight. Nevertheless the possibility is not totally eliminated.

The solution here presented is a broad rule of incompetency, rather than such alternatives as incompetency only as to material matters, leaving the matter to the discretion of the judge, or recognizing no incompetency. The choice is the result of inability to evolve satisfactory answers to questions which arise when the judge abandons the bench for the witness stand. Who rules on objections? Who compels him to answer? Can he rule impartially on the weight and admissibility of his own testimony? Can he be impeached or cross-examined effectively? Can he, in a jury trial, avoid conferring his seal of approval on one side in the eyes of the jury? Can he, in a bench trial, avoid an involvement destructive of impartiality? The rule of general incompetency has substantial support. *See* Report of the Special Committee on the Propriety of Judges Appearing as Witnesses, 36 A.B.A.J. 630 (1950); cases collected in Annot. 157 A.L.R. 311; McCormick § 68, p. 147; Uniform Rule 42; California Evidence Code § 703; Kansas Code of Civil Procedure § 60-442; New Jersey Evidence Rule 42. *Cf.* 6 Wigmore § 1909, which advocates leaving the matter to the discretion of the judge, and statutes to that effect collected in Annot. 157 A.L.R. 311.

The rule provides an "automatic" objection. To require an actual objection would confront the opponent with a choice between not objecting, with the result of allowing the testimony, and objecting, with the probable result of excluding the testimony but at the price of continuing the trial before a judge likely to feel that his integrity had been attacked by the objector.

NOTE BY FEDERAL JUDICIAL CENTER.

The Rule enacted by Congress is the Rule prescribed by the Supreme Court without change; the Rule was not the subject of floor debate.

Rule 606. Juror's Competency as a Witness

ADVISORY COMMITTEE NOTE TO THE 2011 AMENDMENT.

The language of Rule 606 has been amended as part of the restyling of the Evidence Rules to make them more easily understood and to make style and terminology consistent throughout the rules. These changes are intended to be stylistic only. There is no intent to change any result in any ruling on evidence admissibility.

ADVISORY COMMITTEE NOTE.

Subdivision (a). The considerations which bear upon the permissibility of testimony by a juror in the trial in which he is sitting as juror bear an obvious similarity to those evoked when the judge is called as a witness. *See* Advisory Committee's Note to Rule 605. The judge is not, however in this instance so involved as to call for departure from usual principles requiring objection to be made; hence the only provision on objection is that opportunity be afforded for its making out of the presence of the jury. Compare Rule 605.

Subdivision (b). Whether testimony, affidavits, or statements of jurors should be received for the purpose of invalidating or supporting a verdict or indictment, and if so, under what circumstances, has given rise to substantial differences of opinion. The familiar rubric that a juror may not impeach his own verdict, dating from Lord Mansfield's time, is a gross oversimplification. The values sought to be promoted by excluding the evidence include freedom of deliberation, stability and finality of verdicts, and protection of jurors against annoyance and embarrassment. McDonald v. Pless, 238 U.S. 264, 35 S.Ct. 785, 59 L. Ed. 1300 (1915). On the other hand, simply putting verdicts beyond effective reach can only promote irregularity and injustice. The rule offers an accommodation between these competing considerations.

The mental operations and emotional reactions of jurors in arriving at a given result would, if allowed as a subject of inquiry, place every verdict at the mercy of jurors and invite tampering and harassment. *See* Grenz v. Werre, 129 N.W.2d 681 (N.D. 1964). The authorities are in virtually complete accord in excluding the evidence. Fryer, Note on Disqualification of Witnesses, Selected Writings on Evidence and Trial 345, 347 (Fryer ed. 1957); Maguire, Weinstein, et al., Cases on Evidence 887 (5th ed. 1965); 8 Wigmore § 2349 (McNaughton Rev. 1961). As to matters other than mental operations and emotional reactions of jurors, substantial authority refuses to allow a juror to disclose irregularities which occur in the jury room, but allows his testimony as to irregularities occurring outside and allows outsiders to testify as to occurrences both inside and out. 8 Wigmore § 2354 (McNaughton Rev. 1961). However, the door of the jury room is not necessarily a satisfactory dividing point, and the Supreme Court has refused to accept it for every situation. Mattox v. United States, 146 U.S. 140, 13 S.Ct. 50, 36 L. Ed. 917 (1892).

Under the federal decisions the central focus has been upon insulation of the manner in which the jury reached its verdict, and this protection extends to each of the components of deliberation, including arguments, statements, discussions, mental and emotional reactions, votes, and any other feature of the process. Thus testimony or affidavits of jurors have been held incompetent to show a compromise verdict, Hyde v. United States, 225 U.S. 347, 382 (1912); a quotient verdict, McDonald v. Pless, 238 U.S. 264 (1915); speculation as to insurance coverage, Holden v. Porter, 405 F.2d 878 (10th Cir. 1969), Farmers Coop. Elev. Ass'n v. Strand, 382 F.2d 224, 230 (8th Cir. 1967), cert. denied 389 U.S. 1014; misinterpretation of instructions, Farmers Coop. Elev. Ass'n v. Strand, *supra*; mistake in returning verdict, United States v. Chereton, 309 F.2d 197 (6th Cir. 1962); interpretation of guilty plea by one defendant as implicating others, United States v. Crosby, 294 F.2d 928, 949 (2d Cir. 1961). The policy does not, however, foreclose testimony by jurors as to extraneous prejudicial information or influences injected into or brought to bear upon the deliberative process. Thus a juror is recognized as competent to testify to statements by the bailiff or the introduction of a prejudicial newspaper account into the jury room, Mattox v. United States, 146 U.S. 140 (1892). *See* also Parker v. Gladden, 385 U.S. 363 (1966).

This rule does not purport to specify the substantive grounds for setting aside verdicts for irregularity; it deals only with the competency of jurors to testify concerning those grounds.

See also Rule 6(e) of the Federal Rules of Criminal Procedure and 18 U.S.C. § 3500, governing the secrecy of grand jury proceedings. The present rule does not relate to secrecy and disclosure but to the competency of certain witnesses and evidence.

REPORT OF THE HOUSE COMMITTEE ON THE JUDICIARY.

[*Note, that the version of the Rule described in this Report differs substantially from that finally enacted by Congress.*]

As proposed by the Court, Rule 606(b) limited testimony by a juror in the course of an inquiry into the validity of a verdict or indictment. He could testify as to the influence of extraneous prejudicial information brought to the jury's attention (e.g. a radio newscast or a newspaper account) or an outside influence which improperly had been brought to bear upon a juror (e.g. a threat to the safety of a member of his family), but he could not testify as to other irregularities which occurred in the jury room. Under this formulation a quotient verdict could not be attacked through the testimony of a juror, nor could a juror testify to the drunken condition of a fellow juror which so disabled him that he could not participate in the jury's deliberations.

The 1969 and 1971 Advisory Committee drafts would have permitted a member of the jury to testify concerning these kinds of irregularities in the jury room. The Advisory Committee note in the 1971 draft stated that "* * * the door of the jury room is not a satisfactory dividing point, and the Supreme Court has refused to accept it." The Advisory Committee further commented that—

The trend has been to draw the dividing line between testimony as to mental processes, on the one hand, and as to the existence of conditions or occurrences of events calculated improperly to influence the verdict, on the other hand, without regard to whether the happening is within or without the jury room. * * * The jurors are the persons who know what really happened. Allowing them to testify as to matters other than their own reactions involves no particular hazard to the values sought to be protected. The rule is based upon this conclusion. It makes no attempt to specify the substantive grounds for setting aside verdicts for irregularity.

Objective jury misconduct may be testified to in California, Florida, Iowa, Kansas, Nebraska, New Jersey, North Dakota, Ohio, Oregon, Tennessee, Texas, and Washington.

Persuaded that the better practice is that provided for in the earlier drafts, the Committee amended subdivision (b) to read in the text of those drafts.

REPORT OF THE SENATE COMMITTEE ON THE JUDICIARY.

As adopted by the House, this rule would permit the impeachment of verdicts by inquiry into, not the mental processes of the jurors, but what happened in terms of conduct in the jury room. This extension of the ability to impeach a verdict is felt to be unwarranted and ill-advised.

The rule passed by the House embodies a suggestion by the Advisory Committee of the Judicial Conference that is considerably broader than the final version adopted by the Supreme Court, which embodied long-accepted Federal law. Although forbidding the impeachment of verdicts by inquiry into the jurors' mental processes, it deletes from the Supreme Court version the proscription against testimony "as to any matter or statement occurring during the course of the jury's deliberations." This deletion would have the effect of opening verdicts up to challenge on the basis of what happened during the jury's internal deliberations, for example, where a juror alleged that the jury refused to follow the trial judge's instructions or that some of the jurors did not take part in deliberations.

Permitting an individual to attack a jury verdict based upon the jury's internal deliberations has long been recognized as unwise by the Supreme Court. In McDonald v. Pless, the Court stated:

* * * * *

[L]et it once be established that verdicts solemnly made and publicly returned into court can be attacked and set aside on the testimony of those who took part in their publication and all verdicts could be, and many would be, followed by an inquiry in the hope of discovering something which might invalidate the finding. Jurors would be harassed and beset by the defeated party in an effort to secure from them evidence of facts which might establish misconduct sufficient to set aside a verdict. If evidence thus secured could be thus used, the result would be to make what was intended to be a private deliberation, the constant subject of public investigation—to the destruction of all frankness and freedom of discussion and conference.[8]

* * * * *

As it stands then, the rule would permit the harassment of former jurors by losing parties as well as the possible exploitation of disgruntled or otherwise badly-motivated ex-jurors.

Public policy requires a finality to litigation. And common fairness requires that absolute privacy be preserved for jurors to engage in the full and free debate necessary to the attainment of just verdicts. Jurors will not be able to function effectively if their deliberations are to be scrutinized in post-trial litigation. In the interest of protecting the jury system and the citizens who make it work, Rule 606 should not permit any inquiry into the internal deliberations of the jurors.

REPORT OF THE HOUSE/SENATE CONFERENCE COMMITTEE.

Rule 606(b) deals with juror testimony in an inquiry into the validity of a verdict or indictment. The House bill provides that a juror cannot testify about his mental processes or about the effect of anything upon his or another juror's mind as influencing him to assent to or dissent from a verdict or indictment. Thus, the House bill allows a juror to testify about objective matters occurring during the jury's deliberation, such as the misconduct of another juror or the reaching of a quotient verdict. The Senate bill does not permit juror testimony about any matter or statement occurring during the course of the jury's deliberations. The Senate bill does provide, however, that a juror may testify on the question whether extraneous prejudicial information was improperly brought to the jury's attention and on the question whether any outside influence was improperly brought to bear on any juror.

The Conference adopts the Senate amendment. The Conferees believe that jurors should be encouraged to be conscientious in promptly reporting to the court misconduct that occurs during jury deliberations.

NOTE BY FEDERAL JUDICIAL CENTER.

The Rule enacted by Congress is the Rule prescribed by the Supreme Court, amended only by the addition of the concluding phrase "for these purposes." The bill originally passed by the House did not contain in the first sentence the prohibition as to matters or statements during the deliberations or the clause beginning "except."

COMMITTEE NOTE TO 2006 AMENDMENT.

Rule 606(b) has been amended to provide that juror testimony may be used to prove that the verdict reported was the result of a mistake in

---

[8] 238 U.S. 264, at 267 (1944).

entering the verdict on the verdict form. The amendment responds to a divergence between the text of the Rule and the case law that has established an exception for proof of clerical errors. *See, e.g., Plummer v. Springfield Term. Ry.,* 5 F.3d 1, 3 (1st Cir. 1993) ("A number of circuits hold, and we agree, that juror testimony regarding an alleged clerical error, such as announcing a verdict different than that agreed upon, does not challenge the validity of the verdict or the deliberation of mental processes, and therefore is not subject to Rule 606(b)."); *Teevee Toons, Inc., v. MP3.Com, Inc.,* 148 F.Supp.2d 276, 278 (S.D.N.Y. 2001) (noting that Rule 606(b) has been silent regarding inquiries designed to confirm the accuracy of a verdict).

In adopting the exception for proof of clerical mistakes, the amendment specifically rejects the broader exception, adopted by some courts, permitting the use of juror testimony to prove that the jurors were operating under a misunderstanding about the consequences of the result that they agreed upon. *See, e.g., Attridge v. Cencorp Div. of Dover Techs. Int'l, Inc.,* 836 F.2d 113, 116 (2d Cir. 1987); *Eastridge Development Co., v. Halpert Associates, Inc.,* 853 F.2d 772 (10th Cir. 1988). The broader exception is rejected because an inquiry into whether the jury misunderstood or misapplied an instruction goes to the jurors' mental processes underlying the verdict, rather than the verdict's accuracy in capturing what the jurors had agreed upon. *See, e.g., Karl v. Burlington Northern R.R.,* 880 F.2d 68, 74 (8th Cir. 1989) (error to receive juror testimony on whether verdict was the result of jurors' misunderstanding of instructions: "The jurors did not state that the figure written by the foreman was different from that which they agreed upon, but indicated that the figure the foreman wrote down was intended to be a net figure, not a gross figure. Receiving such statements violates Rule 606(b) because the testimony relates to how the jury interpreted the court's instructions, and concerns the jurors' 'mental processes,' which is forbidden by the rule."); *Robles v. Exxon Corp.,* 862 F.2d 1201, 1208 (5th Cir. 1989) ("the alleged error here goes to the substance of what the jury was asked to decide, necessarily implicating the jury's mental processes insofar as it questions the jury's understanding of the court's instructions and application of those instructions to the facts of the case"). Thus, the exception established by the amendment is limited to cases such as "where the jury foreperson wrote down, in response to an interrogatory, a number different from that agreed upon by the jury, or mistakenly stated that the defendant was 'guilty' when the jury had actually agreed that the defendant was not guilty." *Id.*

It should be noted that the possibility of errors in the verdict form will be reduced substantially by polling the jury. Rule 606(b) does not, of course, prevent this precaution. *See* 8 C. Wigmore, *Evidence,* § 2350 at 691 (McNaughten ed. 1961) (noting that the reasons for the rule barring juror testimony, "namely, the dangers of uncertainty and of tampering with the jurors to procure testimony, disappear in large part if such investigation as may be desired is *made by the judge* and takes place *before the jurors' discharge* and separation") (emphasis in original). Errors that come to light after polling the jury "may be corrected on the spot, or the jury may be sent out to continue deliberations, or, if necessary, a new trial may be ordered." C. Mueller & L. Kirkpatrick, *Evidence Under the Rules* at 671 (2d ed. 1999) (citing *Sincox v. United States,* 571 F.2d 876, 878–79 (5th Cir. 1978)).

Rule 607. Who May Impeach a Witness

ADVISORY COMMITTEE NOTE TO THE 2011 AMENDMENT.

The language of Rule 607 has been amended as part of the restyling of the Evidence Rules to make them more easily understood and to make style and terminology consistent throughout the rules. These changes are intended to be stylistic only. There is no intent to change any result in any ruling on evidence admissibility.

ADVISORY COMMITTEE NOTE.

The traditional rule against impeaching one's own witness is abandoned as based on false premises. A party does not hold out his witnesses as worthy of belief, since he rarely has a free choice in selecting them. Denial of the right leaves the party at the mercy of the witness and the adversary. If the impeachment is by a prior statement, it is free from hearsay dangers and is excluded from the category of hearsay under Rule 801(d)(1). Ladd, Impeachment of One's Own Witness—New Developments, 4 U.Chi.L.Rev. 69 (1936); McCormick § 38; 3 Wigmore §§ 896–918. The substantial inroads into the old rule made over the years by decisions, rules, and statutes are evidence of doubts as to its basic soundness and workability. Cases are collected in 3 Wigmore § 905. Revised Rule 32(a)(1) of the Federal Rules of Civil Procedure allows any party to impeach a witness by means of his deposition, and Rule 43(b) has allowed the calling and impeachment of an adverse party or person identified with him. Illustrative statutes allowing a party to impeach his own witness under varying circumstances are Ill.Rev.Stats. 1967, c. 110, § 60; Mass.Laws Annot.1959, c. 233 § 23; 20 N.M.Stats.Annot.1953, § 20-2-4; N.Y. CPLR § 4514 (McKinney 1963); 12 Vt.Stats.Annot.1959, §§ 1641a, 1642. Complete judicial rejection of the old rule is found in United States v. Freeman, 302 F.2d 347 (2d Cir.1962). The same result is reached in Uniform Rule 20; California Evidence Code § 785; Kansas Code of Civil Procedure § 60-420. *See also* New Jersey Evidence Rule 20.

NOTE BY FEDERAL JUDICIAL CENTER.

The Rule enacted by Congress is the Rule prescribed by the Supreme Court without change; the Rule was not the subject of floor debate.

Rule 608. A Witness's Character for Truthfulness or Untruthfulness

ADVISORY COMMITTEE NOTE TO THE 2011 AMENDMENT.

The language of Rule 608 has been amended as part of the restyling of the Evidence Rules to make them more easily understood and to make style and terminology consistent throughout the rules. These changes are intended to be stylistic only. There is no intent to change any result in any ruling on evidence admissibility.

The Committee is aware that the Rule's limitation of bad-act impeachment to "cross-examination" is trumped by Rule 607, which allows a party to impeach witnesses on direct examination. Courts have not relied on the term "on cross-examination" to limit impeachment that would otherwise be permissible under Rules 607 and 608. The Committee therefore concluded that no change to the language of the Rule was necessary in the context of a restyling project.

ADVISORY COMMITTEE NOTE.

Subdivision (a). In Rule 404(a) the general position is taken that character evidence is not admissible for the purpose of proving that the person acted in conformity therewith, subject, however, to several exceptions, one of which is character evidence of a witness as bearing upon his credibility. The present rule develops that exception.

In accordance with the bulk of judicial authority, the inquiry is strictly limited to character for veracity, rather than allowing evidence as to character generally. The result is to sharpen relevancy, to reduce surprise, waste of time, and confusion, and to make the lot of the witness somewhat less unattractive. McCormick § 44.

The use of opinion and reputation evidence as means of proving the character of witnesses is consistent with Rule 405(a). While the modern practice has purported to exclude opinion, witnesses who testify to reputation seem in fact often to be giving their opinions, disguised somewhat misleadingly as reputation. *See* McCormick § 44. And even under the modern practice, a common relaxation has allowed inquiry as to whether the witnesses would believe the principal witness under oath. United States v. Walker, 313 F.2d 236 (6th Cir. 1963), and cases cited therein; McCormick § 44, pp. 94–95, n. 3.

Character evidence in support of credibility is admissible under the rule only after the witness' character has first been attacked, as has been the case at common law. Maguire, Weinstein, et al., Cases on Evidence 295 (5th ed. 1965); McCormick § 49, p. 105; 4 Wigmore § 1104. The enormous needless consumption of time which a contrary practice would entail justifies the limitation. Opinion or reputation that the witness is untruthful specifically qualifies as an attack under the rule, and evidence of misconduct, including conviction of crime, and of corruption also fall within this category. Evidence of bias or interest does not. McCormick § 49; 4 Wigmore §§ 1106, 1107. Whether evidence in the form of contradiction is an attack upon the character of the witness must depend upon the circumstances. McCormick § 49. *Cf.* 4 Wigmore §§ 1108, 1109.

As to the use of specific instances on direct by an opinion witness, *see* the Advisory Committee's Note to Rule 405, *supra.*

Subdivision (b). In conformity with Rule 405, which forecloses use of evidence of specific incidents as proof in chief of character unless character is an issue in the case, the present rule generally bars evidence of specific instances of conduct of a witness for the purpose of attacking or supporting his credibility. There are, however, two exceptions: (1) specific instances are provable when they have been the subject of criminal conviction, and (2) specific instances may be inquired into on cross-examination of the principal witness or of a witness giving an opinion of his character for truthfulness.

(1) Conviction of crime as a technique of impeachment is treated in detail in Rule 609, and here is merely recognized as an exception to the general rule excluding evidence of specific incidents for impeachment purposes.

(2) Particular instances of conduct, though not the subject of criminal conviction, may be inquired into on cross-examination of the principal witness himself or of a witness who testifies concerning his character for truthfulness. Effective cross-examination demands that some allowance be made for going into matters of this kind, but the possibilities of abuse are substantial. Consequently safeguards are erected in the form of specific requirements that the instances inquired into be probative of truthfulness or its opposite and not remote in time. Also, the overriding protection of Rule 403 requires that probative value not be outweighed by danger of unfair prejudice, confusion of issues, or misleading the jury, and that of Rule 611 bars harassment and undue embarrassment.

The final sentence constitutes a rejection of the doctrine of such cases as People v. Sorge, 301 N.Y. 198, 93 N.E.2d 637 (1950), that any past criminal act relevant to credibility may be inquired into on cross-examination, in apparent disregard of the privilege against self-incrimination. While it is clear that an ordinary witness cannot make a partial disclosure of incriminating matter and then invoke the privilege on cross-examination, no tenable contention can be made that merely by testifying he waives his right to foreclose inquiry on cross-examination into criminal activities for the purpose of attacking his credibility. So to hold would reduce the privilege to a nullity. While it is true that an accused, unlike an ordinary witness, has an option whether to testify, if the option can be exercised only at the price of opening up inquiry as to any and all criminal acts committed during his lifetime, the right to testify could scarcely be said to possess much vitality. In Griffin v. California, 380 U.S. 609, 85 S.Ct. 1229, 14 L.Ed.2d 106 (1965), the Court held that allowing comment on the election of an accused not to testify exacted a constitutionally impermissible price, and so here. While no specific provision in terms confers constitutional status on the right of an accused to take the stand in his own defense, the existence of the right is so completely recognized that a denial of it or substantial infringement upon it would surely be of due process dimensions. *See* Ferguson v. Georgia, 365 U.S. 570, 81 S.Ct. 756, 5 L.Ed.2d 783 (1961); McCormick § 131; 8 Wigmore § 2276 (McNaughton Rev. 1961). In any event, wholly aside from constitutional considerations, the provision represents a sound policy.

REPORT OF THE HOUSE COMMITTEE ON THE JUDICIARY.

[Note, that the description of Rule 608(a) which follows is one which assumes that "opinion" testimony will be disallowed. As enacted, Rule 608(a) expressly allows opinion testimony.]

Rule 608(a)

Rule 608(a) as submitted by the Court permitted attack to be made upon the character for truthfulness or untruthfulness of a witness either by reputation or opinion testimony. For the same reasons underlying its decision to eliminate the admissibility of opinion testimony in Rule 405(a), the Committee amended Rule 608(a) to delete the reference to opinion testimony.

Rule 608(b)

The second sentence of Rule 608(b) as submitted by the Court permitted specific instances of misconduct of a witness to be inquired into on cross-examination for the purpose of attacking his credibility, if probative of truthfulness or untruthfulness, "and not remote in time." Such cross-examination could be of the witness himself or of another witness who testifies as to "his" character for truthfulness or untruthfulness.

The Committee amended the Rule to emphasize the discretionary power of the Court in permitting such testimony and deleted the reference to remoteness in time as being unnecessary and confusing (remoteness from time of trial or remoteness from the incident involved?). As recast, the Committee amendment also makes clear the antecedent of "his" in the original Court proposal.

NOTE BY FEDERAL JUDICIAL CENTER.

The Rule enacted by Congress is the Rule prescribed by the Supreme Court, changed only by amending the second sentence of subdivision (b). The sentence as prescribed by the Court read: "They may, however, if probative of truthfulness or untruthfulness and not remote in time, be inquired into on cross-examination of the witness himself or on cross-examination of a witness who testifies to his character for truthfulness or untruthfulness." The effect of the amendments was to delete the phrase "and not remote in time," to add the phrase "in the discretion of the court," and otherwise only to clarify the meaning of the sentence. The reasons for the amendments are stated in the Report of the House Committee of the Judiciary, set forth above.

COMMITTEE NOTE TO 2003 AMENTMENT.

The Rule has been amended to clarify that the absolute prohibition on extrinsic evidence applies only when the sole reason for proffering that evidence is to attack or support the witness' character for truthfulness. *See United States v. Abel,* 469 U.S. 45 (1984); *United States v. Fusco,* 748 F.2d 996 (5th Cir. 1984) (Rule 608(b) limits the use of evidence "designed to show that the witness has done things, unrelated to the suit being tried, that make him more or less believable per se"); Ohio R.Evid. 608(b). On occasion the Rule's use of the overbroad term "credibility" has been read "to bar extrinsic evidence for bias, competency and contradiction impeachment since they too deal with credibility." American Bar Association Section of Litigation, *Emerging Problems Under the Federal Rules of Evidence* at 161 (3d ed. 1998). The amendment conforms the language of the Rule to its original intent, which was to impose an absolute bar on extrinsic evidence only if the sole purpose for offering the evidence was to prove the witness' character for veracity. *See* Advisory Committee Note to Rule 608(b) (stating that the Rule is "[i]n conformity with Rule 405, which forecloses use of evidence of specific incidents as proof in chief of character unless character is in issue in the case . . .").

By limiting the application of the Rule to proof of a witness' character for truthfulness, the amendment leaves the admissibility of extrinsic evidence offered for other grounds of impeachment (such as contradiction, prior inconsistent statement, bias and mental capacity) to Rules 402 and 403. *See, e.g., United States v. Winchenbach,* 197 F.3d 548 (1st Cir. 1999) (admissibility of a prior inconsistent statement offered for impeachment is governed by Rules 402 and 403, not Rule 608(b)); *United States v. Tarantino,* 846 F.2d 1384 (D.C. Cir. 1988) (admissibility of extrinsic evidence offered to contradict a witness is governed by Rules 402 and 403); *United States v. Lindemann,* 85 F.3d 1232 (7th Cir. 1996) (admissibility of extrinsic evidence of bias is governed by Rules 402 and 403).

It should be noted that the extrinsic evidence prohibition of Rule 608(b) bars any reference to the consequences that a witness might have suffered as a result of an alleged bad act. For example, Rule 608(b) prohibits counsel from mentioning that a witness was suspended or disciplined for the conduct that is the subject of impeachment, when that conduct is offered only to prove the character of the witness. *See United States v. Davis,* 183 F.3d 231, 257 n.12 (3d Cir. 1999) (emphasizing that in attacking the defendant's character for truthfulness "the government cannot make reference to Davis's forty-four day suspension or that Internal Affairs found that he lied about" an incident because "[s]uch evidence would not only be hearsay to the extent it contains assertion of fact, it would be inadmissible extrinsic evidence under Rule 608(b)"). *See also* Stephen A. Saltzburg, *Impeaching the Witness: Prior Bad Acts and Extrinsic Evidence,* 7 Crim. Just. 28, 31 (Winter 1993) ("counsel should not be permitted to circumvent the no-extrinsic-evidence provision by tucking a third person's opinion about prior acts into a question asked of the witness who has denied the act.").

For purposes of consistency the term "credibility" has been replaced by the term "character for truthfulness" in the last sentence of subdivision (b). The term "credibility" is also used in subdivision (a). But the Committee found it unnecessary to substitute "character for truthfulness" for "credibility" in Rule 608(a), because subdivision (a)(1) already serves to limit impeachment to proof of such character.

Rules 609(a) and 610 also use the term "credibility" when the intent of those Rules is to regulate impeachment of a witness' character for truthfulness. No inference should be derived from the fact that the Committee proposed an amendment to Rule 608(b) but not to Rules 609 and 610.

Rule 609. Impeachment by Evidence of a Criminal Conviction

ADVISORY COMMITTEE NOTE TO THE 2011 AMENDMENT.

The language of Rule 609 has been amended as part of the restyling of the Evidence Rules to make them more easily understood and to make style and terminology consistent throughout the rules. These changes are intended to be stylistic only. There is no intent to change any result in any ruling on evidence admissibility.

ADVISORY COMMITTEE NOTE.

As a means of impeachment, evidence of conviction of crime is significant only because it stands as proof of the commission of the underlying criminal act. There is little dissent from the general proposition that at least some crimes are relevant to credibility but much disagreement among the cases and commentators about which crimes are usable for this purpose. *See* McCormick § 43: 2 Wright, Federal Practice and Procedure: Criminal § 416 (1969). The weight of traditional authority has been to allow use of felonies generally, without regard to the nature of the particular offense, and of *crimen falsi* without regard to the grade of the offense. This is the view accepted by Congress in the 1970 amendment of § 14-305 of the District of Columbia Code, P.L. 91-358, 81 Stat. 473. Uniform Rule 21 and Model Code Rule 106 permit only crimes involving "dishonesty or false statement." Others have thought that the trial judge should have discretion to exclude convictions if the probative value of the evidence of the crime is substantially outweighed by the danger of unfair prejudice. Luck v. United States, 121 U.S.App.D.C. 151, 318 F.2d 763 (1965); McGowan, Impeachment of Criminal Defendants by Prior Convictions, 1970 Law & Soc. Order 1. Whatever may be the merits of those views, this rule is drafted to accord with the Congressional policy manifested in the 1970 legislation.

The proposed rule incorporates certain basic safeguards, in terms applicable to all witnesses but of particular significance to an accused who elects to testify. These protections include the imposition of definite time limitations, giving effect to demonstrated rehabilitation, and generally excluding juvenile adjudications.

Subdivision (a). For purposes of impeachment, crimes are divided into two categories by the rule: (1) those of what is generally regarded as felony grade, without particular regard to the nature of the offense, and (2) those involving dishonesty or false statement, without regard to the grade of the offense. Provable convictions are not limited to violations of federal law. By reason of our constitutional structure, the federal catalog of crimes is far from being a complete one, and resort must be had to the laws of the states for the specification of many crimes. For example, simple theft as compared with theft from interstate commerce. Other instances of borrowing are the Assimilative Crimes Act, making the state law of crimes applicable to the special territorial and maritime jurisdiction of the United States, 18 U.S.C. § 13, and the provision of the Judicial Code disqualifying persons as jurors on the grounds of state as well as federal convictions, 28 U.S.C. § 1865. For evaluation of the crime in terms of seriousness, reference is made to the congressional measurement of felony (subject to imprisonment in excess of one year) rather than adopting state definitions which vary considerably. *See* 28 U.S.C. § 1865, *supra*, disqualifying jurors for conviction in state or federal court of crime punishable by imprisonment for more than year.

Subdivision (b). Few statutes recognize a time limit on impeachment by evidence of conviction. However, practical considerations of fairness and relevancy demand that some boundary be recognized. *See* Ladd, Credibility Tests—Current Trends, 89 U.Pa.L.Rev. 166, 176–177 (1910). This portion of the rule is derived from the proposal advanced in Recommendation Proposing in Evidence Code, § 788(5), p. 142, Cal. Law Rev. Comm'n (1965), though not adopted. *See* California Evidence Code § 788.

Subdivision (c). A pardon or its equivalent granted solely for the purpose of restoring civil rights lost by virtue of a conviction has no relevance to an inquiry into character. If, however, the pardon or other proceeding is hinged upon a showing of rehabilitation the situation is otherwise. The result under the rule is to render the conviction inadmissible. The alternative of allowing in evidence both the conviction and the rehabilitation has not been adopted for reasons of policy, economy of time, and difficulties of evaluation.

A similar provision is contained in California Evidence Code § 788. *Cf.* A.L.I. Model Penal Code, Proposed Official Draft § 306.6(3)(e) (1962), and discussion in A.L.I. Proceedings 310 (1961).

Pardons based on innocence have the effect, of course, of nullifying the conviction *ab initio*.

Subdivision (d). The prevailing view has been that a juvenile adjudication is not usable for impeachment. Thomas v. United States, 121 F.2d 905, 74 App.D.C. 167 (1911); Cotton v. United States, 355 F.2d 480 (10th Cir. 1966). This conclusion was based upon a variety of circumstances. By virtue of its informality, frequently diminished quantum of required proof, and other departures from accepted standards for criminal trials under the theory of *parens patriae*, the juvenile adjudication was considered to lack the precision and general probative value of the criminal conviction. While In re Gault, 387 U.S. 1, 87 S.Ct. 1428, 18 L.Ed.2d 527 (1967), no doubt eliminates these characteristics insofar as objectionable, other obstacles remain. Practical problems of administration are raised by the common provisions in juvenile legislation that records be kept confidential and that they be destroyed after a short time. While *Gault* was skeptical as to the realities of confidentiality of juvenile records, it also saw no constitutional obstacles to improvement. 387 U.S. at 25, 87 S.Ct. 1428. *See also* Note, Rights and Rehabilitation in the Juvenile Courts, 67 Colum.L.Rev. 281, 289 (1967). In addition, policy considerations much akin to those which dictate exclusion of adult convictions after rehabilitation has been established, strongly suggest a rule of excluding juvenile adjudications. Admittedly, however, the rehabilitative process may in a given case be a demonstrated failure, or the strategic importance of a given witness may be so great as to require the overriding of general policy in the interests of particular justice. *See* Giles v. Maryland, 386 U.S. 66, 87 S.Ct. 793, 17 L.Ed.2d 737 (1967). Wigmore was outspoken in his condemnation of the disallowance of juvenile adjudications to impeach, especially when the witness is the complainant in a case of molesting a minor. 1 Wigmore § 196; 3 *id.* §§ 924a, 980. The rule recognizes discretion in the judge to effect an accommodation among these various factors by departing from the general principle of exclusion. In deference to the general pattern and policy of juvenile statutes, however, no discretion is accorded when the witness is the accused in a criminal case.

Subdivision (e). The presumption of correctness which ought to attend judicial proceedings supports the position that pendency of an appeal does not preclude use of a conviction for impeachment. United States v. Empire Packing Co., 174 F.2d 16 (7th Cir. 1949), cert. denied 337 U.S. 959, 69 S.Ct. 1534, 93 L. Ed. 1758; Bloch v. United States, 226 F.2d 185 (9th Cir. 1955), cert. denied 350 U.S. 948, 76 S.Ct. 323, 100 L. Ed. 826 and 353 U.S. 959, 77 S.Ct. 868, 1 L.Ed.2d 910; and *see* Newman v. United States, 331 F.2d 968 (8th Cir. 1964). *Contra,* Campbell v. United States, 176 F.2d 45, 85 U.S.App.D.C. 133 (1949). The pendency of an appeal is, however, a qualifying circumstance properly considerable.

REPORT OF THE HOUSE COMMITTEE ON THE JUDICIARY.

[*Note, that Rule 609 underwent substantial change in the Senate after this House Report was prepared, particularly with respect to subdivision (a).*]

Rule 609(a)

Rule 609(a) as submitted by the Court was modeled after Section 133(a) of Public Law 91-358, 11 D.C. Code 305(b)(1), enacted in 1970. The Rule provided that:

For the purpose of attacking the credibility of a witness, evidence that he has been convicted of a crime is admissible but only if the crime (1) was punishable by death or imprisonment in excess of one year under the law under which he was convicted or (2) involved dishonesty or false statement regardless of the punishment.

As reported to the Committee by the Subcommittee, Rule 609(a) was amended to read as follows:

For the purpose of attacking the credibility of a witness, evidence that he has been convicted of a crime is admissible only if the crime (1) was punishable by death or imprisonment in excess of one year, unless the court determines that the danger of unfair prejudice outweighs the probative value of the evidence of the conviction, or (2) involved dishonesty or false statement.

In full committee, the provision was amended to permit attack upon the credibility of a witness by prior conviction only if the prior crime involved dishonesty or false statement. While recognizing that the prevailing doctrine in the federal courts and in most States allows a witness to be impeached by evidence of prior felony convictions without restriction as to type, the Committee was of the view that, because of the danger of unfair prejudice in such practice and the deterrent effect upon an accused who might wish to testify, and even upon a witness who was not the accused, cross-examination by evidence of prior conviction should be limited to those kinds of convictions bearing directly on credibility, *i.e.*, crimes involving dishonesty or false statement.

Rule 609(b)

Rule 609(b) as submitted by the Court was modeled after Section 133(a) of Public Law 91-358, 14 D.C. Code 305(b)(2)(B), enacted in 1970. The Rule provided:

> Evidence of a conviction under this rule is not admissible if a period of more than ten years has elapsed since the date of the release of the witness from confinement imposed for his most recent conviction, or the expiration of the period of his parole, probation, or sentence granted or imposed with respect to his most recent conviction, whichever is the later date.

Under this formulation, a witness' entire past record of criminal convictions could be used for impeachment (provided the conviction met the standard of subdivision (a)), if the witness had been most recently released from confinement, or the period of his parole or probation had expired, within ten years of the conviction.

The Committee amended the Rule to read in the text of the 1971 Advisory Committee version to provide that upon the expiration of ten years from the date of a conviction of a witness, or of his release from confinement for that offense, that conviction may no longer be used for impeachment. The Committee was of the view that after ten years following a person's release from confinement (or from the date of his conviction) the probative value of the conviction with respect to that person's credibility diminished to a point where it should no longer be admissible.

Rule 609(c)

Rule 609(c) as submitted by the Court provided in part that evidence of a witness' prior conviction is not admissible to attack his credibility if the conviction was the subject of a pardon, annulment, or other equivalent procedure, based on a showing of rehabilitation, and the witness has not been convicted of a subsequent crime. The Committee amended the Rule to provide that the "subsequent crime" must have been "punishable by death or imprisonment in excess of one year," on the ground that a subsequent conviction of an offense not a felony is insufficient to rebut the finding that the witness has been rehabilitated. The Committee also intends that the words "based on a finding of the rehabilitation of the person convicted" apply not only to "certificate or rehabilitation, or other equivalent procedure," but also to "pardon" and "annulment."

REPORT OF THE SENATE COMMITTEE ON THE JUDICIARY.

[Note, that Rule 609(a) and 609(b) underwent further change in Conference after this Senate Report was prepared.]

Rule 609(a). Impeachment by Evidence of Conviction

As proposed by the Supreme Court, the rule would allow the use of prior convictions to impeach if the crime was a felony or a misdemeanor if the misdemeanor involved dishonesty or false statement. As modified by the House, the rule would admit prior convictions for impeachment purposes only if the offense, whether felony or misdemeanor, involved dishonesty or false statement.

The committee has adopted a modified version of the House-passed rule. In your committee's view, the danger of unfair prejudice is far greater when the accused, as opposed to other witnesses, testifies, because the jury may be prejudiced not merely on the question of credibility but also on the ultimate question of guilt or innocence. Therefore, with respect to defendants, the committee agreed with the House limitation that only offenses involving false statement, or dishonesty may be used. By that phrase, the committee means crimes such as perjury or subornation of perjury, false statement, criminal fraud, embezzlement or false pretense, or any other offense, in the nature of *crimen falsi*, the commission of which involves some element of untruthfulness, deceit or falsification bearing on the accused's propensity to testify truthfully.

With respect to other witnesses, in addition to any prior conviction involving false statement or dishonesty, any other felony may be used to impeach if, and only if, the court finds that the probative value of such evidence outweighs its prejudicial effect against the party offering that witness.

Notwithstanding this provision, proof of any prior offense otherwise admissible under Rule 404 could still be offered for the purposes sanctioned by that rule. Furthermore, the committee intends that notwithstanding this rule, a defendant's misrepresentation regarding the existence or nature of prior convictions may be met by rebuttal evidence, including the record of such prior convictions. Similarly, such records may be offered to rebut representations made by the defendant regarding his attitude toward or willingness to commit a general category of offense, although denials or other representations by the defendant regarding the specific conduct which forms the basis of the charge against him shall not make prior convictions admissible to rebut such statement.

In regard to either type of representation, of course, prior convictions may be offered in rebuttal only if the defendant's statement is made in response to defense counsel's questions or is made gratuitously in the course of cross-examination. Prior convictions may not be offered as rebuttal evidence if the prosecution has sought to circumvent the purpose of this rule by asking questions which elicit such representations from the defendant.

One other clarifying amendment has been added to this subsection, that is, to provide that the admissibility of evidence of a prior conviction is permitted only upon cross-examination of a witness. It is not admissible if a person does not testify. It is to be understood, however, that a court record of a prior conviction is admissible to prove that conviction if the witness has forgotten or denies its existence.

Rule 609(b). Impeachment by Evidence of Conviction of Crime; Time Limit

Although convictions over ten years old generally do not have much probative value, there may be exceptional circumstances under which the conviction substantially bears on the credibility of the witness. Rather than exclude all convictions over 10 years old, the committee adopted an amendment in the form of a final clause to the section granting the court discretion to admit convictions over 10 years old, but only upon a determination by the court that the probative value of the conviction supported by specific facts and circumstances, substantially outweighs its prejudicial effect.

It is intended that convictions over 10 years old will be admitted very rarely and only in exceptional circumstances. The rules provide that the decision be supported by specific facts and circumstances thus requiring the court to make specific findings on the record as to the particular facts and circumstances it has considered in determining that the probative value of the conviction substantially outweighs its prejudicial impact. It is expected that, in fairness, the court will give the party against whom the conviction is introduced a full and adequate opportunity to contest its admission.

REPORT OF THE HOUSE/SENATE CONFERENCE COMMITTEE.

Rule 609 defines when a party may use evidence of a prior conviction in order to impeach a witness. The Senate amendments make changes in two subsections of Rule 609.

A. Rule 609(a)—General Rule.

The House bill provides that the credibility of a witness can be attacked by proof of prior conviction of a crime only if the crime involves dishonesty or false statement. The Senate amendment provides that a witness' credibility may be attacked if the crime (1) was punishable by death or imprisonment in excess of one year under the law under which he was convicted or (2) involves dishonesty or false statement, regardless of the punishment.

The Conference adopts the Senate amendment with an amendment. The Conference amendment provides that the credibility of a witness, whether a defendant or someone else, may be attacked by proof of a prior conviction but only if the crime: (1) was punishable by death or imprisonment in excess of one year under the law under which he was convicted and the court determines that the probative value of the conviction outweighs its prejudicial effect to the defendant; or (2) involved dishonesty or false statement regardless of the punishment.

By the phrase "dishonesty and false statement" the Conference means crimes such as perjury or subornation of perjury, false statement, criminal fraud, embezzlement, or false pretense, or any other offense in the nature of *crimen falsi*, the commission of which involves some element of deceit, untruthfulness, or falsification bearing on the accused's propensity to testify truthfully.

The admission of prior convictions involving dishonesty and false statement is not within the discretion of the Court. Such convictions are peculiarly probative of credibility and, under this rule, are always to be admitted. Thus, judicial discretion granted with respect to the admissibility of other prior convictions is not applicable to those involving dishonesty or false statement.

With regard to the discretionary standard established by paragraph (1) of Rule 609(a), the Conference determined that the prejudicial effect to be weighed against the probative value of the conviction is specifically the prejudicial effect *to the defendant*. The danger of prejudice to a witness other than the defendant (such as injury to the witness' reputation in his community) was considered and rejected by the Conference as an element to be weighed in determining admissibility. It was the judgment of the Conference that the danger of prejudice to a nondefendant witness is outweighed by the need for the trier of fact to have as much relevant evidence on the issue of credibility as possible. Such evidence should only be excluded where it presents a danger of improperly influencing the outcome of the trial by persuading the trier of fact to convict the defendant on the basis of his prior criminal record.

B. Rule 609(b)—Time Limit.

The House bill provides in subsection (b) that evidence of conviction of a crime may not be used for impeachment purposes under subsection (a) if more than ten years have elapsed since the date of the conviction or the date the witness was released from confinement imposed for the conviction, whichever is later. The Senate amendment permits the use of convictions older than ten years, if the court determines, in the interests of justice, that the probative value of the conviction, supported by specific facts and circumstances, substantially outweighs its prejudicial effect.

The Conference adopts the Senate amendment with an amendment requiring notice by a party that he intends to request that the court allow him to use a conviction older than ten years. The Conferees anticipate that a written notice, in order to give the adversary a fair opportunity to contest the use of the evidence, will ordinarily include such information as the date of the conviction, the jurisdiction, and the offense or statute involved. In order to eliminate the possibility that the flexibility of this provision may impair the ability of a party-opponent to prepare for trial, the Conferees intend that the notice provision operate to avoid surprise.

NOTE BY FEDERAL JUDICIAL CENTER.

Rule 609 underwent substantial change at the hands of Congress. They are as follows:

Subdivision (a) of the Rule prescribed by the Supreme Court was revised successively in the House, in the Senate, and in the Conference. The nature of the Rule prescribed by the Court, the various amendments, and the reasons therefor are stated in the Report of the House Committee on the Judiciary, the Report of the Senate Committee on the Judiciary, and the Conference Report, set forth above.

Subdivision (b) of the Rule prescribed by the Supreme Court was also revised successively in the House, in the Senate, and in the Conference. The nature of the Rule prescribed by the Court, those amendments and the reasons therefor are likewise stated in the Report of the House Committee on the Judiciary, the Report of the Senate Committee on the Judiciary, and the Conference Report, set forth above.

Subdivision (c) enacted by the Congress is the subdivision prescribed by the Supreme Court, with amendments and reasons therefor stated in the Report of the House Committee on the Judiciary, set forth above.

Subdivision (d) enacted by the Congress is the subdivision prescribed by the Supreme Court, amended in the second sentence by substituting "court" in place of "judge" and by adding the phrase "in a criminal case."

Subdivision (e) enacted by the Congress is the subdivision prescribed by the Supreme Court without change.

ADVISORY COMMITTEE NOTE TO 1990 AMENDMENT.

The amendment to Rule 609(a) makes two changes in the rule. The first change removes from the rule the limitation that the conviction may only be elicited during cross-examination, a limitation that virtually every circuit has found to be inapplicable. It is common for witnesses to reveal on direct examination their convictions to "remove the sting" of the impeachment. *See e.g.*, United States v. Bad Cob, 560 F.2d 877

(8th Cir. 1977). The amendment does not contemplate that a court will necessarily permit proof of prior convictions through testimony, which might be time-consuming and more prejudicial than proof through a written record. Rules 403 and 611(a) provide sufficient authority for the court to protect against unfair or disruptive methods of proof.

The second change effected by the amendment resolves an ambiguity as to the relationship of Rules 609 and 403 with respect to impeachment of witnesses other than the criminal defendant. *See*, Green v. Bock Laundry Machine Co., 490 U.S. 504, 109 S.Ct. 1981 (1989). The amendment does not disturb the special balancing test for the criminal defendant who chooses to testify. Thus, the rule recognizes that, in virtually every case in which prior convictions are used to impeach the testifying defendant, the defendant faces a unique risk of prejudice—i.e., the danger that convictions that would be excluded under Fed. R. Evid. 404 will be misused by a jury as propensity evidence despite their introduction solely for impeachment purposes. Although the rule does not forbid all use of convictions to impeach a defendant, it requires that the government show that the probative value of convictions as impeachment evidence outweighs their prejudicial effect.

Prior to the amendment, the rule appeared to give the defendant the benefit of the special balancing test when defense witnesses other than the defendant were called to testify. In practice, however, the concern about unfairness to the defendant is most acute when the defendant's own convictions are offered as evidence. Almost all of the decided cases concern this type of impeachment, and the amendment does not deprive the defendant of any meaningful protection, since Rule 403 now clearly protects against unfair impeachment of any defense witness other than the defendant. There are cases in which a defendant might be prejudiced when a defense witness is impeached. Such cases may arise, for example, when the witness bears a special relationship to the defendant such that the defendant is likely to suffer some spill-over effect from impeachment of the witness.

The amendment also protects other litigants from unfair impeachment of their witnesses. The danger of prejudice from the use of prior convictions is not confined to criminal defendants. Although the danger that prior convictions will be misused as character evidence is particularly acute when the defendant is impeached, the danger exists in other situations as well. The amendment reflects the view that it is desirable to protect all litigants from the unfair use of prior convictions, and that the ordinary balancing test of Rule 403, which provides that evidence shall not be excluded unless its prejudicial effect substantially outweighs its probative value, is appropriate for assessing the admissibility of prior convictions for impeachment of any witness other than a criminal defendant.

The amendment reflects a judgment that decisions interpreting Rule 609(a) as requiring a trial court to admit convictions in civil cases that have little, if anything, to do with credibility reach undesirable results. *See, e.g.,* Diggs v. Lyons, 741 F.2d 577 (3d Cir. 1984), *cert. denied,* 105 S.Ct. 2157 (1985). The amendment provides the same protection against unfair prejudice arising from prior convictions used for impeachment purposes as the rules provide for other evidence. The amendment finds support in decided cases. *See, e.g.,* Petty v. Ideco, 761 F.2d 1146 (5th Cir. 1985); Czajka v. Hickman, 703 F.2d 317 (8th Cir. 1983).

Fewer decided cases address the question whether Rule 609(a) provides any protection against unduly prejudicial prior convictions used to impeach government witnesses. Some courts have read Rule 609(a) as giving the government no protection for its witnesses. *See, e.g.,* United States v. Thorne, 547 F.2d 56 (8th Cir. 1976); United States v. Nevitt, 563 F.2d 406 (9th Cir. 1977), *cert. denied,* 444 U.S. 847 (1979). This approach also is rejected by the amendment. There are cases in which impeachment of government witnesses with prior convictions that have little, if anything, to do with credibility may result in unfair prejudice to the government's interest in a fair trial and unnecessary embarrassment to a witness. Fed. R. Evid. 412 already recognizes this and excluded certain evidence of past sexual behavior in the context of prosecutions for sexual assaults.

The amendment applies the general balancing test of Rule 403 to protect all litigants against unfair impeachment of witnesses. The balancing test protects civil litigants, the government in criminal cases, and the defendant in a criminal case who calls other witnesses. The amendment addresses prior convictions offered under Rule 609, not for other purposes, and does not run afoul, therefore, of Davis v. Alaska, 415 U.S. 308 (1974). *Davis* involved the use of a prior juvenile adjudication not to prove a past law violation, but prove bias. The defendant in a criminal case has the right to demonstrate the bias of a witness and to be assured a fair trial, but not to unduly prejudice a trier of fact. *See generally* Rule 412. In any case in which the trial court believes that confrontation rights require admission of impeachment evidence, obviously the Constitution would take precedence over the rule.

The probability that prior convictions of an ordinary government witness will be unduly prejudicial is low in most criminal cases. Since the behavior of the witness is not the issue in dispute in most cases, there is little chance that the trier of fact will misuse the convictions offered as impeachment evidence as propensity evidence. Thus, trial courts will be skeptical when the government objects to impeachment of its witnesses with prior convictions. Only when the government is able to point to a real danger of prejudice that is sufficient to outweigh substantially the probative value of the conviction of impeachment purposes will the conviction be excluded.

The amendment continues to divide subdivision (a) into subsections (1) and (2) thus facilitating retrieval under current computerized research programs which distinguish the two provisions. The Committee recommended no substantive change in subdivision (a)(2), even though some cases raise a concern about the proper interpretation of the words "dishonesty or false statement." These words were used but not explained in the original Advisory Committee Note accompanying Rule 609. Congress extensively debated the rule, and the Report of the House and Senate Conference Committee states that "[b]y the phrase 'dishonesty and false statement,' the Conference means crimes such as perjury, subornation of perjury, false statement, criminal fraud, embezzlement, or false pretense, or any other offense in the nature of *crimen falsi*, commission of which involves some element of deceit, untruthfulness, or falsification bearing on the accused's propensity to testify truthfully." The Advisory Committee concluded that the Conference Report provides sufficient guidance to trial courts and that no amendment is necessary, notwithstanding some decision that take an unduly broad view of "dishonesty," admitting convictions such as for bank robbery or bank larceny. Subsection (a)(2) continues to apply to any witness, including a criminal defendant.

Finally, the Committee determined that it was unnecessary to add to the rule language stating that, when a prior conviction is offered under Rule 609, the trial court is to consider the probative value of the prior conviction *for impeachment*, not for other purposes. The Committee concluded that the title of the rule, its first sentence, and its placement among the impeachment rules clearly establish that evidence offered under Rule 609 is offered only for purposes of impeachment.

COMMITTEE NOTE TO 2006 AMENDMENT.

The amendment provides that Rule 609(a)(2) mandates the admission of evidence of a conviction only when the conviction required the proof of (or in the case of a guilty plea, the admission of) an act of dishonesty or false statement. Evidence of all other convictions is inadmissible under this subsection, irrespective of whether the witness exhibited dishonesty or made a false statement in the process of the commission of the crime of conviction. Thus, evidence that a witness was convicted of a crime of violence, such as murder, is not admissible under Rule 609(a)(2), even if the witness acted deceitfully in the course of committing the crime.

This amendment is meant to give effect to the legislative intent to limit the convictions that are to be automatically admitted under subsection (a)(2). The Conference Committee provided that by "dishonesty and false statement" it meant "crimes such as perjury, subornation of perjury, false statement, criminal fraud, embezzlement, or false pretense, or any other offense in the nature of *crimen falsi*, the commission of which involves some element of deceit, untruthfulness, or falsification bearing on the [witness's] propensity to testify truthfully." Historically, offenses classified as *crimina falsi* have included only those crimes in which the ultimate criminal act was itself an act of deceit. *See* Green, *Deceit and the Classification of Crimes: Federal Rule of Evidence 609(a)(2) and the Origins of* Crimen Falsi, 90 J. Crim. L. & Criminology 1087 (2000).

Evidence of crimes in the nature of *crimina falsi* must be admitted under Rule 609(a)(2), regardless of how such crimes are specifically charged. For example, evidence that a witness was convicted of making a false claim to a federal agent is admissible under this subsection regardless of whether the crime was charged under a section that expressly references deceit (e.g., 18 U.S.C. § 1001, Material Misrepresentation to the Federal Government) or a section that does not (e.g., 18 U.S.C. § 1503, Obstruction of Justice).

The amendment requires that the proponent have ready proof that the conviction required the factfinder to find, or the defendant to admit, an act of dishonesty or false statement. Ordinarily, the statutory elements of the crime will indicate whether it is one of dishonesty or false statement. Where the deceitful nature of the crime is not apparent from the statute and the face of the judgment—as, for example, where the conviction simply records a finding of guilt for a statutory offense that does not reference deceit expressly—a proponent may offer information such as an indictment, a statement of admitted facts, or jury instructions to show that the factfinder had to find, or the defendant had to admit, an act of dishonesty or false statement in order for the witness to have been convicted. *Cf. Taylor v. United States*, 495 U.S. 575, 602 (1990) (providing that a trial court may look to a charging instrument or jury instructions to ascertain the nature of a prior offense where the statute is insufficiently clear on its face); *Shepard v. United States*, 125 S.Ct. 1254 (2005) (the inquiry to determine whether a guilty plea to a crime defined by a nongeneric statute necessarily admitted elements of the generic offense was limited to the charging document's terms, the terms of a plea agreement or transcript of colloquy between judge and defendant in which the factual basis for the plea was confirmed by the defendant, or a comparable judicial record). But the amendment does not contemplate a "mini-trial" in which the court plumbs the record of the previous proceeding to determine whether the crime was in the nature of *crimen falsi.*

The amendment also substitutes the term "character for truthfulness" for the term "credibility" in the first sentence of the Rule. The limitations of Rule 609 are not applicable if a conviction is admitted for a purpose other than to prove the witness's character for untruthfulness. *See, e.g., United States v. Lopez*, 979 F.2d 1024 (5th Cir. 1992) (Rule 609 was not applicable where the conviction was offered for purposes of contradiction). The use of the term "credibility" in subsection (d) is retained, however, as that subdivision is intended to govern the use of a juvenile adjudication for any type of impeachment.

Rule 610. Religious Beliefs or Opinions

ADVISORY COMMITTEE NOTE TO THE 2011 AMENDMENT.

The language of Rule 610 has been amended as part of the restyling of the Evidence Rules to make them more easily understood and to make style and terminology consistent throughout the rules. These changes are intended to be stylistic only. There is no intent to change any result in any ruling on evidence admissibility.

ADVISORY COMMITTEE NOTE.

While the rule forecloses inquiry into the religious beliefs or opinions of a witness for the purpose of showing that his character for truthfulness is affected by their nature, an inquiry for the purpose of showing interest or bias because of them is not within the prohibition. Thus disclosure of affiliation with a church which is a party to the litigation would be allowable under the rule. *Cf.* Tucker v. Reil, 51 Ariz. 357, 77 P.2d 203 (1938). To the same effect, though less specifically worded, is California Evidence Code § 789. *See* 3 Wigmore § 936.

NOTE BY FEDERAL JUDICIAL CENTER.

The Rule enacted by Congress is the Rule prescribed by the Supreme Court without change. Rule 610 is not mentioned in the Report of the Senate Judiciary Committee or the Reports of the House/Senate Conference Committee.

Rule 611. Mode and Order of Examining Witnesses and Presenting Evidence

ADVISORY COMMITTEE NOTE TO THE 2011 AMENDMENT.

The language of Rule 611 has been amended as part of the restyling of the Evidence Rules to make them more easily understood and to make style and terminology consistent throughout the rules. These changes are intended to be stylistic only. There is no intent to change

any result in any ruling on evidence admissibility.

ADVISORY COMMITTEE NOTE.

Subdivision (a). Spelling out detailed rules to govern the mode and order of interrogating witnesses and presenting evidence is neither desirable nor feasible. The ultimate responsibility for the effective working of the adversary system rests with the judge. The rule sets forth the objectives which he should seek to attain.

Item (1) restates in broad terms the power and obligation of the judge as developed under common law principles. It covers such concerns as whether testimony shall be in the form of a free narrative or responses to specific questions, McCormick § 5, the order of calling witnesses and presenting evidence, 6 Wigmore § 1867, the use of demonstrative evidence, McCormick § 179, and the many other questions arising during the course of a trial which can be solved only by the judge's common sense and fairness in view of the particular circumstances.

Item (2) is addressed to avoidance of needless consumption of time, a matter of daily concern in the disposition of cases. A companion piece is found in the discretion vested in the judge to exclude evidence as a waste of time in Rule 403(b).

Item (3) calls for a judgment under the particular circumstances whether interrogation tactics entail harassment or undue embarrassment. Pertinent circumstances include the importance of the testimony, the nature of the inquiry, its relevance to credibility, waste of time, and confusion. McCormick § 42. In Alford v. United States, 282 U.S. 687, 694, 51 S.Ct. 218, 75 L. Ed. 624 (1931), the Court pointed out that, while the trial judge should protect the witness from questions which "go beyond the bounds of proper cross-examination merely to harass, annoy or humiliate," this protection by no means forecloses efforts to discredit the witness. Reference to the transcript of the prosecutor's cross-examination in Berger v. United States, 295 U.S. 78, 55 S.Ct. 629, 79 L. Ed. 1314 (1935), serves to lay at rest any doubts as to the need for judicial control in this area.

The inquiry into specific instances of conduct of a witness allowed under Rule 608(b) is, of course, subject to this rule.

Subdivision (b). The tradition in the federal courts and in numerous state courts has been to limit the scope of cross-examination to matters testified to on direct, plus matters bearing upon the credibility of the witness. Various reasons have been advanced to justify the rule of limited cross-examination. (1) A party vouches for his own witness but only to the extent of matters elicited on direct. Resurrection Gold Mining Co. v. Fortune Gold Mining Co., 129 F. 668, 675 (8th Cir. 1904), quoted in Maguire, Weinstein, et al., Cases on Evidence 277, n.

38 (5th ed. 1965). But the concept of vouching is discredited, and Rule 607 rejects it. (2) A party cannot ask his own witness leading questions. This is a problem properly solved in terms of what is necessary for a proper development of the testimony rather than by a mechanistic formula similar to the vouching concept. *See* discussion under subdivision (c). (3) A practice of limited cross-examination promotes orderly presentation of the case. Finch v. Weiner, 109 Conn. 616, 145 A. 31 (1929). While this latter reason has merit, the matter is essentially one of the order of presentation and not one in which involvement at the appellate level is likely to prove fruitful. *See*, for example, Moyer v. Aetna Life Ins. Co., 126 F.2d 141 (3rd Cir. 1942); Butler v. New York Central R. Co., 253 F.2d 281 (7th Cir. 1958); United States v. Johnson, 285 F.2d 35 (9th Cir. 1960); Union Automobile Indemnity Ass'n v. Capitol Indemnity Ins. Co., 310 F.2d 318 (7th Cir. 1962). In evaluating these considerations, McCormick says:

"The foregoing considerations favoring the wide-open or restrictive rules may well be thought to be fairly evenly balanced. There is another factor, however, which seems to swing the balance overwhelmingly in favor of the wide-open rule. This is the consideration of economy of time and energy. Obviously, the wide-open rule presents little or no opportunity for dispute in its application. The restrictive practice in all its forms, on the other hand, is productive in many court rooms, of continual bickering over the choice of the numerous variations of the 'scope of the direct' criterion, and of their application to particular cross-questions. These controversies are often reventilated on appeal, and reversals for error in their determination are frequent. Observance of these vague and ambiguous restrictions is a matter of constant and hampering concern to the cross-examiner. If these efforts, delays and misprisions were the necessary incidents to the guarding of substantive rights or the fundamentals of fair trial, they might be worth the cost. As the price of the choice of an obviously debatable regulation of the order of evidence, the sacrifice seems misguided. The American Bar Association's Committee for the Improvement of the Law of Evidence for the year 1937–38 said this:

"The rule limiting cross-examination to the precise subject of the direct examination is probably the most frequent rule (except the Opinion rule) leading in the trial practice today to refined and technical quibbles which obstruct the progress of the trial, confuse the jury, and give rise to appeal on technical grounds only. Some of the instances in which Supreme Courts have ordered new trials for the mere transgression of this rule about the order of evidence have been astounding.

'We recommend that the rule allowing questions upon any part of the issue known to the witness . . . be adopted . . . .'" McCormick, § 27,

p. 51. *See also* 5 Moore's Federal Practice § 43.10 (2nd ed. 1964).

The provision of the second sentence, that the judge may in the interests of justice limit inquiry into new matters on cross-examination, is designed for those situations in which the result otherwise would be confusion, complication, or protraction of the case, not as a matter of rule but as demonstrable in the actual development of the particular case.

The rule does not purport to determine the extent to which an accused who elects to testify thereby waives his privilege against self-incrimination. The question is a constitutional one, rather than a mere matter of administering the trial. Under Simmons v. United States, 390 U.S. 377, 88 S.Ct. 967, 19 L.Ed.2d 1247 (1968), no general waiver occurs when the accused testifies on such preliminary matters as the validity of a search and seizure or the admissibility of a confession. Rule 104(d), *supra*. When he testifies on the merits, however, can he foreclose inquiry into an aspect or element of the crime by avoiding it on direct? The affirmative answer given in Tucker v. United States, 5 F.2d 818 (8th Cir. 1925), is inconsistent with the description of the waiver as extending to "all other relevant facts" in Johnson v. United States, 318 U.S. 189, 195, 63 S.Ct. 549, 87 L. Ed. 704 (1943). *See also* Brown v. United States, 356 U.S. 148, 78 S.Ct. 622, 2 L.Ed.2d 589 (1958). The situation of an accused who desires to testify on some but not all counts of a multiple-count indictment is one to be approached, in the first instance at least, as a problem of severance under Rule 14 of the Federal Rules of Criminal Procedure. Cross v. United States, 335 F.2d 987, 118 U.S.App.D.C. 324 (1964). *Cf.* United States v. Baker, 262 F. Supp. 657, 686 (D.D.C. 1966). In all events, the extent of the waiver of the privilege against self-incrimination ought not to be determined as a by-product of a rule on scope of cross-examination.

Subdivision (c). The rule continues the traditional view that the suggestive powers of the leading question are as a general proposition undesirable. Within this tradition, however, numerous exceptions have achieved recognition: The witness who is hostile, unwilling, or biased; the child witness or the adult with communication problems; the witness whose recollection is exhausted; and undisputed preliminary matters. 3 Wigmore §§ 774–778. An almost total unwillingness to reverse for infractions has been manifested by appellate courts. *See* cases cited in 3 Wigmore § 770. The matter clearly falls within the area of control by the judge over the mode and order of interrogation and presentation and accordingly is phrased in words of suggestion rather than command.

The rule also conforms to tradition in making the use of leading questions on cross-examination a matter of right. The purpose of the qualification "ordinarily" is to furnish a basis for denying the use of leading questions when the cross-examination is cross-examination in form only and not in fact, as for example the "cross-examination" of a party by his own counsel after being called by the opponent (savoring more of re-direct) or of an insured defendant who proves to be friendly to the plaintiff.

The final sentence deals with categories of witnesses automatically regarded and treated as hostile. Rule 43(b) of the Federal Rules of Civil Procedure has included only "an adverse party or an officer, director, or managing agent of a public or private corporation or of a partnership or association which is an adverse party." This limitation virtually to persons whose statements would stand as admissions is believed to be an unduly narrow concept of those who may safely be regarded as hostile without further demonstration. *See*, for example, Maryland Casualty Co. v. Kador, 225 F.2d 120 (5th Cir. 1955), and Degelos v. Fidelity and Casualty Co., 313 F.2d 809 (5th Cir. 1963), holding despite the language of Rule 43(b) that an insured fell within it, though not a party in an action under the Louisiana direct action statute. The phrase of the rule, "witness identified with" an adverse party, is designed to enlarge the category of persons thus callable.

REPORT OF THE HOUSE COMMITTEE ON THE JUDICIARY.

Rule 611(b)

As submitted by the Court, Rule 611(b) provided:

A witness may be cross-examined on any matter relevant to any issue in the case, including credibility. In the interests of justice, the judge may limit cross-examination with respect to matters not testified to on direct examination.

The Committee amended this provision to return to the rule which prevails in the federal courts and thirty-nine State jurisdictions. As amended, the Rule is in the text of the 1969 Advisory Committee draft. It limits cross-examination to credibility and to matters testified to on direct examination, unless the judge permits more, in which event the cross-examiner must proceed as if on direct examination. This traditional rule facilitates orderly presentation by each party at trial. Further, in light of existing discovery procedures, there appears to be no need to abandon the traditional rule.

Rule 611(c)

The third sentence of Rule 611(c) as submitted by the Court provided that:

In civil cases, a party is entitled to call an adverse party or witness identified with him and interrogate by leading questions.

The Committee amended this Rule to permit leading questions to be used with respect to any hostile witness, not only an adverse party or person identified with such adverse party. The Committee also substituted the word "When" for the phrase "In civil cases" to reflect the possibility that in criminal cases a defendant may be entitled to call witnesses identified with the government, in which event the Committee believed the defendant should be permitted to inquire with leading questions.

REPORT OF THE SENATE COMMITTEE ON THE JUDICIARY.

Rule 611(b) Mode and Order of Interrogation and Presentation; Scope of Cross-examination

Rule 611(b) as submitted by the Supreme Court permitted a broad scope of cross-examination: "cross-examination on any matter relevant to any issue in the case" unless the judge, in the interests of justice, limited the scope of cross-examination.

The House narrowed the Rule to the more traditional practice of limiting cross-examination to the subject matter of direct examination (and credibility), but with discretion in the judge to permit inquiry into additional matters in situations where that would aid in the development of the evidence or otherwise facilitate the conduct of the trial.

The committee agrees with the House amendment. Although there are good arguments in support of broad cross-examination from perspectives of developing all relevant evidence, we believe the factors of insuring an orderly and predictable development of the evidence weigh in favor of the narrower rule, especially when discretion is given to the trial judge to permit inquiry into additional matters. The committee expressly approves this discretion and believes it will permit sufficient flexibility allowing a broader scope of cross-examination whenever appropriate.

The House amendment providing broader discretionary cross-examination permitted inquiry into additional matters only as if on direct examination. As a general rule, we concur with this limitation, however, we would understand that this limitation would not preclude the utilization of leading questions if the conditions of subsection (c) of this rule were met, bearing in mind the judge's discretion in any case to limit the scope of cross-examination. Further, the committee has received correspondence from Federal judges commenting on the applicability of this rule to section 1407 of title 28. It is the committee's judgment that this rule as reported by the House is flexible enough to provide sufficiently broad cross-examination in appropriate situations in multidistrict litigation.

Rule 611(c). Mode and Order of Interrogation and Presentation; Leading Questions

As submitted by the Supreme Court, the rule provided: "In civil cases, a party is entitled to call an adverse party or witness identified with him and interrogate by leading questions."

The final sentence of subsection (c) was amended by the House for the purpose of clarifying the fact that a "hostile witness"—that is a witness who is hostile in fact—could be subject to interrogation by leading questions. The rule as submitted by the Supreme Court declared certain witnesses hostile as a matter of law and thus subject to interrogation by leading questions without any showing of hostility in fact. These were adverse parties or witnesses identified with adverse parties. However, the wording of the first sentence of subsection (c) while generally prohibiting the use of leading questions on direct examination, also provides "except as may be necessary to develop his testimony." Further, the first paragraph of the Advisory Committee note explaining the subsection makes clear that they intended that leading questions could be asked of a hostile witness or a witness who was unwilling or biased and even though that witness was not associated with an adverse party. Thus, we question whether the House amendment was necessary.

However, concluding that it was not intended to affect the meaning of the first sentence of the subsection and was intended solely to clarify the fact that leading questions are permissible in the interrogation of a witness, who is hostile in fact, the committee accepts that House amendment.

The final sentence of this subsection was also amended by the House to cover criminal as well as civil cases. The committee accepts this amendment, but notes that it may be difficult in criminal cases to determine when a witness is "identified with an adverse party," and thus the rule should be applied with caution.

NOTE BY FEDERAL JUDICIAL CENTER.

Subdivision (a) of the Rule enacted by Congress is the subdivision prescribed by the Supreme Court, amended only by substituting "court" in place of "judge."

Subdivision (b) of the Rule enacted by Congress is substantially different from the subdivision prescribed by the Supreme Court. The nature of the changes and the reasons therefor are stated in the Report of the House Committee of the Judiciary, set forth above.

The first two sentences of subdivision (c) of the Rule enacted by Congress are the same as prescribed by the Supreme Court. The third sentence has been amended in the manner and for the reasons stated in the Report of the House Committee of the Judiciary, set forth above.

Rule 612. Writing Used to Refresh a Witness's Memory

ADVISORY COMMITTEE NOTE TO THE 2011 AMENDMENT.

The language of Rule 612 has been amended as part of the restyling of the Evidence Rules to make them more easily understood and to make style and terminology consistent throughout the rules. These changes are intended to be stylistic only. There is no intent to change any result in any ruling on evidence admissibility.

ADVISORY COMMITTEE NOTE.

The treatment of writings used to refresh recollection while on the stand is in accord with settled doctrine. McCormick § 9, p. 15. The bulk of the case law has, however, denied the existence of any right to access by the opponent when the writing is used prior to taking the stand, though the judge may have discretion in the matter. Goldman v. United States, 316 U.S. 129, 62 S.Ct. 993, 86 L. Ed. 1322 (1942); Needelman v. United States, 261 F.2d 802 (5th Cir. 1958), cert. dismissed 362 U.S. 600, 80 S.Ct. 960, 4 L.Ed.2d 980, rehearing denied 363 U.S. 858, 80 S.Ct. 1606, 4 L.Ed.2d 1739, Annot., 82 A.L.R.2d 473, 562 and 7 A.L.R.3d 181, 247. An increasing group of cases has repudiated the distinction, People v. Scott, 29 Ill.2d 97, 193 N.E.2d 814 (1963); State v. Mucci, 25 N.J. 423, 136 A.2d 761 (1957); State v. Hunt, 25 N.J. 514, 138 A.2d 1 (1958); State v. Deslovers, 40 R.I. 89, 100 A. 64 (1917), and this position is believed to be correct. As Wigmore put it, "the risk of imposition and the need of safeguard is just as great" in both situations. 3 Wigmore § 762, p. 111. To the same effect is McCormick § 9, p. 17.

The purpose of the phrase "for the purpose of testifying" is to safeguard against using the rule as a pretext for wholesale exploration of an opposing party's files and to insure that access is limited only to those writings which may fairly be said in fact to have an impact upon the testimony of the witness.

The purpose of the rule is the same as that of the *Jencks* statute, 18 U.S.C. § 3500; to promote the search of credibility and memory. The same sensitivity to disclosure of government files may be involved; hence the rule is expressly made subject to the statute, subdivision (a) of which provides: "In any criminal prosecution brought by the United States, no statement or report in the possession of the United States which was made by a Government witness or prospective Government witness (other than the defendant) shall be the subject of subpoena, discovery, or inspection until said witness has testified on direct examination in the trial of the case." Items falling within the purview of the statute are producible only as provided by its terms, Palermo v. United States, 360 U.S. 343, 351 (1959), and disclosure under the rule is limited similarly by the statutory conditions. With this limitation in mind, some differences of application may be noted. The *Jencks* statute applies only to statements of witnesses; the rule is not so limited. The statute applies only to criminal cases; the rule applies to all cases. The statute applies only to government witnesses; the rule applies to all witnesses. The statute contains no requirement that the statement be consulted for purposes of refreshment before or while testifying; the rule so requires. Since many writings would qualify under either statute or rule, a substantial overlap exists, but the identity of procedures makes this of no importance.

The consequences of nonproduction by the government in a criminal case are those of the *Jencks* statute, striking the testimony or in exceptional cases a mistrial. 18 U.S.C. § 3500(d). In other cases these alternatives are unduly limited, and such possibilities as contempt, dismissal, finding issues against the offender, and the like are available. *See* Rule 16(g) of the Federal Rules of Criminal Procedure and Rule 37(b) of the Federal Rules of Civil Procedure for appropriate sanctions.

REPORT OF THE HOUSE COMMITTEE ON THE JUDICIARY.

As submitted to Congress, Rule 612 provided that except as set forth in 18 U.S.C. 3500, if a witness uses a writing to refresh his memory for the purpose of testifying, "either before or while testifying," an adverse party is entitled to have the writing produced at the hearing, to inspect it, to cross-examine the witness on it, and to introduce in evidence those portions relating to the witness' testimony. The Committee amended the Rule so as still to require the production of writings used by a witness while testifying, but to render the production of writings used by a witness to refresh his memory before testifying discretionary with the court in the interests of justice, as is the case under existing federal law. *See* Goldman v. United States, 316 U.S. 129 (1942). The Committee considered that permitting an adverse party to require the production of writings used before testifying could result in fishing expeditions among a multitude of papers which a witness may have used in preparing for trial. The Committee intends that nothing in the Rule be construed as barring the assertion of a privilege with respect to writings used by a witness to refresh his memory.

NOTE BY FEDERAL JUDICIAL CENTER.

Rule 612 underwent substantial change at the hands of Congress with respect to the right of the questioner's adversary to inspect and use a writing before he testifies. The Rule was amended by substituting "court" in place of "judge," with appropriate pronominal change, and in the first sentence, by substituting "the writing" in place of "it" before "produced," and by substituting the phrase "(1) while testifying, or (2) before testifying if the Court in its discretion determines it is necessary in the interests of justice" in place of "before or while testifying." The reasons for the latter amendment are stated in the Report of the House

Committee of the Judiciary, set forth above.

Rule 613. Witness's Prior Statement

ADVISORY COMMITTEE NOTE TO THE 2011 AMENDMENT.

The language of Rule 613 has been amended as part of the restyling of the Evidence Rules to make them more easily understood and to make style and terminology consistent throughout the rules. These changes are intended to be stylistic only. There is no intent to change any result in any ruling on evidence admissibility.

ADVISORY COMMITTEE NOTE.

Subdivision (a). The Queen's Case, 2 Br. & B. 284, 129 Eng.Rep. 976 (1820), laid down the requirement that a cross-examiner, prior to questioning the witness about his own prior statement in writing, must first show it to the witness. Abolished by statute in the country of its origin, the requirement nevertheless gained currency in the United States. The rule abolishes this useless impediment to cross-examination. Ladd, Some Observations on Credibility: Impeachment of Witnesses, 52 Cornell L.Q. 239, 246–247 (1967); McCormick § 28; 4 Wigmore §§ 1259–1260. Both oral and written statements are included.

The provision for disclosure to counsel is designed to protect against unwarranted insinuations that a statement has been made when the fact is to the contrary.

The rule does not defeat the application of Rule 1002 relating to production of the original when the contents of a writing are sought to be proved. Nor does it defeat the application of Rule 26(b)(3) of the Rules of Civil Procedure, as revised, entitling a person on request to a copy of his own statement, though the operation of the latter may be suspended temporarily.

Subdivision (b). The familiar foundation requirement that an impeaching statement first be shown to the witness before it can be proved by extrinsic evidence is preserved but with some modifications. *See* Ladd, Some Observations on Credibility: Impeachment of Witnesses, 52 Cornell L.Q. 239, 247 (1967). The traditional insistence that the attention of the witness be directed to the statement on cross-examination is relaxed in favor of simply providing the witness an opportunity to explain and the opposite party an opportunity to examine on the statement, with no specification of any particular time or sequence. Under this procedure, several collusive witnesses can be examined before disclosure of a joint prior inconsistent statement. *See* Comment to California Evidence Code § 770. Also, dangers of oversight are reduced. *See* McCormick § 37, p. 68.

In order to allow for such eventualities as the witness becoming unavailable by the time the statement is discovered, a measure of discretion is conferred upon the judge. Similar provisions are found in California Evidence Code § 770 and New Jersey Evidence Rule 22(b).

Under principles of *expression unius* the rule does not apply to impeachment by evidence of prior inconsistent conduct. The use of inconsistent statements to impeach a hearsay declaration is treated in Rule 806.

NOTE BY FEDERAL JUDICIAL CENTER.

The Rule enacted by Congress is the Rule prescribed by the Supreme Court, amended only by substituting "nor" in the place of "or" in subdivision (a); Rule 613 was not the subject of floor debate.

Rule 614. Court's Calling or Examining a Witness

ADVISORY COMMITTEE NOTE TO THE 2011 AMENDMENT.

The language of Rule 614 has been amended as part of the restyling of the Evidence Rules to make them more easily understood and to make style and terminology consistent throughout the rules. These changes are intended to be stylistic only. There is no intent to change any result in any ruling on evidence admissibility.

ADVISORY COMMITTEE NOTE.

Subdivision (a). While exercised more frequently in criminal than in civil cases, the authority of the judge to call witnesses is well established. McCormick § 8, p. 11; Maguire, Weinstein, et al., Cases on Evidence 303–304 (5th ed. 1965); 9 Wigmore § 2484. One reason for the practice, the old rule against impeaching one's own witness, no longer exists by virtue of Rule 607, *supra*. Other reasons remain, however, to justify the continuation of the practice of calling court's witnesses. The right to cross-examine, with all it implies, is assured. The tendency of juries to associate a witness with the party calling him, regardless of technical aspects of vouching, is avoided. And the judge is not imprisoned within the case as made by the parties.

Subdivision (b). The authority of the judge to question witnesses is also well established. McCormick § 8, pp. 12–13; Maguire, Weinstein, et al., Cases on Evidence 737–739 (5th ed. 1965); 3 Wigmore § 784. The authority is, of course, abused when the judge abandons his proper role and assumes that of advocate, but the manner in which interrogation should be conducted and the proper extent of its exercise are not susceptible of formulation in a rule. The omission in no sense precludes courts of review from continuing to reverse for abuse.

Subdivision (c). The provision relating to objections is designed to relieve counsel of the embarrassment attendant upon objecting to questions by the judge in the presence of the jury, while at the same time assuring that objections are made in apt time to afford the opportunity to take possible corrective measures. Compare the "automatic" objection feature of Rule 605 when the judge is called as a witness.

NOTE BY FEDERAL JUDICIAL CENTER.

The Rule enacted by Congress is the Rule prescribed by the Supreme Court, amended by substituting "court" in place of "judge," with conforming pronominal changes. Rule 614 was not the subject of floor debate.

Rule 615. Excluding Witnesses

ADVISORY COMMITTEE NOTE TO THE 2011 AMENDMENT.

The language of Rule 615 has been amended as part of the restyling of the Evidence Rules to make them more easily understood and to make style and terminology consistent throughout the rules. These changes are intended to be stylistic only. There is no intent to change any result in any ruling on evidence admissibility.

ADVISORY COMMITTEE NOTE.

The efficacy of excluding or sequestering witnesses has long been recognized as a means of discouraging and exposing fabrication, inaccuracy, and collusion. 6 Wigmore §§ 1837–1838. The authority of the judge is admitted, the only question being whether the matter is committed to his discretion or one of right. The rule takes the latter position. No time is specified for making the request.

Several categories of persons are excepted. (1) Exclusion of persons who are parties would raise serious problems of confrontation and due process. Under accepted practice they are not subject to exclusion. 6 Wigmore § 1811. (2) As the equivalent of the right of a natural-person party to be present, a party which is not a natural person is entitled to have a representative present. Most of the cases have involved allowing a police officer who has been in charge of an investigation to remain in court despite the fact that he will be a witness. United States v. Infanzon, 235 F.2d 318 (2d Cir. 1956); Portomene v. United States, 221 F.2d 582 (5th Cir. 1955); Powell v. United States, 208 F.2d 618 (6th Cir. 1953); Jones v. United States, 252 F. Supp. 781 (W.D.Okl.1966). Designation of the representative by the attorney rather than by the client may at first glance appear to be an inversion of the attorney-client relationship, but it may be assumed that the attorney will follow the wishes of the client, and the solution is simple and workable. *See* California Evidence Code § 777. (3) The category contemplates such persons as an agent who handled the transaction being litigated or an expert needed to advise counsel in the management of the litigation. *See* 6 Wigmore § 1841, n. 4.

The amendment is in response to: (1) the Victim's Rights and Restitution Act of 1990, 42 U.S.C. § 10606, which guarantees, within certain limits, the right of a crime victim to attend the trial; and (2) the

Victim Rights Clarification Act of 1997 (18 U.S.C. § 3510).

REPORT OF THE SENATE COMMITTEE ON THE JUDICIARY.

Many district courts permit government counsel to have an investigative agent at counsel table throughout the trial although the agent is or may be a witness. The practice is permitted as an exception to the rule of exclusion and compares with the situation defense counsel finds himself in—he always has the client with him to consult during the trial. The investigative agent's presence may be extremely important to government counsel, especially when the case is complex or involves some specialized subject matter. The agent, too, having lived with the case for a long time, may be able to assist in meeting trial surprises where the best-prepared counsel would otherwise have difficulty. Yet, it would not seem the Government could often meet the burden under Rule 615 of showing that the agent's presence is essential. Furthermore, it could be dangerous to use the agent as a witness as early in the case as possible, so that he might then help counsel as a nonwitness, since the agent's testimony could be needed in rebuttal. Using another, nonwitness agent from the same investigative agency would not generally meet government counsel's needs.

This problem is solved if it is clear that investigative agents are within the group specified under the second exception made in the rule, for "an officer or employee of a party which is not a natural person designated as its representative by its attorney." It is our understanding that this was the intention of the House committee. It is certainly this committee's construction of the rule.

NOTE BY FEDERAL JUDICIAL CENTER.

The Rule enacted by Congress is the Rule prescribed by the Supreme Court, amended only by substituting "court," in place of "judge," with conforming pronominal changes.

ARTICLE VII.
OPINIONS AND EXPERT TESTIMONY
Rule 701. Opinion Testimony by Lay Witnesses

ADVISORY COMMITTEE NOTE TO THE 2011 AMENDMENT.

The language of Rule 701 has been amended as part of the restyling of the Evidence Rules to make them more easily understood and to make style and terminology consistent throughout the rules. These changes are intended to be stylistic only. There is no intent to change any result in any ruling on evidence admissibility.

The Committee deleted all reference to an "inference" on the grounds that the deletion made the Rule flow better and easier to read, and because any "inference" is covered by the broader term "opinion." Courts have not made substantive decisions on the basis of any distinction between an opinion and an inference. No change in current practice is intended.

ADVISORY COMMITTEE NOTE.

The rule retains the traditional objective of putting the trier of fact in possession of an accurate reproduction of the event.

Limitation (a) is the familiar requirement of first-hand knowledge or observation.

Limitation (b) is phrased in terms of requiring testimony to be helpful in resolving issues. Witnesses often find difficulty in expressing themselves in language which is not that of an opinion or conclusion. While the courts have made concessions in certain recurring situations, necessity as a standard for permitting opinions and conclusions has proved too elusive and too unadaptable to particular situations for purposes of satisfactory judicial administration. McCormick § 11. Moreover, the practical impossibility of determining by rule what is a "fact," demonstrated by a century of litigation of the question of what is a fact for purposes of pleading under the Field Code, extends into evidence also. 7 Wigmore § 1919. The rule assumes that the natural characteristics of the adversary system will generally lead to an acceptable result, since the detailed account carries more conviction than the broad assertion, and a lawyer can be expected to display his witness to the best advantage. If he fails to do so, cross-examination and argument will point up the weakness. *See* Ladd, Expert Testimony, 5 Vand.L.Rev. 414, 415–417 (1952). If, despite these considerations, attempts are made to introduce meaningless assertions which amount to little more than choosing up sides, exclusion for lack of helpfulness is called for by the rule.

The language of the rule is substantially that of Uniform Rule 56(1). Similar provisions are California Evidence Code § 800; Kansas Code of Civil Procedure § 60-456(a); New Jersey Evidence Rule 56(1).

NOTES OF ADVISORY COMMITTEE ON 2000 AMENDMENTS.

Rule 701 has been amended to eliminate the risk that the reliability requirements set forth in Rule 702 will be evaded through the simple expedient of proffering an expert in lay witness clothing. Under the amendment, a witness's testimony must be scrutinized under the rules regulating expert opinion to the extent that the witness is providing testimony based on scientific, technical, or other specialized knowledge within the scope of Rule 702. *See generally* Asplundh Mfg. Div. v. Benton Harbor Eng'g, 57 F.3d 1190 (3d Cir. 1995). By channeling testimony that is actually expert testimony to Rule 702, the amendment also ensures that a party will not evade the expert witness disclosure requirements set forth in Fed.R.Civ.P. 26 and Fed.R.Crim.P. 16 by simply calling an expert witness in the guise of a layperson. *See Joseph, Emerging Expert Issues Under the 1993 Disclosure Amendments to the Federal Rules of Civil Procedure*, 164 F.R.D. 97, 108 (1996) (noting that "there is no good reason to allow what is essentially surprise expert testimony," and that "the Court should be vigilant to preclude manipulative conduct designed to thwart the expert disclosure and discovery process"). *See also* United States v. Figueroa-Lopez, 125 F.3d 1241, 1246 (9th Cir. 1997) (law enforcement agents testifying that the defendant's conduct was consistent with that of a drug trafficker could not testify as lay witnesses; to permit such testimony under Rule 701 "subverts the requirements of Federal Rule of Criminal Procedure 16(a)(1)(E)").

The amendment does not distinguish between expert and lay witnesses, but rather between expert and lay testimony. Certainly it is possible for the same witness to provide both lay and expert testimony in a single case. *See, e.g.*, United States v. Figueroa-Lopez, 125 F.3d 1241, 1246 (9th Cir. 1997) (law enforcement agents could testify that the defendant was acting suspiciously, without being qualified as experts; however, the rules on experts were applicable where the agents testified on the basis of extensive experience that the defendant was using code words to refer to drug quantities and prices). The amendment makes clear that any part of a witness's testimony that is based upon scientific, technical, or other specialized knowledge within the scope of Rule 702 is governed by the standards of Rule 702 and the corresponding disclosure requirements of the Civil and Criminal Rules.

The amendment is not intended to affect the "prototypical example[s] of the type of evidence contemplated by the adoption of Rule 701 relat[ing] to the appearance of persons or things, identity, the manner of conduct, competency of a person, degrees of light or darkness, sound, size, weight, distance, and an endless number of items that cannot be described factually in words apart from inferences." Asplundh Mfg. Div. v. Benton Harbor Eng'g, 57 F.3d 1190, 1196 (3d Cir. 1995).

For example, most courts have permitted the owner or officer of a business to testify to the value or projected profits of the business, without the necessity of qualifying the witness as an accountant, appraiser, or similar expert. *See, e.g.*, Lightning Lube, Inc. v. Witco Corp., 4 F.3d 1153 (3d Cir. 1993) (no abuse of discretion in permitting the plaintiff's owner to give lay opinion testimony as to damages, as it was based on his knowledge and participation in the day-to-day affairs of the business). Such opinion testimony is admitted not because of experience, training or specialized knowledge within the realm of an expert, but because of the particularized knowledge that the witness has by virtue of his or her position in the business. The amendment does not purport to change this analysis. Similarly, courts have permitted lay witnesses to testify that a substance appeared to be a narcotic, so long as the foundation of familiarity with the substance is established. *See, e.g.,* United States v. Westbrook, 896 F.2d 330 (8th Cir. 1990) (two lay witnesses who were heavy amphetamine users were properly permitted to testify that a substance was amphetamine; but it was error to permit another witness to make such an identification where she had no experience with amphetamines). Such testimony is not based on specialized knowledge within the scope of Rule 702, but rather is based upon a layperson's personal knowledge. If, however, that witness were to describe how a narcotic was manufactured, or to describe the intricate workings of a narcotic distribution network, then the witness would have to qualify as an expert under Rule 702. United States. v. Figueroa-Lopez, *supra.*

The amendment incorporates the distinctions set forth in State v. Brown, 836 S.W.2d 530, 549 (1992), a case involving a former Tennessee Rule of Evidence 701, a rule that precluded lay witness testimony based on "special knowledge." In *Brown*, the court declared that the distinction between lay and expert witness testimony is that lay testimony "results from a process of reasoning familiar in everyday life," while expert testimony "results from a process of reasoning which can be mastered only by specialists in the field." The court in *Brown* noted that a lay witness with experience could testify that a substance appeared to be blood, but that a witness would have to qualify as an expert before he could testify that bruising around the eyes is indicative of skull trauma. That is the kind of distinction made by the amendment to this Rule.

NOTE BY FEDERAL JUDICIAL CENTER.

The Rule enacted by Congress is the Rule prescribed by the Supreme Court without change. Rule 701 was not the subject of floor debate.

Rule 702. Testimony by Expert Witnesses

ADVISORY COMMITTEE NOTE TO THE 2011 AMENDMENT.

The language of Rule 702 has been amended as part of the restyling of the Evidence Rules to make them more easily understood and to make style and terminology consistent throughout the rules. These changes are intended to be stylistic only. There is no intent to change any result in any ruling on evidence admissibility.

ADVISORY COMMITTEE NOTE.

An intelligent evaluation of facts is often difficult or impossible without the application of some scientific, technical, or other specialized knowledge. The most common source of this knowledge is the expert witness, although there are other techniques for supplying it.

Most of the literature assumes that experts testify only in the form of opinions. The assumption is logically unfounded. The rule accordingly recognizes that an expert on the stand may give a dissertation or exposition of scientific or other principles relevant to the case, leaving the trier of fact to apply them to the facts. Since much of the criticism of expert testimony has centered upon the hypothetical question, it seems wise to recognize that opinions are not indispensable and to encourage the use of expert testimony in nonopinion form when counsel believes the trier can itself draw the requisite inference. The use of opinions is not abolished by the rule, however. It will continue to be permissible for the expert to take the further step of suggesting the inference which should be drawn from applying the specialized knowledge to the facts. *See* Rules 703 to 705.

Whether the situation is a proper one for the use of expert testimony is to be determined on the basis of assisting the trier. "There is no more certain test for determining when experts may be used than the common sense inquiry whether the untrained layman would be qualified to determine intelligently and to the best possible degree the particular issue without enlightenment from those having a specialized understanding of the subject involved in the dispute." Ladd, Expert Testimony, 5 Vand.L.Rev. 414, 418 (1952). When opinions are excluded, it is because they are unhelpful and therefore superfluous and a waste of time. 7 Wigmore § 1918.

The rule is broadly phrased. The fields of knowledge which may be drawn upon are not limited merely to the "scientific" and "technical" but extend to all "specialized" knowledge. Similarly, the expert is viewed, not in a narrow sense, but as a person qualified by "knowledge, skill, experience, training or education." Thus within the scope of the rule are not only experts in the strictest sense of the word, e.g. physicians, physicists, and architects, but also the large group sometimes called "skilled" witnesses, such as bankers or landowners testifying to land values.

NOTES OF ADVISORY COMMITTEE ON **2000** AMENDMENTS.

Rule 702 has been amended in response to Daubert v. Merrell Dow Pharmaceuticals, Inc., 509 U.S. 579 [125 L.Ed.2d 469] (1993), and to the many cases applying *Daubert*, including Kumho Tire Co. v. Carmichael, [119 S.Ct. 1167, 143 L.Ed.2d 238 (1999). In *Daubert* the Court charged trial judges with the responsibility of acting as gatekeepers to exclude unreliable expert testimony, and the Court in *Kumho* clarified that this gatekeeper function applies to all expert testimony, not just testimony based in science. *See also Kumho*, 119 S.Ct. at 1178 (citing the Committee Note to the proposed amendment to Rule 702, which had been released for public comment before the date of the *Kumho* decision). The amendment affirms the trial court's role as gatekeeper and provides some general standards that the trial court must use to assess the reliability and helpfulness of proffered expert testimony. Consistently with *Kumho*, the Rule as amended provides that all types of expert testimony present questions of admissibility for the trial court in deciding whether the evidence is reliable and helpful. Consequently, the admissibility of all expert testimony is governed by the principles of Rule 104(a). Under that Rule, the proponent has the burden of establishing that the pertinent admissibility requirements are met by a preponderance of the evidence. *See* Bourjaily v. United States, 483 U.S. 171 [97 L.Ed.2d 144] (1987).

Daubert set forth a non-exclusive checklist for trial courts to use in assessing the reliability of scientific expert testimony. The specific factors explicated by the *Daubert* Court are: (1) whether the expert's technique or theory can be or has been tested—that is, whether the expert's theory can be challenged in some objective sense, or whether it is instead simply a subjective, conclusory approach that cannot reasonably be assessed for reliability; (2) whether the technique or theory has been subject to peer review and publication; (3) the known or potential rate of error of the technique or theory when applied; (4) the existence and maintenance of standards and controls; and (5) whether the technique or theory has been generally accepted in the scientific community. The Court in *Kumho* held that these factors might also be applicable in assessing the reliability of non-scientific expert testimony, depending upon "the particular circumstances of the particular case at issue." 119 S.Ct. at 1175.

No attempt has been made to "codify" these specific factors. *Daubert* itself emphasized that the factors were neither exclusive nor dispositive. Other cases have recognized that not all of the specific *Daubert* factors can apply to every type of expert testimony. In addition to *Kumho*, 119 S.Ct. at 1175, *see* Tyus v. Urban Search Management, 102 F.3d 256 (7th Cir. 1996) (noting that the factors mentioned by the Court in *Daubert* do not neatly apply to expert testimony from a sociologist). *See also* Kannankeril v. Terminix Int'l, Inc., 128 F.3d 802, 809 (3d Cir. 1997) (holding that lack of peer review or publication was not dispositive where the expert's opinion was supported by "widely accepted scientific knowledge"). The standards set forth in the amendment are broad enough to require consideration of any or all of the specific *Daubert* factors where appropriate.

Courts both before and after *Daubert* have found other factors relevant in determining whether expert testimony is sufficiently reliable to be considered by the trier of fact. These factors include:

(1) Whether experts are "proposing to testify about matters growing naturally and directly out of research they have conducted independent

of the litigation, or whether they have developed their opinions expressly for purposes of testifying." Daubert v. Merrell Dow Pharmaceuticals, Inc., 43 F.3d 1311, 1317 (9th Cir. 1995).

(2) Whether the expert has unjustifiably extrapolated from an accepted premise to an unfounded conclusion. *See* General Elec. Co. v. Joiner, 522 U.S. 136, 146 [139 L.Ed.2d 508] (1997) (noting that in some cases a trial court "may conclude that there is simply too great an analytical gap between the data and the opinion proffered").

(3) Whether the expert has adequately accounted for obvious alternative explanations. *See* Claar v. Burlington N.R.R., 29 F.3d 499 (9th Cir. 1994) (testimony excluded where the expert failed to consider other obvious causes for the plaintiff's condition). *Compare* Ambrosini v. Labarraque, 101 F.3d 129 (D.C. Cir. 1996) (the possibility of some uneliminated causes presents a question of weight, so long as the most obvious causes have been considered and reasonably ruled out by the expert).

(4) Whether the expert "is being as careful as he would be in his regular professional work outside his paid litigation consulting." Sheehan v. Daily Racing Form, Inc., 104 F.3d 940, 942 (7th Cir. 1997). *See* Kumho Tire Co. v. Carmichael, [119 S.Ct. 1167, 1176, 143 L.Ed.2d 238 (1999) (*Daubert* requires the trial court to assure itself that the expert "employs in the courtroom the same level of intellectual rigor that characterizes the practice of an expert in the relevant field").

(5) Whether the field of expertise claimed by the expert is known to reach reliable results for the type of opinion the expert would give. *See* Kumho Tire Co. v. Carmichael, [119 S.Ct. 1167, 1175, 143 L.Ed.2d 238 (1999) (*Daubert's* general acceptance factor does not "help show that an expert's testimony is reliable where the discipline itself lacks reliability, as for example, do theories grounded in any so-called generally accepted principles of astrology or necromancy."); Moore v. Ashland Chemical, Inc., 151 F.3d 269 (5th Cir. 1998) (en banc) (clinical doctor was properly precluded from testifying to the toxicological cause of the plaintiff's respiratory problem, where the opinion was not sufficiently grounded in scientific methodology); Sterling v. Velsicol Chem. Corp., 855 F.2d 1188 (6th Cir. 1988) (rejecting testimony based on "clinical ecology" as unfounded and unreliable).

All of these factors remain relevant to the determination of the reliability of expert testimony under the Rule as amended. Other factors may also be relevant. *See Kumho*, [119 S.Ct. 1167, 1176, 143 L.Ed.2d 238 ("[W]e conclude that the trial judge must have considerable leeway in deciding in a particular case how to go about determining whether particular expert testimony is reliable."). Yet no single factor is necessarily dispositive of the reliability of a particular expert's testimony. *See, e.g.*, Heller v. Shaw Industries, Inc., 167 F.3d 146, 155 (3d Cir. 1999) ("not only must each stage of the expert's testimony be reliable, but each stage must be evaluated practically and flexibly without bright-line exclusionary (or inclusionary) rules."); Daubert v. Merrell Dow Pharmaceuticals, Inc., 43 F.3d 1311, 1317, n. 5 (9th Cir. 1995) (noting that some expert disciplines "have the courtroom as a principal theatre of operations" and as to these disciplines "the fact that the expert has developed an expertise principally for purposes of litigation will obviously not be a substantial consideration.").

A review of the caselaw after *Daubert* shows that the rejection of expert testimony is the exception rather than the rule. *Daubert* did not work a "seachange over federal evidence law," and "the trial court's role as gatekeeper is not intended to serve as a replacement for the adversary system." United States v. 14.38 Acres of Land Situated in Leflore County, Mississippi, 80 F.3d 1074, 1078 (5th Cir. 1996). As the Court in *Daubert* stated: "Vigorous cross-examination, presentation of contrary evidence, and careful instruction on the burden of proof are the traditional and appropriate means of attacking shaky but admissible evidence." 509 U.S. at 595. Likewise, this amendment is not intended to provide an excuse for an automatic challenge to the testimony of every expert. *See* Kumho Tire Co. v. Carmichael, [119 S.Ct. 1167, 1176, 143 L.Ed.2d 238 (1999) (noting that the trial judge has the discretion "both to avoid unnecessary 'reliability' proceedings in ordinary cases where the reliability of an expert's methods is properly taken for granted, and to require appropriate proceedings in the less usual or more complex cases where cause for questioning the expert's reliability arises.").

When a trial court, applying this amendment, rules that an expert's testimony is reliable, this does not necessarily mean that contradictory expert testimony is unreliable. The amendment is broad enough to permit testimony that is the product of competing principles or methods in the same field of expertise. *See, e.g.*, Heller v. Shaw Industries, Inc., 167 F.3d 146, 160 (3d Cir. 1999) (expert testimony cannot be excluded simply because the expert uses one test rather than another, when both tests are accepted in the field and both reach reliable results). As the court stated in In re Paoli R.R. Yard PCB Litigation, 35 F.3d 717, 744 (3d Cir. 1994), proponents "do not have to demonstrate to the judge by a preponderance of the evidence that the assessments of their experts are correct, they only have to demonstrate by a preponderance of evidence that their opinions are reliable . . . . The evidentiary requirement of reliability is lower than the merits standard of correctness." *See also* Daubert v. Merrell Dow Pharmaceuticals, Inc., 43 F.3d 1311, 1318 (9th Cir. 1995) (scientific experts might be permitted to testify if they could show that the methods they used were also employed by "a recognized minority of scientists in their field."); Ruiz-Troche v. Pepsi Cola, 161 F.3d 77, 85 (1st Cir. 1998) ("*Daubert* neither requires nor empowers trial courts to determine which of several competing scientific theories has the best provenance.").

The Court in *Daubert* declared that the "focus, of course, must be solely on principles and methodology, not on the conclusions they generate." 509 U.S. at 595. Yet as the Court later recognized, "conclusions and methodology are not entirely distinct from one another." General Elec. Co. v. Joiner, 522 U.S. 136, 146 [139 L.Ed.2d 508] (1997). Under the amendment, as under *Daubert*, when an expert purports to apply principles and methods in accordance with professional standards, and yet reaches a conclusion that other experts in the field would not reach, the trial court may fairly suspect that the principles and methods have not been faithfully applied. *See* Lust v. Merrell Dow Pharmaceuticals, Inc., 89 F.3d 594, 598 (9th Cir. 1996). The amendment specifically provides that the trial court must scrutinize not only the principles and methods used by the expert, but also whether those principles and methods have been properly applied to the facts of the case. As the court noted in In re Paoli R.R. Yard PCB Litig., 35 F.3d 717, 745 (3d Cir. 1994), "any step that renders the analysis unreliable . . . renders the expert's testimony inadmissible. *This is true whether the step completely changes a reliable methodology or merely misapplies that methodology.*"

If the expert purports to apply principles and methods to the facts of the case, it is important that this application be conducted reliably. Yet it might also be important in some cases for an expert to educate the factfinder about general principles, without ever attempting to apply these principles to the specific facts of the case. For example, experts might instruct the factfinder on the principles of thermodynamics, or bloodclotting, or on how financial markets respond to corporate reports, without ever knowing about or trying to tie their testimony into the facts of the case. The amendment does not alter the venerable practice of using expert testimony to educate the factfinder on general principles. For this kind of generalized testimony, Rule 702 simply requires that: (1) the expert be qualified; (2) the testimony address a subject matter on which the factfinder can be assisted by an expert; (3) the testimony be reliable; and (4) the testimony "fit" the facts of the case.

As stated earlier, the amendment does not distinguish between scientific and other forms of expert testimony. The trial court's gatekeeping function applies to testimony by any expert. *See* Kumho Tire Co. v. Carmichael, [119 S.Ct. 1167, 1171, 143 L.Ed.2d 238 (1999) ("We conclude that *Daubert's* general holding—setting forth the trial judge's general 'gatekeeping' obligation—applies not only to testimony based on 'scientific' knowledge, but also to testimony based on 'technical' and 'other specialized' knowledge."). While the relevant factors for determining reliability will vary from expertise to expertise, the amendment rejects the premise that an expert's testimony should be treated more permissively simply because it is outside the realm of science. An opinion from an expert who is not a scientist should receive the same degree of scrutiny for reliability as an opinion from an expert who purports to be a scientist. *See* Watkins v. Telsmith, Inc., 121 F.3d 984, 991 (5th Cir. 1997) ("[I]t seems exactly backwards that experts who purport to rely on general engineering principles and practical experience might escape screening by the district court simply by stating that their conclusions were not reached by any particular method or technique."). Some types of expert testimony will be more objectively verifiable, and subject to the expectations of falsifiability, peer review, and publication, than others. Some types of expert testimony will not rely on anything like a scientific method, and so will have to be evaluated by reference to other standard principles attendant to the particular area of expertise. The trial judge in all cases of proffered expert testimony must find that it is properly grounded, well-reasoned, and not speculative before it can be admitted. The expert's testimony must be grounded in an accepted body of learning or experience in the expert's field, and the expert must explain how the conclusion is so grounded. *See, e.g.*, American College of Trial Lawyers, *Standards and Procedures for Determining the Admissibility of Expert Testimony after Daubert*, 157 F.R.D. 571, 579 (1994) ("[W]hether the testimony concerns economic principles, accounting standards, property valuation or other non-scientific subjects, it should be evaluated by reference to the 'knowledge and experience' of that particular field."). The amendment requires that the testimony must be the product of reliable principles and methods that are reliably applied to the facts of the case. While the terms "principles" and "methods" may convey a certain impression when applied to scientific knowledge, they remain relevant when applied to testimony based on technical or other specialized knowledge. For example, when a law enforcement agent testifies regarding the use of code words in a drug transaction, the principle used by the agent is that participants in such transactions regularly use code words to conceal the nature of their activities. The method used by the agent is the application of extensive experience to analyze the meaning of the conversations. So long as the principles and methods are reliable and applied reliably to the facts of the case, this type of testimony should be admitted.

Nothing in this amendment is intended to suggest that experience alone—or experience in conjunction with other knowledge, skill, training or education—may not provide a sufficient foundation for expert testimony. To the contrary, the text of Rule 702 expressly contemplates that an expert may be qualified on the basis of experience. In certain fields, experience is the predominant, if not sole, basis for a great deal of reliable expert testimony. *See, e.g.*, United States v. Jones, 107 F.3d 1147 (6th Cir. 1997) (no abuse of discretion in admitting the testimony of a handwriting examiner who had years of practical experience and extensive training, and who explained his methodology in detail); Tassin v. Sears Roebuck, 946 F.Supp. 1241, 1248 (M.D. La. 1996) (design engineer's testimony can be admissible when the expert's opinions "are based on facts, a reasonable investigation, and traditional technical/mechanical expertise, and he provides a reasonable link between the information and procedures he uses and the conclusions he reaches"). *See also* Kumho Tire Co. v. Carmichael, [119 S.Ct. 1167, 1178, 143 L.Ed.2d 238 (1999) (stating that "no one denies that an expert might draw a conclusion from a set of observations based on extensive and specialized experience").

If the witness is relying solely or primarily on experience, then the witness must explain how that experience leads to the conclusion reached, why that experience is a sufficient basis for the opinion, and how that experience is reliably applied to the facts. The trial court's gatekeeping function requires more than simply "taking the expert's word for it." *See* Daubert v. Merrell Dow Pharmaceuticals, Inc., 43 F.3d 1311, 1319 (9th Cir. 1995) ("We've been presented with only the experts' qualifications, their conclusions and their assurances of reliability. Under *Daubert*, that's not enough."). The more subjective and controversial the expert's inquiry, the more likely the testimony should be excluded as unreliable. *See* O'Conner v. Commonwealth Edison Co., 13 F.3d 1090 (7th Cir. 1994) (expert testimony based on a completely subjective methodology held properly excluded). *See also* Kumho Tire Co. v. Carmichael, [119 S.Ct. 1167, 1176, 143 L.Ed.2d 238 (1999)] ("[I]t will at times be useful to ask even of a witness whose expertise is based purely on experience, say, a perfume tester able to distinguish among 140 odors at a sniff, whether his preparation is of a kind that others in the field would recognize as acceptable.").

Subpart (1) of Rule 702 calls for a quantitative rather than qualitative analysis. The amendment requires that expert testimony be based on sufficient underlying "facts or data." The term "data" is intended to encompass the reliable opinions of other experts. *See* the original Advisory Committee Note to Rule 703. The language "facts or data" is broad enough to allow an expert to rely on hypothetical facts that are supported by the evidence. *Id.*

When facts are in dispute, experts sometimes reach different conclusions based on competing versions of the facts. The emphasis in the amendment on "sufficient facts or data" is not intended to authorize a trial court to exclude an expert's testimony on the ground that the court believes one version of the facts and not the other.

There has been some confusion over the relationship between Rules 702 and 703. The amendment makes clear that the sufficiency of the basis of an expert's testimony is to be decided under Rule 702. Rule 702 sets forth the overarching requirement of reliability, and an analysis of the sufficiency of the expert's basis cannot be divorced from the ultimate reliability of the expert's opinion. In contrast, the "reasonable reliance" requirement of Rule 703 is a relatively narrow inquiry. When an expert relies on inadmissible information, Rule 703 requires the trial court to determine whether that information is of a type reasonably relied on by other experts in the field. If so, the expert can rely on the information in reaching an opinion. However, the question whether the expert is relying on a sufficient basis of information—whether admissible information or not—is governed by the requirements of Rule 702.

The amendment makes no attempt to set forth procedural requirements for exercising the trial court's gatekeeping function over expert testimony. *See* Daniel J. Capra, *The Daubert Puzzle*, 38 Ga.L.Rev. 699, 766 (1998) ("Trial courts should be allowed substantial discretion in dealing with *Daubert* questions; any attempt to codify procedures will likely give rise to unnecessary changes in practice and create difficult questions for appellate review."). Courts have shown considerable ingenuity and flexibility in considering challenges to expert testimony under *Daubert*, and it is contemplated that this will continue under the amended Rule. *See, e.g.*, Cortes-Irizarry v. Corporacion Insular, 111 F.3d 184 (1st Cir. 1997) (discussing the application of *Daubert* in ruling on a motion for summary judgment); In re Paoli R.R. Yard PCB Litig., 35 F.3d 717, 736, 739 (3d Cir. 1994) (discussing the use of in limine hearings); Claar v. Burlington N.R.R., 29 F.3d 499, 502–05 (9th Cir. 1994) (discussing the trial court's technique of ordering experts to submit serial affidavits explaining the reasoning and methods underlying their conclusions).

The amendment continues the practice of the original Rule in referring to a qualified witness as an "expert." This was done to provide continuity and to minimize change. The use of the term "expert" in the Rule does not, however, mean that a jury should actually be informed that a qualified witness is testifying as an "expert." Indeed, there is much to be said for a practice that prohibits the use of the term "expert" by both the parties and the court at trial. Such a practice "ensures that trial courts do not inadvertently put their stamp of authority" on a witness's opinion, and protects against the jury's being "overwhelmed by the so-called 'experts'." Hon. Charles Richey, *Proposals to Eliminate the Prejudicial Effect of the Use of the Word "Expert" Under the Federal Rules of Evidence in Criminal and Civil Jury Trials*, 154 F.R.D. 537, 559 (1994) (setting forth limiting instructions and a standing order employed to prohibit the use of the term "expert" in jury trials).

NOTE BY FEDERAL JUDICIAL CENTER.

The Rule enacted by Congress is the Rule prescribed by the Supreme Court without change. Rule 702 was not the subject of floor debate.

Rule 703. Bases of an Expert's Opinion Testimony

ADVISORY COMMITTEE NOTE TO THE 2011 AMENDMENT.

The language of Rule 703 has been amended as part of the restyling of the Evidence Rules to make them more easily understood and to make style and terminology consistent throughout the rules. These changes are intended to be stylistic only. There is no intent to change any result in any ruling on evidence admissibility.

The Committee deleted all reference to an "inference" on the grounds that the deletion made the Rule flow better and easier to read, and because any "inference" is covered by the broader term "opinion." Courts have not made substantive decisions on the basis of any distinction between an opinion and an inference. No change in current practice is intended.

ADVISORY COMMITTEE NOTE.

Facts or data upon which expert opinions are based may, under the rule, be derived from three possible sources. The first is the firsthand observation of the witness, with opinions based thereon traditionally allowed. A treating physician affords an example. Rheingold, The Basis of Medical Testimony, 15 Vand.L.Rev. 473, 489 (1962). Whether he must first relate his observations is treated in Rule 705. The second source, presentation at the trial, also reflects existing practice. The technique may be the familiar hypothetical question or having the expert attend the trial and hear the testimony establishing the facts. Problems of determining what testimony the expert relied upon, when the latter technique is employed and the testimony is in conflict, may be resolved by resort to Rule 705. The third source contemplated by the rule consists of presentation of data to the expert outside of court and other than by his own perception. In this respect the rule is designed to broaden the basis for expert opinions beyond that current in many jurisdictions and to bring the judicial practice into line with the practice of the experts themselves when not in court. Thus a physician in his own practice bases his diagnosis on information from numerous sources and of considerable variety, including statements by patients and relatives, reports and opinions from nurses, technicians and other doctors, hospital records, and X rays. Most of them are admissible in evidence, but only with the expenditure of substantial time in producing and examining various authenticating witnesses. The physician makes life-and-death decisions in reliance upon them. His validation, expertly performed and subject to cross-examination, ought to suffice for judicial purposes. Rheingold, *supra*, at 531; McCormick § 15. A similar provision is California Evidence Code § 801(b).

The rule also offers a more satisfactory basis for ruling upon the admissibility of public opinion poll evidence. Attention is directed to the validity of the techniques employed rather than to relatively fruitless inquiries whether hearsay is involved. *See* Judge Feinberg's careful analysis in Zippo Mfg. Co. v. Rogers Imports, Inc., 216 F. Supp. 670 (S.D.N.Y.1963). *See also* Blum et al., The Art of Opinion Research: A Lawyer's Appraisal of an Emerging Service, 24 U.Chi.L.Rev. 1 (1956); Bonynge, Trademark Surveys and Techniques and Their Use in Litigation, 48 A.B.A.J. 329 (1962); Zeisel, The Uniqueness of Survey Evidence, 45 Cornell L.Q. 322 (1960); Annot., 76 A.L.R.2d 919.

If it be feared that enlargement of permissible data may tend to break down the rules of exclusion unduly, notice should be taken that the rule requires that the facts or data "be of a type reasonably relied upon by experts in the particular field." The language would not warrant admitting in evidence the opinion of an "accidentologist" as to the point of impact in an automobile collision based on statements of bystanders, since this requirement is not satisfied. *See* Comment, Cal.Law Rev.Comm'n, Recommendation Proposing an Evidence Code 148–50 (1965).

NOTES OF ADVISORY COMMITTEE ON 2000 AMENDMENTS.

Rule 703 has been amended to emphasize that when an expert reasonably relies on inadmissible information to form an opinion or inference, the underlying information is not admissible simply because the opinion or inference is admitted. Courts have reached different results on how to treat inadmissible information when it is reasonably relied upon by an expert in forming an opinion or drawing an inference. *Compare* United States v. Rollins, 862 F.2d 1282 (7th Cir. 1988) (admitting, as part of the basis of an FBI agent's expert opinion on the meaning of code language, the hearsay statements of an informant), with United States v. 0.59 Acres of Land, 109 F.3d 1493 (9th Cir. 1997) (error to admit hearsay offered as the basis of an expert opinion, without a limiting instruction). Commentators have also taken differing views. *See, e.g.*, Ronald Carlson, *Policing the Bases of Modern Expert Testimony*, 39 Vand.L.Rev. 577 (1986) (advocating limits on the jury's consideration of otherwise inadmissible evidence used as the basis for an expert opinion); Paul Rice, *Inadmissible Evidence as a Basis for Expert Testimony. A Response to Professor Carlson*, 40 Vand.L.Rev. 583 (1987) (advocating unrestricted use of information reasonably relied upon by an expert).

When information is reasonably relied upon by an expert and yet is admissible only for the purpose of assisting the jury in evaluating an expert's opinion, a trial court applying this Rule must consider the information's probative value in assisting the jury to weigh the expert's opinion on the one hand, and the risk of prejudice resulting from the jury's potential misuse of the information for substantive purposes on the other. The information may be disclosed to the jury, upon objection, only if the trial court finds that the probative value of the information in assisting the jury to evaluate the expert's opinion substantially outweighs its prejudicial effect. If the otherwise inadmissible information is admitted under this balancing test, the trial judge must give a limiting instruction upon request, informing the jury that the underlying information must not be used for substantive purposes. *See* Rule 105. In determining the appropriate course, the trial court should consider the probable effectiveness or lack of effectiveness of a limiting instruction under the particular circumstances.

The amendment governs only the disclosure to the jury of information that is reasonably relied on by an expert, when that information is not admissible for substantive purposes. It is not intended to affect the admissibility of an expert's testimony. Nor does the amendment prevent an expert from relying on information that is inadmissible for substantive purposes.

Nothing in this Rule restricts the presentation of underlying expert facts or data when offered by an adverse party. *See* Rule 705. Of course, an adversary's attack on an expert's basis will often open the door to a proponent's rebuttal with information that was reasonably relied upon by the expert, even if that information would not have been discloseable initially under the balancing test provided by this amendment. Moreover, in some circumstances the proponent might wish to disclose information that is relied upon by the expert in order to "remove the sting" from the opponent's anticipated attack, and thereby prevent the jury from drawing an unfair negative inference. The trial court should take this consideration into account in applying the balancing test provided by this amendment.

This amendment covers facts or data that cannot be admitted for any purpose other than to assist the jury to evaluate the expert's opinion. The balancing test provided in this amendment is not applicable to facts or data that are admissible for any other purpose but have not yet been offered for such a purpose at the time the expert testifies.

The amendment provides a presumption against disclosure to the jury of information used as the basis of an expert's opinion and not admissible for any substantive purpose, when that information is offered by the proponent of the expert. In a multi-party case, where one party proffers an expert whose testimony is also beneficial to other parties, each such party should be deemed a "proponent" within the meaning of the amendment.

NOTE BY FEDERAL JUDICIAL CENTER.

The Rule enacted by Congress is the Rule prescribed by the Supreme Court without change. Rule 703 was not the subject of floor debate.

Rule 704. Opinion on an Ultimate Issue

ADVISORY COMMITTEE NOTE TO THE 2011 AMENDMENT.

The language of Rule 704 has been amended as part of the restyling of the Evidence Rules to make them more easily understood and to make style and terminology consistent throughout the rules. These changes are intended to be stylistic only. There is no intent to change any result in any ruling on evidence admissibility.

The Committee deleted all reference to an "inference" on the grounds that the deletion made the Rule flow better and easier to read, and because any "inference" is covered by the broader term "opinion." Courts have not made substantive decisions on the basis of any distinction between an opinion and an inference. No change in current practice is intended.

ADVISORY COMMITTEE NOTE.

The basic approach to opinions, lay and expert, in these rules is to admit them when helpful to the trier of fact. In order to render this approach fully effective and to allay any doubt on the subject, the so-called "ultimate issue" rule is specifically abolished by the instant rule.

The older cases often contained strictures against allowing witnesses to express opinions upon ultimate issues, as a particular aspect of the rule against opinions. The rule was unduly restrictive, difficult of application, and generally served only to deprive the trier of fact of useful information. 7 Wigmore §§ 1920, 1921; McCormick § 12. The basis usually assigned for the rule, to prevent the witness from "usurping the province of the jury," is aptly characterized as "empty rhetoric." 7 Wigmore § 1920, p. 17. Efforts to meet the felt needs of particular situations led to odd verbal circumlocutions which were said not to violate the rule. Thus a witness could express his estimate of the criminal responsibility of an accused in terms of sanity or insanity, but not in terms of ability to tell right from wrong or other more modern standard. And in cases of medical causation, witnesses were sometimes required to couch their opinions in cautious phrases of "might or could," rather than "did," though the result was to deprive many opinions of the positiveness to which they were entitled, accompanied by the hazard of a ruling of insufficiency to support a verdict. In other instances the rule was simply disregarded, and, as concessions to need, opinions were allowed upon such matters as intoxication, speed, handwriting, and value, although more precise coincidence with an ultimate issue would scarcely be possible.

Many modern decisions illustrate the trend to abandon the rule completely. People v. Wilson, 25 Cal.2d 341, 153 P.2d 720 (1944), whether abortion necessary to save life of patient; Clifford-Jacobs Forging Co. v. Industrial Comm., 19 Ill.2d 236, 166 N.E.2d 582 (1960), medical causation; Dowling v. L. H. Shattuck, Inc., 91 N.H. 234, 17 A.2d 529 (1941), proper method of shoring ditch; Schweiger v. Solbeck, 191 Or. 454, 230 P.2d 195 (1951), cause of landslide. In each instance the opinion was allowed.

The abolition of the ultimate issue rule does not lower the bars so as to admit all opinions. Under Rules 701 and 702, opinions must be helpful to the trier of fact, and Rule 403 provides for exclusion of evidence which wastes time. These provisions afford ample assurances against the admission of opinions which would merely tell the jury what result to reach, somewhat in the manner of the oath-helpers of an earlier day. They also stand ready to exclude opinions phrased in terms of inadequately explored legal criteria. Thus the question, "Did T have capacity to make a will?" would be excluded, while the question, "Did T have sufficient mental capacity to know the nature and extent of his property and the natural objects of his bounty and to formulate a rational scheme of distribution?" would be allowed. McCormick § 12.

For similar provisions *see* Uniform Rule 56(4); California Evidence Code § 805; Kansas Code of Civil Procedure § 60-456(d); New Jersey Evidence Rule 56(3).

NOTE BY FEDERAL JUDICIAL CENTER.

The Rule enacted by Congress is the Rule prescribed by the Supreme Court without change. Rule 704 was not the subject of floor debate.

Rule 705. Disclosing the Facts or Data Underlying an Expert's Opinion

ADVISORY COMMITTEE NOTE TO THE 2011 AMENDMENT.

The language of Rule 705 has been amended as part of the restyling of the Evidence Rules to make them more easily understood and to make style and terminology consistent throughout the rules. These changes are intended to be stylistic only. There is no intent to change any result in any ruling on evidence admissibility.

The Committee deleted all reference to an "inference" on the grounds that the deletion made the Rule flow better and easier to read, and because any "inference" is covered by the broader term "opinion." Courts have not made substantive decisions on the basis of any distinction between an opinion and an inference. No change in current practice is intended.

ADVISORY COMMITTEE NOTE.

The hypothetical question has been the target of a great deal of criticism as encouraging partisan bias, affording an opportunity for summing up in the middle of the case, and as complex and time consuming. Ladd, Expert Testimony, 5 Vand.L.Rev. 414, 426–427 (1952). While the rule allows counsel to make disclosure of the underlying facts or data as a preliminary to the giving of an expert opinion, if he chooses, the instances in which he is required to do so are reduced. This is true whether the expert bases his opinion on data furnished him at secondhand or observed by him at firsthand.

The elimination of the requirement of preliminary disclosure at the trial of underlying facts or data has a long background of support. In 1937 the Commissioners on Uniform State Laws incorporated a provision to this effect in their Model Expert Testimony Act, which furnished the basis for Uniform Rules 57 and 58. Rule 4515, N.Y. CPLR (McKinney 1963), provides:

"Unless the court orders otherwise, questions calling for the opinion of an expert witness need not be hypothetical in form, and the witness may state his opinion and reasons without first specifying the data upon which it is based. Upon cross-examination, he may be required to specify the data . . . ."

See also California Evidence Code § 802; Kansas Code of Civil Procedure §§ 60-456, 60-457; New Jersey Evidence Rules 57, 58.

If the objection is made that leaving it to the cross-examiner to bring out the supporting data is essentially unfair, the answer is that he is under no compulsion to bring out any facts or data except those unfavorable to the opinion. The answer assumes that the cross-examiner has the advance knowledge which is essential for effective cross-examination. This advance knowledge has been afforded, though imperfectly, by the traditional foundation requirement. Rule 26(b)(4) of the Rules of Civil Procedure, as revised, provides for substantial discovery in this area, obviating in large measure the obstacles which have been raised in some instances to discovery of findings, underlying data, and even the identity of the experts. Friedenthal, Discovery and Use of an Adverse Party's Expert Information, 14 Stan.L.Rev. 455 (1962).

These safeguards are reinforced by the discretionary power of the judge to require preliminary disclosure in any event.

NOTE BY FEDERAL JUDICIAL CENTER.

The Rule enacted by Congress is the Rule prescribed by the Supreme

Court, amended only by substituting "court" in place of "judge." Rule 705 was not the subject of floor debate.

ADVISORY COMMITTEE NOTE TO 1993 AMENDMENT.

This rule, which relates to the manner of presenting testimony at trial, is revised to avoid an arguable conflict with revised Rules 26(a)(2)(B) and 26(e)(10) of the Federal Rules of Civil Procedure or with revised Rule 16 of the Federal Rules of Criminal Procedure, which require disclosure in advance of trial of the basis and reasons for an expert's opinions.

If a serious question is raised under Rule 702 or 703 as to the admissibility of expert testimony, disclosure of the underlying facts or data on which opinions are based may, of course, be needed by the court before deciding whether, and to what extent, the person should be allowed to testify. This rule does not preclude such an inquiry.

Rule 706. Court-Appointed Expert Witnesses

ADVISORY COMMITTEE NOTE TO THE 2011 AMENDMENT.

The language of Rule 706 has been amended as part of the restyling of the Evidence Rules to make them more easily understood and to make style and terminology consistent throughout the rules. These changes are intended to be stylistic only. There is no intent to change any result in any ruling on evidence admissibility.

ADVISORY COMMITTEE NOTE.

The practice of shopping for experts, the venality of some experts, and the reluctance of many reputable experts to involve themselves in litigation, have been matters of deep concern. Though the contention is made that court appointed experts acquire an aura of infallibility to which they are not entitled, Levy, Impartial Medical Testimony— Revisited, 34 Temple L.Q. 416 (1961), the trend is increasingly to provide for their use. While experience indicates that actual appointment is a relatively infrequent occurrence, the assumption may be made that the availability of the procedure in itself decreases the need for resorting to it. The ever-present possibility that the judge *may* appoint an expert in a given case must inevitably exert a sobering effect on the expert witness of a party and upon the person utilizing his services.

The inherent power of a trial judge to appoint an expert of his own choosing is virtually unquestioned. Scott v. Spanjer Bros., Inc., 298 F.2d 928 (2d Cir. 1962); Danville Tobacco Assn. v. Bryant-Buckner Associates, Inc., 333 F.2d 202 (4th Cir. 1964); Sink, The Unused Power of a Federal Judge to Call His Own Expert Witnesses, 29 S.Cal.L.Rev. 195 (1956); 2 Wigmore § 563, 9 *id.* § 2484; Annot., 95 A.L.R.2d 383. Hence the problem becomes largely one of detail.

The New York plan is well known and is described in Report by

Special Committee of the Association of the Bar of the City of New York: Impartial Medical Testimony (1956). On recommendation of the Section of Judicial Administration, local adoption of an impartial medical plan was endorsed by the American Bar Association. 82 A.B.A.Rep. 184–185 (1957). Descriptions and analyses of plans in effect in various parts of the country are found in Van Dusen, A United States District Judge's View of the Impartial Medical Expert System, 32 F.R.D. 498 (1963); Wick and Kightlinger, Impartial Medical Testimony Under the Federal Civil Rules: A Tale of Three Doctors, 34 Ins. Counsel J. 115 (1967); and numerous articles collected in Klein, Judicial Administration and the Legal Profession 393 (1963). Statutes and rules include California Evidence Code §§ 730–733; Illinois Supreme Court Rule 215(d), Ill.Rev.Stat.1969, c. 110A, § 215(d); Burns, Indiana Stats.1956, § 9-1702; Wisconsin Stats. Annot.1958, § 957.27.

In the federal practice, a comprehensive scheme for court appointed experts was initiated with the adoption of Rule 28 of the Federal Rules of Criminal Procedure in 1946. The Judicial Conference of the United States in 1953 considered court appointed experts in civil cases, but only with respect to whether they should be compensated from public funds, a proposal which was rejected. Report of the Judicial Conference of the United States 23 (1953). The present rule expands the practice to include civil cases.

Subdivision (a) is based on Rule 28 of the Federal Rules of Criminal Procedure, with a few changes, mainly in the interest of clarity. Language has been added to provide specifically for the appointment either on motion of a party or on the judge's own motion. A provision subjecting the court appointed expert to deposition procedures has been incorporated. The rule has been revised to make definite the right of any party, including the party calling him, to cross-examine.

Subdivision (b) combines the present provision for compensation in criminal cases with what seems to be a fair and feasible handling of civil cases, originally found in the Model Act and carried from there into Uniform Rule 60. *See also* California Evidence Code §§ 730–731. The special provision for Fifth Amendment compensation cases is designed to guard against reducing constitutionally guaranteed just compensation by requiring the recipient to pay costs. *See* Rule 71A(l) of the Rules of Civil Procedure.

Subdivision (c) seems to be essential if the use of court appointed experts is to be fully effective. Uniform Rule 61 so provides.

Subdivision (d) is in essence the last sentence of Rule 28(a) of the

Federal Rules of Criminal Procedure.

NOTE BY FEDERAL JUDICIAL CENTER.

The Rule enacted by Congress is the Rule prescribed by the Supreme Court, amended by substituting "court" in place of "judge," with conforming pronominal changes, and, in subdivision (b), by substituting the phrase "and civil actions and proceedings" in place of "and cases" before "involving" in the second sentence. Rule 706 was not the subject of floor debate.

ARTICLE VIII.
HEARSAY

INTRODUCTORY NOTE: THE HEARSAY PROBLEM.

The factors to be considered in evaluating the testimony of a witness are perception, memory, and narration. Morgan, Hearsay Dangers and the Application of the Hearsay Concept, 62 Harv.L.Rev. 177 (1948), Selected Writings on Evidence and Trial 764, 765 (Fryer ed. 1957); Shientag, Cross-Examination—A Judge's Viewpoint, 3 Record 12 (1948); Strahorn, A Reconsideration of the Hearsay Rule and Admissions, 85 U.Pa.L.Rev. 484, 485 (1937), Selected Writings, supra, 756, 757; Weinstein, Probative Force of Hearsay, 46 Iowa L.Rev. 331 (1961). Sometimes a fourth is added, sincerity, but in fact it seems merely to be an aspect of the three already mentioned.

In order to encourage the witness to do his best with respect to each of these factors, and to expose any inaccuracies which may enter in, the Anglo-American tradition has evolved three conditions under which witnesses will ideally be required to testify: (1) under oath, (2) in the personal presence of the trier of fact, (3) subject to cross-examination.

(1) Standard procedure calls for the swearing of witnesses. While the practice is perhaps less effective than in an earlier time, no disposition to relax the requirement is apparent, other than to allow affirmation by persons with scruples against taking oaths.

(2) The demeanor of the witness traditionally has been believed to furnish trier and opponent with valuable clues. Universal Camera Corp. v. N.L.R.B., 340 U.S. 474, 495–496, 71 S.Ct. 456, 95 L.Ed. 456 (1951); Sahm, Demeanor Evidence: Elusive and Intangible Imponderables, 47 A.B.A.J. 580 (1961), quoting numerous authorities. The witness himself will probably be impressed with the solemnity of the occasion and the possibility of public disgrace.

Willingness to falsify may reasonably become more difficult in the presence of the person against whom directed. Rules 26 and 43(a) of the Federal Rules of Criminal and Civil Procedure, respectively, include the general requirement *289 that testimony be taken orally in open court.

The Sixth Amendment right of confrontation is a manifestation of these beliefs and attitudes.

(3) Emphasis on the basis of the hearsay rule today tends to center upon the condition of cross-examination. All may not agree with Wigmore that cross-examination is "beyond doubt the greatest legal engine ever invented for the discovery of truth," but all will agree with his statement that it has become a "vital feature" of the Anglo-American system. 5 Wigmore § 1367, p. 29. The belief, or perhaps hope, that cross-examination is effective in exposing imperfections of perception, memory, and narration is fundamental. Morgan, Foreword to Model Code of Evidence 37 (1942).

The logic of the preceding discussion might suggest that no testimony be received unless in full compliance with the three ideal conditions. No one advocates this position. Common sense tells that much evidence which is not given under the three conditions may be inherently superior to much that is.

Moreover, when the choice is between evidence which is less than best and no evidence at all, only clear folly would dictate an across-the-board policy of doing without. The problem thus resolves itself into effecting a sensible accommodation between these considerations and the desirability of giving testimony under the ideal conditions.

The solution evolved by the common law has been a general rule excluding hearsay but subject to numerous exceptions under circumstances supposed to furnish guarantees of trustworthiness. Criticisms of this scheme are that it is bulky and complex, fails to screen good from bad hearsay realistically, and inhibits the growth of the law of evidence.

Since no one advocates excluding all hearsay, three possible solutions may be considered: (1) abolish the rule against hearsay and admit all hearsay; (2) admit hearsay possessing sufficient probative force, but with procedural safeguards; (3) revise the present system of class exceptions.

(1) Abolition of the hearsay rule would be the simplest solution. The effect would not be automatically to abolish the giving of testimony under ideal conditions. If the declarant were available, compliance with the ideal conditions would be optional with either party. Thus the proponent could call the declarant as a witness as a form of presentation more impressive than his hearsay statement. Or the opponent could call the declarant to be cross-examined upon his statement. This is the tenor of Uniform Rule 63(1), admitting the hearsay declaration of a person "who is present at the hearing and available for cross-examination." Compare the treatment of declarations of available declarants in Rule 801(d)(1) of the instant rules. If the declarant were unavailable, a rule of free admissibility would make no distinctions in terms of degrees of

noncompliance with the ideal conditions and would exact no quid pro quo in the form of assurances of trustworthiness. Rule 503 of the Model Code did exactly that, providing for the admissibility of any hearsay declaration by an unavailable declarant, finding support in the Massachusetts act of 1898, enacted at the instance of Thayer, Mass-.Gen.L.1932, c. 233 § 65, and in the English act of 1938, St.1938, c. 28, Evidence. Both are *290 limited to civil cases. The draftsmen of the Uniform Rules chose a less advanced and more conventional position. Comment, Uniform Rule 63. The present Advisory Committee has been unconvinced of the wisdom of abandoning the traditional requirement of some particular assurance of credibility as a condition precedent to admitting the hearsay declaration of an unavailable declarant.

In criminal cases, the Sixth Amendment requirement of confrontation would no doubt move into a large part of the area presently occupied by the hearsay rule in the event of the abolition of the latter. The resultant split between civil and criminal evidence is regarded as an undesirable development.

(2) Abandonment of the system of class exceptions in favor of individual treatment in the setting of the particular case, accompanied by procedural safeguards, has been impressively advocated. Weinstein, The Probative Force of Hearsay, 46 Iowa L.Rev. 331 (1961). Admissibility would be determined by weighing the probative force of the evidence against the possibility of prejudice, waste of time, and the availability of more satisfactory evidence. The bases of the traditional hearsay exceptions would be helpful in assessing probative force. Ladd, The Relationship of the Principles of Exclusionary Rules of Evidence to the Problem of Proof, 18 Minn.L.Rev. 506 (1934). Procedural safeguards would consist of notice of intention to use hearsay, free comment by the judge on the weight of the evidence, and a greater measure of authority in both trial and appellate judges to deal with evidence on the basis of weight. The Advisory Committee has rejected this approach to hearsay as involving too great a measure of judicial discretion, minimizing the predictability of rulings, enhancing the difficulties of preparation for trial, adding a further element to the already over-complicated congeries of pretrial procedures, and requiring substantially different rules for civil and criminal cases. The only way in which the probative force of hearsay differs from the probative force of other testimony is in the absence of oath, demeanor, and cross-examination as aids in determining credibility. For a judge to exclude evidence because he does not believe it has been described as "altogether atypical, extraordinary . . . ." Chadbourn, Bentham and the Hearsay Rule—A Benthamic View of Rule 63(4)(c) of the Uniform Rules of Evidence, 75 Harv.L.Rev. 932, 947 (1962).

(3) The approach to hearsay in these rules is that of the common law,

i.e., a general rule excluding hearsay, with exceptions under which evidence is not required to be excluded even though hearsay. The traditional hearsay exceptions are drawn upon for the exceptions, collected under two rules, one dealing with situations where availability of the declarant is regarded as immaterial and the other with those where unavailability is made a condition to the admission of the hearsay statement. Each of the two rules concludes with a provision for hearsay statements not within one of the specified exceptions "but having comparable circumstantial guarantees of trustworthiness." Rules 803(24) and 804(b)(6). This plan is submitted as calculated to encourage growth and development in this area of the law, while conserving the values and experience of the past as a guide to the future.

CONFRONTATION AND DUE PROCESS.

Until very recently, decisions invoking the confrontation clause of the Sixth Amendment were surprisingly few, a fact probably explainable by the former inapplicability of the clause to the states and by the hearsay rule's occupancy of much the same ground. The pattern which emerges from the earlier cases invoking the clause is substantially that of the hearsay rule, applied to criminal cases: an accused is entitled to have the witnesses against him testify under oath, in the presence of himself and trier, subject to cross-examination; yet considerations of public policy and necessity require the recognition of such exceptions as dying declarations and former testimony of unavailable witnesses. *Mattox v. United States*, 156 U.S. 237, 15 S.Ct. 337, 39 L.Ed. 409 (1895); *Motes v. United States*, 178 U.S. 458, 20 S.Ct. 993, 44 L.Ed. 1150 (1900); *Delaney v. United States*, 263 U.S. 586, 44 S.Ct. 206, 68 L.Ed. 462 (1924). Beginning with *Snyder v. Massachusetts*, 291 U.S. 97, 54 S.Ct. 330, 78 L.Ed. 674 (1934), the Court began to speak of confrontation as an aspect of procedural due process, thus extending its applicability to state cases and to federal cases other than criminal. The language of Snyder was that of an elastic concept of hearsay.

The deportation case of *Bridges v. Wixon*, 326 U.S. 135, 65 S.Ct. 1443, 89 L.Ed. 2103 (1945), may be read broadly as imposing a strictly construed right of confrontation in all kinds of cases or narrowly as the product of a failure of the Immigration and Naturalization Service to follow its own rules. *In re* Oliver, 333 U.S. 257, 68 S.Ct. 499, 92 L.Ed. 682 (1948), ruled that cross-examination was essential to due process in a state contempt proceeding, but in *United States v. Nugent*, 346 U.S. 1, 73 S.Ct. 991, 97 L.Ed. 1417 (1953), the court held that it was not an essential aspect of a "hearing" for a conscientious objector under the Selective Service Act. *Stein v. New York*, 346 U.S. 156, 196, 73 S.Ct. 1077, 97 L.Ed. 1522 (1953), disclaimed any purpose to read the hearsay rule into the Fourteenth Amendment, but in *Greene v. McElroy*, 360 U.S. 474, 79 S.Ct. 1400, 3 L.Ed.2d 1377 (1959), revocation of security clearance without confrontation and cross-examination was held unauthorized, and a similar result was reached in *Willner v. Committee on Character*, 373 U.S. 96, 83 S.Ct. 1175, 10 L.Ed.2d 224 (1963). Ascertaining the constitutional dimensions of the confrontation-hearsay aggregate against the background of these cases is a matter of some difficulty, yet the general pattern is at least not inconsistent with that of the hearsay rule.

In 1965 the confrontation clause was held applicable to the states. *Pointer v. Texas*, 380 U.S. 400, 85 S.Ct. 1065, 13 L.Ed.2d 923 (1965). Prosecution use of former testimony given at a preliminary hearing where petitioner was not represented by counsel was a violation of the clause. The same result would have followed under conventional hearsay doctrine read in the light of a constitutional right to counsel, and nothing in the opinion suggests any difference in essential outline between the hearsay rule and the right of confrontation. In the companion case of *Douglas v. Alabama*, 380 U.S. 415, 85 S.Ct. 1074, 13 L.Ed.2d 934 (1965), however, the result reached by applying the confrontation clause is one reached less readily via the hearsay rule. A confession implicating petitioner was put before the jury by reading it to the witness in portions and asking if he made that statement. The witness refused to answer on grounds of self-incrimination. The result, said the Court, was to deny cross-examination, and hence confrontation. True, it could broadly be said that the confession was a hearsay statement which for all practical purposes was put in evidence. Yet a more easily accepted explanation of the opinion is that its real thrust was in the direction of curbing undesirable prosecutorial behavior, rather than merely applying rules of exclusion, and that the confrontation clause was the means selected to achieve this end. Comparable facts and a like result appeared in *Brookhart v. Janis*, 384 U.S. 1, 86 S.Ct. 1245, 16 L.Ed.2d 314 (1966).

The pattern suggested in Douglas was developed further and more distinctly in a pair of cases at the end of the 1966 term. *United States v. Wade*, 388 U.S. 218, 87 S.Ct. 1926, 18 L.Ed.2d 1149 (1967), and *Gilbert v. California*, 388 U.S. 263, 87 S.Ct. 1951, 18 L.Ed.2d 1178 (1967), hinged upon practices followed in identifying accused persons before trial. This pretrial identification was said to be so decisive an aspect of the case that accused was entitled to have counsel present; a pretrial identification made in the absence of counsel was not itself receivable in evidence and, in addition, might fatally infect a courtroom identification. The presence of counsel at the earlier identification was described as a necessary prerequisite for "a meaningful confrontation at trial." *United States v. Wade*, supra, 388 U.S. at p. 236, 87 S.Ct. at p. 1937. Wade involved no evidence of the fact of a prior identification and hence was not susceptible of being decided on hearsay grounds. In

Gilbert, witnesses did testify to an earlier identification, readily classifiable as hearsay under a fairly strict view of what constitutes hearsay. The Court, however, carefully avoided basing the decision on the hearsay ground, choosing confrontation instead. 388 U.S. 263, 272, n. 3, 87 S.Ct. 1951. See also *Parker v. Gladden*, 385 U.S. 363, 87 S.Ct. 468, 17 L.Ed.2d 420 (1966), holding that the right of confrontation was violated when the bailiff made prejudicial statements to jurors, and Note, 75 Yale L.J. 1434 (1966).

Under the earlier cases, the confrontation clause may have been little more than a constitutional embodiment of the hearsay rule, even including traditional exceptions but with some room for expanding them along similar lines. But under the recent cases the impact of the clause clearly extends beyond the confines of the hearsay rule. These considerations have led the Advisory Committee to conclude that a hearsay rule can function usefully as an adjunct to the confrontation right in constitutional areas and independently in nonconstitutional areas. In recognition of the separateness of the confrontation clause and the hearsay rule, and to avoid inviting collisions between them or between the hearsay rule and other exclusionary principles, the exceptions set forth in Rules 803 and 804 are stated in terms of exemption from the general exclusionary mandate of the hearsay rule, rather than in positive terms of admissibility. See Uniform Rule 63(1) to (31) and California Evidence Code §§ 1200–1340.

Rule 801. Definitions That Apply to This Article; Exclusions from Hearsay

ADVISORY COMMITTEE NOTE TO THE 2011 AMENDMENT.

The language of Rule 801 has been amended as part of the restyling of the Evidence Rules to make them more easily understood and to make style and terminology consistent throughout the rules. These changes are intended to be stylistic only. There is no intent to change any result in any ruling on evidence admissibility.

Statements falling under the hearsay exclusion provided by Rule 801(d)(2) are no longer referred to as "admissions" in the title to the subdivision. The term "admissions" is confusing because not all statements covered by the exclusion are admissions in the colloquial sense—a statement can be within the exclusion even if it "admitted" nothing and was not against the party's interest when made. The term "admissions" also raises confusion in comparison with the Rule 804(b)(3) exception for declarations against interest. No change in application of the exclusion is intended.

ADVISORY COMMITTEE NOTE TO RULE 801(a), (b) AND (c).

Subdivision (a). The definition of "statement" assumes importance because the term is used in the definition of hearsay in subdivision (c).

The effect of the definition of "statement" is to exclude from the operation of the hearsay rule all evidence of conduct, verbal or nonverbal, not intended as an assertion. The key to the definition is that nothing is an assertion unless intended to be one.

It can scarcely be doubted that an assertion made in words is intended by the declarant to be an assertion. Hence verbal assertions readily fall into the category of "statement." Whether nonverbal conduct should be regarded as a statement for purposes of defining hearsay requires further consideration. Some nonverbal conduct, such as the act of pointing to identify a suspect in a lineup, is clearly the equivalent of words, assertive in nature, and to be regarded as a statement. Other nonverbal conduct, however, may be offered as evidence that the person acted as he did because of his belief in the existence of the condition sought to be proved, from which belief the existence of the condition may be inferred. This sequence is, arguably, in effect an assertion of the existence of the condition and hence properly includable within the hearsay concept. *See* Morgan, Hearsay Dangers and the Application of the Hearsay Concept, 62 Harv.L.Rev. 177, 214, 217 (1948), and the elaboration in Finman, Implied Assertions as Hearsay: Some Criticisms of the Uniform Rules of Evidence, 14 Stan.L.Rev. 682 (1962). Admittedly evidence of this character is untested with respect to the perception, memory, and narration (or their equivalents) of the actor, but the Advisory Committee is of the view that these dangers are minimal in the absence of an intent to assert and do not justify the loss of the evidence on hearsay grounds. No class of evidence is free of the possibility of fabrication, but the likelihood is less with nonverbal than with assertive verbal conduct. The situations giving rise to the nonverbal conduct are such as virtually to eliminate questions of sincerity. Motivation, the nature of the conduct, and the presence or absence of reliance will bear heavily upon the weight to be given the evidence. Falknor, The "Hear-Say" Rule as a "See-Do" Rule: Evidence of Conduct, 33 Rocky Mt.L.Rev. 133 (1961). Similar considerations govern nonassertive verbal conduct and verbal conduct which is assertive but offered as a basis for inferring something other than the matter asserted, also excluded from the definition of hearsay by the language of subdivision (c).

When evidence of conduct is offered on the theory that it is not a statement, and hence not hearsay, a preliminary determination will be required to determine whether an assertion is intended. The rule is so worded as to place the burden upon the party claiming that the intention existed; ambiguous and doubtful cases will be resolved against him and in favor of admissibility. The determination involves no greater difficulty than many other preliminary questions of fact. Maguire, The

Hearsay System: Around and Through the Thicket, 14 Vand.L.Rev. 741, 765–767 (1961).

For similar approaches, *see* Uniform Rule 62(1); California Evidence Code §§ 225, 1200; Kansas Code of Civil Procedure § 60-459(a); New Jersey Evidence Rule 62(1).

Subdivision (c). The definition follows along familiar lines in including only statements offered to prove the truth of the matter asserted. McCormick § 225; 5 Wigmore § 1361, 6 *id.* § 1766. If the significance of an offered statement lies solely in the fact that it was made, no issue is raised as to the truth of anything asserted, and the statement is not hearsay. Emich Motors Corp. v. General Motors Corp., 181 F.2d 70 (7th Cir. 1950), rev'd on other grounds 340 U.S. 558, 71 S.Ct. 408, 95 L. Ed. 534, letters of complaint from customers offered as a reason for cancellation of dealer's franchise, to rebut contention that franchise was revoked for refusal to finance sales through affiliated finance company. The effect is to exclude from hearsay the entire category of "verbal acts" and "verbal parts of an act," in which the statement itself affects the legal rights of the parties or is a circumstance bearing on conduct affecting their rights.

The definition of hearsay must, of course, be read with reference to the definition of statement set forth in subdivision (a).

Testimony given by a witness in the course of court proceedings is excluded since there is compliance with all the ideal conditions for testifying.

ADVISORY COMMITTEE NOTE TO RULE 801(d)(1)(A).

[Note, that the version of Rule 801(d)(1)(A) which is discussed below was changed before enactment by the action of Congress. See the Congressional Reports set forth below.]

Subdivision (d). Several types of statements which would otherwise literally fall within the definition are expressly excluded from it:

(1) *Prior statement by witness.* Considerable controversy has attended the question whether a prior out-of-court statement by a person now available for cross-examination concerning it, under oath and in the presence of the trier of fact, should be classed as hearsay. If the witness admits on the stand that he made the statement and that it was true, he adopts the statement and there is no hearsay problem. The hearsay problem arises when the witness on the stand denies having made the statement or admits having made it but denies its truth. The argument in favor of treating these latter statements as hearsay is based upon the ground that the conditions of oath, cross-examination, and demeanor observation did not prevail at the time the statement was made and cannot adequately be supplied by the later examination. The logic of the

situation is troublesome. So far as concerns the oath, its mere presence has never been regarded as sufficient to remove a statement from the hearsay category, and it receives much less emphasis than cross-examination as a truth-compelling device. While strong expressions are found to the effect that no conviction can be had or important right taken away on the basis of statements not made under fear of prosecution for perjury, Bridges v. Wixon, 326 U.S. 135, 65 S.Ct. 1443, 89 L. Ed. 2103 (1945), the fact is that, of the many common law exceptions to the hearsay rule, only that for reported testimony has required the statement to have been made under oath. Nor is it satisfactorily explained why cross-examination cannot be conducted subsequently with success. The decisions contending most vigorously for its inadequacy in fact demonstrate quite thorough exploration of the weaknesses and doubts attending the earlier statement. State v. Saporen, 205 Minn. 358, 285 N.W. 898 (1939); Ruhala v. Roby, 379 Mich. 102, 150 N.W.2d 146 (1967); People v. Johnson, 68 Cal.2d 646, 68 Cal.Rptr. 599, 441 P.2d 111 (1968). In respect to demeanor, as Judge Learned Hand observed in Di Carlo v. United States, 6 F.2d 364 (2d Cir. 1925), when the jury decides that the truth is not what the witness says now, but what he said before, they are still deciding from what they see and hear in court. The bulk of the case law nevertheless has been against allowing prior statements of witnesses to be used generally as substantive evidence. Most of the writers and Uniform Rule 63(1) have taken the opposite position.

The position taken by the Advisory Committee in formulating this part of the rule is founded upon an unwillingness to countenance the general use of prior prepared statements as substantive evidence, but with a recognition that particular circumstances call for a contrary result. The judgment is one more of experience than of logic. The rule requires in each instance, as a general safeguard, that the declarant actually testify as a witness, and it then enumerates three situations in which the statement is excepted from the category of hearsay. Compare Uniform Rule 63(1) which allows any out-of-court statement of a declarant who is present at the trial and available for cross-examination.

(A) Prior inconsistent statements traditionally have been admissible to impeach but not as substantive evidence. Under the rule they are substantive evidence. As has been said by the California Law Revision Commission with respect to a similar provision:

"Section 1235 admits inconsistent statements of witnesses because the dangers against which the hearsay rule is designed to protect are largely nonexistent. The declarant is in court and may be examined and cross-examined in regard to his statements and their subject matter. In many cases, the inconsistent statement is more likely to be true than the testimony of the witness at the trial because it was made nearer in time to the matter to which it relates and is less likely to be influenced by the controversy that gave rise to the litigation. The trier of fact has the declarant before it and can observe his demeanor and the nature of his testimony as he denies or tries to explain away the inconsistency. Hence, it is in as good a position to determine the truth or falsity of the prior statement as it is to determine the truth or falsity of the inconsistent testimony given in court. Moreover, Section 1235 will provide a party with desirable protection against the 'turncoat' witness who changes his story on the stand and deprives the party calling him of evidence essential to his case." Comment, California Evidence Code § 1235. *See also* McCormick § 39. The Advisory Committee finds these views more convincing than those expressed in People v. Johnson, 68 Cal.2d 646, 68 Cal.Rptr. 599, 441 P.2d 111 (1968). The constitutionality of the Advisory Committee's view was upheld in California v. Green, 399 U.S. 149, 90 S.Ct. 1930, 26 L.Ed.2d 489 (1970). Moreover, the requirement that the statement be inconsistent with the testimony given assures a thorough exploration of both versions while the witness is on the stand and bars any general and indiscriminate use of previously prepared statements.

REPORT OF THE HOUSE COMMITTEE ON THE JUDICIARY.

[Note, that the version of Rule 801(d)(1)(A) which is discussed below was changed before enactment by the action of the Senate and the House/Senate Conference Committee. See the Congressional Report set forth below.]

Present federal law, except in the Second Circuit, permits the use of prior inconsistent statements of a witness for impeachment only. Rule 801(d)(1) as proposed by the Court would have permitted all such statements to be admissible as substantive evidence, an approach followed by a small but growing number of State jurisdictions and recently held constitutional in California v. Green, 399 U.S. 149 (1970). Although there was some support expressed for the Court Rule, based largely on the need to counteract the effect of witness intimidation in criminal cases, the Committee decided to adopt a compromise version of the Rule similar to the position of the Second Circuit. The Rule as amended draws a distinction between types of prior inconsistent statements (other than statements of identification of a person made after perceiving him which are currently admissible, *see* United States v. Anderson, 406 F.2d 719, 720 (4th Cir.), *cert. denied,* 395 U.S. 967 (1969)) and allows only those made while the declarant was subject to cross-examination at a trial or hearing or in a deposition, to be admissible for their truth. *Compare* United States v. DeSisto, 329 F.2d 929 (2nd Cir.), *cert. denied,* 377 U.S. 979 (1964); United States v. Cunningham, 446 F.2d 194 (2nd Cir. 1971) (restricting the admissibility of prior inconsistent statements as substantive evidence to those made under oath in a formal proceeding, but not requiring that there have been an opportunity for cross-examination). The rationale for the Committee's decision is that (1) unlike in most other situations involving unsworn or oral statements, there can be no dispute as to whether the prior statement was made; and (2) the context of a formal proceeding, an oath, and the opportunity for cross-examination provide firm additional assurances of the reliability of the prior statement.

REPORT OF THE SENATE COMMITTEE ON THE JUDICIARY.

[*Note, that the version of Rule 801(d)(1)(A) which is discussed below was changed before enactment by the action of the Senate and the House/Senate Conference Committee. See* the Conference Report set forth below.]

Rule 801 defines what is and what is not hearsay for the purpose of admitting a prior statement as substantive evidence. A prior statement of a witness at a trial or hearing which is inconsistent with his testimony is, of course, always admissible for the purpose of impeaching the witness' credibility.

As submitted by the Supreme Court, subdivision (d)(1)(A) made admissible as substantive evidence the prior statement of a witness inconsistent with his present testimony.

The House severely limited the admissibility of prior inconsistent statements by adding a requirement that the prior statement must have been subject to cross-examination, thus precluding even the use of grand jury statements. The requirement that the prior statement must have been subject to cross-examination appears unnecessary since this rule comes into play only when the witness testifies in the present trial. At that time, he is on the stand and can explain an earlier position and be cross-examined as to both.

The requirement that the statement be under oath also appears unnecessary. Notwithstanding the absence of an oath contemporaneous with the statement, the witness, when on the stand, qualifying or denying the prior statement, is under oath. In any event, of all the many recognized exceptions to the hearsay rule, only one (former testimony) requires that the out-of-court statement have been made under oath. With respect to the lack of evidence of the demeanor of the witness at the time of the prior statement, it would be difficult to improve upon Judge Learned Hand's observation that when the jury decides that the truth is not what the witness says now but what he said before, they are still deciding from what they see and hear in court.[9]

The rule as submitted by the Court has positive advantages. The prior

---

[9] Di Carlo v. United States, 6 F.2d 364 (2d Cir. 1925).

statement was made nearer in time to the events, when memory was fresher and intervening influences had not been brought into play. A realistic method is provided for dealing with the turncoat witness who changes his story on the stand.[10]

New Jersey, California, and Utah have adopted a rule similar to this one; and Nevada, New Mexico, and Wisconsin have adopted the identical Federal rule.

For all of these reasons, we think the House amendment should be rejected and the rule as submitted by the Supreme Court reinstated.[11]

REPORT OF THE HOUSE/SENATE CONFERENCE COMMITTEE.

[Note, that the version of Rule 801(d)(1)(A) discussed below is the one which Congress enacted.]

The House bill provides that a statement is not hearsay if the declarant testifies and is subject to cross-examination concerning the statement and if the statement is inconsistent with his testimony and was given under oath subject to cross-examination and subject to the penalty of perjury at a trial or hearing or in a deposition. The Senate amendment drops the requirement that the prior statement be given under oath subject to cross-examination and subject to the penalty of perjury at a trial or hearing or in a deposition.

The Conference adopts the Senate amendment with an amendment, so that the rule now requires that the prior inconsistent statement be given under oath subject to the penalty of perjury at a trial, hearing, or other proceeding, or in a deposition. The rule as adopted covers statements before a grand jury. Prior inconsistent statements may, of course, be used for impeaching the credibility of a witness. When the prior inconsistent statement is one made by a defendant in a criminal case, it is covered by Rule 801(d)(2).

ADVISORY COMMITTEE NOTE TO RULE 801(d)(1)(B).

(B) Prior consistent statements traditionally have been admissible to rebut charges of recent fabrication or improper influence or motive but not as substantive evidence. Under the rule they are substantive evidence. The prior statement is consistent with the testimony given on the stand, and, if the opposite party wishes to open the door for its

---

[10] *See* Comment, California Evidence Code § 1235; McCormick, Evidence, § 38 (2d ed. 1972).

[11] It would appear that some of the opposition to this Rule is based on a concern that a person could be convicted solely upon evidence admissible under this Rule. The Rule, however, is not addressed to the question of the sufficiency of evidence to send a case to the jury, but merely as to its admissibility. Factual circumstances could well arise where, if this were the sole evidence, dismissal would be appropriate.

admission in evidence, no sound reason is apparent why it should not be received generally.

ADVISORY COMMITTEE NOTE TO RULE 801(d)(1)(C).

[Note, that originally Congress did not enact the provision discussed below. Several months after enactment of the Rules, however, Congress amended them to add the present Rule 801(d)(1)(C), which is identical to the provision discussed below.]

(C) The admission of evidence of identification finds substantial support, although it falls beyond a doubt in the category of prior out-of-court statements. Illustrative are People v. Gould, 54 Cal.2d 621, 7 Cal.Rptr. 273, 354 P.2d 865 (1960); Judy v. State, 218 Md. 168, 146 A.2d 29 (1958); State v. Simmons, 63 Wash.2d 17, 385 P.2d 389 (1963); California Evidence Code § 1238; New Jersey Evidence Rule 63(1)(c); N.Y.Code of Criminal Procedure § 393-b. Further cases are found in 4 Wigmore § 1130. The basis is the generally unsatisfactory and incon- clusive nature of courtroom identifications as compared with those made at an earlier time under less suggestive conditions. The Supreme Court considered the admissibility of evidence of prior identification in Gilbert v. California, 388 U.S. 263, 87 S.Ct. 1951, 18 L.Ed.2d 1178 (1967). Exclusion of lineup identification was held to be required because the accused did not then have the assistance of counsel. Significantly, the Court carefully refrained from placing its decision on the ground that testimony as to the making of a prior out-of-court identification ("That's the man") violated either the hearsay rule or the right of confrontation because not made under oath, subject to imme- diate cross-examination, in the presence of the trier. Instead the Court observed:

"There is a split among the States concerning the admissibility of prior extra-judicial identifications, as independent evidence of identity, both by the witness and third parties present at the prior identification. *See* 71 ALR2d 449. It has been held that the prior identification is hearsay, and, when admitted through the testimony of the identifier, is merely a prior consistent statement. The recent trend, however, is to admit the prior identification under the exception that admits as substantive evidence a prior communication by a witness who is available for cross-examination at the trial. *See* 5 ALR2d Later Case Service 6.131225–1228 . . . ." 388 U.S. at 272, n. 3, 87 S.Ct. at 1956.

REPORT OF THE SENATE COMMITTEE ON THE JUDICIARY.

[Note, that this Report refers to the proposed version of Rule 801(d)(1)(C), which Congress did not enact along with the balance of the Rules. Congress did, however, add the present Rule 801(d)(1)(C), which is identical to the version originally proposed, at a later date. See

the 1975 Reports from the House and Senate Judiciary Committees below.]

As submitted by the Supreme Court and as passed by the House, subdivision (d)(1)(c) of Rule 801 made admissible the prior statement identifying a person made after perceiving him. The committee decided to delete this provision because of the concern that a person could be convicted solely upon evidence admissible under this subdivision.

1974 REPORT OF THE HOUSE/SENATE CONFERENCE COMMITTEE.

[*Note, that this Report refers to the proposed version of Rule 801(d)(1)(C), which Congress did not enact along with the balance of the Rules. Congress did, however, add the present Rule 801(d)(1)(C), which is identical to the version originally proposed, at a later date. See* the 1975 Reports from the Senate and House Judiciary Committees below.]

The House bill provides that a statement is not hearsay if the declarant testifies and is subject to cross-examination concerning the statement and the statement is one of identification of a person made after perceiving him. The Senate amendment eliminated this provision.

The Conference adopts the Senate amendment.

1975 REPORT OF THE SENATE COMMITTEE ON THE JUDICIARY.

[*Note, that this Report refers to the version of Rule 801(d)(1)(C), which Congress ultimately enacted.*]

STATEMENT.

The Federal Rules of Evidence, as submitted by the Supreme Court and passed by the House of Representatives, included the following provision in Rule 801(d)(1)(C):

A statement is not hearsay if * * * the declarant testifies at the trial or hearing and is subject to cross-examination concerning the statement, and the statement is * * * *one of identification of a person made after perceiving him.* [Emphasis supplied.]

A similar provision was contained in the Preliminary Draft of the Proposed Rules (March 1969), the Revised Draft (March 1971), the Judicial Conference Proposed Draft, and the Supreme Court Draft (November 1972).

Senator Philip A. Hart (for himself and Senators Hruska and McClellan) introduced S. 1549 on April 29, 1975, to add a new subparagraph (d)(1) to Rule 801, Definitions, of Article VIII (Hearsay).

The purpose of the provision was to make clear, in line with the recent law in the area, that nonsuggestive lineup, photographic and other identifications are not hearsay and therefore are admissible. In the lineup case of Gilbert v. California, 388 U.S. 263, 272 n. 3 (1967), the

Supreme Court, noting the split of authority in admitting prior out-of-court identifications, stated, "The recent trend, however, is to admit the prior identification under the exception [to the hearsay rule] that admits as substantive evidence a prior communication by a witness who is available for cross-examination at the trial." And the Federal Courts of Appeals have generally admitted these identifications. *See, e.g.*, Clemons v. United States, 408 F. 2d 1230 (D.C. Cir. 1968) (*en banc*), *cert. denied*, 394 U.S. 964 (1969); United States v. Miller, 381 F.2d 529, 538 (2d Cir. 1967) (Friendly, J.); Edison v. United States, 272 F.2d 684, 686 (10th Cir. 1959). *See also* 4 *Wigmore, Evidence*, Sec. 1130 (Chadbourn rev. 1972) which strongly supports admissibility of prior identifications. Additional authority is collected in Rothstein, *Understanding the New Federal Rules of Evidence*, pp. 385–86, 390, and 669–70 (1975 Supplement).

In the course of processing the Rules of Evidence in the final weeks of the 93d Congress, the provision excluding such statements of identification from the hearsay category was deleted. Although there was no suggestion in the committee report that prior identifications are not probative, concern was there expressed that a conviction could be based upon such unsworn, out-of-court testimony. Upon further reflection, that concern appears misdirected. First, this exception is addressed to the "admissibility" of evidence and not to the "sufficiency" of evidence to prove guilt. Secondly, except for the former testimony exception to the hearsay exclusion, all hearsay exceptions allow into evidence statements which may not have been made under oath. Moreover, under this rule, unlike a significant majority of the hearsay exceptions, the prior identification is admissible only when the person who made it testifies at trial and is subject to cross-examination. This assures that if any discrepancy occurs between the witness's in-court and out-of-court testimony, the opportunity is available to probe, with the witness under oath, the reasons for that discrepancy so that the trier of fact might determine which statement is to be believed.

Upon reflection, then, it appears the rule is desirable. Since these identifications take place reasonably soon after an offense has been committed, the witness' observations are still fresh in his mind. The identification occurs before his recollection has been dimmed by the passage of time. Equally as important, it also takes place before the defendant or some other party has had the opportunity, through bribe or threat, to influence the witness to change his mind.

Both experience and psychological studies suggest that identifications consisting of nonsuggestive lineups, photographic spreads, or similar identifications, made reasonably soon after the offense, are more reliable than in-court identifications. Admitting these prior identifications therefore provides greater fairness to both the prosecution and defense in a criminal trial. *See* McCormick, Evidence, 602 (2d ed. 1972). Their exclusion would thus be detrimental to the fair administration of justice.

That the trier of fact, whether it be judge or jury, cannot properly perform its function if highly probative and constitutional identification evidence is kept from it has been recognized by the Court of Appeals for the District of Columbia Circuit in an *en banc* decision in Clemons v. United States, 408 F.2d at 1243:

> The rationale behind the exclusion of hearsay evidence has little force in the case of witnesses * * * who are available for cross-examination. We also think that juries in criminal cases, before being called upon to decide the awesome question of guilt or innocence, are entitled to know more of the circumstances which culminate in the courtroom identification—an event which, standing alone, often means very little to a conscientious and intelligent juror, who routinely expects the witnesses to identify the defendant in court and who may not attach great weight to such an identification in the absence of corroboration.

For these reasons, evidence of an earlier identification made by a person who is now testifying at the trial should not be treated as inadmissible hearsay.

Again, it should be emphasized that though the rule makes prior identifications admissible, they *still* must meet constitutional muster. In United States v. Wade, 388 U.S. 218 (1967), the Supreme Court held that the Sixth Amendment right to assistance of counsel applied to lineup identifications. Even though the Court held that the right to counsel applied only to post-indictment lineups, Kirby v. Illinois, 406 U.S. 682 (1972), other cases make clear that the Due Process Clause is applicable to *all* pretrial lineups and that it forbids a lineup that is unnecessarily suggestive and conducive to mistaken identification. Stovall v. Denno, 388 U.S. 293 (1967); Foster v. California, 394 U.S. 440 (1969). Having the identifying witness on the stand (which is required by the first clause of Rule 801(d)(1)), coupled with these constitutional safeguards, provide adequate assurances of trustworthiness to warrant the admissibility of such prior identifications.

Finally, the committee notes that several States which have adopted Evidence Codes in the last few years have included a rule which provides for the admissibility of prior identifications. Cal. Evid. Code § 1238 (West 1966); Kan. Civ. Pro. Stat. Ann. § 60-460(a) (Vernon 1964); Nev. Rev. Stat. § 51.035(2)(c) (1973); New Jersey Evidence Rule § 63(1)(c); N.M. Stat. Ann. § 20-4-801(d)(1)(C) (1973); N.Y. Crim. Pro. § 60.25 (McKinney Supp. 1971); Utah Rules of Evidence § 63(1) (1971); Wis. Stat. Ann. § 908.01(1)(a) (Spec. Pamphlet 1974);

Proposed Maine Rules of Evidence § 801(d)(1)(C) (Tent. Draft, Dec. 1974).

1975 REPORT OF THE HOUSE COMMITTEE ON THE JUDICIARY.

[Note, that this Report refers to the version of Rule 801(d)(1)(C), which Congress ultimately enacted.]

BACKGROUND.

The Federal Rules of Evidence govern proceedings in federal courts and before United States magistrates. Article VIII of those Rules deals with hearsay evidence, and Rule 801 provides general definitions for Article VIII. Subdivision (d)(1) of Rule 801 defines certain statements not to be hearsay and therefore not inadmissible under Rule 802, which makes hearsay statements generally inadmissible.

When the Federal Rules of Evidence bill (H.R. 5463) passed the House on February 6, 1974, by a vote of 377 to 13, it contained the following provision:

A statement is not hearsay if . . . the defendant testifies at the trial or hearing and is subject to cross-examination concerning the statement, and the statement is . . . (C) *one of identification of a person made after perceiving him.* [Emphasis added.]

The Senate-passed version of H.R. 5463 omitted the italicized language.

The House-Senate Conference Committee on H.R. 5463 met in December 1974 to iron out the differences between the House and Senate versions of the bill. The Senate strenuously insisted upon its version of Rule 801(d)(1); in fact, it was indicated that any compromise that included the House version of the rule would face extended discussion during the Senate debate. In the face of this, the House Conferees agreed to the Senate version of Rule 801(d)(1).

S. 1549, which is cosponsored in the Senate by Senators Philip A. Hart, John L. McClellan and Roman Hruska, seeks to put back into Rule 801(d)(1) the language that was struck at Conference. In other words, the Senate is now acceding to the House version of Rule 801(d)(1).

ANALYSIS OF THE BILL.

Rule 801(d)(1)(C), as it is proposed to read, has a precondition to the use of the out-of-court statement of identification. The person who made the statement (the "declarant") must testify at the trial or hearing and must be subject to cross-examination concerning the statement. Even if this precondition is met, the out-of-court statement of identification must still meet constitutional standards. If the precondition is satisfied and the constitutional standards are met, then the out-of-court statement of identification is admissible.

A. Constitutional Standards.

Out-of-court statements of identification can be made in different contexts. They can be made at a preindictment or a postindictment lineup. They can be made at a one-person showup that takes place shortly after the crime. They can also be made after being shown a series of photographs.

When there is a postindictment lineup, the Constitution requires that the defendant's counsel be present. United States v. Wade, 388 U.S. 218 (1967). When there is a preindictment lineup, there is no requirement that defendant's counsel be present. Kirby v. Illinois, 406 U.S. 682 (1972). Likewise, when a group of photographs is shown to someone, there is no requirement that the defendant's lawyer be present. Simmons v. United States, 390 U.S. 377 (1968).

Out-of-court identification procedures—including lineups, showups and displays of photographs—must meet the due process standard of the Fifth and Fourteenth Amendments to the United States Constitution. Kirby v. Illinois, 406 U.S. 682 (1972) (preindictment lineup); Foster v. California, 394 U.S. 440 (1969) (preindictment lineup followed by face-to-face showup); Stovall v. Denno, 388 U.S. 293 (1967) (one-person showup); Simmons v. United States, 390 U.S. 377 (1968) (display of photographs). The due process standard requires looking at the totality of the circumstances to determine whether the identification procedure was "unnecessarily suggestive and conducive to irreparably mistaken identification." Kirby v. Illinois, 406 U.S. 682, 691 (1972).

If the identification procedure does not measure up to the Constitutional standard, then the witness' out-of-court statement is not admissible. Furthermore, the witness cannot make an in-court identification unless there is clear and convincing evidence that there is an independent basis for the in-court identification. United States v. Wade, 388 U.S. 218 (1967); Gilbert v. California, 388 U.S. 263 (1967).

B. Case Law.

There was a split among the authorities as to whether out-of-court statements of identification are admissible. *See* Annot., 71 A.L.R.2d 449.

The recent trend, however, is to admit the prior identification under the exception that admits as substantive evidence a prior communication by a witness who is available for cross-examination at trial.

Gilbert v. California, 388 U.S. 263, 272 n. 3 (1967)

Federal courts admit out-of-court statements of identification. *See, e.g.,* United States v. Miller, 381 F.2d 529 (2d Cir. 1967) (photographic display); United States v. Shannon, 424 F.2d 476 (3d Cir. 1970), *cert.*

denied, 400 U.S. 844 (photographic display followed by one-person showup); Bolling v. United States, 18 F.2d 863 (4th Cir. 1927) (on-the-scene identification); United States v. Fabio, 394 F.2d 132 (4th Cir. 1968) (preindictment lineup); United States v. Cooper, 472 F.2d 64 (5th Cir. 1973), *cert. denied*, 414 U.S. 840 (photographic display); United States v. Lincoln, 494 F.2d 833 (9th Cir. 1974) (photographic display); Edison v. United States, 272 F.2d 684 (10th Cir. 1959) (preindictment lineup); Clemons v. United States, 408 F.2d 1230 (D.C. Cir. 1968) (cellblock confrontation).

Thus, Rule 801(d)(1)(C) as proposed in S. 1549 is fully consistent with current Federal case law. Federal case law treats such statements as exceptions to the hearsay rule; Rule 801(d)(1)(C) defines them not to be hearsay. The result is the same in either instance, the statement is admissible if the person who made it testifies and is subject to cross-examination.

C. Rationale.

Courtroom identifications can be very suggestive. The defendant is known to be present and generally sits in a certain location. Out-of-court identifications are generally more reliable. They take place relatively soon after the offense, while the incident is still reasonably fresh in the witness' mind. Out-of-court identifications are particularly important in jurisdictions where there may be a long delay between arrest or indictment and trial. As time goes by, a witness' memory will fade and his identification will become less reliable. An early, out-of-court identification provides fairness to defendants by ensuring accuracy of the identification. At the same time, it aids the government by making sure that delays in the criminal justice system do not lead to cases falling through because the witness can no longer recall the identity of the person he saw commit the crime.

The justification for not admitting out-of-court statements of identification was stated in the Senate Report on the Federal Rules of Evidence bill (H.R. 5463) to be a "concern that a person could be convicted solely upon evidence admitted under this [exception]." Senate Report No. 93-1277, at 16. However, Rule 801(d)(1) is not addressed to the issue of the sufficiency of evidence but to the issue of its admissibility. This was pointed out in Senate Report on the Federal Rules of Evidence in reference to subdivision (A) of Rule 801(d)(1).

It would appear that some of the opposition to this Rule is based on a concern that a person could be convicted solely upon evidence admissible under this Rule. The Rule, however, is not addressed to the question of the sufficiency of evidence to send a case to the jury, but merely to its admissibility.

Senate Report No. 93-1277, at 16 n. 20.

ADVISORY COMMITTEE NOTE TO RULE 801(d)(2).

[*Note that this Advisory Committee's Note refers to the version of Rule 801(d)(2) which Congress did enact, since Congress made no changes.*]

(2) Admissions. Admissions by a party-opponent are excluded from the category of hearsay on the theory that their admissibility in evidence is the result of the adversary system rather than satisfaction of the conditions of the hearsay rule. Strahorn, A Reconsideration of the Hearsay Rule and Admissions, 85 U.Pa.L.Rev. 484, 564 (1937); Morgan, Basic Problems of Evidence 265 (1962); 4 Wigmore § 1048. No guarantee of trustworthiness is required in the case of an admission. The freedom which admissions have enjoyed from technical demands of searching for an assurance of trustworthiness in some against-interest circumstance, and from the restrictive influences of the opinion rule and the rule requiring firsthand knowledge, when taken with the apparently prevalent satisfaction with the results, calls for generous treatment of this avenue to admissibility.

The rule specifies five categories of statements for which the responsibility of a party is considered sufficient to justify reception in evidence against him:

(A) A party's own statement is the classic example of an admission. If he has a representative capacity and the statement is offered against him in that capacity, no inquiry whether he was acting in the representative capacity in making the statement is required; the statement need only be relevant to representative affairs. To the same effect is California Evidence Code § 1220. Compare Uniform Rule 63(7), requiring a statement to be made in a representative capacity to be admissible against a party in a representative capacity.

(B) Under established principles an admission may be made by adopting or acquiescing in the statement of another. While knowledge of contents would ordinarily be essential, this is not inevitably so: "X is a reliable person and knows what he is talking about." *See* McCormick § 246, p. 527, n. 15. Adoption or acquiescence may be manifested in any appropriate manner. When silence is relied upon, the theory is that the person would, under the circumstances, protest the statement made in his presence, if untrue. The decision in each case calls for an evaluation in terms of probable human behavior. In civil cases, the results have generally been satisfactory. In criminal cases, however, troublesome questions have been raised by decisions holding that failure to deny is an admission: the inference is a fairly weak one, to begin with; silence may be motivated by advice of counsel or realization that "anything you say may be used against you"; unusual opportunity is afforded to manufacture evidence; and encroachment upon the privilege against self-incrimination seems inescapably to be involved. However, recent decisions of the Supreme Court relating to custodial interrogation and the right to counsel appear to resolve these difficulties. Hence the rule contains no special provisions concerning failure to deny in criminal cases.

(C) No authority is required for the general proposition that a statement authorized by a party to be made should have the status of an admission by the party. However, the question arises whether only statements to third persons should be so regarded, to the exclusion of statements by the agent to the principal. The rule is phrased broadly so as to encompass both. While it may be argued that the agent authorized to make statements to his principal does not speak for him, Morgan, Basic Problems of Evidence 273 (1962), communication to an outsider has not generally been thought to be an essential characteristic of an admission. Thus a party's books or records are usable against him, without regard to any intent to disclose to third persons. 5 Wigmore § 1557. *See also* McCormick § 78, pp. 159–161. In accord is New Jersey Evidence Rule 63(8)(a). *Cf.* Uniform Rule 63(8)(a) and California Evidence Code § 1222 which limit status as an admission in this regard to statements authorized by the party to be made "for" him, which is perhaps an ambiguous limitation to statements to third persons. Falknor, Vicarious Admissions and the Uniform Rules, 14 Vand.L.Rev. 855, 860–861 (1961).

(D) The tradition has been to test the admissibility of statements by agents, as admissions, by applying the usual test of agency. Was the admission made by the agent acting in the scope of his employment? Since few principals employ agents for the purpose of making damaging statements, the usual result was exclusion of the statement. Dissatisfaction with this loss of valuable and helpful evidence has been increasing. A substantial trend favors admitting statements related to a matter within the scope of the agency or employment. Grayson v. Williams, 256 F.2d 61 (10th Cir. 1958); Koninklijke Luchtvaart Maatschappij N. V. KLM Royal Dutch Airlines v. Tuller, 292 F.2d 775, 784, 110 U.S.App.D.C. 282 (1961); Martin v. Savage Truck Lines, Inc., 121 F. Supp. 417 (D.D.C.1954), and numerous state court decisions collected in 4 Wigmore, 1964 Supp., pp. 66–73, with comments by the editor that the statements should have been excluded as not within scope of agency. For the traditional view *see* Northern Oil Co. v. Socony Mobil Oil Co., 347 F.2d 81, 85 (2d Cir. 1965) and cases cited therein. Similar provisions are found in Uniform Rule 63(9)(a), Kansas Code of Civil Procedure § 60-460(i)(1), and New Jersey Evidence Rule 63(9)(a).

(E) The limitation upon the admissibility of statements of co-conspirators to those made "during the course and in furtherance of the conspiracy" is in the accepted pattern. While the broadened view of agency taken in item (iv) might suggest wider admissibility of statements of co-conspirators, the agency theory of conspiracy is at best a fiction and ought not to serve as a basis for admissibility beyond that already established. *See* Levie, Hearsay and Conspiracy, 52 Mich.L-.Rev. 1159 (1954); Comment, 25 U.Chi.L.Rev. 530 (1958). The rule is consistent with the position of the Supreme Court in denying admissibility to statements made after the objectives of the conspiracy have either failed or been achieved. Krulewitch v. United States, 336 U.S. 440, 69 S.Ct. 716, 93 L. Ed. 790 (1949); Wong Sun v. United States, 371 U.S. 471, 490, 83 S.Ct. 407, 9 L.Ed.2d 441 (1963). For similarly limited provisions *see* California Evidence Code § 1223 and New Jersey Rule 63(9)(b). *Cf.* Uniform Rule 63(9)(b).

REPORT OF THE SENATE COMMITTEE ON THE JUDICIARY.

[Note, that this Report refers to the version of Rule 801(d)(2)(E) which Congress did enact, since Congress made no changes in any part of Rule 801(d)(2).]

The House approved the long-accepted rule that "a statement by a coconspirator of a party during the course and in furtherance of the conspiracy" is not hearsay as it was submitted by the Supreme Court. While the rule refers to a coconspirator, it is this committee's understanding that the rule is meant to carry forward the universally accepted doctrine that a joint venturer is considered as a coconspirator for the purposes of this rule even though no conspiracy has been charged. United States v. Rinaldi, 393 F.2d 97, 99, *cert. denied*, 393 U.S. 913 (1968); United States v. Spencer, 415 F.2d 1301, 1304 (7th Cir. 1969).

ADVISORY COMMITTEE NOTE TO 1997 AMENDMENT.

Rule 801(d)(2) has been amended in order to respond to three issues raised by Bourjaily v. United States, 483 U.S. 171 (1987). First, the amendment codifies the holding in *Bourjaily* by stating expressly that a court shall consider the contents of a coconspirator's statement in determining "the existence of the conspiracy and the participation therein of the declarant and the party against whom the statement is offered." According to *Bourjaily*, Rule 104(a) requires these preliminary questions to be established by a preponderance of the evidence.

Second, the amendment resolves an issue on which the Court had reserved decision. It provides that the contents of the declarant's statement do not alone suffice to establish a conspiracy in which the declarant and the defendant participated. The court must consider in addition the circumstances surrounding the statement, such as the identity of the speaker, the context in which the statement was made, or evidence corroborating the contents of the statement in making its determination as to each preliminary question. This amendment is in accordance with existing practice. Every court of appeals that has resolved this issue requires some evidence in addition to the contents of the statement. *See, e.g.,* United States v. Beckham, 968 F.2d 47, 51 (D.C.Cir. 1992); United States v. Sepulveda, 15 F.3d 1161, 1181–82 (1st Cir. 1993), *cert. denied,* 114 S.Ct. 2714 (1994); United States v. Daly, 842 F.2d 1380, 1386 (2d Cir.), *cert. denied,* 488 U.S. 821 (1988); United States v. Clark, 18 F.3d 1337, 1341–42 (6th Cir.), *cert. denied,* 115 S.Ct 152 (1994); United States v. Zambrana, 841 F.2d 1320, 1344–45 (7th Cir. 1988); United States v. Silverman, 861 F.2d 571, 577 (9th Cir. 1988); United States v. Gordon, 844 F.2d 1397, 1402 (9th Cir. 1988); United States v. Hernandez, 829 F.2d 988, 993 (10th Cir. 1987), *cert. denied,* 485 U.S. 1013 (1988); United States v. Byrom, 910 F.2d 725, 736 (11th Cir. 1990).

Third, the amendment extends the reasoning of *Bourjaily* to statements offered under subdivisions (C) and (D) of Rule 801(d)(2). In *Bourjaily,* the Court rejected treating foundational facts pursuant to the law of agency in favor of an evidentiary approach governed by Rule 104(a). The Advisory Committee believes it appropriate to treat analogously preliminary questions relating to the declarant's authority under subdivision (C), and the agency or employment relationship and scope thereof under subdivision (D).

Rule 802. The Rule Against Hearsay

ADVISORY COMMITTEE NOTE TO THE 2011 AMENDMENT.

The language of Rule 802 has been amended as part of the restyling of the Evidence Rules to make them more easily understood and to make style and terminology consistent throughout the rules. These changes are intended to be stylistic only. There is no intent to change any result in any ruling on evidence admissibility.

ADVISORY COMMITTEE NOTE.

The provision excepting from the operation of the rule hearsay which is made admissible by other rules adopted by the Supreme Court or by Act of Congress continues the admissibility thereunder of hearsay which would not qualify under these Evidence Rules. The following examples illustrate the working of the exception:

FEDERAL RULES OF CIVIL PROCEDURE.

Rule 4(g): proof of service by affidavit.

Rule 32: admissibility of depositions.

Rule 43(e): affidavits when motion based on facts not appearing of record.

Rule 56: affidavits in summary judgment proceedings.

Rule 65(b): showing by affidavit for temporary restraining order.

FEDERAL RULES OF CRIMINAL PROCEDURE.

Rule 4(a): affidavits to show grounds for issuing warrants.

Rule 12(b)(4): affidavits to determine issues of fact in connection with motions.

ACTS OF CONGRESS.

10 U.S.C. § 7730: affidavits of unavailable witnesses in actions for damages caused by vessel in naval service, or towage or salvage of same, when taking of testimony or bringing of action delayed or stayed on security grounds.

29 U.S.C. § 161(4): affidavit as proof of service in NLRB proceedings.

38 U.S.C. § 5206: affidavit as proof of posting notice of sale of unclaimed property by Veterans Administration.

NOTE BY FEDERAL JUDICIAL CENTER.

The Rule enacted by Congress is the Rule prescribed by the Supreme Court, amended by substituting "prescribed" in place of "adopted" and by inserting the phrase "pursuant to statutory authority."

Rule 803. Exceptions to the Rule Against Hearsay—Regardless of Whether the Declarant Is Available as a Witness

ADVISORY COMMITTEE NOTE TO THE 2011 AMENDMENT.

The language of Rule 803 has been amended as part of the restyling of the Evidence Rules to make them more easily understood and to make style and terminology consistent throughout the rules. These changes are intended to be stylistic only. There is no intent to change any result in any ruling on evidence admissibility.

ADVISORY COMMITTEE NOTE.

The exceptions are phrased in terms of nonapplication of the hearsay rule, rather than in positive terms of admissibility, in order to repel any implication that other possible grounds for exclusion are eliminated from consideration.

The present rule proceeds upon the theory that under appropriate circumstances a hearsay statement may possess circumstantial guarantees of trustworthiness sufficient to justify nonproduction of the declarant in person at the trial even though he may be available. The theory finds vast support in the many exceptions to the hearsay rule developed by the common law in which unavailability of the declarant is not a relevant factor. The present rule is a synthesis of them, with revision where modern developments and conditions are believed to make that course appropriate.

In a hearsay situation, the declarant is, of course, a witness, and neither this rule nor Rule 804 dispenses with the requirement of firsthand knowledge. It may appear from his statement or be inferable from circumstances. *See* Rule 602.

Exceptions (1) and (2). In considerable measure these two examples overlap, though based on somewhat different theories. The most significant practical difference will lie in the time lapse allowable between event and statement.

The underlying theory of Exception (1) is that substantial contemporaneity of event and statement negative the likelihood of deliberate or conscious misrepresentation. Moreover, if the witness is the declarant, he may be examined on the statement. If the witness is not the declarant, he may be examined as to the circumstances as an aid in evaluating the statement. Morgan, Basic Problems of Evidence 340–341 (1962).

The theory of Exception (2) is simply that circumstances may produce a condition of excitement which temporarily stills the capacity of reflection and produces utterances free of conscious fabrication. 6 Wigmore § 1747, p. 135. Spontaneity is the key factor in each instance, though arrived at by somewhat different routes. Both are needed in order to avoid needless niggling.

While the theory of Exception (2) has been criticized on the ground that excitement impairs accuracy of observation as well as eliminating conscious fabrication, Hutchins and Slesinger, Some Observations on the Law of Evidence: Spontaneous Exclamations, 28 Colum.L.Rev. 432 (1928), it finds support in cases without number. *See* cases in 6 Wigmore § 1750; Annot. 53 A.L.R.2d 1245 (statements as to cause of or responsibility for motor vehicle accident); Annot., 4 A.L.R.3d 149 (accusatory statements by homicide victims). Since unexciting events are less likely to evoke comment, decisions involving Exception (1) are far less numerouns [*sic*]. Illustrative are Tampa Elec. Co. v. Getrost, 151 Fla. 558, 10 So.2d 83 (1942); Houston Oxygen Co. v. Davis, 139 Tex. 1, 161 S.W.2d 474 (1942); and cases cited in McCormick § 273, p. 585, n. 4.

With respect to the *time element,* Exception (1) recognizes that in many, if not most, instances precise contemporaneity is not possible, and hence a slight lapse is allowable. Under Exception (2) the standard of measurement is the duration of the state of excitement. "How long can excitement prevail? Obviously there are no pat answers and the character of the transaction or event will largely determine the significance of the time factor." Slough, Spontaneous Statements and State of Mind, 46 Iowa L.Rev. 224, 243 (1961); McCormick § 272, p. 580.

Participation by the declarant is not required: a non-participant may be moved to describe what he perceives, and one may be startled by an event in which he is not an actor. Slough, *supra*; McCormick, *supra*; 6 Wigmore § 1755; Annot., 78 A.L.R.2d 300.

Whether *proof of the startling event* may be made by the statement itself is largely an academic question, since in most cases there is present at least circumstantial evidence that something of a startling nature must have occurred. For cases in which the evidence consists of the condition of the declarant (injuries, state of shock), *see* Insurance Co. v. Mosely, 75 U.S. (8 Wall.) 397, 19 L. Ed. 437 (1869); Wheeler v. United States, 211 F.2d 19, 93 U.S.App.D.C. 159 (1953), *cert. denied*, 347 U.S. 1019, 74 S.Ct. 876, 98 L. Ed. 1140; Wetherbee v. Safety Casualty Co., 219 F.2d 274 (5th Cir. 1955); Lampe v. United States, 229 F.2d 43, 97 U.S.App.D.C. 160 (1956). Nevertheless, on occasion the only evidence may be the content of the statement itself, and rulings that it may be sufficient are described as "increasing," Slough, *supra* at 246, and as the "prevailing practice," McCormick § 272, p. 579. Illustrative are Armour & Co. v. Industrial Commission, 78 Colo. 569, 243 P. 546 (1926); Young v. Stewart, 191 N.C. 297, 131 S.E. 735 (1926). Moreover, under Rule 104(a) the judge is not limited by the hearsay rule in passing upon preliminary questions of fact.

Proof of declarant's perception by his statement presents similar considerations when declarant is identified. People v. Poland, 22 Ill.2d 175, 174 N.E.2d 804 (1961). However, when declarant is an unidentified bystander, the cases indicate hesitancy in upholding the statement alone as sufficient, Garrett v. Howden, 73 N.M. 307, 387 P.2d 874 (1963); Beck v. Dye, 200 Wash. 1, 92 P.2d 1113 (1939), a result which would under appropriate circumstances be consistent with the rule.

Permissible *subject matter* of the statement is limited under Exception (1) to description or explanation of the event or condition, the assumption being that spontaneity, in the absence of a startling event, may extend no farther. In Exception (2), however, the statement need only "relate" to the startling event or condition, thus affording a broader scope of subject matter coverage. 6 Wigmore §§ 1750, 1754. *See* Sanitary Grocery Co. v. Snead, 90 F.2d 374, 67 App.D.C. 129 (1937), slip-and-fall case sustaining admissibility of clerk's statement, "That has been on the floor for a couple of hours," and Murphy Auto Parts Co., Inc. v. Ball, 249 F.2d 508, 101 U.S.App.D.C. 416 (1957), upholding admission, on issue of driver's agency, of his statement that he had to call on a customer and was in a hurry to get home. Quick, Hearsay, Excitement, Necessity and the Uniform Rules: A Reappraisal of Rule 63(4), 6 Wayne L.Rev. 204, 206–209 (1960).

Similar provisions are found in Uniform Rule 63(4) (a) and (b); California Evidence Code § 1240 (as to Exception (2) only); Kansas Code of Civil Procedure § 60-460(d)(1) and (2); New Jersey Evidence

Rule 63(4).

Exception (3) is essentially a specialized application of Exception (1), presented separately to enhance its usefulness and accessibility. *See* McCormick §§ 265, 268.

The exclusion of "statements of memory or belief to prove the fact remembered or believed" is necessary to avoid the virtual destruction of the hearsay rule which would otherwise result from allowing state of mind, provable by a hearsay statement, to serve as the basis for an inference of the happening of the event which produced the state of mind. Shepard v. United States, 290 U.S. 96, 54 S.Ct. 22, 78 L. Ed. 196 (1933); Maguire, The Hillmon Case—Thirty-three Years After, 38 Harv.L.Rev. 709, 719–731 (1925); Hinton, States of Mind and the Hearsay Rule, 1 U.Chi.L.Rev. 394, 421–423 (1934). The rule of Mutual Life Ins. Co. v. Hillmon, 145 U.S. 285, 12 S.Ct. 909, 36 L. Ed. 706 (1892), allowing evidence of intention as tending to prove the doing of the act intended, is, of course, left undisturbed.

The carving out, from the exclusion mentioned in the preceding paragraph, of declarations relating to the execution, revocation, identification, or terms of declarant's will represents an *ad hoc* judgment which finds ample reinforcement in the decisions, resting on practical grounds of necessity and expediency rather than logic. McCormick § 271, pp. 577–578; Annot., 34 A.L.R.2d 588, 62 A.L.R.2d 855. A similar recognition of the need for and practical value of this kind of evidence is found in California Evidence Code § 1260.

REPORT OF THE HOUSE COMMITTEE ON THE JUDICIARY.

Rule 803(3) was approved in the form submitted by the Court to Congress. However, the Committee intends that the Rule be construed to limit the doctrine of Mutual Life Insurance Co. v. Hillmon, 145 U.S. 285, 295–300 (1892), so as to render statements of intent by a declarant admissible only to prove his future conduct, not the future conduct of another person.

ADVISORY COMMITTEE NOTE TO EXCEPTION (4).

Exception (4). Even those few jurisdictions which have shied away from generally admitting statements of present condition have allowed them if made to a physician for purposes of diagnosis and treatment in view of the patient's strong motivation to be truthful. McCormick § 266, p. 563. The same guarantee of trustworthiness extends to statements of past conditions and medical history, made for purposes of diagnosis or treatment. It also extends to statements as to causation, reasonably pertinent to the same purposes, in accord with the current trend, Shell Oil Co. v. Industrial Commission, 2 Ill.2d 590, 119 N.E.2d 224 (1954); McCormick § 266, p. 564; New Jersey Evidence Rule 63(12)(c).

Statements as to fault would not ordinarily qualify under this latter language. Thus a patient's statement that he was struck by an automobile would qualify but not his statement that the car was driven through a red light. Under the exception the statement need not have been made to a physician. Statements to hospital attendants, ambulance drivers, or even members of the family might be included.

Conventional doctrine has excluded from the hearsay exception, as not within its guarantee of truthfulness, statements to a physician consulted only for the purpose of enabling him to testify. While these statements were not admissible as substantive evidence, the expert was allowed to state the basis of his opinion, including statements of this kind. The distinction thus called for was one most unlikely to be made by juries. The rule accordingly rejects the limitation. This position is consistent with the provision of Rule 703 that the facts on which expert testimony is based need not be admissible in evidence if of a kind ordinarily relied upon by experts in the field.

REPORT OF THE HOUSE COMMITTEE ON THE JUDICIARY.

After giving particular attention to the question of physical examination made solely to enable a physician to testify, the Committee approved Rule 803(4) as submitted to Congress, with the understanding that it is not intended in any way to adversely affect present privilege rules or those subsequently adopted.

REPORT OF THE SENATE COMMITTEE ON THE JUDICIARY.

The House approved this rule as it was submitted by the Supreme Court "with the understanding that it is not intended in any way to adversely affect present privilege rules." We also approve this rule, and we would point out with respect to the question of its relation to privileges, it must be read in conjunction with rule 35 of the Federal Rules of Civil Procedure which provides that whenever the physical or mental condition of a party (plaintiff or defendant) is in controversy, the court may require him to submit to an examination by a physician. It is these examinations which will normally be admitted under this exception.

ADVISORY COMMITTEE NOTE TO EXCEPTION. (5).

Exception (5). A hearsay exception for recorded recollection is generally recognized and has been described as having "long been favored by the federal and practically all the state courts that have had occasion to decide the question." United States v. Kelly, 349 F.2d 720, 770 (2d Cir. 1965), citing numerous cases and sustaining the exception against a claimed denial of the right of confrontation. Many additional cases are cited in Annot., 82 A.L.R.2d 473, 520. The guarantee of trustworthiness is found in the reliability inherent in a record made while events were still fresh in mind and accurately reflecting them. Owens v. State, 67 Md. 307, 316, 10 A. 210, 212 (1887).

The principal controversy attending the exception has centered, not upon the propriety of the exception itself, but upon the question whether a preliminary requirement of impaired memory on the part of the witness should be imposed. The authorities are divided. If regard be had only to the accuracy of the evidence, admittedly impairment of the memory of the witness adds nothing to it and should not be required. McCormick § 277, p. 593; 3 Wigmore § 738, p. 76; Jordan v. People, 151 Colo. 133, 376 P.2d 699 (1962), *cert. denied*, 373 U.S. 944, 83 S.Ct. 1553, 10 L.Ed.2d 699; Hall v. State, 223 Md. 158, 162 A.2d 751 (1960); State v. Bindhammer, 44 N.J. 372, 209 A.2d 124 (1965). Nevertheless, the absence of the requirement, it is believed, would encourage the use of statements carefully prepared for purposes of litigation under the supervision of attorneys, investigators, or claim adjusters. Hence the example includes a requirement that the witness not have "sufficient recollection to enable him to testify fully and accurately." To the same effect are California Evidence Code § 1237 and New Jersey Rule 63(1)(b), and this has been the position of the federal courts. Vicksburg & Meridian R. R. v. O'Brien, 119 U.S. 99, 7 S.Ct. 118, 30 L. Ed. 299 (1886); Ahern v. Webb, 268 F.2d 45 (10th Cir. 1959); and *see* N. L. R. B. v. Hudson Pulp and Paper Corp., 273 F.2d 660, 665 (5th Cir. 1960); N. L. R. B. v. Federal Dairy Co., 297 F.2d 487 (1st Cir. 1962). *But cf.* United States v. Adams, 385 F.2d 548 (2d Cir. 1967).

No attempt is made in the exception to spell out the method of establishing the initial knowledge or the contemporaneity and accuracy of the record, leaving them to be dealt with as the circumstances of the particular case might indicate. Multiple person involvement in the process of observing and recording, as in Rathbun v. Brancatella, 107 A. 279, 93 N.J.L. 222 (1919), is entirely consistent with the exception.

Locating the exception at this place in the scheme of the rules is a matter of choice. There were two other possibilities. The first was to regard the statement as one of the group of prior statements of a testifying witness which are excluded entirely from the category of hearsay by Rule 801(d)(1). That category, however, requires that declarant be "subject to cross-examination," as to which the impaired memory aspect of the exception raises doubts. The other possibility was to include the exception among those covered by Rule 804. Since unavailability is required by that rule and lack of memory is listed as a species of unavailability by the definition of the term in Rule 804(a)(3), that treatment at first impression would seem appropriate. The fact is, however, that the unavailability requirement of the exception is of a limited and peculiar nature. Accordingly, the exception is located at this point rather than in the context of a rule where unavailability is conceived of more broadly.

REPORT OF THE HOUSE COMMITTEE ON THE JUDICIARY.

Rule 803(5) as submitted by the Court permitted the reading into evidence of a memorandum or record concerning a matter about which a witness once had knowledge but now has insufficient recollection to enable him to testify accurately and fully, "shown to have been made when the matter was fresh in his memory and to reflect that knowledge correctly." The House amended the rule to add the words "or adopted by the witness" after the phrase "shown to have been made," language parallel to the Jencks Act.[12]

The committee accepts the House amendment with the understanding and belief that it was not intended to narrow the scope of applicability of the rule. In fact, we understand it to clarify the rule's applicability to a memorandum adopted by the witness as well as one made by him. While the rule as submitted by the Court was silent on the question of who made the memorandum, we view the House amendment as a helpful clarification; noting, however, that the Advisory Committee's note to this rule suggests that the important thing is the accuracy of the memorandum rather than who made it.

The committee does not view the House amendment as precluding admissibility in situations in which multiple participants were involved.

When the verifying witness has not prepared the report, but merely examined it and found it accurate, he has adopted the report, and it is therefore admissible. The rule should also be interpreted to cover other situations involving multiple participants, e.g., employer dictating to secretary, secretary making memorandum at direction of employer, or information being passed along a chain of persons, as in[13]

The committee also accepts the understanding of the House that a memorandum or report, although barred under this rule, would nonetheless be admissible if it came within another hearsay exception. We consider this principle to be applicable to all the hearsay rules.

ADVISORY COMMITTEE NOTE TO EXCEPTION (6).

Exception (6) represents an area which has received much attention from those seeking to improve the law of evidence. The Commonwealth Fund Act was the result of a study completed in 1927 by a distinguished committee under the chairmanship of Professor Morgan. Morgan et al., The Law of Evidence: Some Proposals for its Reform 63 (1927). With

---

[12] 18 U.S.C. § 3500.

[13] Curtis v. Bradley, 65 Conn. 99, 31 Atl. 591 (1894). *See also* Rathbun v. Brancatella, 93 N.J.L. 222, 107 Atl. 279 (1919). *See, e.g.,* McCormick on Evidence, § 303 (2d ed. 1972).

changes too minor to mention, it was adopted by Congress in 1936 as the rule for federal courts. 28 U.S.C. § 1732. A number of states took similar action. The Commissioners on Uniform State Laws in 1936 promulgated the Uniform Business Records as Evidence Act, 9A U.L.A. 506, which has acquired a substantial following in the states. Model Code Rule 514 and Uniform Rule 63(13) also deal with the subject. Difference of varying degrees of importance exist among these various treatments.

These reform efforts were largely within the context of business and commercial records, as the kind usually encountered, and concentrated considerable attention upon relaxing the requirement of producing as witnesses, or accounting for the nonproduction of, all participants in the process of gathering, transmitting, and recording information which the common law had evolved as a burdensome and crippling aspect of using records of this type. In their areas of primary emphasis on witnesses to be called and the general admissibility of ordinary business and commercial records, the Commonwealth Fund Act and the Uniform Act appear to have worked well. The exception seeks to preserve their advantages.

On the subject of what witnesses must be called, the Commonwealth Fund Act eliminated the common law requirement of calling or accounting for all participants by failing to mention it. United States v. Mortimer, 118 F.2d 266 (2d Cir. 1941); La Porte v. United States, 300 F.2d 878 (9th Cir. 1962); McCormick § 290, p. 608. Model Code Rule 514 and Uniform Rule 63(13) did likewise. The Uniform Act, however, abolished the common law requirement in express terms, providing that the requisite foundation testimony might be furnished by "the custodian or other qualified witness." Uniform Business Records as Evidence Act, § 2; 9A U.L.A. 506. The exception follows the Uniform Act in this respect.

The element of unusual reliability of business records is said variously to be supplied by systematic checking, by regularity and continuity which produce habits of precision, by actual experience of business in relying upon them, or by a duty to make an accurate record as part of a continuing job or occupation. McCormick §§ 281, 286, 287; Laughlin, Business Entries and the Like, 46 Iowa L.Rev. 276 (1961). The model statutes and rules have sought to capture these factors and to extend their impact by employing the phrase "regular course of business," in conjunction with a definition of "business" far broader than its ordinarily accepted meaning. The result is a tendency unduly to emphasize a requirement of routineness and repetitiveness and an insistence that other types of records be squeezed into the fact patterns which give rise to traditional business records. The rule therefore adopts the phrase "the course of a regularly conducted activity" as capturing the essential basis of the hearsay exception as it has evolved and the essential element which can be abstracted from the various specifications of what is a "business."

Amplification of the kinds of activities producing admissible records has given rise to problems which conventional business records by their nature avoid. They are problems of the source of the recorded information, of entries in opinion form, of motivation, and of involvement as participant in the matters recorded.

Sources of information presented no substantial problem with ordinary business records. All participants, including the observer or participant furnishing the information to be recorded, were acting routinely, under a duty of accuracy, with employer reliance on the result, or in short "in the regular course of business." If, however, the supplier of the information does not act in the regular course, an essential link is broken; the assurance of accuracy does not extend to the information itself, and the fact that it may be recorded with scrupulous accuracy is of no avail. An illustration is the police report incorporating information obtained from a bystander: the officer qualifies as acting in the regular course but the informant does not. The leading case, Johnson v. Lutz, 253 N.Y. 124, 170 N.E. 517 (1930), held that a report thus prepared was inadmissible. Most of the authorities have agreed with the decision. Gencarella v. Fyfe, 171 F.2d 419 (1st Cir. 1948); Gordon v. Robinson, 210 F.2d 192 (3d Cir. 1954); Standard Oil Co. of California v. Moore, 251 F.2d 188, 214 (9th Cir. 1957), *cert. denied*, 356 U.S. 975, 78 S.Ct. 1139, 2 L.Ed.2d 1148; Yates v. Bair Transport, Inc., 249 F. Supp. 681 (S.D.N.Y. 1965); Annot., 69 A.L.R.2d 1148. *Cf.* Hawkins v. Gorea Motor Express, Inc., 360 F.2d 933 (2d Cir. 1966). *Contra*, 5 Wigmore § 1530a, n. 1, pp. 391–392. The point is not dealt with specifically in the Commonwealth Fund Act, the Uniform Act, or Uniform Rule 63(13). However, Model Code Rule 514 contains the requirement "that it was the regular course of that business for one with personal knowledge . . . to make such a memorandum or record or to transmit information thereof to be included in such a memorandum or record . . . ." The rule follows this lead in requiring an informant with knowledge acting in the course of the regularly conducted activity.

Entries in the form of opinions were not encountered in traditional business records in view of the purely factual nature of the items recorded, but they are now commonly encountered with respect to medical diagnoses, prognoses, and test results, as well as occasionally in other areas. The Commonwealth Fund Act provided only for records of an "act, transaction, occurrence, or event," while the Uniform Act, Model Code Rule 514, and Uniform Rule 63(13) merely added the ambiguous term "condition." The limited phrasing of the Commonwealth Fund Act, 28 U.S.C. § 1732, may account for the reluctance of some federal decisions to admit diagnostic entries. New York Life Ins. Co. v. Taylor, 147 F.2d 297, 79 U.S.App.D.C. 66 (1945); Lyles v. United States, 254 F.2d 725, 103 U.S.App.D.C. 22 (1957), *cert. denied*, 356 U.S. 961, 78 S.Ct. 997, 2 L.Ed.2d 1067; England v. United States, 174 F.2d 466 (5th Cir. 1949); Skogen v. Dow Chemical Co., 375 F.2d 692 (8th Cir. 1967). Other federal decisions, however, experienced no difficulty in freely admitting diagnostic entries. Reed v. Order of United Commercial Travelers, 123 F.2d 252 (2d Cir. 1941); Buckminster's Estate v. Commissioner of Internal Revenue, 147 F.2d 331 (2d Cir. 1944); Medina v. Erickson, 226 F.2d 475 (9th Cir. 1955); Thomas v. Hogan, 308 F.2d 355 (4th Cir. 1962); Glawe v. Rulon, 284 F.2d 495 (8th Cir. 1960). In the state courts, the trend favors admissibility. Borucki v. MacKenzie Bros. Co., 125 Conn. 92, 3 A.2d 224 (1938); Allen v. St. Louis Public Service Co., 365 Mo. 677, 285 S.W.2d 663, 55 A.L.R.2d 1022 (1956); People v. Kohlmeyer, 284 N.Y. 366, 31 N.E.2d 490 (1940); Weis v. Weis, 147 OS 416, 72 N.E.2d 245 (1947). In order to make clear its adherence to the latter position, the rule specifically includes both diagnoses and opinions, in addition to acts, events, and conditions, as proper subjects of admissible entries.

Problems of the motivation of the informant have been a source of difficulty and disagreement. In Palmer v. Hoffman, 318 U.S. 109, 63 S.Ct. 477, 87 L. Ed. 645 (1943), exclusion of an accident report made by the since deceased engineer, offered by defendant railroad trustees in a grade crossing collision case, was upheld. The report was not "in the regular course of business," not a record of the systematic conduct of the business as a business, said the Court. The report was prepared for use in litigating, not railroading. While the opinion mentions the motivation of the engineer only obliquely, the emphasis on records of routine operations is significant only by virtue of impact on motivation to be accurate. Absence of routineness raises lack of motivation to be accurate. The opinion of the Court of Appeals had gone beyond mere lack of motive to be accurate: the engineer's statement was "dripping with motivations to misrepresent." Hoffman v. Palmer, 129 F.2d 976, 991 (2d Cir. 1942). The direct introduction of motivation is a disturbing factor, since absence of motive to misrepresent has not traditionally been a requirement of the rule; that records might be self-serving has not been a ground for exclusion. Laughlin, Business Records and the Like, 46 Iowa L.Rev. 276, 285 (1961). As Judge Clark said in his dissent, "I submit that there is hardly a grocer's account book which could not be excluded on that basis." 129 F.2d at 1002. A physician's evaluation report of a personal injury litigant would appear to be in the routine of his business. If the report is offered by the party at whose instance it was made, however, it has been held inadmissible, Yates v. Bair Transport, Inc., 249 F. Supp. 681 (S.D.N.Y.1965), otherwise if offered by the opposite party, Korte v. New York, N. H. & H. R. Co., 191 F.2d 86 (2d Cir. 1951), *cert. denied,* 342 U.S. 868, 72 S.Ct. 108, 96 L. Ed. 652.

The decisions hinge on motivation and which party is entitled to be concerned about it. Professor McCormick believed that the doctor's report or the accident report were sufficiently routine to justify admissibility. McCormick § 287, p. 604. Yet hesitation must be experienced in admitting everything which is observed and recorded in the course of a regularly conducted activity. Efforts to set a limit are illustrated by Hartzog v. United States, 217 F.2d 706 (4th Cir. 1954), error to admit worksheets made by since deceased deputy collector in preparation for the instant income tax evasion prosecution, and United States v. Ware, 247 F.2d 698 (7th Cir. 1957), error to admit narcotics agents' records of purchases. *See also* Exception (8), *infra* as to the public record aspects of records of this nature. Some decisions have been satisfied as to motivation of an accident report if made pursuant to statutory duty, United States v. New York Foreign Trade Zone Operators, 304 F.2d 792 (2d Cir. 1962); Taylor v. Baltimore & O. R. Co., 344 F.2d 281 (2d Cir. 1965), since the report was oriented in a direction other than the litigation which ensued. *Cf.* Matthews v. United States, 217 F.2d 409 (5th Cir. 1954). The formulation of specific terms which would assure satisfactory results in all cases is not possible. Consequently the rule proceeds from the base that records made in the course of a regularly conducted activity will be taken as admissible but subject to authority to exclude if "the sources of information or other circumstances indicate lack of trustworthiness."

Occasional decisions have reached for enhanced accuracy by requiring involvement as a participant in matters reported. Clainos v. United States, 163 F.2d 593, 82 U.S.App.D.C. 278 (1947), error to admit police records of convictions; Standard Oil Co. of California v. Moore, 251 F.2d 188 (9th Cir. 1957), *cert. denied,* 356 U.S. 975, 78 S.Ct. 1139, 2 L.Ed.2d 1148, error to admit employees' records of observed business practices of others. The rule includes no requirement of this nature. Wholly acceptable records may involve matters merely observed, e.g. the weather.

The form which the "record" may assume under the rule is described broadly as a "memorandum, report, record, or data compilation, in any form." The expression "data compilation" is used as broadly descriptive of any means of storing information other than the conventional words and figures in written or documentary form. It includes, but is by no means limited to, electronic computer storage. The term is borrowed from revised Rule 34(a) of the Rules of Civil Procedure.

NOTES OF ADVISORY COMMITTEE ON 2000 AMENDMENTS.

The amendment provides that the foundation requirements of Rule 803(6) can be satisfied under certain circumstances without the expense and inconvenience of producing time-consuming foundation witnesses. Under current law, courts have generally required foundation witnesses to testify. *See, e.g.*, Tongil Co., Ltd. v. Hyundai Merchant Marine Corp., 968 F.2d 999 (9th Cir. 1992) (reversing a judgment based on business records where a qualified person filed an affidavit but did not testify). Protections are provided by the authentication requirements of Rule 902(11) for domestic records, Rule 902(12) for foreign records in civil cases, and 18 U.S.C. § 3505 for foreign records in criminal cases.

REPORT OF THE HOUSE COMMITTEE ON THE JUDICIARY.

Rule 803(6) as submitted by the Court permitted a record made "in the course of a regularly conducted activity" to be admissible in certain circumstances. The Committee believed there were insufficient guarantees of reliability in records made in the course of activities falling outside the scope of "business" activities as that term is broadly defined in 28 U.S.C. 1732. Moreover, the Committee concluded that the additional requirement of Section 1732 that it must have been the regular practice of a business to make the record is a necessary further assurance of its trustworthiness. The Committee accordingly amended the Rule to incorporate these limitations.

REPORT OF THE SENATE COMMITTEE ON THE JUDICIARY.

[Note, that the Senate effort to delete references to "business" in the House-passed version of Rule 803(6), described above, did not survive enactment.]

Rule 803(6) as submitted by the Supreme Court permitted a record made in the course of a regularly conducted activity to be admissible in certain circumstances. This rule constituted a broadening of the traditional business records hearsay exception which has been long advocated by scholars and judges active in the law of evidence.

The House felt there were insufficient guarantees of reliability of records not within a broadly defined business records exception. We disagree. Even under the House definition of "business" including profession, occupation, and "calling of every kind," the records of many regularly conducted activities will, or may be, excluded from evidence. Under the principle of *ejusdem generis*, the intent of "calling of every kind" would seem to be related to work-related endeavors—e.g., butcher, baker, artist, etc.

Thus, it appears that the records of many institutions or groups might not be admissible under the House amendments. For example, schools, and hospitals will not normally be considered businesses within the definition. Yet, these are groups which keep financial and other records on a regular basis in a manner similar to business enterprises. We believe these records are of equivalent trustworthiness and should be admitted into evidence.

Three states, which have recently codified their evidence rules, have adopted the Supreme Court version of Rule 803(6), providing for admission of memoranda of a "regularly conducted activity." None adopted the words "business activity" used in the House amendment.[14]

Therefore, the committee deleted the word "business" as it appears before the word "activity." The last sentence then is unnecessary and was also deleted.

It is the understanding of the committee that the use of the phrase "person with knowledge" is not intended to imply that the party seeking to introduce the memorandum, report, record, or data compilation must be able to produce, or even identify, the specific individual upon whose first-hand knowledge the memorandum, report, record or data compilation was based. A sufficient foundation for the introduction of such evidence will be laid if the party seeking to introduce the evidence is able to show that it was the regular practice of the activity to base such memorandums, reports, records, or data compilations upon a transmission from a person with knowledge, e.g., in the case of the content of a shipment of goods, upon a report from the company's receiving agent or in the case of a computer printout, upon a report from the company's computer programmer or one who has knowledge of the particular record system. In short, the scope of the phrase "person with knowledge" is meant to be coterminous with the custodian of the evidence or other qualified witness. The committee believes this represents the desired rule in light of the complex nature of modern business organizations.

REPORT OF THE HOUSE/SENATE CONFERENCE COMMITTEE.

The House bill provides in subsection (6) that records of a regularly conducted "business" activity qualify for admission into evidence as an exception to the hearsay rule. "Business" is defined as including "business, profession, occupation and calling of every kind." The Senate amendment drops the requirement that the records be those of a "business" activity and eliminates the definition of "business." The Senate amendment provides that records are admissible if they are records of a regularly conducted "activity."

The Conference adopts the House provision that the records must be

---

[14] *See* Nev. Rev. Stats. § 15.135; N. Mex. Stats. (1973 Supp.) § 20-4-803 (6); West's Wis. Stats. Anno. (1973 Supp.) w 908.03 (6).

those of a regularly conducted "business" activity. The Conferees changed the definition of "business" contained in the House provision in order to make it clear that the records of institutions and associations like schools, churches and hospitals are admissible under this provision. The records of public schools and hospitals are also covered by Rule 803(8), which deals with public records and reports.

ADVISORY COMMITTEE NOTE TO EXCEPTION (7).

Exception (7). Failure of a record to mention a matter which would ordinarily be mentioned is satisfactory evidence of its nonexistence. Uniform Rule 63(14), Comment. While probably not hearsay as defined in Rule 801, *supra*, decisions may be found which class the evidence not only as hearsay but also as not within any exception. In order to set the question at rest in favor of admissibility, it is specifically treated here. McCormick § 289, p. 609; Morgan, Basic Problems of Evidence 314 (1962); 5 Wigmore § 1531; Uniform Rule 63(14); California Evidence Code § 1272; Kansas Code of Civil Procedure § 60-460(n); New Jersey Evidence Rule 63(14).

REPORT OF THE HOUSE COMMITTEE ON THE JUDICIARY.

Rule 803(7) as submitted by the Court concerned the *absence* of entry in the records of a "regularly conducted activity." The Committee amended this Rule to conform with its action with respect to Rule 803(6).

ADVISORY COMMITTEE NOTE TO EXCEPTION (8).

[Note, that Rule 803(8) was significantly amended on the floor of the House, and that the House-passed amendments were ultimately adopted by Congress in the enacted version of this provision. Those amendments affect clause (b) of Rule 803(8).]

Exception (8). Public records are a recognized hearsay exception at common law and have been the subject of statutes without number. McCormick § 291. *See*, for example, 28 U.S.C. § 1733, the relative narrowness of which is illustrated by its nonapplicability to nonfederal public agencies, thus necessitating resort to the less appropriate business record exception to the hearsay rule. Kay v. United States, 255 F.2d 476 (4th Cir. 1958). The rule makes no distinction between federal and nonfederal offices and agencies.

Justification for the exception is the assumption that a public official will perform his duty properly and the unlikelihood that he will remember details independently of the record. Wong Wing Foo v. McGrath, 196 F.2d 120 (9th Cir. 1952), and *see* Chesapeake & Delaware Canal Co. v. United States, 250 U.S. 123, 39 S.Ct. 407, 63 L. Ed. 889 (1919). As to items (a) and (b), further support is found in the reliability factors underlying records of regularly conducted activities generally. *See* Exception (6), *supra*.

(a) Cases illustrating the admissibility of records of the office's or agency's own activities are numerous. Chesapeake & Delaware Canal Co. v. United States, 250 U.S. 123, 39 S.Ct. 407, 63 L. Ed. 889 (1919), Treasury records of miscellaneous receipts and disbursements; Howard v. Perrin, 200 U.S. 71, 26 S.Ct. 195, 50 L. Ed. 374 (1906), General Land Office records; Ballew v. United States, 160 U.S. 187, 16 S.Ct. 263, 40 L. Ed. 388 (1895), Pension Office records.

(b) Cases sustaining admissibility of records of matters observed are also numerous. United States v. Van Hook, 284 F.2d 489 (7th Cir. 1960), remanded for resentencing 365 U.S. 609, 81 S.Ct. 823, 5 L.Ed.2d 821, letter from induction officer to District Attorney, pursuant to army regulations, stating fact and circumstances of refusal to be inducted; T'Kach v. United States, 242 F.2d 937 (5th Cir. 1957), affidavit of White House personnel officer that search of records showed no employment of accused, charged with fraudulently representing himself as an envoy of the President; Minnehaha County v. Kelley, 150 F.2d 356 (8th Cir. 1945); Weather Bureau records of rainfall; United States v. Meyer, 113 F.2d 387 (7th Cir. 1940), *cert. denied*, 311 U.S. 706, 61 S.Ct. 174, 85 L. Ed. 459, map prepared by government engineer from information furnished by men working under his supervision.

(c) The more controversial area of public records is that of the so-called "evaluative" report. The disagreement among the decisions has been due in part, no doubt, to the variety of situations encountered, as well as to differences in principle. Sustaining admissibility are such cases as United States v. Dumas, 149 U.S. 278, 13 S.Ct. 872, 37 L. Ed. 734 (1893), statement of account certified by Postmaster General in action against postmaster; McCarty v. United States, 185 F.2d 520 (5th Cir. 1950), reh. denied 187 F.2d 234, Certificate of Settlement of General Accounting Office showing indebtedness and letter from Army official stating Government had performed, in action on contract to purchase and remove waste food from Army camp; Morgan v. Pittsburgh-Des Moines Steel Co., 183 F.2d 467 (3d Cir. 1950), report of Bureau of Mines as to cause of gas tank explosion; Petition of W-, 164 F. Supp. 659 (E.D.Pa.1958), report by Immigration and Naturalization Service investigator that petitioner was known in community as wife of man to whom she was not married. To the opposite effect and denying admissibility are Franklin v. Skelly Oil Co., 141 F.2d 568 (10th Cir. 1944), State Fire Marshal's report of cause of gas explosion; Lomax Transp. Co. v. United States, 183 F.2d 331 (9th Cir. 1950), Certificate of Settlement from General Accounting Office in action for naval supplies lost in warehouse fire; Yung Jin Teung v. Dulles, 229 F.2d 244 (2d Cir. 1956), "Status Reports" offered to justify delay in processing passport applications. Police reports have generally been excluded except to the extent to which they incorporate firsthand observations of the officer. Annot., 69 A.L.R.2d 1148. Various kinds of evaluative reports are admissible under federal statutes: 7 U.S.C. § 78, findings of Secretary of Agriculture prima facie evidence of true grade of grain; 7 U.S.C. § 210(f), findings of Secretary of Agriculture prima facie evidence in action for damages against stockyard owner; 7 U.S.C. § 292, order by Secretary of Agriculture prima facie evidence in judicial enforcement proceedings against producers association monopoly, 7 U.S.C. § 1622(h), Department of Agriculture inspection certificates of products shipped in interstate commerce prima facie evidence; 8 U.S.C. § 1440(c), separation of alien from military service on conditions other than honorable provable by certificate from department in proceedings to revoke citizenship; 18 U.S.C. § 4245, certificate of Director of Prisons that convicted person has been examined and found probably incompetent at time of trial prima facie evidence in court hearing on competency; 42 U.S.C. § 269(b), bill of health by appropriate official prima facie evidence of vessel's sanitary history and condition and compliance with regulations; 46 U.S.C. § 679, certificate of consul presumptive evidence of refusal of master to transport destitute seamen to United States. While these statutory exceptions to the hearsay rule are left undisturbed, Rule 802, the willingness of Congress to recognize a substantial measure of admissibility for evaluative reports is a helpful guide.

> Factors which may be of assistance in passing upon the admissibility of evaluative reports include: (1) the timeliness of the investigation, McCormick, Can the Courts Make Wider Use of Reports of Official Investigations? 42 Iowa L.Rev. 363 (1957); (2) the special skill or experience of the official, id., (3) whether a hearing was held and the level at which conducted, Franklin v. Skelly Oil Co., 141 F.2d 568 (10th Cir. 1944); (4) possible motivation problems suggested by Palmer v. Hoffman, 318 U.S. 109, 63 S.Ct. 477, 87 L. Ed. 645 (1943). Others no doubt could be added.

The formulation of an approach which would give appropriate weight to all possible factors in every situation is an obvious impossibility. Hence the rule, as in Exception (6), assumes admissibility in the first instance but with ample provision for escape if sufficient negative factors are present. In one respect, however, the rule with respect to evaluative reports under item (c) is very specific: they are admissible only in civil cases and against the government in criminal cases in view of the almost certain collision with confrontation rights which would result from their use against the accused in a criminal case.

REPORT OF THE SENATE COMMITTEE ON THE JUDICIARY.

[Note, that the amendment to Rule 803(8) described below, which was

proposed by the Senate Judiciary Committee and which would have added a reference to proposed Rule 804(b)(5), was ultimately rejected by the Conference Committee, and did not become part of Rule 803(8) as enacted. The proposed Rule 804(b)(5) was also rejected by Congress, and is not the Rule 804(b)(5) which Congress enacted.]

The House approved Rule 803(8), as submitted by the Supreme Court, with one substantive change. It excluded from the hearsay exception reports containing matters observed by police officers and other law enforcement personnel in criminal cases. Ostensibly, the reason for this exclusion is that observations by police officers at the scene of the crime or the apprehension of the defendant are not as reliable as observations by public officials in other cases because of the adversarial nature of the confrontation between the police and the defendant in criminal cases.

The committee accepts the House's decision to exclude such recorded observations where the police officer is available to testify in court about his observation. However, where he is unavailable as unavailability is defined in rule 804 (a)(4) and (a)(5), the report should be admitted as the best available evidence. Accordingly, the committee has amended rule 803(8) to refer to the provision of rule 804(b)(5), which allows the admission of such reports, records or other statements where the police officer or other law enforcement officer is unavailable because of death, then existing physical or mental illness or infirmity, or not being successfully subject to legal process.

The House Judiciary Committee report contained a statement of intent that "the phrase 'factual findings' in subdivision (c) be. strictly construed and that evaluations or opinions contained in public reports shall not be admissible under this rule." The committee takes strong exception to this limiting understanding of the application of the rule. We do not think it reflects an understanding of the intended operation of the rule as explained in the ADVISORY COMMITTEE NOTES to this subsection. The ADVISORY COMMITTEE NOTES on subsection (c) of this subdivision point out that various kinds of evaluative reports are now admissible under Federal statutes. 7 U.S.C. § 78, findings of Secretary of Agriculture prima facie evidence of true grade of grain; 42 U.S.C. § 269(b), bill of health by appropriate official prima facie evidence of vessel's sanitary history and condition and compliance with regulations. These statutory exceptions to the hearsay rule are preserved. Rule 802. The willingness of Congress to recognize these and other such evaluative reports provides a helpful guide in determining the kind of reports which are intended to be admissible under this rule. We think the restrictive interpretation of the House overlooks the fact that while the Advisory Committee assumes admissibility in the first instance of evaluative reports, they are not admissible if, as the Rule states, "the sources of information or other circumstances indicate lack of trustworthiness."

The Advisory Committee explains the factors to be considered:

* * * * *

Factors which may be assistance in passing upon the admissibility of evaluative reports include: (1) the timeliness of the investigation, McCormick, Can the Courts Make Wider Use of Reports of Official Investigations? 42 Iowa L. Rev. 363 (1957); (2) the special skill or experience of the official, id.; (3) whether a hearing was held and the level at which conducted, Franklin v. Skelly Oil Co., 141 F. 2d 568 (10th Cir. 1944); (4) possible motivation problems suggested by Palmer v. Hoffman, 318 U.S. 109, 63 S.Ct. 477, 87 L. Ed. 645 (1943). Others no doubt could be added.[15]

* * * * *

The committee concludes that the language of the rule together with the explanation provided by the Advisory Committee furnish sufficient guidance on the admissibility of evaluative reports.

REPORT OF THE HOUSE/SENATE CONFERENCE COMMITTEE.

The Senate amendment adds language, not contained in the House bill, that refers to another rule that was added by the Senate in another amendment (Rule 804(b)(5)—Criminal law enforcement records and reports).

In view of its action on Rule 804(b)(5) (Criminal law enforcement records and reports), the Conference does not adopt the Senate amendment and restores the bill to the House version.

ADVISORY COMMITTEE NOTE TO EXCEPTION (9).

Exception (9). Records of vital statistics are commonly the subject of particular statutes making them admissible in evidence, Uniform Vital Statistics Act, 9C U.L.A. 350 (1957). The rule is in principle narrower than Uniform Rule 63(16) which includes reports required of persons performing functions authorized by statute, yet in practical effect the two are substantially the same. Comment Uniform Rule 63(16). The exception as drafted is in the pattern of California Evidence Code § 1281.

ADVISORY COMMITTEE NOTE TO EXCEPTION (10).

Exception (10). The principle of proving nonoccurrence of an event by evidence of the absence of a record which would regularly be made of its occurrence, developed in Exception (7) with respect to regularly

---

[15] H. Rept. 93-1650, at p. 15.

conducted activities, is here extended to public records of the kind mentioned in Exceptions (8) and (9). 5 Wigmore § 1633(6), p. 519. Some harmless duplication no doubt exists with Exception (7). For instances of federal statutes recognizing this method of proof, *see* 8 U.S.C. § 1284(b), proof of absence of alien crewman's name from outgoing manifest prima facie evidence of failure to detain or deport, and 42 U.S.C. § 405(c)(3), (4)(B), (4)(C), absence of HEW record prima facie evidence of no wages or self-employment income.

The rule includes situations in which absence of a record may itself be the ultimate focal point of inquiry, *e.g.* People v. Love, 310 Ill. 558, 142 N.E. 204 (1923), certificate of Secretary of State admitted to show failure to file documents required by Securities Law, as well as cases where the absence of a record is offered as proof of the nonoccurrence of an event ordinarily recorded.

The refusal of the common law to allow proof by certificate of the lack of a record or entry has no apparent justification, 5 Wigmore § 1678(7), p. 752. The rule takes the opposite position, as do Uniform Rule 63(17); California Evidence Code § 1284; Kansas Code of Civil Procedure § 60-460(c); New Jersey Evidence Rule 63(17). Congress has recognized certification as evidence of the lack of a record. 8 U.S.C. § 1360(d), certificate of Attorney General or other designated officer that no record of Immigration and Naturalization Service of specified nature or entry therein is found, admissible in alien cases.

ADVISORY COMMITTEE NOTE TO EXCEPTION (11).

Exception (11). Records of activities of religious organizations are currently recognized as admissible at least to the extent of the business records exception to the hearsay rule, 5 Wigmore § 1523, p. 371, and Exception (6) would be applicable. However, both the business record doctrine and Exception (6) require that the person furnishing the information be one in the business or activity. The result is such decisions as Daily v. Grand Lodge, 311 Ill. 184, 142 N.E. 478 (1924), holding a church record admissible to prove fact, date, and place of baptism, but not age of child except that he had at least been born at the time. In view of the unlikelihood that false information would be furnished on occasions of this kind, the rule contains no requirement that the informant be in the course of the activity. *See* California Evidence Code § 1315 and Comment.

Exception (12). The principle of proof by certification is recognized as to public officials in Exceptions (8) and (10), and with respect to authentication in Rule 902. The present exception is a duplication to the extent that it deals with a certificate by a public official, as in the case of a judge who performs a marriage ceremony. The area covered by the rule is, however, substantially larger and extends the certification procedure to clergymen and the like who perform marriages and other ceremonies or administer sacraments. Thus certificates of such matters as baptism or confirmation, as well as marriage, are included. In principle they are as acceptable evidence as certificates of public officers. *See* 5 Wigmore § 1645, as to marriage certificates. When the person executing the certificate is not a public official, the self-authenticating character of documents purporting to emanate from public officials, *see* Rule 902, is lacking and proof is required that the person was authorized and did make the certificate. The time element, however, may safely be taken as supplied by the certificate, once authority and authenticity are established, particularly in view of the presumption that a document was executed on the date it bears.

For similar rules, some limited to certificates of marriage, with variations in foundation requirements, *see* Uniform Rule 63(18); California Evidence Code § 1316; Kansas Code of Civil Procedure § 60-460(p); New Jersey Evidence Rule 63(18).

Exception (13). Records of family history kept in family Bibles have by long tradition been received in evidence. 5 Wigmore §§ 1495, 1496, citing numerous statutes and decisions. *See also* Regulations, Social Security Administration, 20 C.F.R. § 404.703(c), recognizing family Bible entries as proof of age in the absence of public or church records. Opinions in the area also include inscriptions on tombstones, publicly displayed pedigrees, and engravings on rings. Wigmore, *supra.* The rule is substantially identical in coverage with California Evidence Code § 1312.

REPORT OF THE HOUSE COMMITTEE ON THE JUDICIARY.

The Committee approved this Rule in the form submitted by the Court, intending that the phrase "Statements of fact concerning personal or family history" be read to include the specific types of such statements enumerated in Rule 803(11).

ADVISORY COMMITTEE NOTE TO EXCEPTION (14).

Exception (14). The recording of title documents is a purely statutory development. Under any theory of the admissibility of public records, the records would be receivable as evidence of the contents of the recorded document, else the recording process would be reduced to a nullity. When, however, the record is offered for the further purpose of proving execution and delivery, a problem of lack of first-hand knowledge by the recorder, not present as to contents, is presented. This problem is solved, seemingly in all jurisdictions, by qualifying for recording only those documents shown by a specified procedure, either acknowledgement or a form of probate, to have been executed and delivered. 5 Wigmore §§ 1647–1651. Thus what may appear in the rule, at first glance, as endowing the record with an effect independently of local law and inviting difficulties of an Erie nature under Cities Service Oil Co. v. Dunlap, 308 U.S. 208, 60 S.Ct. 201, 84 L. Ed. 196 (1939), is not present, since the local law in fact governs under the example.

ADVISORY COMMITTEE NOTE TO EXCEPTION (15).

Exception (15). Dispositive documents often contain recitals of fact. Thus a deed purporting to have been executed by an attorney in fact may recite the existence of the power of attorney, or a deed may recite that the grantors are all the heirs of the last record owner. Under the rule, these recitals are exempted from the hearsay rule. The circumstances under which dispositive documents are executed and the requirement that the recital be germane to the purpose of the document are believed to be adequate guarantees of trustworthiness, particularly in view of the nonapplicability of the rule if dealings with the property have been inconsistent with the document. The age of the document is of no significance, though in practical application the document will most often be an ancient one. *See* Uniform Rule 63(29), Comment.

Similar provisions are contained in Uniform Rule 63(29); California Evidence Code § 1330; Kansas Code of Civil Procedure § 60-460(aa); New Jersey Evidence Rule 63(29).

ADVISORY COMMITTEE NOTE TO EXCEPTION (16).

Exception (16). Authenticating a document as ancient, essentially in the pattern of the common law, as provided in Rule 901(b)(8), leaves open as a separate question the admissibility of assertive statements contained therein as against a hearsay objection. 7 Wigmore § 2145a. Wigmore further states that the ancient document technique of authentication is universally conceded to apply to all sorts of documents, including letters, records, contracts, maps, and certificates, in addition to title documents, citing numerous decisions. *Id.* § 2145. Since most of these items are significant evidentially only insofar as they are assertive, their admission in evidence must be as a hearsay exception. *But see* 5 *id.* § 1573, p. 429, referring to recitals in ancient deeds as a "limited" hearsay exception. The former position is believed to be the correct one in reason and authority. As pointed out in McCormick § 298, danger of mistake is minimized by authentication requirements, and age affords assurance that the writing antedates the present controversy. *See* Dallas County v. Commercial Union Assurance Co., 286 F.2d 388 (5th Cir. 1961), upholding admissibility of 58-year-old newspaper story. *Cf.* Morgan, Basic Problems of Evidence 364 (1962), *but see id.* 254.

For a similar provision, but with the added requirement that "the statement has since generally been acted upon as true by persons having an interest in the matter," *see* California Evidence Code § 1331.

ADVISORY COMMITTEE NOTE TO EXCEPTION (17).

Exception (17). Ample authority at common law supported the admission in evidence of items falling in this category. While Wigmore's text is narrowly oriented to lists, etc., prepared for the use of a trade or profession, 6 Wigmore § 1702, authorities are cited which include other kinds of publications, for example, newspaper market reports, telephone directories, and city directories. *Id.* §§ 1702–1706. The basis of trustworthiness is general reliance by the public or by a particular segment of it, and the motivation of the compiler to foster reliance by being accurate.

For similar provisions, *see* Uniform Rule 63(30); California Evidence Code § 1340; Kansas Code of Civil Procedure § 60-460(bb); New Jersey Evidence Rule 63(30). Uniform Commercial Code § 2-724 provides for admissibility in evidence of "reports in official publications or trade journals or in newspapers or periodicals of general circulation published as the reports of such [established commodity] market."

ADVISORY COMMITTEE NOTE TO EXCEPTION (18).

Exception (18). The writers have generally favored the admissibility of learned treatises, McCormick § 296, p. 621; Morgan, Basic Problems of Evidence 366 (1962); 6 Wigmore § 1692, with the support of occasional decisions and rules, City of Dothan v. Hardy, 237 Ala. 603, 188 So. 264 (1939); Lewandowski v. Preferred Risk Mut. Ins. Co., 33 Wis.2d 69, 146 N.W.2d 505 (1966), 66 Mich.L.Rev. 183 (1967); Uniform Rule 63(31); Kansas Code of Civil Procedure § 60-460(cc), but the great weight of authority has been that learned treatises are not admissible as substantive evidence though usable in the cross-examination of experts. The foundation of the minority view is that the hearsay objection must be regarded as unimpressive when directed against treatises since a high standard of accuracy is engendered by various factors: the treatise is written primarily and impartially for professionals, subject to scrutiny and exposure for inaccuracy, with the reputation of the writer at stake. 6 Wigmore § 1692. Sound as this position may be with respect to trustworthiness, there is, nevertheless, an additional difficulty in the likelihood that the treatise will be misunderstood and misapplied without expert assistance and supervision. This difficulty is recognized in the cases demonstrating unwillingness to sustain findings relative to disability on the basis of judicially noticed medical texts. Ross v. Gardner, 365 F.2d 554 (6th Cir. 1966); Sayers v. Gardner, 380 F.2d 940 (6th Cir. 1967); Colwell v. Gardner, 386 F.2d 56 (6th Cir. 1967); Glendenning v. Ribicoff, 213 F. Supp. 301 (W.D.Mo.1962); Cook v. Celebreeze, 217 F. Supp. 366 (W.D.Mo.1963); Sosna v. Celebreeze, 234 F.Supp 289 (E.D.Pa.1964); and *see* McDaniel

v. Celebrezze, 331 F.2d 426 (4th Cir. 1964). The rule avoids the danger of misunderstanding and misapplication by limiting the use of treatises as substantive evidence to situations in which an expert is on the stand and available to explain and assist in the application of the treatise if desired. The limitation upon receiving the publication itself physically in evidence, contained in the last sentence, is designed to further this policy.

The relevance of the use of treatises on cross-examination is evident. This use of treatises has been the subject of varied views. The most restrictive position is that the witness must have stated expressly on direct his reliance upon the treatise. A slightly more liberal approach still insists upon reliance but allows it to be developed on cross-examination. Further relaxation dispenses with reliance but requires recognition as an authority by the witness, developable on cross-examination. The greatest liberality is found in decisions allowing use of the treatise on cross-examination when its status as an authority is established by any means. Annot., 60 A.L.R.2d 77. The exception is hinged upon this last position, which is that of the Supreme Court, Reilly v. Pinkus, 338 U.S. 269, 70 S.Ct. 110, 94 L. Ed. 63 (1949), and of recent well considered state court decisions, City of St. Petersburg v. Ferguson, 193 So.2d 648 (Fla.App.1967), *cert. denied*, Fla., 201 So.2d 556; Darling v. Charleston Memorial Community Hospital, 33 Ill.2d 326, 211 N.E.2d 253 (1965); Dabroe v. Rhodes Co., 64 Wash.2d 431, 392 P.2d 317 (1964).

In Reilly v. Pinkus, *supra*, the Court pointed out that testing of professional knowledge was incomplete without exploration of the witness' knowledge of and attitude toward established treatises in the field. The process works equally well in reverse and furnishes the basis of the rule.

The rule does not require that the witness rely upon or recognize the treatise as authoritative, thus avoiding the possibility that the expert may at the outset block cross-examination by refusing to concede reliance or authoritativeness. Dabroe v. Rhodes Co., *supra*. Moreover, the rule avoids the unreality of admitting evidence for the purpose of impeachment only, with an instruction to the jury not to consider it otherwise. The parallel to the treatment of prior inconsistent statements will be apparent. *See* Rules 613(b) and 801(d)(1).

ADVISORY COMMITTEE NOTE TO EXCEPTIONS (19), (20) and (21).

Exceptions (19), (20), and (21). Trustworthiness in reputation evidence is found "when the topic is such that the facts are likely to have been inquired about and that persons having personal knowledge have disclosed facts which have thus been discussed in the community; and thus the community's conclusion, if any has been formed, is likely to be a trustworthy one." 5 Wigmore § 1580, p. 444, and *see also* § 1583. On this common foundation, reputation as to land boundaries, customs, general history, character, and marriage have come to be regarded as admissible. The breadth of the underlying principle suggests the formulation of an equally broad exception, but tradition has in fact been much narrower and more particularized, and this is the pattern of these exceptions in the rule.

Exception (19) is concerned with matters of personal and family history. Marriage is universally conceded to be a proper subject of proof by evidence of reputation in the community. 5 Wigmore § 1602. As to such items as legitimacy, relationship, adoption, birth, and death, the decisions are divided. *Id.* § 1605. All seem to be susceptible to being the subject of well founded repute. The "world" in which the reputation may exist may be family, associates, or community. This world has proved capable of expanding with changing times from the single uncomplicated neighborhood, in which all activities take place, to the multiple and unrelated worlds of work, religious affiliation, and social activity, in each of which a reputation may be generated. People v. Reeves, 360 Ill. 55, 195 N.E. 443 (1935); State v. Axilrod, 248 Minn. 204, 79 N.W.2d 677 (1956); Mass.Stat. 1947, c. 410, M.G.L.A. c. 233 § 21A; 5 Wigmore § 1616. The family has often served as the point of beginning for allowing community reputation. 5 Wigmore § 1488. For comparable provisions *see* Uniform Rule 63(26), (27) (c); California Evidence Code §§ 1313, 1314; Kansas Code of Civil Procedure § 60-460(x), (y)(3); New Jersey Evidence Rule 63(26), (27)(c).

The first portion of Exception (20) is based upon the general admissibility of evidence of reputation as to land boundaries and land customs, expanded in this country to include private as well as public boundaries. McCormick § 299, p. 625. The reputation is required to antedate the controversy, though not to be ancient. The second portion is likewise supported by authority, *id.*, and is designed to facilitate proof of events when judicial notice is not available. The historical character of the subject matter dispenses with any need that the reputation antedate the controversy with respect to which it is offered. For similar provisions *see* Uniform Rule 63(27) (a), (b); California Evidence Code §§ 1320–1322; Kansas Code of Civil Procedure § 60-460(y), (1), (2); New Jersey Evidence Rule 63(27) (a), (b).

Exception (21) recognizes the traditional acceptance of reputation evidence as a means of proving human character. McCormick §§ 44, 158. The exception deals only with the hearsay aspect of this kind of evidence. Limitations upon admissibility based on other grounds will be found in Rules 404, relevancy of character evidence generally, and 608, character of witness. The exception is in effect a reiteration, in the context of hearsay, of Rule 405(a). Similar provisions are contained in

Uniform Rule 63(28); California Evidence Code § 1324; Kansas Code of Civil Procedure § 60-460(z); New Jersey Evidence Rule 63(28).

ADVISORY COMMITTEE NOTE TO EXCEPTION (22).

Exception (22). When the status of a former judgment is under consideration in subsequent litigation, three possibilities must be noted: (1) the former judgment is conclusive under the doctrine of res judicata, either as a bar or a collateral estoppel; or (2) it is admissible in evidence for what it is worth; or (3) it may be of no effect at all. The first situation does not involve any problem of evidence except in the way that principles of substantive law generally bear upon the relevancy and materiality of evidence. The rule does not deal with the substantive effect of the judgment as a bar or collateral estoppel. When, however, the doctrine of res judicata does not apply to make the judgment either a bar or a collateral estoppel, a choice is presented between the second and third alternatives. The rule adopts the second for judgments of criminal conviction of felony grade. This is the direction of the decisions, Annot., 18 A.L.R.2d 1287, 1299, which manifest an increasing reluctance to reject *in toto* the validity of the law's factfinding processes outside the confines of res judicata and collateral estoppel. While this may leave a jury with the evidence of conviction but without means to evaluate it, as suggested by Judge Hinton, Note 27 Ill.L.Rev. 195 (1932), it seems safe to assume that the jury will give it substantial effect unless defendant offers a satisfactory explanation, a possibility not foreclosed by the provision. *But see* North River Ins. Co. v. Militello, 104 Colo. 28, 88 P.2d 567 (1939), in which the jury found for plaintiff on a fire policy despite the introduction of his conviction for arson. For supporting federal decisions *see* Clark, J., in New York & Cuba Mail S. S. Co. v. Continental Cas. Co., 117 F.2d 404, 411 (2d Cir. 1941); Connecticut Fire Ins. Co. v. Farrara, 277 F.2d 388 (8th Cir. 1960).

Practical considerations require exclusion of convictions of minor offenses, not because the administration of justice in its lower echelons must be inferior, but because motivation to defend at this level is often minimal or nonexistent. Cope v. Goble, 39 Cal.App.2d 448, 103 P.2d 598 (1940); Jones v. Talbot, 87 Idaho 498, 394 P.2d 316 (1964); Warren v. Marsh, 215 Minn. 615, 11 N.W.2d 528 (1943); Annot., 18 A.L.R.2d 1287, 1295–1297; 16 Brooklyn L.Rev. 286 (1950); 50 Colum.L.Rev. 529 (1950); 35 Cornell L.Q. 872 (1950). Hence the rule includes only convictions of felony grade, measured by federal standards.

Judgments of conviction based upon pleas of *nolo contendere* are not included. This position is consistent with the treatment of nolo pleas in Rule 410 and the authorities cited in the Advisory Committee's Note in support thereof.

While these rules do not in general purport to resolve constitutional issues, they have in general been drafted with a view to avoiding collision with constitutional principles. Consequently the exception does not include evidence of the conviction of a third person, offered against the accused in a criminal prosecution to prove any fact essential to sustain the judgment of conviction. A contrary position would seem clearly to violate the right of confrontation. Kirby v. United States, 174 U.S. 47, 19 S.Ct. 574, 43 L. Ed. 890 (1899), error to convict of possessing stolen postage stamps with the only evidence of theft being the record of conviction of the thieves. The situation is to be distinguished from cases in which conviction of another person is an element of the crime, e.g. 15 U.S.C. § 902(d), interstate shipment of firearms to a known convicted felon, and, as specifically provided, from impeachment.

For comparable provisions *see* Uniform Rule 63(20); California Evidence Code § 1300; Kansas Code of Civil Procedure § 60-460(r); New Jersey Evidence Rule 63(20).

ADVISORY COMMITTEE NOTE TO EXCEPTION (23).

Exception (23). A hearsay exception in this area was originally justified on the ground that verdicts were evidence of reputation. As trial by jury graduated from the category of neighborhood inquests, this theory lost its validity. It was never valid as to chancery decrees. Nevertheless the rule persisted, though the judges and writers shifted ground and began saying that the judgment or decree was as good evidence as reputation. *See* City of London v. Clerke, Carth. 181, 90 Eng.Rep. 710 (K.B. 1691); Neill v. Duke of Devonshire, 8 App.Cas. 135 (1882). The shift appears to be correct, since the process of inquiry, sifting, and scrutiny which is relied upon to render reputation reliable is present in perhaps greater measure in the process of litigation. While this might suggest a broader area of application, the affinity to reputation is strong, and paragraph (23) goes no further, not even including character.

The leading case in the United States, Patterson v. Gaines, 47 U.S. (6 How.) 550, 599, 12 L. Ed. 553 (1847), follows in the pattern of the English decisions, mentioning as illustrative matters thus provable: manorial rights, public rights of way, immemorial custom, disputed boundary, and pedigree. More recent recognition of the principle is found in Grant Bros. Construction Co. v. United States, 232 U.S. 647, 34 S.Ct. 452, 58 L. Ed. 776 (1914), in action for penalties under Alien Contract Labor Law, decision of board of inquiry of Immigration Service admissible to prove alienage of laborers, as a matter of pedigree; United States v. Mid-Continent Petroleum Corp., 67 F.2d 37 (10th Cir. 1933), records of commission enrolling Indians admissible on pedigree; Jung Yen Loy v. Cahill, 81 F.2d 809 (9th Cir. 1936), board decisions as to citizenship of plaintiff's father admissible in proceeding for declaration of citizenship. *Contra,* In re Estate of Cunha, 49 Haw. 273, 414 P.2d 925 (1966).

ADVISORY COMMITTEE NOTE TO EXCEPTION (24).

Exception (24). The preceding 23 exceptions of Rule 803 and the first five exceptions of Rule 804(b), *infra,* are designed to take full advantage of the accumulated wisdom and experience of the past in dealing with hearsay. It would, however, be presumptuous to assume that all possible desirable exceptions to the hearsay rule have been catalogued and to pass the hearsay rule to oncoming generations as a closed system. Exception (24) and its companion provision in Rule 804(b)(6) are accordingly included. They do not contemplate an unfettered exercise of judicial discretion, but they do provide for treating new and presently unanticipated situations which demonstrate a trustworthiness within the spirit of the specifically stated exceptions. Within this framework, room is left for growth and development of the law of evidence in the hearsay area, consistently with the broad purposes expressed in Rule 102. *See* Dallas County v. Commercial Union Assur. Co., 286 F.2d 388 (5th Cir. 1961).

REPORT OF THE HOUSE COMMITTEE ON THE JUDICIARY.

[*Note, that the attempt in the House to delete Rule 803(24) below, ultimately failed.*]

The proposed Rules of Evidence submitted to Congress contained identical provisions in Rules 803 and 804 (which set forth the various hearsay exceptions), to the effect that the federal courts could admit any hearsay statement not specifically covered by any of the stated exceptions, if the hearsay statement was found to have "comparable circumstantial guarantees of trustworthiness."

The Committee deleted these provisions (proposed Rules 803(24) and 804(b)(6)) as injecting too much uncertainty into the law of evidence and impairing the ability of practitioners to prepare for trial. It was noted that Rule 102 directs the courts to construe the Rules of Evidence so as to promote "growth and development." The Committee believed that if additional hearsay exceptions are to be created, they should be by amendments to the Rules, not on a case-by-case basis.

REPORT OF THE SENATE COMMITTEE ON THE JUDICIARY.

[*Note, that after the Report set forth below was prepared, Rule 803(24) was again amended to add a notice provision.*]

The proposed Rules of Evidence submitted to Congress contained identical provisions in rules 803 and 804 (which set forth the various hearsay exceptions), admitting any hearsay statement not specifically covered by any of the stated exceptions, if the hearsay statement was found to have "comparable circumstantial guarantees of trustworthiness." The House deleted these provisions (proposed rules 803(24) and 804(b)(6)) as injecting "too much uncertainty" into the law of evidence and impairing the ability of practitioners to prepare for trial. The House felt that rule 102, which directs the courts to construe the Rules of Evidence so as to promote growth and development, would permit sufficient flexibility to admit hearsay evidence in appropriate cases under various factual situations that might arise.

We disagree with the total rejection of a residual hearsay exception. While we view rule 102 as being intended to provide for a broader construction and interpretation of these rules, we feel that, without a separate residual provision, the specifically enumerated exceptions could become tortured beyond any reasonable circumstances which they were intended to include (even if broadly construed). Moreover, these exceptions, while they reflect the most typical and well recognized exceptions to the hearsay rule, may not encompass every situation in which the reliability and appropriateness of a particular piece of hearsay evidence make clear that it should be heard and considered by the trier of fact.

The committee believes that there are certain exceptional circumstances where evidence which is found by a court to have guarantees of trustworthiness equivalent to or exceeding the guarantees reflected by the presently listed exceptions, and to have a high degree of probativeness and necessity could properly be admissible.

The case of Dallas County v. Commercial Union Assoc. Co., Ltd., 286 F.2d 388 (5th Cir. 1961) illustrates the point. The issue in that case was whether the tower of the county courthouse collapsed because it was struck by lightning (covered by insurance) or because of structural weakness and deterioration of the structure (not covered). Investigation of the structure revealed the presence of charcoal and charred timbers. In order to show that lightning may not have been the cause of the charring, the insurer offered a copy of a local newspaper published over 50 years earlier containing an unsigned article describing a fire in the courthouse while it was under construction. The Court found that the newspaper did not qualify for admission as a business record or an ancient document and did not fit within any other recognized hearsay exception. The court concluded, however, that the article was trustworthy because it was inconceivable that a newspaper reporter in a small town would report a fire in the courthouse if none had occurred. *See also* United States v. Barbati, 284 F. Supp. 409 (E.D.N.Y. 1968).

Because exceptional cases like the *Dallas County* case may arise in the future, the committee has decided to reinstate a residual exception for rules 803 and 804(b).

The committee, however, also agrees with those supporters of the House version who felt that an overly broad residual hearsay exception could emasculate the hearsay rule and the recognized exceptions or vitiate the rationale behind codification of the rules.

Therefore, the committee has adopted a residual exception for rules 803 and 804(b) of much narrower scope and applicability than the Supreme Court version. In order to qualify for admission, a hearsay statement not falling within one of the recognized exceptions would have to satisfy at least four conditions. First, it must have "equivalent circumstantial guarantees of trustworthiness." Second, it must be offered as evidence of a material fact. Third, the court must determine that the statement "is more probative on the point for which it is offered than any other evidence which the proponent can procure through reasonable efforts." This requirement is intended to insure that only statements which have high probative value and necessity may qualify for admission under the residual exceptions. Fourth, the court must determine that "the general purposes of these rules and the interests of justice will best be served by admission of the statement into evidence."

It is intended that the residual hearsay exceptions will be used very rarely, and only in exceptional circumstances. The committee does not intend to establish a broad license for trial judges to admit hearsay statements that do not fall within one of the other exceptions contained in rules 803 and 804(b). The residual exceptions are not meant to authorize major judicial revisions of the hearsay rule, including its present exceptions. Such major revisions are best accomplished by legislative action. It is intended that in any case in which evidence is sought to be admitted under these subsections, the trial judge will exercise no less care, reflection and caution than the courts did under the common law in establishing the now-recognized exceptions to the hearsay rule. In order to establish a well-defined jurisprudence, the special facts and circumstances which, in the court's judgment, indicates that the statement has a sufficiently high degree of trustworthiness and necessity to justify its admission should be stated on the record. It is expected that the court will give the opposing party a full and adequate opportunity to contest the admission of any statement sought to be introduced under these subsections.

REPORT OF THE HOUSE/SENATE CONFERENCE COMMITTEE.

The Senate amendment adds a new subsection, (24), which makes admissible a hearsay statement not specifically covered by any of the previous twenty-three subsections, if the statement has equivalent circumstantial guarantees of trustworthiness and if the court determines that (A) the statement is offered as evidence of a material fact; (B) the statement is more probative on the point for which it is offered than any other evidence the proponent can procure through reasonable efforts; and (C) the general purposes of these rules and the interests of justice will best be served by admission of the statement into evidence.

The House bill eliminated a similar, but broader, provision because of the conviction that such a provision injected too much uncertainty into the law of evidence regarding hearsay and impaired the ability of a litigant to prepare adequately for trial.

The Conference adopts the Senate amendment with an amendment that provides that a party intending to request the court to use a statement under this provision must notify any adverse party of this intention as well as of the particulars of the statement, including the name and address of the declarant. This notice must be given sufficiently in advance of the trial or hearing to provide any adverse party with a fair opportunity to prepare to contest the use of the statement.

ADVISORY COMMITTEE NOTE TO **1997** AMENDMENT.

The contents of Rule 803(24) and Rule 804(b)(5) have been combined and transferred to new Rule 807. This was done to facilitate additions to Rules 803 and 804. No change in meaning is intended.

Rule 804. Exceptions to the Rule Against Hearsay—When the Declarant Is Unavailable as a Witness

ADVISORY COMMITTEE NOTE TO THE **2011** AMENDMENT.

The language of Rule 804 has been amended as part of the restyling of the Evidence Rules to make them more easily understood and to make style and terminology consistent throughout the rules. These changes are intended to be stylistic only. There is no intent to change any result in any ruling on evidence admissibility.

No style changes were made to Rule 804(b)(3), because it was already restyled in conjunction with a substantive amendment, effective December 1, 2010.

ADVISORY COMMITTEE NOTE TO THE **2010** AMENDMENT.

Subdivision (b)(3). Rule 804(b)(3) has been amended to provide that the corroborating circumstances requirement applies to all declarations against penal interest offered in criminal cases. A number of courts have applied the corroborating circumstances requirement to declarations against penal interest offered by the prosecution, even though the text of the Rule did not so provide. *See, e.g., United States v. Alvarez*, 584 F.2d 694, 701 (5th Cir. 1978) ("by transplanting the language governing exculpatory statements onto the analysis for admitting inculpatory hearsay, a unitary standard is derived which offers the most workable basis for applying Rule 804(b)(3)"); *United States v. Shukri*, 207 F.3d 412 (7th Cir. 2000) (requiring corroborating circumstances for against-penal-interest statements offered by the government). A unitary approach to declarations against penal interest assures both the prosecution and the accused that the Rule will not be abused and that only reliable hearsay statements will be admitted under the exception.

All other changes to the structure and wording of the Rule are intended to be stylistic only. There is no intent to change any other result in any ruling on evidence admissibility.

The amendment does not address the use of the corroborating circumstances for declarations against penal interest offered in civil cases.

In assessing whether corroborating circumstances exist, some courts have focused on the credibility of the witness who relates the hearsay statement in court. But the credibility of the witness who relates the statement is not a proper factor for the court to consider in assessing corroborating circumstances. To base admission or exclusion of a hearsay statement on the witness's credibility would usurp the jury's role of determining the credibility of testifying witnesses.

ADVISORY COMMITTEE NOTE.

As to firsthand knowledge on the part of hearsay declarants, *see* the introductory portion of the Advisory Committee's Note to Rule 803.

Subdivision (a). The definition of unavailability implements the division of hearsay exceptions into two categories by Rules 803 and 804(b).

At common law the unavailability requirement was evolved in connection with particular hearsay exceptions rather than along general lines. For example, *see* the separate explications of unavailability in relation to former testimony, declarations against interest, and statements of pedigree, separately developed in McCormick §§ 234, 257, and 297. However, no reason is apparent for making distinctions as to what satisfies unavailability for the different exceptions. The treatment in the rule is therefore uniform although differences in the range of process for witnesses between civil and criminal cases will lead to a less exacting requirement under item (5). *See* Rule 45(e) of the Federal Rules of Civil Procedure and Rule 17(e) of the Federal Rules of Criminal Procedure.

Five instances of unavailability are specified:

(1) Substantial authority supports the position that exercise of a claim of privilege by the declarant satisfies the requirement of unavailability (usually in connection with former testimony). Wyatt v. State, 35 Ala.App. 147, 46 So.2d 837 (1950); State v. Stewart, 85 Kan. 404, 116 P. 489 (1911); Annot., 45 A.L.R.2d 1354; Uniform Rule 62(7)(a); California Evidence Code § 240(a)(1); Kansas Code of Civil Procedure

§ 60-459(g)(1). A ruling by the judge is required, which clearly implies that an actual claim of privilege must be made.

(2) A witness is rendered unavailable if he simply refuses to testify concerning the subject matter of his statement despite judicial pressures to do so, a position supported by similar considerations of practicality. Johnson v. People, 152 Colo. 586, 384 P.2d 454 (1963); People v. Pickett, 339 Mich. 294, 63 N.W.2d 681, 45 A.L.R.2d 1341 (1954). *Contra*, Pleau v. State, 255 Wis. 362, 38 N.W.2d 496 (1949).

(3) The position that a claimed lack of memory by the witness of the subject matter of his statement constitutes unavailability likewise finds support in the cases, though not without dissent. McCormick § 234, p. 494. If the claim is successful, the practical effect is to put the testimony beyond reach, as in the other instances. In this instance, however, it will be noted that the lack of memory must be established by the testimony of the witness himself, which clearly contemplates his production and subjection to cross-examination.

REPORT OF THE HOUSE COMMITTEE ON THE JUDICIARY.

Rule 804(a)(3) was approved in the form submitted by the Court. However, the Committee intends no change in existing federal law under which the court may choose to disbelieve the declarant's testimony as to his lack of memory. *See* United States v. Insana, 423 F.2d 1165, 1169–1170 (2nd Cir.), *cert. denied*, 400 U.S. 841 (1970).

ADVISORY COMMITTEE NOTE.

[*Note, that the last sentence in the Note below does not apply to Rule 804 as enacted.*]

(4) Death and infirmity find general recognition as grounds. McCormick §§ 234, 257, 297; Uniform Rule 62(7) (c); California Evidence Code § 240(a)(3); Kansas Code of Civil Procedure § 60-459(g)(3); New Jersey Evidence Rule 62(6)(c). *See also* the provisions on use of depositions in Rule 32(a)(3) of the Federal Rules of Civil Procedure and Rule 15(e) of the Federal Rules of Criminal Procedure.

(5) Absence from the hearing coupled with inability to compel attendance by process or other reasonable means also satisfies the requirement. McCormick § 234; Uniform Rule 62(7)(d) and (e); California Evidence Code § 240(a)(4) and (5); Kansas Code of Civil Procedure § 60-459(g)(4) and (5); New Jersey Rule 62(6) (b) and (d). *See* the discussion of procuring attendance of witnesses who are nonresidents or in custody in Barber v. Page, 390 U.S. 719, 88 S.Ct. 1318, 20 L.Ed.2d 255 (1968).

If the conditions otherwise constituting unavailability result from the procurement or wrongdoing of the proponent of the statement, the requirement is not satisfied. The rule contains no requirement that an attempt be made to take the deposition of a declarant.

REPORT OF THE HOUSE COMMITTEE ON THE JUDICIARY.

[*Note, that the proposed change discussed in the Committee Report below was in fact adopted, and is in Rule 804(a)(5) as enacted.*]

Rule 804(a)(5) as submitted to the Congress provided, as one type of situation in which a declarant would be deemed "unavailable," that he be "absent from the hearing and the proponent of his statement has been unable to procure his attendance by process or other reasonable means." The Committee amended the Rule to insert after the word "attendance" the parenthetical expression "(or, in the case of a hearsay exception under subdivision (b)(2), (3), or (4), his attendance or testimony)." The amendment is designed primarily to require that an attempt be made to depose a witness (as well as to seek his attendance) as a precondition to the witness being deemed unavailable. The Committee, however, recognized the propriety of an exception to this additional requirement when it is the declarant's former testimony that is sought to be admitted under subdivision (b)(1).

REPORT OF THE SENATE COMMITTEE ON THE JUDICIARY.

[*Note, that the position of the Committee set forth below with respect to Rule 804(a)(5) did not prevail. The deposition clause remained in the Rule as enacted.*]

Subdivision (a) of rule 804 as submitted by the Supreme Court defined the conditions under which a witness was considered to be unavailable. It was amended in the House.

The purpose of the amendment, according to the REPORT OF THE HOUSE COMMITTEE ON THE JUDICIARY, is "primarily to require that an attempt be made to depose a witness (as well as to seek his attendance) as a precondition to the witness being unavailable."[16]

Under the House amendment, before a witness is declared unavailable, a party must try to depose a witness (declarant) with respect to dying declarations, declarations against interest, and declarations of pedigree. None of these situations would seem to warrant this needless, impractical and highly restrictive complication. A good case can be made for eliminating the unavailability requirement entirely for declarations against interest cases.[17]

In dying declaration cases, the declarant will usually, though not necessarily, be deceased at the time of trial. Pedigree statements which are admittedly and necessarily based largely on word of mouth are not greatly fortified by a deposition requirement.

---

[16] H. Rept. 93-1650, at p. 15.

[17] Uniform Rule 63 (10); Kan. Stat. Anno. 60-460 (j); 2A N.J. Stats. Anno. 84-63 (10).

Depositions are expensive and time-consuming. In any event, deposition procedures are available to those who wish to resort to them. Moreover, the deposition procedures of the Civil Rules and Criminal Rules are only imperfectly adapted to implementing the amendment. No purpose is served unless the deposition, if taken, may be used in evidence. Under Civil Rule (a)(3) and Criminal Rule 15(e), a deposition, though taken, may not be admissible, and under Criminal Rule 15(a) substantial obstacles exist in the way of even taking a deposition.

For these reasons, the committee deleted the House amendment.

The committee understands that the rule as to unavailability, as explained by the Advisory Committee "contains no requirement that an attempt to be made to take the deposition of a declarent." In reflecting the committee's judgment, the statement is accurate insofar as it goes. Where, however, the proponent of the statement, with knowledge of the existence of the statement, fails to confront the declarant with the statement at the taking of the deposition, then the proponent should not, in fairness, be permitted to treat the declarant as "unavailable" simply because the declarant was not amenable to process compelling his attendance at trial. The committee does not consider it necessary to amend the rule to this effect because such a situation abuses, not conforms to, the rule. Fairness would preclude a person from introducing a hearsay statement on a particular issue if the person taking the deposition was aware of the issue at the time of the deposition but failed to depose the unavailable witness on that issue.

REPORT OF THE HOUSE/SENATE CONFERENCE COMMITTEE.

[*Note, that the resolution of the controversy recommended below was in fact approved.*]

Subsection (a) defines the term "unavailability as a witness." The House bill provides in subsection (a)(5) that the party who desires to use the statement must be unable to procure the declarant's attendance by process or other reasonable means. In the case of dying declarations, statements against interest and statements of personal or family history, the House bill requires that the proponent must also be unable to procure the declarant's testimony (such as by deposition or interrogatories) by process or other reasonable means. The Senate amendment eliminates this latter provision.

The Conference adopts the provision contained in the House bill.

ADVISORY COMMITTEE NOTE.

[*Note, that on the "identity of parties" problem discussed in the last two paragraphs of the Committee's note below, Congress differed, and Rule 804(b)(1) was amended accordingly.*]

Subdivision (b). Rule 803, *supra*, is based upon the assumption that a hearsay statement falling within one of its exceptions possesses qualities which justify the conclusion that whether the declarant is available or unavailable is not a relevant factor in determining admissibility. The instant rule proceeds upon a different theory: hearsay which admittedly is not equal in quality to testimony of the declarant on the stand may nevertheless be admitted if the declarant is unavailable and if his statement meets a specified standard. The rule expresses preferences: testimony given on the stand in person is preferred over hearsay, and hearsay, if of the specified quality, is preferred over complete loss of the evidence of the declarant. The exceptions evolved at common law with respect to declarations of unavailable declarants furnish the basis for the exceptions enumerated in the proposal. The term "unavailable" is defined in subdivision (a).

Exception (1). Former testimony does not rely upon some set of circumstances to substitute for oath and cross-examination, since both oath and opportunity to cross-examine were present in fact. The only missing one of the ideal conditions for the giving of testimony is the presence of trier and opponent ("demeanor evidence"). This is lacking with all hearsay exceptions. Hence it may be argued that former testimony is the strongest hearsay and should be included under Rule 803, *supra*. However, opportunity to observe demeanor is what in a large measure confers depth and meaning upon oath and cross-examination. Thus in cases under Rule 803 demeanor lacks the significance which it possesses with respect to testimony. In any event, the tradition, founded in experience, uniformly favors production of the witness if he is available. The exception indicates continuation of the policy. This preference for the presence of the witness is apparent also in rules and statutes on the use of depositions, which deal with substantially the same problem.

Under the exception, the testimony may be offered (1) against the party *against* whom it was previously offered or (2) against the party *by* whom it was previously offered. In each instance the question resolves itself into whether fairness allows imposing, upon the party against whom now offered, the handling of the witness on the earlier occasion. (1) If the party against whom now offered is the one against whom the testimony was offered previously, no unfairness is apparent in requiring him to accept his own prior conduct of cross-examination or decision not to cross-examine. Only demeanor has been lost, and that is inherent in the situation. (2) If the party against whom now offered is the one *by* whom the testimony was offered previously, a satisfactory answer becomes somewhat more difficult. One possibility is to proceed somewhat along the line of an adoptive admission, i.e. by offering the testimony proponent in effect adopts it. However, this theory savors of discarded concepts of witnesses' belonging to a party, of litigants' ability to pick and choose witnesses, and of vouching for one's own witnesses. *Cf.* McCormick § 246, pp. 526–527; 4 Wigmore § 1075. A more direct and acceptable approach is simply to recognize direct and redirect examination of one's own witness as the equivalent of cross-examining an opponent's witness. Falknor, Former Testimony and the Uniform Rules: A Comment, 38 N.Y.U.L.Rev. 651, n. 1 (1963); McCormick § 231, p. 483. *See also* 5 Wigmore § 1389. Allowable techniques for dealing with hostile, double-crossing, forgetful, and mentally deficient witnesses leave no substance to a claim that one could not adequately develop his own witness at the former hearing. An even less appealing argument is presented when failure to develop fully was the result of a deliberate choice.

The common law did not limit the admissibility of former testimony to that given in an earlier trial of the same case, although it did require identity of issues as a means of insuring that the former handling of the witness was the equivalent of what would now be done if the opportunity were presented. Modern decisions reduce the requirement to "substantial" identity. McCormick § 233. Since identity of issues is significant only in that it bears on motive and interest in developing fully the testimony of the witness, expressing the matter in the latter terms is preferable. *Id.* Testimony given at a preliminary hearing was held in California v. Green, 399 U.S. 149, 90 S.Ct. 1930, 26 L.Ed.2d 489 (1970), to satisfy confrontation requirements in this respect.

As a further assurance of fairness in thrusting upon a party the prior handling of the witness, the common law also insisted upon identity of parties, deviating only to the extent of allowing substitution of successors in a narrowly construed privity. Mutuality as an aspect of identity is now generally discredited, and the requirement of identity of the offering party disappears except as it might affect motive to develop the testimony. Falknor, *supra*, at 652; McCormick § 232, pp. 487–488. The question remains whether strict identity, or privity, should continue as a requirement with respect to the party against whom offered. The rule departs to the extent of allowing substitution of one with the right and opportunity to develop the testimony with similar motive and interest. This position is supported by modern decisions. McCormick § 232, pp. 489–490; 5 Wigmore § 1388.

Provisions of the same tenor will be found in Uniform Rule 63(3)(b); California Evidence Code §§ 1290–1292; Kansas Code of Civil Procedure § 60-460(c)(2); New Jersey Evidence Rule 63(3). Unlike the rule, the latter three provide either that former testimony is not admissible if the right of confrontation is denied or that it is not admissible if the accused was not a party to the prior hearing. The genesis of these limitations is a caveat in Uniform Rule 63(3) Comment that use of former testimony against an accused may violate his right of confrontation. Mattox v. United States, 156 U.S. 237, 15 S.Ct. 337, 39 L. Ed. 409 (1895), held that the right was not violated by the Government's use, on a retrial of the same case, of testimony given at the first trial by two witnesses since deceased. The decision leaves open the questions (1) whether direct and redirect are equivalent to cross-examination for purposes of confrontation, (2) whether testimony given in a different proceeding is acceptable, and (3) whether the accused must himself have been a party to the earlier proceeding or whether a similarly situated person will serve the purpose. Professor Falknor concluded that, if a dying declaration untested by cross-examination is constitutionally admissible, former testimony tested by the cross-examination of one similarly situated does not offend against confrontation. Falknor, *supra*, at 659–660. The constitutional acceptability of dying declarations has often been conceded. Mattox v. United States, 156 U.S. 237, 243, 15 S.Ct. 337, 39 L. Ed. 409 (1895); Kirby v. United States, 174 U.S. 47, 61, 19 S.Ct. 574, 43 L. Ed. 890 (1899); Pointer v. Texas, 380 U.S. 400, 407, 85 S.Ct. 1065, 13 L.Ed.2d 923 (1965).

REPORT OF THE HOUSE COMMITTEE ON THE JUDICIARY.

[Note, that the amendment described below was in fact adopted.]

Rule 804(b)(1) as submitted by the Court allowed prior testimony of an unavailable witness to be admissible if the party against whom it is offered or a person "with motive and interest similar" to his had an opportunity to examine the witness. The Committee considered that it is generally unfair to impose upon the party against whom the hearsay evidence is being offered responsibility for the manner in which the witness was previously handled by another party. The sole exception to this, in the Committee's view, is when a party's predecessor in interest in a civil action or proceeding had an opportunity and similar motive to examine the witness. The Committee amended the Rule to reflect these policy determinations.

REPORT OF THE SENATE/COMMITTEE ON THE JUDICIARY.

[Note, that the "House Amendment" in which the Senate Committee concurred in the Report below was in fact adopted.]

Former testimony.—Rule 804(b)(1) as submitted by the Court allowed prior testimony of an unavailable witness to be admissible if the party against whom it is offered or a person "with motive and interest similar" to his had an opportunity to examine the witness.

The House amended the rule to apply only to a party's predecessor in interest. Although the committee recognizes considerable merit to the rule submitted by the Supreme Court, a position which has been advocated by many scholars and judges, we have concluded that the difference between the two versions is not great and we accept the

House amendment.

ADVISORY COMMITTEE NOTE.

[*Note, that Subdivision (b)(2) as described below would have created an exception for statements of recent perception. This provision was deleted by Congress, and did not become part of Rule 804 as enacted. A qualified version of this exception, available only in civil cases, was approved by the National Conference of Commissioners on Uniform State Laws, and is found in Uniform Rule 804(b)(5). New Mexico, Wisconsin, and Wyoming did adopt an exception for statements of recent perception.*]

Exception (2). The rule finds support in several directions. The well known Massachusetts Act of 1898 allows in evidence the declaration of any deceased person made in good faith before the commencement of the action and upon personal knowledge. Mass.G.L., c. 233, § 65. To the same effect is R.I.G.L. § 9-19-11. Under other statutes, a decedent's statement is admissible on behalf of his estate in actions against it, to offset the presumed inequality resulting from allowing a surviving opponent to testify. California Evidence Code § 1261; Conn.G.S., § 52-172; and statutes collected in 5 Wigmore § 1576. *See also* Va.Code § 8-286, allowing statements made when capable by a party now incapable of testifying.

In 1938 the Committee on Improvements in the Law of Evidence of the American Bar Association recommended adoption of a statute similar to that of Massachusetts but with the concept of unavailability expanded to include, in addition to death, cases of insanity or inability to produce a witness or take his deposition. 63 A.B.A. Reports 570, 584, 600 (1938). The same year saw enactment of the English Evidence Act of 1938, allowing written statements made on personal knowledge, if declarant is deceased or otherwise unavailable or if the court is satisfied that undue delay or expense would otherwise be caused, unless declarant was an interested person in pending or anticipated relevant proceedings. Evidence Act of 1938, 1 & 2 Geo. 6, c. 28; Cross on Evidence 482 (3rd ed. 1967).

Model Code Rule 503(a) provided broadly for admission of any hearsay declaration of an unavailable declarant. No circumstantial guarantees of trustworthiness were required. Debate upon the floor of the American Law Institute did not seriously question the propriety of the rule but centered upon what should constitute unavailability. 18 A.L.I. Proceedings 90-134 (1941).

The Uniform Rules draftsman took a less advanced position, more in the pattern of the Massachusetts statute, and invoked several assurances of accuracy: recency of perception, clarity of recollection, good faith, and antecedence to the commencement of the action. Uniform Rule 63(4)(c).

Opposition developed to the Uniform Rule because of its countenancing of the use of statements carefully prepared under the tutelage of lawyers, claim adjusters, or investigators with a view to pending or prospective litigation. Tentative Recommendation and a Study Relating to the Uniform Rules of Evidence (Art. VIII. Hearsay Evidence), Cal.Law Rev.Comm'n, 318 (1962); Quick, Excitement, Necessity and the Uniform Rules: A Reappraisal of Rule 63(4), 6 Wayne L.Rev. 204, 219–224 (1960). To meet this objection, the rule excludes statements made at the instigation of a person engaged in investigating, litigating, or settling a claim. It also incorporates as safeguards the good faith and clarity of recollection required by the Uniform Rule and the exclusion of a statement by a person interested in the litigation provided by the English act.

With respect to the question whether the introduction of a statement under this exception against the accused in a criminal case would violate his right of confrontation, reference is made to the last paragraph of the Advisory Committee's Note under Exception (1), *supra*.

REPORT OF THE HOUSE COMMITTEE ON THE JUDICIARY.

[*Note, that the position of the Committee described below prevailed. The exception which the Committee deleted never reappeared in Rule 804.*]

Rule 804(b)(2), a hearsay exception submitted by the Court, titled "Statement of recent "perception," read[s] as follows:

A statement, not in response to the instigation of a person engaged in investigating, litigating, or settling a claim, which narrates, describes, or explains an event or condition recently perceived by the declarant, made in good faith, not in contemplation of pending or anticipated litigation in which he was interested, and while his recollection was clear.

The Committee eliminated this Rule as creating a new and unwarranted hearsay exception of great potential breadth. The Committee did not believe that statements of the type referred to bore sufficient guarantees of trustworthiness to justify admissibility.

ADVISORY COMMITTEE NOTE.

[*Note, that the exception for dying declarations, described below as Exception (3), became Exception (2) in Rule 804(b) as enacted. The change in numbering was caused by deletion of the exception for statements of recent perception. The dying declarations exception described below was amended by Congress so as to be available only in civil cases and prosecutions for homicide.*]

Exception (3). The exception is the familiar dying declaration of the common law, expanded somewhat beyond its traditionally narrow limits. While the original religious justification for the exception may have lost its conviction for some persons over the years, it can scarcely be doubted that powerful psychological pressures are present. *See* 5 Wigmore § 1443 and the classic statement of Chief Baron Eyre in Rex v. Woodcock, 1 Leach 500, 502, 168 Eng.Rep. 352, 353 (K.B.1789).

The common law required that the statement be that of the victim, offered in a prosecution for criminal homicide. Thus declarations by victims in prosecutions for other crimes, e.g. a declaration by a rape victim who dies in childbirth, and all declarations in civil cases were outside the scope of the exception. An occasional statute has removed these restrictions, as in Colo.R.S. § 52-1-20, or has expanded the area of offenses to include abortions, 5 Wigmore § 1432, p. 224, n. 4. Kansas by decision extended the exception to civil cases. Thurston v. Fritz, 91 Kan. 468, 138 P. 625 (1914). While the common law exception no doubt originated as a result of the exceptional need for the evidence in homicide cases, the theory of admissibility applies equally in civil cases and in prosecutions for crimes other than homicide. The same considerations suggest abandonment of the limitation to circumstances attending the event in question, yet when the statement deals with matters other than the supposed death, its influence is believed to be sufficiently attenuated to justify the limitation. Unavailability is not limited to death. *See* subdivision (a) of this rule. Any problem as to declarations phrased in terms of opinion is laid at rest by Rule 701, and continuation of a requirement of first-hand knowledge is assured by Rule 602.

Comparable provisions are found in Uniform Rule 63(5): California Evidence Code § 1242; Kansas Code of Civil Procedure § 60-460(e); New Jersey Evidence Rule 63(5).

REPORT OF THE HOUSE COMMITTEE ON THE JUDICIARY.

[Note, that the amendment to the exception for dying declarations described below was to become part of Rule 804(b)(2) as enacted.]

Rule 804(b)(3) as submitted by the Court (now Rule 804(b)(2) in the bill) proposed to expand the traditional scope of the dying declaration exception (i.e. a statement of the victim in a homicide case as to the cause or circumstances of his believed imminent death) to allow such statements in all criminal and civil cases. The Committee did not consider dying declarations as among the most reliable forms of hearsay. Consequently, it amended the provision to limit their admissibility in criminal cases to homicide prosecutions, where exceptional need for the evidence is present. This is existing law. At the same time, the Committee approved the expansion to civil actions and proceedings where the stakes do not involve possible imprisonment, although noting that this could lead to forum shopping in some instances.

ADVISORY COMMITTEE NOTE.

[Note, that the exception for statements against interest, described below as Exception (4), became Exception (5) in Rule 804(b) as enacted. The change in numbering was caused by the deletion of the exception for statements of recent perception. The against-interest exception was amended by Congress prior to enactment.]

Exception (4). The circumstantial guaranty of reliability for declarations against interest is the assumption that persons do not make statements which are damaging to themselves unless satisfied for good reason that they are true. Hileman v. Northwest Engineering Co., 346 F.2d 668 (6th Cir. 1965). If the statement is that of a party, offered by his opponent, it comes in as an admission, Rule 803(d)(2), and there is no occasion to inquire whether it is against interest, this not being a condition precedent to admissibility of admissions by opponents.

The common law required that the interest declared against be pecuniary or proprietary but within this limitation demonstrated striking ingenuity in discovering an against-interest aspect. Higham v. Ridgway, 10 East 109, 103 Eng.Rep. 717 (K.B.1808); Reg. v. Overseers of Birmingham, 1 B. & S. 763, 121 Eng.Rep. 897 (Q.B.1861); McCormick, § 256, p. 551, nn. 2 and 3.

The exception discards the common law limitation and expands to the full logical limit. One result is to remove doubt as to the admissibility of declarations tending to establish a tort liability against the declarant or to extinguish one which might be asserted by him, in accordance with the trend of the decisions in this country. McCormick § 254, pp. 548–549. Another is to allow statements tending to expose declarant to hatred, ridicule, or disgrace, the motivation here being considered to be as strong as when financial interests are at stake. McCormick § 255, p. 551. And finally, exposure to criminal liability satisfies the against-interest requirement. The refusal of the common law to concede the adequacy of a penal interest was no doubt indefensible in logic, *see* the dissent of Mr. Justice Holmes in Donnelly v. United States, 228 U.S. 243, 33 S.Ct. 449, 57 L. Ed. 820 (1913), but one senses in the decisions a distrust of evidence of confessions by third persons offered to exculpate the accused arising from suspicions of fabrication either of the fact of the making of the confession or in its contents, enhanced in either instance by the required unavailability of the declarant. Nevertheless, an increasing amount of decisional law recognizes exposure to punishment for crime as a sufficient stake. People v. Spriggs, 60 Cal.2d 868, 36 Cal.Rptr. 841, 389 P.2d 377 (1964); Sutter v. Easterly, 354 Mo. 282, 189 S.W.2d 284 (1945); Band's Refuse Removal, Inc. v. Fairlawn Borough, 62 N.J. Super. 522, 163 A.2d 465 (1960); Newberry v.

Commonwealth, 191 Va. 445, 61 S.E.2d 318 (1950); Annot., 162 A.L.R. 446. The requirement of corroboration is included in the rule in order to effect an accommodation between these competing considerations. When the statement is offered by the accused by way of exculpation, the resulting situation is not adapted to control by rulings as to the weight of the evidence, and hence the provision is cast in terms of a requirement preliminary to admissibility. *Cf.* Rule 406(a). The requirement of corroboration should be construed in such a manner as to effectuate its purpose of circumventing fabrication.

Ordinarily the third-party confession is thought of in terms of exculpating the accused, but this is by no means always or necessarily the case: it may include statements implicating him, and under the general theory of declarations against interest they would be admissible as related statements. Douglas v. Alabama, 380 U.S. 415, 85 S.Ct. 1074, 13 L.Ed.2d 934 (1965), and Bruton v. United States, 389 U.S. 818, 88 S.Ct. 126, 19 L.Ed.2d 70 (1968), both involved confessions by codefendants which implicated the accused. While the confession was not actually offered in evidence in *Douglas*, the procedure followed effectively put it before the jury, which the Court ruled to be error. Whether the confession might have been admissible as a declaration against penal interest was not considered or discussed. *Bruton* assumed the inadmissibility, as against the accused, of the implicating confession of his codefendant, and centered upon the question of the effectiveness of a limiting instruction. These decisions, however, by no means require that all statements implicating another person be excluded from the category of declarations against interest. Whether a statement is in fact against interest must be determined from the circumstances of each case. Thus a statement admitting guilt and implicating another person, made while in custody, may well be motivated by a desire to curry favor with the authorities and hence fail to qualify as against interest. *See* the dissenting opinion of Mr. Justice White in *Bruton*. On the other hand, the same words spoken under different circumstances, *e.g.*, to an acquaintance, would have no difficulty in qualifying. The rule does not purport to deal with questions of the right of confrontation.

The balancing of self-serving against dissenting aspects of a declaration is discussed in McCormick § 256.

For comparable provisions, *see* Uniform Rule 63(10); California Evidence Code § 1230; Kansas Code of Civil Procedure § 60-460(j); New Jersey Evidence Rule 63(10).

REPORT OF THE HOUSE COMMITTEE ON THE JUDICIARY.

[*Note, that the exception described below for statements against interest was indeed to be amended, but out of the amendments described in the note below, only the deletion of the reference to "hatred, ridicule, or disgrace" and the change requiring "clearly" corroborative circumstances for third party confessions exculpating the accused were to survive.*]

Rule 804(b)(4) as submitted by the Court (now Rule 804(b)(3) in the bill) provided as follows:

Statement against interest.—A statement which was at the time of its making so far contrary to the declarant's pecuniary or proprietary interest or so far tended to subject him to civil or criminal liability or to render invalid a claim by him against another or to make him an object of hatred, ridicule, or disgrace, that a reasonable man in his position would not have made the statement unless he believed it to be true. A statement tending to exculpate the accused is not admissible unless corroborated.

The Committee determined to retain the traditional hearsay exception for statements against pecuniary or proprietary interest. However, it deemed the Court's additional references to statements tending to subject a declarant to civil liability or to render invalid a claim by him against another to be redundant as included within the scope of the reference to statements against pecuniary or proprietary interest. *See* Gichner v. Antonio Triano Tile and Marble Co., 410 F.2d 238 (D.C. Cir. 1968). Those additional references were accordingly deleted.

The Court's Rule also proposed to expand the hearsay limitation from its present federal limitation to include statements subjecting the declarant to criminal liability and statements tending to make him an object of hatred, ridicule, or disgrace. The Committee eliminated the latter category from the subdivision as lacking sufficient guarantees of reliability. *See* United States v. Dovico, 380 F.2d 325, 327 nn.2, 4 (2d Cir.), *cert. denied*, 389 U.S. 944 (1967). As for statements against penal interest, the Committee shared the view of the Court that some such statements do possess adequate assurances of reliability and should be admissible. It believed, however, as did the Court, that statements of this type tending to exculpate the accused are more suspect and so should have their admissibility conditioned upon some further provision insuring trustworthiness. The proposal in the Court Rule to add a requirement of simple corrob[or]ation was, however, deemed ineffective to accomplish this purpose since the accused's own testimony might suffice while not necessarily increasing the reliability of the hearsay statement. The Committee settled upon the language "unless corroborating circumstances clearly indicate the trustworthiness of the statement" as affording a proper standard and degree of discretion. It was contemplated that the result in such cases as Donnelly v. United States, 228 U.S. 243 (1912), where the circumstances plainly indicated reliability, would be changed. The Committee also added to the Rule the final sentence from the 1971 Advisory Committee draft, designed to codify the doctrine of Bruton v. United States, 391 U.S. 123 (1968). The Committee does not intend to affect the existing exception to the Bruton principle where the codefendant takes the stand and is subject to cross-examination, but believed there was no need to make specific provision for this situation in the Rule, since in that event the declarant would not be "unavailable."

REPORT OF THE SENATE COMMITTEE ON THE JUDICIARY.

[Note, that the exception described below for statements against interest was indeed amended by Congress. The Senate view on the reference to "civil liability," described in the third paragraph below, prevailed in the end. So did the Senate view on the sentence which would have put third party confessions implicating the accused beyond reach of the exception.]

The rule defines those statements which are considered to be against interest and thus of sufficient trustworthiness to be admissible even though hearsay. With regard to the type of interest declared against, the version submitted by the Supreme Court included inter alia, statements tending to subject a declarant to civil liability or to invalidate a claim by him against another. The House struck these provisions as redundant. In view of the conflicting case law construing pecuniary or proprietary interests narrowly so as to exclude, e.g., tort cases, this deletion could be misconstrued.

Three States which have recently codified their rules of evidence have followed the Supreme Court's version of this rule, i.e., that a statement is against interest if it tends to subject a declarant to civil liability.[18]

The committee believes that the reference to statements tending to subject a person to civil liability constitutes a desirable clarification of the scope of the rule. Therefore, we have reinstated the Supreme Court language on this matter.

The Court rule also proposed to expand the hearsay limitation from its present federal limitation to include statements subjecting the declarant to statements tending to make him an object of hatred, ridicule, or disgrace. The House eliminated the latter category from the subdivision as lacking sufficient guarantees of reliability. Although there is considerable support for the admissibility of such statements (all three of the State rules referred to *supra*, would admit such statements), we accept the deletion by the House.

---

[18] Nev. Rev. Stats. § 51.345; N. Mex. Stats. (1973 Supp.) § 20-4-804(4); West's Wis. Stats. Anno. (1973 Supp.) § 908-045(4).

The House amended this exception to add a sentence making inadmissible a statement or confession offered against the accused in a criminal case, made by a codefendant or other person implicating both himself and the accused. The sentence was added to codify the constitutional principle announced in Bruton v. United States, 391 U.S. 123 (1968). *Bruton* held that the admission of the extrajudicial hearsay statement of one codefendant inculpating a second codefendant violated the confrontation clause of the Sixth Amendment.

The committee decided to delete this provision because the basic approach of the rules is to avoid codifying, or attempting to codify, constitutional evidentiary principles, such as the fifth amendment's right against self-incrimination and, here, the sixth amendment's right of confrontation. Codification of a constitutional principle is unnecessary and, where the principle is under development, often unwise. Furthermore, the House provision does not appear to recognize the exceptions to the *Bruton* rule, e.g. where the codefendant takes the stand and is subject to cross-examination; where the accused confessed, *see* United States v. Mancusi, 404 F.2d 296 (2d Cir. 1968), *cert. denied*, 397 U.S. 942 (1907); where the accused was placed at the scene of the crime, *see* United States v. Zelker, 452 F.2d 1009 (2d Cir. 1971). For these reasons, the committee decided to delete this provision.

REPORT OF THE HOUSE/SENATE CONFERENCE COMMITTEE.

[*Note, that the compromise described below with respect to the exception for statements against interest prevailed.*]

The Senate amendment to subsection (b)(3) provides that a statement is against interest and not excluded by the hearsay rule when the declarant is unavailable as a witness, if the statement tends to subject a person to civil or criminal liability or renders invalid a claim by him against another. The House bill did not refer specifically to civil liability and to rendering invalid a claim against another. The Senate amendment also deletes from the House bill the provision that subsection (b)(3) does not apply to a statement or confession, made by a codefendant or another, which implicates the accused and the person who made the statement, when that statement or confession is offered against the accused in a criminal case.

The Conference adopts the Senate amendment. The Conferees intend to include within the purview of this rule, statements subjecting a person to civil liability and statements rendering claims invalid. The Conferees agree to delete the provision regarding statements by a codefendant, thereby reflecting the general approach in the Rules of Evidence to avoid attempting to codify constitutional evidentiary principles.

ADVISORY COMMITTEE NOTE.

[Note, that the exception described below for statements of personal or family history survived in the form discussed here. It is referred to as Exception (5), but because of the deletion of the exception for statements of recent perception, the exception for statements of personal or family history ultimately became Exception (4) to Rule 804(b).]

Exception (5). The general common law requirement that a declaration in this area must have been made *ante litem motam* has been dropped, as bearing more appropriately on weight than admissibility. *See* 5 Wigmore § 1483. Item (i) specifically disclaims any need of firsthand knowledge respecting declarant's own personal history. In some instances it is self-evident (marriage) and in others impossible and traditionally not required (date of birth). Item (ii) deals with declarations concerning the history of another person. As at common law, declarant is qualified if related by blood or marriage. 5 Wigmore § 1489. In addition, and contrary to the common law, declarant qualifies by virtue of intimate association with the family. *Id.*, § 1487. The requirement sometimes encountered that when the subject of the statement is the relationship between two other persons the declarant must qualify as to both is omitted. Relationship is reciprocal. *Id.*, § 1491.

For comparable provisions, *see* Uniform Rule 63(23), (24), (25); California Evidence Code §§ 1310, 1311; Kansas Code of Civil Procedure § 60-460(u), (v), (w); New Jersey Evidence Rules 63(23), 63(24), 63(25).

REPORT OF THE HOUSE/SENATE CONFERENCE COMMITTEE.

[Note, that the Senate-proposed Rule 804(b)(5) would have created an exception for records and reports by law enforcement personnel. The Senate Committee's view on this exception is stated in its Report on Rule 803(8), which creates an exception for public records. The Conference Committee Report set forth immediately below recommending against adoption of this exception was to prevail, and no such exception is in Rule 804(b).]

Rule 804(b)(5)—Criminal Law Enforcement Records and Reports

The Senate amendment adds a new hearsay exception, not contained in the House bill, which provides that certain law enforcement records are admissible if the officer-declarant is unavailable to testify or be present because of (1) death or physical or mental illness or infirmity or (2) absence from the proceeding and the proponent of the statement has been unable to procure his attendance by process or other reasonable means.

The Conference does not adopt the Senate amendment, preferring instead to leave the bill in the House version, which contained no such provision.

ADVISORY COMMITTEE NOTE.

[Note, that the catchall exception described below as Exception (6) was renumbered as Exception (5) of Rule 804(b) because of the deletion of the exception for statements of recent perception. The simple provision noted below was amended by Congress.]

REPORT OF THE HOUSE COMMITTEE ON THE JUDICIARY.

[The discussion of Rule 804(b)(5) by the Committee is included with its discussion of the identical catchall exception found in Rule 803(24).]

REPORT OF THE SENATE COMMITTEE ON THE JUDICIARY.

[The discussion of Rule 804(b)(5) by the committee is included with its discussion of the identical catchall exception found in Rule 803 (24).]

NOTE BY FEDERAL CENTER.

The rule prescribed by the Supreme Court was amended by the Congress in a number of respects as follows:

Subdivision (a). Paragraphs (1) and (2) were amended by substituting "court" in place of "judge," and paragraph (5) was amended by inserting "(or in the case of a hearsay exception under subdivision (b)(2), (3), or (4), his attendance or testimony)."

Subdivision (b). Exception (1) was amended by inserting "the same or" after "course of," and by substituting the phrase "if the party against whom the testimony is now offered, or, in a civil action or proceeding, a predecessor in interest, had an opportunity and similar motive to develop the testimony by direct, cross, or redirect examination" in place of "at the instance of or against a party with an opportunity to develop the testimony by direct, cross, or redirect examination, with motive and interest similar to those of the party against whom now offered."

Exception (2) as prescribed by the Supreme Court, dealing with statements of recent perception, was deleted by the Congress.

. . . Exception (2) as enacted by the Congress is Exception (3) prescribed by the Supreme Court, amended by inserting at the beginning, "In a prosecution for homicide or in a civil action or proceeding."

Exception (3) as enacted by the Congress is Exception (4) prescribed by the Supreme Court, amended in the first sentence by deleting, after "another," the phrase "or to make him an object of hatred, ridicule, or disgrace," and amended in the second sentence by substituting, after "unless," the phrase, "corroborating circumstances clearly indicate the trustworthiness of the statement," in place of "corroborated."

Exception (4) as enacted by the Congress is Exception (5) prescribed by the Supreme Court without change.

Exception (5) as enacted by the Congress is Exception (6) prescribed by the Supreme Court, amended by substituting "equivalent" in place of "comparable" and by adding all after "trustworthiness."

ADVISORY COMMITTEE NOTE TO 1997 AMENDMENT.

Subdivision (b)(5). The contents of Rule 803(24) and Rule 804(b)(5) have been combined and transferred to new Rule 807. This was done to facilitate additions to Rules 803 and 804. No change in meaning is intended.

Subdivision (b)(6). Rule 804(b)(6) has been added to provide that a party forfeits the right to object on hearsay grounds to the admission of a declarant's prior statement when the party's deliberate wrongdoing or acquiescence therein procured the unavailability of the declarant as a witness. This recognizes the need for a prophylactic rule to deal with abhorrent behavior "which strikes at the heart of the system of justice itself." United States v. Mastrangelo, 693 F.2d 269, 273 (2d Cir. 1982), *cert. denied*, 467 U.S. 1204 (1984). The wrongdoing need not consist of a criminal act. The rule applies to all parties, including the government.

Every circuit that has resolved the question has recognized the principle of forfeiture by misconduct, although the tests for determining whether there is a forfeiture have varied. *See, e.g.*, United States v. Aguiar, 975 F.2d 45, 47 (2d Cir. 1992); United States v. Potamitis, 739 F.2d 784, 789 (2d Cir.), *cert. denied*, 469 U.S. 918 (1984); Steele v. Taylor, 684 F.2d 1193, 1199 (6th Cir. 1982), *cert. denied*, 460 U.S. 1053 (1983); United States v. Balano, 618 F.2d 624, 629 (10th Cir. 1979), *cert. denied*, 449 U.S. 840 (1980); United States v. Carlson, 547 F.2d 1346, 1358–59 (8th Cir.), *cert. denied*, 431 U.S. 914 (1977). The foregoing cases apply a preponderance of the evidence standard. *Contra* United States v. Thevis, 665 F.2d 616, 631 (5th Cir.) (clear and convincing standard), *cert. denied*, 459 U.S. 825 (1982). The usual Rule 104(a) preponderance of the evidence standard has been adopted in light of the behavior the new Rule 804(b)(6) seeks to discourage.

Rule 805. Hearsay Within Hearsay

ADVISORY COMMITTEE NOTE TO THE 2011 AMENDMENT.

The language of Rule 805 has been amended as part of the restyling of the Evidence Rules to make them more easily understood and to make style and terminology consistent throughout the rules. These changes are intended to be stylistic only. There is no intent to change any result in any ruling on evidence admissibility.

ADVISORY COMMITTEE NOTE.

On principle it scarcely seems open to doubt that the hearsay rule should not call for exclusion of a hearsay statement which includes a further hearsay statement when both conform to the requirements of a hearsay exception. Thus a hospital record might contain an entry of the patient's age based on information furnished by his wife. The hospital record would qualify as a regular entry except that the person who furnished the information was not acting in the routine of the business. However, her statement independently qualifies as a statement of pedigree (if she is unavailable) or as a statement made for purposes of diagnosis or treatment, and hence each link in the chain falls under sufficient assurances. Or, further to illustrate, a dying declaration may incorporate a declaration against interest by another declarant. *See* McCormick § 290, p. 611.

NOTE BY FEDERAL JUDICIAL CENTER.

The Rule enacted by Congress is the Rule prescribed by the Supreme Court without change.

Rule 806. Attacking and Supporting the Declarant's Credibility

ADVISORY COMMITTEE NOTE TO THE 2011 AMENDMENT.

The language of Rule 806 has been amended as part of the restyling of the Evidence Rules to make them more easily understood and to make style and terminology consistent throughout the rules. These changes are intended to be stylistic only. There is no intent to change any result in any ruling on evidence admissibility.

The declarant of a hearsay statement which is admitted in evidence is in effect a witness. His credibility should in fairness be subject to impeachment and support as though he had in fact testified. *See* Rules 608 and 609. There are, however, some special aspects of the impeaching of a hearsay declarant which require consideration. These special aspects center upon impeachment by inconsistent statement, arise from factual differences which exist between the use of hearsay and an actual witness and also between various kinds of hearsay, and involve the question of applying to declarants the general rule disallowing evidence of an inconsistent statement to impeach a witness unless he is afforded an opportunity to deny or explain. *See* Rule 613(b).

The principal difference between using hearsay and an actual witness is that the inconsistent statement will in the case of the witness almost inevitably of necessity in the nature of things be a *prior* statement, which it is entirely possible and feasible to call to his attention, while in the case of hearsay the inconsistent statement may well be a *subsequent* one, which practically precludes calling it to the attention of the declarant. The result of insisting upon observation of this impossible requirement in the hearsay situation is to deny the opponent, already barred from cross-examination, any benefit of this important technique of impeachment. The writers favor allowing the subsequent statement. McCormick, § 37, p. 69; 3 Wigmore § 1033. The cases, however, are divided. Cases allowing the impeachment include People v. Collup, 27 Cal.2d 829, 167 P.2d 714 (1946); People v. Rosoto, 58 Cal.2d 304, 23 Cal.Rptr. 779, 373 P.2d 867 (1962); Carver v. United States, 164 U.S. 694, 17 S.Ct. 228, 41 L. Ed. 602 (1897). Contra, Mattox v. United States, 156 U.S. 237, 15 S.Ct. 337, 39 L. Ed. 409 (1895); People v. Hines, 284 N.Y. 93, 29 N.E.2d 483 (1940). The force of *Mattox*, where the hearsay was the former testimony of a deceased witness and the denial of use of a subsequent inconsistent statement was upheld, is much diminished by *Carver*, where the hearsay was a dying declaration and denial of use of a subsequent inconsistent statement resulted in reversal. The difference in the particular brand of hearsay seems unimportant when the inconsistent statement is a *subsequent* one. True, the opponent is not totally deprived of cross-examination when the hearsay is former testimony or a deposition but he is deprived of cross-examining on the statement or along lines suggested by it. Mr. Justice Shiras, with two justices joining him, dissented vigorously in *Mattox*.

When the impeaching statement was made *prior* to the hearsay statement, differences in the kinds of hearsay appear which arguably may justify differences in treatment. If the hearsay consisted of a simple statement by the witness, e.g. a dying declaration or a declaration against interest, the feasibility of affording him an opportunity to deny or explain encounters the same practical impossibility as where the statement is a subsequent one, just discussed, although here the impossibility arises from the total absence of anything resembling a hearing at which the matter could be put to him. The courts by a large majority have ruled in favor of allowing the statement to be used under these circumstances. McCormick § 37, p. 69; 3 Wigmore § 1033. If, however, the hearsay consists of former testimony or a deposition, the possibility of calling the prior statement to the attention of the witness or deponent is not ruled out, since the opportunity to cross-examine was available. It might thus be concluded that with former testimony or depositions the conventional foundation should be insisted upon. Most of the cases involve depositions, and Wigmore describes them as divided. 3 Wigmore § 1031. Deposition procedures at best are cumbersome and expensive, and to require the laying of the foundation may impose an undue burden. Under the federal practice, there is no way of knowing with certainty at the time of taking a deposition whether it is merely for discovery or will ultimately end up in evidence. With respect to both former testimony and depositions the possibility exists that knowledge of the statement might not be acquired until after the time of the cross-examination. Moreover, the expanded admissibility of former testimony and depositions under Rule 804(b)(1) calls for a correspondingly expanded approach to impeachment. The rule dispenses with the requirement in all hearsay situations, which is readily administered and best calculated to lead to fair results.

Notice should be taken that Rule 26(f) of the Federal Rules of Civil Procedure, as originally submitted by the Advisory Committee, ended with the following:

". . . and, without having first called them to the deponent's attention, may show statements contradictory thereto made at any time by the deponent."

This language did not appear in the rule as promulgated in December, 1937. *See* 4 Moore's Federal Practice ¶ ¶ 26.01[9], 26.35 (2d ed. 1967). In 1951, Nebraska adopted a provision strongly resembling the one stricken from the federal rule:

"Any party may impeach any adverse deponent by self-contradiction without having laid foundation for such impeachment at the time such deposition was taken." R.S.Neb. § 25-1267.07.

For similar provisions, *see* Uniform Rule 65; California Evidence Code § 1202; Kansas Code of Civil Procedure § 60-462; New Jersey Evidence Rule 65.

The provision for cross-examination of a declarant upon his hearsay statement is a corollary of general principles of cross-examination. A similar provision is found in California Evidence Code § 1203.

REPORT OF THE SENATE COMMITTEE ON THE JUDICIARY.

Rule 906 [806], as passed by the House and as proposed by the Supreme Court provides that whenever a hearsay statement is admitted, the credibility of the declarant of the statement may be attacked, and if attacked may be supported, by any evidence which would be admissible for those purposes if the declarant had testified as a witness. Rule 801 defines what is a hearsay statement. While statements by a person authorized by a party-opponent to make a statement concerning the subject, by the party-opponent's agent or by a coconspirator of a party—*see* rule 801(d)(2)(c), (d) and (e)—are traditionally defined as exceptions to the hearsay rule, rule 801 defines such admission by a party-opponent as statements which are not hearsay. Consequently, rule 806 by referring exclusively to the admission of hearsay statements, does not appear to allow the credibility of the declarant to be attacked when the declarant is a coconspirator, agent or authorized spokesman. The committee is of the view that such statements should open the declarant to attacks on his credibility. Indeed, the reason such statements are excluded from the operation of rule 806 is likely attributable to the drafting technique used to codify the hearsay rule, viz. some statements, instead of being referred to as exceptions to the hearsay rule, are defined as statements which are not hearsay. The phrase "or a statement defined in rule 801(d)(2)(c), (d) and (e)" is added to the rule in order to subject the declarant of such statements, like the declarant of hearsay statements, to attacks on his credibility.[19]

REPORT OF THE HOUSE/SENATE CONFERENCE COMMITTEE.

The Senate amendment permits an attack upon the credibility of the declarant of a statement if the statement is one by a person authorized by a party-opponent to make a statement concerning the subject, only by an agent of a party-opponent, or one by a coconspirator of the party-opponent, as these statements are defined in Rules 801(d)(2)(C), (D) and (E). The House bill has no such provision.

The Conference adopts the Senate amendment. The Senate amendment conforms the rule to present practice.

NOTE BY FEDERAL JUDICIAL CENTER.

The Rule enacted by Congress is the Rule prescribed by the Supreme Court, amended by inserting the phrase "or a statement defined in Rule 801(d)(2), (C), (D) or (E)."

ADVISORY COMMITTEE NOTE TO 1997 AMENDMENT.

The amendment is technical. No substantive change is intended.

Rule 807. Residual Exception

ADVISORY COMMITTEE NOTE TO THE 2011 AMENDMENT.

The language of Rule 807 has been amended as part of the restyling of the Evidence Rules to make them more easily understood and to make style and terminology consistent throughout the rules. These changes are intended to be stylistic only. There is no intent to change any result in any ruling on evidence admissibility.

ADVISORY COMMITTEE NOTE.

The contents of Rule 803(24) and Rule 804(b)(5) have been combined and transferred to new Rule 807. This was done to facilitate additions to Rules 803 and 804. No change in meaning is intended.

AUTHORS' NOTE.

Consult the ADVISORY COMMITTEE NOTES and other materials found in this appendix which accompany Rules 803 and 804 for further discussion of the contents of Rule 807.

---

[19] The Committee considered it unnecessary to include statements contained in Rule 801(d)(2)(A) and (B)—the statement made by the party-opponent himself or the statement of which he has manifested his adoption—because the credibility of the party-opponent is always subject to an attack on his credibility.

ARTICLE IX.
AUTHENTICATION AND IDENTIFICATION

Rule 901. Authenticating or Identifying Evidence

ADVISORY COMMITTEE NOTE TO THE 2011 AMENDMENT.

The language of Rule 901 has been amended as part of the restyling of the Evidence Rules to make them more easily understood and to make style and terminology consistent throughout the rules. These changes are intended to be stylistic only. There is no intent to change any result in any ruling on evidence admissibility.

ADVISORY COMMITTEE NOTE.

Subdivision (a). Authentication and identification represent a special aspect of relevancy. Michael and Adler, Real Proof, 5 Vand.L. Rev. 344, 362 (1952); McCormick §§ 179, 185; Morgan, Basic Problems of Evidence 378 (1962). Thus a telephone conversation may be irrelevant because on an unrelated topic or because the speaker is not identified. The latter aspect is the one here involved. Wigmore describes the need for authentication as "an inherent logical necessity." 7 Wigmore § 2129, p. 564.

This requirement of showing authenticity or identity falls in the category of relevancy dependent upon fulfillment of a condition of fact and is governed by the procedure set forth in Rule 104(b).

The common law approach to authentication of documents has been criticized as an "attitude of agnosticism," McCormick, Cases on Evidence 388, n. 4 (3rd ed. 1956), as one which "departs sharply from men's customs in ordinary affairs," and as presenting only a slight obstacle to the introduction of forgeries in comparison to the time and expense devoted to proving genuine writings which correctly show their origin on their face, McCormick § 185, pp. 395, 396. Today, such available procedures as requests to admit and pretrial conference afford the means of eliminating much of the need for authentication or identification. Also, significant inroads upon the traditional insistence on authentication and identification have been made by accepting as at least prima facie genuine items of the kind treated in Rule 902, *infra*. However, the need for suitable methods of proof still remains, since criminal cases pose their own obstacles to the use of preliminary procedures, unforeseen contingencies may arise, and cases of genuine controversy will still occur.

Subdivision (b). The treatment of authentication and identification draws largely upon the experience embodied in the common law and in statutes to furnish illustrative applications of the general principle set forth in subdivision (a). The examples are not intended as an exclusive enumeration of allowable methods but are meant to guide and suggest, leaving room for growth and development in this area of the law.

The examples relate for the most part to documents, with some attention given to voice communications and computer print-outs. As Wigmore noted, no special rules have been developed for authenticating chattels. Wigmore, Code of Evidence § 2086 (3rd ed. 1942).

It should be observed that compliance with requirements of authentication or identification by no means assures admission of an item into evidence, as other bars, hearsay for example, may remain.

Example (1). Contemplates a broad spectrum ranging from testimony of a witness who was present at the signing of a document to testimony establishing narcotics as taken from an accused and accounting for custody through the period until trial, including laboratory analysis. *See* California Evidence Code § 1413, eyewitness to signing.

Example (2). States conventional doctrine as to lay identification of handwriting, which recognizes that a sufficient familiarity with the handwriting of another person may be acquired by seeing him write, by exchanging correspondence, or by other means, to afford a basis for identifying it on subsequent occasions. McCormick § 189. *See also* California Evidence Code § 1416. Testimony based upon familiarity acquired for purposes of the litigation is reserved to the expert under the example which follows.

Example (3). The history of common law restrictions upon the technique of proving or disproving the genuineness of a disputed specimen of handwriting through comparison with a genuine specimen, by either the testimony of expert witnesses or direct viewing by the triers themselves, is detailed in 7 Wigmore §§ 1991–1994. In breaking away, the English Common Law Procedure Act of 1854, 17 and 18 Vict., c. 125, § 27, cautiously allowed expert or trier to use exemplars "proved to the satisfaction of the judge to be genuine" for purposes of comparison. The language found its way into numerous statutes in this country, e.g., California Evidence Code §§ 1417, 1418. While explainable as a measure of prudence in the process of breaking with precedent in the handwriting situation, the reservation to the judge of the question of the genuineness of exemplars and the imposition of an unusually high standard of persuasion are at variance with the general treatment of relevancy which depends upon fulfillment of a condition of fact. Rule 104(b). No similar attitude is found in other comparison situations, e.g., ballistics comparison by jury, as in Evans v. Commonwealth, 230 Ky. 411, 19 S.W.2d 1091 (1929), or by experts, Annot., 26 A.L.R.2d 892, and no reason appears for its continued existence in handwriting cases. Consequently Example (3) sets no higher standard for handwriting specimens and treats all comparison situations alike, to be governed by Rule 104(b). This approach is consistent with 28 U.S.C. § 1731: "The admitted or proved handwriting of any person shall be admissible, for purposes of comparison, to determine genuineness of other handwriting attributed to such person."

Precedent supports the acceptance of visual comparison as sufficiently satisfying preliminary authentication requirements for admission in evidence. Brandon v. Collins, 267 F.2d 731 (2d Cir. 1959); Wausau Sulphate Fibre Co. v. Commissioner of Internal Revenue, 61 F.2d 879 (7th Cir. 1932); Desimone v. United States, 227 F.2d 864 (9th Cir. 1955).

Example (4). The characteristics of the offered item itself, considered in the light of circumstances, afford authentication techniques in great variety. Thus a document or telephone conversation may be shown to have emanated from a particular person by virtue of its disclosing knowledge of facts known peculiarly to him; Globe Automatic Sprinkler Co. v. Braniff, 89 Okl. 105, 214 P. 127 (1923); California Evidence Code § 1421; similarly, a letter may be authenticated by content and circumstances indicating it was in reply to a duly authenticated one. McCormick § 192; California Evidence Code § 1420. Language patterns may indicate authenticity or its opposite. Magnuson v. State, 187 Wis. 122, 203 N.W. 749 (1925); Arens and Meadow, Psycholinguistics and the Confession Dilemma, 56 Colum.L.Rev. 19 (1956).

Example (5). Since aural voice identification is not a subject of expert testimony, the requisite familiarity may be acquired either before or after the particular speaking which is the subject of the identification, in this respect resembling visual identification of a person rather than identification of handwriting. *Cf.* Example (2), *supra*, People v. Nichols, 378 Ill. 487, 38 N.E.2d 766 (1942); McGuire v. State, 200 Md. 601, 92 A.2d 582 (1952); State v. McGee, 336 Mo. 1082, 83 S.E.2d 98 (1935).

Example (6). The cases are in agreement that a mere assertion of his identity by a person talking on the telephone is not sufficient evidence of the authenticity of the conversation and that additional evidence of his identity is required. The additional evidence need not fall in any set pattern. Thus the content of his statements or the reply technique, under Example (4), *supra*, or voice identification under Example (5), may furnish the necessary foundation. Outgoing calls made by the witness involve additional factors bearing upon authenticity. The calling of a number assigned by the telephone company reasonably supports the assumption that the listing is correct and that the number is the one reached. If the number is that of a place of business, the mass of authority allows an ensuing conversation if it relates to business reasonably transacted over the telephone, on the theory that the maintenance of the telephone connection is an invitation to do business without further identification. Matton v. Hoover Co., 350 Mo. 506, 166

S.W.2d 557 (1942); City of Pawhuska v. Crutchfield, 147 Okl. 4, 293 P. 1095 (1930); Zurich General Acc. & Liability Ins. Co. v. Baum, 159 Va. 404, 165 S.E. 518 (1932). Otherwise, some additional circumstance of identification of the speaker is required. The authorities divide on the question whether the self-identifying statement of the person answering suffices. Example (6) answers in the affirmative on the assumption that usual conduct respecting telephone calls furnish adequate assurances of regularity, bearing in mind that the entire matter is open to exploration before the trier of fact. In general, *see* McCormick § 193; 7 Wigmore § 2155; Annot., 71 A.L.R. 5, 105 id. 326.

Example (7). Public records are regularly authenticated by proof of custody, without more. McCormick § 191; 7 Wigmore §§ 2158, 2159. The example extends the principle to include data stored in computers and similar methods, of which increasing use in the public records area may be expected. *See* California Evidence Code §§ 1532, 1600.

Example (8). The familiar ancient document rule of the common law is extended to include data stored electronically or by other similar means. Since the importance of appearance diminishes in this situation, the importance of custody or place where found increases correspondingly. This expansion is necessary in view of the widespread use of methods of storing data in forms other than conventional written records.

Any time period selected is bound to be arbitrary. The common law period of 30 years is here reduced to 20 years, with some shift of emphasis from the probable unavailability of witnesses to the unlikeliness of a still viable fraud after the lapse of time. The shorter period is specified in the English Evidence Act of 1938, 1 & 2 Geo. 6, c. 28, and in Oregon R.S.1963, § 41.360(34). *See also* the numerous statutes prescribing periods of less than 30 years in the case of recorded documents. 7 Wigmore § 2143.

The application of Example (8) is not subject to any limitation to title documents or to any requirement that possession, in the case of a title document, has been consistent with the document. *See* McCormick § 190.

Example (9) is designed for situations in which the accuracy of a result is dependent upon a process or system which produces it. X rays afford a familiar instance. Among more recent developments is the computer, as to which *see* Transport Indemnity Co. v. Seib, 178 Neb. 253, 132 N.W.2d 871 (1965); States v. Veres, 7 Ariz.App. 117, 436 P.2d 629 (1968); Merrick v. United States Rubber Co., 7 Ariz.App. 433, 440 P.2d 314 (1968); Freed, Computer Print-Outs as Evidence, 16 Am.Jur. Proof of Facts 273; Symposium, Law and Computers in the Mid-Sixties, ALI-ABA (1966); 37 Albany L.Rev 61 (1967). Example (9) does not, of course, foreclose taking judicial notice of the accuracy of the process or system.

Example (10). The example makes clear that methods of authentication provided by Act of Congress and by the Rules of Civil and Criminal Procedure or by Bankruptcy Rules are not intended to be superseded. Illustrative are the provisions for authentication of official records in Civil Procedure Rule 44 and Criminal Procedure Rule 27, for authentication of records of proceedings by court reporters in 28 U.S.C. § 753(b) and Civil Procedure Rule 80(c), and for authentication of depositions in Civil Procedure Rule 30(f).

NOTE BY FEDERAL JUDICIAL CENTER.

The Rule enacted by Congress is the Rule prescribed by the Supreme Court, amended in subdivision (b)(10) by substituting "prescribed" in place of "adopted," and by adding "pursuant to statutory authority."

Rule 9023. Evidence That Is Self-Authenticating

ADVISORY COMMITTEE NOTE TO THE 2011 AMENDMENT.

The language of Rule 902 has been amended as part of the restyling of the Evidence Rules to make them more easily understood and to make style and terminology consistent throughout the rules. These changes are intended to be stylistic only. There is no intent to change any result in any ruling on evidence admissibility.

ADVISORY COMMITTEE NOTE.

Case law and statutes have, over the years, developed a substantial body of instances in which authenticity is taken as sufficiently established for purposes of admissibility without extrinsic evidence to that effect, sometimes for reasons of policy but perhaps more often because practical considerations reduce the possibility of unauthenticity to a very small dimension. The present rule collects and incorporates these situations, in some instances expanding them to occupy a larger area which their underlying considerations justify. In no instance is the opposite party foreclosed from disputing authenticity.

Paragraph (1). The acceptance of documents bearing a public seal and signature, most often encountered in practice in the form of acknowledgments or certificates authenticating copies of public records, is actually of broad application. Whether theoretically based in whole or in part upon judicial notice, the practical underlying considerations are that forgery is a crime and detection is fairly easy and certain. 7 Wigmore § 2161, p. 638; California Evidence Code § 1452. More than 50 provisions for judicial notice of official seals are contained in the United States Code.

Paragraph (2). While statutes are found which raise a presumption of genuineness of purported official signatures in the absence of an official seal, 7 Wigmore § 2167; California Evidence Code § 1453, the greater ease of effecting a forgery under these circumstances is apparent. Hence this paragraph of the rule calls for authentication by an officer who has a seal. Notarial acts by members of the armed forces and other special situations are covered in paragraph (10).

Paragraph (3). provides a method for extending the presumption of authenticity to foreign official documents by a procedure of certification. It is derived from Rule 44(a)(2) of the Rules of Civil Procedure but is broader in applying to public documents rather than being limited to public records.

Paragraph (4). The common law and innumerable statutes have recognized the procedure of authenticating copies of public records by certificate. The certificate qualifies as a public document, receivable as authentic when in conformity with paragraph (1), (2), or (3). Rule 44(a) of the Rules of Civil Procedure and Rule 27 of the Rules of Criminal Procedure have provided authentication procedures of this nature for both domestic and foreign public records. It will be observed that the certification procedure here provided extends only to public records, reports, and recorded documents, all including data compilations, and does not apply to public documents generally. Hence documents provable when presented in original form under paragraphs (1), (2), or (3) may not be provable by certified copy under paragraph (4).

Paragraph (5). Dispensing with preliminary proof of the genuineness of purportedly official publications, most commonly encountered in connection with statutes, court reports, rules, and regulations, has been greatly enlarged by statutes and decisions. 5 Wigmore § 1684. Paragraph (5), it will be noted, does not confer admissibility upon all official publications; it merely provides a means whereby their authenticity may be taken as established for purposes of admissibility. Rule 44(a) of the Rules of Civil Procedure has been to the same effect.

Paragraph (6). The likelihood of forgery of newspapers or periodicals is slight indeed. Hence no danger is apparent in receiving them. Establishing the authenticity of the publication may, of course, leave still open questions of authority and responsibility for items therein contained. *See* 7 Wigmore § 2150. *Cf.* 39 U.S.C. § 4005(b), public advertisement prima facie evidence of agency of person named, in postal fraud order proceeding; Canadian Uniform Evidence Act, Draft of 1936, printed copy of newspaper prima facie evidence that notices or advertisements were authorized.

Paragraph (7). Several factors justify dispensing with preliminary proof of genuineness of commercial and mercantile labels and the like. The risk of forgery is minimal. Trademark infringement involves serious penalties. Great efforts are devoted to inducing the public to buy in reliance on brand names, and substantial protection is given them. Hence the fairness of this treatment finds recognition in the cases. Curtiss Candy Co. v. Johnson, 163 Miss. 426, 141 So. 762 (1932), Baby Ruth candy bar; Doyle v. Continental Baking Co., 262 Mass. 516, 160 N.E. 325 (1928), loaf of bread; Weiner v. Mager & Throne, Inc., 167 Misc. 338, 3 N.Y.S.2d 918 (1938), same. And *see* W.Va.Code 1966, § 47-3-5, trademark on bottle prima facie evidence of ownership. *Contra*, Keegan v. Green Giant Co., 150 Me. 283, 110 A.2d 599 (1954); Murphy v. Campbell Soup Co., 62 F.2d 564 (1st Cir. 1933). Cattle brands have received similar acceptance in the western states. Rev.Code Mont.1947, § 46-606; State v. Wolfley, 75 Kan. 406, 89 P. 1046 (1907); Annot., 11 L.R.A.(N.S.) 87. Inscriptions on trains and vehicles are held to be prima facie evidence of ownership or control. Pittsburgh, Ft. W. & C. Ry. v. Callaghan, 157 Ill. 406, 41 N.E. 909 (1895); 9 Wigmore § 2510a. *See also* the provision of 19 U.S.C. § 1615(2) that marks, labels, brands, or stamps indicating foreign origin are prima facie evidence of foreign origin of merchandise.

Paragraph (8). In virtually every state, acknowledged title documents are receivable in evidence without further proof. Statutes are collected in 5 Wigmore § 1676. If this authentication suffices for documents of the importance of those affecting titles, logic scarcely permits denying this method when other kinds of documents are involved. Instances of broadly inclusive statutes are California Evidence Code § 1451 and N.Y.CPLR 4538, McKinney's Consol. Laws 1963.

REPORT OF THE HOUSE COMMITTEE ON THE JUDICIARY.

Rule 902(8) as submitted by the Court referred to certificates of acknowledgment "under the hand and seal of" a notary public or other officer authorized by law to take acknowledgments. The Committee amended the Rule to eliminate the requirement, believed to be inconsistent with the law in some States, that a notary public must affix a seal to a document acknowledged before him. As amended the Rule merely requires that the document be executed in the manner prescribed by State law.

ADVISORY COMMITTEE NOTE.

Paragraph (9). Issues of the authenticity of commercial paper in federal courts will usually arise in diversity cases, will involve an element of a cause of action or defense, and with respect to presumptions and burden of proof will be controlled by Erie Railroad Co. v. Tompkins, 304 U.S. 64, 58 S.Ct. 817, 82 L. Ed. 1188 (1938). Rule 302, *supra*. There may, however, be questions of authenticity involving lesser segments of a case or the case may be one governed by federal common law. Clearfield Trust Co. v. United States, 318 U.S. 363, 63 S.Ct. 573, 87 L. Ed. 838 (1943). *Cf.* United States v. Yazell, 382 U.S.

341, 86 S.Ct. 500, 15 L.Ed.2d 404 (1966). In these situations, resort to the useful authentication provisions of the Uniform Commercial Code is provided for. While the phrasing is in terms of "general commercial law," in order to avoid the potential complications inherent in borrowing local statutes, today one would have difficulty in determining the general commercial law without referring to the Code. *See* Williams v. Walker-Thomas Furniture Co., 350 F.2d 445, 121 U.S.App.D.C. 315 (1965). Pertinent Code provisions are sections 1-202, 3-307, and 3-510, dealing with third-party documents, signatures on negotiable instruments, protests, and statements of dishonor.

REPORT OF THE HOUSE COMMITTEE ON THE JUDICIARY.

The Committee approved Rule 902(9) as submitted by the Court. With respect to the meaning of the phrase "general commercial law," the Committee intends that the Uniform Commercial Code, which has been adopted in virtually every State, will be followed generally, but that federal commercial law will apply where federal commercial paper is involved. *See* Clearfield Trust Co. v. United States, 318 U.S. 363 (1943). Further, in those instances in which the issues are governed by Erie R. Co. v. Tompkins, 304 U.S. 64 (1938), State law will apply irrespective of whether it is the Uniform Commercial Code.

ADVISORY COMMITTEE NOTE.

Paragraph (10). The paragraph continues in effect dispensations with preliminary proof of genuineness provided in various Acts of Congress. *See*, for example, 10 U.S.C. § 936, signature, without seal, together with title, prima facie evidence of authenticity of acts of certain military personnel who are given notarial powers; 15 U.S.C. § 77f(a), signature on SEC registration presumed genuine; 26 U.S.C. § 6064, signature to tax return prima facie genuine.

NOTE BY FEDERAL JUDICIAL CENTER.

The Rule enacted by Congress is the Rule prescribed by the Supreme Court, amended as follows:

Paragraph (4) was amended by substituting "prescribed" in place of "adopted," and by adding "pursuant to statutory authority."

Paragraph (8) was amended by substituting "in the manner provided by law" in place of "under the hand and seal of."

ADVISORY COMMITTEE NOTE.

Paragraphs (11) and (12). Notes of Advisory Committee on 2000 amendments. The amendment adds two new paragraphs to the rule on self-authentication. It sets forth a procedure by which parties can authenticate certain records of regularly conducted activity, other than through the testimony of a foundation witness. *See* the amendment to Rule 803(6). 18 U.S.C. § 3505 currently provides a means for certifying foreign records of regularly conducted activity in criminal cases, and this amendment is intended to establish a similar procedure for domestic records, and for foreign records offered in civil cases.

A declaration that satisfies 28 U.S.C. § 1746 would satisfy the declaration requirement of Rule 902(11), as would any comparable certification under oath.

The notice requirement in Rules 902(11) and (12) is intended to give the opponent of the evidence a full opportunity to test the adequacy of the foundation set forth in the declaration.

Rule 903. Subscribing Witness's Testimony

ADVISORY COMMITTEE NOTE TO THE 2011 AMENDMENT.

The language of Rule 903 has been amended as part of the restyling of the Evidence Rules to make them more easily understood and to make style and terminology consistent throughout the rules. These changes are intended to be stylistic only. There is no intent to change any result in any ruling on evidence admissibility.

ADVISORY COMMITTEE NOTE.

The common law required that attesting witnesses be produced or accounted for. Today the requirement has generally been abolished except with respect to documents which must be attested to be valid, e.g. wills in some states. McCormick § 188. Uniform Rule 71; California Evidence Code § 1411; Kansas Code of Civil Procedure § 60-468; New Jersey Evidence Rule 71; New York CPLR Rule 4537.

NOTE BY FEDERAL JUDICIAL CENTER.

The Rule enacted by Congress is the Rule prescribed by the Supreme Court without change.

ARTICLE X.
CONTENTS OF WRITINGS, RECORDINGS AND PHOTOGRAPHS

Rule 1001. Definitions That Apply to This Article

ADVISORY COMMITTEE NOTE TO THE 2011 AMENDMENT.

The language of Rule 1001 has been amended as part of the restyling of the Evidence Rules to make them more easily understood and to make style and terminology consistent throughout the rules. These changes are intended to be stylistic only. There is no intent to change any result in any ruling on evidence admissibility.

ADVISORY COMMITTEE NOTE.

In an earlier day, when discovery and other related procedures were strictly limited, the misleading named "best evidence rule" afforded substantial guarantees against inaccuracies and fraud by its insistence upon production of original documents. The great enlargement of the scope of discovery and related procedures in recent times has measurably reduced the need for the rule. Nevertheless important areas of usefulness persist: discovery of documents outside the jurisdiction may require substantial outlay of time and money; the unanticipated document may not practically be discoverable; criminal cases have built-in limitations on discovery. Cleary and Strong, The Best Evidence Rule: An Evaluation in Context, 51 Iowa L.Rev. 825 (1966).

Paragraph (1). Traditionally the rule requiring the original centered upon accumulations of data and expressions affecting legal relations set forth in words and figures. This meant that the rule was one essentially related to writings. Present day techniques have expanded methods of storing data, yet the essential form which the information ultimately assumes for usable purposes is words and figures. Hence the considerations underlying the rule dictate its expansion to include computers, photographic systems, and other modern developments.

REPORT OF THE HOUSE COMMITTEE ON THE JUDICIARY.

The Committee amended this Rule expressly to include "video tapes" in the definition of "photographs."

ADVISORY COMMITTEE NOTE.

Paragraph (3). In most instances, what is an original will be self-evident and further refinement will be unnecessary. However, in some instances particularized definition is required. A carbon copy of a contract executed in duplicate becomes an original, as does a sales ticket carbon copy given to a customer. While strictly speaking the original of a photograph might be thought to be only the negative, practicality and common usage require that any print from the negative be regarded as an original. Similarly, practicality and usage confer the status of original upon any computer printout. Transport Indemnity Co. v. Seib, 178 Neb. 253, 132 N.W.2d 871 (1965).

Paragraph (4). The definition describes "copies" produced by methods possessing an accuracy which virtually eliminates the possibility of error. Copies thus produced are given the status of originals in large measure by Rule 1003, *infra*. Copies subsequently produced manually, whether handwritten or typed, are not within the definition. It should be noted that what is an original for some purposes may be a duplicate for others. Thus a bank's microfilm record of checks cleared is the original as a record. However, a print offered as a copy of a check whose contents are in controversy is a duplicate. This result is substantially consistent with 28 U.S.C. § 1732(b). Compare 26 U.S.C. § 7513(c), giving full status as originals to photographic reproductions of tax returns and other documents, made by authority of the Secretary of the Treasury, and 44 U.S.C. § 399(a), giving original status to photographic copies in the National Archives.

NOTE BY FEDERAL JUDICIAL CENTER.

The Rule enacted by Congress is the Rule prescribed by the Supreme Court, amended by inserting "video tapes" in paragraph (2).

Rule 1002. Requirement of the Original

ADVISORY COMMITTEE NOTE TO THE 2011 AMENDMENT.

The language of Rule 1002 has been amended as part of the restyling of the Evidence Rules to make them more easily understood and to make style and terminology consistent throughout the rules. These changes are intended to be stylistic only. There is no intent to change any result in any ruling on evidence admissibility.

ADVISORY COMMITTEE NOTE.

The rule is the familiar one requiring production of the original of a document to prove its contents, expanded to include writings, recordings, and photographs, as defined in Rule 1001(1) and (2), *supra*.

Application of the rule requires a resolution of the question whether contents are sought to be proved. Thus an event may be proved by nondocumentary evidence, even though a written record of it was made. If, however, the event is sought to be proved by the written record, the rule applies. For example, payment may be proved without producing the written receipt which was given. Earnings may be proved without producing books of account in which they are entered. McCormick § 198; 4 Wigmore § 1245. Nor does the rule apply to testimony that books or records have been examined and found not to contain any reference to a designated matter.

The assumption should not be made that the rule will come into operation on every occasion when use is made of a photograph in evidence. On the contrary, the rule will seldom apply to ordinary photographs. In most instances a party *wishes* to introduce the item and the question raised is the propriety of receiving it in evidence. Cases in which an offer is made of the testimony of a witness as to what he saw in a photograph or motion picture, without producing the same, are most unusual. The usual course is for a witness on the stand to identify the photograph or motion picture as a correct representation of events which he saw or of a scene with which he is familiar. In fact he adopts the picture as his testimony, or, in common parlance, uses the picture to illustrate his testimony. Under these circumstances, no effort is made to prove the contents of the picture, and the rule is inapplicable. Paradis, The Celluloid Witness, 37 U.Colo.L.Rev. 235, 249–251 (1965).

On occasion, however, situations arise in which contents are sought to be proved. Copyright, defamation, and invasion of privacy by photograph or motion picture falls in this category. Similarly as to situations in which the picture is offered as having independent probative value, e.g. automatic photograph of bank robber. *See* People v. Doggett, 83 Cal.App.2d 405, 188 P.2d 792 (1948), photograph of defendants engaged in indecent act; Mouser and Philbin, Photographic Evidence—Is There a Recognized Basis for Admissibility? 8 Hastings L.J. 310 (1957). The most commonly encountered of this latter group is of course, the X ray, with substantial authority calling for production of the original. Daniels v. Iowa City, 191 Iowa 811, 183 N.W. 415 (1921); Callamare v. Third Acc. Transit Corp., 273 App.Div. 260, 77 N.Y.S.2d 91 (1948); Patrick & Tilman v. Matkin, 154 Okl. 232, 7 P.2d 414 (1932); Mendoza v. Rivera, 78 P.R.R. 569 (1955).

It should be noted, however, that Rule 703, *supra*, allows an expert to give an opinion based on matters not in evidence, and the present rule must be read as being limited accordingly in its application. Hospital records which may be admitted as business records under Rule 803(6) commonly contain reports interpreting X rays by the staff radiologist, who qualifies as an expert, and these reports need not be excluded from the records by the instant rule.

The reference to Acts of Congress is made in view of such statutory provisions as 26 U.S.C. § 7513, photographic reproductions of tax returns and documents, made by authority of the Secretary of the Treasury, treated as originals, and 44 U.S.C. § 399(a), photographic copies in National Archives treated as originals.

NOTE BY FEDERAL JUDICIAL CENTER.

The Rule enacted by Congress is the Rule prescribed by the Supreme Court without change.

Rule 1003. Admissibility of Duplicates

ADVISORY COMMITTEE NOTE TO THE 2011 AMENDMENT.

The language of Rule 1003 has been amended as part of the restyling of the Evidence Rules to make them more easily understood and to make style and terminology consistent throughout the rules. These changes are intended to be stylistic only. There is no intent to change any result in any ruling on evidence admissibility.

ADVISORY COMMITTEE NOTE.

When the only concern is with getting the words or other contents before the court with accuracy and precision, then a counterpart serves equally as well as the original, if the counterpart is the product of a method which insures accuracy and genuineness. By definition in Rule 1001(4), *supra*, a "duplicate" possesses this character.

Therefore, if no genuine issue exists as to authenticity and no other reason exists for requiring the original, a duplicate is admissible under the rule. This position finds support in the decisions, Myrick v. United

States, 332 F.2d 279 (5th Cir. 1964), no error in admitting photostatic copies of checks instead of original microfilm in absence of suggestion to trial judge that photostats were incorrect; Johns v. United States, 323 F.2d 421 (5th Cir. 1963), not error to admit concededly accurate tape recording made from original wire recording; Sanget v. Johnston, 315 F.2d 816 (9th Cir. 1963), not error to admit copy of agreement when opponent had original and did not on appeal claim any discrepancy. Other reasons for requiring the original may be present when only a part of the original is reproduced and the remainder is needed for cross-examination or may disclose matters qualifying the part offered or otherwise useful to the opposing party. United States v. Alexander, 326 F.2d 736 (4th Cir. 1964). And *see* Toho Bussan Kaisha, Ltd. v. American President Lines, Ltd., 265 F.2d 418, 76 A.L.R.2d 1344 (2d Cir. 1959).

REPORT OF THE HOUSE COMMITTEE ON THE JUDICIARY.

The Committee approved this Rule in the form submitted by the Court, with the expectation that the courts would be liberal in deciding that a "genuine question is raised as to the authenticity of the original."

NOTE BY FEDERAL JUDICIAL CENTER

The Rule enacted by Congress is the Rule prescribed by the Supreme Court without change.

Rule 1004. Admissibility of Other Evidence of Content

ADVISORY COMMITTEE NOTE TO THE 2011 AMENDMENT.

The language of Rule 1004 has been amended as part of the restyling of the Evidence Rules to make them more easily understood and to make style and terminology consistent throughout the rules. These changes are intended to be stylistic only. There is no intent to change any result in any ruling on evidence admissibility.

ADVISORY COMMITTEE NOTE.

Basically the rule requiring the production of the original as proof of contents has developed as a rule of preference: if failure to produce the original is satisfactorily explained, secondary evidence is admissible. The instant rule specifies the circumstances under which production of the original is excused.

The rule recognizes no "degrees" of secondary evidence. While strict logic might call for extending the principle of preference beyond simply preferring the original, the formulation of a hierarchy of preferences and a procedure for making it effective is believed to involve unwarranted complexities. Most, if not all, that would be accomplished by an extended scheme of preferences will, in any event, be achieved through the normal motivation of a party to present the most convincing evidence possible and the arguments and procedures available to his opponent if he does not. Compare McCormick § 207.

Paragraph (1). Loss or destruction of the original, unless due to bad faith of the proponent, is a satisfactory explanation of nonproduction. McCormick § 201.

REPORT OF THE HOUSE COMMITTEE ON THE JUDICIARY.

The Committee approved Rule 1004(1) in the form submitted to Congress. However, the Committee intends that loss or destruction of an original by another person at the instigation of the proponent should be considered as tantamount to loss or destruction in bad faith by the proponent himself.

ADVISORY COMMITTEE NOTE.

Paragraph (2). When the original is in the possession of a third person, inability to procure it from him by resort to process or other judicial procedure is a sufficient explanation of nonproduction. Judicial procedure includes subpoena duces tecum as an incident to the taking of a deposition in another jurisdiction. No further showing is required. *See* McCormick § 202.

Paragraph (3). A party who has an original in his control has no need for the protection of the rule if put on notice that proof of contents will be made. He can ward off secondary evidence by offering the original. The notice procedure here provided is not to be confused with orders to produce or other discovery procedures, as the purpose of the procedure under this rule is to afford the opposite party an opportunity to produce the original, not to compel him to do so. McCormick § 203.

Paragraph (4). While difficult to define with precision, situations arise in which no good purpose is served by production of the original. Examples are the newspaper in an action for the price of publishing defendant's advertisement, Foster-Holcomb Investment Co. v. Little Rock Publishing Co., 151 Ark. 449, 236 S.W. 597 (1922), and the streetcar transfer of plaintiff claiming status as a passenger, Chicago City Ry. Co. v. Carroll, 206 Ill. 318, 68 N.E. 1087 (1903). Numerous cases are collected in McCormick § 200, p. 412, n. 1.

NOTE BY FEDERAL JUDICIAL CENTER.

The Rule enacted by Congress is the Rule prescribed by the Supreme Court without change.

Rule 1005. Copies of Public Records to Prove Content

ADVISORY COMMITTEE NOTE TO THE 2011 AMENDMENT.

The language of Rule 1005 has been amended as part of the restyling of the Evidence Rules to make them more easily understood and to make style and terminology consistent throughout the rules. These changes are intended to be stylistic only. There is no intent to change

any result in any ruling on evidence admissibility.

ADVISORY COMMITTEE NOTE.

Public records call for somewhat different treatment. Removing them from their usual place of keeping would be attended by serious inconvenience to the public and to the custodian. As a consequence judicial decisions and statutes commonly hold that no explanation need be given for failure to produce the original of a public record. McCormick § 204; 4 Wigmore §§ 1215–1228. This blanket dispensation from producing or accounting for the original would open the door to the introduction of every kind of secondary evidence of contents of public records were it not for the preference given certified or compared copies. Recognition of degrees of secondary evidence in this situation is an appropriate *quid pro quo* for not applying the requirement of producing the original.

The provisions of 28 U.S.C. § 1733(b) apply only to departments or agencies of the United States. The rule, however, applies to public records generally and is comparable in scope in this respect to Rule 44(a) of the Rules of Civil Procedure.

NOTE BY FEDERAL JUDICIAL CENTER.

The Rule enacted by Congress is the Rule prescribed by the Supreme Court without change.

Rule 1006. Summaries to Prove Content

ADVISORY COMMITTEE NOTE TO THE 2011 AMENDMENT.

The language of Rule 1006 has been amended as part of the restyling of the Evidence Rules to make them more easily understood and to make style and terminology consistent throughout the rules. These changes are intended to be stylistic only. There is no intent to change any result in any ruling on evidence admissibility.

ADVISORY COMMITTEE NOTE.

The admission of summaries of voluminous books, records, or documents offers the only practicable means of making their contents available to judge and jury. The rule recognizes this practice, with appropriate safeguards. 4 Wigmore § 1230.

NOTE BY FEDERAL JUDICIAL CENTER.

The Rule enacted by Congress is the Rule prescribed by the Supreme Court without change.

Rule 1007. Testimony or Statement of a Party to Prove Content

ADVISORY COMMITTEE NOTE TO THE 2011 AMENDMENT.

The language of Rule 1007 has been amended as part of the restyling of the Evidence Rules to make them more easily understood and to

make style and terminology consistent throughout the rules. These changes are intended to be stylistic only. There is no intent to change any result in any ruling on evidence admissibility.

ADVISORY COMMITTEE NOTE.

While the parent case, Slatterie v. Pooley, 6 M. & W. 664, 151 Eng. Rep. 579 (Exch. 1840), allows proof of contents by evidence of an oral admission by the party against whom offered, without accounting for nonproduction of the original, the risk of inaccuracy is substantial and the decision is at odds with the purpose of the rule giving preference to the original. *See* 4 Wigmore § 1255. The instant rule follows Professor McCormick's suggestion of limiting this use of admissions to those made in the course of giving testimony or in writing. McCormick § 208, p. 424. The limitation, of course, does not call for excluding evidence of an oral admission when nonproduction of the original has been accounted for and secondary evidence generally has become admissible. Rule 1004, *supra*.

A similar provision is contained in New Jersey Evidence Rule 70(1)(h).

NOTE BY FEDERAL JUDICIAL CENTER.

The Rule enacted by Congress is the Rule prescribed by the Supreme Court without change.

Rule 1008. Functions of the Court and Jury

ADVISORY COMMITTEE NOTE TO THE 2011 AMENDMENT.

The language of Rule 1008 has been amended as part of the restyling of the Evidence Rules to make them more easily understood and to make style and terminology consistent throughout the rules. These changes are intended to be stylistic only. There is no intent to change any result in any ruling on evidence admissibility.

ADVISORY COMMITTEE NOTE.

Most preliminary questions of fact in connection with applying the rule preferring the original as evidence of contents are for the judge, under the general principles announced in Rule 1004, *supra*. Thus, the question whether the loss of the originals has been established, or of the fulfillment of other conditions specified in Rule 1004, *supra*, is for the judge. However, questions may arise which go beyond the mere administration of the rule preferring the original and into the merits of the controversy. For example, plaintiff offers secondary evidence of the contents of an alleged contract, after first introducing evidence of loss of the original, and defendant counters with evidence that no such contract was ever executed. If the judge decides that the contract was never executed and excludes the secondary evidence, the case is at an end without ever going to the jury on a central issue. Levin, Authentication and Content of Writings, 10 Rutgers L.Rev. 632, 644 (1956). The latter portion of the instant rule is designed to insure treatment of these situations as raising jury questions. The decision is not one for uncontrolled discretion of the jury but is subject to the control exercised generally by the judge over jury determinations. *See* Rule 104(b), *supra*.

For similar provisions, *see* Uniform Rule 70(2); Kansas Code of Civil Procedure § 60-467(b); New Jersey Evidence Rule 70(2), (3).

NOTE BY FEDERAL JUDICIAL CENTER.

The Rule enacted by Congress is the Rule prescribed by the Supreme Court, amended by substituting "court" in place of "judge," and by adding at the end of the first sentence the phrase "in accordance with the provisions of Rule 104."

Rule 1101. Applicability of the Rules

ADVISORY COMMITTEE NOTE TO THE 2011 AMENDMENT.

The language of Rule 1101 has been amended as part of the restyling of the Evidence Rules to make them more easily understood and to make style and terminology consistent throughout the rules. These changes are intended to be stylistic only. There is no intent to change any result in any ruling on evidence admissibility.

ADVISORY COMMITTEE NOTE.

Subdivision (a). The various enabling acts contain differences in phraseology in their descriptions of the courts over which the Supreme Court's power to make rules of practice and procedure extends. The act concerning civil actions, as amended in 1966, refers to "the district courts . . . of the United States in civil actions, including admiralty and maritime cases . . . ." 28 U.S.C. § 2072, Pub.L. 89-773, § 1, 80 Stat. 1323. The bankruptcy authorization is for rules of practice and procedure "under the Bankruptcy Act." 28 U.S.C. § 2075, Pub.L. 88-623, § 1, 78 Stat. 1001. The Bankruptcy Act in turn creates bankruptcy courts of "the United States district courts and the district courts of the Territories and possessions to which this title is or may hereafter be applicable." 11 U.S.C. §§ 1(10), 11(a). The provision as to criminal rules up to and including verdicts applies to "criminal cases and proceedings to punish for criminal contempt of court in the United States district courts, in the district courts for the districts of the Canal Zone and Virgin Islands, in the Supreme Court of Puerto Rico, and in proceedings before United States magistrates." 18 U.S.C. § 3771.

These various provisions do not in terms describe the same courts. In congressional usage the phrase "district courts of the United States," without further qualification, traditionally has included the district courts established by Congress in the states under Article III of the Constitution, which are "constitutional" courts, and has not included the territorial courts created under Article IV, Section 3, Clause 2, which are "legislative" courts. Hornbuckle v. Toombs, 85 U.S. 648, 21 L. Ed. 966 (1873). However, any doubt as to the inclusion of the District Court for the District of Columbia in the phrase is laid at rest by the provisions of the Judicial Code constituting the judicial districts, 28 U.S.C. § 81 et seq. creating district courts therein, *id.*, § 132, and specifically providing that the term "district court of the United States" means the courts so constituted. *Id.* § 451. The District of Columbia is included. *Id.* § 88. Moreover, when these provisions were enacted, reference to the District of Columbia was deleted from the original civil rules enabling act. 28 U.S.C. § 2072. Likewise Puerto Rico is made a district, with a district court, and included in the term. *Id.* § 119. The question is simply one of the extent of the authority conferred by Congress. With respect to civil rules it seems clearly to include the district courts in the states, the District Court for the District of Columbia, and the District Court for the District of Puerto Rico.

The bankruptcy coverage is broader. The bankruptcy courts include "the United States district courts," which includes those enumerated above. Bankruptcy courts also include "the district courts of the Territories and possessions to which this title is or may hereafter be applicable." 11 U.S.C. §§ 1(10), 11(a). These courts include the district courts of Guam and the Virgin Islands. 48 U.S.C. §§ 1424(b), 1615. Professor Moore points out that whether the District Court for the District of the Canal Zone is a court of bankruptcy "is not free from doubt in view of the fact that no other statute expressly or inferentially provides for the applicability of the Bankruptcy Act in the Zone." He further observes that while there seems to be little doubt that the Zone is a territory or possession within the meaning of the Bankruptcy Act, 11 U.S.C. § 1(10), it must be noted that the appendix to the Canal Zone Code of 1934 did not list the Act among the laws of the United States applicable to the Zone. 1 Moore's Collier on Bankruptcy ¶ 1.10, pp. 67, 72, n. 25 (14th ed. 1967). The Code of 1962 confers on the district court jurisdiction of:

"(4) actions and proceedings involving laws of the United States applicable to the Canal Zone; and

"(5) other matters and proceedings wherein jurisdiction is conferred by this Code or any other law." Canal Zone Code, 1962, Tit. 3, § 141.

Admiralty jurisdiction is expressly conferred. *Id.* § 142. General powers are conferred on the district court, "if the course of proceeding is not specifically prescribed by this Code, by the statute, or by applicable rule of the Supreme Court of the United States . . ." *Id.* § 279. Neither these provisions nor § 1(10) of the Bankruptcy Act ("district courts of the Territories and possessions to which this title is or may hereafter be applicable") furnishes a satisfactory answer as to the status of the District Court for the District of the Canal Zone as a court of bankruptcy. However, the fact is that this court exercises no bankruptcy jurisdiction in practice.

The criminal rules enabling act specifies United States district courts, district courts for the districts of the Canal Zone and the Virgin Islands, the Supreme Court of the Commonwealth of Puerto Rico, and proceedings before United States commissioners. Aside from the addition of commissioners, now magistrates, this scheme differs from the bankruptcy pattern in that it makes no mention of the District Court of Guam but by specific mention removes the Canal Zone from the doubtful list.

The further difference in including the Supreme Court of the Commonwealth of Puerto Rico seems not to be significant for present purposes, since the Supreme Court of the Commonwealth of Puerto Rico is an appellate court. The Rules of Criminal Procedure have not been made applicable to it, as being unneeded and inappropriate, Rule 54(a) of the Federal Rules of Criminal Procedure, and the same approach is indicated with respect to Rules of Evidence.

If one were to stop at this point and frame a rule governing the applicability of the proposed Rules of Evidence in terms of the authority conferred by the three enabling acts, an irregular pattern would emerge as follows:

Civil actions, including admiralty and maritime cases—district courts in the states, District of Columbia, and Puerto Rico.

Bankruptcy—same as civil actions, plus Guam and Virgin Islands.

Criminal cases—same as civil actions, plus Canal Zone and Virgin Islands (but not Guam).

This irregular pattern need not, however, be accepted. Originally the Advisory Committee on the Rules of Civil Procedure took the position that, although the phrase "district courts of the United States" did not include territorial courts, provisions in the organic laws of Puerto Rico and Hawaii would make the rules applicable to the district courts thereof, though this would not be so as to Alaska, the Virgin Islands, or the Canal Zone, whose organic acts contained no corresponding provisions. At the suggestion of the Court, however, the Advisory Committee struck from its notes a statement to the above effect. 2 Moore's Federal Practice ¶ 1.07 (2nd ed. 1967); 1 Barron and Holtzoff, Federal Practice and Procedure § 121 (Wright ed. 1960). Congress thereafter by various enactments provided that the rules and future amendments thereto should apply to the district courts of Hawaii, 53 Stat. 841 (1939), Puerto Rico, 54 Stat. 22 (1940), Alaska, 63 Stat. 445 (1949), Guam, 64 Stat. 384–390 (1950), and the Virgin Islands, 68 Stat.

497, 507 (1954). The original enabling act for rules of criminal procedure specifically mentioned the district courts of the Canal Zone and the Virgin Islands. The Commonwealth of Puerto Rico was blanketed in by creating its court a "district court of the United States" as previously described. Although Guam is not mentioned in either the enabling act or in the expanded definition of "district court of the United States," the Supreme Court in 1956 amended Rule 54(a) to state that the Rules of Criminal Procedure are applicable in Guam. The Court took this step following the enactment of legislation by Congress in 1950 that rules theretofore or thereafter promulgated by the Court in civil cases, admiralty, criminal cases and bankruptcy should apply to the District Court of Guam, 48 U.S.C. § 1424(b), and two Ninth Circuit decisions upholding the applicability of the Rules of Criminal Procedure to Guam. Pugh v. United States, 212 F.2d 761 (9th Cir. 1954); Hatchett v. Guam, 212 F.2d 767 (9th Cir. 1954); Orfield, The Scope of the Federal Rules of Criminal Procedure, 38 U. of Det.L.J. 173, 187 (1960).

From this history, the reasonable conclusion is that Congressional enactment of a provision that rules and future amendments shall apply in the courts of a territory or possession is the equivalent of mention in an enabling act and that a rule on scope and applicability may properly be drafted accordingly. Therefore the pattern set by Rule 54 of the Federal Rules of Criminal Procedure is here followed.

The substitution of magistrates in lieu of commissioners is made in pursuance of the Federal Magistrates Act, P.L. 90-578, approved October 17, 1968, 82 Stat. 1107.

Subdivision (b). is a combination of the language of the enabling acts, *supra*, with respect to the kinds of proceedings in which the making of rules is authorized. It is subject to the qualifications expressed in the subdivisions which follow.

Subdivision (c). singling out the rules of privilege for special treatment, is made necessary by the limited applicability of the remaining rules.

Subdivision (d). The rule is not intended as an expression as to when due process or other constitutional provisions may require an evidentiary hearing. Paragraph (1) restates, for convenience, the provisions of the second sentence of Rule 104(a), *supra*. *See* Advisory Committee's Note to that rule.

(2) While some states have statutory requirements that indictments be based on "legal evidence," and there is some case law to the effect that the rules of evidence apply to grand jury proceedings, 1 Wigmore § 4(5), the Supreme Court has not accepted this view. In Costello v. United States, 350 U.S. 359, 76 S.Ct. 406, 100 L. Ed. 397 (1965), the Court refused to allow an indictment to be attacked, for either

constitutional or policy reasons, on the ground that only hearsay evidence was presented.

"It would run counter to the whole history of the grand jury institution, in which laymen conduct their inquiries unfettered by technical rules. Neither justice nor the concept of a fair trial requires such a change." *Id.* at 364. The rule as drafted does not deal with the evidence required to support an indictment.

(3) The rule exempts preliminary examinations in criminal cases. Authority as to the applicability of the rules of evidence to preliminary examinations has been meager and conflicting. Goldstein, The State and the Accused: Balance of Advantage in Criminal Procedure, 69 Yale L.J. 1149, 1168, n. 53 (1960); Comment, Preliminary Hearings on Indictable Offenses in Philadelphia, 106 U. of Pa.L.Rev. 589, 592–593 (1958). Hearsay testimony is, however, customarily received in such examinations. Thus in a Dyer Act case, for example, an affidavit may properly be used in a preliminary examination to prove ownership of the stolen vehicle, thus saving the victim of the crime the hardship of having to travel twice to a distant district for the sole purpose of testifying as to ownership. It is believed that the extent of the applicability of the Rules of Evidence to preliminary examinations should be appropriately dealt with by the Federal Rules of Criminal Procedure which regulate those proceedings.

Extradition and rendition proceedings are governed in detail by statute. 18 U.S.C. §§ 3181–3195. They are essentially administrative in character. Traditionally the rules of evidence have not applied. 1 Wigmore § 4(6). Extradition proceedings are excepted from the operation of the Rules of Criminal Procedure. Rule 54(b)(5) of Federal Rules of Criminal Procedure.

The rules of evidence have not been regarded as applicable to sentencing or probation proceedings, where great reliance is placed upon the presentence investigation and report. Rule 32(c) of the Federal Rules of Criminal Procedure requires a presentence investigation and report in every case unless the court otherwise directs. In Williams v. New York, 337 U.S. 241, 69 S.Ct. 1079, 93 L. Ed. 1337 (1949), in which the judge overruled a jury recommendation of life imprisonment and imposed a death sentence, the Court said that due process does not require confrontation or cross-examination in sentencing or passing on probation, and that the judge has broad discretion as to the sources and types of information relied upon. Compare the recommendation that the substance of all derogatory information be disclosed to the defendant, in A.B.A. Project on Minimum Standards for Criminal Justice, Sentencing Alternatives and Procedures § 4.4, Tentative Draft (1967, Sobeloff, Chm.). Williams was adhered to in Specht v. Patterson, 386 U.S. 605,

87 S.Ct. 1209, 18 L.Ed.2d 326 (1967), but not extended to a proceeding under the Colorado Sex Offenders Act, which was said to be a new charge leading in effect to punishment, more like the recidivist statutes where opportunity must be given to be heard on the habitual criminal issue.

Warrants for arrest, criminal summonses, and search warrants are issued upon complaint or affidavit showing probable cause. Rules 4(a) and 41(c) of the Federal Rules of Criminal Procedure. The nature of the proceedings makes application of the formal rules of evidence inappropriate and impracticable.

Criminal contempts are punishable summarily if the judge certifies that he saw or heard the contempt and that it was committed in the presence of the court. Rule 42(a) of the Federal Rules of Criminal Procedure. The circumstances which preclude application of the rules of evidence in this situation are not present, however, in other cases of criminal contempt.

Proceedings with respect to release on bail or otherwise do not call for application of the rules of evidence. The governing statute specifically provides:

"Information stated in, or offered in connection with, any order entered pursuant to this section need not conform to the rules pertaining to the admissibility of evidence in a court of law." 18 U.S.C.A. § 3146(f).

This provision is consistent with the type of inquiry contemplated in A.B.A. Project on Minimum Standards for Criminal Justice, Standards Relating to Pretrial Release, § 4.5(b), (c), p. 16 (1968). The references to the weight of the evidence against the accused, in Rule 46(a) (1), (c) of the Federal Rules of Criminal Procedure and in 18 U.S.C.A. § 3146(b), as a factor to be considered, clearly do not have in view evidence introduced at a hearing under the rules of evidence.

The rule does not exempt habeas corpus proceedings. The Supreme Court held in Walker v. Johnston, 312 U.S. 275, 61 S.Ct. 574, 85 L. Ed. 830 (1941), that the practice of disposing of matters of fact on affidavit, which prevailed in some circuits, did not "satisfy the command of the statute that the judge shall proceed 'to determine the facts of the case, by hearing the testimony and arguments.' " This view accords with the emphasis in Townsend v. Sain, 372 U.S. 293, 83 S.Ct. 745, 9 L.Ed.2d 770 (1963), upon trial-type proceedings, *id.* 311, 83 S.Ct. 745, with demeanor evidence as a significant factor, *id.* 322, 83 S.Ct. 745, in applications by state prisoners aggrieved by unconstitutional detentions. Hence subdivision (e) applies the rules to habeas corpus proceedings to the extent not inconsistent with the statute.

Subdivision (e). In a substantial number of special proceedings, *ad hoc* evaluation has resulted in the promulgation of particularized evidentiary provisions, by Act of Congress or by rule adopted by the Supreme Court. Well adapted to the particular proceedings, though not apt candidates for inclusion in a set of general rules, they are left undisturbed. Otherwise, however, the rules of evidence are applicable to the proceedings enumerated in the subdivision.

REPORT OF THE HOUSE COMMITTEE ON THE JUDICIARY.

Subdivision (a) as submitted to the Congress, in stating the courts and judges to which the Rules of Evidence apply, omitted the Court of Claims and commissioners of that Court. At the request of the Court of Claims, the Committee amended the Rule to include the Court and its commissioners within the purview of the Rules.

Subdivision (b) was amended merely to substitute positive law citations for those which were not.

NOTE BY FEDERAL JUDICIAL CENTER.

The rule enacted by the Congress is the rule prescribed by the Supreme Court, amended as follows:

Subdivision (a) was amended in the first sentence by inserting "the Court of Claims" and by inserting "actions, cases, and." It was amended in the second sentence by substituting "terms" in place of "word," by inserting the phrase "and 'court'," and by adding "commissioners of the Court of Claims."

Subdivision (b) was amended by substituting "civil actions and proceedings" in place of "civil actions," and by substituting "criminal cases and proceedings" in place of "criminal proceedings."

Subdivision (c) was amended by substituting "rule" in place of "rules" and by changing the verb to the singular.

Subdivision (d) was amended by deleting "those" after "other than" and by substituting "Rule 104" in place of "Rule 104(a)."

Subdivision (e) was amended by substituting "prescribed" in place of "adopted" and by adding "pursuant to statutory authority." The form of the statutory citations was also changed.

ADVISORY COMMITTEE NOTE TO 1993 AMENDMENT.

This revision is made to conform the rule to changes in terminology made by Rule 58 of the Federal Rules of Criminal Procedure and to the changes in the title of United States magistrates made by the Judicial Improvements Act of 1990.

Rule 1102. Amendments

ADVISORY COMMITTEE NOTE TO THE 2011 AMENDMENT.

The language of Rule 1102 has been amended as part of the restyling of the Evidence Rules to make them more easily understood and to make style and terminology consistent throughout the rules. These changes are intended to be stylistic only. There is no intent to change any result in any ruling on evidence admissibility.

REPORT OF THE HOUSE COMMITTEE ON THE JUDICIARY REPORT ON 28 USCS § 2076.

Subsection (a) sets forth the method by which future amendments may be made to the Rules of Evidence. The present Rules Enabling Acts (18 U.S.C. 3771, 3772, 3402; 28 U.S.C. 2072, 2075), which the Supreme Court invoked as the authority pursuant to which it promulgated the Rules of Evidence, provide that the Court may prescribe rules of "practice and procedure" and submit them to Congress. The rules then take effect automatically either at such time as the Court directs, or after ninety days following their submission. An Act of Congress is necessary to prevent any rule so submitted from taking effect.

The Committee believed that many of the Rules of Evidence, particularly in the privilege and hearsay fields, involve substantive policy judgments as to which it is appropriate that the Congress play a greater role than that provided for in the present Enabling Acts. Accordingly, the Committee concluded that it should provide for a new statutory procedure by which amendments to the Rules of Evidence may be made, designed to insure adequate congressional participation in the evidence rule-making process. Section 2(a) as adopted by the Committee adds a new Section 2076, to title 28, United States Code, permitting the Court to prescribe amendments to the Rules of Evidence, which amendments must be reported to the Congress. However, unlike the situation under the present Rules Enabling Acts, either House of Congress may, by resolution, prevent a rule from becoming operative. Moreover, rather than the ninety-day period allowed in the existing Rules Enabling Acts, a one hundred and eighty day period is prescribed for Congressional action.

The committee considered the possibility of requiring Congressional approval of any rule of evidence submitted to it by the Court, and recognized that a similar judgment inhered in Public Law 93-12, pursuant to which the Court's proposed Rules of Evidence were barred from taking effect until approved by Congress. However, the Committee determined that requiring affirmative congressional action was appropriate to this first effort at codifying the Rules of Evidence, but was not needed with respect to subsequent amendments which would likely be of more modest dimension. Indeed, it believed that to require affirmative Congressional action with respect to amendments might well result in some worthwhile amendments not being approved because of other pressing demands on the Congress. The Committee thus concluded that the system of allowing Court-proposed amendments to the Rules of Evidence to take effect automatically unless disapproved by either House strikes a sound balance between the proper role of Congress in the amendatory process and the dictates of convenience and legislative priorities.

Subsection (b) strikes out Section 1732(a) of title 28, United States Code, since its subject matter is covered in Rule 803(6) relating to records of a regularly conducted business activity.

Subsection (c) amends Section 1733 of title 28, United States Code, since that section is largely, if not entirely, encompassed by Rule 803(8) relating to public records and reports. Because of the possibility that Section 1733 may reach some matters not touched by Rule 803(8), subsection (c) does not repeal Section 1733 but merely provides that the Section does not apply to actions, cases, and proceedings to which the Rules of Evidence are applicable.

REPORT OF THE SENATE COMMITTEE ON THE JUDICIARY REPORT ON 28 USCS § 2076.

The House, in order to clarify the power of the Supreme Court to issue Rules of Evidence or amendments to them, added a new Section 2076 to title 28, United States Code, specifying the Supreme Court's authority. The present Rules Enabling Acts (18 U.S.C. §§ 3771, 3772, 3402; 28 U.S.C. 2072, 2075), which the Supreme Court invoked as the authority pursuant to which it promulgated the Rules of Evidence, provide that the Court may prescribe rules of "practice and procedure" and submit them to Congress. The rules then take effect automatically either at such time as the Court directs, or after 90 days following their submission. An act of Congress is necessary to prevent any rule so submitted from taking effect.

The House believed that the Rules of Evidence involve policy judgments as to which it is appropriate for the Congress to play a greater role than that provided in the present Enabling Acts. Accordingly, the bill provides for a new statutory procedure by which amendments to the Rules of Evidence may be made, designed to insure adequate congressional participation in the evidence rulemaking process. Section 2(a) adds a new section, 2076, to title 28, United States Code, permitting the Court to prescribe amendments to the Rules of Evidence, which amendments must be reported to the Congress. However, three changes were made with respect to the role of Congress. First, any rule, rather than the entire package of rules may be disapproved. Second, either House of Congress, rather than the both Houses acting together, can prevent a rule from becoming operative. Third, rather than the 90-day period allowed in the existing Rules Enabling Acts, a 180-day period is prescribed for congressional action.

In order to augment the power of Congress to review rules of evidence, the committee made two additional amendments. It decided to extend the review period to 365 days—1 full year—and adopted a provision under which either House of Congress can defer the effective date of a rule to permit further study, either until a later date or until approved by Act of Congress. Thus, either House of Congress can disapprove or defer consideration of any proposed rule or combination of rules. The committee also added one clarifying amendment which provides that either a proposed rule or a rule already in effect may be amended by Act of Congress. While this has been generally understood, the committee feels it should be made clear.

The committee considered the possibility of requiring congressional approval of any rule of evidence submitted to it by the Court. We determined, however, that while requiring affirmative congressional action was appropriate to this first effort at codifying the Rules of Evidence, it was not needed with respect to subsequent amendments which would likely be of more modest dimension. Indeed, the committee believed that to require affirmative congressional action with respect to amendments might well result in some worthwhile amendments not being approved because of other pressing demands on the Congress. The committee thus concluded that the system of allowing Court-proposed amendments to the Rules of Evidence to take effect automatically unless disapproved by either House strikes a sound balance between the proper role of Congress in the amendatory process and the dictates of convenience and legislative priorities.

For the same reasons, the committee has deleted an amendment made on the floor of the House providing that no amendment creating, abolishing or modifying a privilege could take effect until approved by Act of Congress. The basis for the House action was the belief that rules of privilege constitute matters of substance that require affirmative congressional approval. While matters of privilege are, in a sense, substantive, and also involve particularly sensitive issues, the committee does not believe that privileges necessarily require different treatment from other rules, provided there are adequate safeguards so that the Congress retains sufficient review power to review effectively proposed changes in this area, as well as in others. By extending the period of review from 90 to 365 days and by providing that any proposed rule may be disapproved or its effective date deferred by either House of Congress, the committee believes that the Congress does, in fact retain sufficient review power to reflect its views on such matters.

Subsection (b) strikes out section 1732(a) of title 28, United States Code, since its subject matter is covered in rule 803(b) relating to records of a regularly conducted activity.

Subsection (c) amends section 1733 of title 28, United States Code, since that section is largely, if not entirely, encompassed by rule 803(8) relating to public records and reports. Because of the possibility that section 1733 may reach some matters not touched by rule 803(9), subsection (c) does not repeal section 1733 but merely provides that the section does not apply to actions, cases, and proceedings to which the Rules of Evidence are applicable.

REPORT OF THE HOUSE/SENATE CONFERENCE COMMITTEE REPORT ON 28 USCS § 2076.

Section 2 of the bill adds a new section to title 28 of the United States Code that establishes a procedure for amending the rules of evidence in the future. The House bill provides that the Supreme Court may promulgate amendments, and these amendments become effective 180 days after being reported to Congress. However, any amendment that creates, abolishes or modifies a rule of privilege does not become effective until approved by Act of Congress. The Senate amendments changed the length of time that must elapse before an amendment becomes effective to 365 days. The Senate amendments also added language, not contained in the House provision, that (1) either House can defer the effective date of a proposed amendment to a later date or until approved by Act of Congress and (2) an Act of Congress can amend any rule of evidence, whether proposed or in effect. Finally, the Senate amendments struck the provision requiring that amendments creating, abolishing or modifying a privilege be approved by Act of Congress.

The Conference adopts the House provision on the time period (180 days) and the House provision requiring that an amendment creating, abolishing or modifying a rule of privilege cannot become effective until approved by Act of Congress. The Conference adopts the Senate amendment providing that either House can defer the effective date of an amendment to the rules of evidence and that any rule, either proposed or in effect, can be amended by Act of Congress. In making these changes in the enabling Act, Conference recognizes the continuing role of the Supreme Court in promulgating rules of evidence.

NOTE BY FEDERAL JUDICIAL CENTER.

The Rule was not included among those prescribed by the Supreme Court. The Rule prescribed by the court as 1102 now appears as 1103.

Rule 1103. Title

ADVISORY COMMITTEE NOTE TO THE 2011 AMENDMENT.

The language of Rule 1103 has been amended as part of the restyling of the Evidence Rules to make them more easily understood and to make style and terminology consistent throughout the rules. These changes are intended to be stylistic only. There is no intent to change any result in any ruling on evidence admissibility.

NOTE BY FEDERAL JUDICIAL CENTER.

The Rule enacted by Congress is the Rule prescribed by the Supreme Court as Rule 1102 without change.

Appendix B

Proposed Federal Rules of Evidence Relating to Privilege

NOTE FROM THE AUTHORS:

The Rules set forth below are the Proposed but Rejected Federal Rules of Evidence 501 through 513, governing the subject of privilege. They were originally drafted with the other Federal Rules of Evidence and approved by the United States Judicial Conference and the Supreme Court of the United States. 56 F.R.D. 183, 230–61. But their passage was blocked by Congress, which elected instead to adopt what is now Federal Rule of Evidence 501. These proposed privilege Rules are therefore not binding on federal judges. Nevertheless, more than any of the other Proposed Rules of Evidence that were never adopted, these proposed privilege Rules are deserving of careful study for several reasons.

Although the proposed privilege rules do not carry the force of law, they were designed largely as a codification of where the common law of privilege stood at the time of their drafting. Consequently, with only a few conspicuous exceptions (such as proposed Rules 505 and 513), they serve as one of the best available statements of modern privilege law. It is no coincidence that many federal courts, including the Supreme Court of the United States, have cited the proposed rules as persuasive precedent on important questions of privilege law, *see, e.g.*, Jaffee v. Redmond, 518 U.S. 1, 14–15, 116 S.Ct. 1923, 1930–31, 135 L.Ed.2d 337 (1996), and often as the starting point of their analysis. Moreover, because Federal Rule of Evidence 501 vests federal judges with discretionary control over the development and refinement of federal privilege law, this is, by design, the one area of evidence law where persuasive precedent carries the most weight.

Rule 501. Privileges Recognized Only as Provided

Except as otherwise required by the Constitution of the United States or provided by Act of Congress, and except as provided in these rules or in other rules adopted by the Supreme Court, no person has a privilege to:

(1) Refuse to be a witness; or

(2) Refuse to disclose any matter; or

(3) Refuse to produce any object or writing; or

(4) Prevent another from being a witness or disclosing any matter or producing any object or writing.

ADVISORY COMMITTEE NOTE

No attempt is made in these rules to incorporate the constitutional provisions which relate to the admission and exclusion of evidence, whether denominated as privileges or not. The grand design of these provisions does not readily lend itself to codification. The final reference must be the provisions themselves and the decisions construing them. Nor is formulating a rule an appropriate means of settling unresolved constitutional questions.

Similarly, privileges created by act of Congress are not within the scope of these rules. These privileges do not assume the form of broad principles; they are the product of resolving particular problems in particular terms. Among them are included such provisions as 13 U.S.C. § 9, generally prohibiting official disclosure of census information and conferring a privileged status on retained copies of census reports; 42 U.S.C. § 2000e-5(a), making inadmissible in evidence anything said or done during Equal Employment Opportunity conciliation proceeding; 42 U.S.C. § 2240, making required reports of incidents by nuclear facility licensees inadmissible in actions for damages; 45 U.S.C. §§ 33, 41, similarly as to reports of accidents by railroads; 49 U.S.C. § 1441(e), declaring C.A.B. accident investigation reports inadmissible in actions for damages. The rule leaves them undisturbed.

The reference to other rules adopted by the Supreme Court makes clear that provisions relating to privilege in those rules will continue in operation. *See*, for example, the "work product" immunity against discovery spelled out under the Rules of Civil Procedure in Hickman v. Taylor, 329 U.S. 495, 67 S.Ct. 385, 91 L.Ed. 451 (1947), now formalized in revised Rule 26(b)(3) of the Rules of Civil Procedure, and the secrecy of grand jury proceedings provided by Criminal Rule 6.

With respect to privileges created by state law, these rules in some instances grant them greater status than has heretofore been the case by according them recognition in federal criminal proceedings, bankruptcy, and federal question litigation. *See* Rules 502 and 510. There is, however, no provision generally adopting state-created privileges.

In federal criminal prosecutions the primacy of federal law as to both substance and procedure has been undoubted. *See*, for example, United States v. Krol, 374 F.2d 776 (7th Cir. 1967), sustaining the admission in a federal prosecution of evidence obtained by electronic eavesdropping, despite a state statute declaring the use of these devices unlawful and evidence obtained therefrom inadmissible. This primacy includes matters of privilege. As stated in 4 Barron, Federal Practice and Procedure § 2151, p. 175 (1951):

> "The determination of the question whether a matter is privileged is governed by federal decisions and the state statutes or rules of evidence have no application."

In Funk v. United States, 290 U.S. 371, 54 S.Ct. 212, 78 L.Ed. 369 (1933), the Court had considered the competency of a wife to testify for her husband and concluded that, absent congressional action or direction, the federal courts were to follow the common law as they saw it "in accordance with present day standards of wisdom and justice." And in Wolfle v. United States, 291 U.S. 7, 54 S.Ct. 279, 78 L.Ed. 617 (1934), the Court said with respect to the standard appropriate in determining a claim of privilege for an alleged confidential communication between spouses in a federal criminal prosecution:

> "So our decision here, in the absence of Congressional legislation on the subject, is to be controlled by common law principles, not by local statute." *Id.*, 13, 54 S.Ct. at 280.

On the basis of *Funk* and *Wolfle*, the Advisory Committee on Rules of Criminal Procedure formulated Rule 26, which was adopted by the Court. The pertinent part of the rule provided:

> "The . . . privileges of witnesses shall be governed, except when an act of Congress or these rules otherwise provide, by the principles of the common law as they may be interpreted . . . in the light of reason and experience."

As regards bankruptcy, section 21(a) of the Bankruptcy Act provides for examination of the bankrupt and his spouse concerning the acts, conduct, or property of the bankrupt. The Act limits examination of the spouse to business transacted by her or to which she is a party but provides "That the spouse may be so examined, any law of the United States or of any State to the contrary notwithstanding." 11 U.S.C. § 44(a). The effect of the quoted language is clearly to override any conflicting state rule of incompetency or privilege against spousal testimony. A fair reading would also indicate an overriding of any contrary state rule of privileged confidential spousal communications. Its validity has never been questioned and seems most unlikely to be. As to other privileges, the suggestion has been made that state law applies, though with little citation of authority, 2 Moore's Collier on Bankruptcy ¶ 21.13, p. 297 (14th ed. 1961). This position seems to be contrary to the expression of the Court in McCarthy v. Arndstein, 266 U.S. 34, 39, 45 S.Ct. 16, 69 L.Ed. 158 (1924), which speaks in the pattern of Rule 26 of the Federal Rules of Criminal Procedure:

> "There is no provision [in the Bankruptcy Act] prescribing the rules

by which the examination is to be governed. These are, impliedly, the general rules governing the admissibility of evidence and the competency and compellability of witnesses."

With respect to federal question litigation, the supremacy of federal law may be less clear, yet indications that state privileges are inapplicable preponderate in the circuits. In re Albert Lindley Lee Memorial Hospital, 209 F.2d 122 (2d Cir. 1953), *cert. denied*, Cincotta v. United States, 347 U.S. 960, 74 S.Ct. 709, 98 L.Ed. 1104; Colton v. United States, 306 F.2d 633 (2d Cir. 1962); Falsone v. United States, 205 F.2d 734 (5th Cir. 1953); Fraser v. United States, 145 F.2d 139 (6th Cir. 1944), *cert. denied*, 324 U.S. 849, 65 S.Ct. 684, 89 L.Ed. 1409; United States v. Brunner, 200 F.2d 276 (6th Cir. 1952). *Contra*, Baird v. Koerner, 279 F.2d 623 (9th Cir. 1960). Additional decisions of district courts are collected in Annot., 95 A.L.R.2d 320, 336. While a number of the cases arise from administrative income tax investigations, they nevertheless support the broad proposition of the inapplicability of state privileges in federal proceedings.

In view of these considerations, it is apparent that, to the extent that they accord state privileges standing in federal criminal cases, bankruptcy, and federal question cases, the rules go beyond what previously has been thought necessary or proper.

On the other hand, in diversity cases, or perhaps more accurately cases in which state law furnishes the rule of decision, the rules avoid giving state privileges the effect which substantial authority has thought necessary and proper. Regardless of what might once have been thought to be the command of Erie R. Co. v. Tompkins, 304 U.S. 64, 58 S.Ct. 817, 82 L.Ed. 1188 (1938), as to observance of state created privileges in diversity cases, Hanna v. Plumer, 380 U.S. 460, 85 S.Ct. 1136, 14 L.Ed.2d 8 (1965), is believed to locate the problem in the area of choice rather than necessity. Wright, Procedural Reform: Its Limitations and Its Future, 1 Ga.L.Rev. 563, 572–573 (1967). Contra, Republic Gear Co. v. Borg-Warner Corp., 381 F.2d 551, 555, n. 2 (2d Cir. 1967), and *see* authorities there cited. Hence all significant policy factors need to be considered in order that the choice may be a wise one.

The arguments advanced in favor of recognizing state privileges are: a state privilege is an essential characteristic of a relationship or status created by state law and thus is substantive in the *Erie* sense; state policy ought not to be frustrated by the accident of diversity; the allowance or denial of a privilege is so likely to affect the outcome of litigation as to encourage forum selection on that basis, not a proper function of diversity jurisdiction. There are persuasive answers to these arguments.

(1) As to the question of "substance," it is true that a privilege

commonly represents an aspect of a relationship created and defined by a State. For example, a confidential communications privilege is often an incident of marriage. However, in litigation involving the relationship itself, the privilege is not ordinarily one of the issues. In fact, statutes frequently make the communication privilege inapplicable in cases of divorce. McCormick § 88, p. 177. The same is true with respect to the attorney-client privilege when the parties to the relationship have a falling out. The reality of the matter is that privilege is called into operation, not when the relation giving rise to the privilege is being litigated, but when the litigation involves something substantively devoid of relation to the privilege. The appearance of privilege in the case is quite by accident, and its effect is to block off the tribunal from a source of information. Thus its real impact is on the method of proof in the case, and in comparison any substantive aspect appears tenuous.

(2) By most standards, criminal prosecutions are attended by more serious consequences than civil litigation, and it must be evident that the criminal area has the greatest sensitivity where privilege is concerned. Nevertheless, as previously noted, state privileges traditionally have given way in federal criminal prosecutions. If a privilege is denied in the area of greatest sensitivity, it tends to become illusory as a significant aspect of the relationship out of which it arises. For example, in a state having by statute an accountant's privilege only the most imperceptible added force would be given the privilege by putting the accountant in a position to assure his client that, while he could not block disclosure in a federal criminal prosecution, he could do so in diversity cases as well as in state court proceedings. Thus viewed, state interest in privilege appears less substantial than at first glance might seem to be the case.

Moreover, federal interest is not lacking. It can scarcely be contended that once diversity is invoked the federal government no longer has a legitimate concern in the quality of judicial administration conducted under it aegis. The demise of conformity and the adoption of the Federal Rules of Civil Procedure stand as witness to the contrary.

(3) A large measure of forum shopping is recognized as legitimate in the American judicial system. Subject to the limitations of jurisdiction and the relatively modest controls imposed by venue provisions and the doctrine of forum non conveniens, plaintiffs are allowed in general a free choice of forum. Diversity jurisdiction has as its basic purpose the giving of a choice, not only to plaintiffs but, in removal situations, also to defendants. In principle, the basis of the choice is the supposed need to escape from local prejudice. If the choice were tightly confined to that basis, then complete conformity to local procedure as well as substantive law would be required. This, of course, is not the case, and the choice may in fact be influenced by a wide range of factors. As Dean Ladd has pointed out, a litigant may select the federal court "because of

the federal procedural rules, the liberal discovery provisions, the quality of jurors expected in the federal court, the respect held for federal judges, the control of federal judges over a trial, the summation and comment upon the weight of evidence by the judge, or the authority to grant a new trial if the judge regards the verdict against the weight of the evidence." Ladd, Privileges, 1969 Ariz.St.L.J. 555, 564. Present Rule 43(a) of the Civil Rules specifies a broader range of admissibility in federal than in state courts and makes no exception for diversity cases. Note should also be taken that Rule 26(b)(2) of the Rules of Civil Procedure, as revised, allows discovery to be had of liability insurance, without regard to local state law upon the subject.

When attention is directed to the practical dimensions of the problem, they are found not to be great. The privileges affected are few in number. Most states provide a physician-patient privilege; the proposed rules limit the privilege to a psychotherapist-patient relationship. *See* Advisory Committee's Note to Rule 504. The area of marital privilege under the proposed rules is narrower than in most states. *See* Rule 505. Some states recognize privileges for journalists and accountants; the proposed rules do not.

Physician-patient is the most widely recognized privilege not found in the proposed rules. As a practical matter it was largely eliminated in diversity cases when Rule 35 of the Rules of Civil Procedure became effective in 1938. Under that rule, a party physically examined pursuant to court order, by requesting and obtaining a copy of the report or by taking the deposition of the examiner, waives any privilege regarding the testimony of every other person who has examined him in respect of the same condition. While waiver may be avoided by neither requesting the report nor taking the examiner's deposition, the price is one which most litigant-patients are probably not prepared to pay.

Rule 502. Required Reports Privileged by Statute

A person, corporation, association, or other organization or entity, either public or private, making a return or report required by law to be made has a privilege to refuse to disclose and to prevent any other person from disclosing the return or report, if the law requiring it to be made so provides. A public officer or agency to whom a return or report is required by law to be made has a privilege to refuse to disclose the return or report if the law requiring it to be made so provides. No privilege exists under this rule in actions involving perjury, false statements, fraud in the return or report, or other failure to comply with the law in question.

ADVISORY COMMITTEE NOTE

Statutes which require the making of returns or reports sometimes confer on the reporting party a privilege against disclosure, commonly coupled with a prohibition against disclosure by the officer to whom the report is made. Some of the federal statutes of this kind are mentioned in the Advisory Committee's Note to Rule 501, *supra. See also* the Note to Rule 402, *supra.* A provision against disclosure may be included in a statute for a variety of reasons, the chief of which are probably assuring the validity of the statute against claims of self-incrimination, honoring the privilege against self-incrimination, and encouraging the furnishing of the required information by assuring privacy.

These statutes, both state and federal, may generally be assumed to embody policies of significant dimension. Rule 501 insulates the federal provisions against disturbance by these rules; the present rule reiterates a result commonly specified in federal statutes and extends its application to state statutes of similar character. Illustrations of the kinds of returns and reports contemplated by the rule appear in the cases, in which a reluctance to compel disclosure is manifested. In re Reid, 155 F. 933 (E.D.Mich.1906), assessor not compelled to produce bankrupt's property tax return in view of statute forbidding disclosure; In re Valecia Condensed Milk Co., 240 F. 310 (7th Cir. 1917), secretary of state tax commission not compelled to produce bankrupt's income tax returns in violation of statute; Herman Bros. Pet Supply, Inc. v. N. L. R. B., 360 F.2d 176 (6th Cir. 1966), subpoena denied for production of reports to state employment security commission prohibited by statute, in proceeding for back wages. And *see* the discussion of motor vehicle accident reports in Krizak v. W. C. Brooks & Sons, Inc., 320 F.2d 37, 42–43 (4th Cir. 1963). *Cf.* In re Hines, 69 F.2d 52 (2d Cir. 1934).

Rule 503. Lawyer-Client Privilege

(a) Definitions. As used in this rule:

(1) A "client" is a person, public officer, or corporation, association, or other organization or entity, either public or private, who is rendered professional legal services by a lawyer, or who consults a lawyer with a view to obtaining professional legal services from him.

(2) A "lawyer" is a person authorized, or reasonably believed by the client to be authorized, to practice law in any state or nation.

(3) A "representative of the lawyer" is one employed to assist

the lawyer in the rendition of professional legal services.

(4) A communication is "confidential" if not intended to be disclosed to third persons other than those to whom disclosure is in furtherance of the rendition of professional legal services to the client or those reasonably necessary for the transmission of the communication.

(b) General rule of privilege. A client has a privilege to refuse to disclose and to prevent any other person from disclosing confidential communications made for the purpose of facilitating the rendition of professional legal services to the client, (1) between himself or his representative and his lawyer or his lawyer's representative, or (2) between his lawyer and the lawyer's representative, or (3) by him or his lawyer to a lawyer representing another in a matter of common interest, or (4) between representatives of the client or between the client and a representative of the client, or (5) between lawyers representing the client.

(c) Who may claim the privilege. The privilege may be claimed by the client, his guardian or conservator, the personal representative of a deceased client, or the successor, trustee, or similar representative of a corporation, association, or other organization, whether or not in existence. The person who was the lawyer at the time of the communication may claim the privilege but only on behalf of the client. His authority to do so is presumed in the absence of evidence to the contrary.

(d) Exceptions. There is no privilege under this rule:

(1) Furtherance of crime or fraud. If the services of the lawyer were sought or obtained to enable or aid anyone to commit or plan to commit what the client knew or reasonably should have known to be a crime or fraud; or

(2) Claimants through same deceased client. As to a communication relevant to an issue between parties who claim through the same deceased client, regardless of whether the claims are by testate or intestate succession or by *inter vivos* transaction; or

(3) Breach of duty by lawyer or client. As to a communication relevant to an issue of breach of duty by the lawyer to his client or by the client to his lawyer; or

(4) Document attested by lawyer. As to a communication relevant to an issue concerning an attested document to which the lawyer is an attesting witness: or

(5) Joint clients. As to a communication relevant to a matter of common interest between two or more clients if the communication was made by any of them to a lawyer retained or consulted

in common, when offered in an action between any of the clients.

ADVISORY COMMITTEE NOTE

Subdivision (a). (1) The definition of "client" includes governmental bodies, Connecticut Mutual Life Ins. Co. v. Shields, 18 F.R.D. 448 (S.D.N.Y.1955); People ex rel. Department of Public Works v. Glen Arms Estate, Inc., 230 Cal.App.2d 841, 41 Cal.Rptr. 303 (1965); Rowley v. Ferguson, 48 N.E.2d 243 (Ohio App.1942); and corporations, Radiant Burners, Inc. v. American Gas Assn., 320 F.2d 314 (7th Cir. 1963). *Contra*, Gardner, A Personal Privilege for Communications of Corporate Clients—Paradox or Public Policy, 40 U.Det.L.J. 299, 323, 376 (1963). The definition also extends the status of client to one consulting a lawyer preliminarily with a view to retaining him, even though actual employment does not result. McCormick, § 92, p. 184. The client need not be involved in litigation; the rendition of legal service or advice under any circumstances suffices. 8 Wigmore § 2294 (McNaughton Rev.1961). The services must be professional legal services; purely business or personal matters do not qualify. McCormick § 92, p. 184.

The rule contains no definition of "representative of the client." In the opinion of the Advisory Committee, the matter is better left to resolution by decision on a case-by-case basis. The most restricted position is the "control group" test, limiting the category to persons with authority to seek and act upon legal advice for the client. *See, e.g.,* City of Philadelphia v. Westinghouse Electric Corp., 210 F.Supp. 483 (E.D.Pa.1962), mandamus and prohibition denied *sub nom.* General Electric Co. v. Kirkpatrick, 312 F.2d 742 (3d Cir.), *cert. denied*, 372 U.S. 943; Garrison v. General Motors Corp., 213 F.Supp. 515 (S.D.Cal.1963); Hogan v. Zletz, 43 F.R.D. 308 (N.D.Okla.1967), aff'd *sub nom.* Natta v. Hogan, 392 F.2d 686 (10th Cir. 1968); Day v. Illinois Power Co., 50 Ill.App.2d 52, 199 N.E.2d 802 (1964). Broader formulations are found in other decisions. *See, e.g.,* United States v. United Shoe Machinery Corp., 89 F.Supp. 357 (D.Mass. 1950); Zenith Radio Corp. v. Radio Corp. of America, 121 F.Supp. 792 (D.Del. 1954); Harper & Row Publishers, Inc. v. Decker, 423 F.2d 487 (7th Cir. 1970), aff'd without opinion by equally divided court 400 U.S. 955 (1971), reh. denied 401 U.S. 950; D. I. Chadbourne, Inc. v. Superior Court, 60 Cal.2d 723, 36 Cal.Rptr. 468, 388 P.2d 700 (1964). *Cf.* Rucker v. Wabash R. Co., 418 F.2d 146 (7th Cir. 1969). *See generally*, Simon, The Attorney-Client Privilege as Applied to Corporations, 65 Yale L.J. 953, 956–966 (1956); Note, Attorney-Client Privilege for Corporate Clients: The Control Group Test, 84 Harv.L.Rev. 424 (1970).

The status of employees who are used in the process of communicating, as distinguished from those who are parties to the communication, is treated in paragraph (4) of subdivision (a) of the rule.

(2) A "lawyer" is a person licensed to practice law in any state or nation. There is no requirement that the licensing state or nation recognize the attorney-client privilege, thus avoiding excursions into conflict of laws questions. "Lawyer" also includes a person reasonably believed to be a lawyer. For similar provisions, *see* California Evidence Code § 950.

(3) The definition of "representative of the lawyer" recognizes that the lawyer may, in rendering legal services, utilize the services of assistants in addition to those employed in the process of communicating. Thus the definition includes an expert employed to assist in rendering legal advice. United States v. Kovel, 296 F.2d 918 (2d Cir. 1961) (accountant). *Cf.* Himmelfarb v. United States, 175 F.2d 924 (9th Cir. 1949). It also includes an expert employed to assist in the planning and conduct of litigation, though not one employed to testify as a witness. Lalance & Grosjean Mfg. Co. v. Haberman Mfg. Co., 87 F. 563 (S.D.N.Y.1898), and *see* revised Civil Rule 26(b)(4). The definition does not, however, limit "representative of the lawyer" to experts. Whether his compensation is derived immediately from the lawyer or the client is not material.

(4) The requisite confidentiality of communication is defined in terms of intent. A communication made in public or meant to be relayed to outsiders or which is divulged by the client to third persons can scarcely be considered confidential. McCormick § 95. The intent is inferable from the circumstances. Unless intent to disclose is apparent, the attorney-client communication is confidential. Taking or failing to take precautions may be considered as bearing on intent.

Practicality requires that some disclosure be allowed beyond the immediate circle of lawyer-client and their representatives without impairing confidentiality. Hence the definition allows disclosure to persons "to whom disclosure is in furtherance of the rendition of professional legal services to the client," contemplating those in such relation to the client as "spouse, parent, business associate, or joint client." Comment, California Evidence Code § 952.

Disclosure may also be made to persons "reasonably necessary for the transmission of the communication," without loss of confidentiality.

Subdivision (b) sets forth the privilege, using the previously defined terms: client, lawyer, representative of the lawyer, and confidential communication.

Substantial authority has in the past allowed the eavesdropper to testify to overheard privileged conversations and has admitted intercepted privileged letters. Today, the evolution of more sophisticated techniques of eavesdropping and interception calls for abandonment of this position. The rule accordingly adopts a policy of protection against these kinds of invasion of the privilege.

The privilege extends to communications (1) between client or his representative and lawyer or his representative, (2) between lawyer and lawyer's representative, (3) by client or his lawyer to a lawyer representing another in a matter of common interest, (4) between representatives of the client or the client and a representative of the client, and (5) between lawyers representing the client. All these communications must be specifically for the purpose of obtaining legal services for the client; otherwise the privilege does not attach.

The third type of communication occurs in the "joint defense" or "pooled information" situation, where different lawyers represent clients who have some interests in common. In Chahoon v. Commonwealth, 62 Va. 822 (1871), the court said that the various clients might have retained one attorney to represent all; hence everything said at a joint conference was privileged, and one of the clients could prevent another from disclosing what the other had himself said. The result seems to be incorrect in overlooking a frequent reason for retaining different attorneys by the various clients, namely actually or potentially conflicting interests in addition to the common interest which brings them together. The needs of these cases seem better to be met by allowing each client a privilege as to his own statements. Thus if all resist disclosure, none will occur. Continental Oil Co. v. United States, 330 F.2d 347 (9th Cir. 1964). But, if for reasons of his own, a client wishes to disclose his own statements made at the joint conference, he should be permitted to do so, and the rule is to that effect. The rule does not apply to situations where there is no common interest to be promoted by a joint consultation, and the parties meet on a purely adversary basis. Vance v. State, 190 Tenn. 521, 230 S.W.2d 987 (1950), *cert. denied*, 339 U.S. 988, 70 S.Ct. 1010, 94 L.Ed. 1389. *Cf.* Hunydee v. United States, 355 F.2d 183 (9th Cir. 1965).

Subdivision (c). The privilege is, of course, that of the client, to be claimed by him or by his personal representative. The successor of a dissolved corporate client may claim the privilege. California Evidence Code § 953; New Jersey Evidence Rule 26(1). *Contra*, Uniform Rule 26(1).

The lawyer may not claim the privilege on his own behalf. However, he may claim it on behalf of the client. It is assumed that the ethics of the profession will require him to do so except under most unusual circumstances. American Bar Association, Canons of Professional Ethics, Canon 37. His authority to make the claim is presumed unless there is evidence to the contrary, as would be the case if the client were now a party to litigation in which the question arose and were represented by other counsel. Ex parte Lipscomb, 111 Tex. 409, 239 S.W. 1101 (1922).

Subdivision (d) in general incorporates well established exceptions.

(1) The privilege does not extend to advice in aid of future wrongdoing. 8 Wigmore § 2298 (McNaughton Rev.1961). The wrongdoing need not be that of the client. The provision that the client knew or reasonably should have known of the criminal or fraudulent nature of the act is designed to protect the client who is erroneously advised that a proposed action is within the law. No preliminary finding that sufficient evidence aside from the communication has been introduced to warrant a finding that the services were sought to enable the commission of a wrong is required. *Cf.* Clark v. United States, 289 U.S. 1, 15–16, 53 S.Ct. 465, 77 L.Ed. 993 (1933); Uniform Rule 26(2)(a). While any general exploration of what transpired between attorney and client would, of course, be inappropriate, it is wholly feasible, either at the discovery stage or during trial, so to focus the inquiry by specific questions as to avoid any broad inquiry into attorney-client communications. Numerous cases reflect this approach.

(2) Normally the privilege survives the death of the client and may be asserted by his representative. Subdivision (c), *supra.* When, however, the identity of the person who steps into the client's shoes is in issue, as in a will contest, the identity of the person entitled to claim the privilege remains undetermined until the conclusion of the litigation. The choice is thus between allowing both sides or neither to assert the privilege, with authority and reason favoring the latter view. McCormick § 98; Uniform Rule 26(2)(b); California Evidence Code § 957; Kansas Code of Civil Procedure § 60-426(b)(2); New Jersey Evidence Rule 26(2)(b).

(3) The exception is required by considerations of fairness and policy when questions arise out of dealings between attorney and client, as in cases of controversy over attorney's fees, claims of inadequacy of representation, or charges of professional misconduct. McCormick § 95; Uniform Rule 26(2)(c); California Evidence Code § 958; Kansas Code of Civil Procedure § 60-426(b)(3); New Jersey Evidence Rule 26(2)(c).

(4) When the lawyer acts as attesting witness, the approval of the client to his so doing may safely be assumed, and waiver of the privilege as to any relevant lawyer-client communications is a proper result. McCormick § 92, p. 184; Uniform Rule 26(2)(d); California Evidence Code § 959; Kansas Code of Civil Procedure § 60-426(b) (d) [*sic*].

(5) The subdivision states existing law. McCormick § 95, pp. 192–193. For similar provisions, *see* Uniform Rule 26(2)(e); California

Evidence Code § 962; Kansas Code of Civil Procedure § 60-426(b)(4); New Jersey Evidence Rule 26(2). The situation with which this provision deals is to be distinguished from the case of clients with a common interest who retain different lawyers. *See* subdivision (b)(3) of this rule, *supra.*

Rule 504. Psychotherapist-Patient Privilege
(a) Definitions.

(1) A "patient" is a person who consults or is examined or interviewed by a psychotherapist.

(2) A "psychotherapist" is (A) a person authorized to practice medicine in any state or nation, or reasonably believed by the patient so to be, while engaged in the diagnosis or treatment of a mental or emotional condition, including drug addiction, or (B) a person licensed or certified as a psychologist under the laws of any state or nation, while similarly engaged.

(3) A communication is "confidential" if not intended to be disclosed to third persons other than those present to further the interest of the patient in the consultation, examination, or interview, or persons reasonably necessary for the transmission of the communication, or persons who are participating in the diagnosis and treatment under the direction of the psychotherapist, including members of the patient's family.

(b) General rule of privilege. A patient has a privilege to refuse to disclose and to prevent any other person from disclosing confidential communications, made for the purposes of diagnosis or treatment of his mental or emotional condition, including drug addiction, among himself, his psychotherapist, or persons who are participating in the diagnosis or treatment under the direction of the psychotherapist, including members of the patient's family.

(c) Who may claim the privilege. The privilege may be claimed by the patient, by his guardian or conservator, or by the personal representative of a deceased patient. The person who was the psychotherapist may claim the privilege but only on behalf of the patient. His authority so to do is presumed in the absence of evidence to the contrary.

(d) Exceptions.

(1) Proceedings for hospitalization. There is no privilege under this rule for communications relevant to an issue in proceedings to hospitalize the patient for mental illness, if the psychotherapist in the course of diagnosis or treatment has determined that the patient is in need of hospitalization.

(2) Examination by order of judge. If the judge orders an examination of the mental or emotional condition of the patient, communications made in the course thereof are not privileged under this rule with respect to the particular purpose for which the examination is ordered unless the judge orders otherwise.

(3) Condition an element of claim or defense. There is no privilege under this rule as to communications relevant to an issue of the mental or emotional condition of the patient in any proceeding in which he relies upon the condition as an element of his claim or defense, or, after the patient's death, in any proceeding in which any party relies upon the condition as an element of his claim or defense.

ADVISORY COMMITTEE NOTE

The rules contain no provision for a general physician-patient privilege. While many states have by statute created the privilege, the exceptions which have been found necessary in order to obtain information required by the public interest or to avoid fraud are so numerous as to leave little if any basis for the privilege. Among the exclusions from the statutory privilege, the following may be enumerated; communications not made for purposes of diagnosis and treatment; commitment and restoration proceedings; issues as to wills or otherwise between parties claiming by succession from the patient; actions on insurance policies; required reports (venereal diseases, gunshot wounds, child abuse); communications in furtherance of crime or fraud; mental or physical condition put in issue by patient (personal injury cases); malpractice actions; and some or all criminal prosecutions. California, for example, excepts cases in which the patient puts his condition in issue, all criminal proceedings, will and similar contests, malpractice cases, and disciplinary proceedings, as well as certain other situations, thus leaving virtually nothing covered by the privilege. California Evidence Code §§ 990–1007. For other illustrative statutes *see* Ill.Rev.Stat.1967, C. 51, § 5.1; N.Y.C.P.L.R. § 4504; N.C-.Gen.Stat.1953, § 8-53. Moreover, the possibility of compelling gratuitous disclosure by the physician is foreclosed by his standing to raise the question of relevancy. *See* Note on "Official Information" Privilege following Rule 509, *infra.*

The doubts attendant upon the general physician-patient privilege are not present when the relationship is that of psychotherapist and patient. While the common law recognized no general physician-patient privilege, it had indicated a disposition to recognize a psychotherapist-patient privilege, Note, Confidential Communications to a Psychotherapist: A New Testimonial Privilege, 47 Nw.U.L.Rev. 384 (1952), when legislatures began moving into the field.

The case for the privilege is convincingly stated in Report No. 45, Group for the Advancement of Psychiatry 92 (1960):

"Among physicians, the psychiatrist has a special need to maintain confidentiality. His capacity to help his patients is completely dependent upon their willingness and ability to talk freely. This makes it difficult if not impossible for him to function without being able to assure his patients of confidentiality and, indeed, privileged communication. Where there may be exceptions to this general rule . . . , there is wide agreement that confidentiality is a *sine qua non* for successful psychiatric treatment. The relationship may well be likened to that of the priest-penitent or the lawyer-client. Psychiatrists not only explore the very depths of their patients' conscious, but their unconscious feelings and attitudes as well. Therapeutic effectiveness necessitates going beyond a patient's awareness and, in order to do this, it must be possible to communicate freely. A threat to secrecy blocks successful treatment."

A much more extended exposition of the case for the privilege is made in Slovenko, Psychiatry and a Second Look at the Medical Privilege, 6 Wayne L.Rev. 175, 184 (1960), quoted extensively in the careful Tentative Recommendation and Study Relating to the Uniform Rules of Evidence (Article V. Privileges), Cal.Law Rev. Comm'n, 417 (1964). The conclusion is reached that Wigmore's four conditions needed to justify the existence of a privilege are amply satisfied.

Illustrative statutes are Cal.Evidence Code §§ 1010–1026; Ga.Code § 38-418 (1961 Supp.); Conn.Gen.Stat., § 52-146a (1966 Supp.); Ill.Rev.Stat.1967, c. 51, § 5.2.

While many of the statutes simply place the communications on the same basis as those between attorney and client, 8 Wigmore § 2286, n. 23 (McNaughton Rev.1961), basic differences between the two relationships forbid resorting to attorney-client save as a helpful point of departure. Goldstein and Katz, Psychiatrist-Patient Privilege: The GAP Proposal and the Connecticut Statute, 36 Conn. B.J. 175, 182 (1962).

Subdivision (a). (1) The definition of patient does not include a person submitting to examination for scientific purposes. *Cf.* Cal.Evidence Code § 1101. Attention is directed to 42 U.S.C. § 242(a)(2), as amended by the Drug Abuse and Control Act of 1970, P.L. 91-513, authorizing the Secretary of Health, Education, and Welfare to withhold the identity of persons who are the subjects of research on the use and effect of drugs. The rule would leave this provision in full force. *See* Rule 501.

(2) The definition of psychotherapist embraces a medical doctor while engaged in the diagnosis or treatment of mental or emotional conditions, including drug addiction, in order not to exclude the general

practitioner and to avoid the making of needless refined distinctions concerning what is and what is not the practice of psychiatry. The requirement that the psychologist be in fact licensed, and not merely be believed to be so, is believed to be justified by the number of persons, other than psychiatrists, purporting to render psychotherapeutic aid and the variety of their theories. Cal.Law Rev. Comm'n, *supra*, at pp. 434–437.

The clarification of mental or emotional condition as including drug addiction is consistent with current approaches to drug abuse problems. *See, e.g.*, the definition of "drug dependent person" in 42 U.S.C. 201(q), added by the Drug Abuse Prevention and Control Act of 1970, P.L. 91-513.

(3) Confidential communication is defined in terms conformable with those of the lawyer-client privilege, Rule 503(a)(4), *supra*, with changes appropriate to the difference in circumstance.

Subdivisions (b) and (c). The lawyer-client rule is drawn upon for the phrasing of the general rule of privilege and the determination of those who may claim it. *See* Rule 503(b) and (c).

The specific inclusion of communications made for the diagnosis and treatment of drug addiction recognizes the continuing contemporary concern with rehabilitation of drug dependent persons and is designed to implement that policy by encouraging persons in need thereof to seek assistance. The provision is in harmony with Congressional actions in this area. *See* 42 U.S.C. § 260, providing for voluntary hospitalization of addicts or persons with drug dependence problems and prohibiting use of evidence of admission or treatment in any proceeding against him, and 42 U.S.C. § 3419 providing that in voluntary or involuntary commitment of addicts the results of any hearing, examination, test, or procedure used to determine addiction shall not be used against the patient in any criminal proceeding.

Subdivision (d). The exceptions differ substantially from those of the attorney-client privilege, as a result of the basic differences in the relationships. While it has been argued convincingly that the nature of the psychotherapist-patient relationship demands complete security against legally coerced disclosure in all circumstances, Louisell, The Psychologist in Today's Legal World: Part II, 41 Minn. L.Rev. 731, 746 (1957), the committee of psychiatrists and lawyers who drafted the Connecticut statute concluded that in three instances the need for disclosure was sufficiently great to justify the risk of possible impairment of the relationship. Goldstein and Katz, Psychiatrist-Patient Privilege: The GAP Proposal and the Connecticut Statute, 36 Conn.B.J. 175 (1962). These three exceptions are incorporated in the present rule.

(1) The interests of both patient and public call for a departure from

confidentiality in commitment proceedings. Since disclosure is authorized only when the psychotherapist determines that hospitalization is needed, control over disclosure is placed largely in the hands of a person in whom the patient has already manifested confidence. Hence damage to the relationship is unlikely.

(2) In a court ordered examination, the relationship is likely to be an arm's length one, though not necessarily so. In any event, an exception is necessary for the effective utilization of this important and growing procedure. The exception, it will be observed, deals with a court ordered examination rather than with a court appointed psychotherapist. Also, the exception is effective only with respect to the particular purpose for which the examination is ordered. The rule thus conforms with the provisions of 18 U.S.C. § 4244 that no statement made by the accused in the course of an examination into competency to stand trial is admissible on the issue of guilt and of 42 U.S.C. § 3420 that a physician conducting an examination in a drug addiction commitment proceeding is a competent and compellable witness.

(3) By injecting his condition into litigation, the patient must be said to waive the privilege, in fairness and to avoid abuses. Similar considerations prevail after the patient's death.

Rule 505. Husband-Wife Privilege

(a) General rule of privilege. An accused in a criminal proceeding has a privilege to prevent his spouse from testifying against him.

(b) Who may claim the privilege. The privilege may be claimed by the accused or by the spouse on his behalf. The authority of the spouse to do so is presumed in the absence of evidence to the contrary.

(c) Exceptions. There is no privilege under this rule (1) in proceedings in which one spouse is charged with a crime against the person or property of the other or of a child of either, or with a crime against the person or property of a third person committed in the course of committing a crime against the other, or (2) as to matters occurring prior to the marriage, or (3) in proceedings in which a spouse is charged with importing an alien for prostitution or other immoral purpose in violation of 8 U.S.C. § 1328, with transporting a female in interstate commerce for immoral purposes or other offense in violation of 18 U.S.C. §§ 2421–2424, or with violation of other similar statutes.

ADVISORY COMMITTEE NOTE

Subdivision (a). Rules of evidence have evolved around the marriage relationship in four respects: (1) incompetency of one spouse to testify for the other; (2) privilege of one spouse not to testify against the other; (3) privilege of one spouse not to have the other testify against him; and (4) privilege against disclosure of confidential communications between spouses, sometimes extended to information learned by virtue of the existence of the relationship. Today these matters are largely governed by statutes.

With the disappearance of the disqualification of parties and interested persons, the basis for spousal incompetency no longer existed, and it, too, virtually disappeared in both civil and criminal actions. Usually reached by statute, this result was reached for federal courts by the process of decision. Funk v. United States, 290 U.S. 371, 54 S.Ct. 212, 78 L.Ed. 369 (1933). These rules contain no recognition of incompetency of one spouse to testify for the other.

While some 10 jurisdictions recognize a privilege not to testify against one's spouse in a criminal case, and a much smaller number do so in civil cases, the great majority recognizes no privilege on the part of the testifying spouse, and this is the position taken by the rule. *Compare* Wyatt v. United States, 362 U.S. 525, 80 S.Ct. 901, 4 L.Ed.2d 931 (1960), a Mann Act prosecution in which the wife was the victim. The majority opinion held that she could not claim privilege and was compellable to testify. The holding was narrowly based: The Mann Act presupposed that the women with whom it dealt had no independent wills of their own, and this legislative judgment precluded allowing a victim wife an option whether to testify, lest the policy of the statute be defeated. A vigorous dissent took the view that nothing in the Mann Act required departure from usual doctrine, which was conceived to be one of allowing the injured party to claim or waive privilege.

About 30 jurisdictions recognize a privilege of an accused in a criminal case to prevent his or her spouse from testifying. It is believed to represent the one aspect of marital privilege the continuation of which is warranted. In Hawkins v. United States, 358 U.S. 74, 79 S.Ct. 136, 3 L.Ed.2d 125 (1958) it was sustained. *Cf.* McCormick § 66; 8 Wigmore § 2228 (McNaughton Rev. 1961): Comment, Uniform Rule 23(2).

The rule recognizes no privilege for confidential communications. The traditional justifications for privileges not to testify against a spouse and not to be testified against by one's spouse have been the prevention of marital dissension and the repugnancy of requiring a person to condemn or be condemned by his spouse. 8 Wigmore §§ 2228, 2241 (McNaughton Rev. 1961). These considerations bear no relevancy to marital communications. Nor can it be assumed that marital conduct will be affected by a privilege for confidential communications of whose existence the parties in all likelihood are unaware. The other communication privileges, by way of contrast, have as one party a professional person who can be expected to inform the other of the existence of the privilege. Moreover, the relationships from which those privileges arise are essentially and almost exclusively verbal in nature, quite unlike marriage. *See* Hutchins and Slesinger, Some Observations on the Law of Evidence: Family Relations, 13 Minn.L.Rev. 675 (1929). *Cf.* McCormick § 90; 8 Wigmore § 2337 (McNaughton Rev. 1961).

The parties are not spouses if the marriage was a sham, Lutwak v. United States, 344 U.S. 604 (1953), or they have been divorced, Barsky v. United States, 339 F.2d 180 (9th Cir. 1964), and therefore the privilege is not applicable.

Subdivision (b). This provision is a counterpart of Rules 503(c), 504(c), and 506(c). Its purpose is to provide a procedure for preventing the taking of the spouse's testimony notably in grand jury proceedings, when the accused is absent and does not know that a situation appropriate for a claim of privilege is presented. If the privilege is not claimed by the spouse, the protection of Rule 512 is available.

Subdivision (c) contains three exceptions to the privilege against spousal testimony in criminal cases.

(1) The need of limitation upon the privilege in order to avoid grave injustice in cases of offenses against the other spouse or a child of either can scarcely be denied. 8 Wigmore § 2239 (McNaughton Rev.1961). The rule therefore disallows any privilege against spousal testimony in these cases and in this respect is in accord with the result reached in Wyatt v. United States, 362 U.S. 525, 80 S.Ct. 901, 4 L.Ed.2d 931 (1960), a Mann Act prosecution, denying the accused the privilege of excluding his wife's testimony, since she was the woman who was transported for immoral purposes.

(2) The second exception renders the privilege inapplicable as to matters occurring prior to the marriage. This provision eliminates the possibility of suppressing testimony by marrying the witness.

(3) The third exception continues and expands established Congressional policy. In prosecutions for importing aliens for immoral purposes, Congress has specifically denied the accused any privilege not to have his spouse testify against him. 8 U.S.C. § 1328. No provision of this nature is included in the Mann Act, and in Hawkins v. United States, 358 U.S. 74, 79 S.Ct. 136, 3 L.Ed.2d 125 (1958), the conclusion was reached that the common law privilege continued. Consistency requires

similar results in the two situations. The rule adopts the Congressional approach, as based upon a more realistic appraisal of the marriage relationship in cases of this kind, in preference to the specific result in *Hawkins*. Note the common law treatment of pimping and sexual offenses with third persons as exceptions to marital privilege. 8 Wigmore § 2239 (McNaughton Rev.1961).

With respect to bankruptcy proceedings, the smallness of the area of spousal privilege under the rule and the general inapplicability of privileges created by state law render unnecessary any special provision for examination of the spouse of the bankrupt, such as that now contained in section 21(a) of the Bankruptcy Act. 11 U.S.C. § 44(a).

For recent statutes and rules dealing with husband-wife privileges, *see* California Evidence Code §§ 970–973, 980–987; Kansas Code of Civil Procedure §§ 60-423(b), 60-428; New Jersey Evidence Rules 23(2), 28.

Rule 506. Communications to Clergymen

(a) Definitions. As used in this rule:

(1) A "clergyman" is a minister, priest, rabbi, or other similar functionary of a religious organization, or an individual reasonably believed so to be by the person consulting him.

(2) A communication is "confidential" if made privately and not intended for further disclosure except to other persons present in furtherance of the purpose of the communication.

(b) General rule of privilege. A person has a privilege to refuse to disclose and to prevent another from disclosing a confidential communication by the person to a clergyman in his professional character as spiritual adviser.

(c) Who may claim the privilege. The privilege may be claimed by the person, by his guardian or conservator, or by his personal representative if he is deceased. The clergyman may claim the privilege on behalf of the person. His authority so to do is presumed in the absence of evidence to the contrary.

ADVISORY COMMITTEE NOTE

The considerations which dictate the recognition of privileges generally seem strongly to favor a privilege for confidential communications to clergymen. During the period when most of the common law privileges were taking shape, no clear-cut privilege for communications between priest and penitent emerged. 8 Wigmore § 2394 (McNaughton Rev.1961). The English political climate of the time may well furnish the explanation. In this country, however, the privilege has been recognized by statute in about two-thirds of the states and occasionally by the common law process of decision. *Id.*, § 2395; Mullen v. United States, 105 U.S.App.D.C. 25, 263 F.2d 275 (1959).

Subdivision (a). Paragraph (1) defines a clergyman as a "minister, priest, rabbi, or other similar functionary of a religious organization." The concept is necessarily broader than that inherent in the ministerial exemption for purposes of Selective Service. *See* United States v. Jackson, 369 F.2d 936 (4th Cir. 1966). However, it is not so broad as to include all self-denominated "ministers." A fair construction of the language requires that the person to whom the status is sought to be attached be regularly engaged in activities conforming at least in a general way with those of a Catholic priest, Jewish rabbi, or minister of an established Protestant denomination, though not necessarily on a full-time basis. No further specification seems possible in view of the lack of licensing and certification procedures for clergymen. However, this lack seems to have occasioned no particular difficulties in connection with the solemnization of marriages, which suggests that none may be anticipated here. For similar definitions of "clergyman" *see* California Evidence Code § 1030; New Jersey Evidence Rule 29.

The "reasonable belief" provision finds support in similar provisions for lawyer-client in Rule 503 and for psychotherapist-patient in Rule 504. A parallel is also found in the recognition of the validity of marriages performed by unauthorized persons if the parties reasonably believed them legally qualified. Harper and Skolnick, Problems of the Family 153 (Rev.Ed.1962).

(2) The definition of "confidential" communication is consistent with the use of the term in Rule 503(a)(5) for lawyer-client and in Rule 504(a)(3) for psychotherapist-patient, suitably adapted to communications to clergymen.

Subdivision (b). The choice between a privilege narrowly restricted to doctrinally required confessions and a privilege broadly applicable to all confidential communications with a clergyman in his professional character as spiritual adviser has been exercised in favor of the latter. Many clergymen now receive training in marriage counseling and the handling of personality problems. Matters of this kind fall readily into the realm of the spirit. The same considerations which underlie the psychotherapist-patient privilege of Rule 504 suggest a broad application of the privilege for communications to clergymen.

State statutes and rules fall in both the narrow and the broad categories. A typical narrow statute proscribes disclosure of "a confession . . . made . . . in the course of discipline enjoined by the church to which he belongs." Ariz.Rev.Stats.Ann.1956, § 12-2233. *See also* California Evidence Code § 1032; Uniform Rule 29. Illustrative of the broader privilege are statutes applying to "information communicated to him in a confidential manner, properly entrusted to him in his professional capacity, and necessary to enable him to discharge the functions of his office according to the usual course of his practice or discipline, wherein such person so communicating . . . is seeking spiritual counsel and advice," Fla.Stats.Ann.1960, § 90.241, or to any "confidential communication properly entrusted to him in his professional capacity, and necessary and proper to enable him to discharge the functions of his office according to the usual course of practice or discipline," Iowa Code Ann. 1950, § 622.10. *See also* Ill.Rev.Stats.1967, c. 51, § 48.1; Minn.Stats.Ann.1945, § 595.02(3); New Jersey Evidence Rule 29.

Under the privilege as phrased, the communicating person is entitled to prevent disclosure not only by himself but also by the clergyman and by eavesdroppers. For discussion *see* Advisory Committee's Note under lawyer-client privilege, Rule 503(b).

The nature of what may reasonably be considered spiritual advice makes it unnecessary to include in the rule a specific exception for communications in furtherance of crime or fraud, as in Rule 503(d)(1).

Subdivision (c) makes clear that the privilege belongs to the communicating person. However, a prima facie authority on the part of the clergyman to claim the privilege on behalf of the person is recognized. The discipline of the particular church and the discreetness of the clergyman are believed to constitute sufficient safeguards for the absent communicating person. *See* Advisory Committee's Note to the similar provision with respect to attorney-client in Rule 503(c).

Rule 507. Political Vote

Every person has a privilege to refuse to disclose the tenor of his vote at a political election conducted by secret ballot unless the vote was cast illegally.

ADVISORY COMMITTEE NOTE

Secrecy in voting is an essential aspect of effective democratic government, insuring free exercise of the franchise and fairness in elections. Secrecy after the ballot has been cast is as essential as secrecy in the act of voting. Nutting, Freedom of Silence: Constitutional Protection Against Governmental Intrusion in Political Affairs, 47 Mich.L.Rev. 181, 191 (1948). Consequently a privilege has long been recognized on the part of a voter to decline to disclose how he voted. Required disclosure would be the exercise of "a kind of inquisitorial power unknown to the principles of our government and constitution, and might be highly injurious to the suffrages of a free people, as well as tending to create cabals and disturbances between contending parties in popular elections." Johnston v. Charleston, 1 Bay 441, 442 (S.C.1795).

The exception for illegally cast votes is a common one under both statutes and case law, Nutting, *supra*, at p. 192; 8 Wigmore § 2214, p. 163 (McNaughton Rev.1961). The policy considerations which underlie the privilege are not applicable to the illegal voter. However, nothing in the exception purports to foreclose an illegal voter from invoking the privilege against self-incrimination under appropriate circumstances.

For similar provisions, *see* Uniform Rule 31; California Evidence Code § 1050; Kansas Code of Civil Procedure § 60-431; New Jersey Evidence Rule 31.

Rule 508. Trade Secrets

A person has a privilege, which may be claimed by him or his agent or employee, to refuse to disclose and to prevent other persons from disclosing a trade secret owned by him, if the allowance of the privilege will not tend to conceal fraud or otherwise work injustice. When disclosure is directed, the judge shall take such protective measure as the interests of the holder of the privilege and of the parties and the furtherance of justice may require.

ADVISORY COMMITTEE NOTE

While sometimes said not to be a true privilege, a qualified right to protection against disclosure of trade secrets has found ample recognition, and, indeed, a denial of it would be difficult to defend. 8 Wigmore § 2212(3) (McNaughton Rev.1961). And *see* 4 Moore's Federal Practice ¶¶ 30.12 and 34.15 (2nd ed. 1963 and Supp.1965) and 2A Barron and Holtzoff, Federal Practice and Procedure § 715.1 (Wright ed. 1961). Congressional policy is reflected in the Securities Exchange Act of 1934, 15 U.S.C. § 78x, and the Public Utility Holding Company Act of 1933, *id.* § 79v, which deny the Securities and Exchange Commission authority to require disclosure of trade secrets or processes in applications and reports. *See also* Rule 26(c)(7) of the Rules of Civil Procedure, as revised, mentioned further hereinafter.

Illustrative cases raising trade-secret problems are: E. I. Du Pont de Nemours Powder Co. v. Masland, 244 U.S. 100, 37 S.Ct. 575, 61 L.Ed. 1016 (1917), suit to enjoin former employee from using plaintiff's secret processes, countered by defense that many of the processes were well known to the trade; Segal Lock & Hardware Co. v. FTC, 143 F.2d 935 (2d Cir. 1944), question whether expert locksmiths employed by FTC should be required to disclose methods used by them in picking petitioner's "pick-proof" locks; Dobson v. Graham, 49 F. 17 (E.D.Pa.1889), patent infringement suit in which plaintiff sought to elicit from former employees now in the hire of defendant the respects in which defendant's machinery differed from plaintiff's patented machinery; Putney v. Du Bois Co., 240 Mo.App. 1075, 226 S.W.2d 737 (1950), action for injuries allegedly sustained from using defendant's secret formula dishwashing compound. *See* 8 Wigmore § 2212(3) (McNaughton Rev.1961); Annot., 17 A.L.R.2d 383; 49 Mich.L.Rev. 133 (1950). The need for accommodation between protecting trade secrets, on the one hand, and eliciting facts required for full and fair presentation of a case, on the other hand, is apparent. Whether disclosure should be required depends upon a weighing of the competing interests involved against the background of the total situation, including consideration of such factors as the dangers of abuse, good faith, adequacy of protective measures, and the availability of other means of proof.

The cases furnish examples of the bringing of judicial ingenuity to bear upon the problem of evolving protective measures which achieve a degree of control over disclosure. Perhaps the most common is simply to take testimony *in camera*. Annot., 62 A.L.R.2d 509. Other possibilities include making disclosure to opposing counsel but not to his client, E. I. Du Pont de Nemours Powder Co. v. Masland, 244 U.S. 100, 37 S.Ct. 575, 61 L.Ed. 1016 (1917); making disclosure only to the judge (hearing examiner), Segal Lock & Hardware Co. v. FTC, 143 F.2d 935 (2d Cir. 1944); and placing those present under oath not to make disclosure, Paul v. Sinnott, 217 F.Supp. 84 (W.D.Pa.1963).

Rule 26(c) of the Rules of Civil Procedure, as revised, provides that the judge may make "any order which justice requires to protect a party or person from annoyance, embarrassment, oppression, or undue burden or expense, including one or more of the following: . . . (7) that a trade secret or other confidential research, development, or commercial information not be disclosed or be disclosed only in a designated way . . . .'" While the instant evidence rule extends this underlying policy into the trial, the difference in circumstances between discovery stage and trial may well be such as to require a different ruling at the trial.

For other rules recognizing privilege for trade secrets, *see* Uniform Rule 32; California

Evidence Code § 1060; Kansas Code of Civil Procedure § 60-432; New Jersey Evidence Rule 32.

Rule 509. Secrets of State and Other Official Information

(a) Definitions.

(1) Secret of state. A "secret of state" is a governmental secret relating to the national defense or the international relations of the United States.

(2) Official information. "Official information" is information within the custody or control of a department or agency of the government the disclosure of which is shown to be contrary to the public interest and which consists of: (A) intragovernmental opinions or recommendations submitted for consideration in the performance of decisional or policymaking functions, or (B) subject to the provisions of 18 U.S.C. § 3500, investigatory files compiled for law enforcement purposes and not otherwise available, or (C) information within the custody or control of a governmental department or agency whether initiated within the department or agency or acquired by it in its exercise of its official responsibilities and not otherwise available to the public pursuant to 5 U.S.C. § 552.

(b) General rule of privilege. The government has a privilege to refuse to give evidence and to prevent any person from giving evidence upon a showing of reasonable likelihood of danger that the evidence will disclose a secret of state or official information, as defined in this rule.

(c) Procedures. The privilege for secrets of state may be claimed only by the chief officer of the government agency or department administering the subject matter which the secret information sought concerns, but the privilege for official information may be asserted by any attorney representing the government. The required showing may be made in whole or in part in the form of a written statement. The judge may hear the matter in chambers, but all counsel are entitled to inspect the claim and showing and to be heard thereon, except that, in the case of secrets of state, the judge upon motion of the government, may permit the government to make the required showing in the above form *in camera*. If the judge sustains the privilege upon a showing *in camera*, the entire text of the government's statements shall be sealed and preserved in the court's records in the event of appeal. In the case of privilege claimed for official information the court may require examination *in camera* of the information itself. The judge may take any protective measure which the interest of the government and the furtherance of justice may require.

(d) Notice to government. If the circumstances of the case indicate a substantial possibility that a claim of privilege would be appropriate but has not been made because of oversight or lack of knowledge, the judge shall give or cause notice to be given to the officer entitled to claim the privilege and shall stay further proceedings a reasonable time to afford opportunity to assert a claim of privilege.

(e) Effect of sustaining claim. If a claim of privilege is sustained in a proceeding to which the government is a party and it appears that another party is thereby deprived of material evidence, the judge shall make any further orders which the interests of justice require, including striking the testimony of a witness, declaring a mistrial, finding against the government upon an issue as to which the evidence is relevant, or dismissing the action.

ADVISORY COMMITTEE NOTE

Subdivision (a). (1) The rule embodies the privilege protecting military and state secrets described as "well established in the law of evidence," United States v. Reynolds, 345 U.S. 1, 6, 73 S.Ct. 528, 97 L.Ed. 727 (1953), and as one "the existence of which has never been doubted," 8 Wigmore § 2378, p. 794 (McNaughton Rev.1961).

The use of the term "national defense," without attempt at further elucidation, finds support in the similar usage in statutory provisions relating to the crimes of gathering, transmitting, or losing defense information, and gathering or delivering defense information to aid a foreign government. 18 U.S.C. §§ 793, 794. *See also* 5 U.S.C. § 1002; 50 U.S.C. App. § 2152(d). In determining whether military or state secrets are involved, due regard will, of course, be given to classification pursuant to executive order.

(2) The rule also recognizes a privilege for specified types of official information and in this respect is designed primarily to resolve questions of the availability to litigants of data in the files of governmental departments and agencies. In view of the lesser danger to the public interest than in cases of military and state secrets, the official information privilege is subject to a generally overriding requirement that disclosure would be contrary to the public interest. It is applicable to three categories of information.

(A) Intergovernmental opinions or recommendations submitted for consideration in the performance of decisional or policy making functions. The policy basis of this aspect of the privilege is found in the desirability of encouraging candor in the exchange of views within the government. Kaiser Aluminum & Chemical Corp. v. United States, 141 Ct.Cl. 38, 157 F.Supp. 939 (1958); Davis v. Braswell Motor Freight Lines, Inc., 363 F.2d 600 (5th Cir. 1966); Ackerly v. Ley, 420 F.2d 1336

(D.C. Cir. 1969). A privilege of this character is consistent with the Freedom of Information Act, 5 U.S.C. § 552(b)(5), and with the standing of the agency to raise questions of relevancy, though not a party, recognized in such decisions as Boeing Airplane Co. v. Coggeshall, 108 U.S.App.D.C. 106, 280 F.2d 654, 659 (1960) (Renegotiation Board) and Freeman v. Seligson, 132 U.S.App.D.C. 56, 405 F.2d 1326, 1334 (1968) (Secretary of Agriculture).

(B) Investigatory files compiled for law enforcement purposes. This category is expressly made subject to the provisions of the Jencks Act, 18 U.S.C. § 3500, which insulates prior statements or reports of government witnesses in criminal cases against subpoena, discovery, or inspection until the witness has testified on direct examination at the trial but then entitles the defense to its production. Rarely will documents of this nature be relevant until the author has testified and thus placed his credibility in issue. Further protection against discovery of government files in criminal cases is found in Criminal Procedure Rule 16(a) and (b). The breadth of discovery in civil cases, however, goes beyond ordinary bounds of relevancy and raises problems calling for the exercise of judicial control, and in making provision for it the rule implements the Freedom of Information Act, 18 U.S.C. § 552(b)(7).

(C) Information exempted from disclosure under the Freedom of Information Act, 5 U.S.C. § 552. In 1958 the old "housekeeping" statute which had been relied upon as a foundation for departmental regulations curtailing disclosure was amended by adding a provision that it did not authorize withholding information from the public. In 1966 the Congress enacted the Freedom of Information Act for the purpose of making information in the files of departments and agencies, subject to certain specified exceptions, available to the mass media and to the public generally. 5 U.S.C. § 552. These enactments are significant expressions of Congressional policy. The exceptions in the Act are not framed in terms of evidentiary privilege, thus recognizing by clear implication that the needs of litigants may stand on somewhat different footing from those of the public generally. Nevertheless, the exceptions are based on values obviously entitled to weighty consideration in formulating rules of evidentiary privilege. In some instances in these rules, exceptions in the Act have been made the subject of specific privileges, *e.g.*, military and state secrets in the present rule and trade secrets in Rule 508. The purpose of the present provision is to incorporate the remaining exceptions of the Act into the qualified privilege here created, thus subjecting disclosure of the information to judicial determination with respect to the effect of disclosure on the public interest. This approach appears to afford a satisfactory resolution of the problems which may arise.

Subdivision (b). The rule vests the privileges in the government where they properly belong rather than a party or witness. *See* United States v. Reynolds, *supra*, p. 7, 73 S.Ct. 528. The showing required as a condition precedent to claiming the privilege represents a compromise between complete judicial control and accepting as final the decision of a departmental officer. *See* Machin v. Zuckert, 114 U.S.App.D.C. 335, 316 F.2d 336 (1963), rejecting in part a claim of privilege by the Secretary of the Air Force and ordering the furnishing of information for use in private litigation. This approach is consistent with *Reynolds*.

Subdivision (c). In requiring the claim of privilege for state secrets to be made by the chief departmental officer, the rule again follows *Reynolds*, insuring consideration by a high-level officer. This provision is justified by the lesser participation by the judge in cases of state secrets. The full participation by the judge in official information cases, on the contrary, warrants allowing the claim of privilege to be made by a government attorney.

Subdivision (d) spells out and emphasizes a power and responsibility on the part of the trial judge. An analogous provision is found in the requirement that the court certify to the Attorney General when the constitutionality of an act of Congress is in question in an action to which the government is not a party. 28 U.S.C. § 2403.

Subdivision (e). If privilege is successfully claimed by the government in litigation to which it is not a party, the effect is simply to make the evidence unavailable, as though a witness had died or claimed the privilege against self-incrimination, and no specification of the consequences is necessary. The rule therefore deals only with the effect of a successful claim of privilege by the government in proceedings to which it is a party. Reference to other types of cases serves to illustrate the variety of situations which may arise and the impossibility of evolving a single formula to be applied automatically to all of them. The privileged materials may be the statement of government witness, as under the *Jencks* statute, which provides that, if the government elects not to produce the statement, the judge is to strike the testimony of the witness, or that he may declare a mistrial if the interests of justice so require. 18 U.S.C. § 3500(d). Or the privileged materials may disclose a possible basis for applying pressure upon witnesses. United States v. Beekman, 155 F.2d 580 (2d Cir. 1946). Or they may bear directly upon a substantive element of a criminal case, requiring dismissal in the event of a successful claim of privilege. United States v. Andolschek, 142 F.2d 503 (2d Cir. 1944); and *see* United States v. Reynolds, 345 U.S. 1, 73 S.Ct. 528, 97 L.Ed. 727 (1953). Or they may relate to an element of a plaintiff's claim against the government, with the decisions indicating unwillingness to allow the government's claim of privilege for secrets of state to be used as an offensive weapon against it. United States v.

Reynolds, *supra*; Republic of China v. National Union Fire Ins. Co., 142 F.Supp. 551 (D.Md.1956).

Rule 510. Identity of Informer

(a) Rule of privilege. The government or a state or subdivision thereof has a privilege to refuse to disclose the identity of a person who has furnished information relating to or assisting in an investigation of a possible violation of law to a law enforcement officer or member of a legislative committee or its staff conducting an investigation.

(b) Who may claim. The privilege may be claimed by an appropriate representative of the government, regardless of whether the information was furnished to an officer of the government or of a state or subdivision thereof. The privilege may be claimed by an appropriate representative of a state or subdivision if the information was furnished to an officer thereof, except that in criminal cases the privilege shall not be allowed if the government objects.

(c) Exceptions.

(1) Voluntary disclosure; informer a witness. No privilege exists under this rule if the identity of the informer or his interest in the subject matter of his communication has been disclosed to those who would have cause to resent the communication by a holder of the privilege or by the informer's own action, or if the informer appears as a witness for the government.

(2) Testimony on merits. If it appears from the evidence in the case or from other showing by a party that an informer may be able to give testimony necessary to a fair determination of the issue of guilt or innocence in a criminal case or of a material issue on the merits in a civil case to which the government is a party, and the government invokes the privilege, the judge shall give the government an opportunity to show *in camera* facts relevant to determining whether the informer can, in fact, supply that testimony. The showing will ordinarily be in the form of affidavits, but the judge may direct that testimony be taken if he finds that the matter cannot be resolved satisfactorily upon affidavit. If the judge finds that there is a reasonable probability that the informer can give the testimony, and the government elects not to disclose his identity, the judge on motion of the defendant in a criminal case shall dismiss the charges to which the testimony would relate, and the judge may do so on his own motion. In civil cases, he may make any order that justice requires. Evidence submitted to the judge shall be sealed and preserved to be made available to the appellate court in the event of an appeal, and the

contents shall not otherwise be revealed without consent of the government. All counsel and parties shall be permitted to be present at every stage of proceedings under this subdivision except a showing *in camera*, at which no counsel or party shall be permitted to be present.

(3) Legality of obtaining evidence. If information from an informer is relied upon to establish the legality of the means by which evidence was obtained and the judge is not satisfied that the information was received from an informer reasonably believed to be reliable or credible, he may require the identity of the informer to be disclosed. The judge shall, on request of the government, direct that the disclosure be made *in camera*. All counsel and parties concerned with the issue of legality shall be permitted to be present at every stage of proceedings under this subdivision except a disclosure *in camera*, at which no counsel or party shall be permitted to be present. If disclosure of the identity of the informer is made *in camera*, the record thereof shall be sealed and preserved to be made available to the appellate court in the event of an appeal, and the contents shall not otherwise be revealed without consent of the government.

ADVISORY COMMITTEE NOTE

The rule recognizes the use of informers as an important aspect of law enforcement, whether the informer is a citizen who steps forward with information or a paid undercover agent. In either event, the basic importance of anonymity in the effective use of informers is apparent, Bocchicchio v. Curtis Publishing Co., 203 F.Supp. 403 (E.D.Pa.1962), and the privilege of withholding their identity was well established at common law. Roviaro v. United States, 353 U.S. 53, 59, 77 S.Ct. 623, 1 L.Ed.2d 639 (1957); McCormick § 148; 8 Wigmore § 2374 (McNaughton Rev. 1961).

Subdivision (a). The public interest in law enforcement requires that the privilege be that of the government, state, or political subdivision, rather than that of the witness. The rule blankets in as an informer anyone who tells a law enforcement officer about a violation of law without regard to whether the officer is one charged with enforcing the particular law. The rule also applies to disclosures to legislative investigating committees and their staffs, and is sufficiently broad to include continuing investigations.

Although the tradition of protecting the identity of informers has evolved in an essentially criminal setting, noncriminal law enforcement situations involving possibilities of reprisal against informers fall within the purview of the considerations out of which the privilege originated.

In Mitchell v. Roma, 265 F.2d 633 (3d Cir. 1959), the privilege was given effect with respect to persons informing as to violations of the Fair Labor Standards Act, and in Wirtz v. Continental Finance & Loan Co., 326 F.2d 561 (5th Cir. 1964), a similar case, the privilege was recognized, although the basis of decision was lack of relevancy to the issues in the case.

Only identity is privileged; communications are not included except to the extent that disclosure would operate also to disclose the informer's identity. The common law was to the same effect. 8 Wigmore § 2374, at p. 765 (McNaughton Rev.1961). *See also* Roviaro v. United States, *supra*, 353 U.S. at p. 60, 77 S.Ct. 623; Bowman Dairy Co. v. United States, 341 U.S. 214, 221, 71 S.Ct. 675, 95 L.Ed. 879 (1951).

The rule does not deal with the question whether presentence reports made under Criminal Procedure Rule 32(c) should be made available to an accused.

Subdivision (b). Normally the "appropriate representative" to make the claim will be counsel. However, it is possible that disclosure of the informer's identity will be sought in proceedings to which the government, state, or subdivision, as the case may be, is not a party. Under these circumstances, effective implementation of the privilege requires that other representatives be considered "appropriate." *See*, for example, Bocchicchio v. Curtis Publishing Co., 203 F.Supp. 403 (E.D.Pa.1962), a civil action for libel, in which a local police office not represented by counsel successfully claimed the informer privilege.

The privilege may be claimed by a state or subdivision of a state if the information was given to its officer, except that in criminal cases it may not be allowed if the government objects.

Subdivision (c) deals with situations in which the informer privilege either does not apply or is curtailed.

(1) If the identity of the informer is disclosed, nothing further is to be gained from efforts to suppress it. Disclosure may be direct, or the same practical effect may result from action revealing the informer's interest in the subject matter. *See*, for example, Westinghouse Electric Corp. v. City of Burlington, 122 U.S.App.D.C. 65, 351 F.2d 762 (1965), on remand City of Burlington v. Westinghouse Electric Corp., 246 F.Supp. 839 (D.D.C.1965), which held that the filing of civil antitrust actions destroyed as to plaintiffs the informer privilege claimed by the Attorney General with respect to complaints of criminal antitrust violations. While allowing the privilege in effect to be waived by one not its holder, *i.e.* the informer himself, is something of a novelty in the law of privilege, if the informer chooses to reveal his identity, further efforts to suppress it are scarcely feasible.

The exception is limited to disclosure to "those who would have cause to resent the communication," in the language of Roviaro v. United States, 353 U.S. 53, 60, 77 S.Ct. 623, 1 L.Ed.2d 639 (1957), since disclosure otherwise, *e.g.* to another law enforcing agency, is not calculated to undercut the objects of the privilege.

If the informer becomes a witness for the government, the interests of justice in disclosing his status as a source of bias or possible support are believed to outweigh any remnant of interest in nondisclosure which then remains. *See* Harris v. United States, 371 F.2d 365 (9th Cir. 1967), in which the trial judge permitted detailed inquiry into the relationship between the witness and the government. *Cf.* Attorney General v. Briant, 15 M. & W. 169, 153 Eng.Rep. 808 (Exch.1846). The purpose of the limitation to witnesses for the government is to avoid the possibility of calling persons as witnesses as a means of discovery whether they are informers.

(2) The informer privilege, it was held by the leading case, may not be used in a criminal prosecution to suppress the identity of a witness when the public interest in protecting the flow of information is outweighed by the individual's right to prepare his defense. Roviaro v. United States, *supra.* The rule extends this balancing to include civil as well as criminal cases and phrases it in terms of "a reasonable probability that the informer may be able to give testimony necessary to a fair determination of the issue of guilt or innocence in a criminal case or of a material issue on the merits in a civil case." Once the privilege is invoked a procedure is provided for determining whether the informer can in fact supply testimony of such nature as to require disclosure of his identity, thus avoiding a "judicial guessing game" on the question. United States v. Day, 384 F.2d 464, 470 (3d Cir. 1967). An investigation *in camera* is calculated to accommodate the conflicting interests involved. The rule also spells out specifically the consequences of a successful claim of the privilege in a criminal case; the wider range of possibilities in civil cases demands more flexibility in treatment. *See* Advisory Committee's Note to Rule 509(e), *supra.*

(3) One of the acute conflicts between the interest of the public in nondisclosure and the avoidance of unfairness to the accused as a result of nondisclosure arises when information from an informer is relied upon to legitimate a search and seizure by furnishing probable cause for an arrest without a warrant or for the issuance of a warrant for arrest or search. McCray v. Illinois, 386 U.S. 300, 87 S.Ct. 1056, 18 L.Ed.2d 62 (1967), rehearing denied 386 U.S. 1042. A hearing *in camera* provides an accommodation of these conflicting interests. United States v. Jackson, 384 F.2d 825 (3d Cir. 1967). The limited disclosure to the judge avoids any significant impairment of secrecy, while affording the accused a substantial measure of protection against arbitrary police

action. The procedure is consistent with McCray and the decisions there discussed.

Rule 511. Waiver of Privilege by Voluntary Disclosure

A person upon whom these rules confer a privilege against disclosure of the confidential matter or communication waives the privilege if he or his predecessor while holder of the privilege voluntarily discloses or consents to disclosure of any significant part of the matter or communication. This rule does not apply if the disclosure is itself a privileged communication.

ADVISORY COMMITTEE NOTE

The central purpose of most privileges is the promotion of some interest or relationship by endowing it with a supporting secrecy or confidentiality. It is evident that the privilege should terminate when the holder by his own act destroys this confidentiality. McCormick §§ 87, 97, 106; 8 Wigmore §§ 2242, 2327–2329, 2374, 2389–2390 (McNaughton Rev.1961).

The rule is designed to be read with a view to what it is that the particular privilege protects. For example, the lawyer-client privilege covers only communications, and the fact that a client has discussed a matter with his lawyer does not insulate the client against disclosure of the subject matter discussed, although he is privileged not to disclose the discussion itself. *See* McCormick § 93. The waiver here provided for is similarly restricted. Therefore a client, merely by disclosing a subject which he had discussed with his attorney, would not waive the applicable privilege; he would have to make disclosure of the communication itself in order to effect a waiver.

By traditional doctrine, waiver is the intentional relinquishment of a known right. Johnson v. Zerbst, 304 U.S. 458, 464, 58 S.Ct. 1019, 82 L.Ed. 1461 (1938). However, in the confidential privilege situations, once confidentiality is destroyed through voluntary disclosure, no subsequent claim of privilege can restore it, and knowledge or lack of knowledge of the existence of the privilege appears to be irrelevant. California Evidence Code § 912; 8 Wigmore § 2327 (McNaughton Rev. 1961).

Rule 512. Privileged Matter Disclosed Under Compulsion or Without Opportunity to Claim Privilege

Evidence of a statement or other disclosure of privileged matter is not admissible against the holder of the privilege if the disclosure was (a) compelled erroneously or (b) made without opportunity to claim the privilege.

ADVISORY COMMITTEE NOTE

Ordinarily a privilege is invoked in order to forestall disclosure. However, under some circumstances consideration must be given to the status and effect of a disclosure already made. Rule 511, immediately preceding, gives voluntary disclosure the effect of a waiver, while the present rule covers the effect of disclosure made under compulsion or without opportunity to claim the privilege.

Confidentiality, once destroyed, is not susceptible of restoration, yet some measure of repair may be accomplished by preventing use of the evidence against the holder of the privilege. The remedy of exclusion is therefore made available when the earlier disclosure was compelled erroneously or without opportunity to claim the privilege.

With respect to erroneously compelled disclosure, the argument may be made that the holder should be required in the first instance to assert the privilege, stand his ground, refuse to answer, perhaps incur a judgment of contempt, and exhaust all legal recourse, in order to sustain his privilege. *See* Fraser v. United States, 145 F.2d 139 (6th Cir. 1944), *cert. denied*, 324 U.S. 849, 65 S.Ct. 684, 89 L.Ed. 1409; United States v. Johnson, 76 F.Supp. 538 (M.D.Pa.1947), aff'd 165 F.2d 42 (3d Cir. 1947), *cert. denied*, 332 U.S. 852, 68 S.Ct. 355, 92 L.Ed. 422, reh. denied, 333 U.S. 834, 68 S.Ct. 457, 92 L.Ed. 1118. However, this exacts of the holder greater fortitude in the face of authority than ordinary individuals are likely to possess, and assumes unrealistically that a judicial remedy is always available. In self-incrimination cases, the writers agree that erroneously compelled disclosures are inadmissible in a subsequent criminal prosecution of the holder, Maguire, Evidence of Guilt 66 (1959); McCormick § 127; 8 Wigmore § 2270 (McNaughton Rev. 1961), and the principle is equally sound when applied to other privileges. The modest departure from usual principles of res judicata which occurs when the compulsion is judicial is justified by the advantage of having one simple rule, assuring at least one opportunity for judicial supervision in every case.

The second circumstance stated as a basis for exclusion is disclosure made without opportunity to the holder to assert his privilege. Illustrative possibilities are disclosure by an eavesdropper, by a person used in the transmission of a privileged communication, by a family member participating in psychotherapy, or privileged data improperly made available from a computer bank.

Rule 513. Comment Upon or Inference from Claim of Privilege; Instruction

(a) Comment or inference not permitted. The claim of a privilege, whether in the present proceeding or upon a prior occasion, is not a proper subject of comment by judge or counsel. No inference may be drawn therefrom.

(b) Claiming privilege without knowledge of jury. In jury cases, proceedings shall be conducted, to the extent practicable, so as to facilitate the making of claims of privilege without the knowledge of the jury.

(c) Jury instruction. Upon request, any party against whom the jury might draw an adverse inference from a claim of privilege is entitled to an instruction that no inference may be drawn therefrom.

ADVISORY COMMITTEE NOTE

Subdivision (a). In Griffin v. California, 380 U.S. 609, 614, 85 S.Ct. 1229, 14 L.Ed.2d 106 (1965), the Court pointed out that allowing comment upon the claim of a privilege "cuts down on the privilege by making its assertion costly." Consequently it was held that comment upon the election of the accused not to take the stand infringed upon his privilege against self-incrimination so substantially as to constitute a constitutional violation. While the privileges governed by these rules are not constitutionally based, they are nevertheless founded upon important policies and are entitled to maximum effect. Hence the present subdivision forbids comment upon the exercise of a privilege, in accord with the weight of authority. Courtney v. United States, 390 F.2d 521 (9th Cir. 1968); 8 Wigmore §§ 2243, 2322, 2386; Barnhart, Privilege in the Uniform Rules of Evidence, 24 OhioSt.L.J. 131, 137–138 (1963). *Cf.* McCormick § 80.

Subdivision (b). The value of a privilege may be greatly depreciated by means other than expressly commenting to a jury upon the fact that it was exercised. Thus, the calling of a witness in the presence of the jury and subsequently excusing him after a sidebar conference may effectively convey to the jury the fact that a privilege has been claimed, even though the actual claim has not been made in their hearing. Whether a privilege will be claimed is usually ascertainable in advance and the handling of the entire matter outside the presence of the jury is feasible. Destruction of the privilege by innuendo can and should be avoided. Tallo v. United States, 344 F.2d 467 (1st Cir. 1965); United States v. Tomaiolo, 249 F.2d 683 (2d Cir. 1957); San Fratello v. United States, 343 F.2d 711 (5th Cir. 1965); Courtney v. United States, 390 F.2d

521 (9th Cir. 1968); 6 Wigmore § 1808, pp. 275–276; 6 U.C.L.A.L.Rev. 455 (1959). This position is in accord with the general agreement of the authorities than an accused cannot be forced to make his election not to testify in the presence of the jury. 8 Wigmore § 2268, p. 407 (McNaughton Rev.1961).

Unanticipated situations are, of course, bound to arise, and much must be left to the discretion of the judge and the professional responsibility of counsel.

Subdivision (c). Opinions will differ as to the effectiveness of a jury instruction not to draw an adverse inference from the making of a claim of privilege. *See* Bruton v. United States, 389 U.S. 818, 88 S.Ct. 126, 19 L.Ed.2d 70 (1968). Whether an instruction shall be given is left to the sound judgment of counsel for the party against whom the adverse inference may be drawn. The instruction is a matter of right, if requested. This is the result reached in Bruno v. United States, 308 U.S. 287, 60 S.Ct. 198, 84 L.Ed. 257 (1939), holding that an accused is entitled to an instruction under the statute (now 18 U.S.C. § 3481) providing that his failure to testify creates no presumption against him.

The right to the instruction is not impaired by the fact that the claim of privilege is by a witness, rather than by a party, provided an adverse inference against the party may result.

INDEX

[References are to sections and to the Federal Rules of Evidence.]

[References are to sections and to the Federal Rules of Evidence.]

[References are to sections and to the Federal Rules of Evidence.]

[References are to sections and to the Federal Rules of Evidence.]

[References are to sections and to the Federal Rules of Evidence.]

[References are to sections and to the Federal Rules of Evidence.]

[References are to sections and to the Federal Rules of Evidence.]

[References are to sections and to the Federal Rules of Evidence.]

**HOSTILE WITNESS, LEADING QUES-
TIONS TO** (See WITNESSES)

HUSBAND AND WIFE
Privileged communication (See PRIVILEGES,
subhead: Spousal)

I

IDENTIFICATION (See AUTHENTICATION
AND IDENTIFICATION)

ILLNESS
Declarant unavailable . . . 804.6; FRE 804(a)(4)

ILLUSTRATIONS (See AUTHENTICATION
AND IDENTIFICATION)

IMMIGRATION LAWS
Applicability of rules to . . . FRE 1101(e)

IMPEACHMENT OF WITNESSES
Generally . . . 607.1; FRE 607-610
Appeal, pendency of, effect . . . FRE 609(e)
Appropriate convictions . . . 609.3; FRE
  609(a)(1)
Bias, exposure of . . . 607.4; FRE 607
Capital offenses . . . 609.2; FRE 609(a)(1)
Character and conduct
  Knowledge . . . 608.3
  Opinion evidence . . . 608.2; FRE 405
  Reputation evidence . . . 608.2; FRE 405;
    FRE 608(a)
  Testimony . . . 405.1; 608.4; FRE
    608(b)(2)
Conduct (See subhead: Character and conduct)
Contradiction . . . 607.5
Conviction of crime
  Generally . . . 609.1; FRE 404(b); FRE
    609
  Annulment, effect of . . . 609.8; FRE
    609(c)
  Appeal, pendency of, effect . . . 609.10
  Introduction of . . . FRE 609
  Introduction of the conviction . . . 609.6
  Pardon, effect of . . . 609.8
  Rehabilitation certificate, effect on witness
    impeachment . . . 609.8
  What constitutes . . . 609.5; FRE 609
  Without regard to penalty . . . 609.4; FRE
    609(a)(2)
Crimen falsi, offenses in nature of . . . 609.4;
  FRE 609(a)(2)
Crimes punishable by imprisonment in excess of
  one year . . . 609.2; FRE 609(a)(1)
Interest, exposure of . . . 607.4
Juvenile adjudications . . . 609.9; FRE 609(d)
Mental capacity, defects . . . 607.6
Operation of FRE 609(a)(2) . . . 609.2
Own witness, impeachment of . . . 607.3; FRE
  607
Pardon, effect of . . . FRE 609(c)
Perception, defects . . . 607.6
Policy, voucher rule rejected . . . 607.2

IMPEACHMENT OF WITNESSES—Cont.
Rehabilitation, certification of . . . FRE 609(c)
Time limit . . . 609.7; FRE 609(b)
Voucher rule rejected . . . 607.2

INCONSISTENT STATEMENTS
Extrinsic evidence . . . 613.3; FRE 613(b)

INDICTMENT, JUROR AS WITNESS (See
JURY)

INSTRUCTIONS TO JURY (See JURY)

INSURANCE (See LIABILITY INSURANCE)

INTEREST
Statements against (See HEARSAY EXCEP-
TIONS)

INTERPRETERS
Generally . . . 604.1; FRE 604
Credibility of . . . 604.3
Jury, function . . . 604.3
Trial judge, function . . . 604.2

INTERROGATION OF WITNESSES
Background . . . 611.1; FRE 611
By court
  Generally . . . 614.1; 614.3; FRE 614
  Calling . . . 614.2
  Objections . . . 614.4; FRE 614(c)
Credibility, cross-examination . . . 611.4; FRE
  611(b)
Cross-examination, scope . . . 611.3; 611.4;
  FRE 611(b)
Discretion of court, mode and order of proof
  . . . 611.2; FRE 611(a)
Leading questions . . . 611.6; FRE 611(c)
Mode, discretion of court . . . 611.2; FRE
  611(a)
Order of proof . . . 611.2; FRE 611(a)
Prior statements (See WITNESSES, subhead:
  Prior statement of)
Purpose . . . 611.1; FRE 611
Self-incrimination, impact of privilege
  . . . 611.5; FRE 611(b)

J

JUDGE
Preliminary questions (See PRELIMINARY
  QUESTIONS)
Witness, competency as (See WITNESSES)

JUDGMENTS (See HEARSAY EXCEPTIONS)

JUDICIAL NOTICE
Generally . . . 201.1; FRE 201
"Adjudicative" versus "legislative" facts
  . . . 201.2; FRE 201(a)
Discretionary versus mandatory . . . 201.5; FRE
  201(c)
Hearings . . . 201.6; FRE 201
Judicial knowledge versus judicial notice
  . . . 201.4; FRE 201
Jury instructions . . . 201.8; FRE 201(f)

[References are to sections and to the Federal Rules of Evidence.]

L

M

N

O

[References are to sections and to the Federal Rules of Evidence.]

PRESEN　　　　　　　　**INDEX**　　　　　　　　**I-12**

[References are to sections and to the Federal Rules of Evidence.]

[References are to sections and to the Federal Rules of Evidence.]

[References are to sections and to the Federal Rules of Evidence.]

[References are to sections and to the Federal Rules of Evidence.]

[References are to sections and to the Federal Rules of Evidence.]

[References are to sections and to the Federal Rules of Evidence.]

X